ERASMUS AND HIS BOOKS

Egbertus van Gulik
at work in the Leiden University Library in 1981
Courtesy of Klaas Koppe, Amsterdam

Egbertus van Gulik

ERASMUS AND HIS BOOKS

Translated by J.C. Grayson

Edited by James K. McConica and Johannes Trapman

University of Toronto Press
Toronto   Buffalo   London

Library and Archives Canada Cataloguing in Publication

Gulik, Egbertus van, 1910–1998, author
Erasmus and his books / Egbertus van Gulik ; translated by
J.C. Grayson ; edited by James K. McConica and Johannes Trapman.

(Erasmus studies)
Manuscripts translated from the Dutch.
Includes bibliographical references and index.
ISBN 978-0-8020-3876-0 (cloth)

1. Erasmus, Desiderius, –1536 – Library.   2. Erasmus, Desiderius, –1536
– Library – Catalogs.   3. Erasmus, Desiderius, –1536 – Books and reading.
I. Grayson, J.C. (J. Chris), translator   II. McConica, James K. (James Kelsey), editor
III. Trapman, Johannes, editor   IV. Title.   V. Series: Erasmus studies.

PA8518.G85 2017   199'.492   C2017-902440-X

University of Toronto Press acknowledges the financial assistance
to its publishing program of the Canada Council for the Arts
and the Ontario Arts Council, an agency of the Government of Ontario.

Contents

Foreword

This study came into being through the dedication of a single scholar, Egbertus ('Bart') van Gulik, who devoted most of his life to assembling the information it contains. It provides the most comprehensive evidence available about the books of Erasmus of Rotterdam – the books he owned and his attitude towards them, when and how he acquired them, how he housed, used, and cared for them, and how, from time to time, he disposed of them.

Part 1, originally intended by the author to be a separate monograph, tells that story. It also opens the door to a new understanding of the more intimate side of Erasmus' daily life as a scholar at home with his books, friends, publishers, and booksellers. Van Gulik's lifelong familiarity with the humanist community known to Erasmus makes of his insights a fresh and engaging introduction to the impact of Italian humanism on the more expressly Christian world of northern Europe. Part 2 is a catalogue, a carefully annotated description of all of the items contained in an inventory that was composed after Erasmus' death in July 1536. Here we find more than 400 books (some containing several works bound together) that belonged to him. They were shipped from Basel by Erasmus' executors around Christmas of that year and consigned to the Polish nobleman Jan Łaski, following the terms of an agreement made with Erasmus in 1525. Łaski acknowledged their receipt in early April 1537. That inventory, cryptic and highly abbreviated in form, is known as the *Versandliste* ('shipping invoice').[1] It is the most comprehensive list surviving of the books in Erasmus' possession at any given time, here fleshed out for the first time by van Gulik. He drew upon his command of bibliographical data and his extensive knowledge of Erasmus' correspondence and related records to propose as precise an identification of each of the titles as the evidence will allow. Van Gulik's annotated catalogue, along with the appendixes, which tell us what can be known of other books in Erasmus' working library and how he used them, will be of interest to students of the northern Renaissance, the history of the book, and the history of learning.

Egbertus van Gulik

Bart van Gulik was born in 1910 in the small provincial town of Hoorn on the Zuiderzee, where he also received his schooling, supplemented with private lessons in the classical languages. Following the death of his father in 1925 and of his older brother two years later, he and his mother moved to Leiden, where he entered the university in 1929. He first came into contact with the work of Erasmus while attending the lectures of Johan Huizinga, and in 1933 he took his first degree. His painstaking perfectionism prolonged his university

---

1 See 5 n11 below.

studies, which concluded only in November 1941 with his *doctoraal* (master's) degree. At
that point a proposed doctorate with a dissertation 'Jefferson's View of Europe' had to be
abandoned. The German occupiers closed the university at Leiden after a student strike,
provoked by a now-famous address on 26 November 1940 by the dean of the Law School,
Professor Rudolph Pabus Cleveringa, protesting the dismissal of Jewish colleagues. With
the assistance of his teachers van Gulik managed eventually to secure a training position in
the library of the Peace Palace at The Hague, where his work on a detailed bibliography of
the works of Hugo Grotius gave him his first experience of the techniques of bibliography.
When, in 1950, the 700-page *Bibliographie des écrits imprimés de Hugo Grotius* was published, van Gulik's name appeared in the Foreword along with those of the compilers.

In 1942, on the recommendation of Huizinga, van Gulik applied for a place in the
University Library at Leiden. After a year of further training there his prospects were such
that in the spring of 1943 he was able to marry Tonny van Beusekom, who, like him, had
been a member of the literary society *Sodalicium Literis Sacrum* ('a society consecrated
to letters') in the university; she eventually taught Dutch at Amsterdam. By the end of
the war, German police were searching everywhere for able-bodied men to supply forced
labour for the Third Reich, and near-starvation conditions prevailed throughout the country. Nevertheless Bart and Tonny van Gulik survived, and in 1946, four years after joining
the library, he was made Keeper of Printed Books. In October 1960 Leiden University appointed him scholarly officer responsible for bibliographical documentation in the field of
general history.

In 1961 van Gulik was placed in charge of the City Library of Rotterdam, a central
library with ten branches and children's libraries, and four lending departments. Within its
holdings of some half-million books was the largest assemblage of Erasmiana in the world.
His predecessor in the post was Cornelis Reedijk, a classical scholar and one of the original
promoters of a new, critical edition of the works of Erasmus.[2] The edition was launched by
the Royal Dutch Academy (Royal Netherlands Academy of Arts and Sciences) in 1963. Van
Gulik, by now an expert bibliographer, started to assemble a bibliography of printed editions of Erasmus in support of the project in the following year. It grew in time to cover the
holdings of nearly 600 libraries. In 1969, to mark the publication of the first volume of the
critical edition, a three-day international congress was held in Rotterdam, which included a
great exhibition in the Boymans-van Beuningen Museum. Van Gulik was largely instrumental in the creation of this exhibition and its invaluable two-volume catalogue, *Erasmus en
zijn tijd*. Among the documents shown there (no 543 in the catalogue) was the *Versandliste*
from the archives of the University Library in Basel. As has been mentioned, this inventory
supplied the titles of some 400 books in very abbreviated form. What was it, exactly? And
what books did Erasmus actually have in his personal collection? These questions were to
occupy van Gulik for the rest of his life. In 1973 he took early retirement to have more time
for scholarly work, chiefly the virtual reassembling of Erasmus' library, and he moved from
Rotterdam to live again near Leiden, at Oegstgeest.

On learning of van Gulik's enterprise from Sir Roger Mynors, a scholarly sponsor of
the new critical edition of Erasmus' *Opera omnia* and also a founding editor and translator
of the Collected Works of Erasmus, this writer paid the first of what was to be a series of

---

2 Earlier editions of the *Opera omnia Desiderii Erasmi Roterodami* had appeared at Basel (1538–40) and Leiden
(1703–6). The Leiden edition is commonly cited as LB. For background to the new edition in question,
see James McConica 'Erasmus in Amsterdam and Toronto.'

visits to van Gulik's apartment at Oegstgeest in October of 1978, bearing the news that the University of Toronto Press would be distinctly interested in publishing his work, by this time already quite far advanced. This encouraging prospect proved insufficient, however, to overcome van Gulik's deeply ingrained caution and perfectionism; there was always something to add. Some time later he broke his hip and had to undergo a succession of four surgeries; the invaluable support of his wife, Tonny, faded as her own health declined, and she succumbed eventually in 1995. It was only with his death in 1998 that the much-revised yet still incomplete version of his edition of the *Versandliste* became available. It runs to more than 1,100 manuscript pages. Other important supporting materials among his extensive papers were subsequently put in order by Johannes Trapman, Secretary of the Council in charge of the critical edition of Erasmus' *Opera omnia*, and yet others were identified by his daughter, Mme Schram-van Gulik, whose patient examination of her father's papers rescued even items of which we had despaired.

The Story of Erasmus and His Books

In the following pages the reader will find the remarkable harvest of Bart van Gulik's perseverance and erudite investigation. In the Introduction he summarizes the background to his work on the *Versandliste* and gives a brief history of the slow dispersal of the books sent to Łaski in the lifetime of their new owner, as Łaski joined the Reform and wandered through Europe. After adding an account of the modern search for books that are identified as formerly in Erasmus' possession – usually through the unmistakable ex libris *Sum Erasmi* (roughly, 'I belong to Erasmus') penned on an endpaper – he outlines his intentions in what follows.

The scope of van Gulik's study is fairly indicated by the successive chapter headings in Part 1, 'The History and Nature of Erasmus' Working Library.' Here the reader will find assembled van Gulik's conclusions, drawn from his years of work on the *Versandliste* and amplified by his extensive experience of Renaissance bibliography and his familiarity with Erasmus' life. He comments upon the focus and range of Erasmus' interest in books, his utilitarian attitude to them (he was no bibliophile), how he and other humanists acquired and exchanged them, how he regarded manuscripts, how he undertook binding and maintenance, how he stored, arranged, and cared for his books, and how he moved them about. The first five chapters give us the evidence to reconstruct Erasmus' library. They are followed at chapter 6, 'Erasmus and the Book: The Humanist at Work,' by a surprisingly intimate portrait of Erasmus among his books and of his working habits and discipline: being read to by his scholar-pupils, keeping up with new publications, dealing with his own publisher, taking his favourite authors – his familiar 'travelling companions' – with him when, as so often, he was on the road. Part 1 concludes with an assessment of Erasmus' collection as representative both of his personal circumstances and of the age in which he lived: it was the working reference library of a Christian humanist in the new age of printing.

The core of van Gulik's research, and of this volume, is contained in Part 2, the annotated catalogue, in which the *Versandliste*, a record of the books in Erasmus' possession at the time of his death, is for the first time amplified with all of the evidence that could be brought to bear upon it. In his Introduction to the annotated catalogue van Gulik describes the procedures he used in approaching the individual works there listed in order to supply as precise an identification of each entry as possible. In the course of doing this, he provides the reader with a wealth of information about the history of the book and the book trade, about Erasmus' attitudes and procedures as a humanist, and about the limits to our knowledge of both.

Supplementing the *Versandliste*/Catalogue are two appendixes. The first, the *Catalogus librorum Erasmi*, is a list compiled after Erasmus' death of 112 mostly unbound works written or edited by Erasmus and probably found by his executors in his final residence in Basel, where they were kept in a chest. The second appendix is a further list, assembled by van Gulik, of 153 works that, judging from his correspondence, were in Erasmus' possession but are not found either in the *Versandliste* or in the *Catalogus librorum*.

JAMES K. MC CONICA

Acknowledgments

In composing this memoir of Drs van Gulik I must acknowledge the invaluable assistance of his daughter, the late Mme M.E. Schram-van Gulik of Wijdenes, the Netherlands. I am also indebted to the *Levensbericht* 'Egbertus van Gulik' by Drs E. Meeldijk in *Jaarboek van de Maatschappij der Nederlandse Letterkunde te Leiden 2000–2001*, and to Dr J.C. Grayson, who translated it; to J.J.M. van de Roer-Meyers, formerly of the Rotterdam City Library; and to Prof Dr H.J. de Jonge, formerly of Leiden University. In the matter of publication, the Conseil international pour l'édition des oeuvres complètes d'Erasme has assisted with a timely and generous subvention. Several colleagues provided generous assistance, especially Prof John N. Grant of the University of Toronto. Finally, this volume's appearance is of itself a tribute to the dedication and meticulous editorial skills of Mary Baldwin of University of Toronto Press.

Illustrations

Erasmus' last will, dated Basel, 12 February 1536

Two pages from the *Versandliste*
University Library Basel MS C VIA 71 (VL / Catalogue nos 197–260)

The bookseller Hainrich Kepner packing books in a barrel for transport

Autograph of the letter, dated Cracow, 5 April 1537, in which Jan Łaski
affirms that he has received Erasmus' library in good order
University Library Basel MS C VIa 71

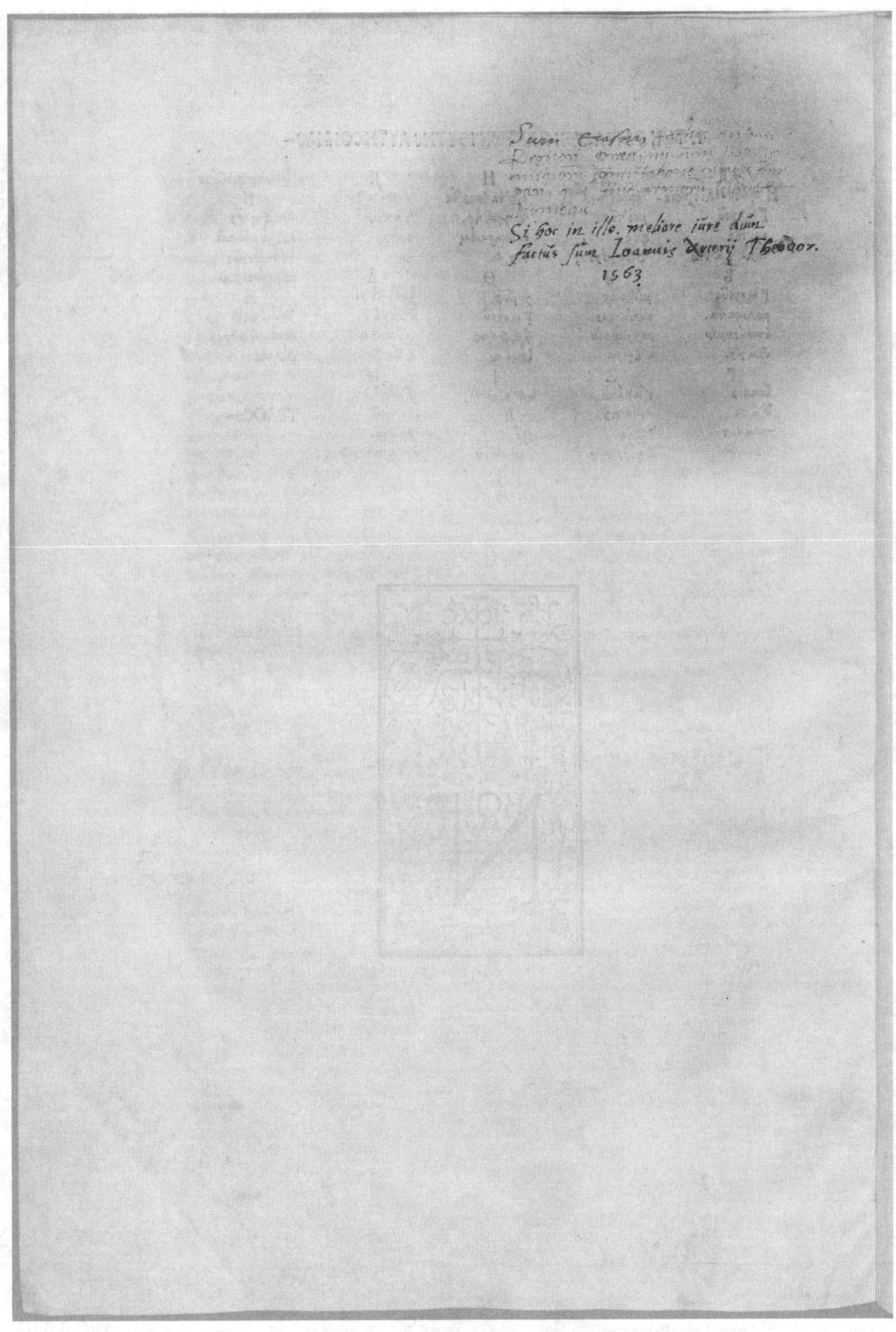

Sum Erasmi: Erasmus' ex libris in his copy of
Galen *Therapeutica* (VL / Catalogue no 138)
Leiden University Libraries

Epistolę ciceronis Ad Atticū, ex Impressione Aldina
vitę posteriorū Imparatorū q Aelium Lampridiū. et alios
Diodorū Siculum.

Homerus ex Impssione florentina
oīā opa Aristotelis grœca
Cōmentatores in Aristotelem grœci omnes.
opa Hermogenis grœca cū alijs.

opa platonis grœca.

opa Xenophontis grœca.

opa Galeni medici grœca.

pindarū grœcū cū alijs.

   Aristidis
orationes Aristidis et aliorū Rhetorū dcīm gurę

Cōmentarij grœci ſ diuersos poetas.

Dioscorides grœcus cū Nicandro.

Epistolas diuersorū grœcas
Aesopus grœcus Aldi cū alijs
Argonautica cū gennis
Et alia oīā que Impreſſit Aldus intra
Nos quatuor ānos proximos, hoc est post
Hermogenē et plutarchum.

An order for books in Erasmus' hand
University Library Basel MS A IX 56

GILBERTVS COGNATVS NOZERENVS, D. ERAS-
mi amanuensis:anno ætatis suæ 26. Christiano uerò 1530.

DES. ERASMVS ROTÆRODAMVS, ANNO
ætatis suæ 70. Christi uerò 1530.

Erasmus in his study in Freiburg with his secretary Gilbert Cousin

De Boeckbinder.

Het oog van 't eewig weesen,   Kan 't boeck uw's herten leesen.

Lach 't weeten heim'lyck in de hoecken,
    Waar dat den Weg ten Heemel leid,
't Was waard de Weereld door te soecken;
    Maar nu 't de Mens word klaar geseid,
In 't Heilig Boeck, van God gegeeven,
Steeckt hem de walg van 't heilig leeven.

A bookbinder
by Jan Luyken (1694)

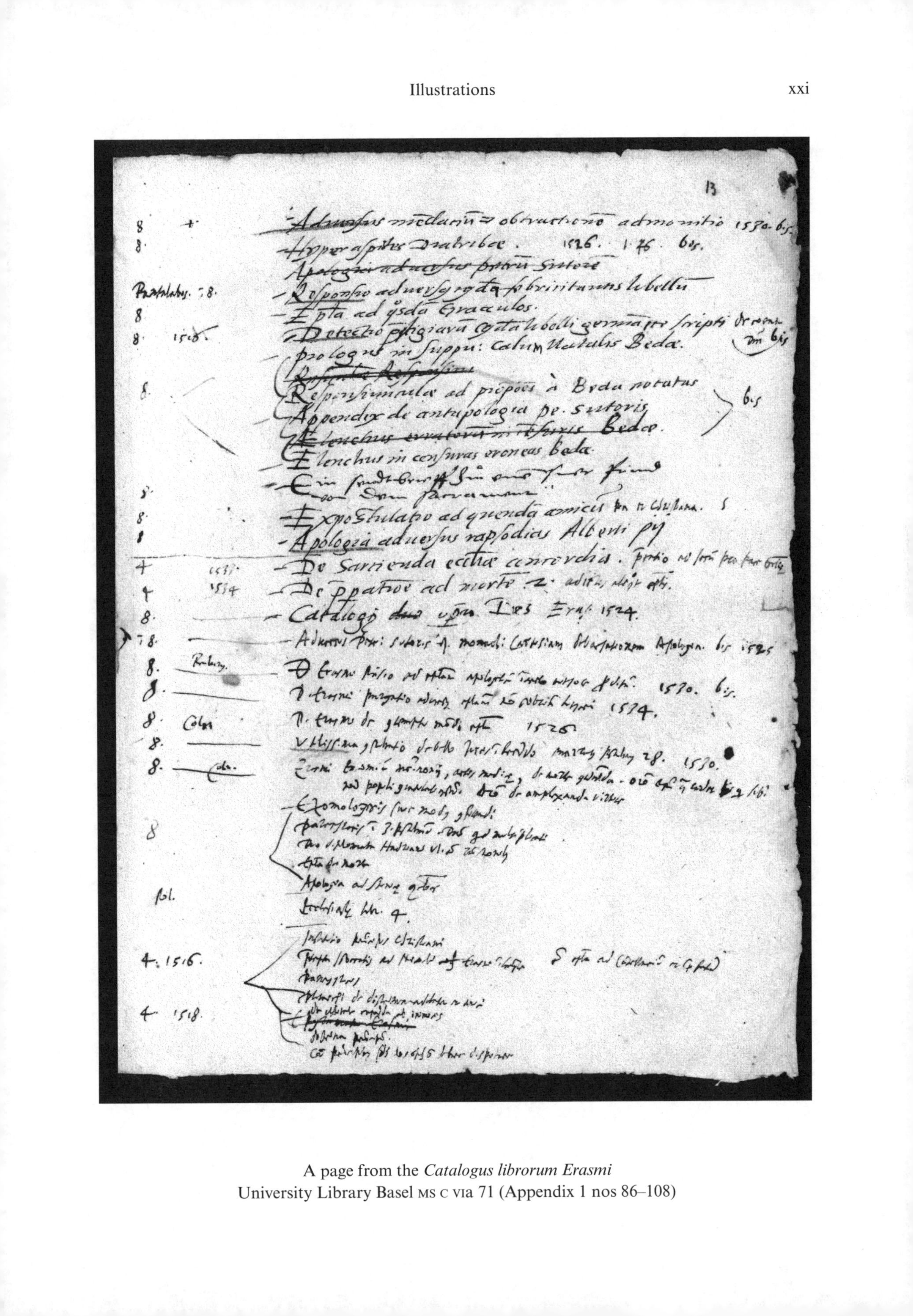

A page from the *Catalogus librorum Erasmi*
University Library Basel MS C VIa 71 (Appendix 1 nos 86–108)

Abbreviations and Works Frequently Cited

Bibliographies and Catalogues

Adams   Adams, H.M. *Catalogue of the Books Printed on the Continent of Europe 1501–1600 in Cambridge Libraries* (Cambridge 1967) 2 vols

Baudrier   Baudrier, H. and J. *Bibliographie Lyonnaise: Recherches sur les imprimeurs, libraires, relieurs et fondeurs de lettres de Lyon au xvie siècle* (Lyon 1895–1921; repr Paris 1964, Geneva 1999) 12 vols plus index volume

BB   *Bibliotheca Belgica: Bibliographie générale des Pays-Bas* ed F. van der Haeghen, re-ed Marie-Thérèse Lenger (Brussels 1964–75; repr Brussels 1979) 7 vols

BE   *Bibliotheca Erasmiana: Répertoire des oeuvres d'Erasme* ed F. Vander Haeghen, 1st series (Ghent 1893)

Benzing *Bibliographie Haguenau*   Benzing, Josef *Bibliographie haguenovienne: Bibliographie des ouvrages imprimés à Haguenau (Bas-Rhin) au xvie siècle* (Baden-Baden 1973)

Benzing *Hutten Bibliographie*   Benzing, Josef *Ulrich von Hutten und seine Drücker: Eine Bibliographie der Schriften Huttens im xvi. Jahrhundert* Beiträge zum Buch- und Bibliothekswesen 36 (Wiesbaden 1956)

Benzing *Lutherbibliographie*   Benzing, Josef, with Helmut Claus *Lutherbibliographie: Verzeichnis der gedruckten Schriften Martin Luthers bis zu dessen Tod* (= *Bibliotheca bibliographica Aureliana* 10, 16, 19) 2nd ed (Baden-Baden 1989, 1994) 2 vols

Benzing *Bibliographie Reuchlins*   Benzing, Josef *Bibliographie der Schriften Johannes Reuchlins im 15. und 16. Jahrhundert* (Bad Bocklet 1955)

Bezzel   Bezzel, Irmgard *Erasmusdrucke des 16. Jahrhunderts in bayerischen Bibliotheken: Ein bibliographisches Verzeichnis* (Stuttgart 1979)

BL *Catalogue*   British Museum/Library *Catalogue of Printed Books*

BL *Catalogue Fifteenth Century*   British Museum/Library *Catalogue of Books Printed in the xvth Century*

BL *Catalogue Italy 1465–1600*   British Museum/Library *Catalogue of Books Printed in Italy 1465–1600*

BN *Catalogue général*   Bibliothèque nationale de France *Catalogue général*

Campbell *Annales*

Campbell, M.F.A.G. *Annales de la typographie néerlandaise au xve siècle* (The Hague 1874)

Cranz

Cranz, F.E. *A Bibliography of Aristotle Editions 1501–1600* 2nd ed rev C.B. Schmitt (Baden-Baden 1984)

GW

Gesamtkatalog der Wiegendrücke (Leipzig 1925–) 11 vols to date

Hain; Hain-Copinger; HCR

Hain, L.F.T. *Repertorium bibliographicum in quo libri ommes ab arte typographica inventa usque ad annum MD typis expressi, ordine alphabetico vel simpliciter enumerantur vel adcuratius recensentur* (Stuttgart 1826–38) 2 vols in 4; Copinger, W.A. *Supplement to Hain's Repertorium bibliographicum* (London 1895–1902) 3 vols; D. Reichling *Appendices ad Hainii-Coperingi Repertorium bibliographicum* (Munich 1905–11; repr Milan 1953) 7 vols with supplement

Koehn

Koehn, Horst 'Philipp Melanchthons Reden, Verzeichnis der im 16. Jahrhundert erschienenen Drucke' *Archiv für Geschichte des Buchwesens* 25 (1984) 1277–1486

Legrand *Bibliographie hellénique*

Legrand, Emile *Bibliographie hellénique des xve et xvie siècles; ou, Description raisonée des ouvrages publiés en grec ou par des Grecs au xve et xvie siècles* (Paris 1885–1906; repr Paris 1962) 4 vols

Meyers

Meyers, Johanna J.M. *Authors Edited, Translated or Annotated by Desiderius Erasmus: A Short-Title Catalogue of the Works in the City Library of Rotterdam* (Rotterdam 1982)

Moreau *Inventaire*

Moreau, Brigitte, d'après les manuscrits de Philippe Renouard *Inventaire chronologique des éditions parisiennes du xvie siècle* (Paris 1972–) 5 vols to date

NK

Nederlandsche bibliographie van 1500 tot 1540 ed Wouter Nijhoff and M.E. Kronenberg (The Hague 1923–71) 3 vols

Panzer

Panzer, G.W. *Annales typographici* (Nürnberg 1793–1803; repr Hildesheim 1963–4) 11 vols

Renouard *Annales des Estienne*

Renouard, Antoine Augustin *Annales de l'imprimerie des Estienne; ou, Histoire de la familie des Estienne et de ses éditions* 2nd ed (Paris 1843; repr New York 1960) 2 vols

Renouard *Bibliographie de Josse Bade*

Renouard, Philippe *Bibliographie des impressions et des oeuvres de Josse Bade Ascensius, imprimeur et humaniste (1462–1535)* (Paris 1908; repr New York 1963) 3 vols

Staehelin *Oekolampad-Bibliographie*

Staehelin, Ernst *Oekolampad-Bibliographie* (Basel 1918; repr Nieuwkoop 1963)

STC

A Short-Title Catalogue of Books Printed in England, Scotland, and Ireland and of English Books Printed Abroad, 1475–1640 ed A.W. Pollard and G.R. Redgrave (London 1926); 2nd ed rev W.A. Jackson et al (London 1976–91) 3 vols de Vreese BER   de Vreese, Willem *Bibliotheca Erasmiana Rotterdamensis catalogus der uitgaven van Desiderius Erasmus' werken aanwezig in de Bibliotheek der Gemeente Rotterdam* (Rotterdam 1936–41) 2 fasc

Walter
  Catalogue Sélestat   Walter, J. *Catalogue Générale de la Bibliothèque municipale de Sélestat, 1e série, 3e partie: Incunables et imprimés du xvie siècle* (Colmar 1929)

Other Sources

AK   *Die Amerbachkorrespondenz* ed Alfred Hartmann and B.R. Jenny (Basel 1942–)

Allen   *Opus epistolarum Des. Erasmi Roterodami* ed P.S. Allen, H.M. Allen, and H.W. Garrod (Oxford 1906–58) 11 vols and index

ASD   *Opera omnia Desiderii Erasmi Roterodami* (Amsterdam 1969–)

BRE   *Briefwechsel des Beatus Rhenanus* ed Adalbert Horawitz and Karl Hartfelder (Leipzig 1886; repr Hildesheim 1966)

CEBR   *Contemporaries of Erasmus: A Biographical Register of the Renaissance and the Reformation* ed Peter G. Bietenholz and Thomas B. Deutscher (Toronto 1985–7) 3 vols

Cosenza
  Italian Humanists   Cosenza, M.E. *Biographical and Bibliographical Dictionary of the Italian Humanists and of the World of Classical Scholarship in Italy, 1300–1800* 2nd ed (Boston 1962–7) 6 vols

CWE   *Collected Works of Erasmus* (Toronto 1974–)

Ferguson *Opuscula*   *Erasmi opuscula: A Supplement to the Opera omnia* ed Wallace K. Ferguson (The Hague 1933; repr Hildesheim/New York 1978)

Förstemann/
  Günther   *Briefe an Desiderius Erasmus von Rotterdam* ed J[oseph] Förstemann and O[tto] Günther xxvii. Beiheft zum *Zentralblatt für Bibliothekswesen* (Leipzig 1904; repr Wiesbaden 1968)

Garanderie
  Correspondance   *La Correspondance d'Erasme et de Guillaume Budé* ed Marie-Madeleine de la Garanderie (Paris 1967)

Hutten *Opera*   *Ulrichi Hutteni equitis germani opera quae reperiri potuerunt omnia* ed E. Böcking (Leipzig 1859–64; repr Aalen 1963) 5 vols with 2 vols supplement

Łaski *Opera*   Johannes a Lasco *Opera tam edita quam inedita* ed A. Kuyper (Amsterdam/The Hague 1866) 2 vols

LB   *Desiderii Erasmi Roterodami Opera Omnia* ed J[ean] Leclerc (Leiden 1703–6; repr 1961–2) 10 vols

Melanchthons Werke   Melanchthon, Philippus *Melanchthons Werke in Auswahl* ed R. Stupperich
                            et al (Gütersloh 1951–75) 7 vols in 9

OCD   *Oxford Classical Dictionary* 3rd ed rev Simon Hornblower and
                            Anthony Spawforth (Oxford/New York 2003)

ODCC2   *Oxford Dictionary of the Christian Church* ed F.L. Cross and E.A.
                            Livingston 2nd ed (Oxford 1974)

Pauly-Wissowa;   Pauly, August F. von *Paulys Realencyclopädie der klassischen*
  Der Kleine Pauly   *Altertumswissenschaft* ed August Friedrich von Pauly and Georg Wissowa
                            (Stuttgart 1893–1972); *Der Kleine Pauly: Lexikon der Antike* (based on
                            Pauly's *Realencyclopädie*) ed Konrat Ziegler and Walther Sontheimer
                            (Stuttgart 1964–75) 5 vols

Phillips *Adages*   Phillips, Margaret Mann *The 'Adages' of Erasmus: A Study with*
                            Translations (Cambridge 1964)

PL   *Patrologiae cursus completus ... series Latina* ed J.-P. Migne, 1st ed
                            (Paris 1844–55, 1862–5; repr Turnhout) 217 vols plus 4 vols indexes. In
                            the notes, references to volumes of PL in which column numbers in the
                            first edition are different from those in later editions or reprints include
                            the date of the edition cited.

Reedijk *Poems*   *The Poems of Desiderius Erasmus* ed Cornelis Reedijk (Leiden 1956)

Rice *Prefatory Epistles*   *The Prefatory Epistles of Jacques Lefèvre d'Etaples and Related Texts*
                            ed Eugene F. Rice (New York 1972)

RM   R.A.B. Mynors material in manuscript in the City Library of
                            Rotterdam

Staehelin BAO   *Briefe und Akten zum Leben Oekolampads* ed Ernst Staehelin, Quellen
                            und Forschungen zur Reformationsgeschichte 10 and 19 (Leipzig
                            1927–34; repr New York/London 1971) 2 vols

Telle *Dilutio*   *Erasmus Roterodamus. Dilutio eorum quae Iodocus Clithoveus scripsit*
                            adversus Declamationem Des. Erasmi Roterodami suasoriam matrimonii
                            ed Emile V. Telle (Geneva 1968)

WA   *D. Martin Luthers Werke: Kritische Gesamtausgabe* (Weimar 1883–1980)
                            60 vols

WA *Briefwechsel*   *D. Martin Luthers Werke: Briefwechsel* (Weimar 1930–78) 15 vols

Zwinglis   *Huldreich Zwinglis Sämtliche Werke 7–11: Zwinglis Briefwechsel* ed
  Briefwechsel   Emil Egli et al, *Corpus Reformatorum* 94–8 (Leipzig 1911–35) 5 vols

Zwinglis Werke   *Huldreich Zwinglis Sämtliche Werke* ed Emil Egli et al, *Corpus*
                            Reformatorum 88–101 (Berlin/Leipzig/Zürich 1905–59; repr 1981) 14 vols

Bibliography

Adelung, Friedrich von *Kritisch-literarische übersicht der Reisenden in Russland bis 1700, deren Berichte bekannt sind* (St Petersburg 1846; repr Amsterdam 1960) 2 vols

[Adrian VI, Pope] *Herdenkingstentoonstelling Paus Adrianus VI. Gedenkboek* (Utrecht/Leuven 1959) exhibition catalogue

Allen, P.S. *The Correspondence of an Early Printing House: The Amerbachs of Basle* (Glasgow 1932)

– *Erasmus: Lectures and Wayfaring Sketches* (Oxford 1934)

Allgemeine Deutsche Biographie (Leipzig 1875–1912) 56 vols

Allgemeines Gelehrtenlexicon. See Jöcher

[Ammianus Marcellinus] *Ammiani Marcellini Rerum gestarum libri qui supersunt* ed Wolfgang Seyfarth (Leipzig 1978) 2 vols

Appelt, T.C. *Studies in the Contents and Sources of Erasmus' Adagia with Particular Reference to the First Edition, 1500, and the Edition of 1526* (Chicago 1942)

Arber, Agnes *Herbals, their Origin and Evolution: A Chapter in the History of Botany, 1470–1670* 2nd ed, rewritten and enlarged (Cambridge 1938; repr 1953)

Arnold, Klaus *Johannes Trithemius (1462–1516)* (Würzburg 1971; rev ed 1991)

Aschbach, Joseph Ritter von *Geschichte der Wiener Universität im ersten Jahrhunderte ihres Bestehens* (Vienna 1865–88; repr Farnborough 1967) 3 vols

Aschmann, Rudolf et al *Der Humanist Heinrich Loriti genannt Glarean, 1588–1563: Beiträge zu seinem Leben und Werk* (Mollis 1983)

Augustijn, C. *Erasmus* (Baarn 1986) / trans J.C. Grayson *Erasmus: His Life, Works, and Influence* (Toronto 1991)

– *Erasmus en de Reformatie; een onderzoek naar de houding die Erasmus ten opzichte van de Reformatie heeft aangenomen* (Amsterdam 1962)

– 'Erasmus von Rotterdam im Galaterbriefkommentar Luthers von 1519' *Luther-Jahrbuch* 49 (1982) 115–32

– 'Hyperaspistes I: La doctrine d'Erasme et de Luther sur la "Claritas Scripturae"' in *Colloquia Erasmiana Turonensia: Douzième stage international d'études humanistes, Tours, 1969* ed J.-C. Margolin (Paris/Toronto 1972) 2 vols II 737–48

– 'Wessel Gansfort's Rise to Celebrity' in *Wessel Gansfort and Northern Humanism* ed F. Akkerman, G. Huisman, and A.J. Vanderjagt, Brill's Studies in Intellectual History 40 (Leiden/New York 1993) 3–21

Aulotte, R. *Amyot et Plutarque, la tradition des Moralia au XVIe siècle* (Geneva 1965)

Bagrow, Leo A. *Ortelii catalogus cartographorum* (Gotha 1928–30) 2 vols

Bainton, R.H. *Erasmus of Christendom* (New York 1969)

Barber, Giles 'Thomas Linacre: A Bibliographical Survey of His Works' in *Essays on the Life and Work of Thomas Linacre, c. 1460–1524* ed Francis Maddison, Margaret Pelling, and Charles Webster (Oxford 1977) 303–4

Barberi, Francesco 'Le edizione romane di Francesco Minizio Calvo' in *Miscellanea di scritti di bibliografia ed erudizione in memoria di Luigi Ferrari* (Florence 1952) 57–98

Bardenhewer, Otto *Geschichte der altkirchlichen Literatur* (Freiburg im Breisgau 1903–24) 4 vols in 2

Baron, Hans 'Aulus Gellius in the Renaissance and a Manuscript from the School of Guarino'
     Studies in Philology 48 (1951) 107–25
Bartel, Oskar *Jan Łaski, czesc I (1499–1556)* (Warsaw 1955) with a summary in English and Russian
– 'Johannes a Lasco und Erasmus von Rotterdam' *Luther-Jahrbuch* 32 (1965) 48–66
Bateman, John J. 'The Text of Erasmus' *De recta latini graecique sermonis pronuntiatione dialogus'*
     in *Acta Conventus Neo-Latini Lovaniensis, Proceedings of the First International Congress of Neo-*
     Latin Studies, Louvain 23–28 August 1971 ed J. IJsewijn and E. Kessler (Leuven/Louvain
     and Munich 1973) 49–75
Becker, August *Christophe de Longueil, sein Leben und seine Briefwechsel* (Bonn/Leipzig 1924)
Bedouelle, Guy *Lefèvre d'Etaples et l'intelligence des écritures* (Geneva 1976)
– *Le Quincuplex Psalterium de Lefèvre d'Etaples: Un guide de lecture* (Geneva 1939)
Die Bekenntnisschriften der evangelisch-lutherischen Kirche ... im Gedenkjahr der Augsburgischen
     Konfession 1930 6th ed (Göttingen 1967)
Béné, Charles *Erasmus et Saint Augustin ou l'influence de Saint Augustin sur l'humanisme d'Erasme*
     (Geneva 1969)
Benzing, Josef and Jean Muller *Bibliographie Strasbourgeoise: Bibliographie des ouvrages imprimés*
     à Strasbourg (Bas-Rhin) au XVIe siècle (Baden-Baden 1981–6) 3 vols
Benzing Josef 'Die deutsche Verleger des 16. und 17. Jahrhunderts' *Archiv für die Geschichte*
     des Buchwesens 18 (1977) 1077–1322
Berg, J. 'Aantekeningen van Erasmus op een exemplaar der editio Aldina van Athenaeus'
     Deipnosophistae' *Het Boek* 10 (1921) 80
Bernouilli, C.A. 'Zur griechischen Uebersetzung von Hieronymus' *De viris illustribus' Theologische*
     Literaturzeitung 20 (1895) 475–6
Berquin. *See under* Erasmus
Beuttenmüller, O. *Vorläufiges Verzeichnis der Melanchthon-Drücke des 16. Jahrhunderts* (Halle 1960)
Bierlaire, F. *La familia d'Erasme: Contribution à l'histoire de l'humanisme* (Paris 1968)
Bietenholz, P.G. *Basle and France in the Sixteenth Century* (Geneva/Toronto 1971)
– 'Erasmus und der Basler Buchhandel in Frankreich' in *Scrinium Erasmianum: Mélanges historiques*
     publiés ... à l'occasion du cinquième centenaire de la naissance d'Erasme ed J. Coppens (Leiden
     1969) 2 vols I 293–323
– *Der italienische Humanismus und die Blütezeit des Buchdrucks in Basel* (Basel 1959)
Biographie nationale (Brussels 1866–)
Biographisch woordenboek van protestantsche godgeleerden in Nederland ed J.P. de Bie et al
     (The Hague 1903–49) 5 vols and 1 fasc
Bloch, Joshua 'Venetian Printers of Hebrew books' *Bulletin of the New York Public Library* 36 (1932)
     71–92
van der Blom, N. 'Erasmus "Carmen votivum" ter ere van Ste-Geneviève' *Hermeneus* 58 (1986)
     191–8
– *Programma van het Erasmiaans Gymnasium voor de cursus 1969/1970* (Rotterdam 1969) 13–20
Blum, Rudolf 'Die Literaturverzeichnung im Altertum und Mittelalter' *Archiv für die Geschichte*
     des Buchwesens 24 (1983) 189–92
Bolgar, R.R. *The Classical Heritage and its Beneficiaries* (Cambridge 1954)
Borst, Arno 'Das Karlbild in der Geschichtswissenschaft von Humanismus bis heute' in *Karl der*
     Grosse: Lebenswerk und Nachleben (Düsseldorf 1965–7) 5 vols IV (1967) 364–402
Boyle, Marjorie O'Rourke '"For peasants, psalms": Erasmus' *editio princeps* of Haymo (1533)'
     Mediaeval Studies 44 (1982) 444–69
Braches, E. 'Boekkunst in de bibliotheek' *Boeken verzamelen* (Leiden 1983) 58–65
Brandi, Karl 'Dantes Monarchia und die Italienpolitik Mercurio Gattinaras' *Deutsches Dante-*
     Jahrbuch 24 (Neue Folge 15) (1942) 1–19
Brann, N.L. *The Abbot Trithemius (1462–1516): The Renaissance of Monastic Humanism* Studies
     in the History of Christian Thought 24 (Leiden 1981)
Brown, Andrew J. 'The Date of Erasmus' Latin Translation of the New Testament' *Transactions*
     of the Cambridge Bibliographical Society 8 (1894) 351–80

[Bucer, Martin] *Correspondance de Martin Bucer* (Leiden 1979–) 10 vols to date
Buck, August 'Der italienische Humanismus' in *Humanismusforschung seit 1945: Ein Bericht aus interdisziplinärer Sicht* ed Deutsche Forschungsgemeinschaft (Bonn-Bad Godesberg 1975) 11–40
– *Die Rezeption der Antike: Zum Problem der Kontinuität zwischen Mittelalter und Renaissance* (Hamburg 1981)
– 'Überlegungen zum gegenwärtigen Stand der Renaissanceforschung' *Bibliothèque d'Humanisme et Renaissance* 43 (1981) 7–38
[Budé, G.] *Guillaume Budé* (Paris, Bibliothèque nationale 1968) exhibition catalogue
Burckhardt, Andreas *Johannes Basilius Herold: Kaiser und Reich im protestantischen Schrifttum des Basler Buchdrucks um die Mitte des 16. Jahrhunderts* (Basel 1966)
Burckhardt, Jacob *Die Kultur der Renaissance in Italien* 18th ed (Leipzig 1928) / *The Civilization of the Renaissance in Italy* trans S.C.G. Middlemore (London 1929). There are many reprints; pages are cited from the Harper Torchbook edition (New York 1958) 2 vols
Burger, H.O. *Renaissance, Humanismus, Reformation; deutsche Literatur im europäischen Kontext* (Bad Homburg/Zürich 1969)
Burmeister, K.H. 'Die Bibliothek des Jakob Spiegel' in *Das Verhältnis der Humanisten zum Buch* ed Fritz Krafft and Dieter Wuttke (Boppard 1977) 163–83
Burscher, J.F. *Index et argumentum epistolarum ad D. Erasmum Roterodamum autographarum quas ab anno 1520 usque ad annum 1536 cardinales, episcopi, ... aliique homines Erasmo familiares exararunt, et quae ... nunc cum nonnullis aliis ex bibliotheca Erasmi autographis adservantur Lipsiae in bibliotheca D. Joa. Frid. Burscheri* (Leipzig 1784)
– *Spicilegium autographarum illustrantium rationem quae intercessit Erasmo Roterodamo cum aulis et hominibus aeui sui praecipuis omnique republica* (Leipzig 1784–1802)
Buschmann, Richard *Das Bewusstwerden der deutschen Geschichte bei den deutschen Humanisten* (Göttingen 1930)
Butzmann, Hans *Corpus agrimensorum romanorum, Codex Arcerianus A der Herzog August Bibliothek zu Wolfenbüttel (Cod. Guelf. 36, 23 A)* (Leiden 1970)
Cambridge History of the Bible III: *The West from the Reformation to the Present Day* ed G.L. Greenslade (Cambridge 1963)
Campbell, Tony *The Earliest Printed Maps 1472–1500* (London 1987)
Catalogus translationum et commentariorum: Mediaeval and Renaissance Latin Translations and Commentaries, Annotated Lists and Guides ed Paul Oskar Kristeller et al (Washington, DC 1960–)
Celenza, Christopher S. (ed) *Angelo Poliziano's* Lamia*: Text, Translation, and Introductory Studies* (Leiden 2010)
Celtis, Konrad *Briefwechsel* ed Hans Rupprich (Münster 1934)
Chastel, André *The Age of Humanism, Europe 1480–1530* (London 1963)
Chomarat, Jacques *Grammaire et rhétorique chez Erasme* (Paris 1981) 2 vols
Choulant, Ludwig *Graphische Incunabeln für Naturgeschichte und Medicin* (Leipzig 1858; repr Hildesheim 1963)
Christ, K. *Die Bibliothek Reuchlins in Pforzheim*, Zentralblatt für Bibliothekswesen, Beiheft 52 (Leipzig 1924)
Christ, Wilhelm von *Geschichte der griechischen Literatur* rev W. Schmid and O. Stählin, 6th ed (Munich 1920–4; repr 1959 and 1961) 2 vols
Christ-von Wedel, Christine *Das Nichtwissen bei Erasmus von Rotterdam* (Basel 1981)
Clemen, Otto 'Hinne Rode in Wittenberg, Basel, Zürich, und die ersten Ausgaben Wesselscher Schriften' in *Zeitschrift für Kirchengeschichte* 18 (1898) 346–72
Clough, Cecil H. 'A presentation volume for Henry VIII: the Charlecote Park copy of Erasmus' *Institutio principis christiani' Journal of the Warburg and Courtauld Institutes* 44 (1981) 199–202
Cochrane, Eric *Historians and Historiography in the Italian Renaissance* (Chicago 1981)
Colish, Marcia 'Seneca's *Apocolocyntosis* as a Possible Source for Erasmus' *Julius Exclusus' Renaissance Quarterly* 29 (1976) 361–8
Congar, Yves 'Bio-bibliographique de Cajétan' *Revue Thomiste* 39 n s 17 nos 86–7 (nov 1934–fév 1935) 3–49

Continental and Russian Books and Manuscripts, Science and Medicine, Sale November 1990
     (Sotheby's London)
Coppens, J. 'Les scolies d'Erasme sur l'epistola de interdicto esu carnium' in *Colloquia Erasmiana
     Turonensia: Douzième stage international d'études humanistes, Tours, 1969* ed J.-C. Margolin
     (Paris/Toronto 1972) 2 vols II 829–36
Crahay, Roland *Editions anciennes d'Erasme: Exposition du cinquième centenaire de la naissance
     d'Erasme* (Bibliothèque centrale universitaire de Mons 1967) exhibition catalogue
–   'Un manifeste religieux d'anticulture: le *De incertitudine et vanitate scientiarum et artium* de
     Corneille Agrippe' in *Acta conventus neo-Latini Turonensis ... 6–10 September 1976* ed J.-C.
     Margolin (Paris 1980) 2 vols II 889–94
Cuspinianus, Johannes *Briefwechsel* ed Hans Ankwicz von Kleehoven (Munich 1933)
Cytowska, Maria 'Erasme de Rotterdam et Marsile Ficin son maître' *Eos* 63 (1975) 165–79
–   'Erasme de Rotterdam, traducteur d'Homère' *Eos* 63 (1975) 341–53
Dalton, Hermann *Lasciana [Denkschriften und Briefe], nebst den ältesten evangelischen Synodal-
     protokollen Polens, 1555–1561* (Berlin 1898; repr Nieuwkoop 1973)
d'Amico, John F. *Renaissance Humanism in Papal Rome* (Baltimore/London 1983)
van Damme, Daniel *Ephéméride illustrée de la vie d'Erasme* (Anderlecht 1936)
Debongnie, Pierre *Jean Mombaer de Bruxelles, abbé de Livry: Ses écrits et ses réformes* (Louvain/
     Toulouse 1927)
Dekkers, R. *Het humanisme en de rechtswetenschap in de Nederlanden* (Antwerp 1938)
Delaruelle, Louis 'Notes biographiques sur Nicole Bérauld, suivies d'une bibliographie de ses oeuvres
     et de ses publications' *Revue des bibliothèques* 12 (1902) 420–45
Delhaye, P. 'Une adaptation du *De officiis* au XIIᵉ siècle: Le *Moralium dogma philosophorum*'
     Recherches de théologie ancienne et mediévale 16 (1949) 227–58
Deutscher Gesamtkatalog ... herausgegeben von der Preussischen Staatsbibliothek (Berlin 1931–)
Dictionary of National Biography (London 1885–1901; repr 1949–50) 63 vols
Dictionnaire de biographie française (Paris 1929–)
Dictionnnaire de spiritualité ascetique et mystique (Paris 1932–95)
Dictionnnaire de théologie catholique (Paris 1908–)
Dilg, Peter 'Die botanische Kommentarlitteratur Italiens um 1500 und ihr Einfluss auf Deutschland'
     in *Der Kommentar in der Renaissance* ed August Buck and Otto Herding (Bonn/Bad Godesberg
     1975) 225–52
Dilke, O.R.W. *The Roman Land Surveyors* (Newton Abbot 1971)
*Dionysiaca: receuil donnant l'ensemble des traductions latines des ouvrages attribués au Denys
     de l'Aréopage* (Paris/Bruges 1937) 2 vols
Dizionario biografico degli Italiani (Rome 1960–)
Dolfen, C. *Die Stellung des Erasmus von Rotterdam zur scholastischen Methode* (Osnabrück 1936)
Doucet, R. *Les bibliothèques parisiennes au XVIᵉ siècle* (Paris 1956)
Douglas, R.M. *Jacopo Sadoleto 1477–1547: Humanist and Reformer* (Cambridge, Mass 1959)
Draguet, R. 'Le maître louvaniste Driedo inspirateur du decret de Trente sur la Vulgate' in
     Miscellanea historica in honorem Alberti de Meyer (Louvain/Brussels 1946) 2 vols II 836–54
[Dürer, Albrecht] *Albrecht Dürer 1471–1971* Ausstellung des Germanischen Nationalmuseums
     Nürnberg 21 Mai bis 1 August 1971 (Munich 1971) exhibition catalogue
Eck, Johannes *Enchiridion locorum communium adversus Lutherum et alios hostes Ecclesiae
     (1525–1543)* ed Pierre Fraenkel, Corpus Catholicorum 34 (Münster 1979)
Eck, Simon Thaddäus *Tres orationes funebres in exequiis Joannis Eckii habitae* ed J. Metzler,
     Corpus Catholicorum 16 (Münster 1930)
Eisenstein, Elizabeth L. *The Printing Press As an Agent of Change: Communications and Cultural
     Transformations in Early Modern Europe* (Cambridge/New York 1979) 2 vols
Elsman, T. 'Albert Rizäus Hardenberg und Johann Molanus in Bremen' in *Wessel Gansfort
     (1419–1489) and Northern Humanism* ed F. Akkerman, G.C. Huisman, and A.J. Vanderjagt,
     Brill's Studies in Intellectual History 40 (Leiden/New York 1993) 195–209
Enciclopedia italiana (Milan 1929–39) 36 vols incl index; supplements 1938–

Encyclopaedia Judaica (Jerusalem 1971) 16 vols
Encyclopedia of the Renaissance ed Paul F. Grendler (New York 1999) 6 vols
Engels, M.H.H. *Auteurs in de bibliotheek van Erasmus: De zogenaamde verzendlijst op persoonsnamen gerangschikt* (Leeuwarden 1997)
– *Catalogus van incunabelen van de Provinciale Bibliotheek van Friesland te Leeuwarden* (Leeuwarden 1977)
– 'Erasmiana in de Franeker academiebibliotheek' in *De vrije Fries* 59 (Leeuwarden 1979) 65–72
– 'Erasmiana in the Old University Library of Franeker' *Erasmus in English* 12 (1983) 19–20
– *Erasmus' handexemplaren: Vijf Griekse Aldijnen in de Franeker collectie van de Provinciale Bibliotheek van Friesland te Leeuwarden* 2nd enlarged ed (Leeuwarden 1994)
– *Olim Erasmi: Homerus en Hesychius uit de bibliotheek van Erasmus in Friesland & Brief van Praedinius over Erasmiana* (Leeuwarden 1997)
– 'Vroeger eigendom van Erasmus' *De Vrije Fries* 80 (2000) 55–80
Epistolarum ab illustribus et claris viris scriptarum centuriae tres coll et ed Simon Abbes Gabbema (Harlingen 1663)
Erasmus and Cambridge: The Cambridge Letters of Erasmus ed H.C. Porter and trans D.F.S. Thomson (Toronto 1963)
Erasmus *Ausgewählte Schriften lateinisch und deutsch* ed Werner Welzig (Darmstadt 1967–80) 8 vols
Erasmus [translated from Latin by le chevalier de Berquin] *Brefve admonition de la manière de prier; Le Symbole des apostres de Jesuchrist [1525]* ed with introduction and notes Emile V. Telle (Geneva 1979)
Erasmus *The Colloquies of Erasmus* trans Craig R. Thompson (Chicago/London 1965)
Erasmus [translated from Latin by le chevalier de Berquin] *La complainte de la paix* ed with introduction and notes Emile V. Telle (Geneva 1978)
Erasmus *Delamatio de pueris statim ac liberaliter instituendis* ed with translation and commentary by J.-C. Margolin (Geneva 1966)
Erasmus [translated from Latin by Louis de Berquin] *Déclamation des louenges de marriage, 1525* ed with introduction and notes Emile V. Telle (Geneva 1976)
Erasmus: Tentoonstelling van Erasmusdrukken bewaard in de Universiteitsbibliotheek te Gent … 4–20 juni 1969 (Ghent 1969) exhibition catalogue
Erasmus en Leuven. See Nauwelaerts, M.A.
Erasmus en zijn tijd Tentoonstelling ingericht ter herdenking van de geboorte, 500 jaar geleden, van Erasmus te Rotterdam in de nacht van 27 op 28 oktober, ed J.C. Ebbinge Wubben et al (Rotterdam 1969) 2 vols (exhibition catalogue)
Erasmus von Rotterdam, Vorkämpfer für Frieden und Toleranz Ausstellung zum 450. Todestag des Erasmus von Rotterdam veranstaltet vom Historischen Museum Basel [26 april bis 7 september 1986] (Basel 1986) exhibition catalogue
Erbse, Hartmut *Scholia graeca in Homeri Iliadem (scholia vetera)* (Berlin 1969)
Essays on the Life and Works of Thomas Linacre ed Francis Maddison, Margaret Pelling, and Charles Webster (Oxford 1977)
Etter, E.L. *Tacitus in der Geistesgeschichte des 16. und 17. Jahrhunderts* (Basel/Stuttgart 1966)
Farge, James K. 'Les procès de Louis de Berquin: Episodes dans la lutte du Parlement de Paris contre l'absolutisme royal' *Histoire et Archives* 18 (2005) 49–77
– *Religion, Reformation, and Repression in the Reign of Francis i: Documents from the Parlement of Paris, 1515–1547* ed with introduction and annotation (Toronto 2015) 2 vols
Febvre, Lucien 'Un secrétaire d'Erasme: Gilbert Cousin et la Réforme en Franche-Comté' *Bulletin de la société de l'histoire du protestantisme français* 56 (1907) 97–148
Febvre, Lucien and Henri-Jean Martin *L'apparition du livre* (Paris 1958; repr 1971)/*The Coming of the Book: The Impact of Printing, 1450–1800* tr David Gerard, ed Geoffrey Nowell-Smith and David Wooton (London 1976; repr 1994, 2010)
Feld, H. 'Der Humanisten-streit um Hebräer 2,7 (Psalm 8,6)' *Archiv für Reformationsgeschichte* 61 (1970) 5–35

Finsler, Georg *Zwingli-Bibliographie: Verzeichnis der gedruckten Schriften von und über Ulrich Zwingli* (Zürich 1897; repr Nieuwkoop 1962)

Firmin-Didot, A. *Alde Manuce et l'hellénisme à Venise* (Paris 1875)

Fokke, Gerard J. *Christus verae pacis auctor et unicus scopus: Erasmus and Origen* (Leuven 1977) 3 vols

Fraenkel, Pierre 'Erste Studien zur Druckgeschichte von Johannes Ecks "Enchiridion locorum communium"' *Bibliothèque d'Humanisme et Renaissance* 29 (1967) 649–78

La France protestante (Paris, Bibliothèque nationale) exhibition catalogue

Freudenberger, T. *Augustinus Steuchus aus Gubbio, Augustinerchorherr und päpstlicher Bibliothekar, 1497–1548, und sein literarisches Lebenswerk* (Münster 1935)

Fueter, Eduard *Geschichte der neueren Historiographie* 2nd ed (Munich 1925)

Gabbema, S. See *Epistolarum ... centuriae tres*

Ganz, P. and Major, E. *Die Entstehung des Amerbachschen Kunstkabinetts und die Amerbachschen Inventare* (Basel 1907)

de la Garanderie, Marie-Madeleine 'Comment parler couramment le latin: un dialogue de Nicolas Bérault (1534)' in *Acta conventus neo-Latini Turonensis ... 6–10 September 1976* ed J.-C. Margolin (Paris 1980) 2 vols I 481–93

– 'Les relations d'Erasme avec Paris au temps de son séjour aux Pays-Bas méridioneaux (1516–1521)' in *Scrinium Erasmianum: Mélanges historiques publiés ... à l'occasion du cinquième centenaire de la naissance d'Erasme* ed J. Coppens (Leiden 1969) 2 vols I 29–54

Garrod, H.W. 'Erasmus and His English Patrons' *The Library* 5th series, 4 (1949) 1–13

Gauthier, R.A. 'Les deux récensions du Moralium dogma philosophorum' *Revue du Moyen-Age Latin* 9 (1953) 170–260

Gavin, J. Austin and Thomas M. Walsh 'The *Praise of Folly* in Context: The Commentary of Gerardus Listrius' *Renaissance Quarterly* 24 (1971) 193–209

Geanakoplos, D.J. 'The Discourse of Demetrios Chalcondyles on the Inauguration of Greek Studies at the University of Padua in 1463' *Studies in the Renaissance* 21 (1974) 118–44

– *Greek Scholars in Venice* (Cambridge, Mass 1962)

Gebhardt, Bruno *Adrian von Corneto* (Breslau 1856)

Gebhardt, Oskar von 'Hieronymus *De viris inlustribus* in Griechischer Übersetsung (der sogenannte Sophronius)' in *Texte und Untersuchungen der altchristlichen Literatur* 14 (1896) 1–62

Gedenkschrift zum 400. Todestage des Erasmus von Rotterdam ed Historische und Antiquarische Gesellschaft zu Basel (Basel 1936)

Geiger, Ludwig *Johann Reuchlin: sein Leben und seine Werke* (Leipzig 1871; repr 1964)

Gerlo, A. 'L'*Opus de conscribendis epistolis*' *Colloquia Erasmiana Turonensia: Douzième stage international d'études humanistes, Tours, 1969* ed J.-C. Margolin (Paris/Toronto 1972) 2 vols I 223–32

– 'The *Opus de Conscribendis Epistolis* of Erasmus and the tradition of the *ars epistolica*' in *Classical Influences on European Culture A.D. 500–1500: Proceedings of an International Conference Held at King's College, Cambridge, April 1969* ed R.R. Bolgar (Cambridge 1971) 103–14

Gerson, Jean *Oeuvres complètes* ed Mgr Palémon Glorieux (Paris 1960–74) 10 vols in 11

Geyer, B. *Die patristische und scholastische Philosophie* (Berlin 1928)

de Ghellinck J. *Patristique et moyen âge* (Gembloux 1946–8) 3 vols

Gibson, R.W. *St Thomas More: A Preliminary Bibliography of His Works and of Moreana to the Year 1750* (New Haven 1961)

Gilbert, Felix 'Biondo, Sabellico and the Beginnings of Venetian Historiography' in *Florilegium historiale. Essays Presented to Wallace K. Ferguson* (Toronto 1971) 276–93

Gilmore, M.P. 'Erasmus and Alberto Pio, Prince of Carpi' in *Action and Conviction in Early Modern Europe, Essays in Memory of E.H. Harbison* ed T.K. Rabb and J. Seigel (Princeton 1969) 299–318

– 'Italian Reactions to Erasmian Humanism' in *Itinerarium Italicum: The Profile of the Italian Renaissance in the Mirror of its European Transformations* ed. H.A. Oberman and T.A. Brady, Jr (Leiden 1975) 61–115

– 'Les limites de la tolérance dans l'oeuvre polémique d'Erasme' in *Colloquia Erasmiana Turonensia: Douzième stage international d'études humanistes, Tours, 1969* ed J.-C. Margolin (Paris/Toronto 1972) 2 vols II 713–36

Glorieux, P. 'Le moralium dogma philosophorum et son auteur' *Recherches de théologie ancienne et médiévale* 15 (1948) 360–6

Godin, A. 'Erasme et le modèle origénien de la prédication' in *Colloquia Erasmiana Turonensia: Douzième stage international d'études humanistes, Tours, 1969* ed J.-C. Margolin (Paris/Toronto 1972) 2 vols II 807–19

– *Erasme lecteur d'Origène* (Geneva 1982)

– 'Jean Vitrier et le "cenacle" de Saint-Omer' in *Colloquia Erasmiana Turonensia: Douzième stage international d'études humanistes, Tours, 1969* ed J.-C. Margolin (Paris/Toronto 1972) 2 vols II 781–805

Goethe, Johann Wolfgang von *Zur Farbenlehre* (Tübingen 1810) 2 vols

Goff, R.R. *Incunabula in American Libraries: A Third Census* (New York 1973)

Goldschmidt, E.P. *Medieval Texts and Their First Appearance in Print* (Oxford 1943)

Graesse, J.G.T. *Trésor des livres rares et précieux* (Dresden 1859–69) 7 vols

Greitemann, N.T.J. 'Erasmus als exegeet' *Studia Catholica* 12 (1936) 294–305, 365–87

Grimm, Heinrich 'Die Buchführer des deutschen Kulturbereichs und ihre Niederlassungsorte in der Zeitspanne 1490 bis um 1550' *Archiv für die Geschichte des Buchwesens* 7 (1965–6) 1153–1772

– *Deutsche Buchdruckersignete des XVI. Jahrhunderts: Geschichte, Sinngehalt und Gestaltung kleiner Kulturdokumente* (Wiesbaden 1965)

Groner, J.F. *Kardinal Cajetan* (Fribourg 1951)

Gumbert, P. 'Over karthuizerbibliotheken in de Nederlanden' in *Studies over het boekenbezit en boekengebruik in de Nederlanden vóór 1600 = Archief-en Bibliotheekwezen in België* extra no 11 (Brussels 1974) 159–86

Gutmann, Elsbeth *Die Colloquia familiaria des Erasmus von Rotterdam* (Basel/Stuttgart 1968)

Hajdukiewicz, Leszek 'Im Bücherkreis des Erasmus' *Studia i Materialy z Dziejów Nauki Polskiej Seria D: Historia Techniki i Nauk Technicznych* (*Studies and Materials for the History of Polish Science* Series D: *History of Technology and Technical Sciences*) 5/2 (1960) 49–102

Hale, David G. 'Aesop in Renaissance England' *The Library* 5th series, 27 (1972) 116–25

Halkin, Léon-E. 'Une édition rarissime des Apologies d'Erasme en 1521' *Bibliothèque d'Humanisme et Renaissance* 45 (1983) 343–8.

– *Erasmus ex Erasmo: Erasme éditeur de sa correspondance* (Aubel 1983)

Hall, Basil *John a Lasco, a Pole in Reformation England* (London 1971)

Hartfelder, K. *Philip Melanchthon als Praeceptor Germaniae* (Berlin 1889)

Heath, M.J. 'Erasmus and the War against the Turks' *Acta conventus neo-Latini Turonensis ... 6–10 September 1976* ed J.-C. Margolin (Paris 1980) 2 vols II 991–9

von Heinemann, Otto *Die Handschriften der herzoglichen Bibliothek zu Wolfenbüttel* part 4: *Die Gudischen Handschriften* IX (Wolfenbüttel 1913)

Heinimann, F. 'Zu den Anfängen der humanistischen Paroemiologie' in *Catalepton: Festschrift für Bernhard Wyss* ed Christoph Schäublin (Basel 1985)

Heller, H. 'The Evangelicism of Lefèvre d'Etaples' *Studies in the Renaissance* 19 (1982) 42–77

– 'Marguerite of Navarre and the Reformers of Meaux' *Bibliothèque d'Humanisme et Renaissance* 33 (1971) 271–310

Helwig, Hellmuth *Das deutsche Buchbinder-Handwerk: Handwerks- und Kulturgeschichte* (Stuttgart 1962–5) 2 vols

Hennig, G. *Cajetan und Luther: ein historischer Beitrag zur Begegnung von Thomismus und Reformation* (Stuttgart 1966)

Herding, Otto 'Isokrates, Erasmus und die *Institutio principis Christiani*' in *Im Dauer und Wandel der Geschichte ... Festgabe für Kurt von Raumer zum 15. Dezember 1965* ed Rudolf Vierhaus and Manfred Botzenhart (Münster 1966) 101–43

Hirsch, E.F. *Damião de Gois* ('s-Gravenhage 1967)

Hirsch, Rudolf *Printing, Selling and Reading, 1450–1550* (Wiesbaden 1967)

Hoefer, J.C.F. *Nouvelle biographie générale* (Paris 1852–66) 46 vols

Holeczek, Heinz *Erasmus Deutsch I: Die volkssprachliche Rezeption des Erasmus von Rotterdam in der reformatorischen Öffentlichkeit 1519–1536* (Stuttgart 1983)

– *Humanistische Bibelphilologie als Reformproblem bei Erasmus von Rotterdam, Thomas More und William Tyndale* (Leiden 1975)

Holfelder, Hans Hermann *Tentatio et consolatio: Studien zu Bugenhagens 'Interpretatio in librum psalmorum'* (Berlin/New York 1974)

Horawitz, A. *Die Bibliothek und Correspondenz des Beatus Rhenanus zu Schlettstadt* (Vienna 1874)

ter Horst, D.J.H. 'Een boek uit de bibliotheek van Erasmus teruggevonden' *Het Boek* 24 (1936–7) 64–70

– 'Nog enkele aanteekeningen over de bibliotheek van Erasmus' *Het Boek* 24 (1936–7) 229–34

Horst, U. 'Der Streit um die hl. Schrift zwischen Cajetan und Ambrosius Catharinus' in *Wahrheit und Verkündigung: Michael Schmaus zum 70. Geburtstag* ed Leo Scheffczyk, Werner Dettloff, and Richard Heinzmann (Munich/Paderborn/Vienna 1967) 2 vols I 551–77

Hoyoux, Jean *Le carnet de voyage de Jérome Aléandre en France et à Liège (1510–1516)* (Brussels/Rome 1969)

Hufstader, Anselm 'Lefèvre d'Etaples and the Magdalen' *Studies in the Renaissance* 16 (1969) 31–60

Hughes, P.E. *Lefèvre: Pioneer of Ecclesiastical Renewal in France* (Grand Rapids, MI 1984)

Huisman, Gerda C. *Rudolph Agricola: A Bibliography of Printed Works and Translations* Bibliotheca bibliographica Neerlandica 20 (Nieuwkoop 1985)

Huizinga, Johan *Erasmus* Verzamelde Werken VI (Haarlem 1924) / trans F. Hopman (New York and London 1924); repr *Erasmus of Rotterdam* (London 1952) and *Erasmus and the Age of Reformation* (New York 1957) with a selection from the letters of Erasmus. References are cited from the reprint.

Hunt, R.W. 'Greek Manuscripts in the Bodleian Library from the Collection of John Stojković of Ragusa' in *Studia patristica VII–IX: Papers Presented to the Fourth International Conference on Patristic Studies Held at Christ Church, Oxford, 1963* ed F.L. Cross, Texte und Untersuchungen zur Geschichte der altchristlichen Literatur 92–4 (Berlin 1966) VII/92 75–82

Husner, Fritz 'Die Bibliothek des Erasmus' in *Gedenkschrift zum 400. Todestage des Erasmus von Rotterdam* ed Historische und Antiquarische Gesellschaft zu Basel (Basel 1936) 228–59

– 'Die Handschrift der Scholien des Erasmus von Rotterdam zu den Hieronymusbriefen' in *Festschrift Gustav Binz* (Basel 1935) 132–46

Hutton, James *The Greek Anthology in France and the Latin Writers of the Netherlands till the Year 1500* Studies in Classical Philology 28 (Ithaca, NY 1946)

– *The Greek Anthology in Italy to the Year 1800* (Ithaca, NY 1935)

Hyma, Albert *The Youth of Erasmus* (Ann Arbor 1930)

Indestege, L. 'Een band teruggevonden uit het bezit van de Antwerpse humanist Peter Gilles' *De Gulden Passer* 33 (1955) 27–35

Indice biografico Italiano compiled by Tommaso Nappo and Paolo Noto (Munich/New York 1993) 4 vols; 2nd ed (Munich 1997) 7 vols

Isaac, Franc *An Index to the Early Printed Books in the British Museum, Part 2: MDI–MDXX, Section 2: Italy, Section 3: Switzerland, Eastern Europe* (London 1938)

Jacob, André 'L'édition "érasmienne" de la liturgie de saint Jean Chrysostom et ses sources' *Italia medioevale e umanistica* 19 (1976) 291–324

Janauschek, L. *Bibliographia Bernardina* (Hildesheim 1959)

Jardine, Lisa 'Distinctive Discipline: Rudolph Agricola's Influence on Methodical Thinking in the Humanities' in *Rodolphus Agricola Phrisius, 1444–1485: Procedings of the International Conference at the University of Groningen 28–30 October 1985* ed F. Akkerman and A.J. Vanderjagt, Brill's Studies in Intellectual Hisory 6 (Leiden/New York 1988) 38–57

– 'Humanism and Dialectic in Sixteenth Century Cambridge' in *Classical Influences on European Culture, A.D. 1500–1700* ed R.R. Bolgar (Cambridge 1971) 141–54

– 'The Place of Dialectic Teaching in Sixteenth-Century Cambridge' *Studies in the Renaissance* 21 (1974) 31–62

Jedin, Hubert *Des Johannes Cochläus Streitschriften De libero arbitrio hominis (1525): Ein Beitrag zur Geschichte der vortridentinischen Theologie* inaugural dissertation (Breslau 1927)

Joachimsen, P. 'Tacitus im deutschen Humanismus' *Neue Jahrbücher für das klassische Altertum, Geschichte und deutsche Literatur und für Pädagogik* year 14 vol 27 (Leipzig 1911) 697–717

Jöcher, C.G. *Allgemeines Gelehrten-Lexicon* (Leipzig 1750–1; repr Hildesheim 1960–1) 4 vols

de Jonge, H.J. 'Aantekeningen van Erasmus in een exemplaar van zijn Apologiae omnes (1522)' *Nederlands Archief voor Kerkgeschiedenis* 58/2 (1978) 176–89

– 'The Date and Purpose of Erasmus' *Castigatio Novi Testamenti*: A Note on the Origins of the *Novum Instrumentum*' in *The Uses of Greek and Latin: Historical Essays* ed A.C. Dionisotti, Anthony Grafton, and Jill Kraye (London 1988) 97–110

– 'Erasmus und die Glossa Ordinaria zum Neuen Testament' *Nederlands Archief voor Kerkgeschiedenis* 56/1 (1975) 51–77

– 'The Relationship of Erasmus' Translation of the New Testament to That of the Pauline Epistles by Lefèvre d'Etaples' *Erasmus in English* 15 (1987–8) 2–7

Jovy, Ernest *François Tissard et Jérôme Aléandre: Contribution à l'histoire des origines des études grecques en France* (Vitry le François 1899–1913; repr Geneva 1971) 3 vols

Jürgens, Henning P. *Johannes a Lasco: Ein Leben in Büchern und Briefen. Eine Ausstellung der Johannes a Lasco Bibliothek vom 15.10 bis 28.11.1999* (Wuppertal 1999) exhibition catalogue

Ker, N.R. 'Oxford College Libraries in the Sixteenth Century' *Bodleian Library Record* 6 (1957–61) 459–515

Keuning, Johannes 'The History of Geographic Map Projections until 1600' *Imago Mundi* 12 (1955) 1–24

Kibre, Pearl *The Library of Pico della Mirandola* (New York 1936)

Kisch, Guido *Gestalten und Probleme aus Humanismus und Jurisprudenz: Neue Studien und Texte* (Berlin 1969)

– *Zasius und Reuchlin: Eine rechtsgeschichtlich-vergleichende Studie zum Toleranzproblem in 16. Jahrhundert* (Constance 1961)

Kline, Michael B. *Rabelais and the Age of Printing* (Geneva 1963)

Knaake, Joachim Karl Friedrich *Bibliothek J.K.F. Knaake: Katalog der Sammlung von Reformations- schriften des Begründers der Weimarer Lutherausgabe* (Leipzig 1906–7; repr Nieuwkoop 1960)

Knepper, Joseph *Jakob Wimpfeling (1450–1528): Sein Leben und seine Werke nach den Quellen dargestellt* (Freiburg 1902; repr Nieuwkoop 1965)

Knod, Gustav C. *Aus der Bibliothek des Beatus Rhenanus* (Schlettstadt 1889)

Knös, Börje *Un ambassadeur de l'hellénisme: Janus Lascaris et la tradition gréco-byzantine dans l'humanisme français* (Uppsala 1945)

– *L'histoire de la littérature néo-grècque, la période jusqu'en 1821* (Stockholm 1962)

Koch, A.C.F. *The Year of Erasmus' Birth and Other Contributions to the Chronology of his Life* (Utrecht 1969)

Köhler, Walther *Huldrych Zwingli* 2nd ed (Stuttgart 1952; rev Ernst Koch Zürich 1984). References are cited from the 1952 edition.

– *Zwingli und Luther: Ihr Streit über das Abendmahl nach seinen politischen und religiösen Beziehungen* I: *Die religiöse und politische Entwicklung bis zum Marburger Religionsgespräch 1529* (Leipzig 1924; repr New York/London 1971)

Kolker, J. *Alardus Aemstelredamus en Cornelius Crocus* (Nijmegen/Utrecht 1963)

Kossmann, F. 'Sporen van Erasmus hand en een afbeelding van den god Terminus' *Het Boek* 24 (1936–7) 59–63

Kramm, H. *Deutsche Bibliotheken unter dem Einfluss von Humanismus und Reformation* (Leipzig 1938)

Kraus, H.P. *Catalogue 83: Incunabula & post-incunabula, 1466–1520* (New York [1955])

Krause, Carl *Helius Eobanus Hessus: Sein Leben und seine Werke* (Gotha 1879; repr Nieuwkoop 1963) 2 vols

Krautter, Konrad *Theologische Methode und humanistische Existenz: Filippo Beroaldo und sein Kommentar zum Goldenen Esel des Apuleius* (Munich 1971)

Krebs, Manfred 'Reuchlins Beziehungen zu Erasmus von Rotterdam' in *Johannes Reuchlin 1455– 1522: Festgabe seiner Vaterstadt Pforzheim zur 500. Wiederkehr seines Geburtstages* ed Manfred Krebs (Pforzheim 1955) 139–55

Kristeller, P.O. 'Erasmus from an Italian Perspective' *Renaissance Quarterly* 23 (1970) 1–14

– 'A Little-known Letter of Erasmus, and the Date of His Encounter with Reuchlin' in *Florilegium historiale: Essays Presented to Wallace K. Ferguson*, ed. J.G. Rose and W.H. Stockdale (Toronto 1971) 52–61

Kronenberg, M.E. 'Albertus Pighius, proost van sint Jan te Utrecht, zijn geschriften en zijn bibliotheek' *Het Boek* 28 (1944–6) 107–58, 226

Krüger, F. *Bucer und Erasmus: Eine Untersuchung zum Einfluss des Erasmus auf die Theologie Martin Bucers* (Wiesbaden 1970)

Labarre, Albert *Bibliographie du Dictionnaire d'Ambrogio Calepino (1502–1779)* (Baden-Baden 1975)

– *Historie du livre* (Paris 1970)

Lauchert, F. *Die italienischen literarischen Gegner Luthers* (Freiburg im Breisgau 1922; repr Nieuwkoop 1972)

Lawton, H.W. *Térence en France au XVIe siècle* (Paris 1926)

Lebègue, Raymond 'Rabelais, the Last of the French Erasmians' *Journal of the Warburg and Courtauld Institutes* 12 (1949) 91–100

Lefèvre, P. 'Martin Davidts, un ami d'Erasme à Bruxelles' *Ephemerides Theologicae Lovanienses* 42 (1966) 628–36

Lehmann, Paul *Johannes Sichardus und die von ihm benutzten Bibliotheken und Handschriften* (München 1911)

Le Long, J. and C.F. Boerner, cont A.B. Masch *Bibliotheca Sacra* II (Halle 1781)

Lemke, A. *Aldus Manutius and His Thesaurus Cornucopiae* (Syracuse, NY 1958)

Lenhart, J.M. *Pre-Reformation Printed Books* (New York 1935)

Levi, A.H.T. 'The Neoplatonist Calculus: The Exploitation of Neoplatonist Themes in French Renaissance Literature' in *Humanism in France at the End of the Middle Ages and in the Early Renaissance* ed A.H.T. Levi (Manchester 1970) 229–48

Lewicka-Kamińska, Anna 'Erazm z Roterdamu w Polsce katalog wystawy w Bibliotec Jagiellońskiej' in *Erasmia Cracoviensia w scolecie wrodzin Erazmu z Roterdamu* (Cracow 1971) 103–24

Lexikon für Theologie und Kirche (Freiburg 1930–8); 2nd edition (Freiburg 1957–68) 14 vols

Lezius, F. 'Der Verfasser des pseudo-cyprianischen Traktates de duplici martyrio' in *Neue Jahrbücher für deutsche Theologie* 4 (1895) 95–110 and 184–243

Libri appendiciarii Bibliothecae Scriverianae ... quae auctione publica distribuentur [8] August 1663 (Amsterdam: S. van Lier 1663)

Linacre Studies: Essays on the Life and Work of Thomas Linacre ed. F. Maddison, M. Pelling, and C. Webster (Oxford 1977)

Lourdaux, W. *Moderne devotie en christelijk humanisme* (Leuven 1967)

Lowry, M.J.C. *The World of Aldus Manutius: Business and Scholarship in Renaissance Venice* (Oxford 1979)

Luchsinger, F. *Der Basler Buchdruck als Vermittler italienischen Geistes 1470–1529* (Basel 1953)

Mack, Peter *Renaissance Argument: Valla and Agricola in the Tradition of Rhetoric and Dialectic* Brill's Studies in Intellectual History 43 (Leiden/New York 1993)

Maffei, Domenico *Allessandro d' Alessandro, giureconsulto umanista (1461–1523)* (Milan 1956)

Maguire, John B. 'Erasmus' Biographical Masterpiece: *Hieronymi Stridonensis vita*' *Renaissance Quarterly* 26 (1973) 265–73

Major, Emil *Erasmus von Rotterdam* (Basel 1926)

Mani, Nicolaus 'Die griechische Editio princeps des Galenos (1525), ihre Entstehung und ihre Wirkung' *Gesnerus* 13 (1956) 29–52

Mansfield, Bruce *Phoenix of His Age: Interpretations of Erasmus c. 1550–1750* (Toronto 1979)

Margolin, J.-C. 'Le cercle humaniste lyonnais d'après l'édition des *Epigrammata* (1537) de Jean Visagier' in *Actes du Colloque sur l'humanisme lyonnais au XVIe siècle, mai 1972* (Grenoble 1974) 151–83

– 'Le "Chant alpestre" d'Erasme: Poème sur la vieillesse' *Bibliothèque d'Humanisme et Renaissance* 27 (1965) 37–79 ; repr in his *Erasme dans son miroir et dans son sillage* (London 1987) article I

– 'Duns Scot et Erasme' in *Regnum hominis et regnum Dei: Acta quarti congressus Scotistici internationalis* ed Camille Bérubé (Rome 1978) 89–112

- 'Erasme commentateur de Boèce: L'adage "Double diapason"' *Latomus* 26 (1967) 165–94
- 'Erasme et Athénée' in *From Wolfram and Petrarch to Goethe and Grass: Studies in Literature in Honour of Leonard Forster* ed D.H. Green, L.P. Johnson, and Dieter Wuttke (Baden-Baden 1982) 213–47
- 'Erasme et Mnémosyne' in his *Recherches érasmiennes* (Geneva 1969) 70–84
- 'Henri Glaréan–Oswald Myconius (1517–1524)' in *La correspondance d'Erasme et l'epistolographie humaniste: Colloque international tenu en novembre 1983* (Brussels 1985)
- 'Łaski lecteur et annotateur du "Nouveau Testament" d'Erasme' in *Scrinium Erasmianum: Mélanges historiques publiés ... à l'occasion du cinquième centenaire de la naissance d'Erasme* ed J. Coppens (Leiden 1969) 2 vols I 93–128

[Martens, Dirk] *Tentoonstelling Dirk Martens 1473–1973* (Aalst 1973) exhibition catalogue

Massa, Eugenio 'Intorno ad Erasmo: Una polemica che si credeva perduta' in *Classical, Mediaeval and Renaissance Studies in Honour of Berthold Louis Ullman* ed Charles Henderson (Rome 1964) 2 vols II 435–54

Massaut, Jean-Pierre *Critique et tradition à la veille de la Réforme en France* (Paris 1974)
- 'Erasme et Saint Thomas' *Colloquia Erasmiana Turonensia: Douzième stage international d'études humanistes, Tours, 1969* ed J.-C. Margolin (Paris/Toronto 1972) 2 vols II 581–612
- *Josse Clichtove, l'humanisme et la réforme du clergé séculier* (Paris 1968) 2 vols

Maurer, W. *Der junge Melanchthon zwischen Humanismus und Reformation* (Göttingen 1967–9) 2 vols
- *Melanchthon-Studien* (Gütersloh 1964)
- 'Reste des kanonischen Rechtes im Frühprotestantismus' *Zeitschrift der Savigny-Stiftung für Rechtsgeschichte* 82, kanonistische Abteilung 51 (1965) 190–253

McConica, James Kelsey *English Humanists and Reformation Politics under Henry VIII and Edward VI* (Oxford 1965)
- 'Erasmus in Amsterdam and Toronto' in *Editing Texts from the Age of Erasmus* ed Erika Rummel (Toronto/Buffalo/London 1996) 81–100

Meeldijk, E. 'Egbertus van Gulik' in *Jaarboek van de Maatschappij der Nederlandse Letterkunde te Leiden 2000–2001* (Leiden 2002) 77–88

Meine, Karl-Heinz *Die Ulmer Geographia des Ptolemäus von 1482: zur 500. Wiederkehr der ersten Atlasdrucklegung nördlich der Alpen* (Ulm 1982) exhibition catalogue

Metzger, Bruce M. *The Text of the New Testament: Its Transmission, Corruption and Restoration* 2nd ed (Oxford 1968)

Metzler, J. *See* Eck, Simon Thaddäus

Miaskowski, Kasimir von *Erasmiana: Die Korrespondenz des Erasmus von Rotterdam mit Polen* I (Posen 1901) and II (Paderborn 1901), originally published in *Jahrbuch für Philosophie und spekulative Theologie* 14 (1900) 331–41 and 15 (1901) 105–24, 195–226, 307–60

Mohlberg, L.C. *Katalog der Handschriften der Zentralbibliothek Zürich I: Mittelalterliche Handschriften* (Zürich 1951–)

Möller, W.E. *Andreas Osiander: Leben und ausgewahlte Schriften* (Elberfeld 1870; repr Nieuwkoop 1965)

Mombello, G. 'Rabelais lecteur de Lorenzo Abstemio?' in *Actes du colloque sur l'humanisme lyonnais au XVIe siècle, mai 1972* (Grenoble 1974) 63–86

Müller, Joseph T. *Geschichte der Böhmischen Brüder* (Herrnhut 1922–31) 3 vols; I (1922) 1400–1528

Muller, Jean *Bibliographie Strasbourgeoise. See* Benzing, Joseph

Muller, S. *Schetsen uit de Middeleeuwen* (Amsterdam 1900)

Munro, John H. 'The Coinages and Monetary Policies of Henry VIII (r 1509–47)' CWE 14 423–76
- 'Money and Coinage in the Age of Erasmus' CWE 1 311–47
- 'Money, Wages, and Real Incomes in the Age of Erasmus' CWE 12 551–699

Nauert, C.G. *Agrippa and the Crisis of Renaissance Thought* (Urbana 1965)

Nauwelaerts M.A. 'Erasme à Louvain: Ephémérides d'un séjour de 1517 à 1521' in *Scrinium Erasmianum: Mélanges historiques publiés ... à l'occasion du cinquième centenaire de la naissance d'Erasme* ed J. Coppens (Leiden 1969) 2 vols I 3–24
- *Rodolphus Agricola* (The Hague 1963)

– *Tentoonstelling Erasmus en Leuven* Leuven Stedelijk Museum 17 nov.–15 dec. 1969 (exhibition catalogue)

– 'Verblijf en werk van Erasmus te Leuven' *Mededelingen van de Geschied-en Oudheidkundige Kring voor Leuven en Omgeving* 9 (1969) 133–60

Neue Deutsche Biographie ed Historische Kommission bei der Bayerischen Akademie der Wissenschaften (Berlin 1953–)

Newald, Richard *Erasmus Roterodamus* (Freiburg im Breisgau 1947)

New Grove Dictionary of Music and Musicians (London 1980)

Nieuw Nederlandsch Biografisch Woordenboek ed P.C. Molhuysen et al, 2nd ed (Amsterdam 1974) 10 vols and Register

Nixon, Howard M. *Five Centuries of English Bookbinding* (London 1978)

Noreña, C.G. *Juan Luis Vives* (The Hague 1970)

Norton, F.J. *Italian Printers, 1501–1520* (London 1958)

Nouvelle biographie générale. See Hoefer, J.C.F.

Nübel, Otto *Pompejus Occo 1483 bis 1537, Fuggerfaktor in Amsterdam* (Tübingen 1972)

Olin, John C. 'Erasmus and His Edition of St Hilary' *Erasmus in English* 9 (1978) 8–11

Oppien d'Apamée *La Chasse* ed Pierre Boudreaux (Paris 1908)

Otto, Carl *Johannes Cochlaeus der Humanist* (Breslau 1874)

Pabel, Hilmar *Conversing with God: Prayer in Erasmus' Pastoral Writings* (Toronto 1997)

Pace, Richard *De fructu qui ex doctrina percipitur (The Benefit of a Liberal Education)* ed and trans F. Manley and R.S. Sylvester (New York 1967)

Parks, George B. 'Did Pole write the "Vita Longolii"?' *Renaissance Quarterly* 26 (1973) 274–85

Paulson, Johannes *Notice sur un manuscrit de Saint Jean Chrysostome utilisé par Erasme et conservé à la Bibliothèque royale de Stockholm* (Lund 1980)

Payne J.F. 'On the "Herbarium" and "Hortus sanitatis"' *Transactions of the Bibliographical Society* 6 (1900–2) 63–126

Payne, John B. 'Erasmus Interpreter of Romans' in *Sixteenth Century Essays and Studies* ed Carl S. Meyer (St Louis, MO 1970–1) 2 vols II 1–35

[Pelagius] *Pelagius's Expositions of Thirteen Epistles of St Paul* ed Alexander Souter (Cambridge 1922–31) 3 vols

Pellechet, M. *Catalogue général des incunables des bibliothèques publiques en France* (Paris 1897–1970) 26 vols

Pellegrin, Elisabeth 'Un ex-libris autographe d'Erasme dans un manuscrit de l'*opus agriculturae* de Palladius (Vat. Reg. lat. 1252)' *Scriptorium* 29 (1975) 162–6

Perosa, Alessandro 'Contributi e proposte per la pubblicazione delle opere latine del Poliziano' in *Il Poliziano ed il suo tempo: atti del IV convegno internazionale di studi sul Rinascimento ... 23–26 settembre 1954* (Florence 1957) 88–100

Petersen, Erik 'Notes on the Erasmus autograph MS Gl. Kgl. Saml. 95, 2°, with a Survey of the Letters' *Cahiers de l'Institut du Moyen Âge Grec et Latin* 54 (Copenhagen 1987) 117–28

– 'Propria manu. Om Erasmus af Rotterdams testamente og hans efterladte papirer' *Fund og Forskning i det Kongelige Biblioteks samlinger* 49 (2010) 7–56

Petitmengin, P. 'Comment étudier l'activité d'Erasme, éditeur de textes antiques?' in *Colloquia Erasmiana Turonensia: Douzième stage international d'études humanistes, Tours, 1969* ed J.-C. Margolin (Paris/Toronto 1972) 2 vols I 217–22

Pfeiffer, R. 'Die Wandlungen der *Antibarbari*' in *Gedenkschrift zum 400. Todestage des Erasmus von Rotterdam* ed Historische und Antiquarische Gesellschaft zu Basel (Basel 1936) 50–68

Phillips, P.L. and C.E. LeGear *A List of Geographical Atlases in the Library of Congress* I (Washington, DC 1909–73)

Pickering & Chatto *Catalogue 677: Sixteenth-century Books* (London 1989)

[Pliny the Younger] *Epistolarum libri decem* ed R.A.B. Mynors (Oxord 1963)

Poel, Marc van der *Cornelis Agrippa: The Humanist Theologian and His Declamationes* (Leiden/ New York/Cologne 1997)

Polain, M.-Louis *Catalogue des livres imprimés au quinzième siècle des bibliothèques de Belgique* (Brussels 1932)

[Poliziano] *Mostra del Poliziano nella Biblioteca Medicea Laurenziana ... Firenze 23 settembre–30 novembre 1954* ed Allesandro Perosa (Florence 1955) exhibition catalogue

Pollard, Graham 'Changes in the Style of Bookbinding, 1550–1830' *The Library* 5th series, 11 (1956) 71–94

Popkin, Richard H. *The History of Scepticism from Erasmus to Descartes* (Assen 1960)

Post, R.R. *The Modern Devotion: Confrontation with Reformation and Humanism* (Leiden 1968)

Potthast, August *Bibliotheca historica medii aevi* 2nd ed (Berlin 1896; repr Graz 1957) 2 vols

[Ptolemy] *Claudius Ptolemaeus: Cosmographia, Ulm 1482* Facsimile ed with introduction by R.A. Skelton (Amsterdam 1963)

Rabil, Albert, Jr *Erasmus and the New Testament: The Mind of a Christian Humanist* (San Antonio 1972)

– 'Erasmus's *Paraphrases of the New Testament*' in *Essays on the Works of Erasmus* ed R.L. DeMolen (New Haven/London 1978) 145–61

Rath, Erich von and Rudolf Juchhoff 'Buchdruck und Buchillustration bis zum Jahre 1600' in *Handbuch der Bibliothekswissenschaft* ed Georg Leyh, 2nd ed (Wiesbaden 1952–66) I 388–533

Rave, Paul Ortwin 'Paolo Giovio und die Bildnisvitenbücher des Humanismus' *Jahrbuch der Berliner Museen* 1 (1959) 119–54

Realencyklopädie für protestantische Theologie und Kirche 3rd ed (Leipzig 1896–1913) 24 vols

Reedijk, C. 'Erasme, Thierry Martens et le *Julius Exclusus*' in *Scrinium Erasmianum: Mélanges historiques publiés ... à l'occasion du cinquième centenaire de la naissance d'Erasme* ed J. Coppens (Leiden 1969) 2 vols II 351–78

– 'Erasmus' Final Modesty' in *Actes du Congrès Erasme ... Rotterdam 27–29 octobre 1969* (Amsterdam 1971) 174–92

– 'Holbeins Erasmus met de pilaster (1523) en de emblematiek' in *Driekwart eeuw historisch leven in Den Haag* (The Hague 1975) 133–50

– 'Das Lebensende des Erasmus' *Basler Zeitschrift für Geschichte und Altertumskunde* 57 (1958) 23–66

– 'The Story of a Fallacy: Erasmus' Share in the First Printed Edition in Greek of Ptolemy's Geography (Basel 1533)' in *Theatrum orbis librorum: Liber amicorum Presented to Nico Israel on the Occasion of His Seventieth Birthday* ed Ton Croiset van Uchelen, Koert van der Horst, and Günter Schilder (Utrecht 1989) 250–76

– *Tandem bona causa triumphat: Zur Geschichte des Gesamtwerks des Erasmus von Rotterdam* (Basel 1980)

– 'Three Erasmus Autographs in the Royal Library of Copenhagen' in *Studia bibliographica in honorem Herman de la Fontaine Verwey* ed S. van der Woude (Amsterdam 1966) 327–49

Reichner, Herbert *Catalogue 27* (Stockbridge, Mass)

Rénaudet, Augustin *Erasme et l'Italie* (Geneva 1954)

– *Etudes érasmiennes (1521–1529)* (Paris 1939)

– *Préréforme et humanisme à Paris pendant les premières guerres d'Italie (1494–1517)* 2nd ed (Paris 1953)

– 'Un problème historique: La pensée réligieuse de J. Lefèvre d'Etaples' in his *Humanisme et Renaissance* (Paris 1956) 201–20

Renouard, Philippe *Imprimeurs et libraires parisiens du XVIe siècle: Ouvrage publié d'après les manuscrits de Philippe Renouard* (Paris 1964[–9]) 5 vols

[Resende, André de] *L'Itinéraire érasmien d'André de Resende (1500–1573)* Textes choisis d'A. de Resende, trans and ann Odette Sauvage (Paris 1971)

Reusch, Franz Heinrich *Der Index der verbotenen Bücher* (Bonn 1883[–1885]; repr Aalen 1967) 2 vols

Rex, Richard *The Theology of John Fisher* (Cambridge 1991)

Reynolds, L.D. and N.G. Wilson *Scribes and Scholars* 2nd ed (London 1974)

van Rhijn, M. *Wessel Gansfort* (The Hague 1917)

Rhodes, D.E. *A Catalogue of Incunabula in All the Libraries of Oxford University Outside the Bodleian* (Oxford 1982)
– 'The Printing of a Group of Greek Books in Rome' *The Library* 5th series, 31 (1976) 242–4
– 'An Unidentified Edition of Galen' in *Festschrift für Claus Nissen* (Wiesbaden 1973) 575–83
Rice, Eugene F. 'Humanist Aristotelianism in France: Jacques Lefèvre d'Etaples and His Circle' in *Humanism in France at the End of the Middle Ages and in the Early Renaissance* ed A.H.T Levi (New York 1970) 132–49
– 'The Humanist Idea of Christian Antiquity: Lefèvre d'Etaples and His Circle' *Studies in the Renaissance* 9 (1962) 126–60
Riemann Musiklexikon, Personenteil I ed Hugo Riemann and Wilibald Gurlitt (Mainz 1959)
Rigo, Georges 'Un recueil de proverbes grecs utilisé par Erasme pour la rédaction des *Adagia*' *Latomus* 32 (1973) 177–84
Ritter, François 'Die Bibliothek des Erasmus, Johannes a Lasco und Gerard Mortaigne in Emden' *Upstalboomblätter für ostfriesische Geschichte, Heimatschutz und Heimatkunde* 13 (1927) 108–14
– *Catalogue des incunables et livres du xvie siècle de la Bibliothèque Municipale de Strasbourg* (Strasbourg 1948)
– *Repertoire bibliographique des livres imprimés en Alsace au xve et xvie siècles* part 2: *Répertoire bibliographique des livres du xvie siècle qui se trouvent à la Bibliothèque nationale et universitaire de Strasbourg* (Strasbourg 1937–55) 4 vols
Rix, Herbert David 'The Editions of Erasmus' *De Copia*' *Studies in Philology* 43 (1946) 595–618
Robinson, Rodney P. 'The Hersfeldensis and the Fuldensis of Ammianus Marcellinus' *The University of Missouri Studies* XI-3 (1936) 118–46
Rodgers, R.H. (ed) *Frontinus: De Aquaeductu Urbis Romae* Cambridge Classical Texts and Studies 42 (Cambridge 2004)
Rodolphus Agricola Phrisius, 1444–1485: Proceedings of the International Conference at the University of Groningen 28–30 October 1985 ed F. Akkerman and A.J. Vanderjagt, Brill's Studies in Intellectual History 6 (Leiden/New York 1988)
Ross, James Bruce 'Venetian Scholars and Teachers Fourteenth to Early Sixteenth Century: A Survey and a Study of Giovanni Battista Egnazio' *Renaissance Quarterly* 29 (1976) 521–60
Roth, Paul 'Die Wohnstätten des Erasmus in Basel' in *Gedenkschrift zum 400. Todestage des Erasmus von Rotterdam* ed Historische und Antiquarische Gesellschaft zu Basel (Basel 1936) 270–82
Rouschausse, Jean *John Fisher, éveque de Rochester, 1469–1535: sa vie et son oeuvre* (Lille 1971)
Rowan, Steven W. 'Ulrich Zasius and John Eck: "Faith need not be kept with an enemy"' *Sixteenth Century Journal* 8 (1977) 79–95
Rudberg, Stig G. 'Welche Vorlage benutzte Erasmus für seine editio princeps der Basilius-Homilien?' *Eranos* 58 (1960) 20–8
Rüdiger, H. 'Die Wiederentdeckung der antiken Literatur im Zeitalter der Renaissance' in Herbert Hunger et al *Geschichte der Textüberlieferung der antiken und mittelalterlichen Literatur* (Zürich 1961–4) 2 vols I 511–80
Rummel, Erika 'An Open Letter to Boorish Critics: Erasmus' *Capita argumentorum contra morosos quosdam ac indoctos*' *Journal of Theological Studies* 39 (1988) 438–59
Ruppel, A.C. 'Die Bücherwelt des 16. Jahrhunderts und die Frankfurter Büchermessen' in *Gedenkboek der Plantin-dagen 1555–1955*, memorial volume of the Plantin-Celebration: Internationaal Congres voor Boekdrukkunst en Humanisme, 4–10 September 1955 (Antwerp 1956) 146–66
Ruysschaert, J. 'Le manuscrit "Romae descriptum" de l'édition érasmienne d'Irénée de Lyon' in *Scrinium Erasmianum: Mélanges historiques publiés ... à l'occasion du cinquième centenaire de la naissance d'Erasme* ed J. Coppens (Leiden 1969) 2 vols I 263–76
Sandys, J.E. *A History of Classical Scholarship* (Cambridge 1906–8; repr 1958) 3 vols
Schirmer, Arno *Das Paulusverständnis Melanchthons 1518–1522* (Wiesbaden 1967)
Schmidt, C.G.A. *Histoire littéraire de l'Alsace à la fin du xve et au commencement du xvie siècle* (Paris 1879; repr Nieuwkoop/Hildesheim 1966) 2 vols
Schmidt, Philipp 'Die Bibliothek des ehemaligen Dominikanerklosters in Basel' *Basler Zeitschrift für Geschichte und Altertumskunde* 18 (1919) 160–254

Schnabel, Paul *Text und Karten des Ptolemäus* (Leipzig 1938)

Scholem, G.G. *Bibliographia kabbalistica* (Leipzig 1927)

Schottenloher, Karl *Pfalzgraf Ottheinrich und das Buch* (Münster 1927)

Schramm, Albert *Der Bilderschmuck der Frühdrücke* (Leipzig 1920–37) 20 vols

Schweiger, F.L.A. *Handbuch der classischen Bibliographie* II (Leipzig 1834); repr *Bibliographisches Lexikon der gesamten Literatur der Römer* (Amsterdam 1962) 2 parts

Screech, M.A. 'Rabelais, Erasmus, Gilbertus Cognatus and Boniface Amerbach: A Link through the Lucii Cuspidii Testamentum' *Etudes rabelaisiennes* 14 (1977) 43–6

Secret, François 'L'édition par Frobenius de la *Chrysopoeia* d'Augurelli' *Bibliothèque d'Humanisme et Renaissance* 38 (1976) 111–12

– *Les kabbalistes chrétiens de la Renaissance* (Paris 1964)

Seebass, G. *Bibliographia Osiandrica* (Nieuwkoop 1971)

Seidel-Menchi, Silvana 'Un opera misconosciuta di Erasmo? Il trattato pseudo-ciprianico De duplici martyrio' *Rivista Storia Italiana* 90 (1978) 709–43

Sicherl, M. 'Die *Editio princeps* Aldina des Euripides und ihre Vorlage' *Rheinisches Museum* 118 (1975) 205–25

– *Johannes Cuno, ein Wegbereiter des griechischen in Deutschland: Eine biographisch-kodikologische Studie* (Heidelberg 1978)

Sieber, L. *Inventarium über die Hinterlassenschaft des Erasmus vom 22. Juli 1536* [edited from Basel MS C VIA 71] (Basel 1889)

Silbernagel, Isidor *Johannes Trithemius: Eine Monographie* (Landschut 1868)

Simone, Franco 'Une entreprise oubliée des humanistes français' in *Humanism in France at the End of the Middle Ages and in the Early Renaissance* ed A.H.T. Levi (Manchester/New York 1970) 106–31

– 'Historiographie et mythographie dans la culture française du XVIe siècle: Analyse d'un texte oublié' in *Actes du colloque sur l'humanisme lyonnais au XVIe siècle, mai 1972* (Grenoble 1974) 125–48

de Smet, A. 'Erasme et la cartographie' in *Scrinium Erasmianum: Mélanges historiques publiés … à l'occasion du cinquième centenaire de la naissance d'Erasme* ed J. Coppens (Leiden 1969) 2 vols I 277–93

Smith, Paul J. 'Thirty-first Annual Erasmus Birthday Lecture: The First French Translations of the *Praise of Folly*' *Erasmus of Rotterdam Society Yearbook* 32 (2012) 7–26

Smith, Preserved *Erasmus: A Study of his Life, Ideals and Place in History* (New York/London 1923)

Souter, Alexander. *See* [Pelagius]

Spahn, Martin *Johannes Cochläus, ein Lebensbild aus der Zeit der Kirchenspaltung* (Berlin 1898; repr Neiuwkoop 1964)

Spangenberg, E. *Einleitung in das Römische- Justinianische Rechtsbuch oder Corpus juris civilis romani* (Hannover 1817)

Spruyt, Bart Jan *Cornelius Henrici Hoen (Honius) and His Epistle on the Eucharist (1525): Medieval Heresy, Erasmian Humanism, and Reform in the Early Sixteenth-Century Low Countries* University of Leiden thesis 1996 (Leiden/Boston 2006)

Stählin, Friedrich *Humanismus und Reformation im bürgerlichen Raum: Eine Untersuchung der biografischen Schriften des Joachim Camerarius* (Leipzig 1936)

Staehelin, Ernst *Das theologische Lebenswerk Johannes Oekolampads* (Leipzig 1939; repr 1971)

Stauffer, R. 'L'influence et la critique de l'humanisme dans le *De vera et falsa religione* de Zwingli' in *L'humanisme allemand (1480–1540): XVIIIe Colloque international de Tours* (Munich/Paris 1979) 427–39

Steffen, C. 'Untersuchungen zum "Liber de scriptoribus ecclesiasticis" des Johannes Trithemius' *Archiv für die Geschichte des Buchwesens* 10 (1969) 1247–354

Stevens, Henry N. *Ptolemy's Geography: A Brief Account of All the Printed Editions down to 1730* (Amsterdam 1972)

Stevenson, R.H. *Codices manuscripti Palatini graeci Bibliothecae Vaticanae* (Rome 1885)

Stintzing, R. *Ulrich Zasius* (Basel 1857)

Stupperich, R. 'Erasmus und die kirchliche Autoritäten' *Annuarium Historiae Conciliorum* 8 (1976) 346–64

– 'Melanchthons Proverbien-Kommentare' in *Der Kommentar in der Renaissance* ed August Buck and Otto Herding (Boppard 1975) 21–34

– 'Zur Biographie des Erasmus von Rotterdam, Zwei Untersuchungen, I: Erasmus und das Corpus iuris canonici' *Archiv für Reformationsgeschichte* 65 (1974) 19–29

Surtz, Edward *The Works and Days of John Fisher: An Introduction to the Position of St. John Fisher (1469–1535), Bishop of Rochester, in the English Renaissance and Reformation* (Cambridge, Mass 1967)

Telle, Emile V. *Erasme de Rotterdam et le septième sacrement: Etude d'évangelisme matrimonial au XVIe siècle et contribution à la biographie intellectuelle d'Erasme* (Geneva 1954)

Thomas, A.H. 'Boekenbezit en boekengebruik bij de Dominikanen in de Nederlanden voor c. 1550' in *Studies over het boekenbezit en boekengebruik voor 1620* (Brussels 1974) 417–75

Thomas, Alan G., bookseller *Catalogue 30* (London 1973)

Thompson Craig R. 'Better Teachers than Scotus or Aquinas' in *Medieval and Renaissance Studies* 2 (Proceedings of the Southeastern Institute of Medieval and Renaissance Studies, Summer 1966) ed John L. Lievsay (Durham, NC 1968) 114–45

– 'Erasmus as a Poet in the Context of Northern Humanism' *De Gulden Passer* 47 (1969) / *Nationale Erasmus-Herdenking: Handelingen / Commmémoration Nationale d'Erasme: Actes* (Brussels 1970) 187–210

– 'Erasmus' Translation of Lucian's *Longaevi*' *Classical Philology* 35 (1940) 397–415

Thomson, D.F.S. 'Linacre's Latin Grammars' in *Essays on the Life and Work of Thomas Linacre c. 1460–1524* ed Francis Maddison, Margaret Pelling, and Charles Webster (Oxford 1977) 24–35

Thorndike, L. *A History of Magic and Experimental Science* (New York 1923–58) 8 vols

Thuis in de late middeleeuwen, het Nederlands burgerinterieur 1400–1535 Tentoonstelling Provinciaal Overijssels Museum, 5 oct.–31 dec. 1980 (Zwolle 1980) exhibition catalogue

Tigerstedt, E.N. 'Joannes Annius and Graecia Mendax' in *Classical, Mediaeval and Renaissance Studies in Honor of Berthold Louis Ullman* ed Charles Henderson (Rome 1964) 2 vols II 293–310

Tocci, L.M. *In officina Erasmi: L'Apparato autografo di Erasmo per l'edizione 1528 degli Adagia e un nuovo manoscritto del Compendium Vitae* (Rome 1989)

Tracy, James D. 'Erasmus Becomes a German' *Renaissance Quarterly* 21 (1968) 281–8

– 'On the Composition Dates of Seven of Erasmus' Writings' *Bibliothèque d'Humanisme et Renaissance* 31 (1969) 355–64

Trapman, Johannes 'Le rôle des "sacramentaires" des origines de la Réforme jusqu'en 1530 aux Pays-Bas' *Nederlands Archief voor Kerkgeschiedenis* 63 (1983) 1–24

– *De Summa der godliker scrifturen (1523)* (Leiden 1978)

Treu, Erwin *Die Bildnisse des Erasmus von Rotterdam* (Basel 1959)

Troje, Hans Erich *Graeca leguntur* (Vienna 1971)

Trillitzsch, W. 'Erasmus und Seneca' *Philologus* 109 (1965) 270–93

Ullman, B.L. *Studies in the Italian Renaissance* (Rome 1955)

Ullman, B.L. and P.A. Stadler *The Public Library of Renaissance Florence: Niccolo Niccoli, Cosimo de' Medici and the Library of San Marco* (Padua 1972)

Vanautgaerden, Alexandre 'Ex bibliotheca Erasmi: Catalogue des 33 ouvrages conservés de la bibliothèque d'Erasme et des 11 ex dono connus à ce jour' in *Le biblioteche private come paradigma bibliografico: Atti del convegno internazionale, Roma, Tempio di Adriano 10–12 ottobre 2007* ed Fiametta Sabba (Rome 2008) 313–62

– '*Ex bibliotheca Erasmi*. Un 34e ouvrage: L'exemplaire des *Epistolae* de Léon Ier (Paris, Josse Bade, 1511) du Cultura Fonds (Dilbeek)' *Bibliothèque d'Humanisme et Renaissance* 74 (2012), 547–62

– 'Item ein schöne Bibliothec mit eim Register: Un deuxième inventaire de la bibliothèque d'Erasme (à propos du manuscript C VI A de la Bibliothèque Universitaire de Bâle)' in *Les humanistes et leur bibliothèque / Humanists and their Libraries: Actes du Colloque international / Proceedings of the*

International Conference, Bruxelles, 26–28 août 1999 ed Rudolf de Smet (Leuven/Paris/Sterling, VA 2002) 59–112

van der Velden, H.E.J.M. *Rudolphus Agricola* (Leiden 1911)

Vernet, André 'Les manuscrits grecs de Jean de Raguse († 1443)' *Basler Zeitschrift für Geschichte und Altertumskunde* 61 (1961) 75–108; repr in his *Etudes médiévales* (Paris 1981) 531–64

Viard, P.E. *André Alciati* (Nancy 1926)

de Vocht, Henry *Acta Thomae Mori* (Louvain 1947; repr Nendeln 1966)

– *History of the Foundation and the Rise of the Collegium Trilingue Lovaniense, 1517–1550* Humanistica Lovaniensia 10–13 (Louvain 1951–5) 4 vols

– *John Dantiscus and His Netherlandish Friends as Revealed by Their Correspondence, 1522–1546* (Louvain 1961)

de Vogel, C.J. 'Erasmus and his Attitude towards Church Dogma' in *Scrinium Erasmianum: Mélanges historiques publiés ... à l'occasion du cinquième centenaire de la naissance d'Erasme* ed J. Coppens (Leiden 1969) 2 vols II 101–34

Voigt, Georg *Die Wiederbelebung des classischen Alterthums* 2nd ed (Berlin 1880) 2 vols

Vos, Alvin 'The *Vita Longolii*: Additional Considerations about Reginald Pole's Authorship' *Renaissance Quarterly* 39 (1977) 324–33

Wachler, A.W.J. *Thomas Rehdiger und seine Büchersammlung in Breslau* (Breslau 1828)

Wackernagel, R. *Geschichte der Stadt Basel, Anmerkungen und Belege* (Basel 1968)

Walsh, James E. 'The *Querela Pacis* of Erasmus: The "lost" French Translation' *Harvard Library Bulletin* 17 (1969) 374–84

Waterbolk E.H. *Een hond in het bad: enige aspecten van de verhouding tussen Erasmus en Agricola* (Groningen 1966); repr in his *Verspreide opstellen* (Amsterdam 1981) 27–44

Wegg, Jervis *Richard Pace, a Tudor Diplomat* (New York 1971)

Weiss, Roberto 'Un allievo inglese del Poliziano, Thomas Linacre' in *Il Poliziano e il suo tempo: Atti del IV convegno internazionale di studi sul Rinascimento ... 23–26 settembre 1954* (Florence 1957) 331–6

– 'Italian Humanism in Western Europe: 1460–1520' in *Italian Renaissance Studies: A Tribute to the late Cecilia M. Ady* ed E.F. Jacob (London 1960) 69–93

– 'Petrarch the Antiquarian' in *Classical, Mediaeval and Renaissance Studies in Honor of Berthold Louis Ullman* ed Charles Henderson (Rome 1964) 2 vols II 199–209

– *The Spread of Italian Humanism* (London 1964)

– 'Traccia per una biografia di Annio da Viterbo' *Italia medioevale e umanistica* 5 (1962) 425–41

Welti, M.E. *Der Basler Buchdruck und Britannien: Die Rezeption britischen Gedankenguts in den Basler Pressen von den Anfängen bis zum Beginn des 17. Jahrhunderts* Basler Beiträge zur Geschichtewissenschaft 93 (Basel 1964)

Westgate, R. Wilfred 'The Text of Valla's Translation of Thucydides' *Transactions of the American Philological Association* 67 (1936) 242–4

Wickersheimer, Ernest *Dictionnaire biographique des médecins en France au moyen-âge* (Paris 1936) 2 vols; facs repr Geneva 1979 with a 3rd supplementary vol

Widmann, Hans 'Die Wirkung des Buchdrucks auf die humanistische Zeitgenossen und Nachfahren des Erfinders' in *Das Verhältnis der Humanisten zum Buch* ed Fritz Krafft and Dieter Wuttke (Boppard 1977) 1–72

Williams, John R. 'The Quest for the Author of the *Moralium Dogma Philosophorum*, 1931–1956' *Speculum* 32 (1957) 736–47

Wilsdorf, Helmut 'Agricola in Italien und seine persönlichen Beziehungen zur angelsächsischen Welt' in *Georgius Agricola 1494–1555* (Berlin 1955) 230–46

Wilson, N.G. 'Erasmus' as translator of Euripides: Supplementary Note' *Antike und Abendland* 18 (1973) 87–8

– 'The Triclinian Edition of Aristophanes' *Classical Quarterly* 12 (1962) 32–47

Wimpfeling, J. *Adolescentia* ed Otto Herding (Munich 1965)

Woods Callahan, Virginia 'The Erasmus-Alciati friendship' in *Acta Conventus Neo-Latini Lovaniensis, Proceedings of the First International Congress of Neo-Latin Studies, Louvain 23–28 August 1971* ed J. IJsewijn and E. Kessler (Leuven/Louvain and Munich 1973) 133–41

Zafarana, Zelina 'Ricerche sul "Liber de unitate ecclesiae conservanda"' *Studi medievali* ser 3, 7 (1966) 617–700
Zambelli, Paola 'Corneille Agrippa, Erasme et la théologie humaniste' in *Colloquia Erasmiana Turonensia: Douzième stage international d'études humanistes, Tours, 1969* ed J.-C. Margolin (Paris/Toronto 1972) 2 vols ɪ 113–59
Żantuan, Konstanty 'Erasmus and the Cracow Humanists: The Purchase of His Library by Łaski' *The Polish Review* 10 no 2 (1965) 3–36
Zickendraht, K. *Der Streit zwischen Erasmus und Luther über die Willensfreiheit* (Leipzig 1909)

Short-Title Forms for Erasmus' Works

Titles following colons are longer versions of the same, or are alternative titles. Items entirely enclosed in square brackets are of doubtful authorship.

Acta: Academiae Lovaniensis contra Lutherum   Ferguson *Opuscula* / CWE 71
Adagia: Adagiorum chiliades 1508, etc (Adagiorum collectanea for the primitive form, when required)   LB II / ASD II-1–9 / CWE 30–6
Admonitio adversus mendacium: Admonitio adversus mendacium et obtrectationem   LB X / CWE 78
Annotationes in Novum Testamentum   LB VI / ASD VI-5–10 / CWE 51–60
Antibarbari   LB X / ASD I-1 / CWE 23
Apologia ad annotationes Stunicae: Apologia respondens ad ea quae Iacobus Lopis Stunica taxaverat in prima duntaxat Novi Testamenti aeditione   LB IX / ASD IX-2
Apologia ad Caranzam: Apologia ad Sanctium Caranzam, or Apologia de tribus locis, or Responsio ad annotationem Stunicae ... a Sanctio Caranza defensam   LB IX / ASD IX-8
Apologia ad Fabrum: Apologia ad Iacobum Fabrum Stapulensem   LB IX / ASD IX-3 / CWE 83
Apologia ad prodromon Stunicae   LB IX / ASD IX-8
Apologia ad Stunicae conclusiones   LB IX / ASD IX-8
Apologia adversus monachos: apologia adversus monachos quosdam Hispanos   LB IX
Apologia adversus Petrum Sutorem: Apologia adversus debacchationes Petri Sutoris   LB IX
Apologia adversus rhapsodias Alberti Pii: Apologia ad viginti et quattuor libros A. Pii   LB IX / ASD IX-6 / CWE 84
Apologia adversus Stunicae Blasphemiae: Apologia adversus libellum Stunicae cui titulum fecit Blasphemiae et impietates Erasmi   LB IX / ASD IX-8
Apologia contra Latomi dialogum: Apologia contra Iacobi Latomi dialogum de tribus linguis   LB IX / CWE 71
Apologia de 'In principio erat sermo': Apologia palam refellens quorundam seditiosos clamores apud populum ac magnates quo in evangelio Ioannis verterit 'In principio erat sermo' (1520a); Apologia de 'In principio erat sermo' (1520b)   LB IX / CWE 73
Apologia de laude matrimonii: Apologia pro declamatione de laude matrimonii   LB IX / CWE 71
Apologia de loco 'Omnes quidem': Apologia de loco taxato in publica professione per Nicolaum Ecmondanum theologum et Carmelitanum Lovanii 'Omnes quidem resurgemus'   LB IX / CWE 73
Apologia qua respondet invectivis Lei: Apologia qua respondet duabus invectivis Eduardi Lei   Ferguson *Opuscula* / ASD IX-4 / CWE 72
Apophthegmata   LB IV / ASD IV-4 / CWE 37–8
Appendix de scriptis Clichtovei   LB IX / CWE 83
Appendix respondens ad Sutorem: Appendix respondens ad quaedam Antapologiae Petri Sutoris   LB IX
Argumenta: Argumenta in omnes epistolas apostolicas nova (with Paraphrases)
Axiomata pro causa Lutheri: Axiomata pro causa Martini Lutheri   Ferguson *Opuscula* / CWE 71

Brevissima scholia: In Elenchum Alberti Pii brevissima scholia per eundem Erasmum Roterodamum   ASD IX-6 / CWE 84

Carmina   LB I, IV, V, VIII / ASD I-7 / CWE 85–6
Catalogus lucubrationum   LB I / CWE 9 (Ep 1341A)
Christiani hominis institutum, carmen   LB V / ASD I-7 / CWE 85–6
Ciceronianus: Dialogus Ciceronianus   LB I / ASD I-2 / CWE 28
Colloquia   LB I / ASD I-3 / CWE 39–40
Compendium vitae   Allen I / CWE 4
Conflictus: Conflictus Thaliae et Barbariei   LB I / ASD I-8
[Consilium: Consilium cuiusdam ex animo cupientis esse consultum]   Ferguson *Opuscula* / CWE 71

De bello Turcico: Utilissima consultatio de bello Turcis inferendo, et obiter enarratus psalmus 28
    LB V / ASD V-3 / CWE 64
De civilitate: De civilitate morum puerilium   LB I / ASD I-8 / CWE 25
Declamatio de morte   LB IV / ASD I-2 / CWE 25
Declamatiuncula   LB IV / ASD IV-7
Declarationes ad censuras Lutetiae vulgatas: Declarationes ad censuras Lutetiae vulgatas sub
    nomine facultatis theologiae Parisiensis   LB IX / ASD IX-7 / CWE 82
De concordia: De sarcienda ecclesiae concordia, or De amabili ecclesiae concordia [on Psalm 83]
    LB V / ASD V-3 / CWE 65
De conscribendis epistulis   LB I / ASD I-2 / CWE 25
De constructione: De constructione octo partium orationis, or Syntaxis   LB I / ASD I-4
De contemptu mundi: Epistola de contemptu mundi   LB V / ASD V-1 / CWE 66
De copia: De duplici copia verborum ac rerum   LB I / ASD I-6 / CWE 24
De delectu ciborum scholia   ASD IX-1 / CWE 73
De esu carnium: Epistola apologetica ad Christophorum episcopum Basiliensem de interdicto
    esu carnium (published with scholia in a 1532 edition but not in the 1540 Opera)   LB IX /
    ASD IX-1 / CWE 73
De immensa Dei misericordia: Concio de immensa Dei misericordia   LB V / ASD V-7 / CWE 70
De libero arbitrio: De libero arbitrio diatribe   LB IX / CWE 76
De philosophia evangelica   LB VI
De praeparatione: De praeparatione ad mortem   LB V / ASD V-1 / CWE 70
De pueris instituendis: De pueris statim ac liberaliter instituendis   LB I / ASD I-2 / CWE 26
De puero Iesu: Concio de puero Iesu   LB V / ASD V-7 / CWE 29
De puritate tabernaculi: Enarratio psalmi 14 qui est de puritate tabernaculi sive ecclesiae christianae
    LB V / ASD V-2 / CWE 65
De ratione studii   LB I / ASD I-2 / CWE 24
De recta pronuntiatione: De recta latini graecique sermonis pronuntiatione   LB I / ASD I-4 / CWE 26
De taedio Iesu: Disputatiuncula de taedio, pavore, tristicia Iesu   LB V / ASD V-7 / CWE 70
Detectio praestigiarum: Detectio praestigiarum cuiusdam libelli Germanice scripti   LB X /
    ASD IX-1 / CWE 78
De vidua christiana   LB V / ASD V-6 / CWE 66
De virtute amplectenda: Oratio de virtute amplectenda   LB V / CWE 29
[Dialogus bilinguium ac trilinguium: Chonradi Nastadiensis dialogus bilinguium ac trilinguium]
    Ferguson *Opuscula* / CWE 7
Dilutio: Dilutio eorum quae Iodocus Clichtoveus scripsit adversus declamationem suasoriam matri-
    monii / *Dilutio eorum quae Iodocus Clichtoveus scripsit* ed Emile V. Telle (Paris 1968) / CWE 83
Divinationes ad notata Bedae: Divinationes ad notata per Bedam de Paraphrasi Erasmi in
    Matthaeum, et primo de duabus praemissis epistolis   LB IX / ASD IX-5

Ecclesiastes: Ecclesiastes sive de ratione concionandi   LB V / ASD V-4–5 / CWE 67–8
Elenchus in censuras Bedae: In N. Bedae censuras erroneas elenchus   LB IX / ASD IX-5
Enchiridion: Enchiridion militis christiani   LB V / ASD V-8 / CWE 66
Encomium matrimonii (in De conscribendis epistolis)
Encomium medicinae: Declamatio in laudem artis medicae   LB I / ASD I-4 / CWE 29

Obsecratio ad Virginem Mariam: Obsecratio sive oratio ad Virginem Mariam in rebus adversis, or Obsecratio ad Virginem Matrem Mariam in rebus adversis   LB V / CWE 69
Oratio de pace: Oratio de pace et discordia   LB VIII / ASD IV-7
Oratio funebris: Oratio funebris in funere Bertae de Heyen   LB VIII / ASD IV-7 / CWE 29

Paean Virgini Matri: Paean Virgini Matri dicendus   LB V / CWE 69
Panegyricus: Panegyricus ad Philippum Austriae ducem   LB IV / ASD IV-1 / CWE 27
Parabolae: Parabolae sive similia   LB I / ASD I-5 / CWE 23
Paraclesis   LB V, VI / ASD V-7
Paraphrasis in Elegantias Vallae: Paraphrasis in Elegantias Laurentii Vallae   LB I / ASD I-4
Paraphrasis in Matthaeum, etc   LB VII / ASD VII-6 / CWE 42–50
Peregrinatio apostolorum: Peregrinatio apostolorum Petri et Pauli   LB VI, VII
Precatio ad Virginis filium Iesum   LB V / CWE 69
Precatio dominica   LB V / CWE 69
Precationes: Precationes aliquot novae   LB V / CWE 69
Precatio pro pace ecclesiae: Precatio ad Dominum Iesum pro pace ecclesiae   LB IV, V / CWE 69
Prologus supputationis: Prologus in supputationem calumniarum Natalis Bedae (1526), or Prologus supputationis errorum in censuris Bedae (1527)   LB IX / ASD IX-5
Purgatio adversus epistolam Lutheri: Purgatio adversus epistolam non sobriam Lutheri   LB X / ASD IX-1 / CWE 78

Querela pacis   LB IV / ASD IV-2 / CWE 27

Ratio: Ratio seu Methodus compendio perveniendi ad veram theologiam (Methodus for the shorter version originally published in the Novum instrumentum of 1516)   LB V, VI
Responsio ad annotationes Lei: Responsio ad annotationes Eduardi Lei   LB IX / ASD IX-4 / CWE 72
Responsio ad Collationes: Responsio ad Collationes cuiusdam iuvenis gerontodidascali   LB IX / CWE 73
Responsio ad disputationem de divortio: Responsio ad disputationem cuiusdam Phimostomi de divortio   LB IX / ASD IX-4 / CWE 83
Responsio ad epistolam Alberti Pii: Responsio ad epistolam paraeneticam Alberti Pii, or Responsio ad exhortationem Pii   LB IX / ASD IX-6 / CWE 84
Responsio ad notulas Bedaicas   LB X / ASD IX-5
Responsio ad Petri Cursii defensionem: Epistola de apologia Cursii   LB X / Ep 3032
Responsio adversus febricitantis cuiusdam libellum   LB X

Spongia: Spongia adversus aspergines Hutteni   LB X / ASD IX-1 / CWE 78
Supputatio: Supputatio errorum in censuris Bedae   LB IX
Supputationes: Supputationes errorum in censuris Natalis Bedae: contains Supputatio and reprints of Prologus supputationis; Divinationes ad notata Bedae; Elenchus in censuras Bedae; Appendix respondens ad Sutorem; Appendix de scriptis Clithovei   LB IX / ASD IX-5

Tyrannicida: Tyrannicida, declamatio Lucianicae respondens   LB I / ASD I-1 / CWE 29

Virginis et martyris comparatio   LB V / ASD V-7 / CWE 69
Vita Hieronymi: Vita divi Hieronymi Stridonensis   Ferguson *Opuscula* / CWE 61

ERASMUS AND HIS BOOKS

Introduction

What became of Erasmus' books? The most famous scholar of his day died in peaceful prosperity and in the company of celebrated and responsible friends. His zeal for useful books was insatiable. Indeed, he had taken care to insure that after his death they would pass to an appreciative noble owner, yet after his death their fate was unknown.

The tale begins as early as November 1547, when Count Ottheinrich of the Palatinate, a zealous bibliophile whose collection became the core of the Bibliotheca Palatina in Heidelberg, sent his agent Christoph Arnold to Basel to find out what had become of the famous scholar's library. As the Chronicle of Zimmern relates, Arnold's mission was prompted by the count's discovery that Erasmus had borrowed some books from the recently dissolved abbey of Lortsch but had never returned them. As he assembled his own collection with fanatical, sometimes unscrupulous, zeal the count took pains to be well informed about the state of many German libraries, and the library at Lortsch had just been carried off in its entirety to his castle in Heidelberg. What had happened to the books Erasmus had borrowed? Eleven years after his death, even Count Ottheinrich was entirely in the dark about the fate of the great humanist's books.[1] But that need not surprise us. Only a small circle of initiates would at first have known that Erasmus had sold his library more than twenty years earlier to the young Polish nobleman, and later Reformer, Jan Łaski. In 1525 Erasmus had transferred the books to Łaski's ownership on condition that he himself might continue to use them until his death. The price was fixed at 300 gold crowns. About half of that sum (200 florins) had been paid to him at the time of the sale; the rest (another 200 florins) was not paid until after Erasmus' death, shortly before the library was dispatched to Poland in December 1536.[2]

The sale of the library first became public knowledge in 1570, when the text of the contract between Erasmus and Łaski was printed at Lausitz.[3] Lausitz lay on the great trade route from Leipzig to Breslau and Cracow, which suggests that the initiative for publication came from the Polish side and that the copy of the original document that had once been in Łaski's possession was the basis of the published text. (Whether this was the same copy that a Polish cleric found in the binding of an old volume at the end of the last century, and later published,[4] is now hard to determine.) The publication in which the text of the

---

1 Schotthenloher *Pfalzgraf Ottheinrich und das Buch* 8–9

2 See Allen Ep 2780:7n. For the agreement of 20 June 1525, reprinted from the earlier sources mentioned below, see Miaskowski I (Anhang II 'Zur Geschichte der Bibliothek des Erasmus') 44–8 ('Vereinbarung betreffs des Verkaufs der Bibliothek des Erasmus an Johannes Łaski') and II 3–5 (no 2); Jürgens *Johannes a Lasco* 94. For the transaction as reflected in Erasmus' first will (1527) see Allen VI 504:38–42 Appendix 19/CWE 12 542:32–5, with n20 on the currency. Cf Allen XI 364:10–14 Appendix 25 'Erasmus' Last Will' and illustrations xii–xiii above.

3 In *Ad rubricam codicis de summa Trinitate, etc., Ederi Georgii* (Lausitz 1570)

4 In the Warsaw *Przeglad Katolicki* 10 July 1897, 460; see Miaskowski I 39n and 44–5.

contract appeared did not attract wide attention. The book appeared in a very small edition and must have been forgotten almost immediately. It was to be nearly 200 years before the transaction of 1525 was 'rediscovered' and the agreement reprinted, this time from the sealed original then among Erasmus' effects but since lost, in the *Vie d'Erasme* of Jean Lévesque de Burigny, which was published at Paris in 1757.[5]

At that date the brief text of this document was all that was known about Erasmus' library. No further details had yet emerged, nor had anything been published about the discovery of books that had once belonged to him. This remained the case for many years: not until the end of the nineteenth century did research on the collection and its fate get under way. It began with the attempt to answer questions about the text of the contract with Łaski and its implementation. Gradually, around the turn of the century, previously unpublished archives, mostly letters, made it possible to reconstruct in outline how the agreement of 1525 had been put into effect, from the financial transaction during Erasmus' lifetime and immediately after his death to the actual transfer of the library to its new owner in early 1537.[6] This investigation, however, got no further than the details of the transfer of ownership. Questions about the library itself, its extent, its composition, and the fate of the books after they came into Łaski's hands, had not yet been asked. In part, this was because only a few books from the collection had been identified,[7] but clearly there was also a lack of interest. Konstanty Żantuan did not exaggerate when he wrote that 'the story of the Erasmus collection remained for the most part beyond the interest of researches.'[8] Typical of this lack of interest was the persistent repetition of the rather surprising assertion, made without any proof in 1850, that Erasmus' library had found its way to Munich via the liquidated University of Ingolstadt and that it was still in existence in the library of the University of Munich. This claim was not checked for many years. As late as 1923 Preserved Smith repeated the tale in his life of Erasmus without the slightest attempt to verify its accuracy.[9] In 1927 Friedrich Ritter gave a spur to research in another direction when he made it clear, from a long-published but unnoticed letter of the Groningen rector Regnerus Praedinius, that Łaski had disposed of part of the library in his lifetime.[10] In 1554 he appears to have transferred to a clerical friend a large number of books, including several that had once belonged to Erasmus; these books were shortly afterwards offered for sale at Emden. This raised a corner of the curtain that had fallen over the fate of Łaski's library after it had been enriched by the more than 400 volumes once owned by Erasmus.

In 1936 the Erasmus quatercentenary gave an impetus to research on the library itself. In the *Gedenkschrift zum 400. Todestages des Erasmus von Rotterdam*, Fritz Husner, then director of the library of the University of Basel, devoted a thorough and solid study to Erasmus'

---

5 The most important of the first three full-length biographies of Erasmus; the two others were those of Samuel Knight (Cambridge 1726) and John Jortin (London 1758–60). On these works see Mansfield *Phoenix of His Age* 268–95.

6 See especially Dalton *Lasciana* 20–1; Miaskowski I 41 (Anhang II); Jürgens *Johannes a Lasco* 96–7. There seems to have been some difference of opinion as to whether Erasmus behaved entirely fairly to Łaski in the financial transaction.

7 Miaskowski (I 44) knew of only one book that been rediscovered, the copy of Reuchlin's *Rudimenta Hebraica* in the library of the Grosse Kirche at Emden; cf 7 below and VL/Catalogue no 280.

8 'Erasmus and the Cracow Humanists: The Purchase of His Library by Łaski' 6

9 *Erasmus* 261. The story was that Erasmus' library had fallen quite soon after 1536 into the hands of Egolph von Knöringen, later bishop of Augsburg, and had been presented by him to the University of Ingolstadt in 1573; for details see Husner 'Bibliothek' 255–7.

10 'Die Bibliothek des Erasmus, Johannes a Lasco und Gérard Mortaigne in Emden.' For the letter, see Gabbema *Epistolarum centuriae tres* 167–73 (Ep 68). See 10 below.

library: 'Die Bibliothek des Erasmus.' Husner undertook to approach the subject from a broader point of view. Without unduly neglecting the transaction of 1525 and its implementation in 1536, of which he gave a brief but adequate account, he drew attention to aspects of the library that had hitherto remained obscure. Within the limits of a short article he discussed both the formation and composition of the library, as well as its housing and the repeated movement of the books from place to place. Husner took a great deal of his documentation from Erasmus' correspondence, which at that time had been published in P.S. Allen's exemplary edition up to the year 1530, but he also made use of unpublished material in the rich collection of manuscripts under his care at Basel. The most important document from this collection, which he brought to light and published in full in his article, was the one to which he gave the name of *Versandliste* ('shipping invoice').[11] This was the inventory of books sent in three large barrels from Basel to their future home in Cracow after the death of Erasmus, around Christmas 1536; they arrived some months later, not without difficulties en route,[12] and Łaski confirmed their safe receipt in early April 1537.[13]

In the last part of his article Husner directed his attention to the fascinating question of the subsequent fate of the books. He made a preliminary attempt to prepare an inventory of the scattered remnants of the collection known to be preserved. He gave a precise description, with many relevant details, of all the books from Erasmus' library that, so far as he could discover, had been traced at that date. Of the more than 500 works contained in the 413 items on the list, this proved to be a disappointingly small number. Husner hoped that the publication of the *Versandliste* would encourage others to undertake further research, for it seemed unlikely to him that no more books with the ex libris *Sum Erasmi* 'I belong to Erasmus' would come to light. But he can scarcely have expected that large connected parts of the collection would be rediscovered. He definitively disproved the tradition that a substantial part of the library was still extant in Munich, hidden among the old collections of the university library. Investigation on the spot made it clear that this assumption must have been founded on a misapprehension.[14] And what Husner was able to deduce about the later vicissitudes of individual books was far from promising: his findings proved conclusively that the library had already begun to disintegrate soon after Łaski had taken possession of it and must have been to a great extent broken up and dispersed before Łaski's death.

After more than half a century Husner's article is still invaluable, and its careful documentation remains the indispensable foundation of all further research. It has been our starting point in the following pages, in which we summarize the circumstances that make the regrettable disintegration of Erasmus' library understandable, and at the same time give an account of the remnants of the library that have come to light since 1936, both by chance and as the result of deliberate search.

---

11 See illustration xiv above. The *Versandliste* had not escaped notice before; Miaskowski (I 45) had drawn attention to its existence in Basel in an inconspicuous note. According to Henning Jürgens the list, composed by Gilbert Cousin, was not made shortly before Erasmus' books were packed and sent to Cracow, but in August 1535, when Erasmus moved from Freiburg to Basel and Cousin was involved in packing his books. Cousin then returned to France. Jürgens thinks it possible that the 1535 list remained in Basel as evidence, and that the books were dispatched together with another list; see Jürgens *Johannes a Lasco* 100; *Erasmus von Rotterdam: Vorkämpfer für Frieden und Toleranz* 120. Since the list includes books printed in 1536, however, Cousin cannot have composed it.

12 Husner 'Bibliothek' 246; AK V 24 Ep 2110; cf illustration xv above.

13 Husner 'Bibliothek' 247; Miaskowski I 47; cf AK V 44–5 Ep 2130 and illustration xvi above.

14 See 4 with n9 above.

Jan Łaski belonged to a distinguished Polish family. Supported by his uncle, the archbishop of Gniezno, he was able to study abroad. He was ordained a priest in 1521, but continued to travel; in 1525, when he lived for six months as a guest in Erasmus' house, he made arrangements to buy Erasmus' library. From the late 1520s civil war in Hungary and its aftermath adversely affected the Łaski family fortunes; at the same time, Jan's ecclesiastical career failed to flourish. During these years he must also have begun to be interested in the Reform movement (he met Melanchthon in Leipzig in 1537). His convictions as a Reformer forced Łaski to live a wandering, and often a fugitive, life.[15] Even before his open breach with the church of Rome he was already inwardly alienated from it, and he left his homeland in the summer of 1539 to seek his salvation in Germany. At first he settled in Frankfurt am Main. It was here, in the city of the great book fair, or perhaps in nearby Mainz, that he met Albert Hardenberg.[16] Hardenberg was later to become a preacher in Emden, but at that time he was still a monk in the Cistercian abbey of Aduard, near Groningen (well known as the place where Rodolphus Agricola and Wessel Gansfort had once met to hold discussions with their learned friends).[17] With Hardenberg, a friend and in many ways a kindred spirit, Łaski left for Leuven, but he could not feel safe or at ease in that bastion of orthodoxy, and in the following year he moved to Emden. There, in late 1542 or early in 1543, he must have committed himself definitively to the Reformation, attracted in particular by the doctrines of Jean Calvin and Heinrich Bullinger. He acted as preacher in the city and at the same time as superintendent of the churches in East Friesland. In the latter capacity he had a considerable share in the reform of the regional ecclesiastical organization. But his unwillingness to endorse the Interim of Augsburg[18] placed him in a difficult situation, and in September 1548 he fled to England. William Turner, a physician and later dean of Wells, whose acquaintance he had made in Emden, recommended him to Archbishop Cranmer, and he stayed at Lambeth House, the London residence of the archbishops of Canterbury.[19] His first stay was short. In the spring of 1549 he was again in Emden, from where he travelled straight on to Danzig and Königsberg, but he was refused permission to enter Poland permanently.

Returning to Emden, he found that he was no longer welcome there either; in early October he was relieved of his post. He spent the winter of 1549–50 in northwest Germany, lodging with Hardenberg at Bremen, and later also visiting Hamburg. In May 1550 he crossed the channel for the second time. He was made welcome in England and appointed superintendent of the church for foreigners by Edward VI, but the accession of the Catholic Mary Tudor brought his fruitful activity in that role to an abrupt end. In September 1553 Łaski and other co-religionists fled to the continent. He landed in Denmark, but since he

---

15 The available literature is often contradictory on the details and dating of Łaski's wanderings. Apart from Husner's article, the following have been consulted: Bartel *Jan Łaski, czesc I (1499–1556)* and 'Johannes a Lasco und Erasmus von Rotterdam'; Hall *John a Lasco, a Pole in Reformation England*; and CEBR II 297–301.

16 On Hardenberg see *Allgemeine Deutsche Biographie* 10 558–60 and *Neue Deutsche Biographie* 87 663.

17 See for example Nauwelaerts *Rodolphus Agricola* 58–9.

18 The so-called Augsburg Interim was a temporary doctrinal agreement enacted by the Diet of Augsburg in May 1548. Framed to provide a basis at a future general council for a negotiated doctrinal concord between German Catholics and Protestants, it was prepared and accepted at the insistence of Charles V, who in 1547 had inflicted an overwhelming defeat on the forces of the Protestant League of Schmalkalden. The Interim became imperial law on 30 June 1548. Conceived by its authors as a compromise, the Interim amounted in practice to the re-imposition of slightly modified Catholic doctrine and worship in the principalities and cities of Germany, including those of Protestant allegiance. It met with both active and passive resistance and was repealed in 1552 following a successful princely uprising against the emperor led by Elector Maurice of Saxony.

19 Hall *John a Lasco* 30; on Turner see *Dictionary of National Biography* 57 363–6.

was unwilling to conform to Lutheranism, he was unable to find asylum there and travelled on to East Friesland. Once again he attempted to find a post, but he met so much opposition from the Lutherans that in 1555 he was forced to move to Frankfurt, where he successfully devoted himself to the organization of a community of Protestant refugees from the Netherlands, which was entrusted to his care in June 1556. Before the end of the year, however, he at last saw a chance to return to Poland. In spite of the restrictions imposed on him, Łaski remained a tireless worker for the cause of the Reformation, moving from place to place in the province of Little Poland until his death in early January 1560.

The fate of Łaski's library during the preceding twenty years, when he moved many times, either by necessity or by choice, largely eludes our observation. To form some idea, we are dependent on the few certain data that have survived. When Łaski went into exile in Germany in 1539, he left almost his entire library behind. At most, he may have taken a few books with him. One of them was Reuchlin's *De rudimentis Hebraicis.* Did he expect that this textbook and vocabulary of Hebrew would soon be of use to him abroad in his biblical studies? If so, this consideration cannot have weighed very heavily with him or for very long, as within a year of his arrival he presented the book, which had once belonged to Erasmus, to Albert Hardenberg on the latter's promotion to doctor of theology in Mainz.[20] Not long afterwards, when they were both in Leuven, Łaski honoured Hardenberg with two more works by Reuchlin that had once belonged to Erasmus.[21] Was this a parting gift when the two men, who had quickly become fast friends, separated again, Hardenberg setting off for the abbey of Aduard, while Łaski went to Emden?

Łaski had left his library in Poland, but during 1541 he arranged to have it brought to Frankfurt. He must have waited impatiently for the arrival of the books, but not because he needed them urgently for his studies. Łaski was no longer intellectually attached to the humanistic scholarly library that only eight years earlier he had claimed would always be his 'greatest treasure.'[22] The wandering Reformer was clearly in need of money, and the books he sent for could help to provide it. From Emden he sounded Hardenberg out on the possibility of taking over duplicates from his collection – works of Greek and Latin authors 'in both sacred and profane literature,' in which his friend, as he recalled, was interested – and suggested that the abbot of Aduard could buy them for the abbey library, for Hardenberg's use. Łaski asked for an early decision, since otherwise, to avoid the heavy costs of carriage, he would do better to have the books sold at once in Frankfurt.[23] It is doubtful whether in fact any of Erasmus' books came into the hands of the abbey of Aduard by this route. All that is certain is that Łaski's library was brought to Emden from Frankfurt via Aduard, for in late December 1541 Hardenberg received a request from his friend to send the books on to an acquaintance in Groningen, who would in turn arrange for the final stage in their transport.[24] Łaski specifically asked Hardenberg to send the books 'in accordance with the catalogue drawn up in my own hand.' From this we may infer that none of his books remained at Aduard. If some books were in fact bought for Hardenberg's use, they

---

20 The book has been preserved; see VL/Catalogue no 280.

21 These works have also been rediscovered, bound in a single volume; see VL/Catalogue no 176.

22 Allen Ep 2862:32–3

23 Łaski *Opera* II 554 Ep 6 (5 August 1541)

24 Łaski *Opera* II 552 Ep 5 ([29 December] 1541). Jerome (Jeroen) was municipal steward at Groningen. He was the son of Wilhelmus Frederici (Willem Frederiks), pastor of St Martin's in Groningen and known as one of Agricola's circle; see CEBR II 55–6 and Nauwelaerts *Rodolphus Agricola* 31 and 58. Kuyper dated the letter 1540, but this cannot be reconciled with the comments of Ep 6 of 5 August 1541, which reports the arrival of the library in Frankfurt.

were probably lost when the abbey was destroyed in 1580.[25] In any case, it is clear that for Łaski, now settled in Emden as a practical Reformer rather than a scholar, the library was no longer an untouchable treasure. He was not especially attached to the books because they had once belonged to Erasmus: in February 1548 he gave away Erasmus' copy (still extant) of an edition of Diogenes Laertius as a gift to an acquaintance, perhaps for the very reason that its illustrious provenance made it more valuable.[26]

The library followed Łaski on his travels, sometimes after considerable delay. Many months after he and his family had arrived in England in the spring of 1550, the books followed him: not until April of 1551 was he able to report that 'the remaining part' of his library had recently reached him in London.[27] What he meant by *reliqua pars* is not entirely clear. Had he perhaps brought most of the books with him in person on the crossing? Or was he only pointing out, perhaps with a pang of regret after all, how his library had shrunk as a result of former losses, which may have been greater than we are aware of? We know of one loss by name: about this time one of the showpieces of Erasmus' collection, the Aldine edition of Aristotle's *Opera* (Venice 1495–8), passed into the possession of the Englishman William Turner, to whom Łaski sold or perhaps gave it. As has been mentioned, Turner had met Łaski in Emden and became a friend.[28] In about 1568 Turner in turn presented the copy of the famous edition to the library of Wells cathedral, where four of the five volumes entered in the *Versandliste* are still in existence.[29]

When Łaski fled England for the continent in 1553, he probably lost some of his books in the storm that drove the ship off course in the channel and forced it to land in Denmark – although, however plausible this may seem, there is no conclusive proof of it.[30] But there is no doubt about the heavy losses that the library suffered soon after Łaski had returned to Emden in early December of that year. In 1554 some of his books were sold. Gérard Mortaigne, a religious exile from Flanders or Brabant, who had become Łaski's friend and had arrived in Emden at the same time, offered for sale a great many named volumes from Łaski's library, including several previously owned by Erasmus. They were sent for viewing to Regnerus Praedinius, rector of St Martin's school in Groningen. It has always been assumed that Mortaigne had taken over Łaski's books but that soon afterwards financial difficulties forced him to dispose of them. Mortaigne's role, however, is still unclear. Is it in fact so certain that he was acting as the new owner of the books and not as a straw man for Łaski, assuming that Łaski wanted to liquidate his library as unobtrusively as possible because he needed money?[31] It does not make a great deal of difference, since the result was the same: towards the end of Łaski's wanderings in western Europe, part of his library – probably a large part, including Erasmus' books – must have passed into other hands and been dispersed. The question is whether he kept many books. For a long time the expectation persisted that if remnants of Erasmus' library were to be found anywhere, it would be in Poland. But in the early 1900s searches undertaken by Kasimir von Miaskowski and Emil Major in the

---

25 Husner 'Bibliothek' 249 n70

26 vl/Catalogue no 305

27 Łaski *Opera* ii 648 Ep 73 (to Heinrich Bullinger)

28 See 6 above.

29 vl/Catalogue no 214

30 cebr ii 300

31 See 4 with n10 above. The assumption, derived from Praedinius' letter to Gérard Camp, that Mortaigne was the owner is not supported by marks of ownership in the printed books offered for sale by him and still preserved (including vl/Catalogue nos 137, 138, 218, and 281); only in the Codex Arcerianus from Erasmus' library does Mortaigne's ex libris appear (see 94 with n6 below).

most important Polish libraries containing old collections proved fruitless. Husner concluded that after his short stay in Frankfurt Łaski returned to Poland without bringing with him,
or having sent on afterwards, anything of consequence from his collection.[32] After World
War II research by Karel Glombiowski, who carried out an investigation in Silesian libraries,
and Jean-Claude Margolin confirmed Husner's conclusion.[33] Only two books once owned
by Erasmus have been found in Poland. It is certain that Łaski gave away one of them, an
edition of Diogenes Laertius, during his stay in East Friesland;[34] it is possible that the other,
the *Etymologicum magnum graecum*, was left behind when he quit his native land in 1539.[35]
Glombiowski's pronouncement may well be definitive: books once owned by Łaski 'must be
sought for everywhere except – alas – in Poland.'[36]

Other survivors of Erasmus' library have come to light in various places over the years.
All told, as we said before, they are a meagre remnant. In 1936 Husner managed to identify
eleven of the books which, according to the *Versandliste*, had passed into new ownership
four hundred years earlier.[37] Besides these, he traced a still extant manuscript that Łaski
must have bought separately from Erasmus' estate,[38] and five printed works that had once
been owned by Erasmus but had been disposed of during his lifetime and had then fallen
into other hands.[39] Since then the number of books from the library that has been rediscovered has more than doubled. In 1936, but too late for Husner to be able to mention it,
the *editio princeps* of Plotinus' *Opera* in the translation by Marsilio Ficino, once owned by
Erasmus, was discovered in the Museum Meermanno-Westreenianum in The Hague.[40] After
the Second World War Erasmus' copy of the *Etymologicum magnum graecum* surfaced in
the Jagiellonian Library in Cracow. The heavy volume, still in its original binding, may well
never have left Cracow; it was presented to the University in 1570, but before that it had
been in the possession of the professor of Greek.[41] The memorial exhibition at Rotterdam
in 1969 drew general attention to Erasmus' copy of Galen's *Therapeutica* (Venice 1500) in
the Leiden University Library, where it had been among the old collections.[42]

The marked growth of interest in Erasmus and the ever more thorough study of his works
in the seventies seem to have been directly or indirectly linked to new finds. A copy of his
Apologiae omnes that contains marginal corrections and additions in his own hand, discovered in the University Library at Cambridge, is almost certainly one of two referred to in the
Versandliste.[43] From the depths of the rich college libraries at Oxford emerged two *editiones
principes* of the Aldine press: one of the Greek grammar of Gaza (1495) in All Souls College
and the other of the tragedies of Euripides in Greek (1503) from Lincoln College. Both
copies contain Erasmus' well-known ex libris, although the *Sum Erasmi* in the first appears
to be forged. A copy of the Greek text and Latin translation of Herodian's history of the

---

32 Miaskowski I 44; Husner 'Bibliothek' 254
33 Margolin 'Łaski lecteur et annotateur du "Nouveau Testament" d'Erasme' 97 with n17
34 The book is now in the United States; see 8 with n26 above.
35 VL/Catalogue no 277
36 In a letter to Margolin dated 22 December 1964; see n33 above.
37 Husner 'Bibliothek' 248–59; VL/Catalogue nos 176 (two titles), 214, 218, 239, 272 (two titles), 280, 281, 305,
    and 389
38 See 93 and n3 below; cf n31 above.
39 Husner 'Bibliothek' 251, 256–8
40 VL/Catalogue no 209
41 Cf n35 above.
42 *Erasmus en zijn tijd* no 545; see VL/Catalogue no 138 and illustration xvii above.
43 See De Jonge 'Aantekeningen van Erasmus in een exemplaar van zijn *Apologiae omnes* (1522),' and cf 101–2
    below and VL/Catalogue nos 332 and 383.

Roman emperors in the Aldine edition of 1524 turned up in the possession of All Souls College. In this the provenance was not confirmed by a *Sum Erasmi*, but the later owner's mark – *Abeli Sylvij Frisij ex libris Erasmi Roterod.* – makes it reasonably plausible that the book belonged to Erasmus.[44] And a manuscript once owned by Erasmus, a twelfth-century codex of Palladius' *Opus agriculturae* that he had received as a gift a year before his death, was discovered in the Vatican Library.[45]

But by far the most important find was made in the Netherlands. The description of the incunabula of the Provincial Library of Friesland at Leeuwarden brought to light for the first time the *editio princeps* of Dioscorides and Nicander in the original Greek, an Aldine edition of 1499, bearing the ex libris *Sum Erasmi nec muto dominum* 'I belong to Erasmus and none other.'[46] According to a catalogue of 1644, the book was already part of the library of the former University of Franeker in that year; two hundred years later the library was incorporated into the Provincial Library of Friesland on its foundation. Could other Erasmiana have ended up in the Provincial Library by the same route? Investigation undertaken by the Keeper, M.H.H. Engels, to answer this question yielded a surprising result: four more Aldine editions of Greek authors once owned by Erasmus: Lucian's *Opera* (1503), Plutarch's *Opuscula 92* (1509) and *Vitae* (1519), Galen's *Opera* in five volumes (1525), and Ermolao Barbaro's *Corollarium in Dioscorides*, part of a volume containing his translation of *De materia medica*.[47] The Aldine edition of Galen was known to have been among the large collection of books offered for sale at Emden in 1554 by Łaski's friend Gérard Mortaigne.[48] Three of those books came, then or in the following year, into the ownership of Regnerus Praedinius, rector of St Martin's School in Groningen, and have been preserved.[49] It is therefore likely that this admirer of Erasmus acquired the *Opera* of Galen, in which he had shown particular interest, from the same source, although he did not confirm this by inserting an ex libris or other note in the volumes. It is equally likely that, along with the Galen edition, the four other Erasmiana found at Leeuwarden also came from the lot that Mortaigne put up for sale: it is not unreasonable to believe that all five books found buyers within a limited radius of Emden and were still in Friesland in the first half of the seventeenth century, in the hands of professors at the University of Franeker. The spectacular discovery in Leeuwarden strengthened Allen's suspicion that a considerable part of Erasmus' library had been dispersed from Emden to the Netherlands in the sale of 1554.[50] Can we go further and assume that almost everything that still remained of the original collection, after the losses of the previous years, changed hands on this occasion? If Łaski returned to Poland two years later with hardly any books, then 1554 would indeed have been the fateful year in which his library, including that of Erasmus, was liquidated, even if some time elapsed before the last book in Mortaigne's keeping found a buyer.

---

44 vl/Catalogue nos 347, 102, and 343; Erasmus' ex libris in no 347 may be forged, and his copy of Herodian (no 343) is now lost.

45 See Pellegrin 'Un ex-libris autographe d'Erasme dans un manuscrit de l'*Opus agriculturae* de Palladius (Vat. Reg. Lat. 1252)'; cf 98 below. On the manuscript discovered earlier see 9 with n38 above.

46 vl/Catalogue no 203

47 vl/Catalogue nos 123, 208, 267, and 137 (the Aldine editions), 201 (*Corollarium*)

48 See 4 and n10, 8 and n31 above.

49 vl/Catalogue nos 138, 218, and 281: Galen *Therapeutica* (Venice 1500), now in the University Library in Leiden; *Plato graece* (Venice 1513), now in the Royal Library in The Hague; and Aulus Gellius *Noctes Atticae* (Venice 1509), now in the City Library of Rotterdam. Cf n10 above.

50 On the basis of even fewer details than we now possess, Allen drew the broad inference that in Łaski's last years the library 'was dispersed in the Netherlands and only a few [books] are now known'; see *The Correspondence of an Early Printing House* 30.

It will never be possible to clarify exactly how the process of disintegration proceeded. The number of Erasmus' books found so far for which the marks of later owners supply some of the links in the chain may have doubled since Husner wrote, but altogether they amount to a tiny percentage of the library as it existed in 1536. It is far too small a sample from which to draw any definite conclusions about the subsequent fate of the collection as a whole. About 95 per cent of the collection has disappeared without trace, and it seems unlikely that this figure will be greatly reduced, both because only a small number of all the books published in Erasmus' lifetime have survived and because books Erasmus once owned may not contain evidence of provenance.

Our muted expectation of new discoveries is based primarily on the recognition that the books entered in the *Versandliste* but not yet rediscovered have for the most part been destroyed. Global estimates of the total number of books printed before 1500 and the number of copies extant tell us that only a very small percentage of the total production of incunabula has been preserved.[51] For the first decades of the sixteenth century, until Erasmus' death in 1536, we should not expect the pattern of survival to be very different: not much more than 5 per cent of the whole book production of these years is likely to have survived. So far as we can determine, of the approximately 500 works noted in the *Versandliste*, fewer than twenty-five, that is, between 4 and 5 per cent, have been identified.[52] It is possible, even probable, that a few others are concealed here and there awaiting discovery. But the hope that the total number of copies traced will ever rise significantly above 5 per cent can be dismissed, for there are no special reasons why Erasmus' collection should have had better chances of survival than the average.

From an early date Erasmus' books were in far from good condition, and during their long wanderings with Łaski they may well have been damaged. In 1554 Regnerus Praedinius spoke plainly about many of the books offered to him, which he was keen to own because they had once belonged to the humanist whom he revered: in each case he already had a copy in better condition. Although as a prospective buyer the Groningen rector had an interest in emphasizing the faults he observed, the examples he gave of incomplete and worn or otherwise damaged copies are too concrete and precisely described to be dismissed.[53] Another factor may have contributed to the disappearance of Erasmus' books: there is nothing to suggest that he possessed a significant number of valuable books, finely printed, perhaps on parchment, and handsomely bound – in short, books whose outward appearance rather than their content might have given them a chance of being treated with special care by their later owners. Nor were their chances of survival favoured by the fact that the library consisted to a very large extent – about 40 per cent of the books entered in the *Versandliste* – of editions of classical and early Christian authors. In the sixteenth and early seventeenth centuries there was a continuing demand for such editions. Printers expanded their capabilities

---

51 The Kommission für den Gesamtkatalog der Wiegendrücke estimated that the number of independent bibliographical units was about 40,000 and the number of known incunabula about 450,000. Juchhoff accepted these figures in his *Handbuch der Bibliothekswissenschaft* (1952) 450. Labarre *Histoire du Livre* (1970) 69 estimated 30–35,000 editions totalling some 20,000,000 copies (assuming an average print run of 600 copies per edition); another estimate (1977) came to 27,000 editions (Widmann 'Die Wirkung des Buchdrucks auf die humanistische Zeitgenossen und Nachfahren des Erfinders' 71–2). Even if one assumes 27,000 editions with an average print run of 400 copies, the 450,000 known incunabula amount to less than 4.2 per cent of the original total printed.

52 Cf 17 n1 below.

53 In the case of the edition of Galen (VL/Catalogue no 137), Praedinius' statements in the letter to Gérard Camp (see n10 above) can be checked, because the book has been preserved; see 84 below.

to meet this demand, and new editions of texts were continually being issued. Though many of them were simply reprints, there were also constantly improved and augmented versions based on more reliable and recently discovered manuscripts and furnished with new commentaries in which the older ones were often incorporated. Moreover, many texts first published separately later appeared again in revised form in the collected works of an author. It would have been entirely natural if the majority of the superseded and obsolete editions from Erasmus' library had been lost, perhaps fairly quickly. The same fate must have befallen another category of books well represented in his library, dictionaries, encyclopaedias, and similar works of reference, that is, books liable to extra wear and tear from frequent use. Very few copies are preserved of one such work, the then popular Latin dictionary of Ambrogio Calepino, of which Erasmus owned one of the roughly fifty editions published, in constantly improved and augmented form, during his lifetime.[54]

Of course, there is still a chance that a few more books may come to light here and there with the ex libris of Erasmus in his characteristic and usually easily recognizable hand on the last page. They may not have been discovered because they were known only to a few initiates and are not mentioned anywhere in the literature. Or they may have escaped attention because the *Sum Erasmi* has faded away completely or has been deliberately erased, so that the quartz lamp or another modern technique must be applied to make it visible again.[55] And there may be books from Erasmus' collection that have been preserved but that we cannot trace because we lack any pointers to their former ownership. Beatus Rhenanus rarely failed to write his name in the books he bought or received as gifts, usually with the year of acquisition.[56] Erasmus was not so methodical and often did not insert his ex libris in newly acquired volumes. We know this from the books that have come to light lacking the *Sum Erasmi* but nevertheless identifiable with reasonable certainty as his former property, sometimes on the grounds of autograph marginalia, as was the case with the edition of Galen found at Leeuwarden, sometimes with the aid of the notes of reliable third parties, as a rule later owners, on the title-page or last page. For example, there is no reason to doubt the accuracy of the precise inscription *Ex bibliotheca Erasmi Roterodami donatum per clarissimum virum D. Joannem a Lasco 1548 penultima februarii* in the edition of Diogenes Laertius now in the Beineke Library at Yale University.[57] But even if they have been preserved, books without an ex libris indicating their provenance can no longer be identified as having belonged to Erasmus.

Their illustrious provenance offered Erasmus' books little protection. After his death there were certainly friends and admirers for whom a book from his library would be a treasured possession. Towards the end of 1536 Claudius Cantiuncula, once professor of law at Basel, asked Amerbach for a book from the library as a memento;[58] eighteen years later Praedinius, as we saw, was eager to acquire a number of books containing Erasmus' ex libris or marginalia. But the provenance of the now scattered books very soon began to work against them. Erasmus' star had already faded by the 1550s, when the dispersal of his library was well under way. He was no longer regarded as a celebrated and admired prince of letters, a great

---

54 VL/Catalogue no 194; the first edition appeared in 1502. It might be added that the large, heavy folio format went entirely out of fashion by the end of Erasmus' life.

55 On the poor quality of the ink that Erasmus sometimes used see Pellegrin (n45 above) 164. Ultraviolet light made it possible to identify Erasmus' copy of the first Greek edition of Plato; see VL/Catalogue no 218.

56 Knod *Aus der Bibliothek des Beatus Rhenanus* viii

57 On the Galen see 10 above and VL/Catalogue no 137; on the Diogenes Laertius see 8 above and VL/Catalogue no 305. Cf no 272.

58 AK IV 467 Ep 2095

authority to whom the world deferred, as he had been at the height of his fame. Gradually, religious strife had overshadowed his reputation and undermined his prestige; the humanist who had wished to maintain his independent but conciliatory middle course in the great conflict had been turned, in spite of himself, into a controversial figure who counted for little in either of the increasingly polarized camps. In his own lifetime, he had been alienated from the Reformers; after his death, the Counter-Reformation gained ground and discredited him among the adherents of the old church. Bruce Mansfield has described the decline of his once unimpeachable reputation in detail. In the Catholic camp, 'by 1550 the mood had changed decisively, the last Erasmian generation had passed away, and the smell of battle was in the air.'[59] The Counter-Reformation no longer admitted any middle way. 'The effect of the Council of Trent could only be to undermine the moderate Catholic judgment of Erasmus.' The attitude of the head of the church was all-important. In 1535 Paul III had been willing to make Erasmus a cardinal, but under Paul IV the Index of Prohibited Books of 1559 placed him 'in the first class of heretics whose whole output was condemned ... "with all his commentaries, annotations, scholia, dialogues, letters, opinions, translations, books and writings, even if these include nothing against or about religion."'[60] Even Luther was spared such wholesale condemnation. In the Reformed world, where, in spite of his always conservative viewpoint, Erasmus had always been able to count on a great deal of sympathy, his reputation also declined, although the reasons for this varied from region to region or even from town to town. On the whole, by the end of the sixteenth century Erasmus' reputation had reached its nadir: 'Those speaking for Erasmus were few.'[61] This negative development meant that books from his dispersed library – those that were not piously cherished by the small band of his remaining loyal adherents and followers – must soon have lost any special attraction for later buyers that their provenance might once have given them. Inevitably, most of them fell into the hands of people wholly uninterested in Erasmus or perhaps even unsympathetic to him. To these owners, evidence of Erasmus' previous ownership may even have seemed undesirable; in an age of increasing intolerance and suspicion, perhaps some preferred not to draw attention to his books and carefully erased the *Sum Erasmi.*

In his article of 1936 Husner confined himself in the main to the outward vicissitudes of Erasmus' library as described in the *Versandliste.* He refrained from analysing or evaluating the contents of the collection, and he did not provide the *Versandliste* with any annotation. He himself regretted that he was not able to do more, but the space at his disposal in the *Gedenkschrift* gave him no opportunity. He could only hope 'to be able to continue elsewhere what had necessarily to be omitted here.'[62] Unfortunately his other studies prevented him from carrying out his intention. His article, however fundamental it remains – and on certain points it has never been superseded – was thus in a sense incomplete. It called for a complementary investigation.

---

59 Mansfield *Phoenix of His Age* 65
60 Mansfield *Phoenix of His Age* 26–7. The first Index was printed in Rome by A. Bladus in 1557 but not published until 1559. The rather more flexible Index of 1564, the so-called Council Index, forbade certain books of Erasmus, including the *Moria,* the *Colloquia,* the *Lingua,* and the *Institutio christiani matrimonii,* while his religious works were forbidden conditionally (that is, unless they were expurgated by the faculties of Paris or Leuven). In 1590 all of Erasmus' works were again placed on the Index issued by Sixtus V. For further details see Reusch *Der Index der verbotenen Bücher*; the summary on Erasmus and the Index in *Erasmus ... Erasmusdrukken uit de Universiteitsbibliotheek te Gent*; Augustijn *Erasmus: His Life, Works, and Influence* 198–9.
61 Mansfield *Phoenix of His Age* 299
62 Husner 'Bibliothek' 237 n53

Such an investigation has been undertaken in this book. To begin with, the author set himself the goal of subjecting the text of the *Versandliste* to a thorough analysis and, so far as possible, identifying the books listed in it so cryptically. But he soon gave up this strictly limited plan. The detective work entailed in expanding the abbreviated descriptions in the list brought to light many interesting details of Erasmus' relationship with his books. Another goal emerged: using the documentation collected for the analysis of the *Versandliste*, it seemed possible to fill out Husner's outline sketch of the library and at the same time to gain an insight into the role that his collection of books had played in Erasmus' life.

The make-up and structure of this book have been dictated by its double objective. The emphasis, at least for the author, lies in its second part, which is entirely taken up by the *Versandliste*, expanded and annotated in detail. In form it is a *catalogue raisonné,* although that term is not precisely accurate in this context, for it is not a catalogue of a collection whose composition is known, but a sometimes highly speculative reconstruction of an incomplete and vaguely described collection, all but a few works of which have perished. The annotated list of titles is preceded by an introduction that discusses the working method followed in this investigation. What was largely a by-product of the exposition of the *Versandliste* has, in the first part of the book, become an account of Erasmus' library that can be read independently. In separate chapters it discusses the formation and growth of the library by purchase and presentation, the owner's efforts to rid his collection of what he felt to be unnecessary ballast, the housing and arrangement of the books, and their upkeep. The manuscripts and books that we know that Erasmus possessed or must have possessed but are not included in the *Versandliste* required separate attention. Another chapter examines both Erasmus' habits of study in his own library and his lifelong engagement with the world of books through correspondence with fellow scholars, conversation with visitors, and a close, often demanding, relationship with his publishers. A summary evaluation of his library is given in the concluding chapter.

PART ONE

The History and Nature of Erasmus' Working Library

1

The Formation and Growth of the Library

The information that may be gleaned from the *Versandliste* concerning the contents of Erasmus' library may be neither complete nor detailed, but it gives us a reasonable overall picture. The annotated catalogue in Part 2 of this book expands, to the best of our ability, the short-title entries in that inventory, taken at his death.

It is extremely difficult, on the other hand, to form any clear idea of the formation and growth of the collection. The surviving books discovered – fewer than twenty-five in all – provide very little information.[1] Only two of them contain handwritten notes showing that they were gifts, but the notes do not include the date of the gift.[2] Erasmus leaves us in the dark about how he acquired his books. Unlike Beatus Rhenanus, who was in the habit of marking each volume with the year of acquisition, thus providing a sound chronological framework for the historian of his library,[3] to judge from the few books preserved, Erasmus was content to sign his new acquisitions *Sum Erasmi*. Nor do the publication dates of the books, where they can be established with any certainty or by bibliographical approximation, offer useful guidance; indeed, they may lead us astray. We can assume that the books dating from the later years of Erasmus' life were mostly acquired or received soon after their publication. But the year of publication of the oldest books – those that might have thrown most light on the formation of the collection – does not tell us anything about when they were acquired. In 1525 Erasmus was still buying works that had appeared before the turn of the century. When we try to reconstruct the origin and growth of the library we are therefore thrown back almost entirely on sources outside the *Versandliste*, chiefly, of course, on Erasmus' correspondence. Scattered within it are numerous – and often surprising – pieces of information about books. Inevitably they are largely casual references; taken as a whole the material is disconnected, with many gaps. We shall never be able, therefore, to arrive at a complete and trustworthy picture of the history of the library. We shall have to be satisfied with an incomplete sketch, in which only the main outlines and a few details can be discerned.

In a letter to Maarten van Dorp written in 1515, Erasmus described the circumstances in which he had written his *Moriae encomium*, conceived while he was crossing the Alps on his return from Italy in the summer of 1509. While lodging with Thomas More in Bucklersbury, kidney pains had forced him to remain indoors for several days; he mentions that his library

---

1 Books mentioned in the *Versandliste* that have survived are marked with an asterisk in the list of 'Books in Erasmus' Library' (152–88 below) that precede the annotated catalogue. Cf Vanautgaerden 'Ex bibliotheca Erasmi: Catalogue des 33 ouvrages' 321–34 and 'Ex bibliotheca Erasmi: Un 34e ouvrage' 554; Vanautgaerden considers twenty-five books to be identical to those on the *Versandliste*.
2 VL/Catalogue nos 176 and 389. Cf nos 280, 305, and 368; see also 33 with n124 below.
3 See 12 with n56 above.

had not yet arrived.[4] This, as far as we can trace, is the first time in his correspondence that he referred to his collection of books as a 'library' (*bibliotheca*). Before that he had merely spoken more modestly of his books. We should not attach too much significance to the choice of words, but the use of the new term at that moment may not have been altogether fortuitous. In the previous years, especially, as we shall see, from about 1511, his collection of books had grown to such an extent that it was no longer an exaggeration to speak of it as a library.

Before his Italian journey, broadly up to the age of forty, Erasmus must have owned few books. His father had supported himself in Italy by copying manuscripts of classical authors,[5] but Erasmus inherited few if any of these, and he could not keep them; he had to use the proceeds of their sale to support himself and his brother. This meant so much to the young Erasmus, then perhaps seventeen, that he even reproached his chief guardian for not selling them quickly enough.[6] During his years in the monastery of Steyn his vow of poverty prevented his forming a serious collection of books, though it need not have ruled out the possession of a few volumes for his own use. Even among the rigorous Carthusians the prohibition of the private ownership of books was evaded by a permanent usufruct;[7] the practice of the Dominican order allowed individual ownership of books,[8] and the Augustinian canons must have been at least as flexible. Erasmus' earliest books may well have included the *Enchiridion* of Augustine on parchment, which he still treasured some years later.[9]

There is nothing to suggest that after Erasmus left Steyn to enter the service of the bishop of Cambrai, Hendrik van Bergen, as his secretary he added much to his presumably meagre collection of books before he was given leave to study in Paris in 1495. The circumstances, though changed, gave him no occasion for this; and even if he had wished it otherwise, chronic shortage of money made it impossible for him to buy many books. Moreover, we may wonder if he really felt the lack of a library of his own as a serious hindrance or disadvantage in his early years. No doubt his hunger for reading matter was insatiable, but at that time his interests were still general and unfocused. As he himself said, he was 'swept ... into liberal studies' by 'a kind of secret natural force' and greedily devoured anything in that field that came his way.[10] From his youth Erasmus must have been in a position amply to satisfy his still unspecialized reading tastes from sources near at hand. That applies to his schooling in Deventer and to his years in the monastery at Steyn.[11] The list of Latin prose and verse authors whom he chose as his models, compiled in 1489, was not short.[12] He may have encountered greater difficulties during the years when he was travelling in the entourage of Hendrik van Bergen, but the bishop owned a library, and Erasmus found others en route. In the monastery of Groenendaal, near Brussels, he was in his element, and he astonished the monks by his tireless reading of Augustine, whose works, probably in manuscript, he even took to his bedchamber.[13] Finally, he found what he needed in the friendly and lettered

---

4 Allen Epp 222:1–24, 337:126–39/cwe Epp 222:1–26, 337 134–46. Erasmus used the term *bibliothecula* a few years later (Allen Ep 807:2), but perhaps more from a fondness for diminutives than from a desire to emphasize how few books he owned.

5 *Compendium vitae* Allen i 47:19–48:24/cwe 4 404:23–30

6 Ep 1, to Pieter Winckel, written when Erasmus was seventeen. In this book it is assumed, based on Koch *The Year of Erasmus' Birth*, that Erasmus was most probably born in 1467.

7 Gumbert 'Over Karthuizerbibliotheken in de Nederlanden' 176

8 Thomas 'Boekenbezit en boekengebruik bij de Dominikanen in de Nederlanden voor c. 1550' 429

9 Allen Epp 123:21–2, 135:44, and 138:120–1/cwe Epp 123:24–5, 135:52–3, and 138:136–7, all to Jacob Batt

10 *Catalogus lucubrationum* Allen i 2:30–2/cwe Ep 1341A:42–4

11 Reedijk *Poems* 47, 49; Huizinga *Erasmus of Rotterdam* 13; Hyma *The Youth of Erasmus* 164–6

12 Allen Ep 20:96–105/cwe Ep 20:95–103

13 Allen i 590 Appendix 5 'Erasmus with the Bishop of Cambray'

milieu of Paris.[14] Thus for a long time the impecunious young Erasmus had no immediate need or spur to buy books for himself.

The situation changed in early 1500 when he threw himself passionately into the study of Greek. The date can be fixed exactly. He had just returned from his first visit to England where, under the influence of Colet's teaching and example, he came to see the study of the Bible and the Fathers of the church as his life's work. What he yearned for above all was to be able to read and interpret the New Testament in its original tongue and to restore the whole text of Jerome, maimed and corrupted by the ignorance of the theologians, including the Greek passages. To achieve this aim he had to master Greek as thoroughly as he could. And for this he needed an adequate number of Greek books and a teacher, preferably a native Greek, who could guide him through his first months as quickly as possible. With his Greek teacher, the only one in Paris and only to be had for an exorbitant fee, he got on so badly that he was soon forced to be his own master.[15]

Finding Greek books was no easier. Even in Italy very few scholars were yet interested in the revival of Greek letters.[16] As a consequence, demand for the original texts was very limited, and the dissemination of printed editions got off to a relatively slow start. While most of the Latin authors had already appeared in print between 1465 and 1475, the *editiones principes* of the most important Greek authors in the original language did not appear until about 1488–1518, and only a few of them predated 1500.[17] Without exception, these were Italian editions, which penetrated north of the Alps only slowly and irregularly. Even in such a centre of the book trade as Paris, there was not a single copy of either of the two current and indispensable Greek grammars for sale in 1501.[18] That frustrating lack of Greek books meant that when the few new editions, especially of texts, reached the French capital, Erasmus had to snap them up as soon as he could. When he returned penniless from England – practically all his savings had been seized by the customs in Dover – he tried to procure money from friends in order, as he said 'to buy some Greek authors; after that, I shall buy clothes.'[19] May we not imagine him making the rounds of the bookshops of Paris in search of the texts he needed? Erasmus always made a point of seeking out printers, publishers, and booksellers in person to be sure of hearing, as far as possible at first hand, what was new on the market. It is characteristic of him that one of the few personal encounters he should have mentioned in his letters during his years at Steyn was with a printer-publisher, Gerard Leeuw. When Leeuw, who had moved his business from Gouda, his native town, to Antwerp, visited his birthplace and the nearby cloister of Steyn in 1489, it was Erasmus who accompanied him on his way back to Gouda as far as the IJssel, undoubtedly listening eagerly to his news of authors and recent books.[20]

---

14 For books he borrowed at that time see for example Allen Epp 67:4–5, 68:7–8, 121:5–6, 122:3–5 / CWE Epp 67:5–7, 68:3–5, 121:6–7, 122:4–8

15 Allen Epp 138:38–48, 139:143–9, 149:56–68 / CWE Epp 138:43–54, 139:166–73, 149:65–79. For more on Erasmus' Greek tutor, Hermonymus of Sparta, see *Catalogus lucubrationum* Allen I 7:22–4 and n / CWE Ep 1341A:226–9 and n44.

16 Bolgar *The Classical Heritage and its Beneficiaries* 276–82; Reynolds and Wilson *Scribes and Scholars* 138–40 and 240 (notes)

17 Sandys *A History of Classical Scholarship* II 104

18 That is, those of Constantine Lascaris and Urbano Bolzani, both of which were available in recent editions from Aldo Manuzio; cf Allen Ep 159:48–50 / CWE Ep 159:54–6. Erasmus complained in a letter from Leuven in September 1502: 'We are very hard up for Greek books here'; Allen Ep 172:13–14 / CWE Ep 172:18.

19 Allen Ep 124:63–4 / CWE Ep 124:72–4; on the 'English disaster' see Allen Ep 119:7n / CWE Ep 119:9n.

20 Allen Ep 32:32–5 / CWE Ep 32:35–9

In Paris the publication of his first works brought Erasmus into contact with several book producers,[21] and very soon he was probably among the regular visitors who frequented the Paris bookshops, the meeting places of the intelligentsia at that time.[22] Clearly he had his favourites. In autumn 1500 his friend Jacob Batt asked him for several books. As he himself had temporarily moved to Orléans to avoid the plague, he sent a messenger to Paris with money for the books, specifying precisely where he could buy them.[23] He had good reason for this, for buying books demanded familiarity with the customs and peculiarities of the trade. Fixed prices did not exist: the bookseller asked what he thought his client could afford.[24] In Paris there were many buyers, and this forced up prices, especially of foreign books, so that an edition from the press of Aldo Manuzio sometimes cost three times as much there as it did in Venice.[25] Erasmus was businesslike enough to be well aware of this price differential. More than ten years later he pointed out to a correspondent the Italian bookseller from whom Aldine editions could be bought more cheaply even than in Rome.[26] Perhaps in Paris he profited from the experience in the book world of Nicolaus Bensrott, his pupil (although perhaps not much younger than himself), and also his friend. Bensrott had studied law at Bologna before he moved to Paris, was well off, and was energetically building up his own library; he was also willing to help his hard-up master with his purchases (although Erasmus' debt to him remained quite small).[27] Erasmus trusted his knowledge of the market and in the summer of 1501, when he was staying with Jacob Batt at the castle of Tournehem, gave Bensrott carte blanche to buy whatever new Greek texts were on the market. 'I would rather pawn my coat than fail to obtain them, especially any Christian works, for example, the Psalms or Gospels.'[28]

The following years saw Erasmus intensively occupied in the study of Greek, and the first results of his efforts were published. He translated three declamations of Libanius, which in 1503 he offered to Nicolas Ruistre, chancellor of the University of Paris and bishop of Arras.[29] On the eve of his journey to Italy, which began in the summer of 1506, he also sent his translations of Lucian and Euripides to the printer.[30] What came of his plans to acquire the Greek texts he needed cannot be traced with any certainty. When the plague forced him to leave Paris in 1501 he spent a short time in Holland and travelled to Haarlem, where he visited Willem Hermans, to 'make a Greek of him,' as he put it. With that aim in view he had brought a large pack of books, presumably editions of Greek texts with perhaps a Greek

---

21 Antoine Denidel (*Carmen de casa natalitia Iesu* [January 1496?]); Johannes Philippi (*Adagiorum collectanea* 1500). Erasmus also edited Willem Hermans *Sylva odarum* and saw it through the press (Guy Marchaut 1497); see Allen and CWE Ep 49 introductions.

22 Cf Allen Ep 522:14–15/CWE Ep 522:15–16.

23 Allen Ep 130:66–74, 104–5/CWE Ep 130:79–88, 122–4

24 Ruppel 'Die Bücherwelt des 16. Jahrhunderts und die Frankfurter Büchermessen'; cf Hirsch *Printing, Selling and Reading 1450–1550* 71.

25 Hoyoux *Le carnet de voyage de Jérôme Aléandre en France et à Liège (1510–1516)* 208 n4; Hutton *The Greek Anthology in France* 3

26 Allen Ep 219:4–6/CWE Ep 219:5–8

27 Allen Ep 158:25–8/CWE Ep 158:31–3. On Bensrott see Allen and CWE Ep 158 introductions; CEBR I 123.

28 Allen Ep 160:6–8, and cf 158:23–4/CWE Ep 160:7–10 and cf 158:28–9. On Erasmus' travels in the spring and summer of 1501 see Allen and CWE Ep 153 introductions; cf Ep 157.

29 Ep 177 is the dedicatory preface. The *Libanii aliquot declamatiunculae* were printed only after a long delay (Leuven: Martens 1519).

30 *Luciani ... opuscula ... ab Erasmo Roterdamo et Thoma Moro in Latinorum linguam traducta* (Paris: Josse Bade 13 November 1506); *Euripidis ... Hecuba et Iphigenia; Latinae factae Erasmo Roterodamo interprete* (Paris: Josse Bade 13 September 1506). See Allen and CWE Epp 187 and 188 introductions.

grammar.[31] On that occasion he may have lent Hermans the Greek fables he asked him to return a year later, when he was still badly off for Greek texts.[32] Could the book have been one of the early editions of Aesop?[33]

Erasmus cannot have managed to acquire many Greek texts in the early years of the century, for as we have said, very few came on to the market outside Italy. On his death he left about twenty Greek books published before 1506. When had he acquired them? At least five of them were on the list of books Erasmus ordered around 1525,[34] and it is very likely that only one or two of the others were among his early purchases. Both his Isocrates and his Suidas (the Suda) had been published in Milan,[35] and because that city had recently fallen into French hands Milanese printings could reach Paris more easily than many other Italian editions. We know that Erasmus was working on Isocrates in 1501;[36] and although he seems not to have had access to an edition of Suidas when he was preparing the *Collectanea adagiorum* he published in 1500, it was to be of great use to him as he added new material in subsequent editions of the *Adages*.[37] We cannot rule out the possibility that the editions of Lucian and Euripides that appear in the *Versandliste* were already among his personal property when he published his translations from them in 1506.[38] And he was anxious to obtain Christian works such as the Gospels and Psalms in Greek.[39] In the case of the Psalms his wish may have been granted very speedily, for in 1502 Pierre de Courtebourne offered to buy a psalter for him. This was a manuscript book, very probably with the Greek text. Erasmus seized the chance eagerly and asked to buy the manuscript, 'so long as it is complete and has a sound text and is reasonably legible,' and guaranteed prompt payment.[40] It is true that the *Versandliste* does not mention a Greek manuscript psalter, but that does not prove that the purchase had fallen through.[41]

Erasmus' early purchases probably included several Latin works as well, for example the 1497 edition of Jerome published by Johannes and Gregorius de Gregoriis in Venice. The copy once in his possession was later presented to a younger friend, so that the title no longer appears in the *Versandliste*.[42] As early as 1500 Erasmus had spoken of scraping together enough money to buy his own copies of the works of Jerome, which he planned to re-edit, restoring the Greek, and to issue with a commentary; he may very well have acquired the two-volume

---

31 Allen Ep 157:38–40 / cwe Ep 157:46–9

32 Allen Ep 172:13–14 / cwe Ep 172:17–18

33 Three editions of the Greek text before 1501 are known, all in quarto: Venice: B. Justinopolitanus et al [c 1498] (gw 312); Milan: B. Accursius [c 1480], with a selection of fables and a Latin translation added to the original text (gw 313); Reggio: D. Bertochus 1497, which contains only the selection added in the Milan edition (gw 314).

34 vl/Catalogue nos 114–15, 116, 198, 203, and 320. See 32 below.

35 vl/Catalogue nos 124 and 344

36 Allen Epp 158:7, 160:4 / cwe Epp 158:10, 160:6

37 asd ii-6 349 56–7n

38 vl/Catalogue nos 123 (Lucian) and 100, 102, and 103 (Euripides)

39 See 20 with n28 above.

40 Ep 169. On the 'psalter' see cwe 6n; on Pierre de Courtebourne, perhaps the bastard brother of Florent de Calonne, Baron de Courtebourne, in whose castle or country house he had just spent a few months, see Allen and cwe Epp 165 and 169 introductions; cebr i 350.

41 Erasmus may have disposed of the manuscript later; see chapter 2 below on how Erasmus cleared 'ballast' from his library.

42 Undoubtedly after the publication of the great Basel edition of Jerome (Froben 1516). Erasmus' copy of this edition, which contains notes by Henricus Glareanus, is now in the Universitätsbibliothek Munich; see vl/ Catalogue no 243 with n9. For the value of the Venetian edition in the preparation of the text of the biblical commentaries in the Froben edition see ak ii 66–7 Ep 551 n2.

Venetian edition current at that time. In the same letter to his friend Jacob Batt in which he first mentioned his work on Jerome and his study of Greek, Erasmus said that he wanted a Plato.[43] None of Plato's works had yet been published in the original Greek, and a manuscript text was not to be had. Erasmus would have had to be content for the time being with the famous Latin translation by Marsilio Ficino, and this is what he probably had in mind. The Venetian edition of the Latin *Opera* of 1491 was almost certainly in his possession on his death;[44] the chances are that he had owned it for many years and had bought it in 1500 or very soon after. It is clear in any case that he not only knew Ficino's version at the time but used it repeatedly and often cited it verbatim,[45] so that the text was evidently at his elbow.

In sum, what we have said about the growth of Erasmus' collection of books in the early 1500s rests to a large extent on unprovable assumptions, but it is not unreasonable to conclude that his purchases of the books he wanted, particularly the Greek books, remained very modest. In the first place, lack of money would have thwarted his determination to acquire them. We must also bear in mind that Erasmus was able to borrow or consult more Greek books in his immediate environment than his laments of their scandalous shortage might suggest. He had access in both France and England to Greek manuscripts, presumably not ancient codices but more recent transcripts. In Paris there were a great many such modern copies, made by Greek emigrants. Erasmus' earliest essays in translation, the *Declamatiunculae* of Libanius, for example, were made from a manuscript. Where and from whom he borrowed it is not known, but in this case too we do know that it was not a venerable ancient codex but 'evidently a recent transcript of a very ordinary kind.'[46]

The growth of Erasmus' library during the time he spent in Italy (autumn of 1506 to mid-July 1509) is equally difficult to reconstruct in any detail, but the fact of its growth is evident. It was books above all that drew Erasmus to Italy and kept him there.[47] It is almost unthinkable that while there he did not acquire any – especially books that he would have considered indispensable and that were much more difficult to obtain north of the Alps, often only at greater expense. As has been mentioned, while he was staying in Thomas More's house after his return Erasmus waited for the arrival of his library. Were these books that he had owned for some time, had perhaps left in storage with friends in 1506 for the duration of his absence, and was now having conveyed to Bucklersbury?[48] Or were they books – perhaps even specific books, as the context of his comment makes plausible – that he had procured in Italy? Years later (in 1527) he made a most unusual reference to a particular purchase of those years: in Siena (this must have been in 1509) he laid hands on a very old, and if he was not mistaken the first, edition of Aulus Gellius.[49] It is irrelevant here that he must later have replaced the edition he had bought then by a more recent one, which has survived.[50]

---

43 Allen Ep 138:38–41 / CWE Ep 138:43–7; cf 19 with n15 above.

44 VL/Catalogue no 217

45 Levi 'The neo-Platonist Calculus' 231 and 246n; Cytowksa 'Erasme de Rotterdam et Marsile Ficin, son maître' 170–2. Erasmus cited Plato's *Cratylus* in the version by Ficino verbatim in his *Collectanea adagiorum* (1500).

46 ASD I-1 177; cf 20 with n29 above.

47 Huizinga *Erasmus of Rotterdam* 62–3, in a brief account of Erasmus' reaction to the Italy of the Renaissance

48 Erasmus was in England from the end of 1505 to early June 1506, mostly in London, though he also paid a brief visit to Cambridge (Allen and CWE Ep 185 introductions; Allen I 591 Appendix 6 'Erasmus at Cambridge in 1506') and may have visited Bedwell in Hertfordshire, not far north of London (Allen Ep 191 introduction). Bucklersbury was in the centre of London near Cheapside.

49 Allen Ep 1824:29–32 / CWE Ep 1824:32–5

50 If Erasmus' purchase really was the *editio princeps* it must have been that of 1469 (Rome: C. Sweynheym and A. Pannartz). For Erasmus' copy of the 1509 edition (Venice: J. de Tridino), see VL/Catalogue no 281.

What matters is that he acquired a copy of the *Noctes Atticae* in Siena, where he cannot have spent more than a short time – one of many indications that in whatever sizeable city Erasmus found himself, he seldom failed to investigate the bookshops in search of something he was interested in. In Italy his searches were not solely for his own benefit. In his very first approach to Aldo Manuzio, in October 1507, he inquired about the works of some less well known authors that the printer and publisher might have in stock, for his learned friends in England had asked him to look out for them;[51] no doubt Erasmus would have been interested in Manuzio's response on his own account as well. Erasmus' longest continuous stay, from November 1506 to October 1507, was at Bologna, where he may have bought his copies of the two important collections of military and agricultural authors edited by Philippo Beroaldo and reprinted in Bologna shortly before his arrival there.[52] But this cannot be more than an inference, for concrete evidence on the date and place of acquisition is lacking. The same is true, with about five or six exceptions,[53] of all the other works published in Italy before about 1509 that appear in the *Versandliste*, including the books that followed Erasmus back across the Alps and were permanently included in his library. Most of them were Venetian editions, which is understandable: Venice was still the dominant centre of printing, and until the first decades of the sixteenth century the most important editions of classical authors, especially the Greeks with whom Erasmus was chiefly concerned, were published there.[54] Current products of the Venetian presses may also have been available in the other great cities Erasmus visited: Bologna, Padua, Florence, and Rome. Nevertheless, we have to assume that Erasmus acquired most of the books he bought or received as gifts in those years in Venice, where he spent eight months living and working in constant proximity to the printing business of Aldo Manuzio and regularly took part in the activities of the learned circle of the New Academy.[55]

The more than forty Italian printings of before 1509 named in the *Versandliste* are chiefly editions of classical texts, both Greek and Latin, but there are several commentaries by Italian humanists as well.[56] If the books that Erasmus acquired during his years in Italy (and that we assume he brought back with him) were similar to those recorded in the *Versandliste*, then we could deduce from them the way in which Erasmus' aspirations for his library expanded. In the first years of the new century he had been determined to acquire the editions of Greek texts he needed for his study of the language. He had every reason to hunt down Greek books in Italy: shortly after his arrival he wrote from Bologna that he had journeyed south above all to gain fluency in Greek.[57] But once in Italy he naturally seized the chance that the highly developed Italian market offered him to expand his collection of books in other directions, even if on a somewhat restricted scale, for he still lacked the funds to do

---

51 Allen Ep 207:47–9 / cwe Ep 207:52–4

52 *Scriptores rei militaris* (Bologna: J.A. de Benedictis 1505) and *Scriptores rei rusticae* (Bologna: B. Hectoris 1504); see vl/Catalogue nos 323 and 324.

53 See vl/Catalogue nos 127–8, 198, 203, 214, and 320. On the order list of 1525 see 32–3 below.

54 The first Greek text editions printed in Rome – the works of Pindar – did not appear until 1515 (see vl/ Catalogue no 107). There were a few exceptions, among them the famous Florentine *editio princeps* of Homer of 1488/9 (see nos 114 and 115) and the Milan editions of Isocrates and Suidas of 1493 and 1499 (see nos 124 and 344).

55 The Aldine press was established by the scholar-printer Aldo Manuzio, whose Greek was sufficient to admit him to the circle of Giovanni Pico della Mirandola and the Florentine Academy. With a view to exploiting the growing demand for Greek texts he established a printing company in Venice in the 1490s and in 1502, the 'New Academy' with statutes (*Neakadamias nomos*). Although his initiative ultimately failed, the humanistic circle it attracted nourished the project of Erasmus' *Adagia*.

56 For example vl/Catalogue nos 279 (two authors) and 285

57 Allen Ep 203:2–3 / cwe Ep 203:3–4

more. He acquired Greek and Latin texts alike, possibly with one or two contemporary commentaries he considered indispensable. In this way he laid the foundations of what became a well-equipped reference library.

After Erasmus' return from Italy we are no longer dependent on guesswork to show that he actively set about building up his still modest library, for now we have conclusive evidence that he began to acquire books on a much greater scale than before. The number of identifiable Paris editions in the *Versandliste* published between 1505 and 1515, especially in 1510 and 1511, is too large to be merely accidental. They were not all extensive works, and many were quartos later bound in combined volumes of three or four titles.[58] There is other evidence of this flood of new purchases. In 1513 Erasmus mentioned the recent extension of his library, which, to use his own words, he owed 'to the extraordinary, the almost incredible, kindness of a man, or rather a great man, who deserves to be remembered to the end of time, William Warham, archbishop of Canterbury and primate of all England.'[59] Erasmus was still highly dependent on protectors. Warham, who had provided him with a prebend in the previous year and soon converted it into a fixed annuity,[60] was his most important benefactor, but the financial support Erasmus received from other friends, especially Lord Mountjoy but also John Colet and Bishop John Fisher, gave him more freedom to buy books on a large scale.[61] In 1511 in particular, Erasmus must have spent heavily on books. H.C. Porter has calculated his expenditure for 1511–14, the years in which he was resident (with interruptions) in Cambridge. He did not live cheaply, and in 1511 he spent considerably more than his annual average.[62] Could at least part of this have been invested in the library? One direct witness confirms his purchases at this time. The young Stephen Gardiner was a member of Erasmus' circle when he was in Paris in spring 1511 and lodged with the Englishman Eden in the Rue Saint-Jean-de-Beauvais.[63] Erasmus was not in Paris, as used to be assumed, to see the *Moria* through the press, but rather to discuss a new edition of the *Adagia* with Josse Bade and to buy books.[64] Some fifteen years later Gardiner, now bishop of Winchester, remembered well how impressed he had been by the large number of books, both Greek and Latin, that Erasmus had acquired.[65] Paris was the best place to find books. In Cambridge Erasmus was on confidential terms with several booksellers, whom he had not forgotten many years later but still counted among his 'old friends' in the city.[66] He may even have stayed a while with one of them, Garrett Godfrey, who was born in Limburg.[67] But neither among his friends in Cambridge nor anywhere else in England would he have had the opportunities that the French capital offered to take advantage of the more broadly based continental book trade.

---

58 For example vl/Catalogue nos 306, 307, and 310
59 Allen Ep 269:72–6/cwe Ep 269:79–83. Ep 269 is the preface to a revised edition of the *Adagiorum chiliades* that appeared in 1515.
60 Allen and cwe Ep 255 introductions
61 See, on Lord Mountjoy, Allen Ep 254:2/cwe Ep 254:2–3; on Colet, Allen Epp 230:43–5, 237:30–69/cwe Epp 230:50–3, 237:37–78; and on Fisher, Allen Epp 227:18–19, 242:4–15/cwe 227:225, 242:5–17.
62 *Erasmus and Cambridge* 69
63 cwe Ep 219 introduction
64 asd iv-3 15–16
65 Allen Ep 1669:23–4
66 Allen Ep 1656:18–20/cwe Ep 1656:21–3 names three: Garrett Godfrey; Nicolaas Spierinck, a bookbinder who who also operated as a bookseller; and Johann Siberch, founder of the first press in Cambridge.
67 Allen Epp 248:44n, 456:281n, 777:29–30 and n/cwe Epp 248:55n, 456:313n, 777:30–1. Erasmus praised him in his *Apologia ad Fabrum*, without naming him and a little apologetically: 'a certain bookseller, not a scholar but a friend' (lb ix 20c/asd ix-3 88/cwe 83 10).

In Paris he could also count on the cooperation of Josse Bade, who had already published his edition of Valla's *Annotationes in Latinam Novi Testamenti interpretationem* in 1505[68] and was now not only printing his *De copia* (published in July 1512) but had also agreed to issue a revised edition of the *Adagia*.[69] During his visit to Paris Erasmus may have begun by going the rounds of the bookshops in person, but the experienced and competent Bade soon seems to have taken over the job of supplying the books that Erasmus wanted. When the bookseller did not deal directly, he acted through a friend and colleague. Some of the purchases were made through Jean-Pierre de Varade, a Milanese who had emigrated to avoid the Italian wars and settled in Paris, where he also acted as agent for the Aldine press. Bade did not hand over all the transactions to others, for he kept a close eye on the new books that Varade received from or via Lyon. The confidence that his principal had in him is shown by the fact that Bade was also trusted to supply, besides the books ordered, others that he thought Erasmus would find worth reading. He also took care of the dispatch of the books bought; in his judgment, it was quite safe to send them to Antwerp, from where they were evidently shipped to England.[70]

Erasmus' orders to Bade gradually fell off after he dropped him as his publisher in favour of Johann Froben. Erasmus' first stay in Basel in connection with the publication of his *Novum Testamentum* and edition of Jerome (August 1514–May 1516) heralded his shift to the Basel book trade. His journey from Basel to England to consult manuscripts for the forthcoming editions, and perhaps also to fetch a manuscript of his Latin translation of the New Testament,[71] provided him with a related experience. On the outward journey in March 1515 he visited the Frankfurt book fair, the event held every year in spring and autumn that was to play such an important part in his future life.[72] From Strasbourg he had travelled for safety with several other visitors to the fair, among them the printer and publisher Matthias Schürer of Strasbourg and Wolfgang Lachner of Basel, the father-in-law of Johann Froben and head of the publishing and bookselling branch of the Froben press.[73] Erasmus has not left us an account of his experiences at this professional meeting of publishers and booksellers. Did he take advantage of the fair to buy anything for himself from Schürer or Lachner? He must have meant to buy something, for he was very aware of how many gold pieces – kept hidden in his leggings during the day – he had with him. One morning he counted the money once again 'to make sure how much [he] could afford to take out for buying books' and discovered, to his dismay, that the previous night a thief had stolen more than twenty gold florins from his purse.[74]

Once in Basel, Erasmus must have realized very soon that the smooth-running book trade there would be of lasting use to him. It was especially fortunate that members of the Froben firm, soon his chief and ultimately his sole printer and publisher, also acted as booksellers; this allowed him to offset the cost of buying books against the fee he expected for his services in preparing his own works for the press. Even after Erasmus left Basel in May 1516

---

68 vl/Catalogue no 364

69 In the end, the revised edition of the *Adagiorum chiliades* was published by Froben in 1515. See cwe Ep 263:22n.

70 Allen Ep 263:50–3/cwe Ep 263:57–60. On Varade, see Allen 50n/cwe 58n; cebr iii 376–7.

71 On the purpose of this voyage see Allen Epp 332 and 384 introductions/cwe Epp 327 and 384 introductions.

72 See 119–20 below.

73 On Schürer see Grimm 'Buchführer' 1448–9, Allen Ep 224:42n, and cebr iii 233; on Lachner Grimm 'Buchführer' 1366–72, Allen Ep 420:18n, and cebr ii 279–80.

74 Kristeller 'A Little-known Letter of Erasmus, and the Date of His Encounter with Reuchlin' in *Florilegium historiale* 56–7/cwe Ep 326b:4–17

and stayed for a time in the Low Countries, Froben and Lachner (who kept a bookshop near the printing works) remained his preferred suppliers, especially of Italian publications.

We know of one interesting example. In the summer of 1517 Erasmus received a visit from Francis Frowick, provincial of the Franciscan Observants in England, who had attended the general chapter of his order in Rome and was passing through Leuven on his way home. During his visit he was able to tell his host a great deal about new books recently published or imminently expected in Italy, and to show him copies of some of them.[75] Erasmus promptly urged Froben and Lachner to buy six of these works at the autumn fair in Frankfurt.[76] Five of them were editions of Greek texts: Strabo's *Geographica*, Plutarch's *Lives*, the speeches of Aristides, and sixteen orations of Gregory of Nazianzus (one of the books that Frowick had shown him), as well as the complete edition of the Bible in Greek nearly ready for publication by the Aldine press;[77] the sixth was a Hebrew grammar.[78] He asked them to state the prices of the books after they had bought them and to value the *exemplaria* of his own works – new manuscripts for publication or printed editions with fresh revisions – he had sent to Basel, so that he could offset them against the cost of the books.[79]

How are we to imagine that such an order was actually carried out? Almost certainly, the books ordered at the Frankfurt fair did not make the detour via Basel but were sent straight from Frankfurt to Leuven, as had been the case shortly before with an edition of Hermogenes.[80] The books were conveyed by Franz Birckmann, a bookseller based in Antwerp who travelled very widely and acted as an agent for Erasmus at about this time.[81] Wolfgang Lachner died in early 1518, leaving the Froben press facing financial and organizational problems. Erasmus lamented his loss, for he had regarded him as the actual head of the firm[82] and at first had a fairly low opinion of the intellectual attainments of his co-proprietor. He apparently doubted that Froben would be able to read his letters correctly, and in the letter he wrote to him about the printing of the revised New Testament Erasmus advised him that he should read it 'with Beatus [Rhenanus] or someone else who knows Latin.'[83] Nor did he trust Froben as a corrector: 'As for Froben,' he wrote to Cuthbert Tunstall, 'nothing more stupid can be imagined.'[84] Again, in consideration of the sum agreed on for his manuscript Erasmus was to receive some books. In this instance he was disappointed in what Birckmann brought to him in Leuven and complained to Froben that he must have lost the list of books he had ordered.[85]

---

75 Allen Epp 642:1–6, 643:23–6 / CWE Epp 642:1–6, 643:25–9

76 Allen Ep 629:12–17 / CWE Ep 629:14–19

77 All but *Orationes Aristidis* (Florence: P. Giunta 1517) are on the *Versandliste*; see VL/Catalogue nos 275, 267, 132, 96, and 221.

78 Allen Ep 629:17 / CWE Ep 629:19: 'Wolfgang Faber on the pointing of Hebrew.' Capito's Greek grammar was not published until January 1518; cf Allen Ep 600:21–2 / CWE Ep 600:25–7.

79 On Erasmus' compensation for his collaboration with the Froben press see CWE Epp 629:7n, 885 introduction.

80 Florence: P. Giunta, July 1515. The book no longer appears in the *Versandliste* and was presumably later replaced by another edition; see VL/Catalogue no 128.

81 On Birckmann and his relationship with Erasmus see Allen and CWE Ep 259:14n; CWE Epp 629:7n, 885 introduction; Grimm 'Buchführer' 1523–8; CEBR I 149–50.

82 Allen Epp 781:8, 794:64 / CWE Epp 781:8, 794:70. For the difficulties of the firm after Lachner's death, see CWE Ep 885 introduction.

83 Above the salutation of Ep 885 to Johann Froben (22 October [1518]) Erasmus wrote: 'Lege hanc epistolam cum Beato aut aliquo qui sciat Latine' (see Allen's introduction).

84 Allen Ep 886:28–9 / CWE Ep 886:30

85 Allen Ep 885:5–8 / CWE Ep 885:6–9

Erasmus continued to order books from Paris even after Froben became his publisher. The trade route from the French capital to Brabant was relatively safe, so that shipments of books usually reached their destinations. In fact, he kept in touch with Bade for some time, and sent him a packet of letters for distribution to various Paris correspondents in April 1518.[86] In these circumstances it is quite easy to imagine that the printer-publisher may still have supplied a few books, perhaps presentation copies from his own press. Paulo Emilio's *De rebus gestis Francorum* of 1516 (or 1517?) may have reached Erasmus directly from Bade's printing house.[87] Perhaps Erasmus' agent Franz Birckmann, who visited Paris regularly, was again of service to him in conveying and paying for these possible occasional acquisitions.

But Erasmus had another, less direct connection with the Paris book trade. Before he settled in Leuven, he spent a good year travelling from one town in Flanders or Brabant to another, but his longest stay was in Antwerp, where he had a pied-à-terre in the house of his friend Pieter Gillis, the town clerk.[88] Gillis kept up personal contact with the book dealers of Paris, including Bade, who even visited him in Antwerp,[89] and Erasmus may have profited from these relationships. He was able to get hold of a couple of older Italian texts, Suetonius and the *Historiae Augustae scriptores*, that Gillis had managed to procure in Paris; if he wanted to have the books, Gillis told him, he must write as quickly as possible and they would be promptly dispatched.[90] Erasmus also asked his friend to buy books for him.[91]

In his years at Leuven (1517–21) Erasmus was in close and regular contact with the only local printer-publisher of any importance, his friend Dirk Martens. Martens brought out many editions of Erasmus' works – more than 40 per cent of his production between 1517 and 1521, including reprints, consisted of works by Erasmus or texts edited by him – and published the first catalogue of Erasmus' writings (1519).[92] He also cared for him with devotion when he lay sick in his house for four weeks in 1518.[93] But there is nothing to suggest that Martens was or could be helpful to him as a supplier of books, except perhaps for a few of the productions of his own press. On the contrary, it is significant that in the same year (1518), when Silvester Prierias Mazzolini's recently published reply to Luther's Ninety-Five Theses was stolen from his travelling bag, Erasmus wrote to one of his Basel friends, Wolfgang Faber Capito, asking him to send another copy.[94] In spite of the presence of the university and the new Collegium Trilingue, to which Martens rendered invaluable service

---

86 Erasmus' last surviving letters to him are Epp 764 and 815. The letters to be distributed (Allen Ep 815:9/CWE Ep 815:10–11) were Epp 813, 814, 816, and 817.

87 VL/Catalogue no 333. On presentation copies sent to Erasmus by printers and publishers see 50–2 below.

88 For Erasmus' movements between May 1516 and July 1517 see CWE Epp 410, 457, 470, and 596 introductions.

89 Allen and CWE Ep 849:15

90 Allen Ep 515:9–12/CWE Ep 515:11–14. The 'Suetonius ... printed some time ago in Italy' cannot be the Aldine edition prepared by Giambattista Egnazio, but must be an older one, perhaps the book entered in the *Versandliste* as *Suetonius cum commenta. Beroaldj* (VL/Catalogue no 262).

91 For example Galen *De sanitate tuenda* translated by Thomas Linacre; Allen Ep 687:26–7/CWE Ep 687:30–1. Erasmus may have acquired another copy of the book through Josse Bade and Thomas Lupset; see Allen Ep 690:8–9/CWE Ep 690:9–11. He later sent a copy of it to Gilles de Busleyden as a present; Allen Ep 971:3–5/CWE Ep 971:4–6.

92 *Lucubrationum Erasmi index*; NK 3502. On Martens see CEBR II 394–6.

93 Allen Ep 867:193–249/CWE Ep 867:207–67

94 Allen Ep 877:36–7; cf Ep 878:6–7/CWE Ep 877:41–2; cf Ep 878:6–8.

by his production of students' books and classical texts, Leuven was no longer the most important city for printing in the southern Netherlands. In the last quarter of the fifteenth century it had excelled Antwerp; between 1501 and 1512, when Martens moved his business entirely from Antwerp to Leuven, it did not even have a printer within its walls.[95] Nor was it a prominent centre of the book trade. Presumably it was in Antwerp, which he visited regularly, rather than in Leuven, that Erasmus sought out any books he especially wanted. The commercial metropolis on the Scheldt was a hive of activity for printing and the book trade, and access to foreign books was reasonably easy. It is certain that Erasmus visited the bookshops there. In 1519, when Maarten Lips, a younger kindred spirit who lived in Leuven and had recently become his friend, was searching without success for a Hebrew book, probably the *Biblia rabbinica* (Venice: D. Bomberg 1518), he immediately offered to buy it for him the next day in Antwerp.[96] Perhaps that was where Erasmus had already acquired his copy of Felice da Prato's translation of the Psalms made directly from the Hebrew, another Bomberg edition (1515).[97]

In these years Erasmus remained determined to acquire the books, especially those printed in Italy, that were of vital importance to him. There were still gaps in his library: he lacked several older but unsuperseded and still authoritative texts of classical writers. Even though the book trade in Antwerp was thriving, Italian books could rarely be supplied quickly, even via such centres as Paris and Basel. Nor were recent editions any easier to procure. It could take a very long time before a new book found its way across the Alps to the study of a scholar in the Low Countries. Erasmus must have wished that he could seek out and buy the books he needed in their country of origin, and for a moment it seemed as if he would have the opportunity. Early in 1518 he was contemplating a journey to Venice to negotiate terms for the second edition of his *Novum Testamentum* with the Aldine press.[98] But he had another motive: he intended to expand his library 'with some good books, for new ones are published in Italy every day.' He needed a considerable sum of money for the journey and to buy books, which he hoped to obtain from his financial protectors, however niggardly he might think them.[99] Nothing came of the plan. The publication of Manuzio's own Greek Bible in February made a visit to Venice superfluous,[100] and the whole journey fell through.

In 1516 Erasmus had an unexpected opportunity, at least so it seemed at first, to expand his library by purchase from a private collection that was said to be for sale. But the transaction did not come about, and the tip he had received would have passed unnoticed if the library had not been that of no less a person than Rodolphus Agricola. Erasmus would certainly have been interested: he thought very highly of the Frisian humanist and had already

---

95 See the catalogue of Martens' printings in *Tentoonstelling Dirk Martens 1473–1973* 261–88 and the catalogue of printers in NK.

96 Allen Epp 1048:7–9, 1049:9–10/CWE Epp 1048:9–11, 1049:11–12. On Lips see Allen and CWE Ep 750 introductions; CEBR II 333–4; and in more detail Lourdaux *Moderne devotie en christelijk humanisme* 149–53, 182–201.

97 VL/Catalogue no 237

98 Erasmus initially hesitated between Froben and the Venetian firm; see Allen and CWE Ep 770 introductions.

99 Allen Epp 781:9–11 (to William Warham?), 786:32–4 (to John Colet)/CWE Epp 781:9–12, 786:34–6. Ep 786 goes on to complain about the stinginess of his protectors.

100 See VL/Catalogue no 221. It may have been the receipt of the presentation copy of the Aldine Bible that made Erasmus choose Froben to print his revised New Testament; see n98 above.

encouraged the collection of his writings for publication.[101] Agricola had bequeathed his books and papers to his physician and friend Adolph Occo. In 1503 the whole collection had passed to Occo's nephew Pompeius Occo, a very wealthy merchant and also the factor of the Fuggers in Amsterdam, where he lived on a lavish scale.[102] At the end of 1516 Alaard of Amsterdam, then in Leuven (where he had been instrumental in the publication of Agricola's chief work, *De inventione dialectica*, the previous year),[103] wrote to Erasmus that Pompeius Occo intended to dispose of all his books, without exception. He did not have a catalogue of them, he explained, but knew for a fact that lying hidden in the merchant's mansion, known as the 'Paradise,' there were more than a thousand books, all eaten away by woodworm, and among them some very old and rare volumes. He had already sent a written request by his courier asking Pompeius Occo to let him have a catalogue for Erasmus. He expected that Occo would comply with this request; but if he did not, it was no great matter. Alaard himself would be in Amsterdam early the next year to resume his ecclesiastical functions and then, he wrote 'I shall be able to bring you without fail anything you want from his library, even if the price is very high.'[104] We do not know how Erasmus reacted to this tip. We do know that even if he had wished to, he could not have acted, for Alaard's report of the imminent sale of the library was premature, to say the least, and clearly based on a misunderstanding. Agricola's manuscripts in any case remained in Pompeius Occo's hands; some years later he generously presented the same Alaard – who had been so scathing about the housing of the collection – with all of Agricola's papers to use in the publication of his *Opera*.[105] Some of the printed volumes in the collection were still in Amsterdam years later. In 1528, thanks to the mediation of Pompeius' son-in-law Haio Herman, Erasmus was able to borrow an old edition of Seneca from Agricola's library to consult in Basel.[106] And Erasmus may have profited in another way from the whole affair. Perhaps to offer some consolation for a premature tip that came to nothing, in the course of 1517 Alaard presented him with the text of what had been published as a letter of Valerianus to Eucherius, bishop of Lyon (d 449), 'on Christian philosophy,' translated from Greek by Agricola. Erasmus identified the letter as written by Eucherius to Valerianus and as a Latin original, not a translation from the Greek, and immediately republished it with his own scholia.[107]

During the last fifteen years of his life, spent in Basel, Freiburg, and then Basel again, Erasmus' library grew considerably. Apart from a separate purchase of a number of mostly older books, to which we shall return, this growth was owed almost wholly to the gradual acquisition of recent publications. Leaving out of account books that can only be conjecturally identified and therefore not certainly dated, it can be stated without exaggeration that

---

101 See VL/Catalogue no 306 #1. On Agricola and Erasmus' attitude to him see Waterbolk *Een hond in het bad*; CEBR I 15–17.
102 See Nübel *Pompejus Occo, 1483 bis 1537, Fuggerfaktor in Amsterdam*; CEBR III 21–2.
103 VL/Catalogue no 19
104 Allen Ep 485:30–47 / CWE Ep 485:28–44
105 [*Opera*] (Cologne: J. Gymnich 1539; repr 1975)
106 See VL/Catalogue no 148, with n5. On Herman, whom Erasmus had met in 1519 at the College of the Lily in Leuven, see Allen Ep 903:12n / CWE Ep 903:14n; CEBR II 157–8.
107 Alaard had presumably sent a copy of *Epistola Valerii episcopi ad propinquum suum ex Greco in Latinum sermonem per magistrum Rodolphum Agricolam traducta* ([Deventer]: J. de Breda [c 1485]); see Allen Ep 676:1n. Erasmus first published his edition, under the title *Eucherii Epistola Lugdunensis ad Valerianum*, at the end of his edition of Cato (Leuven: Martens 1517; NK 535) with an introductory letter to Alaard; see Allen and CWE Ep 676 introductions, and cf VL/Catalogue no 248 with n1.

more than half of the titles in the *Versandliste* refer to books that appeared between 1521 and 1536.

Most of the post-1521 acquisitions were Basel editions, almost exclusively from Froben, with a few exceptions printed by Herwagen, Cratander, and Bebel;[108] the small remainder came from various presses in at least five countries: Germany, France, Italy, England, and the Low Countries. The new acquisitions must have been obtained by purchase or presentation. Among the countless Froben editions several were undoubtedly books presented to Erasmus by his friends, their authors; and the same applied to several of the editions published elsewhere, for example the five London editions and the only Brescia imprint in the *Versandliste*.[109]

Let us leave the positively identifiable presentation copies to one side for the moment. It is striking how few centres of printing are represented by the remaining books, including those Erasmus bought. Apart from the Basel editions, the only cities to yield more than five copies were Paris, Lyon, Venice, and, in Germany, Hagenau, Strasbourg, and Cologne. It is not surprising that Paris and Lyon were so strongly represented. Basel kept up very close relations with them, and both were hugely productive centres of printing, with which there was a lively exchange. Both Paris and Lyon had their 'Écu de Bâle,' a bookshop linked with Basel by direct and indirect family ties and supplied with a wide range of titles from that city. The head of both businesses in 1516 was Johann Schabler, called 'Wattenschnee'; he was both a blood relation of Johann Froben and a former agent of Froben and Froben's father-in-law Wolfgang Lachner. The Paris shop later came into the hands of his nephew Konrad Resch, while another member of the family, Jean Vaugris, ran the business in Lyon.[110] The Lyon book fair, although much less important than the one at Frankfurt, brought with it a more or less permanent seasonal traffic with Basel in which the local 'Écu de Bâle' played an important role. As a result, Erasmus' correspondence with such friends in southern France as Andrea Alciati and Jacopo Sadoleto often passed via the bookshop in Lyon; and Michel Parmentier, its head from 1523, more than once acted as courier, delivering letters from Lyon.[111] These well-established connections made it relatively easy, in spite of the unsafe roads, to obtain books from Paris and Lyon without too much delay; and it must have been just as easy to procure the products of the upper and lower Rhineland presses directly or via Frankfurt. Importing books across the Alps was more troublesome, but still books arrived with some degree of regularity. Venice seems to have been the market par excellence because it too was the seat of a book trade that maintained close ties with Basel: Vincent Vaugris, the brother of Jean, the manager of the 'Écu de Bâle' in Lyon, named his business in Venice 'Al Segno d'Erasmo.'[112] A third brother, Benoît, a bookseller in Constance who had previously worked in Basel, cooperated with his colleagues there and was on good terms with

---

108 See vl/Catalogue nos 120, 121, 131, 271, 313, 403 (Herwagen); 77 (Cratander); 191 (Cratander and Bebel); 195, 215, and 266 (Bebel).

109 vl/Catalogue nos 17, 74, 75, 175, and 368 (London); 158 (Brescia). For other examples see the separate treatment of presentation copies 33–52 below.

110 For the two firms and their owners see Grimm 'Buchführer' sv Johann Wattenschnee (Johann Schabler) (1389–90), Konrad Resch (1391–3), and Jean Vaugris (1345–6); Benzing 'Die deutsche Verleger des 16. und 17. Jahrhunderts' 1241, 1291; Bietenholz 'Erasmus und der Basler Buchhandel in Frankreich' 293–323; CEBR III 215–16 (Schabler), 141–2 (Resch).

111 See for example Allen Epp 2930:3–5, 2972:2–4; cf Bietenholz *Basle and France in the Sixteenth Century* 42.

112 Bietenholz 'Erasmus und der Basler Buchhandel in Frankreich' 296

Erasmus;[113] he made repeated business trips to Venice, as did many other booksellers and publishers from Basel who wished to profit from the friendship of their Italian colleagues. Presumably, then, most of the books imported from Italy by Basel booksellers had been bought in Venice, where many of them will also have been printed, although some books may have been incidentally supplied from other Italian presses.[114]

It is clear, then, that the non-Basel imprints (Paris, Lyon, Rhineland, and Venetian editions) that Erasmus acquired by purchase in later life were publications that were easily available in Basel through the well-used channels of the book trade; some of them will have been in sufficient demand to be kept in stock. In some cases we may wonder whether the attentive Froben or Amerbach supplied books to Erasmus as soon as they appeared, even before he could order them himself. If we bear in mind the nature of his other acquisitions, in particular the Froben editions and the presentation copies, can we avoid the conclusion that after he settled in Basel Erasmus can hardly be said to have pursued an active and independent acquisition policy? The gifts, by definition, formed no part of his policy, and the Froben editions, by far the most numerous category among the acquisitions, if not strictly presentation copies (except perhaps for a few works whose authors were personal friends), were not books ordered in the normal way either.

What then were they? Presumably the great majority were copies sent by the publisher in return for services rendered: Erasmus assisted the Froben press as an adviser, but he also contributed a great deal to the firm's regular output through the stream of editions and new impressions of his own works. We do not know exactly how he was remunerated in kind, but we do know that at a very early stage of his regular dealings with Froben he sought to establish a compensation arrangement on a commercial basis. Perhaps he had a claim to new Froben editions, possibly up to a certain value, fixed or not; in practice this might have meant that he himself chose which titles he wanted and which he did not. Whatever the arrangement, the outcome was clear: for a very important part of his later acquisitions, Erasmus was dependent on Froben's list, extensive and varied as it was.[115] If he also received copies of publications of other presses for his services, which is possible, since some of the books were more or less immediately available in Basel, then as far as we can make out from the *Versandliste* they must have been few.

All in all, therefore, it is fair to say that during the years he spent in Basel and Freiburg Erasmus took a remarkably passive approach towards building his library, which had a negative effect on the quality of the whole. He added books he needed, but important books of those years that he himself praised highly and studied avidly were not found in his collection. Why did he not take the trouble to acquire them? The obvious explanation must be that after he moved to Basel he generally had sufficient opportunity to borrow the books that were indispensable to him from others or to consult them easily elsewhere. Once again Erasmus was in a situation similar to that of his early years, when he had also been able to find the books that interested him in his immediate surroundings and did not feel compelled

---

113 On Benoît Vaugris see Grimm 'Buchführer' 1345–6; CEBR III 380. In 1523 Erasmus made a plea to the Town Council of Basel to remit a fine they had imposed on Vaugris; see Ep 1395.

114 In 1531 Erasmus received Benoît Vaugris, who had just returned from Venice, in Freiburg; Allen Ep 2447:35/ CWE Ep 2447:36. Hieronymus Froben and Johann Herwagen travelled to Venice in 1526 and 1530 respectively; Allen Ep 1707:13–14/CWE Ep 1707:16–17, Allen Ep 2033:58n. Froben and Francesco Giulio Calvo, bookseller/printer of Pavia (and later Rome), exchanged new editions; AK II Appendix 525–7 and Luchsinger *Der Basler Buchdruck als Vermittler italienischen Geistes 1470–1529* 8.

115 Cf 26 above with n79. Of course, remuneration in kind need not exclude further payment in money or some other form.

to possess them and buy them for himself.[116] In principle his attitude remained the same throughout his life. Owning books was not an end in itself, and his purchases rarely went beyond what he had decided he could not do without. This may well mean that of the books on the *Versandliste* from the period 1521–36 rather more than can be strictly documented, perhaps even more than half, were presents, or at least not purchases. This assumption becomes even more credible when we see in how many forms presentation copies reached him.

The picture we have drawn of piecemeal and rather sparing purchases of books in his later years does not seem, at first sight, to tally with a striking and unexpectedly large order that Erasmus placed in 1525 for the purchase of about twenty authoritative Italian editions of classical authors, mostly Greek, some of them published long before. A list of the desired books written in his own hand has been preserved and was published by Allen.[117] He believed this to be a copy of the actual order list given either to Erasmus' servant-pupil Karl Harst or to Jan Łaski, both of whom travelled to Italy in 1525.[118] The list mentioned fifteen specific works, thirteen Greek and two Latin, and also, without specifying them, 'all Greek commentaries on Aristotle' as well as 'the Greek commentaries on the various poets' and finally 'everything that Aldus has printed in the last four years.' The preference for the products of the famous Venetian press was not restricted to the last category, for with one or two exceptions the fifteen named works were also Aldine editions. The order must have been largely filled, for most of the books listed formed part of the library in 1536.[119] Where the books were ordered or by whom they were supplied is not certain, but since both Harst and Łaski visited Venice, it is probable that they gave the order to the bookshop 'Al Segno d'Erasmo,' which was closely linked with Basel. We know nothing about the background to the order, although its primary intention was evident: Erasmus wanted to fill the most glaring gaps in his collection.

The books Erasmus ordered were standard works that a humanist's library would be expected to contain. But why did he acquire them just then in 1525, and why had he not made earlier attempts to do so, gradually if necessary? So far as we can ascertain, these purchases have never been linked with the other important transaction of the same year: the sale of Erasmus' library to Łaski. Yet, if only because they took place in the same year, it seems natural to infer a possible connection. The purchase of the library was coupled with a stipulation that later acquisitions, except for a few valuable manuscripts, should also be included. As it turned out, this worked to Łaski's benefit, but in 1525 it could not yet be foreseen that the collection would grow by almost a third.[120] Moreover, the other terms of the contract, from a strictly business point of view, could not be said to be very advantageous for the Polish humanist. After all, he was not to have the disposal of the books until Erasmus' death and had to pay half of the purchase price immediately without receiving anything in return.[121] All that he received, in fact, was the prospect that he would some day become the owner of the working apparatus of the famous humanist. At that time Łaski certainly prized this highly, but he must also have been aware of the deficiencies in the collection. Erasmus could hardly

---

116 See 18–19, 22 above.

117 Allen VII 547 Appendix 20 'Books Ordered by Erasmus'; Jürgens *Johannes a Lasco* 99; see illustration xviii above.

118 See Allen Epp 1575:7n, 1622:4n / CWE Epp 1575 n2, 1622 n3.

119 VL/Catalogue nos 105, 111, 114, 115, 127–8, 132, 137, 198, 203, 204, 214, 218, and 320. The only specified title known to be missing from the *Versandliste* in 1536 is Apollonius of Rhodes' *Argonautica*, presumably never supplied.

120 On this estimate see 53 below.

121 Cf 3 above. On the reservations Erasmus made in the contract and in his will of 1527 concerning the manuscripts see 92, 97 below.

deny them, and in the discussion on the sale of the library the weak spots may well have been mentioned. If Erasmus gave an unwritten commitment to use part of the half of the price which he was to receive there and then to buy important texts and commentaries to augment his collection, might this have been a way around the problem? Whether or not the purchase of such a large number of specific books all at once was connected with the sale of the library in 1525, as we have assumed, its effect was the same: Erasmus' collection of books gained considerably in quality.[122]

Let us return to the thread of our story. We have mentioned that a surprisingly large part of Erasmus' library must have been made up of presentation copies. We can support this assertion and conclude our attempt to gain a deeper insight into the formation of the library by looking at the various kinds of presents that he received over the years.

Erasmus' correspondence supplies more information about the books he received as gifts than those he bought for himself. He mentioned the latter very rarely.[123] On the other hand his letters allow us to identify dozens of books he received either as gifts or free of charge. Strict proof cannot always be given, and we can only be certain when Erasmus himself confirms the safe arrival of a presentation copy, directly or indirectly, or when the donor's inscription with his name survives in a book that has been preserved.[124] A donor's statement that he has sent the book to Erasmus is not sufficient: such parcels were all too often lost at that time of difficult and dangerous travel. But even if we allow a wide margin for doubtful cases, there are a number of books that we can almost certainly identify as gifts or presentation copies. Some of them can be found in the *Versandliste*, but at least as many are no longer listed in it. To give an undistorted picture of the types and number of books that Erasmus received as presents, we must of course repeatedly refer in the following survey to books that do not appear in the *Versandliste*. Fuller information on these titles can be found in the list of 'Books Found in Erasmus' Correspondence' that follows the annotated *Versandliste*.[125]

As Erasmus' authority came to be recognized in the second decade of the century, and as his fame spread across the world, presentation copies and gifts reached him in growing numbers. He had received gifts of books before, even in his youth, though the donors then were limited to his immediate circle of friends. Once the trickle became a stream it never ceased, even after he had passed the peak of his fame. Books reached him from all quarters,

---

122 Our hypothesis stands or falls by Allen's dating of the order list to 1525. Felix Heinimann doubts the accuracy of this dating, chiefly on the grounds of a passage that Erasmus inserted in his revised *Adagia* of October 1520. In that passage Erasmus cited from an anonymous collection of proverbs added as a supplementary text to the Aldine edition of Aesop (Venice 1505). That was the only edition in which he could have consulted this collection of proverbs. Since the edition of Aesop appears among the books on the order list, Heinimann argues that the copy ordered must already have been in Erasmus' possession before October 1520, so that he could use it in revising his *Adagia*, and that therefore the order must have been given at least five years earlier than Allen's date. But Heinimann leaves open the possibility that Erasmus may have had the opportunity to consult the Aldine Aesop before October 1520 in someone else's library in Leuven, where he was then living; see ASD II-4 109 501–10n. It is also possible that he saw the book in Antwerp, where, as we have seen, he also stayed regularly.

123 Two rare examples of separate purchases documented by the letters are for the works of Chrysostom in 1519 and the *Opera* of Gerson in 1525/6; see VL/Catalogue nos 238 and 169. The only two collective orders known to us are those of 1517 and 1525; see 26 and 32–3 above.

124 At least three such books with donor's inscriptions have survived: the Petit/Bade edition (Paris 1511) of the *Epistolae* of Leo I (see VL/Catalogue no 310 #4); the Aldine edition (Venice 1514) of the *Scriptores rei rusticae* (see 34 below); and a medical work of Simon Reichwein published in Cologne in 1529 (see 'Books Found in Erasmus' Correspondence' no 134). See also 17 n2 above.

125 475–91 below

far and near, and from a variety of donors: princes, ecclesiastical and lay dignitaries, scholarly friends and kindred spirits, printers and publishers, former *famuli* or servant-pupils, and mere admirers like Hugo Bolonius, a self-styled 'laureate of the Muses.' Very little is known for certain about Bolonius, and nothing at all about his relations with Erasmus, but in 1521 he surprised him with a New Year's present of a copy of the Aldine *Scriptores rei rusticae* (Venice 1514).[126] At the other end of the scale, later in the same year 1521 Henry VIII sent Erasmus his famous *Assertio septem sacramentorum*, with an inscription in his own hand.[127] Five years later another of the king's works, like the *Assertio* a polemic against Luther, was given to Erasmus by Duke George of Saxony, possibly the copy of the de luxe edition, not published commercially, which he had just received from the royal author.[128] Duke George had already sent Erasmus several other polemical works, not without ulterior motives.

Erasmus' library was indebted for numerous acquisitions of the most varied character to the authors, both illustrious and obscure, who honoured him with copies of their own works or of texts they had edited. Johann Reuchlin sent him both his *De verbo mirifico* (Tübingen 1514) and his *De arte cabalistica* (Hagenau 1517).[129] From his home in Venice, where he had met Erasmus nine years earlier, the famous philologist Giambattista Egnazio sent a presentation copy of *De caesaribus libri tres* to Erasmus in Leuven in 1517.[130] Around the same time Erasmus must have received the curious work *De fructu qui ex doctrina percipitur* from his younger friend, the English humanist Richard Pace.[131] In 1519 the leader of the humanist circle in Erfurt, Helius Eobanus Hessus, who won fame chiefly as a poet, sent him through two other members of the circle a copy of his *Hodoeporicon*, the versified narrative, published in Erfurt, of his visit to the Dutch scholar in Leuven the previous year.[132] Juan Luis Vives probably sent his *De institutione foeminae christianae* (Antwerp 1524) to Erasmus as a presentation copy; long before it was published the author had announced the work's completion and indicated that Erasmus would soon see it.[133] It is also likely that at the same time the Spanish humanist presented his previous works, the *Opuscula varia* (Leuven 1519) and the *Declamationes Syllanae quinque* (Antwerp 1520), to Erasmus, who had written the letter of recommendation for the latter. Vives may have handed the books over in person, for both men were living in Leuven in those years and were very close friends.[134] If a friend was not only one of his regular correspondents but also well-to-do, Erasmus may have thought a free copy of an expensive edition no more than his due. Sometimes, it seems, he managed to suggest this discreetly: in 1525 he wrote to Willibald Pirckheimer that he had not yet seen his recent edition of Ptolemy, but would try to get hold of a copy soon. Pirckheimer took the hint: he dispatched a copy of the *Geographicae ennarrationes libri octo* to Basel at once,[135] with another appropriate work, Dürer's *Vnderweysung der messung mit dem Zirckel*

---

126 VL/Catalogue no 324

127 VL/Catalogue no 368

128 VL/Catalogue no 74

129 VL/Catalogue no 176. Though we cannot prove it, it remains a possibility that Erasmus did not buy his copy of Reuchlin's Hebrew grammar (VL/Catalogue no 280) but received it as a gift from the author, but not until c 1515.

130 'Books Found in Erasmus' Correspondence' no 52. This presentation copy was probably no longer in the library in 1536; see VL/Catalogue nos 51, 97 #2, and 261.

131 VL/Catalogue no 30 #2

132 VL/Catalogue no 47 #1

133 VL/Catalogue no 155 #2

134 VL/Catalogue nos 25 #2 and 41

135 VL/Catalogue no 134

und Richtscheyt.[136] There is little doubt that Erasmus received his copy of John Longland's *Sermones* from the author.[137] The bishop of Lincoln was a generous patron and shared Erasmus' special interest in the Psalms. He had encouraged Erasmus to undertake commentaries on them; Erasmus in turn dedicated his commentaries on Psalms 4 (1525) and Psalm 85 (1528) to Longland, to whom he sent complimentary copies.[138] Longland could not have chosen a more welcome gift in return than his only published work, which included his Lenten sermons, based on five of the penitential Psalms.

Many of the books Erasmus received from their authors are not found in the *Versandliste*. Not all the donors were friends. On occasion even an opponent could hardly fail to present a scholar of Erasmus' authority and standing with a copy of a work he might be interested in. In the spring of 1518 Erasmus wrote to Johann Maier of Eck, a theologian and professor at Ingolstadt who was known as a champion of papal authority and a grim adversary of Luther. After an early period when he was under humanist influence and had published some small works that were almost anti-scholastic in their theology, Eck changed course and became a fervent champion of Rome and the established authorities in the church. He had been one of the first to publish sharp criticisms of Erasmus' translation of the New Testament (1516). In a letter in which he answers some of Eck's criticisms, Erasmus thanks him for some unnamed works he had received from him.[139] The two men did not get on and Erasmus mistrusted the German scholar throughout his life.

With Adrianus Cornelii Barlandus, however, who was for a short time the first Professor of Latin at the Collegium Trilingue in Leuven and later, until his death, Professor of Rhetoric at the university, we are again in the circle of Erasmus' trusted friends. In 1528 he sent his annotated edition of two unspecified speeches of Cicero to Erasmus in Basel. It was not a valuable gift, but one with a clear background and motive. Eleven years earlier Adrianus had asked the older scholar, then still living in Leuven, for an explanation (which was probably supplied) of a passage in Cicero's *De senectute* on the immortality of the soul, because everything the commentators had written seemed to him to be trifling.[140] Now in the letter accompanying his gift Adrian encouraged his preceptor to write scholia on one or more of the orations of Cicero, just as he had previously written annotations on *De officiis*.[141]

Erasmus must have found a gift he received in the following year particularly welcome: the younger humanist Johannes Alexander Brassicanus, a friend since 1520, sent him his *Proverbiorum symmicta*. This collection of 128 proverbs and eighteen *Pythagorae symbola* was of great use to him in preparing the 1533 edition of the *Adagia*. It allowed him to expand or improve his notes on several of the adages already included, and he also borrowed from it nearly thirty new ones, though without mentioning his source.[142] Erasmus would cer-

---

136 Not in the *Versandliste*; see 'Books Found in Erasmus' Correspondence' no 49.

137 vl/Catalogue no 175

138 See the dedicatory letters, Epp 1535 and 2017.

139 Allen Ep 844:284 / cwe Ep 844:306. On Eck see Allen and cwe Ep 769 introductions; odcc2 441; cebr i 416–19. Eck's *De primatu Petri adversus Ludderum* appears on the *Versandliste*; see vl/Catalogue no 174. See also 'Books Found in Erasmus' Correspondence' nos 50 and 51.

140 Allen Ep 647:6–13 / cwe Ep 647:7–14

141 Allen and cwe Ep 2025:12–24. School editions such as this have often been so intensively read that all the copies of an impression have been lost. Allen was unable to find any of the speeches of Cicero edited by Barlandus; since that time one surviving copy of his edition of the *Oratio pro Marcello* ([Leuven] Dirk Martens [c 1520]) has been found (nk 2660). Cf Allen 12n / cwe nn5 and 7.

142 'Books Found in Erasmus' Correspondence' no 21. Cf asd ii-4 305 547n. 'The Precepts of Pythagoras' was a collection of sayings attributed to the sixth-century philosopher. Erasmus had known the humanist Johannes Alexander Brassicanus of Tübingen since September 1520 when he called on Erasmus in Antwerp.

tainly have been able to count on a presentation copy of the first publication of his protégé Jacobus Ceratinus, *De sono literarum praesertim Graecarum libellus*, published at Antwerp in 1527.[143] This small treatise on the phonetic value of the letters of the alphabet included a prefatory letter to Erasmus, who was much concerned with the subject at the time (he was to bring out his own *Dialogus de recta latini graecique sermonis pronuntiatione* in March the following year).[144] How far Ceratinus wrote his phonetic treatise under the influence of his earlier contact with his patron, who had also guided him in his revision of Craston's Greek dictionary, is hard to determine.[145]

There was no special friendship underlying a present that crossed the Alps in 1530. The Italian scholar Pietro Bembo and Erasmus never met, and it was not until between 1529 and 1535 that they exchanged a few letters, largely formal and businesslike.[146] Nonetheless they respected and appreciated each other's works. In his *Ciceronianus* of 1528 Erasmus devoted a laudatory passage to the brilliant humanist,[147] and a few years later when his Basel friend Ludwig Baer, another emigrant to Freiburg, travelled to Rome, Erasmus urged him to pay a visit en route to Bembo, who was then living in retirement at his villa near Padua, where he devoted himself to art and letters and his garden.[148] In the *libellus* that Bembo entrusted to a friend for safe delivery to Freiburg in 1530 we may see a modest homage to the renown that Erasmus must have enjoyed among the Italian humanists. The book is not described, but according to Allen it was probably a copy of Bembo's dialogues *De Virgilii culice* and *De Guido Ubaldo Feretrio deque Elizabetha Gonzagia Urbini ducibus*, recently published in Venice.[149] Neither work can be found even under an abbreviated or garbled title in the *Versandliste*. We know nothing about the later fate of the presentation copy, but Erasmus would have had no need to keep the *libellus* for its contents, if they were as we have assumed, once he had almost certainly acquired Bembo's *Opuscula aliquot* in the year of publication (1532), since the two dialogues were reprinted in it.[150]

Besides contemporaries such as Bembo, many members of the generation born around the turn of the century presented books to Erasmus when he lived in Freiburg and later in Basel. We have already mentioned Brassicanus and Ceratinus. In 1533 the French poet Nicolas Bourbon, a pupil and close friend of Jacques Toussain, surprised Erasmus with a gift of his *Nugae*, a collection of Greek and Latin odes and epigrams. Several poems were adddressed to Toussain and other friends of Erasmus, but two sets of elegiac verses were also dedicated to Erasmus himself, one of them an epigram singing the praises of his translations from Lucian. Erasmus was very pleased with the gift. He hastened to thank Bourbon for the book and to praise its contents in characteristic style: though he had been feeling

---

The emperor Ferdinand I had crowned Brassicanus poet laureate early in 1518, and in 1522 he succeeded Reuchlin as professor at Ingolstadt. In 1523 the emperor appointed him to the chair in rhetoric at Vienna, where he died in 1539. He published *18 Pythagorae symbola* appended to his *Libellus adagiorum* (Vienna 1529), proverbial sayings quite possibly taken from Iamblichus. See CWE 31 31–2.

143 'Books Found in Erasmus' Correspondence' no 33
144 VL/Catalogue no 352
145 See VL/Catalogue no 186; cf Newald *Erasmus Roterodamus* 270.
146 Nine letters have been preserved, five from Erasmus (letters of recommendation and a request for information about a manuscript) and four from Bembo. On Bembo see Allen and CWE Ep 2106 introductions; CEBR I 120–3.
147 ASD I-2 697–8 / CWE 28 435–6
148 Bembo reported on the meeting in Ep 3026 (20 June 1535), in which his regard and sympathy for Erasmus is evident.
149 Allen Ep 2337:26–9 with 27n / CWE Ep 2337:27–30 with n5
150 See VL/Catalogue no 12 #1.

miserable when it arrived, reading and enjoying Bourbon' poems had 'made him quite himself again instead of a forgetful greybeard.' He promised a fuller letter as soon as he was no longer tormented by kidney stones.[151]

Chief among those of the younger generation who remembered him were his old *famuli* or servant-pupils, who often honoured their revered former master with a present of a book years after they had gone their own way. Sometimes it was one of their own works, but often simply a book that might be expected to interest him. Frans van der Dilft, who stayed in Erasmus' house on three occasions for several months at a time between 1524 and 1529 as his servant-pupil, and who had been the dedicatee of one of Erasmus' translations from Plutarch after his first and longest stay,[152] sent him in 1534 his recently published *Ad Carolum v Hispaniarum regem ob res prospere feliciterque gestas oratio gratulatoria*.[153] He must have been proud to present this work to his old master; the speech, given before the emperor in Barcelona, had procured him the honour of knighthood. Philippus Montanus, another servant-pupil whom Erasmus valued very highly (he left him a legacy of 150 gold crowns in his last will),[154] sent Erasmus a copy of the improved edition of Alciati's famous *Emblematum libellus* soon after it was published by Chrétien Wechel in Paris in 1534.[155] And the Silesian Anselmus Ephorinus, who spent almost six months as a member of Erasmus' household in 1531, gave him a book three years later. It was a collection of bucolic poems by Gratius, Ovid, Nemesianus, and Calpurnius Siculus edited by his friend Georg von Logau from a recently discovered manuscript, supplemented by a recent poem on hunting by Cardinal Adriano Castellesi, and published by the Aldine press in Venice.[156] None of these gifts can be found in the *Versandliste*.

With one exception,[157] translation of his own works that Erasmus received from his friends do not appear on the *Versandliste*. He does not appear to have paid special attention to the countless translations of his works; indeed, he must often have been unaware of them.[158] But he was not completely indifferent when certain works of his appeared in tongues other than Latin. In the summer of 1517 he heard with satisfaction that his *Moria* had been translated into French, for, as he wrote to Thomas More, 'now even the theology professors who know only French understand it.' He did not hesitate to write directly to the translator, Joris, lord of Halewijn and Comines, to ask if he still had a copy available or could at least let him know where one was to be had.[159] The French text, which he saw not long afterwards, perhaps still in manuscript, unfortunately proved a disappointment. Halewijn had added, omitted, and altered so much in the text of the *Moria* that he had produced his own, very different book. Erasmus' reproaches have to be taken with a grain of salt, for he cannot have been very angry with Halewijn about his translation; and he remained on good terms

---

151 'Books Found in Erasmus' Correspondence' no 19; Ep 2789:4–8; see also Allen's introduction. For Toussain see vL/Catalogue no 38 #2. The *Nugae* were reprinted in the same year by Cratander at Basel. Could Erasmus have given a direct or indirect hint urging the reprint?

152 See vL/Catalogue no 151 #1.

153 'Books Found in Erasmus' Correspondence' no 46

154 Allen xi 364:16–17 Appendix 25 'Erasmus' Last Will'

155 'Books Found in Erasmus' Correspondence' no 5

156 'Books Found in Erasmus' Correspondence' no 73. On Castellesi see vL/Catalogue no 21.

157 See 39 below.

158 For example, Erasmus was probably not aware of the Dutch translation of his *Enchiridion militis christiani*, which was published in Amsterdam (Doen Pietersoen 24 July 1523) and reissued at Antwerp (Jan van Ghelden 28 August 1523) see Allen Ep 2165:41n/cwe Ep 2165 n9.

159 Allen Epp 597:15–16, 641:4–7/cwe Epp 597:17–18, 641:6–9

with him.[160] But he made it clear that translation of his works made great demands on the translator; years later (1529) he wrote to Emilio de' Migli, who translated the *Enchiridion* into Italian, that 'it is a rare bird ... who could rise to the challenge in his own language.'[161]

Erasmus saw the French version of his *Exomologesis* by Claudius Cantiuncula, professor of civil law at Basel, at an early stage, perhaps when it was still in manuscript. Besides being fellow townsmen, the author and translator were not unknown to each other. They probably met in Basel in 1518, and in 1523 Cantiuncula delivered to Erasmus a letter in the king's own hand from Francis I assuring Erasmus of a warm welcome in France.[162] Cantiuncula's translation of the *Exomologesis* appeared in Basel under the title *Manière de se confesser*, without any mention of printer or publisher, at the end of April 1524, less than two months after the publication of the Latin text. Since that interval was rather short for the translation to have been written, printed, and published, Allen did not rule out the possibility that it had been made before the *Exomologesis* appeared. Erasmus might have agreed beforehand to the translation from the manuscript or the proofs, to allow the French version to appear in good time. If this was indeed the case, we may assume that Cantiuncula sent a presentation copy of his translation to the author, perhaps delivering it in person, soon after it was printed. Interestingly, François du Moulin, the almoner of the French king, to whom the treatise on confession was dedicated, was presented with a copy in which Erasmus' text and the French translation were bound together.[163]

In March 1526 Erasmus mentions in a letter to the conservative theologian Noël Béda that he had received 'one or two books translated into French' from Louis de Berquin in Paris. A respected humanist and a great admirer of Erasmus, although he also sympathized with Luther, Berquin had first come under suspicion of heresy in 1523.[164] The titles of the books Berquin sent were not specified in Erasmus' letter to Béda, but very likely they were three works printed, probably some time in 1525, without identification of place or publisher or date: the *Declamation des louenges de mariage*, based on Erasmus' *Encomium matrimonii*; *Brefve admonition de la manière de prier*, two translated excerpts from the Paraphrases on Matthew and Luke; and *Le symbole des apostres*, an abbreviated French version of the colloquy *Inquisitio de fide*. They were not complete translations but were made up of translated excerpts in which Berquin had incorporated brief comments of his own, and in two of the works he had interpolated passages borrowed from Luther and Guillaume Farel, a radical Protestant evangelical. It is less likely that Berquin's translation of the *Querela pacis*, made at roughly the same time, was among the gifts, unless it was in manuscript; the only known printed edition of *La complainte de la paix* was not printed until later, after it

---

160 It is not now possible to say whether Halewijn's translation was the first printed edition of the *Moria* in French, *De la declamation de louenges de follie* (Paris: P. Vidoue for G. du Pré 2 August 1520); see CWE Ep 641:6n. If it was in fact the first edition of the *Moria* in French, Erasmus can only have seen the text in manuscript. Or could Halewijn's version have appeared in print, but in a very limited impression, which may well have been totally lost? For Erasmus' opinion of the translation, see Allen Epp 660:6–8, 739:4–7/CWE Epp 1013A:7–10, 739:7–10. For his continued correspondence with Halewijn see Allen Epp 1115, 1269, and cf Epp 1342:254 and 1585:110–11/CWE Epp 1115, 1269, and cf Epp 1342:283 and 1585:25–6. See on this subject Smith 'The First French Translations of the *Praise of Folly*.'

161 Allen Ep 2165:42–3/CWE Ep 2165:46–7

162 Ep 1375. On Cantiuncula see Allen Ep 852:80n/CWE Ep 852:85n; Allen and CWE Ep 997 introductions; CEBR I 259–61.

163 See Ep 1426, the dedicatory letter, with Allen and CWE introductions. On Du Moulin see also Allen Ep 523:7n; CEBR II 411.

164 Allen Ep 1679:54–5/CWE Ep 1679:59. On Berquin see Farge 'Les procès de Louis de Berquin'; CEBR I 135–40; Allen Ep 925 13n/CWE Epp 925:17n, 1579 n44, 1599 introduction and n1.

had already circulated in manuscript for some years. Berquin's translations of the first three works were condemned by the theology faculty of the University of Paris in May 1525, *La complainte de la paix* on 1 June.[165] Erasmus cannot have been very happy about the appearance of Berquin's translations in print. He was bound to fear negative consequences for himself: by their ferocity against the French translator the Sorbonne theologians, and above all their militant spokesman Noël Béda, discredited the author of the original texts. In August Erasmus complained to Berquin that by translating his books he was increasing the theologians' resentment against him.[166] Nonetheless, Erasmus remained well-disposed towards his unfortunate and persecuted admirer. He warned him several times about his unreasonable and incautious behaviour, and appealed to Francis I and his sister Margaret of Angoulême, queen of Navarre, on his behalf, but in 1529 Berquin finally paid for his steadfast religious convictions at the stake.[167]

The Italian translation of Erasmus' *Enchiridion militis christiani*, published in April 1531 by Emilio de' Migli, an educated man who belonged to a well-to-do family in Brescia, was less problematical. The copy of this book that Erasmus received as a gift from its translator was still in his library in 1536, listed in the *Versandliste* as *Enchiri[dion] Hetrusco idiomate*; it was one of only three works not in Latin or Greek to be mentioned in the list.[168] The gift was not a surprise, as the translator had secured the author's consent to his edition in 1529. At the time Erasmus advised him not to include the introductory letter to the Benedictine abbot Paul Volz (Ep 858) that he had prefixed to the 1518 edition, which appeared with almost all later versions of the work; this letter had earlier caused a great commotion among the Dominicans when it was included in the Spanish translation of what Migli called 'a work of pure gold' (*aureum opusculum*). Erasmus also encouraged the translation of some of his other works, 'especially those that are less controversial and more likely to encourage piety,' a few of which he identified by name.[169] Migli took Erasmus' advice and omitted from his translation the letter to Volz. It is quite possible that Erasmus received copies of other translations of his works, even though they can no longer be traced in the *Versandliste* or in his correspondence.

When editions of his works in the original Latin were produced without his knowledge, however, Erasmus could not expect the printers or publishers of pirated editions to send him presentation copies. There must have been a very special reason when a copy of such an unauthorized reprint was presented to him. He received an exceptional gift of this kind when he was living in Leuven: the book, which was probably accompanied by a covering letter, was sent to him as a mark of respect and welcomed as such. It was a present from

---

165 On these translations see Telle's editions, with introductions and commentary; 'Books Found in Erasmus' Correspondence' no 65. See also Allen Ep 1581:750–62 / CWE Epp 1581:835–48, 1599 n1; ASD I-5 353–8 (*Declamation des louenges de marriage*); ASD V-1 118 (*Brefve admonition*); ASD V-1 185–6 (*Le symbole des apostres*); and ASD IV-2 37–8 (*La complainte de la paix*). The only known copy of the book containing the first three works, probably printed by Simon Dubois in Paris, is in the Bibliothèque publique et universitaire de Genève. A complete copy of *La complainte de la paix* is in the Houghton Library of Harvard University; an incomplete copy in the Bibliothèque Royale in Brussels; see Walsh 'The *Querela Pacis* of Erasmus: the "lost" French translation.'

166 Allen and CWE Ep 1599:1–4

167 See, for example, Allen Epp 1599:13–15, 2048:25–9 and 54–7, 2077:16–30 / CWE Epp 1599:13–15, 2048:27–32 and 60–3, 2077:17–34. Cf Epp 1722 (to Francis I), 1854 (to Margaret of Navarre). On Berquin's last trial and execution see Allen Epp 2158:91–120, 2188:12–71 / CWE Epp 2158:94–126, 2188:14–77.

168 VL/Catalogue no 158; for the other two see nos 22 #3 and 256.

169 See Epp 2154 (from Migli) and 2165 (Erasmus' reply). For the titles of the books referred to see VL/Catalogue no 158.

Ludovicus Carinus, who was later to be a member of Erasmus' household (*conviva*) in Basel, where he served as the model for one of the characters in the colloquy *Convivium poeticum*. The gift was a copy of the February 1519 reprint of the *Colloquiorum formulae* by Henri Estienne (for Konrad Resch). Carinus had persuaded the printer to include on the last blank leaf of the book a letter he himself had written extolling the author.[170] Must he not have had in mind how Erasmus himself had first made his name widely known in print with a complimentary letter at the end of Robert Gaguin's 1495 edition of *De origine et gestis Francorum compendium*?[171] The young Carinus could hardly have expected his brief letter, addressed to an unknown English fellow-student, to have the effect achieved by Erasmus' magisterial and detailed letter to Gaguin, but Erasmus was not ungrateful for this homage. During the year Carinus received a gift in return, the Aldine edition of Pliny's *Epistolae* (Venice 1508). We know this by chance, for the book, in which Erasmus wrote a donor's inscription in his own hand, has been preserved.[172]

This was not an exceptional gesture. Erasmus often replied to the gift of a book, if it pleased him, with a gift in return, preferably a presentation copy of one of his own recent works or a text he had edited. For example Richard Sparcheford, chaplain to Bishop Cuthbert Tunstall, who in 1527 sent Erasmus a copy of Thomas Linacre's *De emendata structura latini sermonis*, received in thanks one of Erasmus' editions of Chrysostom.[173] Sometimes, when he had no copy of an appropriate work of his own, Erasmus sent a duplicate, or a book from his collection that had been superseded, or one that was no longer indispensable to him – any of which could still make a suitable present, like the copy of the letters of Pliny he sent to Carinus. And Erasmus and his friends often exchanged their publications on a regular basis. Sometimes it is possible to reconstruct these exchanges from Erasmus' correspondence, which shows, for example, the friendly contact he kept up in his later years with Jacopo Sadoleto and Tommaso de Vio, Cardinal Cajetanus, both learned, well-known and influential prelates of the Roman church, and each in his way reform-minded. In the case of Sadoleto, the frequency of the exchanges in itself is a strong argument to show that some items in the *Versandliste* almost certainly reached Erasmus as presents, even though there is no explicit proof to be found in the letters.

As far as it has been preserved, Erasmus' correspondence with the slightly younger humanist Jacopo Sadoleto, bishop of Carpentras since 1517 and from early 1523 to April 1527 secretary of Pope Clement VII, extended from 1524 (Ep 1511) to the end of 1534 (Ep 2982).[174] It was accompanied by an exchange of publications, probably begun by Erasmus. The bishop, then in Rome, was among the first to receive a copy of his *De libero arbitrio diatribe* in the autumn of 1524.[175] In the following year Sadoleto responded by sending a copy of his newly published *Interpretatio in Psalmum 'Miserere mei, Deus'* through the printer Francesco Calvo. The exegesis was favourably received by Erasmus, who was keen to have the book reprinted in Basel at once.[176] The presentation copy may have ended up elsewhere, for it cannot be found in the *Versandliste*. The list does, however, include three well-known later works by Sadoleto, two biblical commentaries and a work on education, all three sent

---

170 See Allen and CWE Ep 920 introductions (Allen prints the letter); on Carinus see also CEBR I 266–8.
      For *Convivium poeticum* see ASD I-3 344–59 / CWE 39 390–418.
171 Allen Ep 45; see further VL/Catalogue no 319.
172 Ep 1034. Allen found the book in private ownership in England; its present whereabouts are unknown.
173 VL/Catalogue no 75
174 On the gap in the correspondence see Allen Ep 2973:8n.
175 Allen and CWE Ep 1511:19; cf Allen and CWE Ep 1481 introductions.
176 'Books Found in Erasmus' Correspondence' no 137; see Allen and CWE Ep 1586:1–22.

at intervals to Erasmus in Freiburg, where he had moved in the meantime. Early in 1530 Sadoleto sent him his *In Psalmum 93 interpretatio*.[177] The two scholars shared an interest in the Book of Psalms. Shortly before, Erasmus had sent Sadoleto a copy of his earlier (1528) *Concionalis interpretatio in Psalmum 85*, and now he reacted to Sadoleto's exegesis of Psalm 93, which he called a 'little gem of a book,' by presenting him with a copy of his recently published *In Psalmum 22 ennarratio triplex*.[178] In the following years further gifts of books made their way to Carpentras, but Sadoleto's duties as papal secretary left him little time for study and publication, and he was not in a position to respond immediately with works of his own composition. In 1532 Erasmus honoured the bishop by dedicating to him his edition of Basil's works in the original Greek. The delivery of the presentation copy was organized by Bonifacius Amerbach, who also entrusted the carriers with further recent works by Erasmus: his *Enarratio Psalmi 38*, the first edition of the *Declarationes ad censuras Lutetiae vulgatas sub nomine facultatis theologiae Parisiensis*, and other works.[179] It is not clear if Amerbach enclosed these books on his own initiative or on instructions from Erasmus, but even in the first case it is hard to imagine that Erasmus' most trusted friend would have acted entirely without his knowledge and consent in these years. Later in the year he was to send the bishop two more reprinted works, this time demonstrably on Erasmus' instructions: one was the Latin translation of Basil's treatise *De spiritu sancto*, a by-product of the Greek edition he had dedicated to Sadoleto, the other the revised and expanded edition of the *Declarationes ad censuras Lutetiae vulgatas*.[180] Finally, in April of the following year, Erasmus sent a presentation copy of his translation of *Aliquot homiliae ad pietatem summopere conducibiles* of John Chrysostom, and of his own *Explanatio symboli*.[181] Sadoleto's gift in return was delayed until the appearance of his dialogue *De liberis instituendis*. In August 1522 Erasmus received a presentation copy of this humanist educational work, which very probably lies concealed without a title in the *Versandliste* behind the entry naming Sadoleto as the author of one of three works bound together.[182] The present came not from the bishop himself but from his grand-nephew and colleague Paolo Sadoleto, recently appointed his coadjutor in the see of Carpentras with the right of succession. Sadoleto must have staged the presentation of the book with the intention of bringing his young relative, who was devoting himself to the study of the classical authors and the Greek and Latin Fathers of the church, to Erasmus' notice, a purpose to which the book lent itself admirably (Paolo and his uncle were the two interlocutors in the dialogue).[183] Sadoleto's third work, *In Pauli epistolam ad Romanos commentariorum libri tres* of 1535, must undoubtedly have come into Erasmus' possession as a gift from the author. Erasmus had followed its lengthy gestation from the beginning. In 1532 he already knew that it was in preparation, and in August 1533 he became directly involved in the publication when the author sent him by his own courier the draft text in manuscript for his verdict almost two years before the work came from the press.[184] Erasmus responded quickly: he bought an extra copy of Melanchthon's previously published *Commentarii in Epistolam ad Romanos*

---

177 vl/Catalogue no 6

178 Allen Epp 2272:6–7 and 2315:129–31 / cwe Epp 2272:6–7 and 2312a:134–6

179 On these works see vl/Catalogue nos 189, 335, and 337 #1; cf Allen Ep 2648 introduction.

180 Allen Epp 2703, 2765:3n. On these two works see vl/Catalogue no 337.

181 Allen Ep 2775 introduction; for the two works see vl/Catalogue nos 394 and 340 #1.

182 vl/Catalogue no 42 #1

183 Allen Ep 2864:9–10n. On Paolo and his humanist interests see Allen's introduction to this letter; cebr iii 187–8.

184 vl/Catalogue no 404 #1

and sent it to Sadoleto via Amerbach in December. He had given the reformer's commentary a rather cool and unwelcoming reception (not without reason, because he was criticized in covert terms by Melanchthon in various passages). Nevertheless he felt that the bishop could derive some benefit from it if he picked the gold out of the dunghill.[185]

Briefer was Erasmus' contact with his contemporary Tommaso de Vio, called Cajetanus (from his birthplace Gaeta). The humanist who had broken radically with scholasticism might seem to have little in common with the theologian who, though accessible to new ideas, in fact still inhabited a medieval thought-world. Cajetanus entered the Dominican order at fifteen and rose to become its General from 1508 to 1518; during that time he wrote much of his famous commentary on the *Summa theologiae* of Thomas Aquinas, which gave a major impetus to the revival of Thomism in the sixteenth century.[186] He became bishop of his native city in 1519. By the early 1530s the original difference in attitude was no longer a factor in the relationship between Erasmus and Cajetanus. Erasmus had come to appreciate Cajetanus' objections to some of his works, and showed himself willing to accommodate him. A moderate, cautious, and nuanced attitude to the religious strife that was tearing Christendom apart – easily but mistakenly seen as half-heartedness – was characteristic of them both and made them equally suspect in the eyes of the fanatical defenders of the church of Rome.[187] This is illustrated by a work published in 1535 by the Dominican Lancellotto de' Politi, a copy of which was found in Erasmus' library, where it was undoubtedly one of the last acquisitions that he had looked at seriously. In this work, permeated with aversion for Luther and critical of Cajetanus' Bible commentaries, Erasmus and the cardinal were lumped together as alleged promoters of the Lutheran heresy.[188]

Erasmus corresponded with Cajetanus during the last three years before his death in August 1534. Only one letter (Ep 2690) has survived, which he promptly published himself,[189] but references in his correspondence to other letters sent and received make it a plausible assumption that the humanist, now settled in Freiburg, and the bishop of Gaeta must have written to each other fairly frequently. The assumption is supported by the exchange of publications that seems to have accompanied their correspondence. Early in 1532 the cardinal-bishop sent a copy of his collection of treatises 'against the Lutherans,' *De communione sub utraque specie, De integritate confessionis,* and *De invocatione sanctorum,* to Freiburg. Erasmus read them with much pleasure, impressed by their erudite brevity and sobriety in argument, and promptly arranged to make them available to the printers so that a reprint could be published north of the Alps.[190] In his turn he sent Cajetanus a copy of his *De sarcienda ecclesiae concordia* of 1533.[191] Cajetanus was very pleased with the treatise and informed the pope, whom he had allowed to read Erasmus' accompanying letter, of his laudatory opinion. One of the Cardinal's household, Giovanni Danieli, his assistant in the publication of several works including his New Testament commentaries, promised to send Erasmus a copy of the *Quaestiones atque omnia (ut vocantur) quolibeta,* if Erasmus did not already have a copy.[192]

---

185 VL/Catalogue no 14

186 His commentary is still considered 'one of the chief classics of scholasticism' (ODCC2 219).

187 On Cajetanus and his relationship with Erasmus see VL/Catalogue no 177.

188 See VL/Catalogue no 35.

189 In his *Epistolae palaeonaeoi* (Freiburg: September [but already in print at end of August] 1532)

190 'Books Found in Erasmus' Correspondence' no 26; Allen Ep 2619. The reprint that Erasmus envisaged never appeared either in Freiburg or Basel; the present may have lain unused in the printer's workshop, intended as copy for the reprint that never materialized; see Allen Ep 2690 introduction.

191 VL/Catalogue no 340 #2

192 Allen Ep 2935. Cajetanus' commentary was published in 1531 (Venice: L. Giunta).

No short title of this work appears in the *Versandliste* (perhaps Erasmus did not take up the offer); nor does the list mention the three anti-Lutheran tracts. Three other works by Cajetanus, however, are mentioned in the *Versandliste*: his edition with commentaries of the text of the Gospels and the Acts of the Apostles, which in Erasmus' library was bound together with his commentaries on the Epistles; and his *Commentarii in Pentateuchum*.[193] The New Testament commentaries were first published in 1530 in Venice and two years later in a revised edition at Paris; the commentary on the Pentateuch was published at Rome in 1531. How did Erasmus come by these books? There is no direct indication in his correspondence, but in the context of his relationship with the cardinal it is difficult to imagine that they were not presentation copies. In all probability Erasmus bought few books in his later years, and we may exclude the possibility that he would have made an exception for Cajetanus' Bible commentaries. What compelling reason could he have had to buy the three books, especially the commentary on the Pentateuch, which, as it is now practically impossible to find, was probably issued in a very small edition and unavailable north of the Alps except by special order? It is more plausible that Erasmus acquired the commentary on the Pentateuch as a present through the mediation of the papal protonotary Ambrosius von Gumppenberg, a nobleman of South German origin and a protégé of Cajetanus. Gumppenberg's ecclesiastical function took him abroad a great deal and enabled him to act as courier for his closest friends. He repeatedly did so for the cardinal, and also for others in his Roman circle.[194] In early 1532 he procured for Erasmus on behalf of Juan Ginés de Sepúlveda a copy, still preserved, of Sepúlveda's recently published *Antapologia pro Alberto Pio in Erasmum Roterodamum*.[195] The pamphlet, which brought to a close the extended controversy between Erasmus and Alberto Pio, was printed and published by A. Bladus in Rome. The same publisher had brought out Cajetanus' Commentary on the Pentateuch the previous year. Might not Gumppenberg have carried with him in his baggage on his journey from Rome to Freiburg not only Sepúlveda's pamphlet but also Cajetanus'commentary?

Erasmus received many more books as presentation copies. He had such a great share in the coming into being of many books in the *Versandliste* that it is inconceivable that their authors did not thank him for his assistance by presenting him with a copy. He received the most varied manuscripts to read and pass judgement on, beginning in 1516–17 with the *Lucubrationes aliquot* of Udalricus Zasius, a collection of chiefly legal treatises, published in 1518; it was Erasmus, through Bruno Amerbach, who encouraged Froben to print the book.[196] The new Basel edition (Froben 1524) of Crastonus' *Dictionarium graecum* was published over the name of Jacobus Ceratinus but in fact was produced under the constant supervision and with the active cooperation of Erasmus. Ceratinus carried out much of the preparatory work at Erasmus' instigation and received a fee for his labours, but his illustrious patron also wrote the introduction to the new edition and left his mark on it in other ways.[197]

Erasmus' involvement in the prehistory of several works by the humanist Lazare de Baïf, his younger contemporary, is less well known. Long before Baïf's treatise *De re vestiaria* was published by J. Bebel in Basel in 1526, Erasmus had been aware of its nature and of some details of the publication. He was delighted that Baïf was to do for the clothing of the ancients what Budé had done for their coinage. He took it in good part when Baïf

---

193 VL/Catalogue nos 177 (two works) and 254
194 On Gumppenberg see Allen Ep 2619 introduction; CEBR II 154.
195 See VL/Catalogue no 389.
196 VL/Catalogue no 188 #2
197 VL/Catalogue no 186

criticized the accuracy of some of his translations in the *Adagia* of Greek words related to clothing. He frankly acknowledged that he had been wrong and in one case corrected his translation in the next edition, even before *De vestis* was on the market. It must have given Baïf particular satisfaction when the much older and more famous scholar so chivalrously submitted to correction, and it would have been only natural to send Erasmus a copy of the book as soon as it appeared.[198] Five years later, together with the revised edition of *De vestis*, Froben published Baïf's treatise *De vasculis*, on the plate and utensils of the ancients. As soon as Erasmus learned that this work was in preparation he wrote to the author, who was then French ambassador in Venice, offering to have it printed in Basel. And so it was, but Erasmus did not confine himself to acting as go-between; he read the manuscript, sent to him in Freiburg, with great attention and turned it over to the printer only when he had corrected errors that had crept into the text through the ignorance of the copyist.[199] Although Erasmus heard in 1532 that Baïf had begun a third book on the shipbuilding of the Greeks and Romans, he was not involved in its preparation. But in view of the relationship which had grown up between them, it is almost certain that the treatise *De re navali*, issued in August 1536 but registered in the *Versandliste*, was a presentation copy that Baïf, now settled in Paris, sent to Erasmus. Presumably at the time the news of Erasmus' death had not reached the French capital, where the book was printed. The presentation copy must have been conscientiously added to Erasmus' estate by Amerbach or the executors as the last acquisition in the library.[200]

Erasmus was also involved at an early stage in two works by Georgius Agricola, a medical man but chiefly famous as a writer on mining. He had recommended that Froben publish Agricola's dialogue on the silver mines of Joachimsthal in Bohemia, the *Bermannus sive de re metallica*, and when the book appeared in 1530 it contained a complimentary letter by Erasmus recommending the modest author. The *Bermannus* is not named in the *Versandliste*, but Erasmus must have received a presentation copy.[201] In 1536, however, his library did include a copy of another more detailed work by Agricola, his *Libri quinque de mensuris et ponderibus*, published by Froben in August 1533. As soon as he heard that this study of the weights and measures of the Greeks and Romans was under way, Erasmus expressed interest and let it be known that he would be very glad to read the manuscript if it were sent to him. And in fact he must have read it before the work went to press, though we do not know if he made any suggestions to the author. His reading convinced him of the acuity with which Agricola had challenged or refuted several opinions of Guillaume Budé, Leonardus de Portis, and Andrea Alciati.[202]

A few other books in the *Versandliste* can reasonably be assumed to have been presentation copies, even though there is no strict proof. Unlike the works just mentioned, Erasmus had no share in them, so that he could not have expected to receive them as gifts as a matter of course. Sometimes, however, the author was on such good terms with Erasmus at the time of publication that such a personal gesture would not have been too much to expect. Some of the books we have discussed are examples of this, and there are others: Remaclus Arduenna's *Palamedes palliata comedia* (London 1512); the *Opera* of Athanasius edited by Nicolas Bérault (Paris 1519 or 1520); the topical treatise *De libero arbitrio* of Johannes Cochlaeus (Tübingen 1525);

---

198 vl/Catalogue no 73 #1
199 vl/Catalogue no 2 #1
200 vl/Catalogue no 245
201 'Books Found in Erasmus' Correspondence' no 2
202 vl/Catalogue no 78

and the *Psalmorum omnium ... paraphrastica interpretatio* of Jan van Campen (Nuremberg 1532).[203] Sometimes clues in Erasmus' correspondence lead us to suspect that other books were presents: Stephanus Niger's *Dialogus quo quicquid in graecarum literarum penetralibus reconditum*, with the appended translation of the *Heroicus* of Philostratus (Milan 1517); the *Dialogi* of Niccolò Leonico Tomeo (Venice 1524); the so-called Roman legal documents, later unmasked as a fake edition of François Rabelais' *Lucii Cuspidii testamentum; Item contractus venditionis antiquis Romanorum temporibus initus* (Lyon 1532); and Pierre Gilles' selections *Ex Aeliani historiae ... itemque ex Porphyrio, Heliodoro, Oppiano ... libri XVI de vi et natura animalium* (Lyon 1533).[204]

It was not always easy to have a presentation copy delivered safe and sound to its destination in Leuven, Basel, or Freiburg within a reasonable time. Very few of the authors who presented Erasmus with works would have had the opportunity to deliver their gifts in person. Most were dependent on others to deliver them: printers or publishers, professional couriers, or travelling friends and acquaintances.

Some authors were on such good terms with their printers or publishers that they could let them bear the risks of dispatching the presentation copy. Johann Reuchlin simply instructed his printer Thomas Anshelm, who was also a personal friend, to send two copies of his *Ars cabalistica* (Hagenau: March 1517) via the Easter fair at Bergen op Zoom to Erasmus, who had given his address as the house of Pieter Gillis in Antwerp. One of the copies was for Erasmus himself, the other for his friend John Fisher, the bishop of Rochester, whom Erasmus had introduced to the famous Hebraist and humanist at the bishop's request. Reuchlin asked Erasmus to forward the second copy to Fisher, which he punctiliously did.[205] Henricus Cornelius Agrippa of Nettesheim, author of the notorious book *De incertitudine et vanitate scientiarum et artium* (Antwerp 1530), took the same course. He sent the manuscript of his *Apologia contra theologistas Lovanienses*, in which he defended himself against the attack on his earlier book from the orthodox theologians of Leuven, to Andreas Cratander, instructing him to print it. Shortly afterwards, before it was certain that the pamphlet could be published, he asked the Basel printer in advance to send a copy to Erasmus in due course. The request was premature, as Cratander did not dare to publish the pamphlet. The *Apologia* was printed in 1533, with no indication of place or printer (but probably in Cologne by J. Soter), and Erasmus finally received a copy through a friend.[206] Agrippa's request nevertheless shows what sort of service from his printer/publisher an author expected more or less as his due.

Those who could not profit from the convenience of the printers' and publishers' commercial circuit and did not have a friend or acquaintance to act as their personal courier were dependent on professional carriers of whom they knew little. A donor might have to go to a great deal of trouble to send a presentation copy if it involved a long journey or one that followed a less frequented trade route. We hear once or twice about the often tedious preparations for such a consignment. In 1530, the loyal Roman Catholic theologian Conradus Coci de Wimpina, professor of theology and rector of the new university in Frankfurt an der Oder, wished to send Erasmus a copy of his large work against Lutheranism and earlier heresies: *Sectarum errorum, hallutinationum et schismatum ... concisionis Anacephalaeoseos*

---

203 VL/Catalogue nos 364 #1, 187, 10 #1, and 5

204 VL/Catalogue nos 293, 366, 12 #3, 316 (cf no 219)

205 VL/Catalogue no 176 #2; Erasmus told Reuchlin how to reach him (Allen Ep 457:52–4 / CWE Ep 457:58–60), and he sent the book to Fisher via Thomas More (Allen Epp 592:4–7, 593:4–9 / CWE Epp 592:6–8, 593:5–12). On the four Brabant fairs see CWE Epp 562:25n, 468:9–10n.

206 VL/Catalogue no 43. Agrippa gave the copy intended for Erasmus to Tielmannus Gravius, secretary to the chapter of Cologne cathedral and a friend of Erasmus, to forward to Freiburg.

librorum partes tres.[207] Although Wimpina had hoped to have the work printed in Basel, the book was finally published in Frankfurt. How was he to have the copy intended for Erasmus conveyed to Freiburg? Wimpina did not have to spend much of his own time or effort on this; a friend in Leipzig, Jan Horák, offered to handle the transport of the book for him. But it took a while to organize. First Horák enlisted the cooperation of the Leipzig agents of the Augsburg trading firm of Anton and Bartholomäus Welser, who agreed to the use of their carriers. But this got the package no further than Frankfurt am Main. Horák then asked Erasmus to arrange for the book to be collected from the Welser establishment in Frankfurt for the last stage of its journey to Freiburg, as Erasmus could count on Hieronymus Froben to bring the package from Frankfurt to Basel and have it delivered to him in Freiburg.[208] We can no longer trace whether this plan of transport was followed, or if the work ever reached Freiburg at all. Wimpina's book is not mentioned in the *Versandliste*, and although that is no proof, it may well indicate that the thick folio volume (about 390 leaves) was lost en route.

Over the years several other presentation copies promised to Erasmus failed to arrive. He knew the various risks to which books were exposed in transit, and was accustomed to weigh them carefully before he dispatched copies of his own works as presents to his friends and associates. Sometimes they were enough to make him refrain from sending a copy. Immediately after the publication of the first edition of his *Paraphrase on Romans* (Leuven: Dirk Martens 1517), Erasmus sent presentation copies to Thomas More and a number of other people. But he did not send one to Domenico Grimani, even though the book had been dedicated to him (Ep 710), partly because, as he later explained to the cardinal, he knew 'that parcels of any weight do not easily survive so long a journey.' The book cannot have been heavy; it was a quarto of about seventy-five leaves. But Erasmus may have had other reasons to feel that he could not risk sending the book from Leuven to Rome, or at least to fear that it would not arrive safely. Some months later he decided to risk sending Grimani a copy of Froben's reprint, which appeared in January 1518, if he had not already managed to obtain the original edition.[209] Perhaps Froben, who could take advantage of the opportunities open to publishers, arranged to send a copy of this reprint to Rome from Basel or Frankfurt.

At about the same time Erasmus dedicated to Duke Frederick, elector of Saxony, and his cousin, Duke George, his edition of Suetonius with the *Historiae Augustae scriptores* (Basel: Froben, June 1518). Again, he did not send presentation copies to the dedicatee. There were several reasons, as he explained to Elector Frederick: the distance from Basel (at that time Frederick was in Wittenberg); the lack of any reliable person to whom it might safely be entrusted; and the consideration that it might be superfluous to send a copy of a book that was already widely circulated.[210]

Authors among Erasmus' friends and fellow scholars who wished to send him their own works must have faced similar transport problems. Many potential donors must have been deterred from sending a presentation copy of their works by the time and effort required and the high risk of loss en route. It is fair to say that Erasmus would have received many more books as gifts if the books that were actually sent had always reached their destination. In fact it is rather surprising that so many did arrive safely. This was largely thanks to the many

---

207 'Books Found in Erasmus' Correspondence' no 149
208 Allen Ep 2247:24–34 / cwe Ep 2247:25–33; and cf Erasmus' comment in December 1532 to Agrippa: 'If you want something delivered reliably, please give it to Hieronymus Froben' (Allen Ep 2748:5–6).
209 Allen Ep 835:5–7 / cwe Ep 835:5–10
210 Allen Ep 939:12–16 / cwe Ep 939:12–16. The dedicatory letter is Ep 586. For the edition see vl/Catalogue no 261.

ad hoc couriers, that is, not professional carriers but friends or acquaintances of the authors who had the opportunity to do them a service by delivering packets of books to Erasmus. It is clear that numerous presentation copies, from far and near, found their way to Leuven or Antwerp and later to Basel or Freiburg in the hands of such casual couriers.

In 1517 Giambattista Egnazio seized the chance to entrust a copy of his recently published *De caesaribus* to Ulrich von Hutten, who paid his respects to Egnazio in Venice that year; Hutten was given the book to deliver to Erasmus on his return journey.[211] How Eobanus Hessus managed to deliver a copy of his *Hodoeporicon* safely to Erasmus so soon after its publication has already been mentioned; he was able to leave its delivery to two friends from his humanist circle in Erfurt, Justus Jonas and Kaspar Schalbe, who paid a personal visit to Erasmus in Antwerp in May 1519.[212]

Andrzej Krzycki, who had been secretary of King Sigismund I of Poland before he was elected bishop of Przemyśl and in 1529 of Płock, was a fairly frequent correspondent in the last eleven years of Erasmus' life and presented him with several gifts of books, mostly presentation copies of his own works.[213] The prelate, who also won a reputation as a writer and poet, would have had no problem in getting them delivered through the good offices of a friend who was making the journey to the west and including the humanist centre of Basel in his itinerary. In 1524 Hieronim Łaski, himself a leading figure in Polish public life, was sent on an embassy to Francis I and brought with him his younger brothers Jan and Stanisław. He broke his journey in Basel to call on Erasmus.[214] In a letter written in October 1525, Erasmus says that Stanisław and Jan Łaski had shown him two of Krzycki's works: probably *In Luterum oratio*, which was included in a volume of prose and verse with the ironic title '*Praises of Luther*' (*Encomia Luteri*) and *De negotio Prutenico epistola*.[215] Erasmus understood that the books were given on behalf of their author; as a token of his gratitude he sent Krzycki as a gift the treatise *De arte supputandi* by Bishop Tunstall of London.[216] In the spring of 1528, Krzycki sent a protégé, the young Marcin Słap Dąbrówski, to accompany his nephew Andrzej Zebrzydowski on a visit to the west, and the two young men apparently enjoyed Erasmus' hospitality in his house in Basel.[217] Słap returned to the west on two further missions; on both occasions he visited Freiburg, where Erasmus had by then moved, and Erasmus praised him highly in letters to his Polish friends.[218] During his first visit, in 1529, he again spent a night in Erasmus' house. We do not know if he brought any presents from Krzycki on this visit, but in 1530 he had more than letters to deliver; the bishop sent Erasmus a gold ring set with a ruby and a copy of his *De ratione et sacrificio missae* (Cracow 1528).[219]

---

211 'Books Found in Erasmus' Correspondence' no 52; for this work see also VL/Catalogue nos 51, 97 #2, and 261.

212 34 above

213 On Krzycki see Allen and CWE Ep 1629 introductions; CEBR II 275–8.

214 On Hieronim Łaski see Allen Ep 1242:25n/CWE Ep 1242:5n (page 450); CEBR II 294–7. On Stanisław, see CEBR II 301–2. Hieronim's visits are described in *Catalogus lucubrationum* Allen I 31:28–32:38/CWE Ep 1341A:1216–71.

215 Allen Ep 1629:1–6 with 2n and 5n and Krzycki's reply, Ep 1652:54–92/CWE Epp 1629:3–8 with nn2 and 3, 1652:58–97

216 See VL/Catalogue no 17 with n3.

217 On Słap see Allen and CWE Ep 2351 introductions and CEBR III 258–9; on Zebrzydowski, CEBR III 473–4.

218 Allen Epp 2201:58–71 (to Krzycki), 2376:1–6 (to Christoph Szydłowiecki), and 2377:23–30 (to Piotr Tomicki)/CWE Epp 2201:64–78, 2376:3–8, 2377:26–33

219 'Books Found in Erasmus' Correspondence' no 93. On the other works Krzycki sent to Erasmus see ibidem nos 91, 92, and 94. For the ring, see Allen Ep 2375:16–24/CWE Ep 2375:18–27.

One of the presentation copies already mentioned reached Erasmus through a chance courier: in 1530 Pietro Bembo arranged for the son of an acquaintance to deliver a book to Erasmus in Freiburg.[220] Martinus Bovolinus, a doctor of laws and notary from a prominent family of the Mesolcina valley, practised his profession chiefly there and in the adjoining Alpine territories, but he had wider ambitions than the law. He had sought contact with Erasmus before, and was on friendly terms with Bembo in Venice.[221] Bembo was almost certainly aware that Bovolinus' sixteen-year-old son Lazarus had matriculated at the University of Freiburg the previous year and was living with his master Henricus Glareanus, a true friend of Erasmus. (Like him, but a little earlier, Glareanus had migrated to the neighbouring but less turbulent and loyally Catholic city of Freiburg to escape the radical reformers in Basel.) The suggestion to entrust Lazarus with the delivery of the present probably came from his father; but if it came from Bembo, Bovolinus would have seized the opportunity: by doing his illustrious friend a service he could introduce his son to Erasmus and recommend him as a servant-pupil.[222]

While it is possible to use the correspondence to reconstruct in some detail the presentation copies that Erasmus received through professional or occasional couriers, it is difficult to trace the books that were delivered to him in person. Only a few can be identified with any certainty, although there must have been more, for Erasmus received countless visitors from far and near over the years. Some of them may well have called to present their own newly published works; other visitors may simply have wanted the privilege and honour of meeting the famous scholar and may have chosen to offer him a present in the form of a book as a suitable mark of respect. The correspondence seldom refers to those who presented their books to Erasmus in person in his own home, because Erasmus had no need to thank them in writing, although he might recall them afterwards in a letter for some special reason.

In the summer of 1520, two emissaries from the Bohemian Brethren visited Erasmus at Pieter Gillis' house in Antwerp, showed him a statement of their faith, and asked his opinion of it. Erasmus mentions this visit only indirectly. Correspondence with Jan Šlecta and Arkleb of Boskovice had kept him informed about the religious divisions and sects in their country.[223] In the autumn of 1520 Arkleb sent Erasmus a copy of 'the manifesto and rule of life' of the Brethren. In his reply, in January 1521, Erasmus says that he had already received the book 'by way of two Bohemians,' though he had not yet read it through.[224] The book was undoubtedly the *Apologia sacrae scripturae*. Erasmus' summary allusion is not in itself conclusive identification, but a reliable older secondary source removes all doubt. In his account of the Bohemian Brethren published (posthumously) in 1605, Joachim Camerarius described the Antwerp visit in detail. He named the two brothers who had brought the book, discussed their visit and its consequences, and also gave the place and year of publication of the work: it can be definitely identified as the *Apologia sacrae scripturae*, printed in Nuremberg in 1511.[225]

---

220 See 36 above.

221 Ep 2102; on him see Allen and CWE introductions and CEBR I 181.

222 Ep 2337. Lazarus would not receive a stipend, and Bovolinus would pay his room and board.

223 On Jan Šlechta see Epp 950, 1021, and 1039 and CEBR III 259–60; on Arkleb of Boskovice see Ep 1154, CEBR I 174–5.

224 Allen Ep 1183:7–8 / CWE Ep 1183:8–10

225 See 'Books Found in Erasmus' Correspondence' no 145. The episode escaped the notice of Erasmus' biographers until the early 1920s. Allen Ep 1117 introduction quotes Camerarius' account; cf CWE Ep 1039 introduction. Erasmus may have received other works in defence of the Bohemian Brethren from Arkleb of Boskovice; see Allen Ep 1154:8n / CWE Ep 1154 n2.

Another gift delivered to Erasmus in person and recalled later in his correspondence was a work by Damião de Gois, the wealthy Portuguese noble who, despite a difference in age of more than thirty years, was one of Erasmus' most devoted and valued friends in the last years of his life. Gois first visited him in Freiburg in spring 1533, and he discreetly left behind a copy of his *Legatio magni Indorum Imperatoris presbyteri Ioannis ad Emanuelem Lusitaniae regem A.D. MDXIII*, which had been published six months earlier.[226] During the visit Erasmus paid little attention to it. Three months after the meeting in Freiburg, Gois wrote to remind him of the *Legatio* and made it clear that he had left his book, however unobtrusively, for a definite reason. At the end of the book Gois had printed a letter he had sent to the archbishop of Uppsala, Johannes Magnus, a plea on behalf of the Lapps, a people exploited and oppressed by the Swedes. Gois fervently hoped that Erasmus would be willing to put his influence and authority behind the cause of the Lapps, who faced the threat of extermination, either by publishing something himself or by writing a letter that could be published together with Gois' own letter to Archbishop Store.[227] In his reply Erasmus says that until he was able to examine it more closely after his guest left, he was not even aware that the *Legatio* was by Gois himself.[228] He was willing to comply with Gois' request, and in a later conversation with him Erasmus must have undertaken to devote a *iustum volumen* – a pamphlet – to the disastrous fate of the Lapps.[229] He had still not been able to carry out his intention by March 1534 because of problems with the printer, and he was never able to fulfil his promise. He did, however have Gois' *Legatio*, including the letter to the archbishop on the plight of the Lapps, translated into German, and his *Ecclesiastes*, the last major work to appear before his death, included a passage on the subject.[230]

The *Apologia* of the Bohemian Brethren and Gois' *Legatio* are both very rare works; neither appears in the *Versandliste*. It does, however, include the short titles of a number of other works that most probably came into Erasmus' hands in the same way, that is, presented to him personally by their authors. There is no explicit proof in the correspondence or elsewhere, but circumstantial evidence permits the inference that the books were gifts delivered in person, for they are all cases where the authors are known to have paid Erasmus a visit soon after their works appeared.

One example is an edition of a text prepared by Joachim Vadianus, of Watt near St Gallen, the city where he was later active in establishing the reformed church. Vadianus was not a fanatic but a moderate man who never turned against Erasmus as so many other reformers did. After many years work in Vienna, he returned to Switzerland in June 1518 and immediately paid a call on Erasmus, who was then in Basel. In all likelihood Vadianus presented a copy of his edition with commentary of Pomponius Mela's *De situ orbis*, published the previous month, which included two complimentary references to Erasmus.[231] There can hardly be any doubt that Ulrich von Hutten offered Erasmus a copy of his edition of the eleventh-century anti-papal tract, now topical once more, *De unitate ecclesiae conservanda*, published in March 1520, when he visited him in Leuven in June the same year. He left with a flattering

---

226 'Books Found in Erasmus' Correspondence' no 71

227 Allen Ep 2826:31–66

228 Allen Ep 2846:13–15

229 According to Gois' *Deploratio Lappianae* (Leuven 1540) published after Erasmus' death; see Allen Ep 2846:117n.

230 Allen Ep 2914:28–32. Cf *Ecclesiastes* ASD V-4 148:328–36 / CWE 67 359. Chomarat points out (149 329n) that Erasmus based his account largely on the information given by Gois in Allen Ep 2826:31–66.

231 See VL/Catalogue no 321.

letter of recommendation from Erasmus, with whom he was still on good terms, to the imperial court.[232] And it is just as likely that Erasmus received his copy of the 1527 Cologne edition of Valla's *In Pogium Florentinum antidoti libri quatuor* (with his *In errores Antonii Raudensis adnotationes*) from its youthful editor Christoph von Carlowitz, whom he entertained hospitably in Basel in December 1527, the year of publication, possibly lodging him in his house for several days.[233] He was clearly impressed with the intellectually precocious Saxon, for whom he prophesied a promising future in his *Ciceronianus* four months later.

Presentation copies were occasionally sent to Erasmus by printers and publishers. Compared with the many presentation copies that his friends and admirers sent him for personal motives or as marks of attention, they were far fewer. Roughly a quarter of the library as listed in 1536 had been printed by the Froben Press. About half of that number were authorized editions of Erasmus' own works, of which the author received a limited (and varying) number of copies to distribute among his friends.[234] The other half were Froben publications of other authors, most of them published during the years of close cooperation between Erasmus and the Froben firm. Erasmus presumably selected these books himself, and normally they found their way to his house in Basel or Freiburg, as reward in kind for services rendered.[235] In addition, some Froben editions may have been expressly offered to him by or on behalf of their authors, perhaps with a written dedication, as presentation copies.

Two printer-publishers, Matthias Schürer and Josse Bade, not only did considerable work for Erasmus before Froben appeared on the scene but also formed ties of friendship with him.[236] Erasmus also received several publishers' presentation copies in the stricter sense from the Aldine Press in Venice, although after his first major work, the *Adagiorum chiliades* of 1508, they did not publish any further works for him. It must have been a disappointment for the partners in the firm that after this success later lucrative editions went to competing firms. Andrea Torressani, who took over the firm with his son after the death of Aldo Manuzio in 1515, sounded Erasmus out in 1517 about the chair of Greek and Latin that had become vacant in Venice following the departure of Marcus Musurus for Rome. At the same time he sought to obtain his cooperation in the planned new Aldine edition of Terence and in general to win commissions from him.[237] Since Torresani wanted to win Erasmus for his list, it is not impossible that as a mark of his esteem he sent him several new Aldine editions that appear in the *Versandliste*. It was a very natural gesture to honour him the following year with a presentation copy of the Aldine Greek Bible, the first and only printed edition until the appearance of the Complutensian Polyglot.[238] The Greek version of the New Testament it contained was simply taken from Erasmus' *Novum instrumentum* of 1516, but now introduced by a handsome dedication to him by Gianfrancesco Torresani, Andrea's son. Some years later Gianfrancesco complained that he never received copy from Erasmus any more. Erasmus was sympathetic, and in 1523 he seemed willing to bring out a new and revised edition of his *Adagia* in Venice. But when the text was ready Torresani had to let the chance slip, because he needed all of his firm's presses at that time for the great edition of

---

232 See VL/Catalogue no 59.
233 See VL/Catalogue no 153 #2.
234 Usually between ten and twenty copies. See Ruppel 'Die Bücherwelt des 16. Jahrhunderts und die Frankfurter Büchermessen' 155.
235 See 26 above.
236 On Bade, see 25, 27 above. For Schürer's presentation copies of the *Lucubrationes* see VL/Catalogue no 50.
237 Ep 589
238 See 28 with n100 above.

Galen. He could give no better token of his regret than to send a set of the five-volume work to Erasmus in Basel.[239] Torresani sent him another gift book, not named, in 1528. We do not know if it ever arrived.[240]

Other printers may have expressed their gratitude by sending products of their presses to Erasmus in Basel or Freiburg. We know of two from the correspondence. In 1518 Erasmus lent his authority to the important edition of Livy by Johann Schöffer of Mainz by complying with a request to write a commendatory letter to the reader (Ep 919). His eloquent eulogy of Johann Fust, the grandfather of the book's publisher, describes him as chief among the inventors of the art of printing. (Ulrich von Hutten, then still on excellent terms with Erasmus, supplied the actual preface.) Erasmus must undoubtedly have received a free copy of the edition of Livy, but we cannot certainly identify it with any one of the editions of Livy in the *Versandliste*.[241] In the following year Schöffer asked Erasmus for information about the so-called *moles Drusiana*, a Roman monument in the neighbourhood of Mainz, for use in a work on the antiquities of Mainz and its environs that his firm was publishing. He had entrusted the preparation of the text to his corrector Johann Huttich, an acquaintance of Erasmus. This may well explain not only why the request was made to him, but also why Erasmus immediately set to work to comply with it. It is not impossible that a presentation copy of the work was sent to him on its publication as a mark of thanks, but the *Collectanea* do not appear in the *Versandliste*.[242] And as we know from a letter of 1527, Erasmus may also have received a copy of 'a pamphlet written in German containing defamatory illustrations' (*libellum germanice scriptum cum famosis picturis*), a still unidentified work, from Johann Schöffer's brother Peter, who was then active as a printer in Worms.[243]

More traces in Erasmus' library were left by the books presented by Francesco Giulio Calvo, who later changed his middle name to Minuzio. Early in his career as a printer and bookseller he tried to find a new market north of the Alps. He approached Froben in Basel with a proposal to exchange the products of their presses.[244] He was a businessman with many friends among the men of letters of his day, and in 1518 he paid a visit to Erasmus in Leuven, understanding very well that the latter's good will could be of great advantage to him. On that occasion he brought with him as gifts, apart from some fragments of ancient manuscripts, two quite recent and important Greek texts of the Calliergis press: Pindar's Olympian, Nemean, and Pythian Odes and Theocritus' Epigrams, published in Rome in 1515 and 1516.[245] During his visit, Calvo, a cultivated and charming person, persuaded Erasmus to write a letter to the famous bibliophile Jean Grolier. Ep 831, a long and flattering letter to a potential patron, was composed with great care. It became known to the Milanese printer of a work by Stephanus Niger dedicated to Grolier, which suggests that Calvo may have given Erasmus the book entered in the *Versandliste* as 'Stephanus Niger.' This was the first edition of Philostratus' *Heroicus*, preceded by Niger's summary of Pausanius' *Periegesis*

---

239 See cwe Ep 1349 introduction and lines 1–15; cf cwe Epp 1623:5–8, 1628 introduction and the references given there. For the edition of Galen, see vl/Catalogue no 137.

240 It was almost certainly not the Aldine Celsus, as Allen thought (Ep 1989:13n); see vl/Catalogue nos 108 and 192.

241 See vl/Catalogue no 411.

242 'Books Found in Erasmus' Correspondence' no 85; cf 124 below. See Allen Ep 1054:1–5/cwe Ep 1054:3–7; on Huttich see Allen and cwe Ep 550 introductions and cebr ii 220–1.

243 Allen Ep 1804:147–8/cwe Ep 1804:161–2 with n32

244 Allen Ep 581:29–31 with 30n/cwe Ep 581:32–3 with 33n

245 vl/Catalogue nos 107 and 98

in dialogue form.[246] Nor were these gifts the only ones Calvo sent. In 1525 Erasmus wrote a letter thanking him for some 'attractive books.' These probably included the *Libellus de legatione Basilii magni principis Moschouiae ad Clementem VII*, which is mentioned in the *Versandliste*; it was one of Calvo's own publications, printed in 1525 at Rome, where he had moved his business.[247] Erasmus said in his letter that he was impatient to see the others that had been promised to him. Could this further present have included Calvo's edition of *De partu virginis libri III*, a poem by Jacopo Sannazaro (written under the pseudonym Actius Syncerus), which appeared in December 1526? Erasmus mentions the work in a letter of June 1527 and also praises it in his *Ciceronianus*.[248]

Finally it is worth mentioning a few presents received from a printer to whose relationship with Erasmus little or no attention has yet been paid. In 1530 he received from Paris the just published *Comparatio regii potentatus et divitiarum ac praestantiae* of John Chrysostom. The treatise had been translated from Greek by Polidoro Virgilio at the instigation of Erasmus, to whom the edition was also dedicated.[249] It seems obvious that this must have been a presentation copy from the translator. If so, it was presented by the printer-publisher Gerard Morrhy, who was a devoted friend of Virgilio and who had printed it purely as gesture of friendship at his own expense. Morrhy, a native of Kampen in the Low Countries, had a printing shop near the College of the Sorbonne, and Chrysostom's *Comparatio* was one of his earliest productions.[250] Morrhy attached great importance to his contact with Erasmus, and the edition of Chrysostom may not have been his only gift. Not long afterwards Erasmus professed himself extremely interested to know about the author of a book that had just come to his notice, the *Genialium dierum libri VI* of Alessandro d'Alessandro, originally published in Rome in 1522, but reissued in Paris in 1532 by Gerard Morrhy. There can scarcely be any doubt that the *Dies geniales* that appears in the *Versandliste* is this edition, sent to Freiburg as a present by its printer-publisher.[251]

---

246 VL/Catalogue 293, mentioned 45 above
247 Allen Ep 1604:1–3 / CWE Ep 1604:3–5; VL/Catalogue no 370 #2
248 'Books Found in Erasmus' Correspondence' no 138
249 'Books Found in Erasmus' Correspondence' no 88
250 On Morrhy see Ep 2311, which accompanied the gift; CEBR II 465.
251 See VL/Catalogue no 300 #2.

2

The Disposal and Replacement of Books

The arrangement Erasmus made with Jan Łaski when he sold his library in 1525 stipulated that all his future acquisitions should be included except for certain valuable manuscripts.[1] This had a far-reaching consequence for the buyer: the collection transferred to him in 1536 was much more extensive than it had been when he negotiated the purchase agreement. We can be absolutely certain that 115 of the books listed in the *Versandliste* were published after 1525, and virtually certain that about 10 older works were not bought or received as presents until after the transaction in that year.[2] Together these 125 works make up a quarter of the grand total of 500 individual books comprised in the 413 numbered entries in Husner's list. If one also bears in mind that a remarkable number of books named in the *Versandliste* were published in 1525,[3] and that some of them cannot have been acquired until after the sale agreement had been reached in June, one can safely say that the library grew by at least 30 per cent between 1525 and 1536.

The businesslike Erasmus felt it necessary to remind his younger Polish friend afterwards what an advantageous bargain he had made. Twice, in fact, he calculated for him how much the library had increased in value by later acquisitions: in 1528, according to his estimates, by 70 to 80 florins and in 1533 by 100 crowns. On both occasions he substantiated his argument by citing the edition of Galen presented to him by Gianfrancesco Torresani, on its own worth 30 gold florins in its unbound state. He declared himself willing to cancel the transaction if Łaski should regret it. In that case he would refund the first half of the purchase price, which had already been paid.[4] But Łaski did not react to the suggestion and still appeared to be happy with the prospect of his future possession of the valuable library. Erasmus could hardly do anything but accept this, though he continued to keep open the possibility that Łaski could go back on his purchase: 'So far as the library is concerned,' he wrote again in 1534, 'I am still of the same opinion, but the decision shall be yours.'[5]

While the library steadily grew in size over the years through purchase and presentation, some books were lost by deliberate removal. This is more difficult to prove. Erasmus did not allow his collection to grow without limit by simply keeping whatever he had bought or acquired. As we have noted, Erasmus was pragmatic about his books; it is very likely that throughout his life he made an effort to acquire very few books except those he thought

---

1 Miaskowski i 44 and ii 3 (no 2); for the excepted manuscripts see 92–8 below.

2 Chiefly older standard editions of classical authors, which Erasmus purchased in 1525; see 32–3 above.

3 vl/Catalogue nos 7, 8 (possibly two works), 10 (two works), 16, 76, 77, 97 (three works), 134, 137, 152, 172, 204, 358, 370 #2, and possibly 34 (probably several works), 36, 44 (several possibilities), 49 (probably two works), 205, 206, 207, 229 #1, 240, and 381

4 See Allen Epp 2033:15–18 and 2780:7–15/cwe Ep 2033:18–21. On the value of the currency see 3 and n2 above.

5 Allen Epp 2862:30–60, 2911:8

indispensable for his work. He did not make a point of regularly and systematically going through his books to examine them for their permanent usefulness; he had neither the time, given his scholarly work, often performed in haste and under high pressure, nor the patience for this. Undoubtedly he also deliberately left a great many books standing or lying on his shelves more out of sentiment or as mementos than for the real profit he could derive from them.[6] But the careful preservation of some books in such cases did not necessarily rule out the removal on rational grounds of many others, and he must have felt few pangs about disposing of works that were, or had come to seem in his eyes, ballast that merely wasted space.

We can no longer reconstruct in detail exactly how Erasmus set about thinning his library to keep it healthy; ultimately, the evidence is lacking. But in a very few cases we can be certain, either from a reference in his correspondence or, in the rare volumes preserved, from a note on the title-page or flyleaf, that he had once owned a book but later disposed of it. It seems feasible, therefore, by reasoning from the few concrete examples that we know or by using hypotheses, to infer the considerations that led Erasmus regularly to remove books from his collection.

There are indications that in principle Erasmus removed from his library texts and other works that had been superseded by more modern or better editions acquired later. The three copies of Pliny's *Historia naturalis* in his library were almost certainly all Froben editions, the first of which appeared in 1525.[7] The 1496 edition (Venice: de Zannis) he owned now appeared superfluous to him, and he gave it away to his godson Erasmius Froben.[8] He received the original edition of Sepúlveda's *Antapologia pro Alberto Pio* (Rome 1532) from the author when he already owned the Paris reprint of the same year; evidently he disposed of the reprint and kept the original (now in Emden).[9] In the case of Ulrich von Hutten's *Aula* and Giovanni Manardo's *Epistolae medicinales* Erasmus seems to have disposed of the original and kept the reprint.[10] He must have possessed and studied the first two versions of Melanchthon's *Loci communes*, but in the end he kept only one of them.[11] Only one complete copy of his edition of Jerome was still among his books in 1536, the Chevallon edition of 1533, revised with his cooperation.[12] He had only a fragment of one of the two older Froben editions (1516 and 1520) on his shelves, while he had given Glareanus the antiquated Venice edition with which he had first begun his studies of Jerome.[13] His improved edition of Seneca's *Opera*, which appeared in 1529,[14] made it superfluous to keep the original edition published under the title *Lucubrationes*; the latter does not appear in the *Versandliste*. His *Apophthegmata* were first published in 1531 in quarto, and later substantially enlarged in 1532 in folio, but only the third edition of 1535, in octavo, was found in his estate.[15] The number of first editions superseded by later editions still found in Erasmus' collection in

---

6 Cf 127 below.

7 VL/Catalogue nos 205 and 207, both listed as Froben editions, and 412

8 According to an inscription in the copy, which is now in the library of the University of Basel (Inc 483); see Husner 'Bibliothek' 257–8; ASD II-6 427 879n.

9 VL/Catalogue no 389

10 VL/Catalogue nos 4 #1 (Hutten) and 13 #1 (Manardo)

11 VL/Catalogue no 37

12 VL/Catalogue no 405

13 *Opera exegetica in Vetus et Novum Testamentum* (Venice: Giovanni and Gregorio de' Gregori 1497) 2 vols. The books, which are now in the library of the University of Münster, contain the ex libris *Sum Erasmi* and marginal notes; see Husner 'Bibliothek' 256–7.

14 VL/Catalogue no 148

15 VL/Catalogue no 391

1536 is so small, and the examples so random, that it is unlikely he kept them deliberately; they seem rather to have escaped his efforts to weed his library.

Often the disposal of books can be plausibly inferred only from the striking absence of older editions. Both Valla's *Elegantiae* and Cicero's *Opera* were only found in the library in late editions, although it is hard to imagine that Erasmus had not already had earlier editions of both works to hand.[16] His practice of disposing of old editions is indirectly confirmed by the contents of several volumes in which long-superseded editions had been bound with other works that he would not have wanted to dispose of. Erasmus undoubtedly possessed a modern edition of Tacitus, that is, one that included the text of the first five books of the *Annales*, only rediscovered in 1508–9.[17] When he acquired this, it made the older version without these five books redundant. He will already have owned the earlier edition but could not dispose of it because it was bound with an admittedly old but still serviceable text of Appianus Alexandrinus' Roman history that he naturally wished to keep.[18] Similarly, he kept the scholia of Jacques Toussain, published in 1526, on two previously issued collections of Guillaume Budé's letters. Erasmus must certainly have owned those collections as well, but he must have removed them in 1531, when he acquired Toussain's long-awaited edition of Budé's complete correspondence. But he could not dispose of the earlier separate edition of the scholia, which were expanded and incorporated in the new edition, because they had been bound with a text of Chrysostom.[19]

Older editions did not necessarily have to yield to newer ones if there was no difference in quality to justify it. Erasmus evidently found it unnecessary to replace one of the very early editions of the *Scriptores rerum rusticarum* he owned by a later edition that was not much more than a reprint. The Aldine edition of 1514, which he received as a gift from a youthful admirer in 1521 with a dedication 'to the father of true learning and eloquence throughout the world,' was not among the books that went to Łaski in 1536.[20]

Conversely, Erasmus made an effort to acquire for his library older standard editions that had not been superseded by better later editions. In 1525, for example, he acquired the Florentine edition of Homer (1488), which long remained unsurpassed.[21]

The *Versandliste* also mentions several works in two or more editions, which is understandable if we assume that Erasmus did not ask himself every time he acquired a book whether or not it made another book superfluous. Sometimes separately published works, large or small, were included in a volume of collected works acquired later. In some cases that may have been a reason for Erasmus to remove the superseded separate edition; in others there may have been special considerations that led him to keep more than one edition of the same work. Sometimes a modern commentary could be decisive; an important part of typical humanist scholarship was contained in the apparatus of notes to the ancient classical writers. In the case of the 'handbook of medical botany' of Dioscorides, which was still in use, Erasmus kept the Latin translation with the famous *corollarium* ('garland' or 'tribute') of Ermolao Barbaro when he acquired the more recent commentary of the Florentine Marcello Virgilio.[22] The ancillary contents could also play a part. Erasmus already owned the text of Pindar with scholia (Rome 1515), which was highly regarded in his day; why should he have thought it

---

16 vl/Catalogue nos 2 #3 (Valla) and 120–1 (Cicero). See also no 281 (on editions of Aulus Gellius).
17 vl/Catalogue no 269
18 vl/Catalogue no 270
19 vl/Catalogue nos 38 #2 and 289. Cf nos 195 #2 and 229 #2; also no 206.
20 See vl/Catalogue no 324.
21 vl/Catalogue nos 114 and 115
22 vl/Catalogue nos 201 and 202

worth while to acquire the Aldine edition, which was considered to be of inferior quality, unless he wished to have the other Greek texts included in it?[23] The *Versandliste* also contains four editions of the work of Theocritus.[24] Yet another reason may have restrained Erasmus from disposing of a duplicate copy or an edition of a work he already possessed in a better text, that is, his personal marginal notes. Perhaps the two copies of the *Apologiae omnes* in his library are an example of this. One of them has survived and contains notes in his own hand, which were never published by him.[25] Budé's famous work *De Asse*, which appears twice in the list, may well be another example.[26]

Erasmus must have had no scruples about removing superseded or superfluous editions of his own works – both original treatises and editions of texts – from his library. However many authorized revised versions of them there may sometimes have been, they rarely appear in the *Versandliste* in more than one edition. Erasmus' estate also included a special collection of around a hundred of his own works that was kept separate from his other books in a chest near the window. It seems to have been a rather arbitrarily formed collection consisting predominantly of Froben editions, with quite a few duplicates among them. After his death a list of these works was compiled under the title *Catalogus librorum Erasmi*; it has been preserved, and a transcription is included below following the *Versandliste*/Catalogue.[27]

When the *Catalogus* is collated and compared with the *Versandliste*, it becomes clear that the separate collection of Erasmiana consisted for the most part of works that were also present in the library proper, sometimes in the same edition, sometimes in another setting, usually more recent in date. For example, early editions of both the *Querela pacis* and the *Encomium matrimonii* appear in the *Catalogus* under their own titles. But these two short works are not listed as separate publications in the *Versandliste*, where their texts can only be found hidden among the other works printed in a later edition of *De pueris instituendis*.[28] As we have noted, the *Apologiae omnes*, first published in 1521, appear on the *Versandliste*, but the first seven apologies, which had previously been published separately and were now collected in it, do not. Five of the seven original editions, however, were in the special collection.[29] And according to the *Versandliste*, none of the collections of Erasmus' correspondence published before 1529 except the *Opus epistolarum*, which appeared in that year and broadly speaking brought together the contents of all the previous collections,[30] was to be found in the library. It is precisely these older collections, with two exceptions, that are individually listed in the *Catalogus*.[31] Similarly, three adages that were issued separately are listed in the *Catalogus* but are not on the *Versandliste*.[32] Erasmus thus retained more superseded editions of his own works than one might assume from the record in the *Versandliste* alone.

The special collection cannot, however, have been just a deposit for duplicates and superseded editions that Erasmus had removed from his library but had not promptly given away

---

23 VL/Catalogue nos 107 and 105

24 VL/Catalogue nos 98, 99, 106, and 294

25 VL/Catalogue nos 332 and 383; cf *Catalogus librorum Erasmi* no 83. See also 57–8 and 102 below.

26 VL/Catalogue nos 291 and 292

27 452–7 below. See also the discussion of the separate collection 99–103 below.

28 In 1529; see VL/Catalogue no 79. Cf *Catalogus* nos 1, 2, 24, 27, and 31.

29 *Catalogus* nos 43, 25, 60, 32, and 44

30 VL/Catalogue no 226. Cf Allen I 593–602 Appendix 7 'The Principal Editions of Erasmus' Epistolae.'

31 *Catalogus* nos 26, 13, 30, 55, and 23, corresponding to Allen's editions A, C2, D, E, and G. One of the two missing editions was printed at Leuven and not Basel.

32 III iii 1 *Sileni Alcibiadis*; III vii 1 *Scarabaeus aquilam quaerit*; IV i 1: *Dulce bellum inexpertis*; see *Catalogus* nos 47, 48, and 49.

or destroyed, for it also contained a number of his own works for the titles of which one will search the *Versandliste* in vain. What kind of reason can there have been to keep works like his translations from Euripides,[33] his Latin version of Gaza's grammar,[34] the *Modus orandi*,[35] the *Consultatio de bello Turcis inferendo*,[36] the *Spongia*, and several other polemical writings[37] separately in a chest? Presumably the special collection consisted largely or even wholly of unbound books stored in loose quires, an assumption for which we hope to supply plausible arguments in another context.[38] Erasmus definitely did not cherish, collect, and preserve his own works with extra care. We may even wonder if his oeuvre was completely represented in his estate: Erasmus does not even appear to have taken much trouble to ensure that Łaski, by buying the library, would acquire a complete set of his own works. To judge from the *Versandliste* and the *Catalogus librorum Erasmi*, that was not the case; the titles of about twenty works appear in neither list. These include several works whose authorship Erasmus had always stubbornly denied or at least never openly admitted, such as the *Julius exclusus*, the *Acta academiae Lovaniensis contra Luterum*, and the *Axiomata Erasmi pro causa Lutheri*, and it is understandable that he might have been anxious to keep such potentially compromising works out of his house. But the other lacunae are more surprising and not immediately explicable: for example, according to the two inventories both the *Antibarbari* and *De immensa Dei misericordia*, as well as *De vidua christiana*, the *Epistola contra pseudevangelicos* and some other apologetic works were missing from his estate. Could his situation in Basel have made Erasmus rather nonchalant, particularly about his own works? Practically all of them had been published by Froben, and if he had given away or lost his copy of one, he could always fall back on the stock of the bookshop, which was close by. He was spoiled: in 1533, when he could no longer find a copy of his *Responsio ad collationes cuiusdam iuvenis gerontodidascali*, published some years earlier and (highly exceptionally) not in Basel but in Antwerp, Bonifacius Amerbach managed to get it for him, at his request, within a few days.[39]

But there may be another explanation for the absence of some of his own works on either inventory. If they were copies that Erasmus had annotated in his own hand with marginal additions and corrections for a possible new edition, they may have been deliberately removed from his estate after his death, with a view to the planned first edition of his collected works. It was a well-known practice, followed by Erasmus as well, for copies corrected by hand to be made available either directly to the printer-publisher or indirectly to a friendly scholar who would act as editor. This is how the corrected copy of the 1514 edition of *De copia* (Strasbourg: Schürer) came into the hands of Wilhelm Nesen, who helped to prepare the 1517 Froben edition.[40]

We know from Bonifacius Amerbach, the executor of Erasmus' will, that corrected copies of some works were in fact found in the estate in 1536, and it makes sense to assume

---

33 *Catalogus* nos 42 and 79

34 *Catalogus* no 33

35 *Catalogus* no 69

36 *Catalogus* no 103

37 *Catalogus* nos 4, 5, 20, 25, 32, 34, 36, 39, 43, 44, 58, 60, 62, 72, 83, 86, 87, 88, 89, 90, 91, 92, 93, 94, 95, 99, 100, 101, 105 (last title), 109, 112

38 See 76–7 and nn103–4, 80 and n128 below.

39 Allen Epp 2805:15–16 and 2807:81

40 See Husner 'Bibliothek' 254 n90; cf Ep 462. Froben also used Erasmus' corrected copy of the Paris 1514 edition of his translations from Lucian for his own 1517 edition; see Husner 'Bibliothek' 258 and VL/ Catalogue no 118.

that the editor of the Basel *Opera omnia* put them to good use.[41] J.H. Waszink noted that the translations from Euripides in the version of 1540 contained some readings that 'look like the work of a real reviser,' perhaps Erasmus himself; he thought it possible that they had been taken from an annotated author's copy of the edition of 1530.[42] In the separate collection of Erasmiana there were two editions of these translations, that of Aldo Manuzio of 1507 and that of Froben of 1518.[43] Was it perhaps not by chance that the edition of 1530 was missing? In the *Apologia ad annotationes Stunicae* H.J. De Jonge found additions and corrections, most probably inserted by Erasmus in his own hand, that did not appear in print until the posthumous *Opera omnia* of 1540.[44] A.W. Steenbeek found the same thing in the *Apologia ad Fabrum*.[45] In these two cases the editors must almost certainly have used marginal notes inserted by the author in a copy found in his estate. But we may doubt that such corrected copies, removed from the estate for later use as printer's copy in the *Opera omnia*, account for all the copies, possibly the sole copies still in his possession on his death, of the works of Erasmus that are absent from both inventories. In the case of two of the examples cited above, the *Antibarbari* and the *Epistola contra pseudevangelicos*, the 1540 version is practically the same as the text in the last previously published edition authorized by Erasmus.[46] The same holds true for *De immensa Dei misericordia* and *De vidua christiana*.[47] In any case, as further volumes of ASD appear, it will be fascinating to learn if any further surprising discoveries will be made that may put us on the track of one or more of the copies with autograph corrections and additions that Amerbach found in Erasmus' estate.

It is difficult – *a priori* even impossible – to form a complete picture of how Erasmus 'weeded' his library or to identify his criteria for keeping or disposing of books. We do not know about books that once belonged to him but do not appear in the *Versandliste* unless they are mentioned in his letters or writings. Only when Erasmus himself says in so many words that he bought or acquired a particular book can we be certain of his ownership. Even when we know from the letters of donors or third parties that certain presentation copies were sent, we cannot assume that in those turbulent times they reached Erasmus safely. Moreover, if he occasionally cast a critical eye over the contents of his library, judging the interest and usefulness of his books, we may wonder whether many of the books he received as gifts did not end up in a chest or were speedily discarded. And might not Erasmus have deliberately removed works that he no longer needed? Who will not agree that Erasmus must have had a copy of the *Bermannus*, Georgius Agricola's famous dialogue on mining, which he had not only recommended to Froben for publication but had also provided with a complimentary letter?[48] What happened to Andrea Alciati's *Emblemata*, sent to him by Philippus Montanus?[49] Erasmus was not 'attached' to his books and was generous if he knew that he could give a friend pleasure by a gift of a book. He gave Antonius Clava his

---

41 Possibly Sigismundus Gelenius; See Reedijk *Tandem bona causa triumphat* 32, 34. On the possible use of corrected copies cf 101–3 below.

42 ASD I-1 202; Waszink suggests that Beatus Rhenanus may have had a hand in revising the texts also.

43 *Catalogus* nos 42 and 79

44 ASD IX-2 52–3

45 ASD IX-3 56–9

46 For the *Antibarbari* see ASD I-1 31 and Pfeiffer 'Die Wandlungen der Antibarbari'; for the *Epistola contra pseudevangelicos* see 'Books Found in Erasmus' Correspondence' no 61.

47 See the critical apparatus in ASD V-7 31–97 and ASD V-6 263–332.

48 'Books Found in Erasmus' Correspondence' no 2; cf VL/Catalogue no 78.

49 'Books Found in Erasmus' Correspondence' no 5; cf VL/Catalogue no 135.

Herodotus in the original text, because Clava had expressed interest in owning 'Herodotus in Greek'; he would easily be able to find another copy.[50] When he settled in the College of the Lily at Leuven in 1518, Erasmus' library was reasonably housed for the first time, and that gave him the opportunity to subject it to a review. It may have been on such an occasion that he came across the *Carmina* of Gregory of Nazianzus and then gave it to Maarten Lips – another proof that in certain circumstances he was quite ready to give away his own copies. Two years later he had to ask his Leuven friend to look up something in the little book for him.[51] Other letters show that Amerbach too would have had occasion to thank Erasmus for similar small presents.[52]

Erasmus probably owned works that are not mentioned in his correspondence, but we have no evidence to prove it. The *Opus epistolarum* can never offer more than an incomplete and uncertain idea of the presumably numerous books that Erasmus must have possessed at one time or another, although they do not appear in the *Versandliste*. The list of 153 'Books Found in Erasmus' Correspondence' that we have included as an appendix to the *Versandliste*/Catalogue does not pretend to be complete. Nevertheless, it may reveal the typical genre of the works concerned. For the most part they were books in small formats, many of them pamphlets, that were both polemical and ephemeral in character. Such works also formed part of the library inventoried in 1536, several of them often being bound between the same cover. But they were certainly not the heart or backbone of the library.

There is another reason we may never know why some books appear on the *Versandliste* while others do not. Our insight into how the library was weeded of unwanted material is limited. The examples cited may have given the impression that during his lifetime Erasmus deliberately removed from his library all the books he may once have owned that were no longer found in his estate in 1536. He gave away several works of which he had in the meantime acquired more modern editions; he probably removed from his collection books whose subject matter no longer interested him; and it is also possible he did not feel obliged to keep every book sent to him.

If this were a fair representation of Erasmus' policy of ridding the library of unnecessary ballast, then we would have to attach extra significance to what he did wish to retain. But the criteria he used to decide what to keep and what not to keep are not always clear. The polemical literature of the day is poorly represented in his collection; even works that had provoked him into a counter-attack are often missing. One could conclude from this that it interested him only moderately. Then what can have induced him to keep the documentation on a theological polemic that preoccupied the minds of scholars around 1518–19 but is now forgotten: the debate on the question whether one or three Mary Magdalenes played a role in the life of Christ? What moved him to keep small works on soothsaying and astrology? Why do relatively few of his own polemical works appear on the *Versandliste*? Perhaps he discarded the others once the flames of debate had died down, but it is also possible that he stored minor works like pamphlets and polemics, which reached him unbound, in chests, and that later they were not considered, for whatever reason, part of his library. Erasmus refers several times to chests (*scrinia*) full of letters and little books or pamphlets (*libelli*).

We cannot simply assume that Erasmus disposed of all the books once in his possession but not named in the *Versandliste* unless we are certain that the collection of books left on

---

50 Ep 841. See Husner 'Bibliothek' 251 and 258; vl/Catalogue no 272 #1.
51 See Allen Epp 807:2–5 and 1086:4–7/cwe Epp 807:4–8 and 1086:5–8.
52 See Allen Epp 2256:62 and 2368:1–2/cwe Epp 2256:69, 2368:1–2.

his death consisted exclusively of the library that was inventoried and sent to Poland. It has never been made clear, however, whether Erasmus' estate in 1536 also included other books apart from those recorded in the surviving list. If it did, then those books, like the manuscript of Palladius' *Opus agriculturae*,[53] could have remained in Basel with the 'private archive' after Erasmus' library had been sent to Poland. How they became separated from the library and why they were not sent to Łaski, apparently contrary to the agreement of 1525,[54] are not easy questions to answer. For the moment, however, we may let the problem lie; we will return to it in chapter 5, 'What the *Versandliste* Does Not Include.'

---

53 For the manuscript of Palladius see 98 below.
54 In the agreement with Łaski not a single printed book was excluded from the sale.

3

The Housing and Arrangement of the Collection

As we have already seen, after his Italian journey Erasmus' library, before then still fairly modest in size, expanded considerably in quite a short time.[1] The books that he must have brought back across the Alps will explain in part the striking growth of his collection, as do the purchases he began to make around 1511, on a scale to which he had not been accustomed before. Coincidentally, it is only from this time that we find references to his library as a whole, and not only to individual books, in his letters. Erasmus soon began to experience not only the many pleasures of his library, but also the problems it presented. He still led a nomadic life, and was to do so for several years more. As a result, every time he changed residence he faced the problem of what to do with his books. Was he to take them with him or have them sent after him, or would he do better to leave them behind, and if so, under whose protection? Until he settled in Basel, it must often have been a headache for him to arrange for his collection to be conveyed from place to place. No wonder that whenever he mentioned his library in his letters it was mostly to write about the problems of transporting and storing his books. These references are brief and intermittent, so that it is impossible to document every change in location of Erasmus' library in these early years or to describe how his books were housed.

Only in Basel and Freiburg did the accommodation of the library finally take on a more permanent character. Yet that does not mean that we can get a clear picture of how it was housed in those two places either. In his later years Erasmus does not say a word about the sale of his books to Łaski in any of his letters, so far as they have been preserved; clearly he was unwilling to have the transaction publicized. Nor was the library referred to in his correspondence, except cursorily. There are only two explicit references, and on both occasions it was the preparations for the transport of the books that prompted him to mention them: first in 1529, when the books had to be carried from Basel to Freiburg, and again in 1535 on his return to Basel. We owe our knowledge of a few valuable details to these letters, but after the moves, the library, once again installed and in use, unfortunately does not come up again in his correspondence. What we would be so eager to know – how Erasmus arranged his books around him once he was settled in Basel or Freiburg, and how he shelved or stored them in his study or elsewhere in his house – largely eludes our observation. We can say very little with any certainty, and for the most part we must be content with conjecture and assumptions.

We have noted that after his return from Italy in 1509, while he enjoyed the hospitality of Sir Thomas More, Erasmus waited for his library to arrive.[2] What are we to understand by 'library' in this context? We are inclined to think first of the new acquisitions he had

---

1 See 24–9 above.
2 See 17–18, 22 above.

made in Italy, which had been sent after him, rather than of the books he possessed before his journey to the south. Where had these books, still a very modest collection, been kept in the intervening years? The manuscripts of his still unpublished works had accompanied him on his travels in 1506. Their fate is known. Two years later, while in Ferrara on his way to Rome, he gave them to Richard Pace for safekeeping – to his great loss, as it proved, for he was to see little of them thereafter.[3] It is very unlikely that Erasmus took any printed books with him to Italy. Before he crossed to the continent in early June 1506 to begin his long journey, he may have entrusted his books, except for one or two works at most, to the care of his London friends. In that case, he would have had no difficulty in gaining access to them in 1509, so that once his Italian acquisitions arrived he had his entire collection, enlarged but still not very impressive, at his disposal. But where? Allen assumed that until his visit to Paris in the summer of 1511 Erasmus lived mostly at More's house in Bucklersbury, with his friend Andrea Ammonio. There he had the use of a room in which, on his departure for Paris, he had left books borrowed from Colet; he must have had his own books at hand also.[4] As we have seen, his visit to Paris in 1511, though barely two months long, was of great importance for the building of his library. At that time he bought or ordered numerous works that must have found their way to London in one or more consignments.[5]

Erasmus returned to London before the end of June.[6] It is assumed that he no longer lodged with More. After More's second marriage, to Dame Alice, the atmosphere in More's house, once so welcoming, no longer attracted Erasmus or Ammonio.[7] Perhaps he found accommodation with another friend, the Greek scholar William Grocyn,[8] but this is not quite certain and in any case it can only have been for a short time.

As early as mid-August, hardly recovered from the sweating sickness, he left for Cambridge to teach Greek from Chrysoloras' grammar. For the time being he lodged in Queens' College, known to him from an earlier visit.[9] His books followed him, not at once, but at the end of October. Were they in Grocyn's house when they were dispatched, and if not, where were they? Had they perhaps remained at More's? We do not know. We can establish that the books were sent at practically the same time as Ammonio, glad that he no longer needed to see 'the harpy's crooked beak,' as he described More's second wife, moved to another house in the neighbourhood.[10] He knew of the dispatch of the books, and gave the carrier who was to transport them to Cambridge by horse and cart a bottle of Greek wine for his friend.[11] The delivery was anything but faultless. Erasmus had not a good word to say of the carrier. He related to Ammonio how badly the wretched man had fulfilled his instructions. 'What if you had seen my book-chests, battered on all sides? What would you

---

3 See Allen Ep 30:16n/CWE Ep 30:17n.

4 Allen and CWE Ep 218 introductions and lines 19–20/20–1

5 See 25 above.

6 CWE Ep 256:23n

7 During Erasmus' absence More had lost his first wife and had remarried within a month; Allen Ep 221:31n.

8 Allen Ep 241:23n/CWE Ep 241:27–31 with 28n; cf Allen Ep 225 introduction. On Grocyn see Allen Ep 118:22n/CWE Ep 118:26n; CEBR II 135–6.

9 Allen Epp 233:8, 296:134–5/CWE Epp 233:10, 296:141–2; on Chrysoloras' grammar, see VL/Catalogue no 317. On where Erasmus stayed, see Allen I 591 Appendix 6 'Erasmus at Cambridge in 1506.' Later he also lived at other addresses; Allen Ep 248:44n.

10 Ammonio moved from More's house to St Thomas College; Allen Ep 232:4–5 and n/CWE Ep 232:5–6 and n. Cf (with Ammonio's comment) Allen Ep 236:45–8/CWE Ep 236:51–5.

11 Allen Ep 239:19–22/CWE Ep 239:21–4

have said if you had heard his trumped-up story about the horse? And that baldheaded rascal never hove in sight here.'[12]

Erasmus did not remain long in Cambridge. His lectures drew few hearers,[13] and in mid-November, when he voiced his irritation with the carrier, he was already thinking of returning to London. He sounded Ammonio out about a suitable lodging. He was looking for 'some warm hive to hide myself through midwinter,' less poetically but more concretely described as 'an apartment well protected from draughts with a good fire,' preferably not too far from St Paul's. With the help of his friend he soon succeeded in finding suitable accommodation, so that in December or January he was once again able to install himself in London, where he remained through the year 1512.[14] In February and May of that year he made two short visits to Cambridge, one of which may have been concerned with bringing his books to London. We cannot determine how long he spent in London the following year; we know that he was again in Cambridge in July 1513 and hard at work.[15] He had just translated a treatise of Plutarch, and he was beginning to collate the manuscripts of Seneca and especially of Jerome available in Cambridge.[16] He could not work undisturbed. Twice in the latter part of the year he had to take refuge in the countryside, because the plague was claiming victims in the city.[17] Yet he did not intend to quit Cambridge for the time being, for he had had his library, which he must have been without for at least three months, sent there. For this, he made a rapid visit to London, probably in September or October. Alone and in great haste he packed all his books and some other possessions together, and set off again, without even spending a single night in his old room. He left the transport of the load to the bookseller Josse.[18]

Nine months later, in the summer of 1514, Erasmus left England for the continent. He was vague about his plans for the longer term; probably he had already decided to try his fortune in the Netherlands, near the princely court, that is, in Brabant. But his immediate goal was clear: he would go first to Basel, to arrange for the printing of the works of Jerome, the New Testament, and other writings, which were ready for publication.[19] What did he intend to do with his library, once his plans took firmer shape? This time he did not leave it behind for the time being, as he had done before. He left Cambridge in early February.[20] His books must have followed him, for in early July they were in London, where on the eve of his departure for the continent he was able to arrange in person for the shipment of his possessions, chiefly his books. The shipper Antonius was instructed to convey the cases in which everything was packed to Antwerp and to deliver them to Pieter Gillis. There were

---

12 Allen Ep 240:18–21 / cwe Ep 240:19–22

13 See n9 above.

14 Allen Epp 240:45–7, 248:26–8 / cwe Epp 240:51–3, 248:36–7. For Ammonio's efforts see Allen Epp 243:50–62, 249:18–20 / cwe Epp 243:58–72, 249:22–4.

15 Epp 255 (19 February) and 262 (9 May) were written in Cambridge. On 5 January 1513 Erasmus was in London, after which there is a hiatus in his correspondence. Ep 270, from Cambridge, was written in July; see Allen and cwe introductions.

16 The translation of *De discrimine adulatoris et amici* was sent to Henry viii in manuscript; see the dedicatory letter, Ep 272. For references to the editions see Allen Epp 270:58–9, 273:14–17, and 281:3–5 / cwe Epp 270:67–8, 273:15–19, and 281:5–6.

17 See Epp 274–5 (early in September), Allen Epp 276:7, 278:22–3 / cwe Epp 276:8–9 and 278:27–8 (October). Erasmus probably lodged with the schoolmaster William Gonnell at Landbeach, five miles northeast of Cambridge; on him see also cebr ii 118.

18 In London he also felt constantly threatened by the plague; Allen Epp 273:10–11 and 282:22–3 / cwe Epp 273:11–12, 282:26–7. On his visit there to get his books, see Allen Ep 278:13–16 / cwe Ep 278:15–19.

19 Huizinga *Erasmus of Rotterdam* 87; Augustijn *Erasmus of Rotterdam* 40–2

20 cwe introduction to Ep 285, Erasmus' last letter from Cambridge

three cases (*scrinia*) in all, described as follows: 'one square, made of wood and roped; the other two of French type, covered in pigskin.' With the consignment Erasmus sent a letter asking Gillis to store the cases at his home or elsewhere until he arrived. 'Look after my belongings, and regard them as your own,' he urged him.[21] He himself, with his manuscripts in a travelling bag, took another route and crossed from Dover to Calais. He made his way via Saint-Omer, Ghent, Antwerp, Leuven, and Liège through the southern Netherlands to the Rhine, and then followed the river to Basel, which he reached in mid-August. Naturally he visited Gillis in Antwerp, and must then have arranged what was to be done with his books, which were either on their way from England or had already arrived. He had fixed the main lines of his journey at the time. He believed that he would need only a short time in Basel, to settle the publication of his manuscripts with Froben. Afterwards, perhaps before the end of September, he hoped to be able to continue his journey to Italy and in particular to Rome, where he would pass the winter.[22] His plan makes one thing clear: when he sent his books to Antwerp he must already have intended to leave them there, for he could be assured in advance that his devoted friend would keep a watchful eye on them.

Erasmus remained in Basel much longer than he had planned. He soon felt at home there, and he enjoyed his meetings with the German humanists, who gave him an enthusiastic welcome. But what kept him there in the first place was the disappointingly large amount of work that he had to do to make his new publications ready for the press. He worked hard in the printing house, where, as he said himself, he 'got through six years work in eight months.'[23] It is very unlikely that he considered having his books forwarded from Antwerp, even though his stay in Basel lasted longer than he had expected. Apart from the risk of carriage along the often-dangerous roads, his library would not have been of any use to him. For the definitive text of Jerome and the New Testament he wished to consult manuscripts; between March and July 1515 he even made a special journey to England for this purpose.[24] And for the correction and proof-reading of the two works that were ready he had no need, in Basel, of his private collection, which was still very modest. Practically all the printed works he would have wished to consult must have been available to him in the city, which had become a centre of typography and the book trade. In addition, as he wrote with some flattering exaggeration, he was surrounded by many extraordinary scholars: 'They all know Latin, they all know Greek, most of them know Hebrew too.'[25]

In May 1516 Erasmus returned to the Netherlands. Nothing more was said about a visit to Italy. After a rapid journey of less than three weeks he reached Antwerp at the end of May. He lodged with Pieter Gillis, who still had his books. A few days later, recovered from the journey, he went to Brussels to visit Jean Le Sauvage, the chancellor of Brabant, who had managed to obtain for Erasmus the honorific post of counsellor to the ruler, the young Prince Charles. From Brussels he travelled on to spend a few days at Saint-Omer

---

21 Ep 294

22 On the crossing from Dover to Calais Erasmus had the fright of his life when he thought he had lost his travelling bag, 'crammed with [his] writings.' It had ended up on another ship, and he did not find it again until they were at the quayside; Allen Ep 295:4–12/cwe Ep 295:6–15. For the rest of his journey, see his description in Ep 301. For his plan to visit Italy, see Allen Ep 296:225–6/cwe Ep 296:242–3; cf Allen Ep 300:40–1/cwe Ep 300:43–4.

23 Allen Epp 417:3–4, 411:1–2/cwe Epp 417:4–6, 411:2–3

24 See Allen Epp 332 and 337 introductions.

25 Allen Ep 364:8–17/cwe Ep 391A:10–18

with Antoon van Bergen, the abbot of St Bertin.[26] He then returned to Antwerp, where he remained, with only a few short interruptions, in 'Der Spiegel,' as his host's house was called, for much of the next four months. In mid-July he crossed to England, where he worked on his appeal to Rome for the definitive release from his order.[27] Naturally, he also seized the opportunity to meet his old friends.[28] In all, it was six weeks before he set foot on the soil of the continent again, at Calais. He returned via Brussels to Antwerp, where, in the familiar surroundings of his friend Gillis' house, with all his books around him, he would stay until he decided on his future residence as circumstances dictated. This time, however, he did not remain for much more than a month. At the end of September he was ready to follow the call of his new patron, Jean Le Sauvage, and go to Brussels, and he resolved to spend the winter there.[29] On 6 October he wrote to Gillis that he had been able to find a room. It was well situated, close to the court, and, an even greater recommendation, not far from Cuthbert Tunstall, the scholarly cleric who excelled in knowledge of the two ancient tongues. Tunstall, who had been acting as envoy of Henry VIII to Prince Charles in Brussels, strongly attracted Erasmus by his acute judgement, refined taste, and whole style of life. He therefore asked Gillis to have his books sent to his new address, either by boat or by wagon, as soon as possible, even though he had only a very small room.[30] His friend, always ready to do him a service, must undoubtedly have obliged.

Erasmus' stay in Brussels was briefer than he had expected. Winter was only half over when he decided to leave. He could see no further reason to remain in the city of the prince's court, and it was a great disappointment to him when Tunstall, whose company he had regularly enjoyed since his arrival, returned to England in January 1517. 'My life seems to have come to a halt with the loss of Tunstall ... To sit here any longer, I simply have no spirits,' he said. He pondered where he should go. His patron, Lord Mountjoy, he felt, lived too far away. When he was in England in summer 1516, he had considered Leuven as a place to live, and now he did so again, but he felt that this was not a suitable moment to settle there, even though he had more or less reconciled himself to the theologians of the place. The choice he made for the immediate future can hardly surprise us. As so often, he sought refuge with Pieter Gillis and asked if he had a room with a privy to spare. In that case he would go to Antwerp, where, in his friend's house, he could prepare the copy that he wished to send to Basel.[31] And so he did. For about six weeks, from 14 February to the beginning of April, probably without any interruptions, he stayed with Gillis. Once again he had his

---

26 On Erasmus' planned itinerary, see Allen and CWE Ep 410 introductions. On his visit to Jean Le Sauvage, see also Allen Ep 412:51–4/CWE Ep 412:57–60. Epp 413–17 were all written at Saint-Omer. On Jean (I) Le Sauvage see CEBR II 325–6; on Antoon (I) van Bergen, CEBR I 130–1.

27 On the purpose of his petition see Allen and CWE Ep 447 introductions; Huizinga *Erasmus of Rotterdam* 92–3.

28 Thomas More, William Warham, and John Fisher, with whom he lodged in Rochester for about ten days in August; Allen Ep 441 introduction; cf Epp 451:19–20 (More), 452:1–2 (Fisher), 457:42–8 (Warham)/CWE Ep 441 introduction; cf Epp 451:23–4, 452:3–4, 457:47–53.

29 Ep 470; cf Allen and CWE Epp 441 and 457 introductions, Allen Ep 475:12/CWE Ep 475:15.

30 Allen Ep 476:1–6/CWE Ep 476:3–8. The room may have been made available by one of the canons of the collegiate church, Maarten Davidts; Allen Ep 532:32n/CWE Ep 532:35n. On Davidts see also Lefèvre, 'Martin Davidts, un ami d'Erasme à Bruxelles'; CEBR II 378–9. Erasmus had also met Tunstall in early summer; Allen Ep 412:53–4, 63/CWE Ep 412:60, 70. See also his eulogy of Tunstall in Allen Ep 480:5–10/CWE Ep 480:6–11. Pieter Gillis recognized their friendship; Allen Ep 515:7–9/CWE Ep 515:9–11. See also CEBR III 349–54.

31 Allen Ep 516:4–10/CWE Ep 516:5–11; cf Allen Ep 456:5–6/CWE Ep 456:7. Tunstall left towards the end of January; Allen Ep 388:106n/CWE Ep 388:114n. On Mountjoy see Allen and CWE Ep 79 introductions, CWE Ep 301 introduction; CEBR I 154–6. He was at this time residing chiefly at the castle of Hammes near Calais or at Tournai.

books to hand: they had been sent on with his other luggage after he left Brussels.[32] They were housed by his host until early July. Erasmus, however, did not derive much profit from his books in these months, because he was travelling for much of the time. He paid his last visit to England in April, to receive from Ammonio at Westminster the dispensation granted by Pope Leo X, and in June, in his official capacity as a counsellor of the duke of Brabant, he accompanied the court of the young Prince Charles to Ghent and Bruges. Only in May did he spend some time in Antwerp, where he also sat for his portrait; Quinten Metsys painted him with Pieter Gillis in the well-known diptych. Prince Charles travelled from Flanders to Middelburg in Zeeland, where he arrived on 5 July. Two months later he and his suite took ship for Spain at Flushing. Erasmus had previously received an offer to go with them to Spain, but he declined it. Instead of following the prince to Zeeland in early July, he left at about the same time to travel via Antwerp to the city where he had several times announced his intention to settle, and where the Prince had in the meantime commanded him to go: Leuven.[33] As a bulwark of conservative theology, Leuven was still rather suspect in his eyes, but it was the leading centre of scholarship in the Netherlands.

In the years that followed his return from Italy, Erasmus, as we have seen, had at times been forced to do without his library, even for extended periods, as a result of his changes of residence. More than once he had been unwilling to expose his valuable collection to the hazards of transport by unsafe roads and had therefore left it in the care of trusted friends. Even when he had managed to have his books conveyed to his new home without loss or damage, it had often been a long time before they reached him. In short, it cannot be said that his library accompanied him wherever he went. Early in 1517, commenting on the new way of life that had been imposed on Cuthbert Tunstall, he claimed that this was a sine qua non of his existence. Erasmus' English friend had scarcely returned from his diplomatic mission to Brussels when he found himself appointed ambassador to the court of Emperor Maximilian. This required him to follow the court on its travels, whereas his former post at Brussels had allowed him to remain in one place. Erasmus imagined himself in the position of his friend and considered the attractions of Tunstall's new appointment. 'It is a kind of life,' he concluded, 'that I should not altogether dislike, provided my library could accompany me wherever I went'[34] – as if he had not, in his own travels, continually found how impossible it was to fulfil this condition and had not experienced the practical consequences of a peripatetic life. It had been a handicap to his studies that for so much of the time he had been unable to derive any benefit from his library, a handicap that he accepted as inevitable. But it had not occurred to him to change his way of life for the sake of access to his library by settling down in one place. In those years, as Huizinga wrote, he was 'more the victim of his own restlessness than of the disfavour of fate.'[35] The sedentary life of a scholar with his books always to hand would not have been an acceptable alternative at that time.

Erasmus did not regard Leuven as his permanent home. He was still considering what place of residence would be best fitted for the old age that was already knocking at his door.[36]

---

32 See Allen Ep 532:31–3 / CWE Ep 532:34–6. Erasmus sent ten letters from Antwerp during the period from mid-February to mid-March; it is not entirely clear where he spent the second half of March.

33 As he says in Allen Ep 1225:27 / CWE Ep 1225:30–1. On Erasmus' dispensation and his visit to England see Epp 517 and 566. On his travels with the Burgundian court and his refusal to go to Spain, see Allen and CWE Ep 596 introductions; cf Huizinga *Erasmus of Rotterdam* 95. On the Metsys portrait, See Allen Ep 584:6–14 / CWE Ep 584:8–17 with 8n; Treu *Die Bildnisse des Erasmus von Rotterdam* 23–6.

34 Allen Ep 534:70–4 / CWE Ep 534:72–6.

35 *Erasmus of Rotterdam* 91

36 Allen Ep 596:2–3 / CWE Ep 596:2–3

In Leuven, he wrote soon after his arrival, he intended to spend a few months among the theologians, who had given him a friendly reception.[37] Once he had decided to move there, after initial hesitation, he hastened to arrange for the transfer of his library. He did not even wait until he was certain of suitable lodging, although the books could have remained with Gillis, who had no objection, and they would not have been safer anywhere else. In early July he arrived in the coach from Antwerp. M.A. Nauwelaerts points out that he normally used this means of transport when he felt in poor health, but suspects on good grounds that on this occasion Erasmus may have chosen the coach in order to take his books along.[38] In any case, Erasmus leaves us in no doubt that his library was to be with him; he wrote to Oecolampadius very soon after his arrival, 'It seems that Leuven is to be my headquarters, where I keep my library.' He also explicitly reported to his friends that he had removed 'bag and baggage' or, more to the point, 'with all my books.'[39]

Until he found lodging he liked, where he could work, Erasmus stayed with Jean Desmarez, the friend who had provided him with accommodation at the College of St Donatian in Leuven from 1502 to 1504. It was the only feasible solution, although the room at his disposal was not only small but also poorly furnished (he arranged to have one or two chairs sent from Brussels). From his first day in Leuven he was on the lookout for more suitable accommodation, a place where he could, as he said, 'have more room to spread out my books.'[40] Clearly, the library had now become a factor to be taken into account in selecting a place to live. Within two months Erasmus found what he was looking for in the College of the Lily. Another friend, Jan de Neve, was regent of the college and acted as his official host.[41] Around 11 September Erasmus moved into the college, which stood in the centre of the city and had a magnificent garden. He occupied a spacious room on the first floor, which until shortly before had been the residence of the regent.[42] His library must have been installed at the same time.

We know virtually nothing of the furnishing of this room, and we can only conjecture where and how Erasmus arranged his books. At that time, clothes and linens, as well as books, were usually stored in oak chests placed against the wall.[43] Possibly Erasmus kept part of his collection, which had grown substantially, in one or more specially made chests. But perhaps he also kept his books where he could see them, standing or lying on shelves fixed to the wall by a pair of brackets or in a simple open case fastened to or placed against the wall, in the way that is familiar to us from contemporary descriptions and pictures.[44] However Erasmus stored his collection, it seems clear that in his new home he was able to carry out his desire to spread out the books that he needed to have at hand for his current

37 Allen Ep 597:25–6 / CWE Ep 597:28–9; cf CWE Ep 596 introduction and the references given there.

38 'Erasme à Louvain ... de 1517 à 1521' 6

39 Allen Epp 605:7–8, 607:1, 641:8 / CWE Epp 605:10–11, 607:2, 641:10

40 Allen Epp 607:1–2, 616:16–17, 637:11–12, 643:12 / CWE Epp 607:2–3, 616:17–18, 637:13–14, 643:13–14

41 On Neve see Allen and CWE Ep 298 introductions; CEBR II 15.

42 Nauwelaerts *Tentoonstelling Erasmus en Leuven* 234–5. On the dispute that delayed Erasmus' move see CWE Ep 643:14n; on his room see also Ep 651:13n.

43 *Thuis in de late middeleeuwen, het Nederlands burgerinterieur 1400–1535* 34

44 The canons of the Utrecht collegiate churches had in their *studorium*, apart from cupboards with shelves, similar shelves or *richelen* on the wall for their books; Muller *Schetsen uit de Middeleeuwen* 184. In Metsys' diptych with portraits of Erasmus and Gillis (see CWE 4 370–1) one can see in the background recesses in the wall with shelves for books. Similarly, there is a shelf attached to the wall with brackets holding several books in Holbein's 1523 portrait of Erasmus (see Huizinga *Erasmus of Rotterdam* facing 103).

work; a long table was among the pieces of his own that he added to the furnishings of his room in the College of the Lily.[45]

Erasmus had originally said that he would remain in Leuven for a couple of months, but in the end he stayed for four years. Since his days in the cloister at Steyn he had never remained so long in one place. Did his way of life become more regular as a result? In one important respect it certainly did not: between 1517 and 1521 he travelled as frequently as in previous years. Antwerp almost seemed to be his second home. He continued to enjoy the hospitality of Pieter Gillis, with whom he sometimes lodged for a week or two, and in 1519 and 1520 the publication of his responses to Edward Lee's criticism of his edition of the New Testament kept him in Antwerp for lengthy periods.[46] He was also frequently away from Leuven in the summer and autumn of 1520. At the urging of More and Warham he went to Calais in early July, where the famous meetings between the kings of France and England and the king of England and the emperor took place. From Calais he followed the suite of Charles v to Bruges and visited Brussels and Antwerp, perhaps putting in an appearance as an imperial counsellor during the young ruler's visits there in August and September. He may have attended the imperial coronation in Aachen on 23 October in his official capacity, and it is certain that he made a private visit of three weeks to Cologne after the coronation.[47]

Twice in his Leuven years Erasmus stayed for a long period elsewhere. Usually, when he was travelling, he left his library behind in his room in the college, but on these occasions he made special arrangements. In the summer of 1518 he went to Basel for four and a half months (from the beginning of May until 21 September), to prepare the revised edition of his New Testament for the press.[48] At least five weeks before his departure, he already knew precisely what he would do. He had resolved, for the duration of his absence, which he estimated at six to eight weeks, 'to entrust his worldly wealth, that is, [his] books' to Jan Becker of Borsele, 'not only for safe keeping but for use, reckoning that all I have is shared with him.' To none of his fellow residents in the college would Erasmus have dared to entrust his library on loan with more confidence than to Becker. He had corresponded with Becker years before, but it was not until the years in the college of the Lily that he got to know him and learned to value him as 'a most delightful man to live with,' sound, reliable, and someone for whom he 'would undertake to answer ... at every point.'[49] Becker was also appointed, along with Jan de Neve, to look after certain sums of money intended for him that

---

45 *mensam longam*; cf Allen Ep 1355:32–4/cwe Ep 1355:34–7, which also mentions the Brussels chairs and a 'litter' (*lectam*). Dürer's 1526 portrait shows Erasmus with his lectern on one table and books spread out on another close by (cwe 12 263; Huizinga *Erasmus of Rotterdam* facing 246).

46 Erasmus personally assisted Michaël Hillen in preparing for the press his three polemics against Lee, which appeared in the spring of 1520; see Allen Epp 1077, 1086, 1091/cwe Ep 1080 introductions.

47 For Erasmus' movements in these years see especially Nauwelaerts 'Erasme à Louvain ... de 1517 à 1521'; cf Allen and cwe Ep 1155 introductions. See also, on the meetings of the kings, Allen Epp 1118 introduction, 1106:93n/cwe Ep 1106 introduction and lines 97–8; on Erasmus' travels with the court, Allen Epp 1129:1n, Epp 1136 and 1147 introductions/cwe Epp 1129 n1, 1136 introduction; on the coronation and the visit to Cologne, Allen Ep 1512:19/cwe Ep 1512:26.

48 On his itinerary, see Allen and cwe Epp 843 and 867 introductions.

49 On Becker see Allen and cwe Ep 291 introductions and cebr i 115–16. For Erasmus' laudatory comments about him see Allen Epp 687:16–17, 737:7–12, and 805 (recommending him for the Latin chair; lines 19–22 mention the arrangement with him about the books)/cwe Epp 687:18–19, 737:7–13, and 805 (lines 22–4 about the books).

might arrive after he had left Leuven for Basel.[50] It is not surprising that Erasmus should have chosen his official host for this responsibility. Neve was a trusted friend, and Erasmus always spoke favourably of him. But he had his weak points, as Erasmus well knew: in some respects he must have been careless and slapdash, for when he died some years later he left his estate in confusion and encumbered with debts.[51] Perhaps that was why Erasmus did not ask the regent of the college to look after his library for him but preferred to entrust his most cherished possession to Becker's care. Becker would also be at least as able to make good use of the books, for he enjoyed a good reputation as a scholar and teacher. He was an excellent Latinist and for that reason had been chosen as the first occupant of the chair of Latin at the newly founded Collegium Trilingue. Before he left for Basel, Erasmus did his best to make sure of Becker's appointment, which was not yet entirely certain; he pleaded for Becker to be given 'a salary worthy of his merits,' for he foresaw that without it Becker might well accept an offer elsewhere and be lost to Leuven. His fear proved to be not without foundation: at least three months before Erasmus returned to Leuven his trusted friend had moved to Veere, where an attractive benefice awaited him.[52] Hence, little or nothing came of Erasmus' intention to leave his books in his rooms at the College of the Lily under Becker's special care.

Erasmus made a different decision about his books in 1521. He spent the greater part of the summer in Anderlecht, which was then still rural, where he lodged with a friend, the canon Pieter Wichmans. His host's spacious and recently built house, 'De Zwane,' must have offered Erasmus an ideally restful atmosphere for undisturbed study.[53] He worked on the notes to the third edition of the Novum Testamentum and on the edition of Augustine undertaken by Froben;[54] he also composed a lengthy reply to the Spanish theologian Diego López Zúñiga's *Annotationes*, a fierce attack on the Novum Testamentum. Zúñiga's book, published in spring 1520, only reached Erasmus in Anderlecht in June 1521; his *Apologia* in response was published in late September or early October.[55]

Erasmus cannot have expected that it would be easy to have access to enough books for his work in rural Anderlecht; we would not have been surprised to learn that he brought with him from Leuven the texts and works of reference that he knew he would have to consult. But in fact he by no means confined himself to a few books selected with an eye to the work he planned to do. On the contrary, 'I have brought my whole library with me,' he emphatically announced immediately after his arrival. This may indicate that, as in his move from Antwerp to Leuven four years before, he had personally accompanied his books in the coach. In view of the short distance, the transport of the whole collection may not have posed a problem. Nevertheless, the question remains why he should have wished to have all his books, not merely those he knew could be of use to him in the work in hand, with him

---

50 Erasmus also appointed Pieter Gillis and Nicolaas van Broeckhoven in Antwerp; see Allen Ep 794:10–17/cwe Ep 794:12–18.

51 Cf Ep 1355, Allen Ep 2352:23–269/cwe Ep 2352:26–277.

52 See Erasmus' recommendation of Becker in Ep 805. Becker left Leuven to accept the deanery of the collegiate church of the castle of Sandenburg near Veere in June; cf Allen Epp 849:6–7, 852:74–6/cwe Epp 849:7–8, 852:80–1.

53 On Wichmans see Allen and cwe Ep 1231 introductions; cebr iii 442–3. On the house, built in 1515, see Van Damme *Ephéméride illustrée de la vie d'Erasme* 41. Erasmus was absent for about three weeks in August on a visit to Bruges in his capacity as a councillor to Emperor Charles v; see Allen and cwe Ep 1223 introductions.

54 See Allen Ep 1212:43–4/cwe Ep 1212:45–7.

55 Allen Epp 1216:1–2 with 1n, 1235:33/cwe Epp 1216:2 with n1 (page 428), 1235:36; asd ix-2 22. See also 'The Vergara Zúñiga Correspondence' Letter 1 cwe 8 337–40 with n5 (page 454).

in Anderlecht if he intended to stay no longer than three months.[56] The answer appears to lie in his plans for the immediate future. Erasmus was thinking of going to Basel later in the year to see the third edition of the New Testament through the press.[57] He planned to return to Leuven afterwards, possibly in the spring of 1522, though not to occupy his room in the College of the Lily. Before he left for Anderlecht, he had asked Conradus Goclenius to rent a suitable house with a garden for him in Leuven; hardly had he arrived in the countryside than he reminded his friend of the request.[58] In other words, Erasmus had given up his domicile in the college, though some of his furniture and other possessions, perhaps including a few books of little importance, still remained in his old room for the time being.[59]

We last hear of Erasmus in Anderlecht on 14 October 1521. He must then have returned to Leuven, staying for a little less than a week, and made a short visit to Antwerp, where he dined at least once with Gillis and may have spent the night under his roof. On 28 October (his birthday), he set off from Leuven on his intended journey to Basel, where he arrived on 15 November.[60] Though he had not planned it, his stay in Basel was to last seven and a half years. In a milieu that was well disposed to him, he must soon have felt more at home than in Leuven, where in recent years he had become embroiled in several controversies with the theologians. He had foreseen the danger that sooner or later, however unwillingly, he would be manoeuvred into the anti-Lutheran camp, and he drew the consequences. In Huizinga's words: 'It was his mental independence, so dear to him above all else, that he felt to be threatened; and to safeguard that, he did not return to Louvain.'[61]

But the definitive decision to remain in Basel was not taken at once. Almost three months after his arrival Erasmus was still thinking of a short stay and told Conradus Goclenius that he hoped to return to Leuven before Easter.[62] If at first he did not plan to stay in Basel, he probably did not arrange the transport of his library until some time later. Precisely when and by what route Erasmus' books were sent to Basel can no longer be determined. Indeed, the fate of the books after Erasmus' departure from Anderlecht is entirely obscure. Husner and others have assumed that the collection was returned to Leuven and stored in the College of the Lily, under the protection of Neve. They cite as evidence the fact that much later, in early 1523, some of Erasmus' books were still found in the room he had occupied in the college.[63] But is it certain that these books had ever been in Anderlecht and had returned from there? When Neve died unexpectedly in late 1522,[64] Erasmus had enquiries made in Leuven, for there were also pieces of furniture and other personal property of his in the room, which Neve had been occupying. Erasmus was clearly concerned about what would happen to his possessions in the settlement of the regent's estate, and his fears proved

---

56 Allen Ep 1208:7–8 / CWE Ep 1208:9–11. In the event Anderlecht proved to be not entirely without books: Erasmus borrowed from the nearby Carthusian monastery an edition of the Bible with the Gloss; see de Jonge 'Erasmus und die Glossa Ordinaria zum Neuen Testament' 72–3.

57 Allen Ep 1174:15n / CWE Ep 1174 n6

58 See Ep 1209.

59 See n65 below.

60 For a survey of Erasmus' movements between 14 October and 15 November 1521, including the route he took from Leuven to Basel, see Allen and CWE Ep 1242 introductions; for his visit with Gillis, Allen and CWE Ep 1696:21–2.

61 *Erasmus of Rotterdam* 150

62 Allen Ep 1257:10 / CWE Ep 1257:12

63 Husner 232; Allen Ep 1209:4n; Huizinga *Erasmus of Rotterdam* 149; Nauwelaerts 'Verblijf en werk van Erasmus te Leuven' 159

64 See Allen and CWE Ep 1347 introductions.

justified. Joost Vroye, a lawyer and friend, found a few papers that definitely belonged to Erasmus; the Brussels chairs had been sold.[65] But who is to say that Erasmus had not left a few books behind with some of his other household effects in spring of 1521, because they could be of no use to him in Anderlecht? Did he perhaps think them so unimportant that he hardly believed he was stretching the truth when he wrote that he had taken his whole library to Anderlecht? Why should Erasmus have wished his library to be returned from Anderlecht to Leuven, and in particular to the College of the Lily? There is no reason to assume that Erasmus felt his books to be any safer in Leuven during his absence than in the peaceful home of Pieter Wichmans in the suburbs of Brussels. On the contrary.[66] Moreover, as we saw, he had already given up the College of the Lily as his domicile:[67] on his return from Anderlecht, he avoided the college and stayed in a well-known local inn, 'Den Wildeman,' before leaving for Basel.[68] Another interesting detail may indicate that the books followed another route than the one that has hitherto been assumed. Early in 1523 Wichmans mentioned a conversation – clearly recent – he had had with Pieter Gillis about the library.[69] What could Erasmus' host in Anderlecht have had to do with the library if, as is assumed, it had been returned to Leuven when Erasmus left? Must we not consider the possibility that the books did not go to Leuven but were sent directly from Anderlecht to Basel? In that case the conversation between Wichmans and Gillis about the library may well have been concerned with the carriage of the books to Basel. In 1516 Gillis had helped Erasmus to move his books from Antwerp to Brussels;[70] it is very likely that Erasmus appealed again to Gillis' practical cooperation and that it was – as always – generously granted.

It is possible that once he left Brabant Erasmus had to do without the use of his library for a considerable time. In Basel he may not have missed his books too badly to begin with: if he urgently needed a particular book for the work that occupied him in the earliest months of his stay, he could always find a copy in the city, rich in books as it was. Even when it was clear that he was going to stay, he may have had no urgent reason to have his books sent after him from Brabant. For ten months he enjoyed the hospitality of Johannes Froben at his house 'Zum Sessel,' a property in the Totengässlein, which was partly fitted up as a dwelling, the rest being used as the printing works. Of course, there were advantages in being able to live and work on the preparation of his manuscripts for the press under the same roof. But for a longer residence, a house where six or seven printing presses were in continual use had its disadvantages. Was Erasmus able to enjoy the space and the privacy that were his minimum requirements in Froben's house? When, in September 1522, he was able to set up his own household in a part of the complex known as 'Zur alten Treu' (bought by Froben in December 1521, most probably with a view to accommodating his illustrious friend), Erasmus felt as if he had begun a new way of life: 'I have ... set up as an apprentice housekeeper,' he wrote enthusiastically.[71]

---

65 See Allen Ep 1355:19–40/CWE Ep 1355:20–43. On Vroye see Allen Ep 717:21n/CWE Ep 717 22n, CEBR III 419–20. Vroye suggested that Neve had left his fellow lodgers in some uncertainty about the ownership of the books in his rooms, but if Erasmus had afterwards lost important works on account of this, would he not have taken up his pen to satirize the covetous people who had laid hands on his most precious possessions?

66 See 69 and n51 above.

67 See 70 and n58 above.

68 Allen Epp 1244:2–3 and n, 1342:103–5/CWE Epp 1244:1–2, 1342:116–20; Nauwelaerts 'Erasme à Louvain ... de 1517 à 1521' 23. Girolamo Aleandro had also stayed there.

69 Allen Ep 1351:28/CWE Ep 1351:33–4

70 See 65 and nn47, 48, and 51 above.

71 Allen Ep 1316:38–9 and n/CWE Ep 1316:41–2 and n10 (18 October 1522). Erasmus must have moved from 'Zum Sessel' to 'Zur alten Treu' at the end of September; cf Allen Ep 1289:33n/CWE Ep 1289 n14. On the houses, see also Roth 'Die Wohnstätten des Erasmus in Basel' 271–8; AK II 408 Ep 902 with n3 (409).

Indeed it was the ideal solution for him. The group of houses known as 'Zur alten Treu' on the Nadelberg was conveniently near the printing works but in a higher situation, with a wide view over the city. His landlord Froben had had an open hearth installed specially for him in one of the rooms, knowing that Erasmus could not bear the usual heating by an enclosed stove.[72] Erasmus' must have discussed with Froben his need for accommodation elsewhere than at 'Zum Sessel.' The attractive prospect of living on the Nadelberg may even have played some part in his decision to settle in Basel permanently. Perhaps, also, he did not send for his books until he was comfortably installed in his new home.

Erasmus stayed at the house 'Zur alten Treu' for six and a half years (from the end of September 1522 to 13 April 1529), longer than at any other address. Unfortunately we know hardly anything of his style of housekeeping in this period: how he furnished his house and, what interests us particularly, how he arranged and stored his books. It is only an assumption, however plausible it may be, since he refers early in January to taking Hieronim Łaski 'into his library,'[73] that he gathered an important part of his collection around him in a study close at hand for reference. Did he already own any free-standing bookcases for this purpose, as he did later in Freiburg? When he moved to Freiburg in 1529, he sent ahead two wagons filled with household goods, beds, and chests.[74] Bookcases are not specifically referred to (unless they were tacitly included among the 'household goods'), and this may indicate that he had none of his own at his disposal in Basel at the time. This would not be surprising. The use of free-standing cases with shelves exclusively intended for books was still far from normal, and for a library of comparatively modest size, such as that of Erasmus in the 1520s, it would not have been an obvious step, let alone urgently necessary, to acquire such newly fashionable *repositoria*.[75] It therefore seems more likely that in the house 'Zur alten Treu' Erasmus arranged the hundreds of books that made up his collection in the traditional way, that is, not ranged all together but spread out, with some volumes kept open and others shut.[76] In that case, part of the library would have been kept in chests, the most common storage furniture of the time. Erasmus had been accustomed to book chests for years, and the chests he may have used in Basel could have been included among the *scrinia* and *sarcinae* that went with him to Freiburg in 1529. Other books must have been arranged, open and visible, perhaps in small hanging cases fixed to the walls, or in cases in the panelling, but most likely, as was usual at the time, standing or lying on simple boards that were fixed to the walls at suitable heights.[77] If Froben had taken the trouble to have an open fireplace installed for his friend, would he not also have arranged, after discussing it with him, for the future study to be fitted with the necessary shelves to house Erasmus' numerous books? Erasmus also had at least one table on which to lay or stack his books, as he

---

72 Jacobus Nepos writes to Huldrych Zwingli c 12 March 1521 that 'Froben is building an open fireplace for Erasmus'; *Zwinglis Briefwechsel* I Ep 175. On Erasmus' dislike of smoky stoves see CWE Epp 1248 n5, 1258 n18; cf Allen Ep 2112:3–4 and n, 22–3 and n.

73 *Catalogus lucubrationum* Allen I 31:36 (*bibliothecam*); cf 32:11 μουσεῖον *nostrum* / CWE Ep 1341A:1224; cf 1241–2.

74 Allen Epp 2158:48 (*duo plaustra scriniis et lectis*), 2196:73 and 96 (*duo plaustra scriniis et sarcinis onusta ... tota supellectile*), Ep 2202:9 (*sarcinae*) / CWE Epp 2158:49, 2196:73-4 and 98, 2202:10

75 The college libraries of Oxford and Cambridge did not abandon the medieval desk-lectern system for modern bookcases until the end of the sixteenth century; Ker 'Oxford College Libraries in the Sixteenth Century' 470. Owners of larger private libraries may have been forced by lack of space to adopt earlier the most economical method of housing their books: upright alongside each other in cases with a number of shelves.

76 On the size of Erasmus' library at this time cf 53 above.

77 On chests and shelves cf 62, 63–4, and 67 above, 79–80 below.

had in Leuven. In Freiburg he had seven, of which at least two were probably reserved for books. One, fitted with niches, appears to have been specially made for the purpose.[78]

Although all this remains conjecture, and we can form only a vague impression of the room in which Erasmus spent the greatest part of his time – among his books, however they were arranged – one of his letters gives us a glimpse of what his study must have looked like. Writing to John Fisher after he had been living in Basel for almost two years, Erasmus describes some of the concrete requirements that, in his opinion, a comfortable study had to meet. He had learned that Fisher was not well. Erasmus blamed the damp situation of the episcopal palace, and in particular its draughty library, surrounded on all sides by 'glass walls' full of cracks. For the bishop, his library, where he spent hours at a time, was a paradise, but 'if I had spent three hours in such a place,' Erasmus commented, 'I should fall sick.' He recommended to his friend a study 'with a wooden floor and wooden panelling all around the walls,' because 'some sort of miasma issues from bricks and mortar.'[79] This advice and the reasons given for it seem too specific not to be based on personal experience. Had his own comfortable study, with its open hearth, not served him as a model? Furthermore, he must have been so used to the comfort of the open fireplace and the benefits of a wooden floor and panelled walls, and so convinced of their advantages, that when he left Basel he was unwilling to do without them: in the house he bought at Freiburg he at once had one of the rooms rebuilt internally and provided with an open fireplace, a wooden floor, and panelled walls.[80] Erasmus also added decoration to the walls of his study at 'Zur alten Treu,' as we know from letters to Willibald Pirckheimer written early in 1525. Erasmus says that he has received the portrait medallion and another portrait that Pirckheimer had sent and that they now adorn the walls of his room. He hung the cast metal portrait medallion of his friend on the right-hand wall, and on the left his portrait 'painted' (that is, engraved) by Dürer, so that wherever he was in the room, whether he stood to write or walked about, Willibald met his eye, and when friends came to visit they were reminded of him.[81]

After spending nearly seven and a half years in Basel, Erasmus moved to Freiburg in April 1529. His reasons for the move were similar to those that had prompted him to leave Leuven in 1521. At that time he had not wished to be drawn unwillingly into the anti-Lutheran camp; now he felt that his independent position was again under threat, this time from the Reformers in Basel. For some time he had been considering leaving the city and had reviewed various possible places of refuge. Though he had no special preference for Freiburg, he chose the town both because it was nearby and because the strict Austrian regime seemed to offer the best guarantee of repose and independence.[82] He managed to procure an imperial pass from Archduke Ferdinand, the governor of the city for his brother Charles v, while the

---

78 For the table in Leuven, see n45 above. In the visit described in the *Catalogus lucubrationum*, Hieronim Łaski picks up a letter 'lying on the table'; see Allen i 32:6/cwe Ep 1341a:1236. When Erasmus' possessions were inventoried in April 1534 it appeared that his house on the Schiffgasse in Freiburg contained *mensae vii, quarum vna habet nidulos, una duplex*; see Major *Erasmus von Rotterdam* 45, and cf n105 below.

79 Allen Ep 1489:4–13/cwe Ep 1489:5–16

80 See 76 below.

81 Allen Epp 1536:1–2, 1543:6–8, 1558:31–45/cwe Epp 1536:1–3, 1543:6–9, 1558:38–52. Erasmus describes the portrait as *pictum*, but since no portrait of Pirckheimer painted by Dürer is known, it is assumed that he referred to the engraving dated 1524, now in the Kupferstichkabinett, Staatliche Museen, Berlin, (reproduced in cwe 11 24); see *Erasmus en zijn tijd* no 277.

82 The extremist reformers in Basel, led by Oeolampadius, rejected a compromise solution to the growing confessional division by which each citizen should follow the dictates of conscience in attending religious services. In February 1529 the radicals became impatient with the caution of the town council and began a campaign of iconoclasm, smashing images in the cathedral and other churches. Freiburg, in contrast, was a

archduke also spoke in his favour to the city magistrates.[83] And to good effect: the burgomaster put at his disposal (rent-free until Christmas) the first floor of the impressive house 'Zum Walfisch' on the Franziskanergasse, begun in 1516 but not completely finished, and intended to be occupied later by the emperor Maximilian I. Erasmus had prepared his departure, which he wished to keep secret as long as possible, with the utmost care. Probably at the end of February he sent a man he could trust to Freiburg to look at the accommodation offered him.[84] Shortly afterwards he must have taken the definitive decision, which was carried out after a brief delay caused by a cold. He had his valuables sent separately in advance. The rest of his possessions, undoubtedly including his library, followed soon afterwards. They were carried, as we have mentioned, in two wagons laden with furniture and chests. Erasmus himself left on 13 April, accompanied for at least part of the way by Bonifacius Amerbach.[85] The precise date of his arrival is not known.

Our conception of the appearance of Erasmus' study in Freiburg is based on the well-known woodcut in which he and Gilbert Cousin are shown sitting facing each other across a large table, each with a lectern before him, the scholar dictating and his amanuensis writing. Against the left and right walls stand bookcases, while the third visible wall is taken up by windows. The caption dates the scene to 1530. What documentary value may we attach to this picture? The print first appeared in *Effigies Des. Erasmi Roterodami litteratorum principis et Gilberti Cognati Nozereni eius amanuensis*, published by J. Oporinus in Basel in 1553. Probably the print itself originated around that time and the anonymous artist himself never set foot in Erasmus' study. Yet the scene he shows us may not be wholly imaginary. The woodcut goes back to an original painting. Cousin, who had been assisting Erasmus since the summer of 1530, returned to his birthplace, Nozeroy, late in 1535 and spent the rest of his life there.[86] As a souvenir of the hours he had passed in Erasmus' study he commissioned a painting for his canonical residence at Nozeroy, and it was this scene that was later reproduced as a woodcut.[87] The artist may have painted the picture, which is now lost but was still to be seen in 1779, from Cousin's description; in that case it would have been more or less accurate in its depiction of the reality. The same would apply, on the whole, to the woodcut.

With a little good will one can see a resemblance between the façade of the house in the Franziskanergasse, which still exists, and the features of the window wall shown in the print.[88] The accuracy of the depiction of other elements in the room is confirmed, or at least not contradicted, by other sources. The two bookcases that stand facing each other against the left and right walls could indeed have formed part of the furniture of Erasmus' study. In relation to the height of the room they appear to be quite large in the print, but the number of shelves suggests rather that they were fairly low. Could they have been two of the three 'small bookcases' that Erasmus was using in his new house in Freiburg a few years later, according to an inventory of his estate made at that time? The painter and the engraver may have chosen to show the cases with their richly carved doors and frames as more impressive

---

Catholic, imperial city under the protective jurisdiction of the archduke Ferdinand. For Erasmus' reaction to developments in Basel see Ep 2201 from Freiburg (23 July 1529).

83 Allen and CWE Ep 2090 introductions
84 Allen Ep 2112:14–16 and 15n / CWE Ep 2112:14–16 and n4; on the house see also Allen and CWE Ep 2462 introductions.
85 Allen Ep 2158:46–8 / CWE Ep 2158:47–9; cf 72 above. Amerbach went with him by boat as far as Neuenberg and perhaps also on horseback from there to Freiburg; see Allen Ep 2151:9n / CWE Ep 2151 n3.
86 On Cousin see Allen Ep 2381 introduction / CWE Ep 2381 n1; CEBR I 350–2.
87 See Fèbvre 'Un secrétaire d'Erasme, Gilbert Cousin et la Réforme en Franche-Comté' 102; cf illustration xix above.
88 Major *Erasmus von Rotterdam* 22–5

and larger than they really were, just as they turned the armchairs in which Erasmus and Cousin sat into very flamboyant pieces of furniture. The lecterns that the two men have before them on the table are more realistically depicted. Cousin's bears a marked resemblance to the lectern before which Erasmus is sitting in Dürer's portrait of 1526, while Erasmus' simpler lectern could be a folding type, like one of the two mentioned in the inventory.[89]

Of the two bookcases in the woodcut, one is closed and the doors of the other are open. In the open case we can see four shelves. Folio volumes stand on the bottom and the second shelf, while the first and third shelves are occupied by smaller volumes. The handling of perspective is rather clumsy, so that it is not altogether clear how the books are arranged, but some are standing at some distance from one another, with the front or back board visible. This method of arrangement, which allows the often handsome binding to be displayed, was very popular in the fifteenth and early sixteenth centuries among those who did not own too many books, and many paintings and prints of the time bear witness to it. But for larger or still growing collections such an arrangement wasted space and could not be maintained; books had to be shelved in a more economical way. In Freiburg, Erasmus' library was already so large that he had no other choice but to stand most of his books upright next to one another on the shelves. This is clearly the case with the folios that the print shows on the second shelf.

Two of the four shelves shown in the print hold folio volumes, a ratio that tallies approximately with the distribution of Erasmus' books by format as they are recorded in the *Versandliste*. The great age of folio editions was already over by the end of his life. The jurist Andrea Alciati, for example, advised the Basel printer Cratander not, under any circumstances, to print his *Paradoxa* in the archaic – that is, folio – format that Froben had chosen for his edition of Jerome of 1524–6, because Alciati felt that folios were hard to sell in France and Italy.[90] Erasmus himself preferred books in smaller formats, on both practical and aesthetic grounds. From the beginning he welcomed the octavos introduced by Aldo Manuzio, and many of his own works contributed to the increasing popularity of the smaller format. Nevertheless, his private library, when it was inventoried in 1536, still included more folios than quartos and octavos put together.[91]

The woodcut of 1553 was almost certainly accurate in depicting the arrangement of the folios standing upright next to each other on the shelf with the fore-edge facing the observer. This must have been the usual method of shelving books in Germany, the Low Countries, England, and Spain.[92] A brief indication of the author or title written on the fore-edge made it easy to recognize a book quickly. That will often have been the case in Erasmus' library, though no examples have survived: nearly all the preserved books once in his possession have been rebound, so that any writing on the fore-edge disappeared when the pages were trimmed.[93] But indirect evidence suggests that some of the books may indeed have had a title written on the fore-edge. Some of the short titles in the *Versandliste* differ from the real title of the book and give the impression of a name bestowed by Erasmus for his own use, a name that can hardly have been invented by the assistant of Amerbach who compiled the

---

89 The 1534 inventory of Erasmus' household goods mentions *tres parvae repositoriae* [sic] and two lecterns, one a *pluteus versatilis, qui ponitur super mensam*, the other a *pluteus plicatilis*; Major *Erasmus von Rotterdam* 45.

90 Grimm 'Buchführer' 1386 sv Cratander

91 Of the 413 numbers in the *Versandliste*, about 222 refer to works in folio format and about 191 to works in either quarto or octavo. Even allowing for a very wide margin of error in the identification, the folios are in the majority.

92 Pollard 'Changes in the Style of Bookbinding, 1550–1830'

93 Husner 'Bibliothek' (234) writes, though it is difficult to follow him in this, that a title on the fore-edge is visible in the print.

list. The compiler probably simply took over the title he found written on the fore-edge. In two cases it is clear that the markedly different short title originated with Erasmus. Richard Pace's well known work *De fructu qui ex doctrina percipitur* appears in the *Versandliste* as *De fructu studiorum*, the short name by which Erasmus himself usually referred to the work in his correspondence.[94] The other example is even more telling. The addition of τὸ σκότοσ to the abbreviated title of Duns Scotus' commentary on the *Sentences* of Peter Lombard clearly reflects Erasmus' negative opinion of this medieval philosopher.[95] In these cases, and possibly in others, Erasmus himself may have written these identifications in his books.

Erasmus occupied the first floor of the house 'Zum Walfisch' in Freiburg for about two and a half years. Friction both over the rent that he would have to begin paying at Christmas and with his fellow resident in the house, Ottmar Nachtgall – difficulties that he wished to avoid – led Erasmus during 1531 to think of moving to a house of his own.[96] After negotiations that began in June or even earlier, he bought a house in the Schiffgasse 'with a fine-sounding name but for an iniquitous price.'[97] A good deal of repair and rebuilding had to be carried out before he could move into the house 'Zum Kind Jesu' in September. These disagreeable concerns took up his time through the summer. 'Erasmus,' he tells a correspondent, 'who for the whole of his life has put literature before all else, has become a lessee, a buyer, a maker of contracts, a giver of sureties, a builder, and his business is with builders, joiners, smiths, stonemasons, and glaziers instead of the Muses.'[98] He must have gone about it thoroughly. When he took it over, the house, large as it was, had 'not a single corner where he could safely lay his meagre body,' as he put it. He had a room rebuilt and fitted up with an open fireplace, a wooden floor, and wood-panelled walls, just as he had advised Bishop John Fisher to do seven years earlier.[99] Over and above the purchase price, he spent more than a hundred florins on the necessary repairs and renovations of the property.[100] Erasmus probably lived and worked surrounded by all his books in this room. He referred explicitly to 'the room in which his books were,' and his friend Glareanus described its function no less specifically when he wrote that he had 'entered the library.'[101]

As for the arrangement of the books in the house 'Zum Kind Jesu,' the inventory of Erasmus' estate made in 1534 gives us a few concrete pointers to the furniture he could use to store his library. The most important (and at the time the most modern) pieces mentioned were 'three small bookcases.' Although described as 'small,' they could certainly have held at least half of his collection. (A one-metre shelf will hold twenty folio books or thirty quartos or octavos. Three cases one metre wide with four shelves can hold 300 volumes.)[102] Besides these bookcases the inventory mentions 'three large chests and one small,'[103] which may have been meant to hold books, perhaps particular categories of books. In this connection, we may think first of the mostly unbound works in quarto or octavo that Erasmus most

---

94 See VL/Catalogue no 30.

95 See VL/Catalogue no 167.

96 See Allen and CWE Ep 2462 introductions.

97 Allen Ep 2517:27–8; cf also Epp 2518:26, 2528:53–4, and 2534:24–5.

98 Allen Ep 2534:26–9; cf Epp 2517:29–32, 2518:27–34.

99 Allen Ep 2534:31–4; cf 73 above.

100 *super centum florenos*; Allen Ep 3059:10–12

101 Allen Epp 3059:14, 3045:9–10

102 Possibly Erasmus acquired the 'three small bookcases' shortly after his arrival in Freiburg, for his study in the house 'Zum Walfisch,' and if so two of the cases may be depicted in the woodcut of the humanist at work with Gilbert Cousin; see 74–5 above. On the measurements, cf 79 below.

103 *Arcae III et vna parua*; Major *Erasmus von Rotterdam* 45

probably owned but that were not entered in the *Versandliste* of 1536, and then of the copies of his own works, also largely unbound, that he later kept in a separate chest in Basel.[104] Nor was there any lack of tables, then far from the everyday furnishings they were later to become, in Erasmus' house. The inventory mentions seven, so that he had ample opportunity to spread his books out when he needed them for his work. One table was described as specially fitted with niches.[105] We may imagine that he also had the craftsmen fix boards at places where it was convenient for him to keep the books he needed close to hand. 'Zum Kind Jesu' was the only house, after all, where as the owner he could have everything to his liking.

Erasmus was to move house – and transport his library – once more. He left Freiburg im Breisgau without regret for a number of reasons. He owned a well-equipped house on which he had spared neither time nor expense, but running his own household came to be too much for him. Nor, in the end, was he happy in Freiburg. He had no intimate friends there as he had in Basel. Life was not pleasant: he shuddered at the streets, which were like open sewers, and in a more general way he attributed his poor health to the climate of the town.[106] Moreover, he had a compelling motive to return to Basel in 1535: he wished to be on the spot to see his last great work, *Ecclesiastes*, through the press. At the beginning of May he had sent his manuscript to Froben, though it was not yet wholly ready.[107] And behind that reason for leaving Freiburg lay another: he did not intend Basel itself to be his final destination. Though he would find calm restored in the city, which he had left in a rather turbulent state six years before, that did not disguise the fact that the Reformation had been triumphantly enforced. He wished to pass his last years elsewhere, away from religious strife.[108] After completing the *Ecclesiastes* he thought of travelling to Brabant, where the regent, Mary of Hungary, and the whole court had repeatedly invited him.[109] Or perhaps he would go to Burgundy; he had long thought of Besançon as a place where he might end his days. Once he was in Basel he spoke less and less of Brabant, and in October 1535 it seemed that he had chosen Besançon, which was nearer, as his future home.[110] Yet he never wholly gave up the illusion that he could return to Brabant. 'If only Brabant were nearer,' he sighed in the last letter from him that we have, written three weeks before his death, when he was convinced that if he ever left Basel, he would go, not to Brabant but at most to Besançon.[111]

At the end of May 1535 Erasmus, accompanied by his secretary Gilbert Cousin, arrived in Basel, where he took up residence in the house 'Zum Luft' owned by the printer-publisher Hieronymus Froben.[112] Possibly because he assumed that his stay in Basel would only be brief and temporary, he did not bring his library with him, but left it in Freiburg. He did not have his books sent on to his new home until the situation had turned out quite differently from his hopes. Even before his departure from Freiburg his health was deteriorating.[113]

---

104 On the copies of Erasmus' own works, see 99–103, on the other unbound books, 103–6, 110 below.
105 *nidulos*, literally 'little nests'; see n78 above. On tables see for example *Thuis in de late middeleeuwen, het Nederlands burgerinterieur 1400–1535* 26–7.
106 See Allen Epp 3130:26–7, 2897:32–7, 3049:59–63, 90–2; Reedijk 'Das Lebensende des Erasmus' 39–42.
107 Allen Ep 3016:25–6
108 Allen Epp 3049:68–74, 3130:27–8
109 Epp 2820 (from Mary of Hungary), 2850
110 Allen Epp 2759:20n, 3062:4n
111 Allen Ep 3130:28–9. Bonifacius Amerbach and Beatus Rhenanus both felt that Erasmus had to the last persisted in his wish to go to Brabant; Allen Ep 3141:78–87 (Amerbach to Johann Paumgartner), Allen I 69:492–503 (Beatus Rhenanus to Charles V); cf I 53:17–22 (Beatus Rhenanus to Hermann of Wied).
112 Allen Ep 2381 introduction (page 43); the precise date is unknown; cf Ep 3025:18n.
113 Cf Allen Ep 3019:11.

Physically, he was no longer capable of exertion; for the journey to Basel he had had to use a means of transport that he described, half in jest and half in scorn, as typically intended for women.[114] In Basel he did not find the relief he had cautiously hoped for from the change of air, and he was soon suffering from his old complaints. His strength was clearly ebbing, and there were many days on which his hand could hardly guide his pen. He scarcely left his room any more, and in the autumn he was confined to his bed for more than a month by unbearable pain.[115] It was clear that Erasmus, after he had put the final touches to his *Ecclesiastes*, would be in no state to travel to Besançon, still less to Brabant. He foresaw that he would be forced to remain in Basel for some time – the whole of the coming winter, as he predicted, for even a return to nearby Freiburg (which he had not ruled out, since he still owned his house there) soon appeared impossible.[116]

Under these circumstances there was no point in leaving his library unused in Freiburg, and at the end of the summer Erasmus had his books sent to Basel. His decision was probably hastened by an accident: a fierce fire late in August very close to his house in Freiburg, in the stables where a former rector of the university kept his horses. Although Henricus Glareanus, who informed him of the event, at once reassured him that his library had not been in any danger, Erasmus must have been alarmed.[117] At any rate, he chose to have his books fetched to Basel without delay, with the help of his friends. Amerbach, accompanied by Cousin, went to Freiburg and spent at least two days there in early September, making arrangements for the books to be packed and dispatched. Froben organized the actual transport. He sent two carriers to Freiburg, who agreed to be there early on Friday 3 September and load their wagons, so that they could begin the return journey to Basel as early as possible the next morning. Amerbach was afraid that the wagon hired by Froben would not be able to carry everything, and he hired a local carrier to take a separate barrel and case, both full of books, as well as a smaller barrel with sugar loaves, to Basel.[118]

By the time the library arrived, three months had elapsed since Erasmus had been received with demonstrations of honour in Basel. The University offered him delicacies and wine as its welcome gift soon after his arrival at the end of May, while the magistrates, though a little less spontaneously, also held an official reception for him three weeks later.[119] But these outward signs of honour were more than matched by the exceptional care that his close friends showed for him, doing everything in their power to make life comfortable for the old and ailing scholar. In the hope that Erasmus would return to Basel, Hieronymus Froben had rebuilt and adapted a room especially for him in his house 'zum Luft' on the corner of the Bäumleingasse and the Luftgasslein. It 'had been prepared to my taste and set up in a manner that they knew would be convenient for me,' Erasmus wrote after he had been living there, evidently happily, for three months.[120] Did he mean by this that the living and working accommodation at his disposal met his special requirements? Was it equipped with a wooden floor and an open hearth?[121] This is certainly possible, perhaps even probable.

---

114 Allen Epp 3028:17–18 (*carpento muliebri*), 3049:63–4 (*arcera muliebri*)
115 Cf Allen Epp 3049:62–4, 3035:11–13, 3048:94–8, 3077:1–2. Cf also Allen i 69–70:497–508 (Beatus Rhenanus to Charles v) and 53:22–5 (Beatus Rhenanus to Hermann of Wied).
116 Cf Allen Epp 3052:14–15, 3025:18–21, 3043:27–30, 3056:4–5.
117 Ep 3045; cf Allen Ep 2470:24 / cwe Ep 2470:26–7 (on the rector's horses).
118 Allen Epp 3051, 3055:19 and n; ak iv 373–4 Ep 1977 (from Froben to Amerbach)
119 Roth 'Die Wohnstätten des Erasmus' 279–80 n40
120 Allen Ep 3049:65–6; on the history of the house, which Froben had bought with his wife Anna Lachner in 1531, see Roth 'Die Wohnstätten des Erasmus' 278–81.
121 See 73 and 76 above.

When Erasmus wrote, just before his library arrived, that his room suited him, did he also mean that it was already sufficiently fitted up to receive his books without any problem? We may assume that this was almost certainly the case. During September Erasmus sent his secretary Gilbert Cousin to Freiburg to settle certain other matters and at the same time to sell the household effects left behind in his house 'Zum Kind Jesu.'[122] From a later note made by Amerbach on the 1534 inventory of Erasmus' estate in Freiburg, it appears that this commission was carried out. According to this note, all of Erasmus' wooden furniture is said to have been disposed of at the time: his three bookcases, the seven tables, including the one with book-niches, and the chests used for the storage of books.[123] But the chests may not in fact have been sold. Erasmus disposed of his wooden furniture because he no longer needed it in Basel.[124] We can rule out the possibility that he acquired new furniture to house his library in Basel, because the itemized statement of his effects drawn up ten days after his death mentions no bookcases and only one table. The same inventory refers to eight chests and travelling cases, and it is less likely that these were bought in Basel than that they accompanied the library when it was removed from Freiburg. Be that as it may, it is clear that Erasmus was using very little furniture of his own in Basel; the lodging put at his disposal in Froben's house at the end of May must have provided it.[125] Froben, perhaps in cooperation with Amerbach, arranged for adequate accommodation in Erasmus' rooms for the books that were to arrive – several hundred volumes, around half of them folios. For Hieronymus Froben no trouble was too great, for he was eager to retain in Basel the famous scholar who kept his publishing firm almost permanently supplied with work. And Bonifacius Amerbach must have been doing his best from the start to ensure that Erasmus remained in the city.[126]

An estimate of the total space occupied by all the books in Erasmus' lodgings – rather cramped by comparison with Freiburg – can only be approximate. We can use the *Versandliste* to estimate the size of the library in linear metres on the basis of the thickness of the books. The identity of many entries in the list, however, is open to question, so that the total number of pages in the books is equally debatable. Moreover, the bindings must be taken into account, especially for the very numerous folios, the bindings of which were often reinforced with wooden panels. In our calculations there is therefore a wide margin of error. Starting from the text block, the most important factor in the calculation, and assuming an average thickness of 12 millimetres for every hundred pages of text,[127] we reached the following result: standing upright alongside one another, the 413 volumes in the *Versandliste* would have taken up fourteen to sixteen linear metres. It may be possible to draw some useful inferences from this figure. Would Erasmus have been so ready to give up the three bookcases he left

---

122　Ep 3059. The house was soon afterwards sold to the Basel canon Peter Reich (on whom see CEBR III 135–6).

123　Under the heading of 'wooden furniture' (*lignea*), Amerbach wrote 'Sold in Freiburg' (*Vendita Friburgi*); Major *Erasmus von Rotterdam* 45. For the use of these pieces of furniture see 67–8 and 72–3 above.

124　As Amerbach noted: 'Gilbertus Cognatus ... ex supellectili iussu domini quedam illic vendidit minus necessaria'; Major *Erasmus von Rotterdam* 43.

125　See the inventory dated 22 July 1536 in Major *Erasmus von Rotterdam* 52–66. Erasmus' estate included 'VIII trog vnd Reyssladen'; these may well include the 'arcae III et una parva' and the 'scrinia conuestita corio II magna et vnum paruum' of the Freiburg inventory of 1534; both involved the same combination of chests and travelling cases. Apart from the storage chests Erasmus left only two beds and a table. Erasmus must have brought the wall hangings, bench and chair cushions, bed curtains, and a few other things mentioned in the inventory of 1534, for they appear in the inventory of 1536; see Major 44 and 53.

126　AK Ep 1977 (cited n118 above) is characteristic of Froben's collaboration with Amerbach at this period; cf Reedijk 'Das Lebensende des Erasmus' 52 and n.

127　This average is the result of a large number of sample tests made on early sixteenth-century books.

in Freiburg and sell them if he had not found equivalent storage space in Froben's house to replace them? Because tables and chests would hardly have been as useful, we must almost certainly assume that in Basel he was able to arrange most of his books on shelves, as he had been accustomed to do in Freiburg. We can no longer discover where he found the shelf space he needed. The usual shelves, simple boards placed fairly high on the walls on brackets, certainly would not have provided enough room for so many books. There may also have been wall-mounted boxes or recesses left in the panelling. Or should we think rather of a solution that would not have required any carpentry and assume that to compensate for the loss of his *repositoria* Erasmus had the use of similar free-standing cases with shelves in Basel? Most of his books would have stood on the shelves, while the rest could have been spread across chests, tables, or wherever else he found room for them. We know that in the house 'Zum Luft' Erasmus kept copies of a large number of his own works in a separate chest, placed against the window that overlooked the inner courtyard.[128] By specifying the location of this chest so specifically in the inventory he had made of its contents, Amerbach may have meant to distinguish it from other chests, perhaps also used for storing books.

As for how the books were arranged on the shelves, we must fall back upon conjecture. It is difficult to say how far the sequence of titles in the *Versandliste* reflects the actual arrangement of the books. We do not know whether the library was still in its original state in Erasmus' apartment when the list was compiled, nor do we know how Amerbach's assistant went about recording the books. The most we can say with confidence is that he worked through them in groups of folios, quartos, and octavos, or of quartos and octavos mixed together.[129] Within the format groups, he often dealt with books in the order in which he found them, but not consistently, or so it appears. For would the edition of Plautus entered among the editions of Aristotle really have stood or lain so far from its proper place?[130] This is not an isolated case, and the way in which whole series of titles often occur at random in the list might suggest that the compiler paid no attention to the order in which the books were arranged. But that suspicion may be unfounded. The chaotic listing of the titles need not be blamed exclusively on the person who was responsible for the inventory. The library may not have been well organized in Basel. As a result of the move from Freiburg the books may have been in disarray, and Erasmus, tired and sick, may not have had the will or the energy after May 1535 to arrange them in the order to which he had been accustomed.

Given the uncertainty surrounding the making of the *Versandliste*, it is hazardous to draw inferences from it on the way in which the books were arranged in the house 'Zum Luft.' We may however, risk limited presumptions about the simplest and most obvious forms of arrangement, those that concerned only a few books. For example, various editions of the same work or of various works by a single author are often, but not always, recorded together on the list. In these cases the combination of items on paper very likely corresponded to the actual arrangement of the books in the room. It is difficult to imagine that Amerbach's colleague, who had to draw up the summary list in haste,[131] would have brought these books together if he had not found them in combination already. We may therefore safely assume that the three editions of Plato in Erasmus' possession, entered consecutively in the *Versandliste*, were in actual fact placed next to one another. The same applies to

---

128 *in arca aulae versus fenestram*; see *Catalogus librorum Erasmi* 451 below and Husner 'Bibliothek' 237 n54.
129 For the format groups in the *Versandliste*, see the Introduction to the vL/Catalogue 141–3 below.
130 vL/Catalogue no 213
131 Cf the Introduction to the vL/Catalogue 140 below.

his five editions of Aristotle, his three editions of Dioscorides and Diogenes Laertius, his three versions of Plutarch's *Lives*, and the two editions he owned of some other classical authors.[132] Among contemporary authors, Guillaume Budé was represented in the collection by five works, one of them in two editions. Their titles also form a neat group in the list, no doubt because the six folios had been found together: either standing in a row or in a pile somewhere else.[133] In the same way we need not doubt that several small groups of books on a single clearly defined subject that were entered together in the list were arranged together in the library. For example, the books that Erasmus owned on Roman or canon law, which make up an almost complete record of civil and ecclesiastical jurisprudence, must have been kept somewhere en bloc.[134] As for the later medieval theologians, poorly represented though they were, the works listed, with perhaps one or two exceptions, were also kept near one another.[135]

But while we can be fairly confident that some groups of books were kept together in Erasmus' collection, we cannot infer from the *Versandliste* with the same certainty the arrangement of the library as a whole. If there was a guiding principle behind the arrangement of the books, the list gives us only a vague and shadowy reflection of it. Some quite long series of titles cover broadly defined fields of learning. Nearly seventy consecutive entries refer to editions of classical texts and works of humanist philology,[136] while a couple of shorter sequences mention the titles of editions of the Bible and commentaries on it, patristic works, theological works, and ecclesiastical history.[137] We may perhaps see in this an indication that Erasmus classified a considerable number of his books systematically into the two fields that defined his intellectual world: on the one hand classical literature, *bonae litterae*; and on the other the Christian faith, which he wished to reconcile with the spirit of antiquity. But as with the smaller groups of books, titles appear out of place: John Fisher's polemic against Oecolampadius appears among the classical works,[138] and Athenaeus' *Deipnosophistae* turns up between a patristic text and a biblical concordance.[139] As for his own works and the editions of classical and patristic texts that he prepared, most of them appear among the last ninety entries of the *Versandliste*. Of the roughly sixty works of his own that can be shown to have been in his library, three-quarters are among this ninety, while with one exception, all the editions of his New Testament that Erasmus kept, according to the list, are entered there.[140] May we not infer from this that most of Erasmus' own works were placed together somewhere in the room? And if the editions of the *Novum Testamentum* were included among these titles, that would be further evidence of the special place his translation of and annotations on the New Testament occupied in his oeuvre as a whole. The classical and patristic texts Erasmus edited, as distinct from his own works in the stricter sense, were probably allocated a place somewhere else, since it can hardly be a coincidence that only four of

---

132 VL/Catalogue nos 216–18 (Plato); 210–12, 214, and 215 (Aristotle); 201–3 (Dioscorides); 304–6 (Diogenes Laertius); 265–7 (Plutarch); cf eg 130–1 (Demosthenes), 274–5 (Strabo) and 269–70 (Tacitus)

133 VL/Catalogue nos 287–92

134 See VL/Catalogue nos 139–47.

135 See VL/Catalogue nos 159 (Bernard of Clairvaux), 163 (Peter Lombard), 161, 162, 165, and 170 (Thomas Aquinas), 167 (Duns Scotus), 168 (Durandus of St. Pourçain) and 169 (Jean Gerson).

136 VL/Catalogue nos 259–324

137 VL/Catalogue nos 159–85 and 220–43

138 VL/Catalogue no 312

139 VL/Catalogue no 239

140 VL/Catalogue nos 328–31, 342; the exception is no 241.

them appear among the last ninety entries, while all the others are recorded elsewhere in the list, usually in the neighbourhood of similar text editions.[141]

The conclusions we have drawn from the *Versandliste* about the classification of books in Erasmus' library are based on a relatively small part of it. Whole sequences of entries list titles in what seems to be random order. In spite of groups of entries in the *Versandliste* that point to a principle of arrangement, therefore, we do not know how a large part of the library was arranged, and we may not rule out the possibility that after Erasmus moved back to Basel in 1535 his books remained in some disorder.

Would it not have been different in Freiburg? In the house 'Zum Kind Jesu' Erasmus had plenty of room and the freedom to furnish his lodgings himself; he could have arranged his collection entirely as he wished. We may suppose that on the whole the books had been more methodically arranged than they were in the house 'Zum Luft.' Yet we must certainly not assume that the library in Freiburg was a model of organization. The sixteenth-century practice of binding works of the most disparate content in the same covers when it was convenient was an obstacle to any systematic classification of books. From numerous binding combinations in his library it is clear that Erasmus was quite accustomed to this practice and that it did not trouble him, for example, that the index to his 1516 edition of Jerome, which was published later, was combined between the same boards with a legal compilation of Udalricus Zasius.[142] The somewhat disorganized arrangement of the library must also have been aggravated by the motley collection of furniture Erasmus could use to house his books. Works that belonged together by reason of their content could be spread about the room depending on their importance or the amount of use that Erasmus foresaw for them: they might be immediately at hand on one of his tables; within easy reach on a shelf or in a bookcase (*repositorium*); or, more inaccessible, in a book chest.

But regardless of the consequences of binding practice and the lack of uniform storage, would not Erasmus – like most book owners, then and now, of libraries not too extensive to grasp as a whole – know where to find books in his own familiar collection even if they were not very methodically arranged? Possibly Erasmus made a distinction, in part of his collection, between *bonae litterae* and Christian literature. It was an obvious distinction and almost unavoidable in view of the quantity of books involved. But in setting up his library and in shelving new acquisitions, he need not have had any predetermined pattern in mind. It is easier to assume that he placed his books with some freedom and was influenced by various practical or material considerations. He must have found it convenient, for example, to put the classical compilations, the *Scriptores astronomici veteres*, the *Scriptores rei militaris* and the *Scriptores rei rusticae* together, in spite of their disparate subject matter, because they were comparable in their intent.[143] That was to adopt a formal criterion for placing them. But quite subjective associations of ideas may have led him to put certain books next to one another. Sometimes a combination on the shelf that may have originated in this way seems evident in the *Versandliste*. It lists, one after the other, the two commentaries of Jacques Lefèvre d'Etaples on the Gospels and the Epistles of Paul, the collected works issued under the name of Dionysius the Pseudo-Areopagite, and the polemical treatise *Antilutherus*

---

141 For the four exceptions see VL/Catalogue nos 385, 394, 405, and 410. Three of these books were placed among the last ninety entries and not with other text editions because they were recent acquisitions; see 83 below.

142 VL/Catalogue no 188. For more on Erasmus' binding policy see 85–9 below.

143 The three compilations were entered in the *Versandliste* under nos 322–4.

of Josse Clicthove.[144] It is likely that these four books also stood in a row in Basel and quite possibly before that in Freiburg. What at first sight appears a more or less casual grouping would have been a sensible combination for Erasmus. It was easy for him to find, alongside the New Testament commentaries of Lefèvre d'Etaples, the same scholar's edition of Dionysius. The treatise against Luther, in turn, was a suitable companion for the latter. Its author, Clicthove, had contributed a supplementary commentary for the second printing of Lefèvre's edition of Dionysius, the very one in question here. Furthermore, in chapters 5 and 7 of his *Antilutherus* Clicthove asserted, as Lefèvre had done, that the Dionysius Areopagita named in Acts 17:34 was the author of the corpus of mystical theological writings issued under that name. Valla, followed by Erasmus, had disputed this; in chapters 8 and 9 of his extensive polemic Clicthove attempted to refute the arguments they had adduced.[145]

Let us leave the realm of conjecture and close this chapter on firm ground. We have the good fortune to be able to use the *Versandliste* to reconstruct the arrangement of the books in Basel in one concrete particular. The last twenty-six titles entered almost all refer to books that appeared towards the end of Erasmus' life, more precisely after 1531.[146] Ten of them definitely appeared in 1535 or 1536,[147] for some others that is possible if not probable.[148] Nearly fifty books published after 1531 are recorded elsewhere in the list, though scattered through it and interspersed among earlier works, but editions of 1535 and 1536 are not among them. This means that at the end of the list we are dealing with all the books in the library that appeared in these two years. They were all, or nearly all, acquired only after Erasmus had returned from Freiburg to Basel in May 1535 and had installed himself in Froben's house 'Zum Luft.'[149] With a few books from the years immediately preceding, they are entered more or less separately from the rest as a distinct group, on a new page of the *Versandliste*, though the previous page was only three-quarters full.[150] We can hardly doubt that the compiler of the list found them in a separate group. In Erasmus' apartment, the latest acquisitions may have been given a provisional place of their own on a special table or on free shelves set aside for them. In one instance, the provisional character of the placing is obvious. The recently acquired third volume of the medical compilation of Aetius, published in 1535, had clearly been casually put down or set aside without regard for the fact that that the first two volumes, both of which had appeared earlier, in 1533, were kept elsewhere.[151] Among the books added to the library in 1535–6 there were also four of Erasmus' own works, three of them *editiones principes* of recently issued works and the last a reprint, perhaps revised by the author himself, of the *Enchiridion militis christiani*.[152] They are the only entries in the *Versandliste* to state the number of copies present. The duplicates may have been copies given to the author to present to his friends. Erasmus, weak and often bedridden, did not live to do so.

---

144 VL/Catalogue nos 178–81

145 See, in addition to VL/Catalogue nos 180 and 181, Massaut *Critique et tradition à la veille de la Réforme en France* 183.

146 VL/Catalogue nos 388–413. The exception is no 390, a tract from 1484. The dating of nos 411 and 412 remains uncertain.

147 VL/Catalogue nos 388, 391, 393, 396, 397, 399, 400, 402, 404, and 413

148 For example VL/Catalogue nos 395, 401, 406, and 407

149 Nearly all the publications of 1535 were acquired after May of that year; the printing month of VL/Catalogue nos 391, 411, 412, and 413 cannot be determined.

150 VL/Catalogue nos 388–413 are listed on fol 44 verso of the manuscript; fol 44 recto contains only six titles.

151 VL/Catalogue no 413; for the first two volumes see no 133.

152 VL/Catalogue nos 396 (*Precationes aliquot*, four copies), 397 (*Responsio ad Petri Cursii defensionem*, four copies), 400 (*Ecclesiastes*, three copies), and 395 (*Enchiridion*, two copies)

4

Maintenance and Binding

What did Erasmus do to maintain his books? In particular, what care did he devote to their binding? Unfortunately we do not have enough information to give a clear and truly satisfactory answer to these questions. We cannot be sure about the external state of the library Erasmus left in 1536. When Erasmus' books came up for sale in Emden in 1554, Regnerus Praedinius had little good to say about the ones sent to him for inspection.[1] Of all the books he examined, he himself, he wrote, possessed better copies. Some appeared to be incomplete, with either the preliminaries or a part of the text missing. He would not have paid a farthing for Budé's commentary on the Pandects had it not belonged to Erasmus. Hesychius' *Lexicon* was worn and in pieces, and many other books were equally defective. There is no reason why we should not believe him when he gives concrete examples of incomplete or grimy books. In one case his comments can be checked against the surviving copy, and indeed pages are missing, as he had pointed out, from one of the volumes of Galen's *Opera*.[2]

But we cannot take Praedinius' comments without qualification as an accurate description of the state in which Erasmus left his books. In the first place, Praedinius' version of the facts was no doubt coloured by his desire to own the books that had belonged to the humanist he so deeply admired. He wanted them at the most favourable possible price and hoped that he could force it down by emphasizing their various blemishes. Nor does his critical report necessarily describe the state the books were in when Erasmus died. In the eighteen years that had elapsed, the library had come through a great deal and had obviously suffered. Things began to go wrong when it was dispatched to Poland: on the journey one of the three barrels in which the books were packed was found to be full of cracks and had to be replaced in order to avoid damage by rain.[3] Repeated later moves in the wake of the peripatetic Łaski can hardly have done the collection much good. Moreover, Praedinius' emphatically unfavourable verdict does not seem entirely credible when we consider that the surviving books from Erasmus' library – a number of which were also in Praedinius' possession – have on the whole remained in good condition to this day. Two of them, the copies of Aulus Gellius' *Noctes Atticae*, a much consulted book, and Galen's *Therapeutica*, for example, still display an amazing purity and freshness, although the original bindings (like those of the other surviving books) have disappeared.[4] There is no reason to believe either that the library was in perfect condition in 1536 or that it fell into a state of total degradation shortly after.

---

1 Cf 11 above. On the sale see 4 and n10, 8 above.
2 See VL/Catalogue nos 288 (Budé), 297 (Hesychius), and 137 (Galen).
3 AK V 24 Ep 2110
4 See VL/Catalogue nos 281 and 138.

How much importance did Erasmus himself attach to the external state of his books? His attitude was clear enough in theory. Books derived their value exclusively from their content, and when they were of particular interest they ought to be consulted regularly. They did not have to be treated with reverence; they were utilitarian objects and should be handled as such. When he was still in his twenties and had very few books of his own, he sharply rejected misguided, pointless bibliophilia. 'I consider as lovers of books not those who keep their books hidden in their store-chests and never handle them, but those who, by nightly as well as daily use, thumb them, batter them, wear them out, who fill up all the margins with annotations of many kinds, and who prefer the marks of a fault they have erased to a neat copy full of faults.'[5] Later, when he was dealing with books of his own, Erasmus was in one respect consistent with this image of the true book lover: he used them as working material with a pen in his hand. He wrote remarks wherever he pleased and inserted improvements in the margins of the pages. He frequently marked passages in the text or annotations of his own with a figure or drawing, and when it suited him he made the most of blank fly-leaves in order to add more extensive notes.[6]

We may wonder, however, whether Erasmus was as consistently indifferent to the external appearance of his books as the model book lover he described in 1489. Was Erasmus the sort of man to use them negligently and carelessly? His need for cleanliness even in his material life, which Huizinga regarded as one of his characteristics,[7] makes it most unlikely that he should ever have allowed even his most intensively used books to look thumbed, battered, or worn out through any fault of his own. Nor are there any indications that Erasmus deliberately neglected the binding of his books. On the contrary: both his practical sense and his methodical and efficient manner of working lead us to expect that he would conscientiously ensure that unbound books that entered his library were bound if necessary and that the volumes most used and most exposed to wear remained in a reasonably good condition. We can support this hypothesis, however, only by inference.

None of the surviving books from Erasmus' library retains its original binding, and we can only guess at whether the books recorded in the *Versandliste* were all bound. Most of them probably were. The titles of two or more books in the same format and published at more or less the same time listed under a single item undoubtedly indicate books bound together, and we find several such composite volumes in each of the three current formats.[8] Independent folio editions – which, together with the folios bound together, would seem to constitute over half of the 413 volumes – must, as a rule, have stood or lain on the shelves in a binding, simply because a strong binding was an essential condition for the preservation and use of these normally heavy volumes. For the quarto and octavo editions that made up the other half of the collection sent to Łaski,[9] a leather binding was not always necessary, and there were simpler and cheaper solutions. A number of the booklets mentioned in the *Versandliste* of a small or very small size, or of ephemeral interest, were possibly only sewn

---

5 Allen Ep 31:31–5 / cwe Ep 31:35–9

6 For an extensive discussion of a book from his library with numerous marginal notes, Athenaeus' *Deipnosophistae* (Venice 1514), see Margolin 'Erasme et Athénée: le chantier d'un humaniste pressé.' See also Kossman 'Sporen van Erasmus' hand en een afbeelding van den god Terminus' on Erasmus' drawings and notes. vl/Catalogue no 281 (Aulus Gellius) has notes on the flyleaf.

7 *Erasmus of Rotterdam* 117–18

8 About nineteen composite folio volumes, twenty-five quartos, and fourteen octavos

9 On the division into formats see 75 and n91 above.

together and provided with a wrapper.[10] In some cases, perhaps, the shorter pieces of a single author that had appeared over the years were kept in their loose gatherings and simply held together with a piece of string in a bundle (to which new material could be added).[11] Nevertheless, there is a special reason to assume that many of the quarto and octavo books were also bound. Erasmus kept unbound books in the smaller formats apart from the library as it is inventoried in the *Versandliste;*[12] those on the list, therefore, were probably bound.

Examination of the composite volumes on the *Versandliste* can perhaps lead us to another assumption. Most of these volumes contained works published at more or less the same time, and they were mainly books that appeared in Erasmus' later years. By then he obviously made sure that books he intended to keep in his library were bound reasonably soon after he purchased or acquired them. The composite volumes consisting of works that had not appeared at the same time but had been published over a number of years are noticeable exceptions, and it is in these exceptional cases that we also come across earlier books, published before 1510. For example, Erasmus' own edition of Valla's annotations to the Vulgate of 1505 was bound in a single volume with another Valla edition of four years later and a London edition of 1512.[13] Perhaps these exceptions should be seen as an indication that Erasmus only started to devote a serious and systematic attention to the binding of his books a few years after his Italian journey, when improved material circumstances also allowed him to tackle the enlargement of his library with unexpected energy.[14]

In what form, bound or unbound, did Erasmus receive newly acquired books? In order to answer this we must ask a somewhat broader question. How did new books come into circulation in his time? As a rule, they were unbound. The major printer-publishers sent newly printed works to the Frankfurt book fair in loose sheets, packed in barrels.[15] But firms in many countries sometimes also brought new editions onto the market as a completed product – bound, in other words.[16] The individual purchaser thus found some books in the shops ready for use – most likely, perhaps, the best-sellers of the time. But in most cases it was up to the buyer to have books bound. He might have had to arrange this himself, but not always. The booksellers often had a binder at hand or themselves practised binding as an additional commercial activity; in that case the client who ordered a book could immediately arrange whether and how he wished to have it bound.[17] Erasmus would have had to do the same. Even before he moved to Basel there are references in his correspondence to the binding of books he had ordered or bought and to his impatience with the binders' slowness. He complained in February 1517 that he had the greatest difficulty in wresting the augmented edition of Budé's *De asse* (Josse Bade 1516) from the hands of the binders long after he ordered it.[18] He was presumably referring to a binder in Brabant. At about the same time, with Pieter Gillis as an intermediary, he had other books bound there, like the volumes of the 1516 edition of Jerome, which had arrived from Basel in loose sheets. He wrote to Gillis in Antwerp that he wanted to have Jerome's works bound as quickly as possible so that he

---

10 One of the smallest books on the list is vl/Catalogue no 390, a tract by Eusebius Conradus that has only eight folios.

11 vl/Catalogue nos 46 and 47, for example, list the names of authors; no works are specified.

12 See 99–105, 110 below.

13 vl/Catalogue no 364, an edition by Pynson of Remaclus Arduenna

14 See 24–5 above.

15 Ruppel 'Die Bücherwelt des 16. Jahrhunderts und die Frankfurter Büchermessen' 160

16 Helwig *Das deutsche Buchbinder-Handwerk* i 15. The author mentions Germany, Italy, France, and England.

17 Cf 90–1 below.

18 vl/Catalogue no 292. See Allen Ep 531:459–61/cwe Ep 531:512–14.

could add his own annotations. Despite his request the binders took their time and Erasmus, who soon became impatient, set Gillis after the culprits: 'Great heavens, what fate is bad enough for men who are so slow ... do all you can to prod these slowcoaches of yours.'[19]

It is hard to tell whether Erasmus acquired many books that had been bound in advance. He may, on occasion, have purchased a current work already bound in a shop, or have bought a second-hand copy of a book that had been bound by a previous owner. Yet the number should not be overestimated. There was certainly no question of ready-bound second-hand books in his purchase of about fifteen mainly old books in 1525. Many of the works then acquired, some of which were printed before the turn of the century, could probably be obtained from bookdealers in Venice: the publishers normally kept the unsold part of editions that had appeared many years earlier in stock, and always stored them in loose sheets.[20]

There is, however, one category of books that might lead us to expect a different pattern: the many works that Erasmus must have received as presents.[21] Would these gifts not by definition have included numerous books that were attractive externally, not only well bound but sometimes perhaps with boards finely tooled or decorated with gold? This expectation, however, cannot be confirmed with concrete examples. We can establish precisely when several books were presented to him and on what occasion, but we cannot know in what shape they arrived.

We are far better informed about the copies of his own works that Erasmus in turn presented to authorities and friends, books that were dispatched far and wide over what was then the world of culture. It is well worth inquiring about how he sent them, since this may teach us something about the books he himself received. There appears to have been no question of an established practice, and Erasmus acted according to the circumstances. Bound presentation copies seem to have been the exception rather than the rule. In these exceptional cases Erasmus sometimes saw that great pains were taken in the execution of the binding. He had special illuminated pages inserted in the bound presentation volume of the manuscript of his translation of Plutarch's *De discrimine adulatoris et amici*, which was dedicated to Henry VIII and sent to him in 1513. The same was done in the copy of a later edition of the translations from Plutarch bound with the first edition of his *Institutio principis christiani* and *Panegyricus* sent to Henry in 1517. Both books survive; the latter contains a vellum leaf with a fine painting of the royal arms.[22] In 1529 Erard de la Marck, bishop of Liège, received from Erasmus the two volumes of his revised New Testament, 'on parchment, elegantly illuminated, and by no means cheap,'[23] and we know what this meant: another two-volume

---

19 Allen Ep 491:1–3/CWE Ep 491:2–4. Lachner had sent seven complete copies of the *Opera*. Erasmus thought it could be bound in six volumes; Allen Epp 469:9–10, 477:1–3/CWE Epp 469:11–12, 477:3–5.

20 The remains of an edition were often used for a reissue many years later with a new title-page. See VL/ Catalogue no 204 for an example in Erasmus' library; and cf no 273.

21 See 33–52 above.

22 The translation of Plutarch is now in Cambridge University Library (MS Add. 6858). The *Institutio* is now in the library of Charlecote Park, Warwick. Cf Allen and CWE Epp 272 and 657 introductions. On the two gifts see Clough 'A presentation volume for Henry VIII, the Charlecote Park copy of Erasmus' *Institutio principis christiani*.' The painting in the *Institutio* is reproduced in CWE 5 110. Unfortunately the two leaves inserted in the manuscript of the Plutarch translation and presumably decorated in the same way have been cut out. There is a similarly decorated leaf with the coat of arms of Nicolas Ruistre, bishop of Arras, in the manuscript with the Libanius translations that Erasmus dedicated and presented to him in 1503 (Ep 177); it is now in Trinity College Library, Cambridge (MS R.9.26).

23 See *Catalogus lucubrationum* Allen I 43:40–2/CWE Ep 1341A:1718–19.

de luxe edition printed on vellum, also bound according to Erasmus' instructions but at the expense of Cuthbert Tunstall, has survived to this day.[24]

There are, then, examples of finely bound copies of Erasmus' own works that he sent as presents to patrons or friends.[25] But when it came down to it the binding, and a fortiori a particularly fine binding, was of subsidiary importance. Erasmus' primary concern was usually that a newly published work of his should reach the ecclesiastical or secular authorities to whom it was dedicated, or the close friend to whom he wished to send a copy, with as little delay as possible. In order to save the time it took to bind it, he would thus dispatch the book unbound, in loose gatherings. The social status of the recipient made no difference. His correspondent Bishop Sadoleto received the presentation copy of the edition of Basil, which Erasmus had dedicated to him, unbound.[26] Even Archduke Ferdinand, the brother of the emperor and his viceroy in the empire, had to content himself with unbound copies when he was offered the *Paraphrase on John*, which was dedicated to him, together with the earlier *Paraphrase on Matthew* in 1523.[27] Presenting books unbound seems to have become a fully accepted practice. Clement vii himself took no offence when the *Paraphrase on Acts*, which was dedicated to him and dispatched to Rome with great haste, arrived unbound. The pope let Erasmus know that he was delighted with the book, and on his orders 'it was immediately bound that he might all the more enjoy reading it through'; Erasmus was promptly rewarded with two hundred florins.[28] The copy of his *Paraphrase on Mark*, dedicated to Francis I, that Erasmus had sent to the French court by special courier at the end of December 1523 also shows the extreme haste with which books intended for rulers might be dispatched. Before the book came onto the market around March 1524, Froben had an advance copy printed with the title-page predated 1523. The still damp sheets were folded as soon as they came off the press, and we can see even today how the wet ink of the text on the second leaf has blotted onto the blank verso of the title-page.[29] Similarly, in September 1524 Erasmus sent unbound copies of the revised edition of Jerome's letters to his patron Archbishop William Warham 'while the ink was still fresh.'[30]

Besides his haste in dispatching them, another reason would have induced Erasmus to leave his presentation copies unbound, especially when they were of works published in folio. The heavy bindings reinforced with wooden boards were a handicap when it came to having the books transported. Even when they were not bound, presentation copies in a large

---

24 See Allen Ep 848:8–9/cwe Ep 848:8–10 and n; *Erasmus en zijn tijd* no 195. Previously in the library of York Minster, it is now in the possession of The Philips H. and A.S.W. Rosenbach Foundation, Philadelphia.

25 For example his patron Archbishop Warham received the volumes of the 1524–6 revised edition of Jerome 'beautifully bound' and 'decorated in gold'; Allen Epp 1828:76, 1831:5/cwe Epp 1828:84, 1831:7.

26 See vl/Catalogue no 189.

27 Ep 1333 to Ferdinand is the prefatory letter. Erasmus had wanted the books to be given by his patron Bernhard von Cles, Ferdinand's favourite and adviser, probably because he expected to receive a suitable reward. The books were bound later and Erasmus finally received 100 florins from the prince. See *Catalogus lucubrationum* Allen I 44:16–19 and Epp 1357, 1361:12–21, 1376:12–16/cwe Epp 1341A:1738–41, 1357, 1361:12–23, 1376:13–17.

28 Ep 1414 to Clement vii is the prefatory letter. See also Allen Epp 1442:4–6, 1466:3–6/cwe Epp 1442:4–6, 1466:4–7.

29 See Allen and cwe Epp 1400 (the prefatory letter) and 1403 (the covering letter for the presentation copy) line 23n/n6. The courier was Erasmus' servant-pupil Hilarius Bertholf. The book has survived; it is now in the Bibliothèque nationale (Rés A.1138).

30 Allen Ep 1488:36–7/cwe Ep 1488:45–6. Like the first edition of 1516, the revised edition was dedicated to Warham. The prefatory letters to the volumes containing Jerome's correspondence are Epp 1451, 1453, and 1465.

format gave rise to transport problems. 'If he can bear the burden' was Erasmus' significant reservation when he promised to send Leonard de Gruyères, an official of the bishop of Besançon, a copy of his recently published *Ecclesiastes* in 1535 and told him that the work, a bulky folio volume of nearly 500 pages, would be brought to him by his amanuensis Gilbert Cousin.[31] Every time a book was sent, an attempt had to be made to keep the bulk and weight within the narrow limits of the available means of conveyance. It made little difference whether Erasmus applied to an associate of his own, or to another courier who happened to be at hand, or even to travelling book dealers:[32] whoever was responsible for the transport, Erasmus always had to reckon on their preference for unbound copies. On the few occasions when he wanted to dispatch bound copies of one of his works in large format he went to considerable trouble. When all nine volumes of the revised edition of Jerome had been printed, for example, he did not have copies for Warham bound in Basel, where there were plenty of good binders, but sent the loose sheets to Pieter Gillis in Antwerp to have them bound and sent from there.[33]

The dispatch of quarto and octavo books did not, of course, give rise to similar problems, and the pressure to leave them unbound was thus far less. This may be why not only princes or high ecclesiastical officials but also lesser mortals were honoured with a bound presentation copy from Erasmus in a smaller format. Thus François Du Moulin, grand almoner in the service of the French king, received a copy of the octavo *Exomologesis*, which was dedicated to him, bound in a single volume with the French translation, which was published a few weeks later and was perhaps composed from the manuscript.[34]

In sum, Erasmus sent some presentation copies bound, but more unbound, to princes, patrons, and friends. We can assume that by and large, since the conditions of transport cannot have been very different, the same was true of the many books he received from others. In other words, it is probable that Erasmus received a large proportion of the books presented to him in an unbound state. Admittedly this cannot be strictly proved; as we have already mentioned, there is virtually no documentation on the state of the books received. But a single example that can, as it happens, be documented serves to confirm this inference. The 1527 Cologne octavo edition in Erasmus' library containing two polemical works by Lorenzo Valla was almost certainly a present from the youthful Christoph von Carlowitz, who had himself re-edited the two texts. He very probably handed the books to Erasmus in person when he was in Basel. This must have been an unbound copy, for Erasmus had it bound together with one of his own writings a little later.[35]

After what has been said, so much would seem to be sure: Erasmus himself was responsible for the binding of many of his books, whether he bought them or received them as presents. So what do we know about his direct dealings with bookbinders? Very little. During his third stay in England (1509–14) he is said to have been in touch with binders. In Cambridge he probably stayed briefly with the bookbinder and dealer Garret Godfrey in 1511, and his acquaintances there, to whom he sent special greetings many years later, included not only Godfrey but also the better known stationer and bookbinder Nicolaas Spierinck, who (like

---

31 Allen Ep 3063:11–12. On Léonard de Gruyères see Allen and cwe Ep 1534 introductions; cebr ii 141.

32 On the transportation of presentation copies, see 45–8 above. Michel Parmentier from Lyon was one of the many itinerant booksellers who contributed more than once to the conveyance of Erasmus' presentation copies, for example to Bishop Sadoleto in Carpentras; cf ak iv 108–9 Ep 1610.

33 Allen Epp 1740:16–17 and n, 1828:74–6 / cwe Epp 1740:16–17, 1828:83–5; cf n19 above.

34 Cf 38 above.

35 vl/Catalogue no 153 #2

Godfrey) was born in the Low Countries.[36] This tells us little about the commercial aspect of his dealings. Both men could have done some binding for Erasmus at a time when he was buying a fair number of books.[37] But this is a mere supposition, which cannot be confirmed by any concrete evidence. Oddly enough the manuscript containing his translation of Plutarch's *De discrimine adulatoris et amici*, which Erasmus sent to Henry VIII from Cambridge in about July 1513 and which has been preserved in its original binding, appears to have been bound not there but in London.[38]

Erasmus is unlikely to have been actively and directly involved in the binding of his books in the later years of his life. By that time helpful friends relieved him of much of this responsibility. During the years he spent in Brabant his friend Pieter Gillis, whose hospitality he enjoyed regularly, not only when he was on the move but also after he had settled in Leuven, was always ready to assist him. As we have observed, Gillis saw to the binding of the volumes of the great Jerome edition, which came from Basel in loose sheets. Even when Erasmus was living in Basel, he sent Gillis the loose sheets of the revised edition to have bound in Brabant before sending them on to Warham in England.[39]

That Erasmus did not personally have to worry about binding problems in his Basel and Freiburg years is all the more likely when we see how other scholars and men of letters, whether they lived nearby or far away, ordered the bulk of their books in Basel through acquaintances. Some of them were aided by two of Erasmus' very closest friends. Beatus Rhenanus, for example, who remained in Basel until 1526, regularly acted as intermediary for Huldrych Zwingli in Zürich and for Otto Brunfels in Sélestat (then still known as Schlettstadt), as well as for others.[40] He saw to the purchase of the books they had requested and, whenever necessary, also had them bound. In the latter case he took into account the special preferences expressed by his friends concerning the material of the binding: the type of leather to be used for the covering, for example pigskin or calf (*suillis an vitulinis tergoribus*) or the material used for the boards, wood or cardboard. He was also responsible for settling the price, and when a binder appeared to have made a mistake in sewing the gatherings in sequence, he had the error remedied by an expert.[41] Bonifacius Amerbach, who had returned to Basel in 1525, occupied a similar role. He placed numerous book orders for his friends and colleagues, the lawyers Andrea Alciati, who lived in Avignon from 1518 to 1522 and again from 1527 to 1529, and Udalricus Zasius in Freiburg and, when requested to do so, he made sure that the books purchased were bound.[42] He provided the same assistance to his brother-in-law J. Fuchs, who lived in nearby Neuchâtel.[43] Although there was no shortage

---

36 Allen Ep 1656:18–20/CWE Ep 1656:21–3. On Godfrey see Allen Epp 248:44n, 456:280–1 and n/CWE Epp 248:55n, 456:312–13 and n; *Erasmus and Cambridge* 221; Nixon *Five Centuries of English Bookbinding* 26; CEBR II 111–12. On Spierinck see Allen Ep 1656:19n; *Erasmus and Cambridge* 225; Nixon *Five Centuries of English Bookbinding* 28; CEBR III 272.

37 See 24–5 above.

38 Clough 'A presentation volume for Henry VIII …' 199; cf 87 above. For further information on the London binder see Garrod 'Erasmus and his English patrons' 8.

39 See 86–7, 89 above. On a bound book from Gillis' own library, an edition of Silius Italicus printed in Florence in 1515, see Indestege 'Een band teruggevonden uit het bezit van de Antwerpse humanist Peter Gilles' and [Martens, Dirk] *Tentoonstelling Dirk Martens 1473–1973* (exhibition catalogue) 129.

40 Zwingli applied to Beatus Rhenanus on various occasions on behalf of Michael Sanderus, Cardinal Schinner's secretary, among others.

41 See for example BRE 136 Ep 88, 138 Ep 90, 141 Ep 93, 586 Ep 444.

42 See the detailed indexes in AK II–IV.

43 AK IV 167 Ep 1686

of good bookbinders in Basel,[44] the close connection of Beatus Rhenanus and Bonifacius Amerbach with the Froben firm makes it likely that the books they ordered on behalf of others were usually completed by binders in the pay of the firm or by binders who worked for them in a formally autonomous position. They did not always have to deal directly with the binders. If the purchase was one of Froben's own publications, the arrangement was made by the firm; Beatus Rhenanus advised Zwingli to apply directly to Froben for the binding in four or five volumes of the edition of Jerome.[45] Some binders were well known. In the early 1520s one is often mentioned by name, a man obviously reputed for his skill and thus preferred to others. This was Matthias Biermann, whom Amerbach described as 'very skilled in his trade.'[46] He practised as a binder as well as a bookdealer and had regular connections with the Frobens: Wolfgang Lachner, Johannes Froben's father-in-law and, in the last years of his life (he died early in 1518), the manager of the Froben publishing firm, had once been his employer.

If he had wished, Erasmus could easily have had his books expertly bound in any manner he desired close to where he was living. Matthias Biermann, who was so much in demand, lived literally round the corner from his house 'Zur alten Treu' on the Nadelberg, while his bookshop and bindery was on the Fischmarkt. Also on the Fischmarkt was the bookshop with a bindery joined on to it that had been successfully carried on since Lachner's death in 1518 by others.[47] Yet it is doubtful whether Erasmus often dealt with the binding orders himself. It is more likely that Beatus Rhenanus and Bonifacius Amerbach, who were so ready to help scholars living outside Basel (both close friends and others) to purchase books and have them bound, were at all times prepared to perform any service their older and revered friend might require. We may also assume that Erasmus made use of their services whenever he needed to do so (and that, demanding as he could be, he regarded this as his due). Surely Bonifacius Amerbach in particular, Erasmus' intimate friend, who was constantly about the house from 1525 on and who saw to all his needs, occasionally passed on binding orders and kept an eye on their execution. Amerbach's personal intervention was perhaps not always necessary; Erasmus could have reached general agreements directly with Froben about the binding of his own publications. Even so, Amerbach probably conveyed to the printer any additional or more specific requirements. His assistance, on which Erasmus could always count in Basel, was also assured when Erasmus moved to Freiburg. Not only was Amerbach Erasmus' most important correspondent by far between 1529 and 1535 but he also visited him on occasion. He continued to provide a link with the Froben press and, in a broader sense, with the Basel book market. Erasmus had but to name a book he wished to acquire, or simply to consult, to be sure that through the good offices of his friend the work would be lying on his lectern in the shortest possible time.

---

44 In 1475 Basel already had five bookbinders out of a population of 9,000 inhabitants, and between 1501 and 1550 seventeen binders were in the Safranzunft; Helwig *Das deutsche Buchbinder-Handwerk* II 62.

45 BRE 136 Ep 88 (from Zwingli). The copy was intended for Michael Sanderus; see n40 above.

46 AK III 106–7 Ep 1081. On Biermann see AK II 112–13 Ep 611 with n4 and 354 Ep 841 with n1; *Zwinglis Briefwechsel* I 139 n8; and Grimm 'Buchführer' 1383. During Erasmus' first stay in Basel, Biermann's business was made over to Wolf Lorenz Fust, who had very close connections with the Froben firm: Grimm 'Buchführer' 1383. On Lachner see 25 above.

47 After Lachner's death in 1518 the business carried on in the house 'Zum roten Ring' came in time to Johann Schabler (frequently called Wattenschnee), who also had a say in the Froben firm. Subsequently it was run by Konrad Resch; Grimm 'Buchführer' 1391–2.

5

What the *Versandliste* Does Not Include

The books and manuscripts in the *Versandliste* made up by far the largest and most important part of Erasmus' library. But there was more in his collection when he died: manuscripts; 115 of his own works, almost all Froben editions, listed in a separate inventory; and papers and books not thought appropriate for transfer to Łaski and therefore not included in the inventory.

The *Versandliste* is uninformative about Erasmus' manuscripts. A few modern manuscripts were listed, but almost certainly no ancient and valuable codices. And yet we know Erasmus possessed them, for his will of 1527 mentions 'Greek manuscripts on parchment and paper.' After Erasmus' death Łaski showed an interest in three particular manuscripts, and we know that he managed to secure at least one of them, an old Latin codex that must have been sent to Poland after the library as a whole had already arrived. The separate inventory of Erasmus' own works, the *Catalogus librorum Erasmi*, must have been drawn up shortly after his death. Most of the editions can be identified, and it is clear that the books were found in Erasmus' house on his death and formed part of his estate. Finally, it is very likely that the estate also included books that had never been intended for sale and transfer to Łaski and for that reason were excluded from the *Versandliste*. They must have been stored, possibly in chests, separately from the books listed, perhaps because they were still unbound, or perhaps because their special character meant that they belonged more appropriately in what we can call, with some justification, Erasmus' 'private archive' rather than in the library, which was easily accessible to his friends and others.

In what follows we shall try to discover more about these three categories: the manuscripts, the collection of his own works, and the more amorphous residue that presumably remained in Basel after the library proper had been shipped to Łaski in Poland. As far as the scanty evidence permits, we shall examine more closely these components of Erasmus' library and the way in which they were housed.

As we shall see, Erasmus was not rich in manuscripts, and the few he owned were most probably not of any special importance or quality by modern standards, with one spectacular exception: the Codex Arcerianus. This famous manuscript, which is still preserved, eventually came into Łaski's hands even though it was not in the *Versandliste*. He went to some trouble to acquire it. Under the terms of the agreement Erasmus negotiated with Łaski in 1525, future acquisitions were included in the sale of the library but manuscripts, which were very expensive, were explicitly excluded. Two years later, in his first will of 1527, Erasmus repeated this stipulation in slightly different terms: if Łaski wished to acquire the Greek codices on parchment or paper from his library, he must pay for them separately.[1]

---

1 Allen vi 504 Appendix 19 / cwe 12 542 'Erasmus' First Will': 'Excepti sunt libri Graeci calamo descripti in membranis aut chartis pro quibus, si volet habere, numerabit separatim'; cf 53 n1 above.

Erasmus' executors, Bonifacius Amerbach, Nicolaus Episcopius, and Hieronymus Froben, conscientiously adhered to both the letter and the spirit of this clause; in December 1536, after receiving the balance of the purchase price, they sent the library to Poland but kept back what they clearly regarded as the special manuscripts described in the will. Łaski was not satisfied. He laid claim to several particular manuscripts that he felt were his on the grounds of his agreements with Erasmus. Apart from two manuscripts of Chrysostom, not further described, he was eager to obtain three others: *Augustinus de civitate dei litteris Longobardicis in membranis, Chrysostomus in Acta graece maiore forma in membranis scriptus, [praeterea] fragmentum antiquitatum cum picturis in membranis.*[2]

Further discussions seem to have ended in agreement, for one of these three texts, the illustrated *fragmentum antiquitatum*, if this can really be identified with the Codex Arcerianus, came into Łaski's possession. It is an early sixth-century manuscript that contains the earliest and best text of the Roman *agrimensores* or *geomatici* (land surveyors); by modern standards, therefore, it was perhaps the most valuable item in the whole of Erasmus' library. There is no watertight theory about the provenance of the manuscript, though it is generally accepted that it had lain in the abbey of Bobbio, where it was known to Gerbert d'Aurillac, until shortly before Erasmus acquired it.[3] How did Erasmus come to possess it? We shall never know for certain. The old assumption, endorsed by Theodor Mommsen, that he bought or acquired it from the papal secretary Tommaso Inghirami during his visit to Rome in 1509, now appears untenable. Giovanni Mercati thought that Andrea Alciati might have played some part in its acquisition; the famous jurist was living in Milan from 1523 to 1527 and searched for manuscripts for Basel publishers. If Erasmus acquired the manuscript at that time and not in 1509, that would tally with his own list of acquisitions since 1525 on which, according to Łaski, the *fragmentum antiquitatum* appeared.[4]

Mercati's speculation suggests another possibility. Might not the codex have reached Basel in the baggage of Hieronymus Froben, who criss-crossed northern Italy in 1526 looking for manuscripts? Young Froben had previously searched for manuscripts nearer home, and not always very scrupulously; Erasmus wrote rather cynically of this journey, before the event, 'He has gone to your part of the world in search of old manuscripts, which he is prepared to purchase, beg, borrow, or steal.' Hieronymus, who also passed through Milan on his travels, where he visited Alciati, did not return empty-handed, and Erasmus profited

---

2 AK IV 448 Ep 2072 (from Łaski), V 44–5 Ep 2130 (from Łaski), V 116–17 Ep 2214 (from Andreas Frycz Modrzewski, a protégé of Łaski and his agent in this matter)

3 A chief source of information about the Roman land surveyors is the *Corpus agrimensorum*, compiled about the fourth century AD (the late Latin term *geomatici* is less frequently used). The two oldest manuscripts of the *Corpus* are bound in the same volume in the Herzog August Bibliothek in Wolfenbüttel. In 1493 the Acerianus was at Bobbio, where Abbot Gerbert, who was famously interested in ancient science and mathematics, studied it about 981. Gerbert, who became Pope Sylvester II in AD 999, was a scholar and teacher educated at the Benedictine monastery of Aurillac. He later studied at the cathedral school of Reims, where he subsequently became a master. About 982 he was made abbot of Bobbio, a monastery northeast of Genoa founded by St Columbanus in the seventh century and known for its collection of early manuscripts.

4 AK V 117 Ep 2214. The codex actually consists of two uncial manuscripts written in Italy, Arcerianus A, presumably early sixth century, and Arcerianus B, late fifth or early sixth century; the latter 'is inferior to the A in most of its readings and has no illustrations.' On the codex, its importance, and its history see the introduction by Hans Butzmann to the facsimile edition, *Corpus agrimensorum romanorum, Codex Arcerianus A der Herzog August-Bibliothek zu Wolfenbüttel (Cod. Guelf. 36, 23 A)*. Cf also Dilke *The Roman Land Surveyors* 128–9 and 212. On Tommaso Inghirami see Allen Ep 1347:264n / CWE Ep 1347 n42; CEBR II 223–5.

from his searches; we learn in passing that he received two manuscripts of Chrysostom.[5] But that he came into possession of the manuscript of the *agrimensores* at the same time must remain conjecture.

However and wherever he acquired it, there is nothing to suggest that Erasmus ever studied the manuscript seriously, for there are no marginal notes in his hand. We may even wonder if he had more than a superficial interest in it, for he did not bother to write his usual *Sum Erasmi* on the valuable but carelessly treated unbound parchment leaves. Nor did Łaski mark the manuscript with any sign of his ownership. Nevertheless, that both men owned it is certain from the inscriptions of Gérard Mortaigne and Regnerus Praedinius, the two subsequent owners of various other books from Erasmus' library. Mortaigne, a friend and fellow exile of Łaski, wrote his name on the recto of the first leaf, and Praedinius, rector of St Martin's school in Groningen, added his ex libris in the same place, in the year in which he acquired it: *Regneri nunc sum Praedinii 1559* 'I now belong to Regnerus Praedinius 1559.' On the recto of the second leaf he added *Et hic ex bibliotheca Erasmi* 'and it is here from the library of Erasmus.'[6] Some years after Praedinius' death in 1559 the codex came into the hands of his pupil and friend Johannes Arcerius Theodoretus, who was from 1589 to 1604 professor of Greek at the University of Franeker. He was the first to make a thorough philological study of the ancient surveyors' texts, and this earned the manuscript its current and not undeserved name of Codex Arcerianus. In the seventeenth century the manuscript was in the study of the Leiden scholar Petrus Scriverius, and when his estate was sold at auction in 1663 it was bought by Duke August of Brunswick. That was the end of its wanderings: it is still in the old ducal library at Wolfenbüttel.[7]

Łaski probably had less success in his attempt to procure the other two manuscripts he had demanded – Augustine's *De civitate Dei* and Chrysostom's *In Acta Apostolorum*. As soon as the demand came to his notice, Bonifacius Amerbach must have voiced his doubts as to whether the codices had actually belonged to Erasmus. But Łaski thought he could prove that they had been the testator's property and not merely on permanent loan. In 1538 he had his agent show Nicolaus Episcopius a list drawn up by Erasmus in his own hand of the acquisitions that had enriched the library since the sale contract had been concluded; that list, he said, explicitly mentioned the manuscripts. Erasmus had written to him at the time that the manuscript of Augustine was on loan to Goclenius, but that those who had books on loan from his library must be made to return them.[8] The extant correspondence does not tell us how this matter was resolved, but there is reason to assume that Łaski was unlucky, and that Amerbach's doubts were borne out.

The codex of Augustine was probably the same manuscript that Erasmus had lent to Vives in 1521–2 to use in preparing a separate edition of *De civitate Dei*;[9] in 1526, in connection with his own edition of the *Opera omnia* of Augustine, Erasmus sent a message to his friend Pieter Gillis asking him to return the manuscript if he still happened to have it. On this

---

5 Allen Ep 1705:6–8 with 6n / CWE Ep 1705:8–10 with n3; cf Allen Epp 1767:11–12 and n, 1774 / CWE Epp 1767:12 and n, 1774. Johann Huttich commented that in the library of the late Joannes Dalburg at the castle of Ladenburg, Froben 'turned everything upside down'; BRE 373 Ep 264.
6 See Butzmann (n4 above) 2, 5.
7 For the auction, see *Libri appendiciarii Bibliothecae Scriverianae ... quae auctione publica distribuentur [8] Aug. 1663,* MS no 136.
8 AK V 116–17 Ep 2214 (Modrzewski to Amerbach)
9 See VL/Catalogue no 242.

occasion he described the manuscript in the same words as Łaski: 'in Lombardic script.'[10] Erasmus learned through Conradus Goclenius that the 'old manuscript' of *The City of God* had been returned to Cologne, where it evidently belonged.[11] Erasmus must have managed to get it back, for in the fifth volume of the Augustine edition, published in 1529, the title-page announces that he had emended the text of *De civitate Dei* from a manuscript supplied to him by Gillis. Allen assumed that it remained in his possession afterwards.[12]

Something similar happened with the other manuscript Łaski claimed. Łaski described it as *e Patavio allatum*; he must have been referring to a manuscript that had been offered for sale in Padua in 1525 containing Chrysostom's sermons on the Acts of the Apostles in the original Greek. It had come into the possession of Reginald Pole, who had lent it to Erasmus. In the following years Erasmus translated and published several sermons from it, although from the start he had his doubts about their authorship.[13] He kept the manuscript long after an amanuensis had transcribed it, at least until August 1531, when he assured Pole that he would send it back as soon as he had found someone to whom he could entrust it.[14] We do not know if he finally returned it, and if so when.

If Erasmus confused Łaski about the ownership of these manuscripts of Augustine and Chrysostom by suggesting in his list of acquisitions they were his own property, this is less surprising than it appears when we recall the prevailing attitude to handwritten books at that time. The search for good texts of classical and early Christian authors that had begun with humanism brought more and more ancient manuscripts to light in the sixteenth century. As a rule it was not too difficult to penetrate their most frequent hiding places, the rich libraries of monastic houses; the practice of the famous library of the abbey of St Gallen, which was practically inaccessible to outsiders,[15] was not the norm. Ancient manuscripts, apart from the costly and finely illuminated ones, were not regarded as objects of special value in the material sense, and they were often treated with amazing carelessness. When they found that to be the case, the hunters of manuscripts, including professional publishers who scented copy for new editions, seized the opportunity (not always very scrupulously) to relieve the monks of their manuscripts.[16] Bona fide scholars, certainly reputable ones, could count on cooperation and an accommodating attitude as a matter of course. They were allowed to consult an old manuscript in which they were interested on the spot, copy it or have it transcribed, and often even take it home with them or have it sent, without any objection. They were hardly ever bound by a fixed term of loan, or if so, rarely took it seriously.[17] When he died Reuchlin had had a manuscript from the Dominican monastery

---

10 Allen Ep 1758:9–10/cwe Ep 1758:8–10. The phrase *scriptum Longobardicis letteris* in itself says little, because codices thought to be very old were often described in these words.

11 Allen Ep 1778:24–5/cwe Ep 1778:24–6: *apud Machabeitanos Coloniae*, a convent of Benedictine nuns in Cologne, with whose warden Erasmus maintained good contacts; see Allen and cwe Ep 1346 introductions and vl/Catalogue no 193.

12 Allen Ep 1309 introduction

13 ak v 44 Ep 2130 (from Łaski); cf Allen Epp 1623:9–10 and n, 1675:6–8/cwe Epp 1623:11–12 and n3, 1675:9–10 and n4. For Erasmus' translations, in *Chrysostomi lucubrationes* (Basel 1527) and *Opera* (1530), and his doubts about Chrysostom's authorship, see vl/Catalogue nos 150 #1 and 410.

14 Allen Ep 2526:7–8

15 Cf bre 354 Ep 251.

16 For Hieronymus Froben's activity in this field see 93–4 and n5 above. The two most successful manuscript hunters of Erasmus' time were probably Beatus Rhenanus and Johann Sichard. For them see Lehmann *Johannes Sichardus und die von ihm benutzten Bibliotheken und Handschriften*.

17 Cf Kramm *Deutsche Bibliotheken unter dem Einfluss von Humanismus und Reformation* 185: 'Überaus lockere Anschauungen von Eigentum und Leihgut waren während des ganzen Zeitraums ... gang und gäbe.' For the

in Basel for thirty years; it was perhaps only thanks to the casual activity of the last librarian that it returned to its place of origin.[18] The user of a manuscript on long loan (perhaps scarcely missed) whose return was not requested could easily come in the end to feel that he was at least its de facto owner. The original owner would have worried less about the loss if the text had meanwhile been disseminated in print, for in the view of the time this meant that it had lost its original value.

Could this have happened to the codex that Erasmus had procured through the intervention of Lord Mountjoy from the abbey of St Martin at Tournai to use in the preparation of his edition of Suetonius, which was published in 1517? We are not told in so many words that he received the manuscript as a present, but he never restored it to his patron or to the abbey; it remained in his possession until he gave it to Henricus Glareanus shortly before his death.[19] Scholars of the time often behaved in remarkably high-handed fashion with manuscripts lent to them, and Erasmus was no exception. As we shall see, he treated such manuscripts as if they were his own.[20]

As far as the codices of Augustine and Chrysostom were concerned, therefore, we may wonder if it would have made much difference to Erasmus whether he had received them on permanent loan or owned them outright. This makes it easier to understand that he lumped together all the works, both written and printed, that had come into his hands since 1525 and entered them in the same list, without worrying about possible misunderstanding.[21] It seems to us rather thoughtless, or at the very least premature. Did Erasmus assume, consciously or unconsciously, that the owners would no longer care to have the two codices back once the texts had been published in 'modern' printed editions?[22]

Our assumption that Erasmus never owned many exceptional or valuable manuscripts can be substantiated in more than one way. Most important, there is not a scrap of evidence to the contrary. Is it not proof enough that in 1536 Łaski only claimed those codices that seemed worth the trouble, and that two of them were really the property of third parties? Erasmus rarely mentioned any manuscript in his own possession in his correspondence. In 1500 we hear how he took the trouble to have the manuscript of 'Augustine's *Enchiridion*, written on parchment,' which had been left behind in England, packed for shipment to France with another, probably printed, book and some of his clothes.[23] But this need not have been an old manuscript of any value for the textual tradition. It was much more likely to have been a recent transcript of Augustine's little manual, intended for regular reading and therefore written on the most durable material, parchment.

Unlike such contemporaries as Reuchlin or Budé, to say nothing of many Italian humanists, who owned important private collections of manuscripts, Erasmus did not base any of his editions of classical or patristic texts on a manuscript in his own collection, except

---

practice of the library of the Sorbonne, where even in the fourteenth century 'some professors kept out books on indefinite loan,' see Ullman *Studies in the Italian Renaissance* 43.

18 This is the manuscript, also used by Erasmus, of the New Testament (excluding the Apocalypse) now in the Universitätsbibliothek Basel (MS A.N.IV.2, now Cod 1); see Vernet 'Les manuscrits grecs de Jean de Raguse' 84 no 12. See also ASD VI-4 3–4.

19 See Ep 586 (the prefatory letter); VL/Catalogue no 261; Husner 'Bibliothek' 257 n102. The Codex Tornacensis is now lost.

20 See 103 and n59 below. There is no record that Erasmus ever returned the manuscript of Lorenzo Valla's *In Latinam Novi Testamenti interpretationem adnotationes* which he discovered in 1504 and published in 1505 (Ep 182).

21 See 94 above.

22 The *Homiliae in Acta Apostolorum*, although not recognized by Erasmus as the work of John Chrysostom, were published by Froben in 1531, certainly not without his knowledge; see VL/Catalogue no 410.

23 Cf 18 and n9 above.

perhaps his *editio princeps* of the treatise on divine grace and free will of Bishop Faustus of Riez (c 405–c 495). This edition was based on an eighth-century codex discovered in an old library, probably in Spain, by Count Hermann von Neuenahr, who put it at Erasmus' disposal. Erasmus must have been surprised to find this subject, which was once again highly topical, treated in a work more than a thousand years old yet 'Erasmian' in spirit. There is no doubt that it was Erasmus who arranged for the treatise to be printed in 1528 by Joannes Faber Emmeus, then still working in Basel, and he wrote a prefatory letter to Ferry de Carondelet (Ep 2002). But although Erasmus was involved in the first edition of the text, it is an open question whether he formally owned the manuscript at the time. There is no explicit proof that von Neuenahr gave him the manuscript as a gift and not just to use; nor do we know if the manuscript was returned to Erasmus after it had served as printer's copy for Emmeus. All we can be sure of is that it was not lost: unlike so many others that were used in this way, it has survived.[24]

Reference to Erasmus' manuscript collection appears in the text of his first will (1527). As we saw, he included a clause that Łaski might buy, if he wanted them, any 'Greek manuscripts on parchment and paper' that had not been included in the sale of his library, but only for separate payment. If these were manuscripts already in Erasmus' possession when he made his will, then they must have been recent acquisitions. The agreement of 1525 had already stipulated, in similar terms, that Łaski would have to buy valuable manuscripts – not specifically Greek, as in the will – separately from the rest of the library; the provision seemingly referred to manuscripts that Erasmus did not own at the time but might acquire later, perhaps at a high price.[25] Possibly manuscripts acquired between 1525 and 1527, one or more of which Hieronymus Froben may have brought back from Italy, were in fact the first manuscripts that Erasmus possessed, and he wanted to stipulate special payment for them.[26] It is not very likely that the transaction of 1525 included manuscripts Erasmus already owned, which were sold and half paid for at the same time as the rest of the library. If after Erasmus' death Amerbach considered manuscripts transferred to Łaski in the agreement of 1525 to be part of the library, they would have been entered in the *Versandliste* and sent to Poland with the books.

Do manuscripts actually appear in the *Versandliste*? Among the hundreds of printed books there are no more than eight handwritten texts in all. Four of them need not be considered here, because they dated from Erasmus' own times: a handwritten copy of his own *De copia verborum* and a manuscript of an unpublished book by his fellow Augustinian Jan Mombaer, bound with two other works.[27] Only four of Erasmus' manuscripts can be described as old and valuable. Two of them were Greek texts, homilies of John Chrysostom, one an exegesis of the Epistle to the Corinthians, the other of the Epistles to the Hebrews and the Galatians, with other unspecified works. The two others contained texts, either collected or bound in one volume, of Cicero's *De natura deorum* and *De divinatione*. But were all four truly examples of those venerable (*vetusti*) or most venerable (*vetustissimi*) codices, as they were so readily called, which the true humanist hoped to be able to use to emend the corrupt texts handed down to him? A large dose of doubt is appropriate.

---

24 See VL/Catalogue no 13 #2. The manuscript is now in the Bibliothèque nationale in Paris (cod. lat. 2166).

25 See 92 and n1 above.

26 On Froben's search for manuscripts and the possibility that the Codex Arcerianus may have reached Basel at this time, see 93–4 and n5 above.

27 See VL/Catalogue nos 244 and 387 ##2–3; cf 127 below.

Probably the Chrysostom manuscripts were transcripts. Just as the modern researcher has a photocopy or microfilm at his elbow, Erasmus, when he was attentively occupied with his edition of Chrysostom in 1530, had transcripts made, for regular use, of old manuscripts of several of his works. He mentioned some of them in his letters, and one, a copy of Chrysostom's commentary on Romans made by his servant-pupil Nicolaas Kan, whom he praised as an experienced copyist from Greek, has been preserved at Wolfenbüttel. It seems very likely that the two manuscripts of Chrysostom in the *Versandliste* were no more than copies of this kind.[28]

The case of the Ciceronian manuscripts was different, to the extent that Erasmus did not need them for his own edition of the texts, and at first sight there does not seem to have been any other reason why he should have had copies of ancient codices made for his private use. On the other hand it is equally difficult to imagine that he could have acquired any manuscripts of such well-known works as *De natura deorum* and *De divinatione* that were still of interest or value. We must think rather of 'ordinary' copies, which were numerous and widely circulated in the age of the humanists. Perhaps they were a gift from the Augustinian canon and supplier of one of the manuscripts that he had used for his edition of the *Tusculan Disputations*, a man who for pure love of Cicero had copied out almost all his works.[29]

For many years it was thought that the Codex Arcerianus was the only old manuscript from Erasmus' library to survive the ravages of time. But another has now been found in the Vatican Library: a late twelfth-century manuscript of Palladius' *Opus agriculturae* presented to Erasmus in 1535 by Pierre de Mornieu, abbot of the Cistercian abbey at Saint-Sulpice near Chambéry in Savoy. The donor and the year of the gift were revealed by the use of an ultraviolet lamp on the very faded ex libris. The young Mornieu had been a correspondent of Erasmus since at least 1527. He had studied in Basel and presumably made his acquaintance there. Later he invited Erasmus to visit his abbey, and it is a sign of a lasting relationship that he should have presented him, four years later, with the Palladius codex, which was not perhaps indispensable to the abbey library.[30] Łaski certainly never knew of the donation. In 1536 the manuscript, in all probability, remained in Basel, where it surfaced again, in time, in the hands of Professor Henricus Justus. He gave it in 1594 to the printer-publisher Hieronymus Commelin to use in preparing for the press his well-known Heidelberg edition of the *Rei rusticae auctores latini veteres*, published in 1595. The manuscript was bought from Commelin's estate in 1607 by the Leiden scholar Petrus Scriverius, who also managed to secure the codex with the *agrimensores*.[31] Before Scriverius died, not later than 1656, it was in the possession of Queen Christina of Sweden. It has now lain for more than three centuries with the other manuscripts from the queen's collection in the Vatican Library, where it was recognized as the property of Erasmus by Elisabeth Pellegrin.[32] In itself her discovery was unexpected, but no far-reaching conclusion can be drawn from it. Pierre de Mornieu's present was a casual gift and does not mean that Erasmus' library was frequently enriched by such donations. Our assumption that he owned very few manuscripts can stand.

---

28 See VL/Catalogue nos 234 and 235.

29 See VL/Catalogue no 253.

30 Epp 1777 and 2473

31 See 93 above.

32 See 'Un ex-libris autographe d'Erasme dans un manuscrit de l'*Opus agriculturae* de Palladius (Vat. Reg. Lat. 1252).'

In addition to the books that appear on the *Versandliste*, a collection of Erasmus' own works was inventoried separately. We cannot affirm that Erasmus regarded them as part of what he considered to be the library he had sold to Jan Łaski, nor can we prove that they were allocated to Łaski and shipped to Cracow with the rest of the library. The surviving inventory of this collection, the *Catalogus librorum Erasmi*, which lists editions up to the beginning of 1536, was drawn up after Erasmus' death, presumably at about the same time as the *Versandliste*. Amerbach was closely and actively involved, made corrections and comments, and even inserted several titles to complete the list, which was compiled largely by a colleague. Yet years later, when the document fell into his hands again, it seems that he was no longer entirely sure what had happened to these books, for on the last page he deleted his own previous comment and wrote 'List of the books ... of Erasmus sent to Baron Łaski in Poland' (*Index librorum ... Erasmi Lasco Baroni in Poloniam missorum*), but added the words 'if I am not mistaken' (*nisi fallor*). But it does not matter where the books ended up in 1536; the point is that they belonged to Erasmus and were still in the house 'Zum Luft' when he died. Amerbach, as his earliest comment on the reverse of the list shows, knew exactly where they were: 'in a chest near the window overlooking the courtyard' (*in arca aulae versus fenestram*).[33] The contents of the collection are easy to establish, for most of the editions can be accurately identified thanks to the publication dates and formats that Amerbach noted.

Comparison of the *Catalogus* with the titles of Erasmus' own works and editions of texts in the *Versandliste* shows that the separate collection largely consisted of duplicates of works that were already in the 'main library,' although the two collections complemented each other. Several works absent from the *Versandliste* were found in the chest near the window, including several minor works that we might not have expected Erasmus to preserve, since analysis of the *Versandliste* led to the conclusion that Erasmus had little interest in keeping obsolete editions of his works.[34] Among these were two early editions later superseded by more than one corrected reprint: the 1507 Aldine edition of the translations of Euripides, and Erasmus' first printed translation of Plutarch, a London Pynson edition of 1513.[35] Notable among the almost exclusively Latin Froben editions listed in the *Catalogus* is the only German translation of one of his works that can be shown to have been found in his estate, the 'Open letter to one of his good friends concerning the sacrament of the body and blood of Christ' (*Sendtbrieff an einen seiner guten Freunde von dem Sacrament des leybs vnnd bluts Christi*).[36] The original version of this letter from Erasmus to Conradus Pellicanus was circulating in manuscript in October 1525 and must have been printed soon afterwards under the title *Expostulatio ad amicum quendam admodum pia et Christiana*. Only the separate collection contained a copy of this work, listed directly below the *Sendtbrieff*.[37] The two pamphlets, little books of four leaves, were published without any indication of place or publisher, but the *Sendtbrieff* was printed at Hagenau by Farkall in 1526 and the *Expostulatio* at Basel by Froben in 1526. The Froben printing must certainly

---

33 The inventory is in the University Library in Basel (MS C VIA 71 fols 11–14); see the author's transcript of the manuscript and the expanded text 451–74 below. As the error of transcription in no 98 shows, the compiler of the inventory must have known of the imminent or recently published Froben edition of the *Catalogi duo operum Desiderii Erasmi* (1537).

34 See chapter 2 above for Erasmus' policy on ridding the library of 'ballast.'

35 *Catalogus* nos 42 and 82

36 See *Catalogus* no 93.

37 *Catalogus* no 94. Cf Augustijn *Erasmus en de reformatie* 172; ASD IX-1 217, 219. The letter is Ep 1637.

have had Erasmus' full cooperation, for he could not allow the rumour spread by Pellicanus, that his views of the Eucharist agreed with those of Zwingli, to go unchallenged.

The chest by the window overlooking the courtyard also contained works for which Erasmus' share in the authorship has never been clearly determined. The *Consilium cuiusdam ex animo cupientis esse consultum et Romani Pontificis dignitati et christianae religionis tranquillitati* was published anonymously and without the name of the printer in late 1520; this is currently regarded as a 'joint production' of Erasmus and the Dominican Johannes Faber of Augsburg.[38] The equally anonymous and unattributed *Expositio fidelis de morte Th. Mori*, written in the form of a letter from 'P.M.,' was published by Froben in 1535. According to Allen the *Expositio* may originally have been begun by Philippus Montanus but was probably completed, perhaps under Erasmus' guidance, by Gilbert Cousin. According to De Vocht, however, Montanus was only a straw man and Erasmus was the true author of the book, except for the factual report of the trial and execution of More, which was inserted.[39] Another work that Erasmus may have had a hand in is the Froben edition, published in August 1520, of *Epistolae aliquot eruditorum virorum ex quibus perspicuum quanta sit Eduardi Lei virulentia*, a collection of letters in support of Erasmus in the controversy with his critic Edward Lee. The new and greatly enlarged edition may have been instigated without Erasmus' knowledge by his friends in England and Basel, but nevertheless he had a special connection with it: he had been closely and actively involved in the original Antwerp edition some months earlier.[40] Two noteworthy outsiders among all the Froben editions are Cologne printings, one the 1525 edition of *Declamationes quatuor* (*Encomium matrimonii, Encomium artis medicinae, Oratio episcopi*, and *Oratio de virtute amplectenda*) and the other the 1526 edition of *De contemptu mundi*. What induced Erasmus to keep these two unauthorized Cervicornus editions in his separate collection?[41] Finally, the chest contained one pamphlet that was quite out of place, because it was not by Erasmus at all, but about him. It appears twice in close proximity in the inventory, first as *Erasmi meinung vom nachtmal tütsch* and then as *Erasmi de cena d[omi]n[ic]a tütsch*. Both entries undoubtedly refer to the anonymous booklet published in 1526 under the title *Des Hochgelehrten Erasmi von Roterdam und Doctor Luthers maynung vom Nachtmal unsers Herren Jesu Christi*, in which the Zürich preacher Leo Jud tried, as Pellicanus had done, to interpret Erasmus' doctrine of the Eucharist as being in agreement with Zwingli and the Sacramentarian reformers.[42] Erasmus, who at first stubbornly persisted in believing that this pamphlet was also by Pellicanus, reacted to it in his *Detectio praestigiarum*; this too was a minor work not found in the *Versandliste* but only in the chest.[43]

The collection of his own works, which includes those we have described, cannot be dismissed as a negligible component of Erasmus' library as a whole. But why did he keep the collection in a chest while most of his other works or editions were shelved with the rest of his books? One reason may have been the external state of the books. There are indirect

---

38 See *Catalogus* no 110.

39 *Catalogus* no 111. See Allen XI 368–78 Appendix 27 'The Expositio fidelis'; de Vocht *Acta Thomae Mori* 55–91. On Montanus see Allen and CWE Ep 2065 introductions; CEBR II 448–9.

40 *Catalogus* no 72; see also Allen and CWE Ep 1083 introductions; Halkin *Erasmus ex Erasmo* 91.

41 *Catalogus* nos 104 and 102. The ASD editors of *Encomium matrimonii* (I-5 344) and *Encomium medicinae* (I-4 158) devote no special attention to the Cervicornus editions, evidently pirated reprints.

42 *Catalogus* nos 109 and 112. See Augustijn *Erasmus en de Reformatie* 177–9 and ASD IX-1 222–6. It makes little difference whether there were two copies of the same pamphlet or one copy that Amerbach mistakenly listed twice.

43 *Catalogus* no 91. On the *Detectio* see Augustijn *Erasmus en de Reformatie* 182–3 and ASD IX-1 226–30.

hints, to which we shall return in a moment, that at least some of the books in the chest were unbound copies in loose leaves or quires, which it would have been more convenient to keep separate. The collection as a whole may therefore have formed a rather untidy mass of paper, not very easy to survey as a whole, with which Amerbach's helper wrestled without complete success, so that in the end the learned jurist had to finish the inventory himself. He too had some difficulty and sometimes became confused, jotting down a provisional note that he later had to delete.[44] But he set to work seriously, checking the inventory, as far as it went, item by item, correcting the titles or adding to them where necessary, and systematically noting the format in the margin. Amerbach's descriptions of material that had not yet been inventoried are fuller than those of his helper. He carefully specified in the entry for the *Institutio principis christiani* the 'several other works' that were included in early Froben editions of the work but not separately named on the title-page. In the margin, before the titles of the *Institutio* itself and some of the other works he placed the date 1516, with an accolade (that is, marked by a brace), whereas he dated all the rest 1518. This may suggest that he was dealing with a combination of texts he had put together himself from the Froben editions of those two years.[45] Two other titles entered by Amerbach in the list lead to a similar suspicion: they are next to each other and read 'every edition of the New Testament' (*Noui Testamenti omnes editiones*) and 'every edition of the Adages' (*Adagiorum omnes editiones*).[46] It is hard to believe that this really means complete sets of all the authorized editions of the two works. Why would Amerbach's colleague not have itemized each of the five editions of the New Testament or nine editions of the Adages, assuming that they were complete and bound, rather than leaving them aside, when he did enter the last edition of the *Novum Testamentum* (1535) and the 1533 and 1536 editions of the *Adagia* elsewhere in his list?[47] Perhaps instead of complete sets of 'all the editions' we should think rather of sets made up from various editions of the two works, but from copies that were not always complete and possibly composed of loose and disordered sheets or quires. In this case it would be easy to understand if the person who drew up the inventory did not know what to make of the mass of disorganized papers, and was glad to leave it to Amerbach. Other entries in the *Catalogus* support the hypothesis that at least some of the books in the chest were unbound.[48]

Apart from the possible unbound state of the books, Erasmus may have had a very different reason to keep copies of his own works in a special collection. Some of them must have been working copies in which he had written marginal corrections and new material for use in possible future editions.[49] In that case they must have been in the chest by the window.

---

44 See for example *Catalogus* no 9.

45 *Catalogus* nos 107–8 (*Institutio principis christiani … cum aliis nonnullis*). For a detailed list of contents of both editions see BB E 1253 and 1257.

46 *Catalogus* nos 84 and 85

47 *Catalogus* nos 51 (*Novum Testamentum*), 63 and 64 (*Adagia*). Authorized editions of the New Testament appeared in 1516, 1519, 1522, 1527, and 1535. Authorized editions of the *Adagia* appeared in Venice in 1508 and then, in Basel, in 1515, 1517, 1520, 1523, 1526, 1528, 1533, and 1536.

48 See for example *Catalogus* no 7 (*De morte declamatio*) and no 33 (*Gazae Grammaticae institutionis libri duo*). In both cases Erasmus' copies of the Froben editions of which these texts formed only a part were probably incomplete and therefore perhaps unbound. Cf VL/Catalogue nos 395 (*De morte*) and 347 (Gaza).

49 'Ex hisce lucubrationibus universis aliquot post obitum eius inter suos libros repperimus locupletas et recognitas, et ab ipso autore ad novam aeditionem adornatas' (*Catalogi duo operum Des. Erasmi Roterodami ab ipso conscripti et digesti. Cum praefatione D. Bonifacii Amerbachii Iurecons., ut omni deinceps imposturae via intercludatur, ne pro Erasmo quisquam aedat, quod vir ille non scripsit dum viveret* [Basel: H. Froben and N. Episcopius 1537] 84, quoted Reedijk *Tandem bona causa triumphat* 31–2 with n59 and ASD IX-2 53 n210)

This assumption cannot be proved, although there are some plausible arguments for it. It would explain the striking interest Amerbach displayed in the contents of the chest and the great care he took over the inventory as all the books passed through his hands. There is probably no reason to assume that he took such an active part in preparing the books for shipment to Łaski; at least there is nothing in the *Versandliste* to suggest that he had personally checked the books in it as carefully as he did those in the separate collection. Any of Erasmus' own works with his marginalia that may have been present in the main collection thus had every chance of eluding his attention.

In one case this can be demonstrated. If the copy of the *Apologiae omnes* (Basel: February 1522) with marginal notes by the author that is now in Cambridge can be identified with one of the two copies of that work named in the *Versandliste*,[50] then the book must have been sent to Poland with the others in 1536 without Amerbach knowing anything about the marginal notes it contained. Otherwise, with the posthumous edition of Erasmus' *Opera omnia* already in mind, he would almost certainly have kept a copy that was important for the determination of the definitive text. It must be assumed that he kept the others that he found and put them to one side to be used in the preparation of the first complete edition of the collected works.[51]

How many such printer's copies were there? Amerbach speaks of 'some' (*aliquot*).[52] ASD editors have found evidence of two, perhaps three. H.J. de Jonge's edition of the *Apologia respondens ad ea quae Jacobus Lopis Stunica taxaverat in prima Novi Testamenti aeditione* has shown that the Basel collected works of 1540 included a thoroughly revised and previously unpublished text. For this the editor must have had a copy of the *Apologiae omnes* in the enlarged edition of 1522, which opened with the apologia against Zúñiga, improved and supplemented in his own hand by Erasmus. A.W. Steenbeek found similar traces of a corrected copy of the *Apologia ad Fabrum*. Similarly, the translations of Euripides in the Basel version of 1540 contain some readings that do not appear in previous editions, and the ASD editor, J.H. Waszink, cautiously infers that they may have been found in marginal notes in Erasmus' own copy of the Basel edition (Froben 1530) of *Hecuba et Iphigenia*.[53]

If annotated copies of the *Apologiae omnes* and the Euripides translations were among Erasmus' effects, it is very probable that they served as printer's copies in the preparation of the Basel *Opera omnia*. In that case they must have remained in Basel and must have been kept apart for the purpose when Erasmus' estate was liquidated at the end of 1536. This tallies with what we can deduce from the *Versandliste* and the *Catalogus librorum Erasmi*. The *Versandliste* does not mention the translations of Euripides. The two copies of the *Apologiae omnes* on the *Versandliste* were shipped to Poland, and so could not have been used in the preparation of the 1540 edition. These two editions of the *Apologiae* are not listed in the *Catalogus* either. Older editions of the translations of Euripides (Venice: Aldus 1507 and Basel: Froben 1518), are listed,[54] but not the Froben edition of 1530. Could Erasmus' working copy, corrected in his own hand, have been kept originally in the chest and been deliberately removed from it before the inventory of its contents was drawn up after his death? This may seem a premature and gratuitous inference, but if the progress of the ASD edition supports the

---

50 VL/Catalogue nos 332 and 383
51 For the sake of convenience, we refer to the Basel edition as dating from 1540, although only six of the nine
      volumes appeared in that year. For the differences in dates on the title-pages and in the colophons of the
      separate volumes, or even in the different copies of each volume, see Reedijk *Tandem bona causa triumphat* 32.
52 See n49 above.
53 See 57–8 above.
54 *Catalogus* nos 42 and 79

hypothesis that there were more of the annotated working copies that Amerbach mentioned, and if these copies are not listed in the *Catalogus librorum Erasmi*, then the assumption that Erasmus kept in the chest copies of his works in which he inserted corrections and additions would gain in credibility.[55] But real proof can never be forthcoming, because other possibilities have to be kept open. There is a chance that among the other books in the library there were corrected copies that, unlike the working copy of the *Apologiae omnes* shipped to Poland, the executors set aside before the *Versandliste* was drawn up. And who can tell whether or not Erasmus kept the desk copies that he needed for revised editions together and housed them separately, as would have been natural? Amerbach, Erasmus' closest friend and confidant, would certainly have been aware of the existence of such a special collection, and after Erasmus' death he would have secured it for the posthumous edition of the collected works.

Erasmus himself puts us on the track of the last category of books in his possession but not listed in the *Versandliste*. These were the many 'small books' (*libelli*) that he kept with his correspondence, manuscripts, and other papers somewhere in his house, but clearly separate from the bulk of his other books. More and more of this material had accumulated over the years. Towards the end of his life it filled chests and coffers, and he himself says that he had a room stuffed full of letters alone.[56] Altogether it was such a mass of paper that he no longer knew exactly what it contained, and any disturbance to it left him helpless. His move to Freiburg in 1529 was a disaster from this point of view. 'I have so many letters and books and papers,' he commented, 'that I think the emperor must move his court with less fuss.'[57] After the move, his papers, though safely conveyed, were in great disorder. For months he laboured under the consequences of this. Several letters that he would have liked to include in his great *Opus epistolarum* of 1529 had to be omitted because he could not find them in the chaos.[58]

A similar fate befell the manuscript of Alciati's *Contra vitam monasticam*, which had come into his possession about ten years earlier. Alciati, fearing that his polemical work would become known to a wider circle or even be printed, made persistent attempts in 1520 and again in 1529 and 1531 to recover the manuscript or if necessary to have it destroyed. Amerbach interceded for him with Erasmus, who, after he was settled in Freiburg, searched for it again in his private archive but could not find it. According to his reply to Alciati, he had burned the document years before. He may have believed this in good faith, but it was not so: he must have failed to find the manuscript among the mass of his papers, for it was certainly still there; it was found and, albeit very much later, published.[59]

Though much was lost in the move to Freiburg, the opposite was also true: at least one item surfaced again. While burrowing in his hoard of papers Erasmus stumbled across the *Assertio ecclesiasticae translationis* of Diego López Zúñiga, which had appeared five years

---

55 It need not always be proof to the contrary if they are listed, because the special collection of Erasmiana often contained duplicate copies of the same work.

56 Allen and cwe Ep 2299:68

57 Allen Ep 2143:5–7/cwe Ep 2143:6–8

58 See the prefatory letter to the reader, Allen Ep 2203:22–5/cwe Ep 2203:25–8. On this edition see Halkin *Erasmus ex Erasmo* 149–64.

59 Allen Epp 1201 (from Amerbach):14–22 with 15n, 1250 (to Alciati):15–18/cwe Epp 1233A:15–21 and n5, 1250:17–20; cf Allen Epp 2464:1–3, 2467:2–6 (to Amerbach), 2468:192–202 (to Alciati)/cwe Epp 2464:1–4, 2467:1–6, 2468:192–202. The work was published in 1695: *Contra vitam monasticam ad collegam suum Bernardum Mattium* ed Antonius Matthaeus (Leiden: T. Haaring); cf 109–10 below.

earlier; the find now gave him the occasion to answer his old adversary.[60] That Erasmus could have lost Zúñiga's book among his store of papers is in itself a sign of how extensive it must have been and how difficult it was for Erasmus to find his way about in it.[61]

The *libelli*, along with the collection of letters and other manuscripts, were part of this mass of paper. What were they? We referred earlier to the numerous books that must once have been in Erasmus' possession but are not to be found in the *Versandliste*. His letters show that Erasmus gave away some of them during his lifetime; others that we can no longer trace must have been given away because they were of no use to him. But we also took into account the possibility that a great many books not recorded in the *Versandliste* were not disposed of and were still in his house on his death in 1536.[62] Must we not assume that these books were among the *libelli* in the private archive, especially since their form and content make this likely?

As the examples found in a rapid search in Allen show, they were chiefly octavo and quarto books, many of them small pamphlets, in short *libelli*, which if unbound could most easily be stored flat with the manuscripts.[63] And among these octavos and quartos there was a strikingly large number of polemical and controversial works, a category very incompletely and rather arbitrarily represented in the *Versandliste*. It is hard to believe that Erasmus had disposed of all the polemics that are not to be found in the *Versandliste*, for that would not be easy to reconcile with his lasting involvement in the controversies of his time. Admittedly, where the controversies in which he was personally involved were concerned, he usually professed contempt for or indifference to the writings of his opponents. In 1530, for example, Erasmus wrote to Bernhard von Cles that he had decided not to dignify such 'rubbish' by reading or responding to it; later he wrote to Bonifacius Amerbach that he had seen Sepulveda's *Antapologia* in defence of Alberto Pio but that he would not answer it.[64] Such statements may give the impression that Erasmus considered polemical literature a waste of time. But they were just words; in fact, as Myron Gilmore's sober findings show, he did not let slip any opportunity to reply to his critics with verve and in detail, so that his often confessed aversion to engage in polemics cannot be taken very seriously.[65] It was a pretext, a protective pose – and certainly not a motive to clear the mass of polemical works out of his house. The *Versandliste* tells us that in some cases he preserved them very carefully. The pamphlets about the Reuchlin affair were still present in his library in 1536. He was well aware that such material was very hard to replace, so that he had at first been very reluctant to lend his collection of these writings even to his best friends.[66] It also appears from the *Versandliste* that he kept until the end of his life several controversial writings about the Eucharist, among them Oecolampadius' *De genuina verborum Domini 'Hoc est corpus meum' expositione*. He knew that the booklet had become practically unobtainable soon after it was published, and he did not wish to part with his copy.[67]

---

60 Ep 2172, Erasmus' final rejoinder as published in the *Opus epistolarum* of 1529
61 Cf Allen Ep 2161:28–9 / cwe Ep 2161:29–30: '... the recent move has muddled all my papers, with which, as you know, I am bounteously supplied.'
62 See 58–60 above.
63 See 92 above, and 'Books Found in Erasmus' Correspondence' 475–91 below.
64 Allen Epp 2326:11–19, 2652:1–4 / cwe Ep 2326:13–22 (and cf vl/Catalogue no 389)
65 Gilmore 'Les limites de la tolérance dans l'oeuvre d'Erasme' 714; cf Fokke *Erasmus and Origen* I 6.
66 See vl/Catalogue no 22 #2.
67 See vl/Catalogue no 34; cf, for the carefully preserved works on the question of the three Marys, nos 18 and 20.

But there were other groups of polemics from which, if we judge from the *Versandliste* alone, nothing survived in his estate. Would Erasmus really have been so unconcerned that he parted with all of them? If he had sooner or later got rid of the German pamphlets for and against Luther, several of which he must have owned,[68] that would be understandable, although his professions of indifference to them must be taken with a grain of salt. He could not read them because he knew no German, he claimed to Duke George of Saxony, who often sent him recent German pamphlets.[69] Yet he certainly did not neglect pamphlets in the vernacular, and found some of them interesting enough to have them translated by a *famulus*.[70] But what are we to make of the fact that even the fierce polemic provoked by his *Ciceronianus* left not a single trace in the library, although several of the pamphlets exchanged must have been in his possession?[71] In this and similar cases, it is implausible to argue from the silence of the *Versandliste* that all these polemical works had been weeded out. It makes more sense to infer that at least some of them were among the *libelli* he had acquired in the course of the years and kept with his letters and other papers in various chests.

Much of what we have argued concerning the polemical pamphlets also applies to various other works of miscellaneous content. In many of these Erasmus had been so involved in their origin, or had such a close relationship with the author, that it is scarcely imaginable that he could simply have parted with them without hesitation.[72] We know that Erasmus was still occupied with some of his books years after he had acquired them, which may prove that they had remained in his possession because he found their contents important. Thus, in spite of the alleged language barrier, Dürer's *Vnderweysung der messung mit dem Zirckel und Richtscheyt*, given to him by Pirckheimer in 1525, left its mark in a detailed passage of his *De recta pronuntiatione* of 1528.[73] In the same year he gave a characterization in his *Ciceronianus* of Jacopo Sannazaro's *De partu virginis*, the Roman edition of which had been presented to him in 1526.[74] Surely he would have given both works, and others that could probably be traced with a little detective work, a permanent place in his library. Yet we cannot be certain, and in such cases it is best not to draw too hasty conclusions, since Erasmus' legendary memory may have enabled him to quote surprising details or even to cite verbatim from books he had read long before but no longer possessed.[75] Unfortunately, we have no strict proof that there were many books in the house in 1536 that did not appear in the *Versandliste*. To date not one such book has been found with the *Sum Erasmi* or another conclusive proof of origin that had not passed into other hands before his death in 1536.

Our thesis about the *libelli* has this weak point: if there was a 'private archive' of little books, which we assume to have been in the estate but which were not included in the *Versandliste*, what has happened to them? If they remained in relatively safe and peaceful

---

68 See for example 'Books Found in Erasmus' Correspondence' nos 89–90 (Leo Jud) and 103–12 (Martin Luther).

69 See Allen Epp 1313:84–5 and n, 1499:10–12/cwe Epp 1313:93–4 with n16, 1499:10–12.

70 Allen Epp 697:11–13, 713:2–5, 19–20/cwe Epp 697:14–17 with 15n, 713:3–6, 23–4

71 See for example 'Books Found in Erasmus' Correspondence' nos 47 (Etienne Dolet), 96 (Ortensio Lando), 140 (J.C. Scaliger).

72 See for example 'Books Found in Erasmus' Correspondence' nos 3 (Johannes Agricola), 2 (Georgius Agricola), 5 (Andrea Alciati), 7 (Alger of Liège), 137 (Jacopo Sadoleto).

73 asd I-4 37–8 with 786–806n/cwe 26 398. On Dürer's book see Allen Ep 1717:71–2/cwe Ep 1717:82–3; 'Books Found in Erasmus' Correspondence' no 49; cf vl/Catalogue no 134.

74 Allen Ep 1840:75–6/cwe Ep 1840:84–5; cf *Ciceronianus* asd I-2 700–1/cwe 28 437–8.

75 Erasmus could easily have been sneering at the books on the technique of memory that were popular in his time when he wrote that 'memory largely consists in having thoroughly understood something' (*De ratione studii* lb I 522c/asd I-2 118:10–11/cwe 24 671:8–9). Cf the colloquy *Ars notoria* 'The Art of Learning' asd I-3 648–9/cwe 40 934 and, in more detail, Margolin 'Erasme et Mnémosyne.'

Basel in 1536, in the keeping of Erasmus' scrupulously conscientious executors – and there is nothing to suggest that they were sent to Poland – how could they have disappeared without trace? The best way to answer this question is first to examine what happened to the two other components of Erasmus' domestic papers (*supellex chartacea*), the letters and the manuscripts and other written documents.

A very important part of Erasmus' private archive was made up of his correspondence, both incoming and outgoing. Since his youth Erasmus had been careful to keep copies of the letters he wrote to others whenever he regarded them as important.[76] He copied them himself or had his servant-pupils transcribe them into letterbooks. One of these, written in c 1517–18, has been preserved: the Deventer Letterbook, so called from its current home.[77] In later years he had fair copies of his outgoing letters made by a colleague and kept the autograph drafts. Specimens of rough drafts from his estate are found with autographs of other works in a codex now in Copenhagen. Most of the letters in it were published by Erasmus himself. With one exception, he did not send the rough drafts directly to the printer, but revised them and had copies made for the printer.[78] He then kept the drafts carefully in his archive.

With incoming letters Erasmus must have adopted another practice. It cannot be coincidence that out of the hundreds of letters that Erasmus received and published almost none of the originals have survived,[79] except for a very few that were preserved for specific reasons in 1536 and have never left Basel. How are we to explain this? It is quite inconceivable that the executors should have first laboriously collected the originals of the published letters and then destroyed them, simply because in the view of the time manuscripts that had been published had no further value.[80] It is just as difficult to imagine that only those letters that had already been published were later lost (with the very few exceptions to which we referred), while many original unpublished letters survived. We are forced to assume that virtually all of the letters already published were no longer in the estate in 1536. They may have been used as printer's copy in the publication of the many collections; a rough draft written by Erasmus himself, in the Copenhagen manuscript, bears red chalk marks that show it was used by the typesetter when printing the appendix of letters to *De puritate tabernaculi*.[81] But while this draft was returned to Erasmus after use, the originals of many letters addressed to him may very well have remained at the printer's works. That would not have been unusual in the sixteenth century. How many other manuscripts, no longer needed and therefore treated carelessly by the printers, were soon lost? If this is what happened, the very extensive collection of incoming letters found in Erasmus' house after his death must have consisted largely of those not published during his lifetime. We cannot trace in detail what Amerbach and his assistants did with them, but we can reconstruct the main outlines.

---

76 Allen I 593–4 Appendix 7 'The Principal Editions of Erasmus' Epistolae'

77 Athenaeumbibliotheek Deventer, MS 91; for more details see Allen I 603–9 Appendix 8 'The Deventer Letter-book.'

78 See Allen III 630–4 Appendix 13 'The Copenhagen Manuscript'; Reedijk 'Three Erasmus Autographs in the Royal Library at Copenhagen,' especially 329–34. The codex in the Royal Library is MS Gl.Kgl.Saml.95 Fol.

79 This conclusion is based on the data on each letter in Allen. Various collections appeared between 1515 and 1532 and in the appendixes of letters to the *De praeparatione ad mortem* and *De puritate tabernaculi*. On the collections see Allen I 593–602 Appendix 7 'The Principal Editions of Erasmus' Epistolae,' especially the editions A to M described there; and Halkin *Erasmus ex Erasmo*.

80 Cf 95–6 above.

81 At the end of *De puritate* Erasmus added *aliquot epistolae selectae*; see Allen's introductions to Epp 3086 (the preface to *De puritate*) and 3100 (the letter 'to friendly readers' attached to the 'selected letters'). Allen III 633 Appendix 13 'The Copenhagen Manuscript' explains why only this rough draft was used as copy.

Erasmus' executors kept only a small number of published letters, the ones we have already mentioned as an exception and that are still in Basel. Obviously they wanted to keep all the letters that might be important for the liquidation of Erasmus' estate; these included thirty-three letters from Erasmus Schets, who had been his banker in Antwerp,[82] and seventeen from Conradus Goclenius, his close friend in Brabant, to whom he had entrusted not inconsiderable sums of money.[83] These letters, now preserved in two packets, had undoubtedly already been kept together by Erasmus himself.[84] Another group of letters may have already been separated from the rest of the letters Erasmus received before 1536 because either the status of their writer or the importance of their content made them documents of special value to Erasmus: a letter from King Francis I; two letters from Leo x in 1517 granting him the papal dispensation he so needed; two letters, one from Pope Clement vii of 1525 and a letter patent of Charles v of 1530, concerning another strictly personal matter, his will.[85] Finally, there was a small group of letters, not in themselves of any great importance, that remained more or less accidentally in Basel: they dated from the last months of Erasmus' life or were received only after his death; clearly they had not been incorporated in his archive of correspondence.[86]

So much for the incoming letters that remained in Basel. What about the rest of the massive collection of correspondence that was still in the house 'Zum Luft' when Erasmus died? Amerbach and his helpers must have liquidated the estate by finding an appropriate home for them. The many hundreds of original, still unpublished letters must have been divided into several parcels and sooner or later, whether all together or in stages we cannot say, transferred to someone else. The executors probably intended to entrust the letters to friends and associates who could be relied on to treat them with pious respect. An important parcel of at least 162 letters came into the hands of Nikolaus Gerbel (d 1560), who had known Erasmus well and had acted as ad hoc proofreader for the publication of his *Novum Testamentum.* Later they lost contact – perhaps because their approaches to the Reformation differed – but Gerbel had never forsaken him. In 1629 these letters were still in the possession of his granddaughter, but sixteen years later they were sold to a member of the Silesian family of Rehdiger. With the other manuscripts and books of this family, which was rich in bibliophiles, they ended up in due course in the University Library of Wrocław, then known as Breslau, where they still remain, fortunate survivors of the violence of the Second World War.[87]

---

82 On Schets see Allen and cwe Ep 1541 introductions; de Vocht *History of the Foundation and the Rise of the Collegium Trilingue Lovaniense, 1517–1550* iii 358; cebr iii 220–1.

83 On Goclenius and the financial relationship with Erasmus, see Allen and cwe Ep 1209 introductions, cebr ii 109–11; de Vocht *History of the Foundation and the Rise of the Collegium Trilingue Lovaniense, 1517–1550* iii passim; and Allen x 406–24 Appendix 23 'The Donation to Goclenius.'

84 They are in the library of the University of Basel (ms Scheti Epistolae and ms Goclenii Epistolae). See Major *Erasmus von Rotterdam* 54 (the inventory of 1536): 'Item ettlich handtgschrifften herren Erasmi Scheti von Autdorff … Item ettlich handtgschrifften herrn Conradi Goclenii zu löfen …'

85 Basel Universitätsbibliothek mss G2.i.36.10 (Ep 1375, from Francis i); Urk. iia.4 (Ep 517, from Leo x to Andrea Ammonio) and Urk. iia.5 (Ep 518, from Leo x); Epp 1588 (from Clement vii) and 2318 (from Charles v) are also in Basel.

86 Basel Universitätsbibliothek ms Variorum epistolae ad Erasmum (Epp 3105, 3121, 3128, 3132); Nantes, Bibl. dép., mss 674.23 and 674.225 (Epp 3137 and 3138). Epp 3137 and 3138 were in the possession of the Basel University Library until 1841; see Allen Ep 479 introduction and the introductions to the later letters.

87 ms Rehdiger 254. The first letter is dated 6 October 1518 (Ep 866), the last 25 June 1536 (Ep 3129). Allen unravelled their history in a rather inconspicuous note in volume iii xxiv (an addition to i 608 Appendix 8

A second, larger parcel of at least 230 letters, which contains some of Erasmus' autograph manuscripts as well, was by the late eighteenth century in the library of the Leipzig professor of theology Johann Friedrich Burscher, whom we also have to thank for our knowledge of their previous history. He tells us that the letters were first in Amerbach's hands, were then taken to the Netherlands, and later to England. Around 1750 they were in the possession of the Württemberg diplomat Wilhelm Friedrich Schönhau, who died in Italy. After his death the collection changed hands again, before it was acquired by Burscher in Leipzig in 1782. Perhaps the most interesting part of this account is that the first owner after Amerbach was in the Netherlands. To whom could Amerbach have transferred the collection (though the manuscripts need not have followed the same path as the letters)? Could he have thought of Erasmus' friend and confidant Conradus Goclenius, as he did in another case? It is just a guess. The further history of the collection is soon told. Four years after Burscher's death in 1805 his widow presented it to the University Library in Leipzig.[88] Unfortunately the letters, unlike those of the Rehdiger collection, could not be found again after the Second World War and must be assumed to be lost.[89]

But the private archive of letters must have contained more than two parcels. We know from allusions in his correspondence that many letters Erasmus received from his 150 or so correspondents (often several from one correspondent) have not survived;[90] others we cannot know about because Erasmus never referred or alluded to them. There must have been several hundred of these; presumably they too were made up into packets in 1536 but have since been lost or become untraceable.[91]

After his death Erasmus' personal manuscripts were probably divided among those closely involved with the liquidation of his estate. We know that a few came into the hands of his executor Amerbach; these include the autograph with Erasmus' own drawings of the adage *Sileni Alcibiadis*,[92] his translation of Plutarch's *De utilitate capienda ex inimicis*,[93] the definitive version of *Hieronymi Stridonensis vita*,[94] his scholia on the letters of Jerome,[95] and others. In 1662 all these, with other documents originally belonging to Erasmus that had been in Amerbach's possession, were presented to the city of Basel, where they are now in the University Library.[96] Others did not stay so close to home; three bulky codices almost entirely made up of autograph rough drafts wandered from one place to another before they

---

'The Deventer Letter-book'). Cf Wachler *Thomas Rehdiger und seine Büchersammlung in Breslau*. On Gerbel see Allen and CWE Ep 342 introductions; CEBR II 90–1; VL/Catalogue no 360.

88 The collection was formerly MS 0331m in the Universitätsbibliothek Leipzig. The oldest letter is dated 19 February 1520 (Ep 1067) the most recent 11 December 1535 (Ep 3074). Burscher described the contents and prehistory of the collection in his possession in his *Index et argumentum epistolarum ad D. Erasmum Roterodamum autographarum;* he published some of the letters in his *Spicilegium autographorum*. See also the introduction in Förstemann/Günther vii–ix; CWE Epp 1067 and 1254 introductions.

89 Communication from Dr D. Debes, Leiter der Handschriftenabteilung, Bibliothek Universität Leipzig

90 See Allen XII 22 (Index II A) under 'Epistolae, lost.'

91 Allen found no trace of any original letters addressed to Erasmus, apart from the Rehdiger and Leipzig collections, not even any stray odd ones.

92 Universitätsbibliothek Basel MS Erasmuslade D.6; see *Erasmus en zijn tijd* no 130a.

93 Universitätsbibliothek Basel MS A.N.VI.1; see *Erasmus en zijn tijd* no 174; Ferguson *Opuscula* 125–90.

94 Universitätsbibliothek Basel MS A.IX.56^1; see *Erasmus en zijn tijd* no 213.

95 Universitätsbibliothek Basel MS A.IX.56; see *Erasmus en zijn tijd* no 212; Husner 'Die Handschrift der Scholien des Erasmus von Rotterdam zu den Hieronymusbriefen.'

96 Including the important letters received by Erasmus, discussed 107 above. For more on the Amerbachiana see Ganz and Major *Die Entstehung des Amerbachschen Kunstkabinetts und die Amerbachschen Inventare*.

all ended up, though not at the same time, in the Royal Library in Copenhagen.[97] Reedijk has subjected these manuscripts to a close examination and has been able to identify with some certainty the intended destination of one of the three after Erasmus' death. A note that he was able to read by using a quartz lamp showed that the so-called Thott manuscript was once in the possession of the executor Nicolaus Episcopius, who had the collection of rough drafts handsomely bound as a memento of Erasmus for himself and his wife Justina.[98] Were the other two codices allocated to Bonifacius Amerbach and Hieronymus Froben as co-executors? Reedijk did not rule that out, but because there was no proof of it, he also kept open another possibility for one of the two: certain indications suggested that the executors may have presented the drafts, later bound in a codex with a copy of the will, to Conradus Goclenius, professor at the Collegium Trilingue in Leuven and one of Erasmus' closest friends, as a memento.[99]

The Copenhagen manuscripts tell us something about the way in which Erasmus' own autograph drafts and other papers were treated. They seem to have been hastily collected after his death and assembled rather casually. Allen described the contents of the one he saw as 'a congeries brought together almost haphazard by some one desirous of gathering and yet hardly heeding what he gathered,' and Reedijk felt that this was equally applicable to the other two codices.[100] It seems clear that Amerbach, Episcopius, and Hieronymus Froben were all unable or unwilling to examine and arrange the loose papers carefully in the intervals of their own work. But this did not affect the accomplishment of their main objective, demanded by simple piety, to insure that Erasmus' personal manuscripts came safely into the hands of his closest friends.

The executors were not obliged to regard other manuscripts they found in Erasmus' estate with the same reverence; they could dispose of these among a wider circle of interested people. We can only guess how they went about clearing up the material. Perhaps they did not spend much time classifying it, but put the manuscripts that were not in Erasmus' handwriting to one side, intending to come back to them at leisure, to allocate them or destroy them. Whatever they did, a few manuscripts, of very varied contents and nature, can be traced to their new owners. The copy of Chrysostom's Greek commentary on the Epistle to the Romans, made at Erasmus' request by his servant-pupil Nicolaas Kan from an older manuscript, has been preserved at Wolfenbüttel. We do not know who was the first owner of this manuscript, which also contained marginalia by Erasmus; he may even have given it away before his death.[101] Nor do we know the immediate fate of Alciati's *Epistola contra vitam monasticam*, which Erasmus claimed in 1531 that he had already burned but which surfaced again among his papers. In the next century it cropped up in the collection of the Dutch scholar Petrus Scriverius, the owner of numerous papers connected with Erasmus,

---

97 MSS Gl. Kgl. Saml. 95 Fol., Gl. Kgl. Saml, 96 Fol. and Thottske Saml. 73 Fol; the first was acquired by the library between 1663 and 1670, the second perhaps also at that time, and the last in or shortly after 1785.

98 The following words could be deciphered: 'Nicolai Episcopii, successoris <Jo. Frob.> et Justinae <filiae> D. <Erasmi mo>numentum Rot<erodami> …' See Reedijk 'Three Erasmus autographs in the Royal Library at Copenhagen,' especially 339, 348 (the description of the volume).

99 MS Gl. Kgl. Saml. 95 Fol. See Reedijk 'Three Erasmus Autographs' 349; on Goclenius see n83 above.

100 Allen III 632 Appendix 13 'The Copenhagen Manuscript'; Reedijk 'Three Erasmus Autographs' 348. Unlike Allen and Reedijk, Erik Petersen concludes from his research that the Copenhagen manuscript must preserve the arrangement in which the letters were found; see his 'Notes on the Erasmus autograph MS Gl. Kgl. Saml. 95, 2°' and 'Propria manu.'

101 MS Gud gr. fol. no 4197; see von Heinemann *Die Handschriften der herzoglichen Bibliothek zu Wolfenbüttel* part 4: *Die Gudischen Handschriften* IX 5–6. Cf 98 and n28 above.

and later again, in 1695, the text was published in Holland. Clearly when the estate was liquidated, the manuscript was not returned to the person who had the strongest claim to it. Was this negligence on the part of Episcopius or Froben? Or were they both unaware of the previous commotion about the manuscript? In any case it must have changed hands without Amerbach's knowledge, for otherwise he would certainly have made sure that the manuscript of Alciati's youthful indiscretion was safely returned to its author, his great friend, who was afraid of publication and had made persistent attempts to recover it from Erasmus.[102] It is uncertain if the manuscript of Dante's *De monarchia* that Erasmus had received in 1527 from Mercurino Gattinara, the chancellor of Charles v,[103] later found a suitable home in Basel. Erasmus had refrained from acting on the chancellor's invitation to publish the anti-papal tract, and the manuscript may have lain unused among his papers until his death. In 1559 the *editio princeps* of the work was published in Basel by Joannes Oporinus, the son-in-law of Bonifacius Amerbach. It is a natural supposition that the manuscript used as copy was the one in Erasmus' estate, and that it was still in the neighbourhood. Allen raised the possibility in passing, Karl Brandi assumed it almost as certain, and Peter Bietenholz cautiously agreed. Their assumption was not followed later by Andreas Burckhardt, who thinks it more likely that Oporinus used another manuscript received directly from Italy as the basis of his edition, but he cannot supply watertight proof, so the question remains open.[104]

Let us return to the *libelli* in Erasmus' private archive. What is known about the later vicissitudes of the letters and manuscripts in Erasmus' estate gives us some insight into what might have happened to these 'little books.' Amerbach and his colleagues had a big enough job to tackle in sorting Erasmus' papers – one they undoubtedly performed with piety but also in a businesslike manner. Could they be expected to trouble themselves overmuch about the distribution of the printed pamphlets that they found among the manuscripts and other written materials? Though it is not to be ruled out, it is very unlikely that they packed them up and shipped them off to Poland with the rest of the library without noting the titles. In not sending the collection to Łaski, Amerbach and his assistants will not have thought for a moment that they were defrauding him of anything that could be of value to him. For these were small books which, apart from possible donors' dedications or the odd marginal note, had little or nothing to do with Erasmus himself. Many of them were polemical works that had lost all their timeliness. They were numerous, and they did not easily fit in with the humanistic working library, made up largely of manuals and editions of texts, on which Łaski had set his sights when he negotiated the agreement of 1525. And the fact that most of the books were very likely unbound was probably decisive. May we not assume that among the *supellex chartacea* it was the *libelli*, perhaps still unbound, that gave the executors the least trouble: that they took whatever they fancied and simply cleared out the rest?

---

102 Cf 103 above.

103 Allen Ep 1790A with 3n / CWE Ep 1790A with n2; it is assumed here that the manuscript was actually sent and received.

104 *Andr. Alciati de formula Romani imperii libellus, Dantis Florentini de monarchia libri tres, Radulphi Carnotensis de translatione imperii libellus.* See Brandi 'Dantes *Monarchia* und die Italienpolitik Mercurino Gattinaras' 19; Bietenholz *Der italienische Humanismus und die Blütezeit des Buchdrucks in Basel* 106–7; Burckhardt *Johannes Basilius Herold: Kaiser und Reich im protestantischen Schrifttum des Basler Buchdrucks um die Mitte des 16. Jhts.* 198 n25.

6

Erasmus and the Book: The Humanist at Work

In 1489 Erasmus presented an anonymous friend with a copy of the comedies of Terence transcribed in his own hand. The letter from Steyn that accompanied the gift is worth quoting again. Erasmus urged the recipient to study the manuscript diligently and above all not to refrain from using it. For, he continued, 'I consider as lovers of books not those who keep their books hidden in their store-chests and never handle them, but those who, by nightly as well as daily use, thumb them, batter them, wear them out, who fill up all the margins with annotations of so many kinds, and who prefer the marks of a fault they have erased to a neat copy full of faults.'[1] It cannot be denied that this verbose, rather rhetorical passage is the sort of thing that might be composed by a young monk who wished to perfect his Latin by exercises in the epistolary genre. But at the same time it is a strikingly accurate statement of the attitude that was to characterize Erasmus' lifelong relationship with the book, written or printed. Books meant everything to him; they determined the course of his life; but to call him a bibliomane or even a bibliophile would be to misunderstand the nature of his passion for books. That is by no means to say that he cared nothing for their outward appearance. In 1507 he complimented Aldo Manuzio on his type, 'unmatched for elegance,' especially the very small font, which he found the most attractive and in which he would be happy to see his translation of Euripides printed.[2] He was aware of the excellence of the Froben Press' typography and was not indifferent, later, to the make-up of his own books. He sometimes instructed Froben to use the typefaces and format he preferred,[3] and his own design for the title-page of the first volume of the ten-volume edition of Augustine published by Froben (1528–9) has been preserved.[4] But such efforts had a practical rather than an aesthetic object; he was concerned above all to enhance the marketability and thereby the circulation of his books by an attractive presentation aimed at his intended readership. If necessary, he would cater to the taste of others for a handsome volume, and sometimes he gave his benefactors the pleasure of presentation copies of his own works expensively bound or printed on parchment.[5] But everything indicates that for himself it was only the usefulness of books that counted; and that usefulness stood or fell by the quality and currency of the contents. To put it in modern terms, books for Erasmus were no more than media for the transmission and recording of knowledge and wisdom. Books from which no further practical profit was to be drawn lost their value for him. This had clear consequences for the way in which

---

1 Allen Ep 31:29–35 / cwe Ep 31:32–9; cf 85 above.
2 Allen Ep 207:31–3 / cwe Ep 207:36–8
3 Allen Epp 2062:19–20, 2412:8n / cwe Ep 2062:23–4, 2412 n7; cf his earlier comments in Allen Epp 462:6–9, 635:16–19 / cwe Epp 462:10–14, 635:20–4.
4 See vl/Catalogue no 348 n1; for the Augustine edition, see no 258.
5 See 87–8 above.

he built up his own library. He openly criticized the vain display of books, and warned his pupil Christian Northoff, 'Do not be guilty of possessing a library of learned books while lacking learning yourself.'[6]

Having books around him was a vital necessity for Erasmus from his youth. The prospect of 'plenty of books' in the monastery at Steyn was one of the baits used to lure him across the threshold,[7] and the opportunities for reading and study he enjoyed among the Augustinian canons regular may make it easier to understand why so few of his later complaints about the monastic life were voiced at the time. In the first years after he left Steyn, when he had no fixed abode and very little money, the lack of books was always painful. In summer 1500 he complained of his lot to Jacob Batt: 'Where shall I flee, without a rag to my back? What if I fall ill?' But clearly there was an even more worrying question: even if these situations should not arise, what could he achieve in the field of letters without access to books?[8] Batt was his refuge. In July 1501 Erasmus found shelter with him at Tornehem, the castle of Anthony of Burgundy, where his friend was entrusted with the education of the young Adolf of Veere, the grandson and heir of the lord of the castle. There Erasmus enjoyed leisurely conversation with Batt, but also devoted himself wholly to literature, 'lying hidden, as it were, in the innermost retreats of the muses.' For the time being his discontent with his fate had vanished, but one handicap remained; it would have been a life perfectly fit for the gods if only he had had more books.[9]

We can see what it meant for Erasmus to have at hand the books he needed, both from the frustration that just this lack had caused him in his youth, and later from his attachment to the library he built up for himself. The collection, modest at first but gradually growing after his Italian journey into an extremely useful – indeed, almost indispensable – working apparatus, soon became something he could not imagine being without. He began to identify with it. For the sake of his library he could almost have wished for a sedentary life, such as he would later find at Basel and Freiburg. In 1515 Cuthbert Tunstall was appointed English ambassador at the imperial court, which meant that he had no fixed post but had to travel in the suite of the young Prince Charles. When Erasmus imagined himself in his friend's place and considered the attractions of his new sphere of work, he concluded that it was a way of life to which he was not wholly averse, provided that his library could accompany him wherever he went.[10] Given the difficulties and risks of transport at the time, it would not have been easy to meet that condition, but Erasmus certainly meant what he said very seriously. By August 1517 he could say, 'I have moved to Louvain bag and baggage, that is, with all my books.'[11] Having his books within immediate reach began to be an important consideration. A few years later, in 1521, when he spent the summer and early autumn, with a few short breaks, with canon Pieter Wichmans at Anderlecht, he had his whole library brought over from Leuven.[12] Only in his old age did he take a more relaxed attitude to this.

Always busy with books, reading with concentration and an incredible power of absorption or preparing for the press his own works or purified editions of classical or Christian texts, often at breakneck speed – that was Erasmus' way of life, and that was the

---

6 Allen Ep 56:47–8 / CWE Ep 56:55–6
7 Allen Ep 15:2–3, 21–2 / CWE Ep 15:3–4, 22–3; cf *Compendium vitae* Allen I 50:81–6 / CWE 4 407:91–6.
8 Allen Ep 128:21–2 / CWE Ep 128:24–6
9 Allen Ep 161:17–23 / CWE Ep 161:19–25
10 Cf 66 and n34 above.
11 Cf 67 above.
12 Cf 69 above.

way in which he functioned best.[13] His appetite for work was nothing short of amazing. In spite of the feeling of old age that he began to speak of relatively early,[14] and the constant complaints of his poor health and his ailments, until his last days he remained physically and mentally capable of devoting himself intently to productive intellectual work, with very little real relaxation or distraction. He regularly had to work under great pressure on a current project while he put other activities to one side. Sometimes long preparation was followed by a burst of activity in which he put the text down on paper in haste, often under some outside stimulus. His astonishing achievements must often have taxed his powers to the utmost. In Venice he completed the revised edition of his *Adagia*, which in fact was practically new, in only eight months, working like a horse on the many manuscripts, mostly Greek, at his disposal, writing additions to the text amid the din of the printing shop while the printers had already begun to print, and making textual changes right up to the last proof. 'A single frail mortal,' he wrote later, 'had to undertake a mass of work that would be too much for Hercules himself unaided.' If he was not telling the truth then Aldo, Lascaris, Musurus, Egnazio, and Aleandro were there to contradict him, for they had been eyewitnesses.[15] In later years he often took no more than a few days to compose and prepare for press detailed apologies that he wanted to see in print before the next Frankfurt book fair because of their topical nature.[16] But it was not just in exceptional circumstances that he put in such long and exhausting working days. Often, at any rate much more often than agreed with the rule of life he had tried to set himself, he must have had to sacrifice his nightly rest to study and work.

Erasmus made good use of his time. Pliny's saying 'that all the time which one fails to devote to study is wasted' was one after his own heart; he impressed it on his pupils,[17] and he lived up to it himself. After his first voyage to England he threw himself with a feverish passion into the study of Greek and, as he wrote, spent days and sometimes whole nights as well secretly copying Greek books that had chanced to fall into his hands.[18] There is no reason to disbelieve him; and the same applies to his assurance that the edition of the *Adagia* that appeared in 1515, thoroughly revised and once again greatly enlarged, had cost him no fewer nights of effort than the previous edition, the Venice text of 1508.[19] On his travels he carried on working as far as he could. In 1519, when he paid a short visit to some towns in Brabant and Flanders to recover from his long and exhausting studies, he had to leave his library behind, but he took with him enough books to read en route – his 'companions on the journey' he called them – so that if there were no congenial company in the carriage he would have someone to talk to him and pass the time. On this occasion he chose Cicero's *De officiis* and *De amicitia*, Cato, and the *Paradoxa Stoicorum*.[20] Nor, when travelling, did he confine himself to reading. While crossing the Alps on his way to Italy in August 1506 he composed his long poem on the approach of old age, the *Carmen alpestre*, dedicated to Willem Cop. In the daytime, in the saddle, he made notes for it, and then he worked out his

---

13 Cf Huizinga *Erasmus of Rotterdam* 17, 126–7, 134.

14 Ep 596, written in 1517; cf 66 above.

15 Allen and CWE Ep 211 introductions; Allen Ep 269:44–54 / CWE Ep 269:49–60. Cf *Adagia* III i 1.

16 For example *Hyperaspistes 1* (1526) and *Epistola ad quosdam impudentissimos gracculos*; see Allen and CWE Ep 1667 introductions, Ep 2275. Cf 119–20 below.

17 Allen Ep 56:63–4 / CWE Ep 56:74–5; cf Allen Ep 1013:5–8 / CWE Ep 1013:8–12.

18 Allen Ep 149:9–10 / CWE Ep 149:11–13

19 Allen Ep 269:118–19 / CWE Ep 269:130–2

20 Allen Ep 1013:21–31 / CWE Ep 1013:27–38

inspirations in the evening at the inn.[21] The *Moria* was also conceived on horseback, on his return journey from Italy to England in 1509.[22] A ship sometimes offered better opportunity for writing or study than horseback or a jolting coach. In September 1516 Erasmus wrote to William Nesen that he had prepared his revised edition of *De copia* for the press 'while on shipboard, so that even that space of time might not be wholly lost to my programme of work.'[23] And when he went to England from Leuven in April 1517, he took the Roman historian Quintus Curtius as his 'companion on the journey by land and sea' and prepared his edition of the text of the *History of Alexander the Great*.[24]

In his normal everyday life Erasmus tried to follow a sensibly planned and regular routine, because that was the only way to guarantee achieving the optimal amount of work. The handicrafts offered an instructive parallel. 'For a craftsman,' he told his pupil Christian Northoff in 1497, 'usually obeys certain rules of his trade that make it possible for him to produce a given quantity of work, not only more accurately and quickly, but also more easily.' Twenty years later he urged the same argument for the efficient performance of intellectual work in a letter to his friend Pieter Gillis. 'You will find your work less laborious if you arrange your studies on some rational plan.'[25] What was the working method he had in mind? He went into great detail in the good advice he gave to Northoff. 'Divide your day into tasks as it were ... Avoid working at night and studying at unsuitable times and seasons ... Aurora is the Muses' friend: daybreak is an excellent time for study. After lunch take some recreation, or go for a walk, or enjoy gay conversation; reflect that even such activities as these can afford opportunity for studying ... Take a short walk before supper, and again after it. Just before you go to sleep, you should read something of exquisite quality, worth remembering; let sleep overtake you while you are musing upon it and when you awaken try to recall it to mind.' We can supplement this from his advice to Gillis in 1516 when, although he went into less detail, he essentially repeated his earlier plea for a rational allocation of time in the working day. 'Lay down for yourself some definite course of life, deciding what you wish to do at what time of day. Do not pile one task on another until the earlier one is finished; thus you will make the day seem longer, which is now almost entirely wasted.'[26]

Erasmus imposed a similar working method on himself. Or, to put it more accurately, he tried to impose it on himself, for the practicalities of life often made it very difficult, if not impossible, for him to stick to it. But his method of study, in its main outlines and under more or less normal circumstances, exhibits the pattern he recommended and urged on others. In principle he reserved the mornings for his most demanding work. If necessary he also devoted the afternoons to it, though on certain days he set aside an hour or two to receive visitors.[27] He studied texts that interested him, worked on the manuscripts of his books, translated from Greek authors, often dictating as he translated, or arranged and supervised the tasks of his servant-pupils and secretaries. They copied for him and also collated manuscripts, so that he had only to choose between variant readings and provide the commentary.

---

21 Reedijk *Poems* no 83; ASD I-7 and CWE 85–6 no 2; cf *Catalogus lucubrationum* Allen I 4:8–27 / CWE Ep 1341A:97–119. See also Margolin 'Le chant alpestre' 37–9; Thompson 'Erasmus as a Poet in the Context of Northern Humanism' 201–5.

22 Allen Ep 222:1–11 / CWE Ep 222:2–12

23 Allen Ep 462:5–6 / CWE Ep 462:8–10. The edition was published by Froben in April 1517; cf VL/Catalogue no 365.

24 Allen Ep 704:15–16 / CWE Ep 704:17–19

25 Allen Epp 56:36–8, 476:38–9 / CWE Epp 56:42–5, 476:45–6

26 Allen Ep 476:44–7; cf Ep 56:38–63 / CWE Ep 476:51–4; cf Ep 56:45–73.

27 Allen Ep 1805:282–4 / CWE Ep 1805:294–5

He too collated, together with a secretary, while one of them read aloud, the customary practice at the time. In the evenings he abstained from study unless there was 'some urgent necessity.' Sometimes he amused himself with light conversation, for which a partner was easy to find among his friends or the members of his household, though one should not exaggerate this, for according to his own statement he had few table companions in 1528. He did demand that the conversation should be on a respectable level and would never tolerate coarse or unlearned talk.[28] But rather than engaging in conversation he preferred to devote the hours between the evening meal and going to bed to reading. This did not always mean that he read himself. In later years, to spare his eyesight, he often had a *famulus* – one of the educated young men who were his resident pupils and at the same time performed all kinds of services for him – read to him.[29]

Erasmus absorbed the spoken word as thoroughly and as critically as a printed text. When the letters of Pope Clement I and other early popes were read to him he immediately recognized, just by listening, that several lines in a letter alleged to have been written by Pope Anterus had been lifted almost verbatim from the correspondence of Jerome.[30] Shortly after they were published in 1531 he also had his *famulus* read to him every day after dinner from the annotated edition of Budé's collected letters, which he had eagerly anticipated.[31] Nor was it from his own reading that he knew Agrippa's notorious treatise *De incertitudine et vanitate scientiarum et artium*, a verdict on which he had promised to the author. He did not own the book, but received a copy on loan after much delay, and his *famulus* read him selected chapters.[32] It is clear from a letter of 1530 that having someone read to him was his normal practice: to express how ill and miserable and fit for nothing he had been feeling for months, he wrote that he could not 'write or dictate or listen attentively to someone reading to me.'[33]

Erasmus' correspondence brings out another of his peculiarities; he used to walk up and down his room while listening to his *famulus*.[34] Presumably he felt the need to 'stretch his legs' indoors while studying as well. In his colloquy Γεροντολογία 'The Old Men's Chat' he makes Glycion, one of the speakers, relate how, although study gave him the greatest possible enjoyment, he could never spend more than an hour at a time bent over his books. Then he stood up, walked round the room for a few moments, to think over or, if there was anyone nearby, to relate what he had read before returning to his reading. The figure of Glycion reveals several clearly Erasmian traits, so that we can see the author's own habit reflected in these brief interruptions of his work. And while he walked around his room, he could always see a portrait of Pirckheimer.[35]

Was Erasmus perhaps compensating to some extent for the lack of outdoor physical exercise? When he was younger he had been in the habit of taking a short walk after lunch, at least if his advice to Christian Northoff was based on his own practice. In a letter to Jacob Vrood written in 1501 he remarks that he often took a walk after meals because of ill health (as his friend would know, because when Erasmus stayed with him in the fall of 1500 they

---

28 Allen Ep 2073:88–93 / CWE Ep 2073:94–8
29 See eg Allen Epp 1552:4–6 with 5n, 1616:18–19, 1759:55–7, 1790:75–6, 1805:284–5, 1833:13–16 / CWE
      Epp 1552:5–7, 1616:23–4, 1759:59–61, 1790:71–3, 1805:295–6, 1833:17–20.
30 Allen Ep 1790:73–81 / CWE Ep 1790:70–8
31 See VL/Catalogue no 289.
32 Allen Ep 2796:3–5
33 Allen and CWE Ep 2328:6–8
34 Allen Epp 1759:55–7, 2449:76–8 / CWE Epp 1759:59–61, 2449:76–8
35 For the passage in the colloquy, see ASD I-3 380 / CWE 39 453–4. On the portraits of Pirckheimer, see 73 above.

had walked together); on recent such walks he had reread Cicero's three 'truly golden books' *De Officiis*.[36] It is difficult to say precisely how far outdoor exercise was still a fixed part of his daily routine in later years as well; probably he could no longer find the time for regular exercise and certainly his physical state kept him more often in his study. Erasmus had become a 'citizen of the world,' with friends and associates spread far and wide, but his life both in Basel and during the six years he spent in Freiburg was very much confined to one place. He no longer made any long journeys. In September 1522 he made a three-week journey from Basel to Constance, and in spring 1524 he spent nearly as long in Besançon and Porrentruy.[37] His scholarly way of life kept him in a town, but also, with ever fewer interruptions, at home. He took particular pleasure in relaxing in the large and well laid out garden that Froben had bought, on his advice, near the city walls only a short walk from his house. If the season was favourable and the weather tempting, he sometimes spent a few hours there in the afternoon 'to fend off the approach of sleep and relieve the tedium of my interminable labours,' as he writes in 1526. But this made scarcely any break in his established routine, for after a stroll through the garden he could withdraw to the garden house and take up his work of translating Chrysostom again.[38]

By the 1520s Erasmus cannot have had very many afternoons left to spare for wholly undisturbed study or reading. As his fame grew he adapted his daily programme, for he had to make more and more time available for social obligations, answering letters and receiving visitors. Especially after the success of his editions of Jerome and the New Testament, which put him at the centre of the ongoing theological discourse and also made him the pivot of classical learning and the touchstone of literary taste, his correspondence grew enormously in bulk.[39] In 1518, in answer to Colet's complaint that he never wrote, he explained, not without pride, why he wrote 'short and seldom': he was overwhelmed by so many letters from bishops, high dignitaries, scholars, and friends from Italy, Spain, Germany, and France that he could not cope with them even if he had nothing else to do. He could not reply to all of them.[40] As early as 1516 he sometimes wrote a good twenty letters a day; later he gave even larger, almost unimaginable figures.[41] Admittedly, the stream of letters was not always constant. The peak times coincided with the spring and autumn book fairs in Frankfurt, when it was easier to have letters carried and delivered safely. They came in bundles at a time, from all parts of the world.[42] At such periods Erasmus often devoted half of his time to reading and answering his correspondence,[43] setting aside the afternoon for it. Straight after lunch he hurried to his writing desk. He wrote his letters standing, as, according to his own statement, he did much of his other work. In 1526 he tells us in passing that he had been accustomed to write standing for twenty years, and in 1533 he speaks of twenty-five years, from which we can deduce that he did not adopt this position until rather late, when he was already nearing forty. There are several portraits of Erasmus standing and writing at his desk: paintings by

---

36 Allen Ep 152:12–15 / CWE Ep 152:16–19
37 See Allen and CWE Ep 1316 introductions, Allen Ep 1440:4 and n / CWE Ep 1440:4–5 and n4.
38 Allen Ep 1756:4–10 / CWE Ep 1756:5–11
39 Huizinga *Erasmus of Rotterdam* 97
40 Allen Ep 786:5–9 / CWE Ep 786:6–10; cf Ep 873.
41 Allen Ep 480:27 / CWE Ep 480:29–30 (1516) speaks of 20 letters a day. Three letters from 1531 – Allen Epp 2451:11, 2461:1, 2466:242 / CWE Epp 2451:12, 2461:3–4, 2466:246–7 – mention 60, 100, and approximately 90 respectively; Allen Ep 2800:5 (1533) refers to 100.
42 Allen Epp 2315:1–5 with 1n, 2481:2 / CWE Ep 2312A:2–6
43 Allen Epp 1804:64–5, 1985:3–4 / CWE Epp 1804:69–71, 1985:3–4

Quinten Metsys and Hans Holbein, and a copper engraving by Dürer (done from memory or from a drawing made from life a few years earlier).[44]

His many visitors claimed another part of Erasmus' time: friends, fellow scholars, church dignitaries, noblemen and princes, booksellers, and couriers delivering letters or messages. Often his admirers came from great distances, and for them there was no greater honour than to be received and to converse with the celebrity Erasmus had now become. Visitors generally came bearing letters of recommendation, but even so they were not always welcome. Sometimes Erasmus was happier to see them go than arrive; particularly tiresome were those who would not hear of going before they had received a letter from him. Occasionally he could not conceal his irritation when an untimely visitor threw into disarray the daily programme that had cost him so much difficulty to arrange. Helius Eobanus Hessus experienced this in 1518 on his first and only meeting with the humanist he admired so greatly at the time. Erasmus was not well, very busy, and impatient with visitors; Eobanus remembered a reception that did not even pretend to be friendly. He was right: thirteen years later Erasmus himself felt obliged to explain to the poet and Latinist, now estranged from him, why he had greeted him so coolly at the time.[45] Nor were even trusted friends welcome if they disturbed him at his work; someone as close to him as Bonifacius Amerbach could be told tactfully but very clearly that he was expected in the afternoon, after lunch.[46]

In spite of his social obligations, which he must have found time-consuming and therefore burdensome, however closely they were connected with his work, Erasmus in his later years enjoyed great freedom in what he could do and choose not to do. In Basel and Freiburg he had the opportunity to live a life almost approaching his ideal, as Huizinga wrote, free from princely courts, independent of the protection of great lords, constantly devoting all his energy to the work that was dear to him.[47] But was his freedom of action as complete as it seemed? Until the last weeks of his life he was working without interruption for the printing press. Indeed the press tied his hands in his daily life to such an extent that he could hardly be said to be altogether free to allocate his time as he liked.

Erasmus' fame and influence, and the enormous flowering of the art of printing in the first half of the sixteenth century, cannot be imagined without each other. The humanist understood as well as anyone what a prospect printing with movable type had opened up for *bonae litterae*: the massive circulation of good books had become possible at low prices, at least low by comparison with manuscript codices. This was the theme of his dithyramb of 1519 on the 'almost superhuman art' of printing and its inventors – among whom he named as the most notable figure not Johann Gutenberg but his financial backer Johann Fust.[48] Erasmus must have realized very early the opportunities that the medium of print offered him personally, and thanks to the enormous demand for his works he was in a position to make the best use of them. For years the appearance of each new work from his pen was an

---

44 Cf Allen Epp 1759:50–5, 2776:69/cwe Ep 1759:53–9. The Metsys portrait (1517) is in the Galleria Nazionale d'Arte Antica in Rome (see cwe 4 370). One Holbein portrait (1523) is at Longford Castle near Salisbury (see Huizinga *Erasmus of Rotterdam* facing 103); two others, showing Erasmus at a writing desk, are in the Öffentliche Kunstsammlung, Basel (cwe 9 frontispiece) and the Louvre, Paris (Huizinga ibidem facing 207). The Dürer engraving (1526) is in the Cabinet des Estampes, Bibliothèque Royale, Brussels (see cwe Ep 1729:10–13 with n9 and the illustration, page 263).

45 Allen Epp 870 introduction and lines 1–2, 942:25–9, 2495:16–21/cwe Epp 870 introduction and line 3, 942:28–32

46 Ep 1914

47 *Erasmus of Rotterdam* 151

48 Allen Ep 919:1–17/cwe Ep 919:3–18

event in the literary world of the time. Selling them was rarely a problem. On the contrary. His *Paraphrase on the Acts of the Apostles* appeared simultaneously in 1524 in folio and octavo editions, and both editions, in print runs of 3,000 copies each, sold out in a month and a half.[49] In 1533 Hieronymus Froben sold his entire stock of the just-published *Explanatio symboli apostolorum* at the Frankfurt book fair in just three hours, so that later the author himself had some difficulty finding a copy to present to a friend.[50]

Throughout his life the demand for Erasmus' works remained constant. Almost all his books were reprinted after their first publication, sometimes four, five, or even more times, and reprints of his best-sellers appeared from presses in cities all over Europe in rapid succession. This was all the easier since the rights of the author – as of the publisher – were almost unprotected. What is now his most famous work, the *Praise of Folly* (1511), had appeared in thirty-six Latin editions by 1536, and it was far outstripped by *De copia* (1512), in its day an extremely popular schoolbook, which went into more than eighty editions.[51] Then there are the texts Erasmus edited, both his New Testament with Latin translation and the numerous editions of classical authors and Fathers of the church. Including all the reprints, these too amounted to several hundred editions. His popular edition of Cato's *Disticha moralia* with scholia, for example, went into approximately fifty editions within a quarter of a century.[52]

The number of copies of Erasmus' works in circulation during his lifetime was unusually high. Precise contemporary information is rare,[53] and modern estimates of the average print run in the early decades of the sixteenth century vary, but it was most likely a few hundred.[54] Only works of exceptional interest such as Erasmus' *De copia*, the *Moriae encomium*, or the *Colloquies* had print-runs of a thousand or more copies. In April 1515 Beatus Rhenanus informed Erasmus that the original printing of the *Moriae encomium* ran to 1,800 copies, of which only 600 were left;[55] in October 1523, a month after its first publication, Erasmus informed Johannes Fabri that 'a further three thousand of my *Spongia* have been printed.'[56] As we mentioned, in 1524 the *Paraphrase on Acts* appeared in two formats with a joint print

---

49 Allen Ep 1414 introduction; cf Allen Ep 1423:54–5/cwe Ep 1423:57–9; cwe 42 xxv–xxvi.

50 Allen Ep 2845:15–17

51 On the *Moria* see Allen and cwe Ep 222 introductions; asd iv-3 29, 40–60; cwe 27 78. On *De copia* see Allen and cwe Ep 260 introductions; asd i-6 14–15; cwe 24 282–3; Rix 'the Editions of Erasmus' *De copia*.'

52 See vl/Catalogue no 25 #1. The circulation of Erasmus' work was also shown by the numerous translations. His *Precatio dominica*, for example, first published by Froben at the end of 1523, was translated within ten years into Dutch, German, French, English, Spanish, Czech, and Polish. On this 'Paraphrase' on the Lord's Prayer and its reception see Hilmar Pabel *Conversing with God* 112; cwe 69 xvi, 56.

53 Exceptionally, in responding to a court order in 1526, Noel Béda obtained from his printer Josse Bade an impressively precise accounting of the printing and disposition of his *Annotationes Natalis Bede ... in Jacobum Fabrum ... et in Desiderium Erasmum Roterodamum*. Out of a print run of 650 (*integra* 625), Bade had sold or distributed to different cities all but 150 copies; see Farge *Religion, Reformation and Repression in the Reign of Francis I* (*Documents 1515–1543*) 277–8.

54 Reynolds and Wilson *Scribes and Scholars* 138: 'the average number of copies of all publications at this date is thought to have been 250 or a little more'; cf Febvre-Martin *L'Apparition du livre* (1971) 307–10/ *The Coming of the Book* 216–19. Cf also 11 n51 above and Eisenstein *The Printing Press as an Agent of Change* i 11. Even contemporaries could be confused. In a letter of 1529 Erasmus says that he had been told that Simon de Colines in Paris had printed an edition of the *Colloquies* in 24,000 copies (cwe 39 xxxii; cf Allen Ep 2126:139–40/cwe Ep 2126:148–50 and Allen Ep 1875 86n/cwe Ep 1875 n7). The unlikely estimate of the edition's size apparently stems from the circumstance that the edition (9 February 1527) was printed in 24o (vigesimo-quarto); see Moreau *Inventaire* iii no 1200. I am indebted to James K. Farge for this information.

55 Allen Ep 328:46–7/cwe Ep 328:47

56 Allen and cwe Ep 1397:3–4

run of 6,000 copies.[57] Even his last great work, the formidably voluminous *Ecclesiastes*, published in 1535 when the power of Erasmus' words was well past its zenith, was produced in an edition of 2,600 copies.[58]

Without taking these quantities as an index of the influence that Erasmus exerted, for we can no longer sound the depths of that influence, we are still safe in saying that he was for a long time the author in greatest demand in the international book market. When Francesco Giulio Calvo, a printer and bookseller in Italy, placed an order with a northern colleague in 1517, more than a third of it was for works by Erasmus; in 1520 his books made up the same percentage of the sales of John Dorne, a bookseller in Oxford. A detailed investigation of sixteenth-century Paris libraries showed that Erasmus' works were always found in them, often in large numbers.[59] In the German-speaking countries at this time, however, Erasmus had to face the fierce competition of Luther, some of whose works in the vernacular circulated in even larger editions.

If Erasmus gave the printing press a mighty boost, he in turn was in the grip of the explosive new medium: his way of life and above all its tempo were largely determined by it. Like it or not Erasmus had to work for the market, especially once his relationship with Froben had become permanent. In practice that meant that he worked for the Frankfurt market, which was growing by leaps and bounds and would become the unchallenged centre of the book trade in the sixteenth century, not only for Germany but for the whole of Europe.[60] Twice a year, in March and October, countless printer-publishers came to the fair from far and near to sell their latest publications. Besides one another they also met the great booksellers from other parts and sometimes an occasional scholar or writer – Erasmus himself once visited the fair intending to make some purchases.[61] As a good start in sales at the fair was very important, sometimes even decisive, for the success of a book, the spring and autumn fairs were the fixed points around which the lives of the leading publishers with wide sales distribution revolved. That was as true for Froben as it was for others. The planning of his publications was often entirely dictated by the date on which he had to leave for Frankfurt. Erasmus had to take this into account if he did not wish to disturb the production timetable of his printer and publisher or to spoil his own chances of getting a new work onto the market in time. The interests of the author and the printer-publisher ran in parallel, for neither wanted to wait an unnecessary six months or release a book in the interval between fairs, thus diminishing its prospects for wide distribution.

Not all of Erasmus' works appeared in this way, timed with an eye to the Frankfurt fair, but a great many did. This is clear from the dating of his dedications or introductory letters, which as a rule were the last part of the text to be set up in type with the other preliminary matter.[62] The copy for a new work or edition had to be in the printer's hands in good time. Very often Erasmus had no trouble getting it ready, but at other times he met the deadline only with great effort. He began writing his *Exomolegesis* in November 1523. The surviving copies show that some of them were printed in great haste, with an annoying error on the

---

57 See n49 above.

58 Allen Epp 3036 introduction, 3076:7–9; CWE 67 91 with n65

59 On Calvo see CEBR I 245–6; On Dorne see McConica *English Humanists* 89 and Smith *Erasmus, a Study of his Life, Ideals and Place in History* 158. On Paris libraries see Doucet *Les bibliothèques parisiennes au XVIe siècle*, especially 35, 51.

60 Ruppel 'Die Bücherwelt des 16. Jahrhunderts und die Frankfurter Büchermessen' 157

61 See 25 above.

62 For example the *Antibarbari*; see ASD I-1 14, Allen and CWE Ep 1110 introductions.

title-page, for the March 1524 fair, while the rest were finished with corrections in time for the autumn fair later the same year.[63]

Erasmus' polemical works in particular were often produced under enormous pressure. Topicality was a major factor; when he was attacked and wished to respond, Erasmus understood the importance of doing so as promptly as possible, and when the spring or autumn fair was imminent he could work at remarkable speed. In 1525 Erasmus wrote to Alberto Pio, prince of Carpi, about the reports circulating that he and others in Italy were accusing Erasmus of being the source of Luther's errors; Erasmus defended his own position and asked Pio, if the rumours were true, to stop attacking him. At the beginning of 1529 Pio published his criticisms in a letter to Erasmus, the *Responsio paraenetica*. Erasmus received a copy on 9 February. He set to work on his reply immediately. He completed his *Responsio ad epistolam paraeneticam Alberti Pii* in less than a week, he claimed, and the quarto volume of eighty pages was ready just in time for the spring fair.[64] Occasionally in his race with time he only managed half the course. He managed to deal blow for blow against the Spanish Franciscan Luis de Carvajal, who had taken up arms against his *Nugae*, before the Frankfurt fair in March 1529. When Carvajal renewed the attack the following year in a detailed pamphlet, however, Erasmus' reply, the *Epistola ad impudentissimos gracculos* ('shameless jackdaws,' that is, Carvajal and his fellow Franciscans), just made it in time for the spring fair and bore clear signs of the circumstances of its composition: written in great haste, it was an unusually brief – and in Erasmus' own eyes inadequate – piece of barely four pages.[65]

Erasmus was modest in his book purchases, as we noted in our discussion of the formation and growth of his library, but that did not mean that he was not interested in every important and timely new book that came from the presses. His involvement with the world of the book remained undiminished right up to his death. It is incredible how accurately and quickly he was informed of what was being written in the scholarly world and what was about to be published. But however well his information system functioned in general, it stood or fell by the regularity and reliability of the means of communication at his disposal. Naturally it made a great difference to his correspondence whether he could use existing regular connections or fixed channels, such as the network of links between the booksellers, or was forced to use more or less casual couriers. On the whole, his system of informants was exemplary when it concerned the German-speaking countries, Brabant, Flanders, and France; Italy, apart from Venice and Rome, probably remained a weak link. Erasmus did not, for example, have information about the progress of the edition of Chrysostom's commentaries on the Pauline Epistles in the original Greek instigated by Gian Matteo Giberti, the bishop of Verona, and published there in 1529. Erasmus would of course have been interested in this Italian edition, as he was working on Chrysostom himself. The corruption of the original Greek text gave him a great deal of trouble; the manuscript of the commentary on the Epistle to the Romans was so bad and difficult to decipher that in the end the edition of the *Opera* sponsored by Erasmus was published in 1530 without it.[66] Erasmus heard about the Italian edition in September 1530 from Germain de Brie, who was able to tell him that it made use of manuscripts once in the posssession of Cardinal Bessarion. Erasmus could

---

63 Allen Epp 1397:14, 1426 introduction/cwe Ep 1397:15

64 See Allen and cwe Ep 1634 introductions; cwe 84 lxv–lxvii. Cf 122 below.

65 Ep 2275; on Carvajal see Allen Ep 2110 introduction/cwe Ep 2110 n10.

66 See vl/Catalogue no 230; cf nos 58 and 394. For Erasmus' work on Chrysostom see also Allen and cwe Ep 1558 introductions, cwe Ep 1661 n2.

only wish the undertaking and the bishop, its editor and publisher and a scholar with whom he had corresponded, every success.[67]

In Basel, however, Erasmus was in an extremely favourable position, and much unsolicited bibliographical information reached him without difficulty. His very special relationship with the firm of Froben was enough on its own to ensure that practically no news from Europe's most important book market, the Frankfurt fair, escaped him. He was also fully aware of what was on offer in Basel itself. We cannot tell if he still frequented the bookshops in person. As long as his health permitted and the weather was clement, he probably did visit them himself; otherwise he could send one of his *famuli* to keep him informed of the newly published works, just as Syrus in the colloquy *Herilia* 'The Master's Bidding' has to go to the booksellers for his master Rabinius to inquire if new books have arrived and how much they cost.[68] He certainly kept an eye on what was for sale locally. He noted Christophe de Longueil's posthumous *Opera* and Niccolò Leonico Tomeo's *Dialogi* as soon as they were available in Basel in 1526.[69] In May 1531, when Helius Eobanus Hessus' edition of Theocritus, although it had appeared, was not yet in the bookshop, he noted this at once.[70] And friends sometimes asked him to buy something for them: Tunstall was one such.[71]

Erasmus knew of the imminent appearance of many important books, or books that were of interest to him, before they appeared, sometimes long before. Friends and correspondents kept him informed. His truest friend over many years, Bonifacius Amerbach – since 1525 a professor at Basel, a famous jurist, and himself more book-minded than most – must, as an associate of the firm of Froben, have been an invaluable source of information. Amerbach was always ready to help Erasmus, mediated between him and his suppliers and binders, and was an indispensable link with the world of the book. After his return from Avignon, he was a regular visitor and later, while Erasmus was living in Freiburg, he was his most frequent correspondent. Erasmus also owed much of his up-to-date news of books to his visitors from far and near and his far-flung correspondents, who enabled him, like a spider in its web, to follow what was afoot in the world of the printed word. He made use of his prior knowledge, often based on a statement in a letter that might be intended to be confidential, as he saw fit – for which he can hardly be blamed in an age when the letter still had a semi-private and semi-public character.[72] Sometimes he jumped the gun: in his *Ciceronianus* he made the speakers in the dialogue pass a verdict on a work by Ursinus Velius that was indeed planned or perhaps even begun when Erasmus heard of it – he could hardly have imagined that it would not appear before the public until two centuries later.[73]

Some authors with whom he corresponded kept him up to date with news of every important publication they had in hand. That was true, for example, of the scholar Guillaume Budé, the polemicist Ulrich von Hutten, the jurist Udalricus Zasius, or the theologian Jacopo

---

67 Allen Epp 2340:1–11, 2379:6–18 / CWE Epp 2340:2–12, 2379:6–17

68 ASD I-3 160:1125–7 / CWE 39 67:25–7; cf Bierlaire *La familia d'Erasme* 34.

69 Allen Ep 1675:13 and n / CWE Ep 1675:15 and nn7–8; cf VL/Catalogue nos 76 and 366 (Leonico Tomeo's *Opuscula* and *Dialogi*).

70 Allen Ep 2495:41–2

71 Allen Ep 1487:8 / CWE Ep 1487:10

72 See Huizinga *Erasmus of Rotterdam* 97–8.

73 See ASD I-2 689:3–6 with 3n / CWE 28 428; cf Allen Epp 1917 (1527, from Ursinus Velius) and 1977 (1528, to Willibald Pirckheimer). The work, *De bello Pannonico Fernandi I*, was not published until 1762 from the manuscript, which is still preserved (now Vienna MS lat. 7688).

Sadoleto.[74] Erasmus' advance knowledge also extended to books by authors whom he knew only slightly or not at all. He met the well-known mining expert Georgius Agricola not more than once in his life (and even that is not entirely certain), but he followed his progress carefully.[75] He had no personal acquaintance with the jurist Gregorius Haloander, who was known for his critical editions of the texts of the laws of Justinian, but he was well informed about his editions, which broke new ground. He realized the epoch-making character of the undertaking and asked Pirckheimer, who was involved in it, for information some time before the first part, containing the *Digest*, appeared in 1529.[76]

Erasmus sometimes knew about books in progress because he had encouraged his friends to write them or done his best to give a work a push, as was the case for example with Vives' edition of *De civitate Dei* and the *Proverbia* and *De rerum inventoribus* of Polidoro Virgilio.[77] Erasmus also received the first hint of forthcoming or newly published works from third parties, who supplied him with information from far and near. Towards the end of his life, to choose an example at random, he received a hint from Viglius Zuichemus in Padua of a new dictionary of the Latin language that a pupil of Marcus Musurus in Venice was on the point of publishing. He was immediately interested and obtained a copy for himself after it was published.[78]

Suspicious and fearful of possible attacks by his enemies, Erasmus was especially anxious to get prior knowledge of the content of polemics of which he himself was the target. This was not difficult, for kindred spirits and friends were always ready to give him advance warning as soon as they could.[79] Sometimes his opponents were courteous enough to let him know what to expect beforehand. Albert Pio sent Erasmus his *Responsio paraenetica* in manuscript, more for the sake of correctness and to prepare him than to discuss the content. In spite of Erasmus' request to delay publication, it appeared in print.[80] Closer to home little can have escaped him, even what took place among the presses themselves. When Oecolampadius' commentary on Isaiah was still in the press, he managed to procure a secretly printed offprint of part of it. Something similar happened with Pierre Cousturier's *Antapologia*; Erasmus was sent the first four gatherings before the book was published 'by a friend, who had wheedled them out of the printer while the work was being set.'[81]

Freedom of the press was still unknown as an ideal in the early sixteenth century, even though one is amazed by what could appear if those in power had no interest in preventing it. But it is hard to sympathize with Erasmus, who enjoyed unprecedented opportunities to write what he wanted, when he did not shrink from trying to muzzle others. His prior knowledge not infrequently enabled him to delay or even prevent publication of works that displeased him or, if publication was already a fait accompli, to nullify its effect as far as possible. He used his influence both with the chiefs of the Roman curia and with the secular

---

74 On Erasmus' corresondence with Budé see CEBR I 215–16; with Hutten, CEBR II 216–20; with Zasius, CEBR III 471–2; with Sadoleto, 40–2 above and CEBR III 186–7.

75 See VL/Catalogue no 78.

76 Allen Ep 1991:4–6, 67–8/CWE Ep 1991:5–9, 77. See VL/Catalogue no 147.

77 For the Vives edition see VL/Catalogue no 242. On Virgilio see Allen Ep 1210:1–9/CWE Ep 1210:2–9.

78 See VL/Catalogue no 1.

79 See for example Ep 2312 from Bonifacius Amerbach. Erasmus heard from Maternus Hatten about Zúñiga's *Erasmi Roterodami blasphemiae et impietates* (Allen Ep 1289:7–17/CWE Ep 1289:6–16); he obtained a copy of the Paris edition of Carvajal's *Apologia monasticae religionis diluens nugas Erasmi* (Allen Ep 2110:24–30/CWE Ep 2110:24–31; cf n65 above); and he learned about an attack on the *Ciceronianus* by Georg von Logau that was circulating in manuscript (Allen Ep 2961:158–61).

80 Allen Epp 1774:130, 2118:16–24/CWE Epp 1774:138, 2118:19–26. Cf 120 and n64 above; CWE 84 lvii.

81 On Oecolampadius' commentary see VL/Catalogue no 77; on Cousturier's *Antapologia*, no 151 #2.

authorities nearer home.[82] We must not judge him too harshly, for at the time such behaviour was common and more or less tolerated. In one case Erasmus must be exonerated of blame. It is not true that he had his friends buy up all the copies of the second furious diatribe against him by Julius Caesar Scaliger, so that the book disappeared without trace. Joseph Scaliger the son, although he had a great respect for Erasmus, made this claim in his table talk, later to be published as the famous *Scaligeriana*, but he must have been mistaken: the second speech referred to is certainly preserved and was published at the end of 1536, when Erasmus was already dead.[83]

Known as a pre-eminent Latinist from his youth, throughout his life Erasmus received manuscripts to read or criticize and was involved in the publication of many of them. As early as 1489 Cornelis Gerard, his senior and a fellow Augustinian from Lopsen, asked him to criticize his book *De morte*.[84] Later he must have read manuscripts regularly as literary adviser to Froben; he expected as a matter of course that Johannes Alexander Brassicanus would let him see his text of Salvian before submitting the manuscript to the press.[85] Sending manuscripts to friendly critics for their verdict was current practice in the scholarly world of the time, and Erasmus did exactly the same with his own work. Before he reached the summit of his powers he must have felt the need to test his work against the opinion of competent friends. Later, allowing someone to read a manuscript could serve another purpose; in sensitive religious questions Erasmus wished to discover the opinion of those who kept to the old faith.[86] Without seeing the full text of a book, he sometimes corresponded with the author about a particular problem. As a result of Erasmus' advice Hermannus Buschius changed the tone and the title of his famous plea for *bonae litterae*, the *Vallum humanitatis*.[87] Lazare de Baïf's treatise on the clothing of the ancients was published after an indirect exchange of ideas with Erasmus on a number of philological questions; this exchange prompted Erasmus to correct a translation in the next edition of his *Adagia*.[88]

Erasmus' involvement in the publications of other authors often went as far as seeking a printer or supervising publication, even including the technical printing process. The earliest example goes back to 1497, when he returned from Holland with the poems of the friend of his youth Willem Hermans in his luggage. Erasmus ensured that the *Silva odarum* was soon printed in Paris with a prefatory letter of recommendation from Gaguin and a poem of his

---

82 For example, he was delighted when the cardinals forbade the printing or sale of Zúñiga's *Blasphemiae et impietates* (Allen Ep 1302:59–61 / CWE Ep 1302:68–71); Erasmus managed to prevent the circulation of Nicolaus Ferber's attack on him in the Netherlands (Ep 2896); Sebastian Franck was expelled from Strasbourg in 1531 because Erasmus complained to the city government (Allen Ep 2615 introduction).

83 Allen Ep 3005 introduction

84 Allen Epp 19:32–4, 20:106–31 / CWE Epp 19:32–4, 20:104–28

85 Allen Ep 2305:16–18 / CWE Ep 2305:18–19

86 Erasmus asked Gaguin and Colet for their opinion of the *Antibarbari*; see ASD I-1 10 / CWE 23 3, 8–9 and the prefatory letter, Allen Ep 1110:28–34 / CWE Ep 1110:32–6. *De immensa Dei misericordia* (1524) was commissioned by and sent for comment to Bishop Christoph von Utenheim; see Epp 1456, 1464 and CWE 70 70. Henry VIII was asked to comment on *De libero arbitrio* (1524); see Allen Ep 1430:12–19 / CWE Ep 1430:15–22, and cf VL/Catalogue no 376. Erasmus asked for the opinion of Ambrosius Pelargus on his *Declarationes ad censuras Lutetiae vulgatas* (1532); see VL/Catalogue no 337 #1. Erasmus said that his *Epistola de esu carnium* (1524) was published at the request of Bishop von Utenheim after it had been examined by Ludwig Baer; see *Catalogus lucubrationum* Allen I 33:33–9, Ep 1581:717–25 / CWE Epp 1341A:1306–13, 1581:798–807, and cf VL/Catalogue no 341. On the *Apologia adversus monachos* see Epp 1879, 1967 and cf VL/Catalogue nos 352 #2, 153 #1.

87 See VL/Catalogue no 40 #1.

88 See VL/Catalogue no 73 #1; cf 43–4 above.

own.[89] Such a service might be requested, but it could also be offered spontaneously. In 1504 he offered his services to Colet unasked: 'If you would like to have any of your works printed, merely send me the manuscript and for the rest I will see to it that the printed version is quite accurate.'[90] In 1511 he undertook to help another good friend, Andrea Ammonio, who lived in London. Erasmus was in England from the summer of 1509 to July 1514. When he visited Paris in 1511 he took a manuscript collection of Ammonio's poems with him to have them printed.[91] And when Thomas More expressed the wish to publish his *Utopia*, Erasmus took the hint: the famous work first appeared, at Erasmus' instigation, from the press of Dirk Martens in Leuven in 1516.[92] Sometimes it was the printer-publisher, with or without the agreement of the author, who sought his help. The printer Johann Schöffer directed an inquiry, which had presumably been prompted by the author, to Erasmus, who did his best to answer the question.[93]

---

89 *Catalogus lucubrationum* Allen I 49:27 / CWE Ep 1341A:77–8 with n9; Reedijk *Poems* no 40 / ASD I-7 and
    CWE 85–6 no 7. Erasmus also contributed an epigram on the title-page; Reedijk no 43 / ASD I-7 and CWE 85–6
    no 30. Erasmus' dedication of the *Silva odarum* to Hendrik van Bergen (Ep 49) was printed at the end.
90 Allen Ep 181:59–61 / CWE Ep 181:68–70
91 Epp 218–21. Only one copy of this book of poems is known; it is in the Bibliothèque nationale in Paris.
92 See Allen Epp 461:1–3, 474:23–4, 477:5–7 / CWE Epp 461:2–4, 474:26–7, 477:7–9; on the printing, Allen
    Epp 487:1–4, 491:13 / CWE Epp 487:2–5, 491:12.
93 Cf 51 and n242 above.

Conclusion

In his study of Erasmus' editorial work, P. Petitmengin reminds us how unfortunate it is that Erasmus' library, where there must have been many books annotated in his own hand, has been dispersed. It is impossible to reconstitute his workroom, as one can do in the case of Beatus Rheanus or of other scholars – less celebrated, perhaps, but treated more kindly by fate in this respect.[1] If we take it literally, we can hardly quarrel with Petitmengin's discouraging finding, and it is true that nothing makes us more painfully aware of what we have lost through the disappearance of Erasmus' library than a reference to the rich library of Beatus Rhenanus, which is still preserved complete and intact in its historic environment at Sélestat. We cannot enter Erasmus' workroom in Basel (where more material remains recall the humanist than anywhere else), and pick up one by one from their shelves or chests the books that once surrounded him; that experience is denied to us forever. Every trace of his library has vanished, and we have to travel to four countries and visit at least eight collections in order to inspect, as stray and isolated curiosities, the volumes that remain of what was once in his possession.

Yet the defeatism of Petitmengin's statement was not entirely justified. Has not the attempt made in this book to identify the volumes so cryptically listed after his death put us in a position to form a picture of the library, its extent, its content, and its character? It has proved rewarding to enter Erasmus' study in our imagination with the *Versandliste* in hand and to subject the contents of his shelves and book chests to a closer inspection. The result is not a complete or exact reconstruction of his library; it could not be, because the precise identity of too many books remains uncertain. Nevertheless we now have a much clearer idea of Erasmus' collection of books than was formerly possible, an idea that is documented and persuasive, and that on the whole probably does not greatly distort the reality of 1536.

Most of Erasmus' books have disappeared, including the many copies in which we might have expected to find his own marginal notes. But if such annotated copies had survived, would they have told us as much about Erasmus' methods of work as has been thought? In the books preserved – and they include such important authors as Aristotle, Athenaeus, Euripides, and Aulus Gellius, favourites to whom he made frequent references – the autograph marginalia are not abundant; further study must determine if they are really important. The only work of his own authorship to have survived from his library, the collected edition of his *Apologiae*, did indeed contain valuable additions to the printed text, not known from any other source.[2]

The *Versandliste* of books sent to Łaski in Poland gives us a snapshot of Erasmus' library in 1536. But he never saw his library as static; it was dynamic, always subject to change. His

---

1 'Comment étudier l'activité d'Erasme éditeur de textes antiques?' 219
2 See 57–8 and 102–3 above.

consistent policy was to keep his collection of books up to date and to remove anything that seemed to have been superseded by more recent works. This means that the value of the inventory of the library is quite specific: we now know better than before the working equipment Erasmus had within reach in the last years of his life.

An evaluation of Erasmus' library must therefore be confined to examining the most striking characteristics of the collection, and the scope of such an evaluation can only be modest. In general, 'the library of a humanist is a precious record of his culture and intellectual interests, of the arguments and authors which influenced and delighted him';[3] this remains true even if, in Erasmus' case, caution is called for in making connections between the library reconstructed from the *Versandliste* and the personality of its owner.

Erasmus' library, built up, maintained, and carefully looked after as a matter of policy, was not remarkably large. The collections of many contemporaries, some of them much less learned, far outstripped it. We need not make a comparison with the huge collections of the Italian humanists, who strove to achieve a certain completeness, but even north of the Alps several contemporary libraries far exceeded that of Erasmus in size.[4] What is important, however, is that it was never Erasmus' ambition to form an imposing library for its own sake. The motives of the pure bibliophile were simply foreign to him. In this he differed from many Italian humanists; Pico della Mirandola, for example, consciously sought to build up an extensive collection.[5]

Even if Erasmus had shared the ambition of several well-known humanists of the fifteenth and sixteenth centuries to surround himself with an impressive library, rich above all in precious old manuscripts, it would have been materially impossible for him to fulfil such an ambition. Until his forties lack of money kept him from building up his collection, and when he did at length have enough financial freedom to acquire books, especially from the time he settled in Basel, he was able to procure every book that interested him and consult it through the mediation of others.[6]

The striking lacunae in his library often relate to books that appeared in the last years of his life. That there were such gaps is clear from the purchases of 1525.[7] Was it chance that of the three great Greek tragedians, the *editiones principes* of Sophocles and Euripides, published in 1503 and 1506 respectively, were present while the first complete Greek text of Aeschylus, the Aldine edition of 1518, was missing? The Greek text of Epictetus was not published until rather late, in 1528. Erasmus, who for years had owned a Latin translation of Epictetus' *Enchiridion* in the *Opera Politiani* (1498 or 1512),[8] did not go on to acquire the work in its original text.

In Erasmus' years in Basel the possession of books was not an end in itself, and his purchases must seldom have gone beyond the strictly necessary. If this assumption is correct, it is more than likely that very many of the books published at this time and mentioned in the *Versandliste*, perhaps more than can be proved, were gifts and not purchased.[9] Erasmus did not add all such gifts to his library. Many of them he disposed of later, so that we can

---

3 Ullman and Stadler *The Public Library of Renaissance Florence: Niccolo Niccoli, Cosimo de' Medici and the Library of San Marco* 59
4 For example those of F. Colombo, Nicolaus Cusanus, Johann von Dalberg, Beatus Rhenanus, H. Schedel, Jakob Spiegel, Johannes Trithemius, and Johann Reuchlin
5 Kibre *The Library of Pico della Mirandola* 11–16
6 Cf 18–19, 22, 31–2 above.
7 Cf 32–3 above.
8 VL/Catalogue no 285
9 Cf 33–52 above.

say that most of the presentation copies still in his library in 1536 must have been books he consciously valued, for whatever reason, and chose to retain.

More than might perhaps have been thought, Erasmus kept books with which he had an emotional bond. Thus, apart from its function as a primary source of information, his library must also have represented something much more difficult to express in words. On his shelves were books by authors whose work he knew through and through and had himself edited and provided with critical commentaries. There were also the works of authors with whom he had been in direct contact, and gifts presented to him personally by their authors. He prized the Musurus editions for their quality, but at the same time they evoked for him personal recollections of the man himself, whose acquaintance he had made at Padua in the winter of 1508–9. A few lesser known or unknown relationships have been brought to light by books on the *Versandliste* that were almost certainly gifts, as in the cases of Arduenna and Agrippa. Some manuscripts, for example that of Mombaer, also formed part of his library as 'living documents.'[10] Clearly Erasmus felt that he had grown up with his books.

In a study of Pico della Mirandola's library, P. Kibre has noted that the catalogues of private libraries provide a way to ascertain and evaluate their owners' intellectual interests, especially in conjunction with their writings. Even though it cannot be assumed that because someone owned a book he therefore read it, 'its presence and preservation indicate something of the esteem in which it was held.'[11] The value of his library for Erasmus lay in the authors represented and the quality of the editions chosen; examination of the *Versandliste* allows us to form a judgment about Erasmus' interests and what he valued in his books.

What was the most distinctive characteristic of Erasmus' library, as we know it to have been at the end of his life? Beyond doubt, its modern character, in two respects: it was a library of printed books rather than manuscripts, and its contents represented the world of the new learning, not that of medieval scholasticism.

Erasmus' collection breathed the spirit of the new age and was one of the first to exemplify completely the emergence and growing supremacy of the art of printing. It was the first example of a representative library that did not contain a significant number of manuscripts. Reuchlin, who was at most fourteen years older than Erasmus, still owned a very extensive collection of works in manuscript. There is nothing to indicate that Erasmus himself deliberately sought to acquire old manuscripts. The few he had were probably more or less casual acquisitions or manuscripts or transcripts with some personal background. It was not just a question of money, for anyone who wanted them still had the opportunity to acquire old manuscripts for little or no money, as Beatus Rhenanus and Brassicanus proved. Nothing suggests that Erasmus had any ambitions in this field. A library full of precious manuscripts had long been a status symbol for scholars, but for Erasmus, if there was nothing good to be said of the contents of the handwritten books, no matter how beautifully decorated and bound, there was nothing to praise in such a collection. Quite the contrary: in the colloquy *Synodus Grammaticorum* 'A Meeting of the Philological Society' he poked fun at the library of a clerical friend because his library consisted entirely of manuscripts.[12]

---

10 See vL/Catalogue nos 100, 102, 103, 116, 218, 297 and cf cebr ii 472–3 (Musurus); vL/Catalogue no 364 and 44 above (Arduenna); vL/Catalogue no 43 and 45 above (Agrippa). See also vL/Catalogue no 12 #3 and 45 above (Rabelais); no 316 and 45 above (Gilles); vL/Catalogue no 387 #2 (cf no 390 and 97 above (Mombaer).

11 Kibre *The Library of Pico della Mirandola* 21

12 asd i-3 586/cwe 40 834. Lieven Hugenoys had helped Erasmus to acquire a manuscript of the New Testament; in his first will Erasmus bequeathed to him a set of his future *Opera omnia* (Allen vi 505:104/cwe 12 546:98). On him see see Allen Ep 1214 introduction and cebr ii 212.

Erasmus' life coincided with the rise of the printed book, and he himself was a driving force of the new medium. Printing was still in its infancy when he was a young man; by the time of his death it had reached full maturity. Although demonstration is difficult, the printed book completely superseded the manuscript in libraries by the middle of the sixteenth century. The library of Pico della Mirandola, built up at the height of the age of the manuscript book, totalled 1,190 volumes when the catalogue was compiled in 1498; of these 489 – about 40 per cent – were printed books.[13] An investigation of available inventories of French libraries reveals that around 1525 manuscripts made up 25 to 30 per cent of library collections, but that twenty-five years later a manuscript was no more than a relic of the past.[14] How far this conclusion represents a norm and applies to other libraries is perhaps an open question, but it certainly applies to that of Erasmus.

Erasmus' library was also modern in the nature of its books. Typically medieval works are scarcely to be found in it. The Fathers of the church are certainly represented, but they formed a significant part of humanism and were also included in the libraries of the Italian humanists. But everything that breathed the spirit of scholastic learning was kept to a minimum. His own pronouncements offer us no firm basis on which to asses Erasmus' relationship with scholasticism: sometimes he expressed himself favourably about certain scholastics, but on other occasions his general verdict was damning. Yet whatever his deepest feelings about scholasticism may have been, Erasmus was thoroughly at home in the works of a number of prominent figures. The contents of his library support this view: those present include Peter Lombard, John Duns Scotus, Thomas Aquinas, Jean Gerson, and Durandus of Saint-Pourçain. Presumably he consulted few scholastics outside the 'moderns' – that is, the scholastics – whose works he had within reach at home. He claimed more than once to his orthodox opponents that he did not have an unfavourable opinion of the scholastic theologians, urging as proof of this that he named or cited many of them in his works.[15] Those 'many' were not that many: those whom he cited frequently were the very scholars just named and represented in his library. It is worth noting that Durandus was among them, for he is not the most obvious author to expect.[16]

We do not, however, find the encyclopaedic summaries of late medieval learning, typified by the *De proprietatibus rerum* of Bartholomaeus Anglicus (Cologne c 1470) and the *Margarita philosophica* of Gregor Reisch (Freiburg 1503). In Erasmus' library the Elder Pliny's *Naturalis historia* takes their place. Besides Pliny, who alone will furnish an immense amount

---

13 Kibre *The Library of Pico della Mirandola* 112

14 Doucet *Les bibliothèques parisiennes au XVIe siècle* 26

15 See Dolfen *Die Stellung des Erasmus von Rotterdam zur scholastischen Methode* 94. Cf Thompson's remark ('Better Teachers' 132): 'And to say with one eminent scholar [Ferguson *Opuscula* 191] that thereafter Erasmus "ignored" scholastic learning is going too far. He objected to it, he belittled it, but he did not ignore it.' Cf also ASD IV-3 (*Moriae encomium*) 157 498n: Erasmus expressed a certain respect for St Thomas Aquinas, 'in spite of his commanding position among scholastic theologians.' His library contained editions of Peter Lombard's *Sentences* (VL/Catalogue nos 63, 163), Scotus' commentaries on the *Sentences* (no 167), Gerson (no 169), Durandus (no 168), the *Glossa ordinaria* (no 154), and several works of Thomas Aquinas, including the commentaries on Paul (nos 161, 162, 165, and 170).

16 Guillaume Durand, a distinguished French canonist, had studied in Italy and taught at Modena and Bologna. In 1285 he became bishop of Mende. He was born about 1230 and died in 1296, the era of high scholasticism. His *Speculum iudicale*, an authoritative and highly influential text, focused on legal procedure. His *Pontificale*, a codification of liturgical practices, became the standard work throughout the Roman church and was the basis for the first printed Roman *Pontifical* (Rome 1485). A partial revision took place under Pope Pius XII; revision of the remainder was ordained at the Second Vatican Council.

of information, Erasmus recommended in his *De ratione studii* three other late classical guides to literature and culture, namely, Macrobius' *Saturnalia*, Athenaeus' *Deipnosophistae*, and Gellius' *Noctes Atticae*: they might well replace a whole library for those without time or books.[17] In the sixteenth century the boundary between the new humanistic reference works and the old repositories of fantastic and legendary lore was still being explored. The latter, although outdated, were still reprinted and sold; Reisch's *Margarita* was available in Basel in Erasmus' time. Bartholomaeus' *De proprietate rerum* was not, but a century later Shakespeare was still familiar with it.[18]

In the long-accepted manner of his day, Erasmus cited many writers whom he did not know at first hand from compilations. He acquired several Bible commentaries rather late, more or less compelled to do so by his learned conservative opponents, who in their polemics with him appealed to proof texts drawn from such works. Thus he found himself forced to make fairly intensive use of the *Glossa ordinaria* – the *Ordinary Gloss* – which generally enjoyed a great reputation. By making it clear that his *Annotations* on the New Testament were supported by the *Gloss*, 'he tried to stop the mouths of those who objected to him that he introduced innovations or sowed confusion and uncertainty by his criticism.'[19]

Once we understand that Erasmus' library was a study and reference apparatus, we can understand – even predict – the presence or absence of certain books in it. We can conclude with Husner that the core of the library 'belonged to his working equipment, or was close to his heart for some other reason.'[20] It was attuned to his special interests, and because those interests covered such a wide field, it was a many-sided collection with the emphasis very much on standard works. Editions of texts dominated, and there were many reference books comparable to modern and classical encyclopaedic works and dictionaries. Even in areas that were not his preferred domain, Erasmus was careful to have the leading books in his house. In both canon and secular law, for example, he was sufficiently well equipped to find answers to the main questions that might confront him. Three founders of the humanist school of legal scholarship, who applied the historical and philological method to the study of Roman law, Guillaume Budé, Udalricus Zasius, and Andrea Alciati, were each represented by one or more of their most important and most characteristic works.[21]

But the library was most strongly developed in the two fields that reflected the deepest core of Erasmus' being and his ambitions: classical antiquity and Christianity. He possessed the works of the ancient authors in the best editions that existed. Erasmus bought or tried to buy exclusively first-class editions. The Greek texts in his library, taken as a whole, are among the finest products of Aldo Manuzio's press, and he also possessed several of the renowned editions of Calliergis. Similarly, the completeness of his collection of the works of his own time dealing with biblical exegesis – probably the largest group of related books in his library – is particularly striking. All the important commentaries were present: Petrus Mosellanus, Lefèvre d'Etaples, Cajetanus, Oecolampadius, Luther, and Melanchthon, with

---

17 LB I 523B / ASD I-2 120 / CWE 24 673. See Chomarat *Grammaire et rhétorique* I 408 and VL/Catalogue nos 205, 207, 412 (Pliny), 282 (Macrobius), 239 (Athenaeus), and 281 (Gellius).

18 Welti *Basler Buchdruck und Britannien* 68–70

19 de Jonge 'Erasmus und die Glossa Ordinaria zum Neuen Testament' 71

20 Husner 245; cf Braches 'Boekkunst in de bibliotheek' 59.

21 See VL/Catalogue nos 287–92 (Budé); 30 #1, 188 #2, 404 #2 (Zasius), 135 (Alciati). Cf Allen Ep 541:45–59 / CWE Ep 541:51–65.

the commentators who leaned towards the Reformation appearing to be the more numerous.[22] Erasmus remained interested in the circle of Christian humanists around Lefèvre d'Etaples, and all of Lefèvre's important editions were found in his library, not only purely Christian texts but his editions of Aristotle as well. Both scholars were working towards the same goal and were watched with deep suspicion by the conservative theologians. Although they felt a great admiration for each other, a difference of opinion about a commentary on the Epistles of Paul ultimately drove them into controversy.[23] Erasmus also owned the works of Lefèvre's pupil Josse Clichtove, whom he described in 1521 as 'a most copious fount of eloquence.'[24] The impression that Erasmus was consciously building a reference library is reinforced if we are right to assume that a large part of the literature occasioned by current controversies may well have been kept out of the library and was often left unbound.[25]

Of the roughly five hundred titles on the *Versandliste* that can be identified with any certainty, 60 per cent were typical products of the humanist presses. It almost goes without saying that editions of ancient texts made up the lion's share; together they made up almost a third of the library. In view of Erasmus' great preference for Greek we need not be too surprised to find the works of the Greek authors outnumbering those of the Latin authors, though one must bear in mind that at least half of the Greek works were translated into Latin. In many cases Erasmus must have possessed these Latin versions before the *editio princeps* in the original language was published. Everything suggests that he tried to procure these editions as soon as they appeared. The number of *editiones principes* of classical authors that appeared in his lifetime was remarkably large, especially for the Greeks. Knowledge of Greek had grown enormously thanks to the representatives of Byzantine scholarship who had emigrated to Italy, the circle around Bessarion. The number of important editions produced by the members of that circle, including Doukas, Apostolius, Calliergis, and Musurus, is striking. As Geanakoplos put it, 'Greek literature came to the west through the long filter of Byzantium.'[26] Erasmus had acquired a reasonable mastery of Greek by 1502, and he was able to enlarge his knowledge even further in Venice, where he lived for nine or ten months in 1508 and saw the Aldine edition of the *Adagia* through the press.[27]

Erasmus' recognition of the superiority of Italian humanism, whose work had opened up new paths to scholarship, is evident in the remarkably high percentage of books in the library on philology, history, and medicine printed in Italy or prepared by Italians: Lorenzo Valla, Angelo Poliziano, Ermolao Barbaro, Niccolò Leonico Tomeo, Flavio Biondo, and Bartolomeo Platina Sacchi. Erasmus' great admiration for the first three is still shared in the

---

22 VL/Catalogue nos 18 #1 (Mosellanus), 20 #1, 178, 179, 196 and 252 (Lefèvre d'Etaples); 177, 254 (Cajetanus); 34, 77, 188 #1, 357 #1 (Oecolampadius); 10 #2, 44, 52, 97 #3, 173, 369, 381, 406 #2 (Luther); 3, 8, 9, 11, 14, 37, 39, 45, 97 #1 (Melanchthon)

23 On Lefèvre and the controversy see Allen and CWE Ep 315 introductions, Allen Epp 692:21–5, 597:32–40 and nn/CWE Epp 480A:22–6 and 23n, 597:37–45 and nn; and Augustijn *Erasmus* (Baarn 1986) 99–101/(Toronto 1991) 113–15. Goldschmidt calls Erasmus the first great scholar of modern times and Lefèvre d'Etaples the last typical representative of the Middle Ages; see *Medieval Texts and their First Appearance in Print* 54–8.

24 Allen Ep 1212:46–7/CWE Ep 1212:49–50. See VL/Catalogue nos 23, 60, and 181.

25 See 104–5 above.

26 Geanakoplos 'The discourse of Demetrius Chalcondyles on the Inauguration of Greek Studies at the University of Padua in 1463' 144

27 See Allen and CWE Ep 211 introductions. On Erasmus and Greek see also 19–21 above; Allen Epp 172:9–14, 181:34–6, 203:2–3 and I (Beatus Rhenanus to Hermann of Wied) 55:79–83/CWE Epp 172:12–18, 181:39–41, 203:3–4.

twenty-first century: they were 'the humanist teachers of Europe,' and philological humanism reached its zenith with Poliziano and Barbaro.[28]

It may be surprising to find that the works of Pico della Mirandola and Ficino are absent from the library, apart from the former's letters and the latter's extremely important translations of the texts of Plato and Plotinus, because 'Erasmus was, to a much greater extent than is usually realized, a student and disciple of the Italian Renaissance, of its humanism as well as of its Platonism.'[29] His acceptance of Italy's dominant contribution to the revival of ancient culture meant, up to a point, a victory over his own intellectual formation as predominantly 'northern' in spite of his cosmopolitanism. Although once or twice he appeared to accept the situation as self-evident, the element of rivalry was almost always present in his thinking.[30] And though he never made any secret of his debt to some of the Italian humanists, he condemned both their neo-pagan tendencies and their rigid artistic cult of Ciceronianism.[31]

Several of the Italian editions in Erasmus' library included commentaries, for example Filippo Beroaldo's commentary on Suetonius and Niccolò Perotti's commentary on Martial (in his *Cornucopia*). The fact that Erasmus owned three editions of Dioscorides is to be explained by the importance he clearly attached to the different commentaries.[32] To the end of his life Erasmus remained interested in Italian developments and felt a need to keep himself informed of the work of the humanists he had met in Italy.

If we compare the library of Erasmus with those of the Italian humanists of almost a century earlier – leaving aside the mere number of books or the proportions of manuscript and printed works and focusing exclusively on the content of the books – we can see a clear distinction and a clear resemblance.

The obvious distinction is the greater share of Greek texts in Erasmus' library; in the Italian libraries, Latin authors made up the great majority right through the fifteenth century. In their search for manuscripts Italian humanists concentrated on Latin authors; in spite of the gradual emergence of Greek editions, it was an exception for scholars to read Homer or Plato in the original until about 1480. Knowledge and study of Greek remained for a time confined to a small group, and some important collections neglected Greek altogether. In the Gonzaga library there were no Greek manuscripts in 1407, nor did the Este library contain a single work in the language in 1436. The library of San Marco in Florence owned 182 Greek works at the end of the century (6 of them printed) and 1,053 Latin volumes (of which 870 were manuscripts).[33] A Greek work could only find a wide circle of readers if a translation was available. Pico della Mirandola, who in any case owned more patristic and medieval texts than purely classical works, read the Greek historians largely in Latin versions.[34] Niccoli's library was particularly rich in Greek manuscripts, but he himself

28 vl/Catalogue nos 2 #3, 153 #2, 364 ##2 and 3 (Valla); 285 (Poliziano); 201, 279 #1 (Barbaro); 76, 309, 366 (Leonico Tomeo); 264 (Biondo); 302 #2 (Platina). See Weiss *The Spread of Italian Humanism* 88 and 'Italian Humanism in Western Europe, 1460–1520' 72.

29 Kristeller 'Erasmus from an Italian Perspective' 13; cf Tracy 'Erasmus Becomes a German.' For Pico's letters see vl/Catalogue no 285 (and cf nos 12 n2, 24 n6); for Ficino's translations, cf nos 216 and 217 (Plato), 209 (Plotinus). See also ASD I-2 664 3n and 5n.

30 See Ep 397.

31 Buck 'Überlegungen zum gegenwärtigen Stand der Renaissanceforschung' 30; cf CWE Epp 1701:29–31 and n6, 1706:38–45 and n11, 1717:5 and n2, 1719 n18; the introductory note to *Ciceronianus* in CWE 28 328–9.

32 See vl/Catalogue nos 262 (Beroaldo), 384 (Perotti); 201, 202, and 203 (Dioscorides).

33 Ullman and Stadler *The Public Library of Renaissance Florence: Niccolo Niccoli, Cosimo de' Medici and the Library of San Marco* 110–12

34 Bolgar *The Classical Heritage and Its Beneficiaries* 458

seems to have had a shaky grasp of the language.[35] Bessarion was in fact the only humanist who had more Greek than Latin authors in his library. In Spain the library of the college of St Ildefonso, the nucleus of the library of Alcalá University, contained only 14 Greek books in 1512. Comparison of the titles of Greek books in these libraries with those in the *Versandliste* shows that the library of Erasmus was quite up to date.[36]

Apart from the typographical difficulties, there was not enough demand for Greek texts at the time to make an edition pay. A good example is the work of Plato, which was not printed in Greek until 1513, while Ficino's translation had appeared as early as 1485 in an edition of 1,025 copies, an unusually large number compared with the average print run at that time of 250.[37] Analysis of the language of 24,421 incunabula has revealed that 77.42 per cent were written in Latin, while the number of works in Greek was negligible.[38] In 1495 Aldo Manuzio made a start on a complete collection of Greek grammars with the works of Gaza, Apollonius, Herodian, and Apostolius.[39] Although it was to be many years before most of ancient literature was available in print, thanks to the efforts of this printer alone, by around 1516 many Latin authors and a respectable number of the Greeks were in circulation.

Though Erasmus' library differs from those of his Italian contemporaries in that it contained a greater proportion of Greek books, it resembles them in the strong representation, among the authors found in it, of the Fathers of the church. Research since the 1950s has drawn attention to the prominence the humanists gave to the question of the relationship between Christianity and classical antiquity. This was a question to which the Fathers, who respected the ancient authors and enlisted them as their allies, had already supplied an answer. The Fathers were regarded as Christian classics; for the humanists they were authors to be studied, cited as authorities, interpreted, and edited. For Valla the Fathers had even served as literary models, for they had patterned their style on that of the ancients.[40]

Taken as a whole, Erasmus' library was not very different from the collections amassed by his northern contemporaries, yet one may say that Erasmus started to acquire Greek printed texts very early and may be counted among the pioneers. Greek authors were indeed represented in the libraries of northern Europe, albeit sometimes in small numbers and then often in Latin translation. In 1518 most of the books of the young Martin Bucer, then still a Dominican monk who had only recently come into contact with Luther, were works of classical authors. Bucer was clearly inclined towards humanism, as was Jakob Spiegel – but then, who among the cultivated upper strata of the population could be untouched by *bonae litterae*?[41] In 1504 Pirckheimer, who systematically collected them, boasted that he possessed every Greek book that had been printed anywhere in Italy.[42] Reuchlin too procured almost all his books from Italy and owned nearly all the early Aldine editions.[43] The library of Johannes Trithemius, which numbered more than 2,000 volumes in 1505, many of them rare

---

35 Niccolò de' Niccoli (1364–1437), a Florentine humanist active in the learned society around Cosimo de' Medici, was a prominent copyist and collector of manuscripts with an extensive private library.
36 Geanakoplos 'The discourse of Demetrius Chalcondyles on the Inauguration of Greek Studies at the University of Padua in 1463' 110–12
37 Reynolds and Wilson *Scribes and Scholars* 137–8; cf, on print runs, 118 n54 above.
38 Lenhart *Pre-Reformation Printed Books* 36–40
39 Bolgar *The Classical Heritage and Its Beneficiaries* 280
40 Buck 'Der italienische Humanismus' 28–31
41 See Krüger *Bucer und Erasmus: Eine Untersuchung zum Einfluss des Erasmus auf die Theologie Martin Bucers* 44–9; Burmeister 'Die Bibliothek des Jakob Spiegel.'
42 Lowry *The World of Aldus Manutius* 274
43 Christ *Die Bibliothek Reuchlins in Pforzheim* 16–18

and precious, contained a very varied selection of secular and religious literature in many different languages.[44] Unfortunately we do not know the contents of Luther's collection, though we do have his guidelines for the formation of an ideal library.[45] The difference is not in the categories that compose it but in emphasis. Luther was as passionate and tireless a reader as Erasmus, but his interests were clearly different and focused more exclusively on theology. We may expect that classical antiquity was more strongly represented in Erasmus' collection than in Luther's.

We must never forget that Erasmus collected books for use, not for show; he built a reference library to meet his own needs. He studied many works attentively, and this is nowhere more apparent than in the additions he made to revised and enlarged editions of his *Adagia* and his Annotations on the New Testament. He did so on the basis of information in books he had newly acquired. He conscientiously continued this work as long as his health allowed. It is fascinating to see how a presumably rapid glance at a book could sometimes nevertheless leave a trace in his work. How can we explain his ironic allusion in the *Sileni Alcibiadis* of 1515 to the mythical founder of the English royal house, the Trojan Brutus, unless he had been looking at Geoffrey of Monmouth's *Historia regum Britanniae*, a copy of which he must have acquired by then?[46] Erasmus' seeming lack of interest in buying new books for his library in his last years must not be misunderstood; he remained interested in books until his death, and few of his contemporaries were so well informed as was he.

---

44 Brann *The Abbot Trithemius (1462–1516): The Renaissance of Monastic Humanism* 13
45 Burger *Renaissance, Humanismus, Reformation* 457; Ullman and Stadler *The Public Library of Renaissance Florence* 109–10
46 See VL/Catalogue no 315.

Index

PART TWO

The *Versandliste* of Erasmus' Library in 1536:
An Annotated Catalogue

Introduction: Methods and Resources

Various inventories of Erasmus' library were drawn up during his lifetime. His estate included a document that the notary described as 'a Catalogue in which all books are listed in order, compiled some time ago by Erasmus' late servant.'[1] This may have been a register compiled in connection with the sale of the books to Jan Łaski in 1525 and not kept up to date after that. Whether it was sent to Poland together with the library in 1536, as Husner suggests, is difficult to establish.[2] In the settlement of the estate, Andreas Frycz, acting for Łaski, mentions another list, in Erasmus' own hand, of books and manuscripts that had entered his collection after the original agreement. This may have been a survey of acquisitions made since 1525 with the help of which Erasmus could show to what extent the library had increased in value. In 1538 Łaski's solicitor handed the document over to Erasmus' executors in Basel in order to support his claim to three undelivered manuscripts.[3] Finally, Łaski also had at his disposal an inventory that he had left behind after his stay in Basel but asked to have back in 1528.[4] Although it is not certain, it may have been to this inventory that he was referring when he told his friend Hardenberg in 1540 about 'my own catalogue written, as you know, by myself' and sent him this list of books in the following year.[5] All these details are of little relevance, however, since not one of the three book lists mentioned has hitherto come to light. It is thus all the more fortunate that we have the list drawn up in connection with, and shortly before, the dispatch of Erasmus' library to Poland. The *Versandliste*, with its all too summary short titles, may well contain fewer details about individual books than the lost catalogues. It has, however, what for us is the inestimable advantage of being up to date: even the very last acquisition of the library was mentioned in it.[6]

The *Versandliste* consists of eight narrow leaves of paper measuring about 32 x 10 cm; it is now part of the Amerbach Collection in the University Library of Basel (MS C VIa 71 fols 38–45). Three notes added by Bonifacius Amerbach himself remove any doubt about the purpose of the document. The first page bears the heading 'List of the books of Erasmus that were sent to Baron Łaski.' On the last page we read, 'List of the books of Doctor

---

In Part 2, references to Erasmus' letters through Ep 2471 give line or note numbers in Allen and CWE separated by a slash; 'Allen' is specified only when there is no corresponding information in CWE. From Ep 2472 on, references are to Allen.

1 'ein Register, Inn dem all bücher ordentlich bezeichnet, vnd durch D. Erasmus seligen diener vor langist uffgescriben sind'; Sieber *Inventarium* 10

2 Husner 'Bibliothek' 236. After the compilation of the *Versandliste*, the 'Register' would have been superfluous if it had not been kept up to date.

3 AK V 116–17 Ep 2214; cf 92–3 above.

4 Allen Ep 2033:16n. Łaski, writing to Boniface Amerbach, asked for 'descriptum bibliothecae Erasmi indicem quem apud te reliqui' (Dalton *Lasciana* 109 Ep 15).

5 Łaski *Opera* II 553–4 Epp 5 and 6; cf 7 above.

6 See no 245, a book that must have arrived after Erasmus' death.

Erasmus that were sent to the noble Baron Jan Łaski at Christmas 1537,' and lower down on the same page, 'We have sent these books, described in this way shortly before they were put in a barrel, to Łaski.'[7]

The identity of the author of this document has so far eluded us. It is unlikely to have been written by Gilbert Cousin, as some have supposed;[8] Erasmus' erstwhile amanuensis left Basel in October 1535, and the list includes books that first appeared in 1536.[9] Husner thought it might have been written by a clerk in the service of Bonifacius Amerbach.[10] The surviving copy of the *Versandliste* may very well not be the original but a transcript that Amerbach had made for himself and his fellow executors of Erasmus' estate. In this case the original, which was subsequently lost, must have been sent to Łaski, as Allen assumed.[11] However this may be, the man responsible for listing the summary titles emerges as someone with enough education and experience to carry out the task with which he was entrusted. He may indeed have had little or no understanding of some of the books he listed. The *Corpus iuris civilis* was so foreign to him that he changed *Infortiatum*, the name of one of the volumes, into *In Fortiatum* (no 145) – unless the mistake was not in the original but was made by the copyist. Nor does he seem to have kept abreast of Erasmus' recent work; he wrongly ascribed to him the translation of all fifty-three of John Chrysostom's homilies on the Acts of the Apostles (no 410), which were published by Froben in 1531. On the other hand, he did have a rudimentary knowledge of the classical languages and appears to have been quite capable of adapting or paraphrasing the often long and complicated Latin titles without making any grammatical mistakes. Shortage of time obliged him to identify the books as briefly as possible, but in such a way that those who needed to use the list would be able to recognize them. By and large he succeeded. He did not follow a single method; he listed the books with brief titles extempore, as dictated by his practical common sense. He usually based himself on the text of the title-page or the colophon, taking the most essential words for his description and reproducing them literally and in the original sequence. If it was equally clear, however, he used the short title he found written on the fore-edge or the binding of the book, which could be very different from the title-page or colophon.[12] He often, albeit somewhat arbitrarily, listed a book simply under the name of the author, apparently assuming that no man of any education would have been unable to identify the reference works described as 'Calepinus' (no 194) and 'Volaterranus' (no 284). If he found copies of more than one edition of the collected works or of a separate work of an author standing next to or near each other, he listed them under the same heading but sometimes added a clear distinguishing feature: the names of different printers or places of publication, different commentators, or different formats.[13]

All in all the *Versandliste* must have satisfied reasonably well the basic and limited commercial purpose for which it was compiled. The summary list gave Łaski enough information

---

7 'Index Librorum Erasmi wie die dem Herrn von Lasko Zugeschickt ... Das Register von biechern doctoris Erasmi wie die dem wolgepornen Herrn Joanni von Lasko zugeschickt uff Wynacht anno 1537 ... Hos libros Lasko misimus Paulo ante quam in vas clauderenter ita adnotatos.'

8 Hartmann in AK VI 204 Ep 2761 n12; Jenny in *Erasmus Vorkämpter für Frieden und Toleranz* 120

9 Ep 2381 introduction (page 43)/n1. For books published in 1536 see nos 245, 388, 393, 399, 400, 404 #2, and 406 #2.

10 Husner 'Bibliothek' 237

11 Allen XI Appendix 25 'Erasmus' Last Will' 364:10n. In the will (dated 12 February 1536), Bonifacius Amerbach was named legal heir and Hieronymus Froben and Nicolaus Episcopius were appointed executors.

12 See, for example, no 30 (*De fructu studiorum*); for titles on the fore-edge, cf 75–6 above.

13 For example nos 265, 266, and 267 (printer-publishers); 201 and 202 (commentators); 105 and 107, 106 and 98 (formats)

about each item to be able to check the contents of the barrels of books as they arrived, while it gave Amerbach, Froben, and Episcopius a record of the composition of the library in the event any problem arose after the collection reached Poland and was thus out of their reach.

Is it not surprising that the *Versandliste*, which was first published in 1936, has not been subjected to a thorough examination before now? Surely it was important to acquire the greatest possible knowledge of which books Erasmus had in his study, or at least within easy reach in his house? Nevertheless, our hesitation at undertaking such an investigation was understandable. At first sight a faithful reconstruction of the library on the basis of the *Versandliste* seemed a hopeless task, because so little information is given about each book. The *Versandliste* cannot even be described as a short-title list. As was mentioned, many entries give no title, and we had to make do with the name of the author.[14] And what were we to do with the name of a prolific author?[15] In other instances the name of the author is omitted, and titles like *De fructu studiorum* or *Palamedes palliata comoedia* were not immediately transparent.[16] Except in some nine cases, the place of publication is not given;[17] the year of publication is never given; and of the printer-publishers, Aldo Manuzio is mentioned fourteen times, Froben eighteen times, others only sporadically.[18] Finally, the description of the format was almost always omitted.[19] In short, it seemed unduly optimistic to expect that even a painstaking investigation of each of the 413 entries on the *Versandliste* would yield bibliographical results of any precision.

Nevertheless, the time and effort spent have borne fruit. Close study of the *Versandliste* unexpectedly produced information that made it possible to identify a larger number of the works mentioned than could have been predicted and even, allowing for an acceptable proportion of risk, to indicate a precise edition. The first 'hidden key' to the list turned out to be, surprisingly enough, the seldom-mentioned format of the book. A preliminary general survey of the list immediately showed that the author and the title of many books, however incomplete or unclear the description, could easily be identified with the help of some general bibliographical instruments, especially the catalogues of major libraries such as the British Library, the Bibliothèque nationale, and the Library of Congress. It was far more difficult – most of the time impossible – to identify the actual editions. In a very few cases, where the works had appeared in print only once or twice before 1536, the place and date of publication could be established with virtual certainty. But when books had gone through more reprintings before Erasmus' death – and this was true of most of them – all that could be done was to note the various possible editions. For greater precision, the bibliographical format of all the editions taken into consideration was systematically recorded. In this first phase of research no notice was taken of books reprinted so many times before 1536 that there was little point in performing the time-consuming task of gathering all the information about them.

When our first survey, which covered only part of the *Versandliste*, had been completed, we made a surprising discovery. An inspection of the books that had been provisionally identified, roughly in the order in which they appeared in the *Versandliste*, showed that the

---

14 For example nos 284 and 293

15 For example nos 46 and 47

16 See nos 30 #2 and 364 #1.

17 Nos 192, 217, and 237 (Venice), 228 (Rome), 209 (Florence), 260 and 405 (Paris), 225 (Lyon), and 136 (Ulm)

18 Altogether seven works produced by the other four printer-publishers: one, Josse Bade, from Paris (nos 249 and 265), and three from Basel, Johann Herwagen (nos 120–1 and 131), Johann Bebel (nos 215 and 266), and Andreas Cratander (no 191)

19 The four exceptions are nos 105, 106, 391, and 392.

folios, the quartos, and the octavos were not arranged arbitrarily but stood next to each other in adjoining blocks. It suddenly became clear that in listing the books before their dispatch to Poland Amerbach's collaborator entered them in groups by format: groups in which he arranged them himself or in which he found them.

The discovery that the titles on the *Versandliste* had been grouped together according to format not only immediately explained why the same works of a single author were sometimes listed separately from one another and were far apart in the list[20] but also provided an important starting point for all further attempts to identify the editions of the books. By observing the adjacent entries on the list we could often predict the format of a book and thus identify the edition in Erasmus' possession. This 'key' had of course to be handled with caution. The format groups on the list were often arbitrarily interrupted: the folio edition of the *Biblia cum glossa* (no 154), for example, was listed on its own in the middle of a group of books that were undoubtedly of a smaller format. In addition, the octavos and the quartos were sometimes so mixed together that it was impossible to reach a clear conclusion about any one book. Nevertheless, the general arrangement by format provided a working hypothesis that could be depended upon in a number of cases. We find Aristophanes (no 116), for example, listed among a group of folio editions, although in the sixteenth century his *Comoediae* were nearly all published in quarto or octavo. The *editio princeps* of the Greek text with commentary by Marcus Musurus, however, printed just before the turn of the century by Aldo Manuzio, was a folio edition. The Aristophanes edition in Erasmus' possession must thus almost certainly have been the incunable of 1498. Again, the folio format of the adjoining volumes made it virtually certain which edition of Budé's letters stood in Erasmus' bookcase.[21] Our anticipation of the format did not always definitively identify the edition of a particular work, but it always reduced the number of possibilities. Because it appears on the list among a number of folio volumes, it could have been assumed that the Venetian edition of Celsus' *De re medicina* (no 192), was not the octavo Aldine edition of 1528, which Allen thought that Gianfrancesco Torresani might have sent to Erasmus as a present.[22] It must, rather, have been one of the two or three folio editions published in Venice before 1500.

A second 'key,' which could be used in combination with the first for the identification of many books, was hidden in the composite volumes. Often in the *Versandliste* we meet two or three short titles or names of authors listed in the same entry as though they belonged together. Not much imagination was needed to realize that these represent works that were bound together. In Erasmus' time the purchaser had to have his new books bound himself,[23] and we can easily understand his having two or more works of a similar format bound together, regardless of their heterogeneous content, for the sake of convenience. But it had to be proved that the combination of titles in these entries indeed referred to books bound together. This supposition seemed at least reasonable when all the known editions of the works concerned had appeared at more or less the same time. The two quarto works listed under no 370, for example, were on entirely different subjects. One contained the correspondence between Huldrych Zwingli and Andreas Osiander about the Eucharist, while

---

20 For example Ptolemy (nos 134 and 136, both in folio, and 101, in quarto), Suetonius (nos 261, 262, and 263 in folio and 51, presumably in octavo)
21 No 289; cf 144 below.
22 Cf Ep 1989:13n/n7.
23 See 86–7 above.

the other contained Paolo Giovio's report on the embassy that the Grand Prince Basel of Moscow sent to Pope Clement VII. The first was published in Nürnberg in 1527, and the second appeared in Rome in 1525 and was reprinted in Basel in 1527. Similarly, a number of works by Erasmus himself, of which no authorized editions had appeared over a long period and which could consequently be dated within a couple of years, often appeared combined in a single item on the list with works either by himself or by others published at about the same time.[24] This could hardly have been by chance, and it seemed reasonable to assume that the works were simply bound together.

Examples like these led to a more far-reaching hypothesis. If the title combinations in the *Versandliste* indicated books bound together, not only in the cases mentioned but as a rule, then the components to be identified were to be sought among editions that had been published at about the same time. In practice this working hypothesis led to results, even if some were more convincing than others. One that seemed entirely convincing was the explanation of the entry 'Eucherius cum 30 orationibus Nazianzeni interprete Bilibaldo Pirckheimero' (no 248). The only edition of Pirckheimer's translation of the orations of Gregory of Nazianzus was published in Basel by Froben in September 1531. Various editions of Eucherius were known, but could there be any doubt that the work in question was his *Lucubrationes*, published by Froben in the same month of the same year, an edition that included Erasmus' scholia to the *Epistola ad Valerianum de philosophia christiana*? To assume that the reference 'Diodorus Siculus, Paulus Orosius, Berosus et Leonis Papae Epistolae' (no 310) concealed four quarto editions of c 1509–11 simply because the edition of Pope Leo I's letters could almost certainly be identified with a Bade edition of 1511 involved more speculation. But the attribution of the other three works to Parisian presses made good sense, since it could be proved that at about this time Erasmus had purchased books on what for him was a large scale in the French capital.[25] Nor did it seem unjustifiable to presume that, in a library consisting to a large extent of the products of the Froben press, the reference 'Lucianus, Arist. Rhet.' (no 26) covered a combination of octavo editions of Lucian's dialogues in Erasmus' translation and of Aristotle's *Rhetorica* published by the Basel firm in 1532, even if countless other editions of the two works were known – especially since the adjacent books were octavos.

On occasion further evidence proved conclusively that books presumably bound together were correctly identified. There is one particularly good example. Of the two books listed under the heading 'Eras. in monach. Hisp. Val. in Pog.' (no 153), the first could easily be recognized: it was, of course, Erasmus' defence against the accusation of heresy made by the Spanish friars, the *Apologia adversus monachos quosdam Hispanos*, an octavo edition produced by Froben in Basel in 1528, or the reprint of 1529.[26] 'Val. in Pog.' must have referred to a pamphlet by Lorenzo Valla in a notorious fifteenth-century dispute directed against the Tuscan humanist Poggio Bracciolini. The tract had been printed several times. Two editions appeared at about the time Erasmus replied to his Spanish opponents: an octavo was printed by Alopecius in Cologne in 1527 and a quarto by R. Stephanus in Paris in 1529. The Paris edition could be excluded, since a quarto volume could hardly have been bound together with Erasmus' *Apologia* in octavo. All that remained was the Cologne edition. No other octavo edition was to be found, which strengthened our conclusion. It became still

---

24 For example nos 155, 268, 337, 340, 352, and 357
25 See 24–5 above.
26 On why Erasmus probably owned the first edition of 1528 see no 153.

more plausible when further research showed that the Cologne edition was edited by the young philologist Christoph von Carlowitz, who had been in touch with Erasmus at about this time and had visited him in Basel in 1527, possibly offering him on that occasion his recent book.

In this case, the personal background could be gathered from Erasmus' correspondence. Needless to say, Allen's superb edition contributed enormously to the elucidation of the *Versandliste*. Both the content of the letters and the extensive introductions, together with the inexhaustible apparatus of footnotes, provided a wealth of information that, in combination with the results of strictly bibliographical research, made it possible to identify a large number of books with a fair degree of certainty. Suffice it to give a single example. The edition of the *Epistulae Budaei* (no 289) could be identified precisely thanks to the *Opus epistolarum*.[27] Three authorized and constantly augmented editions of the letters of the famous French humanist had to be taken into consideration. All three were published by Bade in Paris, in 1520, 1522, and 1531. Which one was it? The first two editions were in quarto and thus did not fit with the adjoining folios on the list, which were also works by Budé. The folio format already argued for the 1531 edition of the letters. But it did not provide firm proof. This could only be established with the help of Allen: in the middle of March 1531 Erasmus wrote that after his meals, if there was no opportunity for conversation, he had his *famulus* read aloud to him the annotated edition of the letters of Budé. This was communicated as a compliment to Jacques Toussain, who had provided the recent edition of letters with an introduction and scholia. It was thus certain that the edition of the *Epistulae Budaei* Erasmus owned was that of 1531.

In other cases, while it was not possible to identify a particular work in the *Versandliste* with such precision, Erasmus' correspondence provided a means of greatly reducing the number of editions taken into consideration. 'Gerson 1./...2./...3/...4.' on the list (no 169) undoubtedly referred to one of the four-volume editions of the complete works of the great French theologian Jean Gerson that had appeared since 1484–5. But which edition? The *Opus epistolarum* again provided an indication. In 1525 Erasmus was reproached by his unremitting opponent Noël Béda with not being familiar with the work of Gerson. He replied that he had indeed read certain things by him in his youth but admitted that Gerson's works were not in his library. He announced his intention of buying or borrowing them, and less than a year later he could tell Béda that the *Opera Gersonis* were in his possession. This did not of course prove that he had acquired the most recent Paris edition of 1521 or the slightly earlier Basel one of 1518, but the time of the purchase makes the chance that he had to resort to one of the earlier editions at least more remote.

Besides his correspondence, Erasmus' literary, theological, and apologetic works were of some assistance in unravelling the *Versandliste*, but less frequently. When Erasmus referred to, or quoted, other books, he seldom identified the edition he was using. He usually gave only the name of the author or a very general description of the work consulted. He occasionally added the name of the place, the printer, or the editor of a text edition, which was a great help, but never the year of publication. For example, he referred to a passage 'in my two-part Basel edition of Chrysostom' (*in Chrysostomo meo ex gemina editione Basiliensi*); he spoke of Bede's New Testament commentary 'in the edition by Bade' (*in editione Badiana*); and he took a text of Origen 'from an edition prepared by a certain

---

27 Cf 142 above.

Merlin' (*ex Merlini cujusdam editione*).[28] But little precise bibliographical information about the books in his own library could be expected from his works, hardly more than could be derived from the *Versandliste* by the usual bibliographical means.

But this did not mean that all the references in his works that did not seem to offer anything to go by were of no use. The context in which they appeared sometimes made them of considerable indirect assistance. The mere fact that he mentioned or quoted a book for the first time in his works – and this could be in the umpteenth edition of one of his best-sellers – often provided a welcome means of reaching a closer or more certain identification than was possible on the basis of the inadequate description in the *Versandliste*, assuming that Erasmus normally used a recent edition. An interesting example, albeit an extreme one, since the book in question is not even named, occurs in his elucidation of the adage *Sileni Alcibiadis* (III iii 1). Erasmus makes an ironical reference to the legendary founder of the British monarchy, the Trojan Brutus, purported to be the grandson of Aeneas, who landed in Britain as the leader of a group of Trojan fugitives. He must have derived the story from the *Historia regum Britanniae*, the twelfth-century chronicle of Geoffrey of Monmouth, which is based on tradition and still more on fancy. This pseudo-historical work suddenly achieved fame when Bade published the *editio princeps* in 1508 and reprinted it in 1517. Erasmus possessed the book (no 315). But which of the two editions? The textual history of the *Adagia* may answer the question. Brutus Trojanus was first mentioned in a passage inserted in the revised version of his collection of proverbs in 1515, and this makes it at the least likely that Erasmus was using a copy of the original edition of 1508 and not of the 1517 reprint.

This is one of several clues to the identification of the books in Erasmus' library from references in his own works that we owe to the current Amsterdam edition of the *Opera omnia* (ASD). The indexes in the various volumes greatly facilitated their consultation, but the critical apparatus accompanying each text and the thorough annotations, the result of extremely detailed research, often extending to the books Erasmus consulted, were particularly useful. As in the case of the chronicle of Geoffrey of Monmouth, the exemplary edition of the *Adagia* by Felix Heinimann and Emanuel Kienzle made it possible to ascertain how Erasmus constantly made improvements and additions in the many new editions of his collection of proverbs on the basis of books he had become familiar with since the appearance of the previous edition. A number of these books, usually recent, mentioned in the most summary manner in the *Versandliste*, could be closely identified without too many reservations: the *Theocritus graece* published in Rome in 1516 and edited and furnished with scholia by Zacharias Calliergis; the scholia to Homer known as 'scholia minora' or 'scholia Didymi' in the Aldine edition of 1521; the collection of *gnomai* (maxims) edited by Sigismundus Gelenius and printed by Froben in 1532; and other works.[29] We might admittedly have succeeded in identifying these books with some probability via bibliographical channels, and ASD did not always provide us with altogether new information. Nevertheless, when the detailed research performed in connection with this first critical edition confirmed the results of a strictly bibliographical investigation the corroboration was significant.[30]

---

28 See nos 238 (Chrysostom), 160 (Bede), and 222 (Origen).

29 See nos 98 (Theocritus), 108 (Homer), 314 (Callimachus *Gnomai*); also two Basel editions: nos 215 (Aristotle *Opera omnia* published by J. Bebel in 1531) and 304 (Diogenes Laertius *De vitis, decretis & responsis celebrium philosophorum libri decem*, published by Froben in 1533).

30 Heinemann and Keinzle, in their turn, sought support in the *Versandliste*.

Little use has been made of the *Opera omnia* edited by J. Leclerc and published in Leiden in 1703–6 (LB). Although it has in part been definitively superseded by ASD, the old standard edition remains the most accessible text of several works not yet published in the Amsterdam edition. But without any critical apparatus, without notes of any significance, and without a workable index,[31] the Leiden edition was not especially helpful, and in practice only of indirect interest: some of our references to it come from secondary sources; others we owe to the kindness of third parties who drew our attention to them.

To compensate for the lack of a critical apparatus in LB, in exceptional cases we referred back to an original edition. We compared the five authorized editions of the *Annotationes in Novum Testamentum*, for example, in order to check the point at which Erasmus regularly started to mention or to quote certain late medieval theological manuals and works of reference.[32] These enjoyed great popularity and were constantly being republished, especially the works of Peter Lombard, Thomas Aquinas, and Duns Scotus. We hoped to learn more about the editions of the books mentioned in the *Versandliste*. Unfortunately the results barely justified the effort. The references were on the whole too few in number to allow us to reach any clear conclusions. We were left with the hesitant supposition that Erasmus did not possess any very old editions of the scholastic works in question – in any case a category that was scarcely represented in his library – and acquired some of them at a relatively late date.[33] When he did so it was not for any intrinsic value they might have, for he did not usually have a very high opinion of them, but because he could not avoid them in view of the authority they still wielded for certain theologians. Only in the 1520s, for example, does he appear to have obtained Thomas Aquinas' *Catena aurea*, a work he had defended some years earlier against the contemptuous opinion of his friend Colet but which he later took a poor view of himself.[34] This conclusion may seem weak, yet it is neither unfounded nor implausible. In another example of the welcome confirmation provided by the ASD editors, it was reassuring to read that Henk Jan de Jonge, in a thorough article on Erasmus' use of one scholastic work, the standard commentary on the Bible known as the *Glossa ordinaria*, came to a similar conclusion based on far more solid documentation. He writes: 'Erasmus had an aversion to this compilation of disconnected patristic quotations, torn from their original contexts; forced by his adversaries, he began to use it only for the second and later editions of his N[ew] T[estament], with obvious reluctance and mainly to demonstrate that his own interpretations and observations could be backed up with the authoritative commentary of his conservative opponents.'[35]

Finally, to our surprise, the *Versandliste* itself sometimes came to our assistance. Some items on the list, which seemed at first sight to give too little information to fully identify the work indicated, turned out, on closer inspection, to provide bibliographical clues. If entries referred to works by titles worded in a strikingly different way, bibliographical research could conclusively identify the books, even to the edition. The man who compiled

---

31 The *index generalis ad omnia ejus opera excepto III volumine* in vol 10 of LB is virtually useless.

32 See no 331. All the editions (1516, 1519, 1522, 1527, and 1535) can be found in the City Library of Rotterdam.

33 There may have been exceptions. One of the two editions Erasmus owned of Peter Lombard's *Sententiae* may have been a folio edition prior to 1500; see no 163. He perhaps also had in his library an early edition of Thomas Aquinas' commentary to the Pauline Epistles, a work that had attracted his attention at an early stage; see no 161.

34 See no 170.

35 In his edition of Erasmus *Apologia ad annotationes Stunicae* ASD IX-2 79 379n; cf his article 'Erasmus und die Glossa Ordinaria zum Neuen Testament' 77.

the list of books being shipped to Poland was not, as we noted earlier, entirely consistent in how he described them. In identifying them as briefly as possible he sometimes, according to his own discretion, omitted a part, even the greater part, of the full title. But for the key identifying elements of his descriptions he often adopted exactly the same wording that appeared on the title-page or in the colophon. Unusual variants of the titles thus remained recognizable in the *Versandliste*, and this suited our purpose perfectly. The *Rhetorica ad Alexandrum*, for example, which was then attributed to Aristotle but which is now sometimes ascribed to Anaximenes or listed, for the sake of convenience, under the name of [Pseudo-] Aristotle, was identified as 'Vtilissi[ma] ... Rheto[rica]' (no 93). Since the tract was once – altogether exceptionally – published with that title, this edition was almost certainly the one in Erasmus' possession. Similarly, the edition in Erasmus' library of the works of Macrobius (no 282) could be specifically identified by the title given in the *Versandliste*, which was slightly different from the usual one.

With the indications explicitly provided by the list or implicitly provided by the 'hidden keys' we have discussed (the format of the works, and the likelihood that books bound together were published at about the same time), together with the supplementary information derived from external sources (especially Allen's edition of Erasmus' letters and ASD), we have succeeded in identifying with virtually complete certainty a good number of books. But in many cases it was not possible to establish with the same degree of certainty which work or (even more) which edition of a work is concealed behind an item on the list.[36] In all these doubtful cases we have attempted to provide a hypothesis, even if it is simply an enumeration of bibliographical possibilities. Even the most problematic cases were not promptly abandoned as insoluble, and very few led to an admission of defeat: 'the identity of the work mentioned is uncertain,' or 'the edition cannot be established.' We always tried to 'unmask' even the vaguest items, even if this inevitably entailed a speculative approach that was not without risk.

The bibliographical solutions suggested for the problem cases thus often differ greatly in persuasiveness and credibility. We were often strongly tempted to explain and assume, on the basis of difficult or unverifiable premises, more than could be justified by scholarly caution. Nevertheless, even the most speculative solutions were not arrived at without careful study or based on implausible arguments. Let us give an example. One entry in the *Versandliste* reads, 'Bembus, Viues, Cuspidius' (no 12); the three proper names evidently indicate the same number of works, bound together in a single volume. At first sight it seemed completely impossible to indicate even approximately the contents of this composite volume. Both Pietro Bembo and Juan Luis Vives have a number of books to their name. The only solid pointer was the name Cuspidius, which could only refer to the remarkable, and now very rare, booklet containing two fake Roman legal documents originally published in Lyon in 1532 and reprinted in Basel in the same year. For a long time 'The Testament of Cuspidius' was believed to be a forgery in which the Italian humanists Julius Pomponius Laetus and Giovanni Pontano had had a hand, but there is now little doubt that the purported editor of the texts, who was none other than François Rabelais, was also the author. Only one letter has survived from Rabelais to Erasmus (as far as we know, the only one he ever wrote to him); it was written in the same year, 1532. Might the content and background

---

36 Uncertainty prevailed particularly when an entry gave only an author's name – 'Stephanus Niger' (no 293), for example. The collected works of classical authors listed without a title, however, seldom gave rise to problems.

of the letter explain how Rabelais' virtually contemporary Cuspidius booklet made its way into Erasmus' library?

Since November 1531, Erasmus had been pursuing a Greek manuscript of Flavius Josephus' *Bellum Judaicum* for Froben, who was preparing a new edition of it. He had applied to Georges d'Armagnac, bishop of Rodez, in whose possession he had heard it was. D'Armagnac, who had used it, but who appeared not to own it, nevertheless managed to procure it for him thanks to his colleague Jean de Pins, bishop of the neighbouring diocese of Rieux, to whom it really belonged. After having received it from de Pins, the bishop sent the manuscript to Rabelais, who had recently settled in Lyon, requesting him to forward it to Freiburg, where Erasmus was then living. Rabelais complied with the request, delighted to have the chance of introducing himself to the great scholar with a particularly complimentary letter. Might he not also have given the courier a courtesy copy of his Cuspidius, which had recently been published by Gryphius? Or, as is equally possible, did Gryphius himself send Erasmus a copy? The well-known printer and publisher, whose firm in Lyon had turned into a centre of intellectual activity,[37] had every reason to be grateful to Erasmus: pirated reprints of his works were a significant part of his annual production.[38] He undoubtedly knew of the dispatch of the Flavius Josephus manuscript to Freiburg, since Rabelais, who was responsible for it, had had a close commercial connection with him ever since he settled in Lyon. Besides, for the dispatch of letters and packets scholars in southern France and their friends in the Upper Rhineland generally made use of the reliable channels of the publishers and booksellers in Lyon, so that Rabelais may well have found a courier through Gryphius.[39]

For the identification of the works by Bembo and Vives bound together with the 'Testament of Cuspidius' there was only one possible starting point, but this was enough. We could expect them to be books that had appeared at about the same time. Surprisingly enough, an investigation into books by the two authors printed around 1532 yielded only editions published in Lyon. It was hard to believe that this was mere coincidence, and Erasmus' correspondence supported the supposition, at least where Bembo's *Opuscula aliquot* was concerned, that these works were the ones in Erasmus' library. In the spring of 1533 Erasmus wrote that he had recently read Bembo's *adolescentiae progymnasmata*, and particularly his *Aetna*, with great pleasure. The *Opuscula aliquot* contains some of Bembo's early writings, including the *Aetna*. As for Vives, we could only suggest one or more of the tracts published in Lyon in 1532. We have not, therefore, definitively established the contents of this composite volume. We have at most offered a plausible solution, which may or may not convince everyone.

The above entry on the *Versandliste* was particularly difficult to decipher. But even when the descriptions were less problematic, and even when the explanation seemed so plausible as to be virtually certain, in fact the identifications rarely go beyond the declaration of a bibliographical possibility. We knew from the beginning that the reconstruction on paper of Erasmus' library as a whole, with the exception of the extremely small part that has been recovered, had to rest on hypothesis, and hypotheses, however convincingly presented, all too frequently remain open to discussion.

---

37 See Margolin 'Le cercle humaniste lyonnais d'après l'édition des *Epigrammata* (1537) de Jean Visagier' 153.

38 According to the 'union catalogue' of Erasmus editions in the City Library of Rotterdam five or six editions of the same work might have been in circulation at the same time. See www.erasmus.org/ErasmusOnlineDatabase.

39 Various examples of the conveyance of letters and parcels via Lyon between Erasmus, Amerbach, Zasius, and others in Basel and Freiburg and Sadoleto, Alciato, and fellow scholars elsewhere are to be found in AK. Cf 30–1 above.

We set to work on the *Versandliste* using bibliographical and textual resources. The *catalogue raisonné* that follows is the result of our research. The books are discussed in the order in which they appear in the list. We have adhered to the numeration introduced by Husner, even when he mistakenly placed books together under a single number.[40] Each of his 413 numbers is treated according to the following scheme: the summary indication in the *Versandliste* is followed by a more detailed bibliographical description of the work, or of the works that were presumably or possibly bound together, and by an account of the evidence for each identification. Husner's transcription of the list was compared with a photocopy of the manuscript and corrected where necessary. The differences established were few in number and of no great importance, although in a few cases an apparently minute difference could have clear consequences for the interpretation of an entry.[41]

When there was little or no foundation on which to establish the identity of the work in question, we have stated that the identity of the work is uncertain and hazarded a guess in the explanatory discussion.

The bibliographical descriptions do not aim at completeness. Many of the books could have been adequately identified with a short title and reference to a standard bibliography. Some bibliographical information, however, has always been provided. Details concerning foliation and pagination have been omitted as irrelevant to our purpose,[42] but the format turned out to be of decisive assistance in the identification of many editions. Our aim was to establish the content of Erasmus' library as completely and specifically as possible from the bibliographical descriptions. The frequently lengthy titles or subtitles listing all the authors and works in editions containing a number of different works – *Rhetores graeci* (nos 127 and 128), *Scriptores rei rusticae* (no 324), and *Vitae & fabellae Aesopi* (no 198), for example – are thus usually given in full (leaving out, at most, some superfluous verbosity). Sometimes the individual works in such editions are described in the explanatory discussion in greater detail for the sake of clarity. Independent works included in editions of other authors without any special mention on the title-page are likewise identified in those cases that were known to us. How else could we know that, although the grammarians Donatus and Priscian (among others) do not appear in the *Versandliste* under their own names, Erasmus had their principal works in his library hidden in an edition of Diomedes' *Ars grammatica* (no 72)? Or that he was in possession at an early date of a translation of Epictetus' *Enchiridion*,[43] although that work is not listed, concealed in the *Opera omnia* of the translator Angelo Poliziano (no 285)?

In this manner it has been possible to give a reliable survey, without too many gaps, of the content of Erasmus' working reference library. Of course this survey is far from complete. It was impossible to examine personally copies, often extremely rare, of all the works that had been provisionally identified in order to search their contents for works not indicated on the title-page or in the bibliographical tools we used. It must be emphasized in this connection that the descriptions and the supplementary information in the explanatory discussions were only in exceptional cases the result of personal bibliographical activity. As a rule they go back to well-known bibliographies and catalogues, which do indeed rest on autopsy.

---

40 See nos 150 and 406.

41 See, for example, no 65. We thank Professor A. Jolidon of Rennes for correcting certain inexactitudes
     in the transcript that had escaped our attention.

42 We had to consider the foliation or pagination of the books only when we tried to express the extent
     of Erasmus' library at the end of his life per running metre. See 79 above.

43 The *editio princeps* of the *Enchiridion graece* was first published at a late date (Venice 1528). Erasmus appears
     either not to have purchased it or to have acquired it via other channels.

The first purpose of the explanatory notes is to justify the identifications and bibliographical descriptions of the entries in the *Versandliste*. Whenever an entry is problematical, we explain which bibliographical and other data have been used in order to reach a conclusion or to hazard a guess or to admit defeat. The reader can thus decide for himself or herself how plausible the solution suggested is. The annotations have, however, a secondary, no less essential purpose. They include as many details as possible about the manner in which Erasmus obtained a book, by purchasing it or receiving it as a gift; about the part he may have played in its creation; about his relationship with the writer, which sometimes does more to explain the presence of a book in his collection than the interest that the content might have had for him; and about everything that can be considered relevant in the broadest sense of the word for our knowledge of Erasmus' library. The information gathered in the elucidation of the *Versandliste* is the basis of Part 1 of this volume.

The *Versandliste*:
Books and Authors in Erasmus' Library

These two lists are intended to outline in as concise a form as possible the contents of Erasmus' library in 1536 as it has been established in the annotated catalogue. In the transcript of the *Versandliste*, common Latin abbreviations (for example those for *ae, com-, et, -us*) have been silently expanded; other abbreviations have been left as they are in the manuscript. Letters, words, or titles that have been struck through in the manuscript are shown the same way in the transcript. A line break is indicated with a slash or, if the scribe marked it, with a double slash. When an entry contains several lines connected by a brace followed by further identification (for example no 214, where six named works are identified as 'Aristote. graece'), a symbol indicating the brace follows the transcript of the lines; the further identification follows the brace. An asterisk following the VL/Catalogue number indicates that Erasmus' copy of the book has survived. The alphabetical list of authors does not attempt to include every name or title that might be present in a compilation.

Versandliste / Catalogue: Books in Erasmus' Library

folio 39r

1	Apparatus linguae Latinae	Ricci, Bartolomeo *Apparatus latinae locutionis*	Lyon: S. Grphyius 1534 or Strasbourg: M. Apiarius 1535 or Cologne: Gymnicus 1535	octavo or quarto or octavo
2	Bayfius, Iouius, Valla	1/ Baïf, Lazare de *Opus de re vestimentaria; De vasculorum materiis*	Basel: H. Froben, J. Herwagen, and N. Episcopius 1531	octavo
		2/ Giovio, Paulo *De romanis piscibus libellus*	Basel: Froben 1531	octavo
		3/ Valla, Lorenzo *De linguae latinae elegantia* and other works	Lyon: S. Gryphius 1532	octavo
3	Melanch. Annota. in Matth.	Melanchthon, Philippus *Annotationes in evangelium Matthaei*	[Basel: n pr, May 1523] or a pirate edition [Basel: n pr 1523]	octavo
4	Aula Hutteni. Taci. de popu. Germa.	1/ Hutten, Ulrich von *Aula*	Basel: J. Froben, November 1518	octavo
		2/ Tacitus, Cornelius *De moribus et populis Germaniae libellus cum commentariolo ...*	Basel: J. Froben, May 1519	octavo
5	Psalterium Campensis	Campen, Jan van *Psalmorum omnium iuxta Hebraicam veritatem paraphrastica interpretatio*	Nürnberg: J. Petreius, May 1532	octavo
6	Iacobi Sadoleti in Psal. 93. Interpretatio.	Sadoleto, Jacopo *In psalmum xciii interpretatio*	Lyon: S. Gryphius 1530 or pirate edition Basel: Froben 1530	octavo
7	Deutero. Luter.	Luther, Martin *Deuteronomion Mose cum annotationibus*	Wittenberg: H. Lufft 1525 or a pirate edition	octavo
8	Prouer. Melanc.	Melanchthon, Philippus Παροιμίαι, *sive Proverbia Salomonis, cum adnotationibus* and/or *Solomonis sententiae, versae ad Hebraicam veritatem*	Haguenau: J. Setzer 1525 Haguenau: J. Setzer 1525	octavo octavo
9	Melan. in Genesim	Melanchthon, Philippus *In obscuriora aliquot capita Geneseos annotationes*	Haguenau: J. Setzer or Tübingen: U. Morhart 1523	octavo
10	Cochlaei de libe. arbitrio Epistolae Luteri.	1/ Cochlaeus, Joannes *De libero arbitrio hominis adversus locos communes Philippi Melanchthonis*	Tübingen : U. Morhart 1525	octavo

		2/ Luther, Martin *Epistolarum farrago ... cum Psalmorum aliquot interpretatione*	Haguenau: J. Setzer 1525	octavo
11	Melanc. in Prou.	Melanchthon, Philippus *Nova scholia in Proverbia Salomonis*	Haguenau: J. Setzer 1529 or 1531	octavo
12	Bembus, Viues, Cuspidius.	1/ Bembo, Pietro *Opuscula aliquot*	Lyon: S. Gryphius 1532	octavo
		2/ Vives, Juan Luis. One or more tracts published in 1532	Lyon: M. and G. Trechsel 1532	octavo
		3/ [Rabelais, François] *Ex reliquiis venerandae antiquitatis Lucii Cuspidii testamentum. Item contractus venditionis*	Lyon: S. Gryphius 1532 or an undated pirated edition	octavo
13	Menardus, Faust. Episco.	1/ Manardo, Giovanni *Medicinales epistolae*	Strasbourg: J. Schott 17 February 1529	octavo
		2/ Faustus of Riez *De gratia Dei; De fide adversus Arianos*	Basel: J.F. Emmaeus 1528	octavo
14	Melanc. in Epistolam ad Roma.	Melanchthon, Philippus *Commentarii in epistolam Pauli ad Romanos*	Wittenberg: J. Clug October 1532	octavo
15	Bipartitum in Morali Philosophia	probably *Ars moralis introductoria* or *Moralium dogma philosophorum*	Paris: A. Caillaut 1494 (reprinted frequently) — Deventer: R. Pafraet c 1486 or 2d ed Paris J. Bade c 1512	quarto or octavo — quarto
16	De Tralatione Bibliae Petri Sutoris	Cousturier, Pierre *De tralatione Bibliae et novarum reprobatione interpretationum*	Paris: P. Vidoue for J. Petit 28 February 1525	folio
17	Tonstallus de arte supputandi	Tunstall, Cuthbert *De arte supputandi*	[London:] Richard Pynson 14 October 1522	quarto
18	Varia Mosellani. Latomi dialo. Magdale.	1/ Mosellanus, Petrus. Some of his writings, probably including *Oratio de variarum linguarum cognitione paranda*	Leipzig: V. Schumann 1518 or Basel: J. Froben May 1519	quarto
		2/ Latomus, Jacobus *De trium linguarum et studii theologici ratione dialogus*	Antwerp: M. Hillen or Basel: J. Froben 1519	quarto
		3/ One or more writings on the Mary Magdalene controversy		

19	Rodol. Agricola de Inuentione dialec.	Agricola, Rodolphus *De inventione dialectica*	Cologne: H. Fuchs August 1523 or 1528	quarto
20	Magdalenae. Febris hutt. Oratio Mosel.	1/ Some works from the theological polemic about Mary Magdalene, possibly Lefèvre d'Etaples, Jacques *De Maria Magdalena et triduo Christi disceptatio*; *De tribus et unica Magdalena disceptatio secunda*	Paris: H. Estienne 1517 or 1518 Paris. H. Estienne 1519	quarto quarto
		2/ Hutten, Ulrich von *Febris*	[Mainz: J. Schöffer February 1519]	quarto
		3/ Mosellanus, Petrus *De ratione disputandi*	Leipzig: M. Lotter 1519 or Haguenau T. Anshelm [1519 or 1520]	quarto
21	Adria. Cardina. de sermone latino	Castellesi, Adriano *De sermone latino*; *Venatio*; *Iter Julii II*	Basel: J. Froben June 1518 or another edition	quarto
22	De uita et miracu. Ioan. Gerson etc./aliàs Capnionica cum Reuch. augenspiegel	1/ Wimpfeling, Jakob *De vita et miraculis Joannis Gerson* 2/ Writings on the Reuchlin affair, including 3/ Reuchlin, Johann *Augenspiegel*	[Strasbourg: J. Knobloch?] 1506 Tübingen: T. Anshelm 1511	quarto quarto
23	De sacramento Eucha. Iudoci Clichto.	Clichtove, Josse *De sacramento Eucharistiae contra Oecolampadium*	Paris: S. de Colines 9 March 1527	quarto
24	R P. Hoghestratus. Cabala. Mantia	1/ Hoogstraten, Jacob of *Destructio Cabale* 2/ Kabbalistic writings of Paulus Ricius and/or others 3/ Ramyrus *Mantia sive divinatio syderalis*	Cologne: H. Quentel, April 1519 Antwerp: M. Hillen 1518	quarto quarto
25	Cato. Viuis opuscula uaria	1/ Cato *Disticha moralia cum scholiis Erasmi* 2/ Vives, Juan Luis *Opuscula varia*	Leuven: D. Martens [1517] or November 1518 Leuven: D. Martens 1519	quarto quarto
26	Lucianus, Arist. Rhet.	1/ Lucian *Dialogi aliquot* trans Erasmus and Thomas More 2/ Aristotle *De arte rhetorica* trans George of Trebizond	Basel: Froben 1534 Basel: Froben 1534	octavo octavo
27	Titelmanni Collationes 5 super epistolam ad Ro.	Titelmans, Frans *Collationes quinque super Epistolam ad Romanos*	Antwerp: W. Vorsterman, May 1529	octavo

28	Epistolae ad Reuchli.	*Illustrium virorum epistolae, graecae et latinae ad Joannem Reuchlin Phorcensem ... quibus iam pridem additus est liber secundus*	Haguenau: T. Anshelm, May 1519	quarto
29	Phimostomus scripturariorum	Dietenberger, Johann *Phimostomus scripturariorum. Adiectus est Tractatus de divortio*	Cologne: P. Quentel 1532	quarto
30	Varia. scil. Zasij apolog. De fructu studiorum etc.	1/ Zasius, Udalricus *Apologetica defensio contra Joannem Eckium*	Basel: J. Froben, March 1519	quarto
		2/ Pace, Richard *De fructu*	Basel: J. Froben, October 1517	quarto
31	Vita et gesta Caroli Magni.	Einhard *Vita et gesta Karoli Magni*	Cologne: J. Soter 1521	quarto
32	Hutteni Actiones.	Hutten, Ulrich von *Steckelberger Sammlung* and/or *Conquestiones*	Mainz: J. Schöffer September 1519 Strasbourg: J. Schott 1520	
33	Huttenica febris, trias, libertas Germa. etc.	1/ Hutten, Ulrich von *Dialogi: Fortuna, Febris prima, Febris secunda, Trias Romana, Inspicientes*	Mainz: J. Schöffer, April 1520	quarto
		2/ Gebwiler, Hieronymus *Libertas Germaniae*	Strasbourg: J. Schott 1519	quarto
34	Eucharistia Ecolamp. Bilibal.	Oecolampadius, Johannes *De genuina verborum Domini 'Hoc est corpus meum' expositione*;	Strasbourg: n pr 1525	
		Ad Bilibaldum Pyrkaimerum de re Eucharistiae;	Zürich: C. Froschauer, August 1526	
		Responsio posterior ad Bilibaldum Pyrkhaimerum de Eucharistia	Basel: A. Cratander March 1527	
		Pirckheimer, Willibald *De vera Christi carne et vero eius sanguine responsio*;	1525 or 1526	
		Responsio secunda;	Nürnberg: [J. Petreius,] January 1527	
		Epistola de convitiis	[n p 1527]	
35	Ambrosij Catharini in Caietanum	Politi, Lancelotto de' *Annotationes in excerpta quaedam de commentarijs Card. Caietani dogmata*	Paris: S. de Colines, April 1535	octavo

36	Enchiri. locorum Iohan. Eckij	Eck, Johan Maier of *Enchiridion locorum communium adversus Lutteranos*	Landshut: J. Weyssenburger or Rome: F.M. Calvo or another edition 1525 or a later edition	quarto or octavo
37	Loci communes Philip. Melanc.	Melanchthon, Philippus *Loci communes rerum theologicarum seu hypotyposes theologicae*	Wittenberg: M. Lotther 1521 or 2d ed 1522 or a reprint	quarto or octavo
38	Babylas Germa. Brixij. Scholia in Bud.	1/ John Chrysostom *Liber contra gentiles, Babylae ... vitam continens* trans Germain de Brie	Paris: S. de Colines 1528	quarto
		2/ Toussain, Jacques *Annotata in G. Budaei epistolas* (scholia on Budé's letters)	[Paris:] J. Bade 1529	quarto
39	Declamatiunc. in D. Pauli doctrinam.	Melanchthon, Philippus *Declamatiuncula in Divi Pauli doctrinam*	Wittenberg: M. Lotther 1520 or repr Basel: A. Cratander 1520	quarto

folio 39v

40	Vallum Buscij. Magdale. Roff.	1/ Buschius, Hermannus *Vallum humanitatis*	Cologne: N. Caesar 12 April 1518	quarto
		2/ Fisher, John. Works on the identity of Mary Magdalene, possibly *De unica Magdalena libri tres*;	Paris: J. Bade 22 February 1519	quarto
		Confutatio;	Paris: J. Bade 3 September 1519	quarto
		Eversio munitionis	Leuven: Dirk Martens 1518/19	quarto
41	Lod. Viuis declamationes Syllanae	Vives, Juan Luis *Declamationes Syllanae quinque*	Antwerp: M. Hillen, April 1520	quarto
42	Sadol. Cato Octo partes	1/ Sadoleto, Jacopo *De liberis recte instituendis*	Lyon: S. Gryphius 1533	octavo
		2/ Cato *Distica moralia cum scholiis Erasmi*	Lyon: S. Gryphius 1534 or another edition	octavo
		3/ Donatus, Aelius *De octo partibus orationis* or	Lyon: S. Gryphius 1531 or 1535	octavo
		Erasmus *De octo orationis partium constructione*	Freiburg: J. Faber 1533?	octavo
43	Henrici Corn. Agrip. Apologia.	Agrippa, Henricus Cornelius *Apologia adversus calumnias propter declamationem de vanitate scientiarum et excellentia verbi Dei*	[Cologne? J. Soter?] 1533	octavo

44	Luterus in nouum Test.	Luther, Martin *Postilles*	Strasbourg: J. Herwagen?	octavo?
45	Melanc. in Epistolas.	Melancthon, Philippus *Annotationes in Epistolas Pauli ad Rhomanos et Corinthios*	Nürnberg: J. Stuchs 1522 or repr Strasbourg: J. Herwagen 1523–5 or Basel: T. Wolfius 1523	quarto or octavo
46	Glareanus. Beraldus.	1/ Writings of Glareanus, Henricus 2/ Writings of Bérault, Nicolas		
47	Eobanus Hessus. Luscinius.	1/ Writings of Eobanus Hessus, Helius 2/ Writings of Nachtgall, Othmar		
48	Coctus cum Chris. docto. Lute. epistolis	*Annemundi Cocti ad lectorem epistola*; *Martini Lutheri ad principem Carolum Sabaudiae ducem epistola*; *Huldrichi Zuinglij ad Petrum Sebiuillam epistola* ed Anemond de Coct	Zürich: C. Froschauer 1524	quarto
49	Zuinglius de sacramen.	Zwingli, Huldrych *De vera et falsa religione*; *Subsidium sive coronis de Eucharistia*	Zürich: C. Froschauer, March 1525 Zürich: C. Froschauer, 1525	octavo quarto
50	Varia Erasmi. Enchir.	Erasmus *Lucubrationes*	Strasbourg: M. Schürer, September 1515	quarto
51	Suetonius.	Suetonius Tranquillus, Caius XII *Caesares*	Venice: A. Manuzio and A. Torresani August 1516 or May 1521	octavo
52	Libertas Christiana.	Luther, Martin *Epistola ad Leonem x. Tractatus de libertate christiana*	[Wittenberg: J. Grünenberg] 1520 or a reprint	quarto
53	Luciani Tyrannus.	Lucian *Dialogi duo. Charon et Tyrannus* trans Petrus Mosellanus	Haguenau: Anshelm October 1518	quarto
54	Luterus in Galat.	Luther, Martin *In Epistolam S. Pauli ad Galatas commentarius*	[Leipzig: M. Lotther 1519] or a reprint or revised version [Wittenberg: J. Grünenberg, August 1523] or a reprint or expanded version Wittenberg: H. Lufft or Haguenau: P. Braubach 1535	quarto or octavo or octavo

55	Prognostica Alberti Pighij	Pigge, Albert *Adversus prognos-ticatorum vulgus ... astrolo-giae defensio*	Paris: H. Estienne 1518–19	quarto
56	Wesselij Farrago Rerum Theolo. cum Apolo.	Gansfort, Wessel *Farrago rerum theologicarum uberrima emendatio*	Basel: A. Petri, September 1522 or January 1523	quarto
57	Plutarchi opuscula Bud.	Plutarch *Tria opuscula* trans Guillaume Budé and perhaps *De placitis philosophorum libri* trans Guillaume Budé	[Paris:] J. Bade 15 May 1505 Paris: J. Bade for J. Petit 18 March 1505/6	quarto quarto
58	Ioan. Chrysosto. Brix.	John Chrysostom *In epis-tolam divi Pauli ad Romanos homiliae octo priores* trans Germain de Brie	Basel: H. Froben and N. Episcopius, March 1533	quarto
59	De unitate Eccle.	*De unitate ecclesiae conservanda* ed Ulrich von Hutten	Mainz: J. Schöffer, March 152	octavo
60	Propugnaculum Ecclesiae Clichto.	Clichtove, Josse *Propugnaculum ecclesiae adversus Lutheranos*	Cologne: P. Quentel, August 1526 or Cologne: H. Fuchs, September 1526	quarto or octavo
61	Carmen uotiuum Erasmj	Erasmus *Divae Genovefae ... carmen votivum*	Freiburg im Breisgau: J. Emmeus 1532	quarto
62	Argumentum in epistolas Paulj.	Erasmus *Argumenta in omneis epistolas Apostolicas nova* (the second part of the *Ratio*)	Leuven: Dirk Martens, November 1518	quarto
63	Sententi. Textus Magistri Sententiarum.	Peter Lombard *Sententiae*	probably a Paris edition c 1510–20	octavo
64	Paulini Episco. Nolani epistolae etc.	Paulinus of Nola *Epistolae et poemata*	[Paris:] J. Petit and J. Bade, 24 February 1516	octavo
65	Breuiarium. de laude uirtu. psal.	1/ a breviary 2/ Pseudo-Augustine *De laude psalmorum*; *De virtute psalmorum*	Zwolle: P. van Os, November 1486	quarto
66	Mωriac Encomium Eras.	Erasmus *Moriae encomium*	Probably a Froben edition 1516–32	quarto or octavo
67	Epist. Plinij	Plinius Caecilius Secundus, Gaius *Epistolarum libri decem*	Venice: A. Manuzio and A. Torresani 1508 or repr 1518	octavo

68	Pomeranica Commenta. in Psalmos	Bugenhagen, Johann *In librum Psalmorum interpretatio*	Basel: A. Petri, March or (rev ed) August 1524 or a pirate edition	octavo
69	Supputationes errorum	Erasmus *Supputationes errorum in censuris Natalis Bedae*	Basel: J. Froben, March 1527	octavo
70	Longolij Orationes, epistulae etc	Longueil, Christophe de *Orationes duae pro defensione sua*; *Oratio ad Luteranos quosdam iam damnatos*; *Epistolarum libri quatuor*; *Bembus et Sadoletus, Epistolarum liber unus*; *Longolii vita*	Florence: heirs of P. Giunta 1524	quarto
71	Enchir. Institu. prin. et reli. eras.	1/ Erasmus *Enchiridion*, with Basil *In Esaiam commentariolus* trans Erasmus and other works	Basel: J. Froben, July 1518	quarto
		2/ Erasmus *Institutio principis christiani ... cum aliis nonnullis*	Basel: J. Froben, July 1518	quarto
72	Diomedes de arte grammatica	Diomedes *De arte grammatica*	probably a Paris edition	quarto
73	Bayfius de re uestiaria. Libanij decla.	1/ Baïf, Lazare de *De re vestiaria*	Basel: J. Bebel 1526	quarto
		2/ Libanius *Declamatiuculae aliquot graece* trans Erasmus	Basel: J. Froben 1522	quarto
74	Rex Angliae contra Lute.	Henry VIII *Literarum quibus ... Henricus VIII Rex Angliae respondit ad quandam epistolam Martini Lutheri ad se missam, et ipsius lutheranae quoque epistolae exemplum*	London: R. Pynson, 2 December 1526	octavo
75	Linacrus de emendata struc. lati.	Linacre, Thomas *De emendata structura latini sermonis*	London: R. Pynson, December 1524	quarto
76	Leonicj Opuscula uaria	Leonico Tomeo, Niccolò *Opuscula*	Venice: B. Vitalis 1525	quarto
77	Esaias Ecolamp.	Oecolampadius, Johannes *In Iesaiam prophetam ... commentariorum libri VI*	Basel: A. Cratander, March 1525	quarto
78	Geor. Agricolae de pond. et mens.	Agricola, Georgius *Libri quinque de mensuris et ponderibus*	Basel: Froben, August 1533	quarto

79	Varia Erasmi. Libel. nouus etc.	Erasmus *De pueris instituendis, cum alijs compluribus*	Basel: H. Froben, J. Herwagen, and N. Episcopius, September 1529	quarto
80	Natural. Senecae Quaesti. lib. 7.	Seneca, Lucius Annaeus *Quaestiones naturales* ed M. Fortunatus	Venice: A. Manuzio and A. Torresani, February 1523	quarto
81	Tragoediae Senecae.	Seneca, Lucius Annaeus *Tragoediae*	Paris: J. Bade, 7 March 1512 or Venice: A. Manuzio and A. Torresani 1517	octavo

folio 40r

82	Vergilius	Virgil *Opera*	Venice: A. Manuzio 1505?	octavo
83	Terentius	Terence, Publius *Comoediae*		octavo
84	Ouidij Metamor.	Ovid *Opera* I (*Metamorphoses*)	probably Venice: A. Manuzio 1502	octavo
85	Ouidij Fast. Trist. Pon.	Ovid *Opera* III (*Fasti, Tristia, Epistolae ex Ponto*)	probably Venice: A. Manuzio 1502/3	octavo
86	Ouidij Elegiae	Ovid *Opera* II (*Heroidum epistolae ... Elegiae, De arte amandi, De remedio amoris ...*)	probably Venice: A. Manuzio December 1502	octavo
87	Terent. Cato. Ciuilitate	1/ Terence *Comoediae* ed Erasmus	Basel: H. Froben and N. Episcopius 1534	octavo
		2/ Cato *Disticha moralia cum scholiis Erasmi*	Basel: Froben 1534	octavo
		3/ Erasmus *De civilitate*	Basel: Froben 1534	octavo
88	Horatius	Horace *Opera*	Venice: A. Manuzio 1501 or 1509 or a reprint?	octavo
89	Oppianus graece. Eius. de pisci. latinè	Oppian of Corycus *De piscibus* and Oppian of Apamea *De venatione* (with a Latin version of the poem on fishing)	Venice: A. Manuzio and A. Torresani 1517	octavo
90	Hippocratis Praesagia. Calphur.	1/ Hippocrates *Praesagiorum libri tres* and *De ratione victus* trans Willem Cop	[Paris: H. Estienne c 1512]	quarto
		2/ Calphurnius, Franciscus *Epigrammata*	Paris: J. de Marnef n d	quarto
91	L. And. Resendij Genethliacon	Resende, André de *Genethliacon*	Bologna: J.B. Phaelli 1533	quarto
92	Silius Italicus	Silius Italicus *Punica*		quarto or octavo

93	Lucanus. cum Vtilissi. Aristote. Rheto.	1/ Lucan *Bellum civile* 2/ [Aristotle] *Rhetorica ad Alexandrum*	Paris: N. des Prez [c 1506] Paris: G. de Gourmont [c 1507]	quarto quarto
94	Ioan. Aurelij Augurelli Chrysopoeiae	Augurelli, Giovanni *Chrysopoeia*	Venice: S. Luerensis 1515 or Basel: J. Froben 1518	quarto
95	Λειτουργιαι graece cum Ianj Vitalis opusc.	1/ Byzantine liturgies 2/ Vitalis, Janus, one or more minor works	Rome: D. Doukas, October 1526	quarto
96	Nazianzeni Orationes 16. graece.	Gregory of Nazianzus *Orationes*	Venice: A. Manuzio and A. Torresani, April 1516	octavo
97	Melan. orationes. Imperatores. Lute. epistolae	1/ Melanchthon, Philippus *Orationes* 2/ [Huttich, Johann] *Imperatorum romanorum libellus* 3/ Luther, Martin *Epistolarum farrago ... cum Psalmorum aliquot interpretatione*	Haguenau: J. Setzer 1525 Strasbourg: W. Köpfel 1525 Haguenau: J. Setzer 1525	octavo octavo octavo
98	Theocritus graecè εἰδυλλια ἐπιγραμ. etc	Theocritus *Eidyllia, Epigrammata* with the scholia of Z. Calliergis	Rome: Z. Calliergis, January 1516	octavo
99	θεοκριτοσ Latinè et graecè	Theocritus *Idyllia* trans Eobanus Hessus, ed J. Camerarius	Haguenau: J. Setzer November 1530 or Basel: A. Cratander 1530–1	octavo
100	Eurip. Rhesus, troades et reli. graecè	Euripides *Tragoediae* II	Venice: A. Manuzio February 1503	octavo
101	Πτολεμαιου De geographia lib. 8. graecè	Ptolemy *De geographia*	Basel: H. Froben and N. Episcopius 1533	quarto
102*	Tragoediae Eurip. et Soph. cum commen. grae.	1/ Euripides *Tragoediae* 2/ Sophocles *Tragoediae*	Venice: A. Manuzio February 1503 Venice: A. Manuzio, August 1502	octavo octavo
103	Eurip. orestes, phoenissae etc. graece	Euripides *Tragoediae* I	Venice: A.Manuzio February 1503	octavo
104	Επιγραμμα. Florilegium epigram. grae.	*Florilegium diversorum epigrammatum* (the Greek Anthology) ed Janus Lascaris	Venice: A. Manuzio, November 1503 or A. Manuzio and A. Torresani, January 1521	octavo

105	Πινδαροσ graecè in 8°.	Pindar *Odes*	Venice: A. Manuzio and A. Torresani January 1513 or Basel: A. Cratander 1526	octavo
106	Theocritus graece in 4°	Theocritus *Eidyllia*	[Paris:] G. de Gourmont n d or Leuven: Dirk Martens 1520	quarto
107	Πινδαροσ graece cum comment.	Pindar *Olympia, Nemea, Pythia, Isthmia cum scholiis*	Rome: Z. Calliergis 1515	quarto
108	Interpre. in Homerum graece cum Porphy. quaest. grae.	Didymus Alexandrinus *Interpretationes in Homeri Iliada nec non in Odyssea* [sic]; Porphyry *Homericarum questionum liber*	Venice: A. Manuzio and A. Torresani May 1521	octavo
109	Ομηροσ in Iliade [sic] grae.	*Homeri interpres pervetustus*	Rome: A. Collotius, 8 September 1517	small folio
110	Οδυσσεια βατραχο. hymni 32. grae.	Homer *Opera graece* ii	Venice: A. Manuzio 1504 or 1517 or another edition	octavo
111	Ad Atticum M. Tullij Cic. epistolae	Cicero *Epistolarum ad Atticum, ad Brutum, ad Quintum fratrem libri xx*	Venice: A. Manuzio and A. Torresani June 1513	octavo
112	Statij. Syluae, Thebais, Achylleis cum commen.	Statius *Syluae, Thebais, Achilleis,* with commentaries	Venice: B. de Zanis 1494 or J.P. de Quarengis 1498	folio
113	Martialis cum duobus commentis	Martial *Epigrammata,* with the commentaries of Domizio Calderini and Giorgio Merula	Venice: B. de Zanis 1493 or Venice 1495, 1498, 1503, 1510 or Milan 1505	folio
114	Ιλιασ Homeri graece	Homer *Opera graece* ed Demetrius Chalcondyles part i	Florence: B. Nerlius, N. Nerlius, and D. Damilas 1488/9	folio
115	Οδυσσεια Homeri graece	Homer *Opera graece* ed Demetrius Chalcondyles part ii	Florence: B. Nerlius, N. Nerlius, and D. Damilas 1488/9	folio
116	Αριστοφαν. Comoediae 9. cum commen. graece	Aristophanes *Comoediae novem*	Venice: A. Manuzio 1498	folio
117	Terentius cum commentarijs	Terence *Comoediae* ed Erasmus	Basel: H. Froben and N. Episcopius, March 1532 or an earlier edition	folio
118	Lucianus Latine uersus ab Erasmo	Lucian *Dialogues* trans Erasmus and More	Basel: J. Froben, August 1521	folio

119	Quintili. Vallae cum commento	Quintilian *Institutiones* comm Lorenzo Valla, Pomponius Laetus, and Giovanni Antonio Sulpizio	Venice: P. de Pasqualibus, 18 August 1494	folio
120	Ciceronis epistolae. Philosophica. Index. Herua.	Cicero *Opera* III and IV	Basel: J. Herwagen 1534	folio
121	Ciceronis Oratoria ex aeditione Heruagij	Cicero *Opera* I and II	Basel: J. Herwagen 1534	folio
122	Epistolae Cicer./Tullius > opera. M. Tul.	Cicero *Epistolae,* probably from an edition of the *Opera*		folio
123*	Lucianus graece ex offici. Aldi	Lucian *Opera*	Venice: A. Manuzio, June 1503	folio
124	Isocratis opera Graece	Isocrates *Logoi* ed Demetius Chalcondyles	Milan: U. Scinzenzeler 1493	folio

folio 40v

125	Asco. Pedianus in orationes Ciceronis	Asconius Pedianus, Quintus *Commentarii in orationes Ciceronis*		folio
126	Galen. de locis affectis	Galen *De affectorum locorum notitia*	probably Paris: S. de Colines 1520	folio
127	Ρηθορικη [sic] 13. autorum graece. Ald.	*Rhetores graeci* I	Venice: A. Manuzio 1508/9 or 2d ed A. Manuzio and A. Torresani 1523	folio
128	Ερμογεν. et Aphthonius cum commen. graece	*Rhetores graeci* II	Venice: A. Manuzio 1508–9 or 2d ed A. Manuzio and A. Torresani 1523	folio
129	Ioannes grammaticos in lib. de generati. grae.	Philoponus, Joannes. Commentary on Aristotle *De generatione et corruptione*	Venice: A. Manuzio and A. Torresani, September 1527	folio
130	Δεμοσθένησ [sic] orationes 62. graece	Demosthenes *Orationes duae et sexaginta*	Venice: A. Manuzio, November 1504	folio
131	Demost. orationes 62. graece. Heruagij	Demosthenes *Orationes duae et sexaginta*	Basel: J. Herwagen September 1532	folio
132	Orationes Rhetorum 16 graece	*Oratores graeci* I–III	Venice: A. Manuzio and A. Torresani April (I and II) and May (III) 1513	folio

133	Aetius Medicus ex aediti. Frob.	Latin translation of a medical handbook in 3 volumes compiled by Aetius of Amida; probably I and II	Basel: H. Froben and N. Episcopius 1533	folio
134	Ptolemaeus de Geograph. latine	Ptolemy *Geographicae enarrationis libri octo* trans Pirckheimer	Strasbourg: J. Grieningerus, 30 March 1525	folio
135	Alciatus in 16. libris	Alciati, Andrea. A collection of legal studies	Milan: A. Minuziano 1518 or a later edition	folio
136	Ptolomaeus [sic] de geogra. Vlmae excusus	Ptolemy *Cosmographia* trans Jacopo Angeli	Ulm: L. Holle, 16 July 1482 or J. Reger for J. de Albano, 21 July 1486	folio
137*	Galeni prima / Galeni 2. / Galeni 3. / Galeni 4. / Galeni 5.	Galenus, Claudius *Galeni librorum pars prima (–quinta)*	Venice: A. Manuzio and A. Asulani 1525	folio
138*	Γαληνου θεραπευτικησ μεθοδ.	Galen *Therapeutica*; *Ad Glauconem* ed Niccolò Leoniceno	Venice: Z. Calliergis for N. Blastos, 21 October 1500	folio
139	Ινστιτουτα Theophi. Anteces. grae.	*Institutiones iuris civilis in graecam linguam per Theophilum Antecessorem olim traductae* (Greek paraphrase of the Institutes of Justinian by Theophilus Antecessor) ed Viglius Zuichemus	Basel: H. Froben and N. Episcopius, March 1534	folio
140	Sextus Decretalium	Liber Sextus (= *Corpus iuris canonici* III)		folio or quarto
141	Decretalium Gregorij libri .5.	Decretals of Gregory IX (= *Corpus iuris canonici* II)		folio or quarto
142	Decretum pars prima 2ª. 3ª.	Gratian *Decretum* (= *Corpus iuris canonici* I)		folio or quarto
143	Autenticorum seu collationum feudorum libr.	*Volumen parvum* (= *Corpus iuris civilis* V)		folio?
144	Codex Iustiniani libr 9.	*Codex Justiniani* I–IX (= *Corpus iuris civilis* IV)		folio or quarto
145	In Fortiatum [sic] à 24º libro ad 38ᵘᵐ.	*Infortiatum. Digestorum XXIIII-3–XXXVIII* (= *Corpus iuris civilis* II)		folio or quarto

146	Digestum Nouum à 39º libro ad 50ᵘᵐ usque	*Digestum Novum. Digestorum libri XXXIX–L* (= *Corpus iuris civilis* III)		folio or quarto
147	Dige. Vetus 50. librorum pandectarum etc.	*Digestum Vetus. Digestorum libri I–XXIV-2* (= *Corpus iuris civilis* I)		folio or quarto
148	Senecae opera	Seneca *Opera* ed Erasmus (rev ed)	Basel: Froben 1529	folio
149	Ambros. 4./ Ambros. 1.	Ambrose *Opera*; 4 vols plus an extra vol I or vols I and IV	Basel: J. Froben 1527	folio
150	Chrysostomi lucubrationes uersae ab Eras./ ~~Catalogus lucubrationum Erasmj~~	1/ John Chrysostom and Athanasius. A collection of texts translated by Erasmus 2/ Erasmus *Catalogus omnium lucubrationum* [deleted]	Basel: J. Froben, March 1527 Basel: J. Froben, April 1523 or September 1524	folio octavo
151	Lingua. δυσωπ. Sutor in Eras.	1/ Erasmus *Lingua* (probably 2d ed); Plutarch *De vitiosa verecundia* trans Erasmus 2/ Cousturier, Pierre *Antapologia*	Basel: J. Froben February or July 1526 Paris: P. Vidoue June 1526	octavo octavo
152	Latomus de confessione secreta.	Masson, Jacques *De confessione secreta*	Antwerp: M. Hillen 1525 or Basel: A. Cratander 1525	octavo
153	Eras. in monach. Hisp. Val. in Pog.	1/ Erasmus *Apologia adversus monachos* 2/ Valla, Lorenzo *In Pogium* and other works	Basel: Froben 1528 Cologne: H. Fuchs 1527	octavo octavo
154	Index seu Repertorium in Glosam ordin./ Gen. Deut. cum postil. Lyra. et glo. ord./Regum cum glosa ordi. et exposi. Lyrae./Proph. pars 4ª Glosae ordinariae/Iob. Psal. Eccl. 3ª pars glo. ordi./Euan. 5ª pars glo. ord./Epist. Apost. 6ª pars bib. cum glo.	*Biblia: Textus bibliae cum glosa ordinaria et Nicolai de Lyra postilla*	Basel: J. Petri and J. Froben 1506–8 or Lyon: J. Mareschal 1520	folio

| 155 | Tuscula[n]ae. Foemina Christiana. | 1/ Cicero *Tusculanae quaestiones* | Basel: J. Froben, November 1523 | quarto |
| | | 2/ Vives *De institutione foeminae christianae* | Antwerp: M. Hillen 1524 | quarto |

folio 41r

156	Ausonius	Ausonius, Decimus Magnus *Opera*	Paris: J. Bade 1511 or a later Bade edition	quarto
157	Quintilianus Aldi	Quintilian *Institutionum oratoriarum libri XII*	Venice: A. Manuzio and A. Torresani, August 1514 or January 1521	quarto
158	Eras. Enchiri. Hetrusco idiomate	Erasmus *Enchiridion* trans Emilio de' Migli	Brescia: L. Britannico, 22 April 1531	octavo
159	Bernardi opera	Bernard of Clairvaux *Opera*		folio
160	Bedae operum Secundus Tomus	Bede the Venerable *Opera* II (commentaries on Mark, Luke, Acts, the Catholic Epistles, Apocalypse)	[Paris:] J. Bade 1521	folio
161	Thomas de Aquino super epistulas Pauli	Thomas Aquinas *Super epistolas ... Pauli commentaria*	Venice: B. Locatellus for O. Scotus 1498 or Venice: P. Pincius 1510	folio
162	Thomae de Aqui. pars prima	Thomas Aquinas *Summa theologiae prima pars*		folio
163	Sententiae Petri Lombardi	Peter Lombard *Sententiarum libri IV*		folio?
164	Chron. Euseb.	Eusebius of Caesarea *Chronicon*	Paris: H. Estienne and J. Bade, 13 June 1512 or repr 1518	quarto
165	Secun. Secundae sancti Thomae de Aquino	Thomas Aquinas *Summa theologiae. Secundus liber secundae partis*		quarto or folio
166	Chrysost. Ψεγματα Oecolamp.	John Chrysostom *Psegmata quaedam* trans Oecolampadius	Basel: A. Cratander, March 1523 or repr Paris: J. Petit 1524	quarto or folio
167	Τò σκότοσ Scoti Scrip. primum super 1° Sent.	John Duns Scotus. Commentary on the first book of the *Sentences* of Peter Lombard		folio
168	Durandus in 4. Sententiarum libros	Durandus of Saint-Pourçain. Commentary on the Sentences of Peter Lombard ed Jacques Merlin	Paris: J. Bade for J. Petit 1508 or 1515	folio

169	Gerson 1./Gerson 2./Gerson 3/ Gerson 4.	Gerson, Jean *Opera*	Paris: J. Petit and F. Regnault 1521 or Basel: A. Petri for L. Hornken and G. Hittorp 1518	folio
170	Chathena aurea Thomae Aquinatis	Thomas Aquinas *Catena aurea*	Paris: J. Petit 1517 or a pre-1500 edition	folio
171	Homiliae Doctorum in Euan. dominica. de tempore	*Homiliae doctorum ecclesiasticorum* (a collection of sermons for liturgical use compiled by Paul the Deacon)	Basel or Lyon c 1516–20	
172	Canones Apostolorum Decre. pontif. antiquiora etc.	[Dionysius Exiguus] *Canones Apostolorum*; *Veterum conciliorum constitutiones*; *Decreta pontificum antiquiora*; *De primatu romanae ecclesiae* (a collection of documents of church history) ed Johannes Cochlaeus	Mainz: J. Schöffer, April 1525	folio
173	Luteri Operationes in Psalmos.	Luther, Martin *Operationes in Psalmos*	Wittenberg: J.R. Grünenberg 1519–21	quarto
174	Eccius de primatu Petri li. 3.	Johann Maier of Eck *De primatu Petri adversus Ludderum*	Paris: J. Kerver for P. Vidoue, September 1521	folio
175	Sermones Ioan. Longlondi.	Longland, John *Sermones*	[London: R. Pynson? 1527?] or [R. Redman? 1532?]	folio
176*	Reuchlinus de verbo mirifico cum Cabalistica.	1/ Reuchlin, Johann *Liber de verbo mirifico* 2/ Reuchlin, Johann *De arte cabalistica*	Tübingen: T. Anshelm, August 1514 Haguenau: T. Anshelm, March 1517	folio folio
177	Caietani Commentarij super Euan. et acta apo./et super Epistolas Pauli et aliorum apost.	Cajetanus, Tommaso de Vio *Evangelia cum commentariis … castigata*; *Epistolae Pauli et aliorum Apostolorum castigate*	Venice: L. de Giunta 1530 or Paris: J. Bade and J. Petit and J. Roigny, May 1532 [Venice: L. de Giunta 1530?] or Paris: J. Bade and J. Petit and J. Roigny, May 1532	folio folio
178	Commentarij Stapulensis super Euangelia	Lefèvre d'Etaples, Jacques *Commentarii … in quatuor Evangelia*	Meaux: S. de Colines, June 1522 or repr Basel: A. Cratander, March 1523	folio
179	Fabri stapulen. commen. in epistolas.	Lefèvre d'Etaples, Jacques *Epistola ad Romanos …*	Paris: H. Estienne 1512 or [1516]	folio

180	Dionisij coelest. Hierarchia cum Euclide.	1/ Dionysius the Pseudo-Areopagite (the four main works) ed Lefèvre d'Etaples ann Josse Clichtove	Paris: H. Estienne, April 1515	folio
		2/ Euclid *Stoicheia* ed Lefèvre d'Etaples	Paris: H. Estienne [1516]	folio
181	Antilutherus Clichtouei	Clichtove, Josse *Antilutherus*	Paris: S. de Colines 1524	folio
182	Ioan. Driedonis de eccle. doctri. lib. 4.	Driedo, Jan *De ecclesiasticis scripturis et dogmatibus*	Leuven: R. Rescius for B. Gravius, 10 June 1533	folio
183	Opus Cyrilli in Euang. Ioan. Trapezon. interpre.	Cyril of Alexandria *Opus insigne in Evangelium Joannis* trans George of Trebizond	Paris: W. Hopyl, 10 January 1508 or 15 December 1520	folio
184	Lactantij Firmiani opera	Lactantius *Opera*		folio
185	Hilarij opera per Eras. emend.	Hilary of Poitiers *Lucubrationes* ed Erasmus	Basel: J. Froben, February 1523 or rev ed H. Froben and N. Episcopius, August 1535	folio
186	Dictionarius graecus.	Craston, Johannes *Dictionarium graecum* ed Jacobus Ceratinus	Basel: J. Froben, July 1524	folio
187	Athanasij opera.	Athanasius *Opera* ed Nicolas Bérault	Paris: J. Petit 1519 or rev ed 1520	folio
188	Index in opera Hieronymi cum lucubr. Zasij	1/ Oecolampadius, Johannes. Index volume to Erasmus' edition of Jerome	Basel: J. Froben, May 1520	folio
		2/ Zasius, Udalricus *Lucubrationes aliquot* (a collection of mainly juristic treatises)	Basel: J. Froben 1518	folio
189	Basilij Mag. opera Grae. Frob.	Basil the Great *Opera*	Basel: H. Froben and N. Episcopius, March 1532	folio
190	Opera Boetij.	Boethius *Opera*	Venice: J. and G. de Gregoriis 1491–2 or 1497–9	folio
191	Lactantius Cratandrj	Lactantius *Divinae institutiones*; *De ira Dei*; *De opificio Dei*; *Epitome in libros suos, liber acephalus*; *Phoenix*; *Carmen de dominica resurrectione*; *Carmen de passione Domini*	Basel: A. Cratander and J. Bebel 1532	folio
192	Cornelius Celsus Venetijs	Celsus, Aulus Cornelius *De re medicina*	Venice: J. Rubeus 1493 or P. Pinzi for B. Fontana 1497	folio

193	Iosephi Antiquita. libri et de bello Iudaico	Josephus *Antiquitatum judaicarum*; *De bello judaico*		folio
194	Calepinus	Calepinus, Ambrosius *Dictionarium*		folio
195	Clementis libri cum opere Irenaei cont. haeres.	1/ Clement I *Recognitiones*; *Epistolarum pars vetustissimorum episcoporum*	Basel: J. Bebel 1526	folio
		2/ Irenaeus *Adversus haereses*	Basel: J. Froben, August 1526	folio
196	Faber Stapu. in Epistulas	Lefèvre d'Etaples, Jacques *Commentarii in epistolas catholicas*	Basel: A. Cratander, July 1527	folio

folio 41v

197	Apuleius de asino au. cum commen.	Apuleius *De asino aureo* comm Philippo Beroaldo	Bologna: B. Hector, August 1500 or a later edition	folio
198	Aesopus grae. et Latine cum alijs opusc.	Aesopus: *Vita et fabellae Aesopi cum interpretatione latina ...*	Venice: A. Manuzio, October 1505	folio
199	Euclidis opera Latine	Euclid *Opera* trans J. Campanus	Venice: P. de Paganinis, 22 May 1509 or J. Tacuinus 1505 or another edition	folio
200	Plutarchi quaedam opuscula.	Plutarch *Quaedam opuscula* (10 treatises from the *Moralia* translated into Latin)	Paris: J. Bade 1514, 1521, or 1526 or Basel: A. Cratander 1530	folio
201*	Dioscorides cum annota. Egnatij cum / Corollario Hermolai Barbarj.	Dioscorides *De materia medica* trans and comm Ermolao Barbaro, preceded by the annotations of Giovanni Battista Egnazio	Venice: G. de Gregoriis 1516	folio
202	Dioscorides cum annotati. Marcelli.	Dioscorides *De medica materia* trans and comm Marcello Virgilio	Florence: heirs of P. Giunta 1518	folio
203*	Dioscorides et Nicander graece	Dioscorides *De materia medica*; Nikandros *Theriaca*; *Alexipharmaca*	Venice: A. Manuzio, July 1499	folio
204	Xenophontis opera graece	Xenophon *Omnia quae extant*	Venice: A. Manuzio and A. Torresani, April 1525	folio
205	Plinij Natura. Histor. Frob.	Pliny *Naturalis historia*	Basel: J. Froben 1525 or rev ed ann Beatus Rhenanus H. Froben, J. Herwagen, and N. Episcopius 1530	folio

206	Index in Plinium Ioan. Camertis	Ricuzzi, Giovanni, of Camerino *Index in C. Plinii Secundi naturalem historiam*	Basel: Froben 1525 or 1530 or 1535	folio
207	Plin. Natu. hist. Frob.	Pliny *Naturalis historia*	Basel: J. Froben 1525 or rev ed ann Beatus Rhenanus H. Froben, J. Herwagen, and N. Episcopius 1530	folio
208*	Plutarchi opuscu. 92. grae. Aldi.	Plutarchus: *Opuscula LXXXXII* (*editio princeps* of the *Moralia* in Greek) ed Demetrios Doukas	Venice: A. Manuzio and A. Torresani, March 1509	folio
209*	Plotini opera latine. Florentiae	Plotinus *Opera* trans and comm Marsilio Ficino	Florence: A. Miscominus 1492	folio
210	Politi. Economi. etc Aristot. cum commen.	Aristotle *Politica, Oeconomica* ... ed and comm Lefèvre d'Etaples	Paris: H. Estienne 5 August 1506 or 3 April 1511	folio
211	Aristote. quaedam, item Theophr. Gaza interpre.	Aristotle *De natura animalium*; *De partibus animalium*; *De generatione animalium* and Theophrastus *De historia plantarum*; *De causis plantarum* ... trans Theodorus Gaza	Venice: A. Manuzio, March 1504 or 1513	folio
212	Aristotelis opera uarijs interpretibus.	Aristotle *Opera* in various Latin translations	Venice: J. and G. de Gregoriis for B. Fontana 1496 or Venice: P. Pincius for B. Fontana 1505	folio
213	Plauti opera cum interpreta. Bap. Pij.	Plautus *Opera* comm Giambattista Pio	Milan: U. Scinzenzeler, 18 January 1500	folio
214*	Ζῶα / Φυτὰ / Ὄργανα / Προβλήματα / Φυσικα. μετεω. / Ηθικα. πολιτ. } Aristote. graece.	Aristotle *Opera omnia*	Venice: A. Manuzio 1495–8	folio
215	Aristotelis opera graece. Bebelij	Aristotle *Opera omnia*	Basel: J. Bebel 1531	folio
216	Platonis opera tralatione Marsi. Fici.	Plato *Opera omnia* trans Marsilio Ficino ed S. Grynaeus	Basel: Froben 1532 or another edition	folio
217	Platonis opera Venetijs. Latinè	Plato *Opera* trans Marsilio Ficino	Venice: A. Torresani for B. de Choris and S. de Luere 1491 or P. Pincius 1517	folio

218*	Platonis opera graecè. Aldi.	Plato *Omnia opera*	Venice: A. Manuzio and A. Torresani, September 1513	folio
219	Flauij Iosephi opera Frob.	Josephus, Flavius *Opera*	Basel: J. Froben 1524 or Basel: H. Froben and N. Episcopius 1534	folio
220	Biblia Frob.	*Biblia cum pleno apparatu* (with the commentaries, explanatory notes, concordances, and lists of words known as the *plenus apparatus*)	Basel: J. Petri and J. Froben 1509 or Basel: J. Froben 1514	folio
221	Biblia graecè Aldi.	Greek Bible	Venice: A. Manuzio and A. Torresani, February 1518	folio
222	Primus et secun. tomus / Tertius et quar. tom. > operum Orige.	Origen *Opera* (Latin) ed Jacques Merlin	Paris: J. Petit and J. Bade 1512	folio
223	Opera Cypriani	Cyprian *Opera*	probably Rome: C. Sweynheym and A. Pannartz 1471	folio
224	Theophylactus in .4. Euan. Oecolam. interpre.	Theophylact *In quatuor evangelia enarrationes* trans Oecolampadius	Basel: A. Cratander, March 1524 or a reprint	folio
225	Biblia Lugd. excu.	*Biblia cum pleno apparatu*	Lyon: J. Sacon 1506 or a reprint	folio
226	Opus Epistolarum Eras.	Erasmus *Opus epistolarum*	Basel: H. Froben, J. Herwagen, and N. Episcopius 1529	folio
227	Opera Tertulliani Frob.	Tertullian *Opera* ed Beatus Rhenanus	Basel: J. Froben, July 1521 or Froben 1528	folio
228	Origenes contra Celsum. Romae. / excusus Christoph. Persona interprete.	Origen *Contra Celsum* trans C. Persona	Rome: G. Herolt 1481	folio
229	Cypriani et Irenaei opera Frob.	1/ Cyprian *Opera* ed Erasmus 2/ Irenaeus *Adversus omnes haereses* ed Erasmus	Basel: Froben 1530 or 1525 Basel: Froben 1528 or 1534	folio folio
230	Tomus primus / To. 2ᵘˢ. / Tomus 3ᵘˢ / Tomus quartus / To. 5ᵘˢ cum indice } operum Io. Chrysostomj / Frob.	John Chrysostom *Opera*	Basel: Froben 1530	folio

231	Chrysost. in Genesim interprete Oecolam.	John Chrysostom *In totum Genesews librum homiliae 66* trans Oecolampadius	Basel: A. Cratander, September 1523	folio

folio 42r

232	Historiae Eccl. auto. Frob.	*Autores historiae ecclesiasticae* (writers on church history) ed Beatus Rhenanus	Basel: J. Froben, August 1523 or H. Froben and N. Episcopius, March 1535	folio
233	Prima pars/Secun. pars/Ter. pas [sic] } operum Ambrosij	Ambrose *Opera* parts I–III	Basel: J. Amerbach 1492	folio
234	Chrysosto. in Epist. 1. et 2. ad Corin./graece manuscriptus	John Chrysostom on 1 and 2 Corinthians	manuscript	folio
235	Chryso. in epistolas ad Heb. Galatas. Varia,/graece eadem manu scrip.	John Chrysostom on Hebrews and Galatians	manuscript	folio
236	Catalogus scriptorum eccles. Tritenh. Spanheymensis.	Trithemius, Johannes *Liber de scriptoribus ecclesiasticis*	Basel: J. Amerbach 1494 or a later edition	folio
237	Psalterium Felicis. Venetijs excu.	*Psalterium* trans Felice da Prato from Hebrew	Venice: P. Liechtenstein for D. Bomberg 1515	folio
238	Pars prima/Pars altera } operum D. Chrysostomj	John Chrysostom *Opera*	Basel: J. Froben 1517	folio
239*	Athenaeus graecè Aldi.	Athenaeus of Naukratis *Deipnosophistae*	Venice: A. Manuzio and A. Torresani, August 1514	folio
240	Concordantiae maiores Bibliae	*Concordantiae maiores Bibliae*	Basel: Froben, one of many editions	folio
241	Nouum Testamen. Eras. grae. et Lat.	*Novum Testamentum* ed Erasmus with Greek text and Latin translation	Basel: Froben 1516, 1519, 1522, 1527, 1535	folio
242	Augusti. de Ciuitate Dei. Frob.	Augustine *De civitate Dei* ed Vives	Basel: J. Froben, September 1522	folio

243	Pars prima / Pars secun. / Pars ter. / Pars quar. } ope- rum D. Hierony. Frob. / Pars sex. ~~Pars sep.~~	Jerome *Opera* I–IV, VI	Basel: J. Froben 1516 or 1524–6	folio
244	De copia uerborum ~~commen.~~ Eras. commenta // rius, manu scriptus	Erasmus *De copia*	manuscript	
245	Lazarus Bayfius de re nauali, de re uest. / de vasculis. Item Anto. Thyle. de coloribus.	Baïf, Lazare de *De re navali*; *De re vestiaria*; *De vasculis* and Telesio, Antonio *De coloribus*	Paris: R. Etienne, 31 August 1536	quarto
246	Ciceronis Rhet. de Inuen. etc libri 13. Aldi	*[Auctor] ad Herennium*; Cicero *De inventione*; *De oratore*; *De claris oratoribus*; *Oratoriae partitionis*; *De optimo genere oratorum*	Venice: A. Manuzio and A. Torresani 1514 or 1521 or 1533	quarto
247	Annotationes Eras. in Nouum Testa.	Erasmus *In Novum Testamentum annotationes*	Basel: Froben 1519, 1522, 1527, or 1535	folio
248	Eucherius cum 30. orationibus Nazianzeni / in- terprete Bilibaldo Pirckheimero.	1/ Eucherius *Lucubrationes aliquot* ed Brassicanus 2/ Gregory of Nazianzus *Orationes 30* trans Pirckheimer	Basel: Froben, September 1531 Basel: Froben, September 1531	folio folio
249	Hilarij opera. Bad. Ascen.	Hilary of Poitiers *Opera*	Paris: J. Bade 1511	folio
250	D. Basilij Magni opera. Frob.	Basil the Great *Opera*	Basel: H. Froben and N. Episcopius, March 1532	folio
251	Haymonis commen- tarij in Psalmos.	Haymo of Halberstadt *Pia bre- vis ac dilucida in omnes psal- mos explanatio* ed Erasmus	Freiburg im Breisgau: J.F. Emmeus 1533	folio
252	Quincuplex Psalterium Fabri.	*Quincuplex Psalterium: Gallicum, Romanum, Hebraicum, Vetus. Conciliatum* ed Lefèvre d'Etaples	Paris: H. Estienne, 31 July 1509 or 2nd ed 13 June 1513	folio

253	Ciceronis de natura deorum lib .3. Eiusdem de / diuinatione lib. 2. manu scrip.	Cicero *De natura deorum*; *De divinatione*	manuscripts	
254	Caietanus in Pentateuchum.	Cajetanus *Commentarii in Pentateuchum Mosis*	Rome: A. Blado 1531	folio
255	Prima pars Bib. / Altera pars Bib.	A complete Vulgate, bound in 2 vols		folio
256	Herbarius zů teütsche vonn allerhand kreüter.	*Herbarius zu teütsche vnnd vonn allerhand kreüteren* (a German herbal)	Augsburg: J. Schönsperger 1496 or another edition	folio
257	Adagiorum opus D. Erasmj Rot.	Erasmus *Adagiorum opus*	Basel: Froben 1526 or 1528 or 1533	folio
258	Operum Augustini To. primus / Tomus secun. qui complectitur epistolas. / Tomus ter. complectens τὰ διδακτικὰ. / To. quar. compl. reliqua τῶν διδακτικῶν / To. quintus de Ciuitate Dei. / Tomus sextus aduersus haereticos / To. septi. aduersus Donat. et Pelgoianos [sic]. / Tomus octauus in Psalmos / Tomus nonus Tractatuum / To. decimus Sermonum cum Indice omnium operum.	Augustine *Omnia opera* ɪ–x	Basel: Froben 1528–9	folio
259	Titus Liuius Frob.	Livy *Quicquid hactenus fuit aeditum* ... or *Decades tres* ... ann Beatus Rhenanus and S. Gelenius	Basel: H. Froben, J. Herwagen, and N. Episcopius, March 1531 / Basel: H. Froben and N. Episcopius 1535	folio / folio
260	Titus Liuius Paris.	*Que extant decades* ...	Paris: J. Bade 1511 or 1513 or 1516	folio

folio 42v

261 (((	Suetonius cum plurib. alijs auto. Frob.	Suetonius *Historiae Augustae scriptores* with other texts	Basel: J. Froben 1518 or 1533	folio
262 (((	Suetonius cum com- menta. Beroaldj	Suetonius ed Philippo Beroaldo	Bologna: B. Hectoris 1493 (several reprints) or Venice: P. Pincius 1510	folio
263 ((	Sueto. cum plur. alijs auto. Frob.	Suetonius *Historiae Augustae scriptores* with other texts	Basel: H. Froben and N. Episcopius 1533 or 1518	folio
264	Blondi opera. Frob.	Biondo, Flavio *De Roma triumphante*; *De Roma instaurata*; *Italia illustrata*; *Historiarum decades*	Basel: H. Froben, J. Herwagen, and N. Episcopius, March 1531	folio
265	Plutarchi Vitae Lati. Bad.	Plutarch *Vitae* with Aemilius Probus *Vitae*	Paris: J. Bade and J. Petit 1514 or 1520	folio
266	Graecorum uitae auto. Plutar. Bebe.	Plutarch *Graecorum Romanorumque illustrium vitae*	Basel: J. Bebel March 1531	folio
267*	Plutarchi Vitae graece Ald.	Plutarch *Quae vocantur parallela, hoc est vitae illustrium virorum graeci nominis ac latini*	Venice: A. Manuzio and A. Torresani 1519	folio
268	Q. Curtius cum Vuandalia Alber. krantz	1/ Curtius Rufus, Quintus *De rebus gestis Alexandri Magni* ed Erasmus	Strasbourg: M. Schürer, June 1518	folio
		2/ Crantz, Albert *Wandalia*	Cologne: J. Soter, April 1519	folio
269	Cornelius Tacitus	Tacitus *Annales*	Basel: H. Froben and N. Episcopius 1533 (ed Beatus Rhenanus) or an earlier edition, eg Rome: St Guilleret 1515 or J. Froben 1519	folio
270	Tacitus et Appianus Alexandrinus	1/ Tacitus *Opera*	[Venice:] V. de Spira [c 1472] or P. Pincius for B. Fontana 22 March 1497	folio
		2/ Appian *Historia Romana*	Venice: V. de Spira 1472 (part 2) or Venice: C. de Pensis, 20 November 1500 (parts 1 and 2)	folio

271	Procopius et B. Rhen. de Germ.	1/ Procopius *De rebus Gothorum, Persarum ac Vandalorum ...* ed Beatus Rhenanus	Basel: J. Herwagen, September 1531	folio
		2/ Beatus Rhenanus *Rerum germanicarum*	Basel: H. Froben, J. Herwagen, and N. Episcopius, March 1531	folio
272*	Herodotus et Pausanias grae. Aldi.	1/ Herodotus	Venice: A. Manuzio, September 1502	folio
		2/ Pausanias	Venice: A. Manuzio and A. Torresani, July 1516	folio
273	Xenophon, Geor Gemis. Herodianus grae.	Xenophon *Hellenica*; Gemistus, Georgius *Ex Diodori et Plutarchi historiis ... tractatio*; Herodian *Historiarum libri octo*; *Enarratiunculae ... in totum Thucydidem*	Venice: A. Manuzio 1503	folio
274	Strabo de situ orbis	Strabo *De situ orbis* trans Guarino Guarini and Gregorius Tiphernas	perhaps a Venetian edition	folio
275	Strabo de situ orbis grae. Ald.	Strabo *De situ orbis*	Venice: A. Manuzio and A. Torresani, November 1516	folio
276	Thucydides Geor. Gemis. et Herodi. grae.	1/ Thucydides *De bello Peloponnesico*	Venice: A. Manuzio, May 1502	folio
		2/ Gemistus, Georgius, part of the 1503 edition of Xenophon, Gemistus, and Herodian (no 273)	Venice: A. Manuzio 1503	folio
277*	Etymologicon Graecum	*Etymologicum magnum graecum*	Venice: Z. Calliergis for N. Blastus 1499	folio
278	Annotationes doctorum uirorum et/Antiquitatum uariarum uolumina 17.	1/ *Annotationes doctorum virorum ...*	[Paris]: J. Petit and J. Bade, 15 August 1511	folio
		2/ Nanni, Giovanni *Antiquitatum variarum volumina XVII*	[Paris]: J. Petit and J. Bade, 18 January 1512	folio
279	Hermolai Castig. in Plinium cum/Ioannis Tortellij Orthographia.	1/ Barbaro, Ermolao *Castigationes Plinianae*	Rome: E. Silber 1492/3 or Venice: n pr 1493/4 or Cremona C. Darlerius 1495 or Venice: B. de Zanis 1495	folio
		2/ Tortelli, Giovanni *Orthographia*	probably Venice, end 15th or early 16th century	folio
280*	Reuchlini Rudimenta Hebraica	Reuchlin, Johann *De rudimentis hebraicis*	Pforzheim: T. Anshelm, 24 March 1506	folio

281*	Auli Gellij Noctes A	Gellius, Aulus *Noctes Atticae*	Venice: J. de Tridino 20 April 1509	folio
282	Macrobius de Som. Scip. et de Saturn.	Macrobius *De somnio Scipionis nec non de Saturnalibus*	Brescia: A. de Britanicis 1501 or another edition	folio
283	Ludo. Caelij Lectiones antiquae	Ricchiere, Lodovico *Antiquarum lectionum commentarii*	Paris: J. Bade 13 June 1517 or Basel: J. Froben 18 March 1517	folio
284	Volaterranus	Maffei, Raffaele *Commentariorum urbanorum libri XXXVIII*; translation of Xenophon *Oeconomicus*	Paris: J. Bade and J. Petit 1511 or 1515 or another edition	folio
285	Omnia opera Angeli Politiani	Poliziano, Angelo Abrogini *Opera omnia*	Venice: A Manuzio 1498 or Paris: J. Bade 1512	folio
286	Nonius Marcellus, Festus Pompeius Varro.	Marcellus, Nonius *De proprietate sermonum*; Sextus Pompeius Festus *De verborum significatione*; Varro, Marcus Terentius *De lingua latina, De analogia*		folio
287	Comment. Budaei in linguam Graecam	Budé, Guillaume *Commentarii linguae graece*	Basel: J. Bebel, March 1530	folio
288	Annota. Budaei in Pandectas	Budé, Guillaume *Annotationes in ... Pandectarum libros*	[Paris:] J. Bade, 17 November 1508	folio
289	Epistolae Budaei	Budé, Guillaume *Epistolae*	[Paris:] J. Bade, February 1531	folio
290	Philologia Budaei	Budé, Guillaume *De philologia*	[Paris:] J. Bade, November 1532	folio
291	Budaeus de Asse	Budé, Guillaume *De asse*	[Paris:] J. Bade 15 March 1515	folio
292	Assis Budaei	Budé, Guillaume *De asse* (2d ed)	[Paris:] J. Bade 14 October 1516	folio
293	Stephanus Niger.	*Dialogus* (= Pausanias *Periegesis* summarized by Niger in dialogue form); Philostratus *Heroicus* trans Niger	Milan: in off. Minuziano 1517	folio
294	Theocritus cum alijs opusculis graecis	Theocritus *Eclogae* with other Greek works	Venice: A. Manuzio, February 1495	folio
295	Cornucopiae et Horti Adonidis grae. Al.	*Thesaurus cornucopiae et horti Adonidis* (a collection of texts of Greek grammarians)	Venice: A. Manuzio, August 1496	folio
296	Pollux de rerum uocabulis. Aldi	Pollux, Julius *Onomasticon*	Venice: A. Manuzio, April 1502	folio

297	Hesychij dictiona. grae.	Hesychius Alexandrinus *Dictionarium graece*	Venice: A. Manuzio and A. Torresani, August 1514	folio
298	Valerius Maximus cum commento	Valerius Maximus *Facta et dicta memorabilia* comm Oliviero d'Arrignano	probably a Venetian edition late 15th / early 16th century	folio
299	Diony. Halicarnaseus Latine uersus	Dionysius of Halicarnassus *Antiquitatum sive originum Romanarum libri xi. Adiuncta est chronologia*	Basel: Froben, March 1532 or one of the earlier printings	folio
300	Eutrop. Paulus Diaco. de gestis Lan // gobardorum et Alexan. Genial. die. libri	1/ Eutropius *Breviarium historiae Romanae*; Paul the Deacon *De gestis Langobardorum*	Basel: H. Froben and N. Episcopius, August 1532	folio
		2/ Alessandro d'Alessandro *Dies geniales*	Paris: G. Morrhy 1532	folio
301	Rhapsodiae Sabellici pars prima / Pars secunda / Pars tertia.	Sabellico, Marcantonio *Enneades seu rhapsodiae historiarum*	Paris: J. Bade 1509	folio
302	Eusebius de Euang. praeparatione uers. / à Trapezon. et Platynae Historia.	1/ Eusebius of Caesarea *De evangelica praeparatione* trans George of Trebizond	Venice: about 1500	folio
		2/ Sacchi, Bartholomeo Platina *Historia de vitis pontificum*	Venice: P. Pincius 1504 or another Venetian edition	folio
303	Arriani et Hannonis Periplus, Plutar // chus de Flumi. et montibus, Strab. comp. grae.	Arrianus, Flavius and Hanno *Periplus*; Pseudo-Plutarch *De fluminibus et montis*; *Strabonis epitome*	Basel: H. Froben and N. Episcopius 1533	quarto

folio 43r

304	Diogenis Laertij de uitis lib. 10. grae. Frob.	Diogenes Laertius *Vitae philosophorum*	Basel: H. Froben and N. Episcopius 1533	quarto
305*	Diogenes Laertius Latine	Diogenes Laertius *Vitae philosophorum* trans Ambrogio Traversari	Basel: V. Curio 1524	quarto
306	Rodolphi Agricolae nonnulla opuscula, Dioge // nes Laertius, Cice. de Fato cum expla. Geor. Vallae	1/ Rodolphus Agricola *Opuscula nonnulla*	Antwerp: D. Martens, 31 January 1511	quarto
		2/ Diogenes Laertius *Vitae philosophorum* trans Ambrosio Traversari	Paris: J. Petit [1510?]	quarto
		3/ Cicero *De fato* with the explanation of Giorgio Valla	Paris: J. Bade, 12 September 1509	quarto

307	Solinus, Iustinus, Lucius Florus.	1/ Solinus *De memorabilibus mundi*	probably Paris: c 1503–15	quarto
		2/ Justinus *Historia ex Trogo Pompeio*; Annius Florus *Epitome*; Sextus Ruffus *De historia romana*	probably Paris: c 1505–15	quarto
308	Opera Salustij	Sallust *Opera*	probably an early 16th-century edition	quarto
309	Nicolai Leonici de uaria historia lib. 3.	Leonico Tomeo, Niccolò *De varia historia*	Basel: H. Froben and N. Episcopius, August 1531	quarto
310	Diodorus Siculus, Paulus Orosius, Berosus et / Leonis Papae Epistolae	1/ Diodorus Siculus Βιβλιοθήκη (Histories) trans Poggio Bracciolini	Paris: D. Roce for J. Petit c 1510 or another edition	quarto
		2/ Orosius *Historia adversus paganos*	probably Paris: c 1506–17	quarto
		3/ Annius, Johannes (Giovanni Nanni) *Antiquitates*	Paris: J. de Gourmont 1509 or J. Marchant for G. de Marnef 1510 or another edition	quarto
		4/ Pope Leo I *Epistolae*	Paris: J. Bade for J. Petit 1511	quarto
311	Herodoti Nouem Musae à Valla uersae	Herodotus *Novem musae* trans L. Valla	Paris: [J. Marchant] for J. Petit 1510	quarto
312	Roffensis de Eucharistia aduersus Oecolamp.	Fisher, John *De veritate corporis et sanguinis Christi in eucharistia*	Cologne: P. Quentel, March 1527	quarto
313	Heliodori Histo. Aethiop. lib. 10. grae.	Heliodorus *Aethiopika*	Basel: Herwagen, February 1534	quarto
314	Callimachi Hymni, Gnωmae ex diuer. grae.	Callimachus *Hymni*; *Gnomai* ed S. Gelenius	Basel: Froben 1532	quarto
315	De origine et gestis Britannorum.	Geoffrey of Monmouth *Historia regum Britanniae*	Paris: Y. Cavellat for J. Bade 1508 or repr 13 September 1517	quarto
316	Petri Gylij uersiones ex Aeliano, Porphyrio, / Heliodoro Oppiano etc.	Aelianus, Claudius *Historia* and other classical authors on the life of animals trans Pierre Gilles; Gilles, Pierre *De nominibus piscium*	Lyon: S. Gryphius 1533 or repr 1534 or 1535	octavo
317	Grammatica Chrysolorae grae.	Chrysoloras, Manuel *Grammatica*	Paris: G. de Gourmont 1507	quarto

318	Vtopia Mori et Epigrammata Eras.	Thomas More *Utopia*; Erasmus *Epigrammata*	Basel: J. Froben, March 1518	quarto
319	Rober. Gaguinus de gestis Francorum	Gaguin, Robert *De origine et gestis Francorum*	Paris: P. le Dru 1495 or an early reprint	folio
320	Epistolae graecae nouem autorum Ald.	*Epistolae diversorum philosophorum, oratorum, rhetorum sex et viginti*	Venice: A. Manuzio 1499	quarto
321	Pomponius Mela cum commentar. Vadiani	Mela, Pomponius *De chorographia* comm Joachim Vadianus	Vienna: J. Singriener, May 1518 or Basel: A. Cratander, January 1522	folio
322	Astronomicorum libri Iulij Firmici, Manilij,/Arati, Theonis, Procli etc.	[*Scriptores rei astronomicae veteres*]	Venice: A. Manuzio June–October 1499	folio
323	De re militari, Frontini, Vegetij, Aeliani,/et Modesti libri.	[*Scriptores rei militaris*]	Bologna: J.A. de Benedictis, May 1505 or P. de Benedictis 1495/6	folio
324	Res Rusti. Columellae, Varronis,/Catonis etc cum commen. Beroaldi.	[*Scriptores rei rusticae*]	Bologna: B. Hectoris 23 August 1504 or an older edition	folio
325	Arnobius in Psalmos	Arnobius the Younger *Commentarii in psalmos* ed Erasmus; Erasmus *Commentarius in psalmum 2*	Basel: J. Froben, September 1522	folio
326	Saluianus de prouidentia Dei, item Sex./Ruffi Epitome cum Polybij Histo. libris	1/ Salvian *De gubernatione Dei* ed J.A. Brassicanus; *Anticimenon libri III* 2/ Festus (Sextus Rufus) *Epitoma de gestis et assequuto dominio Romanorum*; Polybius *Historiarum libri V* trans N. Perotti	Basel: Froben 1530 Basel: H. Petri 1530	folio folio
327	Egesippus uersus à D. Ambrosio	Pseudo-Hegesippus *Historia de bello judaico*; Josephus *De gestis Machabeorum*	Paris: J. Bade 5 June 1510	folio
328	Nouum Testa. grae. et Lati. Eras.	*Novum Testamentum* ed Erasmus	Basel: Froben 1516, 1519, 1522, 1527, 1535	folio

329	Nouum testa. cum an-notationib. Eras.	1/ *Novum Testamentum* ed Erasmus 2/ *In Novum Testamentum annotationes*	Basel: Froben 1516, 1519, 1522, 1527, 1535	folio
330	Noui testa. textus	*Novum Testamentum*	Basel: Froben 1516, 1519, 1522, 1527, 1535	
331	Noui testa. Annotationes Erasmi	Erasmus *In Novum Testamentum annotationes*	Basel: Froben 1519, 1522, 1527, 1535	folio
332*	Apologiae Erasmi	Erasmus *Apologiae omnes* or *Apologiae ...*	Basel: J. Froben, February 1522 or October 1521	folio
333	Pauli Aemylij de reb. gestis Francorum lib. 4	Emilio, Paulo *De rebus gestis Francorum*	Paris: J. Bade [c 1516]	folio
334	Recognitio Veteris Test. Eugubini	Steuco, Agostino *Recognitio Veteris Testamenti*	Venice: A. Manuzio and A. Torresani 1529 or 2d ed Lyon: S. Gryphius 1531	quarto
335	Enarratio Eras. in Psalmum 38um.	Erasmus *Enarratio in psalmum 38*	Basel: H. Froben and N. Episcopius, March 1532	quarto
336	Enarr. Eras. in psal. trig. tertium.	Erasmus *Enarratio psalmi 33*	Basel: H. Froben, J. Herwagen, and N. Episcopius, March 1531	quarto
337	Declaratio Eras. ad censu. Basilius de Spiritu.	1/ Erasmus *Declarationes ad censuras Lutetiae vulgatas* 2/ Basil *De spiritu sancto* trans Erasmus	Basel: H. Froben and N. Episcopius, September 1532 Basel: H. Froben and N. Episcopius, March 1532	quarto quarto
338	Eras. Hyperaspistae liber secun.	Erasmus *Hyperaspistes 2*	Basel: J. Froben 1527	octavo
339	Apologia Eras. in Pium et alios	Erasmus *Apologia adversus rhapsodias Alberti Pii*	Basel: H. Froben and N. Episcopius 1531	octavo
340	Symbolum Fidei, de Eccles. concordia Eras.	1/ Erasmus *Explanatio symboli* 2/ Erasmus *De concordia*	Basel: Froben, November 1533 Basel: Froben 1533	octavo octavo
341	Apologia Eras. de interdicto esu carnium	Erasmus *De esu carnium* (includes 3 *apologiae* against Zúñiga)	Basel: J. Froben, August 1522	octavo
342	Eras. Nouum testa. Lati.	*Novum Testamentum* trans Erasmus	Leuven: D. Martens 1519 or Basel: J. Froben 1520 or 1522	octavo

343*	Herodianus graece pariter et Latine Aldi	Herodian *Historiarum libri VIII* (Greek text with translation by Angelo Poliziano)	Venice: A. Manuzio and A. Torresani, September 1524	octavo
344	Suidas Mediolani excusus	*Suda* (ed Chalcondyles)	Milan: G. Bissoli and B.M. Dolcibelli 1499	folio
345	Eras. Epistolae Palaeonaej	Erasmus *Epistolae palaeonaei*; *Responsio ad disputationem de divortio*	Freiburg im Briesgau: J.F. Emmeus, September 1532	folio

folio 43v

346	Christiani Matrimonij Insti. Eras.	Erasmus *Institutio christiani matrimonii*	Basel: J. Froben, August 1526	folio
347(*?)	Gazae gram. eiusdem de mensibus, / Apollonij de construc. lib 4. Herod. de nu. / meris	Gaza, Theodorus *Introductivae grammatices* and *De mensibus*; Apollonios Dyskolos *De constructione*; Herodianos, Aelios *De numeris*	Venice: A. Manuzio 1495	folio
348	Chiliades Adagiorum Eras.	Erasmus *Adagiorum chiliades*		folio
349	Paraphrases in Euangelia	Erasmus *Paraphrasis in evangelium Matthaei ... Joannis ... Marci ... Lucae*	Basel: Froben 1522–1524	folio
350	Roffensis confutatio assertionis Luteranae.	Fisher, John *Assertionis Lutheranae confutatio*	Antwerp: M. Hillen 1523	folio
351	Quaestiones in 4^{tum} Sententiarum Hadri // ani Florentij.	Florizoon, Adriaan *Questiones in quartum sententiarum*	Paris: J. Bade 1516 or 1518	folio
352	Eras. de recta pronun. dialo. ciceronia. / item apologia aduersus mona. Hispa.	1/ Erasmus *De recta pronuntiatione*; *Ciceronianus*	Basel: Froben October 1529 or March 1528 or March 1530	octavo
		2/ Erasmus *Apologia adversus monachos*	Basel: Froben [June or July] 1529	octavo
353	Paraphrasis Eras. in Ioan. et Acta.	Erasmus *Paraphrasis in evangelium secundum Ioannem* and	Basel: J. Froben 1523	octavo
		Paraphrasis in Acta Apostolorum	Basel: J. Froben 1524	octavo
354	Paraphrases Eras. in epistolas Pauli mino.	Erasmus *Paraphrases in epistolas minores Pauli*	Antwerp: M. Hillen [November] 1519 or one of the Froben reprints 1520–3	octavo

355	Paraphr. in Lucam	Erasmus *In Evangelium Lucae paraphrasis*	Basel: J. Froben August 1523 or 1523–4	octavo
356	Para. in epistol. ad Rom. et Corin.	Erasmus *Paraphrasis in epistolam Pauli apostoli ad Romanos* and *Paraphrasis in duas epistolas Pauli ad Corinthios*	Leuven: Martens or Basel: Froben 1517–1520	quarto or octavo octavo
357	Demegoriae Oecolamp. Exomolog. Eras.	1/ Oecolampadius, Johannes *In Epistolam Joannis apostolis catholicam primam demegoriae* 2/ Erasmus *Exomologesis; Paraphrasis in tertium psalmum; Apologia ad Stunicae conclusiones*	Basel: A. Cratander June 1524 Basel: J. Froben 1524	octavo octavo
358	Eras. enarrationes in .4. psalmos	Erasmus *Enarratio allegorica in primum psalmum; Commentarius in psalmum 2; Paraphrasis in tertium psalmum; In psalmum quartum concio*	Basel: J. Froben 1525	octavo
359	Eras. de conscrib. epistolis, eiusdem Similia	Erasmus *De conscribendis epistolis; Parabolae*	Basel: J. Froben August 1522	quarto
360	Nouum Testa. grae.	Erasmus' Greek New Testament	Haguenau: T. Anshelm, March 1521 or Basel: J. Bebel 1524 or later	quarto or octavo
361	Colloquia Eras.	Erasmus *Familiarium colloquiorum formulae*	perhaps an authorized Froben edition Basel 1522–4	octavo
362	Eras. Ratio uerae Theologiae	Erasmus *Ratio*	Basel: Froben, February 1520 or 1523 or Antwerp: M. Hillen 1523?	octavo
363	Colloquiorum opus Eras.	Erasmus *Familiarium colloquiorum opus*	Basel: Froben 1526–1533	octavo
364	Palamedes palliata comoedia, annota. / Vallae in nouum testa. Vallae dialectica	1/ Arduenna, Remaclus *Palamedes* 2/ Valla, Lorenzo *In latinam Novi Testamenti interpretationem ... adnotationes* 3/ Valla, Lorenzo *Dialectica*	London: R. Pynson 1512 Paris: J. Bade April 1505 Paris: J. Bade 1509	folio folio folio

365	Eras. Commenta. de duplici Copia	Erasmus *De copia*	Paris: J. Bade, July 1512 or Strasboug: M. Schürer, December 1514 or Basel: J. Froben, April 1517	quarto
366	Nicolai Leonici Dialogi	Leonico Tomei, Niccolò *Dialogi*	Venice: G. de Gregoriis, September 1524	quarto
367	Eras. De ratione studij	Erasmus *De ratione studii*	Strasbourg: M. Schürer 1514 or a reprint	quarto
368	Assertio Sacramentorum Henrici regis	Henry VIII *Assertio septem sacramentorum adversus Martinum Lutherum*	London: R. Pynson July 1521 or January 1522	quarto
369	Contra Henri. regem Angliae Mart. Lut.	Luther, Martin *Contra Henricum Regem Angliae*	Wittenberg: [J. Rhau-Grünenberg] 1522 or repr [Basel: A. Petri] 1522	quarto
370	Epistolae duae, Zuinglij una, Andreae/Osiandri altera: Iouij libel. de legati // one Principis Moschouiae ad Clementem.	1/ Zwingli, Huldrych *Epistola ad Andream Osiandrum*; Osiander, Andreas *Epistola ad Hulderichum Zwinglium apologetica*	Nürnberg: J. Petreius, September 1527	quarto
		2/ Giovio, Paulo *Libellus de legatione Basilii magni Principis Moschoviae ad Clementum VII*	Basel: J. and H. Froben 1527 or Rome: F.M. Calvo 1525	quarto
371	Similia Erasmi	Erasmus *Parabolae*	Strasbourg: M. Schürer 1514 or 1516 or 1518 or Leuven: D. Martens 1515	quarto
372	Eugubinus aduersus Luteranos	Steucho, Agostino *Pro religione Christiana adversus Lutheranos*	Bologna: G.B. Phaelli, May 1530	quarto
373	Alberti Pij responsio ad epistolam Eras.	Pio, Alberto *Responsio paraenetica*	Paris: J. Bade 7 January 1529	quarto
374	Articulorum Luteri damnatorum Ratio	Latomus, Jacobus *Articulorum doctrinae fratris Martini Lutheri per theologos Lovanienses damnmatorum ratio*	Antwerp: M. Hillen 8 May 1521	quarto
375	Opera Prudentij.	Prudentius *Opera*	probably Deventer: R. Paffraet [c 1497]	quarto
376	Diatriba Eras. de Libero arbitrio	Erasmus *De libero arbitrio*	Basel: J. Froben September 1524	octavo

377	Declarationes Eras. ad censu. Paris.	Erasmus *Declarationes ad censuras Lutetiae vulgatas*	Basel: Froben 1532	octavo
378	Responsiones ad propositiones à Beda/notatas, Elenchus in censu. Bedae.	Erasmus *Prologus in supputationem calumniarum Natalis Bedae: Responsiunculae ad propositiones a Beda notatas*; *De Antapologia Petri Sutoris*; *De scriptis Clithovei*; *Elenchus in censuris Bedae*	Basel: J. Froben August 1526 or March 1527	octavo
379	Epitome inscripta Erasmo in Vallam/cum appendice in Copiam uerborum.	Erasmus *Paraphrasis in Elegantias Vallae*	Freiburg im Breisgau: J.F. Emmeus March 1531 or 1534	octavo
380	Eras. de esu car. Item contra Stunicam.	Erasmus *De esu carnium* (includes 3 a*pologiae* against Zúñiga)	Basel: J. Froben, August 1522	octavo
381	Lute. ad Eras. de Seruo arbitrio	Luther, Martin *De servo arbitrio*	Wittenberg: J. Lufft, December 1525 or a reprint	octavo

folio 44r

382	Cleonidae harmonicum introductorium/interprete Georgio Valla: item Vi // truuius Pollio de architectura: item/Iulius Frontinus de aquaeduct. etc.	Kleonides *Harmonicum introductorium* trans G. Valla; Vitruvius *De architectura*; Frontinus *De aquaeductibus*; Poliziano, Angelo *Lamia*	Venice: S. Bivilaqua 1497	folio
383	Apologiae Erasmi	Erasmus *Apologiae omnes*	Basel: J. Froben February 1522 or October 1521	folio
384	Cornucopiae Perot. cum Festo Pompeio etc Aldi	Perotti, Niccolò *Cornucopiae sive linguae Latinae commentarii* with works of Marcus Varro, Sextus Pompeius Festus, and Nonius Marcellus	Venice: A. Manuzio and A. Torresani 1513 or 1517 or 1527	folio
385	Opuscula Eras. ex Plutarcho uersa.	Plutarch *Opuscula* trans Erasmus (2d ed)	Basel: J. Froben, September 1520	quarto
386	Epigrammata Erasmj	Erasmus *Epigrammata*	Basel: J. Froben March or November–December 1518	quarto

387	Regula fratrum minorum cum testa. sancti Fran./Venatorium Canonicorum regularium Item/irregularium, manuscrip.	1/ *Regula fratrum minorum cum testamento sancti Francisci* 2–3/ Mombaer, Jan *Venatorium sanctorum ordinis canonicorum regularium [et] irregularium*	manuscript	

folio 44v

388	Ioachimi Camerarij opuscula aliquot,/ nempe: Erratum, Aeolia, Phaeno // mena, Prognostica, Plan. Disticha	Camerarius, Joachim *Opuscula aliquot*	Basel: B. Lasius and T. Platterus 1536	octavo
389*	Io. Genisij antapologia in Eras.	Sepúlveda, Juan Ginés de *Antapologia pro Alberto Pio*	Rome: A. Bladus 1532	quarto
390	Eusebij Corradi ad Sixtum 4^{tum}/epistola asserens D. Augustinum non/fuisse heremitam.	Conradus, Eusebius *Epistola ad Sixtum IV*	Padua: M. Cerdonis 1484 or another lost edition	quarto
391	Apophtegmatum [sic] opus Eras. in 8°	Erasmus *Apophthegmata*	Basel: H. Froben and N. Episcopius 1535	octavo
392	Nouum testa. Eras. Lati. in 8°	*Novum Testamentum* trans Erasmus	Basel: H. Froben and N. Episcopius 1535	octavo
393	Eras. de Puritate tabern. siue eccles	Erasmus *De puritate tabernaculi sive ecclesiae*	Basel: H. Froben and N. Episcopius 1536	quarto
394	Aliquot Chrysost. Homiliae ab/ Eras. uersae	John Chrysostom *Aliquot homiliae* trans Erasmus	Basel: Froben 1533	quarto
395	Enchir. mili. Christiani 2.	Erasmus *Enchiridion* (with other works)	Basel: H. Froben and N. Episcopius, August 1535	octavo
396	Praecationes aliquot Eras. 4	Erasmus *Precationes aliquot*	Basel: J. Froben and N. Episcopius, August 1535	octavo
397	Eras. responsio ad defensionem Petri/Cursij 4	Erasmus *Responsio ad Petri Cursii defensionem*	Basel: H. Froben and N. Episcopius 1535	quarto
398	Eras. purgatio ad epistolam Luteri.	Erasmus *Purgatio adversus epistolam Luteri*	Basel: H. Froben and N. Episcopius, April 1534	octavo

399	Marcellus de medicamentis empiricis, / Item Galeni libri 9. de uarijs etc.	Marcellus Empiricus *De medicamentis empiricis, physicis, ac rationalibus liber*; Galen on similar subjects	Basel: H. Froben and N. Episcopius, March 1536	folio
400	Eras. Ecclesias. siue Conci. 3	Erasmus *Ecclesiastes*	Basel: H. Froben and N. Episcopius, August 1535 or March 1536	folio or octavo
401	Paraphrases Eras. in Euangel. / epistolas, 4 uoluminibus.	Erasmus *Paraphrases in Novum Testamentum*	Basel H. Froben and N. Episcopius, 1532–5 or 1534	folio or octavo
402	Eras. Ecclesiastes ex prima aedit	Erasmus *Ecclesiastes*	Basel H. Froben and N. Episcopius, August 1535	folio
403	Chronicon Pauli Constantini	Phrygio, Paulus Constantinus *Chronicon*	Basel: J. Herwagen 1533	folio
404	Sadoleti comment. in epistolam ad Romanos / ~~Zasij enarratio in tit. instituti~~ // ~~onum de actionibus.~~	1/ Sadoleto, Jacopo *In Pauli Epistolam ad Romanos commentariorum libri tres* 2/ Zasius, Udalricus *In titulum institutionum de actionibus enarratio* [deleted]	Lyon: S. Gryphius 1535 or rev ed 1536 Basel: 1536	folio folio
405	Opera D. Hieronymi in 9. tom. / digestum, excu. Lutetiae	Jerome *Opera omnia* (9 vols)	Paris: C. Chevallon 1533–4	folio
406	Adagiorum opus / ~~Enchir. catechismi Mart. Lute~~ / ~~Thucydides interprete Lau. Valla~~	1/ Erasmus *Adagiorum opus* or *Adagiorum chiliades* 2/ Luther, Martin *Enchiridion pro pueris instituendis*; *Catechismi brevioris translatio* [deleted] 3/ Thucydides *De bello Peloponnensium Atheniensiumque* trans Valla [deleted]	Basel: H. Froben and N. Episcopius March 1533 or March 1536 Wittenberg: N. Schirlentz 1532 or Strasbourg: W. Rihelius 1536 Paris: J. Bade 1513 or Cologne: E. Cervicornus 1527?	folio octavo folio
407	Opus Paraphraseωv Eras.	Erasmus *Paraphrases*	perhaps Basel: H. Froben and N. Episcopius 1534 or 1532–5	octavo or folio
408	De duplici copia uerborum Eras.	Erasmus *De copia*	Basel: H. Froben and N. Episcopius, August 1534	quarto
409	Eras. de conscribendis epistolis.	Erasmus *De conscribendis epistolis*	Basel: H. Froben and N. Episcopius 1534	octavo

410	Homiliae 55. Chrysost. in acta / Apostolorum Eras. interprete.	John Chrysostom *Commentariorum in Acta Apostolorum homiliae 55*	Basel: Froben May 1531	folio
411	Titus Liuius	Livy *Patavinus historicus ...* or *Decades tres ...* ann Beatus Rhenanus and S. Gelenius	Mainz: J. Schöffer November 1518 or Basel: H. Froben and N. Episcopius 1535	folio
412	C. Plinij Natural. Histo.	Pliny *Naturalis historia* ed Gelenius	Basel: H. Froben, J. Herwagen, and N. Episcopius 1535	folio
413	Aetij Medici lib. 16. interprete / Ioan. Baptista Veronensi	Aetius of Amida (a medical handbook; probably vol III)	Basel: H. Froben and N. Episcopius 1535	folio

Versandliste / Catalogue: Authors in Erasmus' Library

The *Versandliste*:
An Annotated Catalogue

1 Apparatus linguae Latinae

Riccius, Bartholomeus. *Apparatus latinae
locutionis. Ex M.T. Cicerone, Caesare,
Sallustio, Terentio, Plauto, ad Herennium,
Asconio, Celso, ac De re rustica … in suum
ordinem descriptus.* Lugduni: S. Gryphius,
1534 (octavo) or Argentorati: M. Apiarius,
1535 (quarto) or Coloniae: J. Gymnicus,
1535 (octavo).

The Latin dictionary of the ultra-
Ciceronian Bartolomeo Ricci (1490–1569),
pupil of Marcus Musurus and professor
of rhetoric in Venice, is probably the book
meant. It originally came out in Venice (J.
Mantonius and Sabbio brothers) in 1533,
and was immediately reprinted several
times: in Lyon (Gryphius 1534), Strasbourg
(Apiarius 1535), and Cologne (Joannes
Gymnicus 1535). In April 1533, before the
publication of the *editio princeps*, Erasmus
had already heard from Viglius Zuichemus
in Padua that Ricci was preparing a work
de elocutione, 'which the Italians praise
highly.'[1] In his reply Erasmus expressed
interest, saying that he desired to read
Ricci's books, 'if they appear.'[2] but Viglius
did not send him a copy immediately
after the book was published.[3] Probably
Erasmus never acquired the first edition,
a folio volume, but purchased one of the
reprints in octavo; the following numbers
in the inventory are also octavos. In view
of the close relations between booksellers in Basel and Lyon, it was possibly a
copy of the Gryphius octavo edition. But
if he had obtained the work through his

friend Bonifacius Amerbach, it may have
been a copy of the Apiarius quarto; this
is the only edition of the *Apparatus* in the
Amerbach collection now in the University
Library of Basel.[4]

1 Ep 2791:52–3
2 Ep 2810:57
3 Ep 2854:90–3
4 AK IV 238 Ep 1779

2 Bayfius, Iouius, Valla

Baïf, Lazarus. *Opus de re vestimentaria
ab auctore … recognitum. De vasculorum
materiis ac varietate tractatus, antehac
nunquam excusus.* Basileae: H. Frobenius,
J. Hervagius, and N. Episcopius, 1531
(octavo).

probably bound with

Jovius, Paulus. *De romanis piscibus libellus.*
[Basileae:] Off. Frobeniana, 1531 (octavo).

and possibly with

Valla, Laurentius. *De linguae latinae
elegantia libri sex … Eiusdem De reciprocatione sui & suus libellus. Dialogus &
antidotum in Pogium; item Annotationes
in Anton. Raudensem … et alia quaedam.*
[Ed C. Carlowitz.] Lugduni: S. Gryphius,
1532 (octavo).

The second author listed, Paulo Giovio,
was taken as a starting point in the explication of this entry, since two works of his
published before 1536 are known. One, the
*Libellus de legatione Basilii magni Principis
Moschoviae ad Clementem VII,* appears

elsewhere on the *Versandliste* (no 370), so his *Libellus de romanis piscibus* must be the work meant here. If editions published at about the same time were bound together, then the enlarged edition of Lazare de Baïf's *De re vestiaria* is a possible candidate for the first author mentioned; the first edition of this work (1526) and another work printed together with the treatises on the clothing and the pottery of antiquity (1536) are on the *Versandliste* (nos 73 and 245). The third work in this entry cannot be identified with certainty.

1/ On Lazare de Baïf and the first edition of his *De re vestiaria*, printed by Johann Bebel in Basel in 1526, see no 73. A treatise on the pottery of antiquity was added to the reprint of 1531. As early as the spring of 1526 Erasmus was aware that Baïf was working on the piece, and in March 1528 he offered to have the booklet published for him in Basel: 'If you prefer that your book *De vasculis culinariis* be published there [ie Venice], since you are there yourself and "the master's face is better than his back," I approve. But if they dally, we will have it printed here, provided you send a copy that you have examined'[1] Baïf took up the offer, though not until much later. Through the agency of the bookseller Benôit Vaugris of Constance, he sent the manuscript copy of the *commentariolum de vasorum generibus*, together with the text of *De re vestiaria*, which had been improved in several places, to Erasmus. Because of the incompleteness of the work and the carelessness of the copyist, Erasmus did not forward the material directly to the printer. He carefully read through the text, corrected the errors that had crept in through the ignorance of the assistant, and only then turned the manuscript over to Froben.[2]

2/ The treatise on fishes and Roman fishing by the Italian historian Paolo Giovio (1483–1552)[3] was originally published in Rome in 1524 in folio, and reprinted there in 1527 in quarto. The Froben edition in octavo was the only one that could have been bound together with the booklet by Baïf.

3/ Lorenzo Valla's *Annotationes in Novum Testamentum, Dialectica, Antidotum in Pogium,* and his translations of Herodotus and Thucydides appear elsewhere on the *Versandliste*; see nos 364 (2 works), 153 #2, 311, and 406. His best-known work, the *Elegantiae latinae linguae*, however, does not. May we not imagine that this work, for Erasmus the essential guide to pure Latinity, which he had already paraphrased in his years in the monastery at Steyn (no 379), is indicated here? Perhaps it is no accident that the only work of Valla not mentioned elsewhere on the *Versandliste*, of which an edition can be traced in the same format and from about the same time as the two books bound with it, is the *Elegantiae* in the edition of Sebastianus Gryphius (Lyon 1532).[4] In itself this Gryphius edition would not be an exceptional acquisition; Erasmus acquired several products of the same press in the early thirties (cf nos 1, 6, 12, 42, 316, 404). If indeed this entry on the *Versandliste* refers to the Lyon edition of the *Elegantiae*, then the new acquisition might have replaced an earlier, older, and worn-out copy.

1 Ep 1962:13–16/15–18; cf Ep 2046:195–8/ 199–203.
2 Ep 2447:35–43/36–44
3 On Giovio cf no 370.
4 Valla's *De reciprocatione* was included in this edition, but the other works announced on the title-page were not published until later in the year. They were issued separately under the title *Lucubrationes aliquot ad linguae latinae restaurationem spectantes,* which contained *Antidoti in Pogium libri iii; in eundem dialogi ii; in Antonium Raudensem annotationum libellus* and other works (Lyon: Gryphius 1532); see BN *Catalogue général* 199 171; Baudrier viii 65. For Erasmus, however, this supplementary volume would have been of little value; the texts were, directly or indirectly, pirated from the Valla edition prepared by Christoph von Carlowitz and published in Cologne 1527, which was already in his possession; see no 153.

3 Melanch. Annota. in Matth.

Melanchthon, Phil. *Annotationes in Evangelium Matthaei iam recens in gratiam studiosorum editae.* [Basiliae: n pr, May 1523] or later pirate edition [Basileae: n pr, 1523] (octavo).

Philippus Melanchthon's commentary on the Gospel of Matthew was published against his will, based on students' lecture notes from his course during the winter semester of 1519–20 in Wittenberg. The course broke off with chapter 26; the additional exegesis in the edition, on the passion and the resurrection, is not by Melanchthon.[1]

1 *Melanchthons Werke* IV 133

4 Aula Hutteni. Taci. de popu. Germa.

Hutten, Ulrich von. *Aula. Dialogus.* Basileae: J. Frobenius, November 1518 (octavo).

bound with

Tacitus, Cornelius. *De moribus et populis Germaniae libellus. Cum commentariolo vetera Germaniae populorum vocabula paucis explicante* [*Beato Rhenano*]. Basileae: J. Frobenius, May 1519 (octavo).

1/ Erasmus must have acquired the satirical dialogue by Ulrich von Hutten, written at the instigation of and dedicated to Heinrich Stromer, personal physician to the archbishop-elector Albert of Brandenburg, soon after it was published in September 1518.[1] Late in August Jacob Spiegel, chancellor of Emperor Maximilian, had promised him a copy: 'I will send you his dialogue on life at court, as soon as it appears.'[2] In these years Erasmus was still on good terms with Hutten, and he often received a presentation copy of his newly printed works soon after their appearance.[3] Even so, the *editio princeps* probably did not find a lasting place in his library. The Tacitus text bound with the *Aula* in this entry on the *Versandliste* is an octavo,

which seems to indicate that Erasmus did not keep on his bookshelf the original quarto edition but replaced it with the octavo edition reprinted by Froben and dedicated to Thomas More.[4] In April 1519 Erasmus wrote to Hutten about the dialogue, 'Your *Aula* has often been in my hands, but hitherto I have always been forced to drop it by some piece of business which interrupted me when I was longing to read it. What I have read, I like very much; for what is there of yours that I do not like?'[5]

2/ Froben published a folio edition of the complete works of Tacitus in August 1519 (see no 269). At the same time he also brought out a separate edition in octavo of *De moribus et populis Germaniae* with a commentary, the first there is on that work, in which an attempt was made to localize geographically and to explain etymologically the names of peoples and places. From early on this commentary was wrongly ascribed to Henricus Glareanus. Its author was undoubtedly Beatus Rhenanus.[6]

1 Benzing *Hutten Bibliographie* no 73
2 Ep 863:31–2/36
3 Ep 923:18–21/21–5
4 Benzing *Hutten Bibliographie* no 74
5 Ep 951:20–2/21–4
6 Joachimsen 'Tacitus im deutschen Humanismus' 709–10

5 Psalterium Campensis

Campensis, Johannes. *Psalmorum omnium iuxta Hebraicam veritatem paraphrastica interpretatio.* Norimbergae: J. Petreius, May 1532 (octavo).

This work is not a word-for-word translation but a paraphrase verse by verse of the Psalms by Jan van Campen, professor of Hebrew in Busleyden's Collegium Trilingue in Leuven. It was based on the original language and thereby deviated in many places from the Vulgate.[1] His opponents, led by the orthodox theologian Frans

Titelmans and Nicolaus Clenardus, his rival as a Hebraist, succeeded in preventing the publication of the work in Leuven.[2] Campen, however, got a chance to have it printed elsewhere. In 1531 he entered the service of the humanist Johannes Dantiscus, bishop of Kulm (now Chelmno) and Polish ambassador to the emperor. Dantiscus had encouraged the publication from the beginning and was also willing to provide for the expenses. When Dantiscus travelled to Regensburg to attend the diet there, Campen, who had been accompanying him, stayed in Nürnberg to see the *Psalterium* through the press. It appeared in May 1532. Early in July he was able to dispatch the first copies from Regensburg as a present to the king of Poland, to whom the work was dedicated, and to some good friends in authority, both ecclesiastical and secular.[3] Erasmus may have been among them. Erasmus and Dantiscus had recently carried on a friendly correspondence. Moreover, Dantiscus had sent Erasmus plaster medallions of King Sigismund I and of himself; and in April 1532 Erasmus in his turn had dedicated to the bishop-diplomat his translation of St Basil's *De spiritu sancto*.[4] A little over a year later he wrote Dantiscus another letter (now lost), in which he spoke with high praise of Campen.[5] Although his direct relations with Campen were limited, Erasmus had no doubt met the professor, who had been appointed in 1520. In 1527 he was still able to describe him exactly: a man who looked like a Greek, with a dark face and a beard reaching down to his belt.[6]

1 de Vocht *History of the* CTL III 103 and 192
2 de Vocht *History of the* CTL III 169–75. On Titelmans cf no 27; CEBR III 326–7.
3 de Vocht *History of the* CTL III 171, 176, 192. On Dantiscus see Ep 2163:138n / n34; de Vocht *History of the* CTL III 18–23 and *John Dantiscus*; CEBR I 377.
4 Ep 2643
5 Cf Ep 2876:12–13 (to Conradus Goclenius).
6 Ep 1806A:41–2/42–4

6 Iacobi Sadoleti in Psal. 93. Interpretatio.

Sadoletus, Jacobus. *In Psalmum XCIII interpretatio*. Lugduni: S. Gryphius or pirate edition Basileae: Off. Frobeniana, 1530 (octavo).

Jacopo Sadoleto (1477–1547), humanist, theologian, and reform-minded prelate, was secretary (along with his friend Pietro Bembo) to Leo X, and later also to Clement VII. From 1517 on he occupied the see of Carpentras, and under Paul III, who named him a cardinal in 1536, he was closely involved in attempts at ecclesiastical reform and preparations for the Council of Trent.[1] Sadoleto and Erasmus, in many respects kindred spirits, corresponded from 1524 and exchanged publications with each other.[2] Sadoleto sent Erasmus his explication of Psalm 93 immediately after its appearance, with the request that he provide a critique of it, without sparing the author.[3] The elaborate commentary, with its obvious accent on man's free will[4] and its Ciceronian (taken in a favourable sense) articulation of the Christian problematic,[5] met with a very positive reception from Erasmus. He was so taken by the work, he told Sadoleto, that he did not rest before finishing it without stopping for breath. It pleased him even more than Sadoleto's commentary, published in 1525, on Psalm 50 ('Miserere mei, Deus'), though in a later letter he made no distinction when he declared that, if others had not been ahead of him, he would have seen to it that both appeared in print.[6] He probably lamented the fact that Sadoleto had not offered his manuscript to Froben, who in fact pirated the commentary almost immediately. In return for the copy he received of the original edition Erasmus sent his own just published *Enarratio triplex in Psalmum 22* to Carpentras – 'truly,' as he wrote, 'to borrow your modest expression, an exchange of copper for gold.'[7]

1 See Douglas *Jacopo Sadoleto*. Cf Allen and CWE Ep 1511 introductions; CEBR III 183–7.

2 Cf no 404 n1.
3 Ep 2272:10–30 / 10–30
4 Douglas *Jacopo Sadoleto* 86
5 *Ciceronianus* ASD I-2 698 / CWE 28 435–6;
   cf Ep 2315:76–86 / 2312A:81–90.
6 Ep 2315:15–18 / 2312A:17–19, 2443:393–7 / 390–4
7 Ep 2315:129–31 / 2312A:134–6, echoing Sadoleto's
   comparison in Ep 2272:15–18 / 15–18

7 Deutero. Luter.

*Deuteronomion Mose cum annotationibus
Mart. Lutheri.* [Edition?] 1525 (octavo).

In the same year that the *editio princeps* of
Luther's annotations on Deuteronomy was
published (Wittenberg: Hans Lufft 1525),
another five pirated editions appeared: one
in Strasbourg (J. Knobloch); two in Basel
(Adam Petri and Andreas Cratander);
one in Augsburg (S. Ruff); and one in
Nürnburg (J. Petreius).[1]

1 Benzing *Lutherbibliographie* nos 1850–5
   (all octavos)

8 Prouer. Melanc.

Possibly Παροιμίαι, *sive Proverbia Salomonis,
cum adnotationibus Philippi Melanchthonis.*
Haganoae: J. Secerius, 1525 (octavo).

and/or

*Solomonis sententiae, versae ad Hebraicam
veritatem a Phil. Melanchthone.* Haganoae:
J. Secerius, 1525 (octavo).

In the winter of 1524–5 Melanchthon gave
a course on Proverbs at the University of
Wittenberg. An unauthorized edition of
his lectures based on a very mediocre set
of notes was published under the above
title in 1525 by J. Setzer in Hagenau (it
may have been already in circulation late in
1524). Melanchthon was not pleased, and
he attempted to make at least superfluous
the prematurely published commentary by
producing a close Latin translation of the
text of Proverbs.[1] This appeared the same
year under the title *Salomonis sententiae,*

versae ad Hebraicam veritatem; it too was
published by Setzer. It is hard to know
which edition is meant here. One would
expect that Erasmus would prefer the
authorized translation, but since the author
of the *Versandliste* usually copied the main
features of the title-page literally, the desig-
nation '*Prouer.*' points to the unauthorized
edition of the commentary. Or perhaps,
shortly after each appeared from the Setzer
press, the two were joined together in one
volume, as were the copies in the British
Library.[2] Finally, it is also possible that
Erasmus had on his bookshelf one of the
pirate editions of the *Sententiae Salomonis*
that were published under the title
Proverbia Salomonis.[3] See also no 11.

1 *Melanchthons Werke* IV 305; Stupperich
   'Melanchthons Proverbien-Kommentare' 26
2 BL *Catalogue* 17 1065
3 Published n p and n d [1530?] and Nürnberg:
   J. Petreius, 1534

9 Melan. in Genesim

Melanchthon, Phil. *In obscuriora aliquot
capita Geneseos annotationes.* Haganoae:
J. Secer or Tubingae: Ulrich Morhardus,
1523 (octavo).

Melanchthon's commentary on Genesis
came out with a preface by Nikolaus
Gerbel (c 1485–1560), jurist and man of
letters, who worked in Strasbourg from
1515 until his death, initially for the printer-
publisher Matthias Schürer, afterwards
as a legal advisor to the bishop and the
cathedral chapter, despite his sympathy for
the Reformation.[1] In the autumn of 1515
he resided for a short time in Basel to help
Froben with the correction of the proofs of
Erasmus' New Testament. In March 1521
he edited the Greek text only of Erasmus'
New Testament for publication by Thomas
Anshelm in Hagenau (cf no 360).

1 On Gerbel see Allen and CWE Ep 342 introductions; CEBR II 90–1.

10 Cochlaei de libe. arbitrio Epistolae Luteri.

Cochlaeus, Joannes. *De libero arbitrio hominis adversus locos communes Philippi Melanchthonis.* Tubingae: Ulrich Morhardus, 1525 (octavo).

bound with

Luther, Mart. *Epistolarum farrago … cum Psalmorum aliquot interpretatione …* Haganoae: J. Secer, 1525 (octavo).

1/ The learned humanist Johannes Cochlaeus (d 1522) had already written his treatise on free will, directed against Philippus Melanchthon, in the summer of 1522, when Erasmus' work on the same subject was not yet in preparation.[1] It has been suggested that through his humanist contacts he must have known of Erasmus' intention to write against Luther and wanted to offer support in advance.[2] Whatever the truth of this may be, it seems plausible that Cochlaeus sent him a copy of his book when it was published in 1525. It is certainly true that he associated himself closely with Erasmus about this time. His first letter to him dates from the beginning of 1525, and in the same year he also translated (with Hieronymus Emser) the *Diatribe de libero arbitrio*, albeit so freely and faultily that Erasmus held up its publication.[3] They corresponded with each other until Erasmus' death, even though Erasmus occasionally criticized Cochlaeus' almost fanatical stance against Luther and in support of papal authority.

2/ The first and only collection of Luther's letters that appeared during Erasmus' lifetime, published by Vincentius Obsopoeus, the pupil and friend of Melanchthon.[4]

1 Jedin *Des Johannes Cochläus Streitschrift De libero arbitrio hominis (1525)* 12; Spahn *Johannes Cochläus* 345. On Cochlaeus see Allen and CWE Ep 1863 introductions; CEBR I 321–2.
2 Spahn *Johannes Cochläus* 124 and Jedin ibidem
3 An earlier letter, now lost, is mentioned in Ep 1577:10/13.
4 Benzing *Lutherbibliographie* no 65. Erasmus owned another copy; cf no 97 #3.

11 Melanc. in Prou.

Melanchthon, Phil. *Nova scholia in Proverbia Salomonis.* Haganoae: J. Secerius, 1529 or 1531 (octavo).

Although Melanchthon had been dissatisfied with the unauthorized edition of his commentary on the Book of Proverbs (1525; see no 8), it was several years before he himself undertook an edition of it. Only in 1528 did he work up the material from a course on Proverbs that he had given in the previous year in Jena, where the University of Wittenberg temporarily took refuge during an outbreak of plague, into a wholly new work, the *Nova scholia*, which came off the press in May 1529.[1] The abridged indication in the *Versandliste* makes it plausible that the separately published commentary is meant here, not the (unauthorized) text of Proverbs with commentary published earlier.

1 *Melanchthons Werke* IV 305–6; Stupperich 'Melanchthons Proverbien-Kommentare' 27

12 Bembus, Viues, Cuspidius.

Bembo, Pietro. *Opuscula aliquot.* Lugduni: S. Gryphius, 1532 (octavo).

bound with

Vives, Joh. Lud. Possibly one or more tracts, including *De concordia et discordia in humano genere, De pacificatione …; Opuscula aliquot vere catholica …, Introductio ad sapientiam, Satellitium sive symbola, De ratione studii puerilis; Sacrum diurnum de sudore Jesu Christi, Concio de nostro et Christi sudore, Meditatio de passione Christi in Ps. XXXVII; De subventione pauperum.* All four Lugduni: Melchior et Gaspar Trechsel, 1532 (octavo).

and with

[Rabelais, François]. *Ex reliquiis venerandae antiquitatis Lucii Cuspidii testamentum. Item, contractus venditionis antiquis Romanorum temporibus initus.* Lugduni:

S. Gryphius, 1532 or one of the undated pirate editions (octavo).

Of these three works, indicated only by the names of their authors or supposed author, the first can be clearly identified, the third also with certainty except for the edition, but the second only by guesswork.

1/ In answer to a letter from Viglius Zuichemus, who had given him news of Pietro Bembo, Erasmus wrote in May 1533 that he had recently read and enjoyed 'some Exercises he wrote in his adolescence' (*aliquot adolescentiae illius Progymnasmata*) and especially his *Aetna*.[1] By 'Progymnasmata' no publication of Bembo's can be meant other than the *Opuscula aliquot*, and more precisely the pirated Lyon edition, which had been published the year before.[2] The *editio princeps* (Venice: G.A. Sabbio 1530), was in quarto and for that reason can be left out of consideration. The *Opuscula* contains writings of Bembo's youth, and among them is the *Aetna*, his first work, in which he tells his father in the form of a dialogue about an ascent of Mount Etna during his stay in Sicily in July 1493.[3] Pietro Bembo (1470–1547), humanist, poet, and scholar, was for eight years together with his friend Sadoleto secretary of Leo x; after Pope Leo's death he retired into the neighbourhood of Padua, where his villa became a centre of literary and cultural life. In 1529 he assumed the post of official historian in Venice, where before long he also took over the management of the library of San Marco. In 1539 he was made a cardinal and thereafter lived in Rome. Although Erasmus had already spoken highly of Bembo in 1508 in the *Adagia* (ii i 1), they made no contact in writing before the beginning of 1529, and they never met in person.[4]

2/ There is no indication whatever which of Juan Luis Vives' works is meant here.[5] The only pointer towards an identification is offered by the two works bound with it,

one of which was certainly and the other perhaps published in Lyon in 1532. If we suppose that this Vives book appeared at about the same time, the choice seems to be restricted to a few only, of which one was published in Antwerp and four others also in Lyon.

3/ Behind the name Cuspidius undoubtedly hides the small book containing two 'Roman' legal documents published by François Rabelais, the last will and testament of Lucius Cuspidius and a deed of sale executed by him. Both of these had already been unmasked as forgeries before the end of the century, and later they were usually considered to be the handiwork of the well-known fifteenth-century Italian humanists Julius Pomponius Laetus and Giovanni Pontano.[6] Now it is generally accepted that Rabelais himself was guilty of the mystification.[7] The authorship does not concern us here; more important is the year of publication of the book. Rabelais settled in Lyon in 1532, and immediately cooperated with Sebastianus Gryphius as 'corrector' and 'editor';[8] it was in that year that he produced the Cuspidius documents, and it was in that year he came in contact with Erasmus. The earliest and only surviving evidence of that contact is Rabelais' letter of 30 November 1532, the original of which, formerly in Dresden, was unfortunately lost during the Second World War. The letter was accompanied by a Flavius Josephus manuscript, which Erasmus had asked for, that belonged to Jean de Pins. It is tempting to suppose that Erasmus may have received the little book from Rabelais at the same time, although it was not exactly in his sphere of interest.[9] In that case the copy in his library could be identified as the original Lyon edition. There is another argument in favour of the *editio princeps*; about the same time, Gilbert Cousin, Erasmus' *famulus* at Freiburg, sent a copy of it with a handwritten dedication to his former teacher Bonifacius Amerbach in Basel.[10]

1 Ep 2810:71–4
2 Baudrier VIII 66. Beside the *Aetna* (*editio princeps* Venice: Aldo Manuzio 1495), the *Opuscula aliquot* includes among other works Gianfrancesco Pico della Mirandola *Ad Petrum Bembum de imitatione liber* with Bembo's *Responsio ad eundem* [*de imitatione*]; Bembo's *De Culice Vergiliana et Terentii fabulis liber unus*; his *De Guido Vbaldo Feretrio deque Elizabetha Gonzagia Verbini ducibus*; and a number of his letters. Erasmus was already acquainted with the Pico-Bembo correspondence *De imitatione* (1512–13), possibly from Froben's May 1518 edition; see Ep 2088:116–123/123–31 (c January 1529).
3 *Dizionario biografico degli Italiani* 8 134
4 On Bembo see Allen and CWE Ep 2106 introductions; CEBR I 120–3. Cf no 139.
5 On Juan Luis Vives (1492–1540) the distinguished Spanish humanist, cf no 25 n3.
6 Baudrier VIII 63; Kline *Rabelais and the Age of Printing* 9–10
7 *Herbert Reichner Catalogue 27* (Stockbridge, Mass) no 1134, with a full account of the mystification by Paul Kristeller
8 See for example Mombello 'Rabelais lecteur de Lorenzo Abstemio?' 64.
9 Ep 2743; cf no 219. On Rabelais' congeniality with Erasmus as appears from the novels he published in 1532–4 (books 1 and 2 of *Gargantua et Pantagruel*) see Lebègue 'Rabelais, the Last of the French Erasmians.'
10 On this copy with Cousin's dedication on the title-page, now in the Universitätsbibliothek Basel, see Screech 'Rabelais, Erasmus, Gilbertus Cognatus and Boniface Amerbach.'

13 Menardus, Faust. Episco.

Manardus, Joannes. *Medicinales epistolae.* Argentorati: J. Schott, 17 February 1529 (octavo).

bound with

Faustus of Riez. *De gratia Dei et humanae mentis libero arbitrio ... cum D. Erasmi praefatione. Item Faustini episcopi ... de fide adversus Arianos, et de propositis quaestionibus Arianorum.* Basileae: Joannes Faber Juliacensis, 1528 (octavo).

1/ Giovanni Manardo (1462–1536), for some years the personal physician to King Vladislav II of Hungary, and from c 1519 until his death a professor of medicine in his native town of Ferrara, was a pioneer in the field of pharmacy and an independent thinker on medical questions. Erasmus had a high opinion of his *Medicinales epistolae*, a collection of medical observations that also contain many descriptions of medicinal herbs, which was published for the first time in 1521 at Ferrara. Manardo's fellow townsman Celio Calcagnini promised Erasmus in 1525 that he would send him the *Epistolae* as soon as possible in case he had not yet procured it.[1] Perhaps his favourable impression rested on the copy of the work he then received. Erasmus recommended it to the physician Hubertus Barlandus, who had stayed with him for a short time in 1528,[2] and Barlandus immediately arranged for the Strasbourg printer Schott to publish a new edition. Erasmus' laudatory judgment was recorded in the preface.[3] In March 1529 Barlandus sent a copy of the book to Erasmus, which however did not reach him until mid-June.[4]

2/ The tract of Bishop Faustus of Riez (c 405–c 495) on the grace of God and free will ranks as one of the principal works of Semipelagianism. Erasmus obtained the manuscript of this through his friend Count Hermann von Neuenahr, who perhaps discovered it in Spain and brought it back from there.[5] Joannes Faber Emmeus published the text with a prefatory letter of dedication by Erasmus to Ferry de Carondelet, in which he remarked, 'Too bad he did not send it to me before I wrote *De libero arbitrio* against Luther!'[6] Faustus' tract, because of its intermediary position with respect to free will, challenged Catholics as well as Protestants.[7] Presumably Erasmus, fully aware of this, saw to it that another, more orthodox work by the same author, *De fide adversus Arianos*, was included in the book.[8]

1 Ep 1587:287–95 with 288n/303–11 with n52. On Manardo see also Bietenholz *Der italianische Humanismus und die Blütezeit des Buchdrucks in Basel* 145; Bolgar *The Classical Heritage and Its Beneficiaries* 289; Dilg 'Die botanische Kommentarliteratur Italiens um 1500 und ihr Einfluss auf Deutschland' 246; CEBR II 372.

2 Ep 2078:14n/n5; Allen and CWE Ep 2081
  introductions
3 Allen Ep 1587:290n
4 Ep 2172:90–2/96–8
5 On Neuenahr see no 31. The manuscript has been
  preserved and is now in the Bibliothèque nationale
  in Paris (Cod. lat. 2166).
6 Ep 2002:22–3/25–6
7 See for example Ep 2239:26–45/27–47 (from Pierre
  Barbier, 7 December 1529).
8 Renaudet *Etudes érasmiennes* 39; cf Welti *Der Basler
  Buchdruck und Britannien* 41–3.

14 Melanc. in Epistolam ad Roma.

Melanchthon, Phil. *Commentarii in
Epistolam Pauli ad Romanos*. Vitebergae:
J. Clug, October 1532 (octavo).

On 12 and 18 October 1532 Melanchthon
sent two of his colleagues presentation
copies of his commentary on the Epistle
to the Romans, which had just been
published.[1] One week later, on 25 October,
he directed a letter to Erasmus in which
he also mentioned his new book and
went into its background. He called
upon Erasmus to help to allay the church
conflict, which threatened to turn into a
civil war, as far as he was able and pointed to his own counsels, which, he hoped,
would be understood by the moderate
and the prudent: 'I have pared away many
controversies and now I am endeavouring
to clarify in good faith some things that
are necessary for religious piety. I am also
trying to treat suitably the basic principles
of ecclesiastical polity. Whatever happens,
my judgment and wishes will be laid out in
my commentary on Romans, which is now
published. As for you, if you can give any
resources to this tottering commonwealth
… in the last act of your life, as it were, let
the whole world get a special view of your
wisdom.' Is it too much to assume that
a copy of his commentary accompanied
Melanchthon's letter? Perhaps he gave
both to Dietrich Reiffenstein, who was
about to leave for Freiburg, and whom he
warmly recommended in the same letter.[2]
On the other hand, two years later Erasmus
informed Melanchthon that he had bought

three copies of his work; he had sent one
to Christoph von Stadion, the bishop of
Augsburg, one to Jacopo Sadoleto, bishop
of Carpentras, and he had kept the third
for himself.[3] With his new commentary
Melanchthon wanted to distance himself
from the *Annotationes in Epistolas Pauli
ad Romanos et ad Corinthios*, based on one
of his courses, which had been published
without his knowledge in 1522 by Luther
but which no longer reproduced his ideas
precisely or fully.[4] But in the 1532 commentary he covertly took positions on many
points that were opposed to those
of Erasmus, who for his part therefore
reacted rather coolly to the commentary:
'I confess that many things are very well
said. But in many features I am displeased
by it. He twists many statements, he arro-
gantly rejects Origen and Augustine,
he passes over quite a bit of material …
He seems to have acquired some work by
a scholastic theologian whose subject matter he handles.'[5] When he sent a copy to
Sadoleto, he explained to him that he did
not do so to encourage him to imitate the
commentary but rather because many varied opinions were discussed in it. The bishop would know how to choose 'what would
be most helpful in understanding the mind
of Paul' or (to put it more directly) 'to
pick the gold out of the dung.'[6]

1 *Melanchthons Werke* v 17
2 Ep 2732. On Dietrich Reiffenstein cf CEBR III
  136 (sv Johann Reiffenstein).
3 Ep 2970:26–8. On Stadion see CEBR III 274–6;
  on Sadoleto see no 6.
4 *Melanchthons Werke* v 18 and 26n
5 Ep 2818:63–8 (to Bonifacius Amerbach,
  12 June 1533)
6 Epp 2971:21–5 (to Sadoleto), 2818:68–70
  (to Amerbach)

15 Bipartitum in Morali Philosophia

Probably works – which cannot be identified with much certainty – having to do
with the moral philosophy of antiquity
(octavo or quarto).

Something can be said about this entry only through guesswork. The vague description offers little to go on. It could refer to one bipartite work on moral philosophy or to two or more separate works on the subject bound together in two volumes. The adjacent books entered on the *Versandliste* provide a likely, but not certain, indication of size. Nevertheless, within this general context, investigation of bibliographical sources leads to the consideration, almost exclusively, of works having to do with the ethics of antiquity and especially that of Aristotle, and within that field to books published mainly in France shortly before or after the turn of the century and originating with the Paris humanist circle of which Jacques Lefèvre d'Etaples was an outstanding exponent.[1] Two works on the subject in particular achieved striking success at the time: Aristotle's *Nicomachean Ethics* and the commentary paraphrase that Lefèvre had made from it under the title *Ars moralis introductoria*, and an edition of the *Moralium dogma philosophorum*, a twelfth-century compilation of moral maxims.

The *Ethica in Nicomachum* was edited in the translation of Johannes Argyropoulos by the theologian Gillis van Delft (a friend of the Paris humanist Robert Gaguin and later highly esteemed by Erasmus).[2] His text appeared in 1489 (Paris: Jean Higman) and went through many reprints, all of them quartos.[3] Lefèvre d'Etaples made use of it for his own large edition of the ethical writings of Aristotle, the *Decem librorum moralium tres conversiones* (Paris: J. Higman and W. Hopyl 1497), which contained, besides the *Nicomachean Ethics* in the three Latin versions of H. Kosbein (the *antiqua traductio*), Johannes Argyropoulos (with Delft's commentary), and Leonardo Bruni Aretino, the *Magna moralia* translated by Georgio Valla and Bruni's *Isagogicon moralis disciplinae*, considered by Lefèvre to be a suitable substitute for the *Eudemian Ethics*.[4] This edition, however, was in folio

format and for that reason may be left out of account here, since most of the surrounding books on the list are octavos and quartos. But the section containing Argyropoulos' version of the *Ethica ad Nicomachum* was published separately seven years later in quarto (Paris: Jean Granjon). It included Lefèvre's commentary paraphrase; otherwise it was identical to the 1488 edition of Gillis van Delft and bore the same title, *Opus Aristotelis de moribus*.[5] An octavo reprint with a different title came from the press of Henri Estienne in October 1514.[6]

Lefèvre's paraphrase of the *Nicomachean Ethics*, published for the first time in 1494 in Paris by Antoine Caillaut with the title *Ars moralis introductoria*,[7] gained great popularity as a concise handbook of theoretical and practical morals. It was Lefèvre's most frequently reprinted work. Several versions, some under different titles, appeared in quarto and octavo as well as in folio.[8] Moreover, in about 1500, Lefèvre's pupil Johannes Caesarius (later also a friend of Erasmus), published an adaptation of the paraphrase; it was printed for him at Deventer, where for some time he taught at the St Lebuin's school, by J. de Breda, and entitled *Epitome moralis philosophiae in Ethicen Aristotelis introductoria ex Morali Introductione Jacobi Fabri Stapulensis deprompta*.[9] After 1502 several editions of the *Ars moralis introductoria* were published with commentaries by Josse Clichtove, most of them in folio, but some also in quarto.[10]

Another work comes into consideration because of its title, its subject (classical ethics), and its source in the same humanist circle in Paris: The *Moralium dogma philosophorum*, a collection of *sententiae morales* derived mainly from Cicero but also from Seneca, Sallust, Boethius, Horace, Juvenal, Terence, and Lucan. Much has been written about the supposed compiler, but his identity still remains uncertain.[11] The collection was already widely known – over one hundred manuscripts have been preserved – before it appeared in print for the first time from Richard Pafraet in Deventer c 1486.[12] Better known, however, than the *editio princeps* was the second edition, also in quarto, which was printed by Josse Bade c 1512 under the title *Dogma moralium philosophorum compendiose et studiose collectum a Jodoco Clichtoveo*.[13] Josse Clichtove had undertaken the editorial task – his main contribution was to identify the sources of the classical quotations and note them in the margins – at the request of Guillaume Petit, confessor of Francis I, to whom the book was dedicated. Unlike most of the members of his order, this learned Dominican was an advocate of reform and a real humanist. He was a friend of Lefèvre and Budé, and some years later he advised the French king to attach Erasmus to the new *seminarium eruditorum* then being established. He also edited or encouraged others to edit a number of patristic and historical texts; several of these were extant in the library of Erasmus.[14] The *Dogma moralium philosophorum* was reprinted more than once in 1512 and in the following years.[15]

With this report on the possibilities the matter must rest. Although we cannot be certain exactly what book or books 'on moral philosophy' the description in the *Versandliste* points to, the works described seem plausible conjectures. They were well known, and we know that Erasmus was very interested in the editions of Lefèvre d'Etaples and Clichtove, as the arrangement of his library makes clear (cf nos 18, 20, 23, 60, 178–81, 183, 196, and 252).

1 On this circle, see Rice 'Humanist Aristotelianism in France'; and cf Massaut *Josse Clichtove* I.

2 On Gillis van Delft see Ep 456:87n/98n; CEBR I 382–3. For Erasmus' opinion of him see Renaudet *Préréforme et humanisme* 679. Cf Ep 1581:299–30/335–6.

3 *Opus Aristotelis de moribus a Johanne Argyropylo traductum*; GW 2362. Cf on Delft's edition Renaudet *Préréforme et humanisme* 129, 368, 406,

409, and passim. For the reprints see GW 2364–6; Renouard *Bibliographie de Josse Bade* II 47.

4 GW 2359. Cf Renaudet *Préréforme et humanisme* 280–2; Rice *Prefatory Epistles* 48–9 Ep 15 n4 and 548 (bibliography) nos CXXXVIII–CXLII; Bedouelle *Lefèvre d'Etaples et l'intelligence des écritures* 31–3.

5 *Opus Aristotelis de moribus, interprete Joanne Argyropylo cum commento J. Fabri Stapulensis*; see Renaudet *Préréforme et humanisme* LIII (bibliography) no 351b.

6 *Decem libri Ethicorum Aristotelis ad Nicomachum ex traductione Argyropyli, Fabri commentario elucidati ...*; see Renaudet *Préréforme et humanisme* LIII (bibliography) no 351b²

7 GW 9640

8 Renaudet *Préréforme et humanisme* 155; Rice *Prefatory Epistles* 25 Ep 7 n1; on the editions, Renaudet LII (bibliography) nos 346²⁻⁷; Rice 540 (bibliography) nos XLIV–L

9 NK 3012. Cf Hain-Copinger 2392 and Renaudet *Préréforme et humanisme* 155 n2. On Caesarius see Allen and CWE Ep 374 introductions; CEBR I 238–9.

10 See Rice *Prefatory Epistles* 540–1 (bibliography) nos LVI–LXIII.

11 Rice *Prefatory Epistles* 268 Ep 88 introduction. The collection was once attributed to Guillaume de Conches, but more recently in turn to him, to Gauthier de Châtillon, or to Alain de Lille. Cf Glorieux 'Le *Moralium dogma philosophorum* et son auteur'; Delhaye 'Une adaptation du *De officiis* au XIIe siècle: le *Moralium dogma philosophorum*'; Gauthier 'Les deux récensions du *Moralium dogma philosophorum*.' Williams called it 'prudent to regard the authorship of the *Moralium dogma philosophorum* as a riddle awaiting an answer' ('The Quest for the Author of the *Moralium Dogma Philosophorum*' 747).

12 GW 8632

13 Renouard *Bibliographie de Josse Bade* II 408 51

14 Rice *Prefatory Epistles* 268 Ep 88 introduction. On Petit see Ep 522:17n/17n; Renaudet *Préréforme et humanisme* 451–2, 618–19, 653, 687–8, 693–4, and passim; CEBR III 71–2. See also nos 168, 222, 249, 278 #2.

15 Strasbourg: M. Schürer 1512 and 1515 (BB D 194 and D 196); Caen: Pierre Regnault c 1512 (BB D 195); see Massaut *Josse Clichtove* 37–8 and 403.

16 De Tralatione Bibliae Petri Sutoris

Sutor, Petrus. *De tralatione Bibliae et novarum reprobatione interpretationum*. Parisiis: J. Parvus, car. Petri Vidouei, 28 February 1525 (folio).

The Faculty of Theology of Paris condemned as superfluous the Latin and French versions of the New Testament by Erasmus and Lefèvre d'Etaples in August 1523. Early in 1525 the Carthusian Pierre Cousturier, himself a theologian trained at the Sorbonne, joined battle against the new Bible translations.[1] Erasmus had Cousturier's book in his hands almost immediately after its publication and judged it with devastating criticism: 'For sheer lunacy [it] goes beyond anything I have ever read.'[2] In August 1525, possibly at the urging of Nicolas Bérault,[3] he launched a counter-attack with his extremely cutting *Adversus Petri Sutoris ... debacchanationem apologia,*[4] which in its turn invited an equally violent rejoinder from Cousturier (no 151 #2). A folio volume does not fit in with the octavos and quartos entered before and after this item in the *Versandliste,* but no edition in octavo or quarto of Sutor's work can be traced.[5] Might there have been an edition in that format of which – no rare thing – all copies have been lost?

1 Allen and CWE Ep 1571 introductions. On Cousturier see Allen Ep 1591:25n; CWE Ep 1571 n10; CEBR I 352–3.
2 Ep 1585:83/93–4. Cf Epp 1571:27–64/30–69, 1603:33–4/36–7, 1614:1–5/2–6, 1686:56–63/ 63–70.
3 Allen Ep 1687:52n
4 Dedicated to Jean de Selve, Ep 1591. It is not in the *Versandliste.* A copy of it was, however, in the collection of his own works, nearly all Froben editions, that Erasmus kept in a separate chest; see *Catalogus librorum Erasmi* no 4.
5 It is not in Moreau *Inventaire* or in any other obvious bibliography or library catalogue.

17 Tonstallus de arte supputandi

Tunstall, Cuthbert. *De arte supputandi.* [Londini:] Richard Pynson, 14 October 1522 (quarto).

Cuthbert Tunstall's copious work on arithmetic, dedicated to Thomas More, which achieved a great reputation and went through eight reprints during the author's lifetime.[1] Tunstall (1474–1559), diplomat, churchman (from 1522 bishop of London), and a scholar trained in Italy, was a true friend and benefactor to Erasmus. Erasmus on his part remembered the bishop in his first will.[2] no doubt this copy of his book was a gift from the author. In 1525 Erasmus gave a copy of *De arte supputandi* to Andrzej Krzycki, bishop of Przemyśl.[3] The year before, he had made Tunstall an offer to negotiate with Froben, if he wished to have his book reprinted.[4]

1 STC 24319
2 On Tunstall see CEBR III 349–54; on his gifts to Erasmus, see for example Epp 1726, 1750:1–3/1–3, 1781:1–3/1–3, 1783:14–16/13–15, 1866:8–9/8–9, 2072:3–4/3–4, 2115:47–52/48–53, 2159:27–7/30– 1. For the bequest see Allen VI Appendix 19 'Erasmus' First Will' 505:86/CWE 12 544:80.
3 Epp 1629:11–13/13–15, 1652:1–3/3–5
4 Ep 1487:23–4/27–9

18 Varia Mosellani. Latomi dialo. Magdale.

Mosellanus, Petrus. Some of his writings, most probably including *Oratio de variarum linguarum cognitione paranda.* Lipsiae: V. Schumann, 1518 or Basileae: J. Frobenius, May 1519 (quarto).

bound with

Latomus, Jacobus. *De trium linguarum et studii theologici ratione dialogus.* Antwerpiae: M. Hillenius or Basileae: J. Frobenius, 1519 (quarto).

and

One or more writings on the Mary Magdalene controversy.

1/ 'Varia Mosellani' undoubtedly refers to some minor works of Petrus Mosellanus (Peter Schade), who had been professor of Greek at Leipzig since 1519 and spokesman of Erasmian-oriented humanism there.[1] Among these minor writings, especially given the treatise by Latomus bound with it, one must think first of the *Oratio de variarum linguarum cognitione,* his programmatic inaugural lecture at Leipzig. In this he argued that without a knowledge of languages, and in particular a thorough mastery of Greek, Latin, and Hebrew, the practice of scholarship was impossible. He referred to Erasmus several times in his lecture and introduced Jerome speaking in praise of the humanist who had collated the Greek manuscripts of the New Testament. It may be assumed that Erasmus received the address with Mosellanus' letter of early January 1519.[2] He complimented the speaker in enthusiastic terms: 'As soon ... as I had read your oration in defence of the study of classical languages against those who, where the art of writing is concerned, are tongue-tied and in denigrating the humanities are as fluent as you please, I thought your gifts so full of promise that I had hardly ever seen their like – your style is lively, it flows along carrying the reader with it, yet is soundly based on reason.'[3] The correspondence of Erasmus does not contain any further references to other works of Mosellanus in his possession, but several from about the same period and of the same format are eligible for consideration: *Tabulae de schematibus et tropis* (Frankfurt 1516 and later); *Paedalogia in puerorum usum conscripta* (Leipzig 1517 or 1518), a collection of colloquies that Mosellanus used in his teaching; and a number of translations from Greek, including Isocrates' *Oratio de bello fugiendo et pace servanda, P. Mosellano interprete* (Leipzig 1518). Another of Mosellanus' speeches, the *De ratione disputandi ... oratio* of 1520, is very likely on the *Versandliste*; see no 20 #3.

2/ Following the founding of Jérôme de Busleyden's Collegium Trilingue, which, in the Erasmian spirit, concentrated on teaching the three biblical tongues, the Leuven theologian and later professor Jacobus Latomus wrote this dialogue on 'Whether a knowledge of the three languages is necessary for a theologian.'[4] Taking a view opposed to the new philological study of the Bible, he cast doubt on the importance of great linguistic knowledge for the theologian. Although his book was publicly directed only against Petrus Mosellanus' inaugural lecture of 1518 (see above) it was also an indirect attack on the new academic institution at Leuven. Erasmus, who immediately had access to a copy,[5] took up the gauntlet and replied to Latomus in his *Apologia refellens suspiciones quorundam dictitantium dialogum D. Iacobi Latomi de tribus linguis ... conscriptum fuisse adversus ipsum* (Antwerp: J. Theobald 1519).[6]

3/ 'Magdale.' refers to one or more writings in the theological controversy over Mary Magdalene. For this see in more detail no 20 #1.

1 On Mosellanus see Allen and CWE Ep 560 introductions; CEBR II 466–7.
2 Ep 911. Cf de Vocht *History of the* CTL I 309 n4, 312. It is not quite out of the question that Erasmus afterwards exchanged his copy of the *editio princeps* for the Froben edition of May 1519, which the Basel printer may have sent him.
3 Ep 948:4–11 / 7–13
4 On Latomus and the dialogue see Ep 934:3nn / introduction and 4n; de Vocht *History of the* CTL I 324–34; and CEBR II 304–6.
5 See Ep 934.
6 NK 2850; see de Vocht *History of the* CTL I 342–8. It was reprinted in the *Apologiae omnes* (1522); see no 332.

19 Rodol. Agricola de Inuentione dialec.

Agricola, Rodolphus. *De inventione dialectica libri tres, cvm scholijs Ioannis Matthaei Phrissemij.* Coloniae: H. Fuchs, August 1523 or 1528 (quarto).

The chief work of Rodolphus Agricola (1444–85).[1] Though completed in 1479, *De inventione dialectica* was only published thirty-six years later. Nonetheless the Frisian humanist had been during his lifetime and continued to be after his death a man of great reputation. Erasmus paid high tribute to him in a letter of 1489 and extolled him in the *Adages* of 1508 as 'the man in all Germany and Italy most worthy of the highest public honour ... There was no branch of fine learning in which that great man could not vie with the most eminent masters. Among the Greeks, he was the best Greek of them all, among the Latins the best Latin.'[2]

The first edition of *De inventione dialectica* appeared in 1515 at Leuven from the press of Dirk Martens. Alaard of Amsterdam, Maarten van Dorp, and Gerard Geldenhouwer were instrumental in getting it published. The text was based on a fair copy from Agricola's barely legible autograph. Shortly afterwards, Alaard learned about a collection of Agricola's papers that had come into the possession of the Amsterdam merchant Pompeius Occo, who had inherited them from his uncle Adolph Occo of Augsburg, physician and intimate of Agricola and his literary executor. The collection included another fair copy from an autograph of *De inventione dialectica* but with a much better text than the mutilated one on which the 1515 edition was based. Unfortunately Alaard did not have the transcription at his disposal until 1528. He then made up his mind to publish a new and up-to-date edition of Agricola's main work as a companion volume to the *Lucubrationes*, the humanist's minor works, on the preparation of which for the press Alaard was already engaged, and he started preparing and commenting on the text. Difficulty in finding a publisher prevented him, however, from carrying his intention into effect immediately; the two volumes, which together formed for a long time the standard edition of Agricola's works, only appeared in 1539.[4] Erasmus could have known *De inventione dialectica*, therefore, only in the mutilated form of the Leuven *editio princeps*, which he must have acquired and read, interested as he was in Agricola, very soon after its appearance. He certainly had the edition of 1515 in mind when, in October of the following year, he wrote to Budé about his own *De copia verborum*: while other authors had been of little use to him in writing it,

he had found material in Agricola to his purpose that he would have used if *De copia* had not been published three years earlier.[5]

But the edition of 1515, in folio, was perhaps no longer present in Erasmus' library in 1536, for the copy of the work listed under this number in the *Versandliste* is surrounded by quartos. The book on his shelves was probably, therefore, the quarto Cologne edition of Fuchs, published for the first time in 1523 and once again in 1528. The German humanist Johannes Matthaeus Phrissemius had supplied the text with an extensive commentary, which nowadays is much praised and considered to have really made the work useful for teaching in its time.[6] Surprisingly Erasmus, inspecting the Fuchs edition early in 1528, expressed himself rather critically about it to his young Frisian friend Haio Herman precisely because of the scholia of Phrissemius: 'Someone has written a profuse commentary to the work *On Rhetorical Invention*, a young man, as it appears, and not without learning and style. But there are many incidental comments, some of them rather tedious and childishly petulant.' Erasmus preferred learned but relevant explanations and encouraged Haio (the son-in-law of Pompeius Occo), to undertake such a project. If he had not been occupied with so many other things, he revered Agricola's memory so much that he would have wished to write them himself.[7]

1 Huisman *Agricola: A Bibliography* nos 14 and 16. On Agricola see Nauwelaerts *Rodolphus Agricola*; and *Rodolphus Agricola Phrisius, 1444–1485*, a volume containing twenty-six papers read at a conference on Agricola's life and works, which includes an extensive bibliography of sources and secondary literature. In the latter see particularly on his *De inventione dialectica* Jardine 'Distinctive Discipline: Rudolph Agricola's Influence on Methodical Thinking in the Humanities.' See also Mack *Renaissance Argument: Valla and Agricola in the Tradition of Rhetoric and Dialectic*, likewise provided with a comprehensive bibliography. For a brief account see CEBR I 15–17.
2 Ep 23:56–9 with 57n / 57–61 with 58n; *Adagia* I iv 39: *Quid cani et balneo* 'What has a dog to do with

a bath?' ASD II-1 438/CWE 31 348–9. On Erasmus'
admiration for Agricola see Waterbolk *Een hond
in het bad* 27–44; Jardine 'Distinctive Discipline
(n1 above) 44 n26; Mack *Renaissance Argument*
(n1 above) 303–4. From an early date he was
interested in the publication of Agricola's works.
Hence he encouraged Pieter Gillis in 1505 to
collect his minor works. For the result of their
mutual ambition see no 306 #1.

3 NK 45; Huisman *Agricola: A Bibliography* no 11

4 [*Opera* I] *De inventione dialectica libri omnes et
integri & recogniti …, nunc demum ad autographi
exemplaris fidem, per Alardum Aemstelredamum …
accuratius emendati, & additis annotationibus
illustrati.* Coloniae: Joannes Gymnicus, 1539
(Huisman *Agricola: A Bibliography* no 42); [*Opera*
II] *Lucubrationes … nusquam prius aeditae,
caeteráque … opuscula, plusquàm depravatissime
ubique iam olim excusa, nunc demum ad autographorum exemplarium fidem per Alardum
Aemstelredamum emendata, et additis scholijs
illustrata.* Coloniae: Joannes Gymnicus, [1539]
(Huisman *Agricola: A Bibliography* no 2). Alaard
mistook the text of *De inventione* for Agricola's
autograph, as appears from the elaborate title.

5 Ep 480:99–100/104–5

6 Mack *Renaissance Argument* (n1 above) 262;
on the commentary in detail see especially 281–6.
The text with commentary went through nearly
twenty editions in the next two decades.

7 Ep 1978

20 Magdalenae. Febris hutt. Oratio Mosel.

Some works from the theological polemic
about Mary Magdalene, possibly including: Faber Stapulensis, Jacobus. *De Maria
Magdalena & triduo Christi disceptatio.*
Parisiis: H. Stephanus, 1517 or 'secunda
emissio' 1518 (quarto) and *De tribus et
unica Magdalena disceptatio secunda.*
Parisiis: H. Stephanus, 1519 (quarto).

bound with

Hutten, Ulrich von. *Febris, dialogus.*
[Moguntiae: J. Schoeffer, February 1519]
(quarto).

and perhaps

Mosellanus, Petrus. *De ratione dispu-
tandi praesertim in re theologica oratio …*
Lipsiae: M. Lotter, 1519 or Haganoae:
T. Anshelm, s.a. [1519 or 1520] (quarto).

1/ In his *De Maria Magdalena et triduo
Christi disceptatio* the humanist theologian Jacques Lefèvre d'Etaples disproved
the traditional identification of Mary
Magdalene, the follower of Christ who
appears under this name in the Gospels,
with Mary the sister of Martha and
Lazarus and with the anonymous woman
sinner of Luke 7:37–50. He argued that
three different women were referred to. His
little book provoked a violent theological
controversy accompanied by a stream of
writings and ending in the condemnation
of Lefèvre by the Sorbonne in 1521.[1] The
participants in the polemic, to name only
the most prominent, included Marcus de
Grandval, John Fisher, Josse Clichtove,
and Noël Béda. Of these, only Clichtove
stood by Lefèvre, while the others all attacked him vigorously. Erasmus shared
the view of Lefèvre and Clichtove but did
not become openly involved in the war of
words and expressed himself cautiously; he
was unwilling to risk a clash with his friend
Bishop Fisher, the tireless defender of the
traditional view, and was probably more
aware of the relative unimportance of the
whole problem.[2] Nonetheless he must have
followed the debate closely, for writings
on the question in dispute appear at three
places in the *Versandliste* under the heading
'Magdalenae' (cf nos 18 #3 and 40 #2).
It has been clearly established that Erasmus
owned and studied the book that had begun
the whole conflict,[3] and it may be accepted
that he also read and kept the second dis-
quisition (*disceptatio*) of Lefèvre, the reply
to John Fisher's attack. Nor was Clichtove's
Disceptationis defensio (Paris: H. Estienne
1519), which called forth a detailed rejoinder from Bishop Fisher, likely to have
been missing; Clichtove was represented in
Erasmus' library by the best known of his
other controversial writings (see nos 23,
60, and 181). But here and under no 18 we
must resort to surmise as to which works
on the Magdalene controversy may be intended by the entries in the *Versandliste*.[4]

2/ Very probably the original edition of the *Febris*, which Ulrich von Hutten sent to Erasmus on 6 March 1519,[5] with a covering letter and his *Phalarismus*, another dialogue in the spirit of Lucian written two years earlier. The first *Febris* was a biting satire on the corrupt lives of the clergy and the wealthy, directed in particular against the papal legate, Cardinal Cajetanus.[6]

3/ Of the two speeches by Petrus Mosellanus that come into consideration here, one, the *Oratio de variarum linguarum cognitione*, has already been discussed (no 18 #1). The second, an the oration pronounced at Leipzig on 27 June 1519 (on the instructions of the Duke of Saxony) to introduce the dispute of Luther and Karlstadt with Johann Meier of Eck,[7] was very likely in Erasmus' library, although this is not proven. The address was published by the speaker with two appropriate letters of Erasmus, whom he held in great honour, addressed to himself (Ep 948) and to Luther (Ep 980).

1 On the controversy see Surtz *The Works and Days of John Fisher* 5–7, 57–160, and 274–89; Hufstader 'Lefèvre d'Etaples and the Magdalen'; Massaut *Critique et tradition à la veille de la Réforme en France* 67–99; and Bédouelle *Lefèvre d'Etaples et l'intelligence des écritures* 191–6.
2 Cf Ep 1130, his letter to the Leuven canon Jan van Merleberge, with a poem in praise of Mary Magdalene; Reedijk *Poems* no 111 / ASD I-7 and CWE 85–6 no 124; and the interpretation of the poem in Hufstader 'Lefèvre d'Etaples and the Magdalen' 41.
3 In his commentary on Mark 8:31 LB VI 183F–185E / ASD VI-5 400:289–402:347. Cf Reedijk *Poems* 199 (no 21:286–7).
4 For other possibilities see the list of *Magdalenae* in BB 1st series IV C 428 (Josse Clichtove) and the supplements to this in Hufstader 'Lefèvre d'Etaples and the Magdalen' 37–40.
5 Benzing *Hutten Bibliographie* no 91; Ep 923:19–20/ 23
6 For the second *Febris* see no 33 #1. On Cajetanus see no 177.
7 On Eck see *Allgemeine Deutsche Biographie* XXII 359; CEBR I 416–19.

21 Adria. Cardina. de sermone latino

Castellensis, Hadrianus, card. *De sermone latino, et modis latine loquendi. Eiusdem Venatio. Item Iter Julij II.* Basileae: J. Frobenius, June 1518 or another edition (quarto).

Cardinal Adriano Castellesi of Corneto (c 1461–1521) wrote his short treatise *De sermone latino* at the end of 1506 or the beginning of 1507 in Bologna, in consequence of conversations that he held there with some learned men about the elegance of the Latin language. Although it cannot be proved, we can well imagine that Erasmus was included; he was also in Bologna, and a witness of the entry of Julius II. The cardinal was obliged to be present and, though no friend to the pope, celebrated his triumph in the *Iter Julii*. Castellesi acted as the English king's representative at the curia and was bishop of Bath and Wells, though non-resident. Although hyperconservative in ecclesiastical matters, he was a fighter for humanistic Latinity. He also supported Johann Reuchlin in his conflict with the Dominicans of Cologne.[1]

The poem on hunting printed in the Basel volume originally appeared in 1505, published by Aldo Manuzio. In *De copia* (1512) Erasmus mentioned the *Venatio*, which no doubt he had come across in Venice in 1508. Later on, in 1534, he made a reservation concerning Castellesi's authorship of the poem.[2]

The edition cannot be identified with certainty, because the *De sermone latino* together with the *De modis latine loquendi* was reprinted several times before 1536. What is probably the *editio princeps* (Rome: Marcellus Silber 1514/15) does not seem likely, for that would be a folio volume among quartos. Erasmus more likely owned the edition produced by Froben in 1518, dedicated to the literary society of Sélestat; in that year Erasmus stayed in Basel from mid-May till the beginning of September. The Froben edition was supervised by Johann Ruser (d 28 October 1518), a friend of Beatus Rhenanus and, although an inhabitant of Sélestat, often active as corrector for Matthias Schürer. Erasmus met him in Strasbourg in the literary society there and corresponded with him in 1517.[3]

1 On Castellesi see Gebhardt *Adrian von Corneto* (still useful); d'Amico *Renaissance Humanism in Papal Rome*; CEBR I 278–9.

2 ASD I-6 206–7 / CWE 24 581

3 Epp 606 and 633; on Ruser see Ep 302:15n / 16n; CEBR III 179.

22 De uita et miracu. Ioan. Gerson etc. / aliàs Capnionica cum Reuch. augenspiegel

Wimpheling, Jacob. *De vita et miraculis Joannis Gerson.* [Argentorati: J. Knobloch?] 1506 (quarto).

presumably bound with

a number of writings on the Reuchlin affair, including

Reuchlin, Johannes. [*Augenspiegel*] *Warhafftige entschuldigung gegen und wider ains getaufften iuden genant Pfefferkorn … schmachbüchlin.* Tübingae: T. Anshelm, 1511 (quarto).

1/ A defence, preceded by a brief biography, of the famous theologian and chancellor of the University of Paris, Jean Gerson (1363–1429), which took the side of the secular clergy against the monks.[1] Jakob Wimpheling (1450–1528), theologian and leading figure of German humanism, at first taught at Heidelberg, then acted as preacher in Speyer. After 1499 he stayed mainly in Strasbourg, where he was in close contact with Johann Geiler von Kaisersberg and Sebastian Brant, until in 1515 he settled in his birthplace, Sélestat.[2] His earliest relations with Erasmus date from 1511, when, only a few months after the first, unauthorized edition of the *Moria*,

he arranged a reprint of it at Strasbourg by Matthias Schürer, to which he added a letter expressing his support of Erasmus' satire on 'those divines who reduce theology to a mere froth of words and … a wintry mathematics.'[3] Wimpfeling was also the guiding spirit behind the Strasbourg literary society, which gave Erasmus such an illustrious reception in 1514.[4]

2/ The description 'Capnionica' undoubtedly refers to writings related to the Reuchlin affair brought together and probably bound together. The combination with Reuchlin's *Augenspiegel* also points in this direction. Erasmus followed the Reuchlin affair closely and collected the most important documentation on it; as early as March 1517 he was in a position to send 'all the Reuchlin pieces in one volume' to Thomas More for John Fisher, who had asked for them. He was well aware of the difficulty of replacing these fugitive pamphlets; he insisted that Fisher should return the books as soon as he had finished with them, 'for some of them are not to be found anywhere.'[5] It is no longer possible to determine what 'Capnionica' he still had in his library in 1536. The most we can do is identify which tracts he had certainly (or virtually certainly) possessed or had at least read.

(a) Joannes Reuchlin. *Defensio contra calumniatores suos Colonienses.* Tubingae: T. Anshelm, March 1513 (quarto).

Reuchlin's 'Opinion' sent to the Archbishop of Mainz, questioning 'whether one ought to burn all of the books of the Jews,' later reprinted in an expanded form in the *Augenspiegel*, provoked a violent attack from the Cologne theologians. Reuchlin responded with his *Defensio*, which Erasmus declared he had read and encouraged Reuchlin to send to England.[6]

(b) *Epistolae obscurorum virorum ad Magistrum Ortuinum Gratium …* [Haguenau: H. Gran, c October 1515] (quarto) and *Epistolae obscurorum virorum ad Magistrum Ortuinum Gratium* ... [2a pars]. [Speyer: J. Schmidt, at the latest by spring 1517] (quarto).

The *Epistolae obscurorum virorum* (Letters of Obscure Men) supported Reuchlin in satiric style. Wolfgang Angst sent a copy of the first part to Erasmus as a gift in late 1515, probably immediately after its appearance.[7] Erasmus was as little pleased as Reuchlin with the satiric work and deplored its publication.[8] Nonetheless, when the second part of the pamphlet appeared, he asked his friend Pieter Gillis to procure him a copy at once, but unobtrusively.[9]

(c) Georgius Benignus. *Defensio praestantissimi viri Joannis Reuchlin ... per modum dialogi edita.* [Coloniae: E. Cervicornus, September 1517] (quarto).

Giorgio Benigno Salviati, bishop of Nazareth, had been a member of the commission entrusted with the investigation of the orthodoxy of Reuchlin's *Augenspiegel.* His defence of Reuchlin, written in the form of a dialogue, was published with some additional items by Count Hermann von Neuenahr, a friend of Erasmus, to whom two copies were sent in late September, immediately after their publication.[10]

(d) Willibaldus Pirckheimer. *Luciani Piscator seu reviviscentes, Bilibaldo Pirckheymero interprete. Eiusdem epistola apologetica.* Norimbergae: F. Peypus, 2 October 1517 (quarto).

In October Pirckheimer sent Erasmus a copy of the letter he had published in Reuchlin's defence with his translation of the applicable dialogue of Lucian.[11]

(e) Jacobus Hochstraten. *Apologia ... contra dialogum Georgio Benigno ... in causa Joannis Reuchlin ascriptum.* Coloniae: Quentel, February 1518 (quarto).

The reply of the Cologne Dominican and inquisitor Jacob of Hoogstraten to Benigno's *Defensio Reuchlini.* In August 1519 Erasmus wrote that so far he had only read parts of this work.[12]

(f) *Lamentationes obscurorum virorum.* Coloniae: [Peter Quentel, 11 March] 1518 (quarto).

A reply by Ortwinus Gratius to the *Epistolae obscurorum virorum,* using the same techniques of ridicule. All the pieces in the *Lamentationes* were fictitious except 'a letter of Erasmus with his opinion of *De obscuris*' and the papal bull directing that all copies of the *Epistolae obscurorum virorum* must be burned. The letter, addressed to Johannes Caesarius, for many years active at Cologne as a private humanist teacher, is known only from this source. Erasmus expressed his disapproval of the *Lamentationes* as frankly as earlier he had criticized the *Epistolae obscurorum virorum:* 'What could be more misguided or unpleasant or ill-written or malignant?' As for the letter, he admitted his authorship but made clear that its publication was unauthorized (although, in sending his letter to a friend at Cologne he probably had intended it to be circulated there, at least in manuscript).[13] Erasmus wrote the lines quoted above towards the end of April 1518, so he must have set eyes upon the book very soon after its publication (11 March). A copy of the pamphlet may have been forwarded to him directly from the press.

(g) *Epistolae trium illustrium virorum ad Hermannum comitem Nuenarium.* Coloniae: E. Cervicornus, May 1518 (quarto).

The correspondence of Johann Reuchlin, Hermannus Buschius, and Ulrich von Hutten with Count Hermann of Neuenahr, directed against Jacob of Hoogstraten. It was published by Neuenahr with an introduction and a new plea on Reuchlin's behalf. Erasmus wrote to Hoogstraten that he had seen the book in someone's library, but it is open to question whether he is to be taken at his word, as he showed signs of being familiar with the contents.[14] This would not be the only occasion on which he gave the impression that he did not own a book he did not wish to be openly associated with and professed to have seen it elsewhere.

(h) Jacobus Hochstraten. *Apologia secunda … contra defensionem quandam in fauorem Joannis Reuchlin nouissime in lucem editam.* [Coloniae: Quentel], 1519 (quarto).

This second apology was provoked by the correspondence just described, issued by Hermann von Neuenahr (g). Since Erasmus owned Hoogstraten's *Destructio Cabale* (no 24), the presence of this pamphlet in his library is also a possibility.

3/ Among the writings related to the Reuchlin affair the most important item was Reuchlin's own *Augenspiegel*. It was a response to Johann Pfefferkorn, a fanatical advocate of the suppression of Jewish books, and his *Handspiegel*, which included a personal attack on Reuchlin, who had come to the defence of Jewish literature.

Reuchlin's reply comprised a survey of the emotionally charged debate on Jewish books and the texts of all the official documents that referred to it.[15] Published in 1511, the book had been condemned by the theology faculties of Leuven, Cologne, and Paris and was difficult to obtain, but Erasmus managed to get hold of a copy at Mainz in August 1514 when he was on his way to Basel. His reading removed the scepticism with which he had at first interpreted the pronouncement of the bishop of Speyer, who had exonerated the *Augenspiegel* of heresy, and convinced him that Reuchlin was in the right.[16] The *Augenspiegel* was one of the very few non-Latin books in his library (cf nos 158 and 256); apart from an extract, the text was never published in Latin.[17]

1 Ritter *Catalogue des incunables et livres du XVIe siècle de la Bibliothèque Municipale de Strasbourg* no 2227. Cf Knepper *Jakob Wimpfeling* 197.
2 On Wimpfeling see, in addition to Knepper, CEBR III 447–50.
3 Ep 224:25–7/31–2; cf Allen's introduction.
4 Ep 302
5 Ep 543:3–5/5–7
6 Epp 290:1–11/2–14, 300:17–30/19–32, 1006:27–8/29
7 Benzing *Hutten Bibliographie* no 239; Ep 363
8 Epp 622:1–11/1–12, 636:1–11/3–13
9 Benzing *Hutten Bibliographie* no 243; Ep 637:13–14/15–17
10 Verses by Neuenahr himself, among other things; see Allen Ep 877:21n; cf Ep 680:25–8 with 26n/27–9 with 28n. On Neuenahr see no 31.
11 Epp 685:13/13–14, 700:12–13/14
12 Ep 1006:51/54; on Hoogstraten see no 24.
13 See Ep 622 introductions and 1–11/1–12; Ep 830:4–5/6–7.
14 Ep 1006:63–9/67–73
15 Benzing *Bibliographie Reuchlins* no 93. See Geiger *Johann Reuchlin* 240–90. See this biography also for an analysis of all the other writings mentioned having to do with the Reuchlin controversy.
16 Ep 300:12–17/14–19; cf Allen Ep 967:72n.
17 An extract from the text was published in a pamphlet of his adversary Arnold von Tungern; see Benzing *Bibliographie Reuchlins* no 94; cf Ep 615:3n/n9.

23 De sacramento Eucha. Iudoci Clichto.

Clichtoveus, Judocus. *De sacramento Eucharistiae contra Oecolampadium opusculum.* Parisiis: Simon Colinaeus, 9 March 1527 (quarto).

Josse Clichtove, from Nieuwpoort in Flanders, humanist and theologian, was a pupil and later for many years a friend and colleague of Jacques Lefèvre d'Etaples, until the Reformation led them along different intellectual paths.[1] Clichtove became a grim and militant adversary of Luther and a convinced defender of the traditional church. This was by no means a radical about-turn, for he had already taken his stand against certain tendencies in Christian humanism before Luther's writings became widely known. He had for example attacked Erasmus' views on the monastic life, albeit in guarded terms,

in his *De laude monasticae religionis* of
1513.[2] The work considered here was
written as a refutation of Oecolampadius'
*De genuina verborum Domini … exposi-
tione*, published in Strasbourg in 1525 (see
no 34). In the debate then raging over the
Eucharist, Clichtove held fast to the doctrine of the real presence and the dogma of
transubstantiation, which for him was in-
extricably bound up with it.[3] Erasmus too
had begun a work on the Eucharist against
Oecolampadius, but chose not to finish
and publish it; he feared that it would only
provoke uproar, for Oecolampadius was a
masterful personality and had the people
in the palm of his hand. 'Besides,' as he
wrote to Pirckheimer in 1527, 'I heard that
the bishop of Rochester and the Parisians
had girded themselves for this task.'[4] He
referred to Bishop Fisher's book against
Oecolampadius, *De veritate corporis et sanguinis Christi in eucharistia* (no 312); by the
Parisians he must undoubtedly have meant
Clichtove, a theologian at the Sorbonne,
and his treatise.

1 On him see Massaut *Josse Clichtove*; in brief,
  CEBR I 317–20.
2 Massaut *Josse Clichtove* I 348–87
3 Massaut *Josse Clichtove* II 316–17
4 Ep 1893:77–82/83–8; cf Ep 1616:17–18 with
  17n/22 with n2.

24 R P. Hoghestratus. Cabala. Mantia

A composite volume that almost certainly
contained Hochstraten, Jacobus. *Destructio
Cabale seu Cabalistice perfidie ab Joanne
Reuchlin Capnione … edite*. Coloniae:
in edib. Quentilianis, April 1519 (quarto).

and possibly

one or more Kabbalistic writings of Paulus
Ricius and/or others

and perhaps also

Ramyrus Gaditanus. *Mantia sive divinatio
syderalis*. Antwerpiae: M. Hillenius, 1518
(quarto).

1/ It is not clear whether the word 'Cabala'
belongs only with the author's name that
precedes it, 'Hoghestratus,' and is used as
an abbreviated book title, or indicates the
common subject of other, possibly small
and therefore unspecified, writings bound
together in this miscellany. In either case,
Jacob of Hoogstraten's *Destructio Cabale*
must certainly be meant. In it the Cologne
Dominican and inquisitor wished in the
first place to deliver an annihilating blow
against Reuchlin's *De arte cabalistica*
(no 176 #2).[1] But he also seized the opportunity to attack, in passing, Erasmus'
opinions on divorce, as they had been
summarized in the annotations on Matt
19:8 and 1 Cor 7:39 in his New Testament
of 1516. In August 1519 Erasmus took up
the challenge and replied in a long letter (Ep 1006) written, he considered, in a
friendly spirit. Moreover, he expressed his
viewpoint even more precisely in a new and
very extensive annotation on 1 Cor 7:39
in the second edition, then just appearing,
of the *Novum Testamentum*. Although he
did not yield to his opponent in any of the
essential points in this revision, he did make
the gesture of omitting the annotation on
Matt 19:8 that had given offence in the first
edition.[2]

2/ If 'Cabala' is in fact a collective name
for a number of unspecified works on this
subject, what are we to think of? Erasmus
was not especially interested in Kabbalistic
literature. Its esoteric mystical character
was essentially foreign to him, as a ratio-
nalistically oriented humanist. Several
times in 1519 he expressed a negative view
of the Kabbala: 'Personally I have never
felt the attraction of Cabbala or Talmud,'
he wrote, 'whatever they may be, [they]
have never appealed to me'; earlier he had
described himself to Hoogstraten as someone who would be 'unmerciful' towards
the Kabbala.[3] In 1518 he had advised his
Basel friend Wolfgang Faber Capito to
apply himself more to Greek studies than

to Hebrew, citing the nature of the Jewish people: 'I see them as a nation full of most tedious fabrications, who spread a kind of fog over everything, Talmud, Cabbala, Tetragrammaton, *Gates of Light*, words, words, words.' He would, he concluded, much rather see Christians contaminated by Duns Scotus than by the vain fantasies of the Hebrews.[4] He must have seen little purpose in the effort to forge a link between the Kabbala and the doctrines of the Christian faith, and to seek traces of Christianity in the Kabbala.[5] His library appears to reflect this disdainful attitude. Pico della Mirandola, the founder of the Christian Kabbala, who had defended the thesis that no study could provide greater certainty on the divinity of Christ than the magic of the Kabbala, was not represented on his shelves by a single recognizable title.[6] Of the later Kabbalistic literature, which largely built on Pico's work, the *Versandliste* mentioned only the two works of Reuchlin: *De verbo mirifico* and *De arte cabalistica* (no 176).

Erasmus' coolness towards this mystical doctrine, which was making great progress and, especially after the publication of Reuchlin's book in 1517, stimulating many minds, did not, however, prevent him from keeping himself seriously informed about it. He must have read *De arte cabalistica* with interest and was impatient to hear John Fisher's opinion of it.[7] In his dealings with Hebraists like Agostino Giustiniani, who were initiates in a subject that was difficult for outsiders to access, the Kabbala must often have been the subject of conversation.[8] Although there are no signs that Erasmus ever gave up his deeply rooted antipathy, one man at least appears to have succeeded in bringing him to a more considered point of view. This was the converted Jew and able Hebraist Paulus Ricius. Perhaps he also puts us on the track of several small works that may be concealed behind the heading 'Cabala.'

Erasmus first met Ricius in Pavia, probably in September 1506, when he was teaching philosophy there. Later he became personal physician to Emperor Maximilian, at whose request he translated the Talmud into Latin. In 1521 he accepted a professorship of Hebrew, again at Pavia. He is now mainly remembered as one of the architects of the Christian Kabbala.[9] He published several Kabbalist works, one of which must have been in the course of publication when Erasmus made his acquaintance at Pavia.[10] His abbreviated Latin translation of the tractate *Sha'arei Orah* (*de nominibus Dei et 10 Sefiroth*) by the thirteenth-century Spanish Kabbalist Joseph ben Abraham Gikatilla, had a great influence, on Reuchlin among others. It was published in June 1516 by J. Miller in Augsburg under the title *Portae lucis: hec est porta tetragrammaton; iusti intrabunt per eam.* Erasmus' reference to 'Gates of Light' in the letter to Capito quoted above is a clear reference to the book. Did he know it only from Reuchlin, who had used it as a source, or did he also possess a copy of his own? We cannot rule this out. Ten months after its publication Erasmus and Ricius met in Antwerp; as a result of their conversation, Erasmus wrote an exceptionally laudatory comment on Ricius' learning and character and expressed the wish to be able to speak more often and more confidentially to him.[11] Shortly after the *Destructio cabale* was published Ricius entered the lists to defend Reuchlin and the Kabbala against Hoogstraten's attack. His *Apologeticus adversus obtrectatorem Cabalae sermo*, written for this purpose, was probably the book that induced Erasmus to admit that its author had made him a little better disposed towards the Kabbala, 'although before that,' he claimed, he 'was not notably hostile.'[12] Allen assumed that this referred to a text in manuscript; he based this view on the fact that he had not been able to find a printed edition before 1523. But why should the original edition not have been lost or become untraceable, as is the case with many of these little pamphlets? Erasmus remained in contact with Ricius for a while longer; he sent him a remedy against the 'stone' in 1523.[13]

3/ The title '*Mantia*' alone offers few clues, but there are some arguments that allow us to think, however tentatively, of the astrological treatise suggested. Its year of publication is close to the work by Hoogstraten bound with it. In addition, Erasmus stayed more than once and for fairly long periods in Antwerp in 1518, so that the book, which was published by a printer with whom he was friendly, could easily have fallen into his hands. The author of the minuscule pamphlet is wholly unknown, but his name seems to be a pseudonym.[14]

Like Albert Pigge's *Adversus prognosticatorum vulgus*, the only other astrological work in Erasmus library (no 55), Ramyrus' pamphlet took up the struggle against the tremendously popular almanacs with astrological predictions published by the Antwerp physician Jasper (de) Laet van Borchloon.[15] The presence of these critical works in his library need not imply that Erasmus himself rejected astrology entirely. On the contrary, in his way and as a child of his age, he too believed in it, and at exactly this time he was consulting several eminent astrologers to see whether they could give him the key to an understanding of the conflicts in the University of Leuven.[16]

1 See further on the *Destructio* Geiger *Johann Reuchlin* 199.
2 Cf Ep 1022:14–17/11–14. On the annotations see Telle *Erasme et le septième sacrement* 229–30.
3 Epp 967:71/79–80, 1033:35–6/42, 1006:162–3/170–1
4 Ep 798:19–23/20–4
5 On the Christian Kabbala see *Encyclopaedia Judaica* 10 643–4 sv 'Kabbalah.'
6 *Encyclopaedia Judaica* 13 501 sv 'Pico della Mirandola.' Letters from Pico were included in Politian's *Omnia opera*, a copy of which Erasmus had in his library; see no 285.
7 Ep 824:3–4/2–4
8 Giustiniani visited Erasmus in October 1518 in Leuven; cf Ep 886:32–3/33–4.

9 On Ricius see Ep 548:15n/16n; *Encyclopaedia Judaica* 14 163–4; Secret *Les kabbalistes chrétiens de la Renaissance* 87–97 and passim; CEBR III 158–60. For his works see further Scholem *Bibliographica kabbalistica*.
10 *Compendium quo mirifico acumine ... apostolicam veritatem ratione, prophetice, talmudistice, cabalistice plane confirmat* (Pavia: Jacobus de Burgofranco, May 1507)
11 Ep 549:36–47/41–52
12 Ep 1160:1–3/3–5
13 Ep 1558:58–60/66–8
14 See NK 3785.
15 On him see de Vocht *History of the* CTL II 545; NK 3335.
16 Ep 948:15–26/16–27

25 Cato. Viuis opuscula uaria

Cato. *Disticha moralia cum scholiis Erasmi*. Lovanii: T. Martinus, [1517] or November 1518 (quarto).

bound with

Vives Joh. Lud. *Opuscula varia*. Lovanii: T. Martinus, 1519 (quarto).

1/ The edition of the *Disticha Catonis* published by Erasmus and provided with his scholia. Besides other moral texts such as the *Mimi Publiani* and the *Septem Sapientium sententiae*, it also included his poem, translated from Colet, *Hominis christiani institutum*. It first appeared in 1514 from the press of Dirk Martens in Leuven under the title *Opuscula aliquot Erasmo Roterdamo castigatore et interprete*.[1] This schoolbook, which won popularity chiefly through its clear and elegant Latin scholia, was reprinted countless times, so that the possibility of identifying the edition with certainty is ruled out. Since, however, the *Disticha moralia* were bound with a publication of Martens that can be dated to 1519, it seems reasonable to assume that we are dealing with an edition published at about the same time. Perhaps it is not wholly fortuitous that two of the most eligible contemporary editions of Cato were also published by Martens, one in 1517 and the other in November 1518.[2]

2/ A collection of fifteen short religious, philosophical, and philological works, some of them already previously published, for the most part dedicated to the young Cardinal Guillaume (II) de Croy, whose studies Vives guided at Leuven. Among the best known are *Meditationes in septem psalmos poenitentiae, Triumphus Christi Iesu* with, following on from it, *Ovatio Virginis Dei parentis, Fabula de homine,* and *In pseudodialecticos.*[3] The book was undoubtedly a present from the author. The relationship between Erasmus and Vives in 1519, when both of them were living at Leuven, was excellent. Erasmus held the gifts of his twenty-seven-year-old friend in high esteem, and when he was asked about the possibility of becoming the tutor of Ferdinand of Austria but felt that he had to decline the offer, he emphatically recommended Vives for the post. At about this time, Vives acted as mediator between Erasmus and Budé, a testimony to the confidence placed in him, and for his part he included in the reprinted *Triumphus Christi Iesu,* one of the *Opuscula varia,* the wish that Erasmus should accept the tutorship offered to him.[4]

1 NK 534. See Allen and CWE Ep 298 introductions; on the poem see also Reedijk *Poems* no 94/ASD I-7 and CWE 85–6 no 49. Cf nos 42 #2, 87 #2.
2 NK 535 and NK 537
3 NK 2172. See Allen and CWE Ep 927 introductions; CEBR III 409–13; and cf de Vocht *History of the CTL* I 231–4.
4 See Ep 917; cf Ep 1004:9n / 9–11 and n3 (to Budé, written in Greek).

26 Lucianus, Arist. Rhet.

Lucianus. *Dialogi aliquot Des. Erasmo & Thoma Moro interpretibus.* Basileae: off. Frobeniana, 1534 (octavo).

bound with

Aristoteles. *Rhetoricorum ad Theodecten Georgio Trapezuntio interprete libri III.* Basileae: off. Frobeniana, 1534 (octavo).

The surrounding entries on the *Versandliste* practically exclude a folio volume. Among the quarto and octavo editions of Erasmus' and Thomas More's translations from Lucian and of Aristotle's *Rhetoric* that can be imagined as being bound together, the Froben editions named are undoubtedly the most obvious combination.

1/ The last edition of his translations from Lucian to appear in Erasmus' lifetime, reprinted with slight alterations from the Froben edition in *Querela pacis* (Basel: December 1517), with some emendations that probably came from the author.[1] In that case he must have carried out the corrections from Freiburg. On earlier editions see no 118.

2/ Aristotle's *De arte rhetorica* in the translation by the Greek immigrant George of Trebizond was published only in folio during the fifteenth century. The number of sixteenth-century editions in smaller formats of which we are aware is very small: a quarto edition of 1529, also by Froben, two Paris octavos of 1530, by Gerhard Morrhy and Simon de Colines, and the Froben edition in octavo of 1534.[2] We have not considered the Gilles de Gourmont edition of c 1507, with which it is very probable that another edition of the *Rhetoric* mentioned elsewhere in the *Versandliste* is to be identified (no 93 #2).

1 Cf ASD I-1 372, 376–7.
2 Cranz 28

27 Titelmanni Collationes 5 super epistolam ad Ro.

Titelmannus Franciscus. *Collationes quinque super Epistolam ad Romanos.* Antwerpiae: G. Vorstermannus, May 1529 (octavo).

Frans Titelmans (1502–37), who came from Hasselt, studied at Leuven, where he came under the influence of Jacobus Latomus; he then entered the Franciscan order, where he soon made himself known

as a fanatical champion of orthodoxy.
In his *Collationes* on the Epistle to the
Romans the still-young theologian attacked
the new method of textual criticism in
biblical study that had been introduced by
Valla, Lefèvre d'Etaples, and Erasmus and
adhered rigidly to the Vulgate translation
and the traditional exegesis founded on
the Fathers of the church and later writers.[1] Erasmus, whose edition of the New
Testament naturally came under fire, made
an irritated reply to the criticism in two
letters to his friend Johann von Botzheim;
he published them in the new edition of
his letters, the *Opus epistolarum*, in late
1529 (see no 226).[2] He also expanded the
second letter into a formal reply published
separately, the venomous pamphlet *Ad
collationes cuiusdam [iuvenis gerontodidas-
cali] opus recens*.[3] Titelmans' rejoinder to
the two letters to Botzheim was given in his
*Epistola apologetica pro opere Collationum
... ad Desyderium Erasmum*.[4] But that was
not the end of the polemic. The long letter
to Pieter Gillis with which Erasmus accompanied his edition of Xenophon's *Hieron* in
early 1530 was more than half devoted to
an attack on his opponent,[5] while his further correspondence of this period is also
full of bitter sallies against the 'shameless
fellow, inexhaustibly long-winded, unre-
strained in his impudence, who was born
to spit on Erasmus and will stop at nothing
to gain notoriety.'[6]

1 NK 2036. On Titelmans see Allen and CWE Ep 1823
  introductions; de Vocht *History of the CTL* III
  144–53; CEBR III 326–7.
2 Epp 2205 and 2206
3 Antwerp: P. Sylvius, October 1529 (NK 866);
  not in the *Versandliste*
4 Antwerp: W. Vorsterman, January 1530 (NK 2042);
  there are extracts in Ep 2245 (from Titelmans).
5 Ep 2260:145–311/157–335. The edition of *Hieron*
  does not appear in the *Versandliste*.
6 Ep 2263:106–8/114–16 (to Cuthbert Tunstall);
  cf for example Epp 2275:13–14/16–17,
  2277:7/8–9, 2300:27–41/29–44, 2315:269–74/
  2312A:280–4.

28 Epistolae ad Reuchli.

*Illustrium virorum epistolae, graecae et
latinae ad Joannem Reuchlin Phorcensem
... quibus iam pridem additus est liber
secundus nunquam antea editus*. Hagenoae:
T. Anshelmus, May 1519 (quarto).

By publishing in 1514 a number of letters
addressed to himself, Reuchlin wished
to show that he had the support of the
learned world in his controversy with
Pfefferkorn on behalf of Hebrew learning.[1]
A new edition of the collection, supplemented by a second part including five
letters from Erasmus, appeared in 1519.[2]
Erasmus reacted to this enlarged edition in
the afterword to his *Colloquiorum formulae*
(Leuven: Dirk Martens, c November 1519)
with clear displeasure and irritation: his letters had not been intended for publication
and, moreover, the text had been altered.
Above all it annoyed him that his name
stood at the head of the list of Reuchlin
sympathizers included in the book and that
he was described as 'in his masterly works
prepared to defend Reuchlin at all points.'
He was eager to distance himself from the
Reuchlin affair: 'I am no "Reuchlinist."
I belong to no man's party ... Between me
and Reuchlin nothing has passed but the
civilities of ordinary friendship.'[3] We must
assume that Erasmus possessed the later
of the two editions, that of 1519, and preserved it, if only for the sake of four of his
own letters included in it, which he never
chose to include in any of the collections
of correspondence he issued himself.

1 Allen and CWE Ep 300 introductions
2 Benzing *Bibliographie Reuchlins* no 137. The letters
  are Epp 300, 324, 457, 471, and 713.
3 NK 2869. The afterword, in the form of a letter to
  the reader (Ep 1041) is described on the title-page
  as 'Contestatio adversus seditiosas calumnias.'
  For the quotations see lines 1–19 with 11n/2–22
  with n4.

29 Phimostomus scripturariorum

Dietenbergius, Johannes. *Phimostomus scripturariorum. Adiectus est Tractatus de divortio.* Coloniae: P. Quentell, 1532 (quarto).

In a treatise added to his polemic against reformed teachings, written about 1520, the Dominican and inquisitor Johann Dietenberger opposed Erasmus' views on divorce. Erasmus reacted in his *Responsio ad disputationem cuiusdam Phimostomi de divortio* (19 August 1532), which he published again a month later at the end of his *Epistolae palaeonaeoi* (no 345).[1]

1 On Dietenberger see CEBR I 391–2. For further details of the polemic see Telle *Dilutio* 48 and 61; CWE 83 l–liv; ASD IX-4 363–8.

30 Varia. scil. Zasij apolog. De fructu studiorum etc.

A composite volume, containing among other things

Zasius, Ulrich. *Apologetica defensio contra Joannem Eckium ... Super eo, quod olim tractauerat quo loco fides non esset hosti seruanda. Defensa magni Erasmi assertio, quam in ... scholiis super septimo Matthaei capite docuit.* Basileae: J. Frobenius, March 1519 (quarto).

and

Pace, Richard. *De fructu qui ex doctrina percipitur.* Basileae: J. Frobenius, October 1517 (quarto).

For some reason only two of the works bound together in this volume seem to have deserved separate mention.

1/ Johann Maier of Eck (1486–1543), the well-known theologian from Ingolstadt and later a grim adversary of Luther, severely criticized the *Novum Testamentum* in 1517.[1] Erasmus replied in an open letter to Eck,[2] but the jurist Udalricus Zasius also felt the necessity to stand up for his friend, and in particular to defend in the apology with which we are concerned what Erasmus had written on the seventh chapter of St Matthew's gospel.[3] The substance of this pamphlet, however, was made up of Zasius' reply to the attack launched by his former pupil and family friend Eck on his idea that faith need not be kept with an enemy.[4]

2/ Without doubt a present. Erasmus was on friendly terms with Richard Pace, and after reading his book sent him, apparently in return, two of his own writings.[5] He met the English humanist, who lived and studied in Italy for several years, for the first time in Padua, and later paid him a visit in Ferrara in the spring of 1509 on his way to Rome. He entrusted him with the care of his papers, including the manuscripts of the *Antibarbari* and other works.[6]

After his return from Italy, Pace undertook important diplomatic missions in the service first of Cardinal Wolsey and afterwards of Henry VIII, and remained in touch with the world of humanism.[7] His discourse *On the Benefit of a Liberal Education*,[8] finished in Constance while on a diplomatic journey, was a curious book, as confused in composition and careless in details as it was mixed in contents. Pace apologized in advance for its shortcomings: he had written it in haste, at an inn, where he had no access to books.[9] Nevertheless, in the history of civilization it is a remarkable document: 'Pace's chattiness brings to life the day-to-day affairs of the humanist milieu as do few other literary works from the period.'[10] Erasmus, however, cautious as always, was not much attracted by the publication, in which More and he were mentioned several times. 'I could wish that book ... had not been published,' he wrote to Paulo Bombace (who had urged Pace to publish it and had also written a preface).[11] He was especially irritated by a passage referring to his poverty, at a time when he fancied himself 'almost a sort of Midas.'[12] But he was not really angry with Pace, and there was no chill at all in their relations. On the contrary, he went on speaking highly of their friendship; in 1525 he wrote, 'Pace has long been as close a friend as Pylades was to Orestes.[13] *De fructu* was dedicated to John Colet, whom Pace was to succeed in 1519 as Dean of St Paul's.

1 See Ep 769.
2 Ep 844, which was printed in his *Avctarivm selectarvm aliqvot epistolarvm ad ervditos, et horvm ad illvm* (Basel: J. Froben, August–September 1518)
3 Adams z 85. On Zasius cf no 188 #2.
4 See on this controversy Kisch *Zasius und Reuchlin* 8 and 64 and, in more detail, Rowan 'Ulrich Zasius and John Eck: "Faith need not be kept with an enemy."'
5 See Ep 787.
6 Epp 30:16n/17n, 1110:39n/n4. On the papers cf CEBR III 37–8; and nos 244 and 367.
7 On Pace see Wegg *Richard Pace, a Tudor Diplomat.*
8 The title of the edition and translation by Manley and Sylvester
9 Ep 887:7n/7n
10 Pace *De fructu* ed and trans Manley and Sylvester xvi. On *De fructu* see also Welti *Der Basler Buchdruck und Britannien* 128–32.
11 Ep 800:23–4/24–5; cf Epp 776, 796:1–6/2–7.
12 Ep 787:2–4/4–5; cf Ep 800:28–33/30–6.
13 Ep 1626:43–4/48–9; for other letters on which Pace was highly spoken of, see Epp 968:6–11/8–14, 1103:5–22/4–27.

31 Vita et gesta Caroli Magni.

[Einhard.] *Vita et gesta Karoli Magni … per Eginhartum, [Annales regum Francorum Pipini, Karoli, Ludovici ab a. p. Chr. n. 741 usque ad 828].* Coloniae: J. Soter, 1521 (quarto).

The first edition of Einhard's biography of Charlemagne and of the annals of the Frankish kings, supervised by the humanist Count Hermann von Neuenahr and dedicated by him to Charles V. He introduced the work with a 'brief account of the origin and territory of the early Franks,' and demonstrated to the emperor in his dedication that Germany owed as much to the Carolingians as Greece to the Athenians and Italy to the ancient Romans.[1] Special interest in the subject

can hardly have instigated Erasmus to buy this work; it is not unlikely that it was a present from the count to Erasmus. They had been on friendly terms for a long time. Von Neuenahr held Erasmus in esteem and admiration; Erasmus on his side visited the count on his estate, Bedburg, west of Cologne.[2] Just about the time that von Neuenahr was preparing Einhard's *Vita* for the press, he was indebted to his older friend; around the middle of March 1520 Erasmus had published a very complimentary letter to von Neuenahr (Ep 1082) as an introduction to Juan Luis Vives' *Declamationes Syllanae quinque* (no 41).

1 Borst 'Das Karlbild in der Geschichtswissenschaft von Humanismus bis heute' 368
2 See Allen and CWE Ep 442 introductions; CEBR III 14–15.

32 Hutteni Actiones.

Hutten, Ulrich von. Possibly 'actiones' and 'conquestiones' of c 1519/20.

It is difficult to say which works of Hutten were collected here under the broad title of *actiones* ('speeches' or 'indictments'). It may refer to scattered polemical treatises, including the sharply anti-Erasmian *Expostulationes* of 1523, but perhaps one must rather think of several works from the time in which Ulrich von Hutten had still been on good terms with Erasmus and had regularly sent him his latest publications (cf nos 4 #1, 20 #2, 33 #1, and 59). These appeared in 1519 and 1520 under very long descriptive titles that did not lend themselves to abbreviation, so that it would be understandable if they were not individually named but for the sake of simplicity referred to as *actiones*, a name that undoubtedly reflected their character. Two short works appear particularly likely. A book of collected poems, letters, and speeches against Count Ulrich of Wurttemberg on the occasion of the murder of Hutten's cousin Hans, the so-called *Steckelberger Sammlung*, was published by

Johann Schöffer at Mainz in September 1519 and never reprinted.[1] Another possibility is the *Conquestiones* (*Complaints*), open letters written in the Ebernburg addressed to the emperor, the German princes and estates, Cardinal Albrecht of Brandenburg, and the Elector Frederick of Saxony, on the activities of the papal party against Hutten, with a call for help; these were collected in a short book first issued in late 1520 by Johann Schott at Strasbourg and reprinted several times thereafter.[2] The *Steckelberger Sammlung* also contained the text of the dialogue *Phalarismus*, which Hutten had sent to Erasmus in 1519 but which does not appear under its own name in the *Versandliste*.[3] This might be explained if the separately published book was later replaced by a collection that also contained it.

1 Benzing *Hutten Bibliographie* no 120
2 Benzing *Hutten Bibliographie* nos 132–6
3 Ep 923:19–20/23–4

33 Huttenica febris, trias, libertas Germa. etc.

Hutten, Ulrich von. *Dialogi. Fortuna, Febris prima, Febris secunda, Trias Romana, Inspicientes.* Moguntiae: J. Schöffer, April 1520 (quarto).

probably bound with

Gebwiler, Hieronymus. *Libertas Germaniae qua Germanos Gallis neminem vero Gallum a Christiano natali Germanis imperasse, certissimis classicorum scriptorum testimoniis probatur.* Argentorati: J. Scotus, 1519 (quarto).

1/ Hutten's *Trias Romana*, which castigated the weaknesses and faults of Rome, appeared in April 1520, not on its own but included in a collection of dialogues with four others by him: *Fortuna*, *Febris prima* (reprinted here), *Febris secunda* (a continuation of the first *Febris*, which painted a detailed picture of the clergy who lived in concubinage), and *Inspicientes*,

which referred to the Diet of Augsburg.[1] The *Trias Romana* was never reprinted as a separate work at any later date during Erasmus' lifetime. Does it not follow from this that the compiler of the *Versandliste* must have had the *Dialogi* in front of him? He did not, however, list the collection under the main title, which said little about its contents, but took from the title-page the names of the two best-known dialogues. It is highly unlikely that *Trias Romana* refers, in spite of its Latin title, to the anonymous German satire against Rome, published without indication of place or date but very probably around July 1519 by Johann Schöffer at Mainz. At present this anonymous German pamphlet, which certainly served as a model and source for the Latin *Trias Romana*, is also ascribed to Hutten.[2]

Between 1518 and 1520 Erasmus also acquired several more of Hutten's works. Jacob Spiegel sent him the second version of the *Nemo*, although with a special hint that he should have the work reprinted by Froben.[3] Hutten himself still greatly valued his close contact with Erasmus in these years,[4] and regularly sent copies of his writings to Leuven. In March 1519, in the letter in which he tells Erasmus that he is sending his recently published *Febris* and his *Phalarismus*, he says that he has been 'very merry on the subject of court life' and that 'other little things of mine will have reached you lately.'[5] Perhaps these included the pseudonymously published *Triumphus Capnionis*, the *Ad principes Germaniae ut bellum Turcis invehant Exhortatoria* or the *Epistola ad W. Pirckheimer vitae suae rationem exponens*, all three of which were published in the last quarter of 1518.[6] The presentation copies may also have included his popular medical treatise on syphilis, *De Guaiaci medicina et morbo Gallico* of April 1519, in which he says somewhere that he had benefited from a method of treatment recommended to him by Erasmus. It is virtually certain that he sent Erasmus a copy of the text *De unitate ecclesiae conservanda et schismate*, which he published in March 1520.[7] Two of the works mentioned appear elsewhere in the *Versandliste* (nos 20 #2 and 59; cf no 32), but this need not mean that Erasmus disposed of the other copies from his library over the years.

2/ Hieronymus Gebwiler studied at Paris and Basel, and later taught at Breisach and Sélestat, where his pupils included Bonifacius Amerbach and Beatus Rhenanus. From 1509 to 1524 he was attached to the cathedral school of Strasbourg, where he was one of the members of the famous literary society that gave Erasmus such a handsome reception in 1514. It was Gebwiler who pronounced the official speech of welcome on that occasion.[8] When Erasmus passed through Strasbourg four years later on his way to Leuven, he sent his greetings to all his literary friends at Strasbourg, but to three in particular, among them Gebwiler, who had offered to pay his bill at the inn.[9] Gebwiler's *Libertas Germaniae*, published during the contest for the imperial crown, was an anti-French polemic against the imperial aspirations of Francis I. It argued that since the time of Caesar no Gaul had ever reigned over Germany, and that on the contrary it was the Germans who had ruled over Gaul. In Gebwiler's eyes, the Franks who had conquered Gaul had been Germans and were, moreover, the descendants of the Trojans.[10]

It is very possible that 'etc.' at the end of this entry in the list did not refer to the omitted part of the lengthy full title of the *Libertas Germaniae* but indicated that the volume contained more than was specifically stated.

1 Benzing *Hutten Bibliographie* no 122. For the original edition of *Febris* see no 20 #2.
2 Benzing *Hutten Bibliographie* no 253 and pages 142–5
3 Ep 863:28–31/33–6
4 See Ep 1135 introductions. The letter's candour bespeaks a confident familiarity.

5 Ep 923:18–21/21–5
6 See Benzing *Hutten Bibliographie* nos 87–8 (*Triumphus Capnionis*), 85 (*Ad principes Germaniae*), 83 (*Epistola ad Pirckheimer*).
7 Benzing *Hutten Bibliographie* no 103 (*De Guaiaci medicina*; cf Allen VI xx addenda to Ep 867:201/ CWE line 215 and n), and no 219 (*De unitate ecclesiae*).
8 Ep 305:148–53/154–9. On Gebweiler see Ep 302:15n/16n; CEBR II 81–2.
9 Ep 883:7–10/8–12
10 Schmidt *Histoire littéraire de l'Alsace* II 165; Buschmann *Das Bewusstwerden der deutschen Geschichte bei den deutschen Humanisten* 30 and 55

34 Eucharistia Ecolamp. Bilibal.

Probably works bound together or loosely collected on the Eucharist by Johannes Oecolampadius and Willibald Pirckheimer.

For two years Johannes Oecolampadius, the leading reformer at Basel from 1523 to his death, and Willibald Pirckheimer, the Nürnberg humanist, who was a traditionalist in matters of doctrine, kept up a polemic on the subject of the Eucharist and repeatedly harassed each other with publications.[1] The occasion for the controversy was the appearance in 1525 of the treatise *De genuina verborum Domini 'Hoc est corpus meum' expositione*, in which Oecolampadius used patristic texts to defend the view, formulated a little earlier by Karlstadt, that there is nothing in the Eucharist except bread and wine.[2] To escape the censorship of the city magistrates of Basel the book appeared without any indication of place or printer at Strasbourg.[3] Even before its sale in Basel was forbidden, it was already obtainable only with difficulty and clandestinely. Erasmus was therefore very cautious with the copy that he had acquired: 'I would have sent the book,' he wrote to Noël Béda a week after its publication, 'but I only have one copy and it is not on public sale here.'[4] With the theologian Ludwig Baer and the jurists Bonifacius Amerbach and Claudius Cantiuncula, he received a request from the city council to express his opinion on the work. Only a short passage from his report has been preserved, in the *Detectio praestigiarum* of June 1526, the pamphlet in which he went into his relationship with Luther and also gave his verdict on the question of communion.[5]

Oecolampadius' provocative essay soon called forth a detailed counter-attack from Pirckheimer. His *De vera Christi carne et vero eius sanguine responsio*, dated 1526 but perhaps already published at the end of 1525,[6] upheld the real presence of Christ in the Eucharist. About five months later, Erasmus wrote to the author that he was so vexed with a variety of troubles that he had not yet had an opportunity to read it through but that he would do so. Even before this, he had confessed to others that Oecolampadius' book had made an impression on him. The man had buttressed the 'new doctrine' formulated by Karlstadt by so many arguments and witnesses 'that even the elect could be led into the path of error by it.' To Pirckheimer he made his now familiar pronouncement: Oecolampadius' opinion would not displease him if the consensus of the entire church did not stand against it, and from that consensus of the church he could not deviate, and never had deviated.[7] Oecolampadius did not let Pirckheimer's attack go unanswered, and his rejoinder was published as *Ad Billibaldum Pyrkaimerum de re Eucharistiae* (Zürich: Christoph Froschauer, August 1526). Pirckheimer did not yield either, although his *Responsio secunda ...* (Nürnberg: [J. Petreius,] January 1527), a venomous diatribe, produced no new argument. But even this was not the end of the controversy. Oecolampadius followed with his *Responsio posterior ad Bilibaldum Pyrkhaimerum de Eucharistia* (Basel: Andreas Cratander, March 1527) and Pirckheimer had the last word in his *Epistola de convitiis monachi illius qui*

Graecolatine Caecolampadius, Germanice vero Ausshin nuncupatur [n p 1527].[8]

We may assume that Erasmus preserved the two earliest and most important works of the antagonists, which it is clear from his letters he acquired shortly after their publication. They will therefore have formed part of the 'Eucharistia' contained in this volume. So far as the other works mentioned above are concerned, his correspondence contains a fairly clear allusion to Pirckheimer's final contribution to the pamphlet war, his *Epistola de convitiis*.[9]

It cannot be ruled out that this volume in Erasmus' library also contained other works Oecolampadius published on the Eucharist that were not related to his controversy with Pirckheimer. Erasmus was aware of the apologia in which Oecolampadius in 1526 distanced himself from the view of the communion held by another reformer, Theobaldus Billicanus.[10] In 1530 Oecolampadius issued yet another new book in support of his standpoint, probably printed at Basel: *Quid de Eucharistia Veteres tum Graeci tum Latini senserint. Dialogus in quo epistolae Philippi Melanchthonis et Joannis Oecolampadii insertae.*[11] Bonifacius Amerbach thought that Erasmus should read it and sent him a copy. Erasmus, as he reported later to Amerbach, read carefully what Oecolampadius had written against Melanchthon, but he had not been convinced by it.[12]

1 See the summary in Köhler *Zwingli und Luther* I 117–18, 234–40.

2 Staehelin *Oekolampad-Bibliographie* no 113. Cf Epp 1616:19n/n4, 1618:7–10/9–13, 1620:80–5/94–9, 1621:15–24/19–29.

3 AK III 85 Ep 1063 introduction

4 Ep 1620:89–90/104–5; cf Ep 1621:23/25–30.

5 Ep 1674:63–4/72–4. For the fragment preserved see Ep 1636 to the Town Council of Basel. On the *Detectio praestigiarum* (Basel: Froben, June 1526) see Allen and CWE Ep 1708 introductions. Erasmus himself once called the *Detectio* 'my pamphlet on the Eucharist; Ep 1902:26–7/26–7 (to the faculty of theology of Paris, 12 November 1527).

6 Staehelin *Oekolampad-Bibliographie* no 318
7 Ep 1717:1–3, 52–6/1–3, 60–5. For Erasmus' opinion of Oecolampadius' book see the references in n2 above. Cf Köhler *Zwingli und Luther* I 146–7.
8 On the continuation of the controversy see Staehelin *Oekolampad-Bibliographie* nos 131, 140; Köhler *Zwingli und Luther* I 237–9.
9 Ep 1893:51–5 with 51n/57–61 with n21
10 Augustijn *Erasmus en de Reformatie* 177n
11 Staehelin *Oekolampad-Bibliographie* no 164
12 Epp 2372:16–18/16–19, 2631:49–50

35 Ambrosij Catharini in Caietanum

Catharinus, Ambrosius. *Annotationes in excerpta quaedam de commentarijs Card. Caietani dogmata.* Parisiis: Sim. Colinaeus, April 1535 (octavo).

The Sienese jurist Lancellotto de' Politi (c 1484–1553) joined the Dominican Order under the influence of the writings of Savonarola, and then took the name Ambrosius Catharinus Politus. He was an opponent of Luther, on whom he published several attacks. From 1532 till 1537 he lived in France, and there continued his publications in defence of the faith, making by turns Cajetanus, Bernardino Ochino, and Erasmus, 'whom he considered as bad as Luther,' his targets.[1] The book noted here contains another attack on Erasmus, whom he reproached with having promoted the Lutheran cause by his ambiguous attitude, 'so that some people said, "Either Luther Erasmizes or Erasmus Lutherizes." But some said it even more sharply: "Erasmus planted, Luther watered, the devil, however, gave the increase."'[2] Erasmus glanced over the book in the very last year of his life, and in the last but one of his surviving letters he wrote to Melanchthon: 'And now Catarino has published a book in Paris, which appears by its title to be aimed at Cardinal Cajetanus but is virulent throughout in its attacks on me.'[3]

1 Ep 1275:78n/n23; CEBR III 105–6
2 Lauchert *Die italienischen literarischen Gegner Luthers* 63; cf 1 Cor 3:6.

3 Ep 3127:46–7. For a detailed account of the controversy between Cardinal Cajetanus and de' Politi see Horst 'Der Streit um die hl. Schrift zwischen Cajetan und Ambrosius Catharinus.'

36 Enchiri. locorum Iohan. Eckij

Eckius Joannes. *Enchiridion locorum communium adversus Lutteranos.* Landshut: J. Weyssenburger or Romae: Francisco Minuzio Calvo or another edition, 1525 (quarto), or a later edition (in octavo).

Perhaps not the most important but certainly the most widely sold work that Johann Maier of Eck (1486–1543), professor of theology at Ingolstadt from 1510, wrote against the Lutherans. The book was in a sense intended as a refutation of Melanchthon's *Loci communes* (no 37), next to which it stood on Erasmus' shelves, and was reprinted dozens of times in the course of the century, twenty-nine times in its first five years alone. The first edition was published in April 1525 by J. Weyssenburger at Landshut. It was followed in the same year by two unchanged reprints in Cracow, and a revised edition issued by Francisco Minuzio Calvo in Rome. Later Eck revised and added to the text on several occasions.[1] It is difficult to say which of these editions Erasmus owned. Could the *Enchiridion* perhaps have been one of the 'attractive books' that he had received in 1525 as a gift from the publisher Minuzio Calvo in Rome, for which he sent his thanks in August of that year?[2] Erasmus was not on particularly good terms with the author himself, irritated as he was by Eck's sharp criticism of his *Novum instrumentum.* Expressions of respect and presents of books from Ingolstadt did not change this and, although in later years Eck attempted to effect a reconciliation, Erasmus continued to distrust him to the end.[3]

1 For a complete bibliography, see *Johannes Ecks Enchiridion* ed Fraenkel 63*–101*; cf also Fraenkel's 'Erste Studien zur Druckgeschichte von Johannes Ecks *Enchiridion locorum communium.*'

2 Ep 1604:1–2/3–4; cf no 370 #2.
3 See Epp 769 and 844; cf CEBR I 416–19.

37 Loci communes Philip. Melanc.

Melanchthon, Philip. *Loci communes rerum theologicarum seu hypotyposes theologicae.* Wittembergae: M. Lotther, 1521 (quarto) or 2nd ed 1522 (octavo) or one of the reprints (octavo).

Two versions of Melanchthon's chief work were published in Erasmus' lifetime. The *editio princeps* of the earlier form appeared in 1521, and revised and expanded editions of it followed in 1522 and 1525. In 1535 Melanchthon issued a completely new version, for which he had prepared the way in other publications.[1] Erasmus studied both the first and second versions. He must have consulted the first in the original edition of 1521, in one of its reprints, or in the revised edition of 1522. 'I have read your *Loci* all through, he wrote on 6 September 1524 'and saw in it very clearly how fair as well as fertile your mind is,' but in his reading many objections had arisen, on which he would have liked to exchange views 'if we had been able to meet.'[2] Without mentioning Melanchthon by name, he incorporated his critique of the *Loci communes* into his *De libero arbitrio* of the following year.[3] The new version of 1535 also provided matter for polemic. Erasmus appears to have taken offence at the criticism that Melanchthon levelled in the introductory part at the 'academic scepticism so often charged against Erasmus by his opponents – calling the *ludi ambigui opinionum et disputationum* [ambiguous games of opinion and disputation] of this sceptical school a blasphemy which "God punishes with penalties here and hereafter."' Erasmus interpreted this criticism as aimed at him, but Melanchthon managed to disarm this suspicion in such a way that Erasmus could only offer his excuses.[4] The *Loci communes* appears only here in the *Versandliste*. Although it is not possible to identify

with certainty which of the two versions is meant, if we take into consideration that most accessions to the library in the last few years of Erasmus life were noted on the last page of the *Versandliste*,[5] this entry probably refers to one of the early editions. It is possible that Erasmus did not acquire the 1535 edition or receive it as a gift, but that he knew the text from a copy made available to him by one of his Basel friends soon after its publication.

1 Such other publications as Melanchthon's commentary on Colossians (1527/8), an important preparatory work for the *Loci* of 1535, the second and entirely new edition, which was published with an introductory letter to Henry VIII: *Loci communes theologici recens collecti & recogniti* (Wittenberg: Josef Klug 1535; octavo). On the two early versions see *Melanchthons Werke* II-1.
2 Ep 1496: 32–7/37–42
3 Maurer *Melanchthon-Studien* 138
4 Ep 3120 introduction
5 See no 388.

38 Babylas Germa. Brixij. Scholia in Bud.

Johannes Chrysostomus. *Liber contra gentiles, Babylae Antiocheni episcopi ac martyris vitam continens, per Germanum Brixium … latinus factus. Contra Joannis Oecolampadij translationem.* Parisiis: Sim. Colinaeus, 1528 (quarto).

bound with

Tusanus, Jacobus. *Annotata in G. Budaei epistolas tam priores quam posteriores.* [Parisiis:] J. Badius, 1526 (quarto).

1/ Erasmus himself had published John Chrysostom's Life of Babylas of Antioch in the original Greek in 1527,[1] and it was with his knowledge and approval that this Latin translation was made. The Greek text was scarcely, or not yet, in the press when Germain de Brie wrote that he wished to translate the life of Bishop Babylas as soon as he had access to the new edition, because Oecolampadius in his attempt had (as Erasmus himself also thought) fallen so short of accuracy.[2] Erasmus promptly promised, two months before the book appeared, to send Brie a copy: 'Babylas will be visiting you, but he speaks Greek. He wishes to learn Latin from you.'[3] It was not without some *Schadenfreude* that a year later he was to state that 'to the delight of the theologians' Brie had 'launched a full-scale attack' against Oecolampadius and was now ready to translate the rest of the *Psegmata*.'[4]

Germain de Brie (Brixius) studied in Italy, at first in Venice with Janus Lascaris, and then in Padua under Marcus Musurus. He met Erasmus in Venice in 1508; they remained friendly and regularly exchanged letters. On his return to his native France in 1510, Brie entered the service of the chancellor, Jean de Ganay, and was later secretary to Queen Anne of Brittany. Later he retired to the estate he bought at Gentilly near Paris, and devoted himself entirely to the translation of Chrysostom.[5]

2/ These 'scholia,' published separately, belonged to the editions of Budé's 'epistolae priores' and 'epistolae posteriores' (Paris: Josse Bade 1520 and 1522 respectively). Since the annotations of Jacques Toussain (Tusanus) were included and incorporated in the complete edition of Budé's correspondence (Paris: Josse Bade 1531), which Erasmus later included in his library (no 289), the 1526 volume lost its value for him. Erasmus most probably had also possessed the older editions of the letters but disposed of them when they were superseded by the collected edition; he could not do this with the separate scholia because they had in the meantime been bound up with the edition of Chrysostom. Toussain (d 1547), a favourite pupil of Budé, who had once worked for Josse Bade and was later professor of Greek at the Collège de France until his death, corresponded with Erasmus from 1526.[6] Their contact was temporarily interrupted when Toussain took up Budé's cause in the excitement over the 'Ciceronianus,' but they

were reconciled through the mediation of Germain de Brie.[7] Were the two works described here in the *Versandliste* first bound together after this reconciliation, not by chance but almost as a symbolic act?

1 Basel: Froben, August 1527; cf Ep 1856.
2 Ep 1817:43–8/44–8. On Oecolampadius' translation, *Psegmata quaedam* (Basel 1523) see no 166.
3 Ep 1835:9–10/11–12
4 Ep 2062:22–5/26–8. Cf Ep 2052:2–3/4–5; Staehelin BAO II 145–54 nos 555–7.
5 On Brie see Ep 212:1n/2n; CEBR I 200–2. Cf no 58.
6 On Toussain see Ep 810:450n/497n; CEBR III 336–7.
7 Epp 2340:27–101/28–101, 2379:149–65, especially lines 149–74, 243–59, 393–6, 459–65/145–463, especially lines 145–69, 240–56, 391–4, 457–63, 2421 (to Toussain), 2422:80–1/81–2

39 Declamatiunc. in D. Pauli doctrinam.

Melanchthon, Phil. *Declamatiuncula in Divi Pauli doctrinam. Epistola ad Johannem Hessum*. Wittembergae: M. Lotther, 1520 (quarto) or reprint Basileae: Andreas Cratander, 1520 (quarto).

A lecture given in the castle church of Wittenberg on 25 January 1520, the day of the annually commemorated conversion of Paul, who was regarded as the patron of the faculty of theology. In it Melanchthon set Pauline and scholastic theology in opposition to each other.[1]

1 Koehn no 51 (Wittenberg) and 52 (Basel). On the significance of this *declamatiuncula*, see Schirmer *Das Paulusverständnis Melanchthons, 1518–1522* 41–2.

40 Vallum Buscij. Magdale. Roff.

Buschius, Hermannus. *Vallum humanitatis*. Coloniae: N. Caesar, 12 April 1518 (quarto).

bound with

Fisher, John. Works on the identification of Mary Magdalene, possibly *De unica Magdalena libri tres*. Parisiis: J. Badius, 22 February 1519 (quarto) and *Confutatio secundae disceptationis per Jacobum Fabrum Stapulensem habitae.* Parisiis: J. Badius, 3 September 1519 (quarto).

and perhaps *Eversio munitionis quam Jodocus Clichtoveus erigere moliebatur adversus unicam Magdalenam.* Lovanii: T. Martinus, 1518/19 (quarto).

1/ A collection of texts from the classics, the Bible, and the Fathers of the church, with the author's comments, to prove the advantage of a humanistic education. Erasmus compared it to his own *Antibarbari.*[1] Since 1515 he had been in contact with the humanist Hermannus Buschius (Hermann Busch or von dem Busche), like himself a disciple of Alexander Hegius. He esteemed him highly, and put him forward in 1519 as professor of Latin at the Collegium Trilingue in Leuven.[2] He must have been in touch with Buschius very early about the book mentioned here, for he tells us that from the original title it could already be seen to be a sharp attack on the Dominicans. Erasmus' intervention removed some of the sharpness: 'I begged him seriously to change his mind, and when the work appeared it had been revised and was much more moderate, and the title too had been changed.'[3]

2/ John Fisher, bishop of Rochester, took pen in hand three times to contribute to the controversy about the identification of Mary Magdalene with the woman who anointed Christ's feet and with Mary the sister of Martha. Fisher was defending the tradition of the church, which insisted on the existence of one Magdalene, against Lefèvre d'Etaples.[4] His *De unica Magdalena* of the end of February 1519 was in Erasmus' hands only five weeks later. He had only just looked into the work, he wrote to Fisher, but those who had read it acknowledged that the author left the lists as conqueror on this question. Nevertheless he indicated his critical opinion, that he could have wished the book had been more

elegantly printed, and that the labour had been spent on another subject.[5]

With equal speed Erasmus disposed of the *Confutatio,* the work in which half a year later Fisher tried to refute Lefèvre's apologia *De tribus et unica Magdalena disceptatio secunda.* Again, Erasmus' first reaction was non-committal: he had not yet read the book, he said, but was sorry for the excellent Lefèvre, who had suffered greatly from the hatred of the Dominicans in particular because he agreed with Reuchlin. He wished that the bishop would be content with the victory which in the opinion of scholars he had already gained.[6] After thus comparing Fisher's two writings and expressing an opinion on them, he went into the subject no further. In another letter he restricted himself to the statement that the *Confutatio* was more cultivated in style and less violent than *De unica Magdalena,* but he reproached the author for making the question a matter of faith.[7] Perhaps both books were presentation copies.

It is not unlikely, though there is no conclusive evidence in his correspondence, that Erasmus also read and possessed Fisher's third contribution to the discussion, his attack on Josse Clichtove, who had come to Lefèvre's defence.[8]

1 Ep 1110:52–4 / 56–8 (the preface to the *Antibarbari*)
2 On Buschius and the *Vallum humanitatis* see Allen and CWE Ep 830 introductions; CEBR I 233–4; de Vocht *History of the* CTL 481–2.
3 Ep 1196:300–4 / 324–8
4 See nos 18 #3 and 20 #1. On Fisher's standpoint in the controversy, see Rouschausse *John Fisher, évêque de Rochester* 58–67.
5 Ep 936:7–9, 83–8 / 9–11, 92–8
6 Ep 1030:1–8 / 3–11
7 Ep 1068:5–8 / 7–12
8 NK 943; cf Ep 1030:3n / n2, CWE Ep 1068 n3.

41 Lod. Viuis declamationes Syllanae

Vives, Joh. Lud. *Declamationes Syllanae quinque.* Antverpiae: M. Hillenius, April 1520 (quarto).

Five orations in Ciceronian style, put by
Vives into the mouth of one supporter
and three opponents of the dictatorship
of Sulla, and also of the Roman dictator
himself.[1] By way of introduction and recommendation the book was supplied with
a letter from Erasmus to Count Hermann
von Neuenahr (Ep 1082), in which the philosophical qualities of the author were highly spoken of. Vives tells us in the dedication
to Ferdinand of Austria, as rewritten for
a later edition, that his *Declamationes* was
published 'at the suggestion of Erasmus
and other friends.'[2] When Thomas More
wrote praising this work, as well as Vives'
Opuscula varia, which had just been published (no 25 #2), Erasmus expressed his
pleasure in reply that they should be of one
mind concerning the author's talent: 'He is
one of that band of people who will put the
name of Erasmus in the shade ... He has a
wonderfully philosophic mind.'[3] The book
was no doubt a presentation copy from
the author.

1 NK 4062; cf Noreña *Juan Luis Vives* 65.
2 Allen and CWE Ep 1082 introductions. On Juan
   Luis Vives cf no 25 n3; on Neuenahr cf no 31.
3 Epp 1106:21–92/23–96 (from Thomas More)
   and 1107:6–13/8–15 (Erasmus' reply)

42 Sadol. Cato Octo partes

Sadoletus, Jacobus. *De liberis recte instituendis liber*. Lugduni: S. Gryphius, 1533
(octavo).

possibly bound with

Cato. *Disticha moralia cum scholiis Erasmi*.
Lugduni: S. Gryphius, 1534 or another
edition (octavo).

and

Donatus, Aelius. *De octo partibus orationis
libellus. Ad haec D. Erasmi Rot. de constructione opusculum*. Lugduni: S. Gryphius,
1531 or 1535 (octavo) or Erasmus. *De octo
orationis partium constructione libellus*.
Friburgi Brisg.: J. Faber Emmeus, 1533?
(octavo).

1/ There is a good chance that the book in
question here is Sadoleto's *De liberis recte
instituendis*, because two other important
works of the cardinal appear elsewhere in
the *Versandliste* (nos 6 and 404 #1), and
it is certain that Erasmus also owned this
brief educational work, with its plea for the
liberal arts. Bonifacius Amerbach sent him
a copy in August 1533,[1] and not long afterwards he received another copy from Paolo
Sadoleto, a nephew of the cardinal who
was acting as his coadjutor and his partner
in the dialogue that makes up the book.
Erasmus thanked him for the copy in a letter of 30 August 1533, which was published
shortly afterwards in the *editio princeps*
of his *De praeparatione ad mortem* (Basel:
Froben and Episcopius, c January 1534).[2]

2/ Yet another edition of Cato with
Erasmus' annotations. Of the five editions that appeared at approximately the
same time as Sadoleto's work, one was
published, coincidentally or not, at Lyon
by Sebastianus Gryphius, the printer and
publisher who also issued Sadoleto's
De liberis recte instituendis.[3]

3/ The most obvious title suggested by
'octo partes,' Erasmus' *De octo orationis partium constructione libellus*, is not
mentioned elsewhere in the *Versandliste*.
Not long after Sadoleto's pedagogical
treatise was published, a new edition of
De constructione appeared in Freiburg im
Breisgau, where Erasmus was then living,
from the press of Faber Emmeus, who
printed other works for him in these years.[4]
But this was not an authorized edition, and
since Erasmus was not in the habit of keeping routine reprints of his own works, the
Octo partes of the list may refer instead to
another, now rare, book in which his short
syntax had been published with the very
familiar work on the eight parts of speech
by the fourth-century grammarian Aelius
Donatus, the most widely used schoolbook
of the Middle Ages. The book appeared in
1531 and again in 1535 from Sebastianus

Gryphius in Lyon.[5] The assumed combination in one binding of three Lyon editions by the same printer is less far-fetched than it seems. Erasmus and Sadoleto were on excellent terms with each other at just this time. Sadoleto also maintained very good relations with the printer-publisher Gryphius. Regular contacts existed between printers, publishers, and booksellers in Lyon and Basel, and it was through them that Erasmus and Sadoleto kept up their correspondence.[6] All in all, a background against which the possible sending of two books (intended as presents?), besides Sadoleto's *De pueris instituendis*, is not a mere guess, but a plausible suggestion. A supporting argument is found in a similar volume of Lyon imprints (no 2 #3).

1 Ep 2859:19–20
2 Ep 2864
3 Two of the others were printed in Paris and two in Antwerp; see Reedijk *Poems* 373 (Survey of Editions and MS Sources II: Works Edited by Erasmus) nos 44–7. Cf nos 25 #1, 87 #2.
4 Among others, *Paraphrasis in Elegantias Laurentii Vallae* (1531); *Carmen votivum divae Genovefae* (1532); *Epistolae palaeonaeoi* (1532); see nos 379, 61, and 345.
5 There is a copy of the 1531 edition in the Bibliothèque Royale Albert I in Brussels and a copy of the 1535 edition in the University Library, Manchester; neither is listed in Baudrier.
6 See no 404 #1; Introduction: Methods and Resources n39 above.

43 Henrici Corn. Agrip. Apologia.

Agrippa ab Nettesheym, Henr. Corn. *Apologia adversus calumnias propter declamationem de vanitate scientiarum & excellentia verbi Dei, sibi per aliquos Lovanienses theologistas intentatas.* [Coloniae? J. Soter?] 1533 (octavo).

In his *De incertitudine et vanitate scientiarum et artium*, written in late 1526 but not published until 1530, Henricus Cornelius Agrippa of Nettesheim (1486–1535) took a sceptical view of all science and art, put in perspective the value of the Kabbala and magic, which played such

an important part in his main work, the *De occulta philosophia*, published shortly afterwards, and preached a return to the simple faith of the early Christian church. *De vanitate* was also a sharp social satire, which held up secular and ecclesiastical abuses to ridicule, attacked the monks, and did not even leave the authority of monarchy unchallenged. Agrippa reaped the whirlwind: although only recently appointed as imperial historiographer, he fell into disfavour at court, the Sorbonne condemned his work, and the Leuven theologians branded his book as scandalous and heretical.[1] He replied point by point to the attack from Leuven in the *Apologia adversus calumnias* indicated here, written 'modestly, of course, but not without salt and vinegar and even mustard.'[2] He sent the copy of his defence to the Basel printer Cratander with the request that as soon as the book was printed, he should send Erasmus a copy. Cratander did not dare to undertake the publication, and the *Apologia* finally appeared elsewhere without any indication of the printer or place of publication.[3] Erasmus nevertheless received a presentation copy of it through Tielmannus Gravius.[4] Erasmus knew of Agrippa, and had expressed interest in *De incertitudine*.[5] In September 1531, when the dispute over the book had already flared up, Erasmus approached Agrippa in order to introduce a French admirer of his *De occulta philosophia* to him. Agrippa's name, so Erasmus wrote at that time, was on everyone's lips, especially because of his *De incertitudine*. Many scholars who had written to him about it agreed on the bold intention of the book; but for the rest their opinions varied. He himself had not yet seen it, but he would make sure that he obtained a copy as soon as possible and promised that as soon as he had read it through, he would write to Agrippa in detail about it.[6] It was the spring of 1533 before he fulfilled his promise, and then only in part. It does not seem that Erasmus ever acquired or possessed a copy. He only borrowed it for a short time and had select chapters read aloud to him after meals by his *famulus*.[7] He praised the book and told Agrippa that he did not understand why the monks had behaved with such indignation over it; nonetheless he reminded him of the fate of Louis Berquin, who had ended at the stake in 1529 because he had been too free in his contemptuous attitude towards monks and theologians. And he adjured Agrippa not to involve him in this dispute: 'I am already burdened by enough enmity, and that matter will weigh me down and will hinder rather than help you.'[8]

1 On Agrippa and his *De incertitudine* (Antwerp: J. Graphaeus, September 1530; NK 49) see CEBR I 17–19; Nauert *Agrippa and the Crisis of Renaissance Thought* 98, 107–11; Popkin *The History of Scepticism from Erasmus to Descartes* 22–5; Zambelli 'Corneille Agrippa, Erasme et la théologie humaniste'; Crahay 'Un manifeste religieux d'anticulture: Le *"De incertitudine et vanitate scientiarum et artium"* de Corneille Agrippa'; van der Poel *Cornelis Agrippa*. On the *Apologia contra theologistas Lovanienses* see especially de Vocht *History of the* CTL III 143–4.
2 See Nauert *Agrippa* 109 with n13.
3 Epp 2739 introduction, 2790:8–12
4 Cf Ep 2894:59–60. On Tielmannus Gravius see Ep 610:47n/50n; CEBR II 125–6. He was secretary to the chapter of Cologne cathedral and a faithful friend of Erasmus, who dedicated to him (Ep 2103) his edition of Lactantius' *De opificio Dei* (Basel 1529).
5 Ep 2529:11–19
6 Ep 2544:1–6
7 Ep 2800:42–6
8 Ep 2796; cf Ep 2800:41–65.

44 Luterus in nouum Test.

Possibly a Latin version of Martin Luther's *Church Postils* and/or other Latin translations of his exegetical works published by Herwagen (octavo?).

Luther's exegesis of the New Testament, for that is what the vague reference must indicate, was contained not in Latin commentaries but almost entirely in exegetic sermons or other explanatory works in the vernacular. Erasmus professed to know no German,[1] and with two explicable exceptions (nos 22 #3 and 256), the *Versandliste* does not include any German books. Presumably this entry refers to Latin exegetical works. Their number is relatively small. Apart from Luther's commentary on the Epistle to the Galatians, which can be left out of consideration because the edition is entered elsewhere in the list (no 54), these are almost exclusively works, for the most part sermons, translated into Latin. An early collection of postils is an exception; Luther's *Enarrationes epistolarum et evangeliorum quas postillas vocant* (Wittenberg: J.R. Grunenberg 1521 and elsewhere, a quarto) was originally published in Latin and only afterwards in German.[2] A later six-volume collected edition, *Enarrationes in Epistolas & Evangelia ut vulgo vocant* (Strasbourg: Johann Herwagen, 1 February 1525–August 1527, in octavo), contained postils that had already appeared earlier in separate collections in the vernacular.[3] Of the other editions that might be considered, one, the *Exegesis in septimum primae ad Corinthios caput*, was published in Strasbourg by Johann Schott (1525, octavo).[4] The rest were published, also in Strasbourg, by Herwagen: the *Enarrationes in Epistolas D. Petri duas & Judae unam* (1524 and 1525, octavo); the exposition of the Magnificat, Luke 1:46–55 (1525 and 1526, octavo); a sermon on the first Epistle to Timothy (1527, octavo); and some related works.[5] It is noteworthy that most of the writings mentioned appeared from the press of Johann Herwagen between 1525 and 1527. Could it be that editions from his press are concealed behind the words 'Luterus in nouum Test.'? Herwagen, who worked as a printer in Strasbourg from 1523, settled in Basel soon after the publication of his edition of the *Church Postils* mentioned above to continue, in partnership with

Hieronymus Froben and Nicolaus Episcopius, the business of Johann Froben, who
had died at the end of 1527. He married,
probably in early 1528, Gertrud Lachner,
Froben's widow, and thus acquired the
joint ownership of the house Froben had
provided for Erasmus (who still occupied
it at that time) and the garden he bought
at Erasmus' urging. It must have been a
matter of some importance to Herwagen
to establish good relations with Erasmus
quickly, and to recommend himself to him.
Later, when the firm was dissolved and
he operated as an independent printer, he
did his best to bind Erasmus, who had by
now moved to Freiburg, to his publishing
business, but only with partial success;
he never won Erasmus' sympathy.[6]

1 See Epp 1313:85 with n/94 with n16, 1499:11/11–
   12, 2516:114–15 with 115n, 2804 introduction;
   cf Chomarat *Grammaire et rhétorique* I 137–44.
2 Benzing *Lutherbibliographie* no 848; five reprints
   followed in the same year, nos 849–53.
3 Benzing *Lutherbibliographie* no 1148. In 1528
   Herwagen also published a folio edition in one
   volume (Benzing ibidem no 1149).
4 Benzing *Lutherbibliographie* no 17
5 Benzing *Lutherbibliographie* nos 1733 and 1734
   (Epistles of Peter and Jude, translated by Martin
   Bucer), 865–6 (Magnificat), 2221 (1 Timothy),
   2002 (related works). On the Herwagen editions
   cf Muller *Bibliographie Strasbourgeoise* II 260–9.
6 On Herwagen see Allen Epp 2033:58n, 2945
   introduction; CEBR II 186–7; Erasmus mentions
   the garden in Ep 1756:5–6/6–8. On Erasmus'
   relationship with him cf nos 120–1 and 131.

45 Melanc. in Epistolas.

Melanchthon, Phil. *Annotationes in
Epistolas Pauli ad Rhomanos et Corinthios.*
Norimbergae: J. Stuchs, 1522 (quarto)
or one of the reprints, Argentorati: J.
Hervagius, 1523–5 or Basileae: T. Wolfius,
1523 (both octavo).

The short title on the *Versandliste* refers
most probably to Melanchthon's commentaries on the three best-known Epistles
of Paul, which were published – against
Melanchthon's will – with a foreword by

Luther in 1522.[1] The book attracted much
attention, and in the years immediately
following it went into many editions,
revised and expanded, five of them from
the Strasbourg printer Johann Herwagen
alone.[2] The general description 'on the
Epistles' does not exclude the possibility
that other works were bound with or
loosely attached to the *Annotationes* on
Romans and Corinthians. But at most
one or two studies of separate Epistles
of a rather later date are possibilities: the
Scholia in Epistolam Pauli ad Colossenses
of 1527, important both for Melanchthon's
attitude to philosophy (in his lengthy
excursus on Col 2:8) and for his theological
standpoint following the conflict between
Erasmus and Luther on the freedom of
the will;[3] and possibly also the *Dispositio
orationis in Epistolam Pauli ad Romanos*
of 1529–30,[4] not a commentary proper
but a preliminary study for Melanchthon's
Commentarii in Epistolam Pauli ad Romanos
of 1532. This important work may itself be
left out of consideration here, since a copy
of it is entered elsewhere in the list (no 14).

1 Benzing *Lutherbibliographie* no 1252
2 Benzing *Lutherbibliographie* nos 1253–62
3 *Melanchthons Werke* IV 209. Revised and extended
   editions of this work were also published (in 1528,
   1529, and 1534).
4 *Melanchthons Werke* V 16

46 Glareanus. Beraldus.

Presumably a collection of writings, bound
or loosely attached, by Henricus Glareanus
(Heinrich Loriti) and Nicolas Bérault
(Beraldus).

1/ Henricus Glareanus (1488–1563) had
already completed some years of study
at Cologne, where he had been a pupil
of Hermannus Buschius and Johannes
Caesarius, when in 1514 he matriculated
at Basel. There he originally worked for
Froben, but as early as the following year
he began to give lessons at a school that he
had set up himself. In 1517 he moved to

Paris, but only temporarily; he returned to Basel in 1522. Glareanus was a humanist of particularly many-sided talents: poet, philologist, historian, geographer, and musicologist all at once. He was for some years the friend of Huldrych Zwingli and Osvaldus Myconius but eventually felt himself most at home in religious matters among the more conservative humanists; in 1529 he fled the radical Reformation in Basel and migrated, even before Erasmus, to Freiburg im Breisgau.[1] Erasmus made Glareanus' acquaintance at the beginning of his first stay in Basel, which lasted, with an interruption of two months, from August 1514 to mid-May 1516. Their rapport was instant. Erasmus honoured the younger humanist, who was soon a regular visitor at his house, with a *horologium* and in March 1516 recommended him to Urbanus Rhegius for an appointment at Ingolstadt, with a brilliant reference. A little less than a year later Erasmus sent Glareanus an even more detailed and equally glowing reference from Leuven, possibly for the Collège de France then being set up, to Etienne Poncher, bishop of Paris and an influential advisor of the king of France.[2] Given such an intimate friendship, it next to impossible that Glareanus would not have sent Erasmus a copy of his book on Switzerland, the famous versified *Helvetiae descriptio*, published in 1515.[3] The same may be said of his collection of *Elegiae* of November 1516, dedicated to Zwingli, which contained a poem in praise of Erasmus and a poem for Myconius on the occasion of Erasmus' departure from Basel.[4] Erasmus had already received the text of both poems in manuscript, that of the poem of praise at his own special request. But because errors had crept in, Glareanus requested his older friend to destroy the texts he had sent.[5] He will then undoubtedly have sent the printed collection, in which the errors were corrected, to Leuven.

Besides his book on Switzerland and the original musicological work *Dodecachordon*, written between 1519 and 1533 but not published until after the death of Erasmus, two of whose favourite melodies it informs us about,[6] Glareanus also won fame among his contemporaries through his manual *De geographia*, published in 1527 and reprinted very soon after. This brief work on mathematical geography and the production of globes also contained a concise description of the continents and the separate countries, including the newly discovered *regiones extra Ptolemaeum* such as the lands to the west of Spain, to which he gave the name America. Erasmus was closely involved in part of the prehistory of the book. It was at his house that Glareanus showed Jan Łaski the foot, the new measure of length that Budé had deduced from ancient sources, and demonstrated its usefulness for geographical calculations on an astrolabe Łaski had received from the French king.[7] As he himself stated in the foreword, Glareanus dedicated *De geographia* to Łaski at the suggestion of Erasmus, who reported to Łaski the success of Glareanus' lectures on the book: while other scholars appeared before an audience of barely six, that of Glareanus numbered sixty.[8] With Bonifacius Amerbach and Beatus Rhenanus, Glareanus was part of the remarkable and brilliant fellowship (*rara sodalitas sed candida*) – his 'triumvirate' – that made life at Basel so agreeable for Erasmus.[9]

2/ Nicolas Bérault dedicated his life to teaching and study, at first at Orléans and from about 1512 in Paris, where he belonged to the circle around Budé and enjoyed the patronage of Bishop Etienne Poncher and, after the latter's death, of other high ecclesiastical dignitaries; in 1529 he succeeded Paulo Emilio as historiographer royal. Erasmus had been a friend since 1506, when he spent some days in Orléans on his way to Italy and enjoyed Bérault's hospitality. In 1522 he dedicated the first authorized edition of his *De conscribendis epistolis* to him.[10] It is pointless to guess which of Bérault's works were present in Erasmus' library. His most fertile field of activity was the publication of classical and early Christian authors: Lucretius, Pliny (cf no 412), Valerius Maximus, Athanasius (no 187), Appian, and Theophylact (cf no 187), among others. His own works covered a rather varied terrain: philological, juridical, theological, and political.[11] None of them appears to fall within Erasmus' special sphere of interest, unless it is the *Enarratio in psalmos 71 et 130* ([Paris] 1529), or the *Dialogus quo rationes quaedam explicantur quibus dicendi ex tempore facultas parari potest deque ipsa dicendi ex tempore facultate* (Lyon: [Sebastianus Gryphius] 1534). In the latter Bérault advocated a living Latin, a spoken language capable of expressing the realities of modern life, and not the sterile discipline of Ciceronianism, which stifled invention.[12]

1 On Glareanus see Allen and CWE Ep 440 introductions; AK II 20 Ep 505 introduction; CEBR II 105–8; and Ashmann et al *Der Humanist Heinrich Loriti genannt Glarean* (with a complete survey of his works and the text editions he prepared).
2 Epp 305:208–10/214–15, 463:69–71/76–8 (from Glareanus, acknowledging Erasmus' gift), 394 (to Urbanus Rhegius), 529:60–131 (to Etienne Poncher)
3 There were two editions, Basel: A. Petri 1515 and Basel: J. Froben 1519 (with commentary by Myconius). See Margolin 'Henri Glaréan – Oswald Myconius (1517–1524)' 147, 151, 157.
4 *Ad Erasmum Roterodamum inmortale Belgarum decus* ἑκατόστιχον and *Ad Oswaldum Lucernanum Helvetium Elegia Glareani*; cf Epp 440:13nn/16n and 463:67n/74n.
5 Epp 440:13–14/15–16 (to Glareanus), 463:63–9/69–76, 490:10–15/11–28 (both from Glareanus)
6 *Glareani* Δωδεκάχορδον (Basel: [1547]) 120ff and 134ff
7 Maurer *Der junge Melanchthon* I 168–9
8 See Ep 1821:10–11, 67–70/14–16, 74–7.
9 Ep 1910:17–20/19–22; cf Ep 1989:11–12/11–12.
10 On Bérault see Allen Ep 925 introduction; CEBR I 126–8; de la Garanderie 'Les relations d'Erasme avec Paris ... (1516–21)' 39. For *De conscribendis epistolis* see nos 359 and 409. On Emilio see no 333.

11 Delaruelle 'Notes biographiques sur Nicole Bérauld, suivies d'une bibliographie de ses oeuvres et de ses publications'
12 de la Garanderie 'Comment parler couramment le latin: un dialogue de Nicolaus Bérault,' especially 483–7, 490

47 Eobanus Hessus. Luscinius.

Like the preceding number on the list, most probably a collection or bound volume of minor writings by two younger humanists, Helius Eobanus Hessus and Ottmar Nachtgall (Othmarus Luscinius).

1/ Helius Eobanus Hessus (1488–1540), who excelled among the humanists of his generation as a poet, accepted a chair of classical languages at Erfurt, where he had also studied, in 1517. For some years he was the guiding spirit of a circle of young poets and students of literature in this university city who at first were devoted followers of Erasmus but later came under the influence of Luther and the Reformation.[1]

In October 1518 Eobanus Hessus and Johann Werter made a pilgrimage to Erasmus at Leuven, bringing both presents and letters from kindred spirits in Erfurt.[2] Immediately after the visit Erasmus wrote to Eobanus (Ep 874), calling him a Christian Ovid, with reference to his *Heroidum christianarum epistolae* (Leipzig: M. Lotter 1514), the work, inspired by the *Heroides* of Ovid, that had established his fame as a poet. It is possible that Erasmus was already aware of and possessed this collection of verses, but it is perhaps more probable that the book was one of those presented to him. On his way home Eobanus composed a detailed account in verse of his journey and visit to Erasmus, supplemented by five letters Erasmus had given to his Erfurt admirers, which appeared in print in 1519 under the title of *Hodoeporicon*.[3] Erasmus received a copy of the work from the hands of two other representatives of the Erfurt circle, Justus

Jonas and Kaspar Schalbe, who visited him at Antwerp in the course of the same year. This was undoubtedly provided with a similar dedication to that which Eobanus had written in the copy he sent to Beatus Rhenanus, in which the blunders of the printer were pointed out.[4]

Erasmus was so pleased by the *Hodoeporicon* that he at once had it reprinted in Leuven by Dirk Martens, purged of the printer's errors and with some additions, among them a poem in praise of himself by Caspar Ursinus Velius and by Goclenius' metrical version of the Catalogue of Erasmus' works entitled *Lucubrationum Erasmicarum elenchus.*[5] Possibly this edition was still in his library in 1536, and not the presentation copy of the *editio princeps*. He may have had a special reason to preserve the *Hodoeporicon* carefully; the letters from himself included in it were never reprinted in any of the later collected editions of his letters. Eobanus' original boundless admiration for Erasmus was very soon cooled by religious controversy. The brief revival in their correspondence in the early 1530s could not disguise the fact that the convinced Lutheran and the humanist who held fast to the old faith had become alienated from each other. Nonetheless Erasmus kept himself informed of the later literary works of Eobanus. He almost certainly possessed his translation of Theocritus, published in 1531 (no 99), and perhaps also the first collection of his *Epicedia*: he had read his elegies, he wrote to the poet, and none of them with a deeper feeling of grief than that on the death of Pirckheimer.[6]

2/ Ottmar Nachtgall, known as Luscinius (c 1487–1537), jurist, philologist, and musician, came from Strasbourg, where he received his earliest teaching from Jakob Wimpfeling. After a wandering existence in his youth – he studied at Paris but attended at least three other universities and then made a journey through south-eastern

Europe and Asia Minor – he returned to the town of his birth. At the beginning of 1515 he was given an appointment as organist and also began to teach Greek in Strasbourg, the first to do so.[7] Like his old master Wimpfeling, Nachtgall, with Sebastian Brant and Hieronymus Gebwiler, was a member of the literary society, 'that company of all the Muses and the Graces,' which welcomed Erasmus with a display of honour on his visit to the city in 1514. In his letter of thanks for this reception, Erasmus mentioned that Nachtgall's flute playing had 'so ravished [him] that [he] seemed rapt in ecstasy.'[8] But a friendship did not develop between the two men. In later years there was even some doubt whether Nachtgall, a rather volatile person, was well disposed towards Erasmus.[9]

There were also difficulties over the house 'Zum Walfisch' in Freiburg, the first floor of which Erasmus occupied rent-free in April 1529, on his arrival in the city, while Nachtgall had leased another part, but felt that he had a claim to the whole house.[10] Still, these difficulties were resolved, so that they were probably not the primary reason for the cool relationship. Which of Nachtgall's writings Erasmus owned and thought worth keeping cannot be traced from any source. Perhaps they were one or more Strasbourg editions from the time of their meeting in the literary society or shortly afterwards, which, unlike most of Nachtgall's other works, were in quarto format and thus would fit in well with the quarto of Eobanus and the surrounding volumes. Those eligible include, for example, all three works published in Strasbourg: *Collectanea sacrosancta* (J. Schott 1515); *Musicae institutiones* (I. Knoblouch 1515), and *Progymnasmata graecanicae literaturae* (I. Knoblouch 1517).[11]

1 On Eobanus see Allen and cwe Ep 874 introductions; cebr i 434–6; the detailed biography by Krause, *Helius Eobanus Hessus*, is still useful. Cf Reedijk *Poems* 22–3, 81–3.

2 Allen and CWE Ep 870 introductions; Krause
  Helius Eobanus Hessus I 288–99
3 *A protectione ad Des. Erasmum Roterodamum
  Hodoeporicon* (Erfurt: Mattheus Maler 1519).
  For the letters see Epp 870 (to Conradus Mutianus
  Rufus), 871 (to Johannes Draconites), 873
  (to Henrich Bemyng), 874 (to Eobanus), 876
  (to Justus Jonas), all 17–19 October 1518.
4 Allen Ep 870 introduction (page 406); on Jonas
  and Schalbe's visit see Ep 963:1n/6n.
5 NK 764. See Allen Ep 870 introduction (page 406).
6 *Illustrium ac clarorum aliquot virorum memoriae
  scripta epicedia. Epitaphia epigrammata composita
  ab Joachimo Camerario* (Nürnberg: F. Reypus
  1531; octavo); Walter *Catalogue Sélestat* 1140.
  Cf Ep 2495:34–5.
7 On Nachtgall see Ep 302:16n; AK III 380 Ep 1312
  n7; CEBR III 3–4.
8 Ep 305:125–6, 155–60/133, 162–5
9 Ep 2728:41–3
10 Epp 2462 introductions, 2470
11 There is also an edition of Lucian by him from the
  same time: θεῶν διάλογοι, *Deorum dialogi numero
  70, una cum interpretatione ... latina* (Strasbourg:
  J. Schott 1515).

48 Coctus cum Chris. docto. Lute. epistolis

[Coctus, Annemundus, ed.] *In hoc libello
contenta Annemundi Cocti ad lectorem
epistola. Martini Lutheri ad principem
Carolum Sabaudiae ducem epistola.
Huldrichi Zuinglij ad Petrum Sebiuillam
epistola.* [Tigurii: Christ. Froschauer, 1524]
(quarto).

A pamphlet of only eight leaves, with the
text of three contemporary letters, by
Anemond de Coct (d 1525), probably
published early in 1524, during his stay in
Zürich.[1] De Coct, seigneur du Chatelard,
was among the first Lutherans in France.
He came to Wittenberg in 1523, matriculated there at the end of April, and was
soon in personal touch with Luther. It was
he who wrote the severely anti-papist letter
'to the reader' that served as foreword to
the *Commentarii in Regulam Minoritarum*
of his compatriot François Lambert, with
an introduction by Luther himself; this
is the first letter in the book described in
this short title in the *Versandliste*.[2] In the
autumn of 1523 he carried a letter from

Luther to Duke Charles III of Savoy, also
printed in the book.[3] In December he was
back again in Zürich, where Huldrych
Zwingli welcomed him and at his instigation wrote a letter to his supporter in
matters of faith, the former Cistercian
monk Pierre de Sébiville, which is the third
item.[4] On his way back to France he visited
Basel in March 1524, where he met not
only Johannes Oecolampadius but also
Guillaume Farel, the man who had won
him over to the cause of the Reformation,
and who was like himself a native of the
Dauphine. The summer months of 1524 de
Coct spent partly in Paris, but in August he
was back again in Basel and must certainly
have stayed there till February 1525. He
continued his work for the Reformation
along with Oecolampadius, and he kept
up his relationship with Farel, who lived
in neighbouring Montbéliard.[5] It was
probably then too that the plan of Michael
Bentinus to set up a printing office with the
purpose of publishing French translations
of the Gospels took definite shape. The
Fleming Bentinus, who had at first been
employed by Froben and had been drawn
into the correction of the *Adagia* (not
wholly to Erasmus' satisfaction), took
sides with Farel just as de Coct did.[6]

It goes without saying that the presence of
his pamphlet in Erasmus' library is connected with de Coct's stay in Basel and his
activities there. There need not have been
direct contact between the young French
reformer and the humanist. The deepening
religious antagonisms in Basel militated
against such a contact: Erasmus, who had
now put his *De libero arbitrio* on paper,
distanced himself with increasing emphasis
from the reformers, and about June 1524
the dispute with the fanatical Farel, which
led to a complete rupture between the two
men, began.[7] But it is very likely that
Erasmus, who like a spider in its web was
well informed about everything that went
on in his surroundings, found de Coct's

little book in his hands soon after its
publication.

1 Benzing *Lutherbibliographie* no 2005
2 On him see Luther WA *Briefwechsel* III 72 n1;
  Zwingli *Werke* VIII (CR 95) 143 n4; Staehelin BAO I
  272n. Lambert's *Commentarii* had been published
  in 1523 at Strasbourg; Benzing *Lutherbibliographie*
  no 1596.
3 Luther WA *Briefwechsel* III 148–54 (no 657);
  cf Ep 1413:28n/n5.
4 Zwingli *Werke* VIII 142–7 (no 325)
5 Staehelin BAO I 298 n5 and 331 (Ep 228)
6 On Bentinus see Staehelin BAO I 397 Ep 284 n1;
  Ep 1433:2n/n2; CEBR I 123–4.
7 Ep 1510; cf *Catalogus lucubrationum* Allen I
  31:8–17/Ep 1341A:1196–1215 with n305.

49 Zuinglius de sacramen.

Some of Huldrych Zwingli's works on
the sacraments, most probably including

De vera et falsa religione commentarius.
Tiguri: C. Froschauer, March 1525 (octavo).

and

Subsidium sive coronis de Eucharistia.
Tiguri: C. Froschauer, 1525 (quarto).

No work by Zwingli is known under the
title *De sacramentis.* Possibly this heading
groups two or more of the writings in
which the Zürich reformer set out his
opinions on the sacraments, and in
particular on the Eucharist, in 1525–6.
The two works mentioned above are the
most obvious possibilities. The bulky
Commentarius, described by its editor
as the first and also the only systematic
exposition of Zwingli's theology, dealt with
the sacraments in general but went into
great detail on the Eucharist and was the
first statement of Zwingli's mature symbolic view of it.[1] The book came from
the press at the end of March 1525, and
Erasmus must have obtained a copy very
soon, for only two months later Zwingli
was able to relate to a trusted friend what
Erasmus had said of its contents: 'Oh my
good Zwingli, what do you write that

I myself have not written before?' a
pronouncement the reformer set down
to Erasmus' φιλαυτία 'love of self.'[2]

The short *Subsidium* formed a supplement
to the view of the Eucharist in the *Commentarius.* The occasion for its composition
was the debate held in the Council of
Zürich in the spring of 1525 on the
practical reform of communion, in which
the Catholic minority, led by Joachim am
Grüt, was sharply opposed to Zwingli's
symbolic interpretation.[3] In the following
year Zwingli held another disputation
on the question of communion with the
Lutheran Johann Bugenhagen and put his
case in *Ad Joannis Bvgenhagii Pomerani
epistolam responsio* (Zürich: Christoph
Froschauer 1526).[4] In 1530 he formulated
his point of view for the last time in his
Fidei Huldrychi Zwinglij ratio and *De
conuitijs Eccij epistola,* both again published by Froschauer.[5] It is impossible to
establish which of these works may be
concealed behind the general indication
'De sacramentis,' although it seems almost
unthinkable that the fundamental *Commentarius* of 1525 should not have been present
in Erasmus' library. But that book raises
problems because of its format. It was an
octavo edition and for that reason could
not have been bound easily with any of the
other works named, all of them, without
exception, quartos. This difficulty over the
two formats disappears, however, if we
assume that this entry in the *Versandliste*
refers not to a bound volume but to a
number of short books loosely held
together or provisionally sewn together
(cf nos 34, 46, and 47).

1 Finsler *Zwingli-Bibliographie* no 45; Zwingli *Werke*
  III 590–912 (593 for the words cited). See Köhler
  Zwingli und Luther I 80–96.
2 Zwingli *Werke* III 592; VIII 333 Ep 371
3 Finsler *Zwingli-Bibliographie* no 53; Zwingli
  Werke IV 440–504. See Köhler *Zwingli und Luther* I
  99–102.
4 Zwingli *Werke* IV 546–76
5 Zwingli *Werke* VI-2 753–817

50 Varia Erasmi. Enchir.

Possibly Erasmus. *Lucubrationes.*
Argentorati: M. Schürer, September 1515
or one of the other early editions (quarto).

Probably not a volume of writings bound
together with the *Enchiridion militis
christiani* as the principal item, but the
Enchiridion as it was originally published,
that is, not separately under its own name
but preceded by assorted works by Erasmus
under a neutral title. The *Enchiridion* first
appeared in the *Lucubratiunculae aliquot …
perquam utiles adolescentibus* published in
Antwerp by Dirk Martens in February
1503, and was reissued by the same printer
in November 1509.[1] The Strasbourg printer
Matthias Schürer published an expanded
version of the collection in September 1515
under the still shorter title *Lucubrationes.*
The preparation of the text for this edition
was in the hands of Nikolaus Gerbel,
who worked closely with Erasmus and
probably had access to a copy, corrected
by the author, of Martens' 1509 edition of
the *Lucubratiunculae.*[2] The *Lucubrationes*
went into two further unrevised reprints
in June 1516 and November 1517. Among
the *varia Erasmi* from the *editio princeps*
of 1503 onwards were several smaller texts,
including the *De tedio Iesu, De virtute
amplectenda,* and some prayers, with
six poems.[3] The Strasbourg edition of
September 1515 added two further prose
texts, one of which was the *Enarratio in
primum psalmum* with dedicatory preface
addressed to Beatus Rhenanus (Ep 327),
and also doubled the number of poems.[4]
If this collection is meant here – as, since
the adjacent volumes are quartos, the
format seems to indicate – is it not likely
that Erasmus should have kept the most
complete version, the one that had been
prepared with his cooperation, that is,
one of the Schürer editions? Perhaps it
was one of the ten copies of the edition of
September 1515 that Gerbel brought him
fresh from the press on Schürer's behalf.[5]

For other, later, editions see nos 71
and 395.

1 NK 835 and 836. See Epp 93 and 164.
2 Ep 343:6n/7n
3 *De taedio Iesu* was dedicated to John Colet
   (Ep 108); on *De virtute*, written in the form of
   a letter to Adolf of Burgundy, see Ep 93; for the
   poems see Reedijk *Poems* nos 16, 33–7/ASD I-7
   and CWE 85–6 nos 36, 42, 50.
4 Reedijk *Poems* nos 85–90, 92/ASD I-7 and CWE 85–6
   nos 43, 46, 47, 44, 48, 45, 51
5 Ep 352:53–4/58–9

51 Suetonius.

Suetonius Tranquillus, Caius. *XII Caesares.
Sexti Aurelij Victoris … excerpta. Eutropij
de gestis Romanorum lib. x. Pauli Diaconi
lib. VIII ad Eutropij historiam additi.*
Venetiis: aed. Aldi et Andr. Asulani soc.,
August 1516 or May 1521 (octavo).

Besides the three folio editions of
Suetonius that stood next to each other
elsewhere on his bookshelves, Erasmus
also owned the edition listed separately
here because of its different format. It is
impossible to say with any certainty which
edition is referred to. The neighbouring
books are mostly quartos.[1] The *Lives of
the Caesars* (the first twelve emperors from
Julius Caesar to Domitian) had appeared
occasionally in quarto by 1500, in 1471
from N. Jenson in Venice and a few years
later from an unknown printer, probably
either in Venice or Bologna.[2] But would
Erasmus, who was accustomed to dispose
of superfluous books, have kept in his
library until his death an edition that,
besides being so old, had also been superseded, both by one with a commentary by
Filippo Beroaldo (no 262) and by his own
edition of the text in Froben's collection
of *Historiae Augustae scriptores* of 1518
(nos 261 and 263)?

Much later, in 1515, a quarto edition
was published by Matthias Schürer in
Strasbourg.[3] Schürer at that time had
regular personal and business contacts with

Erasmus. He met him in the Strasbourg literary society and travelled in his company from Strasbourg to Frankfurt.[4] He was also responsible for some authorized editions of Erasmus' works, and considered himself eligible for further commissions.[5] It would be wholly understandable if Schürer had sent his friend Erasmus a presentation copy of his edition of Suetonius, to keep their relationship cordial. But one also wonders whether Erasmus would not sooner or later, as was his custom, have disposed of an edition that was an ordinary reprint and did not offer an improved text.

For this item, therefore, we must certainly also consider – even prefer – the edition of Suetonius produced by Giambattista Egnazio and published by the Aldine press in 1516, in spite of its octavo format. Erasmus received a copy of this edition in the summer of 1517.[6] Allen assumed that Ulrich von Hutten, who visited Venice in June 1517, brought it with him in his luggage on his return journey to the north, with its companion volume, Egnazio's own *De caesaribus libri tres*, which included the *Historiae Augustae scriptores* edited by him. The editor had given Hutten a presentation copy of this work intended for Erasmus.[7] Perhaps, but Erasmus was not yet aware of the appearance of Egnazio's *De caesaribus* in August 1517, when the Aldine edition of Suetonius was already on his desk. He could not use Egnazio's Suetonius for the edition of Suetonius' 'xii Caesares' that he himself was preparing at that moment: the text he had edited was practically ready for the press, perhaps already largely set and printed. Erasmus contented himself with inserting a special preface in Froben's 1518 edition, in which he informed the reader of the new Venetian edition and took the opportunity to reject at least some of Egnazio's textual emendations.[8]

The Aldine edition of Suetonius went into a second, augmented impression in 1521,

in which Erasmus' annotations were taken over from the Froben edition published in 1518. It is quite possible that this second edition was in Erasmus' library in 1536, especially if Erasmus' copy of the first edition had served as printer's copy for the epitomes of Aurelius Victor, Eutropius, and Paul the Deacon in the Froben Suetonius / *Historiae Augustae Scriptores* of 1518 (see no 261).

At any rate, Erasmus continued to be interested, even after the appearance of Froben's collection (and possibly with a view to a revised reprint of it), in the latest versions of the two Aldine editions; a few years later he ordered a further copy of the 1519 edition of *De caesaribus* with the *Historiae Augustae scriptores* edited by his friend Egnazio.[9]

Giambattista Cipelli assumed the name of Egnazio when still quite young. He was a pupil of Angelo Poliziano in Florence before he settled permanently in his native city of Venice. There he was an active member of the Aldine literary circle, edited many classical texts for Aldo and after the latter's death for Andrea Torresani, and continued to teach until an advanced age. Erasmus made his acquaintance during his stay in Venice in 1508 and remained friendly with him afterwards.[10] He often sent him copies of his newly published works and must have been able to count on his attentions being reciprocated from time to time by Egnazio.[11]

Egnazio was among the twenty people to whom Erasmus bequeathed in his first will (1527) a set of his *Opera omnia*, which his heirs and executors were to publish.[12]

1 Roughly nos 38–80, with some octavo exceptions
2 Hain-Copinger *15117 and *15113. On the second, BL *Catalogue of Italian Books 1465–1600* reads 'Bologna 1475?'; BN *Catalogue général*, 's.l., n.d. prob. vers. 1472–73.'
3 Ritter *Répertoire bibliographique … de Strasbourg* IV no 2247; repr Lazarus Schürer 1520 (ibidem no 2249)

4 Ep 305:137–47/145–53 and Kristeller 'A
   Little-known Letter of Erasmus'/CWE Ep 326B.
5 *De copia* and *Parabolae* in 1514 (see nos 365 and
   371) and *Lucubratiunculae aliquot* in 1515 (see
   no 50). See also the correspondence with Johann
   Ruser, Epp 606 and 633; Schürer printed Erasmus'
   edition of Curtius Rufus (see no 268 #1).
6 Cf Ep 648:1–3/3–4.
7 Ep 588:55–7/61–2
8 Ep 648 to the reader (probably shortly before 23
   August 1517). Note Erasmus' comment: 'I only
   wish that, having given us Suetonius, Aurelius
   Victor, and Eutropius, he had added Aelius
   Spartianus and the remainder at the same time, in
   whose works I have made many restorations' (lines
   8–11/11–13).
9 Allen VII 547 Appendix 20 'Books Ordered by
   Erasmus'
10 Allen I 55:102–3 (Beatus Rhenanus to Hermann of
   Wied) and 61:161–2 (Beatus Rhenanus to Charles
   V); cf CEBR I 424–5.
11 For example in 1530 his *Epistola contra quosdam
   qui se falso iactant Evangelicos* (Ep 2302:10–11/
   11–12) and in 1533 his edition of St Basil
   (Ep 2871:17–20). The edition of Themisthius
   that Egnazio in 1533 promised to send him on its
   publication (ibidem lines 22–3), does not appear
   in the *Versandliste*.
12 Allen VI Appendix 19 'Erasmus' First Will' 505:96/
   CWE 12 545:90

52 Libertas Christiana.

Luther, Martin. *Epistola Lutheriana ad
Leonem decimum summum pontificem.
Tractatus de libertate Christiana.*
[Wittembergae: J. Grünenberg,] 1520
or one of the reprints (quarto).

A Latin version of the *Von der freyheyt
eynes Christenmenschen*, characterized by
Luther himself as 'a small book, if you
look at the paper, but still containing the
whole sum of a Christian life,' with an
accompanying letter to Pope Leo X.[1] Of
Luther's three sensation-making Reformation works of 1520, *An den christlichen
Adel deutscher Nation, De captivitate
babylonica ecclesiae,* and *De libertate
christiana,* the last is the only one that
appears in the *Versandliste*. Naturally
Erasmus read the other two; in particular
it is difficult to imagine that he did not have

a copy of *De captivitate babylonica ecclesiae,* which appeared to herald Luther's
definitive break with Rome. He repeatedly
expressed in his correspondence his
disappointment and irritation at it.[2]

1 Benzing *Lutherbibliographie* nos 755–63. For
   Luther's description see WA VII 11.
2 For example Epp 1186:7–8/8–10, 1203:24–6/
   29–32, 1218:16/18

53 Luciani Tyrannus.

Lucianus. Possibly *Dialogi duo. Charon
et Tyrannus ... Petro Mosellano interprete.*
Hagenoae: acad. Anshelmiana, October
1518 (quarto).

Lucian's dialogue *Tyrannus* was, so far
as can be ascertained, never published
separately. Possibly this entry refers to
the two dialogues, *Charon* and *Tyrannus,*
edited by Petrus Mosellanus, then active
as lecturer in Greek at the University
of Leipzig.[1] Powerful arguments can
be adduced in favour of this assumption.
In his introduction Mosellanus praised
Erasmus highly for his translations from
Lucian: 'Erasmus has the highest place,
since he has already translated most of
the works of this author.'[2] Moreover, the
book appeared at a time when the Leipzig
humanist was revealing himself in his
words and his writings as one of the most
convinced adherents of Erasmus' ideas.
Erasmus recognized this; in April 1519
he praised Mosellanus' *Oratio de variarum
linguarum cognitione* enthusiastically, since
it expressed so well what he himself was
striving for.[3] If Mosellanus' edition of
Lucian is in fact the one alluded to here,
we must certainly consider the possibility
that it was a presentation copy. He had
very probably sent the printed text of his
lecture as a gift with the letter he wrote
to Erasmus early in January (Ep 911).

1 Benzing *Bibliographie Haguenau* 50
2 ASD I-1 367
3 Ep 948; on the *Oratio* see also no 18 #1.

54 Luterus in Galat.

Luther, Martinus. *In Epistolam S. Pauli ad Galatas commentarius.* [Lipsiae: M. Lotther, 1519] or one of the reprints (quarto); or the revised version [Wittenbergae: J. Grunenberg, August 1523] or one of the reprints (octavo); or the expanded version, Wittenbergae: Hans Lufft or Hagenoae: Peter Braubach, 1535 (octavo).

Luther twice wrote commentaries on the Epistle to the Galatians, a concise version in 1519 and a very detailed one published in 1535. It is doubtful whether Erasmus in the penultimate year of his life was still sufficiently interested in Luther to acquire the completely new version, a thick octavo volume of more than 1,100 pages.[1] It is more likely that Erasmus had in his library the short commentary of 1519, the *editio princeps* of which, a modest little quarto volume of eighty-two folios, appeared at Leipzig from the press of Melchior Lotther; numerous pirated reprints followed both in 1519 and in succeeding years.[2] Erasmus must have read this first edition with special attention and also with some satisfaction, for not only was he mentioned by name twenty times in the text, in references to passages in his *Annotationes* in *Novum Testamentum,*[3] but he was also praised in flattering terms as an exegete – once he was even called *theologicissimus.*[4] The brief commentary on the Epistle to the Galatians was republished in a revised version in octavo in 1523. By then circumstances had changed, and Erasmus' name does not appear.

1 Benzing *Lutherbibliographie* no 3183
2 Ibidem nos 416 (*editio princeps*) and 417 (the reprints)
3 See Augustijn 'Erasmus von Rotterdam im Galatenbriefkommentar Luthers von 1519.' Augustijn found twenty-nine other passages almost certainly based on the *Annotationes,* even though Erasmus' name is not mentioned; see pages 116–17.
4 Maurer *Der junge Melanchthon* II 64

55 Prognostica Alberti Pighij

Pighius Albertus. *Adversus prognosticatorum vulgus qui annuas praedicationes edunt et se astrologos mentiuntur, Astrologiae defensio.* Parisiis: H. Stephanus, 1518 (quarto).

Albert Pigge (c 1490–1542), who came from the town of Kampen in Overijssel, studied at Leuven, where he matriculated in 1507, and later took his doctorate of divinity at Cologne. His teacher of theology at the University of Leuven was Adriaan of Utrecht, who became pope in 1522, and who appointed him chamberlain and counsellor. He held the same confidential position under Clement VII.[1] When Clement wished in 1525 to intervene on behalf of Erasmus, who had been enduring increasingly sharp attacks in Leuven, especially from the Carmelite Nicolaas Baechem of Egmond and the Dominican Vincentius Theoderici, Pigge, although devoted to the humanist, opposed a formal papal brief as too humiliating to the Leuven theologians and wrote instead the official letter admonishing the faculty of theology to compel Erasmus' sharpest critics to moderate their tone (Ep 1589).[2] Pigge had already applied himself to mathematics at Leuven under Jan Driedo, and had won some reputation as an astronomer: he wrote a treatise on the then-current problem of the reform of the calendar, on which Leo X had asked the advice of the University of Leuven. His *Adversus prognosticatorum vulgus* was a pamphlet against a fashionable phenomenon of the time, the annually published popular predictions alleged to be derived from the movements of the stars and planets. He described these as *somnia inanissima* – 'empty dreams' – in contradiction to knowledge based on true astrology, which he defended.[3] M.E. Kronenberg assumed that the word 'Prognostica' referred to another, now lost or untraceable, work by the same author,[4]

but might it not refer to this pamphlet?
Pigge's attack on the 'prognosticators'
(*prognosticatores*), especially the Antwerp
physician Jasper (de) Laet van Borchloon,
a compiler of avidly read almanacs of
predictions,[5] dealt in the broad sense with
portents – *prognostica*. His book, which
had a rather cumbersome title, could easily
be adequately identified by the word
describing its subject.

1 On Pigge see Allen and cwe Ep 1589 introductions; *Dictionnaire de théologie catholique* xii-2
   2094–2104; Godin *Erasme lecteur d'Origène* 544–52;
   and cebr iii 84–5.
2 Cf De Vocht *History of the ctl* ii 268.
3 De Vocht *History of the ctl* ii 545 n2
4 'Albertus Pighius, proost van Sint Jan te Utrecht'
   112
5 Cf no 24 #3 (*Mantia*).

56 Wesselij Farrago Rerum Theolo. cum Apolo.

Gansfort, Wessel. *Farrago rerum theologicarum uberrima emendatio*. Basileae: Adam
Petri, September 1522 or January 1523
(quarto).

A collection of six texts by Wessel Gansfort
(1419–89) was published four times within
the space of one year: at Zwolle by Simon
Corver (quite early in 1522), at Wittenberg
by Melchior Lotther (April 1522) and twice
at Basel by Adam Petri (September 1522
and January 1523). The Zwolle edition
appeared under the title *Farrago … Notulae
aliquot & propositiones*; the three other
editions were entitled *Farrago rerum
theologicarum*. At about the same time as
the *Farrago* the Corver press brought out
a separate volume of *Epistulae* by Wessel,
preceded by a letter of recommendation
from Luther containing the well-known
comment: 'If I had read Wessel earlier
my enemies might think that Luther had
derived everything from him, so closely
do our feelings coincide.'[1]

Erasmus undoubtedly kept in his library
one of the editions of Adam Petri, which

included the letters of Wessel;[2] The Zwolle
edition has a slightly different title, and the
Wittenberg edition lacked the *Epistolae*,
which would have been valuable to him.
Erasmus himself reveals that he not only
owned the *Farrago*, but had also absorbed
its contents. He hardly ever mentioned
Gansfort in his works or letters, but some
years later he quite exceptionally inserted
in his *Epistola ad fratres Inferioris
Germaniae* of 1530 a passage in which he
contrasted Wessel's moderation with the
intemperate behaviour of Luther, Zwingli,
and some of the 'brothers' to whom he was
writing: 'Doctor Wessel has many things in
common with Luther, but how much more
Christian, how much more modest is the
manner in which he states his teachings
than that of many of those men.'[3] Wessel
Gansfort and Rodolphus Agricola, two
well-known scholars of the preceding
generation, were often mentioned together
and met each other in the same circle.
But while Erasmus admired and praised
Agricola, he seems to have more or less
ignored Gansfort. This surely had something to do with his intuitive suspicion
of him. For him Wessel remained, in the
words of Augustijn, 'a meditative theologian, a man of typical late medieval piety,
strongly influenced by the Modern
Devotion.'[4]

The publication history of Wessel's works
in Zwolle and elsewhere has long been
studied in relation to the activities and
travels of Henne Rode, rector of the house
of the Brotherhood of the Common Life at
Utrecht, who was removed from his post in
1522 because of his Lutheran sympathies.
An incoherent, rather chaotic story of the
part he played in the dissemination not
only of Wessel's works but also of a
manuscript text of Cornelis Hoen's *Letter
concerning the Eucharist* was included in
the *Vita Wesseli Groningensis* of Albert
Hardenberg (c 1510–74). He wrote this life
between 1560 and 1565, but it was left in
manuscript on his death and was not

published until forty years later in the first complete edition of Wessel's *Opera* (Utrecht 1614; reprinted at Nieuwkoop in 1966). Hardenberg assumed that Rode had submitted the writings of Wessel, together with Hoen's *Epistola*, in succession to Luther in Wittenberg, to Oecolampadius in Basel, and to Zwingli in Zürich.[5] Thanks to Rode's travels, Hoen's treatise played an important role in the first debates on the Eucharist between Wittenberg and Zürich.

Until recently scholars and experts in the subject did not place much credence in Hardenberg's story. In 1996 the *Vita Wesseli* was rehabilitated to some extent as a source; B.J. Spruyt demonstrated with very thorough documentation the trustworthiness of the main points of Hardenberg's account of Rode's journey. But although the information in the *Vita* may not have been as unreliable as was supposed, most of the original criticism remains valid.

Hardenberg reports that Henne Rode visited Basel, where he is said to have paid his respects to Oecolampadius in January 1522, showing him, besides the writings of Wessel, Hoen's letter on the Eucharist in manuscript. Moreover, Luther had given him a letter addressed to Oecolampadius, asking him for his opinion and encouraging him at the same time to have Wessel's writings printed in Basel. Oecolampadius recognized the importance of Hoen's treatise, but when he learned that Luther disapproved of it he hesitated to express his private opinion and sent Rode with it on to Zwingli in Zürich.

Rode's visit appears to have passed unnoticed in Basel except by the few persons directly involved it. W. Köhler thought that Hoen might possibly have originally intended his *Epistola christiana* for Erasmus, but his argument was based on the assumption, among others, that Zwingli was the editor.[6] More recently, however, bibliographical investigations have shown that the letter was published by the Worms printer Peter Schöffer the Younger in July–August 1525.[7] Trapman has argued that Erasmus became acquainted with Hoen's epistle only through the printed edition (that is, not before 1525).[8] Most probably Erasmus was unaware of Hoen's visit to Basel and was therefore totally ignorant of Hoen's manuscript. He certainly would have disagreed with Hoen, for he never abandoned his belief in Christ's bodily presence in the Eucharist (although in his lifetime Hoen had never done anything that could have led Erasmus to suspect that they held different ideas on the interpretation of the Eucharist, a question still much in dispute).

Erasmus and Hoen were roughly contemporaries. Erasmus may have been the younger; the year of Hoen's birth is unknown but estimated as 1460. Allen thought the report that Hoen had long been a friend of Erasmus was credible; In the words of Spruyt, 'they knew each other, although not personally.' For years they adopted a notably positive attitude to each other. Even before 1499, Erasmus had heard about Hoen, who had recently been attached to the Court of Holland as a lawyer. As such he belonged in The Hague to a circle of lawyers and councillors with outspoken sympathy for Erasmus and his ideas. Ten years later Erasmus received a Diogenes Laertius (no 305) from those humanists, who were still his friends at the time. From a reliable statement it appears that Hoen himself was also favourably disposed to the new learning and had become a fervent student of *bonae litterae*. Erasmus was quickly and fully informed when Hoen was imprisoned at The Hague for a short time early in 1523 on suspicion of heresy, and he stood by him.

The Petri editions may hold the key to another unsolved problem. The *Farrago* is listed in the *Versandliste* with the unspecified addition 'cum Apolo[gia].' Which apology is meant is a matter of guesswork.

We hazard the conjecture that the term 'Apology' may refer to the epilogue added exclusively to the Petri editions of the *Farrago*.[9] The writer, Ulrich Hugwald, a proofreader for the Petri firm, thought highly of Wessel and recommended his works enthusiastically. He saw in him a theologian who vigorously rejected the human traditions, inventions, and regulations in the church, which were, according to the author of the epilogue, the vicious fruits of scholastic theology. He pointed to Wessel as a theologian who taught a middle course, and he depicted him as a biblical humanist, a proto-Erasmus. At the time Hugwald, who later become an Anabaptist, sympathized in many respects with Zwingli, though he was critical of his efforts to carry through a break with bishops and hierarchy. Hugwald and Erasmus were hardly like-minded in their religious attitude, but at the time, 1522, they shared a desire for moderation and shrank from all excessively radical experiments. In short, Erasmus may indeed have read Hugwald's epilogue as an apologia. But this is mere speculation, and it is possible that the addition 'cum Apolo.' has nothing to do with the *Farrago* and refers to some other work of an apologetic character bound with it.

1 WA x-2 317:13–18
2 Erasmus possibly acquired the *Farrago* as a presentation copy from Petri, who had clients in Erasmus' circle.
3 ASD ix-1 405:681–406:683 / CWE 78 349; Wessel Gansfort's name is found neither in the general index in Allen xii nor in the Indices nominum of ASD published up to now.
4 Augustijn 'Wessel Gansfort's Rise to Celebrity' 21
5 Spruyt *Hoen* 5–6
6 Spruyt *Hoen* 173–4; cf Köhler *Huldrych Zwingli* (1952) 175 / (1984) 167.
7 See Spruyt *Hoen* 169–70.
8 See Trapman *De Summa der godliker schrifturen (1523)* 114–15; Spruyt *Hoen* 174, and cf 47.
9 See, for what follows, Augustijn's exposition of Hugwald's epilogue in 'Wessel Gansfort's Rise to Celebrity' 16–20. On Hugwald see also CEBR ii 212–13.

57 Plutarchi opuscula Bud.

Plutarchus. *Ex interpretatione Guillielmi Budei ... tria opuscula.* [Parisiis:] in aed. Ascensianis, 15 May 1505 (quarto).

perhaps bound with

Plutarchus. *De placitis philosophorum libri a Guilielmo Budeo latini facti.* Parisiis: J. Petit ven., J. Badius impr., 18 March 1505/6 (quarto).

The first work that might be described by this entry contained three of Plutarch's treatises translated into Latin by Guillaume Budé: *De tranquillitate animi, De fortuna Romanorum,* and *De fortuna Alexandri.* To these was added Budé's translation of St Basil the Great's letter to Gregory of Nazianzus *de vita per solitudinem transigenda.* Lefèvre d'Etaples introduced the collection in a letter to the translator. Since the entry refers to *opuscula* without limiting them to three, it is possible that the volume also contained Budé's first publication, his translation, issued a little earlier the same year and also printed by Josse Bade, of Plutarch's *De placitis philosophorum.* The assumption that Erasmus acquired the two books soon after their appearance appears entirely plausible. In any case he would have seen and read them very quickly, for he was still in Paris until the end of 1505 and already knew Budé; both men were friends of Fausto Andrelini and pupils of the Greek Georgius Hermonymus.[1] The possibility has even been raised that Erasmus knew the translations earlier, before publication, in manuscript.[2]

1 Renaudet *Préréforme et humanisme* 481–2; Rice 'The Humanist Idea of Christian Antiquity' 144; Rice *Prefatory Epistles* 137–9 Ep 44. The introductory letter of Lefèvre d'Etaples in Budé's translation of Plutarch's tract *De placitis philosophorum* was addressed to Georgius Hermonymus; Rice *Prefatory Epistles* 148–9 Ep 47. Cf Ep 421:25n / 28n.
2 Garanderie *Correspondance* 59 n3

58 Ioan. Chrysosto. Brix.

Joannes Chrysostomus. *In epistolam divi Pauli ad Romanos homiliae octo priores Germano Brixio … interprete.* Basileae: H. Frobenius & N. Episcopius, 1533 (quarto).

Towards the end of August 1526 Erasmus informed his friend Germain de Brie (Brixius) that he had at his disposal seven works in manuscript of Chrysostom (or Pseudo-Chrysostom), namely, homilies or commentaries on some Pauline Epistles and on Acts, among them a commentary on the Epistle to the Romans that he considered genuine.[1] No doubt he was referring to a Greek codex found at Ladenburg castle from the library left by the learned bishop of Worms Johann von Dalberg (d 1503). Probably he had come by the codex partly owing to the intervention of Hieronymus Froben, then twenty-five years old, who in the course of the year had been searching at the castle for manuscripts his father Johann Froben might wish to publish. On Erasmus' recommendation Hieronymus had received permission from the acting administrators of the library to borrow any manuscript.[2] His search at Ladenburg was successful: he returned to Basel with many classic and patristic texts. It is plausible, though not strictly demonstrable, that Hieronymus brought the commentary on the Epistle to the Romans to the notice of Erasmus, who was known to be increasingly interested in the study of Chrysostom at that time. Johann Froben may have instructed Hieronymus to transfer the old codex without more ado to Erasmus.

Three years later, in 1529, Erasmus was actively engaged in seeking out new translators or extant translations, ready to hand and fit for use, for Froben's forthcoming edition of Chrysostom's collected works in Latin (see no 230). He hoped that his intimate friend Conradus Goclenius, professor of Latin in the Collegium Trilingue of Leuven, would be ready to translate the Greek homilies on the Epistle to the Romans or otherwise would persuade willing scholars (he named Frans Cranevelt, Levinus Ammonius, and Nicolaus Clenardus) to do so. To that end the codex, which had been in Erasmus' possession, was transported from Freiburg, his residence since April 1529, to Leuven. The transport of the old codex was carefully arranged by the Froben firm, possibly in cooperation with Bonifacius Amerbach. Nicolaus Episcopius (now a partner) personally delivered it to Goclenius. But Erasmus' plan failed. Goclenius withdrew from the translation of the homilies, and none of the scholars he approached accepted the task, either for lack of time or because of the poor quality of the text and the difficulties presented by the script. By mid-July 1530 Goclenius felt obliged to return the codex to Basel, too late for another translator to be found.[3] Thus the *Opera* of Chrysostom appeared late in 1530 without his commentary on the Epistle to the Romans. The *Opera* were hardly printed when Erasmus sought collaborators in the publication of a supplementary volume in which the homilies, along with some other omissions, could be published.[4]

A year later Erasmus sent a transcript of the codex found at Ladenburg to Brie in Paris (the original remained safe in Basel).[5] Brie accepted the challenge and translated the first eight homilies, based not only on the manuscript but also on the printed text from Gian Matteo Giberti's recent edition of Chrysostom in the original language.[6] The edition of the homilies, which must have been ready for the press by October 1532, included a 'complimentary letter' to Erasmus in which the translator described his struggles with the corrupt text (Ep 2727).[7]

1 Ep 1736:22–8 / 27–35
2 See Epp 1767 (to Theobald Fettich) and 1774 (from Wolfgang of Affenstein, the administrator of the library. On Dalberg and his library, Ep 1774:1n, 19n / n1 and Reedijk 'The Story of a Fallacy.'

3 Epp 2258:6n/n6, 2235:8–9 with 8n/n4 (from
  Amerbach), and 2352:319–29/329–39 (from
  Goclenius)
4 Epp 2359 (to Christoph von Stadion) introductions, 2379:18n/n6 (to Brie)
5 Ep 2258:6n/n6
6 The first three volumes of this edition, which was
  never continued, appeared at Verona (Sabii) in
  1529; see Ep 2340:2n/n2 (from Brie, dated 6 July
  1530). Giberti's version also proved to be corrupt;
  cf Ep 2727:29–30. It is likely that Brie was never
  able to profit from the manuscripts in the Vatican
  library promised to him by Cardinal Agostino
  Trivulzio; cf Allen Epp 2405:37n, 2727:31–4.
7 On Brie see Ep 212:1n/2n; CEBR I 200–2; see also
  no 38 #1.

59 De unitate Eccle.

[Hutten, Ulrich von, ed.] *De unitate
ecclesiae conservanda et schismate quod fuit
inter Henrichum IIII imp. & Gregorium VII
pont. max. cuiusdam eius temporis theologi
liber*. Moguntiae: J. Schoeffer, March 1520
(octavo).

Ulrich von Hutten found the manuscript of
this anti-papal treatise from the investiture
controversy, written by an unknown monk
of Hersfeld in 1086 in defence of the
emperor Henry IV against Pope Gregory VII,
in the library of the abbey of Fulda. He
edited the text with a political intention,
and in his dedicatory letter (probably of
November–December 1519) he tried to
enlist the sympathy of Archduke Ferdinand,
and through him also of Charles V, the
newly elected emperor, in support of his
design to free the German nation from the
yoke of Rome.[1] To champion his cause in
person at the court, he went to the Netherlands in June 1520. In Leuven he first
paid a visit to Erasmus, who wrote to
Melanchthon, 'Hutten is here, and will
leave shortly for Charles' court.'[2] Erasmus
gave him a letter of introduction to Luigi
Marliano, an influential member of the
emperor's council, containing a most
flattering recommendation: 'The bearer of
this letter is Hutten, whose name you will
know as a warrior with a sense of style and

the most warlike of stylists; but he is a very
open-hearted young man and worthy of
your affection, unless I am quite wrong.'[3]
Presumably during his visit Hutten offered
Erasmus his little book, which had just
been published.

1 Benzing *Hutten Bibliographie* no 219. See on this
  tract, which was based on Cyprian's *De unitate
  ecclesiae conservanda*, Zafarana 'Ricerche sul
  "Liber de unitate ecclesiae conservanda."'
2 Ep 1113:36–7/42
3 Ep 1114:10–12/13–16

60 Propugnaculum Ecclesiae Clichto.

Clichtoveus, Jodocus. *Propugnaculum
ecclesiae adversus Lutheranos*. Probably
Coloniae: Petrus Quentel, August 1526
(quarto) or Coloniae: H. Fuchs, September
1526 (octavo).

One of the Cologne editions of Josse
Clichtove's *Propugnaculum* is probably
meant here, as the *editio princeps* (Paris:
S. de Colines 18 May 1526) was in folio.
Although the title names only the Lutherans,
Clichtove openly attacked Erasmus for the
first time in this work.[1] At the end of
book 2 he disputed his opinions on celibacy,
and in the second chapter of book 3, which
dealt with fasts, he also turned against
Erasmus and the Erasmians, 'whom he
regarded as more responsible even than
Luther and the Lutherans for the epicurism
of the time.'[2] Erasmus immediately parried
this onslaught in a short *Appendix de
Scriptis Clithovei* included after the
*Prologus in supputationem calumniarum
Natalis Bedae* (no 378). The apologia he
announced in this 'appendix,' which was
to deal more thoroughly with the criticisms
in Clichtove's *Propugnaculum*, both of his
Encomium matrimonii (1519) and of his
*Epistola apologetica de interdicto esu
carnium* (1522), did not appear for years;
it was finally published in 1532 under the
title *Dilutio eorum quae Iodocus Clithoveus
scripsit adversus declamationem Des.
Erasmu Rot. suasoriam matrimonii*.[3]

1 Massaut *Josse Clichtove* I 436–7; cf nos 23 and 181.
2 Telle *Dilutio* 97 n58
3 The *Dilutio* is not mentioned in the *Versandliste*, but is possibly bound, with its own title-page and signatures, after the octavo edition of the *Declarationes ad censuras Lutetiae* (Basel 1532); see no 377.

61 Carmen uotiuum Erasmj

Erasmus. *Des. Erasmi divae Genovefae praesidio a quartana fabre liberati carmen votivum*. Frib. Brisg.: J. Emmeus, 1532 (quarto).

The only authorized edition of Erasmus' votive hymn to the patron saint of Paris, Ste Geneviève, to whose intercession he had ascribed his recovery from the quartan fever that attacked him in the winter of 1496–7.[1] By writing his poem in honour of the saint many years later, he fulfilled a vow made at the time. Reedijk has explained that a special coincidence of events prompted him to compose the poem. Paris had been threatened in January 1531 in the same way as in January 1497 by the flooding of the Seine, and again, as thirty-four years before, the shrine of Ste Geneviève had been carried in procession to the cathedral of Notre Dame in order to avert another disaster. 'The news of these events may have reached Erasmus in Freiburg and have reminded him of his old vow.'[2]

On his description of the Seine in the poem, which was inspired by Ausonius' *Mosella*, see no 156.

1 Ep 50:3–7/4–8
2 For the dating and background of the *Carmen votivum* see Reedijk *Poems* no 131/ASD I-7 and CWE 85–6 no 88. Cf van der Blom 'Erasmus' "Carmen votivum" ter ere van Ste-Geneviève.'

62 Argumentum in epistolas Paulj.

Erasmus. *Argumenta in omneis epistolas Apostolicas nova*. Lovanii: T. Martinus, November 1518 (quarto).

Erasmus' 'arguments' or introductions to the Epistles form the second part (fols 69–94) of the *Ratio seu methodus compendio perveniendi ad veram theologiam* (Leuven: Dirk Martens, November 1518), which must also have been available separately.[1] While on fol 69a the title reads *Argumenta* …, on fol 71a the title is given in the singular, *Argumentum* …, as is the entry in the *Versandliste*. Erasmus had probably written his Arguments to the Epistles when he was preparing his translation of the New Testament, that is, between 1512 and 1516,[2] although it was only after the encouragement of Bishop Tunstall late in 1518 that he decided to publish them and to include them in the second edition of his *Novum Testamentum*, which was then in preparation.[3] But even before this appeared in 1519 he issued the *Argumenta* separately, in the Martens edition named above, with a dedication to the Benedictine abbot Nicolas de Malaise (Ep 894).

1 See NK 2973 and 861.
2 See Allen and CWE Epp 384, 894 introductions; Brown 'The Date of Erasmus' Latin Translation of the New Testament' 374; de Jonge 'The Relationship of Erasmus' Translation of the New Testament to that of the Pauline Epistles by Lefèvre d'Etaples' 2–3.
3 Ep 886:17–19/18–20

63 Sententi. Textus Magistri Sententiarum.

Petrus Lombardus. *Textus magistri sententiarum in quattuor sectus libros partiales*. Probably a Paris edition c 1510–20 in octavo.

Peter Lombard's *Sentences* (in four books) was the standard manual of Catholic theology in the Middle Ages, only later surpassed by the *Summa theologiae* of Thomas Aquinas.

Of all the scholastic theologians, Peter Lombard was the one for whom Erasmus retained most sympathy.[1] Nevertheless, he had had very little respect for Lombard's main work, which professed to bring together, once and for all, everything connected with the chief subjects of Christian doctrine in order to circumvent disputes. The result was very different, 'for we never find in ths work any resolution of disputes – no deliberation, but rather stormy seas!'[2] As far as can be ascertained, only a few early sixteenth-century French octavo editions of the work bear a title whose opening words (*Textus magistri sententiarum*) parallel the entry in the *Versandliste*. Although the adjacent volumes on the list were almost all quartos, the small format, unusual for the *Sententiae* (which are almost always in folio), lends support to the surmise that we have to do here with one of these French editions.[3] For an early folio edition in Erasmus' library, see no 163.

1 Massaut 'Erasme et Saint Thomas' 584; Margolin 'Duns Scot et Erasme' 96; Christ-von Wedel *Das Nichtwissen bei Erasmus von Rotterdam* 36–8
2 Annotation on Matt 1:19 LB VI 6D / ASD VI-5 78:328–80:335, cited by Massaut (n1 above)
3 For example Paris: N. de Barra 1510 and Paris: J. Petit and F. Regnault 1518; a list of editions from 1468 is given in Goldschmidt *Medieval Texts and Their First Appearance in Print* 16–17.

64 Paulini Episco. Nolani epistolae etc.

Paulinus Nolanus. *Epistolae et poemata.* [Parisiis:] J. Parvus et J. Badius, 24 February 1516 (octavo).

The first partial edition of the extant letters and poems of Paulinus, bishop of Nola (353/4–431), after Prudentius the most important Christian Latin poet of the patristic age. The work was dedicated by the printer Josse Bade to the Dominican humanist Guillaume Petit, the friend of Guillaume Cop. (It was Petit who in 1516, the year of the book's appearance, suggested that Francis I should summon Erasmus to France and appoint him to a college of scholars he was going to establish.)[1] It was undoubtedly to this edition that Erasmus owed his familiarity with the work of Paulinus of Nola, which enabled

him to cast doubt on stylistic grounds on the attribution to the bishop, customary in his day, of a life of Ambrose, which in reality had been written by Paulinus of Milan.[2]

1 On Petit see no 15 n14.
2 In the introduction to his edition of Ambrose (Basel 1527; see nos 149 and 233) where the life is cautiously referred to as *Vita titulo Paulini episcopi ad beatum Augustinum conscripta*; cf Ep 2216:42n / n11.

65 Breuiarium. de laude uirtu. psal.

A breviary

possibly combined with

the texts of pseudo-Augustine appearing in the *Psalterium David bene correctum ... Item Augustinus de laude psalmorum. Item de virtute psalmorum ...* Zwollis: Petrus de Os, November 1486 (quarto)

Examination of the manuscript of the *Versandliste* revealed that there is a full stop after *Breviarium*, which was omitted in the text Husner printed. It is thus highly likely that this item on the list refers to a breviary and one or more other, separate texts. It cannot be proved that the latter are the texts in the Zwolle psalter, but there are arguments supporting a search for the solution to the short title in that direction.

1/ Is there perhaps a breviary in which the texts of the pseudo-Augustine printed with the Zwolle psalter are included? The answer cannot be given with any certainty, but a breviary with the two works could not be found in a sample search, nor were they included in the breviary issued by the printer of that psalter, Pieter de Os, in August 1487, either in folio or in quarto format.[1] The entry may therefore refer to the breviary that accompanied Erasmus throughout the greater part of his life. Could he perhaps have acquired it as a replacement for the one that he lost in early 1499 en route from the castle of Tournehem to Paris?[2]

2/ The words 'de laude uirtu. psal.' seem to be a conflation – understandable to a contemporary – of the titles of two works of Pseudo-Augustine (still attributed to Augustine himself) on the title-page of the Zwolle psalter.[3] So far as can be established (many editions of the psalter have been completely lost), both works were printed only rarely, and except for the edition of the psalter by Pieter de Os, hardly ever in combination.[4]

Why should de Os in Zwolle, and no one else, have published a psalter with these short texts added? The intellectual milieu of the printer might well be the reason. In his *Rosetum exercitiorum spiritualium*, which enjoyed great success among the followers of the *devotio moderna* in Windesheim, Jan Mombaer gave a list of recommended reading in which he mentioned *Tota biblia ... deinde apostolica documenta ... Psalterium potissimum cum explanationibus Augustini, Cassiodori, Hieronymi, et aliorum.*[5] Does not the psalter as de Os printed it in Zwolle correspond exactly to 'the psalter ... with the explanations of Augustine'? The place of printing of a psalter containing these texts cannot be pure coincidence. Zwolle, very near Windesheim, was itself one of the oldest centres of the Modern Devotion, and the publication list of Pieter de Os reflected this. Moreover, Jan Mombaer was probably still active in the monastery at St Agnietenburg near Zwolle in 1486, and he must have known the printer personally; Pieter de Os published his *Rosetum* (under a rather different title and in an abbreviated form) in 1491 and also (under its final title and unabridged) in 1494.[6]

While the abbreviations in this entry on the *Versandliste* might reasonably be taken to refer to the contents of The Zwolle psalter, the difficulty remains that the word *psalterium* is absent from the short title given.

1 GW 5485
2 Ep 95:6/7–8

3 Campbell *Annales* no 539; BL *Catalogue Fifteenth Century* part IX fasc 1 (Holland) 84
4 For editions, separate or otherwise, of the *De virtute psalmorum* see GW 2965, 2967, 3031–8. It is very possible that other editions of these two relatively unimportant works have been lost or overlooked. *De laude psalmorum* appears in several manuscripts (text in PL 40 1135–1138), and also in a Middle Dutch translation under the title *Van den love de psalmen* (information from Dr P.C. Boeren).
5 Debongnie *Jean Mombaer* 328
6 Debongnie *Jean Mombaer* 23–4. See Campbell *Annales* no 715 *Exercitia utilissima* (Zwolle: Pieter de Os, 1491), an octavo (Hain 13994), and no 1224 *Rosetum exercitiorum spiritualium et sacrarum meditationum* n p n d [Zwolle: Pieter de Os] 1494, a folio (Hain *13995). On Mombaer see also nos 387 ##2–3 and 390.

66 Mωriae encomium Eras.

Erasmus. *Moriae encomium.* Probably one of the Froben editions between 1516 and 1532 in quarto or octavo.

There is nothing to show which edition Erasmus chose to keep of the work that most assured his lasting fame. Nor can one build any assumption on the format,[1] since the books which are recorded in this part of the *Versandliste* vary in size. But it is virtually certain that it was not the first edition, published in Paris by Gourmont in 1511, which, as Miller showed from Erasmus' own statements, was not authorized. The work was originally published through the efforts of his friends, and though he was in Paris when it was first printed, it was his protégé Richard Croke who saw the edition through the press. Erasmus complained that the Gourmont edition was set from a faulty and incomplete copy and very badly printed. Not until July 1512 did the first authorized edition appear, from the press of Josse Bade in Paris.[2] Very probably Erasmus kept one of the later authorized Froben editions, as they appeared in more or less definitive form and composition from 1516 on. The edition of 1516 contained not only the latest large newly inserted passage in

the text,[3] but also, for the first time, his
letter to Maarten van Dorp in defence of
the *Moria* (Ep 337).[4] Moreover, it included
the commentary written in part by
Gerardus Listrius and in part by Erasmus
himself.[5] During Erasmus' lifetime five
further editions, none of them radically
revised or expanded, appeared: in 1517,
1519, 1521, 1522, and 1532, of which the
third possibly and the last almost certainly
were corrected by the author himself.[6]
All the Froben editions from 1516 to 1522
included two subsidiary works, which were
'literary analogues … designed to elucidate
and justify the genre and techniques of the
Moria.'[7] The first was Seneca's *De morte
Claudii*, a satiric skit on the apotheosis of
the emperor Claudius, commonly called
the *Apocolocyntosis*, edited with a commentary by Beatus Rhenanus. It has been
suggested that Seneca's satire played an
important role in the genesis of Erasmus'
dialogue *Julius exclusus*.[8] The second was
the *Calvitii laus* by Synesius of Cyrene,
bishop of Ptolemais (c 400) edited in the
original Greek with a commentary by
Beatus Rhenanus and a Latin translation
by John Free. Apart from the book referred
to here, Erasmus also had, in the chest
in which he kept mainly Froben editions
of his own works, a copy of an edition
of the *Moria* from 1517.[9]

1 Until 1521 practically all the eligible editions
  were quartos; after that year, octavos.
2 ASD IV-3 14–16 and 40–2
3 ASD IV-3 30, 46 n138; see also no 75. The 1516 text
  was 17 per cent longer than that of 1511; ASD
  IV-3 29.
4 The letter had already been published in 1515
  in *Jani Damiani Senensis Elegeia* (Basel: Johann
  Froben, August 1515).
5 See ASD IV-3 34–6; Allen and CWE Ep 495 introductions; Gavin and Walsh 'The *Praise of Folly* in
  Context: the Commentary of Gerardus Listrius.'
6 For details on all the early editions of the *Moria*
  see ASD IV-3 29–33 and 40–64. The 1532 edition
  was chosen as the basic text for ASD.
7 ASD IV-3 26
8 Colish 'Seneca's *Apocolocyntosis* as a possible
  source for Erasmus' *Julius Exclusus*'
9 *Catalogus librorum Erasmi* no 61

67 Epist. Plinij

Plinius Caecilius Secundus, Gaius.
*Epistolarum libri decem … Eiusdem
Panegyricus Traiano imp. dictus. Eiusdem
de viris illustribus in re militari et in admin-
istranda Rep. Suetonii Tranquilli de claris
grammaticis et rhetoribus. Julii Obsequentis
Prodigiorum liber*. Venetiis: Aldus et A.
Asulanus Socor, 1508 or reprint of 1518
(octavo).

The letters of Pliny the Younger (61–113)
were edited many times during Erasmus'
life (the *editio princeps* appeared in 1471),
but Aldo Manuzio published the first
complete edition in 1508. It seems most
probable that this is the edition meant here.
When the book was in the press, Erasmus
was living in Venice, was a guest in
Manuzio's household, and cooperated
closely in the work of the printing-house.
He would have known that Aldo had the
use of a manuscript then supposed to go
back to Pliny's own time (though we now
date it around the year 500), from which
he was printing the letters complete for
the first time – the famous codex from
St Victor's in Paris, of which six leaves
still survive in the Pierpont Morgan
Library in New York.[1] It is hard to con-
ceive that he would not have got his hands
on a copy of the new edition as soon as he
could: he was already interested in letter-
writing as a genre, and this was a publication that he valued highly. When, in the
same year, he wants to praise Aldo in the
new edition of his *Adagia* for his merits in
making the original texts of the classics
available, unabridged and freed from errors,
he chose this edition of Pliny's letters as
an example: he suggests that a comparison
between Aldo's text of the letters, which
will shortly be appearing from the press
and of which he has apparently seen
something already, and the current editions
will show the great difference.[2] About 1519
Erasmus presented a copy of Aldo's 1508
edition of the letters to the young

Ludovicus Carinus (later for some time a member of Erasmus' household in Basel)[3] with an inscription in his own hand (Ep 1034). Had he had two copies of it at his disposal until that moment, or did he possess the 1508 edition and give it away as a present after receiving the second Aldine edition of 1518? The latter is perhaps the more probable. The presentation copy was in private hands when Allen published the letter.[4]

1 For this information I am greatly indebted to R.A.B. Mynors. See his edition of Pliny *Epistularum libri decem* vi.
2 *Adagia* II i 1: *Festina lente* 'Make haste slowly' ASD II-3 18:259–62/CWE 33 10
3 On him Allen and CWE Ep 920 introductions; CEBR I 266–8. Carinus is one of the interlocutors in the colloquy *Convivium poeticum* ASD I-3 344–59/CWE 39 390–418.
4 Allen notes in his introduction that at one time the book belonged 'to the late Mr George Dunn of Wooley Hall, near Maidenhead.' Its present location is unknown.

68 Pomeranica Commenta. in Psalmos

Bugenhagius, Joannes. *In librum Psalmorum interpretatio*. Basileae: Adam Petri, March (or revised edition August) 1524 (octavo). Or one of the pirate editions of the same year.

The publication of the Psalms with comments by Johann Bugenhagen (1485–1558), sometimes described as a 'monument to Lutheranism,'[1] was dedicated to Elector Frederick of Saxony and introduced in forewords by Luther and Melanchthon.[2] Luther praised his supporter extravagantly as the first man in the world who deserved to be called a commentator on the book of Psalms.[3] Erasmus also must have rated the work at its true value. In January 1525 he made the point to the members of the Basel town council that if they wished to prevent the printing of Lutheran doctrines, then commentaries that were otherwise of value but incorporated those doctrines here and there could not be allowed to appear, and he mentioned 'Pomeranus' as an

instance.[4] Five years later, when he was writing his own commentary on Psalm 85, he declared that Hilary and Bugenhagen had come into his mind again and again, 'not that I totally trust writers of this sort, but any chance encounter may make a wise man wiser.'[5] Though there is no evidence of direct contact between the two men, Bugenhagen was kindly disposed towards Erasmus for a long time, longer at any rate than his teacher and friend Luther. Indeed Erasmus' influence on his theological way of thinking is beyond doubt.[6]

1 Köhler *Zwingli und Luther* I 355
2 Benzing *Lutherbibliographie* nos 1862 and 1864
3 WA XV 3
4 Ep 1539:77 with n/80 with n3. Bugenhagen was born in Wollin, Pommerania. See on him CEBR I 218.
5 Epp 2315:149–55/2312A:156–61. Erasmus' *Interpretatio in psalmum 85* (Basel: Johann Herwagen and Hieronymus Froben 1528) is not on the *Versandliste*.
6 Staehelin BAO I 319; Holfelder *Tentatio et consolatio* 112–19 and 143

69 Supputationes errorum

Erasmus. *Supputationes errorum in censuris Natalis Bedae*. Basileae: J. Frobenius, March 1527 (octavo).

The only edition of this more detailed elaboration and continuation of the hastily written *Prologus in supputationem calumniarium Natalis Bedae*, published the preceding year (no 378). It also contains at the end four pages with corrections to Erasmus' New Testament *Paraphrases*.[1]

1 Cf Ep 2095:70–1n/n9.

70 Longolij orationes, epistulae etc

Longolius, Christophorus. *Orationes duae pro defensione sua in crimen lesae majestatis... Oratio ad Luterianos. Epistolarum libri quatuor. Bembus et Sadoletus, Epistolarum liber unus. Longolii vita ... ab ipsius amicissimo quodam* [Reginald Pole?]. Florentiae: haer. P. Juntae, 1524 (quarto).

A presentation copy of the original edition of Christoph de Longueil's complete works, which Thomas Lupset gave to Karl Harst in Padua on 23 August 1525 and Erasmus must have received about 21 September.[1] Lupset was at that time the tutor of Reginald Pole, the younger friend and patron of the impoverished Christoph de Longueil, who was for a time a member of Pole's household and died there 11 September 1522. Pole also wrote the biography of Longueil for this posthumous edition.[2] Christoph de Longueil (c 1488–1522), born in Brabant but educated in France and French in his sympathies, went to Rome in 1517, where he studied under Marcus Musurus and Janus Lascaris and was recognized as a convinced Ciceronian in the circle of Bembo and Sadoleto.[3] Erasmus' direct contact with him dates from the beginning of 1519. Shortly before, he had written very highly of him to Paolo Bombace: if he was not mistaken, Longeuil was 'one of those ... who will one day put the name of Erasmus in the shade.'[4] In October 1519 Longueil was his guest for two days at Leuven.[5] But even then their relationship was troubled by a letter Longeuil wrote to the dean of Orléans in late January, in which he questioned why Francis I preferred to appoint Erasmus to the Collège de France rather than Budé – that is, a German rather than a Gaul. In his comparison, Erasmus came off rather less well than Budé. Erasmus, to whom the letter was communicated very soon afterwards, threw oil on the fire by publishing it unchanged, without previous discussion with the author, in the new edition of his correspondence, the *Farrago nova epistolarum* of October 1519.[6]

Longeuil did not forgive him for this, and in his letters of the following year repeatedly directed caustic remarks at Erasmus.[7] The posthumous edition of Longueil's works, in which these letters were included, was thus bound to irritate Erasmus. He took his revenge in his *Ciceronianus*

(no 352 #1). Contemporaries took the figure of Nosoponus in this dialogue as a caricature of Longueil.[8] For Erasmus, Longueil was the prototype of the Ciceronian in the pejorative sense, someone who took Cicero as his yardstick in everything but in his own work achieved no more than an external imitation: 'for what he has written so far has not contributed much to learning, unless we count the elegant gloss of his style.'[9]

Acquaintance with Longueil's posthumously published works influenced Erasmus' opinion in a favourable sense with regard to another Ciceronian. The letters of Pietro Bembo, which were included in the volume, were a revelation to Erasmus: 'I began to esteem and admire Bembo with greater intensity after I read the letters published by Longueil.'[10]

1 Epp 1595:130–2 / 140–2, 1575:7n / n2. On Harst, who acted as a messenger for Erasmus, going to Rome for him in August 1525, see Allen and CWE Ep 1215 introductions; CEBR II 165–6.
2 On Pole see Allen and CWE Ep 1627 introductions; CEBR III 103–5. Pole's authorship of the life of Longueil has been disputed; see Parks 'Did Pole write the *Vita Longolii*?' and Vos 'The *Vita Longolii*: Additional Considerations about Reginald Pole's Authorship.'
3 On him see Becker *Christophe de Longueil*; Allen and CWE Ep 914 introductions; Ep 1675:13–24 and 13n / 15–25 and n7; CEBR II 342–5.
4 Ep 905:19–22 / 21–4
5 Epp 1026:4–5 / 5–6, 1029:25–6 / 29
6 Ep 914; for Erasmus' reaction to the letter see Ep 935 to Longueil.
7 See Becker *Christoph de Longueil* for examples.
8 Allen and CWE Ep 914 introductions; Allen Ep 2632:196n. On Longueil as the model for Nosoponus, see also CWE 28 329–30 and (a differing opinion) Garanderie *Correspondance* 251 n4.
9 Ep 2329:108–10 / 107–8
10 Ep 2059:16–19 / 18–20

71 Enchir. Institu. prin. et reli. eras.

Erasmus. *Enchiridion militis christiani ... Cui accessit nova mireque utilis praefatio et Basilij in Esaiam commentariolus. Cum alijs ...* Basileae: J. Frobenius, July 1518 (quarto).

bound with

Erasmus. *Institutio principis christiani ... recognita cum alijs nonnullis eodem pertinentibus.* Basileae: J. Frobenius, July 1518 (quarto).

This abbreviated entry presumably refers to the two editions named, which not only appeared from the same press in the same month of the same year, but also contained the more or less definitive texts of both works. By 'reli[qua] eras[mi]' is meant the smaller works of Erasmus that are not specified on the title-page but announced as 'some others.'

1/ The first Froben edition of the *Enchiridion militis christiani* was in fact a reissue of the *Lucubrationes* published in September 1515 by Matthias Schürer in Strasbourg (see no 50), but now under the title of the main work included in it, the *Enchiridion militis christiani.* The edition also included two poems and St Basil's *In Esaiam commentariolus,* translated from Greek by Erasmus.[1] Also new was the lengthy and extremely important letter (Ep 858) to Paul Volz (1480–1544), abbot of the Benedictine monastery of Hügshofen near Schlettstadt (Sélestat), which was included in all the later editions.

2/ The second authorized and improved edition of the *Institutio principis christiani,* the base text for all the following editions.[2] Besides the main work, dedicated to prince Charles (Ep 393) and now as well to Chancellor Jean Le Sauvage (Ep 853), the book also included 'other things' (*alia nonnulla*), such as the *Panegyricus ad Philippum,* Isocrates' *De institutione principis,* and Plutarch's *Libellus saluberrimis praeceptis refertus,* two related works that Erasmus translated from Greek.[3]

1 Reedijk *Poems* nos 22 and 36 / ASD I-7 and
  CWE 85–6 nos 1 and 50:157–80. The translation
  of Basil's commentary on Isaiah was dedicated
  to John Fisher; see Ep 229.
2 ASD IV-1 100–1

3 The *editio princeps* of the *Panegyricus* was published by Dirk Martens in 1504 (NK 837). The two translations had already appeared in the *editio princeps* of the *Institutio* (Basel: J. Froben, May 1516).

72 Diomedes de arte grammatica

Diomedes. *De arte grammatica opus utilissimum.* Probably a Paris edition in quarto.

The *Ars grammatica* of Diomedes (fourth century) dealt in three books with the eight parts of speech, the basic concepts of grammar, and metrics; the last book incorporated extracts from Suetonius' lost *De poetis.* In his *De ratione studii,* published in 1511–12 but already written in its first form in 1496–8, Erasmus called him the most important of the older Latin grammarians.[1] So far as his working copy of the book is concerned, the surrounding volumes point to a quarto edition. Very few quarto versions of the *Ars grammatica* can be traced, and the three most eligible all appeared in Paris: the oldest from Ulrich Gehring in c 1480, the two others from Jean Petit (printed by Thielman Kerver) in 1498 and Jean Marchand in 1507. It is possible that Erasmus acquired one of the fifteenth-century editions during his earliest residence in the French capital, or that he bought the Marchand edition in the first years of his return from Italy when he was beginning to expand his library and must have ordered books from Paris.[2] The two identical editions of 1498 and 1507, like virtually all the early editions, also contained other grammatical works: Phocas and Priscian on the noun and the verb, Flavius and Agroecius on orthography, as well as Aelius Donatus' *De octo partibus orationis* and the commentaries on his grammar by Marius Servius Honoratus and Sergius.[3]

1 ASD I-2 114:14 and 117:4 / CWE 24 667, 670. On the
  development of *De ratione studii* see ASD I-2 85–7 /
  CWE 24 662.

2 It was not until then that Erasmus began to enlarge his still modest library. The number of identifiable Paris editions published between 1505 and 1515, especially in 1510 and 1511, on the *Versandliste* bears witness to these purchases.
3 For the contents, see GW 8405. Servius and Sergius are the same (a fourth-century grammarian noted for his commentaries on Virgil); see *Der Kleine Pauly* v 145–6 and OCD 1395–6 sv Servius.

73 Bayfius de re uestiaria. Libanij decla.

Bayfius (Baïf), Lazarus. *Annotationum in 1. vestis, ff. de auro & argento leg., seu de re vestiaria.* Basileae: J. Bebelius, 1526 (quarto).

possibly bound with

Libanius. *Declamatiunculae aliquot graecae, eaedemque latinae per Des. Erasmum. Cum duabus orationibus Lysiae itidem versis, incerto interprete, et aliis nonnullis.* Basileae: J. Frobenius, 1522 (quarto).

1/ The *editio princeps* of Lazare de Baïf's treatise on the clothing of the ancients, which took the form of notes on a chapter in book 34 of the *Digests, De re vestiaria.* Lazare Baïf, a Frenchman by birth, went to Italy as a young man and studied Greek at the same time as Christoph de Longueil under Janus Lascaris at Rome. Later he entered the service of Cardinal Jean of Lorraine, and from 1529 to 1534 he was French ambassador to Venice. He corresponded with such men as Bembo and Sadoleto, and his residence in Venice was a meeting place for artists and scholars.[1] It is virtually certain that the book in question here was a presentation copy. Erasmus had known for a long time that the book was in the press: in August 1524 he wrote to Haio Herman that he was delighted that Baïf had done for clothing what Budé had done for the coinage in his *De asse.* There had also been some indirect contact between the two men on the subject. Baïf had ventured to dispute Erasmus' translation of χλαῖναν by *penulam* in *Adagia* I x 100, and of ἀναξυρίδα by *subligaculum* in *Adagia* III iv 52. Erasmus took the criticism in good

part and immediately acknowledged that Baïf was in the right over χλαῖναν; in the letter to Haio he promised to correct the translation as soon as he had seen a copy of Baïf's book. In the edition of the *Adagia* of 1526, he carried out his promise, a month before the *De re vestiaria* appeared, although he must have been aware of its progress.[2] His high opinion of the work was also expressed in the laudatory mention he made of it in his *Ciceronianus.*[3] His reading of the treatise also left traces in his *Colloquies*: subjects Baïf had discussed were raised by Cornelia in the dialogue 'The Council of Women' (*Senatulus sive Γυναικοσυνέδριον*) which appeared for the first time in the 1529 edition.[4] And finally, Baïf's remark on the translation of ἀναξυρίδα prompted him to insert a supplementary item in the last revised edition of the *Adagia* (1533).[5]

2/ These three declamations on subjects derived from the Greek heroic legends were Erasmus' first essays in translation from Greek. The manuscript from which his texts were taken has not been identified, but it was evidently a recent transcript of a very ordinary kind.[6] The translations, which he had dedicated in 1503 to Nicolas Ruistre, bishop of Arras and chancellor of the University of Leuven, first appeared, with the Greek text and the original dedicatory letter (Ep 177), in 1519, printed by Dirk Martens at Leuven.[7] The name of Libanius did not appear on the title-page on that occasion. It did appear in the second Basel edition (Johann Froben, 1522), perhaps the one meant here, which also contained two of Erasmus' previously published translations from Greek (Isocrates' *Ad Nicoclem regem de institutione principis* and Lucian's dialogues *Tyrannicida* and *Abdicatus*) and Isocrates' *Oratio gravissima ad populum Atheniensem de bello fugiendo et pace servanda* in the version by Petrus Mosellanus. In all these works the Greek text was printed alongside the translation.

1 On Baïf see Allen and CWE Ep 1962 introductions;
  CEBR I 87–8.
2 Ep 1479:4–18/6–21
3 ASD I-2 674:11–14/CWE 28 421
4 Cf ASD I-3 13; CWE 40 905–6.
5 Ep 1479:10n/n6; *Adagia* III iv 52 ASD II-5
  266:602–7 with n (267)/CWE 35 34
6 ASD I-1 177
7 NK 1367. Erasmus offered his versions in a fair
  autograph copy to Ruistre, whose coat of arms
  was painted at the beginning by a professional
  illuminator; the presentation copy has survived
  and since 1657 has been at Trinity College,
  Cambridge (MS R.9.26).

74 Rex Angliae contra Lute.

Henry VIII. *Literarum quibus … Henricus
VIII Rex Angliae respondit ad quandam
epistolam Martini Lutheri ad se missam,
et ipsius lutheranae quoque epistolae
exemplum.* Londini: Richard Pynson,
2 December 1526 (octavo).

The reply of Henry VIII to a letter from
Luther dated 1 September 1525, which is
also printed in the book. The first edition
was published 2 December 1526 by the
London printer Richard Pynson.[1] It has
been suggested that this edition was preceded
by an 'original' one in large octavo, without
place, date, or printer,[2] but in fact this
description fits the Rome edition of 1543,[3]
of which there are still extant copies.[4] The
1526 edition was distributed by the king
among his friends and sympathizers; Duke
George of Saxony, for example, received
a copy.[5] Late in December, the duke in his
turn had his secretary, Hieronymus Emser,
send a copy to Erasmus;[6] it may have been
the duke's own copy, just received from the
king, for on December 25 he can hardly
have had at his disposal in Dresden a copy
of the edition just published in London.
In his *Antwort* to Henry VIII (Wittenberg
1527),[7] Luther accused Erasmus, as the
king's 'best friend,' of having assisted in
drafting his letter. Allen sees no reason
for this suspicion.[8]

1 WA *Briefwechsel* III 562–5 Ep 914; Benzing
  Lutherbibliographie no 2391

2 See WA XXIII 18 and WA *Briefwechsel* III 562.
3 Benzing *Lutherbibliographie* no 2400, in quarto
4 WA Briefwechsel XII 70
5 WA XXIII 18
6 Epp 1773:16–17/17–18, 1776:41–3/46–7
  (from Duke George)
7 Benzing *Lutherbibliographie* nos 2408–10
8 Ep 1773:17n; cf CWE Ep 1773 n7.

75 Linacrus de emendata struc. lati.

Linacre, Thomas. *De emendata structura
latini sermonis libri sex.* Londini: Richard
Pynson, December 1524 (quarto).

The Englishman Thomas Linacre (c 1460–
1524), humanist scholar and physician
(from 1508 court physician to Henry VIII),
was in contact with Erasmus for many
years. His reputation as a grammarian
was based on this Latin syntax, which was
reprinted many times and was regarded
into the seventeenth century as a standard
work.[1] Since he made 'honourable mention'
of Erasmus (as Vives wrote to him) in the
book,[2] Linacre must have considered
presenting him with a copy, but we cannot
prove that one was sent. Three years after
the book was published Erasmus received
a copy from Richard Sparcheford, chaplain
to Bishop Cuthbert Tunstall, with whom,
to judge by his letters, he was on very
friendly terms. In return he sent Sparcheford
one of his recent editions of Chrysostom.[3]
Though Erasmus had a high opinion of
Linacre as a versatile scholar, in 1516 he
added a passage to the *Moria* that was
probably intended to mock, gently, his
grammatical fanaticism.[4]

1 STC 15634. On Linacre see Ep 118:23n/27n;
  Linacre Studies; CEBR II 331–2. On his grammar,
  see in particular Thomson 'Linacre's Latin
  Grammars' 31–2; Barber 'Thomas Linacre:
  A Bibliographical Survey of His Works' 363–4.
  Cf Welti *Der Basler Buchdruck und Britannien* 124.
2 Ep 1513:34–6 with 35n/42–5 with n15
3 Ep 1867. On Sparcheford see Ep 644 introductions; CEBR III 269.
4 Ep 868:62–75/70–84; *Moria* ASD IV-3 46 n138
  and 140:270–83/CWE 27 123

76 Leonicj Opuscula uaria

Leonicus, Nicolaus. *Opuscula nuper in lucem aedita.* Venetiis: Bernardinus Vitalis, 1525 (quarto).

Niccolò Leonico Tomeo (1456–1531), pupil of the Greek scholar Demetrius Chalcondyles, taught philosophy for many years in Padua, where he held the professorship from 1497 till 1504. In 1504 he moved to Venice; later on he returned to Padua, teaching there continuously until his death.[1] Leonico was held in great respect. Sandys said of him that he 'opened a new era in the scholarly study of Aristotle,' though Erasmus called him also 'well trained in Platonic philosophy.'[2] He was a friend of Pietro Bembo, and made contact with Budé through Longueil as intermediary.[3]

He maintained friendly relationships with his many English pupils, all of them also friends of Erasmus: William Latimer, for instance, and Cuthbert Tunstall, Thomas Linacre, Richard Pace, and Reginald Pole; several of his works are dedicated to them.[4] In March 1526 Erasmus mentioned in a letter to Pole that 'Longueil and Leonico are on sale here,'[5] that is to say, are available in the bookshops in Basel; by 'Leonico' he may mean, beside the *Dialogi* published in 1524 (no 366), the *Opuscula nuper in lucem aedita.* This volume contained his translation and exposition of some smaller writings of Aristotle and also, in his own translation, Proclus' *Explicatio Platonis ex Timaeo ubi de animorum generatione agitur.* It has been assumed that when he was living in Venice in 1508 Erasmus must have known Leonico.[6] Yet, even in his sorrowful mention of the philosopher's death, he never claimed to have met him.[7]

1 On Leonico see Ep 1479:180n/70n; CEBR II 323–4.
2 *A History of Classical Scholarship* II 110; Ep 2443:388–9/385–6. Bembo also regarded him as a Platonist.
3 Aulotte *Amyot et Plutarque* 30 n4
4 On Linacre cf no 75; on Pace, no 30 #2. See also, for example, nos 309 (dedicated to Tunstall) and 366 (dedicated to Pole).

5 Ep 1675:13/15
6 Ep 2443:388n/n55
7 Ep 2526:18–21

77 Esaias Ecolamp.

Oecolampadius Johannes. *In Iesaiam prophetam hypomnematωn, hoc est commentariorum ... libri VI.* Basileae: A. Cratander, March 1525 (quarto).

Oecolampadius' commentary on Isaiah, in which the text was included, was dedicated to the Town Council of Basel. The index was compiled by Conradus Pellicanus.[1] While the book was still with the printer, Erasmus, alarmed by what he had heard about it and anxious to distance himself from the Reformation party, complained to Oecolampadius that he referred in his foreword to 'our friend the great Erasmus.'[2] In the dedication to the council as it was finally printed, these words do not occur, and Erasmus is only mentioned in a more neutral sense as the 'the great high-priest of fine literature' who had conferred lustre on Basel. It may be deduced from this either that Oecolampadius responded to the complaint and made an alteration in the final revision of the text or that Erasmus was wrongly informed.

1 Staehelin BAO I 346–52 (Ep 241), 357
2 Ep 1538:8–9 with n, 40n/11–12 with nn1 and 3

78 Geor. Agricolae de pond. et mens.

Agricola, Georgius. *Libri quinque de mensuris et ponderibus.* Basileae: ex officina Frobeniana, August 1533 (quarto).

Erasmus was directly concerned with the publication of two works by Georgius Agricola, first of the *Bermannus sive de re metallica,* the well-known essay in dialogue form on mining and more particularly on the silver mines of Joachimsthal in Bohemia, anticipating his posthumously published *De re metallica libri XXII* (1556), and secondly of the work meant here on the weights and measures of the Greeks and Romans. Erasmus had recommended to Froben the publication of the *Bermannus* at the request of Agricola's friend Petrus Plateanus, rector at the time of the town school of Joachimsthal,[1] and had moreover written an introductory letter for it (Ep 2274). Though he must have received a presentation copy, this small book, published by Froben in 1530, does not figure in the *Versandliste*. Erasmus also showed interest in the work on the weights and measures of antiquity. In 1531, having learned that Agricola was at work on it, he wrote that he would like to read the manuscript as soon as it could be sent to him and predicted that the book would greatly enhance its author's reputation.[2] Petrus Plateanus called on him in March 1533, no doubt in connection with the publication. Through a misunderstanding, Erasmus did not see a manuscript copy, but six weeks later he informed a friend that the book in which Agricola 'acutely establishes many points contrary to the opinion of Guillaume Budé, Leonardo de Porto, and Andrea Alciati' was now in the press.[3] There are indications, albeit only indirect ones, that long before these contacts Agricola had visited Erasmus in Basel in the autumn of 1523.[4]

1 Ep 2216:5–10 / 5–10
2 Ep 2529:20–2
3 Epp 2782:1–2 (to Georgius Agricola), 2803:39–43 (to Johannes Agricola)
4 Wilsdorf 'Agricola in Italien und seine persönlichen Beziehungen zur angelsächsischen Welt' 232

79 Varia Erasmi. Libel. nouus etc.

Erasmus. *Libellus novus et elegans De pueris statim ac liberaliter instituendis, cum alijs compluribus.* Basileae: H. Frobenius, J. Hervagius & N. Episcopius, September 1529 (quarto).

Most probably 'various works of Erasmus,' although named rather strikingly at the head of the short title in the *Versandliste,* do not refer to separate works bound with

the *De pueris instituendis* in a single volume but to the many smaller works that were included in the published version of the educational treatise itself and announced on the title-page as 'several other works' (*alia complura*). They are: *De ratione studii, Concio de puero Iesu, Encomium matrimonii, Declamatio in laudem medicinae, Querela pacis, Virginis et martyris comparatio, Epistola consolatoria in adversis, De contemptu mundi epistola, Liturgia virginis Lauretanae*, and two texts of Ambrose, *Apologia David* and *De David interpellatione*.[1] The book was dedicated to the young Duke William of Cleves (Epp 2189 and 2190), a homage that earned Erasmus a silver cup crowned by a figure of Fortune, which he was to bequeath to Conradus Goclenius.[2]

1 On *De pueris* see especially Margolin's edition of the text with translation and commentary and his edition with introduction in ASD I-2 1–78.
2 Ep 2234:15–18 with 15n / 17–20 with n4 (from Duke William); cf Allen XI Appendix 25 'Erasmus' Last Will' 364:35–6.

80 Natural. Senecae Quaesti. lib. 7.

Seneca, Lucius Annaeus. *Naturalium quaestionum libri VII. Matthaeus Fortunatus, In easdem libros annotationes.* Venetiis: aed. Aldi et Andreae Asulani soc., February 1523 (quarto).

Not much more is known of the editor Matthaeus Fortunatus than that he was a member of the Hungarian embassy to Venice and Rome in 1522 led by István Brodarics (Stephanus Brodericus). En route, during a two-month stop at Padua, he prepared his edition of the *Quaestiones naturales*. In it he used old manuscripts that enabled him to make a considerable improvement on the less soundly based text in Erasmus' 1515 edition of Seneca. In spite of the critical remarks directed against him, Erasmus had a high opinion of the work of Fortunatus: 'I am delighted to learn that that distinguished Hungarian scholar has removed so many errors from the *Naturales quaestiones* of Seneca.'[1] And he praised Fortunatus generously for his work in the lengthy introduction to his revised edition of Seneca's *Opera* (Basel 1529): ' In this I have benefited greatly from the devoted labours of Matthaeus Fortunatus of Hungary, who, as the evidence shows, is a man of precise learning, great industry, and sound and sober judgment. He produced a meticulous edition of the *Naturales quaestiones*; I only wish he had done the same for all the rest. In most cases I have been glad to follow him, though sometimes I disagree, especially where I have found support for my interpretation in the manuscripts.'[2]

1 Ep 1479:89–90/102–4; on Fortunatus see 89n/n43; CEBR II 45–6.
2 Ep 2091:102–8/108–15

81 Tragoediae Senecae.

Seneca, Lucius Annaeus. *Tragoediae.* Possibly Parisiis: in aed. Ascensianis, 7 March 1512 or Venetiis: in aed. Aldi et Andreae soceri, 1517 (octavo).

It is difficult to determine which edition of Seneca's tragedies is meant here. Erasmus had himself worked on the *Tragoediae* during his stay at Venice and had made many improvements to the text, 'not without the help of ancient codices.' On his return from Italy he had gone through the tragedies again in England and then handed over the emended text to Josse Bade, who gratefully accepted the results of his textual criticism.[1] Bade incorporated them with material from other sources in a new edition, *Tragoediae, pristinae integritati restitutae per exactissimi judicii viros*, published in 1514. The title-page mentioned the name of Erasmus, but jointly and in equal rank with those of the other text editors and commentators.[2] Erasmus was probably not greatly pleased with the way in which his work had been absorbed, and later he let it be known that Bade had

acted entirely without his knowledge in mixing his material with other people's.[3] The edition of 1514 was probably not – although it may have been at one time – in Erasmus' library in 1536: it was a folio volume, which would not have fit well with the works in smaller formats recorded in this section of the *Versandliste*. Then which edition did he own at the end of his life? Apart from a pair of French quartos editions published before 1500,[4] only three octavo editions appear eligible for consideration: that of Filippo Giunta (Florence 1506); the edition of Josse Bade jointly with R. de Keysere (Paris and Ghent 7 March 1512, probably based on the Giunta edition)[5] and the 1517 Aldine edition published in Venice.[6] It may have been the 1512 edition of Bade, who was Erasmus' main supplier of books from Paris at the time,[7] or the Venice edition; in 1517 Andrea Torresani was making an effort to win commissions from Erasmus for the Aldine press.[8]

1 *Catalogus lucubrationum* Allen I 13:6–11/ Ep 1341A:443–9, Ep 263:10–17/13–21
2 D. Erasmus, Gerardus Vercellanus, and Aegifius Maserius, text editors and G. Bernardinus Marmita, Daniel Gaietanus and J. Bade, commentators. See Moreau *Inventaire* II 280 (1514 no 967).
3 *Catalogus lucubrationum* Allen I 13:11/ Ep 1341A:448–9
4 Paris, between 1485 and 1489 (Hain-Copinger 14671) and Lyon 1491 (Hain *14665)
5 See Moreau *Inventaire* II 159 (1512 no 450). This edition is not to be confused with Bade's edition of 1514.
6 On another Paris edition printed by Jean Marchand for Jean Petit, *Decem tragediae* ed Gilles de Maizieres (5 February 1511), see Moreau *Inventaire* II 103; cf Ep 263:11n/15n. It can be left out of account because it was in folio.
7 Cf no 72 with n2.
8 Ep 589:30–53/31–56; cf no 83.

82 Vergilius

Vergilius Maro, Publius. *Opera.* Possibly Venetiis: in aed. Aldi, 1505 (octavo).

The only 'handle' with which one can manage this vaguest imaginable title is the format. On the grounds of the neighbouring books it may be assumed as fairly likely that it was an octavo edition. With few exceptions,[1] before 1500 Virgil's works were always printed in folio. Most of the early sixteenth-century editions, such as that of Josse Bade (1501, 1512, 1515), also adhered to that format. The number of relevant editions is thus relatively small.

The oldest octavo appeared from the press of Aldo Manuzio in Venice in 1501. (It was also the first book printed in italic, the fount for which Erasmus had such an admiration.)[2] The second edition, which besides the three main works of Virgil also included the smaller works later referred to as the *Appendix Vergiliana* (taken from the Venice edition of Bartholomew of Cremona) and the so-called thirteenth book of the *Aeneid* by Maffeo Vegio, appeared in 1505; reprints followed in 1514 and 1527. There are other octavo editions; two of them are equally early: [Strasbourg: J. Grununger 1503?] and [Fano: H. de Soncino 1504?], but most are of later date: Florence: heirs of F. Giunta 1520; Paris: S. de Colines 1526; Paris: R. Estienne 1533; and others. If Erasmus acquired his text of Virgil before 1520, which is a reasonable assumption, and if he never replaced it by a more recent edition, then there is a good chance that his working copy of the poet was one of the two early Aldine editions. Perhaps we can go a step further. In the *Adagiorum opus* of 1526 Erasmus inserted a new adage (III x 1: *Quo transgressus etc* 'Where have I transgressed, etc?'), in which he cited the *Carmen de Sapiente* of Ausonius. He must have taken this from the *Appendix Vergiliana*, which was lacking in the Aldine edition of 1501 but was added in the edition of 1505.[3] It is therefore quite probable that the latter edition was in his possession.

1 The most important of them were quarto editions by the Paris printer Gering (1478, 1489, 1494).
2 Ep 207:31–3/36–8
3 ASD II-6 552:32–7 with 33n (553)/CWE 35 356–7 with note and n5; cf ASD II-4 79 414–15n.

83 Terentius

Terentius Afer, Publius. *Comoediae.* Probably an octavo edition.

The edition meant here can only be identified by surmise. More than 225 editions of Terence were published before 1536.[1] The choice is considerably restricted if one proceeds from the assumption that, as with no 87, it was one of the nearly forty octavo editions, virtually all first published after 1500. Only a few of them enjoyed anything more than local circulation. The two that won fame, as is shown by their many reprints, were the 1517 Aldine edition, with a commentary, and the 1526 Paris edition, without commentary but very elegant and convenient, of R. Estienne.

Andrea Torresani, the father-in-law of Aldo Manuzio (d 1515), tried to involve Erasmus in the preparation of the Venice press' edition of Terence. In 1517 he appealed for his collaboration, reminding him of the trouble that Aldo had taken during Erasmus' stay at Venice (1507–8) to produce better editions of Plautus and Terence, and how Erasmus had helped him then with the text of Plautus: 'I beg you ... send me anything you may have in the way of an ancient manuscript, which we can use as a sort of bear leader for the manuscript we have here, or anything else you may have that could help us to put a polish on our work.' The appeal can scarcely have had any effect; the book was published about four months later. This need not have prevented Torresani from honouring Erasmus with a presentation copy of the first Aldine Terence. He had every reason to keep on good terms with him, and the edition of Terence was not his only reason

for writing to Erasmus: in the same letter
he sounded him out concerning the vacant
chair of Greek at Venice and also attempted to get copy for his press from him.[2]

1 Lawton *Térence en France au xvie siècle* gives a list
  of editions.
2 Ep 589; the lines quoted are 47–51 / 50–4.

84 Ouidij Metamor.

Ovidius Naso, Publius. *Metamorphosewn
libri xv*. Probably Venetiis: in aed. Aldi,
1502 (octavo).

Numbers 84, 86, and 85, listed among
mostly octavo volumes, probably refer
to the three-volume Aldine edition in the
same format of Ovid's collected works. The
short titles of nos 84 and 85 correspond
exactly to the contents of the first and third
volumes of this edition. The title given for
no 86 (*Elegiae*) refers to only one of several
works included in the second volume,
but since, so far as can be ascertained,
there was no separate early edition of
the *Elegies*, nor was there another octavo
edition of which they formed a part, it
must be the Aldine edition that is referred
to here also. Possibly the compiler of the
Versandliste only mentioned the work that
most appealed to him in the very long title
summarizing the contents of the second
volume; or perhaps he listed the book from
a shorthand title on the spine or fore-edge.
The Aldine press reprinted its edition of
Ovid twice during Erasmus' lifetime, but
in neither of these editions, of 1515–16 and
1533–c 1527, were the *Elegiarum libri iii*
mentioned under this name on the title-page.

85 Ouidij Fast. Trist. Pon.

Ovidius Naso, Publius. *Fastorum libri vi.
De tristibus libri v. De Ponto libri iiii*.
Probably Venetiis: in Aldi acad., 1502/3
(octavo).

See no 84.

86 Ouidij Elegiae

Ovidius Naso, Publius. *Heroidum epistolae,
Auli Sabini epistolae iii, Elegiarum libri iii,
de arte amandi libri iii, de remedio amoris
libri ii, in Ibin liber unus, ad Liviam epistola
de morte Drusi, de Nuce, de Medicamine
faciei*. Probably Venetiis: in aed. Aldi,
December 1502 (octavo).

See no 84.

87 Terent. Cato. Ciuilitate

Terentius Afer, Publius. *Comoediae opera
Des. Erasmi ... castigatae* (*Argumenta
Philippi Melanchthonis in P. Terentii
comoedias*). Basileae: H. Frobenius &
N. Episcopius, 1534 (octavo).

bound with

Cato, Dion. *Disticha moralia cum scholiis
Erasmi*. Basileae: off. Frobeniana, 1534
(octavo).

and

Erasmus. *De civilitate morum puerilium
libellus*. Basileae: off. Frobeniana, 1534
(octavo).

The three components of this octavo
combination are almost certainly editions
of works by Erasmus published in the same
year by the Froben press.

1/ Since *De civilitate morum puerilium* is
bound with it, we must look first among
editions of Terence's comedies from the
early 1530s. Of these, the one edited by
Erasmus himself and dedicated to the
brothers Jan and Stanisław Boner (Ep 2584)
is the most likely, and then only the octavo
edition of 1534. The first edition of 1532
was a folio (see no 117); it could not have
been bound in one volume with the *De
civilitate*, which always appeared in octavo.

2/ One of many reimpressions of the text
of Cato edited and annotated by Erasmus,

but the only one between 1526 and 1536
to appear from the Froben press.[1]

3/ This new edition of *De civilitate* was
announced on the title-page of the edition
of Cato referred to above and was apparently intended to be circulated and possibly
bound with it; nevertheless the separate
title-page and independent signatures made
its separate sale possible. The *editio princeps*
of Erasmus' popular handbook on good
manners for children, which was to be a
best-seller both in Latin and in translation,
appeared in March 1530, with a dedication
to the young Henry of Burgundy, the son
of Adolph of Veere (Ep 2282). As early
as August it was followed by an edition
revised by the author. The edition of 1534
is the last Froben version that Erasmus
could have prepared for the press.

1 This edition has become exceptionally rare: it was
mentioned in Vander Haeghen (BE I 29), but since
then has been sought in vain; cf Reedijk *Poems*
373 (Survey of Editions and MS Works Edited
by Erasmus) Sources I: no 48. One copy is in
the British Library (BL *Catalogue* 35 515), albeit
without *De civilitate*. Cf nos 25 #1, 42 #2.

88 Horatius

Horatius Flaccus, Quintus. *Opera*. Possibly
Venetiis: in aed. Aldi (octavo).

In view of the adjacent entries in the
Versandliste, this was almost certainly an
octavo. The number of possibilities is thus
relatively restricted, since all the fifteenth-
century editions of Horace, apart from
the oldest known (a quarto),[1] and most of
the early sixteenth-century texts appeared
in folio format. In 1501 Aldo Manuzio
brought out the first octavo edition.
A second edition, supplemented by a
lengthy treatise on Horace's metres by
Aldo himself, appeared in 1509.[2] Reprints
followed in 1519 and 1527, and the handy
octavo was imitated elsewhere: Florence
(Giunta) 1503, 1514, and 1519; Paris (de
Colines) 1528 and 1533; Basel (Curio)
1527; Freiburg (Faber Emmeus) 1533.

By the time the Aldine edition of 1509
went to press Erasmus had probably
already left Venice and Aldo, in whose
house he had found lodging for half a
year (until December 1508), but it is hardly
to be imagined that he should not have
exchanged his thoughts with his host about
the latter's studies in Horatian metres.
Erasmus had felt attracted to Horace in
his boyhood and, if Beatus Rhenanus'
statement is accurate, he had already
learned Horace's poems by heart at that
time.[3] Moreover, Erasmus was a connois-
seur of classical prosody. As Andrea
Torresani recalled in 1517, Erasmus knew
that Aldo had spent a great deal of time
correcting the text of Terence, and he and
Aldo had worked together on the text
of Plautus.[4] Would Erasmus perhaps
have kept the Aldine edition of Horace
in his library?

1 [Venetiis, printer of Basil, 1471?]; Hain 8866,
BL *Catalogue* 5 187
2 Firmin-Didot *Alde Manuce et l'Hellénisme
à Venise* 167–8, 321–3
3 See Reedijk *Poems* 98 / ASD I-7 29 / CWE 85 xxx–xxxi;
Allen I 70:540–1 (Beatus Rhenanus to Charles V).
4 Ep 589:38–46/41–8; cf Reedijk *Poems* 106.

89 Oppianus graece. Eius. de pisci. latinè

Oppianus. *De piscibus libri V. Eiusdem
de venatione libri IIII (graece). Oppiani de
piscibus Laurentio Lippio interprete libri V.*
Venetiis in aed. Aldi et Andr. Asulani
soceri, 1517 (octavo).

There were two Greek didactic poets of
this name, who in Erasmus' day were not
yet distinguished: Oppian (probably) of
Corycus in Cilicia who wrote (c AD 180–90)
the *Halieutica*, a poem on fishing, and
Oppian of Apamea in Syria (c AD 212),
whose *Cynegetica* was devoted to hunting.
The only publication of these works to be
considered here is the Aldine edition of
1517, which contained the Greek of both,
with a Latin version of the *Halieutica* only.
In the Venetian edition of the *Adagia* of
1508, when Erasmus quotes six lines of the

Halieutica in one place and ten in another (because, as he says, 'the author has not been published at all so far'), he must have derived these from a manuscript source.[1] He had probably come to know the work in Venice from one of the manuscripts that Aldo Manuzio and his learned friends – Janus Lascaris, Giambattista Egnazio, Marcus Musurus, Fra Urbano – put so readily at his disposal.[2] Later on, when Musurus was establishing the text for the *editio princeps* of the *Halieutica* (Florence: Filippo Giunta 1515), he used several manuscripts, three of which were in his private possession.[3]

1 *Adagia* II i 1: *Festina lente* 'Make haste slowly' ASD II-3 14:187–15:203 with 187n, 198n, 201n / CWE 33 8 with n27 (340) and III v 38: Ἐκλινίσαι 'To slip through the net' ASD II-5 316:680–704 with 680n (317) / CWE 35 88–9 and n3

2 The manuscript Aldo used for his 1517 edition is perhaps MS Oppian B (Paris, Bibliothèque nationale MS ancien, fonds grec 2736); see Oppian d'Apamée *La chasse* ed Boudreaux 3 and 18.

3 Geanakoplos *Greek Scholars in Venice* 156 n151

90 Hippocratis Praesagia. Calphur.

Hippocrates. *Praesagiorum libri tres. Eiusdem de ratione victus in morbis acutis libri quatuor, interpr. Guilielmo Copo.* [Parisiis: H. Stephanus, c 1512] (quarto).

probably bound with

Calphurnius, Franciscus. *Epigrammata.* Parisiis: J. de Marnef, s.a. (quarto).

1/ Two texts of Hippocrates translated and edited by Guillaume Cop, a respected physician, astronomer, and humanist.[1] Cop, who was born in Basel and had studied at German universities, settled in Paris after taking his doctorate. From 1497 to 1512 he was doctor to the 'German nation' of the Sorbonne and later acted as court physician to Louis XII and Francis I. In his humanist studies, encouraged by Janus Lascaris, Erasmus, and Girolamo Aleandro, he applied himself especially to Greek, and besides translating Hippocrates

he also made translations from Galen (see no 126). Erasmus must have met Cop quite early in Paris, for in the winter of 1496–7 he consulted him during an attack of fever.[2] Their relations were of a friendly nature. Erasmus dedicated his *Carmen de senectute*, written on his journey to Italy in 1506, to Cop,[3] who for his part was involved about ten years later in the attempts to attach Erasmus to the nascent Collège de France.[4] Erasmus also praised his friend and kindred spirit in humanist superlatives in an anecdote about him in the foreword to his edition of Jerome (March 1515).[5]

2/ This collection of epigrams is the only known work of Franciscus Calphurnius, who is almost certainly the author referred to in this abbreviated form. The identification is supported by the year of publication, which can be established quite accurately and corresponds with that of the book bound with it. Who was Calphurnius? His name does not appear in biographical reference works, but the persons to whom he dedicated his epigrams, or whom they dealt with, place him with some probability in contemporary Paris.[6] In two of them he sang of the Paris academic booksellers Josse Bade and J. de Marnef. Several poems also point to relationships with people in ecclesiastical milieus. Three epigrams were dedicated to Michel Boudet, a councillor in the Parlement of Paris who was elected bishop of Langres in 1510; the poet called him 'the sole Maecenas of my studies.'[7] A lament was devoted to Florent d'Allemagne, called shortly before his death to the bishop's throne in Poitiers, which he was never to occupy. Another epigram was dedicated to the abbot of Saint Denis, and yet another to Pierre Tempeste, one of the principals (*provisores*) of the Collège de Montaigu after Jan Standonck. Whether Erasmus also came into contact with Calphurnius in Paris and was thus interested in his poetry cannot be ascertained. Personal contact with him is

not excluded *a priori*, but there is nothing
to indicate it, and perhaps he came into
the possession of the poems more or less
incidentally through one of his connections
among the Paris booksellers, especially
Josse Bade, who was buying books for
him on a large scale at about this time
and sometimes ordered books he himself
thought worth Erasmus' reading.[8]

1 Moreau *Inventaire* II 137. On Cop see Ep 124:16n/
   18n; Wickersheimer *Dictionnaire biographique des
   médecins en France au moyen-âge* I 235–8; CEBR I
   336–7.
2 Cf Ep 50:3n/6n; cf no 61.
3 Reedijk *Poems* no 83/ASD I-7 and CWE 85–6 no 2
4 Epp 522:144–5/158–60, 523 (from Cop),
   531:554–64/618–27
5 Ep 326:28–49/33–57
6 I owe the following details to the kindness of
   Mme J. Veyrin-Forrer, Conservateur de la Réserve,
   Bibliothèque nationale in Paris, who subjected the
   very rare book in the library's possession
   to a close scrutiny for me.
7 Erasmus himself also knew Boudet, but not until
   much later (1525–8); see Epp 1612, 1618, and
   1678. On him see Allen and CWE Ep 1612
   introductions; CEBR I 178–9.
8 Ep 263:51–4/58–60

91 L. And. Resendij Genethliacon

Resendius, Lucius Andreas. *Genethliacon
principis Lusitani ... Eiusdem Epicedion et
ode in raptum Dacorum principem puerum.*
Bononiae: J.B. Phaellus, 1533 (quarto).

A poem on the three days of festivities that
the Portuguese ambassador in Brussels,
Pedro de Mascarenhas, organized in
December 1531 on the occasion of the
birth of Prince Manuel of Portugal.
Together with his countryman Damião
de Gois, the Portuguese Dominican André
de Resende, who had recently entered the
service of the embassy, assisted at the
festivities.[1] Erasmus must have obtained the
Genethliacon not long after its appearance.
From his letter of 11 March 1534 to
Damião de Gois it appears that he had
read it. He praises the descriptive power of
the poem, 'in which he depicts everything
and brings it before our eyes so that I could

see much more in the poem than if I had
been present there,' and inquires sympa-
thetically where Resende now finds himself
and what he is doing, with the intention
of writing in detail as soon as he knows.[2]

The poet and humanist Resende, who
later on also made his name as historian
and historiographer, was a great admirer
of Erasmus. After studying in Alcalá,
Salamanca, and Paris, he travelled to
Leuven, hoping to meet Erasmus in person.
Erasmus, however, had recently moved to
Basel.[3] Years later Resende wrote a long
laudatory poem of 397 verses to the
humanist he admired so much, and
dedicated it to Conradus Goclenius,
his teacher and friend in the Collegium
Trilingue, with a request for a recommendation to Erasmus. Without consulting
Resende and definitely against his intentions,[4] Erasmus passed the manuscript
encomium to Hieronymus Froben, who
published it in 1531 under the title *Carmen
adversus stolidos politioris literaturae
oblatratores.*[5] Although he never met
Resende, Erasmus remained interested
in his younger friend, and as late as 1535
wrote him a letter, which is not preserved,
and which seems to have remained
unanswered.[6]

1 Hirsch *Damião de Gois* 64
2 Ep 2914:10–18
3 On his life see Allen Ep 2500 introduction; de
   Vocht *History of the* CTL II 395–403; CEBR III 144–5.
4 The poem, which criticized the enemies of the
   Collegium Trilingue, compromised Resende, and
   its publication caused some trouble for him from
   his Dominican brethren; de Vocht *History of the
   CTL* III 559.
5 Basel: H. Froben and N. Episcopius, September
   1531; republished in [Resende, André de]
   L'itinéraire érasmien d'André de Resende ed and
   trans Sauvage 37–71
6 Cf Epp 3043:12–17 with 12n, 3076:6n.

92 Silius Italicus

Silius Italicus, Tiberius Catius. *Punicorum
libri XVII.* Probably a quarto or octavo
edition.

An unidentifiable, but probably quarto or octavo, edition of the *Punica*, the epic on the second Punic war, knowledge of which in Erasmus' day was based solely on the manuscript that Poggio Bracciolini had discovered during the Council of Constance. Two quarto editions can be traced, one published in Rome ([after 26 April] 1471), the other in Milan (1481).[1] Octavo editions were published in Florence (Giunta 1513) and Basel (T. Wolfius 1522; edited by Erasmus' contemporary and friend Hermannus Buschius). But the best-known octavo version is the one prepared by Andrea Torresani and published by the Aldine press in 1523, a year of renewed contact between Erasmus and the Venetian printing house, then managed by Gianfrancesco Torresani in partnership with his father Andrea.[2] This edition was the first to contain verses 144–233 of book VIII, not transmitted in any manuscript, the authenticity of which has been disputed.[3]

1 HCR 14734 and 14736
2 Cf Ep 1349 (to Gianfrancesco Torresani).
3 Pauly-Wissowa 2nd series III 79–91 sv Silius Italicus

93 Lucanus. cum Vtilissi. Aristote. Rheto.

Lucanus, Marcus Annaeus. *Bellum civile Pharsalicum nuperrime … recognitum.* Parisiis: N. des Prez, [c 1506] (quarto).

bound with

Aristoteles. *Utilissima rhetorica.* [Parisiis:] Gilles de Gourmont, [c 1507] (quarto).

1/ If the book bound with it is correctly identified, then this entry must refer to a quarto edition of Lucan. His unfinished epic on the civil war between Caesar and Pompey was reprinted countless times before 1536, in the fifteenth century mostly in folio, later usually in octavo, but only very exceptionally in quarto.[1] The Paris edition of c 1506[2] and the Strasbourg edition of 1509[3] were the exceptions. Most probably the first one is meant here.

2/ The *Rhetorica ad Alexandrum* translated by the Italian humanist Francesco Filelfo (1398–1481) is the only edition that could be traced with the unusual title 'Most Useful Rhetoric' (*Utilissima rhetorica*).[4] In the prefatory letter to John More that Erasmus contributed to the second edition of Aristotle's work in Greek (no 215), he voiced his doubts about Aristotle's authorship.[5] This textbook of rhetoric is now usually ascribed to Anaximenes.[6]

1 See Cranz 10.
2 Moreau *Inventaire* I 203 (1506 no 114)
3 *Pharsaliae seu belli civilis libri* ([Strasbourg] J. Prüss 1509); BL *Catalogue* 202 21
4 Moreau *Inventaire* I 218 (1507 no 9)
5 Ep 2432:237–41 / 212–16
4 Pauly-Wissowa I 2086–98 and OCD 86 sv Anaximenes

94 Ioan. Aurelij Augurelli Chrysopoeiae

Augurellus, Johannes Aurelius. *Chrysopoeiae libri III et Geronticon liber primus.* Venetiis: Simon Luerensis, 1515 or Basileae: J. Frobenius, 1518 (quarto).

The allegorical poem *Chrysopoeia*, the subject of which was alchemy and the making of gold, was popular in its time, as appears from the reprints and translations. Giovanni Augurelli (1440/1–1524) lived from 1485 onwards in Venice and neighbouring Treviso.[1] He was friendly with the Bembo family of Venice, including Pietro Bembo, thirty years younger than himself, who sang his praises in his earliest work, the *Aetna* (cf no 12 #1). Aldo Manuzio, who published his *Carmina* in 1505, knew him personally.

There is no direct indication that Erasmus' interest in the *Chrysopoeia* dates back to contact with the poet during his stay in Venice, but the possibility that he met him there need not be excluded. They moved in the same circles and surely had social relationships in common. It was, for example, in the group centred on Aldo Manuzio that Erasmus came to know

Augurelli's young friend, the brilliant and many-sided Paolo Canal (Canalis or Decanalis). It was a short, but more than formal, contact; Erasmus sincerely lamented the premature end of a life of such promise in the 1508 Aldine edition of the *Adagia* (I iii 52; in subsequent editions II iii 48).[2]

Which edition of Augurelli's work Erasmus owned cannot be established with certainty. The *editio princeps* of Venice 1515 is a possibility. But three years later Johann Froben published a pirated reprint and may have presented a copy to Erasmus when the latter stayed with him at Basel from mid-May to September 1518.[3]

1 On Augurelli and his work, see *Dizionario biografico degli Italiani* IV 578–81.
2 ASD II-3 261:3–262:10 with 3–4n/CWE 33 158–9 with n18 (393); on Canal cf Ep 1347:252 with n/271–3 with n38; CEBR I 257.
3 A curious detail: The 1518 edition was provided with a new preface by Johann Froben, which in 1591 the humanist Dominicus Lampsonius in a letter to his friend Justus Lipsius wrongly ascribed to Erasmus. See Secret 'L'édition par Frobenius de la *Chrysopoeia* d'Augurelli' 111–12.

95 Λειτουργιαι graece cum Ianj Vitalis opusc.

Ἀι θεῖαι λειτουργεῖαι. Rome: Demetrios Doukas, October 1526 (quarto).

bound with

Vitalis, Janus. One or more unidentifiable minor works.

1/ The first edition, with privilege of Pope Clement VII, of the Byzantine Liturgies attributed to John Chrysostom and St Basil and of the Liturgy of the Presanctified Gifts attributed to St Germanos. The editor and publisher was the printer-publisher Demetrios Doukas, who had been assisted in the preparation of the text by the archbishop of Nicosia and the metropolitan of Rhodes.[1] The Cretan Doukas (c 1480–c 1527) emigrated to Italy at the beginning of the sixteenth century and settled in Venice, where he worked for the publishing house of Aldo Manuzio. In 1513, at the invitation of Cardinal Francisco Jiménez de Cisneros, he accepted the chair of Greek at the University of Alcalá. In addition he also worked on the Greek New Testament for the Complutensian Polyglot and published Greek texts independently. Around 1526 he must have moved to Rome where, besides his career as a printer and publisher, he also acted as a professor of Greek. After 1527, the year of the sack of Rome, nothing more is known of his life.[2] Erasmus made Doukas' acquaintance during his stay in Venice and probably helped him at that time in the collation of manuscripts for the first edition of the *Moralia* of Plutarch published by the Aldine press (no 208; cf no 127). Erasmus had been interested in the Byzantine Greek liturgy from an early age. Allen thought that the *Officium Chrysostomi* he sent to his friend Colet in September 1511 (at Colet's request) was his Latin translation of the mass of John Chrysostom, made for John Fisher, bishop of Rochester and chancellor of the University of Cambridge. André Jacob, however, has made the plausible suggestion that the translation was made much earlier and dated from the beginning of Erasmus' time in Paris, c 1496–8. He must have based himself then on the Greek text that Georgius Hermonymus had copied, with more than a few changes of his own, from a manuscript in the possession of Janus Lascaris, a diplomat and scholar who had recently come from Italy to enter the service of the king of France. But Erasmus also used the Latin translation that Lascaris had already made of the *Missa*, and it is possible that he had access to a bilingual manuscript that contained both versions (at least three have been preserved).[3] Erasmus' own translation was, according to Jacob, clearly the work of someone who was still inexperienced in Greek, and it is also very much open to question whether the mass was included in the new edition of Chrysostom's *Opera*, published by Chevallon in Paris in the year of Erasmus' death,[4] with his knowledge and approval. In 1537 his translation also appeared separately with the addition of the Greek version by Hermonymus.[5] At present, the Byzantine liturgy of the mass attributed to John Chrysostom is no longer associated with him. Erasmus himself had grave doubts of the attribution. In February 1519 he wrote: 'I have read a liturgy of the Greeks attributed by them to Chrysostom, to whom they are willing to attribute almost anything; that does not seem likely to me.'[6]

2/ It is impossible to determine which work or works of the Sicilian theologian and poet Janus Vitalis, who worked at Rome and was held in high esteem at the papal court,[7] this volume contained. Several of his occasional writings were published at about this time, for the most part also in Rome.[8] Janus Vitalis was an admirer of Erasmus, to whom he wrote two laudatory poems.[9]

1 Legrand *Bibliographie hellénique* I 192–5 no 76
2 On his life see Geanakoplos *Greek Scholars in Venice* 233–55.
3 Ep 227:1n/2n; Jacob 'L'édition "érasmienne" de la liturgie de saint Jean Chrysostome et ses sources.' On Lascaris see Ep 269:51n/55n; Knös *Un ambassadeur de l'hellénisme, Janus Lascaris et la tradition gréco-byzantine dans l'humanisme français*; CEBR II 292–4. Cf nos 102, 104, 109, 115, 314.
4 The mass, entitled *Missa Sancti Joannis Chrysostomi supra complures annos ab Erasmo Roterdamo in gratiam Episcopi Roffensis versa* is in volume V folios 350–4.
5 *Joannis Chrysostomi missa graecolatina D. Erasmo. Roterdamo interprete* (Paris: C. Wechel)
6 Ep 916:52–4/59–61
7 Jöcher *Allgemeines Gelehrtenlexicon* IV 17 col 1651
8 See Cosenza *Italian Humanists* and BL *Catalogue* sv Janus Vitalis.
9 Included in Paolo Giovio (Paulus Jovius) *Elogia virorum literis illustrium* Basel 1577)

96 Nazianzeni Orationes 16. graece.

Gregorius Nazianzenus. *Orationes lectissimae XVI.* [Graece] Venetiis: in aed. Aldi et Andr. Asulani soceri, April 1516 (octavo).

The *editio princeps* of some sixteen orations by the Greek Father of the church Gregory of Nazianzus (329/30–389/90). The text was supervised by Marcus Musurus,[1] who dedicated the work to his former pupil Jean des Pins, the recently appointed French ambassador in Venice.[2]

In August 1517, writing from Leuven, Erasmus instructed Wolfganag Lachner and Johann Froben to buy the book for him at the Frankfurt autumn fair: 'I have seen the works of Gregory Nazianzen in Greek, printed I think by Aldus, not the well-known poems, but the prose works in handy format. Please let me have a copy from the coming fair.'[3] For the *Orationes* translated into Latin by Willibald Pirckheimer and posthumously published with an introductory letter of Erasmus in 1531, see no 248.

Of the other works of Gregory, neither the *Carmina* nor the *Epistolae* figure on the *Versandliste*. Erasmus once had possessed the Aldine edition of the *Carmina* in Greek and Latin (Venice 1504), but in 1508 he had presented his copy to Maarten Lips, canon regular of St Maartensdal at Leuven, in gratitude for a gift, a purse, that he had received from him. The book has been preserved and turned up early in this century in an English private library.[4]

Very probably Erasmus had also owned the *Basilii Magni et Gregorii Nazianzeni epistolae* (Haguenau: J. Setzer 1528), edited by Vincentius Opsopoeus (Obsopoeus) from a manuscript in the possession of Pirckheimer. At any rate, he had the Greek letters of Basil and Gregory at his disposal as soon as they appeared and quoted from them in the revised edition of the *Adagia* published in September of the same year.[5] He intended to translate the letters, but when he realized how badly they had been edited, he abandoned this plan. First he wanted to scan the manuscript himself. He asked Pirckheimer for the loan of it in May and again in August 1528.[6] Notwithstanding this, it is not impossible, according to Allen, that for the benefit of his own edition of Basil in Greek, published by Froben in 1532 (nos 189 and 250), Erasmus may have used Opsopoeus' text and may have sent it to the printer without revision.[7] In that case his copy of the Haguenau edition may have been lost after having served its turn in the printing office.

1 See on him no 116.
2 Ep 928:36n/43n; CEBR III 85–6. Erasmus met him in Bologna c 1507 and was still in correspondence with him during his last years (1532–5).
3 Ep 629:12–14/14–17. In letters to Cuthbert Tunstall Erasmus mentions that Francis Frowick had shown him the book; Epp 642:3–4/3–4, 643:23–4/25–6.
4 Ep 807; cf Allen IV xxviii (addendum to Ep 807:2n). In 1922 it was in the possession of Mr P.M. Barnard of Tunbridge Wells, who lent it to the Bodleian for a short time in 1917; its present location is unknown to me.
5 See for example *Adagia* II vi 14 and II x 49 ASD II-4 29–30:243–8 with 243n and 308:582–4 with n (309)/ CWE 33 298 with n2 (440) and CWE 34 146 with n3 (365).
6 Epp 1997:5–15/5–15, 2028:1–4/1–3
7 Ep 1997:10n. On Opsopoeus see Ep 1997:5n/n2; CEBR III 34.

97 Melan. orationes. Imperatores. Lute. epistolae

Melanchthon, Phil. *Oratio dicta in funere Friderichi Saxoniae ducis. Oratio de legibus. Oratio de gradibus. Praefatio in Aeschinis et Demosthenis orationes. Oratio Critiae contra Theramenem ex Xenophonte.* Haganoae: J. Secerus, 1525 (octavo).

perhaps bound with

Imperatorum romanorum libellus, una cum imaginibus ad vivam effigiem expressis [J. Huttichio auctore.] Argentorati: W. Cephaleus, 1525 (octavo).

and with

Luther, Martin. *Epistolarum farrago … cum Psalmorum aliquot interpretatione …* Haganoae: J. Secerus, 1525 (octavo).

1/ Collections of Melanchthon's speeches were published twice during Erasmus' lifetime, in 1525 and 1533. The earlier of the two is more likely to be meant here because it appeared in the same year and from the same printer as the books of Luther bound with it.[1]

2/ It cannot be proved, but it can be plausibly argued, that 'Imperatores' in this entry refers to the book of portrait medallions of the Roman, Byzantine, and German emperors from Julius Caesar to Charles V, with brief biographies by Johann Huttich appended to the woodcuts, published by W. Köpfel in Strasbourg.[2] Huttich was not unknown to Erasmus, who in 1517 had dedicated his translation of Lucian's *Convivium* to him (Ep 550). The two men had already exchanged letters before that date. Huttich, a follower of Reuchlin and a friend of Beatus Rhenanus (in whose library there was also a copy of this 'little book of Roman emperors')[3] worked for many years as a scholarly corrector for Johann Schöffer of Mainz before moving to Strasbourg in 1521.[4] Schöffer also published, in March 1520, his posthumous edition of Dietrich Gresemund's *Collectanea antiquitatum in urbe atque agro Maguntino repertarum.* Shortly before this book went to press, Erasmus, at the request of the printer-publisher, did his best to obtain data for it on the 'mass of masonry … known as the Drusiana,' that is, the Eigelstein at Mainz.[5] The year of publication of the *Imperatorum Romanorum libellus* is the same as the edition of Luther bound with it, which could be an indication that we are on the right track with Huttich's little work. Perhaps also it is not a coincidence that the book, like the two works bound with it, appeared from an Alsatian press. Another possibility is an edition of the *Historiae Augustae scriptores*, perhaps the Aldine edition of 1519, which Erasmus ordered from Italy in 1525.[6] The year of acquisition could explain why a work of 1519 was bound in the same volume as the Haguenau publications of 1525.

3/ This was the first and only selection from Luther's correspondence to appear during Erasmus' lifetime.[7] There was a second copy in his library, bound with a work by Cochlaeus (no 10 #2).

1 Koehn no 40. The 1533 collection (Haganau: Valentin Kobian, September 1533) was entitled *Orationes aliquot lectu dignissimae, a Philippo Mel[anchthone] atque aliis doctissimis quibusdam in publica Wittenbergensium schola pronunciatae*; see Koehn no 43.
2 Hans Weiditz contributed to the biographies; see Rave 'Paolo Giovio und die Bildnisvitenbücher des Humanismus' 129–30.
3 Walter *Catalogue Sélestat* 403 no 1591
4 On Huttich see Allen and CWE Ep 550 introductions; *Neue Deutsche Biographie* X 160; CEBR II 220–1.
5 Ep 1054:1–5/3–7; cf Allen Ep 919:50n.
6 'Vitae posteriorum Imperatorum per Aelium Lampridium et alios'; Allen VII 547 Appendix 20 'Books Ordered by Erasmus'
7 Benzing *Lutherbibliographie* no 65

98 Theocritus graecè εἰδυλλια ἐπιγραμ. etc

Theocritus. *Eidyllia, Epigrammata cum scholiis cura Zach. Calliergi, graece.* Romae: Zach. Callierges, January 1516 (octavo).

The most important edition yet published of the bucolic poet Theocritus (third century BC), which contained not only some previously unpublished poems but also the first printing of the *scholia*.[1] This entry on the *Versandliste* most probably refers to the copy Erasmus acquired in 1518 from the Italian bookseller-printer Francesco Giulio Calvo, who visited him in Leuven.[2] 'He brought me a Theocritus printed with added commentary,' he writes to Cuthbert Tunstall, 'and Pindar too with notes added by various hands.'[3] The edition of Theocritus he had borrowed from Richard Croke he could then return.[4] For the Calliergis Pindar see no 107; for other editions of Theocritus see nos 99, 106, and 294.

1 Cf on this edition Geanakoplos *Greek Scholars in Venice* 217–18.
2 On Calvo see Ep 581:30n/33n; CEBR I 245–6.
3 Ep 832:29–31/32–4
4 Ep 827:6–7/7–8

99 Θεοκριτοσ Latinè et graecè

Theocritus. *Idyllia triginta sex, latino carmine reddita, Helio Eobano Hesso interprete.* Theocriti idyllia [graece, ed Joachim Camerarius]. Haganoae: J. Secerius, November 1530 or Basileae: A. Cratander, 1530–1, 2 volumes in one (octavo).

A volume in which the Greek text of Theocritus, edited by Joachim Camerarius, and the metrical translation by Helius Eobanus Hessus of 36 idylls, which were published almost simultaneously,[1] are (as is the case with the copies in the Bibliothèque nationale in Paris and the British Library in London) bound together. In March 1531 Erasmus, writing to Eobanus, touched on his translation in passing; the book itself he had not yet obtained, and therefore his critical remarks in advance sound a trifle sour. 'Concerning your translation of Theocritus into Latin verse, I am amazed if you have succeeded in emulating that Sicilian charm. I think you would find Homer easier to handle, but in either case I am afraid that the renown will not correspond to the labour involved. Those who know Greek (for the knowledge of that language is spreading more widely from day to day) prefer to hear such authors singing in their own language. I praise your industry, however, and that will not be defrauded of its praise.'[2] In the middle of May the book was not yet in his possession; in Freiburg it was not for sale yet, he wrote to Hessus, 'but I'll try to get it somewhere else.'[3] Whether he finally acquired the original edition or the reprint by Cratander that came out in the same year, cannot now be determined.[4] Cf nos 98, 106, 294.

1 For further details see Krause *Helius Eobanus Hessus* II 91–5.
2 Ep 2446:134–9/136–42
3 Ep 2495:41–2
4 On the differences between the *editio princeps* and the pirated Basel edition see BN *Catalogue général* sv Théocrite nos 61 and 62.

100 Eurip. Rhesus, troades et reli. graecè

Euripides. *Tragoediae* vol 2.

Together nos 100 and 103 form a copy
bound in two parts of the Aldine edition
of Euripides. This is the second part, which
indeed begins with the *Rhesus*. For details
on this famous edition see no 102, a copy
in which the two parts are bound in one
volume.

**101 Πτολεμαιου De geographia lib. 8.
graecè**

Ptolemaeus, Claudius. *De geographia libri
octo* [Graece.] Basileae: H. Frobenius &
N. Episcopius, 1533 (quarto).

The *editio princeps* of the original Greek
text, published from a manuscript made
available by Theobald Fettich, personal
physician to the Elector Palatine. The
manuscript was copied in the 1430s at
Byzantium for the later Cardinal Johannes
de Ragusis and bequeathed to the
Dominican monastery at Basel with his
other Greek codixes in 1443. The manuscript was given by the monastery in 1482
to Johann Dalberg, bishop of Worms.
After the prelate's death in 1503 his rich
library at the castle of Ladenburg fell into
decay. Later on, Wolfgang von Affenstein,
one of the councillors of the Palatinate,
was commissioned by the then bishop of
Worms to take charge of the neglected
collection and to reorganize it. In performing this duty he was assisted by his medical
adviser Fettich, who may only have been
the intermediary through whom Froben
was allowed to use the Ptolemy codex or
a copy of it,[1] But Erasmus introduced the
edition with a dedicatory letter to him in
which he was the only one thanked for his
collaboration: 'You gave the printer access
to this Greek volume at no charge.' Allen's
successors rightly assumed that, apart from
the dedicatory preface under his name,
Erasmus had nothing to do with the actual
editing of the text.[2] From two marginal

notes and a drawing on the original
manuscript (also adopted in the printed
text), which pointed to a deeper study of
the problems of Ptolemy and were thought
to be in Erasmus' own hand, some scholars
have deduced that Erasmus was more
closely involved in the edition than Allen
assumed. This hypothesis, however, has
been refuted by Reedijk, who failed to
discover any similarity between Erasmus'
handwriting and that of the notes. He
arrived on good grounds at the conclusion
that the anonymous editor of Froben's
Ptolemy was not Erasmus but Sigismundus
Gelenius, and that Gelenius probably also
wrote a first rough draft for the preface
that was to appear under Erasmus' name.[3]

1 Strictly speaking it was von Affenstein and not
   Fettich who in 1526 at Erasmus' urging permitted
   Froben to inspect and borrow any manuscript
   suitable for printing from the Ladenburg library;
   see Ep 1774. On Affenstein see Allen and CWE Ep
   1774 introductions and CEBR I 10–12; on Fettich
   Allen and CWE Ep 1767 introductions and CEBR II
   25–6. On the manuscript see Vernet 'Les manuscrits grecs de Jean de Raguse' 94–5 (no 42);
   de Smet 'Erasme et la cartographie.' The codex,
   which came via the library of the Elector Palatine
   to the Vatican Library (MS Vat. Pal. Gr. 388),
   has been identified as the text used for the *editio
   princeps*; see Schnabel *Text und Karten des
   Ptolemäus* 13. For more detail on the history
   of the *editio princeps*, see Reedijk 'The Story
   of a Fallacy.'
2 Allen Ep 2760 introduction; the quotation is line 8.
3 Cf Schnabel and de Smet (n1 above); Reedijk 'The
   Story of a Fallacy' 253, 266, 269–71. On Gelenius
   see no 149 n1.

**102 Tragoediae Eurip. et Soph. cum
         commen. grae.**

Euripides. *Tragoediae septendecim, ex quib.
quaedam habent commentaria,* [graece].
Venetiis: apud Aldum, February 1503,
2 vols (octavo).

bound with

Sophocles. *Tragoediae septem cum commentariis,* [graece]. Venetiis: in Aldi
Romani Academia, August 1502 (octavo).

1/ The *editio princeps* of eighteen tragedies of Euripides was assumed for a long time to have been published by Marcus Musurus from two manuscripts.[1] Seventeen tragedies are announced on the title-page, but during the printing of the second volume the *Hercules furens* also came to the publisher's knowledge.[2] The work was dedicated by Aldo Manuzio to Demetrius Chalcondylas, 'easily the first among Greeks of his day.' A copy of this edition, with the ex libris *Sum Erasmi* on the last page of the second volume but otherwise without marginal notes in his hand, has, since 1916, been in the library of Lincoln College Oxford, to which it was presented by a member of the college who had himself acquired it in 1870.[3] If this is the copy recorded under this number, then the editions of Euripides and Sophocles originally bound together must have been separated.

Erasmus translated the *Hecuba* and the *Iphigenia in Aulis* from the *Euripides graece* of 1503, the first play before his departure from Leuven at the end of 1504 and the second afterwards in England. Both translations were published by Josse Bade in one volume in September 1506, when Erasmus was already on his way to Italy. In Venice Erasmus prepared a significantly improved edition for the Aldine press, which appeared in print in December 1507.[4] In that milieu he could also have consulted Marcus Musurus on the proper interpretation of the two tragedies.[5] The translations from Euripides do not appear in the *Versandliste*. J.H. Waszink wondered whether for the posthumous but revised text edition of the translated tragedies in the *Opera omnia* of 1540, use might not have been made of a copy of one of the authorized later Froben editions, for example that of 1530, with marginal notes by Erasmus himself. If this were the case then it would explain the absence of the work from his library.[6]

2/ *Editio princeps* of Sophocles' tragedies issued by Marcus Musurus. The text is preceded by a letter from the printer-publisher Aldo Manuzio to the Greek humanist Janus Lascaris, once the teacher of Musurus and later an acquaintance of Erasmus. The commentaries announced on the title-page do not appear in this edition and were not published until 1518, in a separate volume.[7]

1 The manuscripts, Codex Vaticanus Palatinus graecus 287 and Codex Laurentianus Conventi soppressi 172, form two parts of one codex; see ASD I-1 195 n1. Sicherl was the first to reject the theory that Musurus could be considered as the editor. Nor does he believe that the first manuscript named served as the base text for the Aldine edition; see 'Die *Editio princeps* Aldina des Euripides und ihre Vorlagen.'
2 Legrand *Bibliographie hellénique* I no 31 79–82
3 Wilson 'Erasmus as a Translator of Euripides; Supplementary Note'
4 *Catalogus lucubrationum* Allen I 4:28–5:32 / CWE Ep 1341A:120–64 with n28; Epp 188 to William Warham and 198 to the Reader (dedicatory preface to *Hecuba* and preface to *Iphigenia* in the July 1506 edition); Ep 208 to William Warham (preface to the 1507 edition)
5 Cf ASD I-1 197–8 n9.
6 ASD I-1 202. The special collection of his own works in Erasmus' estate did include the Aldine edition of 1507 and its Froben reprint of 1518, but it lacked the later Froben reprint of 1530. See *Catalogus librorum Erasmi* nos 42 and 79.
7 Geanakoplos *Greek Scholars in Venice* 131 n86; On Lascaris see no 95 n3.

103 Eurip. orestes, phoenissae etc. graece

Euripides. *Tragoediae* vol 1.

The first volume of the Aldine edition of Euripides. For the second volume, see no 100; for the work as a whole, the copy bound in one volume listed under no 102. The short title in the *Versandliste* points to an incomplete copy; in the first volume the *Orestes*, the *Phoenissae*, and the rest are preceded by the *Hecuba*. Can it be coincidence that one of the two tragedies that Erasmus translated into Latin is not mentioned in the title? Was it taken from the book? It is not possible to ascertain whether the *Iphigenia Aulidensis*, the other play he translated, was also missing.

104 Ἐπιγραμμα. Florilegium epigram. grae.

Anthologia Graeca. *Florilegium diversorum epigrammatum in septem libros graece.* Venetiis: in aed. Aldi, November 1503 or in aed. Aldi et Andreae Asulani soceri, January 1521 (octavo).

In Erasmus' time the Greek Anthology was still known in the West only in the version of the late thirteenth-century Byzantine monk Maximus Planudes.[1] His collection of epigrams, known later as the *Anthologia Planudea*, was first printed in Florence by Lorenzo di Alopa in 1494, edited by the Greek scholar Janus Lascaris (1445–1535), who was still in the service of Lorenzo de' Medici. The second edition, published by Aldo Manuzio, was in fact a reprint of the *editio princeps* but enriched with an ἐπίγραμμα based on the autograph of Planudes' collection, which Cardinal Bessarion had brought from Byzantium to Venice and presented to the library of San Marco (where it is MS 481). Aldo's 1503 edition was the first to use the traditional translation of the title: *Florilegium diversorum epigrammatum.* The publication of the Anthology was an event in the learned world of the time, and even after 1503 kept the Greek scholars of Venice busy – Janus Lascaris, for example, who acted as French ambassador in Venice from 1504 to 1509. Erasmus made his acquaintance there and enjoyed his co-operation while he was preparing his *Adagiorum Chiliades* for the first edition of 1508.[2] The word 'Florilegium' in the short title almost certainly refers, not to the *editio princeps* of 1494, but to the Aldine supplemented text. Whether Erasmus owned the edition of 1503 or the reprint of 1521 cannot be determined, but it does not matter: the difference between them consisted only in the incorporation in their proper places in the reprint of the

additions and alternative versions found at the end of the 1503 edition. It is highly improbable that 'Florilegium' here refers to the Florentine reprint of Filippo Giunta (1519), which in spite of its promises was an ordinary reprint of the 1503 Aldine edition.

1 For what follows see Hutton *The Greek Anthology in Italy to the Year 1800*; Pauly-Wissowa I 2380–91 sv Anthologia Griechisch; *Der Kleine Pauly* I 375–7 sv Anthologie; OCD 101–2 sv anthology. We have left out of our account the intricate problem of whether and how far the manuscript of the other and older collection of Greek epigrams – afterwards known as the *Anthologia Palatina*, although not published until the end of the sixteenth century – may have been known much earlier to scholars in the West. Sicherl assumes that Marcus Musurus must have had access to the famous codex when he was professor at Padua (where Erasmus made his acquaintance) and later on when he was teaching at the Greek College in Rome (1516/17); see his *Johannes Cuno* 99–100.
2 On Lascaris see no 95 n3.

105 Πινδαροσ graecè in 8º.

Pindarus. *Olympia. Pythia. Nemea. Isthmia. Callimachi hymni qui inveniuntur. Dionysius de situ orbis. Licophronis Alexandra.* [omnia graece] Venetiis: in aed. Aldi et Andreae soc., January 1513 (octavo) or *Olympia, Pythia, Nemea, Isthmia.* [Graece.] Basileae: Andreas Cratander, 1526 (octavo).

This entry may refer to the *editio princeps* of the four books of Pindar's epinician odes and in particular to the copy that Erasmus ordered, with other books, from Italy in 1525.[1] Why he still valued the Aldine edition at that date, when he already possessed the better Calliergis edition (no 107), is not clear, unless he was concerned not only with Pindar but also, or chiefly, with the work of three other Greek poets also printed in the book; the order list does indeed specify a Greek Pindar 'with others' (*Pindarum graecum cum aliis*). But that it was the Aldine edition is by no means certain; strict proof that the order of 1525 was actually filled in Venice is lacking, and the whole edition could have been sold out. One must therefore think of another possibility. Heinimann and Kienzle observed that in the revised edition of the *Adagia* of 1526 Erasmus inserted many new citations from Pindar; this is an indication that he must have examined the poet for his revision. They infer that the stimulus to do so may have been given by the new text of Pindar printed that year by Cratander in Basel, edited from the Calliergis version of 1515 by Ceporinus and Huldrych Zwingli. This edition may also be the one alluded to here. It is true that the book appeared around March, while the revised edition of the *Adagia* had appeared a month earlier, but Erasmus could well have seen it, perhaps in manuscript or proof.[2] The absence of the words 'cum aliis' or 'et alia' in the short title in the *Versandliste* could also be another argument for the Cratander edition, in which the texts of Dionysius Afer and Lycophron from the Aldine edition do not appear.

1 Allen VII 547 Appendix 20 'Books Ordered by Erasmus'
2 ASD II-4 249 711n

106 Theocritus graece in 4°

Theocritus. *Eidyllia*, graece. [Parisiis:] Gilles de Gourmont, s a or Lovanii: T. Martinus, 1520 (quarto).

Four quarto editions of the *Idylls* were published before 1536 and can still be traced: Milan: Bonus Accursius [1480],[1] Paris: Gilles de Gourmont [between 1507 and 1513],[2] and Leuven: Dirk Martens 1520 and 1528.[3] There is no indication which of the three can be meant here. The first mentioned, the *editio princeps*, is probably the least likely and may even be excluded. It was a quarto volume of rather unusual dimensions (the copy in the British Library in London is 275 x 205 mm), which would have been more at home among the folios on the shelves than among the books

in smaller formats. For other editions of Theocritus see nos 98, 99, and 294.

1 Hain 15476
2 Bibliotèque nationale, Paris 1507 or 1508; British Library, London 1513
3 NK 3934 and 2000

107 Πινδαροσ graece cum comment.

Pindarus. *Olympia, Nemea, Pythia, Isthmia. Cum scholiis [graece]*. Romae: Zach. Callierges, 1515 (quarto).

Higher in quality than the Aldine *editio princeps* of January 1513 (no 105) stood the Pindar of Calliergis – the first Greek book printed in Rome – not only on account of the quality of the text, which was based on a better manuscript (the so-called MS B of the Vatican) but also because of the important scholia.[1] The addition 'cum comment.' in the *Versandliste* entry puts it beyond question that this is the edition referred to. When he was on a business visit to Leuven early in 1518 the learned printer and bookseller Francesco Minuzio Calvo offered a copy to Erasmus.[2] It may be noted that while the four great groups of *Odes* are quoted in the *Adagia* some 175 times, only 50 of these are to be found in the first edition of 1508; a few were added in 1523, most in 1526 and 1533.[3]

1 Geanakoplos *Greek Scholars in Venice* 146 and 214
2 Ep 832:29–31/32–4
3 For this information I am indebted to the late R.A.B. Mynors.

108 Interpre. in Homerum graece cum Porphy. quaest. grae.

Didymus Alexandrinus. *Interpretationes ... in Homeri Iliada, nec non in Odyssea* [sic]. Porphyrius. *Homericarum questionum liber. De Nympharum antro in Odyssea opusculum* [graece.] Venetiis: in aed. Aldi et Andreae soc., May 1521, 2 vols (octavo).

These *scholia* on the *Iliad*, handed down with an attribution to the first century BC Alexandrian grammarian Didymus, were printed by the Aldine press from the *editio princeps*, which had been published at Rome in 1517. That too may have been in Erasmus' possession (see no 109). Here they are published in combination with the *Homerika zetemata* of the Neoplatonist philosopher Porphyry (AD 234–c 305). The scholia on the *Odyssey* announced on the title-page do not occur in the edition of 1521 and were not published until 1528, when they appeared separately. It is not possible to deduce from the summary description whether the later publication was bound with the earlier. The publisher of both Greek texts was Gianfrancesco Torresani, who ran the firm with his father Andrea after the death of Aldo Manuzio (1515). He kept up the relationship with Erasmus, but repeatedly complained that he never received copy from him. Erasmus showed some sympathy for the complaint, and although he had by now adapted himself to permanent collaboration with Froben, he was willing to have a new edition of the *Adagia* published at Venice. But Torresani had to let the chance slip, since in 1525 he had his hands full with his great edition of Galen. This made no difference to his relationship with Erasmus, to whom he continued to send now and then a new product of his press.[1] He presented him with the five-volume Galen (no 137) and in 1528 there was talk of a book, not mentioned by name, that he had sent to Basel. Allen took it to be a recently published edition of Celsus, but this is probably a mistake (see no 192). Could it have been Didymus' scholia on the *Odyssey*, which were finally published in that year? Erasmus used this edition of the *scholia minora* for additions to the later editions of his *Adagia* (1528 and 1533).[2]

1 On Gianfrancesco Torresani see Ep 212:2n; CEBR III 333–4. On Erasmus' relations with him and the Aldine press at this time see Epp 1592, 1594, 1595:46–51/50–6, 1623:1–9/2–10, 1628.

2 *Adagia* III ii 48, III iii 33, and III vii 71 ASD II-5 133 667n and 207 8n, ASD II-6 465 812n/CWE 34 242–3 with n8 (397) and 292–3 with n7 (413), CWE 35 262 with nn8–10

109 Ομηροσ in Iliade [sic] grae.

Possibly *Homeri interpres pervetustus, seu scholia graeca in Iliadem.* [Ed cum textu Iliadis Joh. Lascaris.] Romae: in aed. Angeli Collotii, 8 September 1517 (small folio).

On the one hand, the words 'in Iliadem' in this entry point to a commentary, on the other hand the pride of place given to the name Homer in the nominative makes one expect an edition of the text. This apparent contradiction is explained, however, if the 1517 Rome edition, which contained both the scholia on the *Iliad* and the text of the epic itself, is the one meant.[1] The small folio format does not correspond with the octavos listed before and after it, but because another inexplicable break in occurs elsewhere in the *Versandliste* (cf no 16), and because no other commentary on the *Iliad*, so far as can be ascertained, was published separately in Greek before 1536, our assumption may perhaps be upheld.

The scholia in question, now known as the *scholia minora*, or *scholia Didymi* – although Didymus had nothing to do with them,[2] – were published by Janus Lascaris. Born in Constantinople, he first enjoyed the favour of Lorenzo de' Medici in Florence, then entered the service of Charles VIII, and was ambassador of Louis XII to Venice from 1504 to 1509. Erasmus made his acquaintance in Venice in the circle of Aldo Manuzio and the Neakademia, and profited by his knowledge and assistance. In 1513 Lascaris obeyed the summons of Pope Leo X and settled in Rome, which then began to supersede Venice as the centre of Greek learning. He rose to be head of the Greek college and maintained close relations with the so-called Medici press associated with the college and founded mainly at his instigation with the support of the pope. This had been specially set up for the publication of Greek texts and was housed, with the college, in the residence of Angelo Colacci, secretary of the pope and himself a well-known humanist. The scholia on the *Iliad* were the first production of the new press with Colacci's name in the colophon.[3] In April 1518, soon after the publication of the book, Erasmus sounded Lascaris out on possible candidates for the still-open chair of Greek at the recently founded Collegium Trilingue in Leuven, perhaps in the hope that Lascaris himself would be interested in the post offered.[4]

The *scholia minora* were reprinted in 1521 by the Aldine press (see no 108).

1 Legrand *Bibliographie hellénique* I 159–62 no 56
2 Erbse *Scholia graeca in Homeri Iliadem* (*scholia vetera*) I lxvii and xi. Lascaris' edition contained the *editio princeps* of the *scholia minora*.
3 Geanakoplos *Greek Scholars in Venice* 216; on the Medici press, which appears to have been installed in the buildings of the Lyceum Mediceum, see Norton, *Italian Printers* 97–8 and Rhodes, 'The Printing of a Group of Greek Books in Rome' 243–4.
4 Ep 836. On Lascaris cf no 95 n3.

110 Οδυσσεια βατραχο. hymni 32. grae.

Homerus. *Opera graece* vol 2: *Odyssea, Batrachomyomachia, Hymni* XXXII. Venetiis: Aldus, 1504 or 1517 or another edition (octavo).

In view of the format of nos 108 and 111, this book was very probably an octavo. There were several two-volume editions of Homer in this format in which the contents of the second volume agreed with the summary description in the *Versandliste*. The oldest of them is the Aldine edition of 1504 dedicated to Girolamo Aleandro; this was the first new printing of the Greek text after the *editio princeps* of Florence 1488, on which it was based. Reprints appeared in 1517 and 1524. In addition at least three octavo editions were published elsewhere: in Florence by Filippo Giunta in 1519 and in Strasbourg by W. Cephaleus in 1525 and 1534.[1] If we assume that Erasmus would already have had a copy of Homer in his possession before 1517 – he only acquired

the *editio princeps* of 1488 later (see nos 114–15) – then this entry must refer to the Aldine edition of 1504 or its 1517 reprint. Aldo's text of Homer did not stand high in Erasmus' estimation, and he faulted Michael Bentinus for verifying some citations of Homer and Cicero for the 1520 revision of the *Adagia* from the Aldine texts, 'although the Aldine editions are highly corrupt.'[2] But this need not have meant that he paid no attention to the Aldine edition or that he provided himself in 1517 or later with one of the other editions (which were perhaps no better). In practice, Erasmus preferred to use the products of the Venetian firm; in 1525 he ordered without distinction everything that had appeared from its presses in recent years.[3]

1 Quarto editions were also published by Dirk Martens in Leuven in 1523 and Johann Herwagen in Basel in 1535.
2 Ep 1437:162–4/177–9
3 A VII 547 Appendix 20 'Books Ordered by Erasmus'

111 Ad Atticum M. Tullij Cic. epistolae

Cicero, Marcus Tullius. *Epistolarum ad Atticum, ad Brutum, ad Quintum fratrem libri* XX. Venetiis: in aed. Aldi & Andrea soc., June 1513 (octavo).

In the translation of the interpolated Greek passages in this edition (first edition 1513) Aldo Manuzio had been assisted by Marcus Musurus.[1] This entry on the *Versandliste* probably refers to the copy that Erasmus ordered from Italy in 1525.[2]

1 Geanakoplos *Greek Scholars in Venice* 146
2 A VII 547 Appendix 20 'Books Ordered by Erasmus'

112 Statij. Syluae, Thebais, Achylleis cum commen.

Statius, Publius Papinius. *Statii syluae cum Domitii commentariis ... Thebais cum Lactantii commentariis ... Achilleis cum Maturantii commentariis*. Venetiis: B. de

Zanis, 1494 or J.P. de Quarengis, 1498 (folio).

Many editions of the Roman poet Statius (first century AD) appeared after 1470, at first exclusively in folio, and from the Aldine edition of 1502 on also occasionally in octavo. These two Venetian folio editions are, so far as it is possible to discover, the only ones with a title that is exactly reflected in the entry in the *Versandliste*, except for the omission of the names of the commentators.[1]

1 Hain-Copinger *14979 and *14980

113 Martialis cum duobus commentis

Martialis, Marcus Valerius. *Epigrammata. Cum duobus commentis Domitii Calderini et Georgii Merulae.* Venetiis: B. de Zanis, 1493 or Venetiis 1495, 1498, 1503, 1510 or Mediolani 1505 (folio).

After the *editio princeps* of c 1470 the epigrams of Martial (40–102) were republished many times in the last decades of the fifteenth century and the first of the sixteenth, in quarto and folio, and later also in octavo format. The addition *cum duobus commentis* 'with two commentaries,' however, leaves no doubt that one of the five or six folio editions with the commentaries of the Italian humanists Domizio Calderini and Giorgio Merula must be meant. The edition by B. de Zanis de Portesio was followed by four further Venetian editions, in 1493, 1498,[1] 1503 (J. Pentius de Leuco) and 1510 (P. Pincius), as well as by an edition from Milan in 1505 (J.A. Scinzenzeler). Some later editions include the commentaries but do not literally announce 'cum duobus commentis' on the title-page. Erasmus cited Martial in the reading of Domizio Calderini in the first paragraph of *Adagia* IV vi 35: *Auris Batava* 'A Dutch ear.'[2]

1 Hain-Copinger *10823, *10824, and *10825
2 ASD II-8 36:434–5 with n (37)/CWE 36 235 with n3

114 Ιλιασ Homeri graece

Homerus. *Opera graece, a Demetrio Chalcondyla edita* [Pars I: Ilias]. Florentiae: B. Nerlius, Nerius Nerlius, & Demetrius Damilas, 1488/9 (folio).

In contrast with no 109, which is reported between octavos, nos 114 and 115 seem to be placed at the beginning of a series of folios. If this is true – which would make it clear that the Homer editions in the *Versandliste* are separated according to their places in the book shelves – then this entry must refer to the only edition of Homer in folio that appeared before 1536, namely, the famous *editio princeps* of Florence 1488/9 supervised by Demetrius Chalcondyles; it was probably the copy that Erasmus instructed one of his suppliers to buy for him in 1525.[1] Erasmus' purchase as late as 1525 of the first edition in folio, although more manageable later editions (among them probably an Aldine edition) were at his disposal, can be explained by his criticism of the Aldine edition in particular (although it was based on the Florentine); see no 110. In 1524 he mentioned the Homer among the 'highly corrupt' Aldine editions.[2]

1 HCR 8772, BL *Catalogue* 6 678–9. Cf Allen VII 547 Appendix 20 'Books Ordered by Erasmus.'
2 Ep 1437:164/179

115 Οδυσσεια Homeri graece

Homerus. *Opera graece, a Demetrio Chalcondyla edita.* [Pars II: *Odyssea, Hymni.*] Florentiae: B. Nerlius, Nerius Nerlius, & Demetrius Demilas, 1488/9 (folio).

Probably the volume of the *editio princeps* of Homer in the original Greek with the text of the *Odyssey* and the Homeric Hymns; the part with the text of the *Iliad* is entered under the preceding number on the *Versandliste*.[1] The objection – that the two parts of the Florentine edition of 1488 do not have separate title-pages and therefore must have been bound in one volume – need not be decisive. Erasmus, or possibly the former owner, could have had the fairly heavy folio volume split for the sake of convenience and bound in two parts. That would not have been unusual: Janus Lascaris did the same with his annotated copy, which is now in the Bibliothèque nationale in Paris.[2]

The *editio princeps* of Homer was one of several works that remained behind in the Frisian region after the final disintegration of Jan Łaski's library (about 1554). Most of them were afterwards owned by professors of the University of Franeker (founded in 1585), some others by well-read humanist senators (*councillors*) of the influential court of Friesland. It is now known, thanks to Mr Engels' research, that this Florentine incunable from Erasmus' library was sold at auction in Leeuwarden in 1697. In a copy of the auction catalogue a written note was added to the entry on the bipartite work: *hic Codex olim fuit Erasmi Rot.* 'This book once belonged to Erasmus of Rotterdam.' The library auctioned at that time formed part of the estate left by Horatius Knyff, a senator of the court of Friesland. Most probably his copy of the book had previously belonged to Theodorum Saeckma, likewise a senator of the court; he in turn had inherited the library of his father J. Saeckma, who combined the offices of senator of the court and curator of the University of Franeker.[3] Up to the time of writing no other trace of this Homer edition has been found.

1 HCR 8772
2 BN *Catalogue général* 73 188. On Lascaris see no 95 n3.
3 Engels *Olim Erasmi* 4, 5, and 7

116 Ἀριστοφαν. Comoediae 9. cum commen. graece

Aristophanes. *Comoediae novem: Plutus, Nebulae, Ranae, Equites, Acharnes, Vespae, Aves, Pax, Contionantes. [cum scholiis graece editae]*. Venetiis: Aldus, 1498 (folio).

Given the format of the books listed before and after it, the work in question here must be the *editio princeps* of nine of the eleven preserved comedies of Aristophanes.[1] The text was prepared, introduced, and annotated with commentaries in Greek by Marcus Musurus (c 1470–1517), the most influential and most productive of the Cretan refugees who disseminated and promoted the knowledge of Greek in the West.[2] He had studied in Florence with Janus Lascaris, was a collaborator of the scholarly printers Aldo Manuzio and Zacharias Callierges in Venice, and was from 1503 professor of Greek successively at Padua, Venice, and Rome. He edited numerous editions of Greek texts. Erasmus met Musurus at Padua, where, although not formally inscribed as one of his students, he attended his lectures and was on a friendly footing with him in his home. Later in Venice, Erasmus asked his advice more than once and benefited from his assistance in preparing the *Adagiorum chiliades*. Erasmus continued to hold a high opinion of the learned Musurus, who was a little younger; he called him a 'quite extraordinary' Latinist.[3] Most of the texts Musurus edited were in Erasmus' library (nos 96, 102, 218, 239, 272 #2, 277, 297, and 320).

It is not possible to establish when the edition of Aristophanes came into Erasmus' possession. Probably it was not at a very early stage. He did not make intensive use of the work until during his residence in Italy. The comedies are referred to only a few times in the editions of the *Collectanea adagiorum* of 1500 and 1506–7.[4] In these cases Erasmus may have used the original text from one of his Paris friends or have drawn his quotations from a secondary source. The same can be said of a reference to the *Plutus* in a letter of 1505.[5] In the successive editions of the *Adagia* from 1508 on, however, Aristophanes was, after Homer and Plutarch, the most frequently mentioned or quoted Greek author.[6] (In Venice Erasmus was also in a position to inspect the *Lysistrata*, lacking in the 1498 edition, from a manuscript.[7] Thus it is quite plausible that Erasmus acquired his copy of the *editio princeps* of Aristophanes only during or after his residence in Italy. Perhaps he brought the book with him from there.

Erasmus' copy of the 1498 edition of Aristophanes' comedies seems to have been among the books that found their way to Friesland after the decay of Łaski's library (cf nos 115, 123, 137, 138, 201, 203, 208, 218, and 267). Most probably it was the copy in the estate of Johannes Bogerman, the strict Calvinist president of the Synod of Dordrecht and afterwards professor of theology in Franeker, that was sold by auction in 1638 at Leiden; the auction catalogue, preserved in the Royal Library of Copenhagen, specified that the book included a note or notes *cum manu Erasmi* 'in Erasmus' hand.'[8]

1 GW 2333. *Lysistrata* and *Thesmophoriazusae* were missing. They were not included in the Giunta edition of 1525 either, but this is unlikely to be referred to here, since it was a quarto. Both comedies had been published for the first time in an appendix of the preceding Giunta edition of 1515/16. In his revised *Adagia* of 1526 Erasmus quoted the *Thesmophoriazusae* in Greek from this octavo Florentine edition, a copy of which he possibly borrowed from Amerbach; see *Adagia* III ii 22 ASD II-5 119 319n/CWE 34 233 with n2 (393).

2 Most of the scholia were probably not written by Musurus, as was earlier supposed; see Wilson 'The Triclinian edition of Aristophanes.' Cf Geanakoplos *Greek Scholars in Venice* 122; Reynolds and Wilson *Scribes and Scholars* 240.

3 See Ep 1347:239–51/256–70. On his life, see Ep 223:4n/5n; Legrand *Bibliographie hellénique* I cviii–cxxiv and II 394–404; Geanakoplos *Greek*

Scholars in Venice 111–67; CEBR II 472–3. Cf Ep 2447:29–30/30–2; Allen I 55:94–8 (Beatus Rhenanus to Hermann of Wied), 61:170–86 (Beatus Rhenanus to Charles V). He is mentioned in *Adagia* II i i: *Festina lente* ASD II-3 22:390/CWE 33 14.

4 Twice in the 1500 edition (*Collectanea* 18, via Poliziano, and *Collectanea* 835) and once in the proverbs added in 1506–7 (*Collectanea* 722). See ASD II-9 54:410–13, 272:825–8, 243:265–6. Cf Appelt *Studies in the Contents and Sources of Erasmus' Adagia* 116–18.

5 Ep 182:110–11/122–4

6 Phillips *Adages* Appendix III

7 *Adagia* II ix 83 and II x 13 ASD II-4 265 2n and 289 148n/CWE 34 121 with note (357) and 133 with n2 (361)

8 Engels *Erasmus' handexemplaren* 59

117 Terentius cum commentarijs

Terentius Afer, Publius. *Comoediae una cum scholiis ex Donati, Asperi et Cornuti commentariis decerptis ... Studio et opera Des. Erasmi ... Basileae: H. Frobenius & N. Episcopius, March 1532 or an older edition (folio).*

This entry refers either to the 1532 Froben edition with an introduction by Erasmus or to an unidentifiable older folio edition. When in 1527 Johann Froben was thinking of a new edition of Terence 'with notes' (*cum commentariis*), Erasmus at once began to mobilize his friends for it. 'If you can assist us in this project, please do so, but promptly,' he wrote to Goclenius.[1] The death of Froben left the undertaking stranded, and it was not revived and successfully completed until five years later by his son Hieronymus, with Erasmus' help. Erasmus probably had little to do with the publication itself; his collaboration was confined to a short contribution 'on metres' in the preliminary matter, while he also provided a dedicatory letter to the young brothers Jan and Stanisław Boner, sons of the humanistically oriented Polish high official Seweryn Boner (Ep 2584).[2] The suggestion for this had come from the brothers' tutor, Anselmus Ephorinus, who had lived with them in Erasmus' house at

Freiburg from April to September 1531.[3]
A copy of the work was sent to Seweryn
Boner in Cracow but did not reach him
until three years later, after long delays.
As his reward Erasmus received two
specimens of a gold medallion, with the
image of the donor. One of these is now
in the Historisches Museum at Basel.[4]

1 Ep 1890:26–7 / 30–1
2 Ep 2533 introduction; on the members of the
   Boner family see also CEBR I 166–8.
3 Ep 2554:33–9 with 33n. On Ephorinus see Ep 2539
   introduction; CEBR I 436–7.
4 Ep 3010:1–29; *Erasmus … Vorkämpfer für Frieden
   und Toleranz* 113

118 Lucianus Latine uersus ab Erasmo

Lucianus. *Saturnalia. Cronosolon … Des.
Erasmo interprete. Aliquot item ex eodem
commentarii Thoma Moro interprete.*
Basileae: J. Frobenius, August 1521 (folio).

If this entry refers to a book in folio – and
its place in the *Versandliste* points to that
– only two editions of the dialogues of
Lucian translated by Erasmus and More
can be considered: the *editio princeps* of
Josse Bade of 1506 and the Froben edition
of 1521. Probably the latter is meant here.
The first was rendered out of date by the
Bade edition in quarto of 1514, which had
added seven new dialogues translated by
Erasmus to the original selection.[1] Erasmus
must have disposed of the 1506 edition,
or he may have given Bade his copy with
corrections to use in preparing the 1514
edition. Usually he did not keep books,
including his own works, when he acquired
new and better editions. Nor did he retain
the *editiones principes* of his own works for
sentimental reasons. The 1514 Bade edition
of Lucian illustrates what might happen to
Erasmus' copy of an outdated publication.
The book, with the ex libris *Sum Erasmi*
and with corrections in Erasmus' hand,
survives (it is now in the University Library
in Basel), but in 1536 it no longer formed
any part of Erasmus' library. Comparison
of the texts proves that Froben used this,

the author's own copy, for his edition
of the Lucian translations in 1517.[2]
Afterwards the book probably never
returned to its owner but remained at the
Froben press. Later on, in 1634, it came
into the possession of Remigius Faesch,
the Basel collector, and thence it found
its way to the University Library.[3]

For the last edition of the Lucian translations during Erasmus' lifetime see no 26 #1.

1 ASD I-1 370–2, 374–5
2 In 1517 the complete Lucian translations were not
   published independently but were included,
   without being mentioned on the title-page, in
   Froben's quarto *editio princeps* of *Querela Pacis*
   (BB E 1290). A copy of this edition, not recorded
   on the *Versandliste*, and a second copy of the 1521
   folio Lucian translations to which this entry
   probably refers, were found in the separate
   collection of his own works, mainly Froben
   editions, that Erasmus kept in his last Basel
   dwelling; see *Catalogus librorum Erasmi* nos 2
   (1517) and 21 (1521) and cf no 65.
3 Universitätsbibliothek Basel A.N.V. 80; Husner
   'Bibliothek' 258 and *Erasmus … Vorkämpfer für
   Frieden und Toleranz* (exhibition catalogue) 91
   and 197

119 Quintili. Vallae cum commento

Quintilianus, Marcus Fabius. *Institutiones
cum commento Laurentii Vallensis,
Pomponii ac Sulpitii.* Venetiis: Peregrinus
de Pasqualibus, 18 August 1494 (folio).

This entry probably refers to the early
standard edition of the chief work of
Quintilian (c 53–100) with the commentary
of Lorenzo Valla, Pomponius Laetus, and
Giovanni Antonio Sulpizio.[1] In 1406/7 the
Italian humanist Poggio Bracciolini
discovered the first complete manuscript
of the *Institutio oratoria* in the library of
the abbey of St Gallen. His discovery was
the mainspring of the great success that
this work, the most detailed manual of
rhetoric of antiquity, was to have in the
following centuries. Erasmus too was
influenced by Quintilian. In three of his
works the *Institutio oratoria* appears to
have been an important source of

inspiration and information: first in *De ratione studii* (written c 1497, published in 1511–14); later in *De pueris instituendis* (written between 1506 and 1509, published in 1529); and finally in the *Ecclesiastes* (1535).[2] If in fact the *Versandliste* refers to this edition, Erasmus cannot have acquired it before 1500, since in that year he was still obliged to borrow Quintilian's works from Robert Gaguin.[3] When he was preparing his *Adagia* of 1508 in Venice, he consulted another edition of Quintilian with the commentary of Raffaele Regio (Venice: B. Locatellus, 1493),[4] which he no doubt borrowed on the spot. Regio was professor of rhetoric at Padua. It was there, shortly before he moved to Venice to become professor of eloquence in 1508, that Erasmus met him; he recalled him as already an old man, but still vigorous, who, however raw and bad the weather, still went every morning to the Greek lectures of Marcus Musurus.[5]

1 BL *Catalogue* 5 393
2 *De ratione studii* ASD I-2 102–4 / CWE 24 663–4; *De pueris instituendis* ed Margolin 99–100 / CWE 26 293; *Ecclesiastes* ASD V-4 18 / CWE 67 101–5
3 Ep 122:5–7 / 7–8
4 BL *Catalogue* 5 441; ASD II-4 79 411n
5 See CEBR III 134; Ep 1347:231–8 / 248–55.

120 Ciceronis epistolae. Philosophica. Index. Herua.

Cicero, Marcus Tullius. *Opera quae aedita sunt hactenus omnia in tomos distincta quatuor. Tom. III (Opera epistolica) et IV (Opera philosophica).* Basileae: in off. Hervagiana, 1534 (folio).

Nos 120 and 121 together make up the four-volume edition of Cicero which sprang from the initiative of Johann Herwagen, who set up in business on his own account after the break-up of the Froben firm in 1531.[1] The volume here recorded contained volumes 3 and 4 bound together. The publication was achieved under the supervision and with the assistance of Bonifacius Amerbach (1495–1562), who was then a professor in Basel. He had

previously inquired whether any Venetian printing-house was inclined to put a complete Cicero on the market and later attempted to draw Erasmus into the enterprise, asking him to advise Herwagen on the division of the work and also to help if possible with the annotation.[2] He did not have much success: Erasmus was not disposed to become deeply involved and gave explicit advice only on one point: 'There is no difficulty about the division: the first is technique; the second, works; the third, orations; the fourth, philosophy.'[3] This classification was in fact adopted. But apart from some other comments and a vague promise, he dissociated himself from the publication, and also refused doggedly when Herwagen turned to him twice to write a preface, excusing himself on the pretext that it seemed to him improper 'to write a preface concerning a noble author about whom I have written nothing worthwhile.'[4] Herwagen, who aroused tension in the Froben family and in 1531 retired from the firm, was not congenial to him.[5] This is probably not sufficient to account for his unwillingness; Allen believed that 'Erasmus' reluctance to do anything more with Cicero ... was, no doubt, due in part to the fact that Scaliger's book had recently revived the agitation over the *Ciceronianus*.'[6]

1 AK IV 103 Ep 1602 (Herwagen to Amerbach); on Herwagen see Allen Epp 2033:58n, 2945 introduction; CEBR II 186–7.
2 Epp 2753:12–18, 2764:5–13, and 2765:11–19
3 Ep 2768:3–4
4 Epp 2775, 2788:13–14, 47–51 (both to Amerbach)
5 Allen *Erasmus: Lectures and Wayfaring Sketches* 130; cf no 131.
6 Ep 2765:11n. Scaliger's discourse, *Oratio pro M. Tullio Cicerone contra Des. Erasmum*, was published in Paris by G. Gourmont and P. Vidoue in September 1531.

121 Ciceronis Oratoria ex aeditione Heruagij

Cicero, Marcus Tullius. *Opera quae aedita sunt hactenus omnia in tomos distincta quatuor.* Tom. I (*Rhetorica, oratoria et forensia*) & II (*Orationes*). Basileae: off. Hervagiana, 1534 (folio).

Parts 1 and 2 of Herwagen's edition of Cicero. See no 120.

122 Epistolae Cicer./Tullius > opera. M. Tul.

Cicero, Marcus Tullius. Probably the part of the *Opera* in 4 (or 3) volumes containing *Opera epistolica, Epistolarum familiarum libri XVI. Epistolarum ad Brutum liber I,* etc (folio).

The entry in the *Versandliste* probably refers to Cicero's *Epistolae* as a separate part of the *Opera*. Cicero's collected works were often published, from 1498 onwards,[1] in four volumes, one of which contained the letters. Bade produced four editions in this form: the first appeared in 1511 and reprints followed in 1521–2, in 1529, and again in 1531. In 1528 Cratander published the works in three volumes. When Erasmus prepared the revised *Adagiorum opus* of 1533 he quoted Cicero from the new Basel edition.[2] Perhaps he also owned it, although in that case he must have disposed of it after he acquired the Herwagen edition of 1534 (nos 120–1). Neither the new Basel edition nor any other four-volume edition he might have owned before the Cratander edition was published is mentioned on the *Versandliste*. Consequently it cannot be established from which edition he seems to have kept, for some reason, the volume containing the letters.

1 *Opera* ed A. Minutianus (Milan: G. Le Signerre 1498/9; GW 6708

2 *Adagia* III ix 36 ASD II-6 529:326–8 with n/CWE 35 331–2 with n2

123 Lucianus graece ex offici. Aldi

Lucian. *Opera. Icones Philostrati. Eiusdem Heroica. Eiusdem uitae sophistarum. Icones Junioris Philostrati. Descriptiones*

Callistrati [*graece*]. Venetiis: in aed. Aldi, June 1503 (folio).

Erasmus' copy, with his ex libris on the last page and notes in his own hand in the margin of the text, was discovered by M.H.H. Engels in the Provincial Library of Friesland at Leeuwarden, where it was deposited with the library of the University of Franeker, abolished in 1811.[1] As appears from the library catalogue of that year, the book was already in the library of the university in 1644. From two almost identical notes on the title-page and the last page, it appears that it had previously belonged to Menelaus Winsemius, a professor at Franeker from 1616 to 1639, and had then been presented by him to his colleague Andreas Roorda, professor from 1611 to 1621, who died in 1626. Nothing is known of the early owners after Jan Łaski. Erasmus translated Lucian in 1505 and the following years.[2] His autograph marginalia enabled Engels to demonstrate that Erasmus used for his translations, not the *editio princeps* of the Greek Lucian published in Florence in 1496 by Lorenzo de Alopa, but the most recent and most current text then available, the Aldine edition of 1503. A special marginal indication further suggested that his copy of the Aldine edition may have come into Erasmus' possession almost immediately after its publication.

1 Sign. 124 Wsbg. Five other books from Erasmus' library found their way to the University of Franeker and have survived in Leeuwarden; see nos 137, 203, 208, 267, and, cf no 201. See Engels 'Erasmiana in de 'Franeker academiebibliotheek' 68–9, 'Erasmiana in the Old University Library of Franeker' 20, and *Erasmus' handexemplaren* 19–23, 45–7, and 87.

2 He probably began his translation during his stay in England, 1505–6; ASD I-1 370. Cf no 118.

124 Isocratis opera Graece

Isocrates. *Logoi* [*Orationes graece, curante Demetrio Chalcondyla*]. Mediolani: Uldericus Scinzenzeler, 1493 (folio).

'Opera' in this short title cannot mean 'collected works,' because a volume that contained both the speeches and the letters of Isocrates more or less complete did not appear until 1542. In 1513 Aldo Manuzio had published only the speeches, together with those of Alcidamas, Gorgias, and Aristides (no 132). The Aldine press put an enlarged edition of this collection on the market in 1534, under the title *Isocrates nuper recognitus et auctus. Alcidamas, Gorgias, Aristides. Harpocration.* This edition included some letters of Isocrates and of the few editions published before 1536, it therefore comes nearest to the description in the *Versandliste.* Yet this collection cannot be in question here. It is not very likely that Erasmus would still be purchasing Aldine editions in his last years; moreover, it would be surprising if the compiler of the *Versandliste* had not registered the other orators included in the book and explicitly mentioned on the title-page by adding his normal 'cum aliis.' It is much more plausible – we may almost say practically certain – that 'Opera' indicates the only other edition exclusively dedicated to Isocrates that appeared before Erasmus' death: the *editio princeps* of the Λόγοι edited by Demetrius Chalcondyles.[1] The speeches, after all, made up most of the *Opera.* Erasmus probably translated the *Praecepta de regno administrando ad Nicoclem regem* published for the first time in the *editio princeps* (Basel 1516) of his *Institutio principis christiani* from the 1493 Milan edition.[2]

1 Hain 9312, BL *Catalogue* 6 767. For other works edited by Chalcondyles cf nos 114 and 344.
2 On the *Praecepta ad Nicoclem,* which precede the text of the *Institutio principis christiani* in the edition of 1516, see Herding 'Isokrates, Erasmus und die *Institutio principis christiani.*'

125 Asco. Pedianus in orationes Ciceronis

Asconius Pedianus, Quintus. *Commentarii in orationes Ciceronis. Georgius Trapezuntius de artificio Ciceronianae orationis pro Quinto Ligario etc* (a folio edition).

An important and chiefly historical commentary on five of Cicero's orations – *In Pisonem, Pro Scauro, Pro Milone, Pro Cornelio, In toga candida* – written between 54 and 57 AD. The work in its original form was part of a commentary that may have dealt with all the speeches; it survived, albeit with lacunae, in a manuscript discovered by the Italian humanist Poggio Bracciolini in 1416 in the library of the abbey of St Gallen.[1] The manuscript itself was later lost again, but the text was published for the first time from Poggio's transcript in 1477 by J. de Colonia and J. Manthen at Venice,[2] and reprinted more than once. There are no indications that would identify the edition Erasmus owned. It could equally well be the *editio princeps* just mentioned, the Venice edition of C. de Pensis (c 1492)[3] or the more recent edition of P. Vidoue (Paris 1520) prepared by Nicolas Bérault.[4]

1 Pauly-Wissowa II 1524–7 and OCD 188–9 sv Asconius Pedianus
2 GW 2739
3 GW 2740
4 On his relations with Erasmus, see no 46 #2.

126 Galen. de locis affectis

Galenus, Claudius. *De affectorum locorum notitia libri sex, Guilielmo Copo … interprete. Ex secunda recognitione.* Probably Parisiis: S. Colinaeus, 1520 (folio).

Galen's pioneer work in the field of special pathology, translated into Latin and published by the humanist-physician Guillaume Cop, a friend of Erasmus since his Paris days. The oldest edition known (Paris: Henri Estienne 1513) is a quarto volume. The adjacent books on the *Versandliste,* however, point to a folio. Two editions in this format can be traced: one, published with no indication of place or year, has been dated to c 1520 and attributed to the Venetian printer P.

Pincius;[1] the other was published in Paris by Simon de Colines in 1520. Could Erasmus perhaps have received a presentation copy of the 1520 edition from its editor, a friend of long standing?[2]

1 Isaac 14068; see Rhodes 'An unidentified edition of Galen.'
2 Cf Mani 'Die Griechische Editio princeps des Galenos (1525)' 109. On Cop see no 90 #1.

127 Ρηθορικη [sic] 13. autorum graece. Ald.

Rhetores graeci [vol i]. *Rhetores in hoc volumine habentur hi: Aphthonii sophistae Progymnasmata, Hermogenis Ars rhetorica, Aristotelis Rhetoricorum ad Theodecten libri tres. Ejusdem Rhetorica ad Alexandrum. Ejusdem ars Poetica. Sopatri Rhetoris quaestiones de componendis declamationibus in causis praecipuae judicialibus. Cyri Sophistae differentiae statuum. Dionysii Alicarnasei ars Rhetorica. Demetrii Phalerei de interpretatione. Alexandri Sophistae de figuris sensus & dictionis. Adnotationes innominati de figuris Rhetoricis. Menandri Rhetoris diuisio causarum in genere demonstrativo. Aristeidis de ciuili oratione. Ejusdem de simplici oratione. Apsini de arte Rhetorica praecepta.* Venetiis: in aed. Aldi, 1508/9 or second edition in aed. Aldi et Andreae soceri, 1523 (folio).

One of the most important productions of the Aldine press, the first of two substantial folio volumes containing treatises on rhetoric by thirteen (by the cataloguer's count) Greek authors in the original language. Among the three treatises by Aristotle included in the first volume was the *editio princeps* of the *Poetics*. The text had been prepared for the press by Demetrios Doukas (c 1480–c 1527), the Cretan refugee who early in the sixteenth century had settled in Venice and had been received with open arms in the circle of Aldo Manuzio and his Neakademia, which had made its object the spreading of classical Greek texts through printed editions.[1] Erasmus was still in Venice or in

nearby Padua when the first volume of the *Rhetores graeci* appeared in November 1508. In the preceding months he must have made Doukas' acquaintance. It has been supposed that Erasmus and Girolamo Aleandro assisted Doukas in collating the manuscripts for his edition of Plutarch's *Moralia*, issued in March 1509 (no 208). Whether or not they did, their shared philological interests would almost inevitably have brought Erasmus and Doukas into contact. Erasmus himself tells us that while he was working on the *Adagia* in Venice he consulted numerous manuscripts of texts that had not yet been printed, among them 'Aphthonius, Hermogenes with notes, Aristotle's *Rhetoric* with the scholia of Gregory of Nazianzus, the whole of Aristides with scholia.'[2] These same manuscripts must have furnished Doukas at about the same time with the basic texts for his *Rhetores graeci*. In May 1509, just after Erasmus had left Italy, the second volume of the collection, which contained only commentaries on Aphthonius and Hermogenes, was published. It cannot be concluded from the wording of this item on the *Versandliste* that both volumes are meant. More probably it refers only to the first volume, which mentions thirteen authors on the title-page, one of them anonymous (*innominatus*). If this is the case, no 128 may be identified with volume two of Doukas' collection.

1 On Doukas see Geanakoplos *Greek Scholars in Venice* 223–55, especially 226–8 on this work. Cf no 95.
2 *Adagia* ii i 1: *Festina lente* 'Make haste slowly' ASD ii-3 398–400/CWE 33 14

128 Ερμογεν. et Aphthonius cum commen. graece

Rhetores graeci [vol ii]. *In Aphthonii Progymnasmata commentarii innominati autoris. Syriani, Sopatri, Marcellini commentarii in Hermogenis Rhetorica.* Venetiis: in aed. Aldi, 1508–9 or second edition in aed. Aldi & Andreae soc., 1523 (folio).

In August 1517 Erasmus informed Wolfgang Lachner and his son-in-law Johann Froben that the *Hermogenis Rhetorica* sent from Frankfurt had reached him.[1] According to Allen, this referred to the recently published edition of Filippo Giunta (Florence 1515). For two reasons it is unlikely that this entry refers to the book that Erasmus then received. The Florentine edition was an octavo volume and would have been out of place in the group of folios among which it is listed; moreover, it contained the text of Aphthonius and Hermogenes without commentary, while the *Versandliste* specifies an edition 'cum comme[ntariis].' Which work can be alluded to? No independent early edition of either author in folio and with a commentary is known. It is most probable that this entry refers to the second part of the *Rhetores graeci* collected by Demetrios Doukas; for the first part, see no 127. Although this second part did not consist of the writings on rhetoric by Aphthonius and Hermogenes themselves, but only of commentaries on them by others, it is quite plausible that the person who entered the volume in the list took his cue from a misunderstood title on the fore-edge, which might, for example, have read: 'Ἑρμογεν & Aphthonius. Commentarii.' This assumption would explain not only the form of the entry, half in Greek and half in Latin characters, but also the unusual sequence of the authors' names: elsewhere Aphthonius and his *Progymnasmata* always precede Hermogenes on the title-page.[2] It seems justified, therefore, to identify numbers 127 and 128 with the 'Opera Hermogenis greca cum aliis' that Erasmus ordered from Italy in about 1525.[3] But was it the original edition of 1508–9 or the reprint of 1513? It need not necessarily have been the most recent printing that was supplied. It might also have been the *editio princeps*; it would be more natural for the two successively published parts of that edition to have been separately bound, as

in Erasmus' copy, than the simultaneously published parts of the new impression. If in fact Erasmus acquired the Aldine edition of the *Rhetores graeci* around 1525, he might as a consequence have disposed of the Giunta edition of *Hermogenis Rhetorica* that he had bought in 1517. This in turn could explain why the title no longer appears in the *Versandliste*.

1 Ep 629:11–12/13–14
2 Pauly-Wissowa I 2797 sv Aphthonios
3 Allen VII 547 Appendix 20 'Books Ordered by Erasmus'

129 Ioannes grammaticos in lib. de generati. grae.

Philoponus, Johannes. *Joannes grammaticus in libros de generatione et interitu. Alexander Aphrodisiensis in meteorologica etc.* [graece]. Venetiis: in aedibus Aldi et Andreae Asulani soceri, September 1527 (folio).

The learned Byzantine Joannes Philoponus (born c AD 470), who called himself by preference 'Joannes Grammaticus' on account of his work, is also known as the earliest representative of Christian Aristotelianism.[1] In his effort to reconcile Christianity and Aristotelianism he wrote numerous exegetical commentaries on Aristotle's works, among them this one on the *De generatione et corruptione*, which he himself called simply 'scholia.' Possibly Erasmus acquired the book as the continuing result of his instructions of 1525 to buy for him 'all the Greek commentators on Aristotle' (*commentatores in Aristotelem greci omnes*).[2]

1 See on him Pauly-Wissowa IX 1764–99 sv Ioannes Philoponos (on the commentaries on Aristotle, 1772–81); *Der Kleine Pauly* II 1430–1 sv Iohannes Philoponos; OCD 1168–9 sv Philoponos, John.
2 Allen VII 547 Appendix 20 'Books Ordered by Erasmus'

130 Δεμοσθένησ [sic] orationes 62. graece

Demosthenes. *Orationes duae et sexaginta. Libanii sophistae in eas ipsas orationes argumenta. Vita Demosthenis per Libanium. Eiusdem vita per Plutarchum* [Graec. Ed Aldus Manutius et Scipio Fortiguerra (Carteromachus).] Venetiis: in aed. Aldi, November 1504 (folio).

In 1504 Aldo Manuzio published the *editio princeps* of the Greek text of Demosthenes. In his preface to the 1532 Basel edition (no 131) Erasmus praised the master-printer 'Aldo, who was the first to give us this prince among orators,'[1] but did not mention the important part played in the preparation of the text by Scipione Fortiguerra, although to the last days of his life he treasured his memory. Scipione Fortiguerra (also called Carteromachus), a pupil of Poliziano who applied himself particularly to Greek, collaborated closely in Venice with Aldo Manuzio and was in 1500 or 1501 one of the founders of the Neakademia. Erasmus came to know him in the winter of 1506–7 in Bologna and thought him a man of learning in every field, but one who hid his light too modest-ly under a bushel.[2] In the winter of 1508 he met him again in Padua, where the two people he consulted repeatedly when facing any difficult problem were Marcus Musurus and Fortiguerra.[3] Their paths crossed for the third time in Rome in February 1509. In 1535 Erasmus recalled that Fortiguerra 'would often creep into my room unexpect-edly and pass a few hours in the afternoon chatting about literary matters. Nor was it only my table that I often shared with him: sometimes we slept in the same bed.'[4]

1 Ep 2695:87–8
2 On Fortiguerra see Ep 217:2n/4n; CEBR II 44–5; cf Ep 1347:226–30/243–7.
3 Allen I 55:94–6 (Beatus Rhenanus to Hermann of Wied) and I 61:170–86 (Beatus Rhenanus to Charles V); Sicherl *Johannes Cuno* 50
4 Ep 3032:215–18

131 Demost. orationes 62. graece. Heruagij

Demosthenes. *Orationes duae & sexaginta, & in easdem Ulpiani commentarii … Libanii argumenta: tum collectae … ex Des. Erasmi, Guilh. Budaei atque aliorum lucubrationibus annotationes.* Basileae: J. Hervagius, September 1532 (folio).

This translation of Demosthenes contains an introductory letter by Erasmus (Ep 2695), addressed to Johann Georg Paumgartner, a student of law, son of a wealthy Augsberg merchant and patron.[1] At first Erasmus had stubbornly refused to introduce the work, but finally he appears to have yielded to the insistence of Herwagen.[2] Eight years earlier, in 1524, Melanchthon had suggested to Erasmus that he should translate Demosthenes into Latin, but Erasmus then sent the ball back into his court: no one, he said, was better qualified to do this than Melanchthon.[3]

1 On Paumgartner see CEBR III 62.
2 Ep 2686:9–25 (to Bonifacius Amerbach)
3 Epp 1500:67–8/72–3, 1523:207–9/221–3

132 Orationes Rhetorum 16 graece

Oratores graeci: *Orationes horum rhetorum, Aeschinis, Lysiae, Alcidamantis* [etc]; *item Aeschinis vita, Lysiae vita,* graece. *Orationes infra scriptorum rhetorum, Andocidis, Isaei, Dinarchi* [etc]. *Isocratis orationes, Alcidamantis contra dicendi magistros, Gorgiae de laudibus Helenae, Aristidis de laudibus Athenarum, eiusdem de laudibus urbis Romae.* Venetiis: in aed. Aldi et Andreae soc., April (the first and second parts) and May (the third part) 1513 (folio).

This short title refers to a famous collec-tion of Greek orators in the original language, some of them published for the first time. The complete work consisted of three parts, which could probably be bought separately. The second volume was dedicated by Aldo Manuzio to Giambattista Egnazio, a well-known scholar and a friend of Erasmus.[1] In the copies preserved, the first two volumes are often bound together while the third volume, with the orations of Isocrates, is frequently missing;[2] but the three volumes also occur bound in one. The reference to sixteen orators given in the *Versandliste*, although approximate rather than exact, may point to a complete copy with three volumes bound as one. It is possible that Erasmus acquired this collection around 1525 when, together with other books, he ordered from Italy 'Orationes Aeschinis et aliorum rhetorum decem grecae.'[3]

1 On Egnazio see no 51.
2 Cf no 124.
3 Allen VII 547 Appendix 20 'Books Ordered by Erasmus'

133 Aetius Medicus ex aediti. Frob.

Aetius Amidenus medicus. *Libri XVI in tres tomos divisi, quorum primus & ultimus Joanne Baptista Montano Veronensi, secundo Jano Cornario Zuiccaviensi interpretibus latinitate donati sunt. In quo opere cuncta quae ad curandi artem pertinent congesta sunt.* vols 1 and 2. Basileae: H. Frobenius & N. Episcopius, 1533 (folio).

'Sixteen Books on Medicine' compiled from older writers, with a preference for Galen, by Aetius of Amida, a physician who was active at the Byzantine court at the beginning of the sixth century.[1] The Froben edition contained the first complete Latin translation of the work, which won renewed popularity during the Renaissance. It was published in three volumes: the first and third were translated by J. Baptista Montano (1488–1551), an Italian medical man who had also attended the lectures of Marcus Musurus at Padua;[2] the second by Janus Cornarius (c 1500–58), a German scholar who devoted himself to the publication of classical medical authors and had a passing contact with Erasmus during a brief stay at Basel (1528–9).[3] The first and second volumes were published in 1533; the

third appeared in 1535. Very probably this entry on the *Versandliste* refers to the first two volumes, and the third volume is entered under no 413, which makes special reference to 'interprete Ioan. Baptista Veronensi.'

1 Pauly-Wissowa I 703–4 sv Aetios; OCD 30–1 sv Aëtius
2 On Montano see Hoefer *Nouvelle biographie générale* sv; *Encyclopedia italiana* XXIII 728; Cosenza *Italian Humanists* III 2344.
4 On Cornarius see Allen and CWE Ep 2204 introductions; AK III 360 Ep 1295 introduction; CEBR I 339–40. Cf no 399.

134 Ptolemaeus de Geograph. latine

Ptolemaeus, Claudius. *Geographicae enarrationis libri octo Bilibaldo Pirckeymhero interprete.* Argentorati: J. Grieningerus, 30 March 1525 (folio).

The new translation of Ptolemy by Erasmus' friend Willibald Pirckheimer (1470–1530), with the notes of the mathematician-astronomer Johannes Regiomontanus (1436–76) on the earlier translation by Jacopo Angeli.[1] The fifty maps, all but one borrowed from the Strasbourg edition of Laurentius Fries (1522) and printed from the woodblocks used for it, were in reality copies on a smaller scale of the well-known maps in the Ptolemy atlas of 1513, mostly attributed to Martin Waldseemüller; a scaled-down copy of his famous world map of 1507 was also inserted.[2] These maps were modern: for the first time a serious effort was made to incorporate the results of the voyages of discovery of the last few decades. The new image conveyed by the map made Erasmus see the Christian world in a wider context. In his colloquy Ἰχθυοφαγία 'A Fish Diet' of 1526, one of the speakers, a butcher, has recently seen a very large map on canvas in which the whole world was depicted, and he remarks on how small, taken by itself, is the part occupied by the Christians.[3] This is probably an allusion to the world-map of Waldseemüller, which is indeed very large, or to one of the smaller copies derived from it.

The copy of the 1525 edition indicated by this entry must have been a presentation copy from the translator. A few months after its publication Erasmus wrote to Pirckheimer that he had not yet seen the book, but intended to secure a copy. For Pirckheimer the hint was enough, and he sent one to his friend in Basel. Erasmus thanked him in June 1526 not only for his edition of Ptolemy but also for a book of Dürer's that he had received together with the atlas. Allen identified this second gift as Dürer's *Underweysung der messung mit dem Zirckel und Richtscheyt* (Nürnberg 1525), a folio publication dedicated to Pirckheimer.[4] As a companion present for the Ptolemy the book, a manual of instruction for artists, was relevant in so far as it contained examples of projections for maps.[5] Evidently Erasmus did not find permanent space for it in his library, for the title is not to be found in the *Versandliste*.

1 On this edition, see Phillips *Geographical Atlases* I 120.
2 Cf no 321 n2.
3 LB I 792 / ASD I-3 504:349–51 / CWE 40 686:18–20. For more allusions to the *regiones nuper inventas* in the *Colloquies* see ASD I-3 315:46, 380:171, and 398:334–399:369 / CWE 39 330:36, 453:31–2, 479:21–480:21; cf CWE 40 728 n69.
4 Epp 1603:100 / 112–13, 1717:71–2 with 72n / 82–3 with n31
5 Keuning 'The History of Geographic Map Projections until 1600' 6–7

135 Alciatus in 16. libris

Alciatus, Andreas. *Paradoxorum ad Pratum lib. VI. Dispunctionum lib. IIII. In treis lib. Cod. lib. III. De eo quod interest lib. I. Praetermissorum lib. II. Declamatio una.* Mediolani: A. Minutianus, 1518 or a later edition (folio).

A collection of studies devoted in the main to the legislation of Justinian, which established the reputation of Andrea Alciati (1492–1550) as an epoch-making humanistic jurist.[1] Erasmus' attention was drawn to it in October 1519 by Bonifacius Amerbach. Two years later he recalled this in the first letter he wrote to Alciati: 'Amerbach ... has told me much of you, and all of it very greatly to your honour and glory. He has moreover shown me your publication ... and so has caused me to entertain a high respect for your scholarship – almost incredible in one so young.'[2] This shows that he had the *editio princeps* in his hands in Leuven in 1518; possibly he already owned it. Apart from that, Alciati was no stranger to him even before Amerbach's suggestion; for in 1518 the Italian bookseller Francesco Minuzio Calvo, who was a close friend of Alciati, visited Leuven. He had brought with him (without permission) the manuscript of Alciati's *Epistola contra vitam monasticam*, and left it with Erasmus at the end of April.[3] Whether the volume of legal studies indicated here had yet appeared cannot unfortunately be established. Otherwise it would not be too bold to suppose that Calvo, who one the same visit to Erasmus brought several recent publications from Italy, had procured a copy of it for him. Erasmus remained friendly with Alciati and valued him highly; he inserted a very honourable mention in the 1526 edition of the *Adagia* prompted by a suggestion Alciati made in one of the studies in the collection under consideration here.[4] At the end of his life Erasmus received in Freiburg through his former servant-pupil Philippus Montanus another book of Alciati's, the *Emblemata*. This work, later so popular, did not find a permanent place on his shelves; at least, the title does not appear in the *Versandliste*.[5]

1 On him see *Dizionario biografico degli Italiani* II 69–77; Viard *André Alciat*; Allen and CWE Ep 1250 introductions; CEBR I 23–6. On his pioneering treatises, in which for the first time a jurist put his knowledge of Greek to good use in juridical research, cf Troje *Graeca leguntur* 217–32.
2 Ep 1250:1–6 / 2–7; cf Ep 1020:54–61 / 57–74 (from Amerbach).

3 Allen Ep 1201:14–22 / CWE Ep 1233A:14–21;
cf on the affair of the *Declamatio*, which was
not published until 1695, Epp 1250:15–18 / 17–20,
2464:1–3 / 1–4, 2467:2–6 / 1–6. On Calvo see
Ep 581:31n / 33n; CEBR I 245–6; on his visit
to Leuven in 1518 cf Ep 832:29–35 / 32–8.
4 Woods Callahan 'The Erasmus-Alciati Friendship';
Adagia I v 45: *Nihil ad versum* 'Nothing to do with
the verse' ASD II-1 520:43–54 / CWE 31 423:18–29
5 A copy of the 2nd edition (Paris: C. Wechel 1534);
Reedijk 'Holbein's Erasmus met de pilaster (1523)
en de emblematiek' 140 n30. Cf 'Books Found
in Erasmus' Correspondence' no 5.

136 Ptolomaeus [sic] de geogra. Vlmae excursus

Ptolemaeus, Claudius. *Cosmographia.*
Ulmae: Lennardus Holle, 16 July 1482
or Ulmae: J. Reger for Justus de Albano,
21 July 1486 (folio).

Ptolemy's *Cosmographia* translated into
Latin by Jacopo Angeli, a pupil of Manuel
Chrysolaras, with thirty-two woodcut maps
produced by the Benedictine Nicolaus
Germanus.[1] The edition of 1482 was the
first to be published outside Italy; a reprint
appeared in 1486, enlarged with a detailed
index of geographical names.[2] In both
editions twenty-six maps represented the
ancient world as Ptolemy conceived it. To
these rather primitive maps were added six
'modern' ones corresponding with the state
of contemporary knowledge: a world map
(still of the Eastern hemisphere only); four
special maps of Spain, France, Italy, and
Palestine; and one really noteworthy map
that, ten years before Columbus' first
voyage, embraced not only the northern
regions of the Old World, but also part
of the New World (Greenland), including
the legendary 'Vinland,' discovered by the
Scandinavians five hundred years before.[3]
Erasmus' earliest geographical picture of
the world was probably largely based on
this early German Ptolemy atlas. It was
not until 1525 that he came into possession
of another atlas with a greatly increased
number of modern maps that reflected the
results of the voyages of discovery of the
last few decades; see no 134.

1 Hain *15539. The codex used as printer's copy for
the Ulm edition of 1482 has been preserved and is
now in the Waldburg-Wolfeggische Hofbibliothek,
Schloss Wolfegg, Würtemberg. See for detailed
information on the Ulm editions Phillips
Geographical Atlases I 107–9; *Clavdius Ptolemaeus,
Cosmographia, Ulm 1482*, facsimile edition;
Stevens *Ptolemy's Geography* 40–1; Meine *Die
Ulmer Geographia des Ptolemäus von 1482*
(exhibition catalogue) 52 and 61; Campbell *The
Earliest Printed Maps, 1472–1500* 135–8.
2 Hain *15540
3 All the maps from the 1482 edition are reproduced
in Schramm *Der Bilderschmuck der Frühdrucke* VII
3–4 and plates 1–33.

137 Galeni prima / Galeni 2. / Galeni 3. / Galeni 4. / Galeni 5.

Galenus, Claudius. *Galeni librorum pars
prima (–quinta)*. Venetiis: in aed. Aldi
et Andreae Asulani soc., 1525 (folio).

The *editio princeps* of the Greek text of
Galen's works. Erasmus ordered a copy
in the course of 1525.[1] He was already
convinced of the usefulness of the edition:
He wrote to Gianfrancesco Torresani, a
member of the Aldine publishing house in
October that 'the publication of Galen is
causing much excitement in the scholarly
world.' Later he received the five volumes
from him as a gift. He cannot have received
it before the early summer of 1526, for he
did not write his letter of thanks for the
present until September of that year.[2]
By then he had already translated three
general treatises from the first volume of
another copy (the one he had ordered?)
and published them from Froben's press
in May under the title *Exhortatio ad bonas
arteis, praesertim medicinam de optimo
docendi genere, et qualem oporteat esse
medicum*. Thanks to this edition he was
able to insert several novelties in the next
new printing of the *Adagia* (1528).[3] But
once he had used the Greek text on which
several of his friends had worked he had
nothing good to say of it. 'I have never
encountered anything more riddled with
errors,' he wrote; 'the person responsible
for correcting the text hardly seems to

know the first thing about the Greek language' – a damning verdict. And two weeks later, just as unmercifully: 'I have never seen a work more corrupt.'[4]

Erasmus' copy, without his ex libris but with marginal annotations in the first volume unmistakeably in his hand, was rediscovered in the Provincial Library of Friesland at Leeuwarden among the books that came from the former library of the University of Franeker.[5] The Galen already appears in the 1644 catalogue. From another source it was already known that Regnerus Praedinius, the rector of the Latin School at Groningen around the middle of the sixteenth century, had bought the *Opera*, with some other books from Erasmus' library, from Gérard Mortaigne, who went into exile for religious reasons in Emden. Mortaigne had in his turn bought or acquired the books from Łaski.[6]

1 A VII 547 Appendix 20 'Books Ordered by Erasmus'
2 Epp 1628:3/3–4, 1746:1–10/2–12
3 See for example *Adagia* III iii 3 ASD II-5 190:681–5 with 681n (191)/CWE 34 282 with n4 (408) and III vii 76 ASD II-6 468:903–4 with n (469)/CWE 35 266 with n2. For a reference to *De optimo docendi genere* in the 1527 edition of the *Novum Testamentum* see LB VI 376D/ASD VI-6 110:845–7 (on John 8:25).
4 Epp 1707:3–7/6–11, 1713:28–30/29–32
5 Sign. 119 G k. See Engels 'Erasmiana in de Franeker Academiebibliotheek' 67–8, *Erasmus' handexemplaren* 30–3 and 48–50, and 'Erasmiana in the Old University of Franeker' 19–20. For the other books that have survived in Leeuwarden see nos 123, 203, 208, 267, and cf no 201.
6 Gabbema *Epistolarum centuriae tres* 167–73 Ep 68. On the other books Praedinius bought see nos 138, 218, and 281.

138 Γαληνου θεραπευτικησ μεθοδ.

Galenus, Claudius. *Therapeuticorum libri XIV et Ad Glauconem libri II, graece.* Venetiis: [Z. Callierges for] N. Blastos, 21 October 1500 (folio).

The *Therapeutica* was the first text of Galen printed in Greek; it was edited by Niccolò Leoniceno (1428–1524), for many years professor of medicine at Ferrara and a reformer of his profession in the humanistic spirit.[1] He was already eighty years old when Erasmus met him in 1509 in Ferrara and asked him why he taught the science of medicine but did not put it into practice. Leoniceno responded that he accomplished more by teaching all the doctors. Erasmus valued his knowledge highly, and called him the man by whose teaching 'medicine first learnt to speak in Italy.'[2] Erasmus was also acquainted with the learned printer Calliergis (cf no 277).

Erasmus' copy is now in the University Library in Leiden.[3] Two later owners have added their names to the ex libris *Sum Erasmi* on the last page, with the mention of the year in which they acquired the book: *Factus autem Regneri Praedinij anno 1554. Dominorum commutatione magis impari quam fuit armorum Glauci et Diomedis. Si hoc in illo meliore jure dum factus sum Joannis Arcerij Theodor. 1563* 'I became the property of Regnerus Praedinius in 1554 through a change in ownership more unequal than that of the arms of Glaucus and Diomedes. If this was the case with him [Praedinius], it is even more so when I became the property of Johannes Arcerius Theodoretus in 1563.'[4] Regnerus Praedinius (1510–59) was rector of St Martin's school in Groningen. His pupil Johannes Arcerius Theodoretus (1538–1604), later professor of Greek at the University of Franeker, is still remembered for the Codex Arcerianus, a manuscript of the late fifth and early sixth centuries, formerly at Bobbio, containing the text of the *agrimensores*. This famous manuscript also belonged to Erasmus, and is now in the Herzog-August-Bibliothek in Wolfenbüttel. For other books that became Dutch property via Praedinius, see nos 137, 218, and 281.

1 Hain *7426. On Leoniceno see Allen Ep
541:55n / cwe Ep 216a:21n; cebr ii 323. On the
manuscripts of the *Therapeutika* see Mani 'Die
griechische Editio princeps des Galenos (1525)' 38.
2 *Apophthegmata* iii 10 lb iv 156b / asd iv-4
199:59–61 / cwe 37 224; Ep 862:16 / 20–1
3 Sign. 1366 a 2
4 Cf *Adagia* i ii 1: *Diomedis et Glauci permutatio.*

139 Ινστιτουτα **Theophi. Anteces. grae.**

*Institutiones iuris civilis in graecam linguam
per Theophilum Antecessorem olim traductae, nunc ... restitutae et recognitae cura et
studio Viglii Zuichemi Phrysii.* Basileae:
H. Frobenius et N. Episcopius, March 1534
(folio).

A Greek paraphrase of the *Institutes* of
Justinian by the Byzantine jurist Theophilus
Antecessor, edited by Viglius Zuichemus
(Wigle Aytta) from a manuscript that
Cardinal Bessarion had presented to the
library of San Marco in Venice.[1] Viglius
had found it there with the assistance of
the director of the library, Pietro Bembo.
He made a copy and sent it, after preliminary correspondence with Bonifacius
Amerbach in August 1533, to Hieronymus
Froben for publication. Erasmus was kept
fully informed of the discovery and of the
progress of the publication.[2] Before Viglius'
departure for Italy he had seen him and
given him advice, and later on he had
recommended his young friend to Pietro
Bembo, comparing him, with humorous
exaggeration, with Rodolphus Agricola.[3]
When Viglius went to Basel in October
1533 to see the edition through the press,
he paid his respects first to Erasmus in
Freiburg.[4]

1 Dekkers *Het humanisme en de rechtswetenschap
in de Nederlanden* 42–61. The Theophilos paraphrase has been called 'the first great exposition
of Byzantine jurisprudence'; see Troje *Graeca
leguntur* 247–8. On Viglius and his relationship
with Erasmus see Allen and cwe Ep 2101
introductions; cebr iii 393–5.
2 Epp 2716:100–9, 2753:18–20, 2791:57–63 (all from
Viglius); ak iv 169 Ep 1689
3 Ep 2681:5–19
4 Epp 2885, 2888

140 **Sextus Decretalium**

[*Corpus iuris canonici* iii] *Sextus liber
decretalium in concilio Lugdunensi per
Bonifacium viii editus.* Probably a folio
or a quarto edition.

The *Liber sextus,* a collection of decretals
promulgated by Boniface viii in 1298, was
so called because it followed the existing
Decretales Gregorii ix, which consisted
of five books (no 141). The first printed
edition of the *Liber sextus* had appeared
in Strasbourg c 1470,[1] after which the
work was reprinted many times in various
countries. The edition in Erasmus' possession cannot be identified. The great majority of editions published in the sixteenth
century before his death appeared in Paris
and Lyon, and before he settled in Basel
Erasmus had acquired a great many
books from French presses.[2] The sixteenth-
century French editions sometimes included later collections that were counted
as part of the *Corpus iuris canonici:*
the *Clementinae,* the *Extravagantes Joannis
xxii,* and the *Extravagantes communes.*
On Erasmus' concern with canon law
in general, see no 142.

1 Hain-Copinger *7996; Goff *Incunabula in
American Libraries: A Third Census* dates it
c 1470–2.
2 Cf no 72 with n2.

141 **Decretalium Gregorij libri .5.**

[*Corpus iuris canonici* ii] *Decretales Gregorii
ix.* Probably a folio or a quarto edition.

An unidentifiable edition of the collection
of papal decretals compiled and issued in
1234 by Raymond of Peñafort on the
instructions of Gregory ix. This was the
first authentic collection of canon law after
the *Decretum* of Gratian, to which it was
intended as a supplement. For Erasmus'
familiarity with canon law in general see
no 142.

142 Decretum pars prima 2ᵃ. 3ᵃ.

[*Corpus iuris canonici* ɪ] *Decretum Gratiani.*
Probably a folio or a quarto edition.

The collection of conciliar decisions and
papal decretals compiled in the mid-twelfth
century by the Bolognese monk Gratian,
known as the *Decretum Gratiani*, was first
published at Strasbourg in 1471,[1] and
reprinted countless times thereafter.
We cannot identify the copy in Erasmus'
library. The indication in the short title that
it contained three parts does not help: in
the numerous Paris and Lyon editions of
the early sixteenth century (before 1516 for
the most part folio editions but also some
in quarto), the division into three parts was
often stated in the colophon. The *Decretum
Gratiani* was the first part – the foundation
– of the *Corpus iuris canonici*. Since the
two parts that supplement it, the *Decretals
of Gregory* ɪx and the *Liber sextus decretalium* of Boniface vɪɪɪ, were also present in
his library (nos 140 and 141), Erasmus
owned the three most important parts;
or if the edition of the *Liber sextus* in his
possession was augmented, as was often
the case, by the three more recent collections of decretals, then he had the complete
text of the *Corpus iuris canonici*. Erasmus
must have become familiar with the law
books of the church as early as his years
in the monastery. In his *Antibarbari,*
written about 1494–5 but planned even
earlier in the monastery of Steyn, he put
certain passages from the *Decretum* into
the mouth of Jacob Batt, the main speaker
in the dialogue, as arguments against the
enemies of the 'finest arts' (*optimae artes*).
Later the law of the church was to occupy
him repeatedly in connection with his
illegitimacy and his release from some
of the restrictions imposed on him by
his canonical vows.[2]

Wilhelm Maurer thinks that Erasmus
made no small contribution to the new
interpretation of ecclesiastical law that
was emerging at that time, partly under

the influence of humanism. He took
an independent stance with regard to the
problems of canon law. In the *Annotationes*
to the first edition of the New Testament
(1516), the first signs of such an approach
were already evident, but according to
Maurer Erasmus did not apply philological
principles to the text of church law until
the later editions. This, Maurer claims, was
the outcome of his adoption of a clearly
anti-Lutheran position: 'By renewing the
original foundations of canon law, that is,
through a new interpretation of the valid
legal sources, Erasmus tried to mitigate the
consequences of the revolution in canon
law instigated by Luther in order to
neutralize this revolution.'[3]

1 Hain *7883, ʙʟ *Catalogue* ɪ 67
2 For the history of how the *Antibarbari* came into
  being see the editor's introductions in ᴀsᴅ ɪ-1
  7–32 / cwᴇ 23 2–15; for the passage mentioning
  canon law texts, ᴀsᴅ ɪ-1 107:14–111:14 / cwᴇ 23
  86:31–91:14. For Erasmus' early knowledge of
  the *Decretum* and the *Decretales* cf Béné *Erasme
  et Saint Augustin* 67, 73, 84 and passim. See also
  Stupperich 'Zur Biographie des Erasmus von
  Rotterdam. Zwei Untersuchungen. ɪ: Erasmus
  und das Corpus iuris canonici' and 'Erasmus
  und die Kirchlichen Autoritäten.'
3 Maurer 'Reste des kanonischen Rechtes im
  Frühprotestantismus' 199

143 Autenticorum seu collationum feudorum libr.

[*Corpus iuris civilis* v] *Volumen parvum:
Libri autenticorum seu collationum feudorum. Triumque librorum codicis: quos
cesarei iuris interpretes Volumen appellari
voluerunt.* Probably a folio edition.

Perhaps identifiable as an edition of
the fifth part of the *Corpus iuris civilis*.
Two folio editions from Lyon, published by
J. Mareschal in 1509 and 1511, have a title
the beginning of which corresponds in full
to the short title of this item.

The *Corpus iuris civilis*, the codification of
Roman law under the emperor Justinian,
was in the fifteenth and sixteenth centuries

usually collected and published in editions of five volumes, each with its own title, often appearing independently of each other.[1] The first three parts contained together the digests or pandects: the *Digestum Vetus* (books 1–24 title 2), the *Infortiatum* (book 24 titles 3–38), and the *Digestum novum* (books 39–50). The first nine books of the *Codex Justiniani* formed the fourth part. The fifth, known as the *Volumen parvum*, comprised, besides books 10–12 of the *Codex Justiniani*, the Institutes, the *Novellae* (the *Authenticum*), and the *Libri feudorum*. Erasmus presumably owned a complete set of all five parts. The summary descriptions of items 143–7 do not allow us to identify the editions in his library with any certainty, but some of them give grounds to suspect that they were early sixteenth-century French editions.[2]

The Institutes form a part of the *Volumen parvum*. They are often added with a separate title-page after the three sections referred to in the title of the edition suggested – the *Novellae* (the *Authenticum*), the *Libri feudorum* and the *Tres libri codicis*. It is possible that this was also the case with Erasmus' copy; otherwise his set of the *Corpus iuris civilis* would not have been complete.

1 On this method of publication (probably dating from 1475–6) see for example Spangenberg *Einleitung in das Römisch-Justinianische Rechtsbuch oder 'Corpus juris civilis romani'* 659–61; GW VII 79 sv Corpus iuris civilis (introduction).
2 I am grateful to Professor R. Feenstra, Leiden, for his suggestions for the notes to nos 143–7 referring to the *Corpus iuris civilis*.

144 Codex Iustiniani libr 9.

[*Corpus iuris civilis* IV] *Codex. Codex Justiniani libri I–IX*. Probably a folio or a quarto edition.

An unidentifiable edition of the fourth volume of the *Corpus iuris civilis*, containing books 1–9 of the Codex of Justinian. See no 143.

145 In Fortiatum [sic] à 24° libro ad 38um.

[*Corpus iuris civilis* II] *Infortiatum. Digestorum libri XXIIII 3–XXXVIII*. Probably a folio or a quarto edition.

An unidentifiable edition of the second part of the *Corpus iuris civilis*, books 24 title 3–38 of the *Digest*. See no 143.

146 Digestum Nouum à 39° libro ad 50um usque

[*Corpus iuris civilis* III] *Digestum Novum. Digestorum libri XXXIX–L*. Probably a folio or a quarto edition.

An unidentifiable edition of the third part of the *Corpus iuris civilis*, books 39–50 of the *Digest*. See no 143.

147 Dige. Vetus 50. librorum pandectarum etc.

[*Corpus iuris civilis* I] *Digestum Vetus. Digestorum libri I–XXIV 2* ('*Digestum vetus quinquaginta librorum pandectarum primus tomus, XXIII libros continens*'). Probably a folio or a quarto edition.

An unidentifiable edition of the first part of the *Corpus iuris civilis*, Digest books 1–24 title 2, possibly an early sixteenth-century French printing. There is nothing to indicate that Erasmus followed the revival of the study of Roman law in the later years of his life with any greater interest than was to be expected of a humanist of his all-embracing knowledge. In 1529 Gregorius Haloander published a critical edition of the Digest, an enterprise that modern legal historians have described as pioneering: 'a philological achievement of the first rank, to be compared with the Greek New Testament of Erasmus.'[1] Willibald Pirckheimer, and to a lesser extent Philippus Melanchthon, had already spoken forcefully in favour of the work to the town magistracy of Nürnberg, which provided financial support. Erasmus seems to have been aware of the coming publication as early as the spring of 1528, and was able to inform Pirckheimer of the enthusiastic reaction of the Basel jurists and especially of Bonifacius Amerbach. They hoped, he wrote, that 'the Greek version of Justinian' would also be printed.[2] This was a reference to the Greek paraphrase of the Institutes by the Byzantine jurist Theophilos; Viglius Zuichemus' edition was published in 1534 (see no 139). Erasmus' encouragement earned him a copy of the work. With Haloander's edition, on the other hand, Erasmus had no personal connection, and probably never considered purchasing the new edition of the Pandects.

1 Kisch *Gestalten und Probleme aus Humanismus und Jurisprudenz* 201
2 Ep 1991:4–6/5–9; cf Kisch 213–36.

148 Senecae opera

Seneca, Lucius Annaeus. *Opera … per Des. Erasmum ex fide veterum codicum … emendata. Adiecta sunt eiusdem scholia nonnulla.* Basileae: off. Frobeniana, 1529 (folio).

Erasmus' second revised edition of the works of Seneca. The original edition, which appeared in 1515 under the title of *Lucubrationes* (Basel: Johann Froben 1515), does not appear in the *Versandliste*. Erasmus' own copy of it, with handwritten improvements and additions, may have served in the printing of the revised edition, and if that is the case very likely did not return to his library afterwards. Erasmus carried out a great deal of preparatory work on the new edition. At the end of 1525 he asked Robert Aldridge in Cambridge to collate the 1515 edition with a manuscript at King's College.[1] Conradus Goclenius looked for manuscripts for him in Leuven.[2] Even after work had begun on printing in September 1528 he continued, with the aid of his friends, to track down 'exemplaria.' Beatus Rhenanus pointed out

to him a manuscript in the possession of a Basel 'chaplain,'[3] and Udalricus Zasius sent a codex from a monastic library with the text of the letters.[4] On about 1 November a special courier from the Low Countries brought him a copy of Treviso's edition of Seneca of 1478, which had once belonged to Rodolphus Agricola and contained many of his autograph annotations and corrections in the margins.[5] By that time the text had already been largely set in type, and Agricola's notes had to be incorporated in an *Appendix annotationum*. In the course of February 1529 the work came from the press, introduced by Erasmus in a very detailed letter to Piotr Tomicki, bishop of Cracow and chancellor of Poland (Ep 2091). At the end of the month Erasmus sent the borrowed Treviso edition back to its owner, along with two of the only three presentation copies of the new edition that he had received as agreed from the printer.[6]

1 Ep 1656:3–12/5–14
2 Ep 2026:6–7/6–7
3 AK III 358 Ep 1292
4 AK III 367 Ep 1304
5 He received the book on loan from Haio Herman, the son-in-law of Pompeius Occo, a nephew of Agricola's friend Adolph Occo, who had inherited the literary estate of Agricola; Ep 2056:2–3/4–6.
6 Ep 2108:1–3/3–5. On the importance of Erasmus' edition of Seneca see Trillitzsch 'Erasmus und Seneca.'

149 Ambros. 4./Ambros. 1.

Ambrosius. Opera, per eruditos viros … Basileae: J. Frobenius, 1527 (folio).

Probably either a complete set with an extra volume 1 or an incomplete set – volumes 1 and 4 – of the four-volume edition of Ambrose dedicated by Erasmus to Archbishop Jan Łaski, primate of Poland (Ep 1855). His own contribution to the enterprise was modest, as he wrote himself. He did not even read through the text for emendation, and he left part of the editorial work to the corrector

Sigismundus Gelenius, who in 1524 had lodged for some time with Erasmus and had since then continued to work for Froben.[1] The basis of the new publication was Amerbach's three-volume edition of 1492. In contrast to his usual practice of removing out-of-date works from his library, Erasmus kept his copy of the old edition (no 233) as well as the new one.

1 Ep 2033:53–4/58–9 (to Łaski); on Gelenius see Ep 1702:8n/n1; CEBR II 84–5. Cf no 303.

150 Chrysostomi lucubrationes uersae ab Eras. / ~~Catalogus lucubrationum Erasmj~~

Johannes Chrysostomus and D. Athanasius. *Lucubrationes aliquot … uersae & in lucem editae per Erasmum.* Basileae: J. Frobenius, March 1527 (folio).

Erasmus. *Catalogus [novus] omnium Erasmi Roterodami lucubrationum.* Basileae. J. Frobenius, April 1523 or September 1524 (octavo).

Husner mistakenly placed these two titles under the same number. In the manuscript they are clearly written not after each other, but one under the other, and the different format also proves that they were not bound or shelved together.

1/ A collection of texts of Chrysostom and Athanasius for the greater part newly translated by Erasmus. Of the works by Chrysostom only the *Homiliae in epistolam Pauli ad Philippenses duae* and the *De orando Deum conciones duae* had been previously published.[1] The other homilies included had been translated by Erasmus from an eleventh-century manuscript that had come into the possession of Hieronymus Froben during his travels in Italy in May 1525;[2] he dedicated them to King John III of Portugal (Ep 1800). Erasmus had also written sample translations of three homilies from another manuscript that had probably reached the north by the same route, which contained

commentaries by Chrysostom on the Acts of the Apostles. He made no more because he had doubts of the authenticity of the works.[3] He also made room, thus fulfilling a promise, for Chrysostom's *De sacerdotio* in the translation of his friend Germain de Brie.[4] The collection was completed by a number of translated 'lucubrationes' of Athanasius, 'in which there is nothing foreign or previously published,' dedicated by Erasmus to his friend and patron John Longland, bishop of Lincoln (Ep 1790).[5]

2/ The *Catalogus omnium lucubrationum,* a bibliographical survey of Erasmus' works he wrote in the form of a letter to Johann von Botzheim, a canon of Constance, appeared for the first time in April 1523 'with a few other works' (*cum aliis nonnullis*);[6] it was published again, substantially expanded but without the 'other works,' in September 1524. This second edition, entitled *Catalogus novus omnium lucubrationum,* included a list of Erasmus' writings published up to that date, which he divided into ten groups with a view to a future collected edition of his works.[7] Six years later Erasmus compiled a similar and further expanded list for Hector Boece, a friend of his Paris years. He issued this with an accompanying letter, as an appendix to his *Consultatio de bello Turcis inferendo* of 1530.[8] Although it bore the title *Index omnium Erasmi Roterodami lucubrationum,* Beatus Rhenanus later referred to the new list as a *Catalogus lucubrationum* also.[9]

This item of the *Versandliste* no doubt refers to the original 'catalogue,' either the first edition of 1523 or more likely the second of 1524. The words 'Catalogus lucubrationum Erasmi' were deleted from the entry. The title does not appear elsewhere, so the book must have been withdrawn from the library. Why? A satisfactory answer to this question cannot be given. One may imagine that Erasmus kept the *Catalogus* up to date with marginal

amendments and additions and that
the written annotations, which perhaps
contained valuable information for the
later publication of the *Opera omnia*,[10]
prompted Erasmus' executors in 1536 to
keep the book in their own hands. This
assumption, however, cannot be verified.
Early in 1537 Amerbach published
the *Catalogi duo operum Des. Erasmi
Roterodami*,[11] including the unaltered text
of the *Catalogus novus* of 1524 and the
Index omnium lucubrationum compiled
for Boece in 1530 but now revised and
augmented. The list was completed by
interpolating the writings of Erasmus'
last years;[12] moreover, some titles of older
works that had been lacking both in the
text of 1530 and in the *Catalogus novus*
were added. When Amerbach brought
the *Index lucubrationum* up to date he
may have had access to relevant manuscript
material left by Erasmus, but it cannot be
demonstrated that he used any manuscript
annotations found after Erasmus' death in
his personal copy of the *Catalogus omnium
lucubrationum* listed under this number
in the *Versandliste*.

1 Froben published the homilies on Philippians
in Basel in 1526 with Erasmus' prefatory letter
to Polidoro Virgilio (Ep 1734), *De orando Deum*
in 1525 with a dedicatory preface to Maximilian
of Burgundy (Ep 1563). These editions do not
appear separately in the *Versandliste*.
2 On Froben's travels, see Ep 1705:6n/n3. The
manuscript, with the ex libris and a drawing
of a ship by Hieronymus Froben, is now in the
Bodleian Library at Oxford (MS Greek misc 27).
3 Ep 1801 to the reader; see also no 410.
4 See Allen and CWE Ep 1733 introductions.
5 See Allen's introduction. On Longland see also
no 175.
6 Allen I 1–46/CWE Ep 1341A. The 'other works'
were Epp 1342 to Marcus Laurinus and 1301 to
the Leuven theologians, along with the *Libellus …
adversus Jac. Stunicae maledicentiam pro Germania*
of Jakob Ziegler. On Ziegler and the *Libellus*
see Allen and CWE Ep 1260 introductions and
203n/n50, 1330:1–41/2–44.
7 Allen I 38:12–42:10/Ep 1341A:1500–1639
8 Ep 2283. On Boece see Allen and CWE Ep 47
introductions; CEBR I 158. *De bello Turcico*
was dedicated to Johann Rinck; see Ep 2285.

9 Allen I 71:555–7. Allen I 56–71, Beatus Rhenanus'
preface to the *Opera omnia* of 1540, with a sketch
of the life of Erasmus, was addressed to Charles V.
10 For the intricate printing history of the *Opera
omnia* (Basel: Hieronymus Froben and Nicolaus
Episcopius 1538–42, 9 vols), see Allen I 56 (Beatus
Rhenanus to Charles V) introduction and Reedijk
Tandem bona causa triumphat 32.
11 Basel: Hieronymus Frobenius and Nicolaus
Episcopius 1537 (between 1 February and
4 April); see Reedijk *Tandem bona causa triumphat*
54 n57.
12 Allen I 71:565–6 (Beatus Rhenanus to Charles V)

151 Lingua. δυσωπ. Sutor in Eras.

Erasmus. *Lingua … ab autore recognita.
Plutarchus, Libellus elegans … de immodica
verecundia*. Basileae, J. Frobenius, February
or July 1526 (octavo).

bound with

Sutor, Petrus. *Antapologia in quandam
Erasmi apologiam … adversus P. Sutoris
debacchationes*. Parisiis: Petr. Vidoneus,
June 1526 (octavo).

1/ The second or third edition of the
Lingua, Erasmus' treatise on the power of
language for good or evil. Erasmus would
have had no special reason to replace the
February edition by the one issued in July,
as the differences between them are only
slight. It was dedicated to Krzyztof
Szydłowiecki, chancellor of Poland and
prefect of Cracow (Ep 1593), who early in
1526 rewarded the author with a princely
gift of a gold hourglass and a golden fork
and spoon.[1] To the text of the *Lingua* is
added, with a separate title-page (omitted
in the third edition), Erasmus' translation
of Plutarch's Περὶ δυσωπίας (*De vitiosa
verecundia*), dedicated to the young Frans
van der Dilft of Antwerp (Ep 1663), who
had spent some months with him at Basel
in the winter of 1524–5 after his studies
at Leuven.

2/ An answer to Erasmus' *Adversus Petri
Sutoris … debacchationem apologia*, a new
move in the controversy that had begun
the preceding year with Pierre Cousturier's

attack on Erasmus' translation of the New Testament (see no 16). As early as March 1526 Erasmus saw the first four signatures of the book, which a friend had purloined from the printer and sent to him.[2] When he had reason to believe that the polemic against him was on sale he asked Nicolaus Episcopius (Froben's future son-in-law) to send him a copy as soon as possible.[3] After receiving the book, he at once wrote a short rejoinder, which first appeared in the Appendix to his *Prologus in supputationem calumniarum Natalis Bedae* of August 1526 (no 378).

 1 On the gifts see Epp 1660:46–50/43–7 and 1752, Erasmus' letter of thanks; cf *Erasmus … Vorkämpfer für Frieden und* Toleranz (exhibition catalogue) 266.
 2 Perhaps Nicolas Bérault; cf no 16 and Ep 1687:62–6/65–9.
 3 Ep 1714:4–5/4–6

152 Latomus de confessione secreta.

Latomus, Jacobus. *De confessione secreta. De quaestionum generibus quibus ecclesia certat intus et foris. De ecclesia et humanae legis obligatione.* Antverpiae: M. Hillenius, 1525 or *De confessione secreta. Joannis Oecolampadii Elleboron pro eodem Jacobo Latomo.* Basileae: A. Cratander, 1525 (octavo).

The short title given in this entry could refer to either of two editions of Jacobus Latomus' book on secret confession. The first was a publication containing three short treatises with a common preface.[1] In the first, as announced in the foreword, Latomus disputed both Oecolampadius' *De ratione confitendi*[2] and the notes in Beatus Rhenanus' Tertullian (no 227) that referred to confession.[3] But he also covertly attacked the *Exomologesis* of Erasmus (no 357 #2), which dealt with the same subject. Although Latomus' polemic was ostensibly directed only against Luther and his 'fellow culprits,' Erasmus, though not mentioned by name, was clearly a target.

Besides the *Exomologesis,* some passages from the *Colloquia* (quoted verbatim in the text) came under fire.[4] Of course Erasmus saw through this design: 'Latomus … has published three short works which poke fun at me in a sly and underhand way,' he wrote in July 1525, when the collection was hardly out; he had 'just dipped into them.'[5] He greatly resented the Leuven attack, and referred to the book again and again with indignation his correspondence;[6] in his opinion it also paved the way for theological tyranny, because in it the right to repress heresy with physical punishment was accepted.[7]

Erasmus used the original publication, and probably possessed it. As early as August 1525 Cratander published in Basel a reprint of *De confessione secreta.* In this the other works were omitted, but Oecolampadius' answer to Latomus' attack was added.[8] Erasmus immediately reported the publication of this answer to Pirckheimer, although he had not yet seen the text and knew the title *Elleboron* only from hearsay.[9] Whether he admitted the Basel reprint into his library because of the apology of Oecolampadius and discarded the original Antwerp edition cannot be known from the short title in the *Versandliste,* but it is not entirely out of the question.

 1 NK 1325. The beginning and end of the preface are printed in Staehelin BAO I 366–7. On Jacobus Latomus see no 18 #2; CEBR II 304–6.
 2 *Quod non sit onerosa Christianis confessio paradoxon* (Augsburg 1521; Staehelin, *Oekolampad-Bibliographie* no 38). See on this treatise Staehelin BAO I 146 n1.
 3 The text is preceded by an *Admonitio ad lectorem de quibusdam Tertulliani dogmatis,* in which Tertullian's doctrine of penance is discussed.
 4 de Vocht *History of the* CTL II 263
 5 Epp 1581:407–8 with 408n/459–60 with n58, 1585:79–81/89–91
 6 For example Epp 1603:46–7/51–2, 1624:38–41/ 44–7, 1674:29–30/36–7, 1686:47–8/53–4
 7 Ep 1719:55–60/58–64
 8 Staehelin *Oekolampad-Bibliographie* no 112
 9 Ep 1603:47–8/52–4

153 Eras. in monach. Hisp. Val. in Pog.

Erasmus. *Apologia adversus articulos aliquot per monachos quosdam in Hispaniis exhibitos*. Basileae: in officina Frobeniana, 1528 (octavo).

bound with

Valla, Laurentius. *In Pogium Florentinum antidoti libri quatuor* (*et alia*). Coloniae: Hero Alopecius, 1527 (octavo).

1/ There are two authorized editions of Erasmus' *Apologia* against the charge of heresy brought against him by representatives of the Spanish monastic orders, the original of 1528 and a revision with appendix of 1529. Both have two introductory letters addressed to Alonso Manrique, archbishop of Seville (Epp 1879 and 1967). It appears a second time in the *Versandliste*, bound with a different work (no 352 #2). Probably Erasmus kept a copy of both editions and the original of 1528 is meant here. If he had this bound with the work by Valla (which had only recently come into his possession), it would have been impossible to eliminate it from his library later, when the *Apologia* was rendered obsolete by the publication of the revised version – as otherwise in all probability he would have done – without parting from the other work in the same binding.

2/ Two polemical writings by Lorenzo Valla published together with other works. In one he satirized the miserable Latinity of the Tuscan humanist Poggio Bracciolini, who had savagely attacked him in one of the most notorious scholarly quarrels of the fifteenth century;[1] the other was aimed at a treatise by the grammarian and theologian Fra Antonio da Rho or Antonius Raudensis.[2] Since it was bound with the *Apologia*, this book was probably an octavo, and the Cologne edition referred to above is the only one in that size that can be found. There are also other reasons for thinking that this is the edition meant.

The book was edited by Christoph von Carlowitz (1507–78), who was a pupil of Petrus Mosellanus and met Erasmus when he was a young man. Erasmus' friendship and support were of great importance to him, and at the end of 1527 he visited the humanist in Basel. It was perhaps on that occasion that he offered him the Valla edition that he had just published. He must have made an excellent impression; Erasmus immediately saw something to admire in this prematurely learned young man, 'who apart from his age and personal appearance has nothing youthful about him.' From then on Erasmus helped him in his career, and in the *Ciceronianus* he praises his twenty-one-year-old friend highly.[3]

Erasmus was to profit by this publication in the years that followed. In the *Paraphrasis in Elegantias Vallae* (no 379), he borrowed innumerable examples from Valla's criticism of Antonius Raudensis. Although when he was still in the monastery of Steyn he had already made an epitome not only of the *Elegantiae* but of the *Adnotationes*, surely when he was preparing the first version of his *Paraphrasis* he must also have used the printed edition that had come into his possession a short time before. Erasmus mentioned the attack on Poggio only once in the *Paraphrasis*,[4] but in the *Ciceronianus* (1528) Nosoponos appeals to the judgment of Valla on the subject of Poggio's style.[5] Must he not have read the *Antidotum* recently, or at least have reread it? Of Poggio himself he had probably never read a sentence at first hand.[6]

1 On him see ASD I-2 663 4n; CEBR I 182–3.

2 *Paraphrasis in Elegantiarum libros Laurentii Vallae* ASD I-4 192 n6

3 On him see Allen Ep 2010 introduction; CWE Ep 1951 n7; CEBR I 269–70. Cf Epp 1899:100n/n21, 1924:41–6/43–8, *Ciceronianus* ASD I-2 684:9–10 with n/CWE 28 427.

4 ASD I-4 205

5 ASD I-2 663:5–7/CWE 28 415

6 Reedijk *Poems* 101

154 Index seu Repertorium in Glosam ordin./ Gen. Deut. cum postil. Lyra. et glo. ord./ Regum cum glosa ordi. et exposi. Lyrae./ Proph. pars 4ᵃ Glosae ordinariae/ Iob. Psal. Eccl. 3ᵃ pars glo. ordi./ Euan. 5ᵃ pars glo. ord./ Epist. Apost. 6ᵃ pars bib. cum glo.

Biblia: Textus bibliae cum glosa ordinaria et Nicolai de Lyra postilla ... Basileae: J. Petri et J. Frobenius, 1506–8 or Lugduni: J. Mareschal, 1520, 6 vols with *repertorium in glosam ordinariam* (folio).

The analytical description, detailed for the *Versandliste*, makes an identification of this book possible. It is practically certain that we have here an edition of the Bible with the *Glossa ordinaria* and the *Postilles* of Nicholas of Lyra, published in Basel by Petri and Froben in 1506–8[1] or the reprint of this which appeared in 1520 from the press of Jacob Mareschal at Lyon.[2] Both editions consist of six volumes with a volume containing an index (*repertorium*) to the *Glossa ordinaria*. The first Petri/ Froben edition of 1498 is not eligible for consideration since it lacks the *repertorium*.[3] It is not impossible that Erasmus acquired this work only after 1520. During his stay at Anderlecht in 1521, as his annotation on the Epistle to the Philippians shows, he consulted a very early edition of the book at the Carthusian monastery there, 'assuredly the first edition of the work, if I am not mistaken, having both the ordinary and the interlinear gloss added.' He probably had the Strasbourg *editio princeps* before him, which had appeared without any indication of place and year, and was therefore regarded by him, wrongly, as a Mainz printing.[4]

Since Erasmus states that he had had his whole library brought from Leuven to Anderlecht for the duration of his holidays,[5] it could be inferred from his account of the copy he consulted at the monastery that he had not yet bought his own copy of the work in 1521. He had probably not yet

found it urgently necessary to acquire it for the sake of the *Gloss* and the *Postilles* of Nicholas of Lyra alone. So far as the *Gloss* was concerned, 'Erasmus had an aversion to this compilation of disconnected patristic quotations, torn from their original contexts; forced by his adversaries, he began to use it only for the second and later editions of his New Testament with obvious reluctance.'[6] This might make it more understandable that he should have acquired an edition of the bible with *Gloss* only after 1521, by which date the Lyon edition was the most recent.[7] Like Nicholas of Lyra, Hugh of Saint Cher belonged to the newer biblical exegetes, the 'recentioris antiquitatis scriptores' whom Erasmus held in little regard but could not deny as authorities for his conservative opponents.[8] In the 1522 edition of his *Annotationes* he referred for the first time to an 'editio cui sunt adjecti commentarii Carrensis.'[9] This was probably one of two editions of the Bible, both also in six parts with *repertorium*, published in Basel by J. Amerbach (1498–1502) and J. Amerbach, J. Petri, and J. Froben (1504), of which the 'postilla' of Hugh of Saint-Cher formed a part.[10] It would have been easy for Erasmus, certainly when he was in Basel, to have consulted one of these editions when he needed to as well as the *Textus bibliae cum ... Nicolai de Lyra postilla* that was already in his possession.

1 ʙʟ Catalogue
2 Baudrier xi 403–5
3 ɢw 4284
4 Annotation on Phil 4:9 ʟʙ vi 877ᴅ–ᴇ/ ᴀsᴅ vi-9 328:745–9; see de Jonge, 'Erasmus und die Glossa Ordinaria zum Neuen Testament' 71–2 with ᴀsᴅ vi-5 216:582–4.
5 Ep 1208:7–8/9–11
6 de Jonge in ᴀsᴅ ix-2 (*Apologia ad annotationes Stunicae*) 79 379n
7 Cf the eloquent figures in de Jonge, 'Erasmus und die Glossa Ordinaria' 55: there is no reference to the Glossa in the *Annotationes* of 1516; there are two in the 1519 edition; and twenty-seven in the 1522 edition.
8 de Jonge 'Erasmus und die Glossa Ordinaria' 65. See Epp 1171:76–8/81–2, 1687:82–4/87–90, and cf Ep 843:533–8/587–92.

9 Annotation on Acts 14:8 LB VI 488E / ASD VI-6
   268:55–7. I am grateful to Professor de Jonge
   for pointing out this passage to me.
10 GW 4285 and BL *Catalogue*

155 Tuscula[n]ae. Foemina Christiana.

Cicero, Marcus Tullius. *Tusculanae quaestiones*. Basileae: J. Frobenius, November 1523 (quarto).

bound with

Vives, J. L. *De institutione foeminae Christianae*. Antverpiae: M. Hillenius, 1524 (quarto).

1/ Cicero's *Tusculan Disputations*, edited by Erasmus and dedicated to Johann von Vlatten, provost of St Martin's at Kranenburg, to whom he later dedicated his *Ciceronianus* (Ep 1390). He borrowed one of the manuscripts he used from the Augustinian canon Julian Carbo (d c 1523), confessor to the nunnery of Jericho in Brussels; to edit the text took him only a few days. The time-absorbing task of collating the manuscripts he left to secretaries, while he himself chose among the variant readings and added the notes.[1]

2/ Vives' treatise on the perfectly educated woman in girlhood, marriage, and widowhood, dedicated to the English queen Catherine of Aragon and written for the benefit of Princess Mary. The book was probably a presentation copy; Vives had announced its completion and suggested Erasmus would soon see it in a letter to him written in the spring of 1523.[2]

1 Allen and CWE Ep 1390 introductions
2 Ep 1362: 31–2, 69–72 / 32–4, 75–8. On Vives
   see also no 25 #2.

156 Ausonius

Ausonius, Decimus Magnus. *Opera*. Parisiis: J. Badius, 1511 or one of the later Badius editions (quarto).

An edition of the Roman poet and rhetorician Ausonius (c 310–93) that can be identified with a fair degree of certainty. In view of the smaller formats of the adjacent books, it was most probably a sixteenth-century printing; the older editions were all folios, with one rather unimportant exception.[1] The quarto edition of the Venetian printer J. Tacuinus (1507) is left out of consideration (assuming that it was already on sale in the bookshops before Erasmus had started his homeward journey from Italy), because we know that he returned to the north with several works of Greek authors but only a couple of works of Latin authors in his luggage. One well-known edition was the quarto published by Girolamo Aleandro (then still on good terms with Erasmus) in collaboration with Michael Hummelberg in 1511, at the press of Josse Bade. Aleandro had just expounded the poems of Ausonius with great success before a distinguished audience in two lectures at Paris. His edition was so popular that there were new impressions in 1513 and 1517.[2] It is very likely that Erasmus acquired one of them. After his return from Italy, round about 1511, Bade is known to have bought many books for Erasmus.[3] It is altogether plausible that Bade supplied his illustrious client with the just-published edition of Ausonius, perhaps as a presentation copy.

Erasmus' reading of the late Roman poet's work has been shown in one concrete instance. The description of the Seine in his *Carmen votivum* of 1532 (no 61) was inspired not only by his own memories but evidently also by Ausonius' *Mosella*.[4]

1 GW 3090–5. The later editions, those of Venice
   (Aldo Manuzio) and Florence (Filippa Giunta)
   both of 1517, and that of Basel (V. Curio), of
   1523, appeared in octavo format.
2 A. Renaudet, *Préréforme et humanisme* 611 and
   612 n4; Renouard Bibliographie de Josse Bade II
   63–4; Jovy *François Tissard et Jérôme Aleandre* II
   71–3 and 91
3 Ep 263:50–3 / 57–60
4 See ASD I-7 and CWE 85–6 no 88:7–25 with n.

157 Quintilianus Aldi

Quintilianus, Marcus Fabius. *Institutionum oratoriarum libri XII*. Venetiis: in aed. Aldi et Andreae soceri, August 1514 or January 1521 (quarto).

It is impossible to determine whether Erasmus, who probably owned the late fifteenth-century edition of the *Institutio oratoria* with Valla's commentary (no 119), bought or was given the first Aldine edition in or shortly after 1514, or acquired the second Aldine of 1521 at some later date. Erasmus was intently occupied with Quintilian especially when he was working on his *Ecclesiastes* on the art of preaching, begun as early as 1523 but not published until 1535 (see nos 400 and 402). He collected many annotations on the *Institutio oratoria*, and around the year 1529 he still had it in mind to provide a new edition of the text. He asked Johann Lotzer, personal physician of the Elector Palatine, to lend him the manuscript discovered in 1520 by Ulrich von Hutten, which after his death ended up in Lotzer's possession.[1] But the idea of a new edition came to nothing.

1 Ep 2116:7–12/8–13. Cf no 399.

158 Eras. Enchiri. Hetrusco idiomate

Erasmus. *Enchiridion dalla lingua latina nella volgare tradotto per M. Emilio di Emilij Bresciano*. Brescia: Lodovico Britannico, 22 April 1531 (octavo).

One of the very few non-Latin books in Erasmus' library (cf nos 22 #3 and 256), 'hetrusco idiomate' in the *Versandliste* entry meaning the Italian vernacular.[1] Emilio de' Migli (Aemilius de Aemiliis), a well-to-do patrician of Brescia, wrote to inform Erasmus early in 1529 that he had translated the *Enchiridion*, but did not want to publish it without knowing the author's views; he wrote again on 4 May (Ep 2154). Erasmus agreed at once, but he reminded Migli of the 'dreadful uproar from the grackles and magpies' caused by some Spanish translations of his work and advised him, in order to avoid trouble, to suppress the letter to Paul Volz that had appeared as a preface to the *Enchiridion* since the edition of 1518. He also expressed a wish to see translated some of his other works, 'especially those that are less controversial and more likely to encourage piety,' for example, his commentaries on five psalms, *Virginis et martyris comparatio*, *De immensa Dei misericordia*, *Institutio christiani matrimonii*, *De vidua christiana*, and his *Paraphrases* on the Gospels and Epistles of the New Testament (Ep 2165).

1 Cf Ep 1791:57n/n22.

159 Bernardi opera

Bernardus Claravallensis: *Opera*. A folio edition.

An edition that cannot be identified with certainty. The works of Bernard of Clairvaux were published more or less completely in three versions before 1536. The oldest collection of his sermons, letters, and works appeared, with an introduction by Josse Clichtove, in 1508 from the press of André Bocart in Paris. An improved edition, not only introduced by Clichtove but also entirely edited by him, was published in Paris by Jean Petit and B. Rembolt in 1513; this was reprinted by others in 1515, 1517, and 1520. The most accurate text was probably that edited by Lambertus Campester and Laurentius Dantiscenus, printed by J. Clein at Lyon in 1520; this too went into further printings.[1] In his correspondence between 1519 and 1524 Erasmus made relatively frequent references to the 'doctor mellifluus,' both to his writings in general and to his letters in particular as well as other separate works.[2] If this is not mere chance but the reflection of his recent reading, then it may indicate Erasmus' recent acquisition of a copy of Bernard's works. Perhaps it was the last Petit edition, or more likely the Lyon edition of 1520, since that was the first to appear under the title of *Opera omnia*. Dolfen identified references to St Bernard only in Erasmus' later works, which supports the assumption that he owned one of the 1520 editions.[3]

1 On the editions see Janauschek *Bibliographia Bernardina* (nos 350, 379, 388, 402, and 422); cf Massaut *Josse Clichtove* I 37 and 378–9 and Rice *Prefatory Epistles* 180–1 Ep 61, Josse Clichtove to the reader.
2 See the General Index in Allen XII 53. For specific references see, for example, Epp 1206:109–10/118–20 (letters), 1202:16–17/18–19 (*De consideratione*), 1334:136–7/146 (a reference to 'Bernard on the Canticle' added to the prefatory letter to Erasmus' edition of Hilary [1523] in the revised edition of 1535).
3 Dolfen *Die Stellung des Erasmus von Rotterdam zur scholastischen Methode* passim

160 Bedae operum Secundus Tomus

Beda venerabilis. *Secundi tomi operum … commentarii in Evangelium Marci, in Evangelium Lucae, in Acta Apostolorum … in Epistolas catholicas, in Apocalypsim B. Joannis.* [Parisiis:] J. Badius, 1521 (folio).

Erasmus saw the Venerable Bede (672/3–735) less as an ecclesiastical historian, the author of the *Historia ecclesiastica gentis Anglorum*, than as a biblical commentator. Josse Bade's edition of the commentaries on Mark, Luke, Acts, the Catholic Epistles, and Revelation, dedicated to John Fisher, must have come into his hands very soon after its publication. Apart from the reprint of the Bade edition (c 1535) there is no other edition to be considered.[1] In the third edition of his *Annotationes in Novum Testamentum*, published in February 1522, Erasmus referred for the first time to Bede. In the prefatory letter 'to the reader' in this edition he added Bede's name to the list of Fathers of the church whom he had consulted in support of his emendations to the New Testament.[2] But it was not until the fourth edition (1527) that Bede was regularly referred to.[3] The Bade edition is

explicitly mentioned in the fifth and last edition.[4]

1 See Renouard *Bibliographie de Josse Bade* II 148–50.
2 Ep 373:34/38/ASD VI-5 56:36
3 See ASD VI-5 33.
4 Annotation on 1 John 5:7 LB VI 1079D / ASD VI-10 542:279 'in editione Badiana'

161 Thomas de Aquino super epistulas Pauli

Thomas Aquinas. *Super epistolas … Pauli commentaria.* Possibly Venetiis: Bon. Locatellus imp. Oct. Scoti, 1498 or Venetiis: P. Pincius, 1510 (folio).

A commentary repeatedly consulted by Erasmus, but one for which he nevertheless had little esteem.[1] He shared Valla's view that only the Greek text could be the basis for commentary on the New Testament, and Thomas did not know the language. This volume may have been the edition of the commentary that Erasmus had used from the start in annotating the Epistles of Paul. Several references to Thomas already appeared in the first edition of his *Annotationes in Novum Testamentum* (1516).[2] The most recent and current editions of Thomas' commentaries at that time were those published in Venice by B. Locatellus in 1498 and by P. Pincius in 1510. Erasmus could have consulted the more recent of the two, yet it cannot be ruled out that he acquired the 1498 edition it at an early date, around the turn of the century, when he had plunged into the study of Paul. He already possessed a separate manuscript or printed text of the Epistles ascribed to Paul, which he had had sent to him from England in early 1500.[3] In the following year he began to comment on the Epistles himself. He prepared himself thoroughly for this, for he wished to read everything that had been written on the subject by others before him.[4] During his stay at the castle of Courtebourne in late 1501 he asked his friends in the nearby

Franciscan monastery of St Omer to help him gain access to the books which he needed for this purpose: he was thinking in particular of the Fathers, especially Augustine, Ambrose, and Origen, and also of Nicholas of Lyra 'or anyone else who has written a commentary on Paul.'[5]

1 Massaut 'Erasme et Saint Thomas' 599–602
2 See Massaut 'Erasme et Saint Thomas' 609–11; he cites for example the annotations on Eph 3:15, Phil 2:6, and 1 Tim 2:15 LB VI 842F, 868D, and 933C–D/ASD VI-9 208–10:675–6, 292:280–1, and VI-10 54:491–4.
3 Ep 123:22/25
4 Rabil 'Erasmus' *Paraphrases of the New Testament* 149; cf Ep 181:31–41/36–48.
5 Ep 165:7–11/8–14

162 Thomae de Aqui. pars prima

Thomas Aquinas. *Summa theologiae. Prima pars.* A folio edition.

Of the four parts of Thomas Aquinas' chief dogmatic work, known as the *Prima, Prima secundae, Secunda secundae* and *Tertia,* Erasmus possessed the first part, treating of God considered in Himself and as the principle of creation, and the *Secunda secundae* (no 165). As Massaut showed, Erasmus' low esteem for *summae* in general included the *Summa theologiae,*[1] which superseded the *Sentences* of Peter Lombard as the most important manual of theology towards the end of the Middle Ages and even now is considered as 'the highest achievement of medieval theological systematization.'[2] There are many possible editions of the *Prima pars* in folio.

1 Massaut 'Erasme et Saint Thomas' 590–2
2 ODCC2 1371

163 Sententiae Petri Lombardi

Petrus Lombardus. *Sententiarum libri IV.* Perhaps a folio edition.

Besides the edition mentioned under no 63, which was probably an octavo, Erasmus had another copy of the *Sentences* of Peter Lombard. It may have been an older folio,

which he already owned before acquiring the handier octavo volume. Between 1495 and 1498 Peter Lombard must have been familiar reading to him: the *Sentences* and the Bible were the fundamental texts in the three-year bachelor's degree in divinity at the University of Paris.[1] It is usually assumed that Erasmus graduated as a bachelor in 1497 or 1498,[2] though Stupperich thinks that Erasmus could not have obtained the degree: under the statutes of the Sorbonne it was impossible for an illegitimate child to graduate a 'bachelor.'[3] Nevertheless the notes in Listrius' commentary on the *Moria* written by Erasmus testify to his detailed knowledge of the *Sentences.*[4]

1 Thompson 'Better Teachers than Scotus or Aquinas' 129 and 131. Cf Rabil *Erasmus and the New Testament* 27.
2 According to Allen (Ep 64 introduction) c August 1497; according to Thompson, 'Better Teachers than Scotus or Aquinas' 131, about April 1498
3 Stupperich 'Zur Biographie des Erasmus' 31
4 See ASD IV-3 34–5.

164 Chron. Euseb.

Eusebius Caesariensis *Chronicon.* Possibly Parisiis: per H. Stephanum eiusdem & J. Badij expensis, 13 June 1512 or reprint 1518 (quarto).

The epitome with the chronological tables of world history down to 303 by Eusebius (c 260–c 340) bishop of Caesarea, in the Latin adaptation by Jerome. It is difficult to say which of the few editions published before 1536 is referred to here. If the book was a quarto – and this cannot be ruled out, since the format of many of the surrounding books is uncertain – then the edition of E. Ratdolf (Venice, 1483)[1] is less likely than that of Henri Estienne (Paris 1512, reprinted in 1518).[2] Folio editions prepared by Johann Sichard were published by H. Petri in Basel in March 1529 and March 1536.[3] It is not very likely that Erasmus acquired the book so late, but he might have received it as a gift. The printed editions of the *Chronicon* customarily included, besides the continuations by Jerome (to 378) and Prosper of Aquitaine (to 448), modern continuations until recent times, in the Estienne edition carried down to 1512.[4] For Eusebius' *Ecclesiastica Historia*, see no 232.

1 GW 8433. The quarto edition published in Milan (P. de Lavagne c 1474–6; GW 9432) lacks the word *Chronicon* in the title.
2 Renouard *Annales des Estienne* 12 (no 15)
3 On him see Allen Ep 1660:95n; CEBR III 247.
4 GW VIII 112; Renouard *Bibliographie de Josse Bade* II 429

165 Secun. Secundae sancti Thomae de Aquino

Thomas Aquinas. *Summa theologiae. Secundus liber secundae partis.* A quarto or a folio edition.

The *Secunda secundae* of Thomas Aquinas' *Summa theologiae* deals with man's return to God. For another part of the same work see no 162. In his famous letter to Paul Volz introducing the new edition of his *Enchiridion* in 1518, Erasmus criticized current standard theological works in a way that was designed to put in its proper light the true character of his little handbook, intended as it was for a non-academic public and not for the 'wrestling-schools of the Sorbonne.' His criticism was directed in the first place against the content, but he also thought it was deplorable that because of their weight and size they were so impractical to use. He named this part of Thomas' *Summa* as an example: 'Who can carry the *Secunda secundae* of Aquinas round with him?'[1] From about 1463, when it was published by J. Mentelin in Strasbourg,[2] it had indeed circulated in many editions, almost exclusively in folio format. It is not possible to say a great deal about the edition in Erasmus' possession, other than that in view of the quarto format of the two adjacent books, there is a greater chance that it was a quarto than a folio. If this assumption is correct,

then Erasmus would have acquired one of the few quarto editions, which first came on to the market in the second decade of the sixteenth century. Two of them appeared in 1512 and 1520, from the presses of Claude Chevallon in Paris.

1 Ep 858:32–5, 59–60/39–42, 67–8
2 Hain-Copinger *1454

166 Chrysost. Ψεγματα Oecolamp.

Johannes Chrysostomus. *Psegmata quaedam ... a Joanne Oecolampadio in Latinum primum versa.* Basileae: A. Cratander, March 1523 (quarto) or repr Parisiis: J. Parvus, 1524 (folio).

Seventeen texts that Johannes Oecolampadius translated from a ninth- or tenth-century codex in the Basel Dominican monastery while he was staying at the Ebernburg as castle chaplain to Franz von Sickingen in 1522.[1] Twenty-five other texts translated at the same time did not appear until two years later.[2] His translations from Chrysostom had a bad press among those contemporaries who were competent to judge them; Bishop Tunstall later (1529) passed a damning verdict on them.[3] Erasmus too, who knew the Basel codex and probably used it in 1525 as the basis of his own edition of the Greek text of *De Babyla martyre*, was very critical of Oecolamapdius' translation, and therefore immediately agreed with Germain de Brie's proposal to supersede the translation of this text, included in the *Psegmata*, by a better one (see no 38 #1). It would be fairly natural to expect the original Basel edition in quarto in Erasmus' library. But since the surrounding books do not give any clear indication of format, a folio edition cannot be ruled out a priori, so there is a possibility that the short title refers to the 1524 Paris edition of Jean Petit. This was supplemented by further translations from Chrysostom by Theodorus Gaza, Wolfgang Faber Capito, and Oecolampadius himself.

1 Staehelin *Oecolampad-Bibliographie* nos 75 (Basel 1523) and 99 (Paris 1524). See Staehelin BAO I 194 n2 and 210 and *Das theologische Lebenswerk Johannes Oekolampads* 160–1.
2 In the edition of Chrysostom's *Opera omnia* (Basel: A. Cratander 1525)
3 Ep 2226:67–75

167 Τὸ σκότοσ Scoti Scrip. primum super 1° Sent.

Duns Scotus, Johannes. *Scriptum primum Oxoniense super primo sententiarum.*
A folio edition.

The commentary of Duns Scotus (c 1265–1308) on the four books of *Sententiae* of Peter Lombard (cf nos 63 and 163) had appeared in print many times by 1536. In 1519 Bade printed a new edition in four volumes corresponding to the four 'books' of *Sentences*,[1] but since 1472 the commentary on Lombard's first book had repeatedly been issued separately. Erasmus may have owned such a separate edition, but which one cannot be stated with certainty. It could be an argument for the 1515 Venetian edition of G. de Gregoriis that it bears a title analogous to that of the short title in the list of 1536: the ordinal number is used twice and the preposition 'super' governs the ablative (*primo*). The strange-looking word in Greek letters may have been found on the spine or the fore-edge by the man who entered the book in the list. Could Erasmus himself have written the words τὸ σκότοσ in jest? He used to refer to Duns Scotus, for whom he had little regard, as ὁ σκότοσ elsewhere, as in 1516 when he weighed the use of Scotus' *quodlibeta* against his own edition of Cato: 'Nothing could be more trifling than the Cato, on which I spent one short day. But these light pieces, however trifling, I set above Scotus τοῦ σκότου and all his quillets.'[2] Erasmus transliterated the name of the *doctor subtilis* with the intention of denigrating him: τὸ σκότοσ means (like ὁ σκότοσ) 'darkness.' He played on the double meaning of the word *scotus*

again in his dialogue *Epithalamium Petri Aegidii* 'The Epithalamium of Pieter Gillis,' published in 1524 but written earlier.[3] The statement put into the mouth of the pious Eusebius in his dialogue 'The Godly Feast' (*Convivium religiosum*, 1522), that he would rather see all the books of Scotus and his like lost than the books of a single Cicero or Petrarch, was typical of Erasmus' aversion.[4]

1 Renouard *Bibliographie de Josse Bade* II 408
2 Ep 421:91–3 / 99–101
3 ASD I-3 412:24–38 / CWE 39 522:1–16
4 ASD I-3 252:626–7 / CWE 39 192:21–3 with n190 (227–31). On Erasmus' use of the names 'Scotus' and 'Scotist' as 'generic terms for the whole catalogue of scholastic philosophers and theologians,' see also Thompson 'Better Teachers than Scotus or Aquinas' 128.

168 Durandus in 4. Sententiarum libros

Durandus, Gulielmus. *In quattuor sententiarum libros questionum plurimarum resolutiones et … decisiones a Jacobo Merlino recognite.* Parisiis: ex off Ascensiana, ven. ab Joanne Parvo, 1508 or the 1515 edition (folio).

An anti-Thomistic commentary on the *Sentences* of Peter Lombard (see nos 63 and 163). The Dominican Durandus de St Pourçain (c 1270/5–1334), already named *doctor modernus*, was distinguished for his independent critical ideas, which gave him a respected position in later scholasticism along with John Duns Scotus and William of Occam. His thought pointed towards the new age.[1] Durandus' principal work must have found a response in the world of French humanism, in which Erasmus also moved, in the early part of the sixteenth century. It was edited for the first time in 1508 by Jacques Merlin, with the assistance of Guillaume Petit. Merlin, who was an admirer both of Pico della Mirandola and of Origen (see no 222), is supposed to have been influenced by Erasmus,[2] while Guillaume Petit, confessor of Francis I, was the man who in 1516–7 advised the French king to invite Erasmus to join the 'nursery-bed of scholars' that he wanted to establish.[3] This is the background against which we should probably see the presence of the *Resolutiones* in Erasmus' library. In his correspondence, references to 'Durandus' (from whom he sets himself at a distance) are undoubtedly allusions to the writer of the commentary on Peter Lombard and not, as Allen wrongly supposes, to the French canonist and liturgical writer Gulielmus Durandus, who made his name by his *Rationale divinorum officiorum*.[4]

1 On Durandus see Geyer *Die patristische und scholastische Philosophie* 519, 524.
2 Renaudet *Préréforme et humanisme* 594 and 618–19. On Merlin cf Ep 1763:59n/n15; CEBR II 435–6.
3 Renaudet *Préréforme et humanisme* 687–8; Ep 522, especially 37–53/40–58. On Petit see no 15 n14.
4 See Ep 396:90n/101n; cf Epp 844:180/199, 858:82/90, 1211:66/73. Allen's oversight was noted by Greitemann 'Erasmus als exegeet' 385.

169 Gerson 1. / Gerson 2. / Gerson 3 / Gerson 4.

Gerson, Johannes. *Opera* in 4 vols. Parisiis: J. Parvus and F. Regnault, 1521 or Basileae: A. Petri for L. Hornken and G. Hittorp, 1518 or an older edition (folio).

The French theologian Jean Gerson (1363–1429) was the spokesman of a practical, mystical Christianity that nonetheless remained within the bounds of accepted tradition. A tireless fighter for Christian unity and peace, he advocated as well a universal council with powers transcending those of the pope, which would undertake a thoroughgoing reform programme for the church. Gerson's works had been reprinted many times since the first printing at Cologne in 1483. At first they appeared in three volumes, but from the Strasbourg edition of 1502, supplemented by the editor Jakob Wimpfeling with a volume of sermons, in four.[1] It is therefore impossible to say with certainty to which edition the *Versandliste* refers. But we do know when Erasmus acquired

the work. In the war of words with the theological faculty of Paris, Noël Béda, the champion of the university, had in the spring of 1525 urged Erasmus to read a number of passages in Gerson's works. Erasmus replied that as a young man he had read some of Gerson's writings 'and found something in them to admire,' but he recognized the lacuna in his knowledge, and realized that he must fill it. 'I do not have Gerson in my own library, but I shall buy a copy or borrow one from somewhere.' He was in earnest, and in March 1526 he was able to inform his adversary: 'I bought myself the works of Gerson and have begun to read some of them.'[2] He may have bought one of the two most recent editions, Paris 1521 or Basil 1518.

1 On these early editions, see Jean Gerson *Oeuvres complètes* I 7 and 70–1. An exception to the three-volume editions is the *editio princeps* of Cologne 1483–4, which also ran to four volumes.
2 Epp 1579:159–71/185–96, 1581:87–8/96–7, 1596:17–18/20–1, 1679:84/90–1

170 Chathena aurea Thomae Aquinatis

Thomas Aquinas. *Cathena vere aurea: opus … in quattuor evangelia subtilissimo vinculo connexa*. Parisiis: Jean Petit, 1517 or possibly a pre-1500 edition (folio).

Thomas Aquinas himself called his exegetical commentary on the four Gospels *Expositio continua*, though it later became known as *Catena aurea* ('The Golden Chain'). It was composed of excerpts from the commentaries of the Fathers and other writers, linked into a readable whole by connecting text. It went into many editions in the course of the fifteenth and sixteenth centuries. As with the neighbouring books, Erasmus' copy was most likely a folio edition, but which one cannot be established with certainty, although the probable format restricts the possibilities considerably. After 1500 the *Catena aurea* appeared in folio, so far as can be ascertained, only once, in 1517 at Paris, from the press of Jean Petit. On the other hand the fifteenth-century editions, with only a few exceptions, were all folios.

Erasmus had made the Epistles of St Paul a subject of particular study much earlier than he did the Gospels. It would, therefore, not be surprising if he had not felt he needed to have Aquinas' *opus in quattuor evangelia* ('treatise on the four Gospels') by his side for reference, as he had his commentary on the Pauline Epistles (no 161), and had therefore only acquired it after the Paris edition of 1517 appeared. That could also explain the fact that Aquinas' commentary only left traces in Erasmus' *Annotationes in Novum Testamentum* remarkably late: not until the edition of 1527 do clear references, by name, to the *Catena aurea* frequently appear.[1] The only occasion, so far as can be discovered, on which he mentioned the *Catena* in his correspondence was in his sketch of the life of John Colet, of 1521, and that was in a disparaging passage about the *doctor angelicus* ('the Angelic Doctor'). The dean of St Paul's, he relates, had once in a conversation with him shown an even greater aversion to Thomas Aquinas than to Duns Scotus. Erasmus had at that time first come to the defence of Thomas, on the grounds of the impression that 'what they call the *Catena aurea*' had made on him, but since then he read Thomas more carefully and judged him more critically: 'I certainly formed a lower opinion of him than before.'[2] If in fact he had acquired the book not long before, we may imagine that his recollection of the conversation with Colet about Thomas surfaced again when he was writing his biographical sketch.

1 See for example the annotations on Matt 15:5; Luke 10:1, 15:8, and 16:22; John 1:28 and 21:22 LB VI 83D; 272D, 294E, and 298F; 344C and 420D/ ASD VI-5 238:161; ASD VI-5 534:331, 560:54–5, and 565:207; ASD VI-6 58:647–8 and 172:236–174:239.
2 Ep 1211:429–44/467–83. Cf Chomarat *Grammaire et rhétorique* I 570–1 n250.

171 Homiliae Doctorum in Euan. dominica. de tempore

Homiliae doctorum ecclesiasticorum Hieronymi, Ambrosii, Augustini, Gregorii, Origenis, Joannis Chrysostomi, Bede presbyteri, Maximi episcopi et aliorum. Probably a Basel edition or a Lyon edition based on it, c 1516–20.

The collection of sermons, largely by the Fathers of the church, compiled for liturgical use by Paul the Deacon (c 720–c 800) at the request of Charlemagne and later known as the *Homiliarius doctorum*, originally consisted of two parts, a *Pars hiemalis* and a *Pars aestivalis*, each in turn customarily sub-divided into *Sermones de tempore*, to be read at the various feasts of the ecclesiastical year, and *Sermones de sanctis*, to be read on the name-days of the saints.[1] The collection was much used and circulated in print in its original form from c 1475.[2] A new version, mentioning Alcuin (c 740–804) as the compiler, heavily revised in content and arrangement so that the homilies were simply divided into two groups, *De tempore* and *De sanctis*, was first published in Basel in 1493 and was intended more for the use of the lower clergy.[3] Authorized and pirated reprints of it appeared not only in Basel (among others two by Froben, in 1513 and 1516) but also later at Cologne, Paris, and Lyon (two by J. Clein, in 1516 and 1520). Erasmus probably owned the modernized version; it is not possible to identify the edition. The short title 'homiliae' instead of 'homiliarius' may point to one of the more recent editions, especially that by Froben (1516)[4] or Clein (1520).[5] Apparently Erasmus' copy was not complete and included only the *Sermones de tempore*.

1 *Realencyklopädie für protestantische Theologie und Kirche* VIII 310
2 Very few copies of the first edition have been preserved. See an expert and informative description of one of them, in the Prince Arenberg library, which contains only the *Sermones de tempore* of the *Pars hiemalis*, in Kraus *Catalogue*

83: Incunabula & post-incunabula, 1466–1520 50
(no 84).
3 On the Basel version see especially Welti *Der
   Basler Buchdruck und Britannien* 51–2.
4 Panzer VI 197; Adams H 816
5 Baudrier XII 304

172 Canones Apostolorum Decre. pontif. antiquiora etc.

[Dionysius Exiguus.] *Canones Apostolorum.
Veterum conciliorum constitutiones. Decreta
pontificum antiquiora. De primatu romanae
ecclesiae.* [ed J. Vuendelstinus, alias
Cochlaeus]. Moguntiae: J. Schoeffer,
April 1525 (folio).

A collection of documents of church
history, mainly canons of early councils
and decrees of the earliest popes, edited
by Johannes Cochlaeus, with the assistance
of the Mainz scholar Nikolaus Fabri of
Carbach, from three manuscripts procured
for him by the printer Johann Schöffer.
Cochlaeus provided historical prefaces
for the parts and critical notes to the text,
and added a short treatise of his own
against the Lutherans, *De primatu Romanae
ecclesiae*.[1] It was most probably from
this book that Erasmus came to know the
Catalogus Romanorum pontificum and the
name of Pope Anterus, which enabled him
to correct Johann Sichard, editor of the
letters of Clement I and other early popes
(cf no 195 #1).[2] For Cochlaeus' relations
with Erasmus in the year of publication
of this work see no 10 #1.

1 Otto *Johannes Cochlaeus* 156–8
2 Erasmus must have had access to a manuscript;
  see Ep 1790:82n / n22.

173 Luteri Operationes in Psalmos.

Luther, Martinus. *Operationes in Psalmos,
Vittenbergensib. theologiae studiosis
pronunciatae.* Wittenberg: J.R. Grünenberg,
1519–21, 6 parts (quarto).

This entry probably refers to the first
edition of a series of lectures given by
Luther in Wittenberg and printed with a

dedication to the Elector Frederick of
Saxony and an introductory letter by
Melanchthon, who testifies to the obliga-
tion owed by the learned world to Erasmus:
'We are indebted to Erasmus for the study
of Greek and Latin; we also owe him –
to say nothing of most of [his works] –
the elucidation of the text of the New
Testament; we also owe him Jerome.'[1]

In 1526 Erasmus mentioned the
Operationes among some works that
Luther had written on his encouragement
(*meo quidem hortatu*).[2] From the beginning
he had openly spoken of the work with
great appreciation, for already on 30 May
1519 he wrote to Luther himself: 'I have
dipped into your commentary on the
Psalms; I like the look of it particularly
and hope that it will be of great service.'[3]
From this it appears that he saw the
original edition, which was to be published
in six serial parts, almost at once. What he
wrote to Luther in a letter dated by Allen
1 August [1520] must refer to one or more
later parts (the third dates from 1520),
which apparently reached him after long
delay: 'Your commentary on the psalter
has reached me, but after a six-month
wait. I have not yet read it right through,
but what I have read, I like very much
indeed.'[4] Erasmus also expresses a favourable opinion in the well-known letter to
Johann Botzheim, dated 30 January 1523,
which contains a catalogue of his works.[5]

1 Benzing *Lutherbibliographie* no 516; for the
  quotation, Allen Ep 980:53n
2 Ep 1672:66 with n / 67 with n12
3 Ep 980:53–4 / 59–61
4 Ep 1127A:96–8 (Allen VIII xlvii) / 100–2
5 *Catalogus lucubrationum* Allen I 31:41 / CWE
  Ep 1341A:1230

174 Eccius de primatu Petri li. 3.

Eckius, Johannes. *De primatu Petri
adversus Ludderum libri tres.* Parisiis: Petr.
Vidovaeus imp. Joa. Kerver, September
1521 (folio).

Erasmus alluded to this work in April 1522 when he wrote to Jean Glapion, the emperor's confessor,[1] that there was no occasion for him, Erasmus, to make any pronouncement on the primacy of the pope, after what Cajetanus, Silvester Prierias (Silvestro Mazzolini), and Johann Maier of Eck had already urged on the subject. There has been some confusion over the date of publication of Eck's book. Scholars now doubt the existence of the 1520 edition that Allen mentioned and consider the first (and only separate) edition the one published in Paris by P. Vidoue in 1521.[2] Erasmus studied and highly praised Cajetanus' *De divina institutione pontificatus Romani Pontificis super totam Ecclesiam a Christo in Petro* (Rome: M. Silber, March 1521),[3] one of the other works referred to in Ep 1275, and he also owned a copy of Silvestro Mazzolini's *In presumptuosas Martini Luther conclusiones de potestate Pape dialogus* (c February 1518). He did not like the book, but nonetheless he ordered a replacement copy at once when it was stolen from his travelling baggage.[4] Neither work appears on the *Versandliste*.

1 Ep 1275:77–8/85–7
2 Ep 1275:78n/n22; cf Simon Thaddäus Eck *Tres orationes funebres in exequiis Joannis Eckii habitae* ed J. Metzler lxxxv (*Verzeichnis der Schriften Ecks* no 38); Fraenkel 'Erste Studien zur Druckgeschichte von Joh. Ecks *Enchiridion locorum communium*' 653 n2.
3 Ep 1225:198–201/215–18
4 Epp 872:16/18–19, 877:36–7/41–2

175 Sermones Ioan. Longlondi.

Longland, John: *Sermones* ... Perhaps [Londini: R. Pynson? 1527?] or [R. Redman? 1532?] (folio).

Sermons, mostly on the Psalms (including the penitential Psalms, 6, 31, 37, 50, and 101), originally given in English, but published in Latin translation,[1] here perhaps bound together, or collected with a separate added title-page.[2] Certainly a

present. John Longland (1473–1547), bishop of Lincoln from 1521, was a loyal friend of Erasmus, with whom he corresponded regularly. He took a great interest in Erasmus' work and encouraged him to expound the Psalms and to write a commentary on Augustine's *De civitate Dei*.[3] Orthodox in doctrine and suspicious of heresy, Longland had his reservations about the *Colloquia* and seems to have pressed Erasmus to revise the text,[4] but that did not prevent him regularly gratifying his friend with gifts of money.[5] Erasmus was very grateful to his patron. He dedicated to the bishop his commentaries on Psalm 4 and Psalm 85 (Epp 1535 and 2017) and his translation of Athanasius (Ep 1790; see no 150 #1), presented him with a copy of his great edition of Augustine,[6] and named him in his will of 1527 as one of those who were to receive a presentation set of his collected works on their appearance.[7]

1 STC II nos 16790, 16791, 16791.5, 16792, 16793, 16793.5
2 STC II no 16797
3 Cf Epp 1535:1–4/3–6, 2961:31–2. On Longland see Allen and CWE Ep 1535 introductions; CEBR II 341–2.
4 Cf Epp 1704:23–40/24–43, 2037 introduction and lines 13–38/introduction and lines 16–42.
5 See for example Epp 1758:5–6/5–6, 1769:11–12/11–12, 2072:4–6/4–6.
6 Ep 2227:7–9/8–10
7 Allen VI Appendix 19 'Erasmus' First Will' 505:88/CWE 12 544:82

176 Reuchlinus de verbo mirifico cum Cabalistica.

Reuchlin, Johannes. *Liber de verbo mirifico.* Tubingae: Thomas Anshelmus, August 1514 (folio).

bound with

Reuchlin, Johannes. *De arte cabalistica libri tres.* Hagenoae: Thomas Anshelmus, March 1517 (folio).

In 1539 Jan Łaski gave both of these works to his friend Albert Hardenberg, then a Benedictine of the abbey of Aduard;

Hardenberg afterwards became a Protestant and was a clergyman in Emden from 1567 till his death in 1574. The books are still in Emden and have probably formed part of the library of the Grosse Kirche for more than four centuries; the old church was destroyed during the Second World War, but the library was saved and found shelter elsewhere in the city.[1]

On the title-page of *De verbo mirifico* Erasmus wrote 'Ex dono autoris. Sum Erasmi nec muto dominum,' and at the top of the same page Łaski's gift to Hardenberg has been recorded in a five-line ex libris.[2] No indication of the owner is to be found in the copy of *De arte cabalistica,* which could mean that Erasmus received the two books at the same time, put them together, and inscribed them with one ex libris for the two. Erasmus' copies are no longer bound together as they must have been when the *Versandliste* was drawn up but are preserved in a composite volume put together at a later date. Of the four works added, one appeared after Erasmus' death, and the other three, though published before 1536, are nowhere mentioned in the *Versandliste*, and almost certainly formed no part of Łaski's inheritance.

1/ *De verbo mirifico* was the first of Reuchlin's important works to be influenced by the magical-mystical doctrines of the Kabbala. It is written in the form of a dialogue between the Epicurean philosopher Sidonius, the Jew Baruchias, and the Christian Capnio (that is, Reuchlin himself), who were supposed to have met in Pforzheim.[3] The first edition appeared in 1494. Erasmus could have received the second edition of 1514 soon after publication; he had recently begun to correspond with Reuchlin, and proved himself more of a 'Reuchlinist' in the next few years than he admitted later on.[4] But the possibility that it was given to him together with the *De arte cabalistica* must also be taken into account.

2/ Reuchlin's work on the Kabbalistic art, dedicated to Leo x, was also arranged as a dialogue, between the Jew Simon, the Mohammedan Marranus, and the Pythagorean Philolaus, who were together in Frankfurt.[5] In December 1516 Erasmus heard from Gerardus Listrius that the book was in the press. It came out in March 1517, and just at the end of that month Reuchlin instructed his printer-publisher Thomas Anshelm to send Erasmus two copies, one of them intended for John Fisher, the bishop of Rochester, who made contact with Reuchlin through Erasmus. Erasmus forwarded the work to the bishop through Thomas More. More apparently was so much intrigued by the contents that he kept it for a long time; John Colet was slightly annoyed that he had not received a copy, but he succeeded in going quickly through it before it was passed on to Fisher.[6] *De arte cabalistica* caused a sensation in the world of the humanists; and for that very reason, Wilhelm Maurer's supposition that Erasmus perhaps did not read it seems hardly tenable.[7] Although he was not receptive of cabalistic doctrine (cf no 24 #2), it is unthinkable that at the time he could have ignored the work. We can understand therefore that some time later he reminded Bishop Fisher that he was hoping to hear his opinion of it.[8]

1 Husner 'Bibliothek' 248–9; for some corrections and supplementary details I am indebted to Dr H. Fast, former keeper of the Emden church library.

2 *Sum Alberti Hardenbergij ex dono Joannis a Lasco qui nobilis est Baro Jncliti poloniae Regni Regisque ac Regnj Cancellarius primarius, quem unum Erasmus iudicauit dignum cui uenderet suam Bibliothecam eciam tum uiuus. Ex qua nunc mihi dono dedit cum una uiueremus Louanij anno dominj 1539* 'I belong to Albertus Hardenberg thanks to a gift from Jan Łaski, a noble baron of the illustrious Kingdom of Poland, and excellent chancellor of the king and the realm. He was the only one whom Erasmus deemed worthy to sell him his library even in his lifetime, from which he gave it now as a gift to me when we were living together in Louvain in the year 1539.' See Jürgens *Johannes a Lasco* 116.

3 Benzing *Bibliographie Reuchlins* no 23; Geiger
   Johann Reuchlin 179–84
4 The first surviving letter from Reuchlin to
   Erasmus, Ep 290, is dated April 1514; the first
   from Erasmus to Reuchlin, Ep 300, is dated
   August 1514. On Erasmus and Reuchlin see
   also no 28.
5 Benzing *Bibliographie Reuchlins* no 99; Geiger
   Johann Reuchlin 185–97
6 Epp 500:19–20/22–3 (from Listrius), 562:9–
   25/11–29 (from Reuchlin), 593:4–9/5–12 (from
   Colet). On Fisher's interest in Reuchlin see Ep 324.
7 *Der junge Melanchthon zwischen Humanismus
   und Reformation* I 181
8 Ep 824:3–4/2–4

177 Caietani Commentarij super Euan. et acta apo./et super Epistolas Pauli et aliorum apost.

Caietanus, Thomas de Vio. *Evangelia cum
commentariis. In quatuor Evangelia & Acta
Apostolorum castigata.* Venetiis: in aed.
L. Junctae, 1530 or Parisiis: J. Badius and
J. Parvus & J. Roigny, May 1532 (folio).

bound with

Caietanus, Thomas de Vio. *Epistolae Pauli
et aliorum Apostolorum castigate.* [Venetiis:
in aed. L. Junctae, 1530?] or Parisiis:
J. Badius & J. Parvus & J. Roigny,
May 1532 (folio).

An extremely rare copy of the Venetian
edition of Cajetanus' commentaries on
the Gospels is in the British Library in
London. No copy could be located of the
Venetian edition of the commentaries on
the Epistles, but it is taken for granted that
in 1530 L.A. de Giunta published all the
commentaries of Cajetanus on the New
Testament.[1]

These works were perhaps gifts from or on
behalf of the author, whose commentaries
on the Bible, in the eyes of today's reader,
'contain much enlightened criticism of
an unexpectedly "modern kind."'[2] In the
1530s Erasmus kept up a frequent and
friendly correspondence with Cardinal
Tommaso de Vio (1469–1534, usually
called Cajetanus after his birthplace,

Gaeta); only one letter from Erasmus to
Cajetanus (Ep 2690, dated 23 July 1532),
survives.[3]

Erasmus and Cajetanus exchanged several
publications at about this time. Cajetanus
sent a copy of his *De communione sub
utraque specie* (Rome: August 1531) to
Erasmus, who in return later sent the
prelate a copy of *De sarcienda ecclesiae
concordia* (Basel 1533). In 1534, some
months before Cajetanus' death, Giovanni
Danieli, a member of his household who
had assisted him in the publication of
several of his works, including his commentaries on the New Testament, promised
to send Erasmus a copy of the cardinal's
*Quaestiones atque omnia (ut vocantur)
quodlibeta*, in case he had not already
obtained one.[4]

1 See Laurent 'Quelques documents des Archives
   Vaticanes' 112.
2 ODCC2 219. On Cajetanus as a renewer of Thomism
   see Hennig *Cajetan und Luther*.
3 On Cajetanus and his relationship with Erasmus
   see Ep 891 introduction/26n; CEBR I 239–42.
4 Epp 2619:7–14, 2935; cf Ep 2690 introduction.

178 Commentarij Stapulensis super Euangelia

Faber Stapulensis, Jacobus. *Commentarii
initiatorii in quatuor Evangelia.* Meldis:
imp. S. Colinaei, June 1522 or reprint
Basileae: A. Cratander, March 1523 (folio).

Jacques Lefèvre d'Etaples, the herald of the
Reformation in France though he remained
a Catholic himself, after completing his
studies at Paris, made two Italian journeys,
during which he came into contact with
both the Aristotelianism of Ermolao
Barbaro and the Platonism of Giovanni
Pico della Mirandola.[1] He was influenced
by both. On his return to France he made
Aristotle and Dionysius the pseudo-
Areopagite accessible in 'modern' editions
with commentaries (nos 15 and 210, 180
#1). In 1504 he entered the service of
Guillaume Briçonnet, bishop of Lodève,
once his pupil and from then on his great

protector. In 1507 he withdrew to the abbey of Saint-Germain-des-Prés where Briçonnet had recently become abbot, in order to be able to devote himself wholly to biblical study. In 1520 he again followed his friend the bishop and settled at Meaux, where Briçonnet 'wished to restore the church of the apostolic age' in his new diocese.[2] During these years Lefèvre laid out his programme for evangelical renewal by way of a return to the pure doctrine of the ancient Christian sources, in four great works, all present in Erasmus' library: the *Quincuplex Psalterium* of 1509 (no 252), the *Commentarii in Epistolas Pauli* of 1515 (no 179), the *Commentarii in epistolas catholicas* (no 196), and this work, the *Commentarii initiatorii in quatuor Evangelia* of 1522.[3] The spirit of renewal and the covert sympathy for Luther that inspired not only the commentary on the Gospels but also his translation of the New Testament into French, which appeared in 1523, brought Lefèvre into conflict with the Paris theologians. Only the intervention on his behalf of Francis I managed to save him from persecution, but during the captivity of the king he was compelled to flee to Strasbourg.[4]

1 On Lefèvre d'Etaples (Faber Stapulensis) see, besides Allen and CWE Ep 315 introductions, Renaudet *Préréforme et humanisme* 130–45 and passim and 'Un problème historique: la pensée religieuse de J. Lefèvre d'Etaples'; Rice 'The Humanist Idea of Christian Antiquity: Lefèvre d'Etaples and His Circle' and *Prefatory Epistles*; Heller 'The Evangelicism of Lefèvre d'Etaples'; Bedouelle *Lefèvre d'Etaples et l'intelligence des écritures*; Hughes *Lefèvre: Pioneer of Ecclesiastical Renewal in France*; CEBR II 315–18.
2 Renaudet 'Un problème historique' 213
3 On the Meaux edition see Bedouelle *Lefèvre d'Etaples* 99 n46.
4 Ep 1674:70–1 with 70n/80–1 with n27; cf no 196.

179 Fabri stapulen. commen. in epistolas.

Faber Stapulensis, Jacobus. *Epistola ad Rhomanos … Ad has 14: adiecta intelligentia ex Graeco. Epistola ad Laodicenses.*

Epistolae ad Senecam sex. Commentarii libri quatuordecim. Linus de passione Petri et Pauli. Parisiis: H. Stephani, 1512 or the revised edition Parisiis: H. Stephanus, 1515 [= 1516] (folio).

These commentaries on the Epistles of Paul are the best known of the editions of the New Testament Epistles with commentary by Jacques Lefèvre d'Etaples. Erasmus used the two editions named above. At one time he probably owned them both but must have kept only one.[1] The appearance of the *editio princeps* in 1512 caught him by surprise to some extent, for in his friendly conversations with the author he had never heard a word of the work, though it was already in preparation.[2] No doubt Erasmus, interested as he was in Paul (cf no 161), took care to acquire a copy as soon as possible. Although he differed from Lefèvre on certain points, he repeatedly praised the work, for it was wholly in his spirit: 'My friend Jacques Lefèvre d'Etaples some time ago did for Paul what I have done for the whole New Testament.'[3] Apart from the commentaries, the edition also included, in two parallel columns, the text of the Vulgate, which Lefèvre d'Etaples believed was not the work of Jerome, and his own Latin version, entitled *Intelligentia ex Graeco*, in which, like Erasmus, he 'followed [Valla] in altering many passages that were corrupt or wrongly translated.'[4] But in early July 1517, when Erasmus was about to leave for Leuven, a friend drew his attention to the new edition and to the passage in which Lefèvre disputed at length Erasmus' annotation on Heb 2:7 in his recently published *Novum instrumentum*. Erasmus bought the book at once, the predated Paris second edition (1516), according to Feld, and not, as Allen believed, the Regnault edition of 1517. He was indignant at the attack on him made in it, and defended himself in an offended tone in his *Apologia ad J. Fabrum Stapulensem* ([Leuven:] Dirk Martens, [August 1517]).[5]

1 On the editions see Ep 597:32n/37n and 44n,
   cwe Ep 480a:23n.
2 Ep 337:844–9/886–90
3 Epp 337:849–52/890–4, 456:94–6/105–6
4 Rice *Prefatory Epistles* 295–302 Ep 96; for
   Erasmus' statement, see his foreword to the edition
   of Jerome (March 1515) Ep 326:89–90/96–100.
5 *Apologia ad Fabrum* lb ix 17a. See Feld 'Der
   Humanisten-Streit im Hebräer 2:7 (Psalm 8:6)'
   13–23. On the controversy see also asd ix-3 7–15
   and the references in n1 above. The *Apologia ad
   Fabrum* (1517) was included in Erasmus' *Apologiae
   omnes* (1522); see no 332.

180 Dionisij coelest. Hierarchia cum Euclide.

Dionysius [pseudo-] Areopagita. *Coelestis
hierarchia, ecclesiastica hierarchia, divina
nomina, mystica theologia, undecim epistolae. Ignatii undecim epistolae. Polycarpi
epistola una. Cum scholiis Jacobi Fabri
Stapulensis et commentariis Jud. Clichtovei.*
Parisiis: H. Stephanus, April 1515 (folio).

with

Euclides. *Geometricorum elementorum libri
xv. Campani Galli in eosdem commentariorum libri xv. Theonis Alexandrini in xiii
priores commentariorum libri xiii. Hypsiclis
Alexandrini in ii posteriores commentariorum libri ii.* Parisiis: H. Stephanus, [1516]
(folio).

The combination in a single binding of
Dionysius the pseudo-Areopagite and
Euclid would not be merely fortuitous,
but on the contrary perfectly comprehen-
sible if it referred to the editions named
above; not only did they appear in rapid
succession from the same printer, but they
were also both prepared by the French
humanist Jacques Lefèvre d'Etaples.[1]
Another argument in favour of these
editions may be that the volume stood next
to two other works of Lefèvre on Erasmus'
shelves (nos 178 and 179).

1/ Lefèvre's edition of Dionysius – the four
works of the *Corpus Dionysiacum* in the
translation by Ambrogio Traversari,

improved with the aid of a manuscript from
Saint-Denis – was first published in 1498–9
by J. Higman and W. Hopyl in Paris.[2] The
reprint by Estienne was augmented by the
annotation of Josse Clichtove.[3] An ortho-
graphic detail may be decisive evidence that
Erasmus owned the Estienne reprint: the
title of the 1515 edition reads *Coelestis* as
in the *Versandliste*, not *Celestis* as in the
1498–9 edition. Lefèvre, for whom 'next to
the Bible, nothing seemed grander or holier
than the works of Dionysius,'[4] held fast to
the old textual tradition that the author was
to be identified with the convert made by
Paul in Acts 17:34. At first Erasmus too did
not have any doubt of this attribution, as
appears from his *Antibarbari*[5] and the *editio
princeps* of his *Adagiorum collectanea*.[6]
During his first stay in England (summer
1499–late January 1500), he must have
heard much of Dionysius' works in the
circle of John Colet, who was greatly
influenced by him. Erasmus was probably
as little in sympathy with the Neoplatonist
mystical tone of Dionysius at that time as
he was to be later on, so it is not very likely
that he should have hastened to acquire
Lefèvre's recent edition, when there were so
many other books for which he had a more
urgent need.[7] Moreover, the works attributed to the Areopagite were, as Renaudet
remarked, frequently read at Oxford and
easily accessible.[8] Like Lefèvre, Colet was
convinced of the authenticity of the
Dionysian writings, but his friend the
Greek scholar William Grocyn, who also
knew Erasmus well, repudiated the authorship of the New Testament Dionysius,
as Lorenzo Valla had done, in a series of
lectures on the *Hierarchia ecclesiastica*
given in the autumn of 1501.[9] Erasmus
came to agree with Valla and Grocyn,
though exactly when he did so is difficult
to say. It was not until much later that he
pronounced himself on the authorship:
in the annotations on Acts 17:34 in his
edition of the New Testament (1516), in

the second part of his edition of Jerome
(also 1516), in the preface to his *Paraphrasis
in epistolas Pauli ad Corinthios* (1519), and
finally once more in his *Declarationes
ad censuras Lutetiae vulgatas* (1532).[10]
Lefèvre's edition also contained, from its
first impression, the long-disputed letters
of bishop Ignatius of Antioch (c 35–107).
It is difficult to explain how Erasmus could
write, in 1530, that he did not possess these
letters,[11] but it would go too far to infer
from this that this entry in the *Versandliste*
refers to another, earlier, edition of the
pseudo-Dionysius in which the letters
of Ignatius were not included.[12]

2/ The Estienne edition of the *Stoicheia*
of Euclid, in the translation attributed
to Boethius, revised and supplemented by
several ancient and modern commentaries,
was prepared by Jacques Lefèvre d'Etaples
and an assistant.[13] It is noteworthy that
Erasmus also owned a second Latin
version of Euclid (no 199), but notwithstanding his preference for the original
tongue, did not acquire the *editio princeps*
of the Greek text, which appeared from the
press of Johann Herwagen in Basel in 1533,
edited by Simon Grynaeus. Erasmus had
been on close terms with this younger
Greek scholar, a professor at Basel, for
some years.[14] In 1531 he wrote letters of
recommendation for his textual editions
of Aristotle (no 215) and Livy (no 259),
and Grynaeus is said to have been present
at his deathbed. It seems odd that Erasmus
neither received a copy of the *editio princeps*
of the *Stoicheia* from Grynaeus nor
acquired one himself. Perhaps the explanation lies in the relationship between the
two men, which never became a genuine
friendship. Erasmus, irritable and suspicious, occasionally took an unfriendly,
even hostile, attitude towards Grynaeus.
In 1533 he had all kinds of reproaches to
make against him, and accused him of
having dedicated the edition of Euclid to
bishop Cuthbert Tunstall more or less

without his knowledge.[15] Nor was Erasmus
about this time on very good terms with
Herwagen, the printer of the book
(cf nos 120 and 131).

1 On him see no 178 and the literature cited there.
2 GW 8409; Renaudet *Préréforme et humanisme*
   374–5. On Lefèvre's edition in general see Rice
   Prefatory Epistles 66 Ep 20 n1 and 350–3 Ep 111.
3 Renouard *Annales des Estienne* 16 (no 3); Renaudet
   Préréforme et humanisme 665; for a full list of old
   editions see *Dionysiaca* I xxi–xxiv and Rice
   Prefatory Epistles 350 Ep 111.
4 'Et testor … michi nunquam post sancta eloquia
   … quicquam his magni et divini Dionysii operibus
   occurrisse sacratius,' quoted in Renaudet
   Préréforme et humanisme 375 n5
5 ASD I-1 126:25–6 with n / CWE 23 107:23–4 with 24n
6 Renaudet *Préréforme et humanisme* 397 n1; ASD
   II-9 48:287 with n (49)
7 In particular editions of Greek texts; cf Epp
   124:62–4 / 72–4, 160:6–8 / 7–10.
8 Renaudet *Préréforme et humanisme* 397 n1
9 Epp 118:22n / 26n, 1620:67–70 / 78–81 with n11.
   Only the research of modern scholars has
   definitely established their late 5th-century date;
   see ODCC2 407.
10 See the annotation on Acts 17:34 LB VI 503C–F /
   ASD VI-6 288:540–292:584; Erasmus' edition
   of Jerome II part 4 (Basel 1553) 7 (see ASD VI-6
   289:540–584n); the preface to the *Paraphrase on
   Corinthians* LB VII 849–50 / CWE 43 4; *Declarationes
   ad censuras Lutetiae* LB IX 916E–917C / ASD IX-7
   216:18–217:57 / CWE 82 242–4; cf Ep 916:50–2 with
   51n / 56–9 with 56n.
11 Ep 2331:8–10 / 9–11
12 The only early edition of the *Opera* without
   the letters of Ignatius was published in Bruges
   by Colard Mansion c 1480 (GW 8408).
13 Renouard *Annales des Estienne* 18 (no 8); Renaudet
   Préréforme et humanisme LV (bibliography) no 374
   and 665; Rice *Prefatory Epistles* 378–83 Ep 119
14 Allen and CWE Ep 1657 introductions
15 Ep 2878:15–35

181 Antilutherus Clichtouei

Clichtoveus, Jodocus. *Antilutherus tres
libros complectens.* Parisiis: Simon
Colinaeus, 1524 (folio).

In this book Clichtove attacked three of
Luther's works: *De libertate christiana, De
abroganda missa,* and *De votis monasticis.*[1]
But in book 3, which dealt with the

conventual life, he aimed his arrows not only at Luther but also, without mentioning him, at Erasmus.[2] The wording of the text was transparent enough to leave Erasmus in no doubt as to his meaning. In addition Noël Béda, his opposite number at the Sorbonne, did not fail to point out to him the relevant passage.[3] Erasmus gave vent to his feelings in a letter to Nicolaas Everaerts, who at the time was still president of the Court of Holland in the Hague: 'If Josse Clichtove's superstitious books are on sale in your part of the world, please read his *Antilutherus* book 3, chapter 1, section 3. Béda told me in a letter that the passage refers to me. If that is so, surely everyone can see that there is not a grain of sense in that lousy head of his. And yet it is wretches like this that Luther has armed against us!'[4] Erasmus must certainly have got the book, which Emile Telle calls 'of capital importance in the history of the religious controversy,'[5] directly from the press, because shortly after its publication he refers to Clichtove' attack on Luther's *De votis monasticis*.[6] Moreover, the size of the surrounding books leaves no doubt that the *editio princeps* in folio is meant here and not the quarto reprint, which had already appeared in Cologne before the end of 1524.[7]

1 Renaudet *Etudes érasmiennes* 220; Telle *Dilutio* 36; Massaut *Josse Clichtove* I 435

2 Erasmus is mentioned by name, however, in book 1 'on the authorship of the works of Dionysius Areopagita.' See Ep 1620:67–70/78–81 with nn10–11. Cf no 180.

3 Ep 1642:7–10/8–12; Allen 8n prints the passage.

4 Ep 1653:17–22/17–22

5 Telle *Dilutio* 36

6 Ep 1526:232–4/243–6

7 Cologne: P. Quentel 1525

182 Ioan. Driedonis de eccle. doctri. lib. 4.

Driedo, Johannes. *De ecclesiasticis scripturis et dogmatibus libri quatuor*. Lovanii, off Rutgeri Rescij, 10 June 1533 (folio).

In this extensive work, the Leuven professor of theology Jan Driedo (Dridones) of Turnhout (d 1535) took a pragmatic stance in the controversy over the authority of the Vulgate. He did not see in it a divinely inspired translation but a version of the Bible that had to be open to philological textual criticism as it was practised in the Collegium Trilingue; nevertheless he regarded the Vulgate as a text that, free from all heresy, formed as a whole a reliable foundation for the dogmas of the church. During the Council of Trent, his view seems to have had not a little influence on the drafting of the decree *Insuper*, which dealt with the 'the publication and use of sacred books.'[1] Erasmus knew Driedo from his time at Leuven as one of the up-and-coming men in the faculty of theology and saw in him, to judge from some of his letters, a scholarly and moderate controversialist.[2] Thus in 1520 he would have been very pleased to welcome the publication of a book by him which, to his great indignation, Dirk Martens had refused to print.[3] But Erasmus did not trust Driedo entirely, for he also relates how Driedo had once, among a few people and in his absence, raged against him in the most odious way, although the two men, when they met each other a few days later, acted as if nothing had happened. '[Driedo] was most friendly. On my side, I pretended to know nothing of his outpourings.'[4] Erasmus refers to the work of Driedo in his *Ecclesiastes* (nos 400 and 402).[5]

1 See de Vocht *History of the* CTL II 506–7; Draguet 'Le maître louvaniste Driedo inspirateur du decret de Trente sur la Vulgate'; CEBR I 405–6.

2 Cf Epp 1127A:46–8 (Allen VIII xlvi)/48–50, 1163:12–14/14–16, 1164:65–6/77–8, 1167:409–14/460–5.

3 NK 744. Cf Ep 1163:10–11/11; Reedijk 'Thierry Martens et le *Julius Exclusus*' 360.

4 Ep 1165:27–31/32–6

5 LB V 1053–4/ASD V-5 268:520–1 / CWE 68 980; cf ASD IX-2 113 88n (*Apologia ad annotationes Stunicae*).

183 Opus Cyrilli in Euang. Ioan. Trapezon. interpre.

Cyrillus Alexandrinus. *Opus insigne ... in Evangelium Joannis: a Georgio Trapezontio traductum*. Parisiis: W. Hopyl, 10 January 1508 (NS 1509) or 15 December 1520 (folio).

The reference in the *Versandliste* points irrefutably to one of the editions prepared by Josse Clichtove of Cyril's commentary on the Gospel of St John, in the translation by George of Trebizond. The *editio princeps* of 1509 only contained books 1–4 and 9–12, which had been preserved in full. Clichtove, who sought in vain for the manuscripts of the missing books 5–8, which were in fact only handed down in fragments, filled in the lacuna in the second edition of the work (1515) by interpolating texts taken from sermons on the Gospel of John by John Chrysostom and Augustine.[1] An unaltered reprint followed in 1520. It cannot be determined with certainty which of these editions is meant here. A reference to Cyril's commentary on the Gospel of John that Erasmus inserted for the first time in the 1517–18 revised edition of his *Adagia* might indicate that he had acquired and used the edition of 1515 with Clichtove's 'reconstruction' not long before.[2] On the other hand the commentary was only referred to in the 1527 and 1535 editions of his *Annotationes in Novum Testamentum*.

Another work of Cyril, likewise translated by Trebizond, edited by Clichtove, and printed by W. Hopyl in Paris, was his *Praeclarum opus, quod Thesaurus nuncupatur, quatuordecim libros complectens, et de consubstantialitate filii et spiritus sancti cum Deo patre*.[3] Erasmus also used and quoted this *Thesaurus*, a polemical exposition of the doctrine of the Trinity against the errors of the Arians, more than once,[4] but the work is not to be found on the *Versandliste*.

1 Massaut *Josse Clichtove* I 37 and II 19–20. Cf Renaudet *Préréforme et humanisme* 507 n1 and 665 n4; Rice 'The Humanist Idea of Christian Antiquity' 145–6 and *Prefatory Epistles* 182.
2 *Adagia* III iv 67 ASD II-5 273:744–5 with n / CWE 35 42 with n2
3 1513 (NS 1514), repr 1521. See BB C 469 and C 470; Rice 'Humanist Idea' 149 and *Prefatory Epistles* 333–4; Renaudet *Préréforme et humanisme* 639 n4.
4 Ep 1877:160–3 / 170–3; *Apologia ad annotationes Stunicae* ASD IX-2 254:455–63 with nn (255); annotations on John 14:28 and 1 John 5:7 LB VI 400E and 1079B–C / ASD VI-6 144:614 and VI-10 540:257–64

184 Lactantij Firmiani opera

Lactantius, Lucius Caecilius Firmianus. *Opera*. Probably a folio edition.

When Erasmus was preparing his annotated edition of Lactantius' *De opificio Dei* at Leuven in the years between 1516 and 1519,[1] he used as its basis an eighth- or ninth-century manuscript from the abbey of St Amand near Tournai made available to him by his friend the abbot, Willem Bollart. Besides this he also used the new edition of Lactantius' collected works published at Venice in 1515 by the Aldine press.[2] It cannot be ascertained whether he ever possessed his own copy of this edition, but the work, published in octavo format, was not among the books he left in 1536.[3] The edition of Lactantius listed here must almost certainly be a folio. Which one remains uncertain. The works of the 'Christian Cicero'[4] had often been published in collected form since 1465, but almost always under the title of his most important work, *De divinis institutionibus*. Only a few editions bore the name *Opera* on the title-page: the Venetian edition of Joannes Tacuinus of 1502, reprinted in 1509 and 1521, and the Paris edition of Jean Petit, of 1525. Since the *Versandliste* also speaks of 'opera,' one must think first of one of these editions. Yet the other editions of the *De Divinis institutionibus* 'with other small works' (*cum aliis opusculis*) cannot be passed over without comment, for in recording one of them it is quite possible that the compiler of the list, contrary to his usual habit, did not use the title of the book but gave preference to the name 'opera' as a better reflection of the content; he could also have found the title 'opera' on the spine or fore-edge. For a more recent edition of Lactantius, see no 191.

1 This was not published until much later with *De vidua christiana* (Basel: Froben 1529).
2 Ep 2103:9–12/11–14 with n3; on Bollart see Ep 761:40n/43n; CEBR I 162–3.
3 Of course, Erasmus may have borrowed the Aldine edition as well as the manuscript from his friend the abbot, who often stayed at Leuven, where he had a house with a library.
4 The name given to Lactantius by Agricola and also used by Erasmus; Epp 49:100–1/115–16, 3043:50–1

185 Hilarij opera per Eras. emend.

Hilarius. *Lucubrationes.* Basileae: J. Frobenius, February 1523 or revised edition H. Frobenius et N. Episcopius, August 1535 (folio).

This entry refers to the new edition, produced by Erasmus and dedicated to Jean (II) de Carondelet (Ep 1334), of the works of Hilary of Poitiers, designed to take the place of the unsatisfactory edition published by Josse Bade in 1511 (no 249).[1] Nothing is known of the manuscripts Erasmus used, except that one came from Speyer and was borrowed from Maternus Hatten, vicar of the cathedral, or perhaps through him as an intermediary from Thomas Truchses, master of the cathedral school and vicar-general of the bishop, who possessed an important library.[2] The book appeared for the first time in 1523 and again, revised, in 1535. The second edition was enlarged by the addition of a treatise *De Patris et Filii unitate.* It appears from a note by Erasmus printed at the last moment on the verso of the title-page that this was not accepted by him as a work of

Hilary, and was inserted without his knowledge by Froben.[3]

1 On the prefatory letter and the edition see Allen and CWE introductions; Olin 'Erasmus and His Edition of St Hilary.'
2 Ep 1289:18–20/17–19 (from Hatten); on Hatten and Truchsess see Ep 355:14n and 49n/15n and 50n; CEBR II 167–8 and III 347–8.
3 Allen Ep 1334 introduction

186 Dictionarius graecus.

Dictionarius graecus praeter omnes superiores accessiones ingenti vocabulorum numero locupletatus per ... Jacobum Ceratinum. Basileae: J. Frobenius, July 1524 (folio).

A new version, prepared by Jacobus Ceratinus, of the *Dictionarium graecum* of Johannes Craston, which appeared for the first time c 1478 in Milan and had since been republished many times and enlarged by other hands. The title *Dictionarius* in the *Versandliste*, while as far as can be ascertained the book is always called elsewhere *Dictionarium*, makes it nearly certain that Erasmus owned the Basel edition of 1524, which is, moreover, closely connected with his name. The title-page mentions Ceratinus' immense enlargement of the stock of words, but the initiative for the new edition was probably Johann Froben's, and Erasmus lent assistance from the beginning.[1] Erasmus urged Ceratinus to do the preparatory work and instructed Conradus Goclenius in Leuven to pay him twenty-five gold florins for it.[2] Erasmus himself supplied 'a number of words,' and it was he who wrote the introduction, in which he gave an account of the debt owed by the new revision to previous editions (Ep 1460).[3] It was also Erasmus who decided that the voluminous Latin-Greek index, which had been part of the work since the Aldine edition of 1497, should be omitted, 'as serving no purpose except to overload the volume.'

Erasmus was a strong supporter of Jacobus Ceratinus (Jacob Teyng of Hoorn), who died in 1530. He backed, though without success, his application for the professional chair of Latin in Busleyden's Collegium Trilingue in Leuven, and after the completion of the Greek dictionary recommended him as a successor to Petrus Mosellanus as professor of Greek in Leipzig.[4]

1 The following details have been derived mainly from Erasmus' introductory letter, Ep 1460, with Allen's introduction.
2 Ep 1437:157–60/168–73; cf Allen x Appendix 23 'The Donation to Goclenius' A1, 'Acknowledgement by Goclenius of Monies Deposited with Him by Erasmus' 409:14–16.
3 For example a special section, 'De Graecorum numeris,' was taken over from the Gourmont edition (Paris 1523), revised by Guillaume Du Maine and Jean Chéradame.
4 Epp 1561:6–11 with 6n/9–14 with n3, 1564–8. Ceratinus received the appointment but did not occupy the chair; he left in 1526, perhaps having been suspected of Lutheranism. On Ceratinus see Ep 622:31n/34n; de Vocht, *History of the* CTL I 281–2, 294; CEBR I 288–9.

187 Athanasij opera.

Athanasius. *Opera ... olim iam latina facta Christ. Porsena, Ambrosio monacho, Angelo Politiano, Joanne Capnione interpretibus, una cum Erasmi Roterodami Ad pium lectorem paraclesi.* [Ed Nic. Beraldus.] Parisiis: J. Parvus, 1519 or revised edition, 1520 (folio).

In 1519, when he published his edition of Athanasius, which consisted of translations by Italian humanists, Nicolas Bérault was in regular correspondence with Erasmus. He sent letters to him via the printer-bookseller Francesco Giulio Calvo, Wilhelm Nesen, and Haio Herman (Hermannus Phrysius). Erasmus answered them and wrote again after Bérault had successfully intervened in his favour with Maarten van Dorp.[1] Three years later he was to dedicate to his French friend, whom he had known since 1506, the authorized edition of his *De conscribendis epistolis* (Ep 1284; see

no 359). Was this copy of Athanasius' *Opera* a gift? Bérault could certainly count on Erasmus being interested in his publication: indirectly because Bérault's 'sympathies at this period were with freedom of thought (in editing Athanasius he was critical of theologians and thus incurred the hostility of the Paris Faculty);[2] directly because the *Paraclesis* of Erasmus was printed immediately after the text of Athanasius. It is impossible to be sure whether we have to do here with the first edition of 1519 or the second impression of 1520, to which a treatise by Athanasius translated by J. Reuchlin was added.[3] The *Opera* edited by Bérault also included the commentaries on the Epistles of Paul usually attributed to Athanasius, in the translation by Christophorus de Persona (or Porsena). Erasmus was aware by this time that the commentaries were not by Athanasius. While he was preparing the 1518–19 edition of the Annotations on the New Testament, he had compared the *editio princeps* in Persona's translation, published separately at Rome in 1477 (U. Gallus), with a Greek manuscript of Theophylact in the library of the Dominican abbey at Basel, and had discovered that the commentaries ascribed to Athanasius were in fact by Theophylact.[4]

During his retreat at Anderlecht in the summer of 1521 he was of course unable to have the Greek manuscript at his disposal and therefore used the commentaries of Theophylact on Paul in the translation published in Bérault's edition of Athanasius.[5]

For Erasmus' own translations of several texts of Athanasius, see no 150 #1.

1 For their correspondence see Epp 925, 989, 994 (from Bérault), 1002 (answering Bérault, excusing his lapses as a correspondent by an appeal to the 'mass of work' by which he was overwhelmed), 1024 (from Erasmus). Other letters have not survived; cf Epp 1002:2–3/4–5 with n2, 1024:1 with n/2. On Bérault, see no 46 #2.
2 Cf Allen Ep 925 introduction.

3 *De variis quaestionibus*, a treatise previously
published separately at Haguenau in March 1519.
At the end of December 1522 Erasmus promised
to send Jakob Ziegler 'Athanasius in a Latin
version by Reuchlin ... if I can get a copy';
perhaps he had the translation in the 1520
Athanasius in mind; cf Ep 1330:61–2 with
61n/66–7 with n20.

4 Ep 846:8–10 with 8n/9–11 with 9n; ASD IX-2
(*Apologia ad annotationes Stunicae*) 131 437n.
On the manuscript see Vernet, 'Les manuscrits
grecs de Jean de Raguse' 88–9 (no xxvii b). The
manuscript, afterwards used by Erasmus' former
servant-pupil Philippus Montanus for his revised
edition of Theophylactus' *Enarrationes in epistolas
Pauli* (Paris 1552) and long supposed to have been
lost, was preserved and is now in the Bodleian
Library in Oxford (Sign. MS. Auct. E.1.6); see Hunt
'Greek Manuscripts in the Bodleian Library from
the Collection of John Stojkovic of Ragusa' 81.

5 ASD IX-2 193 493n

188 Index in opera Hieronymi cum lucubr. Zasij

Oecolampadius, Johannes. *Index in tomos
omnes operum divi Hieronymi cum interpretatione nominum Graecorum et Hebraeorum.*
Basileae: J. Frobenius, May 1520 (folio).

bound with

Zasius, Udalricus. *Lucubrationes aliquot
(Orationes aliquot).* Basileae: J. Frobenius,
1518 (folio).

1/ Oecolampadius made it his task to
complete Erasmus' edition of Jerome
of 1516 with an index volume. He wrote
to Erasmus in March 1517 that he and a
student of his were working on it. Erasmus
was highly pleased and expressed in his
answer the wish that the index might be
finished as soon as possible; he himself
would profit from it, and many would
be stimulated to start reading Jerome.[1]

2/ The second item in this composite
volume is the *editio princeps* of a collection
of short, mainly juristic, treatises, introduced by a letter of recommendation from
Erasmus (Ep 862), which counts as 'the
first contribution of German scholarship
to the humanistic revival of jurisprudence.'

Udalricus Zasius (1461–1535) had been
professor of law at the university of
Freiburg since 1506. He had an excellent
reputation as a jurist.[2] His friendship with
Erasmus, with whom he stood in high
favour, dated back to 1514 or even earlier.
In mid-December 1516 Zasius sent the
manuscript of the first part of the volume,
the commentaries 'De origine Juris,' to
Erasmus, who urged him to publish it.[3] In
the summer of 1517 Erasmus asked Bruno
Amerbach to encourage Froben to print it:
'Tell Froben he must print Zasius on the
origin of laws; the man well deserves such
an honour.'[4] During his visit to Basel in
1518, Erasmus saw further treatises for
the collection in manuscript. Froben
cannot have received the complete copy
of the *Lucubrationes* until the end of 1518.
The book was then rashly hurried through
the press with hardly any correction, with
the result that the first edition bristled with
mistakes, to Zasius' great annoyance.[5]

1 Epp 563:41–4/46–9, 605:28–30/31–3
2 Allen and CWE Ep 303 introductions; cf AK II 105
Ep 604 n4. On Zasius' life and works see also
Stintzing *Ulrich Zasius* (still unsurpassed); CEBR III
469–73.
3 Epp 376:9–19/9–21, 380:26–9/30–4, 390:9–16/11–
20 (from Zasius), 379 (from Erasmus; cf Ep
859:40–1/ 40–1)
4 Ep 632:3–4/4–5
5 See Ep 862 with Allen and CWE introductions; AK II
145 Ep 642; Allen Ep 904:15n. (In January 1519,
at Zasius' insistence, a sheet of errata was added
to the copies still in stock.)

189 Basilij Mag. opera Grae. Frob.

Basilius. [*Opera, graece.*] Basileae:
H. Frobenius et N. Episcopius, March 1532
(folio).

The *editio princeps* of the works of St Basil
in the original Greek, printed with the new
and larger types that Froben had acquired
a few years earlier at Erasmus' urging.[1]
Although Erasmus refused to assume
responsibility as editor, the edition was in
fact produced under his guidance, and
Froben also followed his lead in not

including the commentaries on Isaiah, the authenticity of which Erasmus had already questioned in 1511. He had then been able to consult the Greek text in a manuscript given to him by his friend William Grocyn, to take with him to Cambridge.[2] Nevertheless, he published his translation of the commentaries in 1518 under Basil's name in the Froben edition of 1518 of the *Enchiridion militis christiani* (no 71 #1). The *Opera* of 1532 lacked the three books *Contra Eunomium*: Erasmus had not succeeded in finding a manuscript of the Greek text.[3] For the homiletic and dogmatic writings, although Erasmus nowhere says anything of this, a manuscript of c 1000 found in the castle library at Tübingen must have served as 'copy' for the printer.[4] For the text of the selection from the correspondence of Basil with Gregory of Nazianzus, Erasmus would have been able to make use of a manuscript in the possession of Pirckheimer, the same manuscript that was the foundation of the edition of this correspondence edited by Vincentius Opsopoeus published in 1528.[5] Because he thought that edition a very poor one, Erasmus at once asked Pirckheimer's permission to borrow the manuscript.[6] In September of the following year he asked his friend the Carthusian monk Levinus Ammonius of St Maartensbos, who knew Greek, to make a transcript of it for him.[7] The edition of Basil was dedicated by Erasmus to Cardinal Jacopo Sadoleto (Ep 2611), who thanked him for it in anticipation in early May 1532 and a month later for the unbound copy that he had received through Amerbach in the meantime.[8]

1 Ep 2062:19–20/23–4
2 Ep 229:4–18/7–20 and Ep 2611 introduction
3 Ep 2611:211–12
4 Rudberg 'Welche Vorlage benutzte Erasmus für seine *editio princeps* der Basilius-Homilien'; the preserved manuscript is now in the Bayerische Staatsbibliothek, Munich (Sign. Monacensis graecus 141). Vernet 'Les manuscrits grecs de Jean de Raguse' 89 assumes that for the nine *Homiliae*

in Hexaëmeron Erasmus most probably used a manuscript from the Dominican monastery at Basel.
5 *Basilii magni et Gregorii Nazanzeni ... epistolae graecae* (Haguenau: J. Secerius 1528). In the same year in which it was published Erasmus mentioned this edition in the new impression of his *Adagia* (III iii 84 ASD II-5 230:552–6/CWE 34 310 and III iii 97 ASD II-5 238:714–19/CWE 35 314–15).
6 Cf Epp 1997:5–15/5–15 and 2028:1–4/1–3.
7 Ep 2214:7n/n4. On Ammonius see Allen and CWE Ep 1463 introductions; CEBR I 49–51.
8 Epp 2648:33–40 and 2656:18–23; AK IV 108 Ep 1610

190 Opera Boetij.

Boethius, Anicius Manlius Severinus. *Opera*. Venetiis: J. et G. de Gregoriis, 1491–2, 2 vols in 1, or 1497–9, 3 vols in 1 (folio).

Perhaps Erasmus owned the more recent of these Venetian editions.[1] Besides the philosophical, theological, and mathematical works of Boethius, including the treatise *De disciplina scholarium* wrongly ascribed to him, it also contained the commentary on the *De consolatione philosophiae* then still attributed to Thomas Aquinas and texts of Aristotle, Cicero, and Porphyry with commentaries by Boethius. When he wrote to Maarten Lips in 1518 defending himself against Edward Lee's criticism of his Annotations on the New Testament, Erasmus expressed doubt that the commentary on *De consolatione* was written by Aquinas.[2] It is not known whether Erasmus bought the work in Italy. We do know that it was this edition (though not necessarily this copy) which he drew on for his commentary on passages in Boethius' *De musica* in *Adagia* I ii 63 ('Double diapason'). It was to his advantage that he had been able to consult the learned physician and humanist Ambrogio Leoni of Nola, whom he probably met in Padua in 1508, in the specialized field of musical theory.[3] Leoni (c 1459–c 1524) was doctor of medicine at Padua and subsequently professor of medicine at Naples. From 1507 he was in Venice acting as physician to Adlo Manuzio's household, and Erasmus first met him there. They immediately became friends. Erasmus valued Leoni's professional skill highly and considered him one of the foremost physicians of the age, along with Thomas Linacre, Guillaume Cop, and Niccolò Leoniceno.[4]

1 GW 4511 and 4512
2 Ep 843:193–5/218–20. The commentator is unknown. 'There is no evidence that Thomas Wallensis is the author, as Allen thought' (CWE 218n; cf Allen 193n).
3 See Margolin 'Erasme, commentateur de Boèce; l'adage "Double diapason."'
4 On Leoni see Allen Ep 854 introduction; CEBR II 322–3. On Linacre see no 75; on Cop, no 90 #1; on Leoniceno, no 138.

191 Lactantius Cratandrj

Lactantius, Lucius Caecilius Firmianus. *Divinarum institutionum libri VII. De ira Dei liber I. De opificio Dei liber I. Epitome in libros suos, liber acephalus. Phoenix. Carmen de dominica resurrectione. Carmen de passione Domini.* Basileae: A. Cratander et J. Bebelius, 1532 (folio).

The Basel printer-publisher Andreas Cratander brought out three editions of the works of Lactantius. Two of them, those of 1521 and 1524, appeared in quarto format. Since all the surrounding works on the *Versandliste* are folios, the edition referred to here must be that of 1532, the only folio published by Cratander in partnership with Johann Bebel. For another edition of Lactantius, see no 184.

192 Cornelius Celsus Venetijs

Celsus, Aulus Cornelius. *De re medicina.* Venetiis: J. Rubeus, 1493 or P. Pinzi, sumpt. B. Fontanae, 1497 (folio).

Possibly one of the two Venetian folio editions of Celsus' medical encyclopaedia.[1] Allen assumed that Erasmus received a copy of the recently published Aldine

edition from Gianfrancesco Torresani as a gift in 1528.[2] But the Celsus of the *Versandliste* cannot be identified with this quarto edition if we assume that it was a folio volume like the books around it. It is not a decisive argument, but at least a supporting one, that the compiler of the list indicated Aldine editions by adding 'Aldi' and never by mentioning the place of publication, 'Venetiis,' as this short title does. Erasmus could have brought the book back from Italy.

1 GW 6458 and 6459
2 Ep 1989:13n/n7

193 Iosephi Antiquita. libri et de bello Iudaico

Josephus, Flavius. *Antiquitatum judaicarum libri XX. De bello judaico libri VII.* A folio edition.

Another edition of Flavius Josephus' works is recorded elsewhere in the *Versandliste* (no 219, a Froben edition). The absence of the addition 'Frob.' is not strict proof, but may well be a strong indication, that this entry refers to the publication of another press. It is, however, impossible to say which one: both the main works of Josephus, his history of the Jews until the Jewish war of 70 AD and its continuation, a history of the war itself, had been reprinted together many times before 1500, and more than once during the early sixteenth century in the translation that was then ascribed to Rufinus.[1]

Erasmus himself had some limited involvement in the first edition in translation of Josephus' Περὶ αὐτοκράτορος λογισμοῦ *liber a D. Erasmo Roterodamo diligenter recognitus ac emendatus*, the account of the martyrdom of the seven Maccabean brothers and their mother. The translation, polished with his collaboration, was published about 1518 in Cologne by Eucharius Cervicornus and edited by Helias Mercaeus, warden of a Benedictine

nunnery in the city. Erasmus read Marcaeus'
Latin text, corrected it, and furnished it
with an introductory letter (Ep 842). This
separate edition must certainly have been in
his library at some time, but it is no longer
present in the *Versandliste*; the book would
have been superfluous once he had access
to the complete works of Josephus, in
which the text was also included. That
could have been, at the earliest, the
Cologne edition, also from Cervicornus,
of February 1524, or the Froben edition,
modelled on it, of September in the
same year.

1 The *editio princeps* appeared in 1470; Hain-
Copinger 9451. 'The author of the 6th-century
Old Latin version … is at present regarded
as unknown' ASD IX-2 117 175n (*Apologia ad
annotationes Stunicae*).

194 Calepinus

Calepinus, Ambrosius. *Dictionarium
ex optimis quibusque authoribus Nonio
Marcello … Tortellioque collectum.
Praeterea ex Suida graeco aliisque complu-
ribus, nullo fere vocabulo cornucopiae [Nic.
Perotti] praetermisso* etc. A folio edition.

The Latin dictionary compiled by the
Augustinian monk Ambrogio Calepino,
first issued in print at Reggio di Calabria
in 1502 and later often reprinted, with
supplements and additions by Calepino
himself and other lexicographers. This
popular work went into countless editions
and was the basis of all Latin dictionaries
before that of Forcellini.[1] During Erasmus'
lifetime it certainly had at least fifty new
editions. The first three of these appeared
at Venice in 1503, 1506, and 1509, and
from 1509 onward Josse Bade and other
Paris printers produced a stream of new
versions, at least seventeen by 1521. At
Basel the two reprints of Adam Petri in
1530 were followed by a thoroughly revised
edition from Valentin Curio. There are
no clues to enable us to identify the edition
Erasmus owned.

1 See Labarre *Bibliographie du Dictionarium
d'Ambrogio Calepino (1502–1779)*; Renouard
Bibliographie de Josse Bade II 254–8; Luchsinger
*Der Basler Buchdruck als Vermittler italienischen
Geistes 1470–1529* 44–5.

195 Clementis libri cum opere Irenaei cont. haeres.

Clemens I papa. *Recognitionum libri x.
Epistolarum pars vetustissimorum episcopo-
rum.* [Ed Johannes Sichardus.] Basileae:
Joannes Bebelius, 1526 (folio).

bound with

Irenaeus. *Opus eruditissimum … adversus
haereses … emendatum opera Des. Erasmi.*
Basileae: J. Frobenius, 1526 (folio).

1/ When Erasmus first made its acquaintance, he had no confidence in this edition
of the writings of Pope Clement I, the third
successor of St Peter, together with letters
attributed to other early popes. He had
asked his *famulus* (so he wrote in March
1527 to Bishop Longland) to read to him
from this book, as was his custom in order
to while away the time between supper and
sleep. When they came to a letter of Pope
Anterus, he found several lines inserted in
the text that had been borrowed almost
verbatim from two letters of St Jerome, to
Heliodorus and Nepotianus. Erasmus had
no doubt that the greatest part of the rest
of the book would be of the same sort.[1]

2/ Irenaeus' major work on the heresies of
Gnosticism, of which Erasmus published
the first edition. He used three manuscripts,
as he says in the dedicatory letter to
Bernhard von Cles (Ep 1738); one was
sent him by Johannes Fabri (Heigerlin)
from Rome, and the other two came
from monastic libraries.[2] In 1528 a second
edition came out at the instigation of the
booksellers,[3] and in 1534 a third Froben
edition followed. Besides this *editio
princeps* Erasmus included one of the later
editions in his library (no 229 #2).

1 Ep 1790:73–85/70–82
2 Ep 1738:111–13/111–14. The manuscript supplied by Fabri, vicar-general and after 1521 suffragan bishop of the diocese of Constance, had been copied from an older manuscript, which has been preserved and is now in the Vatican Library (Vat. lat. 188). One of the monastic manuscripts came from Hirsau but has been lost. On the manuscripts see Ruysschaert 'Le manuscrit "Romae descriptum" de l'édition érasmienne d'Irénée de Lyon.' On Fabri see Allen and CWE Ep 386 introductions, and cf CWE Ep 1690 introduction; CEBR II 5–8.
3 Ep 2007:1–2/3–5

196 Faber Stapu. in Epistulas

Faber Stapulensis, Jacobus. *Commentarii in epistolas catholicas, Jacobi I, Petri II, Joannis III, Judae I.* Basileae. A. Cratander, July 1527 (folio).

Two entries on the *Versandliste* refer to commentaries by Lefèvre d'Etaples 'in Epistulas.' If the first (no 179) refers to the commentaries on the Pauline Epistles, which Erasmus undoubtedly owned, then this entry must refer to the commentaries on the Catholic Epistles (of James, Peter, John, and Jude). Even though Erasmus does not mention them anywhere in his correspondence, their presence in his library would be easy to understand. Heller called this often-neglected work 'the most trustworthy source for fixing the mature religious opinions of Lefèvre.'[1] Completed in 1525 (the foreword is dated April of that year), the commentaries on the Catholic Epistles reflected his views from the last years of his stay at Meaux, the very years in which the ideas of the German and Swiss reformers were penetrating into France. It was fear of strict censorship that delayed the publication of the book, which appeared only in 1527, and then at Basel. In late 1525 Lefèvre had been forced to quit Meaux. For a time he stayed under a false name at Strasbourg until, once again assured of the protection of the king, he returned to France in May 1526. It is often assumed that he visited Basel before his departure, left his manuscript there with the printer Cratander, and at the same time took the opportunity to visit Oecolampadius and Erasmus. But it cannot be proved convincingly that he paid his respects to Erasmus, even if a meeting would have been conceivable at the time.[2] The controversy that had flared up in 1517 had by now clearly died down,[3] and although there could be no further talk of a friendship between the two, their views were so often in harmony that it was possible for their relationship to be marked by mutual understanding. Erasmus, himself the victim of attacks from Pierre Cousturier and Noël Béda, took Lefèvre's part in the precarious situation in which he found himself in 1525 and must have intervened in his favour at Rome.[4] Shortly before the publication of the *Commentarii* Erasmus sought contact with Lefèvre over the request that Lefèvre had received from the king of France to translate Chrysostom's commentaries on the Acts of the Apostles into Latin.[5] On this occasion Erasmus sent him a copy of his own recently issued collection of translations from Chrysostom and Athanasius (no 150 #1). Might he not have received Lefèvre's most recent book as a gift in return three months later?

1 'The Evangelicism of Lefèvre d'Etaples' 48
2 On Lefèvre's travels see Ep 1674:70n/n27; Heller 'Marguerite of Navarre and the Reformers of Meaux' 283–4; Rice *Prefatory Epistles* 486 Ep 141 Appendix II; Bedouelle *Lefèvre d'Etaples et l'intelligence des Ecritures* 110; but Bietenholz *Basle and France in the 16th Century* 181 has doubts about the visit to Basel. The passage cited as evidence (Ep 1713:19/20) is indeed not entirely convincing.
3 Epp 1555:82–5/89–91, 1796:11–15/14–19. On the controversy see no 179.
4 Ep 1650A:15–18 with 16n/16–18 with n4
5 Ep 1795

197 Apuleius de asino au. cum commen.

Apuleius. *De asino aureo. Cum commentariis Philippi Beroaldi.* Bononiae: B. Hectoris, August 1500 or a later edition (folio).

This entry must refer to the folio edition of Apuleius with a commentary by Filippo Beroaldo first published in 1500 by B. Hectoris in Bologna,[1] and frequently reprinted subsequently, almost always in Venice (S. Bevilaqua 1501; B. de Zanis 1504; P. Pincius 1510; and J. Tacuinus 1516) but also exceptionally elsewhere including Paris (Gilles de Gourmont? c 1511;[2] and J. Philippi, at the expense of Ludwig Hornken & Gottfried Hittorp, 1512). When Erasmus arrived in Italy and settled at Bologna for a while, the famous Bolognese humanist Filippo Beroaldo the elder (1453–1505), of whom Erasmus wrote in 1523, 'He was then very famous and warmly remembered,' had just died.[3] Although he could have brought the Bolona edition of Apuleius back from Italy with other books, Erasmus could have bought the work elsewhere later, particularly one of the Paris editions. He acquired a large number of books from Paris after his return from Italy.[4]

1 GW 2305. The text of Apuleius is surrounded by the commentary. On Beroaldo's commentary see Krautter *Philologische Methode und humanistische Existenz; Filippo Beroaldo und sein Kommentar zum Goldenen Esel des Apuleius.*
2 Edited by Robert de Keysere; see Reedijk *Poems* 291–2 (no 85 introduction).
3 Ep 1347:219–21 / 236–7
4 Cf no 72 with n2.

198 Aesopus grae. et Latine cum alijs opusc.

Aesopus. *Vita & fabellae Aesopi* [graece] *cum interpretatione latina. Gabriae* [graece] *cum latina interpretatione etc. etc.* Venetiis: Aldus, October 1505 (folio).

Most probably the 'Aesopus graecus Aldi cum aliis' which Erasmus ordered from Italy around 1525, a folio edition with what was to be the standard text of Aesop for the centuries to come.[1] The later editions that correspond to the description in the *Versandliste* are not appropriate since they were in octavo or quarto format (the

Froben editions of 1518 and later, for example, are all in octavo), and the older fifteenth-century editions, which were published as folios, did not combine the Greek text with the Latin translation or else lacked the other small works the 1505 edition contained. These include, besides the fables of Aesop and Babrias, some other texts more or less connected with the explanation of the fables: Cornutus *De natura deorum*, Palaephatus *De non credendis historiis*, Heraclitus Ponticus *De allegoriis apud Homerum* and Horapollon *Hieroglyphica*. A collection of proverbs, according to the title by Lukillos of Tarrha and Didymos,[2] with supplementary matter from the *Suda* and other compilations, filled the last eighty-six folios of the Greek text. Finally there followed a number of excerpts from Aphthonios, Philostratos, Hermogenes, and Aulus Gellius.

Erasmus must have known and used the 1505 edition as he prepared the greatly enlarged edition of his *Adagia* that appeared from the Aldine press in Venice in 1508, for in it he cited more than once the fables then known under the name of 'Gabrias' from the 1505 edition of Aesop. He also derived a great deal from the collection of proverbs in this edition, which he was accustomed to refer to as Zenobius or Zenodotus, and occasionally cited as the *Collectanea vulgata*.[3] In addition, he referred in his essay on the adage *Festina lente* (II i 1) to a pronouncement of Horapollon, whose speculative allegorical interpretation of hieroglyphic script, which was to win great fame in the course of the century, had appeared in print for the first time not long before, in the 1505 edition of Aesop.[4] Twenty years later, after he had acquired his own copy of that edition, Erasmus devoted a detailed passage to the Egyptian script in a letter to Sigismund I of Poland.[5] It is possible that his renewed contact with Horapollon's treatise had reawakened his interest in this intriguing subject, though what he wrote to the Polish king was certainly not directly or solely inspired by the *Hieroglyphica*. For, apart from other sources of information,[6] Erasmus had at least two works in his library that between them contained the bulk of the then-current knowledge of hieroglyphics: Tortellius' slightly older *Orthographia*, with a detailed excursus on Osiris (no 279 #2), and the commentary on Apuleius of Filippo Beroaldo (no 197), which in chapter 22 collected everything that Diodorus, Pliny, Tacitus, Ammianus Marcellinus, and Macrobius had to say on the subject.[7]

1 Hale 'Aesop in Renaissance England' 118; cf Allen VII 547 Appendix 20 'Books Ordered by Erasmus.'
2 The proverb collections of these two authors are only known from the epitome of them compiled by Zenobios, which in its turn has been handed down only in a later version; see *Der Kleine Pauly* II 11–13 sv Didymos, III 778 sv Lukillos, and v 1493 sv Zenobios; OCD 1115–16 sv paroemiographers. In the Aldine edition of 1505 the name Zenobios, however is not mentioned.
3 ASD II-5 13 n21; see *Adagia* III vi 74 ASD II-6 379 716–17n/CWE 35 162 n1. See also Rigo 'Un recueil de proverbes grecs utilisé par Erasme pour le rédaction des *Adagia*.'
4 ASD II-3 12:128–30 with nn (13)/CWE 33 7 with n22 (340). Horapollon's text first appeared as a separate publication in the Latin translation of P. Fasanini, in 1517.
5 Ep 2034:67–75/70–8
6 In *Adagia* II i 1 Erasmus himself named Macrobius, Plutarch, and the Suda.
7 Krautter *Philologische Methode und humanistische Existenz; Filippo Beroaldo und sein Kommentar zum Goldenen Esel des Apuleius* 159

199 Euclidis opera Latine

Euclides. *Opera, a Campano interprete … tralata.* Venetiis: Paganinus de Paganinis, 22 May 1509 or Venetiis: Jo. Tacuinus, 1505 or another edition in folio.

Since the Paris 1516 edition of Euclid is undoubtedly the one referred to under no 180, this entry probably refers to an earlier edition. The works of Euclid in the translation of J. Campanus had been published frequently before 1516: twice in the fifteenth century, in Venice in 1482 and Vicenza in 1491,[1] and thereafter at least three times again in Venice, by J. Tacuinus in 1505 and 1510, and by Paganinus de Paganinis in 1509. Erasmus could have acquired the work in Italy. The finely produced Tacuinus edition of 1505, which Dürer also acquired during his visit to Venice in 1508,[2] is certainly a possibility. Or Erasmus may have had the chance on his journey to England – he left Rome in the course of 1509 – to buy the Paganinus edition, which had just appeared on 22 May at Venice (to which he did not return).[3] So far as can be ascertained, this was the only edition to bear the title of *Opera*; in the colophon or on the title-page of the other editions the wording is always *Elementorum libri* or *Opus elementorum*.

1 GW 9428 and 9429
2 [Dürer, Albrecht] *Albrecht Dürer 1471–1971* (exhibition catalogue) no 626
3 See Allen and CWE Ep 216 introductions for the chronology of Erasmus' movements in 1509.

200 Plutarchi quaedam opuscula.

Plutarchus. *Opuscula … sedulo undequaque collecta et diligenter recognita.* Parisiis: J. Badius, 1514, 1521, or 1526 or Basileae: off. A. Cratandri, 1530? (folio).

Only one early edition of Plutarch under the title *Quaedam opuscula* can be traced: the collection published in September 1518 by Johann Froben containing ten treatises from the *Moralia* translated into Latin by Erasmus (four), Stephanus Niger (two), Angelus Barbatus, Willibald Pirckheimer (two) and Philippus Melanchthon.[1] Even so, that quarto edition is probably not the one meant here, since the books adjoining this number on the *Versandliste* (nos 174–243) are most probably all folios. For the same reason the 'quaedam opuscula' cannot be a combination of smaller works of Plutarch bound in one volume, since these were almost always quartos or octavos. One edition of Plutarch in folio with the title *Opuscula* seems to be left, the selection from the *opera moralia* in Latin translation published by Josse Bade. The first edition of this work, for which Renouard relies on Graesse's description, appeared in 1514; augmented editions in the same format followed in 1521 and 1526.[2] Finally in 1530 Cratander published an edition modelled on the Paris publication, but with a slightly altered title and a further augmented text, in Basel.[3] The material for the selection had been gathered here and there, and the last edition of Bade and the first of Cratander contained translations by Angelo Poliziano, B. Guarino, Stephanus Niger, J. Regius, Rafaelle Regio (Raphael Regius), Angelus Barbatus, Budé, Erasmus, Pirckheimer, Melanchthon, and others.

The edition of 1514 had not included any contributions from Erasmus. The eight translations that he had probably intended for Bade never reached Paris but were delivered by his agent Franz Birckmann, either in error or by design, to Johann Froben in Basel, who issued them separately in 1514 under the title of *Opuscula* (see no 385).[4] Bade reprinted all eight of them in the second edition of his compilation in 1521. In the third edition of 1526 he added two further versions by Erasmus, which had likewise already been published by Froben (1525): *De non irascendo* and *De curiositate*. Even if it is correct to assume that the *Versandliste* refers here to this anthology of translations from Plutarch, it is difficult to determine which edition Erasmus possessed.

1 Adams P 1653. Erasmus translated nos 3, 6, 7, and 8. A copy of this book was found in the chest containing largely Froben editions; *Catalogus librorum Erasmi* no 46.

2 On all these editions see Renouard *Bibliographie de Josse Bade* III 173–5; cf Graesse *Trésor de livres rares et précieux* V 361.

3 *Opuscula quae quidem extant omnia, undequaque collecta & diligentissime jam pridem recognita*; BL *Catalogue* 191 651; Adams P 1657

4 Ep 283:159–61 / 189–92; ASD IV-2 106. Did Erasmus know or suspect that Bade would include his translations in a compilation, and was he therefore not displeased when they ended up in Basel, where they could appear independently? For a similar case, cf no 81.

201 Dioscorides cum annota. Egnatij cum / Corollario Hermolai Barbarj.

Dioscorides. *Joh. Bapt. Egnatii in dioscoridem ab Hermolao Barbaro tralatum annotamento ... Dioscoridis Anazarbei de medicinali materia ab eodem Barbaro latinitate primum donati libri quinque* [and other works]. *Hermolai Barbari ... corollarium libris quinque absolutum.* Venetiis: Gregoriorum officina, 1516, 2 vols (folio).

Erasmus owned no fewer than three editions of *De materia medica* by Dioscorides (first century AD), which in his time was still considered an authoritative handbook of pharmacology; one with the Greek text, probably not acquired by him until 1525 (no 203), and two with Latin versions (this one and no 202). The edition referred to here contained the work in the translation by Ermolao Barbaro and his commentary, the *Corollarium in Dioscoridem*.[1] The text of Dioscorides was preceded by the annotations of Giambattista Egnazio, with whom Erasmus had been on friendly terms since 1508. The two men often sent each other copies of their newly published books, as is evident from their correspondence. Egnazio's letter of 21 June 1517 says that he gave to Ulrich von Hutten, who had been visiting Venice, his Suetonius and 'other things' to pass on to Erasmus.[2] Perhaps the edition of Dioscorides, which had appeared in the previous year, was one of the 'other things.'

The last part of Erasmus' copy, which contains, with some marginal notes in his handwriting, the *Corollarii [in Dioscoridem] libri quinque non ante impressi* ('in five books not hitherto published') of Ermolao Barbaro, has been discovered in the

Provincial Library of Friesland in Leeuwarden. The *Corollarium*, although announced on the title-page of the whole work, has also its own title-page (without imprint, however) and separate pagination. It was separated from his translation of the Dioscorides texts and Egnazio's commentary and was subsequently bound with another medical work of about equal size of 1517. The new composite volume was acquired between 1644 and 1656 by the library of the Academy of Franeker, the books of which found their way to Leeuwarden in the last century.[3]

1 On Barbaro and Erasmus' esteem for him, see no 279 #1, his best known work, the *Castigationes Plinianae*.
2 Ep 588:55–7/61–2. On Egnazio see no 51 (Suetonius).
3 Engels *Erasmus' handexemplaren* 60–2. I am indebted to Mr Engels, keeper of the Leeuwarden library, for supplementary particulars. Cf nos 123, 137, 203, 208, and 267 for five other books from Erasmus' library that Engels found.

202 Dioscorides cum annotati. Marcelli.

Dioscorides. *De medica materia libri sex, interprete Marcello Virgilio … cum eiusdem annotationibus*. Florentiae: haer. P. Juntae, 1518 (folio).

A translation with commentary, both by Marcello Virgilio (b 1464), pupil of Landino and Angelo Poliziano, and secretary of the Republic of Florence from 1498 till his death in 1521.[1] The extremely detailed commentary discussed both the text and the previous translations of Ermolao Barbaro (no 201) and J. Ruellius (Paris: H. Estienne 1516), but it was confined to linguistic questions and did not throw any essential new light on the medical and botanical content of the work, thereby earning the sharp criticism of Giovanni Manardo.[2] Why did Erasmus, who most probably already possessed the Barbaro/ Egnazio edition, add this version to his library and not the edition of Ruellius, which also dated from 1516 and rapidly

superseded all others? The key to the answer is probably the Lombard printer-publisher and bookseller Francesco Giulio (after 1518 Minuzio) Calvo, who was doing his utmost around 1518 to gain a commercial market north of the Alps. He proposed that Froben and he should exchange publications with each other. He also visited Erasmus at Leuven at the end of April 1518, when Erasmus was on the point of leaving for Basel to work for Froben for a short time. On that occasion he brought with him several presentation copies for Erasmus. Erasmus was prevailed on by his visitor, whom he thought a 'cheerful, scholarly man,' to write a letter to the famous bibliophile Jean Grolier.[3] Could Calvo have discussed his plans for an edition of Dioscorides with Erasmus during this visit? In the summer of 1519 he tried, through Beatus Rhenanus, to induce Froben to produce a new edition of the *Materia medica* revised by Marcello Virgilio and, if desired, augmented by a special contribution from his hand.[4] Calvo seems to have been unsuccessful in this design, but it was certainly through his intervention that various Florentine publications reached Basel: Froben immediately reprinted some of them, among them a speech by Virgilio.[5]

1 On Virgilio see *Catalogus translationum et commentariorum* IV 38. Cf Cosenza *Italian Humanists* I 59.
2 In his *medicinales epistolae*; see no 13 #1. Cf Dilg 'Die botanische Kommentarliteratur Italiens um 1500 und ihr Einfluss auf Deutschland' 244–5.
3 Ep 831. Erasmus' description is in Ep 832:29– 30/32–3. On Calvo see Ep 581:30n (with III xxvii)/ 33n; Ep 3032:581n; CEBR I 245–6. See also Nauwelaerts 'Erasme à Louvain, Ephémérides d'un séjour de 1517 à 1521' 11.
4 BRE 167 Ep 120
5 Luchsinger *Der Basler Buchdruck als Vermittler italienischen Geistes 1470–1529* 88

203 Dioscorides et Nicander graece

Dioscorides. *De materia medica* [graece]. Nicander. *Theriaca. Alexipharmaca* [graece]. Venetiis: Aldus Manutius, July 1499 (folio).

The *editio princeps* of the original Greek text of Dioscorides (for the Latin translation, see nos 201 and 202), here augmented by two didactic poems of Nikandros (second century BC): the *Theriaka* on venemous animals and the wounds they inflict and the *Alexipharmaca* on antidotes to animal, vegetable, and mineral poisons. It was probably the copy he ordered from Italy with other works around 1525.[1] The book has been preserved and is now in the Provincial Library of Friesland at Leeuwarden where it found its way in the last century, with the books of the former University of Franeker.[2] The last gathering, with the scholia on *Nicandri Alexipharmaca*, is missing. On folio 1 verso there is the autograph note: 'Sum Erasmi, nec muto dominum.' On a leaf inserted between the first and second gatherings is the ex libris of one of the later owners, Menelaus Winsemius, professor of medicine at Franeker from 1616 to his death in 1639. Winsemius probably presented or bequeathed it to the university library; it is already listed in the catalogue of 1644.

1 Allen VII 547 Appendix 20 'Books Ordered by Erasmus.' The purchase date may explain why the nearly thirty references to Dioscorides in the *Adagia* are not in Greek, but in Latin; see CWE 31 69 *Adagia* I i 22 7n.
2 With four other books that had belonged to Erasmus; see nos 123, 137, 208 and 267, and cf no 201. See Engels *Catalogus van incunabelen ... te Leeuwarden* 18, 'Erasmiana in de Franeker Academiebibliotheek' 66–7, and *Erasmus' handexemplaren* 18 and 45.

204 Xenophontis opera graece

Xenophon. *Omnia quae extant*. Venetiis: aed. Aldi et Andreae Asulani soc., April 1525 (folio).

Xenophon's works had been published three times in the original Greek before 1536. In 1516 Filippo Giunta published an incomplete and careless *editio princeps* in Florence. In 1525 Aldo Manuzio brought out a much better edition of all of Xenephon's extant works; he used the unsold stock of an edition from his own house of 1503 for the text of the *Hellenica* (see nos 273 and 276). Finally, the firm of Giunta issued another edition, based on that of 1516 but augmented and improved with the aid of the Aldine version. The copy listed here was probably the Aldine edition, which Erasmus ordered from Italy in the year of its publication.[1] An insertion in the 1526 edition of the *Adagia* based on recent reading of the *Hellenica* supports this conclusion.[2]

1 Allen VII 547 Appendix 20 'Books Ordered by Erasmus'
2 *Adagia* III v 59 ASD II-5 327 973n/CWE 35 101 note

205 Plinij Natura. Histor. Frob.

Plinius Secundus maior, Caius. *Historia mundi ex annotationibus Herm. Barbari*. Basileae: J. Frobenius, 1525 or ed. emend. cum annotationibus Beati Rhenani. H. Frobenius, J. Hervagius & N. Episcopius, 1530 (folio).

The Elder Pliny's *Naturalis historia*, because of its encyclopaedic character one of the most often used works of reference of the sixteenth century, went into three Froben editions before 1536. The first, with an introduction by Erasmus in the form of a dedicatory letter (Ep 1544) to Stanislaus Thurzo, bishop of Olomouc (Olmütz), appeared in 1525. The text was based on earlier printed editions, in particular that of Ermolao Barbaro, the author of the famous *Castigationes in Plinium* (no 279), but some manuscripts were also consulted and Erasmus, who had little further direct involvement with the publication, provided a few textual corrections from a codex, now lost, that Froben had probably borrowed from the abbey of Murbach.[1] The second edition of 1530 included the annotations of Beatus Rhenanus, which had first been published separately a year after the original edition. Finally, the third edition of 1535 contained annotations by Sigismundus Gelenius (c 1498–1554), Erasmus' younger friend (who must also have supervized the printing of both previous versions).

Erasmus had nothing good to say of Gelenius' textual alterations: 'Gelenius thinks he has achieved something wonderful; I consider it an unforgivable sin.'[2] Erasmus' library certainly contained two Froben editions of Pliny's *Naturalis historia* (this and no 207), and perhaps even three (see no 412). If no 412 was a copy of the 1535 edition, as there are grounds to suspect, then nos 205 and 207 probably refer to the two earlier editions. It is remarkable that the Froben editions of the *Naturalis historia* are entered in the *Versandliste* under its customary title, although in the 1525 edition the title-page announced a *Historia mundi*. This was Erasmus' preference. As early as his edition of the *Adagia* of 1508 and also in his correspondence, he used the different name, which he probably took from the *Castigationes Plinianae et in Pomponium Melam* of Ermolao Barbaro.[3] Before the appearance of the Froben editions Erasmus had had the old Venetian edition (B. de Zanis 1496) at his disposal. His copy has been preserved and is now in the University Library in Basel (Sign. Inc. 483). Its pages, with wide margins, contain about 1,600 marginal annotations, a great many in Erasmus' hand. The last page bears the well-known owner's mark *Sum Erasmi*. The book does not appear in the *Versandliste*. Presumably Erasmus had already presented it some time before, perhaps not long after he received the new Froben edition, to his godson Erasmius Froben, as appears from an inscription on the fly-leaf: *Sum Erasmii Frobenii ex liberalitate Erasmi Rote*. In the early seventeenth century it passed, with other Erasmiana, from the ownership of the Froben family into the museum of the

Basel collector and bibliophile Remigius Faesch, and afterwards with his books to the University Library.[4] The library also has a second copy of the 1496 edition (C.F.II 19.2) that belonged to Bruno and then to Bonifacius Amerbach; it appears, from numerous marginalia in his hand, also to have been used by Erasmus.

1 Ep 1544:113n/n15. On Thurzo (d 1540) see Allen and CWE Ep 1242 introductions; CEBR III 324–5.
2 Ep 3019:26–7
3 *Adagia* III vii 10 ASD II-6 430:945 with n (431)/ CWE 35 220 with n1
4 On the book and its vicissitudes see Jenny in *Erasmus … Vorkämpfer für Frieden unt Toleranz* (exhibition catalogue) 121–2. It seems to have been sold by the library in 1841 but was bought back from a second-hand bookshop in 1948. On Erasmius Froben see Ep 635:20n/26n; CEBR II 57–8.

206 Index in Plinium Ioan. Camertis

Joannes Camers. *Index in C. Plinii Secundi naturalem historiam ad exemplum Jo. Camertis mutatis quibusdam quae ad hanc aeditionem non congruebant* … Basileae: ex off. Frobeniana, 1525 or 1530 or 1535 (folio).

Probably a separate copy of the detailed subject index from one of the Froben editions of the Elder Pliny (see nos 205 and 207). It was based on the first index published in quarto separately in 1514 by the humanist Giovanni Ricuzzi of Camerino (Johannes Camers), who was working in Vienna, in order to make the *Naturalis historia* more accessible.[1] The index had its own title-page, but is sometimes bound in the Froben editions – usually within the text but sometimes at the beginning.[2] Perhaps Erasmus thought it would be much easier to use the indispensable index separately from the thick and heavy volume containing the text.

1 On Ricuzzi (d 1546) see Cuspinianus *Briefwechsel* 130.
2 As in a copy of the Froben edition of 1530 now in the Bibliothèque nationale in Paris; see *Catalogue général* 139 73.

207 Plin. Natu. hist. Frob.

Plinius Secundus maior, Caius. *Historia mundi.*

See no 205.

208 Plutarchi opuscu. 92. grae. Aldi.

Plutarchus. *Opuscula LXXXXII* [graece]. Venetiis: in aed. Aldi et Andreae soc., March 1509 (folio).

The *editio princeps* of the *Moralia* in Greek, published by the Cretan Demetrios Doukas (c 1480–c 1527) from manuscripts that Cardinal Bessarion had bequeathed to the library of St Mark's in Venice in 1468. It is still assumed by some, although there is no real evidence, that Doukas was assisted in the collation of the manuscripts by Erasmus, who was then in Venice, and by Girolamo Aleandro. Renaudet suggests, more cautiously, that Erasmus probably lent his cooperation to the finely produced (and bulky – more than 1100 pages) edition.[1] He certainly took a lively interest in its preparation even before the completion of his *Adagia* in September 1508: he speaks of the '*Moralia* which began to be printed when my work was nearly finished.'[2] Erasmus' copy, with his autograph marginalia and his ex libris on the last page, is now in the Provincial Library of Friesland at Leeuwarden. Above the *Sum Erasmi* he added the distich ἑπτὰ σοφοί ποτ' ἔγεντο καθ' ἑλλάδα νῦν δὲ παρ' ἡμῖν / Ἄλδος ὁ ῥωμαῖος ὄγδοος ἐξεφάνη 'Once there were seven wise men in Greece, but now Aldus the Roman has appeared as an eighth among us.' The edition of Plutarch is one of five books once owned by Erasmus that have been rediscovered in Friesland. Most probably they had been dispersed from Emden throughout the region and had found their way before 1644 (the year of the appearance of the first catalogue) into the library of the Academy of Franeker, the books of which were transferred to the Provincial Library of Friesland in the last century.[3]

1 Geanakoplos *Greek Scholars in Venice* 229; Aulotte *Amyot et Plutarque, la tradition des Moralia au XVIe siècle* 27 speaks of an edition 'due à la collaboration d'Erasme et de Demetrius Ducas.' Cf Renaudet *Erasme et l'Italie* 85.
2 *Adagia* II i 1 *Festina lente* 'Make haste slowly' ASD II-3 22:397–8 / CWE 33 14
3 Engels 'Erasmiana in de Franeker academiebibliotheek' 69 and *Erasmus' handexamplaren* 24–8, 47. For the other four volumes see nos 123, 137, 203, and 267, and cf no 201.

209 Plotini opera latine. Florentiae

Plotinus. *Opera a Marsilio Ficino latine reddita.* Florentiae: A. Miscominus, 1492 (folio).

The *editio princeps* of the Latin translation with a commentary by Marsilio Ficino (1433–99) of the *Enneads*, the collected works of the originator of Neoplatonism. The original Greek text was not published until 1580. In his *De ratione studii* Erasmus ranked Plotinus among the four most important Greek philosophers – 'Plato, Aristotle, and his pupil Theophrastus will serve as the best teachers of philosophy, and then there is Plotinus who combines both these schools'[2] – although it does not appear that he concerned himself particularly with Plotinus' works. The book is now in the Museum Meermanno-Westreenianum at The Hague. On the verso of the last page, it bears the autograph ex libris *Sum Erasmi*. All that is known of the fate of the volume after 1536 is that it was sold at auction with the library of La Vallire in 1783.[3]

1 Hain 13121
2 ASD I-2 120:12–13 / CWE 24 673:5–7
3 ter Horst 'Nog enkele aanteekeningen over de bibliotheek van Erasmus' 229, 234

210 Politi. Economi. etc Aristot. cum commen.

Aristoteles. *Politicorum libri octo. Oeconomicorum libri duo. Hecatonomiarum libri septem. Oeconomiarum publicarum liber unus. Explanatio Leonardi in Oeconomica.* Parisiis: Stephanus, 5 August 1506 or 3 April 1511 (folio).

After the *Physica* of 1494, the *Moralia* of 1497 (see no 15), and the *Organon* of 1503, this was the fourth edition of a work of Aristotle with commentary by Jacques Lefèvre d'Etaples.[1] Like its predecessors, the collection exemplified Lefèvre's humanist intention to make intelligible the work of the Greek philosopher, which had been obscured by corrupt texts and impenetrable scholastic commentaries, by means of purified texts and brief but clear explanatory notes. For the *Politica* and the first and third books of the *Oeconomica* (wrongly ascribed to Aristotle), Lefèvre made use of his own improved version of the translation by the Italian humanist Leonardo Bruni Aretino. In addition, the edition reflected Lefèvre's own ideas: in the commentary on the eighth book of the *Politics*, he developed for the first time his programme for a Christian-humanist education. Lefèvre dedicated the work to his patron Guillaume Briçonnet, bishop of Lodève. His pupil, Beatus Rhenanus, who acted as corrector in preparing the work for the press, also composed some verses as an introduction to the book. Which edition Erasmus owned cannot be established with any certainty. The *editio princeps* appeared when he was about to leave for Italy or already on his way there. The revised edition of 1511 may be more likely; Erasmus considerably enlarged his library in the years following his return from Italy in 1509, especially with books from Paris.[2]

1 For more detail on this work see Renaudet *Préréforme et humanisme* 484–6; Rice *Prefatory Epistles* 150–7 Epp 49 and 50.
2 Cf no 72 with n2. The Stephanus reprint of 1515–16 is in octavo.

211 Aristote. quaedam, item Theophr. Gaza interpre.

Aristoteles/Theophrastus. *Habentur hoc volumine Theodoro Gaza interprete Aristotelis de natura animalium libri IX ... de partibus animalium libri IV ... de generatione animalium libri V. Theophrasti de historia plantarum libri IX ... de causis plantarum libri VI. Aristotelis problemata ... Alexandri Aphrodisiensis problemata.* Venetiis: Aldus, March 1504 or 1513 (folio).

Theodorus Gaza translated the works of Aristotle and Theophrastus on natural history under the auspices of Pope Nicholas V, who had summoned him to Rome in 1449. He enjoyed a high reputation; Erasmus called him 'of all translators the most successful.'[1] It must also have been on these volumes that Erasmus based his verdict that Gaza excelled as a translator from Aristotle.[2] It is impossible to say with certainty which edition is in question here. Perhaps that of 1513, since the 1515 edition of the *Adagia* includes many new references to or citations from Aristotle and Theophrastus, in Gaza's translation.[3]

1 *Catalogus lucubrationum* Allen I 15:29/CWE Ep 1341A:550–1; cf Ep 2466:234–5/241. On Gaza see *Catalogus translationum et commentariorum* I 130; CEBR II 81.
2 Ep 2432:253–4/230–1
3 See for example *Adagia* III iv 24 ASD II-5 251 239n and 253 246–50n/CWE 35 15–16 with n1 and *Adagia* III vii 1 ASD II-6 405 193–4n, 407 240–1n, 409 301n, 413 426–45n/CWE 35 188 with n53, 190 with n64, 193 with nn87–8, 199–200.

212 Aristotelis opera uarijs interpretibus.

Aristoteles. *Opera nunnulla e graeco in latinum per Johannem Argyropylum, Leonardum Bruni Aretinum et Georgium Valla Placentinum translata, Accedit: Gilbertus Porretanus, De sex principiis ex aed. Herm. Barbari.* Venetiis: Gregorius de Gregoriis, imp. B. Fontanae, 1496 (folio).

or

Aristoteles. *[Quae in hoc volumine conti-
nentur] Vitae Aristotelis ex Plutarcho et ex
Diogene Laertio, Praedicabilia Prophyrii
[sic], Praedicamenta Aristotelis. [In fine]
Aristotelis opera quae a Joanne Argyropylo,
Hermolae Barbaro, Leonardo Aretino et
Georgio Valla: e graeco traducta etc.*
Venetiis: Philippus Pincius, sumpt. Bened.
Fontanae, 12 September 1505 (folio).

Before 1495, the year in which the famous
Aldine edition with the original Greek text
began to appear (see no 214), the works
of Aristotle were only accessible, at least
in print, in translations. As he made clear
in his introduction to the Bebelius edition
of 1531 (Ep 2432), Erasmus had a very low
opinion of these early renderings. In his
eyes, they were, with a few exceptions,
so bad that to understand Aristotle from
them 'was the work, as they say, of a
Delian diver.' He made an exception for
Theodorus Gaza and Leonardo Bruni
Aretino, but not for Argyropoulos (though
he praised him highly elsewhere), since he
believed that Argyropoulos had only begun
to translate Aristotle into Latin after the
Aldine editions had appeared on the
market.[1] It is difficult to understand how
Erasmus' memory had deceived him here.
Argyropoulos could not possibly have set
about translating the Greek philosopher so
late, since he had died in 1474. Moreover,
his translations of Aristotle had been in
circulation for many years.[2]

The 'Opera uarijs interpretibus' entered
in the *Versandliste* under this number
probably alluded to one of the two bulky
volumes of Aristotle's works in Latin
translation.[3] Both collections contained
versions by Italian humanists like Georgio
Valla and Leonardo Bruni, as well as those
of the learned Greek exiles like Johannes
Argyropoulos. Erasmus could have bought
one of these collections during his stay in
Venice. Perhaps the latter, then recently
published, is the most likely.

1 Ep 2432:249–56/225–33 on the earlier translations; for the proverb quoted, cf *Adagia* I vi 29.
2 For example the *Nicomachean Ethics*; see no 15.
3 For the first see GW 2341; the 1505 edition is
known only from Panzer VIII 375 no 302; I have
not been able to trace an existing copy. The edition
of Bernardinus de Vitalibus (Venice 1504) has not
been considered because it was a quarto (according to *Deutscher Gesamtkatalog ... herausgegeben
von der Preussischen Staats-bibliothek* 6 col 603;
Cranz 5 classifies it erroneously as a folio edition).

213 Plauti opera cum interpreta. Bap. Pij.

Plautus, Titus Maccius. *Plautus integer cum
interpretatione Baptistae Pij.* Mediolani:
Uldericus Scinzenzeler, 1500 (folio).

During his stay in Italy Erasmus worked
on Plautus for Aldo Manuzio, although
the edition did not at that time reach
the publication stage. In 1517 Andrea
Torresani, Aldo's father-in-law, reminded
Erasmus of the editorial work he had
already done and appealed for further help
with the planned edition of Plautus, which
he wished to be soundly based on early
manuscripts if possible. Erasmus seems
to have taken no part in the project; in the
Aldine edition of 1522 his name is not on
the title-page, and there is only a casual
mention in the introduction that the work
of Aldo and Erasmus was the basis of
the text.[1] Erasmus did not have a copy of
the edition in his library in 1536. It is not
very likely that Erasmus was engaged in the
Plautus published by Gymnicus in Cologne
in 1530, with added scholia, 'in which
is annotated everything in Plautus that
Erasmus, Budé, and others corrected or
annotated.'[2] Nothing is known of any
relations of Erasmus with the Cologne
printer round about that time.

When Erasmus acquired the edition of
Plautus' comedies with Giambattista Pio's
commentary, published in Milan in 1500,
cannot be determined. Perhaps it was not
at an early date. In the *Adagiorum collectanea*, his first, small collection of proverbs,
which was published at the latest in July

1500, Plautus was by far the most frequently mentioned or quoted classical writer,[3] but that does not necessarily mean that Erasmus already owned a copy of the Milanese edition when he was working on it. All the same, he was undoubtedly aware of the new edition. In his Paris circle of friends he had ample opportunity to skim a copy somewhere, and he may have profited from it occasionally. But he often borrowed his Plautus citations from older editions or took them from secondary sources, including Poliziano's *Miscellaneorum centuria prima*.[4] Moreover, he quoted the comedies again and again from memory.[5] On that account it is quite possible that Erasmus obtained his copy of the 1500 edition only later. Perhaps he brought it back with him from Italy.

Giambattista Pio (c 1460–1540), was a native of Bologna, where he was a pupil of the celebrated humanist Filippo Beroaldo the elder. He taught for many years in his birthplace, but later moved away and was active between 1509 and 1516 in Milan and Rome. After that, he was a teacher again in Bologna and in 1527 also in Lucca.[6] Whether Erasmus met him in Bologna is not clear, but cannot be ruled out.

1 For Erasmus' work on Plautus see Allen i 61:164–5 (Beatus Rhenanus to Charles v) and Epp 1479:96–100 with 96n/110–14 with n46, 589:44–53 with 44n/45–56 with 45n (from Torresani).

2 'in quibus annotantur quaecunque aut castigauit aut annotauit in Plautum Des. Erasmus, G. Budaeus …'; ASD I-2 (*De ratione studii*) 116 2n

3 ASD II-9 29–30; Appelt *Studies in the Contents and Sources of Erasmus' Adagia* 118: 'Three authors are most referred to: Plautus 124, Horace 87 and Terence 73 times' (Appelt does not include hidden quotations; cf ASD II-9 2–3).

4 See for example *Adagia* II ix 71 ASD II-4 259 891n. For another source used (Giambattista Pio's *Annotationes priores*) see *Adagia* II vi 33 ASD II-4 43 note.

5 See for example CWE 31 81 (I i 32 3n), 361 (I iv 60 4n); cf 429 (I i 53 note).

6 On Pio see Allen Ep 256:137n; CEBR III 88.

214 Ζῶα / Φυτὰ / Ὄργανα / Προβλήματα / Φυσικα. μετεω. / Ηθικα. πολιτ. } Aristote. graece.

Aristoteles. *Opera omnia* [graece]. Venetiis: Aldus Manutius, 1495–8, 5 vols in 6 (folio).

Editio princeps of Aristotle's works in the original language, published by Aldo Manuzio and dedicated by him to his pupil and patron Alberto Pio, prince of Carpi. This famous book was already rare by the end of Erasmus' lifetime, and outside of Italy was for sale only at very high prices. Bonifacius Amerbach had to pay twelve crowns for it, while the second edition of the Greek Aristotle, brought out in 1531 by Johann Bebel in Basel (no 215), cost only two crowns.[1] Erasmus does not seem to have procured his Aldine Aristotle until 1525; it was one of many Greek works he ordered from Italy at that time.[2] From the description, with its short table of contents, one can infer that in his copy the five volumes were bound as six, the fourth, which is by far the most bulky, being divided in two. The abbreviated order of contents differs from the chronological sequence in which they were published and are usually described. Ζῶα is volume 3; Φυτὰ is volume 4, part 1 (1–228); Ὄργανα is volume 1; Προβλήματα is volume 4, part 2 (229–520); Φυσικα. μετεω. is volume 2; Ηθικα. πολιτ. is volume 5.[3]

Erasmus' copy, except for the third volume, has been preserved.[4] It is to be found in the cathedral library at Wells, to which it was presented in about 1568 by the dean, William Turner. Whether the third volume was already missing or went astray at a later date cannot now be determined. The original bindings have disappeared and were replaced, probably at the end of the seventeenth or early in the eighteenth century, by those we see today; at that time the division of the fourth volume in two parts was maintained. At the end of each volume, after the closing sentence of the text, Erasmus wrote his mark of ownership in Greek; and he also signed volume 4 on fol 226, which means that it was already bound in two parts. Ἐράσμου εἰμί in volume 5 has been cut off for the benefit, apparently, of a later collector of autographs. Erasmus also provided the volumes with his ex libris in Latin. During rebinding the words *Sum Erasmi* were cut from the flyleaves on which they probably stood originally and pasted inside the new front covers. Perhaps through carelessness on the binder's part, the inscription from the second part of the fourth volume was lost. Under the *Sum Erasmi* in the first half of that volume the gift to Wells Cathedral is still recorded: *Haec ego dona dedi Wellensi bibliothecae / Turnerus nomen cui Gulielmus erat*. Scattered through the work are short annotations written in the margin, often only single words, and in notable quantities only in the first and fifth volumes. Only a few of these are in Erasmus' handwriting.

As for the donor, William Turner, physician and botanist, probably had bought Aristotle's works, or had got them as a present, from Jan Łaski, with whom he had come into contact in Emden in the forties. He had prepared the Polish reformer's first visit to England (1548–9) and his move there with his family in May 1550. In the same year he was appointed to the deanery of Wells, but after the death of Edward VI he left England, as did Łaski, and remained abroad during Mary Tudor's reign.[5]

1 Ep 2432:256–62 with 256–7n / 233–8 with n22; AK IV 36–7 Ep 1518:25–7
2 A VII 547 Appendix 20 'Books Ordered by Erasmus'
3 Cf Hain 1657; GW 2334.
4 For the information that follows I am greatly indebted to Rev Canon T.M. Martin, chancellor of Wells, and to Miss Jane Swingard, ALA, who submitted Erasmus' copy to a detailed investigation on my behalf.
5 On Turner see *Dictionary of National Biography* 57 363–66; for his relation to Łaski cf Hall *John a Lasco* 30. Turner must have been proficient in Greek; in Cambridge he instructed his fellow-student and intimate Nicholas Ridley, afterwards bishop of London, in that language.

215   Aristotelis opera graece. Bebelij

Aristoteles. *Opera omnia*. Basileae: J. Bebelius, 1531, 2 vols (folio).

For this, the second edition of Aristotle in the original Greek (for the first, see no 214), Erasmus wrote a lengthy introductory letter addressed to John More (Ep 2432), and a short Greek dialogue in verse form that was printed, with his name, on the title-page,[1] but he had no further involvement in the production of the work. The man responsible for the text was Simon Grynaeus, who even had a hand in the definitive shaping of the poem on the title-page. Grynaeus was in correspondence with Erasmus even before he became professor of Greek at Basel in 1529, although the relationship never ripened into friendship; some of Erasmus' letters express distrust of the much younger Greek scholar. That Grynaeus was present at Erasmus' deathbed, a tradition still accepted by Allen, cannot be proved.[2] The renewed reading of Aristotle in this Basel text of 1531 gave Erasmus occasion to introduce numerous innovations in the next revised edition of his *Adagia* (1533).[3]

1 Reedijk *Poems* no 130 / ASD I-7 and CWE 85–6 no 87
2 On Grynaeus and Erasmus' relationship with him see Allen and CWE Ep 1657 introductions; CEBR II 142–6; Reedijk, 'Das Lebensende des Erasmus' 63–4 and CWE 40 1125 ('The Return to Basel'). Cf also nos 180 #2 and 216.
3 For example in *Adagia* III ii 15, III iv 1, III iv 2, III iv 4, III iv 71, III vii 55, III vii 61

216   Platonis opera tralatione Marsi. Fici.

Plato. *Omnia opera tralatione Marsilii Ficini emendatione et ad graecum codicem collatione Simonis Grynaei nunc recens … repurgata*. Basileae: off. Frobeniana, 1532 or perhaps another edition (folio).

Although the abbreviation 'Frob.,' often used by the compiler of the *Versandliste*, is absent, the book in question is very probably the 1532 Froben edition of Plato prepared by Simon Grynaeus.[1] It was the first Plato to be published by the Basel press. It is hard to see why Erasmus would have kept another, older edition of Ficino's translation in his library (no 217) and would not have acquired the most recent one, the printer and editor of which were both in constant contact with him. And we know that Erasmus used the new edition. In a letter to Grynaeus he questioned a passage in the text, an intervention that earned him, not an answer to his query but a 'supercilious and acidulous letter,' with a reproach on a quite different matter thrown in for good measure. Erasmus complained bitterly of this to Bonifacius Amerbach.[2] Erasmus' relationship with Grynaeus was often difficult, but was never broken off altogether.

1 On Grynaeus see no 215 n2.
2 Ep 2742

217 Platonis opera Venetijs. Latinè

Plato. *Opera latine interprete Marsilio Ficino cum Vita Platonis ab eodem Ficino.* Venetiis: B. de Choris et Simon de Luere, imp. Andreae Toresani de Asula, 1491 or Philippus Pincius, 1517 (folio).

As far as can be traced, only two editions of Plato's works in the Latin version were published in Venice before 1536: the earlier printed in 1491 by Bernardus de Choris and Simon de Luere for the publisher Andrea Torresani (Asulanus), the other in 1517 by Philippus Pincius.[1] Both used the famous translation of the Florentine Neoplatonist Marsilio Ficino, who made Plato's works known long before the original Greek text was available in print: the *editio princeps* of Plato in Greek did not appear until 1513 (see no 218). It seems plausible that Erasmus should have procured his translation of Plato at a fairly early date; he was already citing from it in the *Adagiorum collectanea* (1500), the *Disputatiuncula de taedio, pavore, tristicia Iesu* (1499–1503?), and the *Enchiridion militis Christiani* (1503).[2] He had become

familiar with Plato during his first exchanges in Oxford with John Colet in 1499; in December he wrote, 'When I listen to Colet, it seems to me that I am listening to Plato himself.'[3] In 1500 he was scraping together a sum of money that would enable him to buy, apart from the complete works of Jerome and some Greek books, a Plato.[4] Might not the copy identified in this entry of the *Versandliste* as 'from Venice' have come into his possession about this time? If so, it must have been the 1491 edition. Erasmus also owned a translation of Plotinus by Ficino (of about the same date, whether by chance or not), the hardly less well known edition of 1492 (no 209).

1 Hain 13063 and Adams P 1442
2 For a literal citation from the *Cratylus* in *Adagia* III i 53: *A fronte pariter atque a tergo* see Cytowska 'Erasme de Rotterdam, traducteur d'Homère' 347. In the *Adagia* of 1508 Erasmus cited the same passage in Greek (in Venice he must have had the Greek text at his disposal in manuscript) and added his own translation. See also Levi *The Neo-Platonist Calculus* 231–2 and 246n; Cytowska 'Erasme de Rotterdam et Marsile Ficin, son maître' 173: 'Dans les rédactions suivantes du recueil *Adagia* parues de 1508 à 1536 on ne trouve presque plus de citations de Platon qui aient été répétées littéralement après Ficin.'
3 Ep 118:21/24–5
4 Ep 138:38–41/43–7

218 Platonis opera graecè. Aldi.

Plato. *Omnia opera [graece].* Venetiis: in aed. Aldi et Andreae soceri, September 1513 (folio).

Editio princeps of the original Greek text of Plato, supervised by Marcus Musurus and Aldo Manuzio and dedicated to Pope Leo X. Preceding the text, besides the dedication, is Musurus' famous Hymn to Plato.[1] The edition must have been planned earlier, for in 1507 Erasmus wrote to Aldo, 'I am told that you are printing a Plato in Greek type; most scholars are already eagerly awaiting it.'[2] Notwithstanding his interest, Erasmus himself seems not to have procured the Greek text till much later, about 1525.[3] What is probably the copy he ordered then is now in the Royal Library in The Hague. The ex libris is defaced, but can still be read by ultraviolet light, with the names of two other owners: *Sum Erasmi. At nunc Regneri Praedini. 1554 ... a Lasco ... Poloniae Jo. Arce. Theodor.*[4] The fate of the Plato seems to have been linked with that of the Galen (no 138) now in the University Library at Leiden, also owned by Praedinus and Arcerius in succession.[5]

1 Geanakoplos *Greek Scholars in Venice* 149–54
2 Ep 207:13–15/15–16
3 Allen VII 547, Appendix 20 'Books Ordered by Erasmus'
4 Ter Horst 'Een boek uit de bibliotheek van Erasmus teruggevonden'
5 Two other books became the property of Dutch owners via Praedinius; see nos 137 and 281.

219 Flauij Iosephi opera Frob.

Josephus, Flavius. *Opera quaedam Ruffino presbytero interprete.* Basileae: J. Frobenius, 1524 (folio) or *Antiquitatum judaicarum libri XX ... De bello judaico libri VII ... Contra Apionem libri II ... De imperio rationis sive de Machabaeis liber unus a Des. Erasmo ... recognitus.* Basileae: H. Frobenius et N. Episcopius, 1534 (folio).

Two Froben editions of the works of Josephus appeared during Erasmus' lifetime: the first in 1524 under the title *Opera quaedam* and the second with the same content in 1534 under a title that enumerates the works included. Although the short title *Opera* in the *Versandliste* suggests the earlier of the two editions, one must certainly bear in mind the possibility that the later may be meant. It was just as complete as the original Froben edition, and if Erasmus' copy bore the title *Opera* on the fore-edge or spine, it could equally well have been described as such by the compiler of the list. Moreover, it is scarcely credible that Erasmus should not have received the 1534 edition from the printer: he had been indirectly involved in its production. For the establishment of the text he supplied Froben with a manuscript, now no longer traceable, of the *Bellum Judaicum*, which, he had heard, had once belonged to the bishop of Rodez, Georges d'Armagnac. In November 1431 he asked the prelate to make this manuscript available for a short time in order to have a transcript made.[1] The owner of the manuscript, however, appears to have been Jean de Pins, bishop of Rieux, to whom d'Armagnac passed on the request he received. Erasmus also applied directly to de Pins, who had lent the manuscript to the Lyon printer Sebastianus Gryphius. On its return he sent it at once to d'Armagnac, who took the responsibility for conveying the valuable document to Freiburg in safety. For this purpose he entrusted the manuscript to Rabelais, who successfully delivered it to Erasmus, accompanied by a personal letter and perhaps also a small gift. Both Froben editions also contained Josephus' account of the martyrdom of the seven Maccabee brothers and their mother; see no 193.

1 Ep 2569. For what follows, see in particular the introduction to this letter. See also Epp 2628:1–14 (to de Pins), 2743:1–7 (from Rabelais); cf no 12 #3. On d'Armagnac see Allen Ep 2569 introduction and CEBR I 72; on de Pins Allen Ep 928:36n and CEBR III 85–6.

220 Biblia Frob.

Biblia cum pleno apparatu summariorum concordantiarum et quadruplicis repertorii sive indicii numerique foliorum distinctione ... Basileae: J. Petri et J. Frobenius, 1509 or Basiliae: J. Frobenius, 1514 (folio).

One of the two folio editions (the surrounding books are all folios) of the Latin Bible with the whole set of commentaries, explanatory notes, concordances, and lists of words known as the *plenus apparatus*,[1] published by Johann Froben. Froben had also published a Bible in a more convenient octavo format, the *Biblia integra*, in 1491. A copy of the *editio princeps* of that Bible, now in the University Library in Basel, was said by the Basel collector R. Faesch (1595–1667) to have belonged to Erasmus and to have been used by him throughout his life. 'This is the same copy,' he wrote in the catalogue of his books, 'that Erasmus of Rotterdam used all his life. Then it came to Froben, Erasmus' heir, and from the Frobens to H. Petri. The names of both Erasmus and Froben are inscribed.' But it is doubtful that the name of Erasmus at the end of the book was an autograph mark of ownership, while it is certain that the numerous manuscript notes in the margin (contrary to Faesch's claim) are not in the hand of Erasmus but that of Froben. The book is in poor condition. The leather of the binding has been heavily worn by frequent use and the corners of the pages have become unusually dirty from fingers greasy with printers' ink. Jenny assumes for this reason that it 'might have been a Bible – at most jointly used and temporarily owned by Erasmus – that was available in Froben's printing office as a permanent reference copy for checking biblical texts.'[2]

1 Le Long and Boerner *Bibliotheca Sacra* II 169–70
2 For these details on the copy see Husner 'Bibliothek' 257 and Jenny in *Erasmus … Vorkämpfer für Frieden und Toleranz* 219.

221 Biblia graecè Aldi.

Biblia. *Sacrae Scripturae veteris, novaeque omnia.* Venetiis: in aed. Aldi et Andreae soceri, February 1518 (folio).

Until the publication of the Complutensian Polyglot in 1521 or 1522,[1] the Aldine edition of 1518 was the first and only edition of the whole Bible in Greek. In it the Septuagint and Erasmus' version of the New Testament were combined. The *Novum Testamentum* of 1516 was reproduced in such a hurry that numerous printer's errors were repeated, even those that Erasmus had rectified in a list of errata.[2] Erasmus' copy may have been a gift from the publisher Gianfrancesco

Torresani, who had dedicated the New Testament section to Erasmus with a handsome introductory letter (Ep 770), although Erasmus had already asked Froben, when he heard in 1517 that the work would be published, to bring him back a copy from the Frankfurt book fair.[3] As he wrote to Maarten Lips more than two years after it was published, the Aldine Bible was difficult to get in the north. Erasmus appeared to be the only one in the vicinity of Leuven who possessed a copy. He was willing to lend it, however, first to the Leuven Franciscans and then to Lips, until he needed it again himself for the revision of his New Testament.[4]

1 The printing of the Greek New Testament was already finished early in January 1514. The publication of the Polyglot Bible, however, had to wait seven or eight years for the pope's sanction.
2 Metzger *The Text of the New Testament* 103
3 Ep 629:16/18–19
4 Epp 1174:14–17/16–19, 1189:4–9/6–11

222 Primus et secun. tomus / Tertius et quar. tom. > operum Orige.

Origenes. *Operum tomi duo priores (tertius et quartus tomi).* Parisiis: ven. in ed. Joannis Parvi et Jodoci Badij (in aed. Ascensianis, 1512) (folio).

Erasmus' special interest in Origen dated from 1501, when he made the acquaintance of Jean Vitrier, guardian of the Franciscan monastery of Saint-Omer and a great admirer of this Father of the church.[1] Origen's work also had a profound and far-reaching influence on Erasmus.[2] One page of Origen, he wrote in 1518, taught him more of Christian philosophy than ten pages of Augustine.[3] In 1527 Erasmus published a fragment of Origen's commentary on the Gospel of Matthew, which he had translated from a Greek codex borrowed from the library at the castle of Ladenburg collected by Johann von Dalberg, bishop of Worms.[4]

Erasmus was much occupied with Origen in the last years of his life, but he did not live to see the completion of the revised edition of Origen's works in Latin translation: it was not published until September 1536, after his death, edited by Beatus Rhenanus, who also wrote a dedicatory letter to Hermann von Wied that included a well-known sketch of Erasmus's life.[5] This entry on the *Versandliste* must refer to the *editio princeps* of Origen's works in Latin translation published in 1512 by Josse Bade and reprinted twice, in 1519 and 1522. Its editor was Jacques Merlin, who also intended, by means of his edition, to free Origen from the charge of heresy.[6] Bade put the work under the protection of the humanist Guillaume Petit, the confessor of Francis I,[7] while Merlin dedicated it to Michel Boudet, bishop of Langes. Boudet was a friend of Budé, and was later to enter into correspondence with Erasmus.[8] The quality of the text was mediocre: for the previously unpublished Περὶ ἀρχῶν Merlin relied on the inaccurate translation of Rufinus and for the other works on older and often very imperfect Italian editions.[9]

Which of the three Bade editions is alluded to here can be determined with some degree of certainty. From notes on the Gospel of Luke and the Acts of the Apostles that appeared for the first time in his *Annotationes* published in March 1519 (but already prepared for the press by the end of August 1518),[10] it is clear that Erasmus had used Bade's text of Origen. At that time this could only have been the original edition of 1512. Even without a source reference, the very numerous citations from and references to Origen in the *Annotationes* in both the 1516 and 1519 editions are a sufficient indication that he had studied this Bade edition intently.[11]

1 On Jean Vitrier (c 1456–1521) see Epp 163:3n/5n, 1211:13–245/16–273; Godin 'Jean Vitrier et la "cénacle" de Saint Omer'; CEBR III 408–9.

2 Godin 'Erasme et le modèle origénien de la prédication' and *Erasme lecteur d'Origène*; Fokke,

Christus verae pacis auctor et unicus scopus: Erasmus and Origen

3 Ep 844:252–4/272–4

4 Ep 1844:93–7/ 101–5; the edition does not appear in the *Versandliste*.

5 *Opera latine, studio et labore D. Erasmi Roterdami partim versa, partim recognita* (Basel: Hieronymus Froben and Nicolaus Episcopius, September 1536; 2 vols). For the biographical sketch in the letter see Allen I 52–6.

6 Renouard *Bibliographie Josse Bade* III 94–9. Volume 3 contains Merlin's *Epistola nuncupatoria in apologiam Origenis*; on Merlin cf no 168.

7 In a letter at the close of volume 4; on Petit cf no 15 n14.

8 In Epp 1612, 1618 and 1678 (1525–6); on Boudet see Allen and CWE Ep 1612 introductions; CEBR I 178–9.

9 Renaudet *Préréforme et humanisme* 619; for Erasmus' late verdict on the edition, see Godin *Erasme lecteur d'Origène* 564.

10 Allen and CWE Ep 864 introductions

11 Cf Erasmus' references in the annotations on Luke 2:35 ('ex Merlini cujusdam editione') and Acts 18:2 ('in voluminibus Origenicis primum a Badio nostro excusis') LB VI 236F and 504C/ASD VI-5 486:112 and ASD VI-6 292:590–1. See Rabil *Erasmus and the New Testament* 116–17; and cf Payne 'Erasmus, interpreter of Romans' 8–9. The *Responsio ad annotationes Lei* (1520) LB IX 140/CWE 72 107 also mentions the Bade edition.

223 Opera Cypriani

Cyprianus, Thascius Caecilianus. *Opera*. Probably Romae: C. Sweynheym and A. Pennartz, 1471 (folio).

In the third impression of his own edition of Cyprian, Erasmus stated that while preparing the text he had made use of three older editions, which Allen identified as those of Rome: Sweynheym and Pannartz 1471; Deventer: R. Pafraet [between 1477 and 1479]; and Paris: B. Rembolt and J. Waterloes 1512.[1] If Erasmus had his own copy of one of these editions, and retained it until his death, then it would most probably have been the Roman *editio princeps*.[2] The Paris edition is not likely since it was a quarto and the surrounding books are all folios, while Erasmus wrote of the Deventer edition that its title escaped him, which seems almost

incredible for a book on his own shelves.
Only the original edition of 1471 would
then be left, but there can be no certainty
about this.

1 Allen Ep 1000 introduction. The letter is the
  dedicatory preface to Lorenzo Pucci.
2 GW 7883

224 Theophylactus in .4. Euan. Oecolam. interpre.

Theophylactus. *In quatuor evangelia
enarrationes Joanne Oecolampadio interprete*. Basileae: A. Cratander, March 1524
or one of the reprints (folio).

The commentaries on the Gospels by
the Byzantine historian and theologian
Theophylact (c 1050–c 1107), archbishop
of Ochryd and later metropolitan of
Bulgaria, were translated into Latin by
Johannes Oecolampadius from a fifteenth-
century manuscript bequeathed to the
Dominican monastery at Basel by cardinal
John of Ragusa on his death in c 1444.[1]
Erasmus too knew and used this manuscript, which is now in the University
Library at Basel. From the parchment label
on its front cover he identified the author
as 'Vulgarius' on the title-page and in the
annotations of his *Novum instrumentum* of
1516; he corrected this to 'Theophylactus'
on the title-page of the 1519 *Novum
Testamentum* and in the annotations
to the 1522 edition.[2] Erasmus quoted
the commentary on John 7:39 from
Oecolampadius' translation in his letter
to Robert Aldridge of 23 August 1527.[3]

1 Staehelin BAO I 270n; Staehelin *Das theologische
  Lebenswerk Johannes Oekolampads* 185–6; Vernet
  'Les manuscrits grecs de Jean de Raguse' 84
2 Sign. A III 15. See Allen Ep 1790:11n and CWE Ep
  1680 n3; cf Ep 846:8n/9n. Cf Payne 'Erasmus
  Interpreter of Romans' 8 n42.
3 Ep 1858:97–106/108–16; the passages cited are
  from fol 175r.

225 Biblia Lugd. excu.

*Biblia cum pleno apparatu summariorum
concordantiarum et quadruplicis repertorii
sive indicii numerisque foliorum distinctione.*
Lugduni: Jacobus Sacon, 1506 or a later
reprint (folio).

One of the countless editions of the
Vulgate that appeared at Lyon in the early
sixteenth century. By far the most famous
and most important printer of Bibles there
was Jacob Sacon, who issued at least nine
folio editions between 1506 and 1522, at
first on his own and later at the expense of
Anton Koberger of Nürnberg (1445–1513)
or his cousin Johan Koberger (d 1543).[1]
One older Lyon folio not from Sacon was
published in 1497 by F. Fradin and J.
Pinard.[2]

1 Le Long and Boerner *Bibliotheca sacra* II 150–8;
  Baudrier XII 318–60
2 GW 4279

226 Opus Epistolarum Eras.

Erasmus: *Opus Epistolarum*. Basileae:
H. Frobenius, J. Hervagius et N. Episcopius,
1529 (folio).

Of the roughly 1,000 letters contained
in this edition,[1] two-fifths had not been
published before and the rest were reprinted from two older collections, the *Epistolae
Erasmi ad diversos et aliquot aliorum ad
illum* of 1521 and the *Selectae aliquot
epistolae nunquam antehac evulgatae* of
1528.[2] The greater part of the *Epistolae
Erasmi ad diversos* consisted in turn of all
the letters, with perhaps a few exceptions,
printed in the five collections that had
appeared between 1515 and 1519.[3] The
Opus epistolarum was thus in effect a
cumulative edition that superseded the
seven preceding collections. Erasmus
clearly thought so, and he removed the
redundant compilations from his working
library; it cannot be coincidence that none

of them is mentioned in the *Versandliste*. There were, however, copies of all but two of the superseded editions in the separate collection of Erasmus' own works that was kept in a chest in his house 'Zum Luft' at the end of his life.[4] See nos 345 and 393 for letters edited by Erasmus after 1529.

1 Allen's edition H; see I 593–602 Appendix 7 'The Principal Editions of Erasmus' *Epistolae*.' Cf on the various volumes of Erasmus' letters Mynors 'The Early Publications of Erasmus' Letters' CWE 3 348–50 and the exhaustive and splendid study of Halkin, *Erasmus ex Erasmo*.
2 Editions F and G
3 Editions A, B, C[1], D[1], E
4 See *Catalogus librorum Erasmi* nos 13, 23, 30, 55, 62, and cf nos 26, 90.

227 Opera Tertulliani Frob.

Tertullianus, Quintus Septimius Florens. *Opera per Beatum Rhenanum e tenebris eruta*. Basileae: J. Frobenius, July 1521 or Basiliae: off. Frobeniana, 1528 (folio).

The complete works of Tertullian, edited for the first time by Beatus Rhenanus from two manuscripts, now lost, in the libraries of the monasteries of Hirsau (west of Stuttgart), and Payene (south of Neuchâtel). The edition was dedicated to Stanislaus Thurzo;[1] it included a *Vita Tertulliani* and an *Admonitio de quibusdam Tertulliani dogmatis* by the editor,[2] while the *Definitiones ecclesiasticorum dogmatum* of Gennadius of Marseilles were added at the end. At the request of Beatus, Conradus Pellicanus compiled the index, as he had previously done for Erasmus' edition of Cyprian. A month after the publication of the edition Erasmus discussed it in a letter to Nicolaas van Broeckhoven of 's Hertogenbosch, master of the Latin School at Antwerp, whom he had known from his youth.[3] It is possible that he did not keep the original edition but the second edition of 1528. Erasmus made fruitless attempts, for the benefit of this second edition, to enlist the help of the Carthusians of Koblenz or his friend

Johannes Cochlaeus of Mainz to trace a manuscript of Tertullian's *De spectaculis*, believed to be part of the estate left by Ulrich Windemacher of Trier.[4]

1 The dedicatory letter contains details on the manuscripts used; see BRE 282–8 Ep 207. For Thurzo, see no 205 n1.
2 To which Jacobus Latomus responded; see no 152 n3.
3 Ep 1232
4 Epp 1946, 1974:1–3/2–4

228 Origenes contra Celsum. Romae./ excusus Christoph. Persona interprete.

Origenes. *Contra Celsum et in fidei Christianiae defensionem liber I (–VIII), Christ. Persona interprete*. Romae: Georgius Herolt, 1481 (folio).

A large part of Origen's *Contra Celsum*, his detailed defence of Christianity against the systematic and fundamental criticism of the pagan philosopher Celsus, has been preserved in a reliable form. In the edition referred to here, the Latin text is preceded by a letter from the Greek scholar Theodorus Gaza to the Italian Hellenist and later custodian of the Vatican library, C. Persona (1416–85), whom he had urged to undertake the translation.[1] In 1504 Erasmus wrote to John Colet that he had read a good part of Origen's works, and there is a possibility that he had become acquainted with the *Contra Celsum* even before his meeting with Jean Vitrier in 1501.[2] In that case he must have seen the work either in a manuscript or in the printed edition of 1481, though of course that need not have been the copy entered under this number in the *Versandliste*. Erasmus spoke enthusiastically in praise of the work, one of the earliest confrontations between the Christian and the pagan thought-worlds, in the dedication of his edition of Irenaeus of 1526 (no 195 #2): 'Celsus the philosopher spewed out blasphemies against Christ, but Origen, a better philosopher, turned his blasphemies to the glory of Christ.'[3]

1 For further details of the edition, see Godin
  Erasme lecteur d'Origène 7. On Gaza cf no 347.
2 Ep 181:38–41/45–8; Fokke *Christus verae pacis
  auctor et unicus scopus: Erasmus und Origen* III 195
  n2. Cf no 222 with n1.
3 Ep 1738:254–6/263–5

229 Cypriani et Irenaei opera Frob.

Cyprianus, Thascius Caecilius. *Opera
ab innumeris mendis repurgata ... [ed.]
Erasmus.* Basileae: off. Frobeniana, 1530
or 1525 (folio).

bound with

Irenaeus. *Opus eruditissimum in quinque
libros digestum in quibus mire retegit et
confutat ueterum haereseon impias opiniones ... emendatum opera Erasmi.* Basileae:
off. Frobeniana, 1528 or 1534 (folio).

1/ The works of Cyprian, bishop of
Carthage (d 258), edited by Erasmus.
In preparing the text Erasmus made use
of three earlier printed editions and two
manuscripts, which he had borrowed from
the abbot of Gembloux; another manuscript from one of the monastic libraries
of Paris may have been made available to
him through the intervention of Lefèvre
d'Etaples.[1] The *editio princeps*, dedicated
to Cardinal Lorenzo Pucci (Ep 1000),
appeared in 1520. Three authorized revised
printings followed, in 1521, 1525, and 1530.
We are probably dealing here with the last
or the penultimate edition.

The last edition contained a hitherto
unpublished treatise *Ad Fortunatum de
duplici martyrio*, which was considered by
later sixteenth-century editors of Cyprian
and by some modern scholars to be a
forgery by Erasmus himself.[2] Allen, however, rejected the idea that Erasmus would
have lent himself to such a fabrication and
suggested that the Basel printers may have
added the treatise, supposedly discovered
'in a very old library,' on their own initiative, just as they did they with the second
edition of Hilary in 1535.[3]

2/ For this edition of Irenaeus' *Adversus
haereses*, edited by Erasmus and dedicated
to the statesman Bernhard von Cles
(Ep 1738), see no 195, under which the first
edition of August 1526 is entered, bound
in one volume with another work. Besides
that copy, Erasmus must have kept one
of the two revised Froben reprints (1528
or 1534).

1 One of the printed texts was probably still in the
  library in 1536; see no 223. On the manuscripts
  see Epp 975 (to Antoine Papin, the abbot) and
  984 (Papin's reply); Allen Ep 1000 introduction
  (page 24); and cf Renaudet *Etudes érasmiennes* 33.
2 Lezius 'Der Verfasser des pseudo-cyprianischen
  Traktates de duplici martyrio' (1895); Otto
  Bardenhewer *Geschichte der altkirchlichen
  Literatur* II (1914) 503; and Seidel Menchi
  'Un'opera misconosciuta di Erasmo? Il trattato
  pseudo-ciprianico *De duplici martyrio*'; cf ASD
  V-3 12–13.
3 Allen Ep 1000 introduction (page 24). Cf no 185.

230 Tomus primus / To. 2ᵘˢ. / Tomus
3ᵘˢ / Tomus quartus / To. 5ᵘˢ cum indice }
operum Io. Chrysostomj / Frob.

Johannes Chrysostom. *Opera, quae
hactenus versa sunt omnia ad Graecorum
codicum collationem multis in locis ...
emendata. Accessere ... aliquot Homiliae
in Acta apostolorum etc.* Basileae: off.
Frobeniana, 1530, 5 volumes with index
(folio).

The initiative for this edition of Chrysostom
most probably came from Froben, who
was looking for a new large work to occupy
several presses after the completion of his
ten-volume edition of Augustine in 1529
(no 258). Erasmus was intimately involved
with the undertaking. Without assuming
heavy editorial responsibilities, he lent his
name to it and introduced the work in
a letter of recommendation addressed to
his friend and kindred spirit the bishop
of Augsburg, Christoph von Stadion
(Ep 2359).[1] Before that he had actively
helped Froben by seeking out translators
and translations. The versions he contributed himself are listed in the catalogue of

his works that Erasmus compiled early in 1530 for Hector Boece and published at the end of his *Consultatio de bello Turcis inferendo*.[2] The edition also contained translations, some old and taken over or reprinted from elsewhere, by Anianus, George of Trebizond, Francesco Griffolini (Aretino), Johannes Oecolampadius, Simon Grynaeus, and Germain de Brie.[3] The edition did not include all of Chrysostom's works, and Erasmus was soon involved in the publication of supplementary volumes (see nos 58 and 394). Dissatisfied with the work as a whole, he also began to take an interest, with Brie, in the new edition of Chrysostom being launched by Claude Chevallon in Paris and supplied it with some sheets of corrections to the Froben text.[4] Chevallon also received Erasmus' previously unpublished translation of the mass attributed to Chrysostom, although it is now doubted whether this can have been with Erasmus' knowledge and approval.[5] The Chevallon edition appeared in the year of Erasmus' death, possibly too late in the year to be included in his library.

1 See Allen and CWE introductions to Ep 2359 on the prehistory of the edition. Since Erasmus was living in Freiburg he had delegated to Simon Grynaeus the task of seeing the edition through the press at Basel; see Ep 2379:71–2/71–2.
2 Ep 2283:156–65/174–83; cf Ep 2263:34–40/36–42.
3 On Oecolampadius' translations, copied anonymously, see Staehelin BAO I 199 (no 135 n3), II 224 (no 597 n39), II 394 (no 702 n11), II 773 (no 982 n2).
4 See Ep 2359 introductions; the five pages in the hand of Gilbert Cousin formerly in the University Library, Leipzig have probably been lost (information from Dr D. Debes, Universitätsbibliothek, Leipzig). For Chevallon's edition of Jerome, also begun about this time with the cooperation of Erasmus, see no 405.
5 On the *Missa Sancti Joannis Chrysostomi* see no 95 #1.

231 Chrysost. in Genesim interprete Oecolam.

Johannes Chrysostomus. *In totum Genesews librum homiliae sexaginta sex*. Ed J. Oecolampadius. Basileae: A. Cratander, September 1523 (folio).

Sixty-six sermons on the book of Genesis, translated by Oecolampadius in not more than two months from two codices bequeathed by Cardinal John of Ragusa to the Dominican monastery at Basel.[1] On other translations from Chrysostom by Oecolampadius and the criticism of them, see nos 38 #1 and 166, and cf no 230 n3.

1 Universitätsbibliothek Basel MS B.II.16, 17. See Staehelin BAO I 205 n8; Vernet 'Les manuscrits grecs de Jean de Raguse' 87 (nos 20 and 21). Oecolampadius also translated Theophylact's commentary on the Gospels from a manuscript that had belonged to John of Ragusa; see no 224.

232 Historiae Eccl. auto. Frob.

Autores historiae ecclesiasticae. Eusebii Pamphili Caesariensis libri IX Ruffino interprete. Ruffini Aquileiensis libri II Item ex Theodoreto Cyrensi, Sozomeno et Socrate Constantinopolitano libri XII … Omnia recognita per Beatum Rhenanum. Basileae: J. Frobenius, August 1523 or Basileae: H. Frobenius and N. Episcopius, March 1535 (folio).

Stanislaus Thurzo, bishop of Olomouc (Olmütz), to whom Beatus Rhenanus dedicated this collected edition of writers on church history, had been in contact with Erasmus since 1521, when he sent him a letter and a gift through Ursinus Velius.[1] Ursinus' visit to Basel was the occasion for Beatus Rhenanus' dedication to Thurzo of his *editio princeps* of Tertullian (no 227). The bishop sent him a golden cup as a mark of gratitude, and four gold pieces for Erasmus at the same time.[2] His assurance that he had read Tertullian in one sitting encouraged Beatus Rhenanus to dedicate his *Autores historiae ecclesiasticae* to his patron as well. Erasmus undoubtedly acquired this important Froben edition immediately after its publication. Some months later, in his preface to the *Paraphrase on Mark*, he cited the *Historia quam Tripartitam vocant*, that is, the work of the early fifth-century authors Socrates scholasticus, Sozomen, and Theodoretus included in the compilation.[3] He likewise cited passages from Eusebius in the foreword to his edition of Irenaeus of 1526, and this too may be the result of his reading or rereading the text in Beatus' collection.[4] Towards the end of his life, he probably used the *Ecclesiastical History* of Eusebius, translated by Rufinus and also published in this collection, as a source for the brief sketch of the life of Origen in his (posthumously published) edition of Origen's *Opera*.[5] Whether Erasmus replaced the 1523 edition a year before his death by the two-volume reprint enlarged with Nicephorus' *Ecclesiastica historia*, Victor's *Historia persecutionis Africanae provinciae*, and another work on church history by Theodoret, bishop of Cyrrhus, cannot be determined.

1 Epp 1242:38–41/42–5, 1243:1–5/3–7. For Thurzo see no 205 n1.
2 Ep 1272:36–8. On the cup, cf Ep 1603:93–9/ 105–12.
3 Ep 1400:209–22/217–32
4 Ep 1738:35–6/38–9
5 *Opera* (Basel 1536) fols 425A–429D; see Godin *Erasme lecteur d'Origène* 632.

233 Prima pars / Secun. pars / Ter. Pas [sic] } operum Ambrosij

Ambrosius. *Operum sancti Ambrosij pars prima (–tertia).* Basileae: J. de Amerbach, 1492 (folio).

Johann Amerbach's edition of Ambrose, which in Allen's opinion undoubtedly served as the basis for Erasmus' own edition (no 149).[1] The titles of the three parts – *Operum sancti Ambrosij pars prima (–tertia)* – tally so exactly with the entry in the *Versandliste* that there is no need to consider either of the Basel reprints of 1516 or 1526. The Basel edition published by J. Petrus de Langendorf in 1506 is likewise not a possibility, in spite of its similar title, because of its quarto format; the surrounding items on the *Versandliste* are folios.

1 GW 1599. See Allen Ep 1855 introduction.

234 Chrysosto. in Epist. 1. et 2. ad Corin. / graece manuscriptus

An otherwise unidentifiable manuscript in folio format containing the Greek text of Chrysostom's commentaries on 1 and 2 Corinthians.

In a letter written in the spring of 1527 Erasmus mentioned a manuscript containing the commentaries on both Epistles to the Corinthians; in August of the previous year he had referred to a manuscript in his possession with the text of the commentary on 2 Corinthians.[1] This entry on the *Versandliste* may refer to one of these, but it cannot be proved. It was most probably not an ancient and valuable manuscript, for such precious codices were not included in the sale agreement with Łaski, although he managed to acquire a single old manuscript from Erasmus' estate after his death.[2] Rather, the manuscripts he referred to in his correspondence must be transcripts that he had had made for his own use. In 1531 or earlier, for example, he caused a copy to be made of an old Greek manuscript with texts of Chrysostom lent to him by Reginald Pole.[3] The manuscript of Chrysostom's *Homiliae in epistolam Pauli ad Romanos* that he put at the disposal of Germain de Brie in 1531 was not an original either, but a copy transcribed for him from a manuscript in the former library of Johann von Dalberg at Ladenburg.[4] He also owned a second copy of the same text, produced for him in 1528 by Nicolaas Kan (Cannius) of Amsterdam, who was then in his service. This copy, with marginal notes in Erasmus' hand, has been preserved and is now in Wolfenbüttel.[5]

1 Epp 1795:15/18, 1736:27–8/33–4
2 The valuable Codex Arcerianus, now in the Herzog August Bibliothek in Wolfenbüttel. In this codex are bound together the two oldest preserved manuscripts (early sixth century and late fifth or early sixth century) of the *Corpus agrimensorum*, a collection of short works that form one of the chief sources of information about Roman land surveyors. Erasmus had probably owned the two manuscripts from about 1526.

3 Ep 2526:7–9; cf Ep 1623:9n/n3 and no 410.
4 See no 58.
5 MS Gud. graec. fol. 4971; see von Heinemann
   *Die Handschriften der herzoglichen Bibliothek zu
   Wolfenbüttel* part 4: *Die Gudischen Handschriften*
   IX 5–6; cf Allen Ep 1832 introduction.

235 Chryso. in epistolas ad Heb. Galatas. Varia, / graece eadem manu scrip.

An otherwise unidentifiable manuscript or collection of manuscripts in folio, with the Greek text of Chrysostom's commentaries on Hebrews and Galatians.

As in the case of the manuscript of Chrysostom's commentaries on 1 and 2 Corinthians, Erasmus mentions in his correspondence of 1526–7 that he had acquired manuscripts of his commentaries on Hebrews and Galatians.[1] For the likelihood that these were not ancient codices but recent transcripts, see no 234.

1 Epp 1736:24–5/30 (Hebrews), 1795:15–16/18–19
   (Galatians)

236 Catalogus scriptorum eccles. Tritenh. Spanheymensis.

Trithemius, Johannes. *Liber de scriptoribus ecclesiasticis*. Basileae: J. Amerbach, 1494 or a later edition (folio).

Johannes Trithemius (1462–1516) was from 1483 to 1505 abbot of the Benedictine abbey of Sponheim near Kreuznach, which under his leadership became a centre of humanist studies, with a library that he built up from nothing to one of the richest of the age. His bibliographical pioneer work, *De scriptoribus ecclesiasticis*, dedicated to the equally passionate collector of books and manuscripts Johann von Dalberg, bishop of Worms, gave a survey of the works, printed or known in manuscript, of 962 authors from the earliest Christian period to the end of the fifteenth century. Belying its title, the work did not confine itself to ecclesiastical writers but also included poets, orators, and authors on a wide variety of scientific subjects.[1]

It is impossible to determine with certainty the edition of Erasmus' copy. So far as the title is concerned, only the quarto edition published by P. Quentell in Cologne in 1531 tallies exactly with the entry in the *Versandliste*, but it seems unlikely that Erasmus should have acquired this indispensable work of reference at such a late date. Moreover, the neighbouring volumes are folios. Perhaps Erasmus owned the *editio princeps*, which had been published in 1494 by Johann Amerbach of Basel under the title *Liber de scriptoribus ecclesiasticis*. In that case the compiler of the *Versandliste* noted the work under a title that may have been current at the time, or, more probably, adopted the title he found on the spine or the fore-edge.

1 On Trithemius see the biographies by Silbernagel
   and Arnold; the articles of Steffen
   'Untersuchungen zum "Liber de scriptoribus
   ecclesiasticis" des Johannes Trithemius' and of
   Blum 'Die Literaturverzeichnung im Altertum
   und Mittelalter'; CEBR III 344–5.

237 Psalterium Felicis. Venetijs excu.

Psalterium ex hebreo diligentissime ad verbum fere tralatum: fratre Felice interprete. Venetiis: in edib. P. Liechtenstein, sumpt. D. Bombergi, 1515 (folio).

The Book of Psalms translated directly from the Hebrew independently of the Vulgate by Felice da Prato, a converted Jew who entered the Augustinian order and obtained permission from Leo x to make a new Latin translation of the Bible. Only the Psalter was completed. The publication, encouraged by Pietro Bembo, was financed by Daniel Bomberg, who had migrated shortly before from Antwerp to Venice, where he was to make a great name as a printer of Hebrew books.[1] Erasmus appears to have acquired the original edition quite early: in August 1516 he mentioned the then still recent publication, which he characterized as a 'new version of the whole Psalter which differs considerably from all its predecessors.'[2]

Perhaps the book had gone on sale in Antwerp quite quickly, thanks to the old business relations of Bomberg; Erasmus bought it there in 1516 on one of his frequent visits.

1 On Felix of Prato and his *Psalterium* see Ep 456:92n/103n; cf Holfelder *Tentatio et consolatio* 93–5. On Bomberg see Bloch 'Venetian Printers of Hebrew Books' 74–6; cf H. Volz 'Hebräische Handpsalter Luthers' in WA x-2 303 n49.

2 Ep 456:92–4 / 102–4

238 Pars prima / Pars altera } operum D. Chrysostomj

Johannes Chrysostomus. [*Opera.*] Basileae: J. Frobenius, 1517 (folio).

Three attempts to publish a collected edition in folio of Chrysostom's works preceded the *Opera* sponsored by Erasmus and published in 1530 (no 230): the first by J. Wolff of Pforzheim and W. Lachner (Basel 1504); the second, more complete, by Johann Froben (Basel 1517); and the third, for the most part based on Froben's text, by Andreas Cratander, in five volumes (Basel 1522).[1] Of these three, Johann Froben's five-volume edition is almost certainly the one listed here. Two years after it appeared, Erasmus wrote to Maarten Lips, 'I have bought the Chrysostom.'[2] It was probably a complete set; other copies of this edition are known in which the five relatively slim volumes have been bound in two parts.[3] The three earlier editions all contained works by Chrysostom in translations that Erasmus criticized very severely when he was helping to prepare the 1530 Froben edition. He was particularly critical of the fifth-century Pelagian deacon Anianus of Celeda and the fifteenth-century Italian Francesco Griffolini (Aretino), a pupil of Lorenzo Valla. Erasmus had never held a favourable opinion of Oecolampadius' translations, but Anianus, Aretino, and others, he wrote in 1530, had sinned much more in their renderings from the Greek than Oecolampadius, who had fallen into error more through excessive

haste than incapacity. The versions by Aretino of which Erasmus was thinking were those of the homilies on 1 Corinthians up to chapter 30, while Anianus' serious deviations from the original in the homilies on the Gospel of Matthew made him sigh that it would almost be easier to translate the whole text anew than to attempt to improve the rendering.[4] Nevertheless, evidently for lack of anything better, he was in the end to include the version of Anianus in the third volume of his edition of Chrysostom in 1530, albeit with corrections.[5]

1 A sixth volume (translated by Oecolampadius) and possibly a seventh appeared in 1525; see Ep 1736:8n/n3. An incomplete copy including *tomus septimus* is in the Bibliothèque municipale de Sélestat; see Walter *Catalogue Sélestat* 279 no 935.

2 Ep 1052:1 / 1

3 In *Responsio ad annotationes Eduardi Lei* Erasmus refers to a passage 'in Chrysostomo meo ex gemina editione Basiliensi' (LB IX 141C / ASD IX-4 105:897). Cf BRE 138 Ep 90 (22 February 1519), in which Zwingli gives instructions for Chrysostom's *Opera* to be bound in two volumes.

4 For Erasmus' comparison of Oecolampadius to other translators, see Ep 2263:42–51 / 44–53. On Aretino, see Ep 2263:51–60 / 53–65, and cf Epp 2291:12–13 / 13–15 and 2359:45–7 / 49–52; on Anianus, Ep 2263:61–5 / 66–70, and cf Epp 1558:187–233 / 202–53, 2359:42–5 / 46–9, and *Adagia* III iv 71 ASD II-5 275:800–276:14 / CWE 35 44–5. For Oecolampadius, see also no 166.

5 Ep 1558: 202n / n22

239 Athenaeus graecè Aldi.

Athenaeus. *Deipnosophistae graece.* Venetiis: Aldus & Andreas soc., August 1514 (folio).

The *editio princeps* of a *symposium* written at the beginning of the third century by Athenaeus of Naukratis: he describes a dinner of scholars who converse on very varied subjects, 'chiefly on cookery (as befits a banquet) but also on music, dances, songs, courtesans, and table-talk of all sorts, including scattered quotations of early poetry.'[1] The work is inexhaustible in its citations from hundreds of classical authors, some of them preserved only in it, and is a source of the greatest importance for our knowledge of late Greek culture and especially the literature of the Alexandrian period. The printed text of 1514 was edited by Marcus Musurus from a transcript of a tenth-century codex brought to Venice from Constantinople in 1423 by Giovanni Aurispa. Erasmus too had used the manuscript of the *Deipnosophistae*, either the ancient codex or a copy, during his stay in Venice, and had drawn from it much material for the 1508 edition of his *Adagia*, in which Athenaeus is one of the most frequently cited authors.[2]

The copy of the first printed edition, once in Erasmus' library, is now in the Bodleian Library at Oxford. The fly-leaf bears his ex libris, *Sum Erasmi Roterodami*, in Latin; it is repeated on the last page in Greek, *Ἐράσμου εἰμί κτῆμα*, with *πολλαὶ μορφαὶ τῶν δαιμονίων*[3] written beneath it in his own hand. From the many other owners' marks it appears that the book was in the Netherlands during the seventeenth and eighteenth centuries. One of its most famous owners in that period was the philologist, poet, and librarian Daniel Heinsius (d 1655). In 1825 the work passed into English hands. From that year it formed part of the library of the well-known collector Richard Reginald Heber. On his death in 1834 it was bought by the Bodleian Library.[4]

Erasmus made intensive use of his copy of Athenaeus, making numerous marginal annotations on the text, mostly for the benefit of the revision of his *Adagiorum chiliades*. The edition of 1517 profited most from this, but his regular rereading of the *Deipnosophistae* also led him to make additions or improvements in later editions of the *Adagia*.[5]

1 Phillips *Adages* 90; Pauly-Wissowa II 2026–33 and *Der Kleine Pauly* I 702 sv Athenaios; OCD 202 sv Athenaeus

2 *Adagia* II i 1: *Festina lente* ASD II-3 22:398 / CWE 33 14; Phillips *Adages* 395

3 'The ways of the gods take many forms' (Euripides *Alcestis* 1159)

4 Sign. Auct. I, R. inf. I.I. See Margolin 'Erasme et Athénée.' One leaf with marginalia (123–4) has been cut out by a collector of autographs and has been preserved since 1875 in the library of the University of Amsterdam; see Berg 'Aantekeningen van Erasmus op een exemplaar der editio Aldina van Athenaeus' *Deipnosophistae*' 80, with additional information in a supplementary note.

5 Margolin 'Erasme et Athénée' 221; for a late addition (1528) see *Adagia* III iii 53 ASD II-5 215–16:203–19 with n / CWE 35 299 with n3 (417).

240 Concordantiae maiores Bibliae

Concordantiae maiores Bibliae. (*Concordantiae Bibliae partium sive dictionum indeclinabilium.*) Basileae: off. Frobeniana, one of many editions (folio).

The first biblical concordance under this title appeared in 1496 at Basel, edited by Sebastian Brant, dedicated to J. Geiler von Kaysersberg, and published by Johannes Petri and Johann Froben.[1] The work consisted of the 'great concordance,' produced in the early fourteenth century from an older concordance by Conrad of Halberstadt, and the 'concordance of indeclinable words' that J. de Segovia had prepared on the instructions of Cardinal John de Ragusa during the Council of Basel. The second printing of this edition appeared in 1506 under a slightly altered title 'printed at the expense of Johann Amerbach, Petrus of Langendorf, and [Johann] Froben of Hammelburg in the city of Basel.' Further reprints, also by Froben, followed in 1516, 1521, 1523, 1525, 1526, and 1531.

1 GW 7422. On this work see *Realencyklopädie für Protestantische Theologie und Kirche* x 699; *Lexikon für Theologie and Kirche* II 361; *Cambridge History of the Bible* III 526.

241 Nouum Testamen. Eras. grae. et Lat.

Novum Testamentum … ab Erasmo Roterodamo recognitum. A folio edition.

Erasmus' famous edition of the New Testament with Greek text and a new Latin translation, actually 'a thorough revision of the traditional Vulgate with the help of Greek manuscripts rather than an entirely fresh translation,'[1] first appeared in February 1516 from the press of Johann Froben under the title of *Novum instrumentum*. During Erasmus' lifetime revised printings were also published by the Froben press under the more current title *Novum Testamentum* in 1519, 1522, 1527, and 1535. One must infer from the *Versandliste* that Erasmus kept three or probably four copies of his *magnum opus* in his library until his death.[2] One of these will presumably have been the revised latest edition of 1535, which included the introductory *Capita argumentorum contra morosos quosdam ac indoctos* (1519).[3]

1 De Jonge 'The Relationship of Erasmus' Translation of the New Testament to that of the Pauline Epistles by Lefèvre d'Etaples' 2. Cf de Jonge 'The Date and Purpose of Erasmus' *Castigatio Novi Testamenti*: a Note on the Origins of the *Novum Instrumentum*.'
2 For the two or three other copies, see nos 328, 329, and 330.
3 Cf Ep 2951:13n. For the *Contra morosos* see Rummel 'An Open Letter to Boorish Critics: Erasmus' *Capita argumentorum contra morosos*.'

242 Augusti. de Ciuitate Dei. Frob.

Augustinus, Aurelius. *Opus absolutissimum de Civitate Dei … emendatum per Joh. Lud. Vivem et per eundem commentariis illustratum*. Basileae: J. Frobenius, September 1522 (folio).

Although it was planned in the context of the great edition of Augustine of 1528–9 (no 258), *De civitate Dei* first appeared separately in 1522 with a letter of recommendation by Erasmus (Ep 1309). The annotated text was prepared by Juan Luis Vives, who based his work largely on three manuscripts. Two of them had been borrowed from Bruges, one from Marcus Laurinus, dean of St Donatian's, and one from the Carmelite monastery; Erasmus had helped him to obtain the third, which

came from Cologne. Vives, who had been living at Leuven since the end of 1518 and was on confidential terms with Erasmus there, must often have discussed the problems of the edition with his older friend before Erasmus left for Anderlecht at the end of May 1521.[1] Froben was unwilling to reprint *De civitate Dei* in the *Opera* because the separate edition had sold poorly. He only did so after long hesitation, and even then omitted Vives' forewords, introduction, detailed notes, and Erasmus' letter of recommendation.[2] Erasmus made some improvements to the text on the basis of a manuscript supplied to him by Pieter Gillis, which was part of his estate on his death in 1536.[3] But the absence of the supplementary matter and the apparatus of notes meant that the separate edition of *De civitate Dei* of 1522 was not superseded. Erasmus kept the volume in his library for that reason and because he did not acquire the Chevallon reprint (Paris 1531) of Augustine's *Opera omnia* (no 258), which included *De civitate Dei* in its unabbreviated version of 1522.

1 On this edition see Allen and CWE Ep 1309 introductions. On the relationship between Erasmus and Vives at this time see nos 25 #2 and 41.
2 Epp 1531:36–8/41–3, 1889:15–18/19–23, 2040:25–32/30–7, 2208:1–10/2–12 with n2
3 Epp 1758:9–10/8–10, 1778:24–5/24–6

243 Pars prima / Pars secun. / Pars ter. / Pars quar. } operum D. Hierony. Frob. / Pars sex. ~~Pars. sep.~~

Hieronymus. *Omnium operum tomus primus (–quartus sextus)*. Basileae: J. Frobenius 1516 or 1524–6 (folio).

An incomplete copy of Froben's nine-volume edition of Jerome. It may contain five single volumes either from the *editio princeps* of 1516 or from the revised second edition of 1524–6, or it may combine volumes from the two editions.[1] Erasmus had taken the letters of Jerome as his province. He also provided Jerome's bibliographical work, the *Catalogus scriptorum ecclesiasticorum* and its continuation, the *Catalogus illustrium virorum* of Gennadius of Marseilles (fl 470), with scholia.[2] Moreover, Erasmus wrote as an introduction to the *Opera omnia* his scholarly *Hieronymi Stridonensis vita*, 'a biography based entirely on original sources and freed from the distortion of legend and myth.'[3] The annotated *Epistolae* filled the greater part of the first four volumes of both the original and the second edition, so that the incomplete copy of the *Opera omnia* noted in this entry contained all the volumes for which Erasmus had been personally responsible. Perhaps he preserved the volumes for the sake of the supplementary written annotations he had made in them, for both the Froben editions lost their textual value for him once the third version of the *Opera omnia*, in which he had revised his scholia on the letters, was brought out by the Paris printer-publisher Claude Chevallon in 1533–4 (no 405). No complete set of either the first or the second edition, which must have been in his possession at one time, appears in the *Versandliste*; the missing volumes had probably been disposed of once they were superseded.

Erasmus' interest in Jerome dated from his early years. At Steyn he was already quite familiar with his letters and later on in Paris, around 1500, he began work upon Jerome, correcting the text and preparing a commentary. Though he had already made up his mind then to edit the letters separately, these plans did not take definite shape until 1511 when he was in Cambridge. Josse Bade at once offered to publish the edition. But by the time the work was ready Erasmus had established a business relationship with the Froben press in Basel, and his work on the letters became part of the great edition that Johann Amerbach had planned, which had already been under way for some years. Preparatory work had been started in 1508 by Conradus Pellicanus and Johann Reuchlin and was later continued by Johannes Cono and Gregor Reisch. After Johann Amerbach's death in 1513, his editorial function was probably assumed for some time by Reisch.[4] The undertaking, under Erasmus' general editorship, was completed in the summer of 1516 by Johann Froben, who had taken over Amerbach's press in conjunction with his three sons. In his letter to Leo x requesting permission to dedicate the edition to him, Erasmus praises all those who collaborated in the edition and noted that 'the greatest contribution of all has been that of the Amerbach brothers, who have shared the expense and the labour with Froben and who are the principals in the whole enterprise.'[5]

Little is known with certainty of the manuscripts Erasmus used for his edition of Jerome's letters. In Queens' College, Cambridge, he collated 'a large number of ancient manuscripts,' probably borrowed from elsewhere, perhaps Peterhouse.[6] Another manuscript was borrowed for him in November 1515 from the monastery of Reichenau. Nevertheless, the basis of his edition was early printed texts; his working copy for private use of the Sacon edition (Lyon 1508) of the *Epistolae* had probably served as a printer's copy in 1516.[7]

In Jerome's *Catalogus scriptorum ecclesiasticorum* the Latin text and the Greek translation are printed in parallel columns. For the Greek translation, wrongly ascribed by him to Sophronios, Erasmus used a twelfth- or thirteenth-century manuscript that has been preserved and is now in the Zentralbibliothek in Zürich. Sicherl has demonstrated that it may be identified as the manuscript of the pseudo-Sophronios translation bequeathed in 1443 by Cardinal John of Ragusa to the monastery of the Dominicans at Basel, which had long been thought to be lost. Evidently the codex, which had been used in the Froben printing office (as appears from Erasmus' autograph instructions for the typesetter in the margin), did not return afterwards to its original possessor.[8]

Before 1516 Erasmus had also owned the older two-volume edition of the works of Jerome (though without his letters), published at Venice by Joannes and Gregorius de Gregoriis in 1497. His copy of that edition, which besides his ex libris *Sum Erasmi* also contained marginal annotations in his own hand, has been preserved and is now in the library of the University of Munich. Since notes by Henricus Glareanus also occur in this copy, it is virtually certain that Erasmus must have lent, given, or handed over this book, which is not in the *Versandliste*, to his younger friend during his lifetime.[9] It is possible that he had bought it himself as early as the beginning of the century: in December 1500 he wrote that he was saving up to buy the complete works of Jerome, on which he was preparing a commentary.[10] In that case he may have borrowed the frequent citations in his *Adagiorum collectanea* from Jerome's *Adversus Rufinum*, which was included in this edition, from his own copy.

Another copy of the 1497 Venetian edition served in 1516 as printer's copy for the text of Jerome's commentaries on the Epistles to the Galatians, the Ephesians, Philemon, and Titus. This copy too, still bearing clear traces of its use in the printing works, has been preserved and is now in the University Library in Basel. It contains numerous manuscript textual variants and improvements in the hands of Johann Amerbach, Reuchlin, and Bruno Amerbach, who were responsible for the preparation of these commentaries.[11] The text used in the 1516 edition for the commentaries on all the Pauline Epistles (except Hebrews), which are not by Jerome but by Pelagius, was based on a transcript made by another collaborator, Gregor Reisch, from an

eleventh-century manuscript at Echternach (now in the Bibliothèque nationale in Paris).[12]

1 On these two editions see Allen and CWE Ep 396 introductions.
2 They are both in volume I, fols 119–41 and fols 156–62.
3 Ferguson *Opuscula* 125; cf Maguire 'Erasmus' Biographical Masterpiece: *Hieronymi Stridonensis vita*'; CWE 61 xxiii–xxiv.
4 AK II 14 Ep 501 n1; on Reisch see CEBR III 137.
5 Ep 335:312–14 / 327–9
6 Ep 273:15–17 / 17–19. See *Erasmus and Cambridge* 41; Allen and CWE Ep 396 introductions. Allen points out that Queens' College was poor in Jerome manuscripts.
7 Husner 'Die Handschriften der Scholien des Erasmus von Rotterdam zu den Hieronymusbriefen' 143–5
8 Codex C 11; Mohlberg *Katalog der Handschriften der Zentralbibliothek Zürich I: Mittelalterliche Handschriften* 19. The text has been edited by von Gebhardt ('Hieronymus *De viris inlustribus*'). See also Vernet 'Les manuscrits grecs de Jean de Raguse' 82; Sicherl *Johannes Cuno* 129–30; Bernouilli 'Zur griechischen Uebersetzung von Hieronymus' *De viris illustribus*' 475.
9 Husner 'Bibliothek' 256–7; on Glareanus, see no 46 #1.
10 Ep 138:38–40 / 43–5
11 Sign. F.L.II.1; see AK II 66–7 Ep 551 n2.
12 MS lat. 9525. See Souter *Pelagius's Expositions of Thirteen Epistles of St. Paul* I 277; *Apologia ad annotationes Stunicae* ASD IX-2 201 620–622n.

244 De copia uerborum ~~commen.~~ Eras. commenta // rius, manu scriptus

Erasmus: *De duplici copia verborum ac rerum commentarii* (manuscript).

It is difficult to determine which manuscript text of the *Copia* this entry on the *Versandliste* refers to. The manuscript of the incomplete version on which Erasmus had worked in Venice remained behind at Ferrara when he made a hasty departure for England in 1509. Erasmus left it in the keeping of his younger friend Richard Pace, with the manuscripts of his *Antibarbari* and *De ratione studii*. When Pace moved from Ferrara to Bologna the manuscripts fell into the hands of the unscrupulous William Thale, who sold them or gave them away, and in the case of *De ratione studii* published an unauthorized edition.[1]

Allen supposed that Erasmus, in spite of strenuous efforts to trace them, never saw his working papers, including the draft of the *Copia*, again, and that when he wished to publish his manual in 1512 at the request of John Colet, who was eager to use it in St Paul's School, it was a new and hastily written manuscript that was sent to Bade for printing.[2] Tracy on the other hand is of the opinion that Erasmus managed to recover the manuscript of *De copia* before 1512 and consequently did not compose the book afresh for Colet: according to him the printed Bade text represents the original draft as revised in 1508 and 1512. Tracy points out that the Frisian Johannes Sixtinus, a friend of Erasmus, had received a copy of the draft of the *De copia* from Thale in Italy. In the autumn of 1511, from Cambridge, Erasmus approached his friend about his lost manuscript (Sixtinus had returned to England and was in London at the time). On that occasion Sixtinus may have returned it to the author. Does the *Versandliste* refer here to this draft returned by Sixtinus? But if this manuscript, after Erasmus revised it, was sent to Bade as printer's copy, it was more likely to have been lost. Or was there yet another copy of the original draft? Tracy considers it possible that Erasmus did not give Pace his only copy of *De copia* in 1509; alarmed as he was by the recent unauthorized edition of his *De ratione studii* he might have been worried, not about losing the work altogether, but about a possible pirate edition.[3]

Erasmus kept two editions of *De copia*; cf nos 365 and 408.

1 Ep 30:16n/17n; Allen and CWE Ep 66 introductions; cf no 367. On Pace see no 30 #2.
2 Allen and CWE Ep 260 introductions; cf ASD I-1 (*Antibarbari*) 11–12.
3 'On the Composition Dates of Seven of Erasmus' Writings' 360–1. Cf Ep 244 with 6n/7n. On Sixtinus see Allen Ep 113 introduction and IV xxi; CEBR III 255–6.

245 Lazarus Bayfius de re nauali, de re uest./de vasculis. Item Anto. Thyle. de coloribus.

Bayfius (Baïf) Lazarus. *Annotationes in legem II de captivis et postliminio reversis in quibus tractatur de re navali. Eiusdem annotationes in tractatum de auro et argento legato quibus vestimentorum et vasculorum genera explicantur. Anthonii Thylesii de coloribus libellus.* Parisiis: R. Stephanus, 31 August 1536 (quarto).

The *editio princeps* of Lazare de Baïf's *De re navali*, a treatise on ships in antiquity in the form of a commentary on the Pandects. Erasmus had heard from Viglius Zuichemus as early as the beginning of 1532 that the work was in preparation,[1] but the complete compilation – besides *De re navali*, it also contained reprints of *De re vestiaria* and *De vasculis*, as well as a treatise by Antonio Telesio on the characteristics and uses of colours[2] – did not appear until 1536, after Erasmus' death. It is not difficult to explain how the book nevertheless came to be present in his library: Baïf was on good terms with Erasmus and had been in close touch with him about his earlier works (see nos 2 #1 and 73 #1); unaware that his older friend had died, he must have sent a copy of his book to Basel immediately after its publication. The copy was conscientiously added to Erasmus' estate by his executor Bonifacius Amerbach.

1 Ep 2594:16–17
2 *Editio princeps* Venice: B. Vitalis 1528; it was the first printed treatise on a subject later to be treated by Goethe, who included Telesio's Latin text in his *Farbenlehre* (1810) II 173–93.

246 Ciceronis Rhet. de Inuen. etc libri 13. Aldi

Cicero, Marcus Tullius. *Rhetoricorum ad C. Herennium lib. IIII. De inventione lib. II. De oratore ad Quintum fratrem lib. III. De claris oratoribus lib. I. Oratoriae partitionis lib. I. De optimo genere oratorum praefatio quaedam*. Venetiis: aed. Aldi et Andreae soc., 1514 or 1521 or 1533 (quarto).

Cicero's works on rhetoric, preceded by the manual of rhetoric then still attributed to him but actually by an unknown author currently described as *Auctor ad Herennium*.[1] Probably but not necessarily the first Aldine edition of 1514. Cf no 111 for an earlier edition of Cicero from the Aldine press, a copy of which Erasmus only bought years after the appearance of the original printing.

> 1 *Der Kleine Pauly* I 728–9 sv Auctor ad Herennium; OCD 1314–15 sv Rhetorica ad Herennium. The attribution, already doubted by Lorenzo Valla, was definitively detached from Cicero's name by Raffaele Regio; *Adagia* I i 2 ASD II-1 107 130n/ CWE 31 45 394n.

247 Annotationes Eras. in Nouum Testa.

Erasmus. *In Novum Testamentum annotationes ab ipso autore … recognitae & ex Graecis codicibus locupletatae*. Basileae: off. Frobeniana (folio).

One of the editions (1519, 1522, 1527, or 1535) of the *Annotationes* published jointly with the text of the *Novum Testamentum* but provided with a separate title-page and here bound independently. For further details see no 331.

248 Eucherius cum 30. orationibus Nazianzeni / interprete Bilibaldo Pirckheimero.

Eucherius. *Lucubrationes aliquot. Ed. I. Alexander Brassicanus*. Basileae: off. Frobeniana, September 1531 (folio).

bound with

Gregorius Nazianzenus. *Orationes xxx, Bilibaldo Pirckheimero interprete*. Basileae: off. Frobeniana, September 1531 (folio).

1/ Erasmus edited and annotated the *Epistola ad Valerianum propinquum de philosophia christiana* by Eucherius

(d 449–450), the fifth-century bishop of Lyon, and published it with a dedicatory letter to Alaard of Amsterdam (Ep 676) at the end of an edition of Cato (Leuven: Dirk Martens, 1517).[1] Later the *Epistola ad Valerianum* with Erasmus' introductory letter was also included in the three editions of Eucherius' collected works that appeared in quick succession at Paris (Chevallon, October 1528), Basel (Cratander, March 1530) and Basel again (Froben, August–September 1531). It is virtually certain that the latter was in Erasmus' library, since the work was bound in one volume with another Froben edition of the same month and year. Its text had been prepared by Alexander Brassicanus, on whom, and his relationship with Erasmus, see no 326 #1.

2/ Erasmus' friend Willibald Pirckheimer died on 22 December 1530. His translation from the Greek of thirty orations by Gregory of Nazianzus appeared posthumously with a dedication and recommendation from Erasmus to Duke George of Saxony (Ep 2493). Cf no 96.

> 1 NK 535; cf no 25 #1.

249 Hilarij opera. Bad. Ascen.

Hilarius. *Opera complura*. Parrhisiis: J. Badius, 1511 (folio).

The first edition of the collected works of Hilary (c 315–67), bishop of Poitiers and a fervent enemy of the Arians and Arianism. Well-known French humanists had been involved in the production of this edition: the commentaries on the Psalms had been purged of errors according to indications given by Jacques Lefèvre d'Etaples; while Guillaume Petit, who later championed Erasmus before Francis I, supplied Bade with the text of two other works.[1] Erasmus had reservations about the quality of the edition and in 1523 he himself reissued the works, improved 'with no little sweat' (see no 185).

Froben's letter to the reader on the title-page leaves no doubt about his opinion: 'We do not condemn the first edition, but by comparing you can see for yourself, dear reader, where they differ.'

1 Renaudet *Préréforme et humanisme* 604 with n1. On the edition of 1511 cf also Rice 'The Humanist Idea of Christian Antiquity: Lefèvre d'Etaples and His Circle' 152–6 (Appendix 2). On Petit see no 15 n14.

250 D. Basilij Magni opera. Frob.

Basilius. [*Opera, graece.*] Basileae: H. Frobenius et N. Episcopius, March 1532 (folio).

Although the usual addition 'graeca' is absent, this must be a second copy (for the other copy, see no 189) of the edition of the Greek text of 1532, since Froben never published the works of Basil in Latin translation, and no other edition of the Greek text is known.

251 Haymonis commentarij in Psalmos.

Haymo. ep. Halberstatiensis. *Pia brevis ac dilucida in omnes psalmos explanatio.* Friburgi Brisg.: J. Faber Emmeus, 1533 (folio).

The *editio princeps* of the commentary on the Psalms attributed, probably erroneously, to the ninth-century bishop Haymo of Halberstadt, a pupil of Alcuin.[1] Erasmus published the text from a manuscript that came from the Augustinian monastery of Marbach, destroyed during the Peasants' War of 1525. He dedicated it to the Carthusian Jan of Heemstede (Ep 2771). It remains unclear how he acquired the manuscript. It has been surmised that it came into his hands through the mediation of his friend Christoph von Utenheim, bishop of Basel, under whose jurisdiction the monastery of Marbach (not to be confused with the Benedictine abbey of Murbach, also in Alsace), was situated.[2]

Probably, however, it was not the bishop who procured the manuscript for him but the suffragan bishop of the diocese, Augustinus Marius. After the reformers had got the upper hand in Basel, he left for Freiburg even before Erasmus did. When the latter arrived at his new residence 'Zum Walfisch' in April 1529 he found Marius already installed in the house.[3] They lived under one roof until the end of the year, and their relations were close at that time. In the spring of 1530 they each published, evidently in concert, an edition of a mediaeval treatise on the same subject, the Eucharistic doctrine: Marius first published *De veritate corporis et sanguinis Christi in eucharistia tres libri* of Guitmund, bishop of Aversa (fl 1088),[4] and shortly afterwards Erasmus brought out his edition of *De veritate corporis et sanguinis Dominici in eucharistia* of Alger of Liège (d c 1131).[5] Though the two works appeared within weeks of one another, Marius must have had his text ready for the printer in late May 1529 (his prefaces are dated 25 and 26 May 1529), more than nine months before Erasmus (Erasmus' preface is dated 15 March 1530). The manuscript Marius used came, just like the Haymo manuscript, from the monastery of Marbach, recovered from the well into which it had been thrown during the Peasants' Revolt.[6] Is it not plausible that Erasmus got his Haymo manuscript through Marius?

1 On the still unsolved question of the authorship see *Dictionnaire de spiritualité* VI-1 97 sv Haymon de Halberstadt and 94 sv Haymon d'Auxerre.
2 Boyle '"For peasants, psalms": Erasmus' *editio princeps* of Haymo (1533)' 457 n80
3 On Marius see Allen and CWE Ep 2321 introductions; CEBR II 391–2.
4 Freiburg im Breisgau: Johannes Faber Emmeus 1530 (octavo)
5 Freiburg im Breisgau: Johannes Faber Emmeus 1530 (octavo). This edition, dedicated to Balthasar Mercklin, bishop of Constance (Ep 2284), does not figure on the *Versandliste*. On it see Oelrich *Der späte Erasmus und die Reformation* 148 and Reedijk 'Erasmus' Final Modesty' 181. Reedijk points out evidence of a gradual return to

orthodox views and of a greater reliance upon the traditions of the church in Erasmus' later writings, a change confirmed in 1530 by his edition of Alger of Liège's treatise on the Eucharist. Both Alger and Guitmund were opposed to the denial of transubstantiation and the spiritualistic interpretation of the Eucharist expounded by Berengarius of Tours (c 1010–88); cf Spruyt *Hoen* 180.

6 Allen Ep 2284:32n

252 Quincuplex Psalterium Fabri.

Quincuplex Psalterium: Gallicum, Romanum, Hebraicum, Vetus. Conciliatum. [Ed Jac. Faber Stapulensis.] Parisiis: H. Stephanus, 31 July 1509 or (second edition) 13 June 1513 (folio).

The *Quincuplex Psalterium* edited by Lefèvre d'Etaples and dedicated to Cardinal Briçonnet contained five Latin versions of the Book of Psalms.[1] First, printed in three columns, the *Psalterium Gallicanum* corrected by Jerome, the *Psalterium Romanum* also corrected by Jerome but at a slightly earlier date, and the *Psalterium Hebraicum* directly translated by Jerome from the Hebrew. The texts were accompanied by explanatory notes and exegetical commentaries. There followed, in two columns: the *Psalterium Vetus*, the text in use in the western churches before Jerome, and the *Psalterium conciliatum*, the harmonized version produced by Lefèvre himself, that is, the Vulgate text (*Psalterium Gallicanum*) corrected in a few places according to Jerome's *Psalterium iuxta Hebraeos*. The work had been eagerly awaited even before publication, and was at once highly praised in all quarters even by so important a person as Cardinal Jiménes de Cisneros, but it was soon put on the Index and was later more than once described as the first book of French Protestantism.[2]

There were two Stephanus editions. Whether Erasmus owned the *editio princeps* of 1509, which had appeared while he was still in Italy, or the enlarged edition of 1513, cannot be determined.

1 See Renaudet *Préréforme et humanisme* 514–17; Rice *Prefatory Epistles* 192–201 Ep 66; and Bedouelle *Le Quincuplex Psalterium de Lefèvre d'Etaples.*
2 *La France protestante* no 1

253 Ciceronis de natura deorum lib .3. Eiusdem de/diuinatione lib. 2. manu scrip.

Nothing further is known of these manuscripts. Erasmus twice edited works of Cicero. Around 1501 his edition of *De officiis* with brief explanatory notes appeared in pocket handbook format from the press of J. Philippi in Paris. The edition of the text was based on collation and emendation of printed editions.[1] For his edition of the *Tusculanae quaestiones*, published by Johann Froben in Basel in November 1523 but probably already begun in his Leuven years, Erasmus had at his disposal manuscripts that his servant-pupils collated for him; his own share was confined to choosing between the variants and adding notes, which, he said, cost him only two or three days' work. He had borrowed one of the manuscripts from the Augustinian canon Julian Carbo (d c 1523) of Herentals, later of Brussels, who had a genuine passion for Cicero and had copied almost all of his works in his own hand.[2] Probably the manuscripts of *De natura deorum* and *De divinatione*, like the manuscripts of Chrysostom (cf nos 234 and 235), were not ancient codices but recent copies. ASD considers that it is not impossible that Erasmus found in this manuscript of *De divinatione* a corrupt textual variant that he cited in the 1515 edition of the *Adagia*.[3]

1 See Ep 152 to Jacob de Voecht, the preface written, but not published, in 1501.
2 Ep 1390:1–18/3–20 and Allen's introduction
3 *Adagia* III iii 38 ASD II-5 208:59–62 with 59n (209)

254 Caietanus in Pentateuchum.

Caietanus, Thomas de Vio. *Commentarii in Pentateuchum Mosis*. Romae: A. Blado, 1531 (folio).

Erasmus' copy of Cajetanus' commentary on the Pentateuch was possibly this extremely rare edition.[1] On Cajetanus and his relationship to Erasmus see no 177.

1 Still mentioned in Panzer VIII 274 no 264. I have not been able to trace a copy. Cf Congar *Bio-bibliographie de Cajétan* nos 86–7, 48; and Groner *Kardinal Cajetan* 72.

255 Prima pars Bib. / Altera pars Bib.

[*Biblia Latine*.] Probably a two-volume folio edition.

Probably a complete Vulgate published and bound in two folio volumes, according to the usual binding practice of the fifteenth century,[1] and perhaps the oldest Bible in Erasmus' library (cf nos 154, 220, 221, and 225). In his *Apologia adversus Petrum Sutorem* of 1525, Erasmus wrote, 'I have at my disposal an edition of both Testaments, printed (as one may conjecture) sixty years ago.'[2] If his estimate was accurate, it was an edition from c 1465, and could have been one of the two editions of Johann Fust and Peter Schöffer, both in two volumes, published in 1462 and in 'line-for-line reprint' in 1472, both without commentary.[3] But that this copy was one of the two editions can be no more than conjecture. Other possible candidates are the Bible printed (without place, name, or date) in two volumes at Mainz or Bamberg c 1458 but not after 1462 and the Bible printed (again without place, name, or date) in two volumes at Basel before 1475 by Berthold Ruppel and Bernhard Richel.[5] It was the general practice of fifteenth-century bookbinders to bind Bibles in two volumes even when the printing shows no two-part division,[6] so that even if we limit the search for the Bible listed here to the year 1475, all nineteen Latin Bibles

printed before then come into consideration.[7] Erasmus says in his apologia against Cousturier that he 'guessed' the age of the old printed Bible he was using; but even if we limit our search to printed Bibles without a date of publication, there are eleven possibilities.[8] The identification of this item on the *Versandliste* and the old Bible mentioned in the apologia against Cousturier – and whether or not the editions are the same – must therefore remain uncertain.

1 Bound as they were printed: Genesis–Psalms in the first part, Proverbs–Apocalypse in the second. See GW IV 67.
2 LB IX 766E. Erasmus also mentioned this edition repeatedly in his *Annotationes in Novum Testamentum*, for example at Matt 27:35 ASD VI-5 340:779–80: *alio quodam vetustae aeditionis typographicae* [sc *codice*] *qui est apud me* (1527); at Mark 2:2 ASD VI-5 364:343: *meus vetustae typographiae* [sc *codex*] (1527); at Mark 8:38 ASD VI-5 403:361: *meo vetustae typographiae* [sc *codice*] (1527); and at Luke 1:45 ASD VI-5 463:503: *velut in meo veteris typographiae* [sc *exemplari*] (1527). I am grateful to Professor H.J. de Jonge, who drew my attention to these passages.
3 GW 4204 and 4211
4 GW 4202
5 GW 4213
6 GW IV 67
7 GW 4201–19
8 GW 4201, 4202, 4203, 4205, 4206, 4207, 4208, 4209, 4213, 4214, 4219

256 Herbarius zů teütsche vonn allerhand kreüter.

Herbarius zu teutsch vnnd von allerhandt kreüteren. Augsburg: J. Schönsperger, 1496 (folio) or one of the other editions by the same publisher.

The herbal *Herbarius zu teutsch* must be distinguished both from the *Herbarius in latino*, of which it was not a translation, and from the *Hortus sanitatis*, a much more extensive work, which dealt not only or chiefly with herbs, but also with animals and minerals.[1] The first edition of the German *Herbarius*, the medical part of which is attributed to the Frankfurt city physician Johann von Cube, appeared at Mainz in 1485 and was followed in the last year of the century by a series of new editions, all from the press of Johann Schönsperger in Augsburg. According to the descriptions in Hain and Choulant, only the editions of 1488, 1493, and 1496 have a title that tallies approximately with the short title in the *Versandliste*.[2] The edition referred to in this entry must be one of these.

One can only guess why Erasmus, whose library consisted almost entirely of books in Latin (for the other exceptions see nos 22 #3 and 158), should have kept a herbal, and that in German. The German *Herbarius* was distinguished from the two other herbals mentioned above not only by its language but also and above all by its illustrations. Whereas the Latin herbals contained primitive prints, sometimes based on mere fantasy, the handsome woodcuts of the *Herbarius zu teutsch* were quite realistic; there were no better illustrations of plants until the appearance of Brunfels' *Herbarum vivae eicones* in 1530. Could the illustrations have been decisive for Erasmus?

1 Payne 'On the "Herbarius" and "Hortus Sanitatis'" (on the "Herbarius zu teutsche" in particular, 89–105); Arber *Herbals, Their Origin and Evolution* 22–8, 28–37
2 Hain 8949–8955; Choulant *Graphische Incunabeln für Naturgeschichte und Medicin* 59 and 60

257 Adagiorum opus D. Erasmj Rot.

Erasmus. *Adagiorum opus D. Erasmi Roterodami per eundem… recognitum & locupletatum*. Basileae: off. Frobeniana, 1526 or 1528 or 1533 (folio).

After the four Froben editions of the *Adagia* under the title of *Adagiorum chiliades*, three more were published under the title of *Adagiorum opus*: in 1526, 1528, and 1533 (cf no 348). One of these three

will be meant here, most probably the last and most complete. The edition of 1533, which was enlarged by 488 new adages and for the first time provided with marginal notes,[1] may be taken as the definitive form of the *Adagia*. The edition of March 1536, which appeared just before Erasmus' death, added nothing essential to its contents. For this edition, again published under the title *Adagiorum chiliades*, see no 406 #1.

An annotated working copy of the 1526 edition of the *Adagiorum opus* that Erasmus gave to Nicolaas Kan, his servant-pupil (especially valued by him as a Greek copyist), has been preserved and is now in the Vatican Library. At the head of the title-page the ownership mark of the new possession is to be found ('Kan is the owner, but thanks to the great Erasmus') and underneath that of Johann Gropper, provost and archdeacon of Cologne, to whom Kan in his turn made a present of the book in 1552 ('Later Kan voluntarily made Gropper the owner'). After the death of Gropper, the volume remained in Germany until it passed into the hands of Fabio Chigi, afterwards Pope Alexander vi, who was papal nuncio at Cologne from 1639 till 1651. The Bibliotheca Chigiana became part of the Vatican Library in 1924. Erasmus wrote numerous autograph corrections and additions in the margins of the volume; a few corrections of minor importance are in Kan's hand. For the most part the additional passages were printed in the subsequent *Adagia* edition of 1528. At the back of the volume some leaves with manuscript material have been added: two leaves contain a contemporary copy of the *Compendium vitae Erasmi*; thirty sheets of paper of different sizes containing annotations mainly in Erasmus' hand have been pasted on nine other leaves.[2]

For a similar working copy of the 1523 edition of the *Adagiorum chiliades*, likewise given by Erasmus to Nicolaas Kan, see no 348.

1 Cf Epp 2726 and 2773.
2 For an extensive description of MS Vaticanus
   Chigianus R. VIII. 62 see Tocci *In officina Erasmi:
   L'Apparato autografo di Erasmo per l'edizione
   1528 degli Adagia e un nuovo manoscritto del
   Compendium vitae.* On Kan see Allen Ep 1832
   introduction and CEBR II 252–3; on Gropper Allen
   Ep 2508:11n and CEBR II 138.

258 Operum Augustini To. primus / Tomus secun. qui complectitur epistolas. / Tomas ter. complectens τὰ διδακτικὰ. / To. quar. compl. reliqua τῶν διδακτικῶν / To. quintus de Ciuitate Dei. / Tomus sextus aduersus haereticos / To. septi. aduersus Donat. et Pelgoianos [sic]. / Tomus octauus in Psalmos / Tomus nonus Tractatuum / To. decimus Sermonum cum Indice omnium operum.

Augustinus, Aurelius. *Omnium operum
primus (–decimus) tomus.* Basileae: off.
Frobeniana, 1528–9 (folio).

In 1517 Froben took the initiative for this
completely revised and annotated new
edition of Augustine, which was to replace
the incomplete and not very accurate text
published in Basel by Johann Amerbach
in 1506. Though at first Erasmus seems
to have advised against it, he approved
of the undertaking and assumed editorial
control. He soon realized, however, that the
immense task would be beyond the powers
of one man and proposed to divide the
editorial work among a team, as had been
done in the case of his edition of Jerome.
Vives was persuaded to take on *De civitate
Dei* entirely as his own responsibility, while
for the other works Erasmus enlisted the
co-operation of Maarten Lips, Conradus
Goclenius, and (possibly) Sigismundus
Gelenius.[1] Nonetheless the enterprise made
sluggish progress and was completed only
after repeated delays and much bad luck.
Erasmus, who had also complained of
the poor quality of the manuscripts used,
felt the edition as a lead weight: 'I am so
weighed down by Augustine, a writer so
inexhaustible that I seem to be supporting

Etna and Athos on my shoulders.' But
he was full of praise for the end result,
ten heavy volumes printed in large type
(as the edition of Jerome was not).[2] In 1531
Claude Chevallon in Paris published a
second edition of the *Opera omnia*, which
was carefully revised with the aid of
manuscripts from the Abbey of St Victor.[3]
Unlike the revised printing of the *Opera
omnia* of Jerome, which appeared two years
later from the same Parisian printer-
publisher, Erasmus does not appear to
have had any involvement in the reissue
of Augustine's works, nor was it present
in his library.

1 For Erasmus' initial opinion of the project see
   Ep 1900:84–6/86–8. On the prehistory of the
   edition see Allen and CWE introductions to Ep 1309;
   Erasmus' foreword to Vives' edition of *De civitate
   Dei,* 1525 (see no 252); and Allen and CWE Ep 2157
   (dedication of the *Opera omnia* to Alfonso Fonseco,
   primate of Toledo, dated May 1529) introductions.
   Cf De Ghellinck *Patrisque et moyen âge* III 378–92.
   For Erasmus' frequent contacts with Lips in the
   early 1520s about manuscripts of Augustine at
   St Maartensdaal, Leuven, and the priory of
   Groenendaal near Brussels, see Epp 1174:17–
   18/19–21, 1189:9–11/11–13, 1473:5–7/7–9,
   and 1547:1–14/3–18.
2 Ep 2049:19–20/21–3 and cf Ep 2038:1–2/2–3
   with n3; Ep 2133:49–51/55–7.
3 Allen and CWE Epp 1309 (page 118/pages 168–9)
   and 2157 (pages 146–7/page 220) introductions

259 Titus Liuius Frob.

Livius, Titus. *Quicquid hactenus fuit
aeditum. Accesserunt autem Quintae decadis
libri quinque. Chronologia Henr. Glareani.*
Basileae: H. Frobenius, J. Hervagius &
N. Episcopius, March 1531 or *Decades tres
… Beati Rhenani & Sig. Gelenij adiunctae
annotationes.* Basileae: H. Frobenius &
N. Episcopius, 1535 (both in folio).

'Frob.' in the *Versandliste* title points to
one of the two Froben editions of Livy's
history of Rome, *Ab urbe condita*: the first
edition of 1531 or the revised edition of
1535. Erasmus was involved in the production of both. In early 1528 he was already

concerned with the hunt for further manuscripts,[1] and he wrote a foreword to the 1531 edition (Ep 2435), which was the first to include books 41–5 from the manuscript found a few years earlier by Simon Grynaeus in the library of the Benedictine monastery of Lorsch near Worms. In the 1535 edition his foreword was reprinted without change from the earlier version, completely ignoring how thoroughly the text had been revised. Beatus Rhenanus and Sigismundus Gelenius had not only added notes to the text, but had also collated new manuscripts; for the first decade, a manuscript from Worms and for the third, one from Speyer.[2] Erasmus acted as intermediary in the search for a manuscript with the first six books of the third decade, which was supposed to be in the possession of Pietro Bembo. Twice, at an interval of four months, he tried in vain to get hold of the supposed manuscript for the editors of the text. Bembo replied that he was unable to be of service to the Frobens because he did not possess any other or better manuscripts of Livy than those already printed by the Aldine press.[3]

If he followed his customary practice, Erasmus would have kept the later, more thoroughly revised edition. But this is only an assumption, and because it cannot be ruled out in advance that the 1535 edition is entered in the *Versandliste* under no 411, this entry may refer to the original edition of 1531. Erasmus also owned a Paris edition of Livy (no 260).

1 Cf Epp 1947, 1974:1–3/2–4.
2 Allen and CWE Ep 2435 introductions, Allen Ep 2925:6–15; cf Pauly-Wissowa XIII-1 820–3 sv Livius. The manuscript Grynaeus found is now in the Österreichische Nationalbibliothek in Vienna (Cod. Pal. Vindobon. phil. Lat. CV); on the year of the discovery, see AK III 191 Ep 1141 n11.
3 Epp 2925:16–20 and 2958:5–6 (to Bembo), 2975:19–23 (Bembo's reply)

260 Titus Liuius Paris.

Livius, Titus. *Que extant decades cum epitome L. Flori in omnes libros. Cum annotationibus M. Antonii Sabellici in eos qui extant ...* Parisiis: J. Badius, 1511 or 1513 or 1516 (folio).

At least five editions of Livy were published at Paris before 1536: by Josse Bade in 1511, 1513, 1516,[1] and 1530,[2] and François Regnault and N. Crespin in 1529. All of them were based on the text previously edited and annotated by Marcantonio Sabellico.[3] This entry presumably refers to one of the early Bade editions from the years in which Erasmus must have considerably expanded his library by purchases in Paris.[4] For other editions of Livy see nos 259 and 411.

1 Renouard *Bibliographie de Josse Bade* III 10–13
2 Adams L 1326
3 On Sabellico see no 301.
4 Cf no 72 with n2.

261 Suetonius cum plurib. alijs auto. Frob.

[Suetonius. Historiae Augustae Scriptores.] *Ex recognitione Des. Erasmi ... C. Suetonius Tranquillus, Dion Cassius Nicaeus, Aelius Spartianus, Julius Capitolinus, Aelius Lampridius, Vulcatius Gallicanus, Trebellius Pollio, Flavius Vopiscus Syracusius. Quibus adiuncti sunt: Sex. Aurelius Victor, Eutropius, Paulus Diaconus, Ammianus Marcellinus, Pomponius Laetus, Jo. Baptista Egnatius.* Basileae: J. Frobenius, 1518 or the 1533 edition (with a different title; see no 263) (folio).

Froben's edition of Suetonius' lives of the Roman rulers from Caesar to Domitian, with a collection of thirty biographies of emperors and usurpers from Hadrian to Numerianus (117–285), currently ascribed to one anonymous author but in Erasmus' day still considered, following the manuscript tradition, as the work of six separate authors.[1] Contrary to the suggestion on the title-page of the first edition of 1518, only the text of Suetonius had been wholly prepared by Erasmus. For that he had access to a 'very old copy' from the monastery of St Martin's near Tournai, which was made available to him by Lord Mountjoy. The manuscript appears to have remained in his hands; shortly before his death he gave it to his friend Glareanus, and later it may have returned to Tournai.[2] For the text of Spartianus and the other five pseudo-authors of the *Historia Augusta* he used a now-lost codex from the monastery of Murbach.[3] The Basel collected edition was also able to profit greatly from two works printed shortly before by the Aldine press, Giambattista Egnazio's edition of Suetonius of 1516 and his concise history of the Roman emperors, *De caesaribus libri tres*, also dated 1516 but not in circulation before June 1517, which did not stop at the fifth century but continued until Emperor Palaeologus in the east and Emperor Maximilian in the west.[4]

The Froben edition of Suetonius was further augmented by three texts of relevance to the imperial period: excerpts from Sextus Aurelius Victor, the epitome of Roman history by Eutropius, and the eighth-century version of Eutropius with a continuation to the year 553 by Paul the Deacon. Egnazio's *De caesaribus* also included his edition of the *Historiae Augustae scriptores*.[5] Egnazio's edition of Suetonius came too late to be of much use to Erasmus for his own edition of the lives of the emperors (see no 51). But various other texts from Egnazio's Suetonius and his *De caesaribus* could be taken over unaltered in the Basel collection. From one Froben unhesitatingly took the epitomes of Sextus Aurelius Victor, Eutropius, and Paul the Deacon, including Egnazio's notes, and from the other he printed in full not only Egnazio's *In Aelium Spartianum, Lampridium et caeteros annotationes* but also his *De caesaribus libri tres*.[6]

Erasmus had received a presentation copy of Egnazio's 'Caesars' directly from the author,[7] but it can no longer be found as an independent title in the *Versandliste*.[8] If Erasmus put it at once at Froben's disposal to be used as printer's copy, it was probably lost. In that case it is likely that many years later, in his commentary on Psalm 28, *Consultatio de bello Turcis inferendo* (1530), Erasmus did not use the original Aldine edition of Egnazio's *De caesaribus* but the reprinted text in the Froben edition of 1518 as his source for the history of the Turks.[9]

Apart from the authors already mentioned, the Froben collection also contained some other texts relating to the imperial age: excerpts from Dio Cassius' Roman history in the translation of Georgio Merula; also books 14–26 of the *Res gestae* of Ammianus Marcellinus, which for lack of a manuscript were taken from a recent (and as it later proved completely unreliable) Bolognese edition edited by P. Castellus (H. de Benedictus 1517), and finally a 'modern' work, the *Romanae historiae compendium ab interitu Gordiani iunioris usque ad Iustinum III* of the Italian humanist Julius Pomponius Laetus.

In 1533 a revised edition of the Froben collection appeared under a slightly different title (see no 263), augmented by Herodian's Roman history from the death of Marcus Aurelius to the accession of Gordian III, in the translation of Angelo Poliziano (see no 343). Sigismundus Gelenius, who had worked as corrector and collaborator at the Froben press on Erasmus' recommendation since 1526, saw the book through the press. He was also responsible for the new version of the *Res gestae* of Ammianus Marcellinus, which now included books 27–30. He was able to base the text on a manuscript of c 900, now lost but for six leaves, from the monastery of Hersfeld.[10] For the edition of 1533, Erasmus subjected the letter of dedication to Dukes Frederick and George of Saxony that had introduced his text of Suetonius to a fairly thorough revision at some points. It may be assumed that of the two copies of the collection in his library which are listed under similar titles (nos 261 and 263), at least one copy will have been of the edition of 1533. It cannot be determined whether the other copy is of the first edition, or a duplicate of the revised edition.

1 *Der Kleine Pauly* II 1191–3 and OCD 713–14 sv Historia Augusta
2 As he says in the dedicatory letter to Dukes Frederick and George of Saxony, Ep 586:56–9/63–6. The Codex Tornacensis, 'in which the entire collation of the Caesars is preserved in Glareanus' manuscript,' has been lost; see Husner 'Bibliothek' 257 n102 and the literature cited there.
3 Allen Ep 586 introduction
4 Egnazio's preface bears the date 10 June 1517; see Allen Ep 588:55n.
5 On the two editions, see Ross 'Venetian Scholars and Teachers, Fourteenth to Early Sixteenth Century: A Survey and a Study of Giovanni Battista Egnazio' 550–2.
6 The content of the Froben editions of 1518 and 1533 is described in Luchsinger *Der Basler Buchdruck als Vermittler italienischen Geistes 1470–1529* 56 and 103–5.
7 Ep 588:55–7/61–2
8 Unless by 'imperatores' under no 97 #2 the edition of 1519 could be meant.
9 Cf *De bello Turcico* ASD V-3 11–14 and 39:228n.
10 Robinson 'The Hersfeldensis and the Fuldensis of Ammianus Marcellinus'; Ammianus Marcellinus *Res gestae* ed Seyfarth I xlix. On Gelenius see no 303.

262 Suetonius cum commenta. Beroaldj

Suetonius Tranquillus, Caius. *Commentationes conditae a Philippo Beroaldo in Suetonium Tranquillum* (with the text of *De vita duodecim Caesarum*). A folio edition.

Most probably the oldest of the four editions of Suetonius in the *Versandliste* (see also nos 51, 261, and 263). The text, edited with a commentary by the Bolognese humanist Philippo Beroaldo (1453–1505), first appeared in 1493 from the press of B. Hectoris in Bologna and was subsequently reprinted several times.[1] In a preface 'to the reader' in his own edition of Suetonius

and the *Historiae Augustae scriptores* of 1518 (see nos 261 and 263), Erasmus referred to a passage in Dio Cassius that according to Allen had first been cited in some anonymous notes added to Beroaldo's commentaries and included in the Venice 1510 edition of P. Pincius.[2] Could this be the one in his library?

1 1493 edition Hain-Copinger *15126; reprints appeared, for example, in Milan in 1494 and Venice in 1496 and 1506.
2 Ep 648:12–26 with 21n/22–9 with 25n.

263 Sueto. cum plur. alijs auto. Frob.

[Suetonius. Historiae Augustae Scriptores.] *Omnia quam antehac emendatiora. Annotationes Des. Erasmi et Egnatij cognitu dignae. C. Suetonius Tranquillus, Dion Cassius, Aelius Spartianus, Julius Capitolinus, Aelius Lampridius, Vulcatius Gallicanus, Trebellius Pollio, Flavius Vopiscus, Herodianus [Angelo] Politiano interpr., Sextus Aurelius Victor, Pomponius Laetus, Jo. Baptista Egnatius, Ammianus Marcellinus quatuor libris auctus.* Basileae: H. Frobenius et N. Episcopius, 1533 or the 1518 edition (with different title; see no 261) (folio).

One of the two Froben editions of Suetonius and the *Historiae Augustae scriptores*. See no 261.

264 Blondi opera. Frob.

Blondus, Flavius (Flavio Biondo). *De Roma triumphante libri X. Romae instauratae libri III. Italia illustrata. Historiarum decades III.* Basileae: H. Frobenius, J. Hervagius & N. Episcopius, March 1531 (folio).

An omnibus of the chief works of the Italian scholar and researcher Flavio Biondo (1392–1463). His *Roma triumphans*, a manual on public and private life in the classical metropolis, was described by Jakob Burckhardt as 'the first great attempt at a complete exposition of Roman antiquity.'[1] For the topography, the ruins, and the monuments of the city and countryside of northern and central Italy, his *De Roma instaurata* and *Italia illustrata* remained indispensable reference works for over a century, while his *Historiarum ab inclinatione Romanorum imperii decades*, which covered the middle ages from 412 to 1440, were also pioneering. The latter were not stylized humanistic history, but to a great extent an accumulation of accurately extracted and thus valuable excerpts from sources. The way in which Erasmus expressed his esteem for Biondo is surprising: in his *Ciceronianus* (1528) Bulephorus, the speaker in the dialogue who often reflects his own standpoint, names him in the same breath as Boccaccio, presenting them as equals (but as the inferiors of Petrarch), 'both in expressive force and in accurate employment of the Roman tongue.'[2]

1 *Die Kultur der Renaissance in Italien* 170/ *The Civilization of the Renaissance in Italy* 187. Weiss 'Petrarch the Antiquarian' 199 calls Biondo 'the father of Roman archaeology.' On Biondo see also Fueter *Geschichte der neueren Historiographie* 107–8, 190; Cochrane *Historians and Historiography in the Italian Renaissance* 34–40 and passim; CEBR I 147–8.
2 ASD I-2 661:21–2/CWE 28 414–15

265 Plutarchi Vitae Lati. Bad.

Plutarchus. *Vitae post Pyladen Brixianum longe diligentius repositae … necnon cum Aemilij Probi vitis*. Parisiis: J. Badius/J. Parvus, 1514 or 1520 (folio).

This edition was of Plutarch's *Lives* with the *Lives* of Aemilius Probus was first published by Josse Bade in 1514 with a dedication to Girolamo Aleandro. A reprint appeared in 1520 with the title *Plutarchi et Aemilij Probi … vitae*.[1] The omission of the reference to Aemilius Probus from the short title in the *Versandliste* may suggest that we are dealing with the original edition, which singled out Plutarch on the title-page, rather than with the later edition, which gave the

two authors equal honour on the title-page. The lives of famous generals (*editio princeps* Venice 1471) long attributed to Aemilius Probus and cited by Erasmus under that name have since the second half of the sixteenth century been ascribed to Cornelius Nepos.[2]

1 Renouard *Bibliographie de Josse Bade* III 175 and 179
2 *Adagia* III ii 67 and III iii 11 ASD II-5 142:893–4 with n (143) and 196:806–8 with n (197)/CWE 34 250 with n2 (400) and 286 with n1 (410)

266 Graecorum uitae auto. Plutar. Bebe.

Plutarchus. *Graecorum Romanorumque illustrium vitae*. Basileae: J. Bebelius, March 1531 (folio).

Erasmus was already in possession of the current Bade edition of the Plutarch's *Parallel Lives* in translation (see no 265) when he acquired this new edition in 1531. Perhaps it was not a purchase but a presentation copy from the publisher. Erasmus had written a long introduction at the end of February 1531 for another of Johann Bebel's publications, the *Opera omnia* of Aristotle (no 215).

267 Plutarchi Vitae graece Ald.

Plutarchus. *Quae vocantur parallela, hoc est vitae illustrium virorum graeci nominis ac latini*. Venetiis: in aed. Aldi et Andreae soc., 1519 (folio).

In August 1519 Erasmus asked Wolfgang Lachner and Johann Froben to buy the first edition of the Greek text of Plutarch's *Lives*, which had just appeared from the press of Filippo Giunta in Florence, at the autumn fair in Frankfurt.[1] Either he never received it and later acquired the Aldine edition, or he disposed of the *editio princeps* when he acquired the better Aldine text. In any case, the latter came into his possession about 1525.[2] His copy with autograph marginalia has been preserved and was

rediscovered in the Provincial Library of
Friesland at Leeuwarden. Notes on fol [III]
recto and the verso of the last leaf, possibly
marks of ownership, are no longer deci-
pherable even with a quartz lamp. Part
of the library of the Academy of Franeker,
the book was transferred to the library in
Leeuwarden with four other Erasmiana,
after the disbanding of the Academy in
1644, as appears from the library catalogue
of that year.[3]

1 Ep 629:15/17–18
2 The *Vitae* were not included in the order for
   Aldine editions; cf Allen VII 547 Appendix 20
   'Books Ordered by Erasmus.'
3 Sign. 482 Gesch. On this discovery, see Engels
   'Erasmiana in de Franeker academiebibliotheek'
   69–70 and *Erasmus' handexemplaren* 29 and 48.
   For the other books see nos 123, 137, 203, and
   208, and cf no 201.

268 Q. Curtius cum Vuandalia Alber. krantz

Curtius Rufus, Quintus. *De rebus gestis
Alexandri Magni. Cum annotationibus
D. Erasmi.* Argentorati: aed. Schurerij,
June 1518 (folio).

bound with

Crantz, Albertus. *Wandalia.* Coloniae:
J. Soter alias Heil ex Bentheim & socii,
April 1519 (folio).

1/ The partially preserved historical work
of Curtius Rufus published by Erasmus
and dedicated to Duke Ernst of Bavaria,
bishop of Passau (Ep 704). En route from
Brabant to England in early 1517, Erasmus
had taken the *De rebus gestis Alexandri
Magni* as reading matter for the journey
and had regretted that the text, in itself so
readable, should have been so incompletely
and corruptly handed down.[1] He had
therefore gone through the text critically
and prepared a new edition for the press.
At the end of October 1517 he sent his
copy – 'revised by myself with index and
preface' – to his friend the Strasbourg
printer Matthias Schürer (who had

recommended himself for work by
Erasmus), and left it to him to decide what
to do with it: to publish or to return it.[2] In
the meantime he had already derived some
profit from his work: in the text of Curtius
Rufus he found material he was immediately able to incorporate into the revised
edition of the *Adagiorum chiliades* that
he was preparing for the press at practically
the same time.[3]

2/ A posthumously published history of
the Wends of the German Baltic coast by
Albert Crantz (c 1450–1517) of Hamburg,
the first German regional historian to
follow the methods of Italian humanist
historiography. He kept his history free
from miracles and legends but at the same
time uncritically (and patriotically) identified the Wends with the Vandals and linked
the collapse of the Vandal kingdom in
Africa with the history of northern
Germany.[4] The *Wandalia* was printed
at Cologne, and this raises the question
whether the book, which seems a little
out of place in Erasmus' library, may
have come into his ownership through
an intermediary or as a gift from one
of his friends in that city, with whom
he was in regular contact around 1519:
from Johannes Caesarius, to whom he
had dedicated his translation of Gaza
some years before (Ep 428), or perhaps
from Hermann von Neuenahr, his host
at Bedburg in September 1518, a man
who was very interested in early medieval
history and was to publish a short treatise
on the Franks with the same publisher two
years later (see no 31).[5]

1 Ep 704:14–20/16–23
2 Cf Epp 612 (from Schürer), 693:1–3/2–4 (from
   Erasmus); cf Ep 633:3–6/5–8.
3 For additions to the November 1517–18 edition
   from Curtius Rufus see for example *Adagia* II
   viii 17, III ii 62, and III vii 100 ASD II-4 161:248–9
   with n, II-5 221 355–7 with n, and II-6 479:142,
   480:150–1 with nn/CWE 34 55 with n3 (335) and
   303 with n2 (419), CWE 35 280–1 with nn1 and 5.
4 See Fueter *Geschichte der neueren Historiographie*
   192–4

5 On Caesarius see Allen and CWE Ep 374 introductions and CEBR I 238–9; on Neuenahr see no 31.

269 Cornelius Tacitus

Tacitus, Cornelius. *Annalium ab excessu Augusti sicut ipse vocat sive Historiae Augustae, qui vulgo receptus titulus est libri sedecim qui supersunt ... recogniti ... per Beatum Rhenanum.* Basileae: H. Frobenius & N. Episcopius, 1533, or one of the earlier editions: *Liber quinque noviter inventi atque cum reliquis ejus operibus editi; Phil. Beroaldus [ed.].* Romae: St Guilleret, 1515 (folio) or *Historia Augusta ... Andr. Alciati annotationes, De situ, moribus & populis Germaniae. Jul. Agricolae vita.* Basiliae: J. Frobenius, 1519 (folio).

It is not possible to identify this edition exactly. But since the other Tacitus in the library must have been a still incomplete edition of the *Opera* (see no 270), this entry most probably alludes to one of the sixteenth-century editions that included the previously unknown books 1–5 of the *Annales* from the ninth-century manuscript found in 1508–9 at the abbey of Corvey and bought by Pope Leo x.[1] The first complete edition to be considered was prepared and annotated by Filippo Beroaldo and appeared in 1515 from the press of S. Guilleret in Rome. The Milan edition published by A. Minutianus in 1517, based on the previous work and with supplementary notes by Andrea Alciati, was issued in octavo format and can therefore hardly be meant here. Two Basel folios followed. The first, published by Johann Froben in August 1519, was for the most part a reprint from the Milan edition but revised, especially so far as the *Germania* was concerned, by Beatus Rhenanus. The second version of this, published by H. Froben and N. Episcopius in 1533, was completely revised by Beatus Rhenanus, who definitively gave the name of *Annales* to the principal work and added to the text a 'thesaurus' of unusual expressions and turns of phrase in Tacitus.[2] Whenever he could, Erasmus wanted to have the latest and most authoritative edition of a famous author. For that reason, and since he also possessed many other Froben editions published in the last years of his life, it is difficult to imagine that the works of Tacitus in the 1533 edition – which was then the best, and moreover by his friend Beatus Rhenanus – should not have been in his library. There is, however, a weak point in this argument: the short title in the *Versandliste* does not include the word 'Frob.' Consequently it is possible that the 1515 edition is meant; the younger Beroaldo was no stranger to Erasmus – they had become friends in Rome in 1506 – and his *editio princeps* of the *Annales* was known for its carefulness.

1 Ep 919:28n/31n. It is now in Florence, MS Laur. 68.I = Mediceus I.
2 On the editions mentioned see Etter *Tacitus in der Geistesgeschichte des 16. und 17. Jahrhunderts* 26–30; Joachimsen 'Tacitus im deutschen Humanismus.'

270 Tacitus et Appianus Alexandrinus

Tacitus, Cornelius. [*Opera ie Historia Augusta (= Annalium et historiarum libri superstites), De situ, moribus et populis Germaniae libellus, et Dialogus de oratoribus clarissimis*]. [Venetiis:] Vindelinus de Spira, [c 1472] (folio) or *Opera a Francisco Puteolano edita acc. Julii Agricolae vita.* Venetiis: P. Pincius, sumpt. B. Fontana, 23 March 1497 (folio).

bound with

Appianus Alexandrinus. [*Historia Romana, pars 2: De bellis civilibus Romanorum interprete Petro Candido*]. Venetiis: Vindelinus de Spira, 1472 (folio) or [*Historia Romana*, partes 1 et 2]. Venetiis: C. de Pensis, 20 November 1500 (folio).

Of the possible combinations in this composite volume, perhaps the *editiones principes* of Tacitus and Appian, which appeared in succession from the same press, is the most likely. Erasmus may have bought the incunabula copies as early as his stay in Italy, but in any case before he acquired the modern edition of Tacitus with all the preserved books of the *Annales*. Later he did not dispose of the superseded and incomplete edition, for he wished to retain the text of Appian that was bound with it, although that contained only the second part of the surviving text.[1]

1/ If one assumes that Erasmus' edition of Tacitus was bound with an edition of Appian of about the same date, then it must have been a fifteenth-century printing. Their number is limited: apart from the Venetian *editio princeps* of c 1472,[2] an edition published without indication of place or date but probably Milan c 1475 and the 1497 Venetian edition are almost the only possibilities. In the older edition of Tacitus, the text of the *Annales* and the *Historiae* was still based on an eleventh-century codex written at Monte Cassino that lacked books 1–5 of the *Annales*.[3] It is highly probable that Erasmus also owned one of the later editions containing the five unknown books, which had meanwhile been rediscovered in another manuscript (see no 269).

2/ The fragmentary remains of the work on Roman history by Appianus Alexandrinus (second century AD), an important source for the civil wars and the only source for the revolutionary movement of the Gracchi, were not published in the original Greek until after Erasmus' death. Before then they were accessible only in the Latin translation of Petrus Candidus. Several editions were published, but only four in folio format: the oldest, also the *editio princeps*, at Venice in 1472, by Vendelinus de Spira; two others in less well known regional printing centres, Reggio nell' Emilia in 1494 and Scandiano in 1495, and a fourth at Venice by C. de Pensis in 1500.[4]

1 GW 2293

2 Hain *15218 dates it wrongly 'c 1469'; see BL *Catalogue Fifteenth Century* v 165: 'undated' and BL *Catalogue of Italian Books 1465–1600* 653: '[1472?].'
3 It is now in Florence, MS Laur. 68.II = Mediceus II.
4 GW 2291–4

271 Procopius et B. Rhen. de Germ.

Procopius. *De rebus Gothorum, Persarum ac Vandalorum libri VII, una cum aliis mediorum temporum historicis*. Basileae: J. Hervagius, September 1531 (folio).

bound with

Beatus Rhenanus. *Rerum germanicarum libri III*. Basileae: H. Frobenius, J. Hervagius et N. Episcopius, March 1531 (folio).

Two works, one edited and the other written by Erasmus' younger friend, Beatus Rhenanus (1485–1547).[1] Beat Bild from Sélestat received his earliest education in the Latin school of his birthplace and then studied at Paris. There he made the acquaintance of Lefèvre d'Etaples,[2] who exercised a great influence on him. After gaining his master's degree in 1505, he was employed as a scholarly proofreader, at first in Paris with Henri Estienne, and later at Strasbourg for Matthias Schürer. In 1511 he settled at Basel, where he was on friendly terms with Bonifacius Amerbach and Froben. From 1526 to his death he again lived in his native city, where his library has been preserved virtually intact.[3] Rhenanus was among the most faithful and devoted friends of Erasmus, who nominated him as one of the editors of his collected works as early as his will of 1527.[4] He was also Erasmus' first biographer. In 1536 he wrote a brief sketch of the humanist's life for Erasmus' posthumously published edition of Origen.[5] Four years later, he elaborated this sketch for his introduction to the *Opera omnia* (Basel: Hieronymus Froben and Nicolaus Episcopius 1533–40).[6] According to tradition he was considered to be the editor of the nine-volume edition, but all concrete proof of this is lacking: Reedijk and Hartmann (earlier, in a casual remark) thought that there were good grounds to regard Sigismundus Gelenius as the actual 'corrector' (*castigator*) of the work.[7] Rhenanus was, however, responsible for preparing many of Erasmus' works for the press during his lifetime.

1/ A collection of sources for the history of the migration of peoples containing, as their most important items, the works of Procopius in the translations by the Italian humanists C. Persona and Raffaele Maffei, here published together for the first time. The collection also included Agathias' *De bello Gothorum*, Leonardo Aretino's *De bello italico adversus Gothos*, largely plagiarized from Procopius,[8] Jordanes' *De origine rebusque Gothorum*, Sidonius Apollinaris' letter on Theodoric II, the king of the Visigoths, and the *editio princeps* of Procopius' *De aedificiis Justiniani*, published in the original Greek by Beatus Rhenanus from a manuscript in the possession of the Augsburg humanist Konrad Peutinger, whose short summary of the history of the migration of peoples was also included. The planned second part of the collection, for which Bonifacius Amerbach applied to Andrea Alciati for new material,[9] never appeared.

2/ Beatus Rhenanus' most important work, his uncompleted history of German history until the time of the Saxon emperors. It was a typical scholarly work of the school of Flavio Biondo, planned on the model of Biondo's *Roma triumphans* (no 264); it had the same merits but also the same defects: the author – without paying too much attention to style and composition – went back to the sources, which he cited with care.[10]

1 On Beatus see Allen and CWE Ep 327 introductions; CEBR I 104–9.
2 On Lefèvre d'Etaples see no 178 with n1.

3 Walter *Catalogue Sélestat*; Horawitz *Die Bibliothek und Correspondenz des Beatus Rhenanus zu Schlettstadt*
4 Allen VI 504:61 Appendix 19 'Erasmus' First Will'/CWE 12 543:53–4
5 Allen I 52–6 (Beatus Rhenanus to Hermann of Wied)
6 Allen I 56–71 (Beatus Rhenanus to Charles V)
7 Reedijk *Tandem bona causa triumphat* 34 with n69 (56), in which the author goes further than his cautiously formulated surmise in ASD I-1 ix (general introduction); Hartmann in AK V 38 Ep 2123
8 Pauly-Wissowa XXIII-1 274–5
9 See Bietenholz *Der italienische Humanismus und die Blütezeit des Buchdrucks in Basel* 102–3
10 Fueter *Geschichte der neueren Historiographie* 191

272 Herodotus et Pausanias grae. Aldi.

Herodotus. *Herodoti libri novem quibus Musarum indita sunt nomina.* [Graece.] Venetiis: in domo Aldi, September 1502 (folio).

bound with

Pausanias. [*Commentarii Graeciam describentes, graece.*] Venetiis: aed. Aldi et Andreae soc., July 1516 (folio).

These two works are now found in one binding in the British Library, which bought them in 1888. On the first flyleaf, an earlier owner wrote, 'notations are found added in the margins in the hand of the great Erasmus.' Under that, in another hand, we read, 'the remaining manuscript notations are added in the hand of Daniel Heinsius.' Daniel Heinsius himself had no special interest in Erasmus, unlike his father, who was an ardent admirer.[1] Did Daniel perhaps inherit this volume from his father?

1/ *Editio princeps* of the Greek text of Herodotus, published by Aldo Manuzio. In April 1518, as he was about to leave for Basel, Erasmus presented his copy of this edition to his friend Antonius Clava of Ghent, a member of the Council of Flanders and a lover of books with a splendid library, full of gilded and richly illustrated volumes. It would be easy, he wrote to him, to find another en route.[2] In fact Erasmus succeeded in finding another copy quite soon, and had it bound with the recent edition of Pausanias. (Or did he speak more liberally than was actually the case, and gave his Herodotus away only after he had acquired the Aldine edition of Pausanias and bound the two together?) In 1529 the donated copy came into the hands of Levinus Ammonius, one of Erasmus' later servant-pupils, who appears from a note at the back of the book to have inherited it from Clava. In our century Allen mentioned it as being in private hands, first in England, then (in 1922) in the United States. Its present location is unknown. The copy bound with Pausanius is now in the British Library.[3]

2/ The *editio princeps* of the famous description of Greece by the second century Greek traveller Pausanias. The text was published after the death of Aldo Manuzio by Marcus Musurus, probably from a manuscript in the library of the learned printer. (Eight years earlier, during his stay at Venice, Erasmus too used Aldo's library, and Pausanius was one of the Greek authors to whom he had access in manuscript there.)[4] Musurus dedicated his edition to his teacher Janus Lascaris in a long introductory letter.[5]

For Erasmus' relationship with Musurus and Lascaris, see nos 116 and 104. In 1522 Vives stated that he had been able to consult the Greek Pausanias in Erasmus' library.[6]

1 Husner 'Bibliothek' 250; ter Horst 'Nog enkele aanteekeningen over de bibliotheek van Erasmus' 233

2 See Ep 841. On Clava see Ep 175:10n/13n; Reedijk *Poems* 348 (no 129 introduction); CEBR I 307. On his library, see Ep 2260:42–4/46–9: 'He was … a great lover of books. All his books had gold on the outside and were decorated on the inside with gold lettering. You would have said they looked more like treasure-chests than books.' Erasmus wrote an epitaph for him, first printed at the end of his translation of Xenophon's *Hieron sive tyrannus* (Basel: Froben 1530; not on the *Versandliste*);

see Reedijk *Poems* no 129/ASD I-7 and CWE 85–6 no 86.

3 Allen Ep 841:1n and IV xxviii: '... now in the library of Mr G.A. Plimpton ... New York'/ CWE Ep 841:3n

4 Allen I 61:175 (Beatus Rhenanus to Charles V); cf *Adagia* I i 90 CWE 31 131.

5 Geanakoplos *Greek Scholars in Venice* 158

6 See Allen Ep 1303:6n.

273 Xenophon, Geor Gemis. Herodianus grae.

Xenophon etc. *Xenophontis omissa, quae et graece gesta appellantur. Georgii Gemisti qui et Pletho dicitur, ex Diodori et Plutarchi historiis de iis quae post pugnam ad Mantineam gesta sunt ... tractatio. Herodiani a Marci principatu historiarum libri octo ..., Enarratiunculae ... in totum Thucydidem* etc. [Graece.] Venetiis: in Aldi Neacademia, 1503 (folio).

There can be no doubt that the title in the *Versandliste* refers to this Aldine edition. Apart from Xenophon's *Hellenica*, it contained the history of Greece from 362–336 BC excerpted from Diodorus Siculus and Plutarch by the Byzantine scholar Georgius Gemistus (1355–1450); the history of Rome from 180 to 238 written by the Greek Herodian, and some scholia on Thucydides (for a later edition of Herodian see no 343). The edition was not a commercial success, and a large part of it remained on Aldo's hands. Later, in about 1525, the then manager of the Aldine press tried to put the copies still in stock to productive use by splitting them into two and bringing the separate parts on to the market again: the first as part of a complete edition of Xenophon's works (see no 204), the second part on its own with a new title-page (see no 276 #2).

When Łaski returned to Poland in April 1555, the book listed here was no longer in his possession but had fallen into the hands of Gerard Mortaigne, his friend, a Flemish religious exile who had spent the winter of 1553–4 with him in Emden. We know that it was offered for sale in 1554 and was sent, with other books derived from the library of Erasmus, to Regnerus Praedinius, rector of St Martin's School at Groningen.[1] After that it disappeared without a trace.

1 Gabbema *Epistolarum centuriae tres* 169 (Ep 68)

274 Strabo de situ orbis

Strabo. *De situ orbis libr. XVII.* Perhaps a Venetian edition (folio).

The *Geography* of Strabo (63 BC–AD 19), no less important for the history than for the geography of the ancient world, appeared in the Latin translation of Chrysoloras' pupils Guarino Guarini of Verona and Gregorius Tiphernas many times from 1469. In the editions published before 1536 it usually went under the title of *Geographiae libri XVII.* The Venetian editions published between 1472 and 1510 are the exception to this rule: in these, the work bore the title *De situ orbis* on the first leaf or the title-page. Erasmus' copy may well have been one of these editions.[1]

1 For example [V. de Spira] 1472; J. [Rubeus] Vercellensis 1494; B. de Zanis 1502; or P. Pincius 1510

275 Strabo de situ orbis grae. Ald.

Strabo. *De situ orbis, graece.* Venetiis: in aed. Aldi et Andreae soceri, November 1516 (folio).

The Aldine *editio princeps* of Strabo's work in the Greek text. Probably the copy that Erasmus asked Wolfgang Lachner and Johann Froben in August 1517 to buy for him with other books at the Frankfurt autumn fair.[1] Vives was to consult the work some years later in the library of his illustrious friend.[2]

1 Ep 629:14–15/17
2 Allen Ep 1303:6n

276 Thucydides Geor. Gemis. et Herodi. grae.

Thucydides. *De bello Peloponnesico* [*graece.*] Venetiis: in domo Aldi, May 1502 (folio).

bound with

Gemistus, Georgius. *Ex Diodori et Plutarchi historiis de iis quae post pugnam ad Mantineam gesta sunt ... tractatio. Herodiani a Marci principatu historiarum libri VIII, Enarratiunculae ... in totum Thucydidem* etc. [Graece.] Venetiis: in Aldi Neacademia, 1503 (folio).

The most obvious candidates here are the two Aldine editions named above.

1/ Aldo Manuzio published the *editio princeps* of Thucydides' history of the Peloponnesian war in the original Greek in 1502. But although according to the imprint the work bound with it was published in 1503, in reality it did not come on to the market until about 1525 (see below). Perhaps Erasmus only acquired his text of Thucydides late; in any case the two books could not have been bound together before 1525.

2/ The book bound in the same volume was part of the 1503 Aldine edition of Xenophon, Gemistus, and Herodian, of which a copy was also included in Erasmus' library (no 273). The sale of this edition had been very poor, so that Gianfrancesco Torresani, then in charge of the business management of the press, decided in about 1525 to use the parts with the text of Xenophon's *Hellenica* for his edition of the complete works of Xenophon (see no 204). He then republished what was left of the remaining copies (the gatherings η–φ) as an independent work, with a new title-page, which, however, did not state the new actual year of publication but the original date, 1503.[1]

1 Cf Adams P 1530.

277 Etymologicon Graecum

Etymologicum magnum graecum. Cum praef. M. Musuri. Venetiis: Zacharias Kallierges sumpt. N. Blasti, 1499 (folio).

The *Etymologicum magnum* was an alphabetically arranged lexicon compiled in the early twelfth century by a Byzantine scholar from older similar works and other sources.[1] It was the first product of the press of the learned Cretan Zacharias Calliergis, who was later (from 1515 to 1523) active at Rome, but at that time was still in Venice.[2] He, and not his friend Marcus Musurus, also seems to have been the actual editor of the work. Musurus' share in the publication was probably restricted to giving advice and writing an introduction.[3] Erasmus met Calliergis at a meal in Musurus' house during his Italian journey in 1508. Much later he recalled this meeting and remembered the printer at that time as 'a young man who was a very good scholar.'[4]

Erasmus' copy of the *Etymologicum magnum* was rediscovered after the Second World War in the Jagiellonian Library in Cracow.[5] A part of the name has been erased from his owner's mark *Sum Erasmi.* The book, which does not contain any autograph marginalia, has been in the uninterrupted possession of the University of Cracow since 1570, when it was bequeathed with 114 other works, mostly of Greek and Byzantine authors, to the library of the Collegium Maius by the Greek scholar Professor Stanisław Grzepski (1524–1570).[6] Whether he had received the book directly from Łaski or had bought it, and if so, when, is unfortunately unknown. While those volumes from Erasmus' library that have been preserved have almost always been rebound, the *Etymologicum*, although heavily restored, still has a part of its original calf binding. The covering of the front and rear boards, blind-stamped with plates, lines, and single

tools, is still intact. With expert assistance it can be established that both boards are stamped with variants of exceptionally large stamps that were in use and popular in France between c 1510 and 1520, although a slight earlier date cannot be ruled out.[7] The binding of the book lends support to the assumption, in itself plausible, that Erasmus acquired the lexicon either in Paris between 1500 and his departure for Italy in 1506, years in which he took great pains to acquire Greek books in particular,[8] or after his return from Italy, perhaps around 1511, when he made large purchases of books in Paris, often from Josse Bade.[9]

1 Pauly-Wissowa VI 815–16 sv Etymologika; OCD 561 sv etymologica
2 GW 9426. On Calliergis see Geanakoplos *Greek Scholars in Venice* 201–22 and passim; CEBR I 244–5.
3 Geanakoplos *Greek Scholars in Venice* 124
4 Ep 1347:250–1 / 269–70
5 Hajdukiewicz 'Im Bücherkreis des Erasmus' 87; Lewicka-Kamińska 'Erazm z Rotterdamu w Polsce katalog wystawy w Bibliotec Jagiellońskiej' 110
6 A note on fol 1 recto reads, *M. Stanislaus Grzepsius maior collega ad bibliothecam Collegii Maioris legauit MDLXX. Oretur pro eo* 'The distinguished colleague Master Stanislaus Grzepsius bequeathed it to the library of the Great College in 1570. One should pray for him.' I owe the further details on this volume to the friendly help of Dr Marian Zwiercan, deputy director of the Bibliothek Jagiellońska.
7 I am grateful to Dr J. Storm van Leeuwen, keeper of bookbindings at the Royal Library in The Hague, who was kind enough to trace the origin of the binding for me, on the basis of a rubbing received from Cracow and extensive comparative material from the professional literature.
8 Cf Epp 124:62–4 / 72–3, 160:6–8 / 7–10.
9 Cf no 72 with n2.

278 Annotationes doctorum uirorum et / Antiquitatum uariarum uolumina 17.

Annotationes doctorum virorum in grammaticos, oratores, poetas, philosophos, theologos et leges. [Parisiis:] J. Parvus and J. Badius, 15 August 1511 (folio).

bound with

Annius, Johannes. *Antiquitatum Variarum Volumina XVII.* [Parisiis:] J. Parvus and J. Badius, 18 January 1512 (folio).

1/ A collection of commentators' notes on classical authors by leading Italian humanists, compiled by the printer-publisher Josse Bade and dedicated by him to Michael Hummelberg (1487–1527), a Greek scholar, active for many years at Paris and a friend of Erasmus.[1] The anthology included texts of varied nature and extent by Angelo Poliziano, Marcantonio Sabellico, the elder Filippo Beroaldo, Domizio Calderini, Giambattista Egnazio, Giambattista Pio, and other scholars.[2]

2/ The collection by the Dominican Johannes Annius (Giovanni Nanni) of Viterbo, originally published in 1498 by E. Silber in Rome, contained so-called newly discovered texts of Greek and Latin authors and purported translations from the writings of the Babylonian priest Berossos and the Egyptian priest Manetho, which were subsequently unmasked as being for the most part fraudulent.[3] The work exhibited a certain Italian patriotism, while a clear anti-Greek sentiment was expressed in the detailed commentaries on the texts.[4] In its time the book also aroused interest outside Italy, especially in France. Five Paris reprints appeared in rapid succession: in 1509, 1510, 1511, 1512, and 1515. It is virtually certain that Erasmus owned one of these – perhaps the edition of 1512, dedicated by Bade to Guillaume Petit,[5] which appeared at about the same time as the *Annotationes doctorum virorum* with which it was bound.

The book did not, however, meet with a uniformly favourable reception. At the beginning of the sixteenth century many scholars, including Sabellico, Raffaele Maffei (Volaterranus), Alciati, Lefèvre d'Etaples, Beatus Rhenanus, and Vives, to name only a few, had begun to have doubts about the authenticity of the texts.[6] Erasmus appears at first to have paid insufficient attention to these doubts; at least he was incautious enough to refer in his annotation on Luke 3:23–38 concerning the genealogy of Christ to the *Liber antiquitatum biblicarum* of the pseudo-Philo, which was included in the book.[7] His appeal to this source earned him a reprimand from his vitriolic opponent Edward Lee. Two years later he passed a less friendly verdict on Nanni as a scholar who, he rather suspected, was 'rash and pompous, and in any case a Dominican.'[8] In the editions of his New Testament that followed, however, he allowed the passage to stand unaltered.

1 On Hummelberg see Ep 263:21n/26n; CEBR II 213–14.
2 For the complete contents see Renouard *Bibliographie de Josse Bade* II 38–9.
3 Weiss 'Traccia per una biografia di Annio da Viterbo'; Cochrane *Historians and Historiography in the Italian Renaissance* 432–5
4 On these aspects and the implications of the work, see Simone 'Une enterprise oubliée des humanistes français' 119 and 'Historiographie et mythographie dans la culture française du XVIe siècle' 133–7; Tigerstedt 'Joannes Annius and Graecia Mendax.'
5 Renouard *Bibliographie de Josse Bade* II 35–6. On Petit see no 15 n14.
6 Cochrane *Historians* (n3 above) 265 and 433
7 Cf ASD VI-5 502:511–506:593.
8 Ep 784:49–50 with 49n/54–5 with 54n; cf Epp 324:14n/17n, 886:77n/81n; Tigerstedt 'Annius' (n4 above) 295. Cf Erasmus' *Apologia* in response to Edward Lee ASD IX-4 27–9:113–14n/CWE 72 8 n39.

279 Hermolai Castig. in Plinium cum/Ioannis Tortellij Orthographia.

Barbarus, Hermolaus. *Castigationes Plinianae … Item emendatio in Melam Pomponium.* Romae: E. Argenteus (Silber), 1492/3 or Venetiis, s n 1493/4 or Cremona: C. Darlerius, 1495 or Venetiis: B. de Zanis, 1495 (folio).

bound with

Tortellius, Joannes. *Orthographia Joannis Tortelli lima quaedam per Georgium Vallam tractatum de orthographia.* Probably a Venetian edition from the end of the fifteenth or the beginning of the sixteenth century (folio).

Two works that cannot be more precisely identified, but that certainly date from the last decade of the fifteenth century or the first of the sixteenth. Erasmus may have brought them from Italy.[1]

1/ Ermolao Barbaro, of aristocratic Venetian descent, not only won fame as a scholar, but also carried out various diplomatic missions and ended his life in the service of the church as patriarch of Aquileia. After his studies in Rome under Pomponius Laetus he accepted the chair of philosophy at Padua in 1477. There he taught and interpreted Aristotle from a Christian viewpoint but in an anti-scholastic spirit.[2] Barbaro enjoyed the esteem both of his own contemporaries and of the younger generation of humanists. Erasmus repeatedly mentioned him in the same breath as the renowned Florentine scholar Poliziano, both of whom he held up as examples to Alaard of Amsterdam.[3] In his dialogue *Ciceronianus,* he did not permit any difference of opinion on Barbaro's greatness to exist between the two participants Bulephorus and Nosoponus.[4] Barbaro's most important work, which has also remained his best known, was his *Castigationes Plinianae,* an inexhaustible collection of textual emendations of the *Naturalis historia.*[5] Budé made fruitful use of it in his *De asse* (nos 291 and 292),[6] and Erasmus was enthusiastic in his praise of the scholar who had rescued the *Naturalis historia* from its textual corruption: 'There can be no question that our greatest debt is to Ermolao Barbaro, not just because he was the first to tackle this noble task, but because none of the others improved the text in so many places.'[7] After the *editio princeps* of 1492/3, three further editions appeared before the end of the century: in Venice (1493/4), Cremona (1495), and again in Venice (1495).[8]

2/ The *Orthographia* of Giovanni Tortelli was first published by N. Jenson in Venice in 1471; it dealt with Latin words derived from Greek and discussed not only their spelling but also their meaning and correct use. The author was a good friend of Lorenzo Valla, secretary of Pope Nicholas v, and the first person to hold the appointment of *praefectus* of the Vatican Library. The work went into many new editions, practically all of them from Venetian printers, around the turn of the century: P. de Pinciis (1493); J. Tacuinus (1495);[9] B. de Zanis (1501 and 1504). In his dialogue on the correct pronunciation of Latin and Greek, Erasmus referred to Tortellius' *Orthographia* as an authority, alongside the ancient writers.[10]

1 As early as his *Adagiorum collectanea* (1500 and 1505) Erasmus derived numerous proverbs, often literally, from Barbaro's *Castigationes Plinianae;* see Heinimann 'Zu den Anfängen der humanistishen Paroemiologie' 170–2; ASD II-4 299 390–2n. But it is quite possible that at that time he used a copy put at his disposal by one of his friends in Paris. He appealed to Robert Gaguin frequently and seldom needed to ask whether a classical text or humanist writing he wanted to consult was in Gaguin's well-furnished library. 'I know there is not a single good author whom you do not own,' he told Gaguin in 1500 (Ep 122:4–5/5–6). Cf no 285 n7.

2 On Barbaro see Ep 126:128n/150n; CEBR I 91–2. On his 'aristotélisme chrétien' see Renaudet *Préréforme et humanisme* 148, 158.

3 Ep 485:1–2/2–3; cf Epp 126:128/150, 471:10–11/12, 3032:224–8. On Poliziano see no 285.

4 ASD I-2 663:9–15/CWE 28 415–16

5 On the *Castigationes* see Heinimann 'Zu den Anfängen der humanistischen Paroemiologie' 170.

6 Garanderie *Correspondance* 75 n14. But Budé did have some criticisms; see Allen Ep 480:134n.

7 Ep 1544:38–41/41–4

8 GW 3340, 3341, and 3342. The last mentioned edition (Venice: B. de Zanis 1495), cannot be found in GW under Hermolaus Barbarus. A copy of it, however, is in possession of the Universitätsbibliothek Basel (C F II.19.2), bound with Pliny's *De naturali hystoria* (1496) from the same press. The volume came from the library of Bruno or Bonifacius Amerbach and was evidently used by Erasmus; it contains numerous marginal notes in his hand. See Husner 'Bibliothek' 258 and *Erasmus ... Vorkämpfer für Frieden und Toleranz* (exhibition catalogue) 122.

9 Hain 15564 (1471), 15572 (1493), and 15574 (1495)
10 *De recta pronuntiatione* ASD I-4 86:401–2 with
   n (87), 90:535–8 with n (91)/CWE 26 452 with n389
   (618), 457 with n416 (620)

280 Reuchlini Rudimenta Hebraica

Reuchlin, Johannes. *De rudimentis hebraicis.* Phorce [Pforzheim]: aed. T. Anshelmi, 24 March 1506 (folio).

There was no occasion for Erasmus, who had already abandoned his attempts to learn Hebrew in 1504,[1] to buy the *Rudimenta hebraica* immediately after its publication in 1506.[2] Nor did he have a personal relationship with Reuchlin at that time. Probably he only acquired the work – a full course in Hebrew, containing a lexicon, a grammar, and reading passages – later, when he had fairly regular contact with Reuchlin and the two men exchanged their writings: that is, broadly from 1514 to 1517 (cf no 176). The book was still available then, for in 1510 almost half of the printing of 1500 remained unsold. Reuchlin relieved the printer-publisher Anshelm of the remainder, which was taken over by Johann Amerbach at the price of one guilder for three copies.[3]

Could this book have been a gift from Reuchlin? In 1516 Erasmus paid the author an indirect but courteous compliment on his excellent work, by telling him the story of the prior of the Carthusian monastery of Saint-Omer, who with the aid of the *Rudimenta* 'had acquired a remarkable knowledge of Hebrew out of your books without a teacher.'[4] He himself had not reached that stage. In March 1515, probably just after his first and only personal meeting with Reuchlin in Frankfurt, Erasmus had confessed to him that 'to Hebrew I make no claim, for I barely set my lips to it.'[5] He therefore availed himself of the assistance of experts for difficulties with Hebrew passages in the two great editions he was then preparing: of the three Amerbach brothers for the edition

of Jerome and of Johannes Oecolampadius for the *Novum instrumentum.*[6]

Erasmus' copy of the *Rudimenta* was given away by Jan Łaski to Albert Hardenberg in Mainz in 1537. It must have passed out of the possession of this scholarly monk, who later went over to the Reformation and from 1567 to his death in 1574 was a pastor in Emden, into the library of the Grosse Kirche of that city, where it still remains. Erasmus' mark of ownership appears twice. On the title-page stands his *Sum Erasmi* and on the inside of the front board *Sum Erasmi nec muto dominum,* next to which Hardenberg wrote *Hoc Erasmi manus est* 'This is the hand of Erasmus' and as the new owner added *Nunc Alberti, nec dominum muto* 'Now I belong to Albert, and I do not change owners.'[7] Hardenberg also added a second ex libris, an autograph note of 1549 on fol 1 recto, which also specified the time and occasion of Łaski's gift.[8]

1 Ep 181:36–8/41–5
2 Benzing *Bibliographie Reuchlins* no 90
3 Geiger *Johann Reuchlin* 132 and Hirsch *Printing, Selling and Reading 1450–1550* 73
4 Ep 471:18–19/19–21
5 Ep 324:31–2/31–2; cf Epp 334:128/135, 396:280/ 300–1. On their meeting see CWE Ep 326B:26–9, Ep 967:71–2 with 72n / 80–1 with 81n; Krebs 'Reuchlins Beziehungen mit Erasmus von Rotterdam' 145.
6 Epp 334:124–9/132–6 and 396:271–83/292–304 (the latter is the dedication to William Warham of the edition of Jerome); Ep 373:66–76/72–83 (preface to the *Novum instrumentum*)
7 After restoration of the worm-eaten boards these autograph notes by Erasmus and Hardenberg are no longer to be found; see Jürgens *Johannes a Lasco* 128.
8 Husner 'Bibliothek' 248; I am grateful to Dr H. Fast, the then keeper of the Emden Church Library, for some essential corrections in Husner's exposition of facts and for further information. The assertion of Elsmann ('Albert Rixäus Hardenberg and Johann Molanus in Priemen' 200–2 n32) that the ex libris *Sum Erasmi, nec muto dominum* only figures in Erasmus' copy of Reuchlin's *De verbo mirifico* (no 176) is refuted by the inscription on the inside of the front board in this copy of the *Rudimenta hebraica.* See, however, the preceding note, added by the editors.

281 Auli Gellij Noctes A

Gellius, Aulus. *Noctium atticarum commentarii*. Venetiis: J. de Tridino, alias Tacuinus, 20 April 1509 (folio).

Erasmus' copy of Aulus Gellius' *Noctes atticae* is now the property of the City Library of Rotterdam.[1] Apart from his ex libris, the customary *Sum Erasmi* written under the colophon, the book also bears more traces of Erasmus' hand: words or jottings in the margin, notes (for example, 'Seneca, de textura') on two flyleaves at the end, and finally, also in the margin, drawings of hands or pointing fingers and four sketches, one of them of the god Terminus. After Erasmus' death the Gellius, along with the rest of his books, was sent to Jan Łaski; it later came into the library of the rector of St Martin's School at Groningen, Regnerus Praedinius, who added to Erasmus' ex libris *Velim mansisses quoad durabit hic mundus, sed postquam fata illum sustulissent, te emi anno 1555, Regnerus Praedinius* 'I would wish that you had remained [in Erasmus' possession] as long as the world shall endure, but after the fates had carried him away, I bought you in the year 1555.'[2]

For Erasmus the *Noctes Atticae* (second century AD) was a storehouse of curiosities, anecdotes, and above all citations from countless classical authors, some of them only known from this source, on which he drew repeatedly from an early date. In the *Adagia* there are 112 references to Aulus Gellius, whose collections Erasmus called 'the most polished and erudite possible,' more than half of them in the first chiliad.[3] Erasmus probably had his own copy of the work from 1509; as he wrote in a letter of 1527, he managed to acquire in Siena, and that must have been in the beginning of 1509, 'a very old edition of Aulus Gellius – the first, if I am not mistaken.'[4] This cannot refer to the Venetian edition now in the City Library of Rotterdam, for that was not yet old in 1509, but had only just

been printed, and had moreover, in a passage discussed in the letter mentioned, a different reading from the one Erasmus had found in his 'very old edition.' Nor was it, as Allen was able to discover from the same reading, the *aeditio prima* of Rome 1469, as Erasmus assumed, or even the second edition of Venice, 1472. It must have been another early printing that he later disposed of after he acquired the more recent Tridino edition. Perhaps the book had been read to tatters after many years of intense study.

We do not know precisely when Erasmus acquired his new edition of Gellius, but it was certainly in his hands when he was preparing the 1528 edition of the *Adagiorum opus*: in a newly inserted passage he cited Ennius with an unusual variant that only appeared in the 1509 edition of the *Noctes Atticae*.[5] He cannot have had it for very long, for otherwise his copy would contain more marginal notes and would show more signs of wear.

In 1527 Erasmus also consulted the Aldine edition of Gellius (1515),[6] which he had probably borrowed from Bonifacius Amerbach, who owned a representative collection of Aldine editions.

1 Husner 'Bibliothek' 253 and Kossmann 'Sporen van Erasmus' hand en een afbeelding van den god Terminus'
2 For other books from Erasmus' library which ended up in Dutch ownership via Praedinius see nos 137, 138, and 218.
3 Phillips *'Adages'* 395 (Appendix III: Analysis of Frequency of Sources); Baron 'Aulus Gellius in the Renaissance and a Manuscript from the School of Guarino' 113; *Adagia* I iv 37 ASD II-1 437:728–9/ CWE 31 346
4 Ep 1824:29–32/32–5
5 *Adagia* III x 79 ASD II-6 577 641–2n/CWE 35 386 n9
6 Ep 1824:37–9/38–40

282 Macrobius de Som. Scip. et de Saturn.

Macrobius, Ambrosius Aurelius Theodosius. *De somnio Scipionis nec non de Saturnalibus libri*. Brixiae: A. de Britanicis, 1501 or another edition (folio).

The works of the Latin philologist and
Neoplatonist Macrobius (late fourth–early
fifth century AD) had often been published
since 1473 and always together; but the
1501 Brescia edition is probably the edition
meant here, for it is the only one in which
the unusual wording of the title – 'De
somnio Scipionis et de Saturnalibus'
– corresponds exactly with the entry
in the *Versandliste*. The title in other
editions reads 'In somnium Scipionis.
Saturnaliorum libri.' The Brescia edition
was obtainable outside Italy: Beatus
Rhenanus bought a copy in 1507 in Paris.[1]
Erasmus may have bought the book there
before his Italian journey. The contents of
Macrobius' work, which compared as a
source of information with the *Noctes
Atticae* of Aulus Gellius and Athenaeus'
Deipnosophistae in the abundance of
subjects dealt with and quotations incorporated, had long been familiar to him. In
1497 he gave his opinion concisely: the
Saturnalia, written in the form of a literary
symposium, attracted him more than the
commentary on Cicero's *Dream of Scipio*;
Aulus Gellius' *Attic Nights*, from which
much of Macrobius had been borrowed,
he valued more highly.[2] But at that moment
he did not yet possess any edition of
Macrobius; and also when he tried to
consult the work three years later, probably
for the first version of the *Adagia*, he had
to appeal to Robert Gaguin to lend it him.[3]

1 Walter *Catalogue Sélestat* 442
2 Ep 61:137–41 / 145–50
3 Ep 121

283 Ludo. Caelij Lectiones antiquae

Rhodiginus (Richerius), Ludovicus Caelius.
Antiquarum lectionum commentarii. Parisiis:
J. Badius, 13 June 1517 or Basileae:
J. Frobenius, 18 March 1517 (folio).

The first edition of this encyclopaedic
work by the Italian philologist Lodovico
Ricchieri (c 1450–1525), who called himself
Rhodiginus, after his birthplace, Rovigo,

appeared in February 1516 from the Aldine
press in Venice and was dedicated to the
bibliophile Jean Grolier. It was reprinted
in the following year by Bade in Paris and,
on the advice of Oecolampadius, by Froben
in Basel.[1] So far as composition and style
were concerned, it did not enjoy a high
reputation – Beatus Rhenanus passed a
damning verdict on it, and advised against
its publication – but thanks to its treasury
of citations from classical texts and from
later writers on such subjects as magic,
the Talmud, and the Kabbala, it formed
a source of information that met a need
of the time.[2] Erasmus' attention was
drawn to the work by Wilhelm Nesen,
when the original edition was offered
at the Frankfurt book fair in the autumn
of 1516.[3] It is not possible to say with
any certainty which edition he acquired.
He drew on the *Antiquae lectiones* for a
supplementary note in the expanded Basel
1517–18 edition of his *Adagia*.[4] Possibly he
owned one of the reprints, either the Paris
edition, which could have reached him at
Leuven around the middle of July 1517
and which gave him occasion to write to
Froben about it, or the Basel edition with
the foreword from the printer to the reader
on the title-page that he had himself
suggested in his letter to Froben.[5] Erasmus
knew Ricchieri from his time at Padua,
where he had met him in 1508. Perhaps
that may explain why he was never as
negative in his comments about Ricchieri's
work as Beatus Rhenanus was. It is true
that Erasmus reproached him with having
repeatedly borrowed without acknowledgment from the *Adagia*, but on his death
he judged him kindly.

1 Renouard *Bibliographie Josse Bade* III 209–10;
   Allen and CWE Ep 602 introductions; AK II 89
   Ep 584 n4
2 Epp 556:27–36 / 27–35, 575:26–31 / 30–4
3 Ep 469:7–9 / 9–11, with 8n / 10n on Ricchieri;
   cf CEBR III 155.
4 *Adagia* I i 2 ASD II-1 90:832–92:856 / CWE 31 34–5;
   Phillips '*Adages*' 123; cf Ep 949 (from Ricchieri):
   10–12 with 11n / 11–12 with 11n.
5 Ep 602

284 Volaterranus

Maffeius, Raphael, Volaterranus.
*Commentariorum urbanorum libri XXXVIII
... Item Oeconomicus Xenophontis ab eodem
latio donatus.* Parisiis: J. Badius / J. Parvus,
1511, or 1515 or another edition (folio).

This short entry undoubtedly refers to
the summary, in thirty-eight books, of
the whole range of knowledge of the time
by Raffaele Maffei (1451–1522), identified
simply as 'Volaterranus,' a name that
described the origin of its author.
Divided into three parts, under the
headings 'Geography,' 'Anthropology,'
and 'Philology,' it was uncritical and lacked
originality but met the need of the time for
information. To understand its importance
as a source of knowledge for the educated
citizen at the beginning of the sixteenth
century, according to Jacob Burkhardt,
one must compare it with all the previous
encyclopaedias.[1] The *editio princeps* was
published in 1506 by Joannes Besicken in
Rome. Josse Bade published the second
edition in Paris in 1511; reprints from his
press followed in 1515 and 1526,[2] and
Froben ventured to bring out yet another
edition in 1530. Erasmus, who probably
never met the author, was familiar with his
publications. Though he says nothing in his
letters about the *Commentaries*, in his *Life
of Jerome* (1516) he criticizes Maffei's
biographical sketch.[3] Moreover, he deals
fairly extensively with Maffei's translation
of the works of St Basil (Rome 1515), of
which he had no high opinion. His preface
(Ep 2611) to the *editio princeps* of Basil's
works in Greek (see nos 189 and 250) is
largely occupied with cataloguing Maffei's
mistranslations in the *Homiliae de laudibus
ieiunii*.[4] Simultaneously Erasmus published
his own, better translation of the two
homilies.[5] In the first edition (Rome 1506)
of the *Commentarii* and later in the Bade
editions, Maffei added a translation of the
Oeconomicus of Xenophon. Erasmus cited
this work several times in his *Institutio*

principis christiani (1516).[6] All of
Xenophon's works had not yet been
published in Greek at that time. Could
Erasmus' attention have been drawn to
the *Oeconomicus* by the translation in the
Bade edition of the *Commentarii*, which
he had perhaps acquired shortly before?

1 *Die Kultur der Renaissance in Italien* 166n / *The
   Civilization of the Renaissance in Italy* 182 n2.
   See also Herding's edition of Jakob Wimpfeling's
   Adolescentia 47–54 and Cochrane *Historians and
   Historiography in the Italian Renaissance* 49–50
   (Cochrane is remarkably favourable in his
   judgment). On Maffei see CEBR II 366–7.
2 Renouard *Bibliographie de Josse Bade* III 384–5
3 Ferguson *Opuscula* 138 / CWE 61 23–4
4 After listing many of the errors of Volaterranus'
   translation he says it would be useless to continue,
   since from these 'it would be abundantly clear
   that there would be as much difference between
   a translation of Basil and his own words as there
   is between a nightingale's song and a crow's
   croaking' (lines 165–7).
5 *Duae homiliae de laudibus ieiunii Erasmo interprete*,
   prefaced with Ep 2617 to Johann Koler (Freiburg:
   J. Emmeus 1532)
6 Cf *Institutio principis christiani* ASD IV-1 133:5–7,
   163:869–70, and 196:897–901 / CWE 27 203, 232,
   and 265.

285 Omnia opera Angeli Politiani

Politianus, Angelus. *Omnia opera et alia
quaedam lectu digna.* Venetiis: in aed. Aldi
Romani, 1498 or Parisiis: J. Badius, 1512
or 1519 (folio).

Angelo Ambrogini Poliziano (1454–94),
scholar, poet, and leading Florentine
humanist, was professor both of Greek
and Latin eloquence, and won high fame;
he enjoyed the friendship and protection
of Lorenzo de' Medici, who entrusted him
with the education of his sons. He made his
name with his *Miscellanea*, first published
in 1489, 'a collection of notes of an
astonishingly rigorous exactitude which
still delights us by the passionate interest
displayed in everything concerning the
reality of the ancient world.' His letters
were also famous, and were described by
Burckhardt, with those of Pietro Bembo,

as 'unrivalled masterpieces, not only of Latin style in general, but also of the more special art of letter-writing.'[1] The 1498 *editio princeps* of his *Omnia opera* contained, besides the *Miscellaneorum centuria prima* and his own letters, those he had received from Giovanni Pico della Mirandola, Ermolao Barbaro, Julius Pomponius Laetus, Battista Guarini, Filippo Beroaldo, Niccolò Leoniceno, Marcantonio Sabellico, and others; his translations from Greek – Plato's *Charmides* (a fragment), Epictetus' *Enchiridion*, Herodian's *Historiae*, the *Problemata* of Alexander of Aphrodisias, Plutarch's *Amatoriae narrationes*, Athanasius on the Psalms; his *praefationes* on classical authors including Homer, Aristotle, Quintilian, Statius, and Suetonius; his essays and his speeches; and finally his poems.[2]

Erasmus probably heard a great deal about Poliziano and his activity in Florence first-hand from his English friends William Grocyn and Thomas Linacre, who had both been his pupils.[3] Erasmus himself had a very high regard for Poliziano, and mentioned him in the same breath as Ermolao Barbaro, as two 'heroic and by common consent quite inimitable figures,' whom he held up as models to Alaard of Amsterdam.[4] He knew Poliziano's work from an early date: not only did he find material in the *Miscellanea* for his *Collectanea*, the first collection of proverbs which he published in 1500,[5] but even before that Poliziano had been for him the modern counterpart of Cicero and the Younger Pliny as a master of the epistolary genre. In his *De conscribendis epistolis*, which, though it was not published until 1529, had been composed in the main as early as 1498 (no 359), he referred many times to the letters of the Florentine humanist.[6] Erasmus probably owned the *editio princeps* of the *Omnia opera* and used it from the year of its publication. But we cannot be certain of this: in Paris, where he

was working on both his *Collectanea* and his handbook on the writing of letters, he could easily have borrowed the book from a literary friend.[7] Thus the possibility remains open that he only later acquired the Bade edition of 1512, which was reprinted in 1519.

1 Chastel *The Age of Humanism* 96; Burckhardt *Die Kultur der Renaissance in Italien* 212 / *The Civilization of the Renaissance in Italy* 239; on Poliziano see also CWE Ep 61:154n; CEBR III 106–8.
2 A summary of the contents is given in Hain *13218 and [Poliziano] *Mostra del Poliziano nella Biblioteca Medicea Laurenziana* (exhibition catalogue) 114 (no 138). On the first edition, see in detail Alessandro Perosa 'Contributi e proposte per la pubblicazione delle opere latine del Poliziano.'
3 Weiss 'Un allieve inglese del Poliziano: Thomas Linacre' 232–3. On Linacre see no 75; on Grocyn, CEBR II 135–6.
4 Epp 531:47–8 / 54–4 (to Guillaume Budé), 485:1–2 / 2–3 (from Alaard of Amsterdam)
5 For example *Adagia* III v 44, III v 75, III vi 62, and III vii 6 ASD II-5 321 838n, 335 note, II-6 375 597n, 429 note / CWE 35 94 note, 110 note, 155 note, 218 note. Cf Heinimann 'Zu den Anfängen der humanistischen Paroemiologie' 181.
6 *De conscribendis epistolis* ASD I-2 265 / CWE 25 44 (and cf *Conficiendarum epistolarum formula* CWE 25 260); see the indexes in ASD I-2 and CWE 26 for the many references to Poliziano's letters. Cf Gerlo 'L'Opus *de conscribendis epistolis*' 228
7 On various books that Erasmus borrowed from the well-stocked library of Robert Gaguin see Epp 67–8 (Valla *Dialectica*; cf no 364 #3), 121 (Macrobius), 122 (George of Trebizond *De rhetoricis praeceptionibus*).

286 Nonius Marcellus, Festus Pompeius Varro.

Nonius Marcellus. *De proprietate sermonum*; Sextus Pompeius Festus. *De verborum significatione*; Marcus Terentius Varro. *De lingua latina*; *De analogia*. A folio edition.

An unidentifiable edition of the works of three Roman grammarians, which were frequently printed together from 1480 on, always in folio. The first edition appeared at Parma;[1] other fifteenth-century editions were printed in Venice. After the turn of the century editions appeared in Milan

(1500 and 1510), Venice (1502), and Paris
(including one in 1511 by E. de Gourmont
and another in 1519 for Jean Petit).
Probably Erasmus already owned the
edition alluded to here before he acquired
the Aldine edition of the *Cornucopia* of
Perotti that also contained the works of the
three grammarians (see no 384). He used
one or both of these editions intensively in
the last years of his life; the eighth edition
of his *Adagia* (1533), includes a remarkable
number of new references to Nonius
Marcellus, Pompeius Festus and, to a lesser
extent, Varro also, particularly in the 488
proverbs added for the first time.[2]

1 Hain 11903
2 Phillips *'Adages'* 393–403 (Appendix III Analysis of
   Frequency of Sources); see for example *Adagia* II
   vii 11, II ix 100, III vii 58 ASD II-4 94:181–5 with
   181n (95) and 278:266–7 with 266n, II-6 455:552–7
   with 556n/CWE 34 8 with n4 (320), 129 with n3
   (359), CWE 35 250–1 with nn1 and 2.

287 Comment. Budaei in linguam Graecam

Budaeus, Gulielmus. *Commentarii linguae
graecae.* Basileae: J. Bebelius, March 1530
(folio).

Guillaume Budé had already collected
materials for his Greek lexicon before 1520.
Erasmus had repeatedly encouraged him in
this: 'You might render a very great service
to Greek studies,' he wrote to Budé in 1524,
'if you were to make a really full lexicon,
not only listing the words but explaining
the idioms and turns of speech peculiar to
Greek when these are not generally known
and obvious.' In 1527, reacting to the still
vague report that the book was to appear,
he writes, 'You have at last begun to do
what I have long wanted you to do.'[1] His
interest in the publication was not dimin-
ished by the breach with Budé caused
by his *Ciceronianus* the following year.
Erasmus awaited the appearance of the
book with all the more excitement because
rumour had it that a 'not very flattering'
reference was made to him in the text.[2]
His fear proved unfounded.

Presumably Erasmus did not possess
the original edition (Paris: Josse Bade,
September 1529). Budé had no reason to
send him a copy after the breach, and the
book was practically unobtainable in the
German-speaking countries.[3] Konrad
Resch, bookseller and publisher at Basel,
managed to ensure, as Erasmus and
Amerbach suspected, that no copies
got through, so that he would have more
chance of success in having Bebel of Basel
reprint the copy he, Resch, had managed
to obtain 'still wet from Bade's press.'[4]
In October 1529 Amerbach sent a specimen of part of the reprint to Erasmus,
who suggested that some errors he had
discovered should be passed on to Bebel.[5]
It was probably Bebel's reprint that was
in Erasmus' library.[6]

1 Epp 1233:163–7 with 166n/179–82 with n26
   (page 442), 1794:2–6/2–7
2 Ep 2052:5–8/7–10; cf Epp 2027:30–3/31–3,
   2077:57–9/66–8.
3 Ep 2221:8–10/8–10
4 Epp 2223:2–3/2–4, 2224:1–5/1–6. On Resch
   see Grimm 'Buchführer' 1391–3; CEBR III 141–2.
5 Epp 2224:5–6/6–7, 2231:72–8/78–85
6 Ep 2379:270–1, 391–2/267–9, 388–90

288 Annota. Budaei in Pandectas

Budaeus, Gulielmus. *Annotationes in
quatuor et viginti Pandectarum libros.*
[Parisiis:] off. Ascensiana, 17 November
1508 (folio).

In 1536 Erasmus probably still owned the
original edition of Guillaume Budé's first
important work. We find the reflection
of his thorough acquaintance with the
text early in his correspondence with the
French Hellenist. 'Your Annotations on
the Pandects and your *De Asse*,' he wrote
in October 1516, 'I regard as oracles, in
which I take refuge when confronted with a
problem on which the usual authorities are
no help.'[1] Budé's attempt to go behind the
glosses of later commentators and reconstruct the pure text of the Pandects from
the manuscripts was entirely in harmony

with Erasmus' own critical ideal of going back to the sources in order to purify the text of the Bible. Erasmus must also have been impressed by the treasure house of lexicographical material collected in the *Annotationes*. He was not blind to the work's weaknesses: he pointed out that numerous digressions wandered too far from the subject and rebuked the author on this point.[2] But this could not detract from his growing admiration for Budé, who, by a happy translation of the text of Luke 1:4 in the *Annotationes*, also gave Erasmus the opportunity to bear enthusiastic witness to it. Beatus Rhenanus had pointed out the passage to him; Erasmus, while the sheets of his *Novum instrumentum* were still coming from the press, hastened to the printing house and made the printer insert in his annotation on the passage of Luke's Gospel not only a reference to Budé's translation but a strikingly enthusiastic dithyrambic eulogy of his French friend.[3] In the 1535 edition of the New Testament, when the breach between the two men had become irreparable, the eulogy is absent.

1 Ep 480:185–8/197–9
2 Ep 531:273–59/303–51
3 Ep 403:25–59/25–62; cf Garanderie
   Correspondance 53–4 n12. For the eulogy, see
   Garanderie 269–70 (Appendix 1)/ ASD vi-5 450–3
   (apparatus criticus).

289 Epistolae Budaei

Budaeus, Gulielmus. *Epistolarum latinarum lib. v. Graecarum item lib. i.* [Parisiis:] J. Badius, February 1531 (folio).

A folio edition that contained the letters of Guillaume Budé, first published in two previous quarto collections (Paris: Josse Bade 1520 and 1522) and a further twenty letters written since then. Erasmus had looked forward to its publication with some anxiety, for he had been told that he was depicted in one or more of the letters as hostile to the French, a charge (perhaps

spread, as he wrote, by people who would be pleased to see him on bad terms with Budé) against which he defended himself at length in anticipation.[1] His fear was premature. After the appearance of the collection of letters, he wrote to Jacques Toussain, praising him for the *scholia* he had added, thanks to which the letters could be read with more profit, and related how his *famulus* read aloud to him after meals while he himself walked about the room.[2] He also wrote to others in praise of the letters.[3]

1 Epp 2261:55–66/61–72, 2291:55–63/61–70
2 Ep 2449:76–81/76–81. The scholia had earlier
   been published separately; see no 38 #2.
3 For example Epp 2453:3–4/5–6 and 2517:4–7
   (both to Caspar Ursinus Velius)

290 Philologia Budaei

Budaeus, Gulielmus. *De philologia.* [Parisiis:] J. Badius, November 1532 (folio).

A treatise that deals with philology in a broader sense than the title suggests and gives a survey of thirty years of humanism in France.[1]

1 [Budé, G.] *Guillaume Budé* (exhibition catalogue)
   28 no 103

291 Budaeus de Asse

Budaeus, Gulielmus. *De asse et partibus eius libri quinque.* [Parisiis:] in aed. Ascensianis, 15 March 1515 (folio).

The *editio princeps* of Budé's best known work, in which an attempt was made 'to define the relative money values of classical and Renaissance times and thereby to determine the conditions of ancient civilization.'[1] For Erasmus the *Annotations on the Pandects* and *On the As* were 'oracles' (cf no 288). But in spite of his admiration for the erudition accumulated in *De asse*, he criticized Budé's use of it. Budé asked him to read parts of the book carefully and tell him what he thought of them. Erasmus complied with the request

and reread the passages. The learned
digressions (which indeed made up
almost a third of the text), like those in the
Annotationes in Pandectas, were too much
for him. He wondered whether an exasper-
ated reader might think, 'This is all very
good and splendid, but what has it to do
with the "as"?'[2]

1 Allen Ep 403 introduction. On Budé and his
  relationship with Erasmus see also CWE Ep 403
  introduction; CEBR I 212–17.
2 Epp 435:45–68/48–73 (from Budé), 480:194–
  265/205–82 (to Budé; the lines quoted are
  257–9/274–5).

292 Assis Budaei

Budaeus Gulielmus. *De asse* … [2a ed.].
Parisiis: in aed. Ascensianis, 14 October
1516 (folio).

Besides the original edition of Budé's *De
asse* (no 291), Erasmus also possessed the
expanded second edition, which had been
provided by Bade, during Budé's absence,
with numerous new marginal *glossemata
et scholia* (glosses and annotations) and
a short list of obscure terms, to make
the work more accessible to the reader.
Erasmus had ordered the new edition long
before he finally managed to extract the
book from the hands of the bookbinders in
February 1517. He proposed to read right
through both editions 'from cover to cover,'
to see more exactly what Budé had altered
or added to the text.[1]

1 Ep 531:459–68/512–21 with 520n; cf Garanderie
  Correspondance 84 n14.

293 Stephanus Niger.

Niger, Stephanus. *Dialogus quo quicquid in
graecarum literarum penetralibus reconditum … in lucem propagatur. His accedunt
Philostrati Heroica latinitate donata [etc].*
Mediolani: in off. Minutiana, 1517 (folio).

No other work in folio of Stephanus
Niger (born c 1475), pupil of Demetrius
Chalcondyles and during the French

occupation for many years professor of
Greek at Milan, can be traced. The
Dialogus, dedicated to Jean Grolier, the
well-known bibliophile who at the time
was treasurer of Milan in the service of
the French government, contained the first
edition of Philostratus' *Heroicus* translated
by Niger, preceded by his summary of
Pausanias' *Periegesis* presented in dialogue
form.[1] Erasmus may not have had direct
connections with Milan at this time, but
a curious coincidence may relate to the
presence of this book in his library. The
bookseller Francesco Giulio Calvo from
Pavia visited Erasmus at Leuven in April
1518, bringing with him a collection of
books published recently in Italy;[2] and it
was on that occasion that he persuaded
him to write a long letter to Jean Grolier
(Ep 831). About this first contact, which
was not continued, the Milanese printer
of Niger's book, Alessandro Minuziano,
was quite well informed. He copied
Erasmus' letter at once into his private
letter-book, and later on had also at his
disposal a copy of Grolier's letter in reply.[3]

1 According to its subtitle it was called *Dialogus,
  in quem quicquid apud Pausaniam scitu dignum
  legitur … congessit Stephanus Niger tam graece,
  quam latine.*
2 Ep 832:29–31/32–4. Cf nos 98 and 107.
3 See Allen IV xxviii, addendum to Ep 831 introduction, page 297; cf Allen Ep 1002:27n.

294 Theocritus cum alijs opusculis graecis

Theocritus. *Eclogae triginta … Catonis
Romani sententiae … Sententiae septem
sapientium … Theognidis sententiae
elegiacae. Sententiae monostichi per capita
ex variis poetis. Aurea carmina Pythagorae.
Phocylidae poema admonitorium. Carmina
sibyllae erythreae de Christo Jesu … Hesiodi
Theogonia. Eiusdem scutum Hercolis …
Georgicon … [omnia graece].* Venetiis: char.
Aldi Manucii, February 1495 (folio).

The words 'cum aliis' in the description of
this book in the *Versandliste* point conclusively to this Aldine edition of 1495/6,[1]

since every other edition of Theocritus has only his name on the title-page or first page (cf nos 98, 99, and 106). Aldo Manuzio dedicated the work to his revered master Battista Guarini, who had also been the teacher of Josse Bade at Ferrara, and if the *Compendium vitae* may be believed, of Erasmus' father Gerard.[2] When Erasmus acquired the book cannot be established. Theocritus is not referred to in the *editio princeps* of his *Adagiorum collectanea* (Paris 1500). He was mentioned or quoted, however, in two of the twenty new proverbs added in the edition of the *Collectanea* published by Jean Petit and Josse Bade (Paris 1506/7).[3] Unless he drew his quotations from some secondary source, therefore, Erasmus was already in a position to make use of the Aldine edition of 1495 before his Italian journey. But that does not necessarily mean that the copy then in his hands was his own. He may have acquired the book only at a later date; perhaps he brought it back from Italy or purchased it afterwards, around 1511, when, with the help of Josse Bade in Paris and his connections in the book trade, he enlarged his library on a considerable scale.[4]

1 Hain-Copinger 15477
2 See Firmin-Didot *Alde Manuce et l'Hellénisme à Venise* 74–7; Allen Ep 183 introduction; *Compendium vitae* Allen I 48:24/CWE 4 404:28–9.
3 ASD II-9 27–8, 269
4 Cf no 72 with n2.

295 Cornucopiae et Horti Adonidis grae. Al.

Thesaurus Cornucopiae et Horti Adonidis. Venetiis: Aldus Manutius, August 1496 (folio).

A collection of texts of Greek grammarians dealing in particular with orthography and accentuation, originally compiled with the collaboration of Poliziano by his pupil Varinus (Guarino) Favorinus and Carolus Antenoreus and now, revised and

augmented, first published by Aldo Manuzio and his friend Urbano Valeriani (Bolzanius).[1] The *Thesaurus*, which, among other things, contained treatises by Aelius Dionysius, Eustathius, Herodianos, Choeroboscus and Johannes Grammaticus, followed the edition of Theodorus Gaza, Apollonius Grammaticus, and Herodianos – also present in Erasmus' library (no 347) – with which Aldo had begun a planned series of editions of all the Greek grammarians in 1495.

1 GW 7571 introduction; Geanakoplos *Greek Scholars in Venice* 172; Lemke *Aldus Manutius and his Thesaurus Cornucopiae of 1496* 13 (Aldo's preface)

296 Pollux de rerum uocabulis. Aldi

Pollux, Julius. *Onomastikon* [graece]. Venetiis: Aldus, April 1502 (folio).

The *editio princeps* of the ten-volume *Onomasticon*, preserved only in excerpts, of Julius Pollux, a Greek sophist who lived at Athens at the time of the emperors Marcus Aurelius and Commodus.[1] Unlike the other Greek dictionaries, the *Onomasticon* is not arranged alphabetically but by subjects (the second book, for example, deals with the human body and the fifth contains the terminology of hunting). The text is preceded by a letter from the Florentine humanist Antonio Franchini to the English physician Thomas Linacre, a friend of Erasmus, on Italian and English humanism. Pollux' work was an invaluable source of information and, like the *Noctes Atticae* of Aulus Gellius and Athenaeus' *Deipnosophistae*, contained fragments of writers now lost. Erasmus refers to the *Onomasticon* in his *De ratione studii* (1511)[2] and in the introduction to his edition of *De copia*.[3] In his *Institutio principis christiani* he took over a long citation in Greek (with translation) from Pollux, on the theme of kings and tyrants.[4] He also used the *Onomasticon* extensively in the *Adagia*.[5]

1 Pauly-Wissowa x-1 773–9 sv Iulius Pollux;
  OCD 1209 sv Pollux, Iulius
2 ASD I-2 123:2–3 / CWE 24 674:6–8
3 Ep 260:47–9 / 53–6; ASD I-6 22 / CWE 24 285:52–6
4 ASD IV-1 121 and 160–2:766–815 / CWE 27 229–30;
  cf Herding 'Isokrates, Erasmus und die "Institutio
  principis Christiani"' 118.
5 *Adagia* I i 4 CWE 31 53 31n

297 Hesychij dictiona. grae.

Hesychius Alexandrinus. *Dictionarium graece*. Venetiis: in aed. Aldi et Andreae soceri, August 1514 (folio).

The dictionary compiled by the grammarian Hesychius of Alexandria (fifth or sixth century AD), based mainly on the older alphabetical lexicon, now lost, of Diogenianus, is the most extensive ancient Greek lexicon that has been preserved.[1] Marcus Musurus edited it from the only surviving manuscript, dating from the fifteenth century, which Aldo Manuzio borrowed on his behalf from a Mantuan nobleman. The manuscript is now in the library of San Marco in Venice.[2] Erasmus must have acquired the book fairly soon after its publication, for when he was preparing the new edition of the *Adagia* to be published in November 1517 he took over his preface to the reader from the previous edition of 1515 unaltered but inserted a passage on the lexicon of Hesychius, which was evidently now at his disposal.[3] In the long run he made good use of it, quoting it about 140 times; but three-quarters of these references were added in the revisions of 1526, 1528, and 1533.[4]

In 1554 Erasmus' copy of Hesychius was offered for sale by Gérard Mortaigne, who had bought it from Jan Łaski, and the lexicon was among the books sent for approval to the rector of the Groningen School Regnerus Praedinius. According to him, the book was 'completely worn out.'[5] Probably Praedinius, a prospective buyer wanting to depress the price, exaggerated. Be that as it may, the lexicon survived and

was sold in 1643 at auction in Leiden, entered in the auction catalogue as '*Lexicon Hesychii Graece*, apud Aldum 1514. Olim exemplar Erasmi.'[6] The book was part of the estate left by J. Lydius, minister at Oudewater and son of Martinus Lydius, from 1588 until 1601 professor of theology in the University of Franeker and there a colleague of J. Arcerius Theodoretus, professor of Greek from 1589 until his death in 1604. The latter, an acknowledged authority in the field of Greek studies, was one of Erasmus' greatest admirers and possessed several books from his library.

1 Pauly-Wissowa VIII 1317–22 and *Der Kleine Pauly*
  II 1120–1 sv Hesychios; OCD 701–2 sv Hesychius
2 Cod. Marcianus gr 522. Cf Geanakoplos *Greek
  Scholars in Venice* 154; CWE 31 11 (*Adagia*
  [Introduction] v) 35n.
3 Ep 269:68–72 / 74–9; on the 1517 addition see
  Allen's introduction and the textual note at line 68.
4 For this information I am indebted to the late Sir
  Roger Mynors.
5 *liber attritus admodum*; Gabbema *Epistolarum
  centuriae tres* 169 (Ep 68)
6 'The *Greek Lexicon* of Hesychius, published by
  Aldus in 1514. Formerly Erasmus' copy.' For the
  catalogue of the auction see Engels 'Vroeger
  eigendom van Erasmus' 60.

298 Valerius Maximus cum commento

Valerius Maximus. [*Facta et dicta memorabilia*] *cum commento Oliverii Arzignanensis Vicentini*. Probably a Venetian folio edition from the late fifteenth or early sixteenth century.

The partly historical and partly anecdotal 'memorable facts and sayings' collected by Valerius Maximus under the Emperor Tiberius, for the use of teaching in the schools of rhetoric, appeared so frequently in print from c 1470,[1] that it is impossible to identify the edition alluded to here with any exactitude. It was very probably a folio, and certainly one with the commentary of the humanist Oliverus Arzignanensis of Vicenza, the earliest version of which appeared in 1487.[2] The entry in the

Versandliste could also refer to one of the editions, almost exclusively Venetian, from the end of the fifteenth and the first years of the sixteenth century, on the title-page of which the work was presented under the identical short title as the one given here, 'Valerius Maximus cum commento,' albeit with the name of the commentator. Editions were published in Venice by B. Locatellus in 1493, B. de Zanis in 1497, A. Rubeus Vercellensis in 1500 and 1503, and Albertus de Lisona in 1503; in Milan, A. Minutianus published an edition in 1505. It would not be surprising if Erasmus had acquired the work, a rich source for him, at an early date and perhaps brought it back with him from Italy. But this cannot be proved; possibly he bought the *Valerius Maximus cum duplici commentario* published by Bade and Petit in 1510 and reissued in 1513, some years later, when he enlarged his library on a considerable scale.[3] The later Petit editions of 1517 and 1522, edited by Erasmus' friend Nicolas Bérault, can probably be left out of consideration, since their title has a completely different wording.

Quotations from Valerius Maximus are found throughout the *Adagia*, though not in great number (twenty-seven in all). But Erasmus had his copy of the popular reference work ready to hand until the last: as late as 1533 he added two sentences from it to the introduction of the latest revision.

1 Hain *15773
2 Hain *15789. On Oliviero d'Arrignano see Cosenza *Italian Humanists* sv; *Indice biografico Italiano* I (1993) 105.
3 Renouard *Bibliographie de Josse Bade* III 316–18; V 90. The second commentator was the learned printer-publisher Josse Bade himself.
4 CWE 31 23 (*Adagia* [Introduction] xii) 59n

299 Diony. Halicarnaseus Latine uersus

Dionysius Halicarnaseus. *Antiquitatum sive originum Romanarum libri XI. Adiuncta est chronologia.* Basileae: off. Frobeniana,

March 1532 or one of the earlier printings (folio).

The work of Dionysius of Halicarnassus, written in Greek, of which about half is preserved, complements Polybius and deals with the earliest history of Rome until shortly before the Punic war. Henricus Glareanus, who re-edited and annotated for Froben the text in the translation of Lapo Birago, sent a copy of the book to King Ferdinand. In order to ensure that the present achieved its aim, Erasmus wrote a letter to Bernhard von Cles, recommending the editor to the king, but not without first having praised the prince in flattering terms; for himself, he wrote, almost too emphatically, he had nothing to ask.[1] The effect was not long delayed. Von Cles, an influential counsellor of the king and a patron of Erasmus, used his good offices and managed to obtain from the king a gift of 50 Rhenish gulden for Glareanus and 150 for Erasmus, to which he himself added a further 50 gulden for Erasmus' use.[2] It may have been from the March 1532 edition that Erasmus added a reference to Dionysius' *Roman History* in the May 1533 edition of the *Adagia*.[3]

1 Ep 2651, especially lines 50–73; see also Ep 2655 (Cles' response).
2 Ep 2801; cf on the payment Ep 2808:2–13.
3 *Adagia* I iv 60 ASD II-1 452:53–5/CWE 31 361 9n

300 Eutrop. Paulus Diaco. de gestis Lan // gobardorum et Alexan. Genial. die. libri

Eutropius. *Romana historia universa … ex diversorum authorum monumentis collecta. Pauli Diaconi de gestis Langobardorum libri VI.* Basileae: H. Frobenius et N. Episcopius, August 1532 (folio).

bound with

Alexandro, Alexander ab. *Genialium dierum libri VI.* Parisiis: Gerardus Morrhius, 1532 (folio).

1/ The first item in this composite volume was the most important work of Paul the Deacon or Paulus Wernefridi (c 739–799?), an incomplete history of the Lombards from 568 to 744. The text, prepared for the press and introduced by Sigismundus Gelenius, corrector for the Froben firm and younger friend of Erasmus,[1] was based on the very careless *editio princeps* of Josse Bade (Paris 1514), though in the meantime Konrad Peutinger had published another excellent edition of the book.[2] The *Historia de gestis Langobardorum* is preceded by Eutropius' *Breviarium historiae Romanae*, a fourth-century compendium up to the year 364, revised by Paul the Deacon and supplemented by him with a sequel to Justinian (553).

2/ Alessandro d'Alessandro (1461–1523), protonotary of the kingdom of Naples and abbot of Carbone, spent his last years in Rome, where he maintained close relations with the world of learning during the pontificate of Leo x.[3] His *Dies geniales*, comparable in its conception with such works as the *Noctes Atticae* of Aulus Gellius and the *Saturnalia* of Macrobius, dealt with Roman antiquities, but at the same time discussed subjects of the most diverse character in confusing abundance.[4] Moreover, notes about his personal encounters with important contemporaries are incorporated into the book. These anecdotes in particular provoked Erasmus' curiosity, and he wanted to know who the author was. 'I wonder who that Alessandro d'Alessandro is,' he wrote in May 1533 to Viglius Zuichemus. 'He knows all the famous men in Italy ... He is familiar with everyone, but no one knows him.'[5] Allen's successors did not understand why Erasmus should be interested in him at that moment; but the explanation may be that a copy of the Paris reissue of the book (the *editio princeps* was published in Rome by I. Mazochius in 1522) had come into his hands shortly before. Probably it was a gift

from the publisher Gerard Morrhy, a native of Kampen and thus a compatriot, and now printer to the Sorbonne, who hoped to make personal contact by sending Erasmus a product of his press.[6] In 1532 he wrote an expansive letter to Erasmus (Ep 2633); it is quite plausible that he wanted to give the *Dies geniales*, a recent publication, to the famous humanist as a special mark of attention.

1. On Gelenius see no 303.
2. See Potthast *Bibliotheca historica medii aevi* II 900.
3. On Alessandro see Allen Ep 2810:110n; Maffei *Alessandro d'Alessandro, giureconsulto umanista*; CEBR I 32.
4. Thorndike *A History of Magic and Experimental Science* V 142–3
5. Ep 2810:109–12
6. Cf Ep 2311:13–15/13–14.

301 Rhapsodiae Sabellici pars prima / Pars secunda / Pars tertia.

Sabellicus, Marcus Antonius Coccius. *Rapsodie historiarum enneadum ab orbe condito ad annum 1504. Pars prima (–tertia)*. Parisiis: in aed. Ascensianis, 1509 (folio).

Marcantonio Coccio (1436–1506), whose pen name was Sabellico, won some fame as a poet – his elegies to Mary were read among German humanists, and Erasmus adopted many phrases and motifs from them, especially in his Paean to St Mary[1] – but is remembered chiefly as an historian. His first great work, the *Rerum Venetarum ab urbe condita libri XXXIII*, though rather uncritical of its sources, quickly written, and no longer highly regarded, earned high praise from the rulers of the city of the doges for its panegyric character and won its author a chair at the school of San Marco in the year of its publication, 1487. From 1487 to his death he was also the head of the library of San Marco. He was the first Italian humanist who ventured, in his *Enneades* listed here, to attempt a history of the world from the earliest times (largely paraphrased from the Old Testament) until his own day, of which he gave only a confused picture: 'the major and minor events of the author's own times' writes Cochrane, 'were thrown in, helter-skelter, as they came across his desk.'[2] The *editio princeps* of the work appeared at Venice in 1498, but the division into three parts, explicitly mentioned in the *Versandliste* entry, makes it a plausible assumption that Erasmus possessed the identical Bade edition of 1509.[3] Erasmus may have acquired it about 1511; he purchased many books in Paris around this time.[4] In the *Ciceronianus* Erasmus acknowledged Sabellico's 'natural gift of eloquence' and his distinction in history.[5]

1 Reedijk *Poems* no 19 / ASD I-7 and CWE 85–6 no 110. Cf Reedijk *Poems* 5 / ASD I-7 31 / CWE 85–6 xxxii. During Erasmus' stay in the monastery at Steyn in 1490, the Deventer printer Pafraet published Sabellico's *In natalem diem divae virginis Mariae.*
2 Cochrane *Historians and Historiography in the Italian Renaissance* 83–6; cf also Fueter *Geschichte der neueren Historiographie* 30–5; Gilbert 'Biondo, Sabellico and the Beginnings of Venetian Historiography.' On Sabellico see also CEBR III 181–2.
3 Adams s 21; Renouard *Bibliographie de Josse Bade* III 222–4
4 Cf no 72 with n2.
5 ASD I-2 668:17–19 / CWE 28 418

302 Eusebius de Euang. praeparatione uers. / à Trapezon. et Platynae Historia.

Eusebius Caesariensis. *De evangelica praeparatione opus interprete Georgio Trapezuntio e graeco in latinum versum.* Venetiis: about 1500 (folio).

bound with

Platina, Bartholomaeus Sacchi de. *Platynae hystoria de vitis pontificum.* Venetiis: P. Pincius, 1504 or another Venetian edition of about the same date (folio).

Two folios, possibly Venetian, of shortly before or after the turn of the century, bound in one volume.

1/ To justify the attitude that the Christians took towards the faith of the Jews, Eusebius of Caesarea (c 260–c 340) in his *Praeparatio evangelica* demonstrated, from Greek and Jewish authors, the superiority of the Hebrew religion over the cosmogony and mythology of the pagans.[1] Many of the citations he discussed were borrowed from lost works of classical writers and thus have a value quite apart from their context. The first edition of this apologetic work appeared in the translation by George of Trebizond in 1470, from the press of N. Jensen in Venice.[2] Around the turn of the century, several new editions followed, practically all of them in Venice, for example: B. Benalius 1497;[3] B. de Zanis 1498–1500;[4] B. Vercellensis 1501.

2/ Bartolomeo Platina Sacchi (1421–81), a pupil of Johannes Argyropoulos, was first the protégé of Pope Pius II and later of Sixtus IV, who appointed him curator of the Vatican Library. In that capacity he wrote his stylistically elegant though rather uncritical lives of the popes, from Christ to Paul II, which later became popular. They were first published in 1479 by J. Manthen in Venice and reprinted many times thereafter.[5] The fifteenth-century editions were always presented as *Vitae pontificum.* Only in some of the early sixteenth-century editions were these words of the title preceded, as in the short title in the *Versandliste,* by the word 'Historia.' Could Erasmus have owned one of these editions? The *Hystoria de vitis pontificum* published by P. Pincio in Venice in 1504 was the first to include, besides the papal biographies, a 'part' containing the minor works of Platina.[6] Two of these were mentioned by Erasmus in his *Ciceronianus* (1529); their language must have made more impression on him than the historical works of their author. Erasmus made Nosoponus say that

Platina, in his dialogue *De optimo cive* and *Panegyricus in Bessarionem*, approached the model of Cicero to some extent, but remained at such a distance from it that he was not entitled to the honourable name of a Ciceronian.[7]

1 von Christ *Geschichte der griechischen Litteratur* II-2 1364
2 GW 9440
3 GW 9444
4 GW 9445
5 Fueter *Geschichte der neueren Historiographie* 47–9 and Cochrane *Historians and Historiography in the Italian Renaissance* 54–5. On Platina see also CEBR III 100–1.
6 The Paris reprint (at the expense of F. Regnault 1505) is in octavo and thus not eligible.
7 ASD I-2 666:9–12 / CWE 28 417

303 Arriani et Hannonis Periplus, Plutar // chus de Flumi. et montibus, Strab. comp. grae.

Arrianus; Hanno. *Arriani & Hannonis periplus. [Pseudo-] Plutarchus de fluminibus & montibus. Strabonis epitome.* [Graece.] Basileae: H. Frobenius & N. Episcopius, 1533 (quarto).

The account of the circumnavigation of the Black Sea by Flavius Arrianus and the narrative of the voyage along the west African coast by the Carthaginian explorer Hanno were published with other Greek geographical texts by Sigismundus Gelenius, partly from a tenth-century manuscript from the Dominican monastery at Basel.[1] Erasmus' copy was undoubtedly a gift, either from the editor or from the publisher, or perhaps from both. The Czech Zikmund Hrubý z Jelení, better known as Gelenius (c 1498–1554), came to Basel in c 1524 after studying at Bologna and Venice. For a time he belonged to the *familia* of Erasmus, and then worked as a scholarly corrector in the Froben press. He enjoyed the complete confidence of Erasmus, who recommended him to Froben and in his will of 1527 not only remembered him with legacies of clothing

and money, but also nominated him as one of the supervisors of the future complete edition of his works. In 1536 Erasmus left him a bequest of 150 ducats.[2] Gelenius was involved as corrector in preparing for the press Erasmus' editions of the texts of Pliny (1525), the *Novum Testamentum* (1527), and Ambrose (1527); the Froben firm later entrusted him with the editing of Paul the Deacon's history of the Lombards (see no 300 #1), published in 1532. Gelenius (and not Erasmus) was also the anonymous editor of the Froben Ptolemy (see no 101). Reedijk has drawn attention to the important part Gelenius must have played in preparing the Froben edition of the *Opera omnia* after Erasmus' death (1538–40).[3]

1 Vernet 'Les manuscrits grecs de Jean de Raguse' 95 (no 43). The codex is now in the Vatican Library; see Stevenson *Codices manuscripti Palatini graeci Bibliothecae Vaticani* 254–7 (MS *398), where it is wrongly said to have once belonged to the library of the monastery of Spanheim.
2 On him see Ep 1702:8n / n1; CEBR III 84–5. Cf Allen VI Appendix 19 'Erasmus' First Will' 504:29–30, 62 / CWE 12 542–3:24–5, 54; Allen XI Appendix 25 'Erasmus' Last Will' 364:23.
3 ASD I-1 ix; Reedijk *Tandem bona causa triumphat* 56

304 Diogenis Laertij de uitis lib. 10. grae. Frob.

Diogenes Laertius. *De vitis, decretis & responsis celebrium philosophorum libri decem.* [Graece.] Basileae: H. Frobenius & N. Episcopius, 1533 (quarto).

The *editio princeps* of the original text of Diogenes Laertius' work on the Greek philosophers and their doctrines, probably compiled towards the end of the third century. Thanks to its more than a thousand citations, many of them not preserved elsewhere, and its excerpts from several hundred authors, it forms, in spite of its anecdotal character, a not unimportant source for the history of Greek philosophy. Only the tenth and last part, which is entirely devoted to Epicurus, contains authentic material.[1] Erasmus clearly made use of the newly available Greek text to rephrase or expand several adages for the revised edition of the *Adagia* that appeared in the same year.[2] For the Latin editions, on which Erasmus was dependent before 1533, see nos 305 and 306 #2.

1 *Der Kleine Pauly* II 45–6 sv Diogenes Laertios; OCD 474–5 sv Diogenes Laertius
2 See for example *Adagia* III ii 4 and III vi 21 ASD II-5 108 with 89n, 91n, 93n (109) and II-6 356 with 209n (357)/CWE 34 226 with note (390) and CWE 35 135 with n2.

305 Diogenes Laertius Latine

Diogenes Laertius. *De vita et moribus philosophorum libri decem*. [Ambrogio Traversari interpr.] Basileae: V. Curio, 1524 (quarto).

Erasmus' copy of this Basel edition of the Latin translation of Diogenes Laertius' *Lives of the Philosophers* has been preserved. Husner stated that in 1936 it was in the possession of Professor Rosenblatt in Cracow and had been bought by him from an antiquarian bookseller in that city.[1] After the Second World War the book found its way to the United States, and not long after the death of its owner in 1947 it was bought for the Beinecke rare book and manuscript library, part of the Yale University Library in New Haven, Connecticut.[2] The *Sum Erasmi* is missing from the book, but an inscription on the last folio reads: *Ex bibliothecae Erasmi Roterodani* [sic] *donatum per clarissimum virum d. Joannem a Lasko. 1548 penultima februarii* 'From the library of Erasmus of Rotterdam, given by the most distinguished Jan Łaski. 28 February 1548.' On the penultimate folio three names are written: 'Gerardus Assendelft Abol de Colstor Jodocus Sasbout.' All three were on good terms with Erasmus as jurists and members of the Court of Holland (the first being its president). Erasmus also saw them as closely associated with each other: in May

1532 he asked Sasbout to regard a letter to him as also being addressed to the two others.[3] It is assumed that his fellow Hollanders presented the edition of Diogenes Laertius to Erasmus as a gift. Nothing is known of the book's vicissitudes between 1536 and 1936. On folio 2 recto there is another owner's mark, but it is largely illegible even under ultraviolet light. The marginalia in the text, less than a dozen words in total, are written in an unknown hand.[4] The volume is exceptional in having retained its sixteenth-century binding. The boards are covered in pigskin, blind-tooled with rolls in concentric frames.[5] Unfortunately it was not possible from the rubbing available to identify and date exactly the typical Renaissance rolls. Perhaps the material provides a pointer to the origin of the volume: pigskin bindings were familiar in the Germanic countries, including Switzerland, but not in the Low Countries.[6] There is quite a good chance, therefore, that the book was bound in Basel. Erasmus probably used this copy of the translation of Diogenes Laertius when he inserted a new passage in revising the text for his edition of the *Adagia* in 1528.[7]

1 Husner 'Bibliothek' 254–5 and 258
2 I am grateful to Mr Francis O. Mattson of the New York Public Library and Mrs Kit Currie of the firm of H.P. Kraus, New York, who helped me to trace the book.
3 Ep 2645:40–7. On Gerrit van Assendelft, see *Nieuw Nederlandsch Biografisch Woordenboek* VII 34–6 and CEBR I 74; on Abel van Colster, Allen Ep 2800 introduction and CEBR I 332; and on Joost Sasbout, *Nieuw Nederlandsch Biografisch Woordenboek* II 1265–6 and CEBR III 196–7.
4 ter Horst 'Enkele aanteekeningen over de bibliotheek van Erasmus' 231
5 I am grateful to Mr Robert Babcock, curator of early books and manuscripts of the Beinecke Library, and Mrs Jane Greenfield of the conservation department for the information they supplied on the owners' marks and marginalia in the volume and on the binding.
6 I am indebted to Dr Jan Storm van Leeuwen in The Hague for this information.
7 *Adagia* III i 32 ASD II-5 58:915–17 with 916n (59)/ CWE 34 194 with n6 (379)

306 Rodolphi Agricolae nonnulla opuscula, Dioge // nes Laertius, Cice. de Fato cum expla. Geor. Vallae

Agricola, Rudolphus. *Opuscula nonnulla collecta a Petro Aegidio.* Antverpiae: T. Martens, 31 January 1511 (quarto).

bound with

Diogenes Laertius. *De philosophorum vita decem libri.* Trad. Ambrosius Traversarius. Parisiis: J. Petit, [1510?] (quarto).

and

Cicero, Marcus Tullius. *De fato. Cum explanatione Georgii Vallae.* Parisiis: J. Badius, 12 September 1509 (quarto).

1/ A collection of Rodolphus Agricola's minor works and translations published by the Antwerp town clerk, Pieter Gillis, and dedicated by him to Maarten van Dorp, a professor at Leuven. From an early date Erasmus had taken pains to acquire the works of his humanist predecessor, whom he held in high esteem. In 1505 he encouraged his friend Gillis to collect everything he could find by Agricola, with a view to publication: 'Get together (from any source you can) the minor works of Rodolphus Agricola, and bring them with you.'[1] The collection that resulted included the Latin translation of the pseudo-Platonic dialogue *Axiochus* and of the *Paraenesis ad Demonicum* of Isocrates (newly collated with the manuscripts by Erasmus and published in an improved version in his edition of Cato);[2] the Latin translation from the French of the letter of Arnold de Lalaing on the meeting of Emperor Frederick and Charles [the Rash or Bold], duke of Burgundy (*de congresu imperatoris Frederici et Caroli Burgundionum ducis*);[3] a letter on the best method of undertaking humanistic studies, later republished separately, under the title of *De formando studio*, in several pedagogical collections; letters to Alexander Hegius and Johannes Agricola; the *Oratio in laudem philosophiae*;

the *Gratulatoria oratio* composed by Agricola, but pronounced by Bishop Johann von Dalberg in 1485 before the new pope, Innocent VIII; and finally some poems.[4]

2/ The identification of the edition of first and the third of the works in this composite volume is virtually certain. About eighteen months separated their dates of publication. If one assumes that the edition of Diogenes Laertius bound with the two other books also dated from about the same time, then only the 1510 Paris edition is likely, and it would have been easy for Erasmus to acquire.

3/ The wording of the entry in the *Versandliste*, 'cum expla. Geor. Vallae,' tallies exactly with the wording on the title-page of the 1509 Bade edition;[5] other editions of *De fato* mention 'cum commentario.'

1   Ep 184:14–15/18–19. Cf the earlier promise of Jacob Faber, master of St Lebuin's school at Deventer: 'I shall see to it that any of Rodolphus Agricola's works that come to hand here are sent on to you, except those that have been published in previous years and are now in the booksellers' shops' (Ep 174:96–8/113–15).
2   See Ep 677. For the edition of Cato see no 25 #1.
3   This may refer to their meeting at Trier in 1473; see CEBR I 225.
4   NK 46. Nauwelaerts *Rodolphus Agricola* 91
5   Renouard *Bibliographie de Josse Bade* II 296

307 Solinus, Iustinus, Lucius Florus.

Solinus, Caius Julius. *De memorabilibus mundi.* Probably a Paris edition, between c 1503 and 1515 (quarto).

bound with

Justinus, Marcus Junianus. *Historia ex Trogo Pompeio XXXIV epithomatis collecta. Lucii Flori Epithoma IV … in decem Titi Livi decadas. Sexti Ruffi De Historia Romana opus.* Probably a Paris edition between c 1505 and 1515 (quarto).

If this composite volume was a quarto, as are the neighbouring books on the *Versandliste*, then the three authors' names given in this entry probably point to the two frequently reprinted early sixteenth-century Paris editions identified above. Perhaps they were among the fairly large-scale purchases Erasmus made two or three years after his return from Italy.[1]

1/ Solinus' collection of geographical, historical, and other *notabilia*, three quarters of it based on the Elder Pliny's *Naturalis historia* and a small part derived from Pomponius Mela's *Chorographia*, dates from the third century AD. Editions of it annotated and printed by Josse Bade were published in Paris, with no year of publication stated, by Jean Petit, Denis Roce, and others; the oldest of them can be dated to about 1503.[2]

2/ Justin's epitome of the lost universal history of Pompeius Trogus, the *Historiae Philippicae*, popular as a school book in the Middle Ages, had since the end of the fifteenth century been repeatedly republished with the panegyric epitome of the history of the Romans by Lucius Florus, now known as Annius Florus. Various Paris publishers, including Jean Petit, Denis Roce, E. Gourmont, and others issued the work without stating the year, but between 1505 and 1515.[3] Sextus Ruffus is the name attached to an abridgement – *Breviarium* – of Roman history dedicated to the emperor Valens, who commissioned it. It was first printed by Sixtus Ruesinger at Rome c 1470.

1 Cf no 72 with n2.
2 Renouard *Bibliographie de Josse Bade* III 260–1
3 See BL *Catalogue*; BN *Catalogue général*; and Adams.

308 Opera Salustij

Sallustius. *Opera. De coniuratione Catilinae, De bello Jugurthino*, etc. Probably an early sixteenth-century edition in quarto.

An edition of the works of Sallust (86–34 BC) that cannot be precisely identified. Probably, like the adjacent volumes, it was a quarto. If this assumption is correct, two well-known editions may be left out of consideration: the *Opera omnia* printed by Josse Bade for Jean Petit in 1504, which appeared in folio format,[1] and the first edition of Sallust brought out by the firm of Aldo Manuzio in 1509 in octavo.

Sallust's works were first printed in 1470, in quarto, and were reprinted many times after that, usually in this format and chiefly in Italy and France. After 1500, nearly all the quartos were published in France, at Paris and more often at Lyon.[2] Could this book perhaps be one of Erasmus' numerous purchases in the French capital around 1511?[3]

1 On the 1504 folio, see Renouard *Bibliographie de Josse Bade* III 227–9.
2 For editions of Sallust from 1470, see the catalogues of the British Library in London, the Bibliothèque nationale in Paris, and the Library of Congress in Washington, DC. Some quarto editions: Paris: Jean Barbier for Jean Petit 13 September 1508; Lyon: Claude d'Avost for Simon Vincent 9 June 1509; and Lyon: Jacques Marechal for Simon Vincent 17 October 1511; Renouard *Bibliographie* III 229–34, 237, 239–40, 243.
3 Cf no 72 with n2.

309 Nicolai Leonici de uaria historia lib. 3.

Leonicus Thomaeus, Nicolaus. *De varia historia libri tres*. Basileae: H. Frobenius & N. Episcopius, August 1531 (quarto).

A compilation by Niccolò Leonico Tomeo containing notes, written many years earlier, on subjects from natural history, mythology, and history, dedicated to Cuthbert Tunstall, bishop of Durham and a former pupil.[1] Froben reprinted the work in the same year the *editio princeps* appeared.[2] For the author, see no 76.

1 Aulotte *Amyot et Plutarque* 30 n4 speaks of commentaries on Pliny, Plutarch, and Pausanias; cf Bietenholz *Der italienische Humanismus und die*

Blütezeit des Buchdrucks in Basel 68. On Tunstall
see no 17.
2 Venice: L.A. Giunta, January 1531 (octavo);
see Allen Ep 1479:180n.

310 Diodorus Siculus, Paulus Orosius, Berosus et / Leonis Papae Epistolae

Diodorus Siculus. [*Historiae a Poggio Florentino in latinum traductae.*] Parisiis: D. Roce for Jean Petit, c 1510 or another contemporary edition (quarto).

bound with

Orosius. *Opus prestantissimum.* Probably a Paris edition published between c 1506 and 1517 (quarto).

and

Berosus Babylonicus. *De antiquitatibus seu defloratio Berosi caldaica.* Parisiis: J. de Gourmont, 1509 or under the title *De his quae praecesserunt inundationem terrarum* … Parisiis: Jean Marchant for Geoffroy de Marnef, 1510 or another edition (quarto).

and

Leo I Papa. *Epistolae.* Parisiis: J. Badius for J. Parvus (Jean Petit), 1511 (quarto).

A combination of four quarto works, of which the last can be identified with a fairly high degree of certainty as a Bade edition of 1511. Probably the others are also Paris editions of about the same date.

1/ The first five books of Diodorus Siculus' Βιβλιοθήκη (*Histories*, usually called *Library of History*) translated by the Italian humanist Poggio Bracciolini (1380–1459) and divided by him into six books. The older editions of this translation are all in folio format. Quarto editions were published in Paris by Jean Petit and D. Roce (printed by W. Hopyl) and others; they do not state any year of publication but may be dated to around 1510. Erasmus may have seen one of these editions before recasting *Scarabaeus aquilam quaerit* for the 1515 Froben edition of his *Adagiorum chiliades.*[1]

It is not clear why he ordered a second Diodorus Siculus in 1525,[2] unless he had the original Greek text in mind and assumed that it must have been printed by then: the *editio princeps* of the Greek text, however, was not to appear until 1539.

2/ Orosius' *Historia adversus paganos libri VI*, written at the urging of Augustine and intended to supplement the latter's *De civitate Dei*, was an apologetic history of the world. All the fifteenth-century editions appeared in folio format. Between 1506 and 1517 at least four editions were published at Paris, the only quartos of this period, by Jean Petit, D. Roce, and P. Lambert.

3/ A short version, published under two different titles, by J. de Gourmont in 1509 and Geoffroy de Marnef in 1510 and 1511, of the *Antiquitates* of Johannes Annius (Giovanni Nanni) of Viterbo. For Annius' compilation see no 278 #2.

4/ *Editio princeps* of 97 (more than half) of the 173 surviving letters of Pope Leo I, prepared for publication by Jacques Lefèvre d'Etaples.[3] A copy of this edition is in the library of the Cultura Fonds at Dilbeek in Belgium.[4] From the inscription on the title-page it appears that this copy was given to Erasmus by Beat Arnold ('Munus D. Beati Arnoldi Erasmo D.D.'). Beat Arnold (1485–1532) was a relative of Beatus Rhenanus and secretary to Maximilian and afterwards to Charles V.[5] In the sixteenth century the book came into the possession of Nikolaus Kratzer (c 1487–after 3 August 1550), a Bavarian scholar who became the astronomer of King Henry VIII,[6] and of the Dalmatian diplomat Jacopo Bannisio (d 19 November 1532), after 1502 secretary to Maximilian.[7]

This copy changed hands several times in the course of the centuries and in 1989 it became part of the library of the Cultura Fonds at Dilbeek.[8] Vanautgaerden formulates two hypotheses on its early history.

Jacopo Bannisio may have first owned the book and then given it to Beat Arnold, who in his turn presented it to Erasmus between 1516 and 1525. Subsequently Łaski may have given the book to Nikolaus Kratzer in London in 1550. Or the book may have first belonged to Beat Arnold, who gave it to Erasmus, who passed it on to Bannisio or Kratzer in 1520, when Erasmus as well as Bannisio and Kratzer were in Antwerp and Brussels. In the latter case the Dilbeek copy cannot be the one described in the *Versandliste*.[9] Moreover, the Dilbeek copy had originally been bound separately, so that it is difficult to connect it with the copy alluded to in the *Versandliste*, which was probably bound with the other three works. Perhaps it was a duplicate that Erasmus, as was his custom, gave away to a friend or acquaintance?

1 *Adagia* III vii 1 ASD II-6 419 593n/CWE 35 206 with n183
2 Allen II 547 Appendix 20 'Books Ordered by Erasmus'
3 See Rice 'The Humanist Idea of Christian Antiquity' 147–8. Cf Renaudet *Préréforme et humanisme* 604 n2.
4 See Vanautgaerden '*Ex bibliotheca Erasmi.*'
5 Ep 399:6n/7n; CEBR I 72
6 CEBR II 273–4
7 CEBR I 90–1
8 Vanautgaerden '*Ex bibliotheca Erasmi*' 553–6
9 Vanautgaerden '*Ex bibliotheca Erasmi*' 553–4

311 Herodoti Nouem Musae à Valla uersae

Herodotus. *Novem musae a Laurentio Valla tralatae [et a Petro Phoenice editae] … (Isocratis Oratio de laudibus Helenae, e graeco in latinum traducta Joanne Petro interprete.)* Parisiis: [Jean Marchant] impr. pro Joanne Parvo, 1510 (quarto).

Since the surrounding volumes are quartos, the identification of this book causes no difficulty: the translation of Herodotus by Lorenzo Valla was only published once in quarto before 1536, by Jean Petit at Paris in 1510.

312 Roffensis de Eucharistia aduersus Oecolamp.

Fisher, John. *De veritate corporis et sanguinis Christi in eucharistia … adversus Johannem Oecolampadium.* Coloniae: P. Quentell, March 1527 (quarto).

John Fisher's point-by-point refutation of Oecolampadius' *De genuina verborum Domini 'Hoc est corpus meum' iuxta vetustissimos authores expositione liber* of September 1525.[1] In the controversy on the Eucharist, John Fisher played off Luther and his followers, who upheld the real presence of the body and blood of Christ in the sacrament, against Oecolampadius and Zwingli, who had come to hold the view that there is nothing in the Eucharist except bread and wine. By this tactical manoeuvre he could draw the Lutherans into the Catholic camp, although he did not conceal their deviation from the traditional ecclesiastical view of the Eucharist, and he described Luther's exegesis of the words 'This is my body' as absurd.[2] Fisher's long-winded treatise, dedicated to Erasmus' older patron Richard Foxe, bishop of Winchester and founder of Corpus Christi College, Oxford, went into three Cologne editions in 1527: two in February and March from P. Quentel, in folio and quarto respectively, and an octavo by Eucharius Cervicornus in April. The format of the adjacent books makes it most probable that Erasmus possessed the quarto edition with Fisher's important 'letter to the reader' on the aim of his work which, unlike the dedication to Foxe, was omitted from the other two editions.[3] Shortly after the appearance of Oecolampadius' book, which he had not yet read, Erasmus declared that he himself had also begun to write something on the Eucharist.[4] But he was in no hurry, and two years later he definitively abandoned the idea of completing it. One of the reasons (or pretexts) he adduced for this was that the bishop of Rochester and the

Parisians had 'girded themselves for this task' in the meantime.[5]

1 See also no 34.
2 See Surtz *The Works and Days of John Fisher* 14 and 346; Köhler *Zwingli und Luther* I 255 n2, 519–30; Rex *The Theology of John Fisher* 136–46.
3 Surtz *The Works and Days of John Fisher* 336. For the dedicatory letter to Bishop Richard Foxe, see Staehelin BAO I 577–81.
4 Ep 1616:17–18 with 17n/22 with n2. Cf Epp 1618:10–12/13–15, 1620:86–7/100–2, 1621:25/31–2, 1624:36–7/41–2, 1679:92/100–1.
5 Ep 1893:77–82/83–8

313 Heliodori Histo. Aethiop. lib. 10. grae.

Heliodorus Emesenus. *Historiae Aethiopicae libri decem [graece]*. Basileae: off. Hervagiana, February 1534 (quarto).

The *editio princeps* of Heliodorus' *Aethiopika*, the last surviving example of the Greek love romance, probably written in the third century AD.[1] The adventurous tale of Theagenes and the Ethiopian princess Charikleia enjoyed great success, thanks in particular to the French translation by Amyot, and was later to inspire Tasso, Cervantes, and Racine. Alas, we do not know what Erasmus thought of Heliodorus' romance; his friend and kindred spirit Alciati had not a good word to say for it and spoke of 'trifles of this kind.'[2] The Greek text was edited by Vincentius Opsopoeus from a manuscript in the library of Matthias Corvinus, king of Hungary, that had survived the sack of Buda in 1526. Opsopoeus, who sympathized with the Reformation and translated various writings of Luther, made a name as a Greek scholar and was the first to publish, besides Heliodorus, Polybius and Diodorus Siculus in the original language.[3] The first of these was not in Erasmus' library, and the second did not appear until 1539.

1 von Christ *Geschichte der griechischen Litteratur* II-2 820–3
2 AK IV 336 Ep 1923
3 Ep 1997:5n/n2

314 Callimachi Hymni, Gnωmae ex diuer. grae.

Callimachus. [Gnomai.] *Callimachi Cyrenaei hymni. cum scholijs nunc primum aeditis. Sententiae ex diuersis poetis oratoribusque ac philosophis collectae non ante excusae.* [Graece]. Basileae: off. Frobeniana, 1532 (quarto).

This edition of the hymns of Callimachus and a collection of Greek *gnomai* was prepared for the press and provided with scholia by Sigismundus Gelenius, a friend of Erasmus and regular collaborator with the Froben press.[1] Separate editions of each had appeared in quick succession in 1495 and 1496, from the printer-publisher Laurentius de Alopa in Florence, both edited by Janus Lascaris.[2] These editions, which, though separate, were connected with each other through their printer and editor, must have inspired Gelenius to combine the hymns of Callimachus and a comparable collection of *gnomai* in one publication. For the text, at least of the hymns, he may have taken advantage of the work of Janus Lascaris, the Byzantine philologist who, after receiving his education at Padua under Demetrius Chalcondyles, had won the favour of Lorenzo de' Medici and was professor of Greek, poetry, and philosophy at Florence at the time when he was preparing the two editions. Later, after the invasion of Charles VIII, he entered the French diplomatic service and from 1503 to 1509 acted as ambassador of Louis XII at Venice. There, in the circle of Aldo Manuzio and the Aldine Neakademia, Erasmus made his acquaintance and learned to esteem him.[3] Might Erasmus have brought back from Italy the two older editions, bound in one volume? The answer must be negative: The words 'ex diuer' in the *Versandliste* are taken literally from the Latin subtitle of Gelenius' edition of 1532 but are not found in the exclusively Greek title of Alopa's edition of the *gnomai*. There is

another indication that the Froben edition
is the one Erasmus owned. The collection
of *gnomai* in it was different from the one
in the Alopa edition. It had been borrowed
from a manuscript put at the disposal
of Froben by Aurigallus, like Gelenius,
a Bohemian.[4] Erasmus read the edition
attentively. In his revision of the *Adagia*
in 1533 he added several citations from the
newly published collection (which included
– anonymously – the first edition of
fragments from Stobaeus' *Gnomologium*)
and many quotations from Menander.[5]

1 On Gelenius see no 303.

2 GW 5917 (Hain 4266) and Hain 7787

3 On Lascaris see Ep 269:51n/55n; CEBR II 292–4.
   For his edition of the Greek Anthology see
   no 104.

4 The manuscript has been identified with a codex
   in the library of the Premonstratensian convent
   Strakov at Prague (cod Strakov DG III ii); see ASD
   II-5 49 659n and II-4 39 464n.

5 Erasmus could consult a manuscript of Stobaeus'
   Gnomologium when he was working on the 1508
   edition of his *Adagia* in Venice; see for example
   Adagia II viii 77 and III vii 53 ASD II-4 199:47n and
   II-6 453 493n/CWE 34 79–80 with n1 (343) and CWE
   35 247–8 with note and n1. For additions to the
   1533 *Adagia* from the collection in the Froben
   edition see for example *Adagia* II ix 16, III i 13, III i
   18, III i 63, III iii 15, III iii 60, III iii 75, III ix 44 ASD
   II-4 227 267n, ASD II-5 49 659n, 53 757n, 75 358n,
   199 85–9n, 221 335n, 227 455n, II-6 532–3/CWE 34
   97 with n2 (349), 186–7 with note (376), 189 with
   n5 (377), 206 with n5 (383), 287 with n6 (411),
   302 with n10 (419), 307 with n4 (421), CWE 35
   335–6 with n3 (Stobaeus); *Adagia* II ix 16 ASD II-4
   227 267n/CWE 34 97 with n2 (349) (Menander).

315 De origine et gestis Britannorum.

Galfridus Monemutensis (Geoffrey of
Monmouth). *Britanniae utriusque regum
et principum origo et gesta insignia ex
antiquissimis Britannici sermonis monumentis in latinum sermonem traducta.* Parisiis:
J. Badius imp. Iuonis Cavellati, 1508 or the
reprint of 13 September 1517 (quarto).

With his chronicle of the pre-Anglo-Saxon
history of Britain (commonly known as
Historia regum Britanniae), in which

tradition, legend, and imagination are
mixed together, Geoffrey of Monmouth
(1100?–54) not only put his stamp on the
conception of the national past for centuries to come but also helped to establish the
Arthurian literary tradition. The chronicle
was printed for the first time in Paris by
Josse Bade in 1508. The man responsible
for the text, based on four manuscripts
from Paris libraries, was Yves Cavellat,
pupil and afterwards collaborator of
Girolamo Aleandro.[1] There is nothing
to suggest how or why Erasmus acquired
the book, apart from his familiarity with
the printer-publisher. Clearly, however,
he did not take seriously all the stories of
Geoffrey's *History*; in the extended version
of *Sileni Alcibiadis* in the 1515 edition
of the *Adagia* he alluded ironically to the
legendary first king of England, the Trojan
Brutus, supposedly a great-grandson of
Aeneas, 'who I rather think never existed.'[2]
We might gather from this comment that
at the time he was already in the possession
of the 1508 *editio princeps* of Geoffrey's
chronicle.

1 Jovy *François Tissard et Jérôme Aléandre* III 30–1

2 *Adagia* III iii 1 ASD II-5 170:233–4 with 233n
   (171)/CWE 34 269 with n44 (407)

316 Petri Gylij uersiones ex Aeliano, Porphyrio,/ Heliodoro Oppiano etc.

Aelianus, Claudius. *Ex Aeliani historia
per Petrum Gyllium latini facti, itemque ex
Porphyrio, Heliodoro, Oppiano, tum eodem
Gyllio luculentis accessionibus aucti libri XVI
de vi et natura animalium. Eiusdem Gyllii
liber … de gallicis et latinis nominibus
piscium.* Lugduni: S. Gryphius, 1533
or a reprint of 1534 or 1535 (octavo).

This anthology was derived from the
pseudo-zoological work of Claudius
Aelianus (c 170–230 AD), supplemented
by extracts from other classical authors
on the life of animals. The texts had been
translated by the French cleric Pierre Gilles
(Petrus Gyllius), who himself contributed

to the volume a treatise on Latin and French fish names.[1] At the suggestion of his old pupil and patron Georges d'Armagnac, bishop of Rodez, Gilles had dedicated his work to Francis I, who in return sent him to the Levant, where he collected manuscripts and explored antiquities.[2] It is very improbable that as late as 1533 Erasmus should have bought this anthology on his own account. We may rather conjecture that the book was a present; a surmise supported by Erasmus' friendly contacts at that time. Shortly before the publication of the book, in 1532–3, Erasmus carried on a correspondence with Georges d'Armagnac and Jean de Pins, bishop of Rieux, whom he knew from his Bologna days, about a manuscript that belonged to the latter and had previously been lent to Gilles.[3]

1 Baudrier VIII 70, 77, 85
2 On Gilles see Allen Ep 2665:32n and CEBR II 98.
3 Cf no 219.

317 Grammatica Chrysolorae grae.

Chrysoloras, Manuel. [*Erotemata.*] *Grammatica.* Parisiis: Egidius Gourmontius, 1507 (quarto).

Manuel Chrysoloras (d 1415), an immigrant from Byzantium and the true founder of Greek studies in Italy, taught Greek at Florence from c 1397 to 1400 and then for some years at Milan and Pavia. Later he accepted diplomatic appointments and finally died in the papal service.[1] His Greek grammar was well known and was reprinted several times from c 1475, albeit at first only in an abbreviated version. The first complete edition appeared c 1496 at Florence, published by Lorenzo di Alopa; this was reprinted c 1498–1500, also in Florence.[2] In 1511 Erasmus supported himself at Cambridge by giving lessons in Greek from the Ἐρωτήματα, but he does not appear to have had many students: 'Up to this moment I have been lecturing on Chrysoloras' grammar, but the audience is small.'[3] Which edition did he use?

Assuming that he was unwilling to be satisfied with the abbreviated version, only three are candidates: the two we have mentioned from before 1500, and the most recent one, published in Paris by Gilles de Gourmont in 1507. Of these, Gourmont's is the only edition with a title that tallies exactly with the entry in the *Versandliste*.

The text of the Gourmont edition had been prepared by François Tissard, who had returned from Italy only a few months before the book appeared. Tissard studied law at Bologna, but later devoted himself entirely to Greek and even undertook to translate three tragedies of Euripides. It is easy to imagine that Erasmus, who was no less interested in Greek and who had also been resident in Bologna since November 1506, must have met him there. Immediately after his arrival in Paris, Tissard settled with Gourmont the terms for the publication of some Greek books (including editions of Homer and Hesiod). He also began to teach Greek at the university, the first person to do so regularly, and was quite successful until the more brilliant Aleandro supplanted him.[4]

It cannot be more than an assumption that on a visit to Paris in the spring of 1511 Erasmus acquired from Aegidius de Gourmont the copy of Chrysoloras' Greek grammar that was to supply him with the material for his lectures at Cambridge later in the year.

1 On Chrysoloras see Ep 233:8n/10n and GW VI 495. The beginning of his activity in Florence has been called 'a key date in Western intellectual history'; Rüdiger 'Die Wiederentdeckung der antiken Literatur im Zeitalter der Renaissance' 562.
2 GW 6694 and 6695. See on his grammar Chomarat *Grammaire et rhétorique* I 311–13.
3 Ep 233:8/10–11
4 Renaudet *Préréforme et humanisme* 501–3, 509–10

318 Vtopia Mori et Epigrammata Eras.

Morus, Thomas. *De optimo reip. statu deque nova insula Utopia libellus. Epigrammata.*

Epigrammata Des. Erasmi ... Basileae:
J. Frobenius, March 1518 (quarto).

A joint publication of Thomas More and
Erasmus with the second authorized
edition of the *Utopia*, in which Erasmus
took an active part.[1] In March 1517 he sent
More from Antwerp a copy of the *Utopia*
so that More could indicate the desired
improvements and urged his friend to
return the corrected text as soon as
possible; in May he had conveyed to
Basel by a special courier the copy for the
Utopia, More's translations from Lucian
and his *Epigrammata*, and his own contributions for the planned edition.[2] He even
concerned himself in Froben's business
management, and proposed, in order to
be sure of a good printing, that Beatus
Rhenanus should again be employed.[3]
But Froben kept the essential decisions
in his own hands: instead of following the
original intention to bring out a combined
edition of More's *Utopia*, Erasmus' *Querela
pacis*, and *Declamatio de morte* in one
volume, with their translations from
Lucian and their *Epigrammata*, he split
the material, which had become too bulky,
in two, and published the *Querela pacis*,
the *Declamatio de morte* and the translations from Lucian first in December 1517.[4]
The rest he kept for a separate edition,
published in March 1518, which is the
one referred to here. He excused the
delay on the grounds that he now had
the opportunity to include with the text
of the *Utopia* Budé's long letter in praise
of it, which had recently been published
in Gourmont's edition.[5]

1 Gibson *St Thomas More: A Preliminary Bibliography* no 3
2 Epp 543:1, 11–13/2, 14–15, 545:5/6, 584:15–16/
   18–19; cf Ep 597:43–6/48–52
3 Ep 594:1n/introduction
4 BB E 1290. Not on the *Versandliste*. A copy was,
   however, in the separate chest with Froben editions
   of his own works that Erasmus kept in his last
   residence in Basel; see *Catalogus librorum Erasmi*
   no 2. Cf Allen and CWE Ep 550 introductions.
5 Epp 664:27n/31n, 785:14–17, 50–3/15–19, 53–6

319 Rober. Gaguinus de gestis Francorum

Gaguin, Robertus. *De origine et gestis
Francorum compendium*. Parisiis: Pierre
le Dru, 1495 or one of the early reprints
(folio).

Robert Gaguin was considered the central
figure among the humanists of the French
capital when Erasmus arrived there in
1495.[1] But his summary manual of French
history hardly breathed the new spirit; in
its design and treatment it strongly recalls
the 'grandes chroniques.'[2] To fill in some
blank pages that the printer had left over
after the book was set in type, a complimentary letter from Erasmus to Gaguin
(Ep 45) was inserted (on fol 136); it made
his name familiar in a wide circle at a
stroke. It was the first text of Erasmus to
appear in print. The edition on his shelves
in 1536 need not necessarily have been
the original. Gaguin himself must have
been rather dissatisfied with the carelessly
printed first version, and he arranged a
new printing, which was published in June
1497 by Johann Trechsel in Lyon. Josse
Bade, then still working in Lyon, had
collaborated in the correction and some
verses by him were also included. The
reprint published at the end of March 1498
by Andreas Bocard in Paris also contained,
besides the verses by Bade, a letter and a
poem by Erasmus' friend Cornelis Gerard
of Gouda.[3] Erasmus himself sent one of
these reprints to the monastic reformer Jan
Mombaer as a present.[4] A fourth edition
appeared in January 1501, also in Paris,
from Thielman Kerver.

1 On Gaguin see Allen and CWE Ep 43 introductions
   and CEBR II 69–70; cf Renaudet *Préréforme et
   humanisme à Paris* 114–16 and passim.
2 Cf Fueter *Geschichte der neueren Historiographie*
   141.
3 On these new editions and their dating see Allen
   Ep 45 introduction.
4 Ep 73:31–2/34–5. On Mombaer see nos 387
   ##2–3 and 390.

320 Epistolae graecae nouem autorum Ald.

Epistolae diversorum philosophorum, oratorum. Rhetorum sex et viginti. [graece] Venetiis: apud Aldum, 1499, 2 vols or only vol 2? (quarto).

Although the adjacent volumes are folios, it is scarcely possible that this entry can refer to any other book than the famous collection of letters by twenty-six classical and early Christian authors issued by Marcus Musurus in a quarto volume.[1] We now know that many of the letters attributed to the Greek authors were much later imitations, though some of them had been written as early as the Hellenistic period.[2] Erasmus ordered a copy of the book directly from Italy in c 1525.[3] The book is entered in the *Versandliste* under the independent title of its second part, in which indeed the letters of only nine authors were included: Basil the Great, Libanius, [Pseudo-] Chion, [Pseudo-] Aeschines, Isocrates, [Pseudo-] Phalaris, M. Junius Brutus, [Pseudo-] Apollonius, and Julian the Apostate. This need not mean that Erasmus possessed an incomplete copy of the work lacking the first volume; the two parts may have been bound in reverse order, as appears to have been the case in several preserved copies,[4] and the compiler of the list may not have noticed. The first part (the title of which, as given above, mentions twenty-six authors) contains letters of Synesius, Demosthenes (doubtful), Plato, Aristotle, Philip of Macedonia, Alexander the Great, [Pseudo-] Hippocrates, [Pseudo-] Diogenes, [Pseudo-] Crates, [Pseudo-] Anacharsis, [Pseudo-] Euripides, the Pythagoreans, Alciphron, Theophylactos, and Aelianus.

1 GW 9367. On the work and Musurus' share in it see Geanakoplos *Greek Scholars in Venice* 122.

2 GW 9367 gives, if the letters are not genuine, the names of the authors to whom they are attributed, with the prefix 'pseud'; we have adopted these prefixes.

3 Allen VI 547 Appendix 20 'Books Ordered by Erasmus'

4 Pellechet *Catalogue générale des incunables des bibliothèques publiques en France* III 309 (no 4613): 'Dans plusieurs exemplaires l'ordre des deux parties a été interverti à la reliure.' Cf Alan G. Thomas, bookseller *Catalogue 30* (London 1973) no 3: 'Part II bound before part I, as usual.'

321 Pomponius Mela cum commentar. Vadiani

Mela, Pomponius. *Libri de situ orbis tres, adjectis Joachimi Vadiani ... in eosdem scholiis.* Viennae Pannoniae: J. Singrenius, May 1518 or perhaps Basileae: A. Cratander, January 1522 (folio).

Pomponius Mela's *De chorographia,* the oldest preserved geographical work of the Romans, written under Emperor Claudius, was published with a commentary by the Swiss Joachim Vadianus (1484–1551), while he was still professor of rhetoric at Vienna. In the year of publication, 1518, he returned to his native country, where he settled at St Gallen. Under the influence of Huldrych Zwingli he became warmly sympathetic to the Reformation, which he helped to introduce as head of the town magistracy of St Gallen.[1] Vadianus was no extremist in religious matters, however, and unlike some of his co-religionists he did not turn away from Erasmus, whom he had always admired. His principal work, begun in 1529, a chronicle of the abbey of St Gallen, contained a eulogy of Erasmus, who was also twice mentioned in honourable terms in two passages of his first edition of Mela (Vienna 1518). The books had scarcely been printed when Vadianus arrived in Switzerland from Vienna, and one of his first acts was to pay a visit to Erasmus at Basel. Could he perhaps have offered him a copy of his book as a gift on that occasion? Vadianus paid Erasmus further compliments in his revised edition of Mela,[2] which was brought out by Cratander in 1522. Erasmus repaid the compliment in a passage inserted in *Adagia* II iv 53 in the 1526 edition.[3]

1 On Vadianus see Ep 1315:9n/n5 and CEBR III 364–5.
2 The revised edition included a reduced copy of the map of the world by Martin Waldseemüller of 1507; Bagrow *A. Ortelii catalogus cartographorum* I 30. Cf no 134.
3 ASD II-3 366:965–8 / CWE 33 218

322 Astronomicorum libri Iulij Firmici, Manilij, / Arati, Theonis, Procli etc.

[Scriptores rei astronomicae veteres.] *Julii Firmici astronomicorum libri VIII. Marci Manilii astronomicorum libri V. Arati Phaenomena Germanico Caesare interprete; eiusdem Phaenomena fragmentum Marco T. Cicerone interprete; eiusdem Phaenomena Ruffo Festo Avieno paraphraste. Arati Phaenomena graece. Theonis commentaria in Arati Phaenomena graece. Procli Diadochi Sphaera graece et latine Thoma Linacro Britanno interprete.* Venetiis, Aldus Manutius, June–October 1499 (folio).

A collection of partly unpublished Greek and Latin astronomical writings with translations of the Greek texts and commentaries.[1] The Latin translation of Proclus' *Sphaera* was by Thomas Linacre (c 1460–1524), the English humanist and physician. Linacre worked in Italy from 1485 to 1499, when he returned to his native land, where Erasmus must have met him for the first time shortly afterwards.[2] Allen considers it possible that a copy of the collection of astronomical works had already reached England in December 1499, and that Erasmus, who praised Linacre for his acuteness, had seen it.[3] Nonetheless it is also possible that Erasmus did not acquire his own copy, or at least become familiar with it, until much later. In 1531, when he expressed his opinion that it was by no means wasted effort for a philologist to translate anew a text which had already been badly translated, in order to approach more closely to the meaning of the author, he named Linacre as an example: 'I see that Thomas Linacre, who translated more correctly the *Sphere* of Proclus, which had been translated

haphazardly by someone else, was of this opinion.'[4]

1 Hain 14559; Polain 3475
2 During his first stay in England; Allen I 59:90 and 62:223 (Beatus Rhenanus to Charles V). On Linacre see also no 75.
3 Allen Ep 118:23n
4 Ep 2422:39–45/40–5. Allen assumed that the reference to 'the German commentator' in Ep 1635 was perhaps an allusion to Germanicus Caesar's prose commentary on Aratus, also included in the collection (see 33n). This identification has been disputed; see CWE Ep 1634A n19.

323 De re militari, Frontini, Vegetij, Aeliani, / et Modesti libri.

[Scriptores rei militaris.] *Sextus Julius Frontinus de re militari. Flavius Vegetius de re militari. Aelianus de instruendis aciebus. Modesti libellus de vocabulis rei militaris. Omnia a Philippo Beroaldo edita.* Bononiae: J. A. de Benedictis, May 1505 or the earlier edition Plato de Benedictis, 1495/6 (folio).

A collection of military works reprinted many times from 1487. It is virtually certain that one of the two editions named above must be involved. Neither the *editio princeps*, which was a quarto, nor the folio edition of Jean Petit, Paris 1515, which lists the authors in a different order on the title-page with Vegetius first, is possible. It may be the edition of 1505, which Erasmus could have bought during his stay in Bologna, a printing centre. Vegetius' *De re militari* was already familiar to him from an earlier edition. In 1497 he cited the work in a reading that at that time appeared only in the Utrecht edition of N. Ketelaer and G. de Leempt (c 1473).[1] Where and how he had seen this edition may be plausibly conjectured. The young Lord Mountjoy possessed a copy – it has been preserved and is now at University College, Oxford[2] – and probably read the text under Erasmus' guidance about 1497–8.

1 Ep 57:1–5/2–6; cf Campbell *Annales* no 1706.
2 Allen IV xx (addendum to Ep 57:1n); on William Blount, fourth Baron Mountjoy see Allen and CWE Ep 79 introductions and CEBR I 154–6.

**324 Res Rusti. Columellae, Varronis, /
Catonis etc cum commen. Beroaldi.**

[Scriptores rei rusticae.] *Opera agricola-
tionum: Columellae, Varronis, Catonisque,
nec non Palladii cum annotationibus Phil.
Beroaldi.* Bononiae: imp. Benedicti
Hectoris, 23 August 1504 or one of
the older editions under the same title,
Bononiae: imp. B. Hectoris, 19 September
1494 or Regii: imp. D. Bertochius,
18 September 1496 or Regii: imp.
F. Mazalis, 20 November 1499 (folio).

It is possible to identify a number of
editions of this well-known collection
of agricultural works that answer to the
description in the *Versandliste*. The probable folio format and the sequence in which
the authors are listed point to one of the
editions from Bologna or Reggio nell'
Emilia. All four contained the commentary
of Pomponius Laetus on Columella from
which Erasmus borrowed a quotation in
the revised 1533 edition of his *Adagia*.[1] Did
Erasmus perhaps buy the still fairly recent
1504 edition during his stay at Bologna?[2]
Years later, in 1521, he also acquired the
Aldine edition (Venice 1514), presented
to him by a youthful admirer with the
dedication 'Hugo Bolonius, the pupil of
the Muses, presented this as a New Year's
gift to Erasmus, the ornament of the world
and the father of good literature, the first
of January 1521.'[3] Because it is practically
certain that that volume, an octavo, is not
referred to here, and because it is not
entered anywhere else in the list, we must
assume that Erasmus did not think it
necessary to retain duplicate texts of the
Scriptores rei rusticae and therefore gave
away the copy he found superfluous, as he
often did (cf nos 243 and 272 #1). There
may have been a reason for him to choose
to keep the older edition instead of the
more recent one: the Aldine, in spite of
using new manuscripts, was less highly
regarded for the purity of its text than its
predecessors.[4] When Allen saw it in early

1912, the book was in the possession of
Worcester College, Oxford. Later it was
acquired by the School of Education
Library at Liverpool University and
then transferred to the University Library.
The text has no marginal annotations of
any kind and the binding is modern.[5]

1 The later editions (Venice: Aldo Manuzio 1514;
   Florence: Filippo Giunta 1515 and 1521; Basel:
   Johann Herwagen 1535) name the authors in
   another order on the title-page (Cato, Varro,
   Columella) and are also in another format, octavo
   instead of folio. For these reasons the assumption
   of the ASD editors of *Adagia* III iii 63 (ASD II-5 223
   370n) that this item on the *Versandliste* was most
   probably the Giunta edition of 1521 has not
   been accepted.
2 Cf no 323.
3 Allen Ep 1178 introduction
4 Schweiger *Handbuch der classischen Bibliographie*
   II / *Bibliographisches Lexikon der gesamten
   Literatur der Römer* 1305
5 I am grateful to Mr M.R. Perkin, Curator of
   Special Collections of the Library of Liverpool
   University, for information on this book, which
   was made available to me through Dr J.C. Grayson,
   Liverpool.

325 Arnobius in Psalmos

Arnobius. *Commentarii … in omnes
psalmos sermone Latino per Erasmum
Roterodamum proditi & emendati.
D. Erasmi … Commentarium in psalmum:
Quare fremuerunt gentes.* Basileae:
J. Frobenius, September 1522 (folio).

The *editio princeps* of the commentaries
on the Psalms by Arnobius the Younger
(d after 451), published by Erasmus from
a manuscript in the Augustinian abbey of
Franckental near Worms and dedicated to
Pope Adrian VI (Ep 1304).[1] Erasmus added
to the work, which he wrongly ascribed to
Arnobius the Elder, a Nubian rhetorician
of the fourth century, his own commentary
on the Second Psalm. The autograph draft
of a first version of his commentary,
slightly shorter than the printed text of
1522, has been preserved and is now in
the Royal Library at Copenhagen.[2]

1 The manuscript is now in the library of the
Vatican (MS Pal. Lat. 160: x^c).
2 Ms Thottske Saml. 73 Fol. (fols 16 recto–45 recto).
See Reedijk 'Three Erasmus Autographs in the
Royal Library at Copenhagen' 341; ASD v-2 91–2.

326 Saluianus de prouidentia Dei, item Sex./Ruffi Epitome cum Polybij Histo. libris

Salvianus Massiliensis. *De vero iudicio
et prouidentia Dei libri VIII cura Jo.
A. Brassicani editi ac scholiis illustrati.
Anticimenon libri III in quibus quaestiones
Veteris ac Novi Testamenti de locis in
speciem pugnantibus incerto autore.* Basileae:
off. Frobeniana, 1530, 2 partes (folio).

bound with

Rufus, Sextus. *Epitoma de gestis et
assequuto dominio Romanorum.* Polybius.
*Historiarum libri v Nicolao Perotto inter-
prete.* Basileae: H. Petri, 1530 (folio).

1/ In his unfinished principal work, usually
called *De gubernatione Dei*, Salvian of
Marseilles (c 390–soon after 480) viewed
the invasions of the barbarians and the
collapse of the western Roman empires as
the justice of God visited on the Romans,
who had proved to be Christians in name
only, and had only their own degeneracy
to blame for the disasters that had befallen
them. The work is of great interest to
cultural history for its many pictures of
the age. Johannes Alexander Brassicanus,
a humanist and philologist who became
a professor at Ingolstadt in 1522 and at
Vienna in 1524, based his edition of the
text on a manuscript from the library of
Matthias Corvinus put at his disposal in
Buda by King Louis II of Hungary (the
edition of Salvian opens with Brassicanus'
well-known description of the library).[1]

Brassicanus met Erasmus, his senior by
more than thirty years, in 1519 for the first
time, and remained on good terms with
him until some coolness later entered their
relationship. He was an admirer, even

describing himself on one occasion 'totus
Erasmicus,'[2] and in 1529 he lectured on one
of the *Colloquies*. In early 1530 he sent the
copy for the edition of Salvian to Froben
in Basel. He also gave his *famulus* a letter
to be delivered to Erasmus at Freiburg.
Brassicanus' letter has not been preserved,
though we have Erasmus' reply, in which
he shows that he had been offended by the
famulus, who had not let him see the text
of Salvian: 'Your servant did not show me
the Salvian, although Froben will not act
on it without my judgment' – a remark that
says much about Erasmus' relationship
with the Froben publishing house.[3] Erasmus
inserted a citation from the book in the
next revised edition (1533) of his *Adagia*.[4]

Some time before Erasmus received
Salvian's *De gubernatione Dei*, published
by Froben in August 1530, Brassicanus
had presented him with a publication of
quite a different kind, his *Proverbiorum
symmicta* (Vienna 1529), a collection of
128 Greek proverbs with commentary and
18 *Pythagorae symbola*. In the letter quoted
above, Erasmus thanked the author for his
gift in words full of praise.[5]

2/ Apart from the résumé of Roman
history by Festus (Sextus Rufus, late fourth
century), this Basel edition contains as its
main constituent books 1 to 5 of Polybius'
Roman history, which covers the period
from 264–216 BC, in the only translation
then current, that by Niccolò Perotti.
Erasmus never acquired the original Greek
text, edited by Vincentius Opsopeus and
published by Setzer of Hagenau in 1530.

1 On Brassicanus see Allen and CWE Ep 1146
introductions and CEBR I 191–2.
2 Bietenholz *Der italienische Humanismus und die
Blütezeit des Buchdrucks in Basel* 122
3 Ep 2305:16–18/18–19
4 *Adagia* III v 1 ASD II-5 297:223–5/CWE 35 67
5 Ep 2305:1–2, 19–49/3–4, 20–50. Erasmus took 27
of the 488 adages added to the March 1533 edition
of his *Adagia* from Brassicanus' collection; see ASD
II-4 305 547n.

327 Egesippus uersus à D. Ambrosio

[Pseudo-] Hegesippus. *Aegesippi historia de bello judaico, sceptri sublatione, Judaeorum dispersione et hierosolymitano excidio a divo Ambrosio ... e graeca latina facta ... Cum Josephi libris etiam De gestis Machabeorum.* Parisiis: J. Badius, 5 June 1510 (folio).

The *editio princeps* of a free, Christianized abridgment of Flavius Josephus' *Jewish War*, then still wrongly ascribed to the second-century author Hegesippus.[1] Lefèvre d'Etaples, who prepared the edition for Josse Bade, also adhered to the traditional, erroneous attribution of the Latin translation to Ambrose. The work was dedicated by Bade to the humanist Guillaume Briçonnet, bishop of Lodève and abbot of St Germain-des-Prés, who offered Lefèvre d'Etaples, his secretary from 1507, a home and the opportunity to study in the famous abbey.[2] It was at St Germain-des-Prés, probably in the summer of 1511, that Erasmus held the 'most friendly conversations' with Lefèvre that he later mentioned.[3] The Greek scholar Michael Hummelberg (1487–1527), active in Paris from c 1504 to 1511 and proctor of the German 'nation' of the university there from 1506, also contributed to the edition: he compiled the epitome of Hegesippus and the tables of concordance between Hegesippus and Josephus' *De gestis Machabeorum*, also mentioned on the title-page. Hummelberg became one of Erasmus' most faithful followers.[4] In 1529 Erasmus wrote to Pelargus that he had not read Hegesippus; in their correspondence about the identification of the apostle Judas, both correspondents appear to be citing Hegisippus from Eusebius' *Ecclesiastical History*.[5]

1 Renaudet *Préréforme et humanisme* 599 with n1; Rice 'The Humanist Idea of Christian Antiquity: Lefèvre d'Etaples and His Circle' 147 and *Prefatory Epistles* 219
2 On Briçonnet see Ep 1407:118n/n33 and CEBR I 198–9.
3 Ep 337:846–7/888

4 On Hummelberg see Allen Ep 263:21n and CEBR II 213–14.
5 Ep 2185:6/9; cf lines 13–19/16–23 and CWE Epp 2184 n9, 2186 54–5 with n10.

328 Nouum Testa. grae. et Lati. Eras.

Novum Testamentum ... ab Erasmo Roterodamo recognito. Basileae: off. Frobeniana. A folio edition.

See no 241.

329 Nouum testa. cum annotationib. Eras.

Novum Testamentum ... ab Erasmo Roterodamo recognitum. Basileae: off. Frobeniana. A folio edition.

bound with

In Novum Testamentum annotationes ab ipso autore ... recognitae ... Basileae: off. Frobeniana. A folio edition.

See nos 241 and 331.

330 Noui testa. textus

Novum Testamentum.

An edition that cannot be identified more closely, unless this and the following number belong together and this entry refers to the text part alone, that is, bound without the *Annotationes*, of one of the editions of Erasmus' New Testament. Cf nos 241, 328, 329.

331 Noui testa. Annotationes Erasmi

Erasmus. *In Novum Testamentum annotationes ab ipso autore ... recognitae, & ex Graecis codicibus locupletatae.* Basileae: off. Frobeniana (folio).

In the *editio princeps* of Erasmus' New Testament, the *Novum instrumentum* of 1516, the *Annotationes* were included after the biblical text without a separate title-page. Rummel has summarized their development: 'In their original form, the *Annotations* were predominantly a philological commentary … Material added to the notes in subsequent editions … broadened their scope considerably. They became a mixture of textual and literary criticism, theological exegesis, spiritual counsel, and polemical asides.' From the second edition of 1519, they were always published with the text, expanded on each occasion, but now with a separate title-page, so that they did not need to be bound with the text part.[1] It is possible that this copy of the *Annotationes* belongs with the text of the New Testament listed under the preceding number in the *Versandliste* and that Erasmus had the two parts bound separately in order to be able to use the volume with the annotations as a handy working copy.

Erasmus continued to work on the *Annotations* and was at pains to complete them and to polish them until the end of his life. Four pages of supplementary notes, preceded by a brief preface to the reader (Ep 1789), were added to the fourth edition (1527), and in the announcement for the fifth and last printing of his *Novum Testamentum* personally corrected by him (1535), he commented to one of his correspondents about the annotations: 'On these I have expended no small amount of sweat – I only wish I had paid proper attention at the beginning!'[2]

1 On the *Annotations* in general see Rummel *Erasmus' Annotations on the New Testament, From Philologist to Theologian* (for the quotation, page vii). For the first version, written for the most part after Erasmus' arrival in Basel in 1514, cf Holeczek *Humanistische Bibelphilologie als Reformproblem bei Erasmus von Rotterdam, Thomas More und William Tyndale* 114–15.
2 Ep 2951:13–14

332 Apologiae Erasmi

Erasmus. *Apologiae omnes*. Basileae: J. Frobenius, February 1522 or *Apologiae …* Basiliae: J. Frobenius, October 1521 (folio).

The entry 'Apologiae Erasmi' appears twice in the *Versandliste*, here and under no 383. At least one of the entries probably refers to the 1522 collected edition of seven of Erasmus' apologies, all but one published separately earlier:[1] *In Jacobum Lopem Stunicam* (1521), *In quendam de loco 'Omnes quidem resurgemus'* (1522; the *editio princeps*), *In Jacobum Fabrum Stapulensem* (1517), *In Jacobi Latomi dialogum* (1519), *In quendam pro declamatione de laude matrimonii* (1519), *De 'In principio erat sermo'* (1520), and *Qua respondet invectivis Eduardi Lei* (1520). A copy once in Erasmus' possession, with seven autograph marginalia by him, survives and is now in the University Library at Cambridge.[2] The book lacks the usual ex libris *Sum Erasmi*, but that does not prove that the book was not his, since the last leaf, on which Erasmus used to write his ex libris, is also missing. The vicissitudes of the copy can be traced back to the end of the seventeenth century, when it was in the possession of the young Amsterdam collector Cornelius Nicolai. It was auctioned with his library in 1698, and then came, perhaps directly, into the hands of the bishop of Ely, John Moore. After Moore's death his collection of books was bought by King George I, who presented it to the University of Cambridge.[3]

Froben published two editions of Erasmus' apologies. The February 1522 edition was preceded by a version bearing a slightly different title, dated on the title-page November 1521, which long remained unnoticed.[4] An extremely rare, if not unique, copy of this original edition, discovered and described by Halkin, is in the Library of the University of Liège.[5] Five of the seven apologies listed above appear in it; the first two are absent. That this *editio princeps* has become practically untraceable can be explained by the fact that shortly after its appearance, Froben used the unsold stock to make up the augmented edition of February 1522.

The text of the first edition, continuously paginated from 1 to 367 with, on the last page, the colophon 'm. Oct 1521,' is preceded by a new title-page, adapted to reflect the expanded contents, with the imprint date 'm. Febr 1522' and forty-eight new pages, unnumbered and provided only with signature markings (Aa, Bb etc), containing the text of the two apologies of 1521 and 1522. Whether one of the two entries in the *Versandliste* may perhaps refer to the original edition cannot be determined.

We can, however, be quite certain about the third version of the *Apologiae* that Erasmus still owned in 1536 but that did not appear in the *Versandliste*. It was part of the special collection of mainly Froben editions of his own works that he kept in a separate chest in his last Basel residence. Amerbach entered this edition in the catalogue of the special collection, compiled after Erasmus' death, as *Apologiarum volvmen 1521*.[6] Since the most likely place to look for information on the date of printing is the title-page (rather than the colophon), Amerbach most probably had in his hands the *editio princeps* of the *Apologiae*, which bore the date November 1521 on the title-page, and not the enlarged edition of February 1522 under the title *Apologiae omnes*. As author, Erasmus would undoubtedly have received the *editio princeps* immediately from the printing office. His copy and the copy today preserved in Liège, the only one known to have survived up to the present, were presumably among the very few copies distributed before Froben blocked the sale of the remaining stock in order to use it for the augmented second edition. It seems an unusual business procedure. Even if the second edition was published before the first had been sold out, Froben need not have been afraid that a second edition of a work of Erasmus, even if only slightly enlarged, would lack buyers. For that reason the question arises how far

Erasmus may have had a hand in Froben's decision: the publication at the same time in one book of seven instead of five apologies might have been of more importance to him than to Froben.

1 The folio format of the adjacent books in the *Versandliste* practically rules out a collection of separate *apologiae* bound in one volume, for they were all published in quarto or octavo.
2 Classmark Adv. a.5.1
3 See de Jonge 'Aantekeningen van Erasmus in een exemplaar van zijn Apologiae omnes (1522)' and his introduction to the apologies against Zúñiga in ASD IX-2 53–5.
4 *Apologiae … quibus respondet iis, qui ex tot ipsius vigiliis, tamquam spectatae fidei monumentis, aliquid tandem quod calumniarentur decerpere conati sunt* (Basel: Johann Froben, November 1521; colophon October 1521)
5 Halkin 'Une édition rarissime des apologies d'Erasme en 1521'
6 See *Catalogus librorum Erasmi* no 83.

333 Pauli Aemylij de reb. gestis Francorum lib. 4

Aemilius, Paulus. *De rebus gestis Francorum libri IV*. [Parisiis:] J. Badius, [c 1516] (folio).

The Veronese Paolo Emilio came to Paris as a young man, studied theology there, and enjoyed the protection first of Cardinal Charles de Bourbon and later of Charles VIII. Erasmus, who was already acquainted with him in Paris around 1500, later spoke of him more than once with approbation.[1] He owned the original edition of Emilio's history of France in four books, intended as a rival to Robert Gaguin's *De origine et gestis Francorum* (no 319). It is often assumed that 1516 was the year of publication of this work, but Erasmus' correspondence points rather to the following year. In February 1517 he had heard that 'Paulo Emilio is at last publishing his history of France,' but it was not until November that he wrote that the book was on sale, and it was January 1518 before a copy of the work reached him in Leuven.[2] The original edition contained the still incomplete text in four books. Pieter Gillis reported to him in June 1518 that Emilio had sent the copy

for the remaining books to the printer.
Erasmus may have acquired these books
also: Bade added in the enlarged edition
five more books without, however, chang-
ing the title-page, which mentioned only
four books.[3]

1 Epp 719:5–6/8, 721:10–12/11–14. On Emilio
see Ep 136:1n/2n and CEBR I 429.
2 Epp 534:53–4/55–6, 719:5–7/7–8, 764:8/11
3 Ep 849:17–19/17–18. On the confused printing
history of the work see Renouard *Bibliographie
de Josse Bade* II 2–3; Rice *Prefatory Epistles* 50
Ep 15 n6; and CWE Ep 849:18n.

334 Recognitio Veteris Test. Eugubini

Steuchus Eugubinus, Augustinus.
*Recognitio Veteris Testamenti ad
Hebraicam veritatem.* Venetiis: in aed.
Aldi et Andreae soc., 1529 or the second
edition, Lugduni: S. Gryphius, 1531
(quarto).

The theologian Agostino Steuco, who
ended his career as librarian of the Vatican,
was in charge of the library of the monastery of San Antonio in Venice from 1525
to 1529. The library had not long before
been enriched by the valuable collection
of books formed by Cardinal Domenico
Grimani.[1] In his *Recognitio Veteris
Testamenti*, a textual-critical commentary
on the Pentateuch but in fact dealing
mainly with Genesis, Steuco defended
the Vulgate text against the attacks of the
humanists, who preferred the Septuagint.
Without mentioning him by name except in
a single instance, he also attacked Erasmus,
who felt himself challenged and reacted,
though without undue haste, in a very long
letter to him written in March 1531
(Ep 2465). As he wrote in the dedication
and the foreword to his work, Steuco had
drawn much of his evidence from Grimani's
library; Erasmus began his letter by relating
his own visit to Rome and the cardinal's
bibliotheca πολυγλωττοτάτη in 1509.
His letter appeared in print in a slightly
modified form, six months after it was sent,
in the *Epistolae floridae* (Basel: J. Herwagen,

September 1531). Steuco's *Recognitio* went
into a second impression in 1531, but
Erasmus still referred in his letter to the
first edition of 1529: the many printer's
errors in it that he criticized had been
largely corrected in the second edition.[2]
In July 1531 Steuco wrote a detailed
answer to Erasmus' letter (Ep 2513) from
Reggio nell' Emilia, where he had become
abbot of the abbey of San Marco. He
included both his own *Responsio* and
Erasmus' letter in his *In psalmum XVIII,
et CXXXVIII interpretatio*, published by
Gryphius at Lyon in 1533. Erasmus did
not respond further, nor does this work
appeal on the *Versandliste*.

1 On Steuco see Allen and CWE Ep 2465 introductions; Freudenberger *Augustinus Steuchus und
sein literärisches Lebenswerk*; CEBR III 285.
2 Freudenberger *Augustinus Steuchus* 77

335 Enarratio Eras. in Psalmum 38[um].

Erasmus. *Enarratio Psalmi trigesimi octavi
multum ab enarratione veterum differens.*
Basileae: H. Frobenius ac N. Episcopius,
March 1532 (quarto).

The only edition of this commentary on
Psalm 38, dedicated to Stanislaus Thurzo
(d 1540), bishop of Olomouc (Ep 2608),
who rewarded Erasmus for the work with
'a gilded bowl.'[1]

1 Ep 2699:13–16. The bowl was bequeathed on
Erasmus' death to Bonifacius Amerbach; Major
Erasmus von Rotterdam 41 and 53.

336 Enarr. Eras. in psal. trig. tertium.

Erasmus. *Enarratio pia ivxta ac docta in
Psalmum XXXIII.* Basileae: H. Frobenius,
J. Hervagius & N. Episcopius, March 1531
(quarto).

The only edition of the commentary
on Psalm 33, which was dedicated to
Konrad von Thüngen, bishop of Würzburg
(Ep 2428), undoubtedly in gratitude for the
golden cup that Erasmus had received from
him in May 1530.[1] The cup had been a

thank-you gift; shortly before, Erasmus had flattered the bishop by presenting him with a copy of his *Enarratio triplex in psalmum 22*. He had entrusted its delivery to Daniel Stiebar, a young nobleman who had lived in his house in Freiburg as servant-pupil for some months in the winter of 1529–30 and who was going to live in Würzburg.[2]

1 Ep 2314:34–40/39–45; for the gold cup decorated with the coat of arms of the bishop, see Major *Erasmus von Rotterdam* 41.

2 Basel: Froben 1530. Not in the *Versandliste*. For the accompanying letter, see Ep 2457; on Stiebar see Allen and CWE Ep 2069 introductions; Allen IV Appendix 14 'Eppendorf's Copy of the *Epistolae ad diversos*' 615; CEBR III 287–8.

337 Declaratio Eras. ad censu. Basilius de Spiritu.

Erasmus. *Declarationes ad censuras Lutetiae vulgatas sub nomine Facultatis Theologiae Pariensis … recognitae & auctae*. Basileae: H. Frobenius & N. Episcopius, September 1532 (quarto).

bound with

Basilius. *Opus argutum ac pium de spiritu sancto ad Amphilochium, Des. Erasmo interprete*. Basileae: H. Frobenius & N. Episcopius, March 1532 (quarto).

1/ In 1532 two editions were published of Erasmus' *Declarationes*, his self-defence against the earlier attacks of the Sorbonne theologians on his work, and in particular against the sharply worded *Determinatio Facultatis Theologiae in schola Parisiensi super quamplurimis assertionibus D. Erasmi Roterodami* of the previous year: the first in octavo without any indication of the month, but probably early February, and the second, a quarto, in September, after Erasmus had asked the Dominican Ambrosius Pelargus to comment on the original text.[1] The combination with the translation of Basil, which was published in quarto, makes it virtually certain that

this entry refers to the enlarged and revised edition of September. See also no 377.

2/ The first translation of this treatise into Latin and a by-product of Erasmus' edition of the works of St Basil in the original Greek published in the same year (nos 189 and 250). The book was dedicated to Johannes Dantiscus (Ep 2643) in thanks for the plaster medallion with portraits of himself and of King Sigismund that Erasmus had received from him.[2] At the end of August 1532 Erasmus instructed Amerbach to send Cardinal Sadoleto a copy of the new edition of the *Declarationes* with one of the translation of Basil, the same combination he had had bound for himself.[3]

1 Ep 2579:57n. For their correspondence on the *Declarationes*, see Epp 2666–77; CWE 82 xxx–xxxii and passim. On Pelargus see Allen and CWE Ep 2169 introductions; CWE 82 xi n4; CEBR III 63–4; ASD IX-7 16–18.

2 On Dantiscus cf no 5.

3 Ep 2703:1–4

338 Eras. Hyperaspistae liber secun.

Erasmus. *Hyperaspistae liber secundus adversus librum Martini Lutheri cui titulum fecit Servum arbitrium*. Basileae: J. Frobenius, 1527 (octavo).

The second part of *Hyperaspistes*, Erasmus' reply to Luther's *De servo arbitrio*, was published at the beginning of September 1527 with a foreword to the reader (Ep 1853). It was the previously announced continuation of the provisional answer that he had written under the same title in 1526 and completed in the shortest possible time in order to be able to bring it out at the Frankfurt book fair in the spring.[1] *Hyperaspistes* part 1, of which a revised reprint followed some months after the *editio princeps*, does not appear in the *Versandliste*, but it is recorded in the list of the separate collection of his own works, mostly Froben editions, that Erasmus kept *in arca aulae versus fenestram* 'in a chest near the window overlooking the courtyard.'[2]

1 See Allen and CWE Ep 1667 (To the Reader) introductions; cf Ep 1683:12–26/15–29. See also no 381 (Luther *De servo arbitrio*).
2 *Catalogus librorum Erasmi* nos 58 and 87. See also Augustijn 'Hyperaspistes I: la doctrine d'Erasme et de Luther sur la "claritas scripturae."'

339 Apologia Eras. in Pium et alios

Erasmus. *Apologia adversus rhapsodias calumniosarum querimoniarum Alberti Pij quondam Carporum principis quem homines male auspicati ad hanc illiberam fabulam agendam subornarunt.* Basileae: H. Frobenius & N. Episcopius, 1531 (octavo).

Alberto Pio did not live to see the effect of his last contribution to the controversy with Erasmus (whom he lumped together with Luther and the Lutherans), namely, the *xxiii libri in locos lucubrationum variarum Erasmi retractandos*, published posthumously by Josse Bade at Paris in early March 1531.[1] Erasmus did not concede his late opponent the last word, and replied in the *Apologia adversus rhapsodias Alberti Pii*. This provoked an 'antapologia' from the Spanish humanist and historian Juan Ginés de Sepúlveda, which was also present in his library (no 389). The addition '& alios' in the *Versandliste* refers to the malevolent individuals – 'homines male auspicati' – alluded to in the title who had encouraged the old and dying prince of Carpi to write his last work.

1 See Epp 2441:64–70/66–73 and 2522:66–9. On the polemic see no 373.

340 Symbolum Fidei, de Eccles. concordia Eras.

Erasmus. *Dilucida et pia explanatio symboli quod Apostolorum dicitur, decalogi praeceptorum et dominicae precationis* (second edition). Basileae: off. Frobeniana, November 1533 (octavo).

bound with

Erasmus. *Liber de sarcienda ecclesiae concordia* (second edition). Basileae: off. Frobeniana, 1533 (colophon 1534) (octavo).

The editions of the two works bound in one volume here can be determined with a great degree of certainty on the grounds of their format: all the adjacent entries in the *Versandliste* refer to octavo books.

1/ The *Explanatio symboli*, a catechism in the form of a dialogue, was written at the request of the English Lord Privy Seal, Thomas Boleyn, and dedicated to him by the author (Ep 2772).[1] It was nonetheless a very personal work, the kind of summary of theology that Erasmus wished to be available to everyone, and one in which he did not at all present himself as a critical reformer but as a faithful defender of the doctrine of the Catholic church of his time.[2] Eight months after the quarto *editio princeps* of March 1533, Froben brought out another edition in octavo.

2/ Erasmus' treatise on the restoration of unity in the church, an exposition of Psalm 83, dedicated to Julius Pflug (Ep 2852), appeared at the beginning of September 1533 in quarto format.[3] An octavo edition authorized by Erasmus followed in quick succession, dated 1533 on the title-page but 1534 in the colophon.

1 On Boleyn see Allen and CWE Ep 2266 introductions and CEBR I 161–2.
2 ASD V-1 183, 195
3 There was a copy in the chest containing Erasmus' own works; see *Catalogus librorum Erasmi* no 96. On Pflug see Allen and CWE Ep 2395 introductions and CEBR III 77–8.

341 Apologia Eras. de interdicto esu carnium

Erasmus. *Ad ... Christophorum episcopum Basiliensem epistola apologetica de interdicto esu carnium.* Basileae: J. Frobenius, August 1522 (octavo).

Erasmus' letter of 24 April 1522 'on the prohibition of eating meat' addressed to Christoph von Utenheim, bishop of Basel, was quickly circulated in manuscript and thereupon published at the instigation of the university and the bishop himself.[1] The edition also contained two apologies of Erasmus: his *Apologia de tribus locis quos ut recte taxatos a Stunica defenderat Sanctius Caranza theologus* and the *Apologia aduersus libellum Stunicae cui titulum fecit Blasphemiae et impietates Erasmi*, with an 'appendix,' *Apologia ad prodromon Stunicae*.[2] The work appears twice in the *Versandliste*, although only one authorized independent edition of it is known.[3] For this reason the second copy (no 380) must have been a duplicate of the original edition or one of the numerous unauthorized reprints (more than ten in two years) that Erasmus wished to preserve, for whatever reason. The *Epistola*, which voiced his opinion on three problems in the context of the Reformation in Switzerland – the rules of fasting, obligatory celibacy of the clergy, and compulsory feast days – and included a few practical proposals for reform, immediately provoked quite a stir; later it ranked with the *Moria* and the *Colloquia* as one of the three works most detested by Erasmus' Catholic enemies.[4]

1 Cf Allen Ep 1274:14n.
2 The first apologia includes Erasmus' response to Sancho Carranza's *Opusculum in quasdam Erasmi Annotationes*; see Ep 1277:1–43/2–45, with the notes. See also the list of works published by Erasmus and Zúñiga during the course of their controversy in Allen IV Appendix 15 'The Heine Collection' 622. On all the polemical works included, see ASD IX-2 24–6, 35–6, and 41–2.
3 The second edition of 1532, provided with scholia (*In epistolam de delectu ciborum scholia*) did not appear independently but in the *Dilutio*. Possibly the *Dilutio* was present in Erasmus' library, bound, as is usually the case, after his *Declarationes ad censuras Lutetiae vulgatas* (Basel 1532); see no 377.
4 Cf Ep 2566:83–4.

342 Eras. Nouum testa. Lati.

Novum Testamentum omne iuxta Graecorum emendata volumina interprete Erasmo Roterodamo. Probably an octavo edition.

The format of the books entered alongside it on the *Versandliste* makes it highly likely that this entry refers to a separate edition of Erasmus' translation of the New Testament in octavo. The edition in this handy format was a success from the start and went into numerous printings. On the basis of the second printing of the *Novum Testamentum* issued by Froben in March 1519, Dirk Martens of Leuven brought out the first Latin version without the Greek text in the same year.[1] Although Erasmus said that the publication was undertaken against his wishes, he nonetheless wrote the foreword to the reader (Ep 1010).[2] In the following year Froben issued the translation separately, with a new preface by Erasmus himself.[3] After he had settled in Basel, he provided the revised Froben edition of July 1522 with two new forewords, both addressed to the reader as before and undated. Two copies of Erasmus' New Testament *latine* are entered on the *Versandliste*; no 392 is described as an octavo. This entry may refer to one of the above-named editions or possibly a rather later, more or less authorized, Froben reprint, while the entry under 392 may allude to the last Froben edition to appear during Erasmus' lifetime.

1 NK 335
2 See Allen's introduction, which discusses in detail the editions of the New Testament translation that followed.
3 *Novum Instrumentum omne ad Graecam veritatem Latinorum codicum emendatissimorum fidem, denuo ... recognitum. Cum nova praefatione Erasmi* (Basel: Froben 1520) The edition is not listed in BE. A copy is in the Universitätsbibliothek Basel; see *Erasmus ... Vorkämpfer für Frieden und Toleranz* (exhibition catalogue) 163. Allen did not know of this edition, and assumed provisionally that the *nova praefatio* appeared for the first time in Cratander's edition of August 1520; but he himself scarcely believed that this was an

authorized edition and thus made the clear reservation, 'unless there is a prior Martens or Froben edition of 1520'; see Ep 1010 introduction.

343 Herodianus graece pariter et Latine Aldi

Herodianus. *Historiarum libri VIII, graece pariter et latine*. Venetiis: in aed. Aldi & Andreae Asulani soc., September 1524 (octavo).

The Greek text of Herodian's history of the Roman emperors from Marcus Aurelius to Gordian II (180–238) was published for the first time by Aldo Manuzio in a collection of Greek historians, which was also present in Erasmus' library (no 273). The second part of the separate and improved edition referred to here also contained the Latin version of the text by Angelo Poliziano, originally published in 1493, and so excellent that it was long believed that Herodian had written in Latin.[1] Erasmus' copy of the work was probably in the possession of John Sparrow, Warden of All Souls College, Oxford.[2] Decisive proof, the *Sum Erasmi*, was missing: the usual place for the ex libris had been so thoroughly erased that even with the aid of the quartz lamp it was not possible to see anything legible. But a sixteenth- or seventeenth-century owner had written on the last leaf, above the Aldine anchor, *Abeli Sylvij Frisij ex libris Erasmi Roterod.* 'the property of Abel Sylvius, Frisian, from the library of Erasmus of Rotterdam.' The Frisian name suggests that this was one of the books that ended up in the northern Netherlands after the dispersal of Łaski's library.[3] Unfortunately, after the death of the warden in 1992 the book was not found in his estate.[4] Its present whereabouts are unknown.

1 Pauly-Wissowa IX 959 sv Herodianus
2 I owe my knowledge of and further details about this copy to the kindness of the late Sir Roger Mynors, sometime Corpus Christi Professor of Latin at Oxford.
3 Cf nos 123, 137, 138, 203, 208, 218, and 267; cf no 201.
4 Kind information from Professor James K. McConica, All Souls College, Oxford and University of Toronto

344 Suidas Mediolani excusus

Suidas. [*Lexicon Graecum.*] Mediolani: impensa et dexteritate Demetrii Chalcondyli, Joannes Bissolus, Benedictus Mangius, 1499 (folio).

The *editio princeps* of the *Suda*, the late tenth-century Greek lexicon wrongly ascribed before c 1930 to an author named Suidas.[1] Erasmus also supposed Suidas to be the compiler's name. It was edited by the Athenian émigré Demetrius Chalcondyles (c 1424–1511), professor of Greek successively at Padua, Florence, and (from 1492), Milan and printed 'at the expense and with the skill of' G. Bissoli and B.M. Dolcibelli. Although primarily lexicographical, the voluminous work – 1,026 pages of 45 lines of print, with about 30,000 entries, in principle alphabetically arranged – also supplies in an encyclopaedic style all manner of historical, geographical, literary, theological, and biographical information.[2] Erasmus, who described Chalcondyles as a 'an honest man and a good scholar' but ranked him lower than his compatriot Theodorus Gaza,[3] did not buy the later Aldine edition (Venice 1514), although it gave an improved text based on additional manuscripts. He could have consulted at least one of these manuscripts himself during his stay in Italy. In the 1508 edition of the *Adages* (published in Venice) he mentions a variant reading from the printed text of Suidas. He must have seen this in Aldo Manuzio's workshop, in a manuscript that was also used for the Aldine Suidas of 1514.[4] When Erasmus acquired the lexicon cannot be documented, but it was probably quite early. He did not yet have access to it when he was collecting material for the *Collectanea* of 1500, but he must have had a copy to hand before 1506. In that year he travelled to Italy with an alphabetically arranged collection of proverbs in his luggage that he had compiled in the preceding years on the basis of the *Collectanea*; the sources he used for this must have included the 1499 edition of Suidas.[5] It is possible that this was the copy entered here.

1 Hain *15135; BL *Catalogue* 6 792
2 On the *Suda* and its sources, see Pauly-Wissowa 2nd series IV-1 675–717 sv Suidas; *Der Kleine Pauly* V 407–8 and OCD 1451 sv Suda; Bolgar *The Classical Heritage and Its Beneficiaries* 72.
3 Ep 428:34–6/39–41; cf 11–17/16–21 on Gaza. On Chalcondeles see 34n/39n and CEBR I 290–1.
4 *Adagia* III vii 61 ASD II-6 456:580–1 with n (457)/ CWE 35 252 with n1
5 *Adagia* III vi 7 ASD II-6 349–51 note/CWE 35 128 note

345 Eras. Epistolae Palaeonaej

Erasmus. *Epistolae palaeonaeoi. Ad haec responsio ad disputationem cuiusdam Phimostomi de divortio.* Friburgi Brisg.: J. Faber Emmeus, September 1532 (folio).

Two years after the publication of the *Opus epistolarum* (no 226), Erasmus sent a number of hitherto unpublished letters to Basel for Johann Herwagen to publish.[1] He was then very busy with his new house at Freiburg, and his selection of the 112 letters was made hastily and rather carelessly, though he revised several of them.[2] After they had appeared in 1531 under the title *Epistolae floridae* he realized and regretted that the collection contained letters and passages from letters that gave offence and might better have been omitted.[3] He tried to repair the damage by issuing under his personal supervision the purged and expanded edition described above, the title of which ('Old-New Letters') speaks for itself. The collection of 1531, thus superseded, does not appear on the *Versandliste*. Added to the *Epistolae palaeonaeoi* was Erasmus' answer to the Dominican Inquisitor Johann Dietenberger, who had attacked his view on divorce (see no 29).

1 On Herwagen see no 44 with n6.
2 Halkin *Erasmus ex Erasmo* 167
3 Those who felt insulted included, among others, Johannes Oecolampadius; cf Ep 2559:26–9.

346 Christiani Matrimonij Insti. Eras.

Erasmus. *Christiani matrimonii institutio.* Basileae: J. Frobenius, August 1526 (folio).

Erasmus' treatise on Christian marriage, dedicated to Catherine of Aragon, the wife of Henry VIII (Ep 1727), appeared simultaneously in two editions, a folio and an octavo. The folio must be meant here.

347 Gazae gram. eiusdem de mensibus,/ Apollonij de construc. lib 4. Herod. de nu./meris

Gaza, Theodorus. *Introductivae grammatices libri quatuor. Eiusdem de mensibus opusculum … Apollonii grammatici De constructione libri quatuor. Herodianus De Numeris.* [Graece.] Venetiis: in aed. Aldi, 1495 (folio).

The *editio princeps* of Gaza's famous Greek grammar, here published with writings of the second-century grammarians Apollonios Dyskolos and Aelios Herodianos.[1] A copy of the first edition has been discovered in the Codrington Library of All Souls College, Oxford, showing the *Sum Erasmi* on the verso of the last leaf (fol 198). Erasmus' ownership of the book is, however, questionable; his ex libris appears to be forged.[2]

Theodorus Gaza, who emigrated from Byzantium to Italy in c 1435, taught Greek successively at Ferrara, Rome, and Naples. Erasmus ranked him highest among the 'modern' Greek grammarians, higher than Constantinus Lascaris.[3] At the end of 1511, after his lectures in Cambridge on the *Erotemata* of Chrysoloras (no 317) had attracted little attention, he proposed to teach from the grammar of Gaza in the hope of drawing a larger audience.[4] Some years later he issued the first and second books of the work in a Latin translation, published by Martens at Leuven.[5] Neither of these editions appears in the *Versandliste*, but a Froben edition containing the two translated books together is entered in the separate inventory of his own works that Erasmus kept 'in arca aulae versus fenestram.'[6] The manuscript of the translation of book 2, sent from Louvain to Basel in August 1517 and used for the Froben edition, is now in the University Library of Basel.[7]

1 Hain-Copinger 7500; BL *Catalogue* 5 553
2 I am grateful to Professor James K. McConica, All Souls College, Oxford and University of Toronto, who informed me of this discovery, and to Mr Simmons, librarian of the Codrington Library, who immediately put photocopies at my disposal. On the ex libris see also Rhodes *A Catalogue of Incunabula* 155 no 812: 'It is not however certain that [what appears to be "Sum Erasmi"] is in Erasmus' hand.' Moreover, Rhodes ascertained that the numerous marginalia in the book are not in his hand either.
3 *De ratione studii* ASD I-2 114:112–13/CWE 24 667:14–16. On Gaza's grammar and Erasmus' translations of books 1 and 2, see Chomarat *Grammaire et rhétorique* I 313–19.
4 Ep 233:8–10/10–12
5 *Primus liber grammaticae institutionis* (Leuven: Dirk Martens 1516; NK 3051) and *De linguae Graecae institutione liber secundus* (Leuven: Dirk Martens 1518; NK 3048)
6 See *Catalogus librorum Erasmi* no 33, which might refer to either the 1518 or the 1520 Froben edition. On the editions see Ep 771 introductions.
7 Allen I Appendix 8 'The Deventer Letter-book' 605; Allen Ep 771 introduction; *Erasmus … Vorkämpfer für Frieden und Toleranz* (exhibition catalogue) 89 and 19

348 Chiliades Adagiorum Eras.

Erasmus: *Adagiorum Chiliades* … A folio edition.

Erasmus' collection of proverbs was originally published in a modest octavo volume as *Adagiorum collectanea* (Paris: J. Philippi 1500; repr 1505 and Paris: J. Bade 1506). It grew into a thick folio, dedicated to William Blount, Baron

Mountjoy (Ep 211) and first published under the title of *Adagiorum chiliades* by Aldo Manuzio at Venice in 1508; Froben in Basel reprinted the Aldine edition in 1513 and then, under the same title, brought out four successive authorized editions, each one enlarged, in 1515, 1517–18, 1520, and 1523. The later editions, from 1526 onwards, appeared with one exception under the title *Adagiorum opus* (see nos 257 and 406 #1). Erasmus appears to have kept one of the old editions, although he normally disposed of superseded versions of a work, including his own. Perhaps he made an exception for the Aldine edition of 1508, which he must have valued highly as a typographical accomplishment, and with which the memory of his fruitful activity in Venice was associated.[1]

A copy of the 1523 edition of the *Adagiorum chiliades*, which Erasmus kept for a long time and subsequently gave to his servant-pupil Nicolaas Kan, was found in 1990 when it surfaced at a Sotheby's auction. Kan's ownership appears from an inscription in the upper margin of the title-page (*Sum Nicol. Cannij senioris & amicor[um]* 'I belong to Nicolaas Kan senior and his friends') and another at the foot of the second page of errata (*Sum nicolai Cannij ex liberalitate praeceptoris mei Erasmi Rotterodami* 'I belong to Nicolaas Kan by the generosity of my teacher, Erasmus of Rotterdam'). This volume was used as a working copy and contains over 240 additional passages of text in Erasmus' own hand and some 160 in an unidentified hand, presumably that of another of his secretaries. Kan's hand in the marginal corrections of typographical errors is identifiable throughout. The majority of the additional passages were worked into the text of the subsequent edition of 1526; a few are printed in the edition of 1528.[2] Almost certainly this copy was not given to the printer: it bears no trace of printer's ink or casting-off marks. The book is now privately owned

again. For a similar working copy of the
Adagiorum opus of 1526, likewise given
by Erasmus to Nicolaas Kan, see no 257.

1 Erasmus clearly took an interest in the typography
of his own works. He wished the second edition
of his Euripides translations to be set in Aldo
Manuzio's italic type, 'that small fount which is the
most elegant of all' (Ep 207:31–3/36–8), for which
the printer had chosen Musurus' handwriting as
his example (ASD I-1 197 8n). In 1516 Erasmus
told Wilhelm Nesen, then employed by the Froben
press as a corrector, to see that the forthcoming
new edition of his *Copia* should be printed 'in
Froben's larger type and as accurate and elegant
as may be. Let [my commentaries on abundance
of style] at least give pleasure by their appearance
if they do not commend themselves to readers by
their learning' (Ep 462:6–9/10–14). Later on it
was at Erasmus' urging that Hieronymus Froben
bought a larger Greek type (Ep 2062:19–20/23–4),
which was used for the first time in the Greek
passages of the 1528 edition of the *Adagia*; his
edition of the Greek text of Basil (no 189) was
set in the new type. A typical specimen of the care
Erasmus bestowed on the typographical appearance of a book is an autograph draft of the title-
page to the first volume of Augustine's *Opera
omnia* (1529), which still exists in the University
Library of Basel (MS Grey-Grynatus II.9.133); see
Erasmus en zijn tijd (exhibition catalogue) no 384.
2 The description of this book has been taken
(almost verbatim) from the auction catalogue;
for further details see *Continental and Russian
Books and Manuscripts, Science and Medicine*.
Sale 20th November 1990, Sotheby's London,
no 297. On Kan see Allen and CWE Ep 1832
introductions and CEBR II 252–3.

349 Paraphrases in Euangelia

Erasmus. *Paraphrasis in Evangelium
Matthaei, in Evangelium Joannis, in
Evangelium Marci, in Evangelium Lucae.*
Folio edition or editions.

Paraphrases on the Gospels could mean
either a combination volume in which
the four folio editions of Erasmus'
Paraphrases issued separately by Froben
in Basel between 1522 and 1524 were
bound together,[1] or the collected edition,
also in folio, of the *Paraphrases* on the
four Gospels and the Acts of the Apostles,
which appeared under its own title in 1524.[2]

1 *Paraphrasis in Evangelium Matthaei* (March 1522
[*editio princeps*] or 1524), dedicated to Charles V
(Ep 1255); *Paraphrasis in Evangelium Joannis*
(February 1523 [*editio princeps*] or 1524), dedicated
to Ferdinand of Austria (Ep 1333); *Paraphrasis
in Evangelium Marci* (1523–4 *editio princeps*),
dedicated to Francis I (Ep 1400); *Paraphrasis in
Evangelium Lucae* (1524), dedicated to Henry VIII
(Ep 1381). For the *Paraphrase on Luke* cf no 355.
2 *Tomus primus Paraphraseon ... in Novum
Testamentum, videlicet in quatuor Euangelia et
Acta Apostolorum; quarum bona pars nunc recens
nata est, omnes ab ipso autore non oscitanter
recognitae* (Basel: Johann Froben 1524); each
Paraphrase has its own title-page and its own
pagination.

350 Roffensis confutatio assertionis Luteranae.

Fisher, John. *Assertionis Lutheranae
confutatio.* Antverpiae: M. Hillenius, 1523
(folio).

The papal bull *Exsurge domine* of 15 June
1520, which stigmatized and condemned
forty-one pronouncements in his work as
heretical, provoked Luther to defend
himself in his *Assertio omnium articulorum
per bullam Leonis X novissimam damnatorum*. The foreword to the *Assertio* was
dated 1 December 1520; Luther burned
the bull and the papal decretals in public
on 10 December. It was in refutation of
the *Assertio* that Fisher wrote this exhaustive work, which has been called his *opus
magnum* against Luther. It goes into the
disputed propositions with scrupulous care
and cites Luther's apology verbatim from
beginning to end.[1] For that reason,
Erasmus would not have needed to keep
Luther's *Assertio* in his library, if he had
ever possessed it. In writing his *De libero
arbitrio* he used John Fisher's book,
especially those parts in which the bishop
had disputed Luther's statements on
freedom of the will in his *Assertio*.[2]

1 Surtz *The Works and Days of John Fisher* 8, 309
2 Zickendraht *Der Streit zwischen Erasmus und
Luther über die Willensfreiheit* 17, 42–5, 183–5

**351 Quaestiones in 4ᵗᵘᵐ Sententiarum Hadri
// ani Florentij.**

Florentius, Hadrianus. *Questiones in
quartum sententiarum presertim circa
sacramenta.* Parisiis J. Badius, 1516 or 1518
(folio).

A commentary by Adriaan Floriszoon,
later Pope Adrian vi, on the fourth book
of the *Sentences* of Peter Lombard (see
nos 63 and 163), which dealt chiefly with
the sacraments. The book was published
without the permission or knowledge of
the author, who was then in Spain, from
a very defective text, so that it contained
countless errors and even some complete
misrepresentations.[1] Erasmus nevertheless
recognized it as having a certain authority,
and in 1531 he asserted, albeit with the
qualification 'if I am not mistaken,' that
the commentary had contributed greatly
to Adriaan's being raised to the cardinalate
by Leo x and subsequently 'to the triple
crown.'[2]

1 See [Adrian vi, Pope] *Herdenkingstentoonstelling
  Paus Adrianus vi. Gedenkboek* (exhibition
  catalogue) 119 no 138
2 Ep 2522:133–6

**352 Eras. de recta pronun. dialo. ciceronia. /
item apologia aduersus mona. Hispa.**

Erasmus. *Dialogus de recta latini graecique
sermonis pronuntiatione. Dialogus cui
titulus Ciceronianus … cum aliis nonnullis,
quorum nihil est non novum.* Basileae: off.
Frobeniana, October 1529 or March 1528
or March 1530 (octavo).

bound with

Erasmus. *Apologia adversus articulos
aliquot per monachos quosdam in Hispaniis
exhibitos.* Basileae: off. Frobeniana,
[June or July] 1529 (octavo).

1/ The first work described in this entry on
the *Versandliste* contained two of Erasmus'
dialogues. *The Right Way of Speaking
Latin and Greek*, which in spite of its title

devotes its first part to the general problem
of education and teaching, was dedicated
to the thirteen-year-old Maximilian of
Burgundy (Ep 1949), son of Adolf of
Veere, to whose favour Erasmus had
previously recommended himself.[1] The
Ciceronianus, his satire against exaggerated
Latin purism, was dedicated to a personal
friend, Johann von Vlatten (Ep 1948), who
had for some years been a counsellor of
the duke of Cleves; he sent Erasmus a
silver goblet in thanks for this gesture.
In 1536 this was bequeathed to Bonifacius
Amerbach, who in turn gave it to Henricus
Glareanus as a memento of Erasmus.[2]
The dialogues were published three times
in a single volume by Froben; as *editiones
principes* in March 1528, enlarged and
improved in October 1529,[3] and then, with
no further substantial revision, in March
1530.[4] It is possible that Erasmus replaced
the original edition with the revised version
of October 1529 but did not replace this
by the later reprint.

2/ Of the two copies that Erasmus preserved of his apology against the Spanish
monastic orders that suspected him of
heresy, one, probably the first edition of
[March] 1528, was bound in combination
with an edition of Valla from the preceding
year; see no 153 #1. It may be assumed that
this entry refers to the revised edition of
[June or July] 1529, to which an appendix
with its own title-page was added containing corrections to several works of recent
years: *Loca quaedam in aliquot Erasmi
lucubrationibus per ipsum emendata.*[5]

1 Epp 93 and 266
2 Ep 1964:17 with n/18–19 with n3. On Vlatten
  see Allen and cwe Ep 1390 introductions and
  cebr iii 414–16.
3 It was the second authorized edition of the
  De recta pronuntiatione, but the third authorized
  version of the *Ciceronianus*, a revised second
  edition of which had already been published
  in March 1529 jointly with a new edition
  of the *Colloquia*.
4 Collation of the March 1530 text of the
  Ciceronianus with the October 1529 text yields

only a few minor differences. The *De recta pronuntiatione* of March 1530 was composed of the unsold sheets of the previous edition except the final gathering (sign H), which had to be reset in order to incorporate a long list of errata and a new colophon; see Bateman 'The Text of Erasmus' *De recta latini graecique sermonis pronuntiatione dialogus*' 61.

5 See Ep 2095, the foreword to the *Loca quaedam*.

353 **Paraphrasis Eras. in Ioan. et Acta.**

Erasmus. *Paraphrasis in Evangelium secundum Ioannem*. Basileae: J. Frobenius, 1523 (octavo).

and

Erasmus. *Paraphrasis in Acta Apostolorum,* Basileae: J. Frobenius, 1524 (octavo).

Erasmus dedicated his *Paraphrase on the Gospel of John*, published in February 1523 by Froben in folio, to Ferdinand of Austria (Ep 1333). He presented an unbound copy of the *editio princeps* to the archduke at the end of April. Subsequently he sent a properly bound copy, to which Ferdinand responded with a gift in acknowledgment of one hundred florins. The *Paraphrase on the Acts of the Apostles*, dedicated to Clement VII (Ep 1414), appeared early in 1524 from Froben simultaneously in folio and octavo, each issue numbering 3,000 copies. Erasmus dispatched a copy of the octavo to the pope, who rewarded him at once with a handsome present of money.[1]

Does this entry on the *Versandliste* refer to two octavo editions bound together? Froben editions of the *Paraphrase on John* in this format are known from March and April 1523, (described as 'now printed for the first time'), another from 1523 without month-date (similarly described), and another from 1534 (described as 'revised by the author'), which was included in the collected *Paraphrases in Novum Testamentum*. Octavo editions of the *Paraphrase on Acts* are known from [c February] 1524, another from 1524, and another dated 4 July 1524 ('from Erasmus'

second revised edition'), and from 1534, included in the collected Paraphrases. In this part of the *Versandliste*, unlike the section at the end,[2] only a few works of Erasmus' later years appear, so that this entry may refer to two of the early editions.

1 See Allen Epp 1333 and 1414 introductions, with a review of subsequent editions. For the *Paraphrase on John* see also Adams E 766, 767, 769, 771 (1524).
2 See no 407.

354 **Paraphrases Eras. in epistolas Pauli mino.**

Erasmus. *Paraphrases in epistolas minores Pauli (ad Timotheum duas, ad Titum unam & ad Philemonem unam)*. Antverpiae: M. Hillenius, [November] 1519 or one of the Froben reprints, 1520–3 (octavo).

The *editio princeps* of this work, dedicated to Philip of Burgundy, bishop of Utrecht (Ep 1043), appeared late in 1519 from Michaël Hillen at Antwerp in octavo.[1] Later Froben reprinted the *Paraphrases* on the minor Epistles several times, both in folio and in octavo, sometimes as the second part of the *Paraphrases in omnes epistolas Pauli*. This entry may refer either to the original edition or to one of Froben's octavos – March 1520, March and July 1521, 1522, and 1523.[2] The 1534 edition is left out of account; cf no 353.

1 Allen was unable to trace this edition (see his introduction to Ep 1043) but a copy, unfortunately incomplete, has been discovered in the library of Aachen cathedral; there is a photocopy of it in the City Library of Rotterdam.
2 See Allen Ep 1043 introduction; for the March 1520 edition see also Adams E 791 and for the March and July 1521 editions, see the 'union catalogue' of Erasmus editions in the City Library of Rotterdam: www.erasmus.org/ ErasmusOnlineDatabase.

355 **Paraphr. in Lucam**

Erasmus. *In Evangelium Lucae paraphrasis*. Basileae: J. Frobenius, August 1523 or 1523–4 (octavo).

The *Paraphrase on the Gospel of Luke*, dedicated to Henry VIII (Epp 1381, 1385), was reissued several times both in octavo and folio format, but as the adjacent books practically exclude a folio volume in this case, one of the (authorized) octavo editions must be meant here: either the *editio princeps* of August 1523[1] or the Froben edition of 1523 (colophon 1524), described on the title-page as 'revised by the author.'[2] The 1534 edition is left out of consideration; cf nos 353 and 354.

1 Adams E 755
2 Adams E 756; Allen Ep 1381 introduction

356 Para. in epistol. ad Rom. et Corin.

Erasmus. *Paraphrasis in epistolam Pauli apostoli ad Romanos*. A quarto or octavo edition.

and

Erasmus. *Paraphrasis in duas epistolas Pauli ad Corinthios*. A quarto or octavo edition.

The short title in the *Versandliste* could refer to a combination of separately issued quarto editions or to an octavo edition that included both paraphrases.

Separate quarto editions of the *Paraphrase on the Epistle to the Romans* appeared in Leuven (Dirk Martens, November 1517; the *editio princeps*) and in Basel (Johann Froben, January and November 1518),[1] as also did the *Paraphrase on 1 and 2 Corinthians* (Leuven: Dirk Martens, c February 1519, *editio princeps* and Basel: Johann Froben, March 1519).[2] A combined octavo edition of the two Paraphrases also included the *Paraphrase on the Epistle to the Galatians* (Basel: Johann Froben, January 1520).[3]

1 The Froben edition of April 1519 was an octavo. See for the Leuven edition NK 846 and for the Basel edition Allen Ep 710 (dedicatory letter to Domenico Grimani) introduction
2 NK 844 and Allen Ep 916 (dedicatory letter to Erard de la Marck) introduction
3 Adams E 790

357 Demegoriae Oecolamp. Exomolog. Eras.

Oecolampadius, Johannes. *In Epistolam Joannis apostoli catholicam primam demegoriae, hoc est homilae una et xx*. Basileae: A. Cratander, June 1524 (octavo).

bound with

Erasmus. *Exomologesis sive modus confitendi*. Basileae: J. Frobenius, 1524 (octavo).

1/ Sermons on the First Epistle of John by Oecolampadius given after his return to Basel during Advent 1523 and published early in the next year with a dedication to the bishop of Basel, Christoph von Utenheim, and his coadjutor Nikolaus von Diesbach.[1] In one of them, not naming him but citing him literally, he criticized Erasmus, who had earlier commented on the style of John. He had Erasmus in mind in another sermon as well, in which he made a sharp attack on the modern Pelagians. Erasmus reacted to the criticism at the end of January 1525 in a letter to Oecolampadius himself (Ep 1538).

2/ The *editio princeps* of Erasmus' little book on confession, dedicated to François Du Moulin, grand almoner to Francis I (Ep 1426). It also contained, besides four letters,[2] the first publication of his *Paraphrasis in tertium psalmum*, dedicated to Melchior of Vianden (Ep 1427),[3] and his *Apologia ad Stunicae conclusiones*, dedicated to Johannes Fabri (Ep 1428).[4] The second Froben printing of the *Exomologesis* (1530), although described by its title-page as 'revised with care and enlarged,' does not appear in the *Versandliste*.

1 Staehelin BAO I 285–9. For the first edition see Staehelin *Oekolampad-Bibliographie* no 95. A second edition 'denuo per authorem recognitae' appeared from Cratander in January 1525; ibidem no 105.

2 Ep 1310, a letter sent to Adrian VI with a
 presentation copy of the edition of Arnobius;
 Ep 1324, Adrian's reply; Ep 1329, the letter
 dedicating *Exomologesis* to Adrian; and Ep 1347,
 Epistola Iodoco Gavero de morte, a letter lamenting
 the death of Jan de Neve.
3 A transcript of Erasmus' autograph of this
 paraphrase had been preserved and is now in
 the Town Library at Gouda; ASD V-2 92.
4 The *Apologia* was not subsequently reprinted;
 see Allen Ep 1428 introduction; ASD IX-2 26–8
 and 42. Erasmus kept a copy of the 1524 edition
 of *Exomologesis* in *arca aulae versus fenestram*;
 see *Catalogus librorum Erasmi* nos 3 and 105.

358 Eras. enarrationes in .4. psalmos.

Erasmus. *In primum et secundum psalmum
… enarrationes, in tertium paraphrasis, iam
denuo per autorem recognitae. His accessit
in psalmum quartum concio.* Basileae:
J. Frobenius, 1525 (octavo).

The only known authorized edition of
Erasmus' commentaries on Psalms 1–4.
The *Sermon on the Fourth Psalm*, dedicated
to John Longland (Ep 1535) appeared here
for the first time and had its own title-page;
the commentaries on the others had
already been published, though not
independently: *An Exposition of the First
Psalm* in the *Lucubrationes* (Strasbourg:
Matthias Schürer 1515; see no 50),
A Commentary on the Second Psalm in
Arnobius Commentarii in omnes psalmos
(Basel: Johann Froben 1522; see no 325),
and *A Paraphrase on the Third Psalm* in the
Exomologesis (Basel: Johann Froben 1524;
see no 357).

359 Eras. de conscrib. epistolis, eiusdem
   Similia

Erasmus. *Opus de conscribendis epistolis …
recognitum & locupletatum. Parabolarum
sive similium liber … recognitus.* Basileae:
J. Frobenius, August 1522 (quarto).

Almost certainly this title describes the first
authorized edition of Erasmus' treatise on
the writing of letters, which was also the
only edition to include the *Parabolae sive*

similia. Froben reissued both works in
octavo format in 1534, but independently
and not in a combined volume. The two
later editions, bound together, could be
referred to here, but that is not very likely:
in the first place, because the *De conscribendis epistolis* of 1534 appears elsewhere in the *Versandliste* (no 409); and
secondly because the edition of the
Parabolae of that year was produced
without any active collaboration of
Erasmus and reproduced the text of
one of the early editions, in which the
'not unimportant addition,' consisting
of sixteen new *parabolae* added to the
Froben edition of 1522, was still lacking.[1]

Erasmus was forced to issue this edition
of *De conscribendis epistolis* when in 1521,
without his knowledge, John Siberch in
Cambridge published a *Libellus de conscribendis epistolis, autore D. Erasmo*, very
carelessly prepared and based on a circulating copy of his short manuscript draft of
c 1498.[2] He dedicated the greatly enlarged
and much revised – indeed practically new
– version to his French friend, Nicolas
Bérault (Ep 1284).[3]

The revised edition of the *Parabolae* of
1522 occupies an important position in the
textual history of the work because of the
additions, which were omitted in most of
the later printings, including that of Froben
of 1534.

1 ASD I-5 27–8 and 31. On the early editions
  see no 371.
2 See Ep 71 introductions; on the Siberch and the
  1522 Froben editions see ASD I-2 166–73 / CWE 25
  2–6. On the original manuscript and the copy
  of it made by a secretary, which Erasmus kept,
  see Ep 3100:30n.
3 On Bérault see no 46 #2.

360 Nouum Testa. grae.

Novum Testamentum graece [Ed. Nic.
Gerbelius]. Hagenoae: in aed. Thomae
Anshelmi, March 1521 (quarto) or Basileae:
J. Bebelius, 1524 or later (octavo).

In 1521 Thomas Anshelm of Hagenau published the first edition of Erasmus' New Testament in the original Greek without the accompanying translation into Latin. That edition followed, with only minor differences, the second edition of Erasmus' text (1519).[1] The editor was Nikolaus Gerbel, who in 1515 had assisted Oecolampadius in the correction of the proofs of the *Novum instrumentum*.[2] Erasmus did not have a very high opinion of that collaboration, but three years later when he visited Strasbourg and was the guest of the literary society there, Gerbel did him many kindnesses, so that later Erasmus thanked his Strasbourg friends through Gerbel for the welcome he had received.[3]

If this entry refers to a quarto volume, then it must almost certainly be the Gerbel edition, but since the surrounding volumes do not clearly indicate the format, one of the later octavos of the Greek Testament, printed separately, may also be eligible. The Basel printer Johann Bebel, using Erasmus' third version of the New Testament (1522) as a basis, published an edition in 1524 corrected by J. Ceporinus and introduced by an 'Exhortation to the reading of Holy Scripture' by Oecolampadius, which he reprinted without change in 1531 and 1535. Other editions appeared from the presses of Wolfgang Cephalaeus in Strasbourg (1524) and Simon de Colines in Paris (1534), the latter also founded on Erasmus' Greek version of 1522 but distinguished 'by the adopting of many readings from ancient sources.'[4]

1 BL *Catalogue* 18 1216
2 Cf Allen Ep 373 introduction (page 164), Allen and CWE Ep 384 introductions (page 183/216), and Epp 351:1n/2n, 358 5n/7n, 417:5n/6n. On Gerbel see also Celtis *Briefwechsel* 620–1 note; CEBR II 90–1.
3 Epp 797:8–10/9–11, 867:23–5/26–7, 883
4 On all these editions see BL *Catalogue* (n1 above); on Anshelm's 1524 edition see also Staehelin *Das theologische Lebenswerk Oekolampads* nos 186–7.

361 Colloquia Eras.

Erasmus. *Familiarium colloquiorum formulae*? Perhaps one of the authorized Froben editions, Basel 1522–4, in octavo.

Erasmus *Colloquies* were published before 1526 under the title of *Familiarium colloquiorum formulae* and after that date as *Familiarium colloquiorum opus*. The work appears twice in the *Versandliste*. Under no 363 it is explicitly recorded as *Colloquiorum opus*. Perhaps the short form *Colloquia* is deliberately used here to indicate one of the older Froben editions, which Erasmus may have kept. But that cannot be proved, and which of the editions of the *Formulae* could in that case be referred to is pure conjecture. The *Formulae*, originally a short collection of phrases and idioms for young students of polite Latin conversation, were first published by Froben in November 1518, without the author's knowledge or approval and edited by Beatus Rhenanus from a careless copy of c 1498. It is unlikely that Erasmus would have kept this unauthorized edition, out of all the others. He was rather indignant about its publication, and an amended edition appeared within a few months, printed by Dirk Martens of Leuven in March 1519.[1] This was the first authorized version. The first edition to be fully recognized by Erasmus, an octavo, was published by Froben in March 1522. This edition, dedicated to his godson Johannes Erasmius Froben (Ep 1262), the printer's six-year-old son, was of particular importance for another reason: the new dialogues included in it gave the originally didactically conceived work the satirical and polemical character it was to keep.[2] The edition of March 1522 was followed in quick succession by four authorized editions, in the same format and with the same title, each including new dialogues: in July–August 1522, August 1523, March 1524 and August–September 1524.[3] For the later editions under the title of *Familiarium colloquiorum opus*, see no 363.

1 Allen Ep 56 introduction, Ep 130:92n/108–9n, and Ep 909, Erasmus' preface to the reader for the Martens 1519 edition. A copy of this edition, which Erasmus gave as a present to Johann Froben, is now in the library of Beatus Rhenanus in Sélestat; see Walter *Catalogue Sélestat* 3 (no 1171) and *Erasmus … Vorkämpfer für Frieden und Toleranz* 185 (E9.3).
2 ASD I-3 8
3 The edition of September 1524 had a new introduction, Ep 1476. On the various editions of the *Colloquies* see ASD I-3 3–20 (introduction); Gutmann *Die Colloquia Familiaria des Erasmus von Rotterdam* 3–64; CWE 39–40 xx–xxvii, 1137–8.

362 Eras. Ratio uerae Theologiae

Erasmus. *Ratio sev compendium theologiae.* Probably an octavo edition.

The *Ratio verae theologiae* originally formed a part of the preliminary matter to Erasmus' edition of the New Testament. It appeared in its embryonic form (under the title of *Methodus*) in the *editio princeps* of 1516 and was subsequently considerably enlarged in the second edition of 1519; it was omitted in later editions of the *Novum Testamentum*. The expanded version had already been published separately before 1519 in November 1518, by Dirk Martens of Leuven, in a quarto volume, with two letters preceding the text, one from and the other to Albert of Brandenburg, archbishop of Mainz (Epp 661 and 745). This entry on the *Versandliste* probably does not refer to that independent edition, since the surrounding volumes are octavos. The augmented Froben edition of February 1520 is a possibility.[1] But the authorized revised edition that appeared in 1523, with a new prefatory letter from Erasmus to Albert of Brandenburg (Ep 1365) replacing the two letters originally included, is more likely. Could it perhaps have been the Antwerp edition of Michaël Hillen, which Erasmus himself explicitly named in his *Catalogus lucubrationum* as the definitive text of the *Ratio* but of which no copy

appears to have been traced to this day?[2] It is known that of the smaller formats Hillen published practically only octavos at around this time.

1 In a letter to Albert Erasmus refers to this edition, 'enriched with considerable additions'; Ep 1033:265–6 with 265n/289–1 with n39. A copy of the 1520 edition was in the separate collection of his own works, mainly Froben editions, which Erasmus kept 'in a chest in the hall, near the window'; see *Catalogus librorum Erasmi* no 77. In the same collection (no 17) Erasmus also kept a copy of the semi-authorized quarto edition of the *Ratio* (Froben, January 1519), which had as a preface a letter from Beatus Rhenanus to Johannes Fabri (dated 10 January 1519) instead of the letters from and to Albert of Brandenburg. In issuing this edition Beatus was 'acting, no doubt, on the general instructions by which Erasmus had given him a free hand in the publication of his works'; see Allen Ep 745 introduction.
2 Allen I 40:29–30/CWE Ep 1341A:1579–80. It appears neither in BE nor in the bibliographical apparatus of the City Library of Rotterdam (www.erasmus.org/ErasmusOnlineDatabase).

363 Colloquiorum opus Eras.

Erasmus. *Familiarium colloquiorum opus … ab auctore recognitum.* Basileae: off. Frobeniana. An octavo edition.

The *Colloquiorum familiarium formulae* were first published under the title of *Familiarium colloquiorum opus* by Froben in February 1526 (see no 361). Under this new title, the Basel printing house issued six further authorized editions until Erasmus' death, each one enlarged: in June 1526, 1527, March and September 1529, September 1531, and March 1533. The title *Colloquiorum opus* appears in the *Versandliste* only once, which suggests that as each new edition was published, Erasmus removed its predecessor from his library. Thus, this entry may refer to the edition of March 1533, the last to be enlarged with new dialogues and the standard text after Erasmus' death, which was to be the basis for countless impressions of the complete *Colloquia*. But this is of course pure conjecture.

364 Palamedes palliata comoedia, annota./ Vallae in nouum testa. Vallae dialectica

Arduenna, Remaclus. *Palamedes palliata comedia*. Londini: R. Pynson, 1512 (folio).

bound with

Valla, Laurentius. *In latinam Novi Testamenti interpretationem … adnotationes*. Parisiis: J. Badius, April 1505 (folio).

and

Valla, Laurentius. *Dialectice libri tres*. Parisiis: J. Badius, 1509 (folio).

1/ There are two undated editions of Arduenna's *Palamedes*, the supposed *editio princeps* in folio printed in London by Pynson and a quarto printed by Gourmont in Paris, both c 1512. The size of another book bound in the same volume makes it probable that Erasmus possessed the original edition. Remaclus Arduenna, humanist poet and magistrate, was a native of Florennes near Namur. He studied in Paris and Cologne at the beginning of the century, and published a volume of *Epigrammata* in Cologne. He taught at a London school, perhaps St Paul's, in 1512. Next he went to Paris, and later returned to the Low Countries, where about 1517 he became a member, and soon after secretary, of the privy council of the governor, Margaret of Austria. During his stay in Paris he must have known the poet Fausto Andrelini (c 1462–1518), whose influence can be seen in his love-poems. In London, perhaps influenced by Maarten van Dorp's *Dialogus in quo Venus et Cupido omnes adhibent versutias*, he wrote his allegorical-didactic prose comedy *Palamedes*, which he published together with some spiritual poems on the life of Christ and the Assumption of the Blessed Virgin and dedicated to his patron, a collector of papal revenues in England, Pietro Griffi. Among his older friends and patrons were Jérôme de Busleyden and Joris van Halewijn, both of whom enjoyed good relations with Erasmus.[1] Erasmus and Arduenna were on friendly terms. Where and when they came into contact we do not know. Perhaps they met in Paris in the circle of Fausto Andrelini, one of Erasmus' first friends in the French capital. In 1512 they were both in London, and Remaclus may have made a present of his *Palamedes* to Erasmus at that time. In 1516 Erasmus was still corresponding with him, but afterwards there must have been a chill in their friendship; in the *Acta Academiae Lovaniensis contra Lutherum*, attributed to Erasmus, Remaclus is described as an accomplice of Girolamo Aleandro and a 'notorious and unprincipled glutton.'[2]

2/ The only edition of Lorenzo Valla's philological annotations on the Vulgate translation of the New Testament, edited by Erasmus from the manuscript he had discovered in the abbey of Parc at Leuven in 1504 and dedicated by him to Christopher Fisher (Ep 182). As Bainton has pointed out, 'Valla's annotations … contain nothing especially exciting. They are just philological notes … But that the New Testament should be subjected to the same sort of philological scrutiny as any other book may well have stimulated Erasmus to undertake his own translation and annotations.'[3]

3/ 'For some time I have been in need of Lorenzo Valla's *Dialectica*,' wrote Erasmus in 1498 to Robert Gaguin, 'if you have it, I beg you to lend it to me; or if not, to suggest whom I should ask.'[4] He alludes to the quarto edition that had appeared about this time (without year-date or publisher's name).[5] It was not until later that he obtained the book for himself, a folio volume like the two other works bound with it; for this reason it must have been the Bade edition of 1509.

1 On Remaclus Arduenna see Allen and CWE Ep 411 introductions; *Biographie nationale* XIX 8–11; de Vocht *History of the* CTL I 6, 207, and 220; CEBR III 140; *Dictionnaire de biographie française* III, 446;

Ellinger *Geschichte der neulateinischen Lyrik in
den Niederlanden* 15; IJsewijn 'The Coming of
Humanism to Low Countries' 279. On Griffi see
Ep 243:60n/69n and CEBR II 131–2. On Busleyden
see Ep 205 introductions and CEBR I 235–7. On
Halewijn see Allen Ep 641 introduction and
CEBR II 158–9.
2 Ferguson *Opuscula* 324/CWE 71 104; cf Allen
Ep 411 introduction.
3 *Erasmus of Christendom* 65
4 Ep 67:4–5/5–6
5 Hain 15828

365 Eras. Commenta. de duplici Copia

Erasmus. *De duplici copia verborum ac rerum
commentarii.* Possibly one of the early
authorized editions: Parisiis: J. Badius,
July 1512; or Argentorati: M. Schürer,
December 1514; or Basileae: J. Frobenius,
April 1517 (quarto).

Erasmus' *De copia*, a manual designed to
help beginners in Latin composition by
supplying them with an abundance of
words and phrases, was dedicated to John
Colet (Ep 260). Soon adopted as a textbook of rhetoric throughout northern
Europe, it had been reprinted nearly a
hundred times by 1536. Any attempt to
identify the edition Erasmus kept in his
library might therefore seem futile. Yet,
if it was a quarto volume – and the nine
following entries in the list could point in
that direction – and if pirated reprints can
be left out of consideration, then only a
few editions, all of them early, are possibilities. The oldest of them is the *editio
princeps*, published by Bade in 1512, which
also contained the *Concio de puero Jesu*
and some poems, besides the first version
of the *De ratione studii* to be acknowledged
by the author.[1]

Matthias Schürer of Strasbourg twice
reprinted the Bade text, but he also
brought out a revised and enlarged edition
of *De copia* in December 1514, with a
preface by Erasmus addressed to him
(Ep 311). This was the first to contain the
correspondence between Erasmus and

Jakob Wimpfeling occasioned by the visit
he had paid to Sélestat and Strasbourg in
the summer of that year. Also added were
laudatory poems on the three Alsatian
humanists Sebastian Brant, Thomas
Vogler, and Johannes Sapidus, whom
Erasmus had met there.[2] After *De copia*,
though with its own title-page, the *editio
princeps* of the *Parabolae* was included
(cf no 371). Reprints of this edition were
issued by Schürer in February and October
1516, respectively with and without the
Parabolae.

A new version of *De copia* appeared from
Froben at Basel in April 1517, dedicated by
the author to Froben's corrector Wilhelm
Nesen (Ep 462), who was responsible for
seeing it through the press. Erasmus had
revised the text, at Nesen's request, while
journeying down the Rhine in May 1516.
It was assumed that he used as his guide a
copy of the Bade edition of July 1512 that
has been preserved and is now in the
Stadt- und Universitätsbibliothek of
Frankfurt-am-Main, but this has been
questioned by Betty I. Knott.[3] The 1517
edition once again included the text of
the *De ratione studii*, and from it Froben
produced two quarto reprints, published
in March 1519 and February 1521 respectively. After 1523 *De copia* was brought out
only very rarely in quarto. The authorized
Froben edition of May 1526, an octavo,
may therefore be left out of consideration.
The greatly expanded last authorized
Froben edition of August 1534, though
one of the rare exceptions in quarto
format, may likewise be left aside for
another reason: most probably this edition
is listed elsewhere on the *Versandliste*
(no 408). There are thus only three quarto
editions that are likely to be meant here,
because of Erasmus' direct concern with
them: the *editio princeps* of 1512, the
Schürer edition of 1514, and the Froben
edition of 1517. Which of them Erasmus
kept in his library cannot be ascertained.

1 For the poems see Reedijk *Poems* nos 85–90/
ASD I-7 and CWE 85–6 nos 43, 46, 47, 44, 48, 45;
for *De ratione studii* cf no 367.
2 Cf Epp 302 (from Wimpfeling) and 305 (Erasmus'
reply); Reedijk *Poems* nos 95–7/ASD I-7 and CWE
85–6 nos 54, 55, 3.
3 Sign. Einbd. Slg. 611 no 1. Husner 'Bibliothek'
254 n90 wrongly mentions the Schürer edition
of 1514; cf ASD I-6 17 with n49.

366 Nicolai Leonici Dialogi

Leonicus, Nicolaus Thomaeus. *Dialogi
nunc primum in lucem editi*. Venetiis: G.
de Gregoriis, September 1524 (quarto).

A direct reflection of Erasmus' reading of
this collected edition of Niccolò Leonico
Tomeo's dialogues, which was dedicated
to Reginald Pole, is found in Erasmus'
letter to Jacopo Sadoleto of March 1531.
In it he mentions one of the dialogues, the
Sadoletus sive de precibus, and expresses
his admiration by saying, 'If I had read
this dialogue (I would have read it if my
friends had sent it to me in time), then
my little book on praying would have been
a little less jejune and crawling along the
ground'[1] In the previous year Erasmus had
written to Luca Bonfiglio, the secretary of
Cardinal Campeggio, that he would be very
glad to read Leonico's book, which he had
clearly only just acquired, 'for I know that
nothing comes from the pen of an erudite
and pious man that is not learned and
pious.' Allen thought that this was a
reference to the dialogue *Bembus sive de
essentia animi*, also published separately at
Venice. But why should Erasmus not have
meant Leonico's collection, which, as is
evident from his letter to Sadoleto, he had
first read at about this time? Is it too daring
to speculate that he had received a copy of
the book from Bonfiglio, who set particular
store by Erasmus' friendship and who
presumably was also keen to bring the
dialogues to his attention? For Bonfiglio, a
good friend of Leonico Tomeo (who had
dedicated a translation of Aristotle to
him), appeared himself as a leading

character in the dialogue *Alverotus sive
de tribus animorum vehiculis*, also included
in the book. Erasmus' letter gives the clear
impression of being a letter of thanks,
beginning with a reference to a gift and
ending with the words 'I thank you for
your kind sentiments towards me. I
promise in all sincerity to reciprocate
them.'[2] Apart from the dialogues already
named, the collection also included
*Trophonius sive de divinatione, Peripateticus
sive de nominum inventione, Sannutus sive
de compescendo luctu, Severinus sive de
relativorum natura, Phoebus sive de aetatum
moribus, Bonominus sive de Alica*, and
Sannutus sive de ludo talario.

1 Ep 2443:387–93/384–90, echoing Horace *Epistles*
2.1.251. Froben published *Modus orandi Deum*
on October 1524. On Leonico Tomeo see no 76.
2 Ep 2347:1–2 with 1n, 11–12/2–4 with n1, 14–15.
On Bonfiglio see Allen and CWE introductions.

367 Eras. De ratione studij

Erasmus. *De ratione studii ac legendi
interpretandique auctores libellus aureus.
Officium discipulorum ex Quintiliano. Qui
primo legendi, ex eodem … Ex recognitione
auctoris*. Argentorati: M. Schürer, 1514
or one of the reprints (quarto).

In October 1511, without Erasmus'
knowledge, an abbreviated version of his
De ratione studii, based on a manuscript
that had fallen into the hands of William
Thale, was published in Paris as a supplement to a collection of letters from the
Italian humanist Agostino Dati.[1] Robert
de Keysere and Matthias Schürer also
published the work in this form, with
some other Erasmiana, at Paris (or Ghent)
and Strasbourg respectively, before the
first text acknowledged by the author and
more fully elaborated was published by
Josse Bade in Paris in July 1512, in the
editio princeps of *De copia* (cf nos 244,
365).[2] Further reprints of this last version
were produced by Dirk Martens in Leuven
and Matthias Schürer in Strasbourg, in

October 1512 and August 1513. Bade's edition had been prepared in haste, and showed several shortcomings. In the summer of 1514, when Erasmus visited Strasbourg,[3] he took the opportunity to help Schürer prepare an improved text of *De ratione studii* for the press. The new edition, which appeared in August and was reprinted by Schürer in 1516, 1518, and 1519, also contained the 'alia' that had been included in his unauthorized editions of 1512 and 1513.[4] Must it not have been this Strasbourg edition, with the definitive version of *De ratione studii*, that Erasmus left in 1536? It is difficult to imagine that he would have preserved one of the early pirated reprints. On the other hand, the Bade text included in the 1512 *De copia* would not have been entered under its own title, so that the compiler of the *Versandliste* would have seen no title-page. The likely format – all the adjacent books are quartos – makes the possibility very slight that one of the later editions, all octavos from 1520, is referred to.

1 *Augustini Dathi Senensis Pancarpie Epistolae … Praeterea Herasmi Roterodami Ratio studii ac legendi interpretandique auctores* (Paris: G. Biermans for Jean Granjon 20 October 1511)
2 On the history of the text and the early editions, see ASD I-2 83–96. The Strasbourg edition appeared in July 1512.
3 On the visit see Epp 302 and 305 to Jakob Wimpfeling.
4 For the poems included in it see Reedijk *Poems* 84–90 / ASD I-7 and CWE 85–6 nos 52, 43, 46, 47, 44, 48, 45.

368 Assertio Sacramentorum Henrici regis

Henry VIII. *Assertio septem sacramentorum adversus Martinum Lutherum*. Londini: R. Pynson, July 1521 or January 1522 (quarto).

Henry VIII's *Assertio septem sacramentorum* was directed against Luther, in particular against the doctrine of the sacraments set out in his *De captivitate babylonica*; it immediately earned the king his title of

'Defender of the Faith' from Pope Leo X. Erasmus probably kept in his library the copy with the king's dedication in his own hand that William Tate had sent to him.[1] At Bruges, where he was staying in August 1521 during the negotiations between the emperor and Cardinal Wolsey, the papal nuncio had let him have a glimpse of the book, but Erasmus had yet not received the copy repeatedly promised him by Wolsey.[2] The presentation copy from the court appears not to have reached him until late, so that it is possible that he only received the second Pynson edition. Some contemporaries thought that Erasmus had composed the text of the *Assertio*. He denied the suspicion and sought the grounds for it in his influence on the king's style: 'For the king when he was a boy read nothing more diligently than my writings, and from them he may perhaps have picked up something of my style, if indeed there is anything of mine in his book.'[3]

1 Ep 1246:26–7 / 30–1; cf Ep 1342:860–5 / 949–52.
2 Epp 1227:5–6, 28–30 / 7–8, 32–4, 1342:835–68 / 921–55
3 Ep 1275:85–7 / 94–6; cf Ep 1342:868–71 / 953–9.

369 Contra Henri. regem Angliae Mart. Lut.

Luther, Martinus. *Contra Henricum Regem Angliae*. Wittembergae: [J. Rhau-Grunenberg,] 1522 or the reprint, [Basileae: Adam Petri] of the same year (quarto).

Luther's answer to the *Assertio septem sacramentorum* of Henry VIII; see no 368. In the summer of 1522 Luther had prepared both the Latin text and 'a reply in German,' which in fact appeared slightly earlier.[1] Beatus Rhenanus had only seen this German version in Basel on 12 October.[2] The Latin text must have become available not much later, for Adam Petri reprinted it before the end of the year. In Henry VIII's circle, the suspicion arose that Erasmus had had something to do with its publication. To clear himself of this charge, Erasmus sent his pupil and helper Lieven Algoet to England at the end of April 1523 with letters (no longer extant) for the king and Cardinal Wolsey. The mission achieved its purpose. Erasmus received letters in return: 'The king exonerates himself, and so does the cardinal.' His friends presented his *famulus* with thirty gulden. Bishop Tunstall was delighted with the letters Erasmus had written, but also expressed the expectation and wish of his friends that Erasmus would write something against Luther, as the pope had asked him, and suggested a subject: the freedom of the will.[3]

1 Benzing *Lutherbibliographie* nos 1225 and 1226; for the 'Antwort deutsch,' no 1228
2 Ep 1308:9 with n/9–10 with n3
3 Epp 1383:25–9/28–32 (to Pirckheimer) and 1367:1–14 with 1n/3–16 with n1 (from Tunstall)

370 Epistolae duae, Zuinglij una, Andreae/ Osiandri altera: Iouij libel. de legati // one Principis Moschouiae ad Clementem.

Epistolae duae, una Hulderichi Zwinglii ad Andream Osiandrum…, altera Andreae Osiandri ad eundem Hulderichum Zwinglium, apologetica … Norimbergae: J. Petreius, September 1527 (quarto).

bound with

Jovius, Paulus. *Libellus de legatione Basilii magni Principis Moschoviae ad Clementem VII Pont. Max.* Basileae: J. et H. Frobenius, 1527 or Romae: F. Minutius Calvus, 1525 (quarto).

1/ In the Eucharistic controversy the Nürnberg reformer Andreas Osiander chose the side of Luther, and in 1526 he openly attacked the opinions of Zwingli in his sermons. The Zürich reformer, who saw his writings banned in Nürnberg, responded in May 1527 in an arrogant and challenging letter to his colleague.[1] Osiander was highly indignant at the tone and content of this letter and replied in September in a detailed letter that was

equally violent and hostile.[2] He republished the two letters, which contributed little positive to the controversy on the disputed doctrine, in the work referred to above.[3] Erasmus must have acquired and read a copy very soon, for he referred to it early in December, when he expressed to Martin Bucer his dismay at the way in which Zwingli, Luther, and Osiander attacked each other in such biting polemical works.[4]

2/ A brief description of the Muscovite empire – the country and its people, their manners, customs, and means of livelihood – by the historian Paolo Giovio (1483– 1552), compiled from information related to him by a member of the embassy of the Grand Prince Vasily III to Pope Clement VII.[5] Erasmus may have owned either the *editio princeps*, published in August 1525 by Francesco Minuzio Calvo at Rome, or Froben's Basel 1527 reprint. The Basel edition seems the obvious choice, especially since Osiander's pamphlet, the work with which it is bound, also dated from 1527. But Erasmus and Calvo were occasionally in direct contact. In 1517 Erasmus received some Greek books from him (see nos 98 and 107), and in 1525 he thanked him 'on behalf of the general cause of learning' for some 'attractive books' that he had received.[6] Giovio's little work may well have been among them. But even so, it may not have been the presentation copy from Calvo that he had bound after 1527. Perhaps he gave the original edition to Froben to reprint, and later received a copy of the reprint in return.

1 Zwingli *Werke* IX 127–30
2 Zwingli *Werke* IX 232–76
3 Seebass *Bibliographia Osiandrica* 45 (no 14). Cf Moller *Andreas Osiander* 88–97.
4 Ep 1901:35–8/38–41
5 Adelung *Kritisch-literarische Übersicht der Reisenden in Russland* II 187; Barberi 'Le edizione romane di Francesco Minuzio Calvo' 79 no 65
6 Ep 1604:1–2/3–4

371 Similia Erasmi

Erasmus. *Parabolarum sive similium liber*. Possibly one of the editions Argentorati: ex. aedib. Schurerianis, 1514 or 1516 or 1518 or Lovanii: T. Martinus, 1515 (all quarto).

If this book, like most of those listed from no 365 to no 375, was a quarto, then only a few of the early editions of the *Parabolae* need be considered. The *editio princeps* appeared in quarto format, at the same time as the revised *De copia*, in December 1514. Erasmus must have settled the terms for publication of this work, dedicated to his friend Pieter Gillis, the town clerk of Antwerp (Ep 312), with Matthias Schürer in the summer of that year, when he spent a short time at Strasbourg en route to Basel; cf nos 365 (*De copia*) and 367 (*De ratione studii*). Copies of these editions of *De copia* and *Parabolae* are usually found bound in one volume. The *Parabolae* were announced on the title-page of *De copia*, but they had their own title-page as well, and thus were also circulated separately. A second edition, likewise in quarto, appeared from the press of Dirk Martens at Leuven in June 1515; it was most probably revised by Erasmus and produced under the supervision of Gerard Geldenhouwer, who was then still on good terms with him.[1] Also in quarto were the Schürer reprints that came out in February and November 1516 and July 1518, the first of them seen through the press by Nikolaus Gerbel, who had attempted in vain to involve the author actively in the work of revision.[2]

In the meantime, at the suggestion of Erasmus himself, who sent him a revised copy of Schürer's edition, Josse Bade put in hand a new version provided with a glossary of uncommon words that he himself had compiled.[3] This, however, appeared in small octavo format (in Bade's words 'reduced … to a handy form') and thus may be left out of consideration here,

if our assumption that the entry refers to a quarto is correct. The same applies even more strongly to the small octavos published by Johann Froben without the author's knowledge in February 1518, February 1519, and July 1521, from the Schürer or Bade text.[4] After 1520, no further editions of the *Parabolae* appeared in quarto with a single exception: the authorized Froben printing, important for the textual history of the work, of August 1522, which, however, is very probably entered elsewhere in the list (no 359). Erasmus drew the substance of the *Parabolae* from three classical authors: from Plutarch, whose *Moralia* was the source of half the parallels; from Seneca, mainly from the *Epistolae morales*; and from the Elder Pliny, whose *Naturalis historia* (see nos 205, 206, and 412) may also frequently have been the indirect source of extracts from Aristotle's *Historia animalium* and Theophrastus' *Historia plantarum* and *De causis plantarum* (cf no 211). A negligible number of similes was derived from Lucian, Xenophon, and Demosthenes.

1 NK 838. On this edition, see ASD I-5 13–15/CWE 23 125. On Geldenhouwer see Allen and CWE Ep 487 introductions and CEBR II 82–4.
2 Cf Epp 369 and 383 from Nikolaus Gerbel; ASD I-5 15–18. The three quarto Schürer editions were practically page-for-page reprints of the *editio princeps*. The February 1521 Schürer edition is in octavo.
3 See Epp 434 and 472, with Allen and CWE introductions; ASD I-5 18–22; CWE 23 126. Remarkably enough, Erasmus had still not received a copy from Bade more than a year after its appearance; Ep 764:1–4/3–7.
4 ASD I-5 23–4/CWE 23 126

372 Eugubinus aduersus Luteranos

Steuchus Eugubinus, Augustinus. *Pro religione Christiana adversus Lutheranos*. Bononiae: J.B. Phaellus, May 1530 (quarto).

In his book in defence of the Christian religion against the Lutherans, dedicated to Cardinal Alessandro Farnese (later Pope

Julius II), Agostino Steuco directed his polemic not only against Luther, as the title suggests, but also against Erasmus and the 'pernicious' ideas contained, above all, in his *Colloquies*. (Steuco's *Recognitio Veteris Testamenti*, a defence of the Vulgate text of the Pentateuch against humanist textual criticism, was also in Erasmus' library; see no 334.) Steuco saw in Erasmus the man who had prepared the way for Luther and, lumping the two together, spoke of the *principes* 'leaders' of the religious controversy. In the second part of his book he defended the doctrine of the primacy of papal power, and consequently also the genuineness of the so-called Donation of Constantine, which had long been dismissed as a forgery on convincing grounds by Laurenzo Valla. Steuco roused ill-feeling through the violent attacks in his book on Germans and German scholarship.[1]

1 For an analysis of the content of the book see Freudenberger *Augustinus Steuchus und sein literarisches Lebenswerk* 265–300.

373 Alberti Pij responsio ad epistolam Eras.

Pius, Albertus. *Ad Erasmi … expostulationem responsio accurata et paraenetica Martini Lutheri et asseclarum eius haeresim vesanam magnis argumentis et iustis rationibus confutans*. Parisiis: J. Badius, 7 January 1529 (quarto).

Alberto Pio, prince of Carpi, had been brought up under the guidance of Aldo Manuzio, and the lasting friendship between master and pupil is evident from the numerous Aldine editions dedicated to Pio (among them the Greek Aristotle; see no 214).[1] It was also in Venice, in Aldo's circle, that Erasmus met Pio in 1508. From 1510, the prince played an important role as a diplomat both in French and in imperial service. He was from the start a fanatical anti-Lutheran, and he held Erasmus to a great degree responsible for the religious unrest. Informed of this in reports from Rome, Erasmus wrote to Pio in October 1525 to explain his point of view (Ep 1634). Pio's reaction was his *Responsio paraenetica*, dated 15 May 1526, which Erasmus saw in manuscript in the summer of that year. He hesitated to reply, and the work circulated in manuscript for two more years before Pio prepared it for the press and had it printed by Josse Bade in January 1529. Towards the end of February Erasmus noted that Pio had published the book and commented that 'in it he does two things: he tries to persuade us that I was responsible for all the trouble that has arisen in the world; and he refutes the teachings of Luther, but with such feeble arguments that I do not think he has thought deeply about the matter.'[2] Erasmus, who had tried to prevent publication, wrote a reply of eighty quarto pages within four days of receiving the pamphlet. This was published a few weeks later by Froben as the *Responsio ad epistolam paraeneticam Alberti Pii*.[3] But the duel was not over, nor did the posthumously published rejoinder of Pio prevent Erasmus from having the last word; see no 339 and cf no 389.[4]

1 On Pio see Firmin-Didot *Alde Manuce et l'hellénisme à Venise*; CWE 84 xvii–xxxviii; Allen and CWE Ep 1634 introductions; CEBR III 86–8.
2 Ep 2110:31–6 / 32–8
3 The *Responsio* does not occur in the *Versandliste*, but a copy was in the separate chest of Froben editions of Erasmus' works; see *Catalogus librorum Erasmi* no 20.
4 On the whole polemic see Gilmore 'Erasmus and Alberto Pio, Prince of Carpi,' 'Les limites de la tolérance dans l'oeuvre polémique d'Erasme' 725–31, and 'Italian Reactions to Erasmian Humanism'; ASD IX-6 1–65 / CWE 84 xl–cxxx.

374 Articulorum Luteri damnatorum Ratio

Latomus, Jacobus. *Articulorum doctrinae fratris Martini Lutheri per theologos Lovanienses damnatorum ratio*. Antverpiae: M. Hillenius, 8 May 1521 (quarto).

The Leuven theologians pronounced their condemnation of Luther's writings on

7 November 1519; the faculty of theology of Cologne had already done so on 30 August. Luther reacted to both pronouncements at the same time in his *Responsio ad condemnationem doctrinalem … per … Lovanienses et Colonienses factam* (1520). A justification of the Leuven condemnation appeared in reply, in the form of the work referred to above, the *Articulorum … ratio* by Jacobus Latomus, who appears to have assumed the leadership of the conservative-orthodox Leuven theologians after the death of Jan Briart of Ath. His apology provoked a rejoinder from Luther, the *Rationis Latomianae confutatio* of June 1521.[1] Erasmus followed the controversy closely. On 28 April 1520 he sent a copy of the Cologne and Leuven condemnations to Ulrich von Hutten, and he read Luther's first defence with approval.[2] He too had to endure attacks from the Leuven theologians at this time, which led him to reply to them in a letter in the summer of 1521 (Ep 1217). Of all the polemics mentioned, Erasmus seems to have preserved only that of Latomus.

1 On the condemnation see Ep 1030:16n/n7. On Luther's *Responsio*, see Benzing *Lutherbibliographie* no 627; Ep 1113:33n/n15; on his *Rationis Latomianae confutatio*, Benzing ibidem no 944. On Latomus see no 18 #2; on his position in Leuven at this time cf Allen and CWE Ep 1059 introductions.
2 Ep 1113:33–4/38–9

375 Opera Prudentij.

Prudentius, Aurelius Clemens. *Opera.* Probably Daventriae: R. Paffraet, c 1497 (quarto).

Erasmus might have owned one of two editions of Prudentius: the *editio princeps* published in Deventer by Richard Pafraet between 1490 and 1498, a quarto,[1] and the edition published by Andreas Cratander in Basel in 1527, an octavo. The *Opera* also appeared with the work of some other poets in 1501, in the first part of the Aldine collection *Poetae christiani veteres*, but

since the *Versandliste* names only Prudentius and does not add 'cum aliis,' this is almost certainly not the one alluded to. It is an argument against the later Cratander edition that the *Versandliste* entry neither gives its title – *Psychomachia, Cathemerinon etc.* – nor mentions the *scholia* it contains, although the compiler of the list rarely used the fictitious title *Opera* without some special reason and elsewhere often specified commentaries. The first page of the Deventer edition, however, reads *Prudentii Opera* – the title given in the *Versandliste*. This is not of course a strict proof that the older edition must be meant, but there is another reason to consider it. Reedijk has pointed out that among the early Christian poets Erasmus was especially attracted to and influenced by Prudentius (348–505), and Vredeveld has pointed out countless verses that imitate and adapt Prudentius in Erasmus' early poems, written between 1488 and 1499.[2] Reedijk thinks it possible that Erasmus had become acquainted with Prudentius as early as his youth in Deventer, because there are indications that the poet was included in the curriculum of the school there. That could have been a reason for him to acquire the first edition of the collected poems quite early.

1 Hain 13432 dates it to c 1490; BL *Catalogue* 9 59 'not after 20 April 1498'; and Campbell *Annales* no 1456 'vers 1497.'
2 Reedijk *Poems* 100; ASD I-7 506–15/CWE 85–6 166–79 'Index of Patristic, Medieval, and Renaissance References' under Prudentius

376 Diatriba Eras. de Libero arbitrio

Erasmus. *De libero arbitrio diatribe sive collatio.* Basileae: J. Frobenius, September 1524 (octavo).

In spite of the impression, created by Erasmus himself, that he would publish his treatise directed against Luther somewhere other than Basel, partly because no printer there would be found willing to print an anti-Lutheran work,[1] it is currently generally accepted that of the three editions that appeared in 1524, without any indication of the month but in rapid succession, at Basel, Antwerp, and Cologne, the Froben edition was nevertheless the original.[2] The date on which the *Diatribe* must have appeared in 1524 can be determined quite accurately: the letters Erasmus wrote to authorities and friends to accompany the presentation copies were probably written in advance and sent – dated 2 September and the following days – when the books were ready.[3] He himself would have kept a copy of this first and only authorized edition.

1 Epp 1385:11–13/15–17, 1430:15–18/18–22
2 Allen Ep 1419 introduction
3 Ep 1481 introductions

377 Declarationes Eras. ad censu. Paris.

Erasmus. *Declarationes ad censuras Lutetiae vulgatas sub nomine Facultatis Theologiae Parisiensis.* Perhaps bound with *Dilutio eorum quae Iodocus Clithoveus scripsit adversus Declamationem suasoriam matrimonii. Epistola … de delectu ciborum … In Elenchum Alberti Pii brevissima scholia.* Basileae: off. Frobeniana, 1532 (octavo).

Froben published two editions of the *Declarationes* in 1532: the first in octavo and the second, revised and enlarged, in quarto. The quarto edition is listed under no 337, and this entry, in view of the octavo format of the adjacent volumes, must refer to the octavo. Another work by Erasmus printed in octavo appeared at the same time as the *Declarationes*, his *Dilutio eorum quae Iodocus Clithoveus scripsit adversus Declamationem suasorium matrimonii*, often published with a (slightly) revised version with scholia of the *Epistola apologetica de interdicto esu carnium*, and his *In Elenchum Alberti Pii brevissima scholia*. Although it has its own title-page and signatures, the *Dilutio* is often found

bound after the *Declarationes* because, as Telle says, its content belongs with them 'as a logical complement'.[1] It cannot be deduced from the entry in the *Versandliste* whether the *Dilutio* and the other works were also bound in Erasmus' copy of the *Declarationes*.

1 See Telle *Dilutio*, especially 19 and 60; Telle wrongly supposed that there are two 1532 editions; see ASD IX-1 62 n74. See on the *Dilutio* also no 60 (Clichtove's *Propugnaculum*). *De esu carnium* appears twice on the *Versandliste* (nos 341 and 380); on it and the scholia see ASD IX-1 19–50 and 65–89. On the scholia cf also Coppens 'Les scolies d'Erasme sur *l'Epistola de interdicto esu carnium.*' On the *Brevissima scholia*, see ASD IX-6 663–89 / CWE 84 cviii–cix.

378 Responsiones ad propositiones à Beda / notatas, Elenchus in censu. Bedae.

Erasmus. *Prologus in supputationem calumniarum Natalis Bedae. Responsiunculae ad propositiones a Beda notatas. Appendix De antapologia Petri Sutoris, & scriptis Iodoci Clithovei, quibus addatur Elenchus erratorum in censuris Bedae …* Basileae: J. Frobenius, August 1526 or March 1527 (octavo).

The first and preparatory part of Erasmus' defence against the attacks launched by the faculty of theology of Paris and in particular its syndic Noël Béda on supposed heresies in his works.[1] It preceded the elaboration and continuation of this defence that was to appear in March 1527 as *Supputationes errorum in censuris Natalis Bedae* (no 69). After the *Prologus*, which took the form of a point-by-point answer to Beda's criticism,[2] two appendixes were included, one a reply to Sutor's *Antapologia* (cf no 151 #2) and the other a treatise *De scriptis Clithovei* (answering Josse Clichtove's attack on a number of Erasmus' positions); finally there was a further answer to Béda, the *Elenchus in censuras Bedae*, also mentioned in the short title given in the *Versandliste*. The first edition of the *Prologus* appeared in August 1526; a second came out in March 1527, at the same time as the *Supputationes*, with which it is frequently bound.

1 On the controversy, see Allen and CWE Epp 1571 and 1664 introductions; ASD IX-5 1–13. Clichtove is mentioned several times in Erasmus' correspondence with Béda; see for example Epp 1609:53–7/ 63–9 with n8, 1620:67–70/78–81 and n10, 1679:84–91/91–9 with nn21–2.
2 In his *Annotationes* (Paris: Josse Bade, May 1526); cf Allen Ep 1679:39n and CWE Ep 1664 n1.

379 Epitome inscripta Erasmo in Vallam / cum appendice in Copiam uerborum.

Erasmus. *Paraphrasis seu potius epitome inscripta D. Erasmo Roterodamo luculenta iuxta ac brevis in Elegantiarum libros Laurentii Vallae ab ipso iam recognita. Cui addita est et Farrago sordidorum verborum … per Cornelium Crocum.* Friburgi Brisg.: J. Faber Emmeus, March 1531 or 1534 (octavo).

The epitome that Erasmus had made at Steyn in about 1488 from Valla's *Elegantiae linguae latinae* and *In errores Antonii Raudensis adnotationes* was published without his knowledge, through the intervention of Alaard of Amsterdam, by Johann Gymnicus of Cologne, in 1529.[1] Here, as is evident from the words 'epitome inscripta,' taken verbatim from the title-page, the reference is to the authorized edition published in 1531 or to the further expanded version of 1534.[2] In spite of his sharp criticism of the 1529 edition, which he did not acknowledge, Erasmus also kept the *Hotchpotch of Latin Barbarisms* by the Amsterdam priest and schoolmaster Cornelius Croock in his improved 'official' edition.

1 On the prehistory of the *Paraphrasis*, see the introduction to the edition of the text in ASD I-4 191–205; van der Blom *Programma von het Erasmiaans Gymnasium voor de cursus 1969/1970* 13–20. Cf also no 153 #2.
2 We have not considered the practically unaltered third edition (Freiburg 1536), which was not revised by Erasmus and perhaps not published until after his death; cf ASD I-4 202.

380 Eras. de esu car. Item contra Stunicam.

Erasmus. *Ad … Christophorum episcopum Basiliensem epistola apologetica de interdictu esu carnium.* Basileae: J. Frobenius, August 1522 (octavo).

See no 341.

381 Lute. ad Eras. de Seruo arbitrio

Luther, Martinus. *De servo arbitrio ad Des. Erasmum.* Wittembergae: J. Lufft, December 1525 or one of the reprints (octavo).

Luther's reply to Erasmus' *De libero arbitrio diatribe* (no 376), long awaited, was not ready until the end of 1525. Sometime in February 1526 Erasmus received a copy, sent to him by chance by a friend in Leipzig, most probably Simon Pistoris. Erasmus saw his opponent's ill will behind the fact that he had not received a copy earlier: clearly his opponents had wished to prevent him from being able to produce a reply before the spring book fair in Frankfurt. This design, if it existed, failed. Erasmus managed, by incredible exertion, to have his provisional answer, the first part of *Hyperaspistes*, written and in print within two weeks. By keeping six presses available for a whole week, Froben helped to carry off this tour de force.[1]

1 On *De servo arbitrio* see Benzing *Luther-bibliographie* nos 2201–9. On the delay in its publication see Ep 1519:50–4 with 53–4n/53–7 with n18. On its publication and the speed with which Erasmus' response, *Hyperaspistes 1*, was printed see Allen and CWE Ep 1667 introductions, Epp 1678:16–22 with 19n/19–24 with n9, 1679:73–8/80–4, 1683:12–26/15–29 with n5.

382 Cleonidae harmonicum introductorium / interprete Georgio Valla: item Vi // truuius Pollio de architectura: item / Iulius Frontinus de aquaeduct. etc.

Cleonides etc. *Cleonidae harmonicum introductorium interprete Georgio Valla. L. Vitruuii Pollionis de architectura libri decem. Sexti Julii Frontini de aquaeductibus liber unus. Angeli Policiani in priora analytica praelectio cui titulus est Lamia.* Venetiis: S. Papiensis dictus Biuilaqua, 1497 (folio).

Erasmus may have bought the only edition of this compendium during his stay in Italy. Vitruvius' ten books *On Architecture*, which makes up two-thirds of the contents, is preceded by the translation of the Εἰσαγωγὴ ἁρμονική ascribed to Kleonides (fl second century AD), a compendium based on the musical theory of Aristoxenes. The collection also included Frontinus' treatise on the aqueducts of ancient Rome and Poliziano's famous *Lamia*, the opening oration in his course on Aristotle's *Prior Analytics*.[1]

1 GW 7123. See, on the authors named: *The New Grove Dictionary of Music and Musicians* IV 491 and Riemann *Musiklexikon, Personenteil* I 934; Ebhardt Die 10 *Bücher der Architektur des Vitruvius und ihre Herausgeber*; Rodgers (ed) *Frontinus: De Aquaeductu Urbis Romae*; Celenza *Angelo Poliziano's* Lamia: *Text, Translation, and Introductory Studies.* For Poliziano's *Opera omnia* see no 285.

383 Apologiae Erasmi

Erasmus. *Apologiae omnes.* Basileae: J. Frobenius, February 1522 or *Apologiae …* Basileae: J. Frobenius, October 1521 (folio).

See no 332.

384 Cornucopiae Perot. cum Festo Pompeio etc Aldi

Perottus, Nicolaus. *Cornucopiae sive linguae Latinae commentarii … M. Terentii Varronis de lingua latina libri tres, IV, V, VI. Eiusdem de analogia libri tres. Sexti Pompeii Festi XIX librorum fragmenta. Nonii Marcelli compendia.* Venetiis: aed. Aldi et Andreae soc., 1513 or 1517 or 1527 (folio).

The *Cornucopia* of the prelate and philologist Niccolò Perotti, first published posthumously (Venice: P. Paganini 1489), was originally intended as a commentary on Martial, but grew in later impressions into a sort of thesaurus of the Latin language and Roman history and mythology.[1] The much-consulted work also served as a basis for the lexicon of Ambrogio Calepino (no 194). During Erasmus' lifetime four Aldine editions were issued: in 1499, 1513, 1517, and 1527. The reference here can only be to one of the last three, since the 1499 edition lacked the works of Nonius Marcellus, Sextus Pompeius Festus, and Marcus Varro. It must have been the text of Festus from this edition of the *Cornucopiae* that gave Erasmus, very shortly before his death, the occasion to remark disparagingly of some of the Aldine editions of texts by classical authors: 'The Venetian press has given us a terribly corrupt Pompeius Festus in a dreadfully corrupted form. I do not blame Aldus. It is his usual practice to entrust such work to some schoolmaster.'[2] For another, perhaps older, edition of the three Roman grammarians, see no 286.

1 Hain 12697; on Perotti and his work, see Ep 117:42n/49n and ASD I-2 114–15 15n. Cf on the *Cornucopiae* Heinimann 'Zu den Anfängen der humanistischen Paroemiologie' 162.
2 Ep 3100:46–8; cf no 110 n2.

385 Opuscula Eras. ex Plutarcho uersa.

Plutarchus. *Ex Plutarcho versa per Des. Erasmum … Recognita per eundem ex collatione Graecorum voluminum.* Basileae: J. Frobenius, September 1520 (quarto).

Translations by Erasmus from the *Moralia* of Plutarch appeared for the first time in August 1514, from Froben, under the title of *Opuscula.* Of the eight translations, the first was dedicated to Henry VIII (Ep 272) and the second to Cardinal Thomas Wolsey (Ep 297). The manuscript had reached Froben at the same time as the corrected copy of the *Adagiorum chiliades* that was the basis of the new edition of that work in 1515. Erasmus had at first more or less promised Josse Bade permission to publish both works, but then, whether or not through a misunderstanding, the Antwerp bookseller Franz Birckmann passed the material he had been given into Froben's hands instead of delivering it to Paris.[1] In September 1520 Froben issued a second edition of the *Opuscula*. This one announced on its title-page *Ex Plutarcho versa per Des. Erasmum*; on the verso of the title-page, the heading of the contents read *Opuscula Plutarchi*. The wording of the short title in the *Versandliste* suggests that Erasmus kept the revised edition of his work. He later published three more translations from Plutarch. Two of them, *De non irascendo* and *De curiositate*, were printed with the Greek text in a *libellus* dedicated to Alexius Thurzo (Ep 1572) and published separately by Froben in May 1525. This book does not appear in the *Versandliste*. Did Erasmus fail to keep it because he came into the possession, a year later, of another collection of works by Plutarch in which both translations were included (cf no 200)? The third translation, *De vitiosa verecundia*, was added as an appendix to the February 1526 edition of *Lingua* (cf no 151 #1).

1 Ep 283:152–64/181–96

386 Epigrammata Erasmj

Erasmus. *Epigrammata*. Basileae: J. Frobenius, March or November– December 1518 (quarto).

This entry probably refers to the *Epigrammata* of Erasmus as they appeared in the Froben edition of Thomas More's *Utopia*, published in March 1518 and reprinted in December of the same year (no 318). They follow More's own epigrams and form the last part of the book, but although the signatures are continuous, they have a separate title-page and were also issued separately. *Varia epigrammata* had also made up the second part of the Bade-Petit edition of the *Adagiorum*

collectanea in 1506–7, and that too is sometimes found separately, although it has no title-page of its own.[1] It is, however, rather unlikely that this earlier collection of poems, all of which reappeared in the considerably enlarged collection of 1518, can be meant here.

1 On these editions see Reedijk *Poems* 367–8 (Survey of Editions and MS Sources I: Editions of Erasmus' Works) nos 164 and 165, 361 no 3; ASD I-7 47–9/CWE 85–6 li–liii.

387 Regula fratrum minorum cum testa. sancti Fran./Venatorium Canonicorum regularium Item/irregularium, manuscrip.

Regula fratrum minorum cum testamento sancti Francisci. Probably a printed edition.

and

Mauburnus, Johannes (Jan Mombaer). *Venatorium Sanctorum ordinis canonicorum regularium. Item Venatorium canonicorum irregularium* (manuscript; format unknown).

All but certainly the last two titles, entered in the *Versandliste* on a new line, were mistakenly combined with the *Regula fratrum minorum* in Husner's transcript.[1] If so, the addition 'manuscrip.' relates only to the *canonicorum regularium*, and *Regula fratrum minorum* may refer to a printed work.

1/ The *regula bullata*, the rule of the Franciscan order, in its final wording as confirmed in 1223 by a bull of Pope Honorius III, and the last will of St Francis of Assisi appeared in print together in Erasmus' time more than once.[2]

2/ *Venatorium sanctorum ordinis canonicorum regularium* was the name of a hagiographical work of the last years of the fifteenth century, never published but preserved only in manuscript, on the Augustinian order of regular canons.[3] Its author, Jan Mombaer, traced back the origin of the order to the evangelist Mark and the apostle James, argued that the order was held in greater respect than all the others, and enumerated the saints and illustrious men produced by the order. He paid special attention to the authors of the Windesheim Congregation, and was one of the first to attribute the *Imitatio Christi* to Thomas à Kempis.[4] Erasmus might well have possessed a manuscript of the *Venatorium*. Mombaer, a native of Brussels, entered the monastery of Augustinian canons at Agnietenberg near Zwolle, where he wrote his *Rosetum exercitiorum spiritualium et sacrarum meditationum*, a manual for the ascetic and contemplative life that was a characteristic expression of the late *Devotio moderna* and circulated widely.[5] In 1496, at the urging of Jan Standonck, director of the Collège de Montaigu in Paris, Mombaer came to France, where he and the canons who came with him hoped to reform Augustinian priories in the Paris region in the spirit of Windesheim. They succeeded at the abbey of Château-Landon near Fontainebleau but failed at St Victor. He overcame all difficulties at Livry and died in 1501 at the head of that abbey. During his stay in the French capital, Erasmus was on friendly terms with him. Soon after Mombaer arrived, he sent him as a gift copies of his own *Carmen de casa natalitia Jesu* and of the little volume of poems, *Sylva odarum*, by Willem Hermans, the friend of his youth; a year later he presented him with Gaguin's *De origine et gestis Francorum compendium*. His letters revealed affection: he would like to visit him or write to him daily, and wished that Mombaer might be to him a second Willem Hermans. They belonged to the same order and wore a common habit, and he noted a considerable similarity in their dispositions, though the other was more inclined to virtue! Erasmus was all the more kindly disposed towards the Windesheim canon for his reforms of monastic life. He gave him

encouragement: Mombaer must not mind if 'everything still goes forward at a snail's pace, since it is always an uphill task to dis-accustom those who are accustomed to something.' At the same time he proposed to commemorate his friend's achievements in some literary memorial as soon as he should have time.[6] It is very difficult to gauge the sincerity of such utterances. Erasmus had come to know the Windesheim asceticism in its most rigid form in Standonck's house for poor students at the Collège de Montaigu, and he later looked back with horror on the time he spent in the Collège. Renaudet, however, saw no contradiction, holding the view that during his first Paris years Erasmus' spiritual orientation was still very unsettled, and that before his encounters with John Colet in Oxford and Jean Vitrier in Saint-Omer he was not at all insensible to the ideas of Mombaer, whose influence for a moment even 'seemed to reawaken in him the ascetic ideals of the Windesheim Congregation.'[7]

Two versions of Mombaer's work on the regular canons have come down to us, one, the more detailed, under the title *Investigatorium*, and the other, more concise, under the title *Venatorium*. Comparison of the two texts brought Debongnie to the conclusion that the shorter version must be considered definitive.[8] The short title in the *Versandliste* entry indicates that this version was the one in Erasmus' possession.

3/ Presumably the third short title in this entry does not mean a separate work. Supposing that *Item irregularium* stands for *Venatorium canonicorum irregularium*, it may refer to the appendix to Mombaer's work, which dealt with the saints among the canons who came from churches or religious houses founded or inhabited originally by regular canons who later changed their status and became secular canons.[9]

1 Husner 'Bibliothek' 244
2 For example NK 3741
3 The following discussion is based on Debongnie
   Jean Mombaer (on the *Venatorium* 45–67);
   Renaudet *Préréforme et humanisme* 219–20,
   254, 279–80, 288–9; and cf CEBR II 447–8.
4 Debongnie *Jean Mombaer* 66
5 Cf Post *The Modern Devotion* 542–3.
6 Epp 52 (lines 18–19/20–1 mention the gift) and 73
   (lines 31–2/34–5 mention the 'histories'; CWE 35n
   identifies the book)
7 Renaudet *Préréforme et humanisme* 700; cf de
   Vogel 'Erasmus and His Attitude Towards Church
   Dogma' 107.
8 Debongnie *Jean Mombaer* 56–7. There is a copy
   of this in Brussels, Royal Library MS 11973,
   a seventeenth-century copy from the priory
   of Corsendonck.
9 Debongnie *Jean Mombaer* 61–2

388 Ioachimi Camerarij opuscula aliquot,/ nempe: Erratum, Aeolia, Phaeno// mena, Prognostica, Plan. Disticha

Camerarius, Joachimus. *Opuscula aliquot
elegantissima nempe: Erratum … Aeolia …
Phaenomena … Prognostica. Planetae
ac menses duplices. Disticha.* Basileae:
B. Lasius & T. Platterus, 1536 (octavo).

The last page of the *Versandliste* contains
entries 388–413. Except for no 390, these
books, divergent in content and in different
formats, were all published between 1531
and 1536, most of them after 1533. The
majority were Erasmus' works, or his
editions or translations of texts; some were
works by other authors. In the last years
of his life Erasmus must have provisionally
put presentation copies from publishers
or authors somewhere – on a shelf or table
in his apartment in Basel where there
was room for them – and never arranged
them according to subject or format.

Joachim Camerarius (1500–1574), philologist, pedagogue, and theologian, studied
at Erfurt, where he belonged to the circle
of admirers of Erasmus around Helius
Eobanus Hessus; he soon came under the
influence of the Reformation.[1] He was
personally acquainted with Luther at

Wittenberg and delivered a letter from him
to Erasmus in 1524 (Ep 1443).[2] Camerarius
drifted away from Erasmus' theological
opinions: Luther relates in one of his
Tischreden that his young adherent gave
him the final impetus to put the *De servo
arbitrio* on paper.[3] In 1526, on the recommendation of Melanchthon, Camerarius
was appointed rector of the new Lutheran
and humanistic gymnasium (grammar
school) of Nürnberg, where he found his
old teacher Eobanus among the masters.
Erasmus, relying on information from
Pirckheimer, wrote in somewhat unfriendly
terms of the initially rather unpromising
state of affairs at the school in his *Responsio
ad epistolam apologeticam ad fratres
Germaniae inferioris* (1530), embroidering
the theme that the Reformation had put
humane studies under pressure. It caused
some bitterness when, in 1531, he included
in his *Epistolarum floridarum liber* a critical
letter on the subject from his correspondence with Eobanus Hessus, thus giving
the school fresh negative publicity.
Camerarius, who was also hurt because
Erasmus had spoken slightingly of his
literary activities,[4] took his characteristi-
cally 'courteous' revenge for this attack
in the collection referred to above. In the
first item, the *Erratum*, to the great delight
of Eobanus, he showed with a vast display
of learning how all great men, from Homer
to Erasmus, had fallen into error.[5] The
copy in Erasmus' library was a reprint;
the *editio princeps* (Nürnberg: J. Petreius
1535) bears a different title.

1 On Camerarius see Allen and CWE Ep 1501
   introductions and CEBR I 247–8.
2 Erasmus wrote to Melanchthon that when
   Camerarius came he had been weakened by illness
   and had hardly been able to bear the effort of
   a conversation; Ep 1496:209–11/233–5.
3 WA *Tischreden* IV no 5069
4 Ep 2495:35–8
5 Krause *Helius Eobanus Hessus, sein Leben und
   seine Werke* II 87; Stählin *Humanismus und
   Reformation im bürgerlichen Raum* 3–4

389 Io. Genesij antapologia in Eras.

Sepulveda, Joannes Genesius de.
*Antapologia pro Alberto Pio in Erasmum
Roterodamum.* Romae: A. Bladus, 1532
(quarto).

Erasmus' copy of the *editio princeps* of
Juan Ginés de Sepúlveda's *Antapologia* is
now in the Johannes a Lasco Bibliothek in
Emden. The book has not been preserved
in its original state but in a later binding,
with two other works that need not have
belonged to Erasmus.[1] Erasmus had
received the pamphlet from the author
through Ambrosius von Gumppenberg,
apostolic protonotary and a protégé of
Cardinal Cajetanus; Gumppenberg's
donor's inscription is on the title-page.[2]
Even before the packet from Rome with
its accompanying letter from the author
(Ep 2637) was delivered to him, Erasmus
was already in possession of the Paris
reprint of the same year.[3] It appears that
he disposed of the latter and retained the
original edition. The *Antapologia* was the
last salvo in the polemic between Erasmus
and Albert Pio. When in 1531 Erasmus
reacted in *Apologia adversus rhapsodias
Alberti Pii* (no 339) to a work by Pio
directed against him but published posthumously, *Responsio paraenetica* (no 373),
the Spanish humanist and historian Juan
Ginés de Sepúlveda took up the cause
of his deceased older friend and wrote his
Antapologia.[4] The pamphlet was couched
in moderate terms. Nonetheless Erasmus,
who considered that Pio's last polemic had
also largely been the work of Sepúlveda,
was highly irritated, although he was
no longer inclined to answer it; he wrote to
Bonifacius Amerbach: 'It is mere nonsense.
I do not think it deserves any response.
I have more important things to do.'[5]
He did not see, he wrote to the author
himself, what else could come of this
mutual inflammation in polemical pamphlets, except discord, of which there was
already enough in the world.[6] Eighteen

months later the 'remarkably stupid and
insulting book' was still an irritant.[7] Yet
the controversy did not lead to personal
enmity. For Erasmus, Sepúlveda was also
the man who had fostered the study of
literature in Spain, and he continued to
correspond with him: in the following
years, they exchanged letters on the
Greek manuscript of the Bible known
as Vaticanus B or 03, to which Sepúlveda
had drawn Erasmus' attention.[8]

1 Husner 'Bibliothek' 249. Dr H. Fast informs me
  that the copy in Emden is bound with Erasmus'
  Responsio ad Petri Cursii defensionem (Basel:
  Froben 1535) and J. Apellus *Methodica dialectices
  ratio, ad iurisprudentiam adcommodata* (Nürnberg
  F. Peypus 1535).
2 Jürgens *Johannes a Lasco* 134–5 (with a photo-
  graph of the title-page). On Gumppenberg see
  Allen Ep 2619 introduction and CEBR II 154.
3 Paris: A. Augereau 22 March 1532; Ep 2652:1–2
4 See Allen Ep 2637 introduction; on Sepúlveda
  cf CEBR III 240–2.
5 Ep 2652:3–4
6 Ep 2701:6–8
7 Ep 2906:16–19
8 Ep 2873:19–34; cf Epp 2905:37–46, 2938:69–102.

390 Eusebij Corradi ad Sixtum 4[tum] / epistola asserens D. Augustinum non / fuisse heremitam.

Conradus, Eusebius. *Ad Sixtum quartum
pontificem maximum pro auferendo de
ecclesia errore scribentium Sanctum
Augustinum ecclesie doctorem fuisse
heremitam.* Padue: M. Cerdonis, 1484
(quarto) or another lost edition.

In the controversy that raged at the end of
the 1470s between the Augustinian hermits
and the Augustinian regular canons
'concerning the habit and manner of life
of St Augustine,' the Milanese jurist and
theologian Eusebius Conradus (d 1500),
himself a regular canon and later prior
of a monastery in Parma, acted as one
of the foremost champions of his order.[1]
In the tract referred to here, dedicated to
Pope Sixtus IV, he disputed the assertion
that St Augustine had been a hermit.[2]

After the death of the pope, who shortly before had attempted to impose silence on the two parties in a bull, the controversy flared up again. Among the younger polemicists who took up the cause of the regular canons was Jan Mombaer of Brussels. He wrote a couple of short apologetic works in favour of the canons and, to the greater glory of their order, a *Venatorium sanctorum* which was never published but of which Erasmus possessed a manuscript copy (no 387 ##2–3).[3] Mombaer was fully aware of the writings of his predecessor, and it was certainly not a coincidence that the manuscript from the monastery of Corsendonck in which one of his polemical works is preserved also contained a transcript of Eusebius Conradus' *Brevis annotatio in errores scribentium S. Augustinum fuisse heremitam*, to which he also referred at the beginning of his own work.[4]

Mombaer's familiarity with Eusebius Conradus may perhaps help to explain the presence of the *Epistola ad Sixtum iv* in Erasmus' library. Mombaer, who was active in the Paris region as a monastic reformer in the spirit of Windesheim from 1496 to his death in 1501, was on friendly terms with Erasmus when he was in Paris in 1497 and 1498. It is quite likely that Erasmus acquired the book through Mombaer. So far as the question at issue in Eusebius Conradus' booklet is concerned, Erasmus appears in later life to have continued to share Conradus' opinion. 'Read Augustine's letter to Aurelius, which is number 76,' he wrote in 1518 to his young friend Maarten Lips, who was very interested in Augustine. 'It is clear enough from that that Augustine was not a monk.'[5]

1　On Conradus see Debongnie *Jean Mombaer* 45–67; GW VII 12.
2　The way in which his name is written may indicate that the 1484 Padua edition of this tract (GW 2923) is in question here, for only there does it appear (on fol 1b) as Corradus, as in the *Versandliste*; in his other works on the same subject it is always given as Conradus.

3　On the apologetic works see Debongnie *Jean Mombaer* 48–9.
4　Bruxelles, Bibliothèque Royale MS 858–61, fol 376ff; cf Debongnie *Jean Mombaer* 64, 46 n2.
5　Ep 901:9–11/12–13. Augustine's letter is now numbered 60.

391　Apophtegmatum [sic] opus Eras. in 8°

Erasmus. *Apophthegmatum libri octo.* Basileae: H. Frobenius et N. Episcopius, 1535 (octavo).

The *editio princeps* of the six books of *Apophthegmata* dedicated by Erasmus to the young Duke William of Cleves (Ep 2431) was issued, at his own suggestion, in 1531 in the same format as the *De pueris instituendis* of 1529, that is, in quarto.[1] The second printing, augmented by two new books and a second preface addressed to Willian (Ep 2711), appeared in folio at the end of 1532.[2] Only the third printing of 1535 was an octavo, which is what this entry title specifies, and so must be the one referred to here. The *Apophthegmata* was a compilation of anecdotes borrowed for the most part from Plutarch's *Apophthegmata Laconica* and *Regum et imperatorum apophthegmata*.[3] Other sources from which Erasmus drew copiously for sayings of famous men of antiquity were Diogenes Laertius (nos 304, 305, 306), Suetonius (nos 51 and 262), and the *Scriptores Historiae Augustae* (nos 261 and 263), besides Athenaeus (no 239), Stobaeus (cf no 314), and Xenophon (nos 204 and 273).[4] Dozens of other classical authors supplied him incidentally with material for his collection, virtually all of whom he had consulted over the years for his *Adagia*. He knew Plutarch's *Apophthegmata* in the fifteenth-century translation of Francesco Filelfo,[5] and the more recent version by Raffaele Regio.[6] He had met Regio in Padua and had been in Venice with him in 1508, when his translation was published there. If Erasmus ever owned these Latin versions, they no longer appear on the *Versandliste*. He was rather critical of both renderings, and in his dedicatory letter he made it clear that in his own work he had also another aim in view than that of his Italian predecessors. While they confined themselves strictly to the translation of the Greek text, he made his *Apophthegmata* an original work. To almost all of the apophthegms he attached a commentary to explain the moral. His collection thus acquired the character of what Cytowska called a 'sixteenth-century manual of Christian morality' and enjoyed great popularity (about eighty editions in many languages appeared before the end of the century).[7]

1 Ep 2412:9–10/10–12 (to Hieronymus Froben); *De pueris instituendis* had also been dedicated to the duke (see no 79).

2 A copy of the folio edition *Apophthegmatum opus* was in the chest with mainly Froben editions of Erasmus' works in his last residence in Basel. See *Catalogus librorum Erasmi* no 54.

3 The following discussion owes much to Cytowska 'Apophthegmata d'Erasme de Rotterdam, manuel de morale chrétienne du XVIe siècle' and Rummel *Erasmus as a Translator of the Classics* 120–5.

4 In 1508 Erasmus had had access to a manuscript of Stobaeus in Venice. And in 1531, although he was then living in Freiburg, Erasmus could have seen the proofs of a collection of *gnomai* published in the following year at Froben's press by his younger friend Gelenius, in which the *Gnomologium* of Stobaeus was included anonymously; see ASD II-5 49 659n and II-6 453 493n. See also no 314 with nn4 and 5.

5 *Apophthegmata … Philelfo interprete* ([Deventer:] R. Pafraet 1499; Campbell *Annales* no 1424). Allen Ep 2431:70n mentions another edition ([Utrecht: Ketelaer and Leempt 1473]; Campbell *Annales* no 1423).

6 *Apophthegmata regum et imperatorum; Laconica apophthegmata* (Venice: G. dei Rusconi 1508). Under a similar title, a new edition of Regio's translation had appeared from the press of Simon de Colines (Paris 1530), shortly before Erasmus' compilation.

7 Cf BE 1st series 15–19.

392 Nouum testa. Eras. Lati. in 8°

Novi Testamenti aeditio postrema, per Des. Erasmum Roterodamum. Basileae: H. Frobenius et N. Episcopius, August 1535 (octavo).

Like no 342, the edition of the separately issued Latin translation of the *Novum Testamentum* referred to here cannot be further identified. Since the final entries in the *Versandliste* mainly list acquisitions of Erasmus' last years (see no 388), it might be to the then most recent edition, published in Basel in 1535, sent to Erasmus by Froben as a publisher's presentation copy.[1]

1 See the 'union catalogue' of Erasmus editions in the City Library of Rotterdam, www.erasmus.org/ ErasmusOnlineDatabase sv Novum Testamentum (no 4902): 'NT, Lat., Basel Froben 1535, 8°, copies Oxford Bodleian and Erasmus House Anderlecht.'

393 Eras. de Puritate tabern. siue eccles

Erasmus. *De puritate tabernaculi sive ecclesiae Christianae*. Basileae: H. Frobenius et N. Episcopius, 1536 (quarto).

The exposition of Psalm 14, written for and dedicated to Christoff Eschenfelder (Epp 3081, 3086), customs officer for the archbishop of Trier at Boppard on the Rhine, with whom he had been acquainted since 1518, was Erasmus' last work.[1] It also included nineteen previously unpublished letters.[2]

1 On Eschenfelder see Ep 867:46–55/50–60; Allen and CWE Ep 879 introductions; CEBR I 443.

2 Allen I Appendix 7 'The Principal Editions of Erasmus' Epistolae' 601; Halkin *Erasmus ex Erasmo* 195–203

394 Aliquot Chrysost. Homiliae ab/ Eras. uersae

Johannes Chrysostomus. *Aliquot homiliae ad pietatem summopere conducibiles*. Basileae: off. Frobeniana, 1533 (quarto).

Eight translated homilies, among them *De Davide et Saule deque tolerantia*, which were not included in the great edition of Chrysostom of 1530 (no 230) and were intended by Erasmus as a supplement to it. He translated them from a codex that he described as 'beautifully written, magnificently illuminated with colours and golden letters' and dedicated them to the wealthy

Catholic Augsburg merchant Johann Paumgartner (Ep 2774).[1]

In 1890 Johannes Paulson identified a manuscript now in the Royal Library of Stockholm that answers quite well to Erasmus' description, although it is badly damaged. His argument that this codex, like the manuscript on which the edition of Ptolemy in Greek was based, belonged to Theobald Fettich, cannot be maintained.[2] But Fettich may well have been instrumental in putting it at Erasmus' disposal. After the death of Johann von Dalberg, bishop of Worms, in 1503, his rich library at Ladenburg was neglected. Wolfgang von Affenstein, one of the councillors of the Palatinate, was commissioned to reorganize it, and Theobald Fettich assisted him. Fettich was an erudite man in touch with humanist circles, and so it was he to whom Erasmus wrote late in 1526 praising Johann Froben for publishing 'the best authors' and asking permission for Froben's son Hieronymus to search for manuscripts that might serve as the basis for new editions (Ep 1767). The formal reply to his request came from von Affenstein: Froben was allowed to look around the library and to borrow any manuscript that was of interest to him (Ep 1774).[3]

Froben must have returned to Basel with a number of manuscripts on loan. One of these, the manuscript of Ptolemy's *De geographia*, was turned over to Sigusmundus Gelenius, who edited it for Johann Froben (see no 101). Another, very probably, contained Chrysostom's homilies on Paul's Epistle to the Romans. Erasmus was increasingly absorbed in the study of John Chrysostom at this time and in 1525 and 1526 had published several of his minor works (some in Greek editions, some with translations).[4] Froben was equally interested; it even seems likely that the idea of the *Opera* in Latin originated with him.[5] When, or whether, Hieronymus Froben found the manuscript of Chrysostom's

homilies on Paul's Epistle to the Romans that Erasmus mentioned in a letter to Germain de Brie in August 1526 cannot be demonstrated. But it was then in Erasmus' hands, although the first eight of the homilies, translated by Brie, were not published until 1533. In his preface Brie described the text he translated as a transcript made for Erasmus from a manuscript found in Dalberg's library at Ladenburg (see no 58).

The edition of the Greek text of Ptolemy's *Geography* and the first eight of Chrysostom's homilies on Romans translated by German de Brie were based on manuscripts discovered at Ladenburg; like Erasmus' translation of eight *Homiliae ad pietatem summopere conducibiles*, the book we are considering here, they were published by Hieronymus Froben and Nicolaus Episcopius in 1533. Is it too far-fetched to guess that the manuscript from which Erasmus translated these eight homilies also came from the Dalberg library and was placed at Erasmus' disposal around 1526?

1 On the manuscript, see Ep 2774:61–114; on Paumgartner see Allen Ep 2603 introduction and CEBR III 60–1. Erasmus also dedicated a book to his son; see no 396.
2 See his *Notice sur un manuscrit de Saint Jean Chrysostome utilisé par Erasme et conservé à la Bibliothèque royale de Stockholm*. Paulson notes that the ornamentation at the beginning of each homily and the initial letters are blue and gold. He points out that from his preface to Ptolemy's *Geographia* (Ep 2760) it is clear that Erasmus (whom Paulson assumed was the editor) mistook Fettich for the owner of the codex. Since Froben published Ptolemy's *Geography* and the eight homilies of Chrysostom almost simultaneously in the early spring of 1533, Paulson assumed that most probably the Stockholm codex of the homilies also belonged to Fettich.
3 Johann Huttich, who visited Ladenburg in 1527, reported that Froben had turned the library upside-down; Allen Ep 1767:11n/CWE Ep 1774 n4. In 1527 Froben published Erasmus' translation from a codex from Ladenburg of a *Fragmentum commentariorum Origenis in Evangelium secundum Matthaeum*, and Erasmus acknowledged von Affenstein's help in procuring it (Ep 1844).

4 For example *De sacerdotio* (Froben, May 1525;
the Greek text); *De orando Deum libri duo* (Froben,
April 1525; translation with the Greek text
appended); *Conciunculae sex de fato et providentia
Dei* (Froben, February 1526; Greek text); *In
epistolam ad Philippenses homiliae duae* (Froben,
August 1526; translation with the Greek text
appended)

5 See Ep 2359 introductions.

395 Enchir. mili. Christiani 2.

Erasmus. *Enchiridion militis Christiani …
Cui accessit libellus De praeparatione ad
mortem, per autorem recognitus. Cum alijs.*
Basileae: H. Frobenius ac N. Episcopius,
August 1535 (octavo).

The figure added to the short title in nos
395, 396, 397, and 400 of the *Versandliste*
must refer to the number of copies found
of the books in question. The last three are
works by Erasmus first published in 1535,
which explains the presence of multiple
copies in his library: the author had them
in hand to send to friends and patrons but
had not yet been able to do so before he
died. It may be assumed that the fourth
case is similar and that of the countless
editions of the *Enchiridion militis christiani*,
this entry refers to the last Froben edition
of 1535.[1] Another circumstance supporting
this conclusion is that the books listed in
this section of the *Versandliste* all seem to
be editions published towards the end of
Erasmus' life (see no 388). The *Enchiridion*
of 1535 included, besides the items already
inserted in the authorized Froben edition
of 1518 (no 71 #1), the *Declamatio de
morte* and, with its own title-page, the
De praeparatione ad mortem.[2] For one
of the earlier editions of the *Enchiridion*,
which Erasmus had preserved, see no 50.

1 BB E 1044

2 The *Declamatio* was originally published in the
Querela pacis edition of 1 December 1517; this is
not on the *Versandliste*, but a copy was in the chest
of Froben editions (*Catalogus librorum Erasmi*
no 2). It appeared again, but without the preface,
in the Basel 1522 edition of *De conscribendis
epistolis* (no 359). The *editio princeps* of *De

praeparatione ad mortem appeared independently
in early 1534; it does not appear in the *Versandliste*,
but a copy was in the special collection of Froben
editions; see *Catalogus librorum Erasmi* no 97.

396 Praecationes aliquot Eras. 4

Erasmus. *Precationes aliquot novae
ac rursus novis adauctae …* Basileae:
H. Frobenius et N. Episcopius,
August 1535 (octavo).

Four copies of the only authorized edition
of these prayers, which were dedicated to
David Paumgartner (Epp 2994 and 2995),
the young son of the Augsburg merchant
Johann Paumgartner. Erasmus had done
the father the same honour two years
earlier, in a collection of 'homiliae ad
pietatem conducibiles' translated by
him from Chrysostom (no 394).

397 Eras. responsio ad defensionem Petri/ Cursij 4

Erasmus. *Responsio ad Petri Cursii defensionem nullo adversario bellacem.* Baileae:
H. Frobenius et N. Episcopius, 1535
(quarto).

Four copies of Erasmus' reply to Pietro
Corsi, who had accused him of an anti-
Italian attitude, which took the form
of a letter to his friend Johann Koler
of Augsburg (Ep 3032).[1] Erasmus had
received Corsi's *Defensio pro Italia ad
Erasmum Roterodamum* (Rome: A. Bladus
1535) in or before the first week of May
1535, but the book does not appear in
the *Versandliste*. Did Erasmus find it not
worth the trouble of preserving? He had,
he wrote, not read the book, merely glanced
at some sections and understood what it
was about.[2] Nonetheless, Erasmus spoke
with respect of Corsi, who was especially
admired by his contemporaries as a poet,
in his *Responsio*.

1 On Corsi see Allen Ep 3007:54n and CEBR I 344.

2 Ep 3015; cf Ep 3016:17–18.

398 Eras. purgatio ad epistolam Luteri.

Erasmus. *Purgatio adversus epistolam non sobriam Martini Lutheri*. Basileae: H. Frobenius et N. Episcopius, April 1534 (octavo).

Early in 1534 Luther unexpectedly stirred up the dispute with Erasmus in a letter of invective addressed to Nicolaus von Amsdorf. This appeared in print with the letter from Amsdorf to Luther about Erasmus that prompted it, as *Epistolae Domini Nicolai Amsdorfii et D. Martini Lutheri de Erasmo Roterodamo* (Wittenberg: J. Lufft, [March] 1534).[1] Erasmus reacted instantly in his *Purgatio*.[2] The book was reprinted in the same year at Antwerp, Cologne, Augsburg, Cracow, and Paris, but the Froben edition was the only authorized text.

1 Benzing *Lutherbibliographie* no 3118
2 Allen Ep 2918 introduction; on the work see Augustijn in *Erasmus en de Reformatie* 271–6 and ASD IX-1 429–40.

**399 Marcellus de medicamentis empiricis, /
Item Galeni libri 9. de uarijs etc.**

Marcellus Empiricus. *De medicamentis empiricis, physicis, ac rationalibus liber. Item Claudii Galeni libri novem*. Basileae: H. Frobenius & N. Episcopius, March 1536 (folio).

The *editio princeps* of a fourth-century book of medical lore. Janus Cornarius (c 1500–1558) lectured on Greek medical authors at Basel in about 1528–9 (he preferred the Greek tradition to the Arab) and edited and translated several medical writers. He prepared the text of Marcellus for Froben from a ninth-century manuscript.[1] An edition of Marcellus had been on Froben's programme as early as 1529; at that time Erasmus had tried in vain to obtain another manuscript (a part of the so-called Fulda manuscript) from the Heidelberg physician Johann Lotzer, who

had acquired it from the legacy of Ulrich von Hutten.[2]

1 Now MS Par. Lat. 6880. See Pauly-Wissowa XIV-2 1499 sv Marcellus. On Cornarius see Ep 2204 introductions and CEBR I 339–40.
2 Ep 2116:15–17 with 15n / 16–18 with nn4–6

400 Eras. Ecclesias. siue Conci. 3

Erasmus. *Ecclesiastes sive de ratione concionandi libri quatuor*. Basileae: H. Frobenius & N. Episcopius, August 1535 (folio) or March 1536 (octavo).

As no 402 refers to the *editio princeps* in folio of the *Ecclesiastes*, this entry most probably refers to three copies of the smaller octavo edition of the work that appeared in March 1536. Erasmus sent some familiar acquaintances presentation copies of the folio edition, but with difficulty, as the volume was heavy. He wanted to have one brought to his friend Léonard de Gruyères in Besançon, for example, by his secretary Gilbert Cousin 'if he could bear the burden.'[1] Though the octavo volumes would have made distribution easier, Erasmus died three months after the 1536 edition had appeared, and three copies remained behind in the library after his death.

1 Ep 3063:11–12. Copies were sent, for example, to Piotr Tomicki, bishop of Cracow (Ep 3049:187–9), and to his friend Paul Volz (Ep 3069:1–2).

**401 Paraphrases Eras. in Euangel. /
epistolas, 4 uoluminibus.**

Erasmus. *Paraphrases in Novum Testamentum*. Basileae: H. Frobenius et N. Episcopius, 1532–5 (folio) or 1534 (octavo).

A complete, or nearly complete, set of the New Testament *Paraphrases*, bound in four volumes, and probably, as is the case with most of the entries at the end of the *Versandliste*, a set from the last years of Erasmus' life. In the early 1530s the Froben press brought out two editions of the collected *Paraphrases*, one in folio format in 1532–5 and the other in octavo in 1534. Both editions were split into two parts, entitled *Tomus primus paraphraseon in Novum Testamentum, videlicet in quatuor Evangelia et Acta apostolorum* and *Tomus secundus continens Paraphrasim in omneis epistolas apostolicas*. The *Paraphrases* on the Gospels and on Acts each had separate pagination and a separate title-page, so that they could be bought and sold independently. The second 'tome,' on the other hand, which contained the *Paraphrases on the Apostolic Epistles*, had continuous pagination and no separate title-pages. A complete copy of one of these editions, either in folio or in octavo, is most probably the *Opus Paraphraseωv* entered as no 407 in the *Versandliste*. Although the title given in the *Versandliste* for this entry is different, it may refer to the same edition in folio or octavo of the complete *Paraphrases*. Whether in that case it is an identical and complete copy cannot be determined. In the short title the *Paraphrase on the Acts of the Apostles* does not appear. The omission may be an error, but it may also point to an incomplete copy. Copies of the collected *Paraphrases* that have been preserved, especially the first 'tome' – let alone the different mixtures of the separable parts – are often more or less incomplete: sometimes one of the separate title-pages or even the text of one of the *Paraphrases* on the Gospels or on Acts is missing. Be that as it may, the set of the *Paraphrases* referred to here was at any rate sufficiently complete for it to be worthwhile to have it bound in four volumes, as was usual for a perfect copy.[1]

1 On the editions of the collected *Paraphrases*, see Mynors 'The Publication of the Latin *Paraphrases*' in CWE 42 xxvi–xxvii. The twenty or so sets of the collected *Paraphrases* that Sir Roger Mynors examined, containing material from 1532 through 1538, exhibited eleven different mixtures. A striking example of an imperfect copy of *Tomus primus paraphraseon* of the earlier folio edition of 1524 is described in Crahay *Editions anciennes d'Erasme* (exhibition catalogue) 50 (no 62). Froben provided

the *Tomus secundus paraphraseon* of the 1524 octavo edition with a second title-page, *In aliquot epistolas Pauli*, after Galatians, so that a purchaser could bind the book conveniently in two parts.

402 Eras. Ecclesiastes ex prima aedit

Erasmus. *Ecclesiastes sive de ratione concionandi libri quatuor*. Basileae: H. Frobenius & N. Episcopius, August 1535 (folio).

The *editio princeps* in folio of the *Ecclesiastes* of Erasmus, dedicated to Christoph von Stadion, bishop of Augsburg (Ep 3036). Erasmus had worked on the book for many years, though not continuously.[1] The edition of 2,600 copies, very large for the time, was rapidly sold out. Before that point was reached, Froben, clearly expecting demand to continue for some time, prepared a second edition in octavo, which appeared in March 1536. Allegedly 'newly revised by the author,' it was practically unchanged and simply a handier and cheaper version;[2] see no 400. Five months later (August 1536) another Froben reprint followed.

1 The genesis of the *Ecclesiastes* is summarized in Bené *Erasme et Saint Augustin* 372–7. On the work in general, see Chomarat *Grammaire et rhétorique* II 1053–1153. The first sections of this study are reproduced, with little modification, in the introduction to his edition in ASD V-4 3–27. See also CWE 67 78–237.
2 Epp 3036 introduction, 3076:7–9

403 Chronicon Pauli Constantini

Constantinus, Paulus. *Chronicum regum regnorumque omnium catalogum et perpetuum ab exordia mundi temporum, seculorumque seriem complectens*. Basileae: J. Hervagius, 1533 (folio).

The author of this now forgotten chronicle, the theologian Paulus Constantinus Phrygio, knew Beatus Rhenanus and Michael Hummelberg from his youth, belonged to the literary society of his birthplace, Sélestat, and was on close terms with Jakob

Wimpfeling, Johannes Sapidus, and Paul
Volz, all friends of Erasmus. Unlike them,
however, he chose the party of the Reformation and became the first Protestant
pastor of the Peterskirche in Basel. In
1532 he accepted the professorship of Old
Testament in Basel, and from 1535 he was
professor of New Testament in Tübingen.[1]
Phrygio wrote his *Chronicon*, which
appeared in the year he assumed rectorship
of the University of Basel, at the instigation of Simon Grynaeus. In March 1533
he explained the aim of his work in a letter
to Beatus Rhenanus, whose collaboration
he invoked.[2] That request cannot have
been very welcome, since Beatus found
him insufficiently competent to undertake
the work and even made some rather
disparaging comments about the intended
publication.[3] Erasmus may have met
Phrygio briefly during his short visit to
Sélestat in August 1514.[4] In the *Encomium
Selestadii*, which he composed on the
occasion of that visit, he mentioned
him by name with other humanists from
the town.[5] But nothing is known of any
contact between them after that date.

1 On Phrygio see Ep 1285:15n/n4; AK I 342
  Ep 372 introduction; CEBR III 79–80.
2 BRE 414–15 Ep 289
3 AK IV 206 Ep 1737
4 Ep 305:171/176–7
5 Reedijk *Poems* no 98:24/ASD I-7 and CWE 85–6
  no 53:24

**404 Sadoleti comment. in epistolam ad
    Romanos/~~Zasij enarratio in tit.
    instituti~~//~~onum de actionibus.~~**

Sadoletus, Jacobus. *In Pauli Epistolam
ad Romanos commentariorum libri tres.*
Lugduni: S. Gryphius, 1535 or revised
edition 1536 (folio).

and

Zasius, Udalricus. *In titulum institutionum
de actionibus enarratio.* Basileae: 1536 (folio).

Husner wrongly included these two books
under one number. In the manuscript of

the *Versandliste*, the titles are clearly
distinct. The deletion of Zasius' work,
which must have been withdrawn from
the collection for unknown reasons after
the inventory was made, also rules out a
combination with Sadoleto's commentary
in one binding.

1/ Erasmus' copy of Sadoleto's commentary on the Epistle to the Romans was
undoubtedly a gift from the author.
Sadoleto had received at least six works
of Erasmus as presents in the years before
it was published.[1] But this was not merely
a reciprocal gesture. Erasmus knew in 1532
that Sadoleto's commentary was in preparation, and he had been directly involved
in its production: he had received the
manuscript by special courier, to give his
verdict on it, before it went to the printer.[2]
When the bishop did not react at once to
the criticisms he had made, Erasmus feared
that they had not been well received, but
Sadoleto later wrote that he had derived
great benefit from the improvements
Erasmus suggested in the first book,
and wished that his friend had also read
through the two other books. Nevertheless,
Sadoleto did not follow his original plan to
have his book printed by Froben through
the mediation of Erasmus;[3] it appeared at
Lyon. Its Semipelagian tendency provoked
some opposition both at the Sorbonne and
in the Curia. Erasmus was not surprised
by this. He had had a premonition, so
he wrote to a friend, and had warned the
bishop. A new edition of the commentary
appeared in 1536, which was intended to
meet the objections but in fact retained
the essence of the original text.[4] It is not
possible to establish whether Erasmus,
in the last months of his life, acquired
the new edition to replace the old one in
his library; it cannot be ruled out *a priori*,
but it is not very likely.

2/ A posthumously published legal treatise
with Erasmus' epitaph in verse for his friend
Zasius,[5] who had died at Freiburg on

24 November 1535. Undoubtedly one of the last acquisitions, if not the last, in his library (apart from the special case of no 245).

1 Epp 1511:16 with n/19 with n5, 2272:6–7/6–7, 2315:129–31/2312A:134–6, 2648 introduction, 2765:3n, 2775:4–6. Cf no 14, Melanchthon's commentary on Romans, a copy of which Erasmus sent to Sadoleto.
2 Epp 2616:14–15, 2648:11–33, 2816 introduction, 2865:13–14
3 Epp 2816 introduction, 2973:22–5, 2648:23–5; cf Douglas *Jacopo Sadoleto* 223–4.
4 Douglas *Jacopo Sadoleto* 85–91; Ep 3076:9–12
5 Reedijk *Poems* no 135/ASD I-7 and CWE 85–6 no 92

405 Opera D. Hieronymi in 9. tom./ digestum, excu. Lutetiae

Hieronymus. *Opera omnia quae exstant.* Parisiis: C. Chevallonius, 1533–4, 9 vols (folio).

The third authorized edition of Jerome with revised scholia by Erasmus and a new foreword, also by him (Ep 2758); for the two previous editions see no 243. For the text the Paris printer Claude Chevallon, with whom Erasmus had come into contact after the death of Johann Froben, had made use of manuscripts from the abbey of St Victor near the French capital.[1] Erasmus' share in the edition, as in earlier printings, was confined to the preparation of the three volumes containing Jerome's letters, although he devoted a great deal of attention to them: in the long announcement on the general title-page, it is stated that the *scholia* to the letters had been revised and extended in so many places that *vt videri, si cum ante excusis conferas, noua fetura possint* 'if compared with those previously printed, they may seem a new offspring.' Erasmus also referred, in his letters to his friends, to the effort that the revision had cost him.[2]

1 See the general title-page (there is also a special title-page for the section with the *Epistolae*). On Erasmus and Chevallon cf Allen *Erasmus: Lectures and Wayfaring Sketches* 130–2.
2 Epp 2734:47–8, 2735:33–4, 2776:59–61

406 Adagiorum opus/~~Enchir. catechismi Mart. Lute/Thucydides interprete Lau. Valla~~

Erasmus. *Adagiorum chiliades.* Basileae: H. Frobenius & N. Episcopius, [probably] March 1533 or March 1536 (folio).

and

Luther, Martinus. *Enchiridion pro pueris instituendis. Cui addita est nova Catechismi breuioris translatio.* Wittenbergae: Nickel Schirlentz, 1532 or Argentorati: Wendelinus Rihelius, 1536 (octavo).

and

Thucydides. *De bello Peloponnensium Atheniensiumque libri VIII, Laurentio Vallensi interprete.* Edition?

The compiler of the *Versandliste* listed here three works in different formats, their titles written independently of each other and underneath each other; they were therefore rather misleadingly brought together by Husner under one number. Why the second and third titles were deleted, the books thus indicated apparently withdrawn from the library, can no longer be discovered. It seems quite plausible that, like other books in this section of the *Versandliste*, these were acquired during Erasmus' last years; see no 388.

1/ The *Adagiorum opus* listed here was probably one of the last two Froben editions before Erasmus' death. The edition of 1536 added nothing essential, apart from five adages and a new dedication (Ep 3092),[1] to its predecessor of 1533 (cf no 257). As had been the case before 1526, the title was once more *Adagiorum chiliades*. The book is entered here as *Adagiorum opus* (the title under which the 1533 edition had appeared), but that need not rule out a reference to the 1536 edition: in the written inventory of the separate collection of his own works left by Erasmus, the 1536 edition is also entered under the then apparently completely naturalized name *Adagiorum opus*, which had in fact been used by the author himself in 1514.[2] For the edition of March 1536, Erasmus inscribed autograph dedications in presentation copies.[3]

2/ The first Latin translation of Luther's *Kleiner Katechismus* appeared in 1529, some months after the *editio princeps* of the German text.[4] But only the above-mentioned later editions of 1532 and 1536 bear titles from which the short entry in the *Versandliste* can be easily derived.[5] Both editions contained some Psalms translated from Hebrew by Melanchthon. It is merely an educated guess that the book became part of Erasmus' library shortly before his death because of this new material: perhaps there is a connection between his acquisition of it and the resumption at that time, in a spirit of reconciliation, of his correspondence with Melanchthon.

3/ An edition, difficult to identify, of Laurenzo Valla's translation of Thucydides, although there are few eligible versions. Was it, like many of the adjacent entries on the *Versandliste*, a late acquisition of a recently published work? There is a 1535 Paris edition in octavo by C. Wechel; but why would Erasmus have bought it at that time or who would have wished to do him the kindness of sending it to him as a gift? Unless a more likely edition of 1536 or shortly before can be traced, we must consider one of the older folio versions, one issued in Paris by Josse Bade in 1513 and dedicated by him to Erasmus' bosom friend Pieter Gillis, and the other in Cologne by Eucharius Cervicornus in 1527, 'now revised by Konrad Heresbach from a Greek original.'[6] The latter is the more likely. The Greek scholar Heresbach (1496–1576) was a confidant of Erasmus, who had assisted him to find a post as tutor to the young Duke William of Cleves. At the court of Cleves he became friendly with another

of Erasmus' intimates, Johann von Vlatten, counsellor of the reigning Duke Johann III. It was at Heresbach's suggestion that Erasmus dedicated his *De pueris instituendis* of 1529 to the young Duke William (see no 79), and Erasmus corresponded with him to the end of his life.[7] In this context of close friendly relations, a present from Heresbach of his edition of Thucydides would be most appropriate. And towards the end of his life Erasmus must have made use of a Thucydides edition. Of the only two (or possibly three) references to the Greek historian in *De copia*, two were inserted in the last authorized revised edition of 1534,[8] and a reference in *Adagia* II ix 72 was inserted in 1533.[9]

1 To Charles Blount. William Blount, Baron Mountjoy, to whom all the previous editions of the *Adagia* had been dedicated, had died in 1534; see Allen's introduction.
2 *Catalogus librorum Erasmi* no 64; Allen Ep 305:222
3 See the facsimile of the title-page of the copy dedicated to Bonifacius Amerbach in AK VII facing 256, the image on the left.
4 *Parvus catechismus pro pueris in schola* (Wittenberg: Georg Rhau 1529; Benzing *Lutherbibliographie* no 2598)
5 Benzing *Lutherbibliographie* nos 2633a and 2633b (*Enchiridion Catechismi Martini Lutheri pro pueris instituendis*); cf WA XXX-1 700. On the *Enchiridion* see also the introduction to *Explanatio symboli* in ASD V-1 194 and *Die Bekenntnisschriften der evangelisch-lutherischen Kirche* XXIX–XXXI
6 Westgate 'The Text of Valla's Translation of Thucydides.' The Heresbach edition was reprinted in Paris in September 1528 'sub praelo Ascensiano.'
7 On William of Cleves, see Allen and CWE Ep 2189 introductions and CEBR I 316–17; on Heresbach see Allen and CWE Ep 1316 introductions and CEBR II 183–4.
8 ASD I-6 205 247n / CWE 24 580:17
9 ASD II-4 258 902n / CWE 34 117

407 Opus Paraphraseων Eras.

Erasmus. *Tomus primus paraphraseon in Novum Testamentum, videlicet in quatuor Evangelia et Acta apostolorum, nunc postremum ab autore … recognitus. Tomus secundus continens Paraphrasim in omneis epistolas apostolicas ... denuo ab autore recognitam emendatamque ...* Basileae: H. Frobenius & N. Episcopius, 1534 (octavo) or 1532–5 (folio).

It is possible to identify some of the reissues of Erasmus' own works that appear in this section of the *Versandliste* with a high degree of probability; see no 388. Thus this entry of a collected edition under one title of his New Testament *Paraphrases* probably does not refer to the first folio edition published in 1523–4[1] but to the folio edition of 1532–5, or to the octavo edition of 1534. For further details on the collected *Paraphrases*, see no 401.

1 *Tomus secundus* of the first edition of the complete *Paraphrases* in octavo was published in 1523, but whether the Gospels and Acts appeared in 1524 as *Tomus primus* is uncertain; see Ep 1472:11n/ n2 and CWE 42 xxvi.

408 De duplici copia uerborum Eras.

Erasmus. *De duplici copia verborum ac rerum commentarii due.* Basileae: H. Frobenius & N. Episcopius, August 1534 (quarto).

Given the position of this entry in the *Versandliste* (see no 388), the edition of *De copia* meant here is probably the last authorized edition of August 1534, described by Erasmus himself in a contemporary letter as 'greatly enlarged,' in which new material was added in many places.[1] For an earlier edition, see no 365.

1 Ep 2961:20. See the introductions to the text in ASD I-6 16–17 and CWE 24 282.

409 Eras. de conscribendis epistolis.

Erasmus. *Opus de conscribendis epistolis ex postrema autoris recognitione.* Basileae: H. Frobenius & N. Episcopius, 1534 (octavo).

In all probability this entry refers to the 1534 Froben edition of *De conscribendis epistolis*, with textual improvements and additions by Erasmus himself.[1] It was the second authorized edition after the first of 1522, which is entered elsewhere in the *Versandliste* (no 359).

1 See the introduction in ASD I-2 175, 196–7, and 202; cf CWE 25 6.

410 Homiliae 55. Chrysost. in acta/ Apostolorum Eras. interprete.

Johannes Chrysostomus. *Commentariorum in Acta Apostolorum homiliae quinquaginta-quinque.* Basileae: off. Frobeniana, May 1531 (folio).

The addition 'Erasmo interprete' in the *Versandliste* does not appear on the title-page of this Latin version of John Chrysostom's commentary on Acts, and is only partly accurate: Erasmus was responsible for the translation of the first four homilies only, the other fifty-one being the work of Johannes Oecolampadius.[1] Erasmus knew the original Greek text of all fifty-five sermons from a manuscript that had been offered for sale at Padua in 1525.[2] Reginald Pole, presumably the new owner, had immediately placed it at Erasmus' disposal. He translated three homilies from it, issuing them in 1527 with several others from another source under the title of *Lucubrationes Chrysostomi* (see no 150 #1). Even then he was suspicious of the authenticity of the sermons on stylistic grounds: 'There was something clipped and abrupt about the writing that seemed out of keeping with the style of Chrysostom' – although on the other hand there were many points of agreement as well. Erasmus was therefore unwilling to rely on his own judgment, but translated only three sermons provisionally, with the intention of letting others follow 'if scholars think the work worthy of Chrysostom.'[3] His friend Bishop Tunstall later urged him to complete the translation of the whole collection.[4] Erasmus did in fact go through the manuscript again when preparing his great five-volume edition of Chrysostom of 1530 (no 230). He translated a further homily, which was given a place in the new edition, with the three mentioned above. But that was all. Erasmus continued to have his doubts, and his verdict was even more unfavourable than before: 'I have never read anything so foolish,' he wrote to Tunstall, 'I could write better in a drunken stupor.'[5]

Against this background, the edition of 1531, with all fifty-five sermons on the Acts of the Apostles, is rather surprising. Erasmus must have been aware of the coming publication through his very special relationship with the Froben press and his involvement with the publication of supplements to the Chrysostom *Opera* (cf no 58). How could he have agreed that the sermons should be published without qualification under the name of Chrysostom when less than six months before he had deliberately excluded all but four of them from the edition of Chrysostom's works, also a Froben publication? Perhaps he raised objections but the proprietors of the firm pushed through the edition in the belief that they could do so without coming into too serious a conflict with their illustrious adviser.

Erasmus would not have disapproved of the publication of the homilies themselves; he found them worth reading. He only doubted, on grounds of style, whether they were by Chrysostom. The defective translations by Oecolampadius, assuming that they were already available in 1530, may also have persuaded him against publication.[6] The publishers would have had a different point of view. They would not have troubled themselves about the problem of authorship but, as good businessmen, would have seen an advantage in an edition of all fifty-five sermons, as long as the name of Chrysostom, under which they had been (rightly or wrongly) handed down in the manuscript, appeared

on the title-page. Such an edition would be an attractive and easily saleable complement to the recently published *Opera* of Chrysostom.

Contemporaries undoubtedly took the collection at its face value: in the libraries of Trinity Hall and Pembroke College Cambridge, the copies are bound with the *Opera* of 1530.[7] The presentation of the book was very subtle. On the title-page no mention was made of either Erasmus or Oecolampadius as translators. The preliminary matter shed no light on and gave no justification for the publication. The text was preceded by the same typographically unobtrusive short foreword, literally unchanged, which Erasmus had written for the three homilies he had translated for the *Lucubrationes* of 1527. The heading of the actual text, which was composed largely of renderings by Oecolampadius, read: SANCTI JOANNIS CHRYSOSTOMI COMMENTARIUM IN ACTA APOSTOLORUM, DES. ERASMO ROTERODAMO INTERPRETE 'St John Chrysostom's Commentary on the Acts of the Apostles, translated by Erasmus.' This suggestive title, in capital letters, probably also led the compiler of the *Versandliste* astray, and caused him to attribute the work entirely to Erasmus in his short title.

1 Staehelin *Das theologische Lebenswerk Johannes Oekolampads* 621; cf his *Oekolampad-Bibliographie* 80–1 and BAO II 582.
2 Ep 1623:9n/11–15 with n3
3 Ep 1801; cf Ep 1795:3–9/4–11.
4 Ep 2226:63–5; cf Ep 2379:48–51 (to Germain de Brie).
5 Ep 2263:34–8/36–40; cf Epp 2291:8–10/9–11 and 2359:58–64/62–8.
6 For criticism of Oecolampadius' translations of Chrysostom, see Ep 2226:70–5 (from Cuthbert Tunstall). They were subsequently revised 'ad Graeca' by Erasmus' younger friend Sigismundus Gelenius.
7 See Adams under C 1515.

411 Titus Liuius

Livius, Titus. *Patavinus historicus duobus libris auctis cum L. Flori epitome …* Moguntiae: J. Scheffer [sic], November 1518 (folio) or *Decades tres … Beati Rhenani & Sig. Gelenij adiunctae annotationes.* Basileae: H. Frobenius & N. Episcopius, 1535 (folio).

Of the three editions of Livy in the *Versandliste*, the two entered elsewhere mention their place of publication (Paris; see no 260) or printer's name (Froben; see no 259). There is no comparable pointer to an edition here. Could it be the important Schöffer edition of 1518 (de facto 1519), which Erasmus, although he was not concerned in the preparation of the text, had blessed with his authority? The text was based on a manuscript rediscovered a little earlier in the library of Mainz cathedral, which included two hitherto unknown parts of books 33 and 40 of the *Historiae*. Ulrich von Hutten was closely involved in the publication and composed the introduction for it. Erasmus, then still on good terms with him, wrote a letter of recommendation for the work (Ep 919), praising the young printer and, at the end, naming the three men to whom particular thanks were due for the appearance of the new edition. All three belonged to Hutten's circle: Theoderich Zobel, a canon of Mainz, vicar-general of the archbishop, and scholaster of the cathedral chapter; Nikolaus Fabri of Carbach, the scholar who had discovered the manuscript and prepared it for publication; and Wolfgang Angst, a corrector for Johann Schöffer, who had seen it through the press. In September 1518 Erasmus had met Angst in Mainz and dined with him and his Franconian friends, perhaps Zobel and Carbach.[1] Given this milieu, it is virtually impossible to imagine that he should not have possessed the Schöffer edition. It can also be shown that he used it in his work: in a newly inserted passage in the 1526 edition of the *Adagiorum opus*, he cited the Mainz text.[2]

After he had acquired the more complete text of Livy published by Froben, why should Erasmus have regarded the Schöffer edition bearing his own letter of recommendation (not reprinted in any of the collections of letters he compiled) as superseded and disposed of it, when he kept the much more outdated Bade edition? But if this Livy, like most of the other books at the end of the *Versandliste*, was a work published in Erasmus' last years (see no 388), then an edition of 1518 would not be the one referred to here, and the revised Froben text of 1535 would be the most likely alternative among the editions we know of.

1 Ep 881:7–8/6–7; cf CWE Ep 919:58n. On Angst see Allen and CWE Ep 363 introductions with Allen's addendum (II xix); CEBR I 58–9.
2 ASD II-5 211 87n

412 C. Plinij Natural. Histo.

Plinius Secundus maior, Caius. *Historia mundi denuo emendata non paucis locis … nunc primum animadversis castigatisque quemadmodum … in Sigismundi Gelenii annotationibus operi adnexis apparet.* Basileae: H. Frobenius, J. Hervagius & N. Episcopius, 1535 (folio).

The editions of the Elder Pliny published by Froben and sponsored by Erasmus entered under nos 205 and 207 could be identified thanks to the abbreviated printer's name in the short title of the *Versandliste*. Since 'Frob.' is missing from this entry, one would expect another folio edition. Could it have been one of those to which Erasmus implicitly alluded in his foreword to the Froben version when he listed the scholars to whom thanks were due 'that we now possess a Pliny much freer from error than at any time before'?[1] For Erasmus, Ermolao Barbaro unquestionably stood at the forefront of these scholars. Barbaro's famous *Castigationes*

Plinianae (no 279 #1) had been incorporated in a new edition of the text of the *Naturalis historia* that appeared posthumously in 1496 and was reprinted several times thereafter.[2] But Erasmus also praised three other critics of the text: Guillaume Budé, Nicolas Bérault, and Johannes Caesarius. Budé's involvement with Pliny did not, however, lead him to bring out an edition of his own, as the two others did.[3] Bérault, a friend of Erasmus, prepared an edition in 1516 with notes by Marcantonio Sabellico, Rafaelle Maffei, Filippo Beroaldo, Erasmus, Budé, and Gisbertus Longolius. How Bérault came by Erasmus' notes remains unclear.[4] More recent was the improved text of the *Naturalis historia* with scholia brought out in 1524 by the Cologne humanist Joannes Caesarius, also a good friend of Erasmus.[5]

Erasmus may well have owned one of the versions he praised before 1525, the year in which the first Froben edition was published. We know from the preserved copy containing hundreds of annotations in the wide margins, to a large extent in Erasmus hand, that he still possessed at that time the Venetian edition of 1496 that he had used for many years as his desk copy. But we must take another real possibility into consideration. Like most of the books in this last section of the *Versandliste*, all recently published books that were shelved together, Erasmus may have acquired the edition of Pliny alluded

to here towards the end of his life. If that is the case, practically the only likely candidate is the third revised Froben edition of 1535 edited by Gelenius (see no 205).

1 Ep 1544:36–51 / 39–55
2 *Naturalis historia … a castigationibus Hermolai Barbari quam emendatissime edita* (Venice: B. Benalius 1496)
3 Budé's textual critical notes were included in his *De asse* (nos 291 and 292); Ep 1544:43n / n7
4 Paris: R. Chalderius 1516; cf Allen Ep 1544 introduction. On Bérault see no 46 #2.
5 Cologne: Eucharius Cervicornus 1524. On Caesarius see Allen and CWE Ep 374 introductions and CEBR I 238–9.

413 Aetij Medici lib. 16. interprete / Ioan. Baptista Veronensi

Aetius Amidenus medicus. Libri XVI in tres tomos divisi quorum primus & ultimus Joanne Baptista Montano Veronensi, secundus Jano. Cornario Zuiccaviensi interpretibus latinitate donati sunt. In quo opere cuncta quae ad curandi artem pertinent congesta sunt. Tom. 3. Basileae: H. Frobenius & N. Episcopius, 1535 (folio).

There can be no doubt that this entry on the *Versandliste* refers to the third and last part of Aetius' great medical compilation in Latin translation. The two previous volumes had appeared in 1533; the third, published in 1535, clearly failed to find its correct place alongside them on Erasmus' shelves in the last year of his life; see no 133.

Appendix 1:
Catalogus librorum Erasmi

The *Catalogus librorum Erasmi* (Catalogue of the Books of Erasmus) lists the titles of the works written, translated, or edited by Erasmus that were found in a chest near the window (*in arca aulae versus fenestram*), presumably in the house 'Zum Luft' in Basel, his last residence.[1] The manuscript is undated, but the list, which comprises chiefly Froben editions, was probably compiled by a clerk acting for Bonifacius Amerbach or in his employ towards the end of 1536; it is written in an unknown hand (not that of the *Versandliste*). Amerbach carefully checked the inventory after it was made. As can be seen on the folio (13r) reproduced on page xxi above, he must have had the books in his hands as he went through the list item by item, since he seems to have drawn lines checking off single titles and braces connecting groups of titles in the left margin. He also corrected titles where necessary, supplemented them with bibliographical details such as the format, and added many titles the compiler had overlooked. We may be fairly certain that the chest contained unbound works, probably kept for the most part in loose quires and not always complete. It must have been difficult for the compilers of the inventory to deal with such an untidy collection. For a discussion of this separate collection of Erasmus' works see Part 1 chapter 5, 'What the *Versandliste* Does Not Contain,' 99–103 above.

The author submitted his transcript of the *Catalogus*, with the often illegible additions of Amerbach, to Dr C. Vischer, at the time librarian of the University Library in Basel, who arranged for Dr B.R. Jenny, the expert on Amerbach's handwriting, to examine it. Dr Jenny read the transcript with care, supplementing and correcting it in many places. The author would like to express his gratitude to both scholars for their assistance.

In the transcript printed here, common Latin abbreviations (eg those for *ae, com-, cum-, -um, -us, -orum, epistola, responsio, propositio*) have been silently expanded; other abbreviations have been left as they are in the manuscript. Editorial remarks appear in square brackets. Titles or words that are struck through or underlined in the manuscript are shown the same way; Amerbach's additions (which he sometimes indicated with a caret) and his braces (shown with lines, parentheses, or brackets) are in bold-face type. The printed transcript does not, however, reproduce the periods in the clerk's usual format for writing dates (.1.5.28.), occasionally inserted after a title, or used (not consistently) by Amerbach in his notes and corrections. In order to facilitate comparison with the more detailed list that follows, the editor has numbered the items in the right margin.

An expanded description, with full titles, of the editions referred to follows the transcript of the *Catalogus*. Titles joined by a brace in the manuscript appear under the same number in that list. For explanation of the short titles cited as references, see the Works Frequently Cited and the Bibliography (xxiii–xxvi, xxvii–xliv above). If the same edition of a work appears in the *Versandliste*, this is always mentioned.

---

1   University Library Basel MS CVIa71, fols 11–14; paper, 29 x 26 cm

Catalogus librorum Erasmi

[fol 11r]

4°	/	Querela pacis }		[1]
	/	De morte declamatio } anno MDXVIII		
	\	Encomium matrimonij }		
	\	Encomium artis medicae }		

~~folio~~ 4   Lucianica 1517 **Querela pacis   de morte declamatio**   [2]

8°   Exomologesis siue modus confi. 1524   [3]

8   Aduersus petrum sutorem 1525 Apologia   [4]

8	/	Prologus in suputationem Bedae }		[5]
	/	Responsiunculae ad propositiones Bedae } 1526		
	\	Elenchus erratorum in Caesa. [sic] bedae }		

ad Rom. Corinth et Galatas
8   Paraphrases in epistolas pauli ^ 1520   [6]

4   De morte Declamatio   [7]

4   Plutarchi Chaeronesis 15~~13~~ **18 uersus Anno 18 uersus anno 20**   [8]

Principis   ter
4   Institutio ~~militis~~ Christiani ~~ter~~ bis 1518 ~~in 4 Institutio principis~~   [9]
                                                           ~~Christiani 1516~~
                                                           ~~bis~~

Principis
4   Institutio ~~militis~~ Christiani 1516 **bis**   [10]

4   Syntaxis 1517   [11]

8   Praecationes 1535   [12]

4   Aliquot epistolae elegantes 1518   [13]

~~Consultatio de bello turcis inferendo 1530~~   [14]

4   **Ratio sive methodus compendio perveniendi ad ueram theologiam**   [15]
            cum paraclesi 1520

~~In epistolam pauli ad Galatas 1519~~   [16]

4   **cum paraclesi**
            Compendium verae theologiae ^ 1519   [17]

4   Explanatio symboli apostolorum 1533   [18]

4   De puritate Tabernaculi <u>1536</u>   [19]

4	/	<u>Responsio</u> ad epistolam paraeneticam **Alberti Pij**	[20]
	\	Notaciunculae ad Naenias Bedaicas 1529	

folio   **Luciani versa 1521**   [21]

                                   (**Enchiridion militis Christiani cum praefatione ad Volzium**   [22]
                                   (**Disputatio de tedio ac pavore Christi**
4 Ann. 1518   (**Basilius in Esaiam. Epistola ad capessendam virtutem precatio ad**
                                   (**Jesum Paean Virginis Concio de puero Jesu**
                                   (**Enarratio psalmi 1   Ode casa natalicia Expostulatio Jesu Hymni**

[fol llv]

4   Selectae aliquot epistolae   1528   [23]

                                         Encomium matrimonij   1528   [24]

4   Apologia de tribus linguis   1519   [25]

                                   (Epistola ad Leonem x pon.   )   [26]
)   (Epistola ad D. Grimannum cardi.   )
4) 1515   (Epistola ad Raphaelem Rearium   )
)   (Epistola ad Martinum Dorpium   )
                                   (**carmen**
                                   (Panegyricum in laudem Selestadij   )   1515

4   (Encomium matrimonij   }   [27]
                                   (Encomium artis medicae } 1518   **bis**

                                         Erasmi
4   ~~Quaedam~~ Epigrammata   1518   [28]

4   Adhortatio ad Christianae philosophiae studium   1519   [29]

4   Auctarium selectarum epistolarum   1518   [30]

                                         ~~Quaerela pacis~~   [31]
                                         ~~De morte declamatio~~

4   Apologia In principio erat sermo   1520   [32]

4   Theo. Gazae gramma. Insti. lib. duo   1516   [33]

8   Spongia   1523   [34]

8   Colloquia   1~~524~~ **22**   [35]

8   De libero arbitrio   1524   [36]

                                                                   Et Prvdentij dvos hymnos
8   <u>Commentarius</u> in Nucem Ouidij ^ 1524   [37]

8   Paraphrasis in Euang. Joannis   1523   [38]

                                         ~~Responsio ad epistolam apologeticam   1530~~   [39]

8   Colloquia 15~~32~~ **22**   [40]

[fol 12r]

                                                                   et de curiositate adiectis graecis
8   <u>Plutarchi</u> Chaeronei de non Irascendo   1535   [41]

Ald. 8   /   Hecuba et Iphigenia Euripidis   }   [42]
                        /   Ode eiusdem de laude Britanniae   }
                        \   Ode de senectutis incommodis   15 } 07

4   Apologia ad Jacobum fabrem [sic] stapulensem   1518   [43]

4   (Responsio ad annotationes Eduardi Lei   }   [44]
Eduardi Lei   (Apologia In principio erat sermo   } 1530 **20**
  annotat. _______(_______________   }
in testamentum   (Epistolae illustrium virorum   }
  Erasmi   (

4   Ex Plutarchi versa   **1520**   [45]

                                             versa a variis
4   Plutarchi Chaeronensis opuscula   1518   [46]

4   Sileni Alcibiadis   1517   [47]

4   Scarabeus   1517   [48]

4   Bellum   1517   [49]

folio   Paraphrasis in Euang. Ioannis   1533 **23**   [50]

folio   /   Nouum testamentum ex 5 recog.   1535   [51]
                        \   Annotationes in Nouum testamentum ex 5 recog.   1535

                                Aliquot Homiliae Chrysostomi   1533   [52]

folio   Institutio Matrimonij   1526   [53]

folio   Apophtegmatum [sic] opus   1532   [54]

folio   Farrago noua Epistolarum   1519   **Frobenius 33**   [55]

8   (Lingua   1526   [56]
                        (**Plvtarchus de viciosa verecvndia**

8   /   De recta pronunciatione Grecae linguae   }   [57]
                        /   Latinae   } 1528
                        \   Dialogus Ciceronianus   }

8   Hyperaspistes diatribae   1526   [58]

4   **Paraphrasis in epistolam ad Timothevm Titvm Philemonem   1520**   [59]

4   ~~Declamatio~~ **Apologia pro declamatione ...** [illegible abbreviation   [60]
                                    deleted] **de laude matrimonij   1519**

4   **Moriae Encomium cum Lystrij commentarijs et ludo Senecae**   [61]
                                    et Dorpij epistola   1517

[fol 12v]

fol   ————   Epistolae palaeonaeoi }   1532   **friburgi**   [62]
                        \   Responsio De divortio }

fol	Adagiorum opus 1533	[63]
fol	Adagiorum opus 1536	[64]
	Lucianica 1521	[65]
	Plutarchi Chaeronensis opuscula 1513	[66]
	Paraphrasis in epistolas pauli ad { Romanos } { Corinthios } 1520 { Galatas }	[67]
	Morias Encomium 1517	[68]
8	Modus orandi 1524 **Basileae**	[69]
	~~Methodus perueniendi ad veram theo. 1520~~	[70]
	Paraphrasis ad Christianae philosophiae studium 1519	[71]
	Epistolae aliquot eruditorum virorum 1520	[72]
4	**dvas** Paraphrasis in epistolas pauli ad Corinthios 1519	[73]
4	Paraphrasis in epistolam pauli ad Gallatas 1519	[74]
4	Paraphrasis in epistolam pauli ad Romanos 1518	[75]
	Institutio principis Christiani 1516	[76]
8	Methodus perueniendi ad veram theo. **cum Paraclesi** 1520	[77]
8	Similia 1518	[78]
Frob. 8	Hecuba et Iphigenia Euripidis 1518	[79]
8	Colloquia 1518	[80]
4	**Chrysostomi homiliae 8 1533**	[81]
4	**Plutarchi de tuenda bona valetudine praecepta Eras. 1513**	[82]
folio	**Apologiarum volvmen 1521**	[83]
fol	**Nouui [sic] testamenti omnes editiones**	[84]
fol	**Adagiorum omnes editiones**	[85]
[fol 13r]		
8	<u>Aduersus</u> mendacium et obtractionem [sic] admonitio **1530 bis**	[86]
8	Hyperaspistes Diatribae **1526 1 pars bis**	[87]
	~~Apologia aduersus petrum Sutorem~~	[88]
Pantalabvs in 8	<u>Responsio</u> aduersus cuiusdam febricitantis libellum	[89]

8   Epistola ad quosdam Gracculos   [90]

8 1516   <u>Detectio</u> praestigiarum cuiusdam libelli germanice scripti **de coena**   [91]
                                 Domini   bis

                   /   (Prologus in suppu. calu**m** Natalis Bedae   [92]
                   /   (~~Responsiunculae Responsine~~ [?]
8   /   (Responsiunculae ad propositiones à Beda notatas \
                   \   (Appendix de antapologia Pe. Sutoris   \ **bis**
                   \   (~~Elenchus erratorum in censuris Bedae~~   /
                   \   (Elenchus in censuras eroneas Bedae   /

8   Ein Sendtbrieff fur einen siner freund von dem sacrament   [93]

8   Expostulatio ad quendam amicum **pia et Christiana**   [94]

8   <u>Apologia</u> aduersus rapsodias Alberti pij   [95]

4 1533   De sarcienda ecclesiae concordia **precatio ad Jesum pro pace ecclesiae**   [96]

4 1534   De praeparatione in mortem 2 **adiectis aliquot epistolis**   [97]

8   Catalogus [corrected from Catalogi] ~~duo~~ operum Des Eras   **1524**   [98]

8   **Aduersus Petri Sutoris etc. monachi Cartvsiani debachationem**   [99]
                                 Apologia   bis   1525

8 Friburg.   **D. Erasmi responsio ad epistolam apologeticam incerto avthore**   [100]
                                 proditam   1530   bis

8   **D. Erasmi purgatio aduersus epistolam non sobriam Lvteri   1534**   [101]

8 Colon   **D. Erasmi de contemptu mundi epistola   1526**   [102]

8   <u>**Vtilissima**</u> **consultatio de bello Turcis inferendo enarratus psalmus 28**   [103]
                                 1530

8 Colon.   **Erasmi Encomivm matrimonij, artis medicae, de morte contemnenda**   [104]
                                 Oratio episcopi qua respondet iis qui sibi nomine popvli gratulati
                                 essent Oratio de amplexanda virtute

8   /   **Exomologesis sive modus confitendi**   [105]
                       /   **Paraphrasis in 3 Psalmum Domine quid mvltiplicati**
                       /   **Dvo diplomata Hadriani** vi, **cum responsionibus**
                       \   **Epistola de morte**
                       \   **Apologia ad Stvnicae conclusiones**

fol   **Ecclesiastae libri 4**   [106]

                   /   **Institutio principis Christiani**   [107]
4 1516   /   **Precepta Isocratis ad Nicoclem ...** [illegible abbreviation deleted]
                   \   **Erasmo interprete   Cum epistola ad Cancellarium et praefatione**
                   \   **Panegyricus**
                   \

	\	**Plutarchi de discrimine adulatoris et amici**	[108]
	\\	**de utilitate capienda ab inimicis**	
4 1518	|	~~**Epigrammata Erasmi**~~	
	\	**doctrina principum**	
	\	**Cum principibus philosophum debere disputare**	

[fol 13v]

Erasmi meinvng vom nachtmal tütsch [109]

Consilivm cuiusdam ex animo cupientis esse consvltum et pontificis [110]
    dignitatj et Christianae religionis tranquillitati

Expositio fidelis mortis Thomae Mori [111]

Erasmi de cena dominica tütsch [112]

[fol 14r]   [blank]

[fol 14v]

~~**Erasmica a Frobenio seorsim**~~
~~**et successu temporum impressa**~~
~~**in arca aulae versus fenestram**~~
        nisi fallor
Catalogvs librorum ^ Erasmi
Lasco ~~(**nisi fall.**~~ **Baroni**
in Poloniam missorum.

1 **4°**   Querela pacis / De morte declamatio / Encomium matrimonij / Encomium artis
medicae / anno MDXVIII

*Querela pacis undique gentium eiectae profligataeque. In genere consolatorio de morte
declamatio. Encomium matrimonii. Encomium artis medicae.* Basel: J. Froben,
November 1518 (quarto). BB E 1294; Bezzel 1668

See also nos 2, 7, 24, 27, and 31 (which was crossed out).

2 ~~folio~~ **4**   Lucianica   1517   **Querela pacis   de morte declamatio**

*Querela pacis undique gentium eiectae profligataeque. Cum quibusdam aliis, quorum
catalogum proxima reperies pagella.* Basel: J. Froben, December 1517 (quarto).
BB E 1290; Bezzel 1666; Meyers 114; RM 738

Cf no 1. This edition contains the complete Lucian translations; cf nos 21 and 65.

3 **8°**   Exomologesis siue modus confi.   1524

*Exolomogesis sive modus confitendi … opus nunc, primum et natum et excusum cum
aliis lectu dignis, quorum catalogus reperies in proxima pagella.* Basel: J. Froben 1524
(octavo). Bezzel 1060; Adams E 373; RM 439; Halkin *Erasmus ex Erasmo* 136–8

Perhaps the same copy that Amerbach entered with full list of contents under no 105

VL/Catalogue no 357 #2

4 **8**   Aduersus petrum sutorem   1525   Apologia

Adversus Petri Sutoris … debacchationem apologia. Basel: J. Froben, August 1525
(octavo). BB E 302; Bezzel 156

See also nos 88 (deleted) and 99 (added by Amerbach).

5 **8**   Prologus in suputationem Bedae / Responsiunculae ad propositiones
Bedae / Elenchus erratorum in Caesa. [sic] bedae / 1526

*Prologus in supputationem calumniarum Natalis Bedae. Responsiunculae ad propo-
sitiones a Beda notatas. Appendix De antapologia Petri Sutoris, & scriptis Jodoci
Clithovei, quibus addatur Elenchus erratorum in censuris Bedae.* Basel: J. Froben,
August 1526 (octavo)

Perhaps an incomplete copy; this entry does not mention the *Appendix de antapologia
Petri Sutoris.* The *Catalogus* includes a complete copy at no 92.

VL/Catalogue no 378; cf VL/Catalogue no 69.

6 **8**   Paraphrases in epistolas pauli ^ **ad Rom. Corinth et Galatas**   1520

Paraphrases in epistolas Pauli apostoli ad Rhomanos, Corinthios et Galatas. Basel:
J. Froben, January 1520 (octavo). Bezzel 1163

See also no 67.

7 **4** De morte Declamatio

Presumably the text in loose quires from one of the editions of the *Querela* (Froben, November 1518 or December 1517; see nos 1 and 2). The only independent edition published in quarto before 1536 (Basel: A.Cratander et S. Crustanus, October 1518) is most probably not the copy in question here.

8 **4** Plutarchi Chaeronesis 15~~13~~ **18 uersus Anno 18 uersus anno 20**

Plutarchus. *Opuscula quaedam.* Basel: J. Froben, September 1518 (quarto). Adams P 1653

Contains ten treatises from the *Moralia* translated by Erasmus (four), Stephanus Niger (two), Angelus Barbatus, Pirckheimer (two) and Melanchthon.

Cf nos 46 and 66, and vl/Catalogue no 200.

and

[Opuscula] Ex Plutarcho versa per Des. Erasmum. Basel: J. Froben, September 1520 (quarto). Adams P 1654

Froben had first published Erasmus' translations from Plutarch's *Moralia* in 1514. Cf nos 45 and 66.

vl/Catalogue no 385

9 **4** Institutio ~~militis~~ **Principis** Christiani ~~ter~~ ~~bis~~ **ter** 1518 ~~in 4 Institutio/principis/Christiani 1516/bis~~

Institutio principis christiani … recognita cum aliis nonnullis eodem pertinentibus, quorum catalogum in proxima reperies pagella. Basel: J. Froben, July 1518 (quarto). bb e 1257; Bezzel 1246

See also no 108 (added by Amerbach), and nos 10, 76, and 107 (the 1516 edition, also added by Amerbach).

vl/Catalogue no 71 #2

10 **4** Institutio ~~militis~~ **Principis** Christiani 1516 **bis**

Institutio principis christiani saluberrimis referta praeceptis … cum aliis nonnullis eodem pertinentibus, quorum catalogum in proxima reperies pagella. Basel: J. Froben, May 1516 (quarto). bb e 1253; Bezzel 1245; asd iv-1 96 (title-page)

A duplicate of no 76; cf also nos 107 and 108 (added by Amerbach).

11 **4** Syntaxis 1517

Absolutissimus de octo orationis partium constructione libellus. Basel: J. Froben, September 1517 (quarto). Bezzel 644

This edition is not on the *Versandliste*, but see vl/Catalogue no 42 #3.

12 **8**   Praecationes   1535

Precationes aliquot novae. Basel: H. Froben and N. Episcopius, August 1535 (octavo)

VL/Catalogue no 396

13 **4**   Aliquot epistolae elegantes   1518

Aliquot epistolae sane quam elegantes. Basel: Froben, January 1538 (quarto).
Bezzel 1014; Halkin *Erasmus ex Erasmo* 45–53

14 ~~Consultatio de bello turcis inferendo 1530~~

See no 103, added by Amerbach.

15 **4   Ratio sive methodus compendio perveniendi ad ueram theologiam cum
paraclesi   1520**

Ratio seu methodus compendio perveniendi ad veram theologiam. Basel: J. Froben,
March 1520 (quarto). Bezzel 1693

The *Ratio* is followed by the *Paraclesis.*

Cf nos 17 and 77; no 70 was deleted.

16 ~~In epistolam pauli ad Galatas   1519~~

See no 74.

17 **4**   Compendium verae theologiae ^ **cum paraclesi**   1519

Ratio seu compendium verae theologiae. Basel: J. Froben, January 1519 (quarto).
BB E 1126; Bezzel 1688

and

Paraclesis, id est adhortatio ad … Christaniae philosophiae studium. Basel: J. Froben,
February 1519 (quarto). Bezzel 1396; Adams E 728

Cf nos 15, 77.

18 **4**   Explanatio symboli apostolorum   1533

Dilucida et pia explanatio symboli quod Apostolorum dicitur … Basel: H. Froben and
N. Episcopius, March 1533 (quarto). Bezzel 714

Cf VL/Catalogue no 340 #1: 'Eight months after the quarto *editio princeps* of
March 1533, Froben brought out another edition in octavo' (Bezzel 715).

19 **4**   De puritate Tabernaculi   <u>1536</u>

*De puritate tabernaculi sive ecclesiae christianae. Cum aliis nonnullis lectu non indignis,
nova omnia.* Basel: H. Froben and N. Episcopius 1536 (quarto). Bezzel 1660

VL/Catalogue no 393

20 **4** <u>Responsio</u> ad epistolam paraeneticam **Alberti Pij** / Notaciunculae ad Naenias Bedaicas 1529

Responsio ad epistolam paraeneticam … Alberti Pii Carporum principis. Eiusdem notatiunculae quaedam extemporales ad Naenias Bedaicas. Basel: Froben, March 1529 (quarto). Adams E 827; Bezzel 1781; RM 802

21 **folio Luciani versa 1521**

Lucianus [Dialogi et alia] Des. Erasmo interprete. Aliquot item ex eodem commentarii Thoma Moro interprete … Basel: J. Froben, August 1521 (folio). ASD I-1 374–5 (edition D).

Added by Amerbach; see also no 65.

VL/Catalogue no 118

22 **4 Ann. 1518 Enchiridion militis Christiani cum praefatione ad Volzium / Disputatio de tedio ac pavore Christi / Basilius in Esaiam. Epistola ad capessendam virtutem precatio ad Jesum Paean Virginis Concio de puero Jesu / Enarratio psalmi 1 Ode casa natalicia Expostulatio Jesu Hymni**

Enchiridion militis Christiani … Cui accessit nova mireque utilis Praefatio. Et Basilii in Esaiam commentariolus. Cum aliis … Basel: J. Froben, July 1518 (quarto). BB E 1003; Bezzel 852; RM 322

23 **4** Selectae aliquot epistolae 1528

Selectae aliquot epistolae. Basel: J. Herwagen and H. Froben 1528 (quarto). Bezzel 1022; Halkin *Erasmus ex Erasmo* 141–8

24 Encomium matrimonij 1528

Encomium matrimonii. Encomium artis medicae. Basel: J. Froben, November 1518 (quarto). Bezzel 1668

'1528' must be an error; there is no 1528 edition and no independent Froben edition at all except that of 1518. See no 1; see also nos 27 and 31 (deleted).

25 **4** Apologia de tribus linguis 1519

Apologia refellens suspiciones quorundam dictitantium dialogum D. Jacobi Latomi de tribus linguis & ratione studii theologici conscriptum fuisse adversus ipsum. De trium linguarum & studii theologici ratione dialogus per Jacobum Latomum [Basel: J. Froben, May 1519] (quarto). Bezzel 191; RM 43

26 **4 1515** Epistola ad Leonem X pon. / Epistola ad D. Grimannum cardi. / Epistola ad Raphaelem Rearium / Epistola ad Martinum Dorpium / Panegyricum **carmen** in laudem Selestadij 1515

Jani Damiani Senensis ad Leonem x. Pont. Max. de expeditione in Turcas elegeia. Epistola Pisonis ad J. Coritium. Erasmi Roterodami epistola ad Leonem x. Ad

Grimannum. Ad Raphaelem Rearium. Ad Martinum Dorpium. In laudem urbis Selestadii panegyricum carmen. Basel: J. Froben 1515 (quarto). Bezzel 1010; cf Allen I 599 Appendix 7 (edition A); Halkin *Erasmus ex Erasmo* 27–36.

27 **4**   Encomium matrimonij/Encomium artis medicae   1518   **bis**

See no 24; cf no 31.

28 **4**   ~~Quaedam~~ **Erasmi** Epigrammata   1518

Epigrammata. Basel: J. Froben, March 1518 (quarto). Bezzel 912 or 913

Also mistakenly listed, and deleted, by Amerbach in no 108

29 **4**   Adhortatio ad Christianae philosophiae studium   1519

Paraclesis, id est adhortatio ad … Christianae philosophiae studium. Basel: J. Froben, February 1519 (quarto). Bezzel 1396

See also nos 17, 71 (both February 1519).

30 **4**   Auctarium selectarum epistolarum   1518

Auctarium selectarum aliquot epistolarum ad eruditos. Basel: J. Froben 1518 (quarto). Bezzel 1015 (August 1518); Halkin *Erasmus ex Erasmo* 55–67

31 ~~Quaerela pacis/De morte declamatio~~

See nos 1 and 2.

32 **4**   Apologia In principio erat sermo   1520

Apologia refellens quorundam seditiosos clamores apud populum, qui velut impium insectabantur, quod verterit, In principio erat sermo … Basel: J. Froben 1520 (quarto). Bezzel 1773(a)

One part of the composite work listed at no 44, printed with a separate title-page

33 **4**   Theo. Gazae gramma. Insti. lib. duo   1516

Theodorus Gaza. *Grammaticae institutionis libri duo … translati per Erasmum Roterodamum. Colloquiorum familiarum incerto autore libellus Graece & Latine …* Basel: J. Froben 1518 or 1520 (quarto).

Dirk Martens first published Gaza book I in Leuven in October 1516 (NK 962) and book II in 1518 (NK 3052). In the Froben edition of 1518 (books I and II) the old colophon (October 1516) was maintained, as it was also in the Froben edition of August 1520. See Allen Epp 771 introduction, 629:1–3; Meyers 80–1.

Cf VL/Catalogue no 347.

34 **8**   Spongia   1523

Spongia Erasmi adversus aspergines Hutteni. Basel: J. Froben 1523 (octavo).
Bezzel 1804 (September 1523) or 1805 (October 1523); ASD IX-1 113

35 **8**   Colloquia   15~~24~~ **22**

Familiarum colloquiorum formulae non tantum ad linguam puerilem expoliendam
utiles, verum etiam ad vitam instituendam. De ratione studii epistola paraenetica.
Basel: J. Froben, [March] 1522 (octavo). Bezzel 451

36 **8**   De libero arbitrio   1524

De libero arbitrio διατριβή *sive collatio.* Basel: J. Froben, September 1524 (octavo).
Bezzel 1263

VL/Catalogue no 376

37 **8**   <u>Commentarius</u> in Nucem Ouidij ^ **et Prvdentij dvos hymnos** 1524

Commentarius Erasmi Roterodami in Nucem Ovidii. Eiusdem commentarius in duos
hymnos Prudentii. Basel: J. Froben 1524 (octavo). Meyers 125; RM 1398

38 **8**   Paraphrasis in Euang. Joannis   1523

Paraphrasis in Evangelium secundum Joannem … nunc primum excusa. Basel: J. Froben
1523 (octavo)

One of the 1523 octavo editions of the *Paraphrase on John* (Bezzel 1481, 1483,
or 1484)

39 ~~Responsio ad epistolam apologeticam   1530~~

See no 100.

40 **8**   Colloquia   15~~32~~ **22**

Familiarum colloquiorum formulae … non tantum ad linguam puerilem expoliendam
utiles, verum etiam ad vitam instituendam … Basel: J. Froben, March or [c August]
1522 (octavo). BB E 441 or 443; Bezzel 451 (March 1522) or perhaps 450 (1522 without
month)

41 **8**   <u>Plutarchi</u> Chaeronei de non Irascendo **et de curiositate adiectis graecis**   1535

Plutarchus. *Libellus perquam elegans, De non irascendo. Eiusdem De Curiositate.*
Perquam latinus Des. Erasmo Rot. interprete. Adiecti sunt iidem Graeci, quo vel praelegi
possint, vel certe legi a Graecanicae literaturae studiosis. Basel: J. Froben, May 1525
(octavo). ASD IV-2 262 (title-page); Meyers 133

'1535' must be an error; the 1525 edition is the only possibility.

42 **Ald. 8**   Hecuba et Iphigenia Euripidis / Ode eiusdem de laude Britanniae / Ode de senectutis incommodis   1507

Euripides. *Hecuba & Iphigenia in Aulide … Tragoediae in latinum tralatae Erasmo Roterodamo interprete. Eiusdem Ode de laudibus Britanniae, Regisque Henrici VII ac regiorum liberorum eius. Eiusdem Ode de senectutis incommodis.* Venice: Aldo Manuzio, December 1507 (octavo). ASD I-1 194 (title-page)

43 **4**   Apologia ad Jacobum fabrem [sic] stapulensem   1518

Apologia ad Jacobum Fabrum Stapulensem. Basel: J. Froben, February 1518 (quarto). ASD IX-3 xiii (title-page); BB E 299; Bezzel 166

44 **4**   Responsio ad annotationes Eduardi Lei / Apologia In principio erat sermo / **Eduardi Lei annotat. in testamentum Erasmi** / Epistolae illustrium virorum   1530 **20**

Responsio ad annotationes Eduardi Lei. Apologia Eras, de In principio erat sermo. Eduardi Lei annotationes in Novum Testamentum Erasmi. Epistolae aliquot illustrium virorum, Lei temerariam loquacitatem tractantium detestantiumque quorum cui quisque scripserit, proxima indicat pagella. Basel: J. Froben, August 1520 (quarto). ASD IX-4 72 (title-page); Bezzel 1773; Adams E 412

Erasmus *Apologia de 'In prinipio erat sermo,'* Edward Lee's *Annotationes* on Erasmus' New Testament, and *Epistolae illustrium virorum* have separate title-pages.

Cf nos 32, 72.

45 **4**   Ex Plutarchi versa   **1520**

Plutarchus. Ex Plutarcho versa per Des. Erasmum. Recognita per eundem ex collatione Graecorum voluminum. Basel: J. Froben, September 1520 (quarto). Meyers 130

Cf nos 8 (second entry) and 66, and VL/Catalogue no 385.

46 **4**   Plutarchi Chaeronensis opuscula **versa a variis**   1518

Plutarchus. *Opuscula quaedam.* Basel: J. Froben, September 1518 (quarto). Adams P 1653

Cf nos 8 (first entry) and 66, and VL/Catalogue no 200.

47 **4**   Sileni Alcibiadis   1517

Sileni Alcibiadis, cum scholiis. Basel: J. Froben, April 1517 (quarto). BB E 259; Bezzel 150

See also no 48.

48 **4**   Scarabeus   1517

Scarabeus, cum scholiis [Beati Rhenani]. Basel: J. Froben, May 1517 (quarto). BB E 274; Bezzel 150

Part of no 47 (folios e–k4), but with its own title-page

49 4 Bellum 1517

Bellum. Basel: J. Froben, April 1517 (quarto). BB E 212; Bezzel 134

The oldest separate edition of *Dulce bellum inexpertis* (*Adagia* IV i 1)

50 folio Paraphrasis in Euang. Ioannis 1533 **23**

Paraphrasis in Evangelium secundum Ioannem. Basel: J. Froben, February 1523 (folio).
Bezzel 1482

Cf VL/Catalogue no 401.

51 folio Nouum testamentum ex 5 recog. 1535 / Annotationes in Nouum testamentum
ex 5 recog. 1535

Novum testamentum … recognitum a Des. Erasmo … cum annotationibus eiusdem …
locupletatis. Basel: H. Froben and N. Episcopius 1535 (folio). Meyers 157–63

and

In novum testamentum annotationes ab ipso autore … recognitae ac locupletatae.
Basel: Froben 1535 (folio). Meyers 163

See VL/Catalogue nos 241, 247, 328–31.

52 Aliquot Homiliae Chrysostomi 1533

Johannes Chrysostomus. *Aliquot homiliae ad pietatem summopere conducibiles.*
Basel: Froben 1533 (quarto)

Amerbach made no note on the format of this title. Perhaps he did not find the book
here when he was going through the list; it may be the same copy of the collected
sermons of Chrysostom that he added (and identified as a quarto) at no 81.

VL/Catalogue no 394

53 folio Institutio Matrimonij 1526

Christiani matrimonii institutio. Basel: J. Froben, August 1526 (folio). Bezzel 344

VL/Catalogue no 346

54 folio Apophtegmatum [sic] opus 1532

Apophthegmatum opus cum primis frugiferum, vigilanter ab ipso recognitum autore,
e Graeco codice correctis aliquot locis in quibus interpres Diogenis Laertii fefellerat,
locupletatum insuper quum variis … accessionibus, tum duobus libris … adiectis,
per Des. Erasmum Roterodamum. Basel: H. Froben and N. Episcopius 1532 (folio).
De Vreese BER fasc 1 73; Bezzel 195

On editions of the *Apophthegmata*, see VL/Catalogue no 391.

55 folio   Farrago noua Epistolarum   1519   **Frobenius 33**

Farrago nova epistolarum Des. Erasmi Roterodami ad alios, et aliorum ad hunc; admixtis quibusdam, quas scripsit etiam adolescens. Basel: J. Froben, October 1519 (folio). Allen I 600 Appendix 7 (edition E); Halkin *Erasmus ex Erasmo* 69–88 (title-page 71); Adams E 851

56 8   Lingua   1526/**Plvtarchus de viciosa verecvndia**

Lingua … ab autore recognita. Plutarchus, Libellus elegans … de immodica verecundia. Basel: J. Froben, February or July 1526 (octavo)

VL/Catalogue no 151

57 8   De recta pronunciatione Grecae/Latinae linguae/Dialogus Ciceronianus   1528

De recta latini graecique sermonis pronuntiatione dialogus. Dialogus cui titulus Ciceronianus, sive de optimo genere dicendi. Cum aliis nonnullis quorum nihil est non novum. Basel: Froben, March 1528 (octavo). Bezzel 1763; ASD I-4 1, ASD I-2 582 (title-page)

VL/Catalogue no 352 #1 (probably the 1529 edition)

58 8   Hyperaspistes diatribae   1526

Hyperaspistes diatribae adversus servum arbitrium Martini Lutheri [book 1]. Basel: J. Froben, [March?] or July 1526 (octavo). Bezzel 1116 (no month-date) or Bezzel 1117 (July); Adams E 673 or E 675

Also listed at no 87

Cf VL/Catalogue no 338, *Hyperaspistes 2* (1527); Bezzel 1122 (1527).

59 4   Paraphrasis in epistolam ad Timothevm Titvm Philemonem   1520

Paraphrasis in epistolas Pauli ad Timotheum duas, ad Titum unam et ad Philemonem unam. Basel: J. Froben, March 1520 (quarto). Bezzel 1457

Froben also published an octavo edition in March 1520. *Versandliste* no 354 is probably an octavo. At about this time Froben also published quarto editions of the Paraphrase of the Epistles to the Romans and the Galatians.

60 4   ~~Declamatio~~ Apologia pro declamatione … [illegible abbreviation deleted] **de laude matrimonij   1519**

Apologia pro declamatione de laude matrimonii. Basel: J. Froben, May 1519 (quarto). BB E 1238; Bezzel 186

61 4   Moriae Encomium cum Lystrij commentarijs et ludo Senecae et Dorpij epistola   1517

Moriae Encomium … cum Listrii commentariis & aliis complusculis libellis [etc]. Basel: J. Froben, November 1517 (quarto). Bezzel 1305; BB E 849

A page-by-page reprint of the Froben 1516 edition (ASD IV-3 46–7, no 11)

Cf no 68.

On editions of the *Moria*, see VL/Catalogue no 66.

62 **fol**   Epistolae palaeonaeoi / Responsio De divortio   1532   **friburgi**

Epistolae palaeonaeoi. Ad haec responsio ad disputationem cuiusdam Phimostomi de divortio. Freiburg: J. Faber Emmeus, September 1532 (folio). Allen I Appendix 7 601 (edition K); Halkin *Erasmus ex Erasmo* 177–83 (title-page 179); Bezzel 1028 or 1029

The *Responsio* is mentioned on the title-page.

VL/Catalogue no 345

63 **fol**   Adagiorum opus   1533

Adagiorum opus ... exquisitiore quam antehac unquam cura recognitum ... Basel: H. Froben et N. Episcopius, March 1533 (folio). BB E 101; Bezzel 79

64 **fol**   Adagiorum opus   1536

Adagiorum chiliades ... tum auctiores, tum emendatiores. Basel: H. Frobenius and N. Episcopius, March 1536 (folio). BB E 102; Bezzel 80

VL/Catalogue no 406 #1

65   Lucianica   1521

Lucianus. [Dialogi et alia] Des. Erasmo interprete. Aliquot item ex eodem commentarii, Thoma Moro interprete ... Basel: J. Froben, August 1521 (folio); ASD I-1 374–5, edition D

There is no indication of the format in this entry. It is possibly the same copy or a duplicate of the copy recorded by Amerbach under no 21.

VL/Catalogue no 118

66   Plutarchi Chaeronensis opuscula   1513

An edition (or perhaps parts of several editions) of translations from Plutarch that is impossible to identify. See no 8, an edition also misdated 1513. There Amerbach altered '1513' to '1518,' the year in which the *Opuscula quaedam* appeared, and added under the same entry the September 1520 edition of [*Opuscula*] *Ex Plutarcho versa per Des. Erasmum.* See also nos 46 (1518) and 45 (1520).

67   Paraphrasis in epistolas pauli ad Romanos / Corinthios / Galatas   1520

Paraphrases in epistolas Pauli apostoli ad Rhomanos, Corinthios et Galatas. Basel: J. Froben, January 1520 (octavo). Bezzel 1163

There is no indication of the format here. Presumably this is the same copy as the one added by Amerbach at no 6.

68 Morias Encomium   1517

Joannes Frobenius lectori. Habes iterum Morias Encomium ... Basel: J. Froben,
November 1517 (quarto). BB E 849; Bezzel 1305; ASD IV-3 46–7, no 11

There is no indication of the format here. Presumably this is the same copy as the one
added by Amerbach at no 61.

69 **8** Modus orandi   1524   **Basileae**

Modus orandi Deum. Basel: J. Froben, October 1524 (octavo). Bezzel 1284; ASD V-1 118

This is the *editio princeps.*

70 ~~Methodus perueniendi ad veram theo.~~   ~~1520~~

See no 15 (added by Amerbach).

71 Paraphrasis ad Christianae philosophiae studium   1519

Paraclesis, id est adhortatio ad ... Christianae philosophiae studium. Basel: J. Froben,
February 1519 (quarto)

Mangled title of *Paraclesis*; cf nos 17, 29.

72 Epistolae aliquot eruditorum virorum   1520

*Epistolae aliquot eruditorum virorum, ex quibus perspicuum quanta sit Eduardi Lei
virulentia.* Basel: J. Froben, August 1520 (quarto)

Part, with separate title-page, of *Responsio ad Annotationes Eduardi Lei*; see no 44.

73 **4**   Paraphrasis in **dvas** epistolas pauli ad Corinthios   1519

Paraphrasis in duas Epistolas Pauli ad Corinthios. Basel: J. Froben, March 1519
(quarto). Adams E 789

Possibly the *editio princeps* (Leuven: Martens, [January–March] 1519; NK 844),
but more probably Froben's reprint; cf Ep 916 introductions.

74 **4**   Paraphrasis in epistolam pauli ad Gallatas   1519

In epistolam Pauli ad Galatas paraphrasis. Basel: J. Froben, August 1519 (quarto).
Adams E 787

Froben's reprint of the *editio princeps* (Leuven: Martens, May 1519; NK 845)

Cf no 16, which was deleted.

75 **4**   Paraphrasis in epistolam pauli ad Romanos   1518

In epistolam Pauli Apostoli ad Romanos paraphrasis. Basel: J. Froben, January
or November 1518 (quarto). BE 143 (both editions)

76 Institutio principis Christiani   1516

Institutio principis christiani saluberrimis referta praeceptis ... cum aliis nonnullis eodem pertinentibus, quorum catalogum in proxima reperies pagella. Basel: J. Froben, May 1516 (quarto). BB E 1253; Bezzel 1245; ASD IV-1 96 (title-page)

A duplicate of no 10; cf also no 107 (added by Amerbach).

77 **8**   Methodus perueniendi ad veram theo. **cum Paraclesi**   1520

Ratio seu methodos compendio perveniendi ad veram theologiam. Basel: J. Froben, February 1520 (octavo). Bezzel 1692

Cf no 15.

Cf VL/Catalogue no 362.

78 **8**   Similia   1518

Parabolae sive similia. Basel: J. Froben, February 1518 (octavo). Bezzel 1365

The frst (unauthorized) edition

79 **Frob. 8**   Hecuba et Iphigenia Euripidis   1518

Euripides. *Hecuba et Iphigenia Erasmo interprete.* Basel: J. Froben, February 1518 (octavo). ASD I-1 212

80 **8**   Colloquia   1518

Familiarium colloquiorum formulae, et alia quaedam. Basel: November 1518 (octavo). BB E 405; Bezzel 430

81 **4   Chrysostomi homiliae 8   1533**

Johannes Chrysostomus. *Aliquot homiliae ad pietatem summopere conducibiles.* Basel: Froben 1533 (quarto). BE 35

Cf no 52.

VL/Catalogue no 394

82 **4   Plutarchi de tuenda bona valetudine praecepta Eras.   1513**

Plutarchus. *De tuenda bona valetudine precepta Erasmo Roterodamo interprete.* London: R. Pynson, July 1513 (quarto). STC 20060

A Martens reprint is dated November 1513 (NK 1743). The Froben 1513 edition (BE 45) is a 'ghost' edition.

83 **folio   Apologiarum volvmen   1521**

Apologiae omnes. Basel: J. Froben, October 1521 (folio). ASD IX-3 xv (title-page)

Possibly a rare copy of the *editio princeps* of the *Apologiae omnes* dated on the title-page November 1521 and in the colophon October 1521. The only known specimen to date was discovered by Halkin in Liège; see vl/Catalogue nos 332 and 383.

84 fol   Nouui [sic] testamenti omnes editiones

Presumably not complete copies but unidentifiable loose quires or gatherings of several authorised editions of Erasmus' *Novum Testamentum*

85 fol   Adagiorum omnes editiones

Like the previous entry, presumably not complete copies but unidentifiable parts of different editions of the *Adagia* in loose quires or gatherings

86 8   Aduersus mendacium et obtractionem [sic] admonitio   1530   bis

Adversus mendacium et obtrectationem utilis admonitio. Freiburg im Breisgau 1530 (octavo). Bezzel 155

No other copy of this work is listed in the *Catalogus.* Amerbach's *bis* must mean 'two copies.'

87 8   Hyperaspistes Diatribae   1526   1 pars   bis

Hyperaspistes diatribae adversus servum arbitrium Martini Lutheri [book 1]. Basel: J. Froben, [March?] or July 1526 (octavo). Bezzel 1116 (no month-date) or Bezzel 1117 (July); Adams e 673 or e 675

A duplicate of no 58

88   ~~Apologia aduersus petrum Sutorem~~

See nos 4 and 99, the latter added by Amerbach.

89 Pantalabvs in 8   Responsio aduersus cuiusdam febricitantis libellum

Adversus febricitantis cuiusdam libellum responsio. Basel: Froben, March 1529 (octavo). be 175; Bezzel 154; Adams e 829

Amerbach's marginal note 'Pantalabus' is the name given by Erasmus to Luis Carvajal, against whom the *Responsio* was directed (Ep 2110 introduction / n10).

90 8   Epistola ad quosdam Gracculos

Epistola ad quosdam impudentissimos gracculos. [Freiburg: J. Faber Emmeus c 1530] (octavo). Bezzel 937; Ep 2275

There is a rare copy in the Library of Sélestat; see Walter *Catalogue Sélestat* no 1245.

91 **8 1516**   <u>Detectio</u> praestigiarum cuiusdam libelli germanice scripti **de coena Domini   bis**

Detectio praestigiarum cuiusdam libelli germanice scripti ficto authoris titulo, cum hac inscriptione, Erasmi et Lutheri opiniones de coena Domini. Basel: J. Froben, June 1526 (octavo). ASD IX-1 212 (title-page), 230; Bezzel 702

No other copy of this work is listed in the *Catalogus*. Amerbach's *bis* must mean 'two copies.'

92 **8**   Prologus in suppu. calu**m** Natalis Bedae/~~Responsiunculae Responsine~~ [?]/ Responsiunculae ad propositiones à Beda notatas/Appendix de antapologia Pe. Sutoris/ ~~Elenchus erratorum in censuris Bedae~~/Elenchus in censuras eroneas Bedae   **bis**

Prologus in supputationem calumniarum Natalis Bedae. Responsiunculae ad propositiones a Beda notatas. Appendix De antapologia Petri Sutoris, & scriptis Jodoci Clithovei, quibus addatur Elenchus erratorum in censuris Bedae iampridem excusus. Basel: J. Froben, August 1526 (octavo). ASD IX-5 ix (title-page 1526 edition) and xii (title-page 1527 edition).

This entry is marked as a duplicate; see no 5 (an incomplete copy).

VL/Catalogue nos 378 and 69

93 **8**   Ein Sendtbrieff fur einen siner freund von dem sacrament

Sendtbrieff an einen seiner guten freunde von dem Sacrament des leybs vnnd bluts Christi. [Hagenau: Farckall 1526] (octavo)

Translation of no 94, published shortly after the Latin text. The translator is unknown. See Holeczek *Erasmus deutsch I* 196–7; *Erasmus von Rotterdam, Vorkämpfer für Frieden und Toleranz* 208, G 10.1

This title is written in a different hand from the rest of the original list.

94 **8**   Expostulatio ad quendam amicum **pia et Christiana**

Expostulatio ad quendam amicum admodum pia et Christiana [Basel: J. Froben 1526] (quarto?)

Erasmus' letter to Conradus Pellicanus on the Eucharist (Ep 1637, c 15 October 1525), which had first circulated in manuscript; see Allen's introduction. See also ASD IX-1 217–18; *Erasmus von Rotterdam, Vorkämpfer für Frieden und Toleranz* 208, G 10.

95 **8**   <u>Apologia</u> aduersus rapsodias Alberti pij

Apologia adversus rhapsodias calumniosarum querimoniarum Alberti Pii … Basel: H. Froben and N. Episcopius 1531 (octavo). BB E 306; Bezzel 179

96 **4 1533**   De sarcienda ecclesiae concordia **precatio ad Jesum pro pace ecclesiae**

Liber de sarcienda ecclesiae concordia deque sedandis opinionum dissidiis, cum aliis nonnullis lectu dignis. Basel: H. Froben and N. Episcopius 1533 (quarto). Bezzel 1785; BE 116; Adams E 385; RM 479

The *aliis nonnullis* include the *Precatio ad dominum Jesum pro pace ecclesiae* and
several letters. The *Precatio* does not have a separate title-page. There is a copy
in the City Library, Rotterdam.

vl/Catalogue no 340 #2

97 **4 1534**   De praeparatione in mortem 2 **adiectis aliquot epistolis**

*Liber cum primis pius, de praeparatione ad mortem, nunc primum et conscriptus et
aeditus. Accedunt aliquot epistolae serijs de rebus, in quibus item nihil est non novum
ac recens.* Basel: H. Froben and N. Episcopius, January 1534 (quarto). Bezzel 1578;
bb e 1150; Halkin *Erasmus ex Erasmo* 185–93

Cf vl/Catalogue no 395.

98 **8**   Catalogus [corrected from Catalogi] ~~duo~~ operum Des Eras   **1524**

*Catalogus novus omnium lucubrationum Erasmi Roterodami cum censuris & digestione
singularum in suos tomos.* Basel: J. Froben, September 1524 (octavo). Adams e 517;
for the full title see de Vreese ber fasc 2 page 136.

The change in the title from *Catalogi duo* to *Catalogus* shows that the compiler must
already have known of the imminent publication by H. Froben and N. Episcopius of
the *Catalogi duo* (Bezzel 311), which is dated 1537 on the title-page (with 1536 in the
colophon). Amerbach's dedicatory letter to Paumgartner is dated 1 February 1537.

99 **8   Aduersus Petri Sutoris etc. monachi Cartvsiani debachationem
Apologia   bis   1525**

Adversus Petri Sutoris … debacchationem apologia. Basel: J. Froben, August 1525
(octavo). bb e 302; Bezzel 156

A duplicate. See no 4 and cf no 88 (deleted).

100 **8 Friburg.   D. Erasmi responsio ad epistolam apologeticam incerto avthore
proditam   1530   bis**

*Responsio ad epistolam apologeticam incerto autore proditam, nisi quod titulus, forte
fictus, habebat: per ministros verbi, ecclesiae Argentoratensis.* Freiburg: J. Faber
Emmeus 1530 (octavo). Bezzel 1777; asd ix-1 312 (title-page)

Added by Amerbach as a duplicate; cf no 39 (deleted).

101 **8   D. Erasmi purgatio aduersus epistolam non sobriam Lvteri   1534**

Purgatio adversus epistolam non sobriam Martini Luteri. Basel: H. Froben and
N. Episcopius, April 1534 (octavo). be 164; Bezzel 1656; asd ix-1 428 (title-page)

vl/Catalogue 398

102 **8   Colon   D. Erasmi de contemptu mundi epistola   1526**

De contemptu mundi epistola. Cologne: E. Cervicornus 1526 (octavo). Bezzel 688

103 8 <u>Vtilissima</u> consultatio de bello Turcis inferendo enarratus psalmus 28   1530

Utilissima consultatio de bello Turcis inferendo & obiter enarratus Psalmus xxviii.
Basel: Froben 1530 (octavo). Bezzel 1809; ASD V-3 2 (title-page)

Cf no 14 (deleted).

**104 8 Colon.   Erasmi Encomivm matrimonij, artis medicae, de morte contemnenda
Oratio episcopi qua respondet iis qui sibi nomine popvli gratulati essent   Oratio de
amplexanda virtute**

*Declamationes quatuor, I Encomium matrimonii; II Encomium artis medicae; III De
morte contemnenda; IV Orationem episcopi qua respondet iis qui sibi nomine populi
gratulati essent, continet. Eiusdem de amplexanda virtute oratio* ... [Coloniae]:
E. Cervicornus 24 January 1525 (octavo). BB E 1230; Bezzel 906; RM 364

**105 8   Exomologesis sive modus confitendi / Paraphrasis in 3 Psalmum Domine quid
mvltiplicati / Dvo diplomata Hadriani vi, cum responsionibus / Epistola de morte /
Apologia ad Stvnicae conclusiones**

Exolomogesis sive modus confitendi ... *opus nunc, primum et natum et excusum cum
aliis lectu dignis, quorum catalogus reperies in proxima pagella.* Basel: J. Froben 1524
(octavo). Bezzel 1060; Adams E 373; RM 439; Halkin *Erasmus ex Erasmo* 136–8

Cf no 3; this may be the same copy or a duplicate.

A complete copy, which includes the *Paraphrasis in tertium Psalmum*, two letters
to Adrian VI with the answers, the *Epistola Iodoco Gavero de morte* (Ep 1347),
and the *Apologia ad Stunicae conclusiones*

VL/Catalogue no 357 #2

106 fol   Ecclesiastae libri 4

Ecclesiastae sive de ratione concionandi libri quatuor, opus recens ... Basel: H. Froben
et N. Episcopius, August 1535 (folio). Bezzel 820; ASD V-4 2 (title-page)

VL/Catalogue no 402

107 4 1516   Institutio principis Christiani / Precepta Isocratis ad Nicoclem ... [illegible
abbreviation deleted] **Erasmo interprete   Cum epistola ad Cancellarium et
praefatione / Panegyricus**

Institutio principis christiani ... *cum aliis nonnullis eodem pertinentibus, quorum
catalogum in proxima reperies pagella.* Basel: J. Froben, May 1516 (quarto).
BB E 1253; Bezzel 1245

Cf no 108. Both editions contain, besides the *Institutio*, the *Praecepta Isocratis ad
Nicoclem*, the *Panegyricus ad Philippum*, and four named translations from Plutarch
(*De discrimine adulatoris et amici; De utilitate capienda ex inimicis; De doctrina principum; Cum principibus maxime philosophum debere disputare*). Presumably these two
entries describe texts in loose quires, some belonging to the 1516 edition and some
to the 1518 edition. See also nos 10 (marked by Amerbach as a duplicate) and 76.

**108   4 1518   Plutarchi de discrimine adulatoris et amici / de utilitate capienda ab inimicis /
~~Epigrammata Erasmi~~ / doctrina principum / Cum principibus philosophum debere
disputare**

*Institutio principis christiani ... recognita cum aliis nonnullis eodem pertinentibus,
quorum catalogum in proxima reperies pagella.* Basel: J. Froben, July 1518 (quarto).
BB E 1257; Bezzel 1246

See no 107. See also no 9.

For the *Epigrammata*, mistakenly listed and deleted here, see no 28.

109   Erasmi meinvng vom nachtmal tütsch

*Jud, Leo. Des Hochgelernten Erasmi von Roterdam, vnd Doctor Luthers Maynung vom
Nachtmal vnsers Herren Jesu Christi neuwlich aussgangen auff den XVIII. tag Aprellens.*
[Zürich, C. Froschauer, April 1526]. ASD IX-1 222

The second part of this publication (folios A2 verso–A6 recto) contains the *Maynung
von Nachtmal*, attributed by the author to Erasmus; Erasmus contested this in his
Detectio praestigiarum (Basel: J. Froben, June 1526); cf no 91.

**110   Consilivm cuiusdam ex animo cupientis esse consvltum et pontificis dignitatj
et Christianae religionis tranquillitati**

*Consilium cuiusdam ex animo cupientis esse consultum et Roman. Pontifici dignitati
et Christiani religionis tranquillitati* [Cologne 1520]

The first edition of this 'joint production' of Johannes Faber of Augsburg and
Erasmus was published shortly after November 1520; four Latin editions followed.
See Ep 1149 introductions; see also Ferguson *Opuscula* 343, 349–51.

111   Expositio fidelis mortis Thomae Mori

*Expositio fidelis de morte D. Thomae Mori et quorundam aliorum insignium virorum
in Anglia.* [Basel: Froben] 1535 (quarto)

The original author may perhaps have been Philip Montanus; it is likely that Gilbert
Cousin, perhaps under Erasmus' direction, prepared the Basel edition of 1535; see
Allen XI 368 Appendix 27 'The Expositio fidelis' introduction; Bietenholz 'Erasmus
und der Basler Buchhandlung in Frankreich' 300.

112   Erasmi de cena dominica tütsch

A duplicate of no 109

Appendix 2:
Books Found in Erasmus' Correspondence

The following list of works includes both those that Erasmus' correspondence shows that he received or that were sent to him and those whose presence is in his library is highly probable because of Erasmus' relationship with their authors. Among them are some that are not included either in the *Versandliste* or in the *Catalogus librorum Erasmi*. The list makes no claim to completeness; it may be assumed that many other works, particularly ephemeral topical books or pamphlets, were in Erasmus' possession at one time or another. For explanation of the short titles cited as references, see the Works Frequently Cited and the Bibliography xxiii–xxvi, xxvii–xliv above.

1 Afinius, Henricus. *Questiones tres elegantissime nuper in publico liberalium disciplinarum gymnasio in ... Lovaneniensium Academia disputatae.* Antwerp: W. Vorstermann, 4 April 1517 (quarto); NK 42

   Prefaced by Ep 542

2 Agricola, Georgius. *Bermannus sive de re metallica.* Basel: Froben 1530 (octavo)

   Printed with Erasmus' commendatory letter, Ep 2274

3 Agricola, Johannes. *Scholia copiosa in therapeuticam methodum, id est, absolutissimam Claudii Galeni Pergameni curandi artem.* Augsburg: Philip Ulhart, March 1534 (probably 1533) (folio)

   Printed with a prefatory letter from Erasmus, Ep 2803

4 Alber, Erasmus. *Iudicium Erasmi Alberi de Spongia Erasmi Roterodami, adeoque quatenus illi conveniat cum M. Lutheri doctrina.* Haguenau: Johann Setzer for Johann Schott in Strasbourg [c July 1524]

   Epp 1397 introductions, 1437:36–8 with 37n/40–2 with n17, 1466:26 and n/29 and n19, 1477:46–7/55–7, 1496:98, 137–8/105–6, 152

5 Alciati, Andrea. *Emblematum libellus.* Paris: C. Wechel 1534 (octavo)

   Allen Ep 2065 introduction

6 [Aleandro, Girolamo]. *Racha.* Paris, Bibliothèque nationale MS Lat. 3461

   Epp 1717:33–41 with 33n/38–48 with n18, 1719:37–51/39–54, 1744:131–4/138–42, 1804:248–9/274–5, 2443:289–97. This text aimed against Erasmus was never published but circulated in manuscript. See Massa 'Intorno ad Erasmo: una polemica che si credeva perduta,' and cf Gilmore 'Italian Reactions to Erasmian Humanism' 67–9 and Erasmus' annotation on Matt 5:22 ASD VI-5 139 676–726n.

7   Alger of Liège. *De veritate corporis et sanguinis Dominici in Eucharistia.* Freiburg: Johannes Faber Emmeus 1530 (octavo)

Ep 2284, Erasmus' prefatory letter to his edition. Cf no 75 below, Guitmund of Aversa's treatise on the same subject.

8   Ammonio, Andrea. *Carmina.* Paris: [Gilles Gourmont?] 1511 (quarto)

For Erasmus' involvement in this publication see Epp 218, 219, 220, 221, 234.

9   Amsdorf, Nicolaus von and Martin Luther. *Epistolae Domini Nicolai Amsdorfi et D. Martini Lutheri, de Erasmo Roterodamo.* Wittenberg: J. Lufft 1534 (octavo)

Ep 2918

10   Anthoniszoon, Jacob, of Middelburg. *De precellentia potestatis imperatoriae.* Antwerp: Dirk Martens, 1 April 1503 (quarto); NK 120

Printed with Erasmus' complimentary preface, Ep 173

11   Apollonius of Rhodes. *Argonautica.* Venice: Aldine press 1521 or 1523

See Allen VII 547 Appendix 20 'Books Ordered by Erasmus'; presumably he never received the book.

12   Apostolius, Arsenius. *Praeclara dicta philosophorum, imperatorum, oratorumque et poetarum.* Rome: [Monte Cavallo Press], c 1519 (octavo). Legrand *Bibliographie hellénique* I 169 no 62

CWE Ep 1232A:18–19 with n2. See Geanakoplos *Greek Scholars in Venice* 182; Knös *L'histoire de la littérature néo-grèque, la période jusq'en 1821* 301

13   Basil the Great and Gregory of Nazianzus. *Basilii magni et Gregorii Nazanzeni theologorum Epistolae Graecae nunquam antea editae.* Haguenau: J. Secerius 1528 (octavo)

Ep 1997:5–6 with 5n/n3; ASD II-4 29 and 309; ASD II-5 230–1 and 238–9

14   Beatus Rhenanus. *In C. Plinium.* Basel: Froben, March 1526

Epp 1544 introductions, 1674:73–4/84–5

15   Becichemo, Marino. *Elegans ac docta in C. Plinium praelectio.* [Ed Nicolas Bérault]. Paris: P. Vidoue for R. Resch, 23 July 1519 (folio)

Ep 1016 was first printed as a preface in this book; cf Epp 1594:83n/n19, 1626:47 and n/52–3 and n17.

16   Béda, Noël. *Annotationum … in Jacobum Fabrum Stapulensem libri duo, et in Desiderium Erasmum Roterodamum liber unus.* Paris: Josse Bade, 28 May 1526 (folio)

Epp 1571 introductions and 71–2/75–6, 1596:3–4/5–7, 1664 introduction/n1, 1679:39–42/44–8, 1685:14–24/17–29

17 Béda, Noël. *Apologia adversus clandestinos Lutheranos*. Paris: Josse Bade, 1 February 1529 (quarto)

Epp 1571 introductions and 2110:23–4/23–4

18 Bembo, Pietro. Perhaps *De Virgilii culice et Terentii fabulis* liber. Venice: G.A. Sabio and brothers 1530

or

De Guido Ubaldo ... deque Elisabetha Gonzaga Urbini ducibus. Venice: G.A. Sabio and brothers 1530

Ep 2337:26–9 with 27n/27–30 with n5

19 Borbonius, Nicolaus. *Nugae*. Paris: M.Vascosanus 1533 (octavo)

Ep 2789. The work includes two sets of elegaic verse addressed to Erasmus.

20 Brassicanus, Johannes Alexander. *Musae et gratiae scholiis illustratae, Orphei statua ex Callistrato graeco latina facta*. Vienna: J. Singrenius, 9 July 1524

Ep 1146 introductions. The letter (dated 26 September 1520) was printed as a preface in this book. See also von Aschbach *Geschichte der Wiener Universität* Nachträge I-1 88.

21 Brassicanus, Johannes Alexander. *Proverbiorum symmicta*, Vienna, H. Vietor, March 1529

Ep 2305. Erasmus used this collection of proverbs, without actually naming it, for his 1533 edition of the *Adagia*; see ASD II-4 305 547n; ASD II-8 14.

22 Brie, Germain de. *Antimorus*. Paris: P. Vidoue 1519 (quarto)

Ep 1045:31/32

23 Brunfels, Otto. *Pro Ulricho Hutteno defuncto, ad Erasmi Roterodami Spongiam Responsio*. Strasbourg: J. Schott [1524]

Epp 1405 introductions; 1432:46–52/50–7; ASD IX-1 111. Brunfels' work was printed with a corrected edition of Hutten's *Expostulatio*. Cf no 84 below.

24 Bucer, Martin. *Defensio adversus axioma catholicum, id est criminationem R.P. Roberti episcopi Abrincensis*. Strasbourg: M. Apiarus 1534 (octavo)

Epp 3127:21–32 with 21n, 2972:12–14

25 Bucer, Martin. *Epistola apologetica ad syncerioris Christianismi sectatores per Frisiam orientalem et alias inferioris Germaniae regiones*. Strasbourg: P. Schaefer and J. Apronianus 1530

Epp 2238 introductions, 2312:1–3 with n/1–3 with n2

26 Cajetanus, Tommaso de Vio, Cardinal. *De communione sub utraque specie. De integritate confessionis. De satisfactione. De invocatione sanctorum.* Rome: A. Bladus 1531
(quarto)

Epp 2619:7–14, 2690 introduction; Groner *Kardinal Cajetan* 72

27 Cajetanus, Tommaso de Vio, Cardinal. *De divina institutione pontificatus Romani
pontificis super totam ecclesiam a Christo in Petro.* Rome: M. Silber, 22 March 1521
(quarto)

Ep 1225:198–201 with 198n/215–18 with n47

28 Calcagnini, Celio. *Libellus elegans de libero arbitrio ex philosophiae penetralibus.* Basel:
J. Froben 1525

Ep 1578 was written as an introduction. See Luchsinger *Der Basler Buchdruck* 125.

29 Capito, Wolfgang Faber. *Hebraicarum institutionum libri duo.* Basel: J. Froben, January
1518 (quarto)

In Ep 629:14–17/16–19 Erasmus asked Wolfgang Lachner and Johann Froben to send
him 'Wolfgang Faber on the pointing in Hebrew.' Cf Epp 556:26–7 with 26n/26–7n,
561:15/17, 575:54–5/58–9.

30 Carranza, Sancho. *Opusculum in quasdam Erasmi annotationes.* Rome: A. de Trino
1522

Ep 1303:44–5/52–3; cf Epp 1277:22n/n8, 1281:34–40, 55–6/34–40, 55–7.

31 Carvajal, Luis. *Apologia monasticae religionis diluens nugas Erasmi.* Salamanca 1528

Epp 2110 introduction/n10, 2126 introductions and 1–5/2–6, 2300:22–3/23–4,
2301:1–13/2–15, 2892:165–8

32 Carvajal, Luis. *Dulcoratio amarulentiarum Erasmicae responsionis ad Apologiam ...
Lodovici Carvaiali.* Paris: S. de Colines 1530 (octavo)

Presumably received by Erasmus in manuscript. Epp 2110 introduction/n10, 2275
introductions and 61–2/67–8, 2300:8–9, 77–8/10–11, 83–4, 2301:10–11/12–13

33 Ceratinus, Jacobus. *De sono literarum, praesertim Graecarum, libellus.* Antwerp:
J. Graphaeus 1527 (octavo); NK 2623

Ep 1843 was printed as a preface to this treatise.

34 Charles v. *Ad duo Clementis septimi ... brevia Responsio in qua ab ipso Pontifice
appellat, petitque Generalis Christianorum omnium Concilii congregationem.* Alcalá:
M. de Eguía, 10 April 1527

Ep 1863:8–10 with 8n/10–12 with n5; R. Stupperich 'Erasmus und die kirchliche
Autoritäten' 358

35 Chierigati, Francesco. *Oratio habita Nurimbergae in senatu Principum Germaniae. xiii Cal. Decembris, m.d.xxii.* [Nürnberg: F. Peypus 1522] (quarto)

Ep 1336:1 with n/3 with n1

36 Cicero. *Oratio pro Marcello cum annotationibus H. Barlandi* [Leuven]: Dirk Martens [c 1520] (quarto); NK 2660

An oration with scholia by Adrianus Cornelii Barlandus; Ep 2025:12–13 with 12n/n5

37 Ciołek, Erazm (Erasmus Vitellius). *Oratio in celeberrimo Augusten. conventu ... regis Poloniie Sigismundi habita ... die xx. Aug. 1518.* Augsburg: J. Miller [1518] (quarto)

Ep 863, a preface by J. Spiegel to the *Oratio*

38 Cleves-Mark-Jülich-Berg, John III, duke of. *Erklärung zur Kirchenordnung,* 8 April 1533

Epp 2804 and 2845:18–21

39 Cochlaeus, Johannes. *Dialogus de bello contra Turcas, in antilogias Lutheri.* 30 June 1529

M.J. Heath 'Erasmus and the War against the Turks' 995 with n25

40 Cochlaeus, Johannes. *De matrimonio ... Henrici VIII. Congratulatio disputatoria ... ad Paulum III.* Leipzig: M. Blum, February 1535 (quarto)

Ep 3001:7 with n

41 Cochlaeus, Johannes. *Fasciculus calumniarum, sannarum et illusionum Martini Lutheri.* Leipzig: V. Schumann 1529

Epp 2120:102–3 with 103n/102–4 with n29, 2143:1–4 with 1n/2–5 with n1

42 Colet, John. *Oratio habita a D. Ioanne Colet, decano Sancti Pauli, ad clerum in convocatione, Anno M.D.XI.* London: R. Pynson n d

Ep 258:15 with n/15–16 with 16n. The oration was delivered 6 February 1512.

43 Corvinus, Antonius. *Quatenus expediat aeditam recens Erasmi de sarcienda Ecclesiae concordia Rationem sequi, tantisper dum apparatur Synodus, Iuditium.* Wittenberg: N. Schirlentz 1534 (octavo)

Epp 2993:77–83 with 80n, 3127:36–7; Augustijn *Erasmus en de Reformatie* 281–2

44 Corsi, Pietro. *Defensio pro Italia ad Erasmum Roterodamum.* Rome: A. Bladius 1535 (quarto)

Epp 3007:54–76 with 54n, 3015, 3016:17–18, 3032 (Erasmus' *Responsio ad Petri Cursii defensionem*); cf CWE 28 334.

45 Decius, Jodocus Ludovicus. *Sendbrieff von der grossen schlacht vnd sigg so Kü. Ma.*
Von Poln volk in Litten am XXVII *tag Ianuarii des 1527. Jars mit den vnglaubigen Tartern*
gehabt hat. n p, n d

Ep 1803:39–44 with 43n / 39–44 with n11

46 Dilft, Frans van der. *Ad Carolum* V *Hispaniarum regem ob res prospere feliciterque*
gestas oratio gratulatoria. Leuven: S. Zassenus, November 1533 (quarto); NK 4329

Ep 2904 introduction and line 30

47 Dolet, Etienne. *Dialogus de imitatione Ciceroniana adversus Desiderium Erasmum*
Roterodamum, pro Chistophoro Longolio. [Lyon: S. Gryphius 1535] (quarto)

Ep 3052:26–9 with 26n

48 Dorp, Maarten van. *Oratio in praelectionem epistolarum divi Pauli.* Antwerp: M.
Hillen, 27 September 1519; NK 739 and Basel: J. Froben, January 1520 (quarto)

Ep 438, a congratulatory letter from Erasmus, was printed at the beginning.

49 Dürer, Albrecht. *Underweysung der Messung, mit dem Zirckel und Richtscheyt.*
Nürnberg: [Hieronymus Andreae] 1525 (folio)

Ep 1717:71–2 with 72n / 82–3 with n31; [Dürer, Albrecht] *Albrecht Dürer, 1471–1971*
(exhibition catalogue) 352 no 640

50 Eck, Johann Meyer of. *In summulas Petri Hispani explanatio.* Augsburg: J. Miller,
May 1516 (folio)

Ep 844:284 / 306; cf Ep 769:110–13 with 113n / 126–9 with 128n.

51 Eck, Johann Meyer von. *CCCCIV articuli … partim … ex scriptis pacem Ecclesiae*
perturbantium extracti. Ingolstadt : n pr [31 May] 1530 (quarto)

Epp 2365:16–18 with 16n / 18–21 with n5, 2406:1–22 / 3–25

52 Egnazio, Giambattista. *De caesaribus libri* III *a dictatore Caesare ad Constantinum*
Palaeologum, hinc a Carolo Magno ad Maximilianum caesarem. Eiusdem in Spartiani,
Lampridiique vitas et reliquorum annotationes, etc. Venice: Aldine press [1517] (octavo)

Ep 588:55–8 with 55n / 61–3 with 61n. The colophon is dated 1516. Cf no 80 below.

53 Emser, Hieronymus. *Apologeticon.* n p 1525

Ep 1566:11 / 12; cf Ep 1551:3n / n1

54 Emser, Hieronymus. *In Euricii Cordi medici Antilutheromastigos calumnias expurgatio*
pro Catholicis. n p [c Spring 1526]

Ep 1683:32–5 with 32n / 36–40 with n8

55 Enríques, Alonzo (Alphonsus Henriquez). *Defensiones pro Erasmo*. Naples 1532

Published in a volume dedicated to Charles v that contained another short treatise and Ep 2614, a commendatory letter to Erasmus from Johann Albrecht Widmanstetter.

56 Eobanus Hessus, Helius. *Heroidum christianarum epistolae*. Leipzig: M. Lotter [1514]

Epp 871:14 with n/15–16 with 16n, 874:6–7/8

57 Eobanus Hessus, Helius. *Hodoeporicon*. Erfurt: M. Maler [1519] (quarto)

Epp 870 introductions, 963:1n/6n

58 *Epistolae atque libelli aliquot, continentes controversiam quae inter ... D. Georgium Saxoniae Ducem etc. et M. Lutherum ... versata est, de mandato eiusdem Ducis Georgii iam recens e germanico in latinum traducti*. Leipzig: M. Lotter 1529

Ep 2338:10–15 with 14n, 74–8/11–16 with n5, 78–82. Publications of this kind were usually quartos or octavos.

59 Eppendorff, Heinrich. *Ad D. Erasmi ... libellum cui titulus, adversus mendacium & obtrectationem utilis admonitio iusta querela*. Hagenau: J. Secerius, February 1531 (octavo)

Ep 2438:8–9 with n/8–9 with n5

60 Erasmus. *Adagiorum omnium tam Graecorum quam Latinorum Aureum flumen ... ex D. Erasmi Roterodami aeditione brevi commentariolo, secundum ordinem alphabeti, per Theodoricum Cortehoevium selectum*. Antwerp: M. de Keyser for G. van der Haeghen, 16 February 1530; NK 772

Ep 2265, a dedicatory preface by Theodoricus Cortehoevius dated 1 February 1530

61 Erasmus. *Contra quosdam qui se falso iactant Evangelicos. Epistola ... iam recens edita, & scholiis illustrata* [by Gerard Geldenhouwer]. n p [1530]

Ep 2289:1–3 with 1n/1–3 with n2, and cf Epp 2238 introductions, 2293:1–8/2–9 with n2; ASD IX-1 313–14

62 Erasmus. *Epistolae aliquot selectae ex Erasmicis per Hadrianum Barlandum*. Leuven: Dirk Martens, December 1520 (quarto); NK 820

Printed with Erasmus' cooperation. Cf Allen III 627–9 Appendix 12 'The *Epistolae selectae per Barlandum*, 1520'; Halkin *Erasmus ex Erasmo* 91–5.

63 Erasmus. *Familiarum Colloquiorum formulae*. Paris: H. Etienne, at the expense of C. Resch, February 1519 (quarto)

Ep 920 introductions. Erasmus may have received a copy of this reprint of the unauthorized edition of the *Colloquies*.

64 Erasmus. *In omnes ... Adagiorum chiliadas epitome ad usum studiosorum utrius linguae conscripta per Hadrianum Barlandum*. Leuven: Dirk Martens, June 1521 (quarto); NK 2844

Ep 1204, an introductory letter by Erasmus

65 Erasmus, translations by Louis Berquin:

Brefue admonition de la maniere de prier: selon la doctrine de Jesuchrist. Avec une brefue explanation du Pater noster. Extrait des paraphrases de Erasme sur sainct Matthieu et sur sainct Luc. n p, n d (octavo); ASD v-1 118

Declamation des louenges de mariage [Paris: S. Dubois, c 1525] (octavo); ASD i-5 354

Le symbole des apostres quon dict vulgairement le Credo. Contenant les articles de la foy: par manière de dialogue ... La pluspart extraict dung traicte de Erasme de Rotterdam intitule Deuises familieres. n p, n d; ASD v-1 185

Querela Pacis (in manuscript); ASD iv-2 37

The *Brefue admonition* and *Le symbole* have nothing to do with the *Modus orandi Deum* and the *Explanatio symboli.*

66 Eucherius. *Epistola Valerii Episcopi ad propinquum suum ex Greco in Latinum sermonem per magistrum Rodolphum Agricolam traducta.* [Deventer]: J. de Breda [1485] (quarto); NK 535

Ep 676 introductions and Allen 1n

67 Ferber, Nikolaus, of Herborn. *Enarrationes Evangeliorum per sacrum quadragesimae tempus occurrentium.* Antwerp: M. Hillen 1533 (octavo); NK 1055

Sent by Cornelius Graphaeus to Erasmus; Epp 2896:12–13 with 12n, 3053:1–4, 25–8

68 Galen. *De sanitate tuenda.* Translated by Thomas Linacre. Paris: G. Rubens, 22 August 1517

Epp 502:15–16 with 15n / 17–19 with 17n, 534:58–9 / 60–2, 664:26 / 29–30, 687:26–7 / 30–1, 726:2–4 / 3–5, 868:62–8 / 70–7, 971:3–7 / 4–8

69 Geldenhouwer, Gerard. *D. Erasmi Roterodami Annotationes in leges pontificias et caesareas de haereticis. Epistolae aliquot Gerardi Noviomagi de re evangelica & haereticorum poenis.* Strasbourg: C. Egenolphus 1529 (octavo)

or

Ejn Antwort des ... D. Erasmi von Roterdam, die ersuchung und verfolgung der Ketzer betreffend, disser zeyt allen Fürsten, Herren, Ratherren, Richtern und allen gewalthabern fast nötig zu wissen. [Strasbourg: C. Egenolphus], autumn 1529

Ep 2238; cf Ep 2219:11–14 with 11n / 10–14 with n4; ASD ix-1 271–3.

70 Geldenhouwer, Gerard [Gerardus Noviomagus]. *Epistola ... de triumphali ingressu illustrissimi principis Philippi de Burgundia, electi et confirmati Ecclesiae Traiectensis, in ditionem suam,* Leuven: Dirk Martens [1517] (quarto); NK 977

Published with Ep 645, a commendatory letter from Erasmus dated 31 August 1517

71 Gois, Damião de. *Legatio magni Indorum Imperatoris presbyteri Ioannis ad Emanuelem Lusitaniae regem, A.D. MDXIII.* Antwerp: J. Grapheus, September 1532 (octavo); NK 680

Ep 2826 introduction and 31–2 with 31n

72 Gratius, Ortwinus. *Gemma prenosticationum ponderata supra orizontem generalem et specialem.* Cologne 1517

Ep 526:8–12 with 8n/9–13 with 10n

73 Gratius, Ortwinus *De venatione;* Ovidius *Halieuticon;* Nemesianus *Cynegeticon;* idem *Carmen bucolicum;* Calphurnius *Bucolica;* Adrianus card. *Venatio.* (Ed Georg van Logau). Venice: Aldine Press 1534 (octavo). Adams P 1704

Ep 2953:96–8 with 97n; cf Ep 2568 15n.

74 Gregory Thaumaturgus. *In Ecclesiastem Salomonis metaphrasis ... interprete Oecolampadio.* Augsburg: S. Grimm and M. Wirsung 1520

Ep 1158:18 with n/21 with n4

75 Guitmund, bishop of Aversa. *De veritate corporis et sanguinis Christi in Eucharistia tres ... libri.* Freiburg im Breisgau: J. Faber Emmeus 1530 (octavo)

Ep 2284:32n/n5. This edition by Augustinus Marius (Ep 2321) of a manuscript from the ruined monastery of Marbach was published, by the same printer, almost at the same time as Erasmus' own edition of Alger of Liège; see no 7 above.

76 Hasard, Jacques. *Apologia.* Leuven: Dirk Martens 1520 (quarto); NK 3142

Ep 1165:18–20/21–3

77 Hegius, Alexander. *Carmina et gravia et elegantia cum ceteris eius opusculis.* Deventer: R. Paffraet, 29 July 1503 (quarto); NK 1041

Ep 174, the dedicatory preface to Jacobus Faber's edition of this work. On its contents see 65n/77n.

78 Hermans, Willem. *Sylva odarum.* Paris: G. Marchand 1497 (quarto)

Ep 49, printed at the end of Hermans' work, which Erasmus edited and had published

79 Hippocrates. *Octoginta volumina ... per M. Fabium Calvum ... latinitate donata.* Rome: F.M. Calvus 1525 (folio)

Sent by Johann von Vlatten; see Ep 1912:1–2/1–2 with n1. Cf Ep 1810:60–2 with 61n/65–7 with n18.

80 *Historiae Augustae scriptores.* Ed Giovanni Battista Egnazio. Venice: Aldine press [1517] (octavo)

Ep 588:55–8 with 55n/61–3 with 61n. The book, containing *De caesaribus libri III* and other works from the 'Augustan History,' has a colophon dated 1516, but Egnazio's preface is dated 10 June 1517.

Cf no 52 above and VL/Catalogue nos 51 and 261.

81 *Hochstratus ovans, Dialogus festivissimus.* Cologne: n pr 1520 (quarto)

Ascribed to Hutten (Allen Ep 1165:22 with n, and cf Ep 1083:23n/n8); as well as to Hermannus Buschius (Bucer *Correspondance* I 121); cf CWE Ep 1165:25–6 with n11.

82 Hoen, Cornelis. *Epistola Christiana admodum ab annis quatuor ad quendam, apud quem omne iudicium sacrae Scipturae fuit, ex Bathavis missa, sed spreta, longe aliter tractans coenam Dominicam quam hactenus tractata est.* [Worms: Peter (II) Schöffer] 1525

Cf Ep 1621:18–20 with 18n/23–5 with n12; VL/Catalogue no 56.

83 Horák, Jan. *Ad Luderanorum famosum libellum recens Wittenbergae editum responsio* n p [30 September 1528]

Epp 2143:1–4 with 4n/2–5 with n2, 2247 introductions

84 Hutten, Ulrich von. *Cum Erasmo Roterodamo … expostulatio.* [Strasbourg: J. Schott, June 1523] (octavo)

Catalogus lucubrationum Allen I 27:4–5/CWE Ep 1341A:1020–1 with n283; ASD IX-1 100–8. Cf no 23 above.

85 Huttich, Johann. *Collectanea antiquitatum in urbe atque agro Moguntino repertarum.* Mainz: J. Schöffer, March 1520

Ep 1054

86 *In Eduardum Leeum quorundam e sodalitate literaria Erphurdien. Erasmici nominis studiosorum epigrammata.* (Ed Peter Eberbach [Petreius Aperbacchus]). Erfurt: J. Knapp 1520 (quarto) or Mainz: J. Schöffer 1520 (quarto)

Ep 1123:19–20 with 20n/24–5 with n12; Cf Allen Ep 998:66n, CWE Ep 1083 introduction; ASD IX-4 10–11.

87 Irenicus, Franciscus (Franz Friedlieb). *Germaniae exegesis.* Hagenau: T. Anshelm for J. Koberger, August 1518 (folio); Adams I 164

Ep 877:1–4 with 1n/2–6 with 2n

88 John Chrysostom. *Comparatio regii potentatus et divitiarum ac praestantiae, ad monachum in verissima Christi philosophia acquiescentem.* Paris: G. Morrhy, March 1530 and Basel: n pr 1533 (octavo)

Ep 2019 from Polidoro Virgilio is printed as the preface to his translation of Chrysostom's *Comparatio*.

89 [Jud, Leo]. *Des hochgelerten Erasmi von Roterdam unnd Doctor Martin Luthers maynung vom Nachtmal unnsers herren Ihesu Christi.* n p [c 1526] (quarto)

Epp 1708 introduction and 1n/n1, 1737:5–6 with 5n/6–8 with n2, 1804:148–59/161–72

90 Jud, Leo. *Uf entdeckung Doctor Erasmi von Roterdam der dückischen arglisten eynes tütschen büchlins, antwurt und entschuldigung.* [Zürich: C. Froschauer] 1526 (octavo)

Epp 1737:1 with n/1 with n1, 1744:7–12/8–13, 1804:148–59/161–72

91 Krzycki, Andrzej (Andreas Critius). *De afflictione Ecclesiae, commentarius in Psalmum xxi.* Cracow: H. Vietor 1527 and Rome: [F.M. Calvus] 1527 (quarto)

Epp 1629:7–8n, 1810:85–7 with 86n/90–2 with n22, 1822:1–2/3–4, 1825:35–6/42

92 Krzycki, Andrzej (Andreas Critius). *De negotio Prutenico epistola.* Cracow: H. Vietor 1525

Ep 1629:4–6 with 5n/5–8 with n3; cf Ep 1652:82–7/87–92

93 Krzycki, Andrzej (Andreas Critius). *De ratione et sacrificio missae.* Cracow: M. Scharffenberg 1528

Ep 2375:1–9 with 1n /3–11 with n1

94 [Krzycki, Andrzej (Andreas Critius) and others]. *Encomia Luteri.* [Cracow: H. Vietor] 1524

Includes Andrzej Krzycki's *In Luterum oratio*; see Epp 1629:2n/n2, 1652:54–5/58–60

95 *Lamentationes obscurorum virorum non prohibite per sedem apostolicam. Epistola D. Erasmi Roterodami, quid de obscuris sentiat.* Cologne: [H. Quentel, c March] 1518; repr August 1518 (quarto)

Ep 622

96 [Lando, Ortensio (Hortensius Landus)]. *Cicero relegatus et Cicero revocatus.* Venice 1534 or Lyon 1534 (octavo)

Epp 3005:11–12 with 11n, 3019:43–4 with 43n

97 Lascaris, Janus. *Epigrammata.* Paris: Josse Bade 1527 (octavo); Renouard *Bibliographie de Josse Bade* iii 3–4

Ep 2027:26–7 with 27n/27–8 with n14; cf Epp 2038:19–23/19–22, 2040:21–4/25–8, 2048:17–19/18–20, 2077:13–14/14–15

98 Latomus, Bartholomaeus. *Oratio de studiis humanitatis.* Paris: F. Gryphius 1534

Ep 3029:16–27

99   Lee, Edward. *Annotationes in Annotationes Novi Testamenti Desiderii Erasmi*. Paris: [Gilles de Gourmont for Konrad Resch, c 15 February 1520] (quarto)

Ep 1037, a preface published with Lee's *Annotationes*

100   López Zúñiga, Diego (Jacobus Lopis Stunica). *Annotationes contra Erasmum Roterodamum in defensionem tralationis Novi Testamenti*. Alcalá: Arnao Guillén de Brocar 1520 (folio)

Ep 1216:1–2 with 1n/2 with n1, and cf Ep 1128:3n/n2; ASD IX-2 35

101   López Zúñiga, Diego (Jacobus Lopis Stunica). *Assertio ecclesiasticae translationis Novi Testamenti a soloecismis quos illi Erasmus Roterodamus impegerat. Loca quae ex Stunicae annotationibus illius suppresso nomine, in tertia editione Novi Testamenti Erasmus emendavit*. Rome: n pr 1524 (quarto)

Two pamphlets 'published surreptitiously'; Epp 1466:35/38–9 with n23, 1470:38/47. Cf Allen IV 622 Appendix 15 'The Heine Collection' nos 9 and 10; ASD IX-2 37 nos 8 and 9.

102   Lucian. *Piscator seu reviviscentes*. Translated by Willibald Pirckheimer. Nürnberg: F. Peypus, 2 October 1517

Epp 685:13 with n/13 with n, 694:1/2. Cf no 128 below.

103   Luther, Martin. *Ad Leonem X ... resolutiones disputationum de virtute indulgentiarum ...* n p October 1518 (quarto); Benzing *Lutherbibliographie* 205 and 206

Epp 785:37/39, 904:18–19 with 19n/20–1 with 20n

104   Luther, Martin. *Antwortt deutsch auff König Henrichs von Englland Buch*. Wittenberg: N. Schirlentz 1522; Benzing *Lutherbibliographie* 1228

Ep 1313:84–5/93–4; cf Ep 1308:9n/n3.

105   Luther, Martin. *Condemnatio doctrinalis librorum Martini Lutheri, per quosdam magistros ... Lovanienses & Colonienses. Responsio ad condemnationem doctrinalem per Lovanienses & Colonienses facta*. Wittenberg: M. Lotter 1520 (quarto); Benzing *Lutherbibliographie* 627

Ep 1113:33–4 with 33n/38–9 with n15; cf Ep 1030 16n/n7. The Condemnation and Luther's Response were printed together. There are six other 1520 editions: Antwerp, Augsburg, Schlettstadt, Leipzig, Paris, and Vienna; see Benzing *Lutherbibliographie* 628–32a.

106   Luther, Martin. *De votis monasticis iudicium*. Wittenberg: [M. Lotter 1521] (quarto); Benzing *Lutherbibliographie* 1008. There are two 1522 editions: Basel: [Petri] and Wittenberg: J. Grünenberg; see Benzing 1009 and 1010.

Epp 1503:10–11 with 11n/12–13 with n2, 1526:232–3/243–5

107 Luther, Martin. *Eine Heerpredigt widder den Turcken.* Wittenberg: N. Schirlentz 1529 or 1530, or one of the reprints of 1530 (quarto); Benzing *Lutherbibliographie* 2711–17

Ep 2338:41–8 with 41n/44–50 with nn14–16. Allen and CWE disagree about the identification of the 'palinode.' According to Allen it is this book. CWE suggests *Vom Kriege widder die Türcken* (no 109 below).

108 Luther, Martin. *Tesseradecas consolatoria pro laborantibus et onerantibus.* Wittenberg: J. Grünenberg 1520; Benzing *Lutherbibliographie* 591

Ep 1332:56n/n13

109 Martin Luther. *Vom Kriege widder die Türcken.* Wittenberg: H. Weiss 16 April 1529; Benzing *Lutherbibliographie* 2701–6

Ep 2279:1–2 with n/1–2 with n1, CWE Ep 2338:44–50 with nn14–16. There is no Latin edition.

110 Luther, Martin. *Von beyder Gestallt des Sacraments zu nehmen vnd ander newrung.* Wittenberg: J. Grünenberg [c 20 April] 1522; Benzing *Lutherbibliographie* 1156

Ep 1298:22–9 with 24n/26–33 with n4

111 Luther, Martin. *Von heimlichen vnd gestolen brieffen … widder Hertzog Georgen zu Sachsen.* Wittenberg: H. Lufft 1529; Benzing *Lutherbibliographie* 2667–70

Ep 2338:10–40 with 14n/11–43 with n5; cf Ep 2124:40–3 with 42n/42–5 with n9

112 Luther, Martin. *Wider den falsch genantten geystlichen Stand des Babst und der Bischoffen.* Wittenberg: N. Schirlentz 1522; Benzing *Lutherbibliographie* 1196

Ep 1298:22–9 with 24n/26–33 with n4

113 Mantuanus, Baptista (Giovanni Battista Spagnolo). *Fastorum libri.* [Ed J. Wimpfeling]. Strasbourg: M. Schürer, August 1518 (quarto)

Ep 385:5–6 with 5n/6–7 with 7n

114 Marliano, Luigi. *In Martinum Lutherum oratio.* Rome [1520] and three reprints in Germany

Epp 1198:39–45 with 39n/44–50 with n5, 1199:18/22

115 Melanchthon, Philippus. *Articuli de quibus egerunt per visitatores in regione Saxoniae.* Wittenberg: N. Schirlentz, August 1527

Ep 1944:1 with n/1 with n1

116 Melanchthon, Philippus [Didymus Faventinus]. *Oratio pro Martino Luthero.* Wittenberg: n pr [1521]

Epp 1199:23–30 with 24n/28–35 with n6, 1167:408n/n73

117   More, Thomas. *Epistola ad Germanum Brixium.* London: R. Pynson 1520 (quarto)

Ep 1087 introductions

118   Nauclerus, Johannes. *Memorabilium omnis aetatis et omnium gentium chronici com-mentarii.* Tübingen: T. Anshelm, March 1516, 2 vols (folio)

Ep 397, a commendatory letter from Erasmus to the printer Thomas Anshelm writ-ten for this edition

119   Nausea, Fridericus. *Ad ... Carolum v ... pro sedando plebeio in Germania adversus ecclesiasticum equestremque ordinem tumultu oratio.* Vienna: n pr 3 May 1525 (octavo)

Ep 1632:1 with n/2 with n1

120   Nausea, Fridericus. *Ad magnum Erasmum Roterodamum, ut is proximo in Spira sacri Rhomani Imperii principum statuumque conventui intersit oratio.* Vienna: J. Singriener 1524 (quarto)

Ep 1577:1 with n/3 with n1

121   Nausea, Fridericus. *Tres Evangelicae veritatis homiliarum centuriae.* Cologne: P. Quentel 1532

Ep 2847:17–18 with 17n

122   Nesen, Konrad. *Dialogus sane quam festivus bilinguium ac trilinguium, sive de funere Calliopes.* [Paris: printed for Konrad Resch 1519] (octavo)

Ep 1519:83–7 with 83n/88–92 with n26. On the authorship of this work, sometimes ascribed to Erasmus, see Allen Ep 1061:505n, Ferguson *Opuscula* 206–24; cwe 7 330–3, the introductory note to an English translation.

123   Nidepontanus, Johannes and Laurentius Frisius. *Sudoris Anglici exitialis pestiferique morbi ratio, praeservatio et cura.* Strasbourg: J. Knoblouch [c October] 1529 (quarto)

Ep 2256:62 with n/69 with n28

124   Pelargus, Ambrosius. *Opuscula.* Cologne: J. Gymnicus, August 1534 (octavo)

Ep 2970:23–5 with 23n

125   Pfefferkorn, Johann. *Streydt puechlyn vor dy warheit und eyner warhafftiger historie Joannis Pfefferkorn Vechtende wyd den falschen Broder Doctor Joannis Reuchlyn, und syne jungernn Obscurorum virorum ...* [Cologne: Heinrich von Neuss] 1516 (quarto)

Ep 697:11–13 with 12n/14–17 with 15n; Geiger *Johann Reuchlin* 383–4

126   Pio, Alberto. *Tres & viginti libri in locos lucubrationum variarum D. Erasmi ... quos censet ab eo recognoscendos & retractandos.* Paris: Josse Bade 9 March 1531 (folio)

Epp 2261:69–71 with 70n/75–7 with n29, 2414:8–13/10–14, 2441:64–8/66–71, 2522:66–72 ; asd ix-6 40–4

127 Pirckheimer, Willibald. *De convitiis Monachi illius qui graecolatine Caecolampadius, germanice vero Ausshin nuncupatur, ad Eleutherium suum epistola.* [Nürnberg: J. Petreius 1527] (octavo)

Ep 1893:51–2 with 51n/57–8 with n21

128 Pirckheimer, Willibald. *Epistola apologetica.* Nürnberg: F. Peypus, 2 October 1517

Published with Pirckheimer's translation of *Luciani piscator*; cf no 102 above. Epp 685:13 with n/13 with n, 694:21–2, 108–10/22–3, 114–16, 700:12–13/14.

129 Plutarch. *De his qui tarde a numine corripiuntur.* Nürnberg: F. Peypus, 30 June 1513 (quarto)

Epp 362:3–4 with 3n/5–6 with 5n, 375:3–8/3–8

130 Prierias, Silvester (Silvestro Mazzolini). *In presumptuosas Martini Luther conclusiones de potestate Pape dialogus.* n p [c February 1518] (quarto)

Epp 872:16 with n/18–19 with 19n, 877:36–7/41–2; cf Ep 878:6–7/6–8.

131 Proba. *Probe coniugis Adelphi Cento Virgilii vetus et novum continens testamentum.* [Ed J. Canter]. Antwerp: Gerard Leeuw, 12 September 1489

Ep 32:36–8 with 37n/40–1 with n

132 Resende, André de. *Carmen eruditum et elegans ... adversus stolidos politioris literaturae oblatratores.* Basel: H. Froben, September 1531

Ep 2500:1–9 with 4n

133 Ringelberg, Joachim van. *Institutiones astronomicae.* Basel: V. Curio, 31 October 1528 and Paris: C. Wechel 1530 (octavo)

Printed with one (Basel) and two (Paris) epigrams of Erasmus; Reedijk *Poems* nos 118 and 119/ASD I-7 nos 76 and 77/CWE 85–6 nos 76 and 77

134 Riquinus, Simon (Reichwein). *De novo hactenusque Germaniae inaudito morbo ... sudatoria febri, quem vulgo sudorem Britannicum vocant ... iudicium doctissimum.* Cologne: J. Soter, October 1529 (quarto)

Ep 2246:40 with n/41 with n10. This copy has been preserved and can be found in the University Library Basel (L e VI 21 7); see AK VII 258 Ep 3168.

135 Rivieren, Eustacius van der. *Apologia pro pietate in Erasmi Roterodami Enchiridion canonem quintum.* Antwerp: W. Vorsterman 1531 (octavo); NK 2988 and 2989

Epp 2264 introductions, 2522:81–92 with 86n

136 Rothmann, Bernhard. *Von der Rache.* Münster: December 1534

Ep 3060:22–5 with 23n

137 Sadoleto, Jacopo. *Interpretatio in Psalmum Miserere mei.* Rome: F.M. Calvus 1525 (quarto)

Epp 1586:1–22 with nn/introduction, 1–22 with n1, 1604

138 Sannazaro, Jacopo. *De partu Virginis.* Rome: F.M. Calvus, December 1526 (octavo)

Ep 1840:75–8 with 75n/84–7 with n23; *Ciceronianus* ASD I-2 700–1/CWE 28 437 with n822. The Aldine press in Venice published an octavo edition in August 1528.

139 Schatzgeyer, Kaspar. *Scrutinium divinae scripturae pro conciliatione dissidentium dogmatum.* [Augsburg 1522]

The preface is signed by Conradus Pellicanus.

140 Scaliger, Julius Caesar. *Oratio pro M. Tullio Cicerone contra Des. Erasmum Roterodamum.* Paris: G. Gourmont and P. Vidoue, September 1531 (octavo)

Epp 2564:1–4 with 2nn, 2574:1–2, 2577

141 *Selecta epigrammata graeca latine versa ex septem epigrammatum Graecorum libris.* [Ed Janus Cornarius]. Basel: J. Bebelius, 1529 (octavo)

A selection of Greek epigrams translated by Alciati, Luscinius, More, Lily, Erasmus, Sleidan, Ursinus Velius, and Cannius. Ep 2356:28–31 with 28n/30–3; ASD II-5 93 775n

142 Theoderici, Vincentius. *Apologia in eum librum quem ab anno Erasmus Roterodamus de Confessione edidit, per Godefridum Ruysium Taxandrum theologum. Eiusdem libellus quo taxatur Delectus ciborum sive liber de carnium esu ante biennium per Erasmum Roterodamum enixus.* Antwerp: S. Cocus and G. Nicolaus, 12 March 1525 (octavo); NK 1840

Ep 1571:65–8 with 65n/70–3 with n14; cf Epp 1196 introductions, 1608, 2045:111–49/120–60.

143 Titelmans, Frans. *Epistola apologetica pro opere Collationum ... ad Desyderium Erasmum Roterodamum.* Antwerp: W. Vorsterman, January 1530 (octavo); NK 2042

Ep 2245 (selections); cf Ep 1823 introductions.

144 Titelmans, Frans. *Libri duo de authoritate libri Apocalypsis.* Antwerp: M. Hillen 1530 (octavo); NK 2035

Ep 2417 (the preface); cf Epp 1823 introductions, 2245:51–7 with 52n/56–61 with n6.

145 [Unitas Fratrum]. *Apologia sacrae scripturae.* [Ed Mikuláš Klaudyán]. Nürnberg: H. Hoeltzel 1511 (quarto); Panzer VII 449 no 72

Allen Ep 1117 introduction, CWE Ep 1039 introduction, Epp 1154:7–10 with 8n/7–10 with n2, 1183:7–9/8–10; Müller *Geschichte der Böhmischen Brüder* I 395 and 558

146 Virgilio, Polidoro. *De rerum inventoribus.* Basel: J. Froben, July 1525

Ep 1702:1–2 with 1nn/2–3; cf Ep 1494:6–10 with 7n/7–11 with n6. This work was reprinted from *Polidori Vergilii Adagiorum liber. Eiusdem de inventoribus rerum libri octo*. Basel: J. Froben, July 1521. Cf Adams v 442; Luchsinger *Der Basler Buchdruck* 50–1, 97–9.

147 Virgilio, Polidoro. *Proverbiorum libellus*. Venice: C. de Pensis, 10 April 1498 [or 6 November 1500] (quarto)

Epp 1175 introductions, 2773; ASD II-5 91 749–50n

148 Vives, Juan Luis. *De europe dissidiis, & republica*. Bruges: H. de Croock December 1526 (octavo); NK 2164

Epp 1847:34 with n/37 with n9. Erasmus was clearly familiar with Vives' writings, but it is difficult to identify individual titles that he might have had in his library. Cf Epp 1792:23n/n8, 1889:11–12 with 11n/15–16 with n6. A book containing three works printed in 1524 is another possibility: *Introductio ad sapientiam. Satellitium sive Symbola. Epistolae duae de ratione studii puerilis*. Leuven 1524 (octavo); NK 2168

149 Wimpina, Conradus Coci de. *Sectarum, errorum, hallutinationum, et schismatum ab origine ... ad usque hec nostrae tempora concisioris Anacephalaeoseos ... librorum partes tres*. Frankfurt an der Oder: [J. Hanau] 1528 (folio)

Ep 2247:24–44 with 26n/25–41 with n7

150 Witzel, Georg. [A book published c 1533–4]

Ep 2918:44–5 with 44n. In the letter, dated around the beginning of April 1534, Erasmus says that Johannes Cochlaeus has sent him 'Witzel's book.' Witzel published several books at about this time; it is not possible to identify which one is meant.

151 Ziegler, Jakob. *Libellus ... adversus Iacobi Stunicae maledicentiam, pro Germania*. Basel: J. Froben, April 1523 (octavo)

Published with *Catalogus lucubrationum D. Erasmi*; see Epp 1260:201–4 with 203n, 265–70/224–7 with n50, 296–302, 1330:3–4/4–6.

152 Zwingli, Huldrych. *Apologeticus Archeteles adpellatus* [Zürich: C. Froschauer 1522] (quarto)

Ep 1315

153 [Zwingli, Huldrych]. *Suggestio deliberandi super propositione Hadriani pontificis Romani Nerobergae facta ad principes Germaniae*. [Zürich: C. Froschauer, c November 1522]

Ep 1327:6–9 with 6n/7–9 with n1